October 16-19, 2011
Santa Barbara, CA, USA

Association for
Computing Machinery

Advancing Computing as a Science & Profession

UIST'11

Proceedings of the 24th Annual ACM Symposium on
User Interface Software and Technology

Sponsored by:

ACM SIGCHI & ACM SIGGRAPH

Supported by:

Autodesk, Bloomberg, Microsoft, Perceptive Pixel, Google, Synaptics, WaCom, Grand Graphics, Animation & New Media, Adobe, Disney Research, Nokia, IBM Research, & FXPal

Association for Computing Machinery

Advancing Computing as a Science & Profession

The Association for Computing Machinery
2 Penn Plaza, Suite 701
New York, New York 10121-0701

Notice to Past Authors of ACM-Published Articles
ACM intends to create a complete electronic archive of all articles and/or other material previously published by ACM. If you have written a work that has been previously published by ACM in any journal or conference proceedings prior to 1978, or any SIG Newsletter at any time, and you do NOT want this work to appear in the ACM Digital Library, please inform permissions@acm.org, stating the title of the work, the author(s), and where and when published.

ISBN: 978-1-4503-0716-1

Additional copies may be ordered prepaid from:

ACM Order Department
PO Box 30777
New York, NY 10087-0777, USA

Phone: 1-800-342-6626 (USA and Canada)
+1-212-626-0500 (Global)
Fax: +1-212-944-1318
E-mail: acmhelp@acm.org
Hours of Operation: 8:30 am – 4:30 pm ET

ACM Order No: 609112

Printed in the USA

Chairs' Welcome

Welcome to UIST 2011, the Twenty-Fourth Annual ACM Symposium on User Interface Software and Technology.

UIST is the premier forum for the presentation of research innovations in the software and technology of human-computer interfaces. Sponsored by ACM's special interest groups on computer-human interaction (SIGCHI) and computer graphics (SIGGRAPH), UIST brings together researchers and practitioners from many areas, including web and graphical interfaces, new input and output devices, information visualization, interactive displays, tangible computing, and computer supported cooperative work. The single-track schedule, intimate size, and location in Santa Barbara, "the American Riviera", make UIST 2011 an ideal place to exchange results and to forge future collaborations.

We received 262 paper submissions from more than 20 countries. After a thorough review process, the program committee accepted 67 papers (25%). Each anonymous submission was reviewed by a primary program committee member and two external reviewers. If any of the three reviewers deemed a submission to pass a rejection threshold we asked a secondary committee member to write a fourth review of the paper. Authors then received all the reviews and if their paper passed the rejection threshold they had the opportunity to write a short rebuttal. The program committee met in person in San Francisco on June 17-18, 2011, to examine each submission and select the top papers. Submissions were finally accepted only after the authors provided a final revision addressing the committee's comments.

In addition to the presentations of accepted papers, this year's program includes keynotes by Ge Wang (Stanford professor and co-founder of Smule) on computers and music and by Dan Jurafsky (another Stanford professor and MacArthur Fellow) on computational linguistics. Posters, demos, the eighth annual Doctoral Symposium, and third annual Student Innovation Content (this year focusing on Microsoft's new TouchMouse) complete the program.

Jeff Pierce
UIST'11 General Chair
IBM Research, USA

Maneesh Agrawala
UIST'11 Program Chair
University of California, Berkeley, USA

Scott Klemmer
UIST'11 Program Chair
Stanford University, USA

Table of Contents

Session 3: Social Learning

Session Chair: Sep Kamvar *(Stanford University)*

Session 4: With a Little Help

Session Chair: Joel Brandt *(Adobe)*

Keynote Address 1

Session 5: Development

Session Chair: Michael Terry *(University of Waterloo)*

Session 6: Tactile

Session Chair: Jeff Bigham *(University of Rochester)*

Session 7: Tangible

Session Chair: Michel Beaudouin-Lafon *(University of Paris)*

Session 8: Patterns

Session Chair: Bjoern Hartmann *(University of California, Berkeley)*

UIST 2011 Conference Organization

General Chair:	Jeff Pierce *(IBM Research, USA)*
Program Chairs:	Maneesh Agrawala *(University of California, Berkeley, USA)* Scott Klemmer *(Stanford University, USA)*
Treasurer:	Christine Robson *(IBM Research, USA)*
Sponsorship Chairs:	Roel Vertegaal *(Queen's University, Canada)* Daniel Wigdor *(University of Toronto, Canada)*
Poster Chairs:	Shamsi Iqbal *(Microsoft Research, USA)* Amy Karlson *(Microsoft Research, USA)*
Demo Chairs:	Otmar Hilliges *(Microsoft Research, USA)* Christian Holz *(University of Potsdam, Germany)*
Doctoral Symposium Chair:	Steven Feiner *(Columbia University, USA)*
Student Innovation Contest Chairs:	Kayur Patel *(University of Washington, USA)* Chris Harrison *(Carnegie Mellon University, USA)* Nick Chen *(University of Maryland, USA)*
Student Volunteer Chairs:	Katrina Panovich *(Massachusetts Institute of Technology, USA)* Elena Agapie *(Harvard University, USA)*
Registration Chairs:	Kevin Li *(AT&T Labs, USA)* Sean White *(Columbia University, USA)*
Proceedings Chairs:	Clifton Forlines *(Draper Laboratory, USA)* Ari Rapkin Blenkhorn *(Perceptive Pixel, USA)*
Publicity Chairs:	Rafael Tico Ballagas *(Nokia Research, USA)* mc schraefel *(University of Southampton, UK)*
Madness Chair:	Hyunyoung Song *(University of Maryland, USA)*

Program Committee:

Caroline Appert *(LRI, France)*
Rafael Tico Ballagas *(Nokia Research Center, USA)*
Michel Beaudouin-Lafon *(University of Paris, France)*
Jeff Bigham *(University of Rochester, USA)*
Michael Bernstein *(Massachusetts Institute of Technology, USA)*
Joel Brandt *(Adobe, USA)*
Stu Card *(Stanford University, USA)*
Ed Chi *(Google Research, USA)*
Michael Cohen *(Microsoft Research, USA)*
Steve Feiner *(Columbia University, USA)*
Tovi Grossman *(Autodesk, Canada)*
Francois Guimbretiere *(Cornell University, USA)*
Ken Hinckley *(Microsoft Research, USA)*
Jim Hollan *(University of Calfornia, San Diego, USA)*
Shamsi Iqbal *(Microsoft Research, USA)*
Sep Kamvar *(Stanford University, USA)*
Amy Karlson *(Microsoft Research, USA)*
Andy Ko *(University of Washington, USA)*
Jeff Nichols *(IBM Research, USA)*
Tapan Parikh *(University of California, Berkeley, USA)*
Shwetak Patel *(University of Washington, USA)*
Eric Paulos *(Carnegie Mellon University, USA)*
mc schraefel *(University of Southampton, UK)*
Michael Terry *(University of Waterloo, Canada)*
Gina Venolia *(Microsoft Research, USA)*
Andy Wilson *(Microsoft Research, USA)*
Jacob Wobbrock *(University of Washington, USA)*
Stephen Voida *(University of California, Irvine, USA)*
Shumin Zhai *(Google Research, USA)*

Doctoral Symposium Committee:

Takeo Igarashi *(University of Tokyo, Japan)*
Rob Jacob *(Tufts University, USA)*
mc schraefel *(University of Southampton, UK)*

UIST'11 Reviewers

Salman Ahmad, *Stanford University,* USA
Paul André, *University of Southampton,* UK
Lisa Anthony, *Lockheed Martin Advanced Technology Laboratories,* USA
Ryosuke Aoki, *NTT Corporation,* Japan
Caroline Appert, *Université Paris-Sud, CNRS,* France
Jorge Aranda, *University of Toronto,* Canada
Daniel Ashbrook, *Nokia Research Center Hollywood,* USA
Mark Ashdown, *Thales UK,* UK
Daniel Avrahami, *Intel Labs Seattle,* USA
Maribeth Back, *FX Palo Alto Laboratory,* USA
Rafael Ballagas, *Nokia Research Center,* USA
Shumeet Baluja, *Google,* USA
Connelly Barnes, *Princeton University,* USA
Alexis Battle, *Stanford University,* USA
Olivier Bau, *Disney Research Pittsburgh,* USA
Patrick Baudisch, *Hasso Plattner Institute,* Germany
Michel Beaudouin-Lafon, *Université Paris-Sud,* France
Steffi Beckhaus, *University of Hamburg,* Germany
Benjamin Bederson, *University of Maryland,* USA
Nikolaus Bee, *Augsburg University,* Germany
Blaine Bell, *Schrodinger,* USA
Victoria Bellotti, *PARC,* USA
Hrvoje Benko, *Microsoft Research,* USA
François Bérard, *CLIPS-IMAG,* France
Michael Bernstein, *Massachusetts Institute of Technology,* USA
Xiaojun Bi, *University of Toronto,* Canada
Timothy Bickmore, *Northeastern University,* USA
Jacob Biehl, *FX Palo Alto Laboratory, Inc.,* USA
Jeffrey Bigham, *University of Rochester,* USA
Mark Billinghurst, *University of Canterbury,* New Zealand
Marco Blumendorf, *TU-Berlin,* Germany
Mark Bolas, *USC,* USA
Jan Borchers, *RWTH Aachen University,* Germany
Sebastian Boring, *University of Calgary,* Canada
Cati Boulanger, *Microsoft,* USA
Doug Bowman, *Virginia Tech,* USA
Andrew Bragdon, *Brown University,* USA
Joel Brandt, *Stanford University,* USA
A. J. Brush, *Microsoft Research,* USA
Xiang Cao, *Microsoft Research Asia,* P.R. China
Stuart Card, *PARC,* USA
Sheelagh Carpendale, *University of Calgary,* Canada
Géry Casiez, *LIFL & INRIA Lille, University of Lille,* France
Anna Cavender, *University of Washington,* USA
Olivier Chapuis, *Université Paris-Sud & CNRS,* France
Jilin Chen, *University of Minnesota,* USA
Kuang Chen, *University of California, Berkeley,* USA
Nicholas Chen, *University of Maryland, College Park,* USA
Yinpeng Chen, *Arizona State University,* USA
Marshini Chetty, *Georgia Institute of Technology,* USA
Ed Chi, *Google,* USA
Parmit Chilana, *University of Washington,* USA
Karen Church, *Telefonica Research,* Spain
Jesse Cirimele, *Stanford University,* USA
James Clawson, *Georgia Institute of Technology,* USA
Andy Cockburn, *University of Canterbury,* New Zealand
Michael Cohen, *Microsoft Research,* USA
Gabe Cohn, *University of Washington,* USA
Sunny Consolvo, *Intel Labs Seattle,* USA
Henriette Cramer, *Mobile Life Centre & Swedish Institute of Computer Science,* Sweden
Laura Dabbish, *Carnegie Mellon University,* USA
Richard Davis, *Singapore Management University,* Singapore
David Dearman, *University of Toronto,* Canada
Rob DeLine, *Microsoft Research,* USA
Anind Dey, *Carnegie Mellon University,* USA
Nicholas Diakopoulos, *Rutgers University,* USA
Paul Dietz, *Microsoft Corporation,* USA
Judith Donath, *Massachusetts Institute of Technology,* USA
Mira Dontcheva, *Adobe Advanced Technology Labs,* USA
Pierre Dragicevic, *INRIA,* France
Steven Drucker, *Microsoft Research,* USA
Tom Drummond, *Monash University,* Australia
Lucy Dunne, *University College Dublin,* Ireland
James Eagan, *Télécom-ParisTech,* France
Keith Edwards, *Georgia Tech,* USA
Umer Farooq, *The Pennsylvania State University,* USA
Gregg Favalora, *Optics for Hire,* USA
Steven Feiner, *Columbia University,* USA
Pablo Figueroa, *Universidad de los Andes,* Colombia
Leah Findlater, *University of Washington,* USA
Danyel Fisher, *Microsoft Research,* USA
George Fitzmaurice, *Autodesk,* Canada
James Fogarty, *University of Washington,* USA
Clifton Forlines, *Mitsubishi Electric Research Laboratories,* USA
Jodi Forlizzi, *Carnegie Mellon University,* USA
Adam Fourney, *University of Waterloo,* Canada
Jan-Michael Frahm, *UNC CH,* USA
Robert Futrelle, *Northeastern University,* USA
Krzysztof Gajos, *Microsoft Research,* USA

Pierre Garrigues, *IQ Engines, Inc.,* USA
William Gaver, *Goldsmiths College,* UK
Rich Gossweiler, *Google,* USA
Saul Greenberg, *University of Calgary,* Canada
William Griswold, *University of California, San Diego,* USA
Tovi Grossman, *Autodesk Research,* Canada
Francois Guimbretiere, *Cornell University,* USA
Sidhant Gupta, *University of Washington,* USA
Sean Gustafson, *Hasso Plattner Institute,* Germany
Mark Guzdial, *Georgia Tech,* USA
Martin Hachet, *LaBRI-INRIA University of Bordeaux,* France
Michael Haller, *Media Interaction Lab,* Austria
Tracy Hammond, *Texas A&M University,* USA
Mark Hancock, *University of Waterloo,* Canada
Chris Harrison, *Carnegie Mellon University,* USA
Björn Hartmann, *University of California, Berkeley,* USA
Jeffrey Heer, *Stanford University,* USA
Rorik Henrikson, *University of Toronto,* Canada
Otmar Hilliges, *Microsoft Research Cambridge,* UK
Ken Hinckley, *Microsoft Research,* USA
Steve Hodges, *Microsoft Research,* UK
Eve Hoggan, *University of Helsinki,* Finland
James Hollan, *University of California, San Diego,* USA
Paul Holleis, *DoCoMo Euro-Labs Munich,* Germany
Tobias Hollerer, *University of California, Santa Barbara,* USA
David Holman, *Queen's University,* Canada
Reid Holmes, *University of Washington,* USA
Christian Holz, *Hasso Plattner Institute,* Germany
Lichan Hong, *Google,* USA
Elaine Huang, *Georgia Institute of Technology,* USA
Scott Hudson, *Carnegie Mellon University,* USA
Stephane Huot, *Université Paris-Sud,* France
Amy Hurst, *Carnegie Mellon University,* USA
Dugald Hutchings, *Elon University,* USA
Takeo Igarashi, *The University of Tokyo,* Japan
Kori Inkpen, *Microsoft Research,* USA
Shamsi Iqbal, *Microsoft Research,* USA
Pourang Irani, *University of Manitoba,* Canada
Hiroshi Ishii, *Massachusetts Institute of Technology,* USA
Poika Isokoski, *University of Tampere,* Finland
Shahram Izadi, *Microsoft Research Limited,* UK
Robert Jacob, *Tufts University,* USA
Yvonne Jansen, *Université Paris-Sud,* France
Lahiru Jayatilaka, *Harvard University,* USA
Michael Johnson, *Google,* USA
Sergi Jorda, *Universitat Pompeu Fabra,* Spain
Eric Kabisch, *University of California, Irvine,* USA
Maryam Kamvar, *Google,* USA
Sep Kamvar, *Stanford University,* USA
Shaun Kane, *University of Washington,* USA
Amy Karlson, *University of Maryland,* USA
Thorsten Karrer, *RWTH Aachen University,* Germany
Joseph 'Jofish' Kaye, *Nokia,* USA
Caitlin Kelleher, *Washington University,* USA
Kibum Kim, *Queen's University,* Canada
Aniket Kittur, *Carnegie Mellon University,* USA
Jeff Klingner, *Stanford University,* USA
Andrew Ko, *University of Washington,* USA
Joseph Konstan, *University of Minnesota,* USA
Aleksandra Korolova, *Stanford University,* USA
Matthias Kranz, *Technische Universität München,* Germany
Per Ola Kristensson, *University of Cambridge,* UK
Adrian Kuhn, *University of Bern,* Switzerland
Alexander Kulik, *Bauhaus-Universitaet Weimar,* Germany
Anand Kulkarni, *University of California, Berkeley,* USA
Manu Kumar, *K9 Ventures,* USA
Ranjitha Kumar, *Stanford University,* USA
Andrew Kun, *University of New Hampshire,* USA
Gordon Kurtenbach, *Autodesk,* Canada
Shyong Lam, *University of Minnesota,* USA
James Landay, *University of Washington,* USA
Edward Lank, *University of Waterloo,* Canada
Thomas LaToza, *Carnegie Mellon University,* USA
Celine Latulipe, *University of North Carolina at Charlotte,* USA
Tessa Lau, *IBM Almaden Research Center,* USA
Joseph LaViola, *University of Central Florida,* USA
Edith Law, *Carnegie Mellon University,* USA
Eric Lecolinet, *Telecom ParisTech,* France
Johnny Lee, *Microsoft - Applied Sciences,* USA
Jonathan Lester, *University of Washington,* USA
Kevin Li, *AT&T Labs - Research,* USA
Wilmot Li, *University of Washington,* USA
Yang Li, *Google Research,* US
Greg Little, *Massachusetts Institute of Technology,* USA
Shixia Liu, *Microsoft Research Asia,* China
Ying Liu, *Nokia Research Center,* China
Sara Ljungblad, *Sics,* Sweden
Kent Lyons, *Intel Research,* USA
Blair MacIntyre, *Georgia Tech,* USA
Wendy Mackay, *INRIA,* France
Lena Mamykina, *Columbia University,* USA
Cristina Manresa Yee, *University of Balearic Islands,* Spain
Nicolai Marquardt, *University of Calgary,* Canada
Anthony Martinet, *LIFL & INRIA Lille - University of Lille,* France
Winter Mason, *Yahoo! Research,* USA
Joe McCarthy, *University of Washington, Tacoma,* USA

Daniel McFarlane, *Lockheed Martin Advanced Technology Laboratories,* USA
Joanna McGrenere, *University of British Columbia,* Canada
Michael McGuffin, *École de technologie supérieure,* Canada
Indrani Medhi, *Microsoft Research Labs India,* India
Jan Meskens, *Hasselt University,* Belgium
Andrew Miller, *University of Central Florida,* USA
Rob Miller, *Massachusetts Institute of Technology,* USA
Neema Moraveji, *Microsoft Research Asia,* China
Carlos Morimoto, *University of São Paulo,* Brazil
Daniel Morris, *Microsoft Research,* USA
Robert Morris, *Massachusetts Institute of Technology,* USA
Tomer Moscovich, *INRIA,* France
Max Mühlhäuser, *TU Darmstadt,* Germany
Sean Munson, *University of Michigan,* USA
Brad Myers, *Carnegie Mellon University,* USA
Miguel Nacenta, *University of St Andrews,* UK
Kumiyo Nakakoji, *Software Research Associates, Inc.,* Japan
Mark Newman, *University of Michigan,* USA
Tao Ni, *Virginia Polytechnic Institute & State University,* USA
Jeffrey Nichols, *IBM Research,* USA
Laurence Nigay, *University of Grenoble 1,* France
Natasha Noy, *Stanford University,* USA
Rodrigo de Oliveira, *Telefonica Research,* Spain
Dan Olsen, *Brigham Young University,* USA
Alex Olwal, *Royal Institute of Technology (KTH),* Sweden
Margaret Orth, *International Fashion Machines, Inc.,* USA
Antti Oulasvirta, *Helsinki Institute for Information Technology HIIT,* Finland
Dan Overholt, *Aalborg University,* Denmark
Sharon Oviatt, *Incaa Designs,* USA
Katrina Panovich, *Massachusetts Institute of Technology,* USA
Joseph Paradiso, *Massachusetts Institute of Technology,* USA
Aditya Parameswaran, *Stanford University,* USA
Tapan Parikh, *University of California, Berkeley,* USA
Kurt Partridge, *PARC,* USA
Nirmal Patel, *Georgia Institute of Technology,* USA
Shwetak Patel, *University of Washington,* USA
Fabio Paternò, *ISTI-CNR,* Italy
Sharoda Paul, *The Pennsylvania State University,* USA
Eric Paulos, *Carnegie Mellon University,* USA
Ken Perlin, *New York University,* USA
Emmanuel Pietriga, *INRIA,* France
Anne Marie Piper, *University of California, San Diego,* USA
Benjamin Poppinga, *OFFIS - Institute for Information Technology,* Germany
Ivan Poupyrev, *Sony Computer Science Laboratories,* Japan
Pernilla Qvarfordt, *FX Palo Alto Laboratory, Inc.,* USA
Hayes Raffle, *Google,* USA
Gonzalo Ramos, *Microsoft Corporation,* USA
Naomi Ramos, *Northrop Grumman,* USA
Ramesh Raskar, *MERL,* USA
Katharina Reinecke, *Harvard University,* USA
Jason Reisman, *Perceptive Pixel,* USA
Jun Rekimoto, *University of Tokyo & Sony CSL,* Japan
Tom Rodden, *University of Nottingham,* UK
Michael Rohs, *LMU Munich,* Germany
Roni Rosenfeld, *Carnegie Mellon University,* USA
Daniela Rosner, *University of California, Berkeley,* USA
Anne Roudaut, *Hasso Plattner Institut,* Germany
Enrico Rukzio, *University of Duisburg-Essen & Lancaster University,* Germany
Kimiko Ryokai, *Massachusetts Institute of Technology,* USA
Alireza Sahami, *University of Duisburg Essen,* Germany
T. Scott Saponas, *Microsoft Research,* USA
Eric Saund, *Palo Alto Research Center,* USA
Christopher Scaffidi, *Carnegie Mellon University,* USA
Chris Schmandt, *Massachusetts Institute of Technology,* USA
Albrecht Schmidt, *University of Duisburg-Essen,* Germany
Dominik Schmidt, *Lancaster University,* UK
m.c. schraefel, *University of Southampton,* UK
James Scott, *Microsoft Research,* UK
Abigail Sellen, *Microsoft Research,* UK
Orit Shaer, *Tufts University,* USA
Aneesh Sharma, *Twitter, Inc.,* USA
Eli Shechtman, *Adobe Systems,* USA
Chia Shen, *Harvard University,* USA
Frank Shipman, *Texas A&M University,* USA
Takaaki Shiratori, *Carnegie Mellon University,* USA
Linda Sibert, *Naval Research Laboratory,* USA
Beth Simon, *University of California, San Diego,* USA
Barton Smith, *IBM Research Division,* USA
Joshua Smith, *University of Washington,* USA
Erin Solovey, *Tufts University,* USA
Hyunyoung Song, *University of Maryland, College Park,* USA
Robert St. Amant, *North Carolina State University,* USA
Thad Starner, *Georgia Tech,* USA
Jürgen Steimle, *Darmstadt University of Technology,* Germany
Amanda Stent, *AT&T Labs - Research,* USA
Wolfgang Stuerzlinger, *York University,* Canada
Sriram Subramanian, *University of Bristol,* UK
Jay Summet, *Georgia Institute of Technology,* USA
Leila Takayama, *Willow Garage,* USA
Chew Lim Tan, *National University of Singapore,* Singapore
Anthony Tang, *Georgia Institute of Technology,* USA
John Tang, *Microsoft Research,* USA

Craig Tashman, *Georgia Institute of Technology,* USA
Jaime Teevan, *Microsoft Research,* USA
Michael Terry, *University of Waterloo,* Canada
Anuj Tewari, *University of California, Berkeley,* USA
William Thies, *Microsoft Research India,* India
Michael Toomim, *University of Washington,* USA
Khai Truong, *University of Toronto,* Canada
Theophanis Tsandilas, *In Situ, INRIA Saclay, LRI Université Paris-Sud,* France
Joe Tullio, *Motorola Labs,* USA
Michael Twidale, *University of Illinois at Urbana-Champaign,* USA
Brygg Ullmer, *Louisiana State University,* USA
Matt Uyttendaele, *Microsoft,* USA
Anton van den Hengel, *University of Adelaide,* Australia
Max Van Kleek, *Massachusetts Institute of Technology,* USA
Gina Venolia, *Microsoft Research,* USA
Roel Vertegaal, *Queen's University,* Canada
Daniel Vogel, *Mount Allison University,* Canada
Juergen Vogel, *SAP Research,* Switzerland
Stephen Voida, *University of California, Irvine,* USA
Luis von Ahn, *Carnegie Mellon University,* USA
Julie Wagner, *InSitu, Univ. Paris-Sud, INRIA,* France
Jingtao Wang, *University of Pittsburgh,* USA
Martin Wattenberg, *IBM Research,* USA
Mark Weal, *University of Southampton,* UK
Nadir Weibel, *University of California, San Diego,* USA
Malte Weiss, *RWTH Aachen University,* Germany
Brandyn White, *University of Maryland, College Park,* USA
Sean White, *Nokia Research Center,* USA
Steve Whittaker, *Sheffield University,,* UK
Daniel Wigdor, *University of Toronto,* Canada
Doug Wightman, *Queen's University,* Canada
Amanda Williams, *University of California, Irvine,* USA
Andrew Wilson, *Microsoft Research,* USA
Chadwick Wingrave, *UCF,* USA
Jacob Wobbrock, *University of Washington,* USA
Woontack Woo, *GIST,* Korea
Leslie Wu, *Stanford University,* USA
Svetlana Yarosh, *Georgia Institute of Technology,* USA
Koji Yatani, *University of Toronto,* Canada
Tom Yeh, *University of Maryland, College Park,* USA
Robert Zeleznik, *Brown University,* USA
Shumin Zhai, *Google Research,* USA
Shengdong Zhao, *National University of Singapore,* Singapore

UIST 2011 Sponsors & Supporters

UIST 2011 gratefully acknowledges our sponsoring SIGs and the support of the following corporations:

Sponsors

SIGCHI

ACMSIGGRAPH

Platinum Supporters

Autodesk

Bloomberg

Microsoft

Gold Supporters

PERCEPTIVE PIXEL

Silver Supporters

Google

wacom

Synaptics

GRAND — Graphisme, animation et nouveaux médias — Graphics, Animation and New Media

Bronze Supporters

Disney Research

Adobe

NOKIA

IBM Research

FXPAL — PALO ALTO LABORATORY

PlateMate: Crowdsourcing Nutrition Analysis from Food Photographs

Jon Noronha, Eric Hysen, Haoqi Zhang, Krzysztof Z. Gajos
Harvard School of Engineering and Applied Sciences
33 Oxford St., Cambridge, MA 02138, USA
{noronha,hysen,hqz,kgajos}@seas.harvard.edu

ABSTRACT

We introduce PlateMate, a system that allows users to take photos of their meals and receive estimates of food intake and composition. Accurate awareness of this information can help people monitor their progress towards dieting goals, but current methods for food logging via self-reporting, expert observation, or algorithmic analysis are time-consuming, expensive, or inaccurate. PlateMate crowdsources nutritional analysis from photographs using Amazon Mechanical Turk, automatically coordinating untrained workers to estimate a meal's calories, fat, carbohydrates, and protein. We present the Management framework for crowdsourcing complex tasks, which supports PlateMate's nutrition analysis workflow. Results of our evaluations show that PlateMate is nearly as accurate as a trained dietitian and easier to use for most users than traditional self-reporting.

ACM Classification: H5.2 [Information interfaces and presentation]: User Interfaces. - Graphical user interfaces.

General terms: Design, Human Factors

Keywords: Human computation, Crowdsourcing, Mechanical Turk, Nutrition, Remote Food Photography

INTRODUCTION

The majority of Americans perceive healthy eating as complicated [5]. Seeking comprehensible and actionable advice, Americans spend over $40 billion each year on diets and self-help books [18], but achieve little success: the majority eventually regain any lost weight and more [13].

There are many factors that may impact successful long-term change in eating habits. Our work is based on the observation that food intake monitoring is a popular component of many diets. For people who make a commitment to changing their eating habits, accurate logs of what they eat may help in monitoring progress toward set goals [11]. Currently, food logging is typically done by hand using paper diaries, spreadsheets, or a growing number of specialized applications. This process is both time-consuming and error-prone [17, 6]. Nutritionists have explored alternative methods such as daily interviews with trained experts. While these methods improve accuracy, they are costly and still require substantial time investment.

Our work is inspired by the *Remote Food Photography Method* (RFPM) [16], a novel approach from the nutrition literature. Rather than remembering foods or writing down records, users take two photographs of each meal: one at the beginning of the meal and one at the end documenting the leftovers. These images are analyzed by a third party, making logging easier and discouraging self-deception. The challenge is in finding a qualified third party without prohibitive costs. Expert nutritionists are scarce and costly, limiting the system to wealthy users or patients with particular conditions.

To make accurate food logging easier and more affordable, we introduce *PlateMate*, a system for crowdsourcing nutritional analysis (calories, fat, carbohydrates, and protein) from photographs of meals using Amazon Mechanical Turk. Complex tasks like this are hard problems for crowdsourcing, as workers may vary drastically in experience and reliability. To achieve accurate estimates, we propose a workflow in which the overall problem is decomposed into small, manageable, and verifiable steps. PlateMate uses this workflow to assign tasks to contributors, to validate and combine results, and to appropriately route tasks for further processing.

This paper makes three main contributions:

1. We present PlateMate, an end-to-end system for crowdsourced nutrition analysis from food photographs.
2. We discuss the results of a two-part evaluation, which suggests PlateMate can be as accurate as experts and self-report methods, and more usable than manual logging for everyday use.
3. We introduce the Management framework—inspired by the structure of human organizations, it provides effective support for managing crowdsourcing of complex heterogeneous tasks.

PlateMate implements the first step in the Remote Food Photography Method. In the last section we suggest how it can be extended to also support the second step: the analysis of photographs of food waste.

In the next section we review relevant prior work. We then describe the design and implementation of the PlateMate system and its components. Next, we discuss our Management framework. We then present an evaluation of the accuracy and usability of PlateMate and discuss the results. Finally, we consider future extensions to PlateMate.

RELATED WORK

Nutritionists have established several methods for measuring food intake. One prominent approach is 24-hour recall, in which a trained dietitian interviews a subject about her consumption over the previous day [16]. Accuracy depends on the subject's memory and honesty, and the technique requires a costly expert to conduct analysis. The main alternative is food journals, in which subjects record meals and estimate portions themselves, usually with pen and paper.

Both methods require significant time and self-reports also suffer from limited accuracy. A review of nine studies found error rates from -76% (underestimates) to $+24\%$ (overestimates) [19]. Prior work also suggests a dangerous bias in self-report methods. Most subjects selectively underreport fat intake, and obese people underestimate portions much more than leaner ones [17, 6]. These errors imply a larger problem of self-deception, especially in vulnerable groups.

A number of online interfaces exist to simplify the process of food logging. Smartphone applications and online calorie databases improve on earlier methods by performing calculations automatically. However, they still require tedious logging that discourages recording. Self-reports using these interfaces are no more accurate than pen and paper [2, 21].

The Computer Science community has explored additional alternatives, such as automatic analysis of chewing sounds [1] and scanned grocery receipts [12]. These methods, while potentially more scalable and less time-consuming than current approaches, remain inaccurate.

Martin et al. recently suggested an alternative approach called the Remote Food Photography Method (RFPM) [16]. Rather than typing names of foods and estimating portions, users take photographs of their plates both at the beginning of the meal and at the end to accurately capture how much food was actually eaten. Trained dietitians identify the pictured foods remotely and estimate portions. The results of laboratory studies showed that dietitians using RFPM underestimated calories by 5-7% compared to the ground truth obtained by directly weighing the foods [16].

RFPM thus combines the accuracy of direct observation by experts with the convenience of free-living conditions. Users of the method found it extremely satisfying and easy to use [16]. The problem is cost. RFPM relies on experts to analyze each photograph, limiting the system's accessibility and potential scale.

Kitamura et al. attempted to use computer vision to cheaply implement RFPM [7]. They were successful in algorithmically detecting if a photograph contained food and in estimating amounts of general categories of food, such as meats, grains, and fruit. They did not attempt to identify the specific foods in a photo or provide actual intake totals.

The cost of experts and limitations of computer vision suggest an opportunity for crowdsourced nutritional analysis. Prior research indicates that the most difficult part of nutritional analysis is estimating portion size [16], and that trained amateurs have low bias but high variance [15]. The "wisdom of crowds" is ideally suited to these situations, since the average of amateur estimates often beats a single expert [20].

A recent iPhone application demonstrates, however, that naive approaches to crowdsourcing for nutritional analysis are not sufficient. In April, 2011, the fitness website Daily Burn released Meal Snap, which allows users to photograph foods and receive calorie estimates by so-called "pure magic."[1] Meal Snap creates a single Mechanical Turk task for each image. Workers provide a free text description of food, and the application appears to match this description with a database of average consumption to estimate a range of possible calories. This approach is appealing, but critics have accused it of failing to provide useful data[2] and our evaluation showed that Meal Snap's results do not correlate with the meal's actual caloric content.

PhotoCalorie[3] is a recent on-line tool that encourages users to upload photographs of their meals, but it uses them just to illustrate the user's personal photo journal. The apparent similarity to PlateMate is superficial because to obtain calorie estimates, users have to enter short descriptions of the contents of the meals and manually estimate the amounts eaten.

PLATEMATE

PlateMate allows users to upload food photographs and receive nutrition estimates within a few hours. The estimates consist of a list of foods in the photograph, with associated measurements of serving size, calories, fat, carbohydrates, and protein for each food item. The information is displayed to the user via the user interface shown in Figure 1.

Estimates are generated from a series of tasks on Amazon Mechanical Turk. Crowdsourcing nutritional analysis presents several challenges in interface and workflow design. First, Turkers are inexperienced, and may thus produce unreliable estimates. Second, most Mechanical Turk tasks are simple, and Turkers may be unaccustomed to performing complex operations like nutritional analysis if presented as a single, complex task. Finally, any individual Turker may be biased in their estimates or have trouble recognizing certain foods contained in a photograph, making it necessary to select from or combine the outputs of multiple workers.

To best design a workflow for crowdsourcing nutritional analysis, we started by observing a dietitian as she determined nutritional data from several photographs. Her process consisted of three distinct steps: identifying foods in each image, estimating their portions, and then calculating the corresponding nutrition data. The final step can be fully computerized, but PlateMate implements the first two with

[1] `http://mealsnap.com/`, accessed July 5, 2011
[2] `http://www.mobilecrunch.com/2011/04/05/too-lazy-to-count-calories-now-you-can-just-take-a-picture-of-your-meal/`
[3] `http://photocalorie.com/`, accessed on July 5, 2011

DINNER

	kcal	fat (g)	carbs (g)	protein (g)
	1573.2	72.9	84	138.9
Yellow Corn (0.50 cup)	303	3.9	61.6	7.8
barbeque chicken breast				
Chicken Breast Meat and Skin (Broilers or Fryers) (1.00 breast, bone removed)	249	13.4	0	30.2
Barbeque Sauce (Low Sodium, Canned) (0.14 cup)	26.6	0.6	4.5	0.6
Beef Steak (0.92 medium steak (yield after cooking, bone removed))	471.3	28.1	0	51.0
Hominy (White, Canned) (0.44 cup)	52.8	0.6	10.4	1.1
Ketchup (2.00 tbsp)	30	0.1	7.5	0.5
Beef Steak (0.86 medium steak (yield after cooking, bone removed))	440.5	26.2	0	47.7

+ Add Food

Delete this photo

Figure 1: The PlateMate user interface. Users upload photographs of their meals, which are processed through Mechanical Turk to produce a list of foods, serving sizes, and nutrition information.

crowdsourcing. Following Soylent [3], we also add an input decomposition stage at the start to parallelize work.

The result is a workflow with three major stages, shown in Figure 2. *Tag* takes photos and labels them with boxes drawn around distinct foods on a plate. *Identify* matches each box to one or more foods in a commercial nutrition database. *Measure* returns portion estimates for each identified food.

Step 1: Tag

The goal of the Tag stage is to find every food item in a photograph. One picture may depict several plates, and each plate might contain several distinct foods. Tag discovers these foods and distinguishes them by drawing a rectangle around each. The result is a group of boxes overlaid on the picture. Each box corresponds to a single food item, like a sandwich.

This step has the same benefits as the Find stage in Soylent's Find-Fix-Verify pattern [3]. Results can be surfaced more naturally in the user interface, and this makes estimates easier to understand and correct. Parallel work can also be combined more carefully, since we know which identifications describe each pictured food. Finally, the Tag step encourages completeness, preventing "Lazy Turkers" from ignoring or forgetting to match certain foods.

Drawing Boxes Tag's first Human Interactive Task (HIT) asks workers to draw boxes around each food in the picture. Workers need cultural background knowledge to understand how foods on a plate fit together. Pure computer vision can detect edges and boundaries, but it cannot recognize that an open-faced hamburger with half of the bun off to the side is in fact one item. The HIT relies on Turkers' general intuition about food items, and provides examples of sandwiches, salads, and pasta with vegetables as appropriate items.

Similarity Comparison and Voting Two Turkers are asked to tag each photo, and a combination of machine and human computation is used to select the better box group. Once both assignments are completed, they are algorithmically compared in the number, size, and position of boxes. If the two groups are sufficiently similar, one is picked at random as the final answer.

If the box groups differ significantly, three additional Turkers are shown each set overlaid on the photo and asked to select the better option, using similar guidelines. The box group receiving more votes is returned as the final result.

Step 2: Identify

The Identify step matches a tagged box to one or more food entries in a commercial nutrition database. While each box output from Tag should only contain one food, some composite items do not exist in the database. For example, if "ham and cheese sandwich" is missing, Identify should choose "wheat bread," "sliced ham," and "American cheese."

There are two main challenges in this stage. Identifications must be correct, and when several correct identifications exist, the most compact one should be used in order to simplify measurement and eventual presentation of data to end users.

In an initial pilot study, Identify was performed in a single HIT. Workers used an autocomplete text input to list each food in the box. Their answers were frequently incorrect or incomplete. Workers appeared to type a one-word description of the picture, like "chicken," and then select the first option regardless of how closely it fit. Like the "Lazy Turkers" in [3], they performed the minimal work necessary to get paid and nothing more.

These problems also occurred because the interface asked Turkers to perform two conceptually different tasks sequentially but only produce one final output. Turkers first had to identify the food in their own minds, and then locate the corresponding entries in the database. To correct for this, we developed a workflow that contained two simpler HITs. The first asks workers to describe the food in their own words. The second asks them to match this description to items in the database.

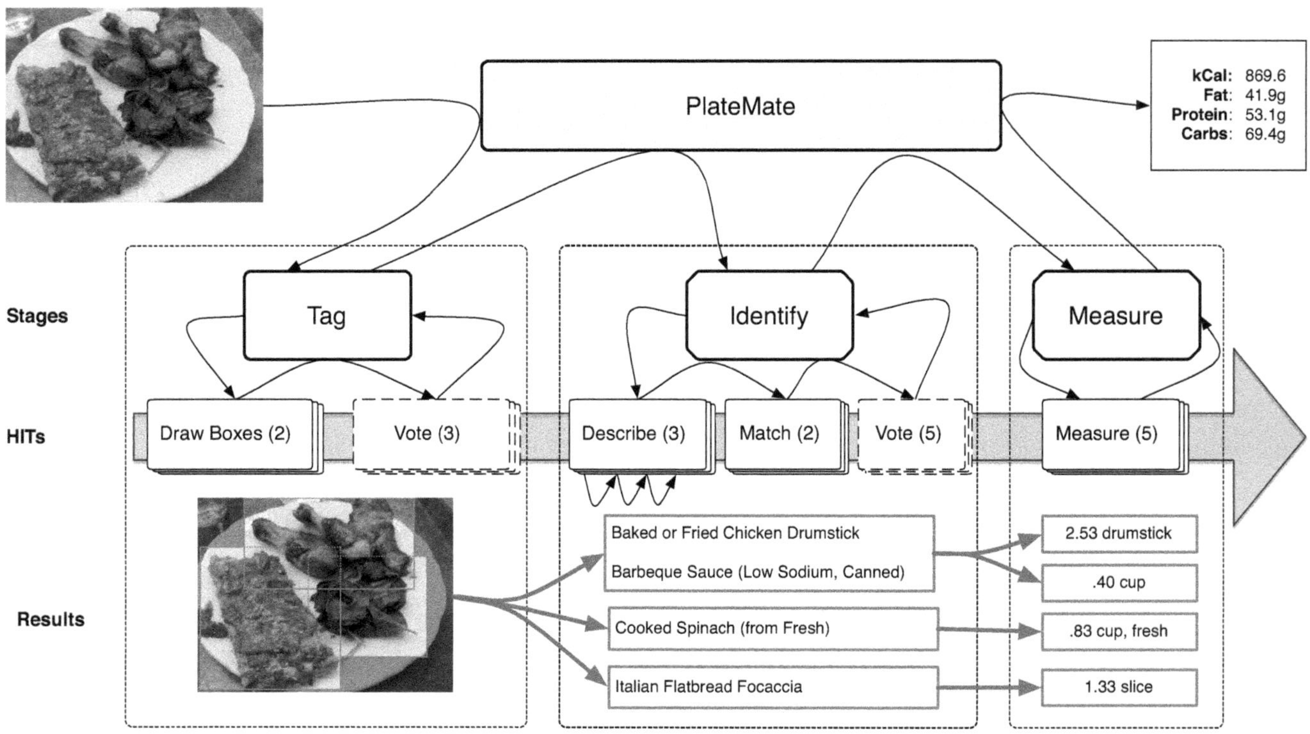

Figure 2: The PlateMate system. Work travels between stages and Human Intelligence Tasks (HITs) along the black arrows, starting from the input on the left and concluding with the output on the right. The system takes submitted photos and creates Tag tasks to annotate these photos with boxes. Each box becomes the input to a series of Identify tasks which end with a list of foods from a commercial food database. Each individual food is then input to a Measure task, which produces a unit and amount. Dashed boxes represent optional stages, which may be skipped during routing.

Describing Items In this HIT, Turkers see a box on a photo. One question asks "What is this food?", requesting one-line descriptions like "pepperoni pizza" or "salad with chicken." Another asks "What is it made of?", providing a free-form text field where workers can list component parts. For simple foods like broccoli these fields will be identical, but for composite foods the fields should have different answers that are each useful.

Following successful prior experiments in describing images [9], we made this step *iterative*. One worker starts from blank boxes. Her answer becomes input to another HIT, where the next Turker is asked to improve on it by correcting mistakes and adding detail. This process is well-suited to the "Eager Beavers" of [3], who provide minute details and list many possibilities. It also handles "Lazy Turkers" well, since terse descriptions are progressively expanded.

Matching Foods After three iterations, the output of the Describe task is fed into a Match HIT. Here, workers see the photo and the final descriptions. They are asked to select the best entry or set of entries in the database to match the box, with the descriptions as a suggestion for what to search. Workers first attempt to locate the description of the box as a whole in the database. If they find no good match, they search for each part. For example, workers should first search for "salad with chicken and tomatoes." If this fails, they should look for "chicken breast", "romaine lettuce", and "cherry tomatoes."

The search interface is modified from a standard autocomplete. Search results display below the input box, but the keyboard cannot be used for quick selection. Turkers must use the mouse to click the correct items to add. The interface also makes it clearer that multiple items can be selected through several searches. These changes negate the instinct of "Lazy Turkers" from the pilot study to select the first item they see.

This decomposition makes each step manageable for Turkers moving rapidly through HITs. The results of the Describe step are not necessary for the end goal of calculating nutrition information, but the generated descriptions reduce the mental work required for the Match step. We can then ask Turkers working on Match HITs to find the simplest representation in the database, using the Describe results as a guide.

Agreement Detection and Voting Two workers are asked to complete each Match HIT. If each returns a list pointing to the exact same item or items in the food database, then that list is used. Otherwise, five workers complete a Vote HIT to decide between them.

Step 3: Measure

The Measure step produces an estimated portion size for each food matched in Identify. Following this stage, the nutrition data for a photo can be calculated by multiplying the per-unit nutrition breakdown from the food database with the estimated measurement for each identified food.

Measure uses only one HIT, which shows Turkers a photo with a box highlighted along with the name of one food in that box. They are asked to first select a measurement unit and then provide a numeric estimate in terms of that unit. The units provided by the food database are specific to each food. "Pepperoni pizza" includes options like "slice, large" or "whole pie, medium," while "white rice, cooked" uses cups or ounces.

Measurement is considered the most difficult step of this process for amateurs [16], so the Measure stage uses a number of techniques to produce accurate results. Presenting multiple measurement options is helpful, since many of these only require counting rather than estimating a weight or volume. For example, it is much easier to count florets than to estimate grams of broccoli.

Not every food can be measured by counting. To help in cases where weight or volume estimates are necessary, HITs include a portion guide which provides common approximations for different measurements. For example, 3oz of meat looks like a deck of cards, and a quarter cup is roughly the size of a golf ball. These approximations are more error-prone than simple counting, but they allow workers to estimate portions without any training.

The interface also warns Turkers who appear to be making common errors. Pilot testing revealed that measurements in weight were significantly less accurate than those using volume or counting, so a warning is presented when Turkers choose grams, ounces, or pounds. Testing also indicated that some workers misunderstood the serving types. For example, for "chicken nuggets," one worker selected "serving, 6 nuggets" and then entered 6 as the value. This indicated 6 servings of 6 nuggets each for 36 total.

To reduce these errors, the interface generates a calorie estimate on the fly and asks workers to eyeball their answer. They are given common calorie ranges for different meals and shown warnings if the count becomes unusually low or high. These warnings cannot prevent all errors, but they encourage Turkers to double-check their answers.

Aggregating Measurements Five Turkers are presented with Measure HITs. The results from these HITs can be compared in the common units of calories. This means estimates can be aggregated without any additional human computation like voting. Drawing on the principle that averaging many high variance by low bias estimates can lead to accurate results [20], we remove outliers and then return the mean of the remaining estimates.

Turker Qualifications

After several iterations during pilot testing, we decided to accept only Turkers located in the United States who had previously completed at least 200 HITs and had a 98% HIT acceptance rate. We chose to require American Turkers due to the unique cultural context required for most elements of the process. Pilot tasks with foreign workers showed common mistakes like identifying the ketchup on a hamburger bun as strawberry jam, showing the necessity of cultural context.

THE MANAGEMENT FRAMEWORK

In this section, we introduce a programming framework for solving problems with crowds based on a human organizational hierarchy. This approach differs conceptually from prior work, which has focused on creating "crowd programming languages" that combine human and machine computation. For example, TurKit [9] lets requesters program crowds in JavaScript, Qurk [14] integrated crowds into SQL, and CrowdForge [8] parallelized work with MapReduce scripts. In each case, these toolkits have attempted to make working with crowds more like working with computers. This approach emphasizes computation as the natural glue for combining individual worker contributions and the resulting artifact is a computer program with some of the primitive operations implemented as "functional calls" to human workers [9].

Because PlateMate relies primarily on human work, divided into a number of heterogenous and interacting tasks, and because the issues of worker skill and motivation were central to our design process, we found it conceptually helpful to use human organizational hierarchies as the metaphor for designing our system. Specifically, we observe that in the real world, expert-level work (e.g., building a table) can be reproduced by less skilled workers—each working on a specific part of the process—supervised by managers who are not necessarily skilled craftsmen themselves, but who know how to assign tasks, route work among workers, and verify the quality of the work.

Thus, to implement division of labor for crowdsourcing, we created a new framework organized around objects called *managers*. Managers communicate with their supervisors and their *employees* using asynchronous message passing: managers assign tasks by placing them in inboxes of lower level managers and communicate with their superiors by placing results of completed tasks in their own outboxes. This hierarchical message-passing approach allows programmers to implement workflows by decomposing problems into progressively smaller steps.

As illustrated earlier in Figure 2, the root of this tree is a *chief* manager, which gathers new inputs and produces completed outputs. In PlateMate, the chief has three employees: Tag, Identify, and Measure. Each of these are in turn managers and have their own employees, corresponding to the individual HITs described above.

This hierarchical structure creates a flexible workflow consisting of modules connected by higher-level managers. Managers can route work intelligently among their employees, and may dynamically alter the sequence of steps in the process depending on a situation. For example, PlateMate's Tag manager compares the outputs from its DrawBoxes employee. If they are sufficiently different, they are sent to the VoteBoxes manager to decide between them. Otherwise, one answer is chosen randomly and sent up the hierarchy as Tag's completed output. All managers work in parallel, each processing its own stream of work.

When multiple tasks are submitted, processing is done just-in-time: for example, as soon as one photograph is tagged, the Identify manager begins the process of finding out what foods are present in each of the boxes without waiting for the remaining photographs to be tagged.

At the lowest level of the hierarchy are managers whose employees are the crowd workers. Managers at this level create jobs (such as asking for the food in one tagged box on a photo to be identified) and receive responses. Programmers create HIT templates and validation functions which are used by the framework to create HITs and approve work. Managers simply assign work to the crowd and receive validated outputs that can be passed up the tree.

Of course, the Management Framework *is* a computational framework, and it naturally supports a number of the recently introduced design patterns for programming the crowds. For example, the Tag step is an analog of the map step in MapReduce and the Describe step (part of Identify, see Figure 2) relies on iterative refinement [10] to improve the level of detail of the descriptions.

Management is implemented as an extension of Django, a web application framework for Python. It builds on several useful features from Django, including an HTML template language for defining HIT instructions, examples, and interfaces. It also uses Django's object-relational mapper, which automatically stores Python objects in a MySQL database. This means that the precise state of the system is always stored, including managers' inboxes and outboxes, active HITs and completed assignments, and intermediate inputs and outputs. This simplifies later analysis, since requesters can go back and query responses from each stage in the workflow. It also protects completed work from program errors or service outages; after crashes, execution simply resumes from the last good state.

EVALUATION

Our evaluation focused on PlateMate's feasibility as a replacement for traditional food logging. We considered three broad criteria:

1. **Accuracy.** How accurate were crowdsourced estimates compared to current alternatives? Could users trust them?

2. **Usability.** How much effort or discomfort would users experience in photographing food, uploading the photos, and correcting errors in PlateMate's estimates?

3. **Robustness.** How well does the PlateMate system fare with "real world" photographs?

We designed two experiments to answer these questions. In the first, nutrition data returned from PlateMate was compared with ground truth, expert dietitian estimates, and a recent commercial application. In the second study, ten participants used PlateMate and a manual food-logging system for four days.

Figure 3: Examples of photos from the study of PlateMate's accuracy.

Evaluation of Accuracy

Our first study had two goals. The first was to determine the accuracy of PlateMate with ground truth data obtained from manufacturers or preparers. The second was to compare PlateMate's performance with two alternative approaches to remote food photography: analysis by experts and results from Meal Snap. Because Meal Snap only returns calorie information and to make the task manageable for our expert participants, we limited our comparison to estimated calories even though PlateMate generates reports that also include fat, protein, and carbohydrates.

Method We conducted the experiment with a sample of 18 photographs showing 36 distinct foods. Some depicted individual foods or packages, while others showed complex plates containing many items, as shown in Figure 3. Each pictured food had nutritional data available through the manufacturer or preparer, and foods were weighed when necessary to ensure accuracy. These foods were selected to span a variety of meals and sources, including restaurants, cafeterias, and grocery items. We also included a mix of simple foods and composite items like salads and sandwiches.

We recruited three professional dietitians to provide expert estimates: one was a private nutrition counselor, and the other two were employed by a hospital. They received compensation for their time and provided estimates from their own offices. They were encouraged to use any aids, like books and calorie databases, that they would typically use for a similar task.

Our third set of estimates came from Meal Snap, a recent commercial application. Meal Snap returns a range of calories rather than a definitive answer, so we used the mean of its high and low values.

Results In terms of mean absolute error on calorie estimates, PlateMate was not significantly different from the human experts or the Meal Snap application. Figure 4 illustrates the results in detail. As expected, trained dietitians

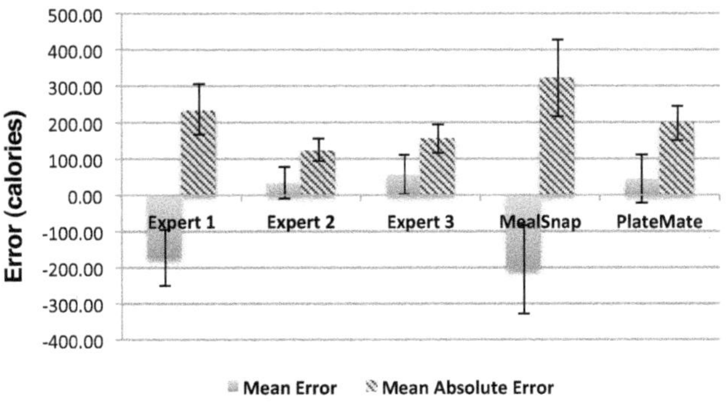

Figure 4: Mean errors (i.e., overall bias) and mean absolute errors (average magnitude of an error) for estimates made by the human experts, the Meal Snap application, and PlateMate compared to data provided by manufacturer or preparer. Error bars correspond to standard error.

were the most accurate on average. Their mean absolute error rates were 39.4%, 20.8%, and 26.1%, for an average of 172.0 calories or 28.7% per photograph. The best expert was off by just 124.5 calories, on average. PlateMate was close behind with a mean absolute error rate of 198 calories, or 33.2%. MealSnap was farther behind, with an average error rate of 322.8 calories or 53.9%.

Absolute error rates reflect the average magnitude of the error, but not the biases in each method. To understand how estimates from each source would add up over time, we also measured mean error without taking absolute values. The best expert overestimated by just 32.75 calories on average, for a mean error rate of +5.5%. The other two experts had error rates of +9.2% and −27.5%.

In comparison, PlateMate had a mean error rate of +44.1 calories, or +7.4%, which was much closer than Meal Snap's −34.4%. Expert and PlateMate results are significantly correlated with the ground truth data ($r^2 = .8626$, $.9062$, and $.9378$ for the experts, and $r^2 = .8622$ for PlateMate, all with $p < .0001$), while Meal Snap results were not correlated with the actual nutritional content of the meals ($r^2 = .2352$, $p = .3475$).

PlateMate's error rate compares favorably to amateur self-reports, where error rates can be greater than 400 calories/day and range from −76% to +24% [19, 4]. It also lacks the systematic bias towards underestimation in self-reports, especially among vulnerable users. These results indicate that PlateMate's answers, while imperfect, can be a useful nutritional guide.

Error Analysis Most errors in the study corresponded to single failures in specific parts of the pipeline. In the Tag stage, boxes were sometimes drawn improperly, leading to missing or duplicate identifications. In one photo of a brownie and banana on a small plate, only one box was drawn covering the entire banana and most of the brownie. As a result, the workers at the Identify stage omitted the brownie. On a photo of a hamburger with mushrooms, overlapping boxes were drawn over the burger and topping. In this case, the mushrooms were identified in both boxes.

Most errors occurred in the Identify stage. Turkers had trouble distinguishing similar types of a food, which sometimes had large nutrition differences. A plate of vegetarian baked beans was identified as regular baked beans, tripling the calorie count. Branded foods also caused problems: a relatively low-calorie chicken sandwich was identified as a sandwich from the restaurant Chili's, which had over twice as many calories. Another common situation involved duplication with both a composite item and one or more foods included in that composite both being selected. A slice of pizza with pepperoni and olives was identified as "Pizza with Meat and Vegetables," "Pepperoni," and "Black Olives," duplicating the toppings.

During measurement, many very small quantities were overestimated, especially when a small amount of a food was spread over a large area. A dash of parsley on a sandwich was overestimated as .27 cups, for example. Other errors occurred when one food appeared in several boxes. This led to a hamburger bun being counted as two buns when each half of the bun was seen in its own box.

User Study

Our second study looked at the subjective experience of using PlateMate as an end-to-end system for nutritional monitoring, compared to manual logging. We looked for insights about the system's usability, in terms of the inconvenience of taking photographs and the effort required to correct errors. Finally, we wanted to observe how robustly PlateMate functioned in the "real world," without any constraints on the types of photographs submitted to the system.

Method We recruited 10 participants (4 male, 6 female) via advertisements posted on several university email lists. Seven of the participants were undergraduates, two were graduate students, and one was a faculty member.

To help us evaluate the quality of the nutritional estimates generated by PlateMate and by the participants in this study, we recruited four dietitians employed at a local hospital. Two of them had also participated in the experiment evaluating the accuracy of PlateMate, where they produced the most accurate results. Participants and dietitians were compensated for their time.

Users were interviewed before and after the experiment. In the first interview, we discussed prior experiences tracking meals and trained participants on using the system. In the exit interview, we discussed their experiences using both logging methods.

During the study, we asked the participants to take photographs of their meals for four days and upload them to PlateMate once a day. For two of the days, participants received estimates generated by PlateMate and could correct those estimates. For the other two days, participants were not shown estimates and manually logged their food. Half of the participants used the manual system first and half used PlateMate first. We designed the interface for manual logging and

Figure 5: Example user photos. PlateMate handled (a) - (c) well, while (d) - (f) caused problems. In (d) the pasta with sauce in the middle was hard to see; in (e) there is no sense of scale to determine the size of the bag; and in (f) the type of milk is unclear.

correcting estimates to resemble existing commercial tools for manual food logging.

In order to assess the results produced by PlateMate compared to current consumer best practices, we used PlateMate to generate hidden estimates for participants' photos from the two days of manual recording. Participants only saw this data during the exit interviews, when they were asked to compare their own logging with the automatic estimates.

Findings from the Initial Interviews Our pre-interviews with participants confirmed that existing methods of logging food are cumbersome. All but one of the 10 had tried logging their food at some point, but most gave up after a few days or weeks. Only two participants still tried, and neither reported doing so consistently or reliably. They recalled their attempts to keep track of food as "annoying," "inconvenient," and "tedious." One subject recalled six separate failed attempts, each lasting just a few days. Some reported success when they were required to log for athletics or class projects, but recording lapsed when those commitments ended.

Despite these challenges, participants found nutritional information valuable. Eight participants reported looking at nutrition labels on packaged foods. Several reported looking up new foods out of curiosity. One participant reported revelations like "Oh wow, that's a lot of calories in dressing," and another now dilutes her juice with water after discovering how much sugar it contains.

Exit Interview Reactions We asked all ten participants their preference between using PlateMate for automatic estimates and logging manually (by any method). Seven participants said they would prefer using PlateMate in the future, citing its ease of use and the convenience of "having someone else do that for me rather than guess myself." One subject explained, "My answers were closer to guesswork; this felt more like science." The three subjects who did not prefer PlateMate felt that they could not trust it or that the process of taking photos and correcting the estimates was too cumbersome.

Subjects were divided in their perceptions of PlateMate's accuracy. Seven of 10 found the answers at least as good as their own and of these four found PlateMate's estimates to be more accurate than self reports. After seeing his own estimates and PlateMate's for the same meals, one subject said the exercise "confirmed my suspicions that you guys were more accurate than I was. The tendency is always to say 'oh, I didn't have that much.'" Three others found their own estimates and PlateMate's basically equivalent.

The other three subjects all found PlateMate less accurate than their own estimates. One said that PlateMate's answers were close, "like 80-90%, but not perfect. I want to be sure." Another still preferred PlateMate even though she could not fully trust its results. She explained, "For some people if it's not perfect they'll never use it. But for me it was great...Even if it is only half of them correct, that is fewer I have to enter manually, and the happier I am." Another user disagreed, feeling that it took more effort to correct PlateMate estimates than "do it right myself the first time."

In total, seven users said that PlateMate required less effort than manual logging, which most of these users considered unpleasant and tedious. They called it "annoying", "boring," and "not excruciating but not insignificant either." These participants said PlateMate was "definitely easier" and "much simpler," concluding that it "definitely saves me time and effort." They also found receiving the results exciting. One user explained, "it was more fun...I got the email, and my friend was like, 'Oh! Do we get to see it now?'" Another was discouraged by the difficulty of manually estimating portions, so she found it "really helpful to have someone else do that for me rather than guess myself."

PlateMate Performance Next, we analyze PlateMate's performance on photographs collected by our users. We wanted to investigate the system's robustness given a broad variety of meals and realistic variations in photograph quality. Ideally, the PlateMate estimates and manual logging data from the user study could be compared to ground truth to determine accuracy, but such data were clearly not available.

Instead, we first looked at the differences between participant and PlateMate estimates. Comparing results from 112 photos for which we had both participant and PlateMate estimates, we found the two sets of results to be positively correlated ($r^2 = 0.62$, $p < .0001$). PlateMate's estimates were slightly higher than participants', with a mean difference of $+41.0$ calories (median $+18.8$) or $+11.5\%$ that was not statistically significant (Wilcoxon $z = 686$, *n.s.*).

To gain further insight into relative accuracies of PlateMate and our participants, we presented 50 of these photographs together with both sets of nutritional estimates to 4 professional nutritionists. The nutritionists worked in pairs. Each pair was presented with a photo and two sets of numbers representing total calories, protein, fat, and carbohydrates. One of these sets came from a participant and one from PlateMate, and the experts were blind to the source of the data. They were then asked to pick the more accurate set, taking as much time as necessary and using any necessary tools and references. The dietitians in each pair were allowed to talk to each other and could choose to agree on one data set as more accurate, disagree, or say they were unable to pick one data set as more accurate.

Of the 50 user study photos, the first pair could not decide which set of nutritional estimates was more accurate in 5 cases and the second pair could not in 12 cases. Out of the decisive photos, PlateMate data was selected as more accurate 44.4% and 47.4% of the time by the two pairs. These results suggest that neither method was obviously more accurate, especially since nearly half (49.2%) of photos had estimates within 100 calories of each other.

When disagreements did happen, PlateMate's estimates were larger 63.5% of the time. This is consistent with our finding in the first study that PlateMate slightly overestimates and prior research that suggests a strong bias in manual recording towards underestimation. [17, 6]. PlateMate's estimates for daily energy intake were +229.8 calories higher than self-reports on average, a difference equivalent to four Oreo cookies every day.

Error Analysis Many of the errors seen from the user study results were similar to those already discussed from the ground truth study, but some new issues emerged. In measurement, we saw difficulty estimating portions when extreme close-up photos were taken with no sense of scale. Turkers could not agree if a bag of potato chips (Figure 5) was a portion or large bag. Scale was also a problem in identification: a small tangerine was identified as a larger orange. Other identification errors occurred when foods with nearly correct names but vastly different nutrition were selected, like "grapefruit juice" and "juice concentrate," which has eight times the calories. One Subway chicken sandwich was identified as "Subway Roasted Chicken Patty," which could be interpreted as the whole sandwich but in fact just contained the chicken.

Human errors during manual logging mostly occurred when participants forgot to log a certain food. In photo (f) of Figure 5 the participant only recorded the milk and forgot to log the muffin, which represented most of the photo's calories. In a photo of french fries, a participant forgot to record the dipping sauce next to the fries. Similar errors occurred when participants sought to simplify their recordings to save time. One subject ate a bowl of several types of fruit but recorded the entire bowl as raspberries, while PlateMate correctly identified each fruit.

Cost and Wait Times During the course of both evaluations we analyzed 262 photos using PlateMate, generating 1,553 HITs that were assigned to 199 total Turkers 4,332 times. The average cost of a single photo was $1.40. The mean time to complete analysis was 94.14 minutes, with 73% of photos completing in less than 2 hours and all photos completing in less than 6 hours.

DISCUSSION AND FUTURE DIRECTIONS

The results from our evaluations of PlateMate suggest that through careful coordination, untrained workers can approach experts in their accuracy in estimating nutrition information from photographs of meals. These estimates are close to those logged by the people who actually ate the meals. However, several issues which became apparent during the course of our evaluations could be addressed through future work.

PlateMate consistently struggled to produce good results on liquids like beverages and salad dressing. One participant drinks a low-fat latte each morning, but PlateMate consistently identified it as coffee with cream. Another only used low-fat salad dressings, which were identified as their full-fat versions. These issues could be addressed by introducing personalization mechanisms. For example, the interface could give users access to images of foods they eat frequently—instead of taking a picture of today's latte, a user would simply select a picture of last week's, ensuring correct logging and obviating the need for engaging the crowd. Statistical methods could also be used to adapt the Turker interface to emphasize the foods most common in a user's diet and thus most likely to appear in their photos. These approaches could result in improvements to both reliability and cost.

Geolocation capabilities available in many mobile devices could be used to further improve accuracy of the crowd-sourced analysis of restaurant meals. Photos could be annotated with the cuisine of the restaurant in which they were taken, providing Turkers with helpful context while maintaining the privacy of user's actual location. Integrating with existing local "check-in" applications like Foursquare[4] would make it even simpler to associate meals with their places of origin.

Permitting optional textual annotations by users (e.g., "skim latte", "mango curry") would naturally further improve accuracy and reduce cost. So would employing computer vision and machine learning for parts of the process: over time and continued use, PlateMate could build a large database mapping tagged sections of photographs to specific foods and portions. An algorithmic approach could be taken to analyze new photos for similarity with previously processed images. This could result in fully computerized analysis based on the prior crowdsourced work, extending the vision approach in [7], or these potential similar items could be surfaced in alternate HIT interfaces to Turkers as a way of skipping unnecessary stages of the PlateMate process.

This work was done on the assumption that lowering the barrier to monitoring one's food intake may result in a larger number of people persisting in their attempts to alter their eating habits. We are aware, however, that making the process too easy may reduce the opportunities for reflection. Ultimately, PlateMate's success depends on the users' willingness to engage with the information it provides. But if they do, PlateMate can help its users correct misconceptions about nutritional content of the foods they consume and to improve their ability to estimate portion sizes.

The Remote Food Photography Method relies on two images of each meal: a photograph of the original portion and a photograph of any food that was left uneaten. We have explored the first part of the process and we expect that the second can

[4] `https://foursquare.com/`

be performed in a similar manner. A major difficulty in analyzing images of leftovers is likely to be in identifying the foods in the photo. But as such foods are already identified in the first part of the process, a reasonable approach to extend PlateMate may be to display an annotated image of the original plate next to the photograph of the leftovers, and ask Turkers to identify portions of the second image where the original foods are present and, in the subsequent step, to estimate the amounts of the leftover foods. Our future work will aim to test the efficacy of such an approach and to thus fully implement the Remote Food Photography Method.

CONCLUSION

This paper presents PlateMate, which allows users to take photos of their meals and receive estimates of the meals' nutrition content. PlateMate builds on a concept of remote food photography developed recently by the nutrition community. While the original method relies on expert dietitians providing the estimates, PlateMate uses Amazon Mechanical Turk to make this approach more affordable and scalable.

Through careful decomposition of the process into small and verifiable steps, PlateMate achieves accuracy comparable to trained dietitians: the results of our evaluation demonstrate that PlateMate overestimated caloric content by $+7.4\%$ on average, while the best of three trained dietitians overestimated by $+5.5\%$. In our user study, which compared PlateMate to the currently most common practice of manual self-logging of meals, most participants found PlateMate easier and faster to use and at least as accurate. Four dietitians were unable to differentiate between nutrition estimates produced by PlateMate and those manually logged by our study participants, further suggesting parity with the current methods.

Overall, PlateMate is an attractive alternative to existing solutions because it reduces user effort compared to manual logging, achieves good accuracy, is affordable, and can be conceivably deployed to support a large number of users.

We suggest ways in which the accuracy can be further improved and cost reduced by combining crowdsourcing with machine learning, computer vision, personalization and location information.

PlateMate is one of the first complex crowdsourcing systems to combine—in a real world application—several of the recently introduced design patterns for programming the crowds. In the process of building PlateMate, we have developed the Management framework, a modular software framework inspired by the structure of human organizations. The Manager abstraction conveniently supported hierarchical problem decomposition as well as modular development and debugging. The choice of message passing as the main communication mechanism cleanly supports asynchronous just-in-time processing of sub-tasks. PlateMate may serve as a useful case study for future developers of complex crowd-based applications.

REFERENCES

1. Amft, O., Stäger, M., Lukowicz, P., and Tröster, G. Analysis of chewing sounds for dietary monitoring. In *Ubicomp*. Springer, 2005, volume 3660 of *Lecture Notes in Computer Science*, 56–72.
2. Ann Yon, B., Johnson, R., Harvey-Berino, J., and Gold, B. The use of a personal digital assistant for dietary self-monitoring does not improve the validity of self-reports of energy intake. *Journal of the American Dietetic Association, 106*, 8 (2006), 1256–1259.
3. Bernstein, M., Little, G., Miller, R., Hartmann, B., Ackerman, M., Karger, D., Crowell, D., and Panovich, K. Soylent: a word processor with a crowd inside. In *Proc. UIST'10*. ACM, 2010, 313–322.
4. Champagne, C., Bray, G., Kurtz, A., Monteiro, J., Tucker, E., Volaufova, J., and Delany, J. Energy intake and energy expenditure:: A controlled study comparing dietitians and non-dietitians. *Journal of the American Dietetic Association, 102*, 10 (2002), 1428–1432.
5. Dinkins, J. Beliefs and attitudes of americans towards their diet. US Department of Agriculture Center for Nutrition Policy and Promotion (2000).
6. Goris, A., Westerterp-Plantenga, M., and Westerterp, K. Undereating and underrecording of habitual food intake in obese men: selective underreporting of fat intake. *The American journal of clinical nutrition, 71*, 1 (2000), 130.
7. Kitamura, K., de Silva, C., Yamasaki, T., and Aizawa, K. Image processing based approach to food balance analysis for personal food logging. In *IEEE International Conference on Multimedia and Expo (ICME)*. IEEE, 2010, 625–630.
8. Kittur, A., Smus, B., and Kraut, R. *CrowdForge: Crowdsourcing Complex Work*. Technical Report CMU-HCII-11-100, CMU (2011).
9. Little, G., Chilton, L., Goldman, M., and Miller, R. Turkit: human computation algorithms on mechanical turk. In *Proc. UIST'10*. ACM, 2010, 57–66.
10. Little, G., Chilton, L. B., Goldman, M., and Miller, R. C. Exploring iterative and parallel human computation processes. In *Proc. ACM SIGKDD Workshop on Human Computation*. ACM, New York, NY, USA, 2010, HCOMP '10, 68–76.
11. Locke, E. and Latham, G. Building a practically useful theory of goal setting and task motivation. *American Psychologist, 57*, 9 (2002), 705–717.
12. Mankoff, J., Hsieh, G., Hung, H. C., Lee, S., and Nitao, E. Using low-cost sensing to support nutritional awareness. In *Proc. UbiComp '02*. Springer-Verlag, London, UK, 2002, 371–376.
13. Mann, T., Tomiyama, A., Westling, E., Lew, A., Samuels, B., and Chatman, J. Medicare's search for effective obesity treatments: Diets are not the answer. *American Psychologist, 62*, 3 (2007), 220.

14. Marcus, A., Wu, E., Karger, D., Madden, S., and Miller, R. Crowdsourced databases: Query processing with people. In *CIDR*. 2011.

15. Martin, C., Anton, S., York-Crowe, E., Heilbronn, L., VanSkiver, C., Redman, L., Greenway, F., Ravussin, E., and Williamson, D. Empirical evaluation of the ability to learn a calorie counting system and estimate portion size and food intake. *British Journal of Nutrition*, *98*, 02 (2007), 439–444.

16. Martin, C., Han, H., Coulon, S., Allen, H., Champagne, C., and Anton, S. A novel method to remotely measure food intake of free-living individuals in real time: the remote food photography method. *British Journal of Nutrition*, *101*, 03 (2009), 446–456.

17. Pikholz, C., Swinburn, B., and Metcalf, P. Under-reporting of energy intake in the 1997 national nutrition survey. *The New Zealand Medical Journal*, *117*, 1202 (2004).

18. Reisner, R. and Thompson, D. The diet industry: A big fat lie. *BuisinessWeek* (2008).

19. Schoeller, D., Bandini, L., and Dietz, W. Inaccuracies in self-reported intake identified by comparison with the doubly labelled water method. *Canadian journal of physiology and pharmacology*, *68*, 7 (1990), 941.

20. Surowiecki, J. *The wisdom of crowds: why the many are smarter than the few and how collective wisdom shapes business, economies, societies, and nations.* Doubleday, 2004.

21. Yon, B., Johnson, R., Harvey-Berino, J., Gold, B., and Howard, A. Personal digital assistants are comparable to traditional diaries for dietary self-monitoring during a weight loss program. *Journal of behavioral medicine*, *30*, 2 (2007), 165–175.

Instrumenting the Crowd: Using Implicit Behavioral Measures to Predict Task Performance

Jeffrey M. Rzeszotarski, Aniket Kittur
Human-Computer Interaction Institute
Carnegie Mellon University
Pittsburgh, PA
{jeffrz, nkittur}@cs.cmu.edu

ABSTRACT

Detecting and correcting low quality submissions in crowd-sourcing tasks is an important challenge. Prior work has primarily focused on worker outcomes or reputation, using approaches such as agreement across workers or with a gold standard to evaluate quality. We propose an alternative and complementary technique that focuses on the way workers work rather than the products they produce. Our technique captures behavioral traces from online crowd workers and uses them to predict outcome measures such quality, errors, and the likelihood of cheating. We evaluate the effectiveness of the approach across three contexts including classification, generation, and comprehension tasks. The results indicate that we can build predictive models of task performance based on behavioral traces alone, and that these models generalize to related tasks. Finally, we discuss limitations and extensions of the approach.

ACM Classification: H5.2 Information interfaces and presentation (e.g., HCI) --- User Interfaces: Evaluation / methodology, Theory Methods;

General terms: Human Factors, Measurement

Keywords: Crowdsourcing, Mechanical Turk, Event Logging, User Logging, User Behavior, Performance

INTRODUCTION

Crowdsourcing markets like Amazon's Mechanical Turk (MTurk) allow users to rapidly disseminate large quantities of small tasks to a large pool of willing workers. This empowers researchers to assemble large datasets of human labeled corpora, corporations to outsource simple data processing, and even one day to have individuals utilize crowdworkers to complete tasks in their own word processors [1, 2]. The ability to quickly and effectively reach a willing microtask work force has the potential to change the way work is done in society.

However, the distributed nature of such markets can pose challenges for employers. Because tasks are typically small, short, and high volume, workers can expend minimal effort or even cheat on jobs as their output often blends in with the crowd. This is especially true for subjective tasks or those with multiple valid answers, which can attract cheating rates of over 30% [15]. Adding to this issue is the limited reputation system in MTurk which only tracks the total percentage of work a worker has had accepted; cheaters can slip through and even maintain high reputations by accepting tasks they are unlikely to get rejected for. Even if workers are not cheating, there can be high variability in the quality of their work due to differences in effort or skill [2].

Significant research efforts have been made to develop ways to detect and correct for low quality work in order to improve the overall quality of the resulting data. Researchers have proposed a variety of approaches to address this issue, ranging from using gold standards to post-hoc weighting based on worker agreement or reputation [2, 4, 12]. Most of these approaches rely on a single aspect of the workflow in human computation markets: the end products. With only the end products of the work process and some minimal reputation metrics about the workers involved, employers must make difficult tradeoffs depending on the quality control method they use. For example, methods based on worker agreement rely on multiple redundant worker judgments, while gold standards require some percentage of labeled data.

We present an alternative and complementary technique for evaluating task performance on crowdsourcing markets: examining the way the workers work, rather than the products they produce. The work process itself may provide information as to the effort, skills, and behavior of the worker which may be useful for predicting their output quality. For example, imagine two different workers tasked with tagging an image. The lazy worker, after accepting the task, may immediately scroll to the text fields, type their first tag, tab to the second field, and without delay enter their second tag. The conscientious worker, after accepting the task, may pause while inspecting the image, scroll to the text fields, type their first tag, scroll back to the image, pause again, and then type their second tag. An employer presented only with the behavioral patterns of each worker might be able to tell the conscientious worker from the lazy worker, and weight their judgments accordingly.

In this paper we examine whether crowdworkers' behavioral traces as they complete work can actually be used to predict the quality of their final product. We propose a technique we call *task fingerprinting* to collect and analyze such behavioral traces in online task markets (though the technique may generalize to other settings as well). We describe a prototype implementation of task fingerprinting on the Amazon Mechanical Turk market, and test its efficacy in three different task contexts. Our results demonstrate how workers' behavioral traces can be used to make inferences about their task performance, including identifying cheaters, estimating output quality, and predicting errors. Finally, we discuss some limitations and extensions of the task fingerprinting approach, and explore applications beyond the crowdsourcing context.

TASK FINGERPRINTING

A task involves a worker performing some actions on an input (typically provided by the employer) resulting in some output. The input might be an image to tag, a document to summarize, or even just a set of guidelines for open response. Using this input, the worker engages in a series of cognitive and motor actions that result in changes in their web browser (e.g., mouse movements, scrolling, keystrokes) and produces an end product for the requester. This process can be represented as:

$$f_{worker}(\text{input}_{task}) = \text{output}_{task,\ worker}$$

where the input is given by the employer, some sequence of cognitive and motor actions are performed by the worker (f_{worker}) on the input, generating some output that is consumed by the employer. Common methods for quality control alter the design of the input or evaluate the output side of the function, since the cognitive effort and skills of the worker (in f) are not directly observable. Yet, if evaluation based on the *process* of generating results were effective, it would result in a number of benefits. In contrast to gold standard approaches, one could make inferences about the quality of the output even without labeled data; or even having to inspect the output at all. And unlike output agreement approaches, predictions of quality could be made without many redundant judgments from different workers. Furthermore, assuming workers are consistent in their behaviors across tasks (which we examine in more detail later), we could use information about their work process on one task to make inferences about their work on other tasks. For example, we could identify workers that ignore the guidelines of one task so that we could flag all of their work across all tasks for closer examination.

We propose *task fingerprinting* as a means to capture the process that crowdworkers use to complete a task, as embodied by their interactions with their computer interface. By logging what workers do in their interface while working on the task, we can develop a quantitative description of their process which will allow us to compare workers and evaluate end products, make inferences about worker cognition, and determine how effective a worker pool is at a given task and set of data.

Task fingerprints can assume a variety of structures to quantitatively describe what workers do. In their raw form, they are sequential logs of interface events; what the workers did, and when. The sequences encode valuable information, such as the order of operations, time delays between actions, and patterns of labor. Refining this raw data, we can gather summary statistical data, such as counts of different actions or the occurrence of outlier behaviors like copy-pasting, that can be used to compare workers. Machine learning based on the input and fingerprint can be used to infer characteristics of the output such as its probable quality or the likelihood that the worker was cheating. Visualization of the fingerprints might enable human outlier and pattern detection in large sets of workers.

RELATED WORK

Our work is related both to evaluation efforts in crowdsourcing and to user event logging.

Evaluating Crowdsourcing Outcomes

There are at least two general approaches researchers have explored for obtaining good data from crowdworkers. Pre-task approaches focus on designing tasks so that they are resistant to poor responses (e.g., von Ahn and Dabbish). For example, in the context of MTurk, Kittur et al. propose that tasks be designed in such a way that performing poorly or cheating is as costly as contributing in good-faith [15]. Other approaches include promoting intrinsical motivation [18], splitting larger tasks into small, fault-tolerant subtasks [1, 19], incorporating randomness in cooperative task designs [23], financial manipulation and tweaking outcome measures [10, 16]. While these can be effective strategies, they require that tasks be specially tailored for the approach.

Other researchers address the low quality data problem using a post-hoc approach, controlling or correcting for workers' outputs. One common way is to use validated gold standard data to sort out good workers from bad [2, 5]. However gold standard data is not always available or applicable, as is the case in some generative tasks like tagging and summarization. Other work calculates relationships between worker answers or identifies erroneous workers using trends to reduce bias [2, 4, 12, 20]. A congruent approach is to have workers rate other workers in a verification step [1]. While these techniques can be effective, they also have drawbacks; for example, approaches based on worker agreement require a number of redundant judgments, may be susceptible to gaming or majority effects, and may not work well when there are a broad range of valid answers or most answers are unique.

Our methodology of harnessing workers' implicit behaviors provides a number of advantages over the above approaches. First, models of user behavior can generalize across tasks. Second, collecting additional data about the worker's behavior has the potential to improve predictions beyond the theoretical limits of just using a worker's identity and their end products. Third, our method doesn't require knowledge of 'correct' answers, and supports having

Diligent	S_{191px}	M_{33x52y}	C_{Tag1}	$D_{1.1s}$	$K_{OUTSIDE}$	$S_{=198px}$	$D_{1.8s}$	S_{89px}	C_{Tag2}	$K_{PLAYING}$	S_{40px}	C_{Submit}
Lazy	S_{185px}	M_{44x51y}	C_{Tag1}	$K_{MAN<tab>}$	K_{DOG}	S_{50px}		$D_{5.3s}$				C_{Submit}

S=Scroll$_{Amount}$ M=Mouse Movement$_{Distance}$ D=Delay$_{TimePassed}$ C=Click$_{Target}$ K=Keypress$_{Key}$

Figure 1: Example refined event logs for tagging an image with both 'lazy' and 'diligent' workers. The lazy worker quickly writes simplistic tags, while the diligent worker takes time to think and check the source image between tags.

a range of valid answers. Fourth, it can scale down to a small worker pool, making judgments even about individual workers.

On the other hand, our technique falls victim to some of the same problems that affect post-hoc analysis, including majority effects and automated task completers. The method can be improved by combining it with other techniques (e.g. including gold standard data), and we will discuss additional ways to improve our technique in the limitations section.

User Event Logging

HCI researchers have spent considerable effort on capturing and analyzing event logs, primarily for the purposes of evaluating usability [9]. Kim et al. used event logs from video games to remove player frustrations by identifying game components that were causing trouble [14]. Chi et al. used simulated logs to visualize the usability of web pages [3]. Ivory and Hearst evaluated a large number of automation systems, concluding that although automated logging is still not widely implemented, it has cost benefits and allows for quick design comparisons [13].

Event logs have also been used to predict cognitive and user outcomes, for example detecting gender differences in problem solving [6], survey logging [21], predicting age and cognitive impairment [11], and skill levels of users for adaptive interfaces, and estimating the complexity of tasks [7, 17].

Other research applies event logs to process mining. Rather than log small granular actions, workflow and process mining examines logs of larger transactions. These systems allow users to model behavioral patterns among workers and determine worker processes necessary to complete certain tasks [22].

The previous findings indicate that not only do user event logs encode information about performance, but also about skill and user behavior. Our work extends this research to examine the feasibility of using user event logs in a crowdsourcing context across different types of tasks, with a focus not on the usability of the system but instead on predicting the quality of task outcomes.

IMPLEMENTATION

We prototyped a task fingerprinting system that uses Javascript and the jQuery library to monitor user activity on crowdsourcing market web pages. Each time the user clicks within the page, presses a key, scrolls, changes focus, or moves their mouse, an event is triggered and recorded to a list along with a unique user hash, a page hash, event information such as mouse position or which key pressed, and a timestamp (to the millisecond). After completing the task, the user uploads the collected log to a server through an opt-in button. The server uses the Django web framework to record each event in the usage data as a row in an SQLite database for later analysis. The system is portable and able to log users on any website, however the database must be hosted by the web site, as cross site scripting limitations make uploading log data very difficult otherwise.

Event logs are discretized on the server to facilitate analysis, with sequences of scrolling and mouse movement encoded into individual events for each 200 pixels total moved or scrolled. We found it useful to make two refinements to the above approach. First, repeated sequential events, such as mouse movements or scrolling, are encoded into individual events with aggregate information (total mouse movement from start to end, total scrolled position); this avoids simple "spoofing" attacks such as extended scrolling or mouse movement without other activity (Figure 1). Second, discretization may miss significant delay information (for example, if the user scrolls, then reads without moving their mouse, then scrolls again). To address this, we use *delay* events to encode temporal information into the log: if a user waits longer than a specific time threshold (here we use 200 milliseconds) a delay event is encoded, with further delay events added for every 200 milliseconds the user waits.

In addition, we also collect information that characterizes the user's behavior in a holistic sense (see Table 1). Firstly, we generate summary data, such as the total time the system was logging activity, the counts of different types of events, the total amount of scrolling and mouse movement, and the lengths of the raw and collapsed event logs. These allow us to get a general sense of what a user is doing in the environment. Secondly, we collect more specific information about the events, such as the number of time certain special keys like tab and backspace were used, the number of times a user pastes text, a total count of the number of unique keys a user presses, and how many form fields were accessed. This information can help expose users with especially unique behavioral patterns. Finally, we collect information about the delays the user introduces into their work. We determine how long the user spent 'off focus' from the page, the cumulative time they spent before they started typing in a form field, and the cumulative time they spent between keystrokes in a form field. We can use these features to make higher level judgments about user deliberation and attention in tasks. For crowdsourcing markets such as Mechanical Turk, we incorporate the time the mar-

General Information

Raw Log Length	Assignment ID
Refined Log Length	Worker ID
Discretized Log Length	

Timing

Total Task Time	Before Typing Delay
On Focus Time	Within Typing Delay
Recorded Time Disparity	

Action Counts

Total Clicks	Total Keypresses
Total Mouse Movement	Total Pastes
Total Scrolled Pixels	Total Tabs
Total Fields Accessed	Total Backspaces
Total Focus Changes	Count of Unique Characters

Table 1: Aggregate data collected by the prototype

ket reports they spent on the task, and their unique worker identification.

Our implementation exposed several limitations in event logging using Javascript. Foremost, cross-browser compatibility, despite many standardization efforts, remains poor. Some browsers accurately report when the user focus changes from a window, others provide no feedback whatsoever. Some browsers report keystrokes accurately, others provide questionable information about special characters. Likewise, browser extensions that prevent JavaScript from running, such as NoScript, completely inhibit logging. Latency is also an issue, as sending events as they occur to the server proved to be less reliable than a one-shot upload at the end of the task. As implemented presently, there is little to no latency in our logging scheme since the user data is uploaded at the end of the task. In future work we will explore more reliable means of periodic updating. Finally, user logging has privacy implications, as such a script can send sensitive user data without any signals to the user. Our decision to use an opt-in approach addressed both the latency and privacy issues in a way that fit the Mechanical Turk market; however the technique does not require this be the case.

EXPLORATION AND EVALUATION

To evaluate the utility of task fingerprinting, we examined collections of workers performing a series of tasks on Amazon's Mechanical Turk crowdsourcing market. Mechanical Turk is a rich arena for studying tasks, as workers are willing and able to complete jobs ranging from the minute, like identifying parts of speech, to the complex, like comprehending a passage or composing a summary. Further, there are enough workers on Mechanical Turk that one is likely to get a good sample of worker behaviors for a given task [15, 20].

We conducted three different experiments on Mechanical Turk designed to highlight a variety of cognitive tasks that crowdworkers may do and the applications task fingerprinting has in such work. Our first experiment has Turkers identify words that are nouns in a list. This task relies on simple word recognition, and can therefore be performed rapidly and workers can complete multiple tasks in quick succession. We can evaluate the results simply by counting labeling errors. Our second experiment has Turkers generate keyword tags for four different images. Since this task is generative, there is a large spectrum of results that a worker can produce, which we evaluate by both the quantity of tags and the descriptive value of the tags. Our final experiment has Turkers read a passage and answer reading comprehension questions. The evaluation, based on correct answers, provides insight into the worker's understanding of the text. For each experiment we solicit workers on Mechanical Turk, capture their behavior using our prototype, validate that our observations align with their end products, develop a task fingerprint using our observations, and apply the task fingerprint to the evaluation of the task using Weka, a machine learning toolkit [8].

Classification Tasks

We had Mechanical Turk workers perform data labeling, a type of task often used on human computation markets. Workers were presented with a HIT (Human Intelligence Task) that presented them with a list of 40 words and asked them to check boxes for words that were nouns and leave non-nouns unchecked. On average, each HIT had 11 nouns and 29 verbs, adjectives, or adverbs between 4 and 9 characters selected from the Moby and Wordnet databases intersected with an English as a second language dictionary so as to choose easier words. Payment was set at $0.05, somewhat high for a task of its magnitude, in order to encourage cheating as well as unscrupulous behavior. We

Task	Input Type	Submissions	Evaluation Measures
Classification	word ☑	185	Noun identification accuracy
Content Generation	tag	114	Rated quality, 'cheated' label
Comprehension	A ○ B ◉	63	Question answering accuracy

Table 2: Experimental conditions

solicited a total of 5 instances of each of 40 different labeling tasks, totaling 200 requests. Of those 200 requests, 15 were excluded because their browsers did not relay event logs. 21 unique participants generated the remaining 185 points in this task.

We evaluated participants based on the number of 'correct' answers they gave, where a correct answer meant checking a noun and leaving a non-noun unchecked. On average people correctly classified 83% of words (*SD*=14.1), compared to an average of 73% if they had left the form completely blank. Because the participant average is below even what would be the case if they only checked half the nouns and left the rest blank (86%), it is likely that a fair percentage of workers put forward a minimum amount of effort.

Results: Task Time

While task time can be a useful metric for identifying non-compliant workers, as researchers using Mechanical Turk are well aware, task times reported by the system can be dramatically different from the actual time a worker spent on completing a task [15]. Workers may often accept multiple tasks and leave them open while finishing others. Our data enables us to examine how large the discrepancy is between reported and actual work time for tasks. Examining all of the worker logs, which averaged 32.7 refined events, we discover that workers spent on average 1 minute, 13 seconds completing the task and clicked on checkboxes 9.5 times. The time of task completion recorded by Mechanical Turk's system was off by an average of 21.1 seconds from recorded on-task time. As shown in Figure 2, this disparity is unevenly distributed, with a few tasks accepted but not worked on for a long time period. Interestingly, tasks with high reported vs. actual time discrepancies may also tend to be of lower quality. In our later reading comprehension task, higher time disparity was marginally correlated with more errors ($F(1,62) = 3.28$, $p=0.075$) This suggests that although the raw reported time from Mechanical Turk may not be dependable as a measure of effort (as workers may accept and queue tasks), using the disparity between reported and actual time may actually offer some information about the quality of the work.

Results: Accuracy

We used machine learning to predict our quantitative evaluation of the labels each Turker provided using the task fingerprints. After removing non-essential features such as keyboard presses and delays (since there was no typing),

First, we investigated a binary prediction task, using a pass/fail threshold of 80% (where "pass" corresponds to a generous threshold of identifying 3 nouns accurately with no non-nouns checked; 69 of 185 participants fail this milestone and 116 pass). This threshold also is consistent with the 30% cheating ratio found by other crowdsourcing researchers [1, 15]. After identifying the most predictive features, we used Weka to generate decision trees to predict

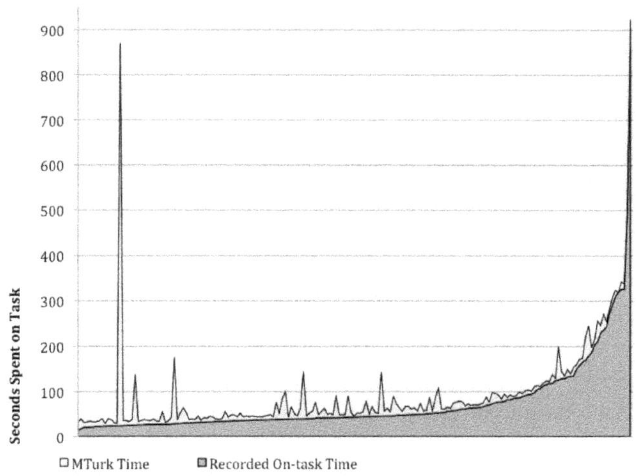

Figure 2: Time disparity between our logged 'on task' time and MTurk's recorded task time (in seconds) on the word classification task.

our pass/fail classification[1]. We limited the number of features used in these trees to maximize generality and avoid overfitting. Our initial tree utilized the number of clicks, checkboxes accessed, and the difference between the Turk recorded time and our event log time. Using 10-fold cross-validation, the model predicted our pass/fail evaluation for the 185 data points with 83.2% accuracy, a kappa of 0.608, and an F-measure of 0.823. This suggests such a model could highlight points of interest for exclusion or human inspection. However, since many of the checkboxes were correct in their default unchecked form, we considered the possibility that the number of fields accessed may be too directly tied to our choice of leaving nouns in the minority. Removing those fields, we generated a decision tree that utilized the total amount a user scrolls and moves the mouse as well as the disparity between recorded task times. This model, using only summary statistics about the user's behavior, classified the points with 78.3% accuracy, a kappa of 0.534, and an F-measure of .784, reinforcing our suggestion that even with limited fingerprint data, a model could highlight questionable points in a large sample of end products.

Beyond classifying workers' products as suspect, we investigated whether we could predict the raw accuracy score of a given worker using only their fingerprint. Using support vector regression, we trained models from the fingerprints and accuracy scores. Under 10-fold cross-validation, our model significantly correlated with the actual accuracies we recorded ($r=0.3289$, $p<0.001$). This suggests the model may be suitable for identifying high quality work in a large sample of completed submissions. By incorporating worker

[1] We initially tested our data with both decision trees and SVMs and found that they both provided similarly high levels of accuracy. We chose decision trees because their small set of features is easy to interpret and describe with respect to user behavior.

Image	Quality Rating	Predicted Rating	Tags
	4.5	4.799	Orange, Storm, Mountain, Night, Clouds, Sky
	3	3.33	Tree, Cloud, Sky
	1	1.02	<no tags, with comment 'he he he!!!!'>

Table 3: Rated quality versus model predicted quality with tags for one of the four images tagged by the worker

identity we further improved the model, boosting the correlation higher (r=0.8926, p<0.001). Similarly, adding worker identity and predicting a pass/fail score using a decision tree without clicks classifies better than our previous classifier, having an accuracy of 85.4%, a kappa of 0.681, and an F-measure of 0.856. Examining the trees, it is clear that accounting for intra-worker variance has significant benefits, since workers seem to produce similar quality work across multiple iterations of the task.

In summary, we found that task fingerprinting is able to predict the outcomes of simple labeling tasks in Mechanical Turk, even when cheating and low-quality results represent a large proportion of the data. Moreover, limiting the task fingerprint to simple features such as cumulative mouse movement and scrolling is effective. However, human computation tasks are not limited to binary labeling. Next we examine a more complex task with a different set of evaluation criteria.

Content Generation Tasks

To investigate content generation HITs on Mechanical Turk, we had Turkers supply three to five keyword tags for each of four images. We generated three different sets of images based on three themes: art, pets, and landscapes. For each of the themes, we solicited 20 submissions. To gather more variance, we generated a duplicate set of the series of tasks, this time explicitly asking for workers to pretend they were clever cheaters. Their new task was to try to complete the same tagging task with the minimum of effort needed to avoid being caught by an inattentive requester. We requested a similar group of 20 submissions for each image set under this condition. Our examinations of the end products revealed that this 'cheating' group in fact produced many acceptable submissions, suggesting that some of the workers may not have comprehended the nature of the cheating task or that "clever" cheating may actually have been more difficult than doing the task in good faith [15]. As a result, we combined the two datasets into one that represented a broader range of work quality. Of the 120 submissions, we excluded 6 from which we did not receive event logs. The remaining 114 points represent the work of 52 unique participants.

Unlike in the noun identification task, we did not have gold standard images and tags to provide a quantitative evaluation. Instead, we had two raters examine each group of tags with respect to the set of images and judge them on two five point scales. The first scale concerned the *quantity* of work done, where a value of 1 represented clear cheating or no work completed, 3 meant an adequate amount of work according to the HIT directions, and 5 represented exceptional effort. The second scale concerned the *descriptiveness* of completed work, where 1 corresponded to poor quality, specious, or empty tags, 3 represented tags that accurately described the images, and 5 meant exceptionally descriptive tags. The raters rated the 114 points with high interrater reliability (Spearman's ρ = 0.7541, 0.7636; p<0.001, p<0.001 respectively). The two scales are correlated, suggesting they indeed measure an innate *quality* aspect of the task results, as confirmed by their high item reliability (Cronbach's α = 0.8248). As a result we averaged the results of the two scales into one rating for general performance, and of the 114 points, the rating for submissions averaged to 3.5 out of 5 (SD=1.13). We also had the raters decide by consensus from the submitted tags whether a submission represented cheating. Of our points, 17, or 14.1%, were identified as clear cheats. This proportion is smaller than in our previous experiment likely because the task was more complex and there were a small number of tasks to complete in series, thus making them less attractive to potential cheaters.

We constructed task fingerprints as before from the logs, which averaged 107.9 events. On average, the workers spent 2 minutes, 32 seconds on the task, spending in total an average of 39.7 seconds before they typed a tag in a field, and 30.3 seconds typing their tags. On average they used 20.5 different characters and typed 105.8 keystrokes. The Mechanical Turk system reported times that were on average 27.1 seconds longer than our recorded on-task time.

We investigated whether the fingerprints for image tagging could predict whether a person cheated or not using a logistic decision tree. The resulting tree weighted primarily for the number of unique ASCII characters used and the total time spent on the task. Under 10-fold crossvalidation it achieved 93.0% accuracy, a kappa of 0.655, and an F-measure of 0.930 using only those two attributes. The tree structure suggests that cheaters might use fewer unique keyboard keys (leading to fewer distinct tags) and take less time to complete the task than non-cheaters.

Given this success, we also used support vector regression on the task fingerprints to predict the rated quality of the results. The resulting model significantly predicts quality (correlation with actual ratings: r = .5874, p<0.001). It suggests that the more fields accessed, more unique characters, fewer total keypresses, more clicks, and more total time spent predict higher scores. In summary, the model can suggest how good tags will be without knowledge of the tags themselves.

We also examined whether our system could predict high quality outcomes, as opposed to just cheaters and low quality output. After filtering the data to only acceptable submissions and higher, we applied support vector regression to the remaining 81 high scoring points. Once again, our model was highly correlated with the actual scores ($r=0.4598$, $p<0.001$). Thus, given only high quality data, we can still predict the quality rating of submitted tags.

Our results suggest that for even qualitative, generative tasks like image tagging, task fingerprints encode information that can help identify cheaters and predict the quality of the tags produced. The predictions relied on low-fidelity statistical information, such as the number of unique keys used and the total time on task. One can imagine quality ratings from the predictions functioning as confidence values for the set of tags produced. From there, tags from many jobs could be ranked cumulatively by order of quality. Yet, while generative tasks represent another area of human computation, there still remain more complex tasks. Does task fingerprinting function in tasks where cognitive processing may be less evident through the keyboard?

Comprehension Tasks

We chose reading comprehension for our evaluation of task fingerprinting in complex cognitive work on Mechanical Turk. We gave workers a passage from an online test preparation booklet in English and had them read the text and then answer questions based on their reading. We ascertained their level of comprehension through 9 questions: 8 multiple-choice, and 1 short response sampled from the same test preparation booklet. Of the 8 multiple-choice questions, we added one question that could be answered easily using only the text from another question without even examining the passage. This allowed us to evaluate whether a Turker was even paying attention to the questions they were answering, or were clicking random answers. We solicited 35 responses for each of two different passages, one corresponding to the physicist Marie Curie, the other expositing on the circumnavigation of the globe. Of the 70 Mechanical Turk results, we received 63 unique event logs from 45 different participants. Only 4 submissions failed the test question, suggesting that by and large the Turkers were at least reading and understanding the questions. On average the workers got 5.32 questions correct out of 9 (SD=1.97). Examining the task fingerprints, workers spent an average of 6 minutes, 2.9 seconds on the task, and their task time as reported by Mechanical Turk differs from our recorded on-task time by an average of 37.4 seconds. Refined logs averaged 298.6 events because of scrolling and mouse moment.

As in the previous cases, we used the task fingerprints to predict the performance of workers on the task. In this case, our performance measure is the number of correct answers a worker entered, which approximates their overall learning and comprehension from the passage. Using support vector regression, task fingerprints significantly predicted the comprehension level of Turkers ($r=0.260$, $p=0.0393$). The predictive model depended largely on the time spent on focus, the difference between the recorded HIT time and our event log time, the total mouse and scroll movement, the number of clicks, and the delay between typing characters in the short response. The typing delay might relate to the fact that many successful submissions copy-pasted their answer to the short answer question from the passage. This produces a zero typing delay, which explains the negative relation between delay and number correct. Mouse movement and scrolling might capture the behavior of workers that often refer to the passage when answering questions. Based on these findings, we suggest that task fingerprints indeed hold predictive value for higher cognitive tasks and functions in crowd workers.

Avoiding Manual Labeling

In the previous experiments we utilized fully labeled data. It is likely to be the case that the data used for crowdsourcing is neither perfect nor gold standard. More often than not, it is likely to be unlabeled and hard to evaluate by hand. Given our previous experiments' reliance on predicting labels based on an entire scored dataset, we now investigate three different means to reducing the burden on requesters in actually applying task fingerprinting to crowdsourced tasks.

We conducted test runs of our image tagging and word identification data training on only small randomly selected proportions of the total labeled data points. We posit that if we are able to predict the rest of the dataset with reasonable accuracy, then it is likely that requesters need not label their entire dataset. Rather, they need only label a small subset to provide the necessary training for a task fingerprint predictor. In the case of image tagging, we trained a qualitative performance rating support vector regression model using 5% through 60% of the data, in increments of ten percent, averaging 20 runs that use a different random selection of data points each time. Although the model cannot significantly predict performance using 5% and 10% of the data, for 20% of the data (23 points) and above the model predictions significantly correlate to the actual ratings. There is enough data in the task fingerprints that a small sample and a generalized machine learning model can provide good accuracy. Running a similar prediction for accuracy in our word identification task reinforces this: Once again, from 20% of the data (37 points) onwards the model's predictions correlated with significance to the actual accuracy values. Thus, one way to avoid being overburdened with labeling is to simply label a selection of random points, create a classifier using the task fingerprints, and examine selected results to ensure it is behaving appropriately.

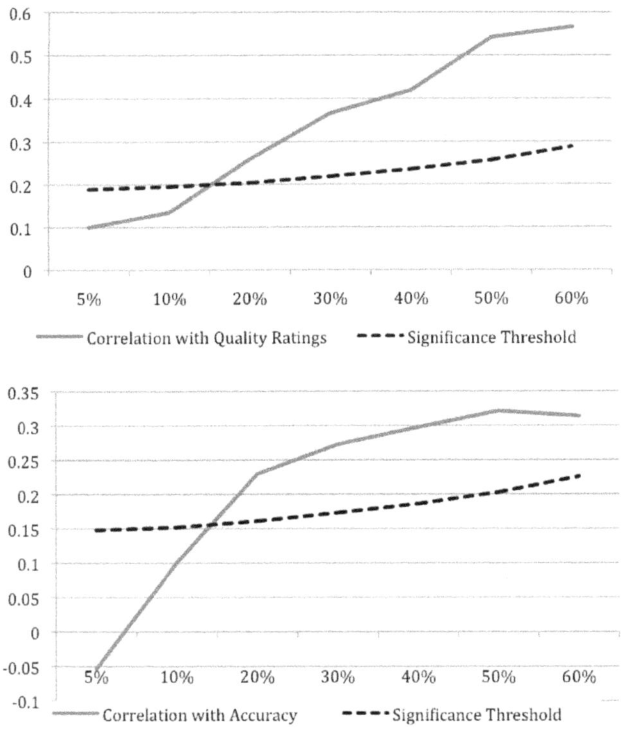

Figure 3: Model prediction correlation with actual ratings as training set size increases for image tagging and word identification

However, labeling data may not be possible for all datasets and tasks. Yet, some tasks are similar to other tasks in Mechanical Turk. For instance, our reading comprehension task involved workers examining a passage and then clicking on multiple choice boxes. Would such a model port over to our word identification task, which asks workers to examine words and click to make a judgment on whether it is a noun? After we normalized all of the task fingerprint values for both reading comprehension and word identification, we trained a support vector regression model on all of the normalized counts of correct answers in the reading comprehension problem. We then applied this model to the entirety of the word identification dataset, predicting its normalized count of correct answers. The model was able to significantly predict correct answers in the new dataset ($r=0.4948$, $p<0.001$). Thus, if one had gold standard data for a congruent task, one may be able to gather task fingerprints for the benchmark job and then apply the model to evaluate a related different task without labels. It is particularly surprising how well the model generalized given the fundamental differences in the nature of the tasks: reading a passage and answering multiple choice questions versus identifying nouns in a word list. Building up a toolbox of archetypal task fingerprints for model training may enable prediction for a variety of tasks and evaluations.

It is possible that even in the absence of any labeled data, a mixed-initiative approach starting with unsupervised clustering could be used to bootstrap the system. By visualizing

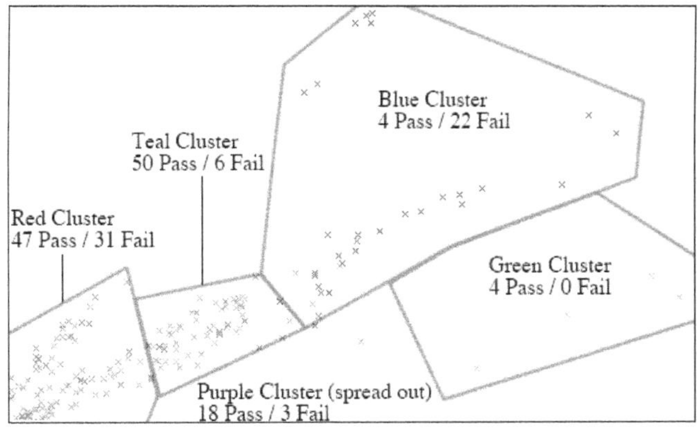

Figure 4: Word identification task fingerprint clusters graphed based on the number of fields each user accessed (x) versus the length of their collapsed event log (y). Notice that the blue and teal clusters discriminate between pass and failure well. The red cluster encapsulates borderline points, while the diffuse purple cluster gathers diffused 'pass' points.

features that differ between clusters (e.g., number of fields clicked on, time on task) employers could identify potential outliers and after investigation label the cheaters; such labels could then be leveraged by the system for the unlabeled data. Prior research using unsupervised clustering techniques for finding differences in problem solving skills between users using event logs demonstrate the potential viability of such an approach [6], suggesting this may be a profitable area for future research.

We conducted a preliminary investigation into the feasibility of unsupervised clustering of task fingerprints. Using the word identification task, we stripped the points of labels and used expectation maximization to identify 5 clusters of fingerprints. Four of the clusters corresponded to high likelihoods of either high or low performance workers, while one cluster was split, warranting manual inspection. Figure 4 shows a visualization of the clusters on two dimensions (fields accessed and collapsed log length); this suggests the potential for a mixed initiative system in which the user could inspect representative cluster samples and outliers, bootstrapping the classification process.

CONCLUSION

This paper introduces and evaluates task fingerprinting, a method for capturing crowdworker behavior and making inferences about their task performance. We demonstrate that by analyzing a worker's procedure in a generalizable way, we can develop event logs and behavioral statistics that can predict outcome measures such as task accuracy, content quality, or comprehension. Furthermore, we find that models trained on one task can predict performance on other related tasks.

We prototyped task fingerprinting by gathering event logs for Amazon Mechanical Turk workers and post-processing the data to extract statistical information about the workers' processes. We applied this prototype to image tagging, part of speech classification, and passage comprehension experimentally. Training machine learning models on the fingerprints, we were able to accurately predict outcome measures such as qualitative ratings of tags, noun identification accuracy, and passage comprehension, even when training using a small proportion of rated end products.

Future work remains to be done in several areas. Investigating how task fingerprinting might affect 'botting', or automated task completion on markets might be identified using event log pattern detection, for example examining the variance of the workers' behavior (e.g., using string comparison methods like minimum edit distance on refined event logs, or temporal variance measures). This approach could be even more powerful if requesters shared the fingerprints of known bots as they emerged (as antivirus companies do with virus hashes). More varied tasks, including ones where workers might spend significantly different amounts of time and effort on a task might be tested to reinforce the consistency and comparability of fingerprints across workers and tasks. Clustering of task fingerprints not based on statistical data, but rather the conformation of the event log strings using bioinformatics algorithms might also yield useful behavioral information. Moreover, there remains much work to be in visualizing task fingerprints for human inspection and analysis.

Finally, it may be advantageous to combine task fingerprints with other forms of task performance predictors. Our approach has both advantages and drawbacks that are complementary to other approaches to improving crowd worker output, including both task design methods and post-hoc approaches based on gold standards or worker agreement or reputation. Exploring appropriate ways to combine these metrics is an important area for future work.

ACKNOWLEDGMENTS

We would like to thank Jen Mankoff for her valuable feedback and the Carnegie Mellon Social Computing Lab for their support. This work was supported by NSF grants OCI-0943148 and IIS-0968484, and the Center for the Future of Work, Heinz College, Carnegie Mellon University

REFERENCES

1. Bernstein, M.S., Little, G., Miller, R.C., et al. Soylent: a word processor with a crowd inside. *Proceedings of the 23nd annual ACM symposium on User interface software and technology*, ACM (2010), 313–322.
2. Callison-Burch, C. Fast, cheap, and creative: Evaluating translation quality using Amazon's Mechanical Turk. *Proceedings of the 2009 Conference on Empirical Methods in Natural Language Processing: Volume 1-Volume 1*, Association for Computational Linguistics (2009), 286–295.
3. Chi, E.I., Pirolli, P., and Pitkow, J. The Scent of a Site : A System for Analyzing and Predicting Information Scent , Usage , and Usability of a Web Site. *2*, 1 (2000).
4. Dekel, O. and Shamir, O. Vox populi: Collecting high-quality labels from a crowd. *COLT 2009: Proceedings of the 22nd Annual Conference on Learning Theory*, Citeseer (2009).
5. Downs, J.S., Holbrook, M.B., Sheng, S., and Cranor, L.F. Are your participants gaming the system?: screening mechanical turk workers. *Proceedings of the 28th international conference on Human factors in computing systems*, ACM (2010), 2399–2402.
6. Fern, X., Komireddy, C., Grigoreanu, V., and Burnett, M. Mining problem-solving strategies from HCI data. *ACM Transactions on Computer-Human Interaction 17*, 1 (2010), 1-22.
7. Ghazarian, A. and Noorhosseini, S.M. Automatic detection of users' skill levels using high-frequency user interface events. *User Modeling and User-Adapted Interaction 20*, 2 (2010), 109-146.
8. Hall, M., Frank, E., Holmes, G., Pfahringer, B., Reutemann, P., and Witten, I.H. The WEKA data mining software: an update. *ACM SIGKDD Explorations Newsletter 11*, 1 (2009), 10–18.
9. Hilbert, D. and Redmiles, D. Extracting usability information from user interface events. *ACM Computing Surveys (CSUR) 32*, 4 (2000), 384-421.
10. Huang, E., Zhang, H., Parkes, D.C., Gajos, K.Z., and Chen, Y. Toward Automatic Task Design : A Progress Report. *Proceedings of the ACM SIGKDD workshop on human computation*, ACM (2010), 77–85.
11. Hurst, A., Hudson, S., Mankoff, J., and Trewin, S. Automatically detecting pointing performance. *Proceedings of the 13th*, (2008), 11.
12. Ipeirotis, P.G., Provost, F., and Wang, J. Quality management on amazon mechanical turk. *Proceedings of the ACM SIGKDD workshop on human computation*, ACM (2010), 64–67.
13. Ivory, M. and Hearst, M.A. The state of the art in automating usability evaluation of user interfaces. *ACM Computing Surveys (CSUR) 33*, 4 (2001), 470–516.
14. Kim, J., Gunn, D., Schuh, E., and Phillips, B. Tracking real-time user experience (TRUE): a comprehensive instrumentation solution for complex systems. *Proceedings of the twenty-sixth annual SIGCHI conference on Human Factors in Computing Systems*, (2008), 443-451.
15. Kittur, A., Chi, E., and Suh, B. Crowdsourcing user studies with mechanical Turk. *Proceedings of the twenty-sixth annual SIGCHI conference on Human Factors in Computing Systems*, (2008), 1509-1512.
16. Mason, W., Street, W., and Watts, D.J. Financial Incentives and the " Performance of Crowds ."*SIGKDD Explorations 11*, 2 (2009), 100-108.

17. Rauterberg, M. and Aeppli, R. Learning in Man-Machine Systems : the Measurement of Behavioural and Cognitive Complexity. *Systems, Man and Cybernetics, 1995. Intelligent Systems for the 21st Century., IEEE International Conference on*, IEEE (1995), 4685–4690.

18. Rogstadius, J., Kostakos, V., Kittur, A., Smus, B., Laredo, J., and Vukovic, M. An Assessment of Intrinsic and Extrinsic Motivation on Task Performance in Crowdsourcing Markets. (2011).

19. Shahaf, D. and Horvitz, E. Generalized task markets for human and machine computation. *Proc. 24th AAAI Conference on Artificial Intelligence*, (2010).

20. Snow, R., O'Connor, B., Jurafsky, D., and Ng, A.Y. Cheap and fast—but is it good?: evaluating non-expert annotations for natural language tasks. *Proceedings of the Conference on Empirical Methods in Natural Language Processing*, Association for Computational Linguistics (2008), 254–263.

21. Stieger, S. and Reips, U.-D. What are participants doing while filling in an online questionnaire: A paradata collection tool and an empirical study. *Computers in Human Behavior 26*, 6 (2010), 1488-1495.

22. Vanderaalst, W., Vandongen, B., Herbst, J., Maruster, L., Schimm, G., and Weijters, a. Workflow mining: A survey of issues and approaches. *Data & Knowledge Engineering 47*, 2 (2003), 237-267.

23. Von Ahn, L. and Dabbish, L. Labeling images with a computer game. *Proceedings of the SIGCHI conference on Human factors in computing systems*, ACM (2004), 319–326.

Real-time Crowd Control of Existing Interfaces

Walter S. Lasecki[1], *Kyle I. Murray*[1], *Samuel White*[1], *Robert C. Miller*[2], *and Jeffrey P. Bigham*[1]

University of Rochester, Computer Science[1]
Rochester, NY 14627 USA
{wlasecki,jbigham}@cs.rochester.edu
{kyle.murray,samuel.white}@rochester.edu

MIT CSAIL[2]
Cambridge, MA 02139 USA
rcm@mit.edu

ABSTRACT

Crowdsourcing has been shown to be an effective approach for solving difficult problems, but current crowdsourcing systems suffer two main limitations: (i) tasks must be repackaged for proper display to crowd workers, which generally requires substantial one-off programming effort and support infrastructure, and (ii) crowd workers generally lack a tight feedback loop with their task. In this paper, we introduce Legion, a system that allows end users to easily capture existing GUIs and outsource them for collaborative, real-time control by the crowd. We present mediation strategies for integrating the input of multiple crowd workers in real-time, evaluate these mediation strategies across several applications, and further validate Legion by exploring the space of novel applications that it enables.

ACM Classification: H5.2 [Information interfaces and presentation]: User Interfaces. - Graphical user interfaces.

General terms: Human Factors, Experimentation

Keywords: real-time crowd control, real-time human computation, crowdsourcing, remote control

INTRODUCTION

Crowdsourcing has been shown to be effective at solving problems that are beyond the capabilities of current automated approaches [2, 3]. However, current crowdsourcing systems suffer from two main limitations: (i) tasks must first be repackaged for proper display to crowd workers, which generally requires substantial one-off programming effort and corresponding support infrastructure; and (ii) crowds generally participate asynchronously, without a tight feedback loop between workers and their task. This paper considers a new approach to crowd computing that surpasses both limitations by using existing graphical user interfaces and putting the crowd in control of the mouse and keyboard. We introduce Legion, a system that allows end users to easily capture existing GUIs and outsource them for collaborative, real-time control by the crowd.

To use Legion, users first select a portion of their desktop interface that they would like the crowd to control, provide a natural language description of the task for the crowd to perform, and offer a price that they are willing to pay (Figure 2). Legion then forwards a video feed of the interface to the crowd and forwards key presses and mouse clicks made by the crowd back to the interface. To improve reliability, multiple workers are recruited to collaboratively complete the task. A fundamental question that we explore in this paper is how to effectively mediate crowd work to balance reliability with the desire for real-time control of the interface. Legion coordinates task completion by recruiting crowd workers, distributing the video feed, and providing a flexible mediation framework to synthesize the input of the workers.

Legion lets end users leverage crowdsourcing in ways previously not possible. Our original motivation was to provide a quick way of bootstrapping highly-robust, intelligent assistive robots. Such systems usually require significant (and costly) training to work automatically, are prone to errors, and so can often be controlled remotely by experts. We imagined a hybrid system in which robots could operate mostly automatically, but in which new tasks could be crowdsourced on demand for real-time control. Legion supports the flexible control of such existing remote-control interfaces.

We have used Legion to turn an inexpensive robot into one that intelligently follows natural language commands. We have outsourced bits of office work using a word processor or spreadsheet. We have used it to fill in for us while playing games requiring constant attention while we got a drink. We have used it to provide the intelligence of a predictive keyboard to make its suggestions quicker and more accurate. As we will highlight, not all of these use cases currently work flawlessly, but they illustrate the broad possibilities of outsourcing existing interfaces and motivate our work on real-time crowd control.

Legion supports experimentation with different ways of combining the input of multiple crowd workers in real-time while retaining reliability guarantees. Although there are numerous approaches that could be taken, we have implemented five *mediation strategies* in Legion that we compare in this paper: (i) control by a single crowd worker, (ii) mob rule in which all input from all workers is serialized and forwarded to the interface, (iii) voting over small time windows in which only the most popular input is forwarded to the interface, (iv) dynamically choosing a random worker to put in control, switching only when they become inactive, and (v) using crowd-agreement to dynamically elect leaders whose input is immediately forwarded to the interface and whose time in control is a function of their reputation built over time. The most appropriate mediation strategy is context dependent, as we will demonstrate with experiments across several different types of applications and tasks.

Our contributions are the following:

- We articulate the idea of real-time crowd control of existing interfaces, and describe considerations for the design of applications in this space.
- We present a system, Legion, that lets end users easily outsource existing interfaces to the crowd and exposes a framework for mediating the inputs of crowd workers.
- We formulate several mediation strategies for aggregating the input of multiple crowd workers, and investigate these strategies in experiments with a diverse set of applications.
- We further validate Legion by showing several new types of applications that we created that illustrate interactive crowd assistance, programming by demonstration, and the mash-up of several desktop applications.

BACKGROUND

Individual users have controlled interfaces remotely as long as networked systems have existed, dating back to early terminals that allowed users to log in and control time-sharing systems. With graphical user interfaces came remote display protocols such as the X Window System [18], and Virtual Network Computing (VNC) [17] became popular. Remote control has also been used to compensate for limitations in mobile browsers. For instance, Highlight runs a full browser on its server, which is remote controlled by the mobile browser [14]. Specialized remote control systems even allow aircraft to be piloted remotely (Figure 1). The main difference between these prior systems and Legion is the idea that multiple workers could collectively control the end user's interface directly.

Real time groupware allows remote users to collaborate in shared online spaces [8], and many online games and multi-user dungeons (MUDs) likewise allow users to play or interact in the same space with one another. In contrast, Legion synthesizes the input of multiple workers to act as a single controller of existing interfaces. A few web-based games allow multiple users to control a single interface. For example, Massively Multiplayer Pong allows all of the current players to control the paddle [13]. Its interface displays both the "real" paddle position and the user-specific paddle position. Maynes-Aminzade *et al.* have brought these techniques into the real world by enabling large audiences to collectively control a projected interface with collective actions like leaning to the left or right [12].

In machine learning, meta-learners combine multiple *weak* learners for better performance [16]. A specific class of meta-learners called arbiters learn to combine the input of multiple base classifiers in order to arrive at a final decision in a supervised manner and can work in an online fashion [4]. Legion is able to use the metric of crowd agreement that we have defined to learn how to combine crowd input in an unsupervised manner.

Figure 1: Cockpit control center for a Predator UAV. A pilot and several sensor experts collaboratively control the aircraft remotely, although their effort is split between different functions. The unofficial role of the observers is to ensure that the pilot has everything that he needs so that he doesn't need to leave the controls. *Image courtesy of Bryan William Jones.*

Prior work has considered how graphical user interfaces could be controlled automatically. Early work in this area used operating system APIs, but these projects quickly ran into problems because limitations in the APIs meant that many interfaces could not be correctly interpreted and manipulated in this way. The CoScripter [11] web automation system leverages the openness of the web to reliably interpret and manipulate the web interface, affording the freedom to focus on high-level problems like end user programming and intelligent interfaces for interface automation. Recent projects have taken a more robust low-level, pixel-based approach to interpreting and manipulating GUI components [23, 7]. Legion crowdsources not only the interpretation and manipulation of GUI components but also higher-level planning, allowing greater flexibility in how end users decide to automate their interfaces and what can be automated.

Human computation was introduced to integrate people into computational processes to solve problems too difficult for computers to solve alone, but has not been applied to real-time control problems. Human computation has been shown useful in writing and editing [2], image description and interpretation [3, 22], and protein folding [6], among many other areas. Existing abstractions focus on obtaining quality work, and generally introduce redundancy and layering into tasks so that multiple workers contribute and verify results at each stage. For instance, guaranteeing reliability through answer agreement [22] or the find-fix-verify pattern of Soylent [2]. Unfortunately, this takes time, which makes these approaches unsuitable for real-time control. Naive solutions like recruiting a single online worker may allow for real-time control, but would subvert existing methods of achieving reliability and are not robust to workers leaving (common in the crowd). As a result, new abstractions are necessary.

Several systems have explored how to make human computation interactive. As an example, VizWiz [3] answers visual questions for blind people quickly. It uses quikTurkit to pre-queue workers on Amazon's Mechanical Turk so that they will be available when needed. Legion needs multiple users to be available at the same time in order for its input mediators to work correctly. Prior systems have also needed multiple workers to be available. For instance, the ESP Game encouraged accurate image labels by pairing players together and requiring them both to enter the same label, although ESP Game players could also be paired with simulated players [22]. Seaweed reliably got Mechanical Turk workers to be available at the same time to play economic games by requiring the first worker to arrive to wait (generally for a few seconds) [5]. Legion similarly utilizes the input of multiple workers and asks workers to wait until enough workers have arrived, but engages workers for longer control tasks.

Prior systems have enabled real-time control from the web, most often in the context of robotics [19]. Osentoski *et al.* used a web-based interface to a robot to crowdsource a substantial amount of training data that they then used to train a system for automatic real-time control of a robot [15]. Goldberg *et al.* enabled groups of web users to collectively control a web cam [20] and make navigation decisions for a human actor [9] by interactively choosing regions of interest in captured images. Such systems are generally created only for the control of a particular system, whereas Legion can be used to control a variety of interfaces that were not originally intended to be crowdsourced. Legion might help researchers train other types of systems for real-time control.

THE CROWD

We define *the crowd* as a dynamic pool of anonymous workers of varying reliability. Because the pool is dynamic, workers come and go, and no specific worker can be relied upon to be available at a given time or to continue working on a job for a set amount of time. Workers cannot be relied upon to provide high-quality work of the type one might expect from a traditional employee for various reasons including misunderstanding of task directives, laziness, or even maliciousness. Finally, workers may experience delays that are beyond their control, such as network bandwidth variability.

For enabling real-time control, the dimensions of the crowd that are most relevant are (i) the time each recruited worker continues working on the task and (ii) the quality of the worker's output. These can be measured empirically for a specific crowd source, but are expected to be task-dependent [21]. A related dimension is the latency required to recruit workers to a particular job. For this paper, we assume that workers can be made available quickly, recruited and kept available using systems like quikTurkit [3].

Our experiments are run on Amazon's Mechanical Turk because of the ease by which workers can be recruited. Nevertheless, our framework is compatible with worker pools from other marketplaces, volunteers drawn from social networks, or any other group of workers available.

CONTROL CONSIDERATIONS

Legion can control a variety of applications, but several dimensions are especially important for enabling real-time crowd control. As we explain later in this paper, Legion synthesizes input from multiple workers by identifying when workers in the crowd provided the same input at the same time. To recognize when multiple inputs agree, Legion requires the input to be discrete, and, to associate input over time, Legion uses fixed time windows. As we will see, this does not mean worker input needs to be delayed until the end of a window.

The input space is defined by the application that is being controlled. GUI applications vary from being controllable by a few discrete keys to using the full continuous input of a pointing device. Key presses are already discrete. Pointer clicks are also discrete in the space of the pixel locations. Legion reduces the size of this space to a fixed grid in order to aggregate clicks. Legion does not currently handle other pointer interactions, such as movement paths or dragging.

Many tasks have several correct ways of completing them. For instance, if the task is to navigate a robot around an obstacle to a specified location there are at least two reasonable, high-level paths (going left around the obstacle or going right). Applications can be characterized by the number and degree of these decision points. Crowd input can be expected to diverge more at such decision points.

To correlate worker inputs over time, we divide time into discrete windows called *epochs* and associate inputs received in the same epoch together. Tasks with more decision points may be more easily solved by mediation strategies that allow for longer term strategies over multiple epochs.

LEGION

Legion is comprised of (i) an end user client application for capturing and controlling interfaces with the crowd, (ii) a server-side framework for recruiting and mediating input from crowd workers, and (iii) a web-based front end on which crowd workers complete the specified task (Figure 2).

End User Client Application

The Legion client allows users to select a portion of their screen to be controlled by the crowd by drawing a box around it. We chose to allow users to flexibly choose the region of the screen to export, instead of choosing a particular window, because it allows users to (i) exercise control over the information shared with the crowd, (ii) expose simpler interfaces for workers comprising only necessary interface components, and (iii) create new mash-ups by sharing pieces of multiple applications arranged next to one another (discussed later). Smaller regions also lower the required bandwidth.

Users provide a natural language description of the task that they would like the crowd to complete, and create a legend of keys that the crowd can use and where they are able to click. To simulate mouse clicks and keyboard events locally, Legion uses the OS X Application Services framework to post Quartz events into the event stream at specific screen locations. The CamTwist library[1] captures video from the user's screen and sends it to the server. Only specified keys and mouse clicks in the defined region are simulated (we use a white list). This does not completely ensure security, but reduces what workers are able to control on the client GUI. Future work may explore how to further isolate crowd input.

[1] http://www.allocinit.com

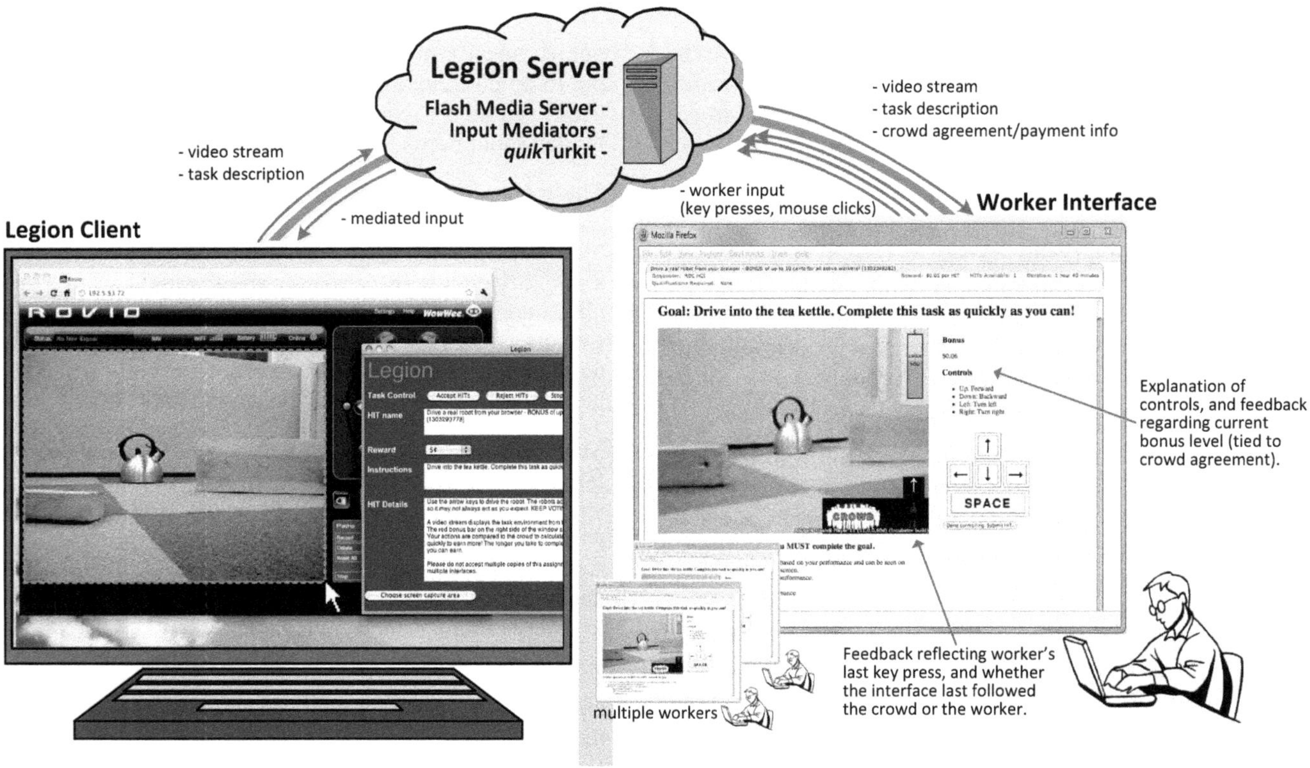

Figure 2: Legion is a framework that allows existing interfaces to be outsourced to the crowd. In this example, a user has outsourced control of her Rovio robot. The Legion client allows end users to choose a portion of their screen to send to crowd workers, sends a video stream of the interface to the server, and simulates events (key presses, mouse clicks) when instructed by the server. The Legion server recruits workers, aggregates the input of multiple crowd workers using flexible input mediators, and forwards the streaming video from the client to the crowd workers. The web interface presents the streaming video, collects worker input (key presses and mouse clicks), and gives workers feedback.

Users decide when the crowd is done, and decide whether the crowd as a whole successfully completed their given task.

Server-Side Framework

The Legion server is a Java application that recruits multiple workers from the crowd; collects, mediates, and forwards worker key presses and mouse clicks to the client application; and pays workers for their work. To recruit workers, Legion uses quikTurkit, a script for the TurKit platform [10], that maintains an active pool of workers. The HITs are described using the short task description provided by the end user. Workers can either be recruited on-demand or automatically when the user opens the application in anticipation of future need. If workers arrive early they are paid to wait. quikTurkit was able to satisfactorily maintain the dynamic pool of at least 3-5 workers needed for Legion.

The Legion server also includes Flash Media Server (FMS)[2]. Video is streamed from the client application to FMS, which supports multiple workers receiving the stream via their web browsers. The video is compressed using On2.VP6 and sent using the User Datagram Protocol (UDP), which unlike TCP, allows packets to be dropped. As a result, if bandwidth is temporarily reduced between our server and the workers, frames will drop instead of being queued, helping to ensure that the frame currently being shown is the most recent one.

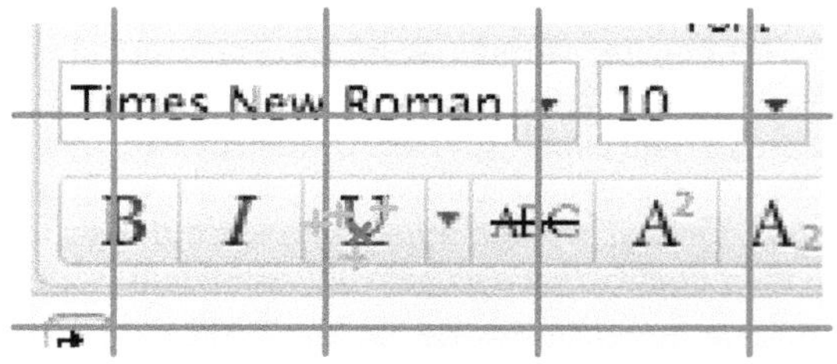

Figure 3: Our method for discretizing mouse clicks. The screen is split into a grid without knowledge of the interface beneath it, and so some inputs that are semantically the same will be discretized into different grid cells (as here). When simulating the click, Legion either uses the coordinate directly or averages the positions of each, depending on the input mediator.

Worker key presses and mouse clicks are sent to the server, which aggregates them and uses one of several input mediators to choose which events to send to the client. The server framework allows inputs to be analyzed, aggregated and filtered in a number of ways. It includes a number of procedures for deciding which inputs to pass through, for blocking or allowing inputs only from certain workers, or for analyzing inputs over time windows. End users will neither write these procedures nor need to decide between them, but the flexibility of the framework may provide opportunities for researchers looking to evaluate different strategies for mediating input from multiple crowd workers controlling an interface in real-time.

[2]http://www.adobe.com/products/flashmediaserver/

The input mediators require input to be discrete. This is straightforward for key presses. To discretize mouse clicks, we divide the screen into a grid and use the grid cell in which the click occurred (Figure 3). For instance, the event descriptor *mc_12_20* refers to a mouse click in the grid cell at (12,20). Later, this can be generalized by clustering the mouse clicks in order to find a discrete set of possible actions to select from. Discrete inputs allow the input mediators to compare the inputs of crowd workers.

The input mediators that we have implemented are described in the next section.

Worker Web Page

Workers control the interfaces via a web page hosted by the Legion server. This web page displays the live video feed of the client interface, and collects the key presses that workers make and sends them back to the client. As workers are queued, they play a simple game in which they are shown a letter and asked to type what it says. Although we don't currently, we could use this as a simple test to weed out workers who provide bad input or whose latency is too high.

Providing good feedback is difficult because a worker's input may not always be followed. In the robot control case, for instance, a worker may tell the robot to turn right, but the robot may go left because that action is preferred by other workers. As users press keys or click the mouse, their input is reflected back to them visually in the interface (Figure 2). They also see whether their input or the crowd's input was last sent to the client. We explored showing the workers the chosen input (e.g. the *m* key), but workers quickly learned to mimic it to improve their crowd agreement score. Workers are shown their current crowd agreement score in a power meter, a fractional value serving as a multiplier against the maximum bonus they can receive (in our case 10 cents). Workers are not told directly whether they are the current leader (in input mediators that support it), but they may be able to infer their status.

CROWD CONTROL

Legion aggregates the control input from all of the workers in the crowd into a single input that is forwarded to the interface as if it was sent by a single user. We developed the five input mediators described below. Each has strengths and weaknesses, which we expect to be application dependent and compare later in the paper. The input mediators each balance reliability and latency differently. For example, the *solo* input mediator recruits a single worker to directly control the interface. Latency will be low but so will reliability.

Mob The mob input mediator simply serializes the inputs from each of the workers and sends the single stream of actions to the interface. Each input from a worker is immediately sent to the interface being controlled. This approach may work for systems in which large numbers of redundant inputs are either ignored or handled gracefully. In this case, the 'wisdom' of the crowd is preserved by the fact that the majority of the inputs to the system will be those most agreed upon by the crowd. For applications in which excess or redundant input leads to loss of accuracy, such as editing a document, this style of mediation will perform poorly.

Vote The vote input mediator attempts to address the problem of unreliable individual crowd workers. We use a weighted vote, in which each user has a corresponding weight that acts as an influence measure. At the end of each epoch, individual worker's most recent inputs are collected as votes and scaled based on the weight of the worker who cast the vote, then summed to find the action with the highest weighted value amongst all participating workers. This action is then sent to the client and the weights of each worker w_i are recomputed according to the following formula:

$$w_i^{(t+1)} = \alpha w_i^{(t)} + (1-\alpha)\frac{\sum_{j=1}^{N_{A_i}} w_j^{(t)}}{N} \quad (1)$$

Where t is the current epoch, N_{A_i} is the number of workers that voted for selected action A_i and N is the total number of workers casting votes. α is a discount factor selected such that $\alpha < 1$. Its effect is that a worker's influence is affected more by recent agreement with the crowd than historical agreement.

We expect that using worker inputs as votes will improve accuracy, but at the cost of slowing down response time. This is because the votes of crowd workers will not be temporally synchronized, meaning that epoch windows can only be reduced so far before corresponding votes start falling into different epochs, thus skewing the vote. We used an epoch of 1 second in our experiments.

Leader In order to reduce the latency inherent in gathering votes over the span of an epoch, the *leader* input mediator selects the highest influence worker at the beginning of each epoch to assume direct control for its duration. This means that each input entered by the leader is immediately forwarded to the interface being controlled. Since the leader is elected based on weight, they serve as leader for as long as they remain in agreement with the crowd, on average.

The leadership model provides a means for real-time responses to feedback from the system without sacrificing the benefits of crowd agreement and enables longer term plans. For example, suppose a navigation task requires a decision to be made as to which path to take in order to avoid an obstacle. In the *vote* or *mob* input mediators, close crowd decisions can result in actions belonging to disparate plans being performed in a sequence because of crowd weight and participation fluctuations. This may lead to a course of action which is not in alignment with any individual worker's plan. In the navigation example, this may result in colliding with the obstacle. Electing a single leader allows them to take consecutive actions coinciding with their individual plan.

Worker weights are calculated using a *bag-of-votes* model to choose a leader after each epoch. These weights are calculated by comparing the normalized actions of each worker to the actions of the crowd with the vector-cosine as follows:

$$VC(a_i, c) = \frac{a_i \cdot c}{||a_i|| * ||c||} \quad (2)$$

where a_i a vector of the proportion of votes cast for each action by the ith worker and c is the same dimension vector computed for the whole crowd. We then recompute the

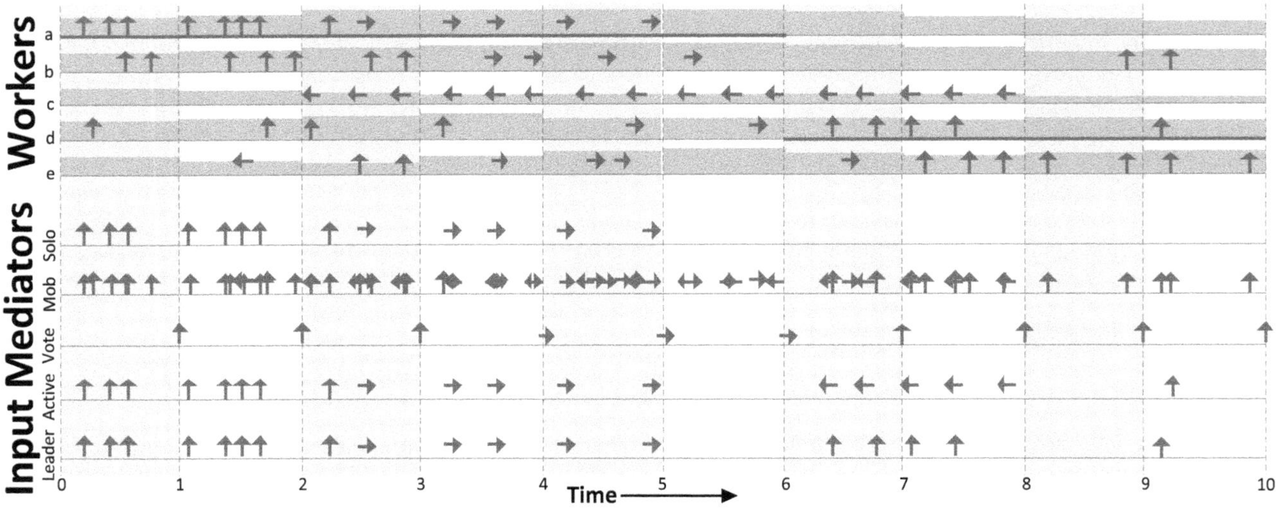

Figure 4: A visual depiction of the five input mediators. The application is controlled using only the left, right, and up arrow keys. We assume the "best" strategy to be *up* for epochs 0-3, *right* for epochs 4-5, and then *up* again from 6-9. Workers *a, b, d, e* all generally exercise this strategy, although none vote during every epoch. Worker *c* misunderstands the task, is malicious, or is trying to solve the task in a different way by pressing only *left*. The shading indicates the worker's crowd agreement level for the given epoch. *solo* chooses worker *a* at random and accepts input only from that worker, which works well until that worker stops providing input. *mob* serializes and passes through all input, without considering crowd agreement. *vote* issues the single most popular input over an epoch at the end of the epoch. *active* works like *solo* but switches to a new worker when the chosen worker does not vote during an epoch. *leader* dynamically chooses the worker with the highest crowd agreement level at the beginning of each epoch and passes their input through immediately.

worker's weight after each epoch similar to before, but use the vector-cosine as the new crowd agreement metric:

$$w_i^{(t+1)} = \alpha w_i^{(t)} + (1-\alpha)VC(a_i^{(t)}, c) \quad (3)$$

where $\alpha < 1$ is the same discount factor as in Eq. 1.

Active The *active* input mediator is variation on *leader* that we created in order to tease apart the two benefits of *leader*: (i) control by a single worker in the crowd, and (ii) the selection of a worker that has been shown to agree the most with the crowd. The *active* input mediator randomly selects a worker, who maintains control as long as they continue to provide input. If they fail to provide input during some number of consecutive epochs (here we used 5), a new random worker is selected.

Mediation Strategies Not Explored There are clearly a number of mediation strategies beyond the five described here. In particular, we did not explore hierarchical input mediators in which different workers have different roles. For instance, some workers could be responsible for controlling the interface and a separate group of workers could vote whether (or even which of) the workers were doing a good job. Our input mediators also do not allow workers to indicate their confidence in the actions they suggest, for instance determining that they are so confident of an action that they would like to wager that it will end up being a good action to take in the long run. We could imagine variations on the strategies above that allow limited communication between workers to help them devise and exercise long-term plans.

MEDIATOR EVALUATION

We evaluated our mediation strategies on two applications: robot navigation and data entry into a spreadsheet. These applications varied in characteristics that we hypothesize will manifest in the mediation strategies. Specifically, the robot task has a small input space and is designed such that workers can follow only one general path to complete it. The spreadsheet entry task has a large input space (all keys and mouse clicks) and can reasonably be completed in different orders.

We paid workers 5 cents per task in our experiments if the crowd completed the task. Workers could earn up to 10 more cents based on their crowd agreement level and the total time taken to complete the task. We waited for at least 3 workers to be available before starting the task, which generally took less than one minute.

As an initial feasibility test, we used Legion to control the web application in Figure 5 to measure latency. The application displayed a random key, crowd workers typed it, and then repeated. They were not shown the latency measurements. Timing is done in the web application, which we ran on our machine, and sums both system and human latency on this simple task. On average the recorded latency was 854.6 milliseconds (SD=743.0). This gives a sense of the lowest overall latency supported by Legion on Mechanical Turk, although realized latency may be task dependent.

Robot Navigation

Robot control is natural as a motivating task because it exercises three main contributions of Legion: robots need to be controlled in real-time, creating a new robot control interface for web workers would require significant one-off programming effort, and no obvious way previously existed for multiple crowd workers to simultaneously, collectively control robots in real-time. Robot control is difficult, so enabling even simple navigation tasks can require substantial

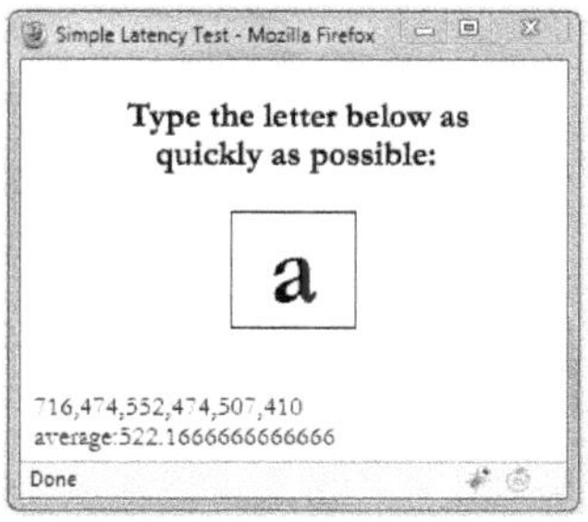

Figure 5: Web application used to measure latency.

customization for the robot and the environment. Even relatively simple tasks can become complex - the robot we used drifts severely to the left when told to go straight. Completing tasks with a robot can require longer-term strategies to be executed, e.g. it may need to go around a barrier, moving farther from its goal before reaching it. Finally, tasks naturally take some time to complete, and so workers available at the start might leave before the end. Eventually, our aim is to use crowds to control assistive robots that both navigate through and manipulate the environment.

We used an inexpensive remote-controlled mobile webcam called Rovio[3] as a platform for experiments with robot navigation. This device can be controlled over wifi via its web-based interface (Figure 2). Although it is marketed as a "robot," it does not contain any functionality for automatic decision-making or navigation. By connecting the Rovio to the crowd with Legion, we created an intelligent mobile robot that accepts natural language commands.

The navigation task was to drive the robot from a start position into a tea kettle a few feet away. Although the goal could be seen from the start of the task, the direct path to it was obstructed by various objects (Figure 2). Legion captured video at 320x240 resolution. As a baseline, we asked three local students to complete the robot navigation task three times as quickly as possible. On average these local workers required 46.3 seconds (SD=12.4) to complete the task.

We ran 10 trials for each of the five mediation strategies. The total unique voters (those who voted at least once) varied from 1 to 14 per task, although on average 3.1 workers voted during each epoch. These numbers highlight the highly dynamic nature of the crowd on Mechanical Turk. There were not detectably significant differences in the number of engaged workers across conditions. We ended trials that lasted more than 10 minutes.

In both the *active* and *leader* conditions, all trials were successfully completed, as compared to 8/10 successful trials with *vote* and *mob*, and only 4/10 successful trials with *solo* (Figure 7). Few trials were completed successfully with *solo* because workers who did not quickly complete the task disconnected. The crowd seemed unable to exercise a consistent strategy with the *vote* and *mob* input mediators. *vote* was further hampered by its slow rate of issuing actions.

We also considered task completion time (Figure 6). When the chosen worker completed the task, *solo* was the fastest, averaging just 56.0 seconds (SD=12.9). Trials in the *leader* condition were completed faster than trials in the *active* condition, 101.7 seconds (SD=81.0) vs 165.7 seconds (SD=166.3), a significant difference ($F_{1,9}$=6.96, $p < .05$). This suggests that choosing the leader based on crowd agreement, rather than randomly, leads to better results. *vote* performed no better than *mob*, 232.4 seconds (SD=110.5) vs. 205.8 seconds (SD=140.1), a difference that was not statistically significant.

[3]http://www.wowwee.com/en/support/rovio

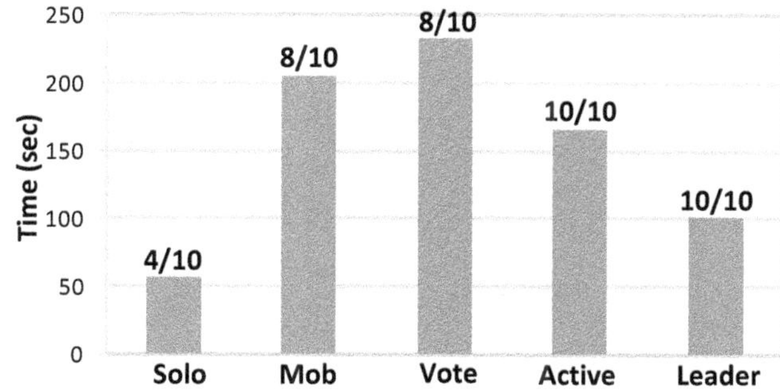

Figure 6: The average time required to complete the robot navigation task for each of the input mediators, along with the fraction of successful runs. *solo* was the fastest but only completed 4 of 10 runs, whereas *leader* was close in time and completed all runs. Choosing leaders based in crowd agreement in *leader* outperformed *active*, which chooses leaders randomly.

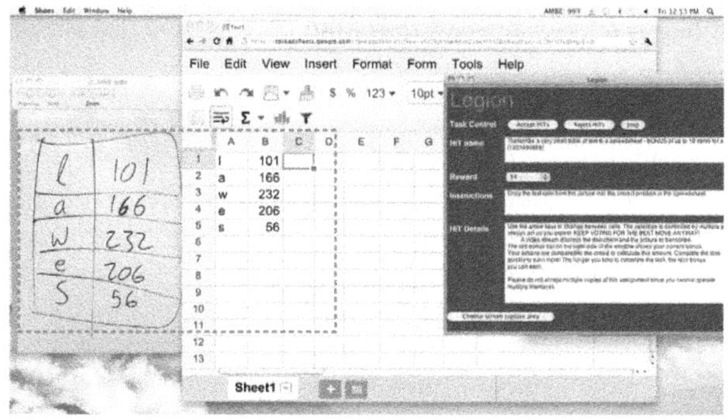

Figure 8: User view of spreadsheet transcription task.

Spreadsheet Transcription

Our next experiment explored the *vote*, *active*, and *leader* mediators on a simple spreadsheet transcription task (Figure 8). Prior work has demonstrated the value and feasibility of crowd assistance in word processing tasks [2]. In this experiment, we used Legion to capture both a Google spreadsheet and a picture of a table scribbled on a whiteboard (the timing results from the robot navigation task), and workers were asked to transcribe the table into the spreadsheet. Legion captured video at 640x480 resolution. This task is interesting because of the large input space (numbers, letters, arrow keys, and mouse clicks), which makes it more difficult for the crowd to agree. Furthermore, while Google spreadsheets already enable collaborative use, there is no protection against malicious users. As such, it is not suitable for collaborative use by the crowd.

We again conducted 10 trials of each of the input mediators, and ended trials lasting more than 10 minutes. Trials were deemed successful when all of the labels and numbers were entered into the spreadsheet correctly.

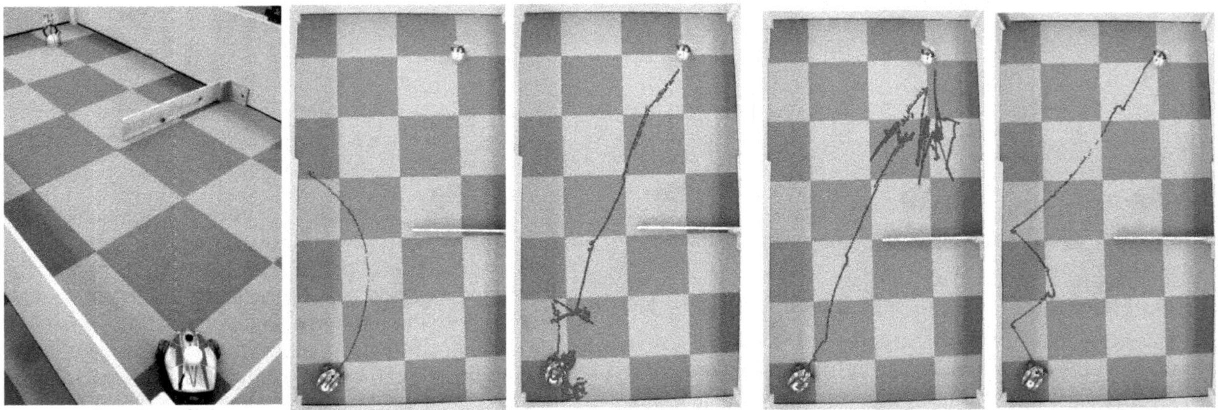

Figure 7: Example traces from the robot navigation trials. *solo* starts well but ends before reaching the goal, *vote* makes shaky progress slowly toward the goal, *active* goes toward the goal but fails to reach it when the worker in control drives back and forth near it, and *leader* goes mostly straight toward the goal (the robot tends to go left).

None of the *vote* trials were successful, whereas 9 of 10 trials with both *active* and *leader* were successful. With the *vote* input mediator, it was particularly difficult for the crowd to converge on a single plan. We did not test the *mob* mediator because we expected similar performance, and we expect the *solo* mediator to again perform like *active* but with fewer successful completions. Task completion times were again lower for the *leader* condition as compared to *active*, 78.2 seconds (SD=72.3) vs. 100.0 seconds (SD=74.8), although this difference was not statistically significant.

VALIDATION IN NEW TYPES OF APPLICATIONS

Legion enables end users to flexibly and creatively apply crowdsourcing to their existing interfaces. In this section, we explore several new types of applications enabled by Legion that we created using the framework. Although additional work is necessary to fully evaluate the utility of these applications, we present them here as a demonstration of the broad set of possibilities Legion opens up.

Interactive End User Assistance

Most of our discussion of Legion has assumed that a user will outsource full control of her interface to the crowd, but Legion can be used much more flexibly to provide interactive assistance to end users.

User Support Legion enables end users to outsource certain functions to the crowd who then can work cooperatively with them as they work. We used this idea to help make a crowd-powered predictive keyboard out of an existing predictive keyboard software program called KeyStrokes[4]. On-screen keyboards are used by many people with motor impairments, who use trackballs, head pointers, and other devices to type. Because typing in this way can be slow, KeyStrokes predicts what word the user is likely trying to type and displays suggestions that can be selected with a mouse click. We used Legion to outsource the selection of suggestions in order to bring human intelligence to prediction and possibly make typing faster (Figure 9). When using this application, we found workers would often disrupt our typing by choosing suggestions prematurely; applications of this type clearly need to manage the initiative between users and the crowd.

Co-Pilot Mode In co-pilot mode, the end user controls the interface herself with the crowd standing by in case she needs to temporarily attend to something else. We implemented this in the Legion framework by creating a modified version of the Legion client that captures and sends local user input to the server, a modified version of the server that can accept input from the local user in addition to the crowd, and a modified *Leader* input mediator that artificially gives the end user a weight high enough that she will always be the leader.

The result is that a user can control her interface as she normally would, but the system will automatically and quickly transition control to the crowd when she leaves. This mode may be particularly useful in real-time gaming or other applications that require continuous attention and control. Currently, users must stay at their computers, or signal they will be away from keyboard (afk).

The Co-Pilot Apprentice An interesting extension of co-pilot mode is for the end user to train the crowd to control an interface. Because the end user is always the leader through an artificially high weight, the best way for the crowd to increase their agreement score (and receive a higher bonus) is to mimic what the end user does. The co-pilot application can thus be used to program the crowd by demonstration.

Programming by Demonstration

We used Legion to enable basic programming-by-demonstration across diverse applications. The eventual goal is for automatic systems to learn to complete new tasks with existing interfaces by watching the crowd complete those tasks, but as a proof of concept we implemented a simple recording mechanism on the Legion server that can capture the inputs provided by the crowd and then replay them. We successfully recorded and replayed tasks with both the Rovio robot and Google spreadsheet.

[4]http://www.assistiveware.com

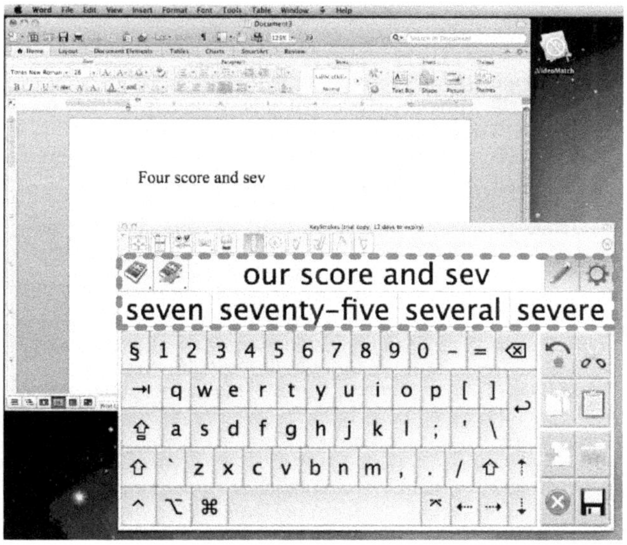

Figure 9: In this Legion use case, suggestion selection in a software keyboard is crowdsourced while the user continues to control the software keyboard.

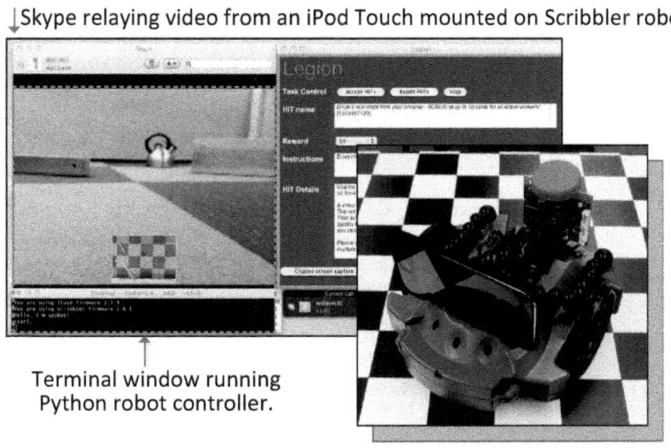

Figure 10: A crowd-powered robot created by mounting an iPod Touch to a Scribbler robot. Legion crowdsources the Skype video and the controller terminal.

Mash-Ups of Desktop Applications:

Finally, we explored how Legion could be used to create a novel type of desktop mash-up in which pieces of multiple existing interfaces are sent to the crowd for control.

We have already seen an example of this in the second experiment in the previous section, in which we combined a simple photo viewer and Excel to enable the crowd to fill in a spreadsheet with the numbers sketched on a whiteboard.

As a second example, we created a new video-enabled robot by combining a remote-controlled Scribbler[5] robot and an iPod Touch running Skype (Figure 10)[6]. The Scribbler driving platform was controlled over bluetooth from a terminal window. To construct the robot, the iPod was simply taped to the platform. On the desktop, we moved the Skype and terminal windows close together and then used the Legion end user interface to select the relevant parts of both of these windows. This mash-up allowed workers to see where the robot was going, and type commands to control it.

DISCUSSION

We have introduced Legion, a system for real-time crowd control of existing interfaces. Although Legion can control a wide variety of interfaces, our experiments highlighted the fact that different input mediators may be appropriate for different types of applications. Applications with a large input space, such as the spreadsheet, proved most difficult for the input mediators that did not select a single individual. Tasks in which the crowd was presented with multiple reasonable courses of action and a large input space made it especially difficult to achieve high crowd agreement levels.

The input mediator that did consistently well was the *leader* input mediator, which elects a leader who has direct control over the interface as long as he remains in power. This would go against the notion of the *wisdom of the crowds*, if the leader had not been elected by the crowd. Nevertheless, input mediators that allow a single crowd worker to control an existing interface trade expediency for trust. As a result, applications in domains in which errors have consequences may need to trade higher latencies for reliability.

It was clear that the crowd faced challenges related to missing feedback. Because multiple workers were controlling the same interface, a worker's actions would not always be reflected in the behavior of the interface. We received several emails from workers wanting to let us know that they had been trying to control the application as instructed but that it did not seem to be following their instructions. These concerns may dissipate as workers become accustomed to interacting in this way, but we may also need to find ways to give better feedback via the interface. Such concerns may have real implications, as we suspect that workers who felt that they were not being listened to quit the task earlier. Our current interface shows workers when the crowd decision was taken over their own, but it would be nice to give users the impression that the interface followed their input.

Legion does not support communication between workers, which is unusual for collaborative systems. Early experiments that showed workers what action the crowd chose resulted in poor quality input as workers mimicked what the crowd was already doing. Nevertheless, watching the crowd seem to struggle against one another to complete tasks suggests that a form of limited communication may be helpful.

Our experiments show that it is possible to have multiple crowd workers collaboratively control an existing interface in real-time. Our experiments were conducted on Amazon's Mechanical Turk, and many of our workers came from countries other than the United States. We expect that other crowds would face fewer technological limitations.

FUTURE WORK

Future work may explore how to better enable group work in Legion. For instance, new input mediators may help facilitate consistency. Our *leader* input mediator enables a consistent strategy as long as the same leader remains in control. Intelligent input mediators might be able to automatically cluster input into distinct strategies, allowing leaders to

[5]http://www.parallax.com/tabid/455/Default.aspx
[6]This robot actually performed better than the Rovio.

be replaced by other workers likely to execute similar plans. Other promising approaches include allowing workers limited communication, or to enforce a management hierarchy.

We are currently working on ways of extending Legion to more robustly and automatically adjust to different domains. It may be useful, for example, to dynamically switch between multiple input mediators. For instance, the *mob* could normally provide control with the benefit of a collective crowd voice, but *leader* could take over at a decision point at which the collective voice might not agree.

Complex applications may be better controlled by multiple specialized groups (Figure 1). For instance, an assistive robot requires control for both navigation and manipulation; each function may be best handled by different sets of crowd workers. For some tasks, limited communication between workers may facilitate collaboration. Finding effective ways of moderating communication to avoid excessive or malicious messaging in this context is ongoing.

As explored briefly in this paper, Legion can be used as a basis for interactive programming by demonstration. Future work may look to better support end users training a crowd to help them on their tasks, or new input mediators that will continue to reward the crowd for exercising control similar to what the end user demonstrated even after the user has left.

Workers often found the feedback provided by Legion confusing. Because the control input sent to the interface is based on the crowd, an individual may find that the interface does not do what they tell it. It may be interesting to explore how to allow different users to take different paths. In some systems with real-world consequences this would not be possible, e.g. in the robot domain, but for many others it may be possible to simulate the effects of different actions being sent to the interface. For instance, copies of the application could be run simultaneously in virtual machines and only merged when the crowd's consensus was clear. We also plan to explore giving workers more information about their current status, for instance whether they are the current leader.

CONCLUSION

We have presented Legion, a system that enables real-time control of existing interfaces by the crowd. Prior approaches to crowdsourcing require programmers to encapsulate tasks into new interfaces, cannot be used for continuous control, and use abstractions for reliability that introduce additional latency. We have implemented and evaluated several ways of combining input from multiple workers in real-time, and have demonstrated how letting the crowd control existing interfaces allows for several new kinds of applications.

ACKNOWLEDGMENTS

The authors would like to acknowledge the contributions of Craig Harman and Robin Miller.

REFERENCES

1. J. Allen, N. Chambers, G. Ferguson, L. Galescu, H. Jung, M. Swift, and W. Taysom. Plow: a collaborative task learning agent. In *Proc. of the national Conf. on Artificial intelligence - Volume 2*, 1514–1519. AAAI Press, 2007.
2. M. S. Bernstein, G. Little, R. C. Miller, B. Hartmann, M. S. Ackerman, D. R. Karger, D. Crowell, and K. Panovich. Soylent: a word processor with a crowd inside. In *Proc. of the ACM Symp. on User Interface Software and Technology*, UIST '10, 313–322, 2010.
3. J. P. Bigham, C. Jayant, H. Ji, G. Little, A. Miller, R. C. Miller, R. Miller, A. Tatarowicz, B. White, S. White, and T. Yeh. Vizwiz: nearly real-time answers to visual questions. In *Proc. of the ACM Symp. on User Interface Software and Technology*, UIST '10, 333–342, 2010.
4. P. Chan, and S. Stolfo. Learning Arbiter and Combiner Trees from Partitioned Data. In *KDD 1995*, 39–44, 1995.
5. L. Chilton. Seaweed: A web application for designing economic games. Master's thesis, MIT, 2009.
6. S. Cooper, F. Khatib, A. Treuille, J. Barbero, J. Lee, M. Beenen, A. Leaver-Fay, D. Baker, Z. Popovic, and F. Players. Predicting protein structures with a multiplayer online game. *Nature*, 466(7307):756–760, 2010.
7. M. Dixon and J. Fogarty. Prefab: implementing advanced behaviors using pixel-based reverse engineering of interface structure. In *Proc. of the Intl. Conf. on Human Factors in Comp. Systems*, CHI '10, 1525–1534, 2010.
8. S. Greenberg and D. Marwood. Real time groupware as a distributed system: concurrency control and its effect on the interface. In *Proc. of the ACM Conf. on Computer supported cooperative work*, CSCW '94, 207–217, 1994.
9. K. Goldberg, D. Song and A. Levandowski. Collaborative teleoperation using networked spatial dynamic voting. In *Proceedings of the IEEE*. 91(3): 403-439, 2003.
10. G. Little, L. B. Chilton, M. Goldman, and R. C. Miller. Turkit: human computation algorithms on mechanical turk. In *Proc. of the ACM Sypm. on User Interface Software and Technology*, UIST '10, 57–66, 2010.
11. G. Little, T. A. Lau, A. Cypher, J. Lin, E. M. Haber, and E. Kandogan. Koala: capture, share, automate, personalize business processes on the web. In *Proc. of the Conf. on Human Factors in Comp. Systems*, CHI '07, 943–946, 2007.
12. D. Maynes-Aminzade, R. Pausch, and S. Seitz. Techniques for interactive audience participation. In *Proc. of the Intl. Conf. on Multimodal Interfaces*, ICMI '02, 15–, 2002.
13. Massively multiplayer pong. collisiondetection.net, 2006.
14. J. Nichols, Z. Hua, and J. Barton. Highlight: a system for creating and deploying mobile web applications. In *Proc. of the ACM Symp. on User Interface Software and Technology*, UIST '08, 249–258, 2008.
15. S. Osentoski, C. Crick, G. Jay, and O. C. Jenkins. Crowdsourcing for closed loop control. In *Proc. of the NIPS Workshop on Computational Social Science and the Wisdom of Crowds*, NIPS 2010.
16. D. Opitz, and R. Maclin. Popular Ensemble Methods: An Emperical Study. In the *Journal of Artificial Intelligence Research*, 11: 169–198, 1999.
17. T. Richardson, Q. Stafford-Fraser, K. Wood, and A. Hopper. Virtual network computing. *Internet Computing, IEEE*, 2:33–38, Jan/Feb 1998.
18. R. W. Scheifler and J. Gettys. The X Window System. *ACM Trans. Graph.*, 5:79–109, April 1986.
19. D. Schulz, W. Burgard, A. B. Cremers, D. Fox, and S. Thrun. Web interfaces for mobile robots in public places, 2000.
20. D. Song, A. Pashkevich and K. Goldberg. ShareCam Part II: Approximate and Distributed Algorithms for a Collaboratively Controlled Webcam. In *Proc. of the IEEE Conf. on Intellignet Robots and Systems*, IROS '03, 1087-1093, 2003.
21. M. Toomim, T. Kriplean, C. Prtner, and J. A. Landay. Utility of human-computer interactions: Toward a science of preference measurement. In *Proc. of the ACM Conf. on Human Factors in Comp. Systems (CHI 2011)*, CHI '11, 2275–2284, 2011.
22. L. von Ahn and L. Dabbish. Labeling images with a computer game. In *Proc. of the SIGCHI Conf. on Human Factors in Comp. Systems*, CHI '04, 319–326, 2004.
23. T. Yeh, T.-H. Chang, and R. C. Miller. Sikuli: using gui screenshots for search and automation. In *Proc. of the ACM Symp. on User Interface Software and Technology*, UIST '09, 183–192, 2009.

Crowds in Two Seconds: Enabling Realtime Crowd-Powered Interfaces

Michael S. Bernstein[1], Joel Brandt[2], Robert C. Miller[1], and David R. Karger[1]
[1] MIT CSAIL
Cambridge, MA 02139
{msbernst, rcm, karger}@csail.mit.edu
[2] Adobe Systems, Advanced Technology Labs
San Francisco, CA 94103
joel.brandt@adobe.com

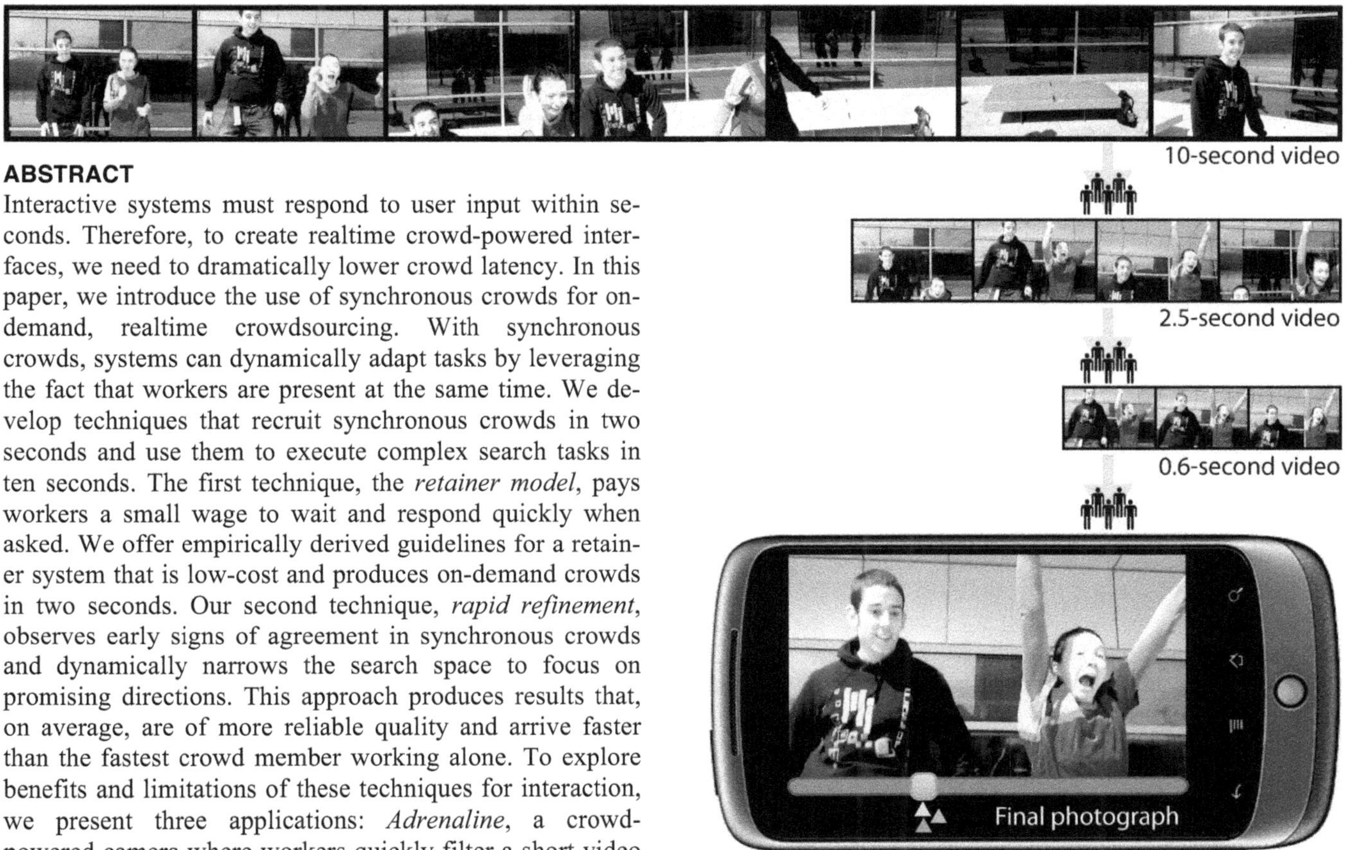

Figure 1. Adrenaline is a camera that uses crowds to find the right moment for a picture by capturing ten-second movies. It looks for early agreement to filter the timeline down quickly to a single frame. A photo is typically ready about one second after the user reviews the movie.

ABSTRACT
Interactive systems must respond to user input within seconds. Therefore, to create realtime crowd-powered interfaces, we need to dramatically lower crowd latency. In this paper, we introduce the use of synchronous crowds for on-demand, realtime crowdsourcing. With synchronous crowds, systems can dynamically adapt tasks by leveraging the fact that workers are present at the same time. We develop techniques that recruit synchronous crowds in two seconds and use them to execute complex search tasks in ten seconds. The first technique, the *retainer model*, pays workers a small wage to wait and respond quickly when asked. We offer empirically derived guidelines for a retainer system that is low-cost and produces on-demand crowds in two seconds. Our second technique, *rapid refinement*, observes early signs of agreement in synchronous crowds and dynamically narrows the search space to focus on promising directions. This approach produces results that, on average, are of more reliable quality and arrive faster than the fastest crowd member working alone. To explore benefits and limitations of these techniques for interaction, we present three applications: *Adrenaline*, a crowd-powered camera where workers quickly filter a short video down to the best single moment for a photo; and *Puppeteer* and *A|B*, which examine creative generation tasks, communication with workers, and low-latency voting.

ACM Classification: H5.2 [Information interfaces and presentation]: User Interfaces — Graphical user interfaces.

General terms: Design, Human Factors

Keywords: Crowdsourcing, Human computation

INTRODUCTION
Crowd-powered interfaces have demonstrated the potential to revolutionize interactive applications [2,3], but they are limited by the problem of crowd latency. Paid crowdsourcing markets like Amazon Mechanical Turk allow us to embed human intelligence inside applications like word processors [2], question-answering services [3] and image search [28], but today crowdsourcing is only a reasonable choice if the user can wait a minute or more for a response. Existing "nearly realtime" techniques on average produce a single, unverified answer to a question in 56 seconds [3]. More complex workflows require 22 minutes or longer [2].

Users are not used to waiting, and will abandon interfaces that are slow to react. Search engine usage decreases linearly as delays grow [21], and Jakob Nielsen argues that ten seconds is the maximum delay before a user loses focus on the interaction dialogue [20]. The much longer delays with crowdsourcing make it difficult for crowds to help with

UIST'11, October 16–19, 2011, Santa Barbara, CA, USA.

tasks in the moment-to-moment workflow. For example, using crowds to create a smarter copy-paste command would be difficult: one minute waits between copying and pasting drive users away. We need new approaches if we want to realize the vision of the user pushing a button and seeing a crowd-powered result just seconds later.

In this paper, we introduce recruitment strategies, algorithms, and applications for *realtime crowdsourcing*. Our goal is to complete non-trivial crowdsourced computation within seconds of the user's request — fast enough to feed back into an interface before the user loses focus. Realtime crowdsourcing can open up a broad new class of applications for crowd-powered interfaces.

Our core contribution is to introduce *on-demand synchronous crowds* as a key to realtime crowdsourcing. In synchronous crowds, all crowd members arrive and work simultaneously. While prior work has focused on recruiting individual crowd members quickly (e.g., [3]), we believe that *minimizing recruitment time is not enough*. Even fast workers may not produce a first result for tens of seconds [3], and complex workflows require several minutes [23,28]. Worse, fast workers may not be available, and unpredictable wait times hurt user experience. With synchronous crowds, we can reliably execute complex search tasks within ten seconds of request. However, to do so, we need to recruit synchronous crowds on-demand and guide them to complete tasks effectively.

To recruit on-demand synchronous crowds, we present the *retainer model* and a set of empirically derived guidelines for its use. It hires crowd members in advance, then places them on hold for low cost and alerts them when a task is ready. Our most effective design results in a majority of workers returning within two seconds and 75% within three seconds. The retainer model's performance is striking in that it approaches human limits on the cognitive recognize-act cycle and motor reaction times [4]. It nearly zeroes out wait times, which in previous work ranged from twenty seconds [3] to twenty minutes [2]. Most importantly, however, it makes on-demand synchronous crowds available as a new resource for crowdsourcing.

Developers need ways to guide or program synchronous crowds for realtime results. We introduce *rapid refinement,* the first design pattern for synchronous crowds, which focuses on low-latency, reliable work. The fundamental insight behind rapid refinement is that *synchronicity enables an algorithm to recognize crowd agreement early*. The rapid refinement design pattern quickly reduces a large search space by focusing workers' attention to areas they are beginning to agree on independently (Figures 1 and 4). Repeatedly narrowing the search space to an agreement region encourages quality results because it is built around independent agreement. It also allows the interface to provide incremental, trustable feedback before a final answer is available. Critically, rapid refinement leads to fast results: faster than approaches that keep workers separate, and faster on average than even the fastest individual worker.

We use the retainer model and rapid refinement to explore new avenues for realtime crowd-powered interfaces through a system called *Adrenaline*. Adrenaline is a smart camera shutter powered by crowd intelligence: it finds the right moment to take a photo. Instead of taking a single shot, Adrenaline captures a short video — allowing the user to move around the scene, the subject to strike multiple poses, or action in the scene to unfold unpredictably — then uses rapid refinement to identify the best moment as a still photo about ten seconds later. Low latency means that users can preview and share photos they just took, like they would with any other digital camera.

To investigate the larger design space of realtime crowd-powered interfaces, we also present two other systems, *Puppeteer* and *A|B*. Puppeteer focuses on large-scale creative generation tasks, allowing a graphic artist or designer to fill a page with a large collection of crowd-posed figures (for example, a stadium of excited concert attendees or a full dance floor). The designer interacts directly with the crowd as they work, and sees the first results 2.1 seconds after request. A|B focuses on extremely low latency responses for A-or-B questions, allowing users to ask which clothes to wear, which font looks better, or which version of a sentence reads more clearly. A|B returns a histogram of five votes to the user in 5–7 seconds.

This paper carries realtime crowdsourcing from recruitment, through programming patterns, to applications. We make the following contributions:

1. The *retainer model*, which produces synchronous crowds by recruiting workers in advance and alerting them when work is available. We present empirically derived design guidelines for retainer systems.
2. The *rapid refinement* programming pattern, which looks for emerging agreement in synchronous crowds to narrow down a large search space to a single result.
3. *Adrenaline*, a realtime crowd-powered camera that crowdsources the selection of the best photographic moment in a short movie in roughly ten seconds. Puppeteer and A|B extend these ideas into creative design tasks, opinion tasks, and online feedback to workers.

We implement these ideas on Amazon's Mechanical Turk platform. However, we also suggest ways that realtime crowdsourcing techniques might impact future platforms.

The remainder of this paper proceeds as follows. We first survey related work on systems and studies that gather crowds for quick results. We then introduce the retainer model and describe several experiments exploring its effectiveness. We introduce Adrenaline, and use it to motivate and explain the rapid refinement design pattern. We evaluate Adrenaline to test the effectiveness of our approach, and finally introduce Puppeteer and A|B to demonstrate the reach of realtime crowd-powered interfaces.

RELATED WORK

The work presented in this paper builds upon research on low-latency crowdsourcing, synchronous crowds, and crowd-powered interfaces.

Latency in Crowdsourced Tasks

An important thread of work models and influences wait times on crowdsourced task markets. We use several of these techniques, then push beyond single workers to crowds and from half-minute results to 5–10 second results.

Reducing task completion time has become one of crowdsourcing's holy grails. Increased payment leads to higher work output, which translates to faster completion times [19]. Task type (e.g., audio transcription vs. product review) impacts completion time in long-running tasks, but time of day and day of week have a much weaker effect [27]. quikTurKit recruits workers in advance to solve old tasks, then replaces the old tasks with new work when requests arrive. It also re-posts tasks to keep them near the top of the "most recent" ordering, which is a popular view that workers use to find tasks [5]. We adopt versions of both these techniques in Adrenaline, then introduce new techniques to gather crowds simultaneously, reduce variance in lag times, and reduce wait times by a factor of ten — without added cost.

No work to our knowledge has investigated ways to reduce latency once workers arrive. This is the focus of the rapid refinement algorithm.

Synchronous Crowds

In addition to low-latency crowdsourcing, researchers have begun investigating synchronous, collaborative crowds. Our work introduces the notion that low-latency crowds can enable synchronous crowds on demand, and that algorithmic designs can coordinate synchronous crowds through complex workflows quickly.

The ESP Game pioneered the use of multiple individuals working simultaneously on human computation tasks [26]. Our work adopts the game's notion of simultaneous independent agreement, as well as the idea of replaying old episodes when there are no collaborators.

Synchronous online experiments have gathered some of the largest simultaneous crowds so far. One approach is to build a panel of workers prior to the study, e-mail the night before the study, and recruit three times as many workers as needed [18]. The retainer model is a more sustainable, shorter-term variant of the waiting room in this approach. Our work recruits somewhat smaller crowds, but needs orders of magnitude less time to do so.

Finally, synchronous crowds open up the possibility for crowd collaboration. For example, Mao et al. used Mason and Suri's techniques to recruit crowds to solve distributed problems like graph coloring [17]. Kittur used collaborative text authoring software to enable collaborative text translation, finding that workers would coordinate and communicate with each other while working [13]. The Shepherd system likewise recognizes that workers overlapping in time could provide synchronous peer feedback [7]. The retainer model can bring crowds of this kind together relatively quickly, further enabling this kind of work. Many of these techniques draw on synchronous group collaboration research (e.g., [8,11]).

Crowd-Powered Interfaces

Our work aims to break ground on a new class of realtime interactivity in crowd-powered interfaces. There are currently two approaches to managing latency in crowd-powered interfaces: streaming and batching results. Streaming is used by VizWiz [3] and CrowdSearch [28]: they return work to the user, unfiltered, as soon as it is available. Streaming returns work relatively quickly. However, because the system does not have time to aggregate answers, it cannot perform much quality control via redundancy, and it tends not to use complex workflows. Soylent [2] takes a second approach, batching: it waits longer, but has the time to execute a multi-stage workflow and combine all results into a single interface. Our work is closer to a batching approach, but it shortens batch time to a few seconds. High-frequency batching enables workflows while still providing feedback to the user every few seconds.

Adrenaline, Puppeteer and A|B use the crowd to expand on previous applications. Adrenaline shares the goals of the Moment Camera [6] by recording continuously and using crowds to make the hard semantic decision of what is a good photo. The Moment Camera and Adrenaline complement each other: computational photography can check whether subjects' eyes are open and can tune camera settings, but it is only trained on certain classes of images and it is much harder to train an algorithm to make subjective judgments. Puppeteer gives the crowd a rigid shape deformation tool [10], then relies on the crowd to generate plausible deformations based on a text description. It is inspired by projects like The Sheep Market [14], and introduces crowd assistance as part of the tight loop of the creative process. Furthermore, it allows the user to interact with the workers as they explore. A|B gathers opinions quickly from multiple independent people, as suggested by Surowieki [24], though it focuses on subjective assessment rather than guesses at factual questions. Toomim [25] used crowds to evaluate alternatives more thoroughly, though with much longer latency.

ADRENALINE: A REALTIME CROWD-POWERED CAMERA

"You must know with intuition when to click the camera. That is the moment the photographer is creative. [...] The Moment! Once you miss it, it is gone forever."
— Henri Cartier-Bresson [1], 1957

Novice photographers often struggle to capture what Cartier-Bresson called *The Decisive Moment.* The instant when the shutter opens, the subject might have broken into an awkward smile, the angle might be poor, or the decisive moment might have passed. As a result, photos taken by novices can feel stilted or 'off'. Experienced photographers learn to compensate by taking many photographs — tens of photos rather than one — then sorting through them later to find the gem. They try multiple angles, capture photos over several seconds, or ask subjects to strike different poses.

Adrenaline is a realtime crowd-powered camera that aims to find the most photogenic moment by capturing many alternatives. Rather than taking a single photo, Adrenaline captures a ten-second movie and recruits a crowd to quickly find the best photographic moment in the movie (Figure 1). Within five seconds after the movie is captured, the user can see crowd members exploring the timeline (colored triangles in Figure 1). A few seconds later, the user can see that the crowd has narrowed down to a small fraction of the timeline, then again to a few adjacent frames, and finally to a final photo in a total of about eleven seconds. This means that a final photo is ready just moments after the user finishes reviewing the movie they just captured.

Adrenaline's goal is to mimic the instant-review capabilities of cameras today. Seeing a photo quickly means that users can take another photo if they want, show it instantly to friends, or post it to the web. The visceral thrill of novice photography can be lost when the photo is not available for minutes or days. Many novices never review the pile of extra photos, so we believe that is extremely important to complete the image selection process while Adrenaline still has the user's attention.

Existing crowdsourcing techniques cannot support Adrenaline's goal of 10–12 second latency. To achieve this, we introduce the use of synchronous crowds via the *retainer model* for recruitment, and the *rapid refinement algorithm* to guide the search process quickly and reliably.

RETAINER MODEL

To power realtime applications like Adrenaline, we need to gather not just one individual but an entire crowd quickly: a synchronous, 'flash' crowd. We would like the crowd to turn their attention to our task as soon as it is available, and to do so without paying for more tasks than necessary.

While it was clear from our explorations that workers would respond more quickly when paid money, it was not certain that they could respond fast enough for an interactive system. How should a retainer system be designed to 1) guarantee a fast response time, 2) be cheap enough to scale, *and* 3) maintain that response time after a long wait?

In this section, we introduce the *retainer model* for synchronous crowdsourcing and empirically derived design guidelines for its use. This approach solves all three issues by placing workers on retainer — signed up to do work when it is available — for a small fee, then allowing them to pursue other work while they wait. When the user makes a request, the retainer model alerts the workers. Our designs result in a majority of workers returning two seconds after request, all together, enabling synchronous crowds.

Retainer Design and Wait Time

Workers agree to be put on retainer by accepting the task. They are given task instructions and an example, and told that they will be alerted when a task is ready. We scale the task price up by expected wait time, usually 0.5¢–1¢ per minute on retainer. After workers agree, they are free to leave the browser tab open and pursue other work.

The worker's browser polls a work server to see if tasks are available. When a user posts a task, the work server notifies the client, and the client's browser issues a Javascript `alert()` and an audio chime to signal the worker. Optionally, the work server may also offer a small bonus to reward quick responses. Workers dismiss the alert when they arrive, then begin the task. If no new tasks are ready by the end of the retainer period, the retainer model gives workers an old task to perform. As work arrives more consistently, however, the chances of this happening become lower.

Retainer Field Experiments

Can workers react quickly enough to support a realtime application, especially when they may be distracted with other tasks? This section describes field experiments of the retainer model that investigate its effectiveness.

We created a benchmark Mechanical Turk task that instructed workers to click on all the verbs in a random paragraph from a blog or a book. Workers were told that the task would be ready within a specific retainer time limit, then the web page began an invisible countdown that sampled randomly between zero seconds and the maximum retainer time. When the countdown finished, the page alerted the worker and showed a task. We prevented workers from accepting more than one of our tasks at a time.

Study 1: Retainer Time

To test how long we could keep workers primed, we experimentally manipulated retainer time to vary between 0.5, 1, 2, 5, 10, and 30 minutes. We scaled payment roughly linearly with retainer time: 2¢, 3¢, 4¢, 7¢, 12¢, and 32¢. We hypothesized that worker response time would increase after 1–2 minutes, as workers stopped monitoring the page.

To reduce the chance that workers would see multiple price points for the same task, we posted each set at different hours. We ran the experiment over a period of six days, in six separate one-hour periods each day, and randomized the order of conditions. A total of 280 workers completed 1545 tasks. We removed and rejected 103 tasks because they disagreed significantly with our ground truth.

Results. For retainer times under ten minutes, 46–61% of workers dismissed the alert within two seconds and 69–84% of workers dismissed the alert within three seconds. These curves in Figure 2 asymptote to a completion rate of 83–87%: the rest of the workers never returned to complete the task. Retainer times of ten minutes or more resulted in much lower completion rates, 49–66%. The median time between dismissing the alert and completing the first incremental piece of work (clicking on a verb) was 3.35 seconds across all conditions.

These results suggest that for wait times under ten minutes, we could expect to produce a crowd in two seconds, and a larger crowd in three seconds. In the next study, we investigate how to improve response time and completion rates further through retainer designs.

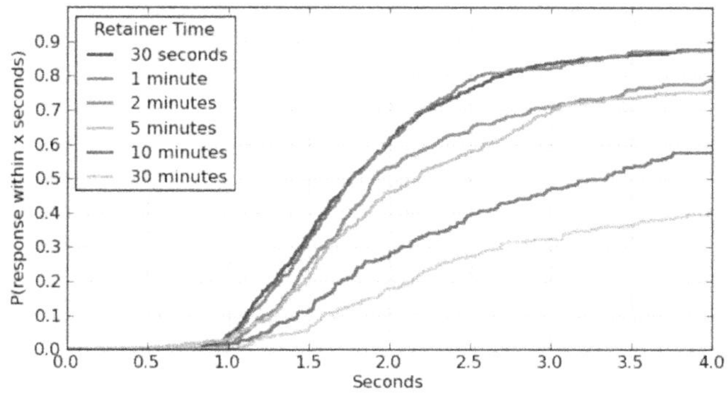

Figure 2. For retainer times under ten minutes, a majority of workers responded to the alert within two seconds and three-quarters responded within three seconds. N=1442.

	30 sec	1 min	2 min	5 min	10 min	30 min
Median	1.77 s	1.77 s	1.91 s	2.18 s	3.34 s	10.32 s
3rd quartile	2.44 s	2.39 s	3.46 s	3.75 s	—	—
Completion	86.6%	87.2%	82.9%	75.1%	66.4%	49.4%

Table 1. A tabular representation of Figure 1.

Study 2: Alert Design

While Study 1's results are already good enough to get a crowd quite quickly, can we improve on them by changing the reason that workers would pay attention? Can we incentivize the slow workers to move more quickly?

We investigated design and financial incentives to shift the curve so that more workers came within the first 2–3 seconds. We used the 12¢ 10-minute retainer condition from Study 1, which exhibited a low completion rate and a slower arrival rate. The *alert* condition functioned as in Study 1, with a Javascript alert and audio chime. Bonuses can be powerful incentives [19], so we designed a *reward* condition that paid workers a 3¢ bonus if they dismissed the alert within two seconds. Two seconds is short enough to be challenging, but not so short as to be out of reach. To keep workers' attention on the page, we created a *game* condition that let workers optionally play Tetris during the waiting period. Finally, to isolate the effectiveness of the Javascript alert, we created a *baseline* condition that displayed a large Go button but did not use an audio or Javascript alert. We hypothesized that the bonus and game conditions might improve response time and completion rate.

For Study 2, we implemented a between-subjects design by randomly assigning each worker to a condition for the same verb-selection task. We posted tasks for four hours per day over four days. Workers completed 1913 tasks — we removed 90 for poor work quality.

Results. Paying a small reward for quick reactions had a strong positive impact on response time (Figure 3). In the reward condition, 61% of workers responded within two seconds vs. 25% in the alert condition, and 74% responded within three seconds vs. 50% in the alert condition. Roughly speaking, the ten-minute retainer with reward had similar performance to the two-minute retainer without reward. In addition, workers in the reward condition completed 2.25 times as many tasks as those in the alert condition (734 vs. 325), suggesting that the small bonus has a disproportionately large impact on work volume. Predictably, the baseline condition without the alert dialog performed poorly, with 19% returning within three seconds. The game was not very popular (5.7% of completed tasks cleared a row in Tetris), but had a small positive impact on reaction times.

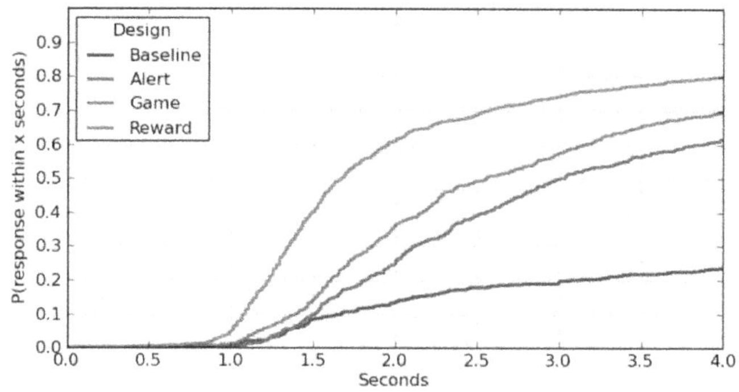

Figure 3. A small reward for fast response (red) led workers in a ten-minute retainer to respond as quickly as those on a two-minute retainer without reward (Figure 2, red). N=1913.

	Baseline	Alert	Game	Reward
Median	36.66 s	3.01 s	2.55 s	1.68 s
3rd quartile	—	6.92 s	5.01 s	3.07 s
Completion	64.2%	76.5%	76.7%	85.5%

Table 2. A tabular representation of Figure 2.

Retainer Model Discussion

Our data suggest that the retainer model can summon a crowd two seconds after the request is made. In exchange for a small fee, the retainer model recalls 50% of its workers in two seconds and 75% in three seconds. Though reaction times worsen as the retainer time increases, a small reward for quick response negates the problem. Our experiment commonly produced 10–15 workers on retainer at once, suggesting that users could fairly reliably summon a crowd of ten within three seconds. Applications with an early indication that the user will want help (for example, a mouseover on the icon or an "Are You Sure?" dialog) can eliminate even this delay by alerting workers in advance.

The cost of the retainer model is attractive because it pays workers a small amount to wait, rather than spending money to repeat old tasks. The cost of the retainer model depends on the desired arrival time t, the empirical arrival distribution $P(arrive \leq t)$ as in Figure 2, and the desired workers w. The number of retainer workers r needed is:

$$r = \frac{w}{P(arrive \leq t)}$$

For example, to recruit 5 workers within 3 seconds in the ten-minute retainer with reward, the system should place 8 workers on retainer (rounded from 7.8), then expect that 7 will return to complete the task and 4 will earn rewards.

Assuming that we set the retainer length longer than the expected time period between requests T, the hourly (60-minute) cost of the retainer model depends on the retainer wage per minute c_r, and the base cost for the task c_t:

$$cost = r\left(\frac{60}{T}c_t + 60c_r\right)$$

Paying a half-cent per minute on retainer and with no wasted tasks, one worker on retainer costs 30¢ per hour.

RAPID REFINEMENT: COORDINATING SYNCHRONOUS CROWDS FOR FAST RESULTS

Once recruitment times are negligible, slow work time dominates the user experience. Even straightforward tasks like question-answering can take thirty seconds under good conditions [3], and the wait can be much longer before there are enough answers to make a clear judgment.

The problem is not just one of minimum response time, but also one of variance. Time variance means that wait time will not be reliable: it will depend on whether the system happened to recruit a fast worker. That worker may also produce low quality results. Worse, nontrivial human computation algorithms (e.g., [16]) often wait for several results before proceeding: it is even less likely that a system would recruit multiple fast workers. We could require workers to finish within a short time limit, but our experience is that this is stressful to workers and leads to poor results.

To complete nontrivial crowdsourcing tasks in realtime, we must develop new algorithms and programming patterns to return quality results quickly and reliably. Like traditional randomized algorithms, we may be willing to sacrifice some amount of comprehensiveness for faster runtime.

The insight behind our solution is that *low-latency crowds are synchronous crowds*: all workers are working simultaneously. Synchronous crowds can interact with, influence, and communicate with each other and the user. In most on-demand crowdsourcing approaches, workers do not overlap in time enough for synchronous designs to make sense. However, the retainer model makes it practical to assume, for the first time, that the crowd is all present simultaneously a few moments after request. So, rather than waiting for all results in order to continue, a realtime algorithm has the opportunity to influence the process *as it takes place*.

We take advantage of synchronous crowds by recognizing potential agreement early on, while workers are still exploring, and then focusing workers' attention on the area of agreement. The insight is that the majority of Turkers who are efficient satisficers [22] can guide the process: these workers decide on the gist of the solution quickly, but can take time to commit to a final answer. Rapid refinement recognizes when several workers are *likely to* agree and commits for them by focusing the task on that area. Fast workers will still find an answer quickly and contribute to the vote, whereas slow workers benefit from the focus on a smaller search space. In the next section, we will describe the rapid refinement algorithm that implements this idea.

Algorithm Design

The rapid refinement algorithm repeatedly narrows down a search region to a fraction of its existing size when it senses that workers independently agree on the subregion (Figure 4). It is appropriate for a variety of search-oriented human computation tasks.

Figure 4. Rapid refinement repeatedly shrinks the working area for all workers when it detects that several independent workers are exploring the same area.

Rapid refinement begins with the entire search space available and workers initialized to a random position. The algorithm takes place in *phases* where each phase narrows to a smaller search region. Workers trigger a new phase by independently focusing on the same area for a period of time. The algorithm depends on three values: the agreement range r, agreement time t, and agreement amount a. If a fraction a of the workers stayed within a range less than a fraction r of the existing search area for at least t seconds, rapid refinement declares agreement. It then shrinks the search space to match the agreement range and begins a new phase. Workers are no longer able to explore the out-of-bounds area, and must try to agree within the new region. This process repeats until convergence. To approve or reject work, rapid refinement looks at whether the worker agreed with at least one phase change.

In Adrenaline, the algorithm begins with the entire video timeline. Workers vote on a good photo using their timeline slider. They cannot see others' sliders, which encourages independent agreement [24]. When at least 33% of the workers have been in the same 25% of the timeline for at least 2 seconds, Adrenaline declares agreement. These values can be adjusted to trade off delay for false positives. With these values, Adrenaline converges in 3–4 phases per video. The first phase is the slowest, and agreement accelerates as workers' attention is focused on one area.

The rapid refinement algorithm has several benefits aside from speed. First, it produces preliminary results that can be returned to the user early. Early results reduce interface latency and allow the user to provide feedback on the process. Second, it combines work and verification into one stage, which saves cost and time for a separate verification step. Third, workers tailor their votes toward what someone else might think, which minimizes individual bias [9].

Rapid refinement makes tradeoffs. First, the algorithm may focus too early on a single part of the search space, especially if the low quality workers are the first to respond. With four or more workers, it is possible to fork the crowd into two simultaneous groups to help avoid this problem. Forking the crowd has the additional benefit that the algorithm can explore multiple promising paths at the same time. Second, it may stifle individual expression: talented workers might be forced to agree with the majority. A future system could recognize such workers and give them more weight in the votes.

A slight modification to the algorithm can guarantee convergence. In particular, systems can increase the agreement fraction r as time passes in each phase. Then, given at least three workers, the algorithm will always converge.

EVALUATION

We have argued that the retainer model and rapid refinement combine in Adrenaline to produce a realtime crowd-powered interface by controlling variance in wait time and quality. In this section, we report on an evaluation of Adrenaline that evaluated this claim, stress-tested the retainer model and rapid refinement, and investigated whether end users understand the system.

Method

We recruited 24 participants through e-mail lists in exchange for a $20 gift certificate. Fourteen were male and ten were female, and the median age was 25. About half had taken a photograph on a cell phone camera or consumer camera in the past month, and five had taken pictures on a DSLR camera in the past month. The typical participant was a young, technically competent student who had a moderate interest in photography as a hobby (median Likert response: 4/7). Participants arrived to the study in pairs.

We gave each participant a smartphone with Adrenaline installed and introduced them to the application. We did not allow participants to immediately see the still photos that Adrenaline chose, so that we could compare rapid refinement to other approaches. Participants began by taking a video portrait of their partner. Then, the pair spent fifteen minutes in a public area capturing videos of people, actions, or landscapes. Finally, participants chose two videos in addition to the portrait to submit for the evaluation.

On a weekend afternoon, we generated candidate photographs using the following computational, expert, and crowdsourced approaches:

- *Rapid Refinement:* we required five workers to be on retainer before labeling each video.
- *Generate-and-Vote:* a standard crowdsourcing approach [15] in two stages. First, five retainer workers independently selected a frame in the video. Then, keeping the fastest three results returned, we use eight retainer workers to vote on the best photo of the three.
- *Generate-One*: using the same dataset as Generate-and-Vote, this condition simulated stopping the process as soon as the first worker submitted a photo.
- *Photographer:* a professional photographer labeled the best still frame in each video.

	Delay Median	Mean	Quality 9pt Likert
Computer Vision	–	–	4.9 σ=2.2
Generate and Vote	41.9	45.3 σ=14.0	6.6 σ=2.1
Generate One	13.6	16.3 σ=9.8	5.9 σ=2.6
Professional Photographer	–	–	6.4 σ=2.3
Rapid Refinement	11.6	12.6 σ=4.3	5.8 σ=2.2

Table 3. Rapid Refinement was the fastest algorithm and had the lowest timing variance, though it sacrificed slightly on quality compared to Generate-and-Vote.

- *Computer Vision:* the still frame selection algorithm on YouTube, which uses recent computer vision research algorithms [12].

We used the quikTurKit technique to repeatedly post tasks and keep work near the top of the Mechanical Turk task list, then implemented a five-minute retainer and a 2¢ bonus for quick response. We paid 4.5¢ on average for a rapid refinement or generate task (quikTurKit posts tasks at multiple price points simultaneously), and 3.5¢ on average for a vote task. Including bonuses and removing one worker on average who never responded to the retainer, these costs added up to 4(4.5¢) base + 2(2¢) bonus = 22¢ per video for the rapid refinement and generate tasks. Voting added eight workers: we estimated 7 would appear and 3 would earn the bonus, for an additional 31¢. So, rapid refinement and generate-one cost 22¢ per video, and generate-and-vote cost 53¢ per video. In a live system, it would be feasible to use fewer workers and pay closer to 10¢ rather than 22¢. On Mechanical Turk, we posted half of the videos first in the rapid refinement and generate-and-vote conditions to compensate for order effects.

We then contacted all of our participants and asked them to rate each still photo on a 9-point Likert scale. We instructed participants to ignore aspects of the picture like contrast and color that could be computationally improved.

Results

We used the retainer model to post each video as soon as there were five workers on retainer, stress-testing the volume of the retainer model. Adrenaline had enough workers to label a video every 45 seconds (median). Worker arrivals were bursty, but the median time between retainer arrivals was 6.3 seconds. The median time between unique worker arrivals was 48.8 seconds. These numbers are dependent on the current workforce state of Mechanical Turk, and will change as the market grows or more tasks use retainers.

Timing. Table 3 lists our results. Rapid refinement returned the fastest results, with a median total time of 11.6 seconds (μ=12.6, σ=4.3). Generate-One, which used the first available photo was a few seconds slower, with a median time of 13.6 seconds (μ=16.3, σ=9.8). Generate-One's timing standard deviation was nearly twice that of rapid refinement. These variances are significantly different from each other, $F(71, 71)=5.17, p<0.001$.

The timing data is non-normal, so we square-root transformed it to satisfy normality assumptions. An ANOVA comparing the delay for the three human computation algorithms is significant $F(2, 213) = 278.11, p < .001$, and post-

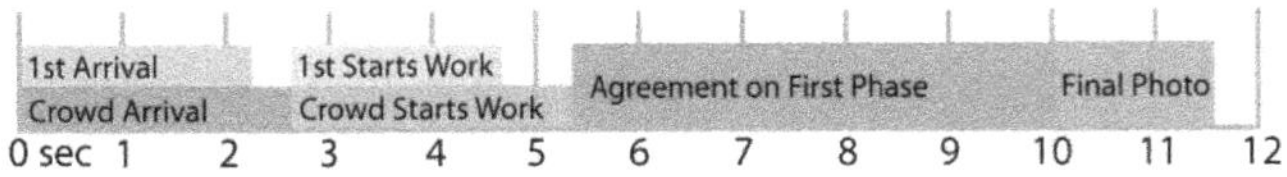

Figure 5. Timeline of the median Adrenaline execution.

hoc pairwise Tukey comparisons confirmed that all conditions were significantly different than each other (all $p <$ .05), confirming that rapid refinement is fastest.

Figure 5 outlines the median timing distributions of a rapid refinement process. One worker typically arrived 2.2 seconds after the video was uploaded, and the second and third came within 2.6 seconds. At least two workers were moving their sliders by 5.3 seconds after request. After the crowd began exploring, agreement took 4.7 seconds in the first phase. The median first phase completed a total of 10.05 seconds after request (μ=10.65, σ=3.0). The following phases lasted 0.75 seconds each, typically. These phases moved more quickly because workers were often already agreeing on a small area when the first phase completed.

Quality. Quality ratings tell an unexpected story. Participants' ratings had high variance, making it difficult to draw statistical conclusions (Table 3). However, Generate-and-Vote appears to match or beat the Photographer condition. While we believe that a photographer would take better pictures given the opportunity to operate the camera, it appears that an unskilled crowd may be equally talented at selecting good moments. Generate-One also performed better than expected, roughly matching Rapid Refinement. As with timing, however, Generate-One was less reliable and had a higher variance. The Computer Vision approach was the least successful, which suggests that using crowds in a subjective photo quality task is a good match.

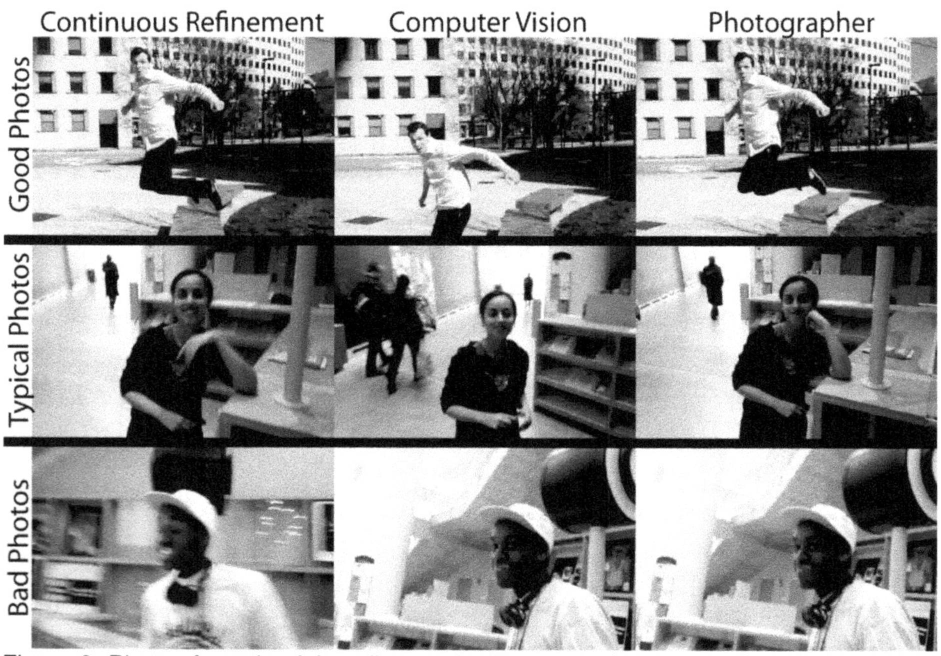

Figure 6. Photos from the Adrenaline study. The examples are good, typical, and bad photos that rapid refinement recommended. The computer vision and photographer columns demonstrate how other approaches performed on the same movie.

Study Discussion

This study suggests that rapid refinement guides crowds of two to five people to select a good photo faster than even the fastest member of a similar-size group. We might expect that workers would conflict, stalemate and disagree with each other. However, bottlenecks were uncommon, especially with more than two crowd workers. This result suggests that, rather than interfering with each other, synchronous crowds may hold significant promise for exploring new forms of cooperation and collaboration (e.g., [13]).

Quality may be the most salient issue with rapid refinement: its photos were of reasonable quality, but it did not match Generate-and-Vote. One common source of error was too-fast agreement in the later phases. Sometimes the algorithm decided that workers agreed in the second phase before they had adequate time to explore the timeline and make a decision. We have prototyped designs to compensate for this: for example, requiring that workers explore a minimum fraction of the range before their votes are counted, or requiring a minimum time lapse between phases. These approaches empower the designer to trade off increased lag in exchange for better quality.

A second issue is that rapid refinement uses constants that may depend on task, crowd size and the number of items being explored. For example, constants that work well for small crowds of 3–5 may act differently when 10–15 crowd members arrive. A more principled approach would treat workers' locations as populating a probability density function over frames. Then, measures of distribution peakedness, like kurtosis, would likely ease this problem.

The retainer model was more aggressive than necessary. Often workers joined midway through the process, resulting in more workers than needed. Given a sufficiently busy system, we might re-route latecomers from a retainer into a different task. Alternatively, there may be design patterns that place latecomers into a complementary role in the computational process, like vetting.

OTHER REALTIME APPLICATIONS

In this section, we expand the design space of realtime crowd-powered interfaces beyond Adrenaline. We introduce two applications, Puppeteer and A|B, to explore questions of creative content generation and even lower latency.

Puppeteer: Creativity and Creation in Seconds

Realtime crowds can thread creation tasks into user interfaces as well. Puppeteer (Figure 7) works in conjunction with Adobe Photoshop to support large-scale content generation and synchronous feedback

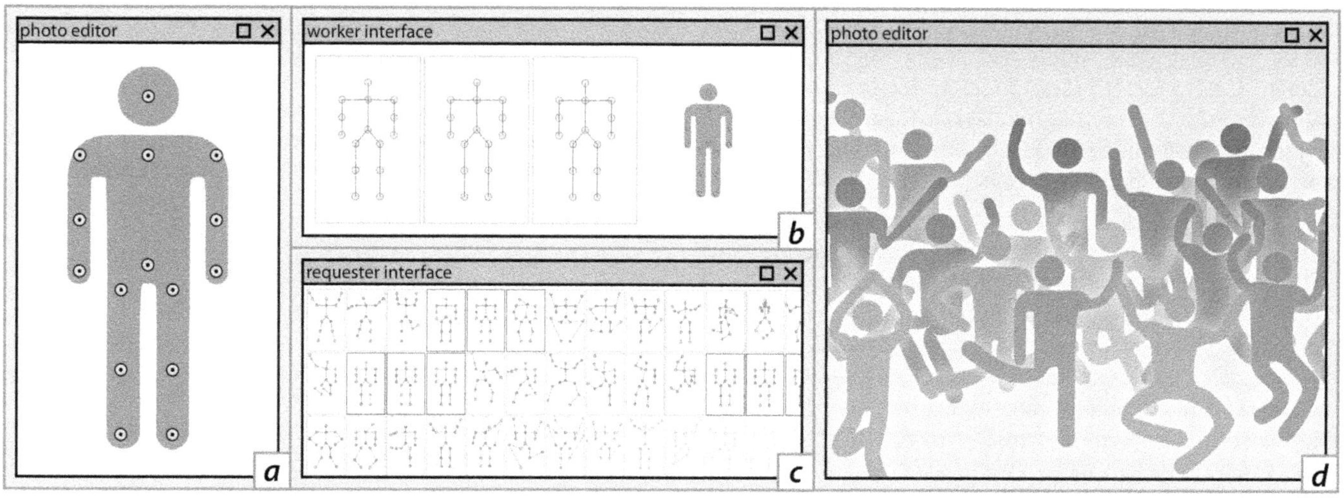

Figure 7. Puppeteer allows an artist or designer to generate a group of articulated figures quickly, and to interact with workers as they work. a) The user demonstrates control points. b) Workers move control points to match a request, like "make the person look excited!" c) The user watches incoming results and interacts with workers. d) The final result in Photoshop.

to workers. Artists often want to create a large number of believably varying objects, like an excited audience at a concert or flowers in a field. Algorithmic techniques to generate poses may not be realistic, semantically meaningful, or generalizable to new objects.

Puppeteer users specify control points on an image using Photoshop's Puppet Warp tool [10] (Figure 7a). Users give a textual description of their goal (*e.g.*, "Make the person look like he is dancing"), then workers each pose three figures to match the goal. As workers progress, the user observes them through a small multiples interface (Figure 7c). Then, because of the realtime nature of the application, the user can communicate with workers (*e.g.*, "Can you make another one more like your first?") These poses can be imported back into Photoshop to arrange the final result.

As an illustrative example, we simulated a user request to a large number of Puppeteer workers that they pose a human stick figure so that it looked excited. After they finished two puppets, we programmatically prompted workers with a request to make the third figure look like it is jumping. Anecdotally, the message was quite effective — the majority of workers' third puppets appeared to be jumping whereas the first and second puppets were rarely doing so.

To understand the latency and total throughput of Puppeteer, we repeated the "excited" task, but removed the prompt. We began the task when there were 8 workers on retainer, received the first control point movement 2.1 seconds later, and received the first completed figure in 25.0 seconds. The first worker completed the entire task (3 puppets) in 46.1 seconds. Workers completed 300 puppets in 16 minutes and 35 seconds, or one puppet every 3.3 seconds. Work output rate was relatively constant throughout.

A/B: Instant Crowd Feedback

It can be hard to escape from our own biases when we try to predict what others will think. Crowds are certainly good at having opinions, but high latency makes them less useful for snap decisions. A|B is our lowest-latency crowd feedback platform. The user asks a question and takes two pictures, then a histogram of crowd feedback appears moments later. A user might try on two different sweaters, take pictures of each, and ask which one looks better; an artist might sketch two different versions of a character and ask which one looks more engaging; a designer might want fast aesthetic feedback on a sketch.

In our tests with eight workers on retainer, A|B returned five opinions in as little as five seconds.

DISCUSSION

In this section we explore the implications and limitations of realtime crowdsourcing.

Synchronous crowds and rapid refinement open the door to many applications and techniques. Crowdsourcing has largely been confined to divide-and-conquer tasks, but synchronous crowds enable coordination and collaboration on a new set of problems. Such crowds can edit documents simultaneously (e.g., [13]), work on team tasks, and distribute large tasks in new ways. Rapid refinement also has applications in other search tasks. For example, rapid refinement might power a predictive mobile web browser that uses crowds to search the page for the user's next action and offer swipe-to-complete for that action, or redesign Soylent's Find task [2] as a synchronous, parallel process.

Larger, non-visual search spaces are another avenue for future work. If it is harder for workers to skim the items or the search space is very large, agreement will be sparser. We are interested in separating tasks into overlapping segments to address this problem. The core interface insight is to stop workers from worrying about deciding on one right answer and instead quickly call out promising areas.

We envision a future where crowdsourcing markets are designed for quick requests. A centralized system could use queueing theory to manage the worker pool and decide when to hire. Queueing theory makes assumptions about the distribution of worker arrivals, request arrivals and work times that would imply how many workers to put on retainer in advance. Workers could *follow* tasks they liked, saving them time searching the task list, and be on call for several tasks simultaneously. The system could then route workers to tasks where they are needed most.

Until we have such a large-scale realtime crowdsourcing platform, scale remains an issue. Our experiments in April 2011 found it relatively straightforward to recruit 8–15 workers on retainer, but if thousands of users began using Adrenaline, it might exhaust the worker pool. Given sufficient demand, however, more workers would likely enter the market in exchange for higher wages. Successful realtime services might eventually recruit their own full-time crowds like ChaCha [www.chacha.com].

CONCLUSION

This paper introduces techniques for realtime crowdsourcing and its applications in user interfaces. Where the fastest crowd-powered interfaces used to be limited by a median response time of nearly a minute [3], we show that it is possible to recruit a crowd within two seconds, get that crowd to answer a simple query within five seconds, and complete a complex search in roughly ten seconds. We presented Adrenaline, a realtime crowd-powered mobile phone camera that captures several seconds of video, then uses the crowd to quickly find the best still photo in the set.

Our solution is to introduce on-demand synchronous crowds, where workers arrive and work simultaneously. To create on-demand synchronous crowds, we present the retainer model of recruitment, which pays workers a small amount to come quickly when asked, and a set of empirically derived design guidelines for its use. With synchronous crowds, algorithms can identify regions of likely agreement before workers would normally select a final answer. This intuition led to rapid refinement, a design pattern that focuses the search space on areas of emerging agreement to quickly narrow complex search tasks. The combination of these two ideas enable reliably fast turnarounds for Adrenaline — ten seconds to a preview and the final photo a second or two later. This speed is on average faster than even the fastest individual worker. Finally, we extended the design space of realtime crowd-powered interfaces with A|B and Puppeteer, which achieved an even lower latency of five seconds to five responses and embedded crowd contributions directly in an authoring interface.

ACKNOWLEDGMENTS

Special thanks to Katrina Panovich, Jeff Bigham, our colleagues at MIT and Adobe, and the workers on Amazon Mechanical Turk. This work was funded in part by Quanta Computer via the T-Party Project. Additional funding provided by Adobe and a NSF Graduate Research fellowship.

REFERENCES

1. Bernstein, A. The Acknowledged Master of the Moment. *Washington Post*, 2004.
2. Bernstein, M.S., Little, G., Miller, R.C., et al. 2010. Soylent: A Word Processor with a Crowd Inside. *UIST '10.*
3. Bigham, J.P., Jayant, C., Ji, H., et al. 2010. VizWiz: Nearly Real-time Answers to Visual Questions. *UIST '10.*
4. Card, S.K., Moran, T.P., and Newell, A. 1983. *The psychology of human-computer interaction.* Lawrence Erlbaum.
5. Chilton, L.B., Horton, J.J., Miller, R.C., and Azenkot, S. 2010. Task search in a human computation market. *HCOMP '10.*
6. Cohen, M.F. and Szeliski, R. 2006. The moment camera. *Computer 39*, 8, 40–45.
7. Dow, S.P., Bunge, B., Nguyen, T., et al. 2011. Shepherding the Crowd: Managing and Providing Feedback to Crowd Workers. *Ext. Abs. CHI '11.*
8. Greenberg, S. and Bohnet, R. 1991. GroupSketch: A multi-user sketchpad for geographically-distributed small groups. *Graphics Interface'91.*
9. Hacker, S. and Von Ahn, L. 2009. Matchin: eliciting user preferences with an online game. *CHI '09.*
10. Igarashi, T., Moscovich, T., and Hughes, J.F. 2005. As-rigid-as-possible shape manipulation. *ACM Transactions on Graphics (TOG)*, 1134–1141.
11. Ishii, H. and Kobayashi, M. 1992. ClearBoard: a seamless medium for shared drawing and conversation with eye contact. *CHI '92.*
12. Ižo, T. and Yagnik, J. 2009. Smart Thumbnails on YouTube. *Google Research Blog.*
13. Kittur, A. 2010. Crowdsourcing, collaboration and creativity. *XRDS 17*, 2, 22–26.
14. Koblin, A.M. 2009. The sheep market. *C&C '09.*
15. Little, G., Chilton, L., Goldman, M., and Miller, R.C. 2010. Exploring iterative and parallel human computation processes. *HCOMP '09.*
16. Little, G., Chilton, L., Goldman, M., and Miller, R.C. 2010. TurKit: Human Computation Algorithms on Mechanical Turk. *UIST '10.*
17. Mao, A., Parkes, D.C., Procaccia, A.D., and Zhang, H. 2011. Human Computation and Multiagent Systems: An Algorithmic Perspective. *AAAI '11.*
18. Mason, W. and Suri, S. 2010. A Guide to Conducting Behavioral Research on Amazon's Mechanical Turk.
19. Mason, W. and Watts, D.J. 2009. Financial Incentives and the "Performance of Crowds." *HCOMP '09.*
20. Nielsen, J. 1993. *Usability engineering.* Morgan Kaufmann.
21. Schurman, E. and Brutlag, J. 2009. Performance related changes and their user impact. *Velocity 2009.*
22. Simon, H.A. 1956. Rational choice and the structure of the environment. *Psychological review 63*, 2, 129.
23. Sorokin, A., Berenson, D., Srinivasa, S.S., and Hebert, M. 2010. People helping robots helping people: Crowdsourcing for grasping novel objects. *IROS '10.*
24. Surowiecki, J. 2005. *The Wisdom of Crowds.* Random House, New York.
25. Toomim, M., Kriplean, T., Pörtner, C., and Landay, J.A. 2011. Utility of Human-Computer Interactions: Toward a Science of Preference Measurement. *CHI '11.*
26. Von Ahn, L. and Dabbish, L. 2004. Labeling images with a computer game. *CHI '04.*
27. Wang, J., Faridani, S., and Ipeirotis, P.G. 2011. Estimating the Completion Time of Crowdsourced Tasks Using Survival Analysis Models. *CSDM '11.*
28. Yan, T., Kumar, V., and Ganesan, D. 2010. CrowdSearch. *MobiSys '10.*

CrowdForge: Crowdsourcing Complex Work

Aniket Kittur *Boris Smus* *Susheel Khamkar* *Robert E. Kraut*
Carnegie Mellon University
5000 Forbes Ave, Pittsburgh, PA 15213
nkittur@cs.cmu.edu, boris.smus@gmail.com, susheelkhamkar2@gmail.com, robert.kraut@cs.cmu.edu

ABSTRACT
Micro-task markets such as Amazon's Mechanical Turk represent a new paradigm for accomplishing work, in which employers can tap into a large population of workers around the globe to accomplish tasks in a fraction of the time and money of more traditional methods. However, such markets have been primarily used for simple, independent tasks, such as labeling an image or judging the relevance of a search result. Here we present a general purpose framework for accomplishing complex and interdependent tasks using micro-task markets. We describe our framework, a web-based prototype, and case studies on article writing, decision making, and science journalism that demonstrate the benefits and limitations of the approach.

ACM Classification: H5.m. Information interfaces and presentation (e.g., HCI): Miscellaneous.

General terms: Algorithms, Design, Economics, Human Factors.

Keywords: crowdsourcing, Mechanical Turk, human computation, distributed processing, MapReduce, coordination.

INTRODUCTION

Crowdsourcing has become a powerful mechanism for accomplishing work online. Hundreds of thousands of volunteers have completed tasks including classifying craters on planetary surfaces (clickworkers.arc.nasa.gov), deciphering scanned text (recaptcha.net), and discovering new galaxies (galaxyzoo.org). Crowdsourcing has succeeded as a commercial strategy for accomplishing work as well, with companies accomplishing work ranging from crowdsourcing t-shirt designs (Threadless) to research and development (Innocentive).

One of the most interesting developments is the creation of general-purpose markets for crowdsourcing diverse tasks. For example, in Amazon's Mechanical Turk (MTurk), tasks range from labeling images with keywords to judging the relevance of search results to transcribing podcasts. Such "micro-task" markets typically involve short tasks (ranging from a few seconds to a few minutes) which users self-select and complete for monetary gain (typically from 1-10 cents per task). These markets represent the potential for accomplishing work in a fraction of the time and money required by more traditional methods [5][14][22][25].

However, the types of tasks accomplished through MTurk have typically been limited to those that are low in complexity, independent, and require little time and cognitive effort to complete. The typical task on MTurk is a self-contained, simple, repetitive, and short one, requiring little specialized skill and often paying less than minimum wage. Amazon calls its tasks HITs, for human intelligence tasks. During February 2010, we scraped descriptions of 13,449 HIT groups posted to Mechanical Turk. The modal HIT paid $0.03 US. Examples of typical tasks include identifying objects in a photo or video, de-duplicating data, transcribing audio recordings, or researching data details, with many tasks taking only a fraction of a minute to complete.

In contrast to the typical tasks posted on Mechanical Turk, much of the work required in many real-world work organizations and even many temporary employment assignments is often much more complex, interdependent, and requires significant time and cognitive effort [18]. They require substantially more coordination among co-workers than do the simple, independent tasks seen on micro-task markets. The impact of micro-task markets would be substantially greater if they could also be applied to more complex and interdependent tasks.

Consider for example the task of writing a short article about a locale, a newspaper, a travel guide, or a corporate retreat or an encyclopedia. This is a complex and highly interrelated task that involves many subtasks, such as deciding on the scope and structure of the article, finding and collecting relevant information, writing the narrative, taking pictures, laying out the document and editing the final copy. Furthermore, if more than one person is involved, they need to coordinate in order to avoid redundant work and to make the final product coherent. Many kinds of tasks ranging from researching where to go on vacation to planning a new consumer product to writing software share the properties of being complex and highly interdependent, requiring substantial effort from individual contributors. These challenges are exacerbated in crowdsourcing markets such as MTurk, in which tasks must be simple enough for workers to easily learn and complete and workers have low commitment and unknown expertise and skills.

Here we present the CrowdForge framework and toolkit for crowdsourcing complex work. Our first contribution is conceptualizing a framework for accomplishing complex and interdependent tasks from many small contributions in crowdsourcing markets. The framework provides a small set of task primitives (partition, map, and reduce) that can be combined and nested to address many crowdsourcing problems. Our second contribution is implementing the framework in a software toolkit, and using this toolkit to investigate the applicability, strengths, and weaknesses of the framework across a diverse range of tasks.

MECHANICAL TURK

Amazon's Mechanical Turk is a "marketplace for work that requires human intelligence" in which employers post generally small and self-contained tasks that workers across the globe can complete for monetary reward. MTurk encompasses a large and heterogeneous pool of tasks and workers; Amazon claims over 100,000 workers in 100 different countries, and as of the time of writing there were approximately 80,000 tasks available. There has been an increasing amount of research on Mechanical Turk recently. A large number of studies have examined the usefulness of MTurk as a platform for collecting and evaluating data for applications including machine translation [4] image databases [7], and natural language processing [22]. There have also been studies examining the use of MTurk as a platform for experiments in perception [5][11], judgment and decision making [13], and user interface evaluation [14]. Sorokin & Forsyth used Mechanical Turk to tag images in computer vision research and suggested voting mechanisms to improve quality [25]. Little et al. **Error! Reference source not found.** introduced TurKit, discussed later in this paper, a toolkit for iterative tasks in MTurk.

APPROACH

Our goal is to support the coordination dependencies involved in complex work done using micro-task markets. Most tasks on these markets are simple, self-contained, and independent. The audio transcription tasks posted by Castingwords.com are a rare exception. Castingwords breaks up an audio stream into overlapping segments, and workers

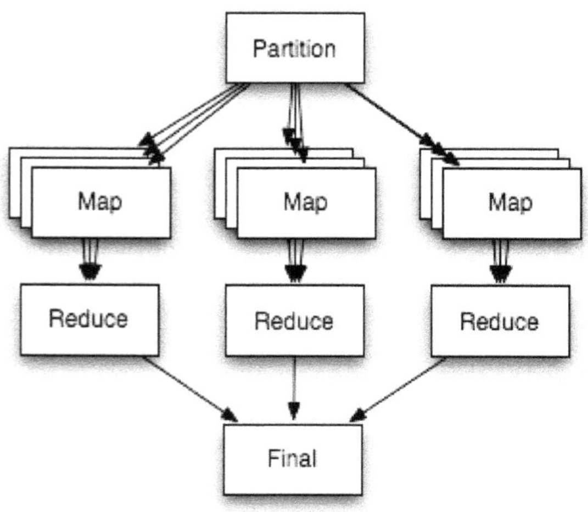

Figure 1: Overview of framework for splitting up and recombining complex human computation tasks.

are employed to generate transcriptions from each audio segment. These transcriptions are then verified by other workers, whose work is later automatically put together into a complete transcription. Unlike the standard micro-market task, the disaggregation of an audio file into smaller transcription tasks and the use of a second wave of workers to verify the work done by the transcriptions involves the producer/consumer dependency identified in [18]. It also provides a simple model for many of the elements of our approach. For example, the transcription task can be broken up into the following elements:

- A pre-specified partition that breaks up the audio into smaller subtasks
- A flow that controls the sequencing of the tasks and transfer of information between them
- A quality control phase that involves verification of one task by another worker
- Automatic aggregation of the results

The TurKit toolkit for MTurk **Error! Reference source not found.** extends some of these elements by enabling task designers to specify iterative flows. Little and colleagues use as an example a text identification in which the results of multiple workers' outputs are voted on and the best sent to new workers, whose work is then voted on, and so forth. This can also be characterized as a producer/consumer dependency [18], with a flow between a production task (text identification) and a quality control task (voting) that serves to aggregate the results.

Our goal is to generalize these elements into a framework that supports the crowdsourcing of highly complex work. Specifically, our framework aims to support:

- Dynamic partitioning so that workers themselves can decide a task partition, with their results in turn generating new subtasks (rather than the task designer needing to fully specify partitions beforehand)
- Multi-level partitions in which a task can be broken up by more than one partition
- Complex flows involving many tasks and workers
- A variety of quality control methods including voting, verification, or merging items
- Intelligent aggregation of results both automatically and by workers.
- A simple method for specifying and managing tasks and flows between tasks

To accomplish these goals our approach draws on concepts from both organizational behavior [18] and distributed computing [1][24]. Malone and Crowston [18] note the general parallels between coordination in human systems and computer systems. Key challenges in both organizations and distributed computing include partitioning work into tasks that can be done in parallel, mapping tasks to workers/processors, managing the dependencies between them, and maintaining quality controls [1][2][18][24]. Crowdsourced labor markets can be viewed as large distributed systems in which each person, such as a worker on Mechanical Turk, is analogous to a computer processor that can solve a task requiring human intelligence. In this way a crowdsourcing market could be seen as a loosely coupled distributed computing system [1]. This suggests that some solutions to managing distributed computing may be profitably applied to crowdsourcing as well.

Our approach builds on the general approach to simplified distributed computing exemplified by systems such as MapReduce [6] of breaking down a complex problem into a sequence of simpler subtasks using a small set of subtask types (e.g., Maps and Reduces) and managing the dependencies between them. MapReduce was inspired by functional programming languages in which a large array of data is processed in parallel through a two step process: first, key/value pairs are each processed to generate a set of intermediate key/value pairs (the Map phase). Next, values with identical intermediate keys are merged (the Reduce phase). Although we use MapReduce terminology as a convenient analog here, our work builds on a larger tradition of simplified distributed computing (e.g., [11][21]). We define three types of subtasks as:

- Partition tasks, in which a larger task is broken down into discrete subtasks
- Map tasks, in which a specified task is processed by one or more workers
- Reduce tasks, in which the results of multiple workers' tasks are merged into a single output

CrowdForge, our prototype system, abstracts away many of the programming details of creating and managing subtasks by treating partition/map/reduce steps as the basic building blocks for distributed process flows, enabling complex tasks to be broken up systematically and dynamically into sequential and parallelizable subtasks.

In partition tasks, workers are asked to create a high level partitioning of the problem, such as creating an outline of an article with section headings or a list of criteria for buying a new car. In CrowdForge the partitioning is made an explicit part of the task itself, with subtasks dynamically created based on the results of the partition step. Importantly, this means that the task designer does not have to know beforehand all of the subtasks that will be generated. Defining the division of labor and subtask design are shifted to the market itself, a key advantage that is novel and unique to human computation.

In map tasks, a specified processing step is applied to each item in the partition. In micro-task markets, these tasks should be simple enough to be completed by a single worker in a short amount of time. For example, a map task for article writing could ask a worker to collect one fact on a given topic in the article's outline. Multiple instances of a map tasks could be instantiated for each partition; e.g., multiple workers could be asked to collect one fact each on the topic in parallel.

Finally, reduce tasks take all the results from a given map task and consolidate them, typically into a single result. In the article writing example, a reduce step might take facts collected for a given topic by many workers and have a worker turn them into a paragraph.

Any of these steps can be iterative. For example, the topic for an article section defined in a first partition can itself be partitioned into subsections. Similarly, the paragraphs returned from one reduction step can in turn be reordered through a second reduction step.

CASE STUDIES

Before describing implementation details of the system we first provide examples and evidence of how the system works in practice through two case studies: article writing and researching a purchase decision.

Article writing

The first complex task we explored was writing an encyclopedia article. Writing an article is a challenging and interdependent task that involves many different subtasks: planning the scope of the article, how it should be structured, finding and filtering information to include, writing up that information, finding and fixing grammar and spelling, and making the article coherent. While there are examples of collaborative writing on the Internet, notably Wikipedia, previous work has shown that the success of harnessing a large group of contributors is often dependent on a small core of leaders that do a large proportion of the work and organize the contributions of others [15][16]. This poses a challenge in micro-task markets where individuals may not be willing to spend the large amount of effort needed to be a leader and may not be able to com-

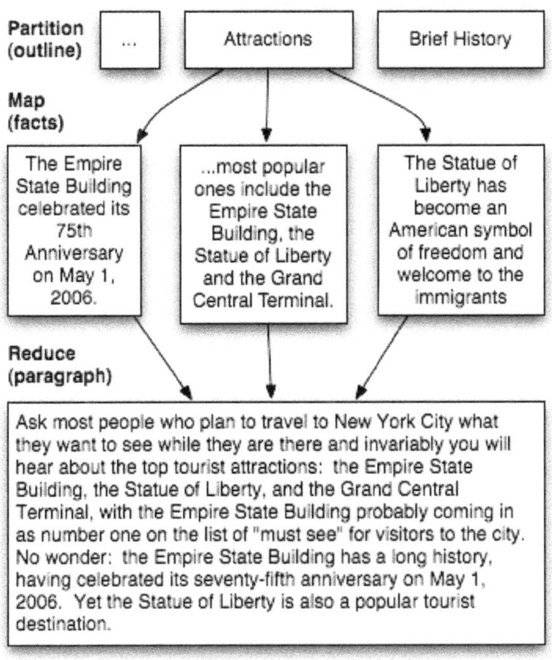

Figure 2: Partial results of a collaborative writing task.

municate with others in order to coordinate or influence their behavior. Furthermore, many of the subtasks involved, such as assembling the relevant information or doing the actual writing, can be time consuming and complex. These characteristics make article writing a challenging but representative test case for our approach.

To solve this problem we created a simple flow consisting of a partition, map, and reduce step (see Figure 2). The partition step asked workers to create an article outline, represented as an array of section headings such as "History" and "Geography". In an environment where workers would complete high effort tasks, the next step might be to have someone write a paragraph for each section. However, the difficulty and time involved in researching and writing a complete paragraph for a heading is a mismatch to the low work capacity of micro-task markets. Thus we broke the task up further, separating the information collection and writing subtasks. Specifically, each section heading from the partition was used to generate map tasks in which multiple workers were asked to submit a single fact about the section (workers were also asked to submit a URL reference to the source of the fact to encourage high quality fact collection).

Next, the reduction step asked other workers to create a paragraph for each section based on the facts collected in the map step. By separating the collection of information and writing into two stages we could significantly decrease the cost of each stage, making the task more suitable for micro-task workers. In addition, we benefit from other effects such being able to collect more diverse information. Finally, since the resulting paragraphs were relatively independent, they were themselves reduced into an article by simply concatenating them[1].

We used this approach to create five articles about New York City. Articles cost an average of $3.26 to produce, and required an average of 36 subtasks or HITs, each performed by an individual worker. Partition-workers identified 5.3 topics per article in the partition step. The average number article included 658 words. A fragment of a typical article is shown in Figure 2; this article consisted of 955 words and 7 sections: brief history, getting there, basic layout, neighborhoods, getting around, attractions and ethnic diversity. It was completed via 36 different HITs for a total cost of $3.15.

To verify the quality of these collaboratively written articles, we compared them to articles written individually by workers and to the entry from the Simple English Wikipedia on New York City [28]. To produce a comparison group of individually written articles, we created eight HITs which each requested one worker to write the full article. To control for motivations associated with reward, we paid these individuals $3.05, approximately the same amount as the average group payment. The resulting articles consisted of an average of 393 words, approximately 60% the length of the collaborative written articles.

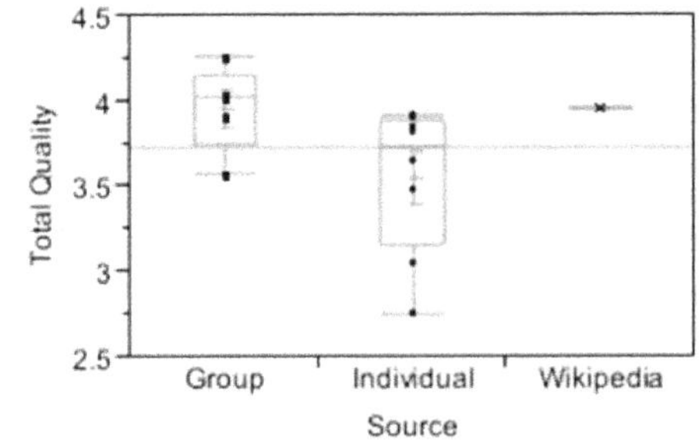

Figure 3: Rated quality of articles about New York City produced by Mechanical Turk workers acting individually or as a group using our framework compared to the quality of the same article on the Simple English Wikipedia.

We then evaluated the quality of all articles by asking a new set of workers to each rate a single article based on four dimensions: use of facts, spelling and grammar, article structure, and personal preference. Fifteen workers rated each article on five-point Likert scales. We averaged the ratings of the 15 raters across the four dimensions to get an overall quality score for each article.

On average the articles produced by the group were of higher quality than those produced individually (see Figure 3: mean quality for group-written articles = 4.01 versus 3.75 for individually-written ones, $t(11)=2.17$, $p=.05$). The average quality for the group-written articles was roughly the same as the Simple English Wikipedia article (Wikipedia quality=3.95). Not only was the average quality of the group articles higher than the individually written ones, but as Figure 3 also shows, the variability was lower as well ($t(11)=-2.43$, p=.03), with a lower proportion of poor articles.

Overall, we found that using CrowdForge to crowdsource the complex and interdependent task of article writing worked surprisingly well. Despite the coordination requirements involved in managing and integrating the work of dozens of workers, each contributing only a small amount of work, the group-produced articles were rated higher and had lower variability than individual-produced articles -- even though individuals were paid the same amount as the whole group and did not have to deal with coordination challenges -- and similar in quality to corresponding Simple Wikipedia articles.

Quality Control

In the above study each partition task was completed by a single worker. This creates the possibility that a single bad partition (i.e., outline) could have a large negative effect on the whole task. We found this did occur in one of the group articles, with a bad outline's effects cascading down the task chain. It is remarkable that despite this brittleness, we still found a robust advantage of the group condition over the individual condition, speaking to the strength of the

[1] For other kinds of articles there could be another crowdsourced reduce phase that integrates the paragraphs.

approach. However, in many cases we would like to minimize the likelihood of any task failing due to a single low quality worker by combining multiple workers' results.

Our approach to dealing with this challenge is to utilize additional Map or Reduce tasks to supporting fault tolerance and quality control. For example, to represent Castingwords transcription flow, described earlier, in the CrowdForge framework, workers verifying the results of other workers' outputs can be represented as a Map task that applies a verification function to each value. Other kinds of quality control processes can also be applied; for example, voting on the best choice can be represented as a Reduce task in which a single output is chosen from multiple workers' outputs based on the vote. Other kinds of human intelligence tasks could also be used, such as a Reduce task in which workers combine the best aspects of other workers' outputs rather than choosing a single best output. An advantage of this approach is that quality control steps are treated the same as other kinds of subtasks, minimizing added complexity.

A particularly interesting question is whether more complex quality control methods that require human intelligence -- such as combining the best aspects of multiple workers' outputs -- would work better than methods such as simple voting. Merging results (in this case, article outlines) could have a number of advantages over voting. The likelihood of a poor outline could be reduced, since at the very least – if workers did no merging at all – the best of the outline options should be chosen. It is also possible that the merged outlines could be better than the initial outlines, if the best aspects of each of multiple outlines were combined, or if seeing multiple outlines at once facilitates comparison between them and thus leads to better outlines.

To test these hypotheses we ran an experiment on quality control of article outlines. In the first phase we asked 20 workers to each independently generate an outline for an article on the recent Gulf of Mexico oil spill using the same procedure as in the article writing case study above. We then took these 20 outlines and randomly assigned them to 20 different sets of three outlines (outlines could be in more than one set). Each set was given to a different worker, who was asked to create a new outline for the article using elements from the 3 outlines in his or her set (i.e., a Reduce task). Workers were instructed to use any elements from any of the outlines they had available, but were not allowed to add new elements. This resulted in 20 merged outlines.

For evaluation we crossed the 20 initial and 20 merged outlines, and asked workers to choose which outline would result in a better article. To ensure that workers evaluated both outlines, they were also required to identify matching elements in the two outlines, following best practices outlined in [14]. Merged outlines were rated higher than the initial outlines: 61% of merged outlines were chosen compared to 39% of initial outlines. A binomial test revealed the difference in choice preferences were statistically significant ($p < .001$). Histograms of choice preferences for

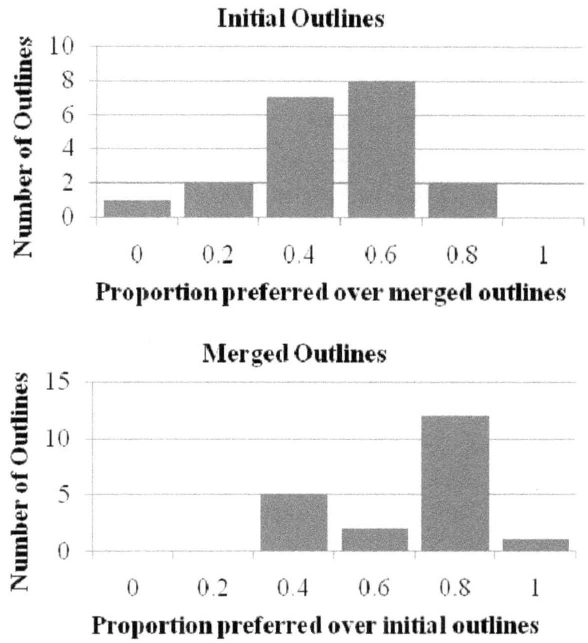

Figure 4. Histograms of participants preference choices for initial and merged outlines.

individual outlines are shown in Figure 4. Merged outlines also had fewer poor outlines: while 7 of the initial outlines were preferred 35% or less of the time, no merged outlines had preference values lower than 35%. Furthermore, the best merged outlines were considered better than the best initial outlines: the best initial outline was preferred 74% of the time, while 3 merged outlines were preferred more than that with the highest preferred 90% of the time. Together these results suggest that complex quality control tasks such as combining the results of multiple workers' outputs can be more effective than simple voting. CrowdForge makes such quality control tasks simple to implement as Reduce tasks.

Researching a purchase

We also investigated a different task— researching purchase decisions—in order to test the generality of the framework. Specifically, we applied our framework to commission decision matrices, in this case to help consumers compare automobiles. This example extends the framework by showing how one can partition the initial task on multiple dimensions (or, equivalently, repartition each element of the original partition). In the partition HIT for this problem, one worker was given a short description of a consumer (a hypothetical suburban family that drives their two children to and from school and enjoys occasional road trips) and asked to submit criteria they would evaluate a car on (e.g., reliability, safety). Another worker was given the same description and asked to submit a list of potential competitors (e.g., Honda Odyssey, Ford Escape). Combining the resulting lists yielded a matrix resembling a product comparison table. In the map step, workers were asked to submit facts for one cell in the table, for example evidence relevant to safety ratings for the Honda Odyssey they might find from an online review of the car. Finally, in the reduce step workers were given all the facts for a cell collected by workers in the map step, and were asked to write a single sentence consolidating them.

The entire task was completed in 54 different HITs for a total cost of $3.70. An excerpt from the resulting product comparison table is shown in Figure 5. We had no success getting even a single worker to generate a similar product comparison chart individually, even when offering more money than we paid the entire group, suggesting some complex tasks may not be amenable to completion in micro-task markets without appropriate decomposition.

PROTOTYPE

We implemented a software prototype to test our approach by allowing task designers to indirectly use MTurk to solve complex problems. It was this prototype that generated the HITs used in the experiments described above. The prototype allows task designers to break complex problems down into sub-problems, to specify the relationship between the sub-problems, and to generate a solution using MTurk. The system consists of a web user interface for the task designer, and a backend server which interfaces with Amazon's MTurk servers. The web user interface in Figure 6 allows users to define each step in the problem solving process and to specify the flow between each step. The server-side component creates MTurk HITs, consumes their results, and generates new HITs as needed. The prototype is written in Python using Django [8], a high-level web framework for rapid application development. Boto [3], a Python interface to Amazon Web Services, is used to communicate with MTurk. Source code for the prototype is available at https://github.com/borismus/crowdforge.

The system abstracts the entire process as a *problem*, which tracks the state of the current complex task. A problem references multiple *HIT Templates* (which may be either partitions, maps, or reduces), and a *flow* that defines the dependencies between the HIT Templates. The prototype allows multiple problems to exist in parallel, each one tracking its own currently active HIT Template. HIT Templates are parameterized templates used to create HITs on MTurk, specifying basic parameters like title, HTML body and compensation amount. Finally, flows manage the sequential coordination between HITs, as well as transferring data between HITs. When a user creates a new problem, they specify which flow to use to solve that problem.

	Honda Odyssey	Ford Escape	Nissan Pathfinder
Safety Rating	Honda's Odyssey scored 5 stars for front and side impact in tests conducted by the NHTSI, and features anti-lock brakes for added stability in turns when braking.	Ford's Escape model scored high marks in front and side crash testing, with a safety rating of 9.9 and pretensioner seatbelt feature that tightens automatically in a crash.	Nissan's Pathfinder gets high marks for safety in NHTSI tests and scored 4 stars for front crash test and is offered in a couple different body styles.

Figure 5: An excerpt from the product comparison table

Flows are implemented as python classes which have the **on_stage_completed**(self, stage): method. When all of the hits for the given hit type have been completed, CrowdForge calls the problem's flow's **on_stage_completed** method. Users can create a new flow by implementing a subclass of **crowdforge.flows.Flow** and registering it with **crowdforge.flows.register**. CrowdForge comes with several pre-built flows, such as the **SimpleFlow** which supports the simple partition-map-reduce scenario we used in generating NYC articles, and partition selection and verification flows that include additional verification steps.

The system uses a notification-based flow control mechanism to manage which tasks and templates are posted. Every few minutes the system monitors active problems for four kinds of events, and fires notifications as needed. The *result retrieved* notification fires when the system detects a new result from MTurk. The *HIT expired* notification fires when a HIT that was posted by the prototype expires due to the HIT lifetime running out. The *HIT complete* notification fires when all instances of a HIT were completed by workers. The *stage complete* notification fires when all HITs of the currently active HIT Template are completed or expired. Often, steps in CrowdForge require user submitted data from previous steps. Since CrowdForge is constantly polling MTurk to get newly submitted results, we have all of the results from previous submissions in the Results table in the database. All of these results are linked to the hit, and the hit type. The flow code can fetch these results using django's object relational model API.

For example, the simplest predefined flow (Figure 1) starts with a partition HIT Template, the result of which is fed into a map HIT Template, the results of which are fed into a reduce HIT Template. Transitions between these three HIT Templates occur when the *stage complete* notification fires. In the article writing example, this flow takes the article outline generated by a worker completing a partition HIT, and creates map HITs to collect facts for each heading in the outline. Note that this process is dynamic: the number of headings does not need to be specified beforehand by the task designer. Once all map HITs for a heading are complete, the flow posts a reduction HIT to consolidate all facts collected in the map HITs into a paragraph.

COMPLEX FLOWS

The example of article writing assumed a simple linear flow from partitioning to mapping to reduction, which may not be powerful enough to represent some tasks. For more general cases, subtasks can be themselves be broken down into partition, map and reduce phases (Figure 7). For example, in journalism, writing headlines and leads and soliciting quotes themselves can be broken into parallelizable partition, map and reduce phases. The notification-based architecture of the CrowdForge prototype allows this kind of nesting to be implemented as a custom flow (future work will allow the creation of nested flows using GUI tools).

Below, we discuss a case study involving a much more complex flow.

Crowdsourcing Science Journalism

We chose to address the complex problem of crowdsourcing the science journalism process; i.e., turning a paper published in an academic venue (such as *Science*) into a newspaper article for the general public. This task is challenging for a number of reasons. Just reading a complete academic paper may require more motivation and expertise than any single crowd worker possesses, let alone any subsequently writing. However, seeing only a portion of the article might not provide workers with the whole story; thus, it is unsuitable for the simpler partitioning used in the encyclopedic article case study. Furthermore, a science article has a particular structure to it that the crowd output would need to adhere to; enforcing this structure provides additional constraints. Finally, the task may simply require more expertise than available in the task market. Thus we chose this task in the spirit of a "grand challenge", hoping that even if the process failed we would learn about where the CrowdForge approach would break down.

To help us shape this the task we partnered with two professional journalists interested in the question of whether science journalism could be crowdsourced. We started by choosing an article published in *Science* examining the role of social influence in determining popularity in an artificial music market [22]. Although the research was complex and moderately technical, we believed that crowd workers would be able to understand it.

We worked with the journalists to identify a typical structure for a popular science article, including creating a news lead, describing what scientists did, what they found, getting a quote from a relevant expert and an author of the study, and describing implications and future work. For each of these sections we worked to develop subflows that would produce them. Some of the subflows required iteration and trying several different approaches. In total our

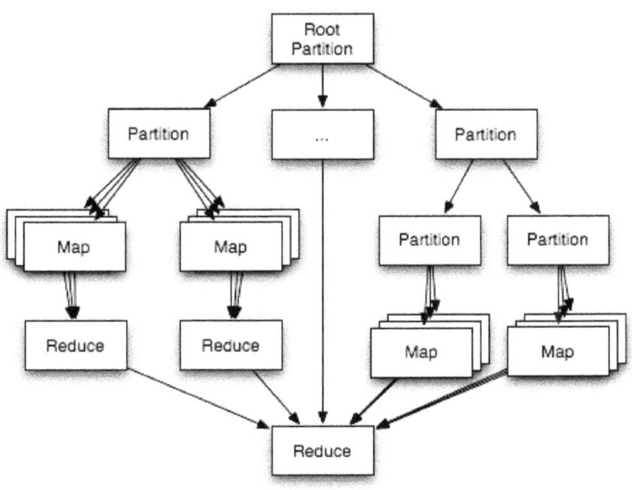

Figure 7. Nested subtasks forming a complex flow.

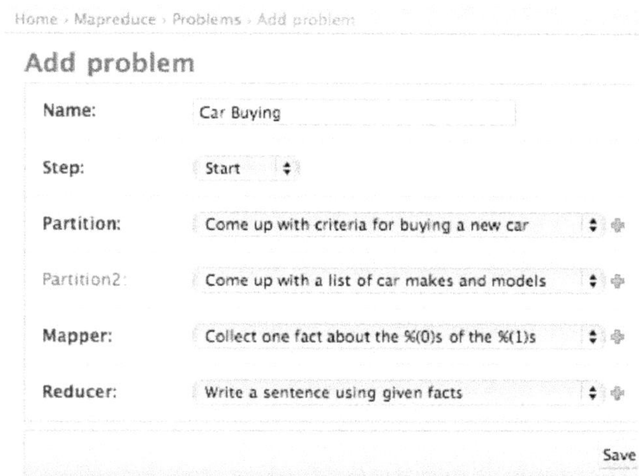

Figure 6: Creating a problem with the web user interface.

article generation task involved 11 subflows comprising 31 subtasks, which represent 262 worker judgments and a total cost of approximately $100. To give an idea of the tasks involved we will describe two interesting subflows in more detail below: generating a news lead and describing what the researchers did.

Generating a news lead requires quickly and succinctly conveying what the article is about in an engaging way that draws the reader in. To do this we initially provided workers with the article and asked them to tell us the single most important thing that a general reader needs to know about the finding in the paper. However, this task proved to be too large a chunk for workers to complete. Through several iterations we discovered task characteristics which made the process more amenable to workers. First, we used a "consolidate" process pattern in which the results of a large set are consolidated down to an input that better matches the limited attention profile of the worker. A simple example is presenting workers with the abstract of a scientific paper, in which the article authors have already consolidated the paper the paper down to the key points; however, we used various forms of consolidation throughout the process, including generating tags describing key terms from the abstract (to help find relevant experts) and extracting pieces of the article for different tasks (in the description of research, discussed below). Second, we provided workers with concrete examples of what we desired from them, e.g., in the form of an abstract and news lead from an exemplar article. This "exemplar" pattern proved particularly useful throughout many tasks, as mapping the sample input and output to the target article made the desired outcome much clearer than instructions could.

We used similar task patterns ("consolidation" + "exemplar") in the flow for generating a description of the research procedures, although with a slightly different instantiation. First, a partition task asked workers to extract the sections from the article that corresponded to different experiments. Then, for each experiment workers were asked to summarize what the researchers actually did, again providing them with a sample experiment and description.

Evaluation

To evaluate the quality of the resulting items we enlisted experts with complementary skills, including a professional journalist, the first author of the *Science* paper, a graduate student doing research on social computing, and one of the authors of this study. Each rater was given a survey asking them to rate each of 16 news leads and 8 research descriptions on a 7-point Likert scale. Items were arranged in one of two randomized orders to control for order effects. Raters were in moderate agreement across items (alpha = .74).

Overall, the results were surprisingly good. According to the author of the paper, "it was a bit below what you would see in a high-quality publication like the NY Times, but the best were not totally different (although the worst were pretty bad)." The professional journalist had a similar reaction: "I'm really impressed by the quality of the answers. The abstract from the Salganik paper is not that technical by the standards of scientific literature, but the key news point -- that social influence helps determine success -- is contained in just one line. Yet 7 of the 10 workers who did the task put that point in their lead."[2] Ratings for the news leads ranged from 6.25 to 1.25 (higher being better), with a standard deviation of 1.3. Research descriptions fared less well, ranging between 4.4 and 1.8 (*SD* = .93). To provide some insight into the range of content created, the best rated (6.25) and worst rated (1.25) news leads are shown below:

> "Blockbusters, bestsellers, hit songs - the main variable that makes these things more popular than their lesser-known counterparts is not quality differences, according to a recent study. The answer lies in social influence - the more people know a certain movie is the one to watch, the more likely it will become popular." (Best)

> "The psychology of song preference. Song quality isn't the best predictor of song success." (Worst)

As indicated in the quotes above the results, while good, were not perfect. The resulting article would not be likely to win a Pulitzer, for example, which is not surprising given that workers were not trained nor expert writers. This suggests their output might be best used as part of a work flow in which professional editors or writers subsequently massage the crowdsourced work. Their value in this regard was supported by the journalist, who said: "An editor does not require that a reporter (or in this case a Turker) produce beautifully polished copy. But editors do need to be confident that the copy captures the main points of the story, because editors don't expect to have to do any additional reporting themselves. From that point of view, the replies are impressive. The quality of the writing is variable and in some cases a little muddled, but it is more important to note that many of the workers produced leads that captured the newsworthy element of the paper."

[2] This quote was from a time when only 10 leads were collected.

Perhaps more concerning, none of the leads or descriptions mentioned the important finding that there was high unpredictability about which items became popular. However, upon discussion the article author noted that "lots of the 'real' reporters missed the unpredictability part too", while the journalist raised the point that this might actually be due to differences in audience rather than missing the point: "the disagreement arises because the two are writing for different audiences: a journalist for lay readers and an academic for other researchers. The two audiences often care about different things."

Together these results suggest that despite the lack of expertise, limited time and effort, and limited context provided by crowd workers, assembling the output of many small judgments through the proper coordination can result in highly complex artifacts of surprisingly good quality.

LIMITATIONS

While we have demonstrated some of the strengths of the CrowdForge approach, here we discuss some limitations. First, the system currently does not support iteration or recursion, requiring the task designer to specify each stage in the task flow (though workers can define their own partitions and thus what future tasks will be). While CrowdForge is compatible with iteration, the strength of existing crowdsourcing toolkits that focus on iteration (e.g., TurKit) led us to focus our contribution elsewhere. We plan to merge both approaches in future work; this would enable, for example, one stage (e.g., a vote) to determine if another (e.g., a further partition) is necessary.

Second, and more fundamentally, CrowdForge is based on the idea that complex work can be broken up into relatively small and independent pieces with the system managing the coordination dependencies between those pieces. However, these assumptions can be violated. For example, it is possible that some work may not be easily decomposable into units small enough to match the task capacity of the workforce. We approached these limits with the science journalism task: although we had workers extract each experiment in the article separately to minimize the work, they still needed to read and summarize an entire experiment in order to complete the task; had the experiments been larger or more complex this step would not have succeeded as well. Another possibility is that the decomposition and recomposition of tasks, along with necessary intermediate quality control steps, could introduce more overhead and cost than they are worth. For example, it is likely not worth decomposing an article into independent sentences and requiring workers to merge arbitrary sentences into paragraphs. Finally, in situations where tasks really cannot be decomposed, selecting another task market where individuals have higher skill or motivation (e.g., oDesk, TopCoder) may be necessary.

Another violation of the assumptions may occur if subtasks are not independent. For example, while the diversity provided by multiple judgments was sufficient for the map phase of the New York City article to succeed, CrowdForge provided no guarantee that workers would not select diverse information. Providing them information about other workers' outputs could be valuable in preventing workers from all returning the same results. However, the advantages of providing additional context need to be weighed against the costs of increased task load (since workers need to process more information) and the potential for seeing other workers' judgments leading to negative consequences such as cognitive tunneling, information cascades, and production blocking [8][29]. This suggests that in some contexts (e.g., brainstorming) independent generation and subsequent merging of output may be superior to iteration on others' work, which in others exposure to others' outputs could improve the final product as workers could build on each others' work or reduce the bias of an individual. Understanding the appropriate times and ways to provide context and visibility into the work of others is an important area for future crowdsourcing research.

CONCLUSION

In this paper we presented a general-purpose framework for solving complex problems through micro-task markets. The framework manages the coordination between workers so that complex artifacts can be effectively produced by individuals contributing only small amounts of time and effort. Based on concepts from coordination science and distributed computing, the CrowdForge framework provides a systematic and dynamic way to break down tasks into subtasks and manage the flow and dependencies between them.

We demonstrate through three case studies and multiple experiments how the framework can break down complex tasks such as writing an article or researching a purchase decision into flows of partition, map, and reduce subtasks. In the article writing case we showed that CrowdForge-produced articles were rated more highly and had lower variability than individual-produced articles, despite the coordination requirements of managing and integrating dozens of workers, and were rated of similar quality as Simple Wikipedia articles. In an extension to this example, we showed how to insert a quality control step in the flow and demonstrated the value of combining the best aspects of multiple workers' outputs rather than simple voting. In the purchase decision case we were unable to get even a single individual to complete the task given the high effort involved, but could accomplish the goal using CrowdForge with low monetary costs. Finally, we explored more complex flows and subtasks using the domain of science journalism, demonstrating how a popular press article could be created despite crowdworkers having limited expertise, time and effort, and context. In this example we also discuss useful patterns for subtask design, such as the "consolidate" and "analogy" patterns. Finally, we discuss limitations of and fundamental challenges for the approach.

Furthermore, as the nature of work itself becomes more distributed, such an approach has the potential to change the way that work gets done, enabling many more people to be involved in solving complex problems ranging from business intelligence to writing software. However, markets don't work well for complex tasks when the employer cannot define exactly what they want in advance or if the contract is difficult to pre-define. The CrowdForge framework reduces this need for predefinition by allowing for subtasks to be dynamically generated by the market itself. It also supports scaling up complex tasks to involve many workers by managing the coordination dependencies between them.

As general purpose markets continue to evolve, there is a growing need to be able to solve a wider range of tasks of increasing complexity and coordination requirements. Although our framework draws from ideas in distributed computing such as MapReduce, using humans instead of machines as processors provides both distinct benefits and challenges. For example, our human-driven partition step is novel and unique to human computation. However, the unreliability and unknown expertise of each worker necessitates more complex and nested flows for quality control. Here we provide a conceptual framework and vision that we hope will inform and inspire future researchers and task designers in taking on more complex and even "grand challenge" tasks that will push the limits of what can be crowdsourced.

There are a number of directions we are exploring for future work. Most immediately, one challenge is extending our GUI to support more complex, nested flows so that task designers with no programming experience can complete arbitrarily complex work that involves high coordination dependencies. Looking further ahead, we are interested in exploring the possibilities of the CrowdForge framework in very different kinds of task markets. Although in this paper we implemented systems for two different platforms (MTurk and CrowdFlower), both have similar worker characteristics (indeed, many CrowdFlower tasks are posted on MTurk). If the framework was applied to a market in which the expertise of individual workers was better known (e.g., in a corporation) there might be greater opportunities for managing resource allocation of workers to appropriate tasks. Feedback about the selection and quality of their past work could also be useful for improving resource allocation if the system had a shared memory of individual workers' history across tasks.

ACKNOWLEDGMENTS

This work was supported by NSF grants OCI-0943148 and IIS-0968484, and the Center for the Future of Work, Heinz College, Carnegie Mellon University.

REFERENCES

[1] Bal, H.E., Steiner, J.G. and Tanenbaum, A.S. Programming languages for distributed computing systems. ACM Computing Surveys (CSUR) (1989) vol. 21 (3).

[2] Becker, G.S. and Murphy, K.M. The division of labor, coordination costs, and knowledge. The Quarterly Journal of Economics (1992) vol. 107 (4) pp. 1137-1160

[3] Boto, http://code.google.com/p/boto/

[4] Callison-Burch, C. Fast, cheap, and creative: evaluating translation quality using Amazon's Mechanical Turk. In *Proceedings of the 2009 Conference on Empirical Methods in Natural Language Processing: Volume 1* (2009) pp. 286-295

[5] Cole, F., Sanik, K., DeCarlo, D., Finkelstein, A., Funkhouser, T., Rusinkiewicz, S., and Singh, M. How well do line drawings depict shape? In *ACM SIGGRAPH* (2009), 1–9.

[6] Dean, J. and Ghemawat, S. Map Reduce: Simplified data processing on large clusters. *Communications of the ACM*, 51, 1 (2008), 107-114.

[7] Deng, J., Dong, W., Socher, R., Li, L.J., Li, K., Fei-Fei, L. "ImageNet: A large-scale hierarchical image database," cvpr, pp.248-255, *IEEE Conference on Computer Vision and Pattern Recognition* (2009).

[8] Diehl, M. and Stroebe, W. Productivity loss in brainstorming groups: Toward the solution of a riddle. *Journal of personality and social psychology* 53, 3 (1987), 497–509.

[9] Django, http://www.djangoproject.com

[10] Ipeirotis, P. (2010, Mar 3). The New Demographics of Mechanical Turk. http://behind-the-enemy-lines.blogspot.com/2010/03/new-demographics-of-mechanical-turk.html. Retrieved 9-21-20

[11] Isard, M., Budiu, M., Yu, Y., Birrell, A., and Fetterly, D. Dryad: distributed data-parallel programs from sequential building blocks. *Proceedings of the 2nd ACM SIGOPS/EuroSys European Conference on Computer Systems 2007*, (2007), 59–72.

[12] Heer, J. and Bostock, M. Crowdsourcing graphical perception: using mechanical turk to assess visualization design. In *Proceedings of CHI* (2010). ACM, New York, 203-212.

[13] Horton, J. J., Rand, D.G. and Zeckhauser, R.J., The online laboratory: Conducting experiments in a real labor market (2010). NBER Working Paper Series, Vol. w15961.

[14] Kittur, A., Chi, E., Suh, B. Crowdsourcing User Studies With Mechanical Turk. In *Proceedings of CHI* (2008).

[15] Kittur, A., Lee, B., Kraut, R. E. Coordination in Collective Intelligence: The Role of Team Structure and Task Interdependence. In *Proceedings of CHI* (2009). ACM, New York.

[16] Kittur, A. and Kraut, R. E. Harnessing the wisdom of crowds in wikipedia: quality through coordination. In *Proceedings of CSCW* (2008). ACM, New York.

[17] Little, G., Chilton, L.B., Goldman, M., and Miller, R.C. Turkit: human computation algorithms on mechanical turk. In *Proceedings of UIST* (2010), ACM, New York, 57–66.

[18] Malone, T. and Crowston, K. The interdisciplinary study of coordination. *ACM Computing Surveys*, 26, (1994), 87-119.

[19] Malone, T., Yates, J. and Benjamin, R. Electronic markets and electronic hierarchies. *Communications of the ACM*, 30 (6). 484-497.

[20] Mintzberg, H. 1979. The Structuring of Organizations.Prentice-Hall, Englewood Cliffs, N.J.

[21] Olston, C., Reed, B., Srivastava, U., Kumar, R., and Tomkins, A. Pig latin: a not-so-foreign language for data processing. In *Proceedings of the 2008 ACM SIGMOD international conference on Management of data*, (2008), 1099–1110.

[22] Salganik, M.J., Dodds, P.S., & Watts, D.J. Experimental study of inequality and unpredictability in an artificial cultural market. *Science, 311* (2006), 854.

[23] Snow, R., O'Connor, B., Jurafsky, D., and Ng, A.Y. Cheap and fast---but is it good?: evaluating non-expert annotations for natural language tasks. In *Proceedings of the Conference on Empirical Methods in Natural Language Processing, Association for Computational Linguistics* (2008), 254-263.

[24] Skillicorn, D.B., Talia, D. Models and languages for parallel computation, *ACM Computing Surveys* 30(2) (1998) 123–169.

[25] Sorokin, A., Forsyth, D. Utility data annotation with Amazon Mechanical Turk, *First IEEE Workshop on Internet Vision at CVPR* (2008).

[26] Van de Ven, A., Delbecq, A. and Koenig, R. Determinants of coordination modes within organizations. *American Sociological Review*, 41 (1976), 322-338.

[27] Williamson, O. Transaction-Cost Economics: The Governance of Contractual Relations. *The Journal of Law and Economics, 22* (2). 233.

[28] Wikipedia Simple entry on New York City, http://simple.wikipedia.org/wiki/New_York_City

[29] Woods, D. & Cook, R. 1999. Perspectives on human error: Hindsight biases and local rationality. In F. Durso (Ed.), Handbook of applied cognition. NY: John Wiley.

The Jabberwocky Programming Environment for Structured Social Computing

Salman Ahmad saahmad@stanford.edu
Alexis Battle ajbattle@stanford.edu
Zahan Malkani zahanm@stanford.edu
Sepandar D. Kamvar sdkamvar@stanford.edu

ABSTRACT

We present Jabberwocky, a social computing stack that consists of three components: a human and machine resource management system called Dormouse, a parallel programming framework for human and machine computation called ManReduce, and a high-level programming language on top of ManReduce called Dog. Dormouse is designed to enable cross-platform programming languages for social computation, so, for example, programs written for Mechanical Turk can also run on other crowdsourcing platforms. Dormouse also enables a programmer to easily combine crowdsourcing platforms or create new ones. Further, machines and people are both first-class citizens in Dormouse, allowing for natural parallelization and control flows for a broad range of data-intensive applications. And finally and importantly, Dormouse includes notions of real identity, heterogeneity, and social structure. We show that the unique properties of Dormouse enable elegant programming models for complex and useful problems, and we propose two such frameworks. ManReduce is a framework for combining human and machine computation into an intuitive parallel data flow that goes beyond existing frameworks in several important ways, such as enabling functions on arbitrary communication graphs between human and machine clusters. And Dog is a high-level procedural language written on top of ManReduce that focuses on expressivity and reuse. We explore two applications written in Dog: bootstrapping product recommendations without purchase data, and expert labeling of medical images.

ACM Classification: H5.2 [Information interfaces and presentation]: User Interfaces. - Graphical user interfaces.

General terms: Languages, Human Factors

Keywords: social computing, crowdsourcing

INTRODUCTION

In the last few years, there has been a heightened interest in human computation, where tasks that are difficult for computers (such as image labeling or transcription) are split into microtasks and dispatched to people. Human computation has been used to address large-scale goals ranging from labeling images [23], to finding 3-D protein structures [3], to creating a crowdsourced illustrated book [8], to classifying galaxies in Hubble images [1].

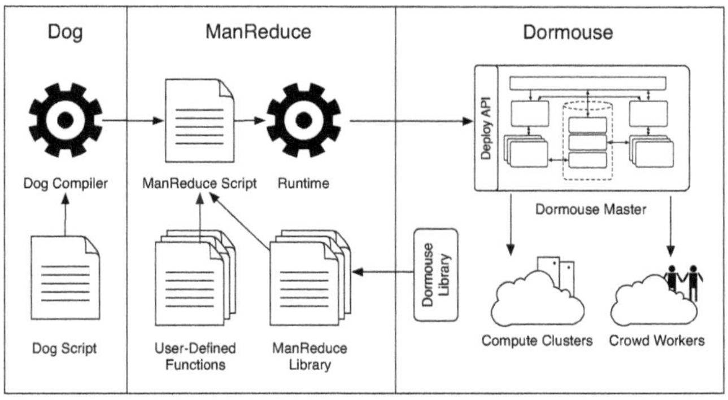

Figure 1: Overview of Jabberwocky

In existing paradigms, human workers are often treated as homogeneous and interchangeable, which is useful in handling issues of scale and availability. However, the limited notions of identity, reputation, expertise, and social relationships limit the scope of tasks that can be addressed with these systems. Incorporating real identities, social structure, and expertise modeling has proven valuable in a range of applications, for example, in question-answering with Aardvark [11]. Building general frameworks for human computation that include these notions will enable complex applications to be built more easily.

A second drawback of existing platforms is that each defines a stand-alone system with rigid structure and requirements, and thus demands significant work in order to integrate human computation into larger applications. Each new application may require building a pipeline from the ground up, and in many cases, a new community. Particularly for complex applications, which may involve several steps of human computation using different crowdsourcing platforms interleaved with machine computation, constructing such a pipeline can be a tedious effort. In practice, complex systems are discouraged, and most uses of human computation avoid multiple interleaved processing steps.

To address these issues, we designed Jabberwocky, a social computing stack that consists of Dormouse, ManReduce, and Dog. Dormouse is the "virtual machine" layer of the Jabberwocky stack, consisting of low-level software libraries that interact with both people and traditional computing machines. Dormouse maintains real identities, rich user profiles, and social relationships for the people who comprise the system, and allows end users to define arbitrary person-level properties and social structures in the system. Further, Dormouse allows programmers to interact with several different crowdsourcing platforms using the same primitives. This enables the development of cross-platform programming languages for social computing. And finally, because Dormouse defines communications protocols for both people and machines, programmers can very naturally interact with both in unified control flows even for complex parallel processing tasks.

On top of Dormouse, we built ManReduce, a programming framework inspired by MapReduce [4] (and related to CrowdForge [13]) to facilitate complex data processing tasks. ManReduce, like MapReduce, gives the programmer the ability to specify *map* and *reduce* steps, but allowing either step to be powered by human or machine computation. The data flow, resource allocation, and parallelization necessary for each step are handled by ManReduce with no onus on the programmer. In addition to combining machine and human computation, ManReduce also provides the ability to choose particular types of people to complete each task (based on Dormouse), and allows arbitrary dependencies between multiple *map* and *reduce* steps. Many interesting social computing applications fit naturally into this paradigm, as they frequently involve the need for parallelization of subtasks across people or machines, and subsequent aggregation such as writing a summary or averaging ratings. As a simple example, conducting a survey and tabulating summary statistics for each question (breaking down according to a variety of demographics) can be expressed using a human *map* step that sends the survey in parallel to many people, and one or more machine *reduce* steps on the output that aggregate the responses keyed by question and/or user demographic.

While ManReduce offers flexibility and power, it can be too low-level for several classes of applications. In many cases, it is useful to trade some flexibility for expressivity, maintainability, and reuse. To that end, we designed Dog, a high-level scripting language that compiles into ManReduce. Inspired by the Pig [19] and Sawzall [21] languages for data mining, Dog defines a small but powerful set of primitives for requesting computational work from either people or machines, and for interfacing with workers (and their properties) through Dormouse. In addition, it defines simple interfaces for using, creating, and sharing functions (human or machine) and microtask templates, making it easy to quickly implement a wide range of applications.

Together, the components of the Jabberwocky stack allow programmers to implement applications in a few lines of code that would otherwise require writing large amounts of ad hoc infrastructure. We explore several such applications in this paper, including a journal transcription application that maintains the privacy of the journal-writer, a recommender system that requires no pre-existing co-occurrence data, and a medical image tagging application that allows experts to leverage low-cost generalists (and generalists to learn from experts).

DORMOUSE

The lowest level of the Jabberwocky stack is Dormouse, a "virtual machine" layer that enables cross-platform social computation. Similar to process virtual machines (such as the Java Virtual Machine) in traditional computing, Dormouse sits on top of existing crowdsourcing platforms, providing a platform-independent programming environment that abstracts away the details of the underlying crowdsourcing platform. Importantly, Dormouse also enables programmers to seamlessly create new crowdsourcing communities and add social features (such as worker profiles and relationships) to existing ones.

Design Goals

Our design goals for Dormouse are to:

Support cross-platform programming languages for social computing. Programming languages run on Dormouse can work with any crowdsourcing platform that hooks into Dormouse, and can support execution across several platforms in the same program. For example, a programmer may, in one step, routes tasks to a large number of inexpensive workers from one crowdsourcing platform, and in a next step, routes tasks to a smaller number of vetted experts from another platform, without the needing to learn the separate (and often complex) API calls from multiple platforms.

Make it easy for programmers to build new crowdsourcing communities. In addition to being able to reside on top of existing crowdsourcing platforms, Dormouse makes it easy for programmers to create new worker communities given a set of e-mail addresses.

Enable rich personal profiles and social structures. Programming languages run on Dormouse allow the programmer to route tasks based personal properties such as expertise and demographic, and also to set and modify expertise levels based on task performance. Further, programmers may route tasks based on social structure (for example, an application that matches technical papers to reviewers may route papers to computer science graduate students to review, and then to their advisor to validate the review).

Combine human and machine computation into a single parallel computing framework. Programming languages run on Dormouse allow the programmer to allocate machines and people in similar ways, leading to more natural control flows for parallelization.

Make it easy for programmers to create and reuse human tasks. Dormouse has a straightforward mechanisms to create new templates for human tasks, and importantly, to reuse those created by others. This minimizes redundant work and allows programmers to focus on control flows rather than creating and optimizing task templates.

Architecture

Dormouse is implemented as a set of software components that reside on a *Dormouse master* machine. These components communicate with one another, as well as an external Dormouse machine cluster and a set of human workers. These software components are described below and shown in Figure 2.

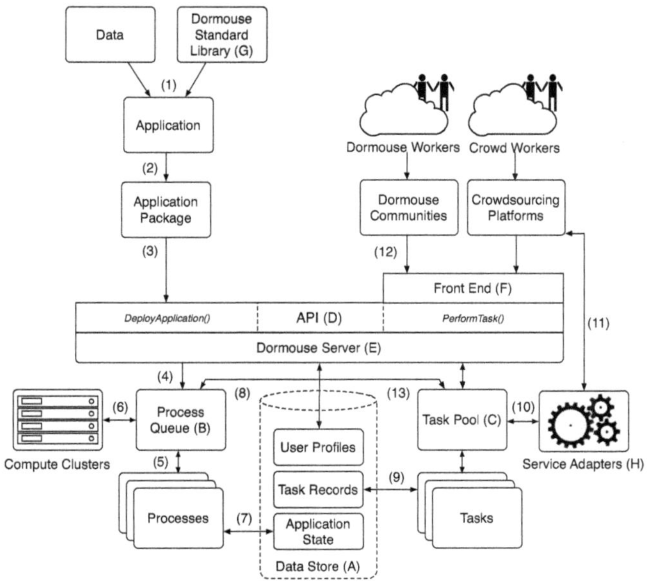

Figure 2: Internal Architecture of Dormouse

The *Dormouse Data Store (A)* is a set of distributed SQL databases that store user profiles, community information, and application-specific information and data for each running process.

The *Dormouse Process Queue (B)* schedules the top level control flow of an application, as well as any computational steps that require the Dormouse machine cluster. All Dormouse applications are registered with the Process Queue.

The *Dormouse Task Pool (C)* maintains a set of tasks that are waiting to be performed by human workers. Each task in the pool is annotated with specifications for the type of workers that are eligible to complete the task. Worker specifications are predicates represented by a binary expression tree and encoded using JSON.

The *Dormouse API (D)* is a low-level API that contains functions to process and update Dormouse system resources (for example, to register a task, to update a profile, to terminate an application, etc.).

The *Dormouse Server (E)* is a continuously running service that manages programs as they are executed, human tasks as they are dispatched, people as they join or leave, etc., by calling Dormouse API functions when appropriate. For example, when the Dormouse Server gets a request to run a new Dormouse package, it calls `add`, which adds the package to the Process Queue.

The *Dormouse Front End (F)* is a Ruby on Rails web application that serves as a UI for both workers and developers. Workers use the Frontend to manage profile information, view tasks for which they are eligible, and select and complete tasks. Developers can use the interface to manage their developer accounts and deploy their applications.

The *Dormouse Standard Library (G)* provides runtime hooks that communicate between an application and Dormouse, a set of human tasks (e.g. `Label` and `Compare`), and a set of common computational steps (e.g. `Average` and `Sum`) that can be called from any Dormouse application. A human task is an object that consists of a UI template[1], input parameters, and a return value. A computational step is an object that includes a method that is designed to run in parallel over a set of key-value inputs on a Dormouse machine cluster.

The *Dormouse Service Adapters (H)* manage communication between Dormouse and other crowdsourcing platforms, such as Mechanical Turk. To hook into Dormouse, a crowdsourcing platform need only provide an API that minimally allows for the posting of tasks. The Task Pool uses these adapters to invoke the target service's API to post tasks.

Process Deployment

To show how these components interact with one another, we walk through deploying an application on the Dormouse architecture. Figure 2 illustrates the process.

The developer begins by writing an application that links to the Dormouse Standard Library (1), packaging the application using the Dormouse Command-line Utility (2), and deploying the package through the Dormouse Server (3).

The Dormouse Server unpacks the application, reads the manifest file to find the main executable (the program that contains the top-level control flow of the application) and sends that executable to the Process Queue (4).

The Process Queue begins running the executable (5), which may pause for one of two reasons: it either needs access to machine resources to perform a computational step over a set of key-value pairs or it needs to ask human workers to perform a task. In either case, the executable automatically saves its state to the Dormouse Data Store using the Dormouse Standard Library serialization routines (7), and temporarily terminates.

The Process Queue exploits the parallelism in computational steps by running them over a compute cluster (6). It does this by copying the application package to each node in the cluster and invoking the runtime hooks provided by the Dormouse Standard Library to selectively execute a single step over a subset of key-value input parameters. Once all of the steps from all the different nodes are finished, the results are sent back to the Process Queue, and then to the executable, which starts to run again.

When the executable reaches a point where no further work can be done without human input, it saves its state, terminates, and outputs a list of human tasks using JSON. The executable will be started again once the human tasks are complete.

The Process Queue takes the JSON output and sends information to the Task Pool (8). The Task Pool creates a record that includes a link back to the process, worker specification information, and the name of the Service Adapter, if any, that should be used to post tasks (9). The Task Pool invokes the "submit" method on the specified Service Adapter (10), which performs the steps necessary to post each task on

[1]written in ERB, a template language used by Ruby on Rails

the appropriate crowdsourcing platform (11). If no Service Adapter is provided, the tasks will be available on Dormouse to existing users (12).

Once a task is completed, the Task Pool sends the answer back to the Process Queue (13). When all needed human tasks are finished, the process is re-executed, starting up from where it left off. The process continues until it once again needs human input or it finishes running. When the process is finished, it outputs a return code signaling the Process Queue to mark it as done and sends the developer a notification, which includes a download link to a JSON file containing the results.

MANREDUCE

In order to make Dormouse readily usable for complex data-intensive applications, we specify a programming framework called ManReduce, based on the simple functional programming paradigm and resource management scheme used by MapReduce [4]. ManReduce shares some conceptual similarities with the independently conceived CrowdForge [13], but ManReduce has some important advantages to both MapReduce and Crowdforge that we discuss below.

Design Goals

With ManReduce, while providing power and flexibility, we aimed to maintain a conceptually simple design that can be rapidly understood and easily used. In addition, ManReduce has three key features that, in combination, allow us to develop a wide range of applications for social computation: the ability to dispatch jobs both to machines and people, to utilize social structure and choose which people to whom to send jobs, and to introduce arbitrary dependencies between multiple *map* and *reduce* steps. These features, in particular, are absent in both CrowdForge and MapReduce. We discuss each core contribution below.

Conceptual simplicity and ease of use. We begin with a clean conceptual foundation for our framework. Like in MapReduce, a program is broken down into steps that are each written as a *map* or a *reduce* . A ManReduce *map* step consists of a set of small, equivalent chunks of work, performed in parallel when possible on independent inputs, producing outputs in the form of key-value pairs. A *reduce* step collects several input items (according to a shared key), and performs some computation over all of them to produce a final output. These two steps can be used to encode a wide range of parallelized computational applications.

In addition to the conceptual simplicity, our particular implementation is easy to use and allows a programmer to create full applications in few lines of code. The ManReduce framework is written in Ruby[2]. Internally, *map* and *reduce* are convenience wrappers that instantiate a Ruby `Step` object that accepts an anonymous function. A simple ManReduce script, shown in Figure 3, conducts a survey (utilizing the Dormouse function Survey). In this example, a *map* step `survey_map` sends the survey to human workers, and a *reduce* step `avg_reduce` takes the mean of their responses to each question. Notice that the user does not need to write

[2] We are also working on Python and Java implementations.

```
map :name => "survey_map" do |key, value|

  task = Survey.prepare
    :task_name => "Respond to survey",
    :replication => 1000

  task.ask do |answer|
    for a in answer
      emit(a["question"], a["response"])
    end
  end
end

reduce :step =>"Average",:name =>"avg_reduce"
```

Figure 3: Survey ManReduce Script.

any scaffolding code, such as parsing input or writing output. The appendix includes the full source code of `Survey` and `Average`

ManReduce can be run simply on the command line, and it is then deployed it on the Dormouse server. Once all the tasks have been completed, ManReduce will write the output to a destination file and terminate the process. Note that ManReduce automatically serializes all worker answers, allowing us to re-run (and even debug) a script many times, automatically using the available answers to compute new (or corrected) statistics without re-doing human tasks. Thus, designing, coding, and executing ManReduce programs is straightforward.

MapReduce with both humans and machines. In the ManReduce framework, either people *or* machines can perform the work necessary for both *map* and *reduce* steps. This allows users to implement complex applications which interleave both human and machine steps.

Many computation tasks fit naturally into this hybrid ManReduce paradigm. For example, ManReduce makes it easy to specify a human-assisted information extraction system. This application has a variety of uses for large corpora of documents, where automatic information extraction cuts down on human work significantly, but alone does not always provide sufficient accuracy. A machine *map* step could specify automatic information extraction of facts from a set of scientific papers, such as genetic and environmental risk factors for a set of candidate diseases. Then, a human *reduce* step could aggregate the proposed facts about each disease, check their accuracy and convert them into a summary. The ManReduce code for this example is shown in Figure 4.

In the example explored in Figure 4, the reduce step includes asking people to aggregate and summarize a set of facts. As shown on line 12, this was accomplished by instantiating a Dormouse Task object in Ruby and calling the ask method. Custom human *map* and *reduce* steps can include any of the human tasks available through the Dormouse libraries, or custom human functions. Likewise, machine *map* and *reduce* steps can call functions from existing Ruby libraries and custom libraries, as used on line 2. In addition, the ManReduce libraries include a range of pre-defined *map* and *reduce* steps, including image labelling, ranking items from a list,

```
map :name => :extract_disease_facts do |key, value|
  facts = RiskExtractor.extract (value)

  for fact in facts do
    emit (fact["disease"], fact["risk_factor"])
  end

end

reduce :name => :summarize do |key, values|

  task = SummarizeFacts.prepare
    :task_name => "Summarize disease risks: #{key}"
  task.facts = values

  task.ask do |answer|
    emit (key, answer)
  end

end
```

Figure 4: Human-Assisted Information Extraction

and free text-entry. The built-in libraries, and the ability to define and share custom steps, provide a large and growing codebase with which to easily create new ManReduce scripts.

Utilization of social structure through Dormouse. ManReduce takes advantage of the social structure and worker profiles provided by Dormouse, finding people whose attributes match those needed for a particular task. This is a natural extension from MapReduce, which allows specification of machines by their properties, such as processor speed or memory. Using functionality from Dormouse, we can specify that certain *map* or *reduce* tasks be dispatched only to people with graduate degrees in biology, or expertise in computer science, or simply to people under 25.

Adding identities and relationships opens many possibilities in human computation. For instance, accurately tagging people in photographs is important for image search engines. Using current techniques, search engines can identify a set of images and candidate names associated with each, but many pictures contain multiple people and many names correspond to several real people. The people in these photos can, however, be identified quickly and accurately by their friends. By identifying Facebook users according to each name, we could define a *map* step that asks friends of each user to judge whether an image contains their friend.

A user specification is used in ManReduce by simply setting the worker predicate and namespace properties of a Task object before it is asked. The specification is created using a Predicate object, as shown in Figure 5.

Complex ManReduce dependency graphs. Going beyond the original MapReduce model, ManReduce allows arbitrary chaining of *map* and *reduce* steps, similar to the Dryad (machine computational) framework [12]. Not only can a programmer specify multiple *map* and *reduce* steps in arbitrary

```
task = ImagePersonTask.prepare
    :task_name => "Tag person: #{key}",
    :replication => 5

task.worker_namespace = "facebook"
task.worker_predicate = Predicate.parse(["friends CONTAINS ?", key])
```

Figure 5: User Specification with Predicate

```
map :name => "collect_survery" do |key,value|
  ...
end

reduce :name => "sort_by_gender", :from => "collect_survey"
  ...
end

reduce :name => "sort_by_age", :from => "collect_survey"
  ...
end
```

Figure 6: Complex ManReduce Dependencies

order, she can also specify several different *reduce* steps that operate on the output of a single *map* step, or have a *map* step follow a *map* step directly. The ability to define functions on a generalized graph rather than a single *map* and *reduce* holds particular importance in the social computing domain. For instance, even a simple case like two sequential *map* steps may not fit naturally into single *map*, if a human step follows a machine step, or if a one human step is followed by another with different worker expertise constraints.

In ManReduce, each Step (*map* or *reduce*) may have multiple parents and multiple children. A step receives inputs from its parents and sends its output to each of its children. By default, ManReduce infers dependencies by the order in which they are defined – each Step's parent is assumed to be the Step immediately preceding it in the source code. To specify complex dependencies, we provide the `from` specifier in the `man` and `reduce` declarations, which specifies the name of the step whose output to use as input, as shown in Figure 6.

An interesting example with complex control flow is privacy-preserving journal transcription. Many researchers and designers keep handwritten notebooks, which would be useful to digitize and make searchable. Since OCR has limited accuracy with handwriting, we use human transcription, but split each page up into small chunks to make the tasks manageable and reduce the likelihood of revealing sensitive content. A ManReduce program for this application begins with a machine *map* step that "shreds" each scanned page into small overlapping images, each of which contains just a few words. A human *map* step then classifies the snippet as to whether it contains text, an image, or an equation. The result is sent to three human transcription map steps, one which is public and operates on the text, and two that are sent to people who are proficient in latex or illustrator to transcribe figures and equations. A human reduce step then votes on

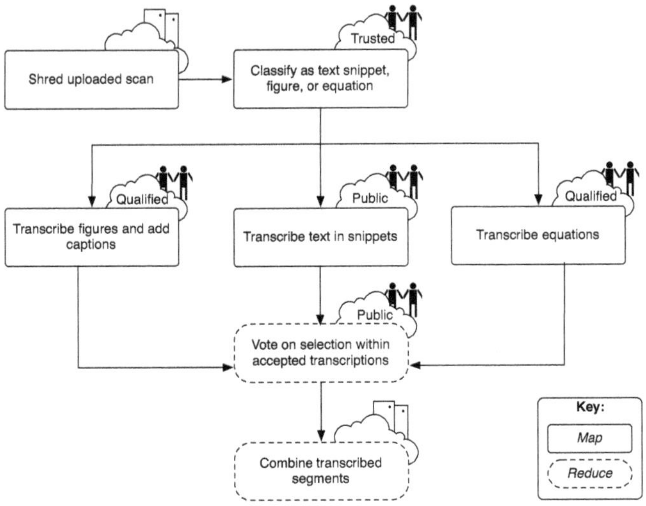

Figure 7: Illustration of dependency graph in the Journal Transcription Application

the best transcription for each snippet, and a machine *reduce* step then pastes the chunks from a single page back together into a PDF. Optionally, a final human *reduce* step, perhaps restricted to a trusted set of workers (e.g. people from your own institution or even just yourself) is used to rapidly verify the complete output of several pages at a time and output the final document. The control flow for this application is shown in Figure 7.

Discussion

While ManReduce takes inspiration for its name from MapReduce, it takes inspiration for its design from a number of parallel programming frameworks, including MapReduce, Dryad [12], and GPU shader languages [22]. Each of these frameworks was developed in an environment characterized by data-intensive applications and the availability of parallel computing resources. This characterization also holds for many applications in human computation, for example, in image processing or machine learning.

At the same time, there are some applications where ManReduce is not suitable, for example, for using a single worker in the crowd to control a robot [14]. Data-processing applications are well-suited to ManReduce, while real-time or single-worker sequential applications are not.

In fact, while we believe MapReduce-based models are compelling for variety of human computation applications, we recognize that other paradigms may be more appropriate for certain tasks, or preferred by some programmers. Dormouse makes it possible to implement other such frameworks, and we hope to see a variety of paradigms for social computation implemented for use with Dormouse. These programming paradigms could take advantage not only of the features provided by Dormouse, but also the wide array of human tasks that are written for Dormouse[3].

[3]As an analogy, languages like Scala [18] and Clojure [10] are implemented for use with the Java Virtual Machine, allowing these languages to make use of the platform independence of the JVM as well as the function libraries written for Java.

DOG

While ManReduce is flexible and powerful, one drawback is that it can be too low level for many applications. ManReduce requires programmers to think in terms of explicit *map* and *reduce* steps, even in common cases where it is more natural to think in terms of reusing and assembling basic building blocks. It also requires some knowledge of advanced programming constructs (for example, ManReduce uses callback functions for human steps).

To address these issues, we developed Dog, a high-level procedural programming language that sits on top of ManReduce and focuses on reusability, maintainability, and ease-of-use. Our approach of writing a high-level language that compiles into ManReduce is inspired by similar techniques in the large-scale data-processing world. For example, Pig [19] and Sawzall [21] are high-level languages built on top of MapReduce, and Nebula [12] and DryadLINQ [24] are high-level languages built on top of Dryad.

Design Goals

In creating Dog, we had three main design goals. First, we wanted to make Dog a highly expressive language, so that even people with little knowledge of programming languages could understand and write a Dog program. This is an especially appropriate design goal for a social computing language, where many of the constructs involve specifying people and asking them to do something. Such constructs are understood even by non-programmers, and having a language that reflects the natural way that people express these requests would make social computation accessible to a broad audience.

Our second goal was reusability. In traditional MapReduce, many programs are written by combining pre-existing maps and reduces in ad hoc ways. In human computation, there are a large number of common patterns, for example, human verification, human voting, machine summarization of human inputs. We wanted to make it very easy for Dog programmers to express and combine these common patterns.

And finally, we wanted to achieve these goals without diminishing the efficiency, power and flexibility of ManReduce.

We achieve the first two goals as follows. We define a large number of library functions that express common human and machine functions, such as the human functions Vote, Label, Compare, Extract, and Answer, and the machine functions Histogram, Filter, Median, and Sort. Dog then contains a set of easily-understandable primitives for (a) human and machine resource allocation and (b) and parameterization and execution of these library functions.

This approach abstracts away not only the code for parallelization, but also the code for defining human or machine functions, and lets the programmer focus on defining the control flow. This is an exciting feature of Dog that will become apparent in the code samples later in this paper. Dog scripts are very easily readable and writable. Even with just the functions that are included in default Dog libraries, a programmer can write a large number of powerful programs simply and compactly.

To achieve our third goal of maintaining the power and flexibility of ManReduce, we allow programmers to write their own libraries of human and machine functions in ManReduce, and import those libraries into Dog programs. In this sense, our design of Dog gives the same power of ManReduce behind the scenes, while still achieving our goals of expressivity and reuse.

The Dog compiler is implemented as a recursive descent parser that parses Dog programs and generates ManReduce code. The Dog standard library functions are simply wrappers around mappers and reducers in the ManReduce standard library. The Dog command-line utility includes convenience methods to compile and deploy Dog programs in a single step.

Language Specification

At its core, Dog is organized around four high-level language primitives:

`PEOPLE`, which specifices the type of people to perform some function
`ASK`, which asks a group of people to perform some human function
`FIND`, which instantiates those people
`COMPUTE`, which asks a set of machines to perform some function
as well as default libraries that include a number of human tasks (such as `Label`) and computational steps (such as `Histogram`).

For example, a simple Dog program to review UIST submissions and compute a tag cloud on words in the reviews can be written:

```
students = PEOPLE FROM facebook WHERE university =
    'mit' AND degree = 'computer science'
reviews = ASK students TO Review ON
    uist_submissions USING payment = 0 and
    replication = 3
words = COMPUTE Split ON reviews
histogram = COMPUTE Histogram ON words
```

People

The `PEOPLE` command returns a specification of people. The common use case for the `PEOPLE` command is to specify a certain type of people to perform a given task. `PEOPLE` requires a `FROM` clause that specifies the Dormouse community or crowdsourcing service from which the people will be selected. For example:

```
workers = PEOPLE FROM mechanical_turk;
```

will return a specification for mechanical turk workers.

Each Dormouse community defines properties on the people in the community, and these properties can be accessed through the `WHERE` clause. For example, a Dog programmer may write:

```
workers = PEOPLE FROM gates WHERE expertise
    CONTAINS 'theory' AND advisor='don knuth'
```

Note that the `PEOPLE` command doesn't return actual person ids; it returns a worker specification, stored internally as a predicate. The specification is instantiated when `ASK` or `FIND` is called on the specification.

Ask

The `ASK` command executes a human function. It takes as arguments a human task, a specification of people to perform it, and (optionally) a set of parameters for the human task, and (optionally) a data set on which the human task should operate.

So for example, a Dog programmer may write:

```
labels = ASK workers TO Label ON image_data USING
    layout='game'
```

Each human function has default parameters, so unless a programmer wants to change these default parameters, she can omit the `USING` clause. Further, programmers can omit the `ON` clause for human tasks that don't take input data.

Dog inherits a number of human tasks from Dormouse, for example: Vote, Label, Compare, and Answer. Programmers may also create libraries of other human functions for their own use and reuse by others in Dormouse, and import them into Dog.

Compute

The `COMPUTE` command executes a machine function. `COMPUTE` takes as its arguments a machine function, a data set upon which the function acts, and (optionally) any additional parameters required by the function. For example:

```
tag_cloud = COMPUTE TagCloud ON words USING
    color_scheme = 'random'
```

Like human tasks, the Dog standard libraries inherit a number of machine functions from Dormouse, including `Histogram`, `Average`, and `Filter`. Additionally, Dog programmers may create libraries of machine functions for their own use and reuse by others using Dormouse or ManReduce.

Find

In some cases, a Dog programmer may want to instantiate a specification of people independently of the `ASK` function. For example, she may be interested in computing summary demographic information on a given Dormouse community. The `FIND` command does this. For example, the code snippet:

```
workers = PEOPLE FROM gates WHERE expertise
    CONTAINS 'machine learning'
ids = FIND workers
```

returns the Dormouse ids of machine learning experts in the `gates` community. `FIND` may also be used to return people who have successfully performed a task. For example:

```
workers = PEOPLE FROM facebook
labels = ASK workers TO Label ON data
workers_who_labeled = FIND PEOPLE FROM labels
```

Data Model

Dog is designed to support sequential transformations on large-scale data, either by parallel human or machine functions. Dog is also designed to make it easy to express control flows that involve selecting people and specifying tasks for them to perform.

As such, Dog supports two primary data types: people specifications and data maps. A *people specification* is returned by the `PEOPLE` command, and is stored internally as a predicate[4].

A *data map* in Dog is expressed as a wrapper around a key-value store. Key-value stores lend themselves naturally to parallelism, and crowdsourcing is by its nature parallel. They also lend themselves well to serialization, which is an important part of Dog, especially as human steps can be expensive to re-run, and intermediate steps are often too big to fit in memory. And finally, having all data items be a key-value store helps our goal of simplicity, as new human and machine functions can be easily written in ManReduce, and the output of any data transform can be used as the input to any other data transform.

An important design feature of Dog is that all data returned by human functions retains information about who performed that function. This is a useful feature in a number of contexts, including reputation updating and routing data based on social relationships.

Routing Tasks

A key feature of Dog is the ability to route tasks to workers based on expertise, demographic, or social structure. While `FROM` handles basic routing, some applications require routing based on properties of each *individual* task or data item. The `SUCH THAT` clause enables such routing. In the following example, we show a program where students are asked to review papers in their areas of expertise, and their advisors are asked to validate them, matching the particular reviewer with her advisor for each paper.

```
students = PEOPLE FROM gates
reviews = ASK students TO Review ON
    uist_submissions SUCH THAT uist_submission.
    topic IS IN student.areas_of_expertise
reviewers = FIND PEOPLE FROM reviews
advisors = PEOPLE FROM gates WHERE advisees
    CONTAINS reviewers
validated_reviews = ASK advisors TO Validate ON
    reviews SUCH THAT review.reviewer = advisor.
    student
```

Function Libraries and Input Data

To create a library, a programmer simply creates a directory with a .doghouse extension that contains the appropriate Dormouse and ManReduce program files that define the human and machine functions. To import a library, a Dog programmer uses the `REQUIRE` command in the header, followed by a path to the Doghouse file, as well as an optional library namespace. For example:

```
REQUIRE "/dog/lib/statistics.doghouse" AS stats
```

To import a data file, a programmer uses the `IMPORT` command in the header:

```
IMPORT "/dog/lib/image_file.js" AS images
```

[4]For example, the Dog code `PEOPLE FROM facebook WHERE gender = "female"` is equivalent to the Ruby code: `Condition.new(["facebook","gender"],"female","=")`

Other Dog Features

Dog supports a number of other commands as well. Joining of communities and data is supported through the `MERGE`, `SHIFT`, `UNSHIFT`, and `CROSS` commands. The `PARAMETERS` command is a convenience command that encapsulates parameters for the `ASK` function. The `PRINT` command prints variable values, and the `INSPECT` command prints a small selection of large maps for debugging purposes.

A convenient feature of Dog is that the primitives are composable, allowing Dog programmers to produce compact, readable code. For example, the following code snippet

```
workers =  PEOPLE FROM mechanical_turk
preferred_candidates = ASK workers TO Vote ON
    candidates
```

can be rewritten as:

```
workers = ASK PEOPLE FROM mechanical_turk TO Vote
    ON candidates
```

Composability can be arbitrarily complex, and entire programs can be written in one line:

```
COMPUTE ranking ON (ASK PEOPLE FROM
    mechanical_turk TO Vote ON candidates)
```

Debugging Environment

A challenge when writing programs with human tasks is that it can be expensive to test and debug, as human workers may need to be paid, or may get frustrated by errors in their task templates. This discourages programmers from iterative improvements to their programs. A second challenge to debugging is that many times, programs will need to run over large amounts of input data (for example, labeling a large image corpus) that take time. What programmers will often do is create separate truncated input data sets for debugging, which requires additional work.

The Dog command-line utility has a debug mode that addresses both of these issues in simple but effective ways. In debug mode, Dog programs are deployed on a local version of Dormouse, which uses the programmer's local machine as the Dormouse master, and routes tasks to the programmer or whomever the programmer specifies. Second, in debug mode, input data is automatically truncated to a reasonable size based on a number of heuristics.

This allows programmers to easily test out their control flow and human functions on a small set of people and data before deploying.

EXAMPLES

Bootstrapping Recommendations

As a case study of the Dormouse framework, we developed a prototype pipeline for personalization of product offerings (such as Groupon deals). Based on evaluating demographic preferences for deals, this pipeline would enable significantly improved targeting of deals to people, but without the need for large amounts of proprietary usage data. Small companies and brand-new services rarely have access to the volume of usage data needed for standard personalization approaches such as collaborative filtering, making this an exciting use of human-powered computation.

Figure 8: Deals Application

For this use case, we used the `facebook` community through Dormouse, allowing us to easily access demographic information (location, gender, and age) for each of the people contributing preferences, in addition to the friendship graph for people. We collected a set of 500 Groupon deals, and paired them randomly, creating 12,500 total pairs. We asked workers from the `facebook` community to state which of the two deals in a pair they preferred, and why. Three hundred workers performed an average of 42 comparisons each. Note that soliciting ratings of individual deals would be problematic, as there is no absolute scale of quality or interest. Soliciting preferences between pairs is a simple and robust way around this problem. At the end, we collected a set of preferences for any subset of people (of a certain age group, for instance), and using ordering by the number of "wins" for each item, produce an approximate ranking of all deals for that demographic. We showed ManReduce code in Figure 6 illustrating components of this pipeline, so here we show a simple Dog script that could be used, requiring even fewer lines of code (Figure 10).

This pilot study demonstrated the convenience and simplicity of the Jabberwocky framework. With just a few lines of code and minimal setup, we specified the entire pipeline. In addition, we gained evidence that product targetting could benefit from such a system, as the preferences did indeed vary noticeably by demographic. For example, the top five deals prefered by males over females, and the top five deals prefered by females over males, are shown in the table at the end of this section. Anecdotally, we noticed that the female raters preferred many deals related to beauty, fitness, and home improvement, while the male raters often preferred dining and hobbies. We also note that the male and female rankings showed low Spearman correlation ($r = 0.24$), compared with correlation between rankings segregated by a random split ($r = 0.71$). The difference between these empirical correlations is highly significant ($p < 1e-4$).

To target deals to a particular individual, we can combine the preferences according to each relevant demographic (such as "male" and "18-25" and "San Francisco") using a probabilistic noisy-or model [5]. This would combine the probability of each demographic segment liking a deal with the probabilities that an individual will agree with each of their demographics. Also, we can can incorporate a feedback loop, in which deals with uncertain ranking are re-submitted for further user feedback. Additionally, and importantly, we can incorporate the friend graph directly, asking users which deals they believe their friends would prefer, and up-weighting agreements[5].

Male-preferred	Female-preferred
Artisan Cheese Experience **	Manicure or Deluxe Mani/Pedi **
Shooting range, Dinner, Drinks **	Paddleboard Rental and Lesson **
Chiropractic, Massage, or Allergy Treatment **	Keratin Treatment **
Panoramic Wall Mural **	RedAwning.com (Vacation)**
Wine Tour and Tasting **	Custom Massage *

Figure 9: Deal preferences by gender. ** $p < .01$; * $p < .05$ by Fisher's exact method.

Medical Image Analysis

A second application of Jabberwocky is to use people to improve the performance and evaluation of a machine learning framework for complex medical data. This case study explores the role of expertise in human computation.

In medicine, a common method of clarifying the subcellular location of proteins is immunohistochemical staining, where flourescently tagged antibodies are introduced into a tissue, binding with the protein the scientist wants to localize. The resulting images are then evaluated by pathologists. This technique is used in a wide range of applications, from exploring gene function in Parkinson's [25] to diagnosing cancerous tumors.

There are large quantities of immunohistochemical stains generated each year. Because of this, some researchers have started to explore image-recognition techniques to analyze these stains. However, these techniques are not often used in practice, because the idiosyncracies in how staining methods work make it difficult for a single image-recognition algorithm to work across many different stains.

We used Dog to write a program that routes IHC stains to generalists to localize the stains via a human image-segmentation function in Dormouse (Figure 11), and then routes those non-expert localizations to experts to perform a faster validation step. The expert validation feedback was then rerouted to the original generalists, who could use the feedback to improve. The validated localizations can then be used as input into a machine learning algorithm. An extension of this would be that as the generalists got more right, they increased in reputation in the system.

What is interesting is that what we originally built as a tool to aid machine learning ended up also aiding human learn-

[5]reminiscent of the Newlywed Game.

```
#!/usr/bin/env dog

IMPORT "deals.js" AS deal_pairs
REQUIRE "rank_deals.doghouse"

CONFIG title = "Compare Deals"
CONFIG description = "..."

answers = ASK PEOPLE TO RankDeals ON
    deal_pairs

age = COMPUTE Projection ON answers USING
    key_name = "age" AND value_name = "deals"
gender = COMPUTE Projection ON answers USING
    key_name = "gender" AND value_name = "
    deals"
ethnicity = COMPUTE Projection ON answers
    USING key_name = "ethnicity" AND
    value_name = "deals"
education = COMPUTE Projection ON answers
    USING key_name = "education" AND
    value_name = "deals"

age_ranking = COMPUTE PairwiseRank ON age
gender_ranking = COMPUTE PairwiseRank ON
    gender
ethnicity_ranking = COMPUTE PairwiseRank ON
    ethnicity
education_ranking = COMPUTE PairwiseRank ON
    education
```

Figure 10: Deals Application in Dog

ing. One can imagine that such systems can get even more nuanced, with active learning algorithms that have input as to what labeling tasks to route to which people. We call this *social machine learning*, where social learning systems interact with the machine learning systems, and both benefit from the other. We believe that this will be an area with much opportunity.

RELATED WORK

A number of programming frameworks for human computation have been introduced in recent years. Crowdforge [13], a MapReduce-inspired framework that was developed simultaneously but independently from ManReduce, defines *partition*, *map*, and *reduce* steps, and allows nested *map* and *reduce* steps. TurKit [16] is a toolkit for deploying iterative tasks to Mechanical Turk that maintains a straighforward procedural model. Soylent [2], a word-processing interface that calls Mechanical Turk workers to edit parts of a document on demand, introduces the Find-Fix-Verify crowd programming pattern, which splits tasks into a series of generation and review stages. Each of these specifies and implements a design pattern rather than building a full stack, and are platform dependent.

Recently, a trio of declarative query languages for human computation have been proposed: hQuery [20], CrowdDB [6], and Qurk [17]. These languages view crowdsourcing services as databases where facts are computed by human processors. These languages are different from Dog in that they are declarative rather than imperative. The imperative model of Dog is particularly important for social computation, where we want the programmer to be able to specify the type of person who will compute the result, not just the desired outcome.

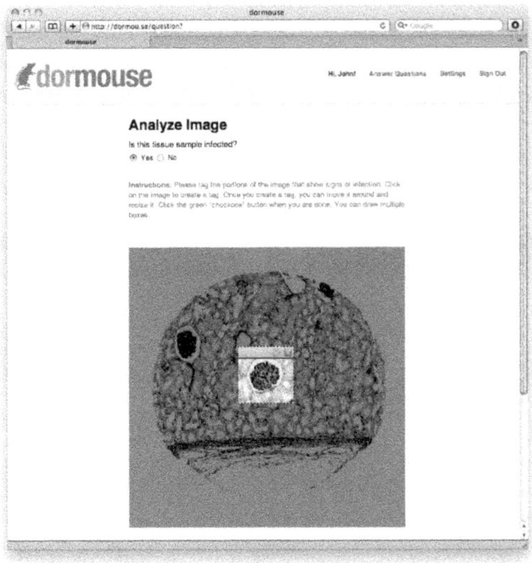

Figure 11: Immunohistochemical Staining Application

Heymann et. al propose hProc [9], a programming environment that focuses on modularity and reuse. It shares with Dormouse the notions of easy reuse of human function templates, and of abstracting out the specific crowdsourcing service through its marketplace drivers. However, there are also many key differences; for example, hProc does not have mechanisms for interleaving human and machine computation or abstracting away details of parallel processing. More substantively, since hProc has not been implemented, the design decisions are described as high-level proposals.

Much of the Jabberwocky software stack has taken its inspiration from related constructs in traditional and parallel computing. The Dormouse Virtual Machine is inspired in part from the Java Virtual Machine [15], a platform-independent execution environment that converts Java bytecode into machine language and executes it. In practice, Dormouse is not a true virtual machine in that it operates on top of crowdsourcing platforms rather than microprocessor architectures. In this sense, it is perhaps more reminiscent to Google's Global Workqueue, or some of the cluster management protocols used in scientific computing such as Parallel Virtual Machine [15] or MPI [7]. ManReduce takes its inspiration from MapReduce [4], Dryad [12], and GPU shader languages [22]. And Dog takes its inspiration from Pig [19], Sawzall [21], Nebula [12] and DryadLINQ [24]. The popularity of these existing tools suggests that the paradigms we present here will be useful and natural for many programmers.

CONCLUSION

To date, the programming frameworks for crowd computing have been single-platform frameworks. Further, the programming frameworks for crowdsourcing have viewed the crowd as a collection of largely independent and interchangeable workers, rather than an ecosystem of connected, heterogeneous people. And finally, despite a clearly differentiated domain, no domain-specific programming languages have been developed for social computing, requiring programmers to define control flows for people in languages designed for computers.

The Jabberwocky software stack represents a step forward in the tools available to programmers for social computation. A programmer may deploy a non-trivial application in Dog without having to build labor-intensive sociotechnical infrastructure, allowing developers to easily tap into people and their heterogeneous skillsets in an organized manner. Jabberwocky puts a wide range of possibilities for data-intensive applications within reach of a broad class of developers, and we believe it holds the potential to change the way programmers interact with people using code.

REFERENCES

1. S Bamford and et al. Galaxy Zoo.
2. M. Bernstein, G. Little, R.. Miller, B. Hartmann, M. Ackerman, D. Karger, D. Crowell, and K. Panovich. Soylent: a word processor with a crowd inside. In *Proc. UIST (2010)*.
3. S Cooper, F. Khatib, A. Treuille, J. Barbero, J. Lee, M. Beenen, A. Leaver-Fay, D. Baker, and Z. Popovic. Predicting protein structures with a multiplayer online game. *Nature*, June 2010.
4. J. Dean and S. Ghemawat. MapReduce: simplified data processing on large clusters. *Communications ACM*, January 2008.
5. FJ Diez. Parameter adjustment in bayes networks. the generalized noisy or-gate. In *Proc. UAI (1993)*.
6. Michael J. Franklin, Donald Kossmann, Tim Kraska, Sukriti Ramesh, and Reynold Xin. CrowdDB: answering queries with crowdsourcing. In *Proc. SIGMOD (2011)*, pages 61–72.
7. William Gropp, Ewing Lusk, Nathan Doss, and Anthony Skjellum. A high-performance, portable implementation of the MPI message passing interface standard. *Parallel Computing*, 1996.
8. B. Hartmann. Amazing but True Cat Stories. http://bjoern.org/projects/catbook/, April 2009.
9. P. Heymann and H. Garcia-Molina. Human processing. Technical report.
10. R. Hickey. The clojure programming language. In *Proc. DLS (2008)*.
11. D. Horowitz and S.D. Kamvar. The anatomy of a large-scale social search engine. In *Proc. WWW (2010)*.
12. M. Isard, M. Budiu, Y. Yu, A. Birrell, and D. Fetterly. Dryad: distributed data-parallel programs from sequential building blocks. *SIGOPS Operating Systems Review*, March 2007.
13. A. Kittur, B. Smus, and R. E. Kraut. CrowdForge: Crowdsourcing Complex Work.
14. W. Lasecki, K. Murray, S. White, R. Miller, and F. Bigham. Legion: closed-loop crowd control of existing interfaces. In *Proc. UIST (2011)*.
15. T. Lindholm and F. Yellin. *Java Virtual Machine Specification*. Addison-Wesley Longman Publishing Co., Inc., 2nd edition, 1999.
16. G. Little, L. Chilton, M. Goldman, and R. Miller. TurKit: Tools for Iterative Tasks on Mechanical Turk. In *Proc. HCOMP (2009)*.
17. A. Marcus, E. Wu, S. Madden, and R. C. Miller. Crowdsourced Databases: Query Processing with People. In *Proc. CIDR (2011)*.
18. M. Odersky, P. Altherr, V. Cremet, B. Emir, S. Maneth, S. Micheloud, N. Mihaylov, M. Schinz, E. Stenman, and M. Zenger. An overview of the Scala programming language. Technical report, EPFL Lausanne, Switzerland.
19. C. Olston, B. Reed, U. Srivastava, R. Kumar, and A. Tomkins. Pig Latin: A Not-So-Foreign Language for Data Processing. In *Proc. SIGMOD (2008)*.
20. A. Parameswaran and N Polyzotis. Answering Queries using Humans, Algorithms and Databases. Technical report.
21. R. Pike, S. Dorward, R. Griesemer, and S. Quinlan. Interpreting the data: Parallel analysis with Sawzall. *Scientific Programming*, October 2005.
22. D. Tarditi, S. Puri, and J. Oglesby. Accelerator: using data parallelism to program GPUs for general-purpose uses. *SIGOPS Operating Systems Review*, October 2006.
23. L. von Ahn. Games with a Purpose. *Computer*, June 2006.
24. Y. Yu, M. Isard, D. Fetterly, M. Budiu, Ú. Erlingsson, P. Gunda, and J. Currey. DryadLINQ: a system for general-purpose distributed data-parallel computing using a high-level language. In *Proc. OSDI (2008)*.
25. L. Zhang, M. Shimoji, B. Thomas, D. Moore, S. Yu, N. Marupudi, R. Torp, I. Torgner, O. Ottersen, T. Dawson, and V. Dawson. Mitochondrial localization of the Parkinson's disease related protein DJ-1. *Human Molecular Genetics*, June 2005.

Appendix

The source code of `Survey` and `Average` from Figure 3.

survey.rb:

```
class Survey < ManReduce::Task
  def render
    include_file("survey.erb")
  end

  def process_response(response)
    answers = []
    answers << {"rating" => response["rating"]}
    answers << {"length" => response["length"]}
    return answers
  end
end
```

survey.erb:

```
<label>
  How long have you been using the service?
</label>
<input type="text" name="length">

<label>
  How is the quality of your service?
  (10 is good, 0 is bad)
</label>
<input type="text" name="rating">
```

average.rb:

```
class Average < ManReduce::Reduce
  def reduce(key, values)
    count = values.length
    sum = values.inject(0) {|sum, x| sum += x}
    if count == 0 then
      emit(key, 0)
    else
      emit(key, sum / count)
    end
  end
end
```

Proactive Wrangling: Mixed-Initiative End-User Programming of Data Transformation Scripts

Philip J. Guo, Sean Kandel*, Joseph M. Hellerstein†, Jeffrey Heer**

*Stanford University
{pg, skandel, jheer}@cs.stanford.edu

†University of California, Berkeley
hellerstein@cs.berkeley.edu

ABSTRACT
Analysts regularly wrangle data into a form suitable for computational tools through a tedious process that delays more substantive analysis. While interactive tools can assist data transformation, analysts must still conceptualize the desired output state, formulate a transformation strategy, and specify complex transforms. We present a model to proactively suggest data transforms which map input data to a relational format expected by analysis tools. To guide search through the space of transforms, we propose a metric that scores tables according to type homogeneity, sparsity and the presence of delimiters. When compared to "ideal" hand-crafted transformations, our model suggests over half of the needed steps; in these cases the top-ranked suggestion is preferred 77% of the time. User study results indicate that suggestions produced by our model can assist analysts' transformation tasks, but that users do not always value proactive assistance, instead preferring to maintain the initiative. We discuss some implications of these results for mixed-initiative interfaces.

ACM Classification: H5.2 [Information interfaces and presentation]: User Interfaces – Graphical user interfaces.

General terms: Design, Human Factors

Keywords: Data transformation, data cleaning, end-user programming, mixed-initiative interfaces, data analysis

INTRODUCTION
The increasing scale and accessibility of data — including government records, web data, and system logs — provides an under-exploited resource for improving governance, public policy, organizational strategy, and even our personal lives [23]. However, much of this data is not *suitable* for use by analysis tools. Data is often stored in idiosyncratic formats or designed for human viewing rather than computational processing (e.g., cross-tabulations within spreadsheets).

These hurdles require that analysts engage in a tedious process of data transformation (or *data wrangling*) to map input data to a form consumable by downstream tools. Both prior work [3] and our own conversations with analysts indicate that wrangling is one of the most time-consuming aspects of analysis. As a result, domain experts regularly spend more time manipulating data than they do exercising their specialty, while less technical audiences may be excluded.

Analysts typically wrangle their data by writing scripts in programming languages such as Python or Perl or by manually editing the data within spreadsheets. To assist this process, researchers have developed novel interactive tools. Potter's Wheel [21] and Google Refine [11] are menu-driven interfaces that provide access to common data transforms. Wrangler [13] extends this approach by (a) automatically suggesting applicable transforms in response to direct manipulation of a data table and (b) providing visual previews to aid transform assessment. Each of these tools enable skilled practitioners to rapidly specify transformation workflows; however, they fall short in helping users formulate data transformation strategies. Given an input data set, what is the desired output state? What operations are possible and which sequence of operations will result in suitable data?

One complication is that there is no single "correct" output format. A data layout amenable to plotting in Excel is often different than the format expected by visualization tools such as Tableau. That said, one format is required by many database, statistics and visualization tools: a relational data table. In this format, each row contains a single data record and each column represents a variable of a given data type.

In this paper, we augment the Wrangler transformation tool [13] to aid transform discovery and strategy formation. We take a mixed-initiative [10] approach to end-user programming: we generate **proactive suggestions** to improve the suitability of a data set for downstream tools. In other words, we want the computer to help analysts get data into the format that computers expect. We make three contributions:

A model of data table *"suitability"* that enables generation of proactive transform suggestions. We introduce a metric that indicates the degree to which a table adheres to a relational format usable by downstream tools. We use this metric to guide automated search through the space of possible operations. As the search space is too large to evaluate at interactive rates, we couple our metric with empirically-derived heuristics for pruning the space of candidate transforms.

An analysis of algorithm behavior assessing the strengths and limitations of our suggestions. Across a set of realistic transformation tasks, we find that our method suggests over

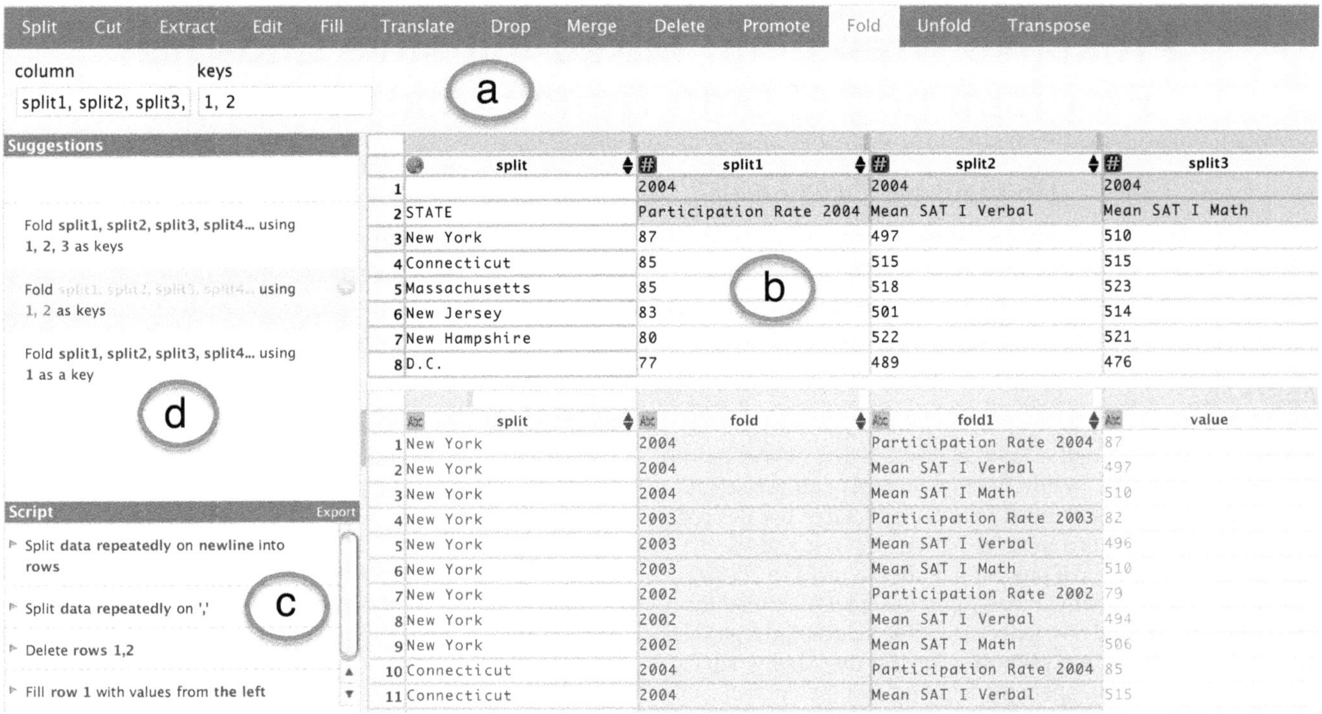

Figure 1: The Wrangler User Interface. Clockwise from the top: (a) tool bar for transform specification, (b) data table display, (c) history viewer containing an exportable transformation script, (d) suggested transforms. The effect of the selected *Fold* transform is previewed in the data table display using before (top) and after (bottom) views.

half (53%) of the steps used in "ideal" transformations. In these cases our suggestions exhibit high precision: the top-ranked suggestion is the preferred option 77% of the time.

A user study examining how end users apply proactive suggestions. We find that our method can help users complete transformation tasks, but not always in the manner that we expected. Many users express a desire to maintain control and roundly ignore suggestions presented prior to interaction with the data table. However, users do not express similar concerns when suggestions generated by our proactive model are inserted among "reactive" suggestions specific to an initiating interaction. User assessment of suggestions appears to improve when users see themselves as the initiators.

We also present a redesign of the Wrangler interface to better surface the space of available data transforms and parameters. The resulting interface enables manual specification or refinement of transforms and facilitates learning from the examples provided by automated suggestions.

RELATED WORK

Researchers have proposed numerous strategies for simplifying programming tasks, including domain-specific languages [18], visual programming [1], keyword programming [17], and programming-by-demonstration [2]. Myers et al. [20] provide a survey of these approaches. Here, we review prior work in end-user programming tools for data transformation.

Menu-Driven Data Transformation

Both database and HCI researchers have devised graphical interfaces [6, 11, 21] for reformatting and cleaning data. Each of these tools share a similar design: a data table view and a set of menu-accessible transformation operators. Google Refine [11] combines menu-driven commands with faceted histograms for data profiling and filtering. Ajax [6] similarly provides an interface for transform specification with advanced facilities for entity resolution. Potter's Wheel [21] is a graphical interface for authoring statements in a declarative transformation language and offers extensible facilities for data type inference. Each of these tools enable skilled practitioners to transform data more rapidly. However, each imposes a learning curve: users must learn both the available operations and how to combine them to achieve common data transformation needs.

Programming-by-Demonstration Systems

Another class of targeted data manipulation tools rely on programming by demonstration (PBD) techniques [2]. Potluck [12] uses simultaneous editing [19] to help users perform data integration. Karma [22] infers text extractors and transformations for web data from examples entered in a table. Vegemite [16] extends CoScripter [15] to integrate web data, automate the use of web services, and generate shareable scripts. Dontcheva et al. [4] use PBD techniques to enable extraction, integration, and templated search of web data. Gulwani [8] introduces an algorithm for learning expressive string processing programs from input-output examples. PADS [5] infers nuanced data parsers from a set of positive examples. Though well-suited for their intended tasks, these systems are insufficient for the more general demands of data wrangling. For example, while text extraction and mass editing are quite valuable for data transformation, the above tools lack other needed operations such as table reshaping, aggregation, and missing value imputation.

Closely related to our current work is Harris and Gulwani's [9] system for learning table transformations from an example input-output pair. Given input and output tables, the system can infer a program that filters, duplicates, and/or reorganizes table cells to generate the output table. These resulting programs can express a variety of table reshaping operations.

Our work differs in multiple respects. First, the approach of Harris and Gulwani treats table cells as atomic units, and thus has limited expressiveness. For example, it does not support transformations involving text editing or extraction. Second, their approach requires that a user specify both input and output examples, and thus know the details of the desired output in advance. In the case of large tables, creating the output example may be tedious. On the other hand, providing a small example from which the proper transformation can be inferred may require significant insight. Third, the actual mechanics of the resulting transformation are opaque, potentially limiting user skill acquisition. In contrast, our approach does not accept an output example but instead leverages the assumption that the user desires a relational data table with homogeneous columns. This enables our system to offer proactive suggestions in the context of a full-featured data transformation environment.

DATA WRANGLER

In this work, we introduce extensions to *Data Wrangler* [13], a system that combines multiple end-user programming strategies to facilitate specification of data transformation scripts. Underlying Wrangler is a *declarative domain-specific language* that includes a comprehensive set of transformation operators and enables code-generation of reusable programs (e.g., Python and JavaScript code). Wrangler provides natural language descriptions and *visual previews* with which users can assess and verify transform behaviors. Wrangler uses *programming-by-demonstration methods* (c.f., [8, 19]) to specify regular expression patterns and row predicates. In addition, Wrangler generates *automatic transform suggestions* in response to user interactions with a data table.

The Wrangler Transformation Language

The transformation scripts produced by Wrangler consist of a linear sequence of individual transforms, expressed in an underlying declarative language. The transforms support common data cleaning and reformatting tasks such as splitting or extracting text values, deleting or merging columns, batch text editing, interpolating values, and reorganizing cell layout (table *reshaping*). Table 1 summarizes the most common transforms surfaced in the user interface. The language is the direct descendant of the Potter's Wheel language [21] and draws on concepts introduced in SchemaSQL [14]. This prior work [14, 21] also provides formal proofs of the language's expressiveness, showing it is capable of expressing any one-to-one or one-to-many transform of cell values.

In addition, the declarative nature of the language facilitates implementation across a variety of platforms. Thus the Wrangler tool can generate executable code for multiple runtimes, including Python and JavaScript. For example, we often wrangle a data subset within the user interface and then export a resulting Python script to transform much larger databases (millions or more rows) on a server machine.

Transform	**Description**
Cut	Remove selected text from cells in specified columns.
Delete	Remove rows that match given indices or predicates.
Drop	Remove specified columns from the table.
Edit	Edit the text in each cell of the specified columns.
Extract	Copy text from cells in a column into a new column.
Fill	Fill empty cells using values from adjacent cells.
Fold	Reshape a table into columns of key-value sets; selected rows map to keys, selected columns to values.
Merge	Concatenate multiple columns into a single column.
Promote	Promote row values to be the column names.
Split	Split a column into multiple columns by delimiters.
Translate	Shift the position of cell values by a given offset.
Transpose	Transpose the rows and columns of the table.
Unfold	Reshape a table by mapping key-value sets to a collection of new columns, one per unique key.

Table 1: The Wrangler Transformation Language. Each transform accepts as parameters some combination of enumerable values and text, row, or column selection criteria. For further discussion, see [13, 21].

	Boys	Girls
Australia	1	2
Austria	3	4
Belgium	5	6
China	7	8

Australia	Boys	1
Australia	Girls	2
Austria	Boys	3
Austria	Girls	4
Belgium	Boys	5
Belgium	Girls	6
China	Boys	7
China	Girls	8

Figure 2: An example of table reshaping. A *Fold* operation transforms the table on the left to the one on the right; an *Unfold* operation performs the reverse.

A critical feature of the language design is its compactness: with only a dozen operators, analysts can complete a wide variety of data cleaning tasks. Moreover, most operators accept identical parameter types, namely row, text and column selections. The compact language design is intended to facilitate exploration and learning by limiting the number of possible operations considered. An additional benefit is that this reduced set of formally-defined operators lends itself to computational search over operation sequences.

The Wrangler User Interface

The Wrangler user interface (shown in Figure 1) allows analysts to specify transforms in the underlying language. The interface contains four primary components: along the top of the display is a tool bar for transform specification, the right panel contains an interactive data table display, and the left panel contains both automated transform suggestions (top) and an interactive history viewer describing the current script (bottom). Similar to other transformation tools [11, 21], a transform can be specified manually by selecting a transform type from the tool bar and then entering in desired parameter values. However, Wrangler provides additional facilities to aid transform specification and verification.

Automated Transform Suggestions

Wrangler's data table display supports a set of common interactions, such as selecting rows and columns by clicking their headers or selecting and manipulating text within table cells. While these actions can be used to specify parameters for a selected transform type, manual specification can be tedious and requires that users have a firm command of the available transforms. To facilitate rapid specification, Wrangler infers applicable transforms directly from an initiating interaction.

After the user makes a selection on the data table, Wrangler generates automatic suggestions in a three-phase process. First, Wrangler infers a set of possible parameter values in response to the user's selection. Example parameters include regular expressions matching selected text substrings and row predicates matching selected values, generated using programming-by demonstration methods [13, 19]. Second, Wrangler enumerates a list of transforms that accept the inferred parameters. Third, Wrangler filters and ranks the resulting transforms according to historical usage statistics and heuristics intended to improve result quality. These transforms then appear as a ranked list of suggestions in the interface, where users can preview their effects and modify their parameters. For more details regarding the Wrangler inference engine, we refer interested readers to Kandel et al. [13].

Assessing Transform Effects

When creating data transformation scripts, users often find it difficult to understand a transform's effect prior to executing it [13]. To aid in transform assessment, Wrangler presents suggestions using natural language descriptions to aid quick scanning of the suggestions list. When a transform is selected, Wrangler uses visual previews to enable users to quickly evaluate its effects without executing it. When feasible, Wrangler displays in-place previews in the data table, drawing users' attention to the effect of the transform in its original context. For complex reshaping operations, Wrangler shows before and after images of the table and uses color coding to help users perceive the correspondence of cells between the two states (Figure 1b).

Design Issues and Opportunities

Wrangler's automated suggestions and visual assessment features help analysts iteratively hone in on a desired transformation. A user study by Kandel et al. [13] finds that these mechanisms can accelerate specification and facilitate discovery of applicable transforms. However, the initial Wrangler design also suffers from some shortcomings.

Surfacing Transform Parameters

While natural language descriptions enable users to scan suggestions, they provide little guidance for how to specify parameters manually. This disconnect constitutes a missed opportunity: in addition to accelerating specification, suggested transforms might serve as *instructive examples* of more advanced system use. The initial Wrangler design also buries transforms within hierarchical menus, limiting visibility.

In response, we redesigned the Wrangler user interface to better surface available transforms and their parameters. The tool bar along the top of the user interface makes all transforms immediately visible, and the parameters for a current transform appear directly below. As users preview suggested transforms, the complete parametrization is now visible in the tool bar. We apply linked highlighting between parameters in natural language descriptions and those in the tool bar. In terms of Green's Cognitive Dimensions of Notation [7], this redesign is intended to improve the *visibility* of options and decrease the *viscosity* of manually tuning inferred parameters. In terms of Horvitz's principles for mixed-initiative interaction [10], the design provides a *shared working memory* by which users can more directly observe (and thus hopefully learn from) system-initiated actions.

Specifying Transforms and Formulating Strategies

Observing user activity with Wrangler reveals that analysts may have difficultly formulating data cleaning strategies [13]. Novice users are often unsure which target data state is the one best suited for subsequent analysis. Even when the target data state is known, users are often unsure which sequence of operations is needed to reach that state. We have observed that both novice and expert users may consequently resort to blind exploration of the available transforms. This process is hampered by the fact that some operations remain difficult to specify despite the aid of automated suggestions. In particular, reshaping operations that significantly alter the arrangement of table cells are hard to conceptualize and apply. However, it is exactly these operations that are often necessary to map input data to a format usable by analysis tools.

We attempt to address these issues by extending Wrangler to provide *proactive suggestions* in addition to "reactive" suggestions initiated by user actions. Our proactive suggestions are intended to lead users towards effective cleaning strategies and facilitate the specification of complex reshaping operations. After describing the details of our proactive suggestion algorithm, we go on to analyze the behavior of our algorithm and evaluate our approach in a user study.

PROACTIVE DATA WRANGLING

We now describe extensions to Wrangler to automatically generate proactive suggestions. In addition to the previous method of suggesting transforms in response to user-initiated actions (e.g., selecting a row or column), *Proactive Wrangler* continually analyzes the current state of the data table and provides suggestions to make the table more suitable for import into a relational database or analytic tool. These suggestions are intended to both accelerate the work of experts and guide novices towards a desired outcome. For example, we wish to surface complex reshaping operations (*fold* and *unfold*) within a "recognition" task, rather than a harder "recall" task in which the user needs to determine which operation they require and manually initiate its specification.

A Proactive Data Cleaning Scenario

To give a sense of how proactive suggestions ease the data cleaning process, Figure 3 illustrates a complete scenario where a user transforms data imported from an Excel spreadsheet (Table 1 within Figure 3) into a dense relational format (Table 6). First, Wrangler analyzes the initial table state and makes 3 proactive suggestions. The user ignores them and instead manually selects and deletes the first two rows, turning Table 1 into Table 2. Then the user chooses to execute the 2nd suggestion (shown in **bold**), *Split column 2 on ':'*, which transforms the data into Table 3. Wrangler continues proactively suggesting additional transforms, and the user can simply pick the desired ones from the list.

1.

Bureau of I.A.	
Regional Director	Numbers
Niles C.	Tel: (800)645-8397
	Fax: (907)586-7252
Jean H.	Tel: (918)781-4600
	Fax: (918)781-4604
Frank K.	Tel: (615)564-6500
	Fax: (615)564-6701

Manually select and delete the first two rows

Proactive suggestions (none chosen):
1. Fill column 1 from above
2. Split column 2 on ':'
3. Delete empty rows

2.

Niles C.	Tel: (800)645-8397
	Fax: (907)586-7252
Jean H.	Tel: (918)781-4600
	Fax: (918)781-4604
Frank K.	Tel: (615)564-6500
	Fax: (615)564-6701

Proactive suggestions:
1. Fill column 1 from above
2. **Split column 2 on ':'**
3. Delete empty rows

3.

Niles C.	Tel	(800)645-8397
	Fax	(907)586-7252
Jean H.	Tel	(918)781-4600
	Fax	(918)781-4604
Frank K.	Tel	(615)564-6500
	Fax	(615)564-6701

Proactive suggestions:
1. **Delete empty rows**
2. Fill column 1 from above

4.

Niles C.	Tel	(800)645-8397
	Fax	(907)586-7252
Jean H.	Tel	(918)781-4600
	Fax	(918)781-4604
Frank K.	Tel	(615)564-6500
	Fax	(615)564-6701

Proactive suggestions:
1. **Fill column 1 from above**

5.

Niles C.	Tel	(800)645-8397
Niles C.	Fax	(907)586-7252
Jean H.	Tel	(918)781-4600
Jean H.	Fax	(918)781-4604
Frank K.	Tel	(615)564-6500
Frank K.	Fax	(615)564-6701

Proactive suggestions:
1. Unfold column 1 on column 3
2. **Unfold column 2 on column 3**

6.

	Tel	Fax
Niles C.	(800)645-8397	(907)586-7252
Jean H.	(918)781-4600	(918)781-4604
Frank K.	(615)564-6500	(615)564-6701

Result: cleaned table ready for DB import

Figure 3: Using Proactive Wrangler to reformat raw data from a spreadsheet. The proactive suggestion chosen at each step is highlighted in **bold**. In the Wrangler UI, proactive suggestions are displayed in the suggestions panel (Figure 1d).

Although the above example is small, it is indicative of a common usage pattern when cleaning data with Proactive Wrangler. In particular, cleaning often involves executing a mix of human-initiated and proactively-suggested transforms. Here the user must recognize that rows 1 and 2 are extraneous headers that should be deleted, but Wrangler proactively suggests all other necessary transforms. In the remainder of this section, we describe how Wrangler generates, filters and ranks these proactive suggestions.

A Metric for Data Table "Suitability"

We define a *suitable* data table as one that can be loaded and effectively manipulated by an analytic tool or relational database. These tools often expect data in a relational format where each row contains a single data record and each column represents a variable of a given data type. Although the raw data in Table 1 of Figure 3 is human-readable, it is not suitable for analytic tool or database import because of its irregular structure: it contains extraneous header rows, empty rows, and telephone/fax numbers are located in cells mixed with other strings, separated by a colon delimiter (e.g., "Tel: (800)645-8397"). In contrast, the compact relational result in Table 6 is more usable by downstream tools.

We created a metric that assesses how amenable a table is for import into downstream tools. Our metric rewards column type homogeneity (H), fewer empty values (E), and lack of delimiters (D). A *lower* score indicates a more suitable table. A homogeneous, dense, delimiter-free table (e.g., Table 6 in Figure 3) has a "perfect" score of zero; tools expecting relational tables should be able to import it.

For a table T with rows R and columns C, we define the table suitability S as

$$S(T) = \left(1 - \frac{\sum_{c \in C} H_c(T)}{|C|}\right) + \frac{E(T) + D(T)}{|R|\,|C|} \qquad (1)$$

where $|R|$ is the number of rows, $|C|$ is the number of columns, and each component function is defined as follows.

H_c is the **homogeneity** of column c, the sum of squares of the proportions of each data type $Type$ present in that column:

$$H_c = \sum_{Type} \left(\frac{|i \in R : c_i \in Type|}{|R|}\right)^2 \qquad (2)$$

Wrangler parses each cell's contents into the most specific possible type, which can be a built-in like *number* or *date*, a user-defined type like *zip code* or *country name*, or a generic *string* type for those that fail to match a more specific type (for more details regarding Wrangler's type inference, see Kandel et al. [13]). If 75% of values in a column are numbers and 25% are dates, then the column's homogeneity is $(0.75)^2 + (0.25)^2 = 0.625$. If 50% are numbers and 50% are dates, then the column is less homogeneous: $(0.5)^2 + (0.5)^2 = 0.5$. A column that contains only values of a single type has the maximum possible homogeneity score of 1. Our table suitability score averages the homogeneity of all columns and subtracts that average from 1, so that higher homogeneity leads to a *lower* (more "suitable") score.

E is the count of **empty cells**. We favor denser tables, as missing values may indicate a sub-optimal data layout possibly containing replicated values in adjacent columns.

D is the count of **delimiters**. A delimiter is a comma, colon, pipe, or tab character. We favor tables with fewer delimiters, as those tables are more likely to consist of atomic data rather than compound elements that could split into specific values.

Our suitability score is invariant of table size, since its terms are all normalized by the numbers of rows and columns. However, one of its limitations is that it does not penalize *data loss*. In the extreme pathological case, deleting all cells except for one can lead to a perfect score of 0 (assuming that last cell contains no delimiters). In the next section, we describe how we designed Proactive Wrangler to avoid suggesting such undesirable transforms.

Poor scores in each component of Equation 1 make a table ill-suited for tool import. In databases and analytic tools, a column with a mixture of data types typically can only be imported as uninterpreted strings. A column with many delimiters may be treated as strings rather than composite values of more specific types. A column with many empty cells often indicates replicated values in adjacent columns. All these situations can limit downstream analyses.

Generating Candidate Transforms

Proactive Wrangler automatically suggests transforms that improve a table's suitability score by first generating candidate suggestions, and then evaluating, filtering, and ranking these candidates before presenting them to the user.

One way to avoid suggesting undesirable lossy transforms is to explicitly penalize data loss when ranking suggestions; however, this suffers from efficiency problems because all possible suggestions must still be generated, evaluated, and ranked. Instead, we adopt a simpler approach: we prune the space of suggestions to ensure that Proactive Wrangler never makes suggestions that involve significant data loss. We limit lossy transforms to deletions of mostly-empty rows (which often appear in spreadsheet headers or footnotes). We contend that data deletion should be left to the user's discretion, and so Proactive Wrangler should only help to compact (fill and delete empty cells), parse (split on delimiters), and reshape (fold and unfold) the table. Thus, it generates the following types of transforms as candidates at each step:

- **Fold** columns $C_1, \ldots, C_n$ using rows $R_1, \ldots, R_n$ as keys
- **Unfold** column C_1 on column C_2
- **Split** column C into multiple columns using a delimiter (comma, colon, pipe, or tab)
- **Fill** all empty cells of row R with values from the left
- **Fill** all empty cells of column C with values from above
- **Delete** all mostly-empty rows ($\geq 75\%$ empty cells)
- **Delete** all empty rows
- **Delete** all empty columns

Since most of these transforms take row and/or column indices as parameters, enumerating all possibilities is both infeasible and undesirable. Assuming that a table has $|R|$ rows and $|C|$ columns, there are $O(|R|)$ possible row fills, $O(|C|)$ possible column fills and splits, $O(2^{|R|} \cdot 2^{|C|})$ possible folds, and $O(|C|^2)$ possible unfolds. It would take far too much time to evaluate all possible parameterizations, precluding interactive response rates. Even if efficiency were not a concern, many parameterizations are undesirable since they trigger degenerate cases of certain transforms.

Informed by our data cleaning experiences and empirical observations from a corpus of public data sets (described in the next section), we developed rules to reduce the set of transform parameters and eliminate undesirable candidates:

Fill. Proactive Wrangler only generates *fill* candidates if the majority ($\geq 50\%$) of cells in a given row or column are empty. This type of transform is useful for filling in sparse key rows (or columns) before doing a fold (or unfold).

Fold. Proactive Wrangler only generates *fold* candidates using all columns except for the leftmost one (i.e., Columns 2 through $|C|$), and using at most the first 3 rows as keys (i.e., Row 1, Rows 1–2, or Rows 1–3).

The above rule reduces the number of possible folds from $O(2^{|R|} \cdot 2^{|C|})$ to 3 and covers the majority of observed use cases for transforming a cross-tabulation into a relational format. To quantify our intuition, we manually inspected all 114 tables in the 2010 OECD Factbook, an annual publication of world socioeconomic data sets from `oecd.org`. For all except for 2 of the tables, the *only* sensible fold used columns 2 through $|C|$, and for all except for 1 table, the only sensible fold used at most the first 3 rows as keys. A cursory inspection of cross-tabulation data sets from Wikipedia, US Bureau of Justice, and `data.gov` showed no tables that could be sensibly folded using columns other than 2 through $|C|$ or using more than the first 3 rows as keys.

Also, Proactive Wrangler only generates fold candidates if the leftmost column contains all unique and non-null values in rows other than the key row(s); otherwise the folded table will have conflicts. For example, if there were a duplicate "Australia" row in the table on the left of Figure 2, then the results of a fold would be ambiguous.

Unfold. Proactive Wrangler only generates *unfold* candidates of the form "Unfold C_1 on C_2" if all columns except for C_2 are completely homogeneous (single-typed) and non-empty; otherwise the headers in the resulting cross-tab will not be well-typed. (The values in C_2 become the data matrix at the core of the resulting table, so it can have empty cells.) Also, Proactive Wrangler only generates unfold candidates if the table has exactly 3, 4, or 5 columns, which corresponds to 1, 2, or 3 key columns, respectively. Our intuition for imposing this limit is similar to why we only restrict folds to using at most the first 3 rows as keys: it covers the majority of use cases, as indicated by our data corpus.

The aforementioned rules reduce the number of candidate transforms from $O(2^{|R|} \cdot 2^{|C|})$ to $O(|R| + |C|)$. At each step (e.g., in Figure 3), Proactive Wrangler generates all of these candidates at once and then evaluates, filters, and ranks them before presenting them to the user.

Ranking and Presenting Proactive Suggestions

After Proactive Wrangler generates a set of candidate transforms, it executes each of them on the current table and calculates the suitability score for the resulting table. It removes all candidates that result in tables with scores higher ("worse") than the current table. We use a slightly modified scoring method for *unfold* transforms. The operation "Unfold C_1 on C_2" transforms the values in column C_2 into a 2D data matrix at the core of the resulting table. Thus, that matrix should be scored as an atomic unit rather than as disparate columns. Proactive Wrangler calculates the score improvement of an unfold by the change in homogeneity and density between C_2 and the resulting data matrix.

Proactive Wrangler then presents the remaining candidates to the user in the suggestions panel (Figures 1d and 3), sorted by the amount of improvement ($-\Delta S$). A user can preview and execute one of these proactive suggestions or can choose to ignore them, and instead make a selection on the data table to surface the ordinary context-dependent suggestions.

CHARACTERIZING PROACTIVE ALGORITHM BEHAVIOR

To assess the quality of our proactive suggestions, we analyzed the behavior of our algorithm across a collection of diverse data sets. For each, we compared the suggestions produced by our algorithm with "ideal" transformation scripts constructed by hand. As there is often more than one feasible "clean" goal state, we strove to transform each data table into a relational format amenable for import into a database or analytic tool and also sought to remove extraneous tokens from fields (e.g., parentheses, leading dashes, etc.).

We compared 20 distinct data sets in our analysis. While this collection is relatively small, each data set was chosen because it is representative of a much larger class of data we have collected. For example, although we only included three tables from the 2010 OECD Factbook of world socioeconomic data, all 114 tables from that source had a format that matched one of these three canonical tables. Although we cannot claim that our corpus is a representative sample of all data that users might want to clean, we strove to select data of diverse origins, formats, and complexity:

Origins. Our corpus consists of a mix of government and NGO data (e.g., OECD, US Department of Justice, data.gov), scientific data (e.g., flower classifications, audiology experiments) and data scraped from websites (e.g., Wikipedia reference tables, Craigslist apartment rental listings).

Format. Data formats range over cross-tabulations (e.g., left half of Figure 2), Excel reports intended for human consumption (e.g., Table 1 in Figure 3), line-oriented records with custom token separators and ad-hoc formats generated by scientific experiments.

Complexity. The most concise cleaning script we constructed for data sets in our corpus ranged from 1 to 7 transforms in length (i.e., some data sets were noticeably "dirtier" than others). The mean script length was 3.6 transforms.

We now summarize the results of using Proactive Wrangler to transform the 20 data sets in our corpus. When available, we always selected the highest-ranking proactive suggestion that would lead us towards the goal state; otherwise we initiated a selection on the data table and chose to execute the appropriate context-specific suggestion. Of all executed transforms, 53% (39/73) were proactive suggestions; the remaining 47% (34/73) resulted from human-initiated actions. When appropriate proactive suggestions appeared, the top-ranked (#1) suggestion was the preferable choice 77% of the time (30/39). The lowest rank of any chosen proactive suggestion was 6, and the mean rank was 1.6.

For reference, in the ideal case 100% of all executed transforms would come from the top-ranked proactive suggestion. In reality, our scoring metric is not perfect and there are certain classes of transforms that Proactive Wrangler is designed specifically *not* to offer. For our corpus, the following transforms required human intervention: splitting on non-standard delimiters, extracting and cutting substrings, and deleting non-sparse rows and columns. Across our collection, 6 of the corpus tables can be cleaned solely using proactive suggestions, 9 require a mix of human-initiated selections and proactive suggestions, and 5 require exclusively human selections. We now discuss each category in turn.

Fully Proactive

Six of the data tables in our corpus (30%) exhibited the best-case performance for Proactive Wrangler: all of the required transforms appear as proactive suggestions. This typically occurs for tables whose individual elements are properly formatted but the table itself requires re-structuring.

For example, all 114 tables in the 2010 OECD Factbook and all 50 state-level crime data sets from the Department of Justice are cross-tabulations embedded within Excel spreadsheets. Even though we only included a few samples in our corpus, the rest of the tables from those sources are identically formatted. For all of these tables, Proactive Wrangler suggests to delete the mostly-empty title and footnote rows, fill in the header key row(s), and then perform the appropriate fold to get the data into a relational format.

Hybrid

In the common case (9/20 tables, 45%), data must be cleaned using a combination of user-initiated transforms and proactive suggestions. For these kinds of tables in our corpus, 55% of executed transforms (23/42) came from proactive suggestions. By design, Proactive Wrangler does not offer certain types of suggestions, namely of transforms that lead to data loss. This limitation causes Wrangler to sometimes get "stuck" at a local optimum point when it cannot generate any more proactive suggestions. In those cases, human intervention can allow Wrangler to escape local optima and resume generating useful proactive suggestions.

For example, in a veteran's hospital dataset, we first chose a proactive suggestion to delete all empty rows, but then we had to manually delete an unnecessary column and remove (cut) the trailing '%' character from all numbers representing percentages. After those user-initiated clean-ups, Wrangler proactively offers the proper fold suggestion, which we executed to complete our cleaning task.

Manual

Wrangler cannot offer useful proactive suggestions for data that require extensive string parsing within individual cells, which occurred in a quarter of our examples (5/20 tables, 25%). These data sets all require the user to perform custom string splits, cuts, or extracts. For two of these data sets, Wrangler "stayed out of the way" and did not offer any proactive suggestions. For the other three, Wrangler offered on average two (unhelpful) proactive suggestions. Our findings from the user study (see next section) indicate that users find it easy to ignore such unhelpful suggestions.

For example, each line in a Craigslist apartment listings dataset is a string in this format:

```
$2475/2br - Superb location - (palo alto) pic
```

To create a table of rental prices, bedroom count, and locations, one can split each line on the '/' character, cut the '$' from the price to make it into an integer, and extract the location (e.g., "palo alto") from within the parentheses. These types of string manipulations are easier for a human to initiate using Wrangler's reactive suggestions; it is difficult for an algorithm to suggest these manipulations *a priori* with both high precision and recall. Consequently, Wrangler does not currently attempt to make proactive suggestions for them.

USER STUDY

We conducted a user study comparing versions of Wrangler with and without proactive suggestions. We originally hypothesized that proactive suggestions would simplify specification of commonly-used, but hard-to-specify reshaping transforms (e.g., fold, unfold), while causing limited distraction to users specifying other types of transforms. Furthermore, we hypothesized that by lowering the cost of finding applicable transforms, users would more quickly complete data cleaning tasks requiring multi-step transformations.

As we will discuss, our results indicate that suggestions generated by our proactive model can help users discover applicable transforms, but not always in the manner we anticipated. Users often dismissed proactive suggestions presented prior to an initiating interaction, but made use of those exact same suggestions when presented later in the session.

Participants

We recruited 16 participants (11 male, 5 female) who had never used Wrangler before. All were university students with at least moderate experience programming and using data analysis tools such as Microsoft Excel or Matlab; all came from Computer Science or related majors. Participants received a $15 gift certificate for one hour of their time.

Methods

We evaluated the impact of proactive suggestions by comparing Proactive Wrangler to a baseline version that only generates suggestions in reaction to user-initiated interactions. First, we guided each subject through a 15-minute tutorial of Wrangler, highlighting both proactive and reactive modes.

Next, we had each subject perform data cleaning tasks on four data sets that were miniature versions of data sets from our corpus. We designed each task so that, in proactive mode, helpful proactive suggestions were available at most but not all steps (the "Hybrid" category from the algorithm behavior study). We imposed a 10-minute limit per task. The four cleaning tasks were divided into two pairs, each requiring structurally similar transformations. We gave participants a paper printout of the desired goal table state for each task. For a given pair of tasks, we assigned subjects one task using Proactive Wrangler and the other task using the baseline "reactive" Wrangler. We counterbalanced task order and Wrangler versions across subjects.

After completing the four tasks, we asked subjects to describe their preferences for reactive versus proactive suggestions. Each study session was administered on a 15" MacBook Pro laptop and recorded using screen capture software.

The first eight subjects used a version of Proactive Wrangler that displayed proactive suggestions only when there was no active selection on the data table; as soon as the user makes a selection, the proactive suggestions were replaced by the standard reactive suggestions. However, we observed that most subjects largely ignored the proactive suggestions in this configuration. After interviewing those subjects about their rationale, we updated Wrangler to append the top three proactive suggestions to the list of reactive suggestions normally generated from a user interaction. In other words, Wrangler now displayed proactive suggestions regardless of how the user interacted with it. This modified *embedded proactive* interface was seen by the last eight subjects.

Results

We initially expected subjects to complete tasks faster using Proactive Wrangler, but in fact we found no significant difference in completion times between proactive, embedded, or reactive variants ($F_{2,51} = 0.059$, $p = 0.943$ according to repeated measures ANOVA). We compared within individual tasks and controlled for the effects of task order, but found no significant differences. The average task completion time was 231 seconds; in only one instance did a user fail to complete a task by going over the 10-minute time limit.

Upon reviewing the usage logs, we found that subjects made sparing use of proactive suggestions. Most users (11/16, 69%) executed a proactive suggestion at least once. However, the total number of such transforms was small: in proactive conditions, subjects executed 1.16 proactive suggestions per task on average, compared to an average of 4.9 reactive suggestions on those same tasks.

To understand why subjects were reluctant to use the proactive suggestions, we reviewed our recorded experiment sessions to identify critical incidents. We identified three recurring patterns: subjects ignoring useful proactive suggestions, previewing but dismissing suggestions, and viewing suggestions as a last resort. We now discuss each.

Ignoring proactive suggestions

Nearly one-third of the subjects (5/16) simply never previewed any proactive suggestions, despite having used them in the tutorial. All of these subjects ignored at least one proactive suggestion that they later executed after making a selection and choosing an *identical* reactive suggestion. For example, after 137 seconds of work, one subject was almost done with a task and only needed to perform a final unfold. The necessary unfold was displayed as the sole proactive suggestion, but the subject ignored it and spent the next 86 seconds experimenting with selecting columns and specifying various folds and unfolds. He finally chose the correct unfold and completed his task, at which point he said, *"A proactive suggestion would have really helped me here!"*

Once we integrated proactive suggestions among reactive suggestions, 4 out of the 8 subjects who used the embedded version ignored a useful proactive suggestion only to click on it immediately after selecting an unrelated part of the table. One subject wanted to do a fold when in fact he needed an unfold (which was proactively suggested but ignored). When he selected some columns and attempted a fold, he noticed the proactive unfold suggestion at the bottom of the list and realized he needed to unfold, so he selected it and completed his task. This unfold would not have surfaced if he had not been using the embedded proactive interface.

Previewing, then ignoring, proactive suggestions

Almost half of our subjects (7/16) actually previewed the effects of a useful proactive suggestion, dismissed it, and a short time later made a selection and executed the *identical* reactive suggestion. As a typical example, one subject previewed a proactively-suggested unfold transform for a few seconds. But instead of executing it, he immediately selected the two columns in the table necessary to have Wrangler reactively suggest the *same* unfold. He then navigated directly to that unfold transform, previewed, and executed it.

Proactive suggestions as a last resort

Three subjects used proactive suggestions only when they ran out of ideas for triggering reactive suggestions. For example, out of the 167 seconds that one subject spent on a task, she was stuck staring at the table for 60 seconds (36% of total time) before she looked at the top-ranked proactive fold, previewed, and then executed it. This was the first (and only) time that she paused for long enough to actually consider using proactive suggestions; for the remainder of her session, she was continually making selections on the table, which surfaced reactive suggestions and hid the proactive ones.

Study Limitations

All subjects had some programming background, and this might make them more likely to want to explore rather than immediately follow proactive suggestions. One subject remarked, *"Maybe it's just me, but I like to try [initiating Wrangler actions] myself to see how they work."*

We provided specific target end states to subjects and timed them. Although many analysts have some end state in mind when working with data, discovering an appropriate end state is often an exploratory task. Several subjects reported that given a more ambiguous task, they believe they would be more likely to explore proactive suggestions, since these may inform what types of end states are possible.

Summary

Our user study largely disconfirms our original hypotheses. Users initially ignored proactive suggestions and on average did not complete tasks more quickly with them. However, proactive suggestions did aid the transformation process. Over two-thirds of subjects executed a proactive suggestion at least once. Suggestions generated by our proactive model proved helpful when embedded among reactive suggestions and when users failed to complete tasks by other means. At minimum, proactive suggestions are occasionally helpful and do not disrupt users. Moreover, our results raise some future research questions for the design of mixed-initiative interfaces. We discuss these in the next section.

DISCUSSION

In this paper, we presented a metric for table "suitability" that we apply to generate suggested data transforms. When compared with idealized transformation scripts, our model produces helpful suggestions for a majority of transform steps and ranks the preferred suggestion highly. In our own use, we have found proactive suggestions to be of great assistance: we regularly use the tool for data wrangling and find proactive suggestions to be a valuable complement. As a result, we believe our proactive suggestion model helps advance the state-of-the-art in interactive data transformation.

However, our user study results cast a shadow on our initial motivations. We find little evidence that proactive suggestions help novice users complete transformation tasks more quickly or learn data cleaning strategies. Upon review of our notes and recordings, we hypothesize multiple factors shape the observed usage patterns: *attentional blindness* to proactive suggestions, users' desire to *sustain initiative*, and *insufficient expertise* to recognize the value of suggestions.

Attention Blindness

Some subjects reported that they did not attend to proactive suggestions, even after using them in the tutorial. Many instead clicked on the table to initiate reactive suggestions. On the one hand, subjects expressed appreciation that proactive suggestions did not interrupt their workflow: annoying distractions are a classic complaint for mixed-initiative interfaces. However, insufficient visibility also seems to be a problem. Wrangler and similar tools might benefit from cues that emphasize suggested operations. For instance, subtle animation or colored backgrounds might draw attention to high-confidence suggestions without interrupting users' flow.

User Agency and Sustained Initiative

Many users expressed a pre-existing disdain for proactive interfaces. One said: *"I hate suggestions popping up at me on the computer ... I just want to get them out of my way."* Users described a distrust of automated suggestions in productivity software, citing examples like the infamous Microsoft Office 'paper clip'. Another user, describing his reluctance to use Wrangler's proactive suggestions, stated *"I knew what I wanted to do with the data, so I just did it myself."* Ironically, users voiced no such qualms regarding reactive suggestions, which were regularly employed to transform data.

During the first half of our study, only 4/8 subjects (50%) executed proactive suggestions. After we deployed the embedded proactive interface, 7/8 subjects (88%) executed suggestions generated by our proactive model, including those inserted into reactive suggestions. It is possible that user assessment of suggested transforms improves when users perceive of themselves as the initiator. We observed several instances of subjects making a selection, choosing an embedded proactive suggestion, and executing it *after* the same suggestion had already been proactively presented and viewed.

Subjects seem to value suggestions more when they are offered in response to an initiating action, even if the suggestions are generated independently. While speculative, this observation suggests that future research might examine not only the utility of suggestions to the stated task goal [10], but also how interface design and turn-taking affects user receptiveness to those suggestions. What design decisions might help sustain users' sense of control in mixed-initiative UIs?

Expertise for Transform Assessment

Our own internal use of Proactive Wrangler and the results of our study with novice users are at a disconnect. In our experience, proactive suggestions can reduce the cognitive effort and also the time required to specify transformations. Initially we hypothesized that proactive suggestions can speed transformation by casting transform specification as a "recognition" task, in which users recognize a desired transform among the list of suggestions. Our user study results suggest otherwise. Prior knowledge of transformation strategies may be needed to rapidly "recognize" the value of a transform. Thus, proactive suggestions may actually be more effective for expert users than for novices. New preview mechanisms might better facilitate user assessment of suggestions. For example, thumbnails of a transform's effects might be easier to comprehend than the current textual descriptions.

More sophisticated approaches may be needed to foster learning of multi-step transformation strategies. In most cases subjects followed a greedy approach to discovering an appropriate chain of transformations. Some complex transformations may require steps in which it is difficult to gauge progress from an intermediate state (e.g., a fold transform followed by a subsequent unfold). Subjects stated that they were worried that proactive suggestions might lead them down the wrong path. However, they often did later select and execute transforms that were identical to those previously suggested by Proactive Wrangler. By this point the subject had explored more alternatives and used interactions to communicate their intent. It is unclear which of these two factors gave the user more trust in the system.

Ultimately, users may be the most successful once they are able to articulate and evaluate their own transformation strategies. Towards this aim, future work might examine alternative approaches to fostering expertise. Tutorial generation may be one means. Another possibility is to examine the effects of multi-step suggestions. New user interface techniques for suggesting and previewing multiple steps may aid these situations; can a different design prompt multi-step reasoning rather than greedy search? More broadly, designing mixed-initiative interfaces to foster expertise through example presents a compelling challenge for future work.

ACKNOWLEDGMENTS

The authors thank all the participants in the user study. This research was supported in part by NSF grant CCF-0964173, the Boeing Company, and Greenplum/EMC.

REFERENCES

1. M. Burnett. Visual programming. In J. G. Webster, editor, *Encyclopedia of Electrical and Electronics Engineering*. John Wiley & Sons Inc., 1999.
2. A. Cypher. *Watch What I Do: Programming by Demonstration*. MIT Press, 1993.
3. T. Dasu and T. Johnson. *Exploratory Data Mining and Data Cleaning*. John Wiley & Sons, Inc., New York, NY, 2003.
4. M. Dontcheva, S. M. Drucker, D. Salesin, and M. F. Cohen. Relations, cards, and search templates: user-guided web data integration and layout. In *ACM UIST*, pages 61–70, 2007.
5. K. Fisher and D. Walker. The Pads project: An overview. In *International Conference on Database Theory*, March 2011.
6. H. Galhardas, D. Florescu, D. Shasha, and E. Simon. Ajax: an extensible data cleaning tool. In *ACM SIGMOD*, page 590, 2000.
7. T. R. G. Green. Cognitive dimensions of notations. In *British Computer Society, Human-Computer Interaction Specialist Group on People and Computers V*, pages 443–460. Cambridge University Press, 1989.
8. S. Gulwani. Automating string processing in spreadsheets using input-output examples. In *ACM POPL*, pages 317–330, 2011.
9. W. Harris and S. Gulwani. Spreadsheet table transformations from examples. In *ACM PLDI*, 2011.
10. E. Horvitz. Principles of mixed-initiative user interfaces. In *ACM CHI*, pages 159–166, 1999.
11. D. Huynh and S. Mazzocchi. Google Refine. `http://code.google.com/p/google-refine/`.
12. D. F. Huynh, R. C. Miller, and D. R. Karger. Potluck: semi-ontology alignment for casual users. In *ISWC*, pages 903–910, 2007.
13. S. Kandel, A. Paepcke, J. Hellerstein, and J. Heer. Wrangler: Interactive visual specification of data transformation scripts. In *ACM CHI*, 2011.
14. L. V. S. Lakshmanan, F. Sadri, and S. N. Subramanian. SchemaSQL: An extension to SQL for multidatabase interoperability. *ACM TODS*, 26(4):476–519, 2001.
15. G. Leshed, E. M. Haber, T. Matthews, and T. Lau. CoScripter: automating & sharing how-to knowledge in the enterprise. In *ACM CHI*, pages 1719–1728, 2008.
16. J. Lin, J. Wong, J. Nichols, A. Cypher, and T. A. Lau. End-user programming of mashups with Vegemite. In *IUI*, pages 97–106, 2009.
17. G. Little and R. C. Miller. Translating keyword commands into executable code. In *ACM UIST*, pages 135–144, 2006.
18. M. Mernik, J. Heering, and A. M. Sloane. When and how to develop domain-specific languages. *ACM Comput. Surv.*, 37(4):316–344, 2005.
19. R. C. Miller and B. A. Myers. Interactive simultaneous editing of multiple text regions. In *USENIX Tech. Conf.*, pages 161–174, 2001.
20. B. A. Myers, A. J. Ko, and M. M. Burnett. Invited research overview: end-user programming. In *ACM CHI Extended Abstracts*, pages 75–80, 2006.
21. V. Raman and J. M. Hellerstein. Potter's wheel: An interactive data cleaning system. In *Proc. VLDB*, 2001.
22. R. Tuchinda, P. Szekely, and C. A. Knoblock. Building mashups by example. In *ACM IUI*, pages 139–148, 2008.
23. H. Varian. Hal Varian on how the Web challenges managers. In *McKinsey Quarterly*, Jan 2009.

MUSE: Reviving Memories Using Email Archives

Sudheendra Hangal *Monica S. Lam* *Jeffrey Heer*
Computer Science Department
Stanford University
{hangal, lam, jheer}@cs.stanford.edu

ABSTRACT

Email archives silently record our actions and thoughts over the years, forming a passively acquired and detailed life-log that contains rich material for reminiscing on our lives. However, exploratory browsing of archives containing thousands of messages is tedious without effective ways to guide the user towards interesting events and messages. We present MUSE (Memories USing Email), a system that combines data mining techniques and an interactive interface to help users browse a long-term email archive. MUSE analyzes the contents of the archive and generates a set of cues that help to spark users' memories: communication activity with inferred social groups, a summary of recurring named entities, occurrence of sentimental words, and image attachments. These cues serve as salient entry points into a browsing interface that enables faceted navigation and rapid skimming of email messages. In our user studies, we found that users generally enjoyed browsing their archives with MUSE, and extracted a range of benefits, from summarizing work progress to renewing friendships and making serendipitous discoveries.

Keywords: Life-logging, Email, Data mining, User interfaces, Visualization.

ACM Classification: H.5.2 Information Interfaces and Presentation.

General terms: Algorithms, Design, Human Factors.

INTRODUCTION

Email is one of the Internet's most enduring "killer applications" with over 1.8 billion users and 2.9 billion accounts worldwide, as of 2010 [26]. Given the availability of free email services with virtually unlimited storage, we expect that millions of mainstream users will amass large email repositories, perhaps spanning over half a century, across their lifetimes. Already, it is common to find people with email archives spanning several decades.

In much of the wired world, email is used for many daily activities, for everything from setting up meetings to processing business workflow; from making purchases on the Internet to sending emotional messages of love, joy, and condolence; from sending oneself reminders to sharing an interesting web link with friends, and so on. Unlike blogs, diaries and journals, email archives silently capture our experiences *in situ*, as they arise in our communication, with no additional action needed to record them. Indeed, email has become a de facto medium of record; many people consciously deposit important information into email, knowing they can look it up later, and thereby use their email account as an informal backup device. Therefore, email archives contain or reflect memories that are extremely valuable for the purposes of reminiscence. We surmise that for a significant fraction of computer users, more characters are typed into email than into any other application, and these characters, accumulated over a lifetime, can provide a powerful window into history.

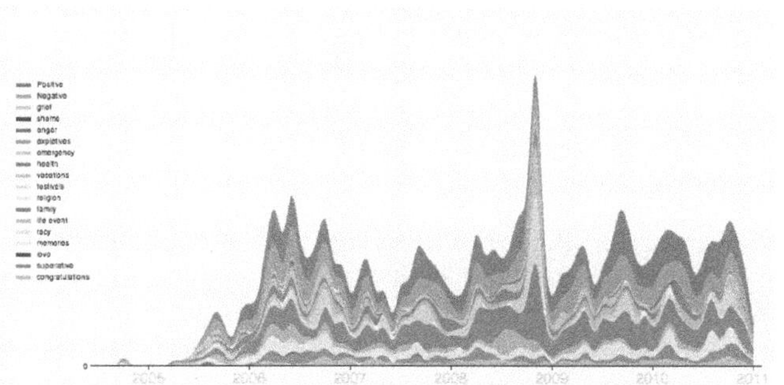

Figure 1: A MUSE visualization of email sentiment. A stacked graph shows the number of email messages reflecting a particular sentiment category over time.

An email archive is one example of a life-logging device that captures and stores different forms of personal data across a long period of time [10]. Ironically, while service providers routinely mine email and other personal data for advertising purposes, there are relatively few tools to help individuals make sense of their own digital assets. Even if all personal data is captured, as Petrelli et al. remark: "*This may be the fate of lifelog data, stored somewhere and ignored, if the owner is not given tools for sorting, clearing and distilling what is of value*" [24].

However, distilling valuable information is a difficult problem in practice, particularly in a domain like email that consists mainly of free-form text along with some metadata and attachments. What kinds of information do users find valuable when detailed, day-by-day records of their communication are available? What techniques enable users to conveniently browse their life-logs and identify valuable information? How do these techniques interact with the user's own knowledge and memory? We believe email is a good platform for studying these questions, as many people already have archives spanning relatively long periods of time.

While email archives contain a wealth of valuable information, they are also voluminous; a life-long archive can easily run into tens or hundreds of thousands of messages. Traditional email clients allow users to examine one message at a time, and to filter and to issue search queries. These clients are ill-suited for browsing a large-scale archive, where a user may not know exactly what to look for. Like others before us [35], we see a two part solution to this challenge. First, we can automatically generate cues likely to orient the user towards messages of interest. Second, once the user has acquired a cue, we can encourage exploration of the messages related to that cue and to other related cues. Such exploration mirrors the natural organization of episodic memory of autobiographical events [32].

To explore the efficacy of different types of cues and browsing techniques, we have built a program called MUSE, for *Memories USing Email*[1]. MUSE processes the contents of a user's email archive and generates several types of cues. It also provides a browsing environment that enables the user to follow these cues by rapidly skimming related messages and forking off other trails of exploration. As an illustration, Figure 1 shows how Muse presents a timeline summarizing the sentiments expressed in the archive.

Contributions

In this paper, we make the following research contributions:

1. Based on iterative design and user feedback, we identify four types of cues useful for reminiscence: communication activity with inferred social groups, a summary of recurring named entities over time, occurrence of sentimental words, and image attachments.

2. We propose specific and relatively lightweight mining techniques to identify, organize and present these cues, as well as techniques to enable rapid and exploratory browsing of associated messages and other related cues.

3. We discuss some of the memories evoked by MUSE in users reminiscing with their own email archives, and present insights about the efficacy of different cues. Our studies uncover a range of benefits for exploratory browsing with MUSE, from summarizing work progress to renewing old friendships and identifying milestones.

To date, MUSE has been used to explore email archives containing up to 50,000 messages.

RELATED WORK

While there has been much prior work in various forms of email analysis, there are relatively few usable systems that let end users explore large scale email archives. MUSE draws on several lines of research, summarized below.

Email Analysis

The closest related work to MUSE is Themail [35], which aims to help users reflect on the dyadic relationship with each one of their contacts. Themail visualizes single words that have a high TF-IDF score in emails exchanged with a contact over time. Our starting point for generating important name cues in MUSE was similar to Themail; however, we found that this approach tended to generate noisy words lacking any context and was inefficient when browsing thousands of contacts accumulated in a long-term archive. MUSE solves these problems with its use of named entities and automatic inference of social groups, and introduces additional types of cues; it also provides a more sophisticated exploratory browsing environment.

Other related work includes research on "email rhythms" to provide insights about patterns of communication [19, 23, 33, 34]. SocialFlows [17], GroupGenie [25] and ContactMap [36] help to organize a user's social contacts. These tools are focused on messaging patterns and not the actual message contents.

There is much interest in helping users become more effective in email correspondence. Examples include Xobni (xobni.com), Rapportive (rapportive.com), SNARF [21] and Gmail's Priority Inbox and People Widget. However, these systems do not target interactions with email archives.

Life-logging

Many life-logging systems today are geared towards active life-logging, which involves deliberate actions by the user and/or the use of specific hardware, software or services[2]. Pensieve actively solicits input from the user by periodically emailing personal questions and attempts to create a repository of reminiscences [22]. In personal finance, mining spending data [28] is an example of analyzing a passively captured life-log. MUSE shares this focus on passive life-logging, but works in the domain of email communication.

Legal Discovery and Intelligence Analysis

There are some similarities between MUSE and systems used for legal discovery and intelligence analysis. Users of these systems also need to spot cues and peruse large-scale, loosely organized datasets, often including emails. MUSE shares techniques with such tools; for example, extraction of key entities as in Jigsaw [30], and the need for pre-built views of intelligence corpora [3]. However, the use case for discovery tools (trained analysts making sense of unfamiliar corpora in order to spot suspicious activity) is starkly different from that of MUSE (mainstream consumers using their own email for reminiscence). This leads to different design considerations for MUSE.

Text Analysis and Visualization

The TIARA system integrates text analytics and interactive visualization of email [15], and was tested with users performing focused tasks on a short-duration email corpus belonging to another person. The Parallel Tag Clouds visualization [4] highlights the presence as well as absence of significant terms across the parallel text corpora of different circuit courts. MUSE has somewhat similar requirements for identifying key term in email messages across time, though it detects only the presence of terms, not their absence. Themeriver is a system for visualization of text content acquired

[1] MUSE is publicly available at http://mobisocial.stanford.edu/muse.

[2] See http://personalinformatics.org for a list of life-logging systems.

over time, such as news articles [12]. Work in the topic detection and tracking (TDT) area tends to focus on clustering and labeling the textual content of messages (e.g. [31]). Unlike MUSE, all of the above systems do not target the task of reminiscence, and do not take advantage of personal and social context (such as cohesive groups, sentimental messages and images). However, there are possible synergies between the text analysis techniques used by MUSE and these systems.

Interaction Techniques

Many systems use faceted navigation to support exploratory browsing (e.g., Flamenco [38], Phlat [5] and Stuff I've Seen [6]). MUSE employs similar ideas in the domain of email, where the facets are people, months, years and automatically inferred groups and sentiments. Systems like Cyclostar have demonstrated the effectiveness and versatility of elliptical gestures [18]; the MUSE jog dial we describe in later sections is a simplified form of such an interface.

Sentiment Analysis

There is much work on sentiment analysis of tweets and reviews for the purposes of inferring public reaction to a product (e.g., [1]). We Feel Fine is a visualization of sentiments expressed in public blog posts and has been used to generate hypotheses about sentiments at a societal level [13]. MUSE tracks sentimental words in the personal communication of a single user across time and can potentially be used by an individual to examine hypotheses about herself.

Memory and Archiving Practices

There are several studies that take an ethnographic approach to understanding family memories and archiving practices (e.g., [14]). Elsweiler et al's work on understanding human memory in the context of email refinding concludes that "*...although people generally remember quite a lot about their emails, there are situations in which people remember less and in these situations it may be more difficult to refind the information required with existing tools*" [7]. Zalinger's dissertation explores the role of Gmail as storyworld, and its intensive participant interviews confirm the richness of narratives that are embedded in email [39]. These studies establish the value of personal and family archives and provide motivation for experimental systems such as MUSE.

USING MUSE

To run MUSE, a user typically downloads it to her own computer and launches it using Java Webstart. This reassures users about confidentiality, which is important given that email archives frequently contain highly sensitive information, from love letters to financial documents. MUSE starts up an embedded web server in the background, and launches a browser window for the user to interact with it. This interface choice means users can use their favorite browser and its familiar features like multiple tabs and windows, navigation buttons, bookmarks and browser plugins.

The user specifies one or more sources of email to MUSE, including online POP/IMAP servers or mbox format files stored on a local file system. The user can select folders to analyze from each source and optionally apply filters by date range, or tell MUSE to only analyze their sent messages. Focusing on sent messages is a useful heuristic for reminiscence because they are handcrafted by the user and reflect the user's thoughts and actions. In contrast, the INBOX tends to be much larger (on average, 2.5 times as many messages involving 4.8 times as many people, according to an anonymized dataset provided to us for research purposes by Xobni). Much incoming email is delivered via mailing lists, which are sometimes scanned casually or even ignored entirely. Since access to online email providers can be slow, MUSE caches messages once fetched, though the cache can always be cleared under user control.

Once MUSE has fetched the user's messages, it processes and indexes their contents and attachments, and builds an address book of contacts. Typical processing speed on a current-generation laptop or desktop computer is about 1,000 messages per minute. MUSE performs entity resolution by unifying names and email addresses in email headers when either the name or email address (as specified in the RFC-822 email header) is equivalent. This is essential since email addresses and even name spellings for a person are likely to change in a long-term archive. Name equivalence is tested by ignoring case differences and equating commonly used variations in naming, e.g., with or without a middle initial, "Firstname Lastname", "Lastname, Firstname" and "Firstname Lastname - Department". Once the address book is available, MUSE infers social groups based on a grouping algorithm, described in the next section. The user can specify the number of groups to be inferred, but 20 is a reasonable default. Users can also refine the inferred groups manually.

Next, MUSE allows the user to browse four different kinds of cues and the messages associated with them. These cues are described in detail in the next two sections. Since users' tend to become highly engaged while exploring their archives containing years or decades of messages, it is not uncommon for them to spend several hours with MUSE. To allow them to split this time across multiple sessions, MUSE lets users save session state and reload it later without having to reprocess the archive.

MEMORY CUES FOR BROWSING EMAIL ARCHIVES

In this section, we discuss a set of memory cues for browsing email archives and techniques for generating them. We discovered these cues by observing users interact with early versions of MUSE on their archives and analyzing why they appeared to be useful. For each type of cue, we present the intuition, some details of its implementation, and the presentation technique used.

Automatically generated cues do not have to be fully precise or complete; rather, they should work hand-in-hand with a user's memory and the actual content of the messages. In practice, we expect that many cues will be ignored by a user because they are obvious, redundant, noisy or overshadowed by other, stronger cues. However, for the system to be engaging it should surface a relatively high fraction of useful cues that lead to valuable memories and avoid flooding the user with misleading or irrelevant cues. We also prefer techniques that are sufficiently lightweight to run on end-users' own machines and do not require server-class hardware.

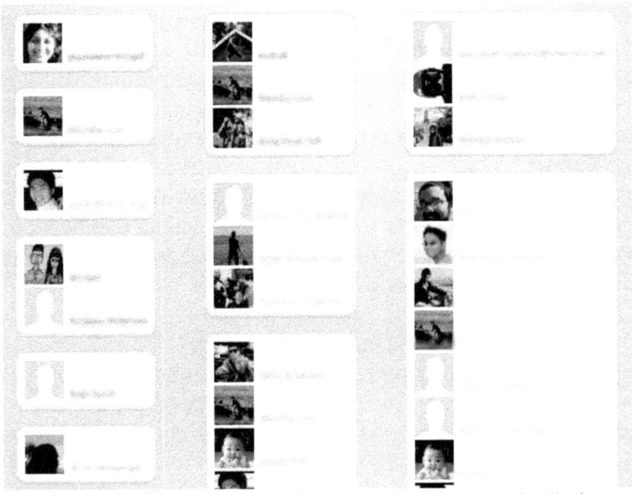

Figure 2: The groups editor showing automatically inferred groups that can be refined by the user. Names are blurred to preserve user privacy.

Group Cues

People routinely interact with thousands of contacts in the course of a few years over email. Since it is difficult to visualize messages, topics, and communication activity with so many individuals, MUSE groups these contacts automatically and lets users explore their communication with the group as a whole. This approach mirrors the way people mentally chunk their contacts into groups like family, colleagues, classmates, neighbors, and so on.

MUSE automatically discovers likely groups by analyzing co-recipiency in messages. It employs a group mining algorithm [25] that satisfies several properties that are important in social contexts. First, a group may consist of people who do not all appear together in any single message (e.g., a user's extended family.) Second, within a group, there may be important subgroups with a significant identity of their own (e.g., siblings as an important subset of extended family). Next, the same person could belong to multiple groups (e.g., a colleague at work may also be part of a hiking group.) And finally, a significant "group", for the purposes of organization, could consist of just one very important person with a high communication volume, such as a spouse or close friend.

Users can optionally refine the inferred groups manually using a drag-and-drop editor. The editor lets users move people between groups and create, clone or delete groups. Users can see the name of each person in a group, but if their browser supports the W3C contacts API [37], they also see the contacts' pictures, if available. For example, Mozilla's Contacts plugins for Firefox can fetch photographs for friends from networks like Facebook, LinkedIn and Gmail. Fig. 2 shows a screenshot of the groups editor with this plugin.

To present the cues associated with groups, MUSE generates a stacked graph visualization with one layer per group as shown in Fig. 3. This visualization lets users spot relative patterns of communication with each group over time, and to correlate them with total communication volume. Most users find that this visualization tells a story of when they started

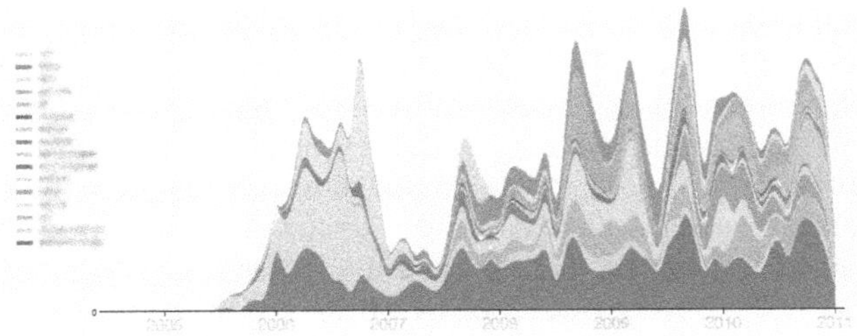

Figure 3: A stacked graph representation of communication with each group over time. Group names are blurred to preserve user privacy.

and stopped interacting with various groups, reflecting different phases of their lives. Users can click at any point on the stacked graph to launch into a view containing all the messages exchanged with that group. The view is initialized to the point in time along the X-axis that was clicked. Each group is also assigned a color, which is used to code important terms, as described below.

Name Cues

To provide a quick overview of an archive, MUSE creates a summary of important terms on a monthly basis. Terms that make the best cues are often names of various kinds, including people, places, organizations and so on, because names generally tend to carry rich associations in the user's episodic memory [32]. Hence MUSE first extracts named entities from message contents and analyzes these terms. We apply the Named Entity Recognition package from the Stanford NLP toolkit [9], using the default training model. This decision was informed by early experiments using the standard TF-IDF (Term Frequency by Inverse Document Frequency) metric with single words, similar to Themail. The results with this metric were very noisy, despite using appropriate stop-word lists and other heuristics like factoring word commonality into ranking.

Fig. 4 illustrates the difference on an example corpus: a portion of the email archive of noted American poet Robert Creeley, which is hosted at Stanford University Libraries [8]. Using word-based TF-IDF, the top-scoring terms, shown in Fig. 4(a), include generic words like *best*, *lovely*, *say* and *touch* which are unlikely to be useful, and in fact tend to waste the user's time as she tries to understand the context in which they arise[3]. However, we observe from this list that the terms most likely to be interesting are the named entities such as *Waldoboro*, *Helen*, etc. Fig. 4(b) shows the results of first extracting named entities from the message contents, and scoring only these terms. The overall results already appear to be better cues to memory.

We also experimented with 2 other options for identifying key terms: scoring multi-word phrases, and scoring noun phrases extracted with linguistic parsing. We found that users generally react better to named entities since names tend to have deeper associations in the user's memory compared to phrases, which may still lack context.

Time-based TF-IDF To score terms, we use a metric based on TF-IDF scoring of the named entities, using the *ntn* vari-

[3]While the Themail program is not available to us, from the screenshot in the paper, it appears to suffer from the same problem.

Figure 4: Comparison of top-ranked terms for the same month on a portion of the Robert Creeley archive. (a) single words, (b) named entities, and (c) named entities color coded and clustered by group.

ation described by Manning et al [20]. This variation corresponds to natural term frequency, the regular definition of inverse document frequency and no TF normalization. High TF-IDF scores are associated with terms that are specific to a particular document (in our case, the messages for a month) compared to the rest of the corpus.

To further improve term scoring, we introduce a simple, novel variant for *time-based* TF-IDF. The traditional IDF factor penalizes the score of terms that appear across many documents in the entire corpus. In contrast, we compute the IDF factor for a term T in a document D based on the number of documents *preceding* D that contain T.

Intuitively, it makes sense to identify the most significant terms at a particular point in time without knowledge of the future. We have observed that people tend to find the onset of a new term particularly memorable; such scenarios are promoted by the time-based TF-IDF. Examples of terms that benefit from this metric include the name of a newborn family member, or a name like *Obama*, that emerges at some point in time and subsequently becomes commonplace. As time goes by with repeated use of the new term, the IDF score slowly reduces, making the term less prominent.

A concrete example from one of the authors' email archives illustrates this point. MUSE highlighted terms related to music in the first two months after he started taking music lessons. Thereafter, the music conversations continued, but these terms disappeared from the monthly summaries because they become relatively common. With the regular version of TF-IDF, these terms do not show up at all because of a relatively low IDF score across the entire corpus.

To present these terms to the user, MUSE lists the top named entities for each month in a month-by-month view, similar to a calendar. Users can ask for more or less terms to be displayed (the default is set to 30 terms for each month). MUSE clusters and color-codes the terms by the inferred group they are most closely associated with. Terms assigned to the same group (and therefore the same color), are displayed together, and are further sorted by descending score. This is useful because terms belonging to a group tend to be related to each other and the user can quickly scan them together; users frequently have varying levels of interest in different groups. An early round of user testing with five users showed that organizing and color coding terms by group was unanimously preferred over just sorting terms by score. Terms not assigned to any group are colored gray and displayed last. The color encoding also makes it easy to scan all terms related to a particular group across different months. Fig. 4(c) shows the names view actually displayed by MUSE for this example.

To avoid the problem of over-representation from a single message, we throttle the number of terms displayed that belong to a single message. After a preset threshold is reached (empirically, four works well), other terms from the message are suppressed, unless they are also present in a different, non-maximally represented message.

Sentiment Cues

During our experiments with early versions of MUSE, we found that many of the messages that engaged users the most during the reminiscence process were those that reflected significant turning points in their life and deep emotions, such as love, joy, grief and anger. There is much evidence that emotional episodes tend to be well-remembered, both for positive and negative emotions [27]. MUSE therefore uses simple sentiment analysis techniques to let users quickly browse messages by the sentiment associated with them.

Figure 5: Attachment wall using the PicLens viewer.

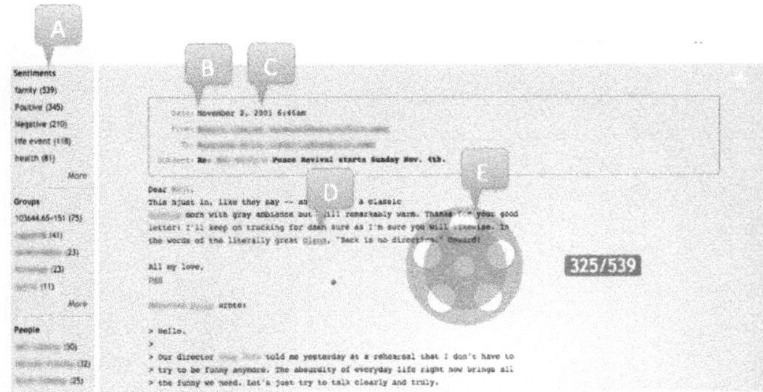

Figure 6: The messages view in MUSE, with 539 messages loaded. (A) Facet panel for sentiments, groups and people. (B) Link to all messages for month and (C) for year. (D) Hyperlink inserted into message contents. (E) Jog dial for rapid skimming. Some details blurred to protect privacy.

The most commonly used tools for sentiment analysis such as SentiWordnet [2] and LIWC [16] use word lists to detect sentiment. We have generated our own (English language) lexicon, that consists of 20 categories with terms covering various emotions, family, health, life events, expletives, etc. that may be useful for our domain of reminiscence with email archives. These terms are matched (modulo stemming) with the contents of the message. Significant emotions that can be detected with high certainty, such as congratulations, are assigned their own category. Other kinds of emotions that can be classified with less certainty are grouped into two broad categories for positive (gratitude, pride, joy, humor, etc.) and negative (disappointment, anxiety, worry, etc.) sentiment.

MUSE depicts the frequency of messages reflecting these sentiment categories across time using a stacked graph (see Fig. 1); each layer represents a particular sentiment category. Users can click on a layer to launch into a view containing all the messages reflecting that sentiment; the view is initialized to the point in time along the X-axis that was clicked. Users can also examine how their sentiment graphs vary across different social groups.

We have found that while sentiments are among the noisiest cues provided by MUSE, they are also often the most engaging. Users are curious about interpreting the sentiments graph, especially when exploring their sent messages. Even if a detected sentiment is due to a language artifact, it often gives users a new view into their own use of language.

Picture Cues

Picture attachments in email messages are useful because the vividness of images provides strong cues to memory. Further, pictures are often taken for the explicit purpose of later remembrance and hence may be worth recalling.

MUSE extracts picture attachments from messages (and optionally PDF documents, which are converted to thumbnails) and displays them on the PicLens photo wall (from cooliris.com) which provides a 2.5D zoomable and draggable interface. The images are arranged in reverse chronological order and it is easy for the user to rapidly scan pictures, and pan to different areas of the wall without waiting for the whole wall to render chronologically.

We find that users are often pleasantly surprised to rediscover pictures from their email attachments. While many more pictures are shared through formal mechanisms such as photo sharing sites, the memory of pictures sent in email attachments is not refreshed since it is not easy to browse email attachments. Therefore there is a sense of novelty in re-discovering a long forgotten picture.

From the photo wall, users can click on an attachment to go to a view containing the message(s) with that attachment. From that point, the user can continue exploratory browsing using the usual facets such as people, groups, and sentiments. The browsing interface is described in the next section.

EXPLORATORY BROWSING

Generating interesting cues is often merely a step on the way to browsing the actual messages which hold the memorable details. In practice, most users spend more time browsing messages than browsing cues. Therefore it is important to support rapid exploratory browsing of a large set of messages. When a user follows up on a cue, e.g., by clicking on a name in the monthly summaries, or by selecting a point in a stacked graph visualization, MUSE opens a *message view* for the associated messages. The message view displays the actual message header and contents, along with thumbnails of any attachments for the message at the bottom. Multiple views can be simultaneously active in different browser windows or tabs to encourage multiple chains of exploration.

Skimming with an on-screen jog dial

Our original implementation of the message view displayed all the messages in the view, one below the other. This tended to create long pages, and we found that when there were more than about 10-15 messages, users would get bored and stop scanning messages part of the way down the page. While following cues, however, some views (for example, all messages for a group or person) can consist of hundreds of messages and are tedious to click or scroll through.

To alleviate the tedium of scrolling down a long page, we load multiple messages into the browser but display only one message at a time in a fixed message frame. This has the advantage that it fixes the on-screen locations of the message headers and the beginning of the message contents, which are often the most important for sensing the relevance of a message. To enable rapid scanning of messages in the view, we provide a translucent on-screen circular jog dial that is summoned on the spot and dismissed by clicking anywhere in the message frame. The operation of the dial is similar to the physical dial on iPod music players: moving clockwise to the next octant causes the frame to display the next message; moving counter-clockwise displays the previous message. Fig. 6 shows the message view with the jog dial visible. Apart from being somewhat playful, the dial allows fast interactive performance through the use of client-side Javascript – in our experience, users can rapidly rotate the dial to approach a skimming speed of 150 messages a minute while still being able to monitor the content passing by.

The dial affords finer-grained control than keyboard navigation, as users can slow down and speed up as they wish, depending on their interest level in the phase of messages. The jog dial lets them travel relatively long distances (scanning through a few hundred messages is common) without the need for precise cursor positioning, mouse clicks, key presses, or switching gaze from the message view. The circularity of the gesture avoids the need to periodically reposition the cursor, and is a general advantage of elliptical gestures. For fast travel in extremely long views, we also provide the option of tabbing backwards or forwards to move month by month. Of course, the user can always use the keyboard right or left arrows keys to scroll through messages.

It is important to manage browser load for a view with thousands of messages. MUSE maintains a sliding window of pages around the page currently being displayed, and keeps only the pages in that window loaded in the browser. As the user moves along, the Javascript "pages in" new messages to maintain the window around the current page, while retiring pages outside the window. In practice, we find that a default window size of 100 pages (60 pages ahead and 40 pages backward) is adequate for good user experience with no stalls and is easily handled by current browsers.

While we have not formally evaluated the jog dial with respect to alternatives, it is a popular feature with many users of MUSE. We designed the dial to operate primarily with a trackpad, but users have also reported relatively high satisfaction rates with a mouse. We plan to perform detailed standalone evaluation of this interface element in future.

Facets and Hyperlinks

We encourage users to follow top-level cues by using links to related facets and annotating the message contents with the named entities identified as top level name cues. For example, if a name cue is mentioned in a message, we insert a hyperlink for that name to a view containing all the messages with that name. Users can optionally open this new view in a different browser tab without disturbing the current chain of exploration. Similarly, ordered lists of groups, sentiments and people associated with the messages in the current view are shown in a facets panel on the left (see Fig. 6). From any message, the user can click on the month or year in the message header to launch a new view containing all the messages in that time unit. When a message view is generated by querying for a term or sentiment, that term is highlighted in the text of the message.

Throughout the interface, clicking on the name or email address of a person, or the description of a group, can be used to launch a message view containing all the associated messages. Similarly it is possible to launch an attachment wall consisting of all pictures in the messages in the current view. Finally, in addition to browsing facets, users can always type in their own search terms.

USER STUDY

Throughout the development of MUSE, we conducted surveys and formative studies to inform our design. We also conducted two formal studies (with a total of 13 users), as well as other informal testing with early users. The findings led to the current version of MUSE. We now report on a small study with 6 users to test this version.

Methodology

In this study, we recruited 6 participants (P1–6) who had access to relatively long-term email archives. We required them to have at least 5,000 messages (preferably sent by the user), acquired over at least 5 years. We invited three professionals from our university library to participate in this study because they could offer us expert-level feedback based on their experience in dealing with archival material. Two were professional archivists who dealt with special collections, both physical and digital, and the third was a historian and professional curator for the library. The remaining three participants were working professionals. Participants had between 10 and 30 years of work experience, and had all been using email throughout their working lives for both professional and personal purposes. Two of the participants were female, and only one had used an early version of MUSE before this study. Participants were compensated with a $10 gift coupon.

We conducted a pre-study meeting with each user to ascertain the state of their email archives. Without exception, all users had email archives in multiple accounts or sources (online service providers, company account, files on a hard drive, etc.) Some users had archives in older formats (like Eudora) and no longer had the program to read it; in these cases we wrote scripts to help them convert their archives to the mbox format which MUSE can read. There were frequently discrepancies between what users thought they had in which folders, and what material was actually present, pointing to the difficulty of maintaining consistent foldering practices, across time and different accounts, even for professional archivists. In general, it remains a challenge for ordinary users to access their decades old email. Further some service provides like Hotmail support only the POP email protocol, which allows access only to the Inbox folder. One user had a significant number of messages in a Hotmail account; we helped him import the Hotmail messages to Gmail for better access via IMAP. The problem of maintaining access to email in historical formats is well-known to archivists [11], and they pointed us to commercial software that they frequently use to convert from one email format to another.

In the actual study, we gave participants a 5-minute tour of the different types of cues and browsing features of MUSE.

We then asked them to spend 30 to 45 minutes examining the cues and following them to generate memories. At the end, we asked them to fill out a detailed survey with 41 questions (5 of the 6 users asked for more time to browse their archives, or if they could return the survey after running MUSE on other parts of their archives, in which case we let them do so). The survey asked them to rate the usefulness of different kinds of cues, and to rate different aspects of the user interface such as the jog dial and faceted navigation. Other questions asked for feedback on sentiment categories that were useful or noisy, and for general comments about the automatically inferred social groups.

Results

Most users thought MUSE provided useful cues to jog their memory and remind them of past incidents, which they had otherwise forgotten. While Musing, people were deeply engrossed in their past. They were reminded of both high-level patterns (P5: *"That year is full of Europe for me, I traveled so much."*) and specific episodes (P1: *"I had to go to the DMV when I moved to a new city."*). Users were often surprised by the extent of material in their archives (P4: *"Wow – I'm writing a book on Warcraft, and I didn't realize my email had stuff about it back in 1999!"*), and generally enjoyed discovering long-forgotten messages.

Broadly, all four cue types got good ratings from users. On a 5-point scale, the attachments cues were rated the highest with an average of 4.25, closely followed by a tie between monthly terms and sentiments at 4.17 each. The groups cues got an average rating of 3.83. While our sample size is too small to be conclusive, comments from other users of MUSE are consistent with these findings.

Two participants remarked that the monthly terms view was what they would use the most. The picture cues were also popular. One user found valuable pictures of her son's first year lying in her archives. P3: *"I've been looking for these and thought they were lost. Let me save them while I can..."*

While we expected that the names and attachments cues would be highly evocative for the user, we were somewhat surprised that users responded well to the simple sentiment cues. The sentiment cues achieved the same average rating as the name cues, which took considerably more time and effort on our part to generate and prioritize. P1 remarked, *"I just keep coming back to the sentiments view, it's so much fun."* Users also took the sentiment graphs fairly seriously. P5: *"I am relieved to see that 'positive' outweighs 'negative' by a considerable margin, especially in recent years!"*

When we asked users which sentiment categories were accurate, and which ones were not, the responses varied. P5: *"I thought positive and negative were pretty accurate, the negative and angry ones did capture some uncomfortable exchanges with a former roommate (there was money involved)"*, and P3: *"The congratulatory messages are pretty useful."* Users also experienced noisy or incorrect sentiments. P1: *"It thinks there is a lot of religion in my life because I used to work in a theology library... well, you know, maybe that's right"* (laughs), or P6: *"I deal a lot with 'Born Digital' documents, so MUSE thinks I have a lot of life events."* For the most part, users ignored misclassifications and focused on the categories that did work well for them. Our observation is that the simplicity of the sentiment categorization has the advantage of being extremely *transparent*, which allows users to easily ignore any parts that do not work well. A surprise to us was that four of our six users voluntarily mentioned that they would like to be able to edit the lexicon and put in their own terms. Perhaps this should not be so surprising seeing the popularity of tools like Google's N-gram viewer that allow people to ask simple questions about the evolution of language.

While the social groups were rated lower than other cues, we noted that the activity graphs with groups straightaway told a story. Most users would look at the graph and say, *"Oh yeah, that makes perfect sense."* Further, users would often enter group views from the faceted browsing interface (by clicking on a particularly important group or person) and may not have realized that they were following group cues.

Although it was not an explicit goal of this study, we were curious about how users would react to potentially unpleasant memories being brought up. One user volunteered a reaction that was particularly interesting. P1: *"This reminded me of the stress of looking for a job, how much work goes into a cross-country move, and how hard it was to sell my house after I moved. That sounds unpleasant, but being reminded of these things wasn't a bad experience – it made me reflect on how much I've been through over the past six years, and how glad I am that certain experiences are behind me."*

While browsing, some users switched into the mode of looking for what their conversations were about at specific points in time. P5: *"Let's see, does Obama show up in the monthly terms around November 2008? Oh yes, he does. Cool!"*

On the interface questions, the average rating of the jog dial was 3.6 on a scale of 5. This rating is somewhat skewed by one user giving a rating of 1; she found it hard to use on her new desktop with trackpad that she was unfamiliar with. Surprisingly, 2 users with a mouse gave the jog dial a 5 rating. In hindsight, mouse vs. trackpad is a condition that we should have controlled for in our study, but we let users choose whatever computer they had available. Making the jog dial more robust and easier for first timers to use, and understanding design issues for mice may be areas of future study. The faceted browsing interface was generally liked (average rating 4.00) as was the fact that a regular web browser could be used to interface to MUSE (average rating 4.25).

In the rest of this section, we present further insights obtained by feedback from people who have used MUSE outside the context of this study.

Summarizing work progress. Several of our users remarked after using MUSE that they would find it useful to summarize their year when writing an annual report or performance review. A user commented: *"I wish I had this system at project reviews to quickly scan all the project group messages since the last meeting."*

Extraction and organization. One user suggested that it would be useful to form a group of all personal contacts and use it to take personal email out with her when leaving a job. She said, *"My husband was leaving the newspaper company he worked at, and spent two days printing out all the personal emails in his work account"*, as she rolled her eyes.

A user who is a software entrepreneur said that he had saved his email mainly because it had important documents embedded in it, such as *"company ownership spreadsheets, benefits packages, legal agreements – stuff that's nowhere else."* MUSE can be used to extract these documents and organize them better.

Family groups. A consistent pattern (also noted by Viégas et al. [35]) was that users tended to spend much of their time browsing messages exchanged with their family group(s), perhaps more than any other group. This may have been due to the long-lived nature of such relationships, which makes introspection on them particularly valuable. In addition, it is common for people to tell distant family members about important milestones and events in their lives, such as job promotions and new romances. One user suggested that we allow editing of results so he could clean them up and share his memories with his family.

Picking up forgotten threads. A few users remarked after using MUSE that they were reminded of unfinished work or projects. For example: *"I'd like to remind my friend that we were planning this trip – wonder why it got dropped and we never went."* Our hypothesis is that users may also find such life-browsing useful as a reminder of high level goals and ambitions they once had. Interestingly, one user reported that she felt a renewed sense of confidence by looking at her past achievements, an observation also made by Kirk and Sellen [14].

Renewing relationships. Multiple users remarked after reviewing old conversations that they felt bad they were no longer in touch with people who had been very close some years ago: *"I had forgotten that we were such close friends, but then I moved, and we stopped talking"* and *"Wow! I had forgotten how nice one friend was in offering me a temporary place to stay (I ended up staying elsewhere) but she has been a little grumpy lately but I can forgive that a bit now that I remember that incident."*

Serendipitous discovery. One user when browsing messages noticed that her son's name was part of a message and had a hyperlink. Clicking on the link brought up a view with 224 messages with her son's name. As she skimmed through the messages, she remarked: *"Wow, this offers a pretty complete history of my first son's milestones. There is no other record of this. I've been trying to remember his milestones to compare with my other son's."*

All users said that MUSE revived their memories of topics that they had otherwise forgotten about. Sometimes these were topics in themselves, and sometimes they were satellite topics around other events that they did remember: *"I had forgotten about that lunch we organized right before my thesis defense."* This suggests that MUSE can add color and detail even to such "flashbulb" memories of significant and well-remembered events. Further, the archives add concrete evidence to the event; it is well known that even flashbulb memories are prone to incorrect recall with high confidence [27].

Summary

What struck us, as we saw our users' reaction to MUSE, was the variety of ways in which users derived utility and benefits from a system that jogs their memory, from summarizing work to renewing friendships and serendipitous discovery. Though our initial goal with MUSE was only to support the task of reminiscence, the stories above include an example of each one of the "5R's" described by Sellen and Whittaker [29]: recollection, reminiscing, retrieving, reflecting, and remembering intentions. Further, it suggests that browsing and remembering the past can affect the future.

The expert users from our library were also very interested in using MUSE to enable browsing of archives of famous people whose papers they help to acquire and organize. P6: *"We have so many donors wanting to donate their documents (including email) to us, we don't have enough people to look through all the materials."*

CONCLUSIONS

Millions of people have email archives that are rich in sentiment and meaning to them, forming a passively acquired life-log. Users are surprised by the extent of information directly or indirectly reflected in their archives, and broadly enjoy discovering forgotten topics. We have identified and evaluated four types of cues that are useful, yet lightweight to compute: communication with inferred social groups, recurring named entities, sentimental words, and image attachments. We have found that users derive many different types of benefits from reflecting on their email archives. Further, we found that MUSE can potentially be useful to archivists and other curators of digital content. We discovered that users spend most of the time with the actual message content, so it is necessary to integrate cues with effective browsing of messages. MUSE can be publicly accessed along with supplementary materials for this paper at the URL: http://mobisocial.stanford.edu/muse.

FUTURE WORK

We have made MUSE publicly available and intend to scale our current user study by recruiting diverse users via the web. We plan to improve its usability and features based on feedback from users, and conduct detailed user studies of specific user-interface elements. A limitation of our current user studies is that we do not measure recall, i.e., we do not know what important topics and events were not picked up by MUSE. A controlled experiment to identify such topics may suggest possible improvements.

Acknowledgements

We thank Stu Card, Peter Chan, Phuong Ly, Diana MacLean and Jason Zalinger for useful discussions and feedback on this paper, Stanford University Libraries for access to the Robert Creeley corpus, and Peter Monaco from Xobni for providing us an anonymized email data set. Users of all versions of MUSE have provided us valuable feedback. We also thank our anonymous reviewers for useful feedback. This research was funded in part by NSF POMI (Programmable Open Mobile Internet) 2020 Expedition Grant 0832820 and the Stanford MobiSocial Computing Laboratory.

REFERENCES

1. S. Asur and B. A. Huberman. Predicting the future with social media. *CoRR*, abs/1003.5699, 2010.
2. S. Baccianella, A. Esuli, and F. Sebastiani. SentiWordNet 3.0: An enhanced lexical resource for sentiment analysis and opinion mining. In *Proceedings of Language Resources and Evaluation (LREC'10)*. European Language Resources Association, May 2010.
3. G. Chin, Jr., O. A. Kuchar, and K. E. Wolf. Exploring the analytical processes of intelligence analysts. In *Proceedings of CHI-2009*. ACM, 2009.
4. C. Collins, M. Watternberg, and F. Viegas. Parallel tag clouds to explore and analyze faceted text corpora. In *Proceedings of VAST '09*. IEEE, 2009.
5. E. Cutrell, D. Robbins, S. Dumais, and R. Sarin. Fast, flexible filtering with Phlat. In *Proceedings of CHI '06*. ACM, 2006.
6. S. Dumais, E. Cutrell, J. Cadiz, G. Jancke, R. Sarin, and D. C. Robbins. Stuff I've Seen: a system for personal information retrieval and re-use. In *Proceedings of SIGIR '03*. ACM, 2003.
7. D. Elsweiler, M. Baillie, and I. Ruthven. Exploring memory in email refinding. *ACM Trans. Inf. Syst.*, 26(4):1–36, 2008.
8. Email archives. Robert Creeley Papers, M0662. Dept. of Special Collections, Stanford University Libraries, Stanford, CA.
9. J. R. Finkel, T. Grenager, and C. Manning. Incorporating non-local information into information extraction systems by gibbs sampling. In *Proceedings of ACL '05*. Association for Computational Linguistics, 2005.
10. J. Gemmell, G. Bell, and R. Lueder. MyLifeBits: a personal database for everything. *CACM*, 49(1), 2006.
11. A. Goethals and W. Gogel. Reshaping the repository: The challenge of email archiving. In *Proceedings of the 7th International Conference on Preservation of Digital Objects*, 2010.
12. S. Havre, E. Hetzler, P. Whitney, and L. Nowell. Themeriver: visualizing thematic changes in large document collections. *IEEE Transactions on Visualization and Computer Graphics*, 8(1):9–20, 2002.
13. S. D. Kamvar and J. Harris. We Feel Fine and searching the emotional web. In *Proceedings of WSDM-2011*. ACM, 2011.
14. D. S. Kirk and A. Sellen. On human remains: Values and practice in the home archiving of cherished objects. *ACM TOCHI*, 17(3):10:1–10:43, 2010.
15. S. Liu, M. X. Zhou, S. Pan, W. Qian, W. Cai, and X. Lian. Interactive, topic-based visual text summarization and analysis. In *Proceedings of CIKM '09*, pages 543–552, 2009.
16. LLWC Inc. Linguistic Inquiry and Word Count. `http://www.liwc.net`.
17. D. MacLean, S. Hangal, S. K. Teh, M. S. Lam, and J. Heer. Groups without tears: mining social topologies from email. In *Proceedings of IUI-2011*. ACM, 2011.
18. S. Malacria, E. Lecolinet, and Y. Guiard. Clutch-free panning and integrated pan-zoom control on touch-sensitive surfaces: the cyclostar approach. In *Proceedings of CHI '10*. ACM, 2010.
19. M. Mandic and A. Kerne. Using intimacy, chronology and zooming to visualize rhythms in email experience. In *Proceedings of CHI '05 (extended abstracts)*. ACM, 2005.
20. C. D. Manning, P. Raghavan, and H. Schutze. *Introduction to Information Retrieval*, page 127. Cambridge University Press, 2008.
21. C. Neustaedter, A. Brush, M. A. Smith, and D. Fisher. The social network and relationship finder: Social sorting for email triage. In *Proceedings of CEAS '05*, 2005.
22. S. T. Peesapati, V. Schwanda, J. Schultz, M. Lepage, S. Jeong, and D. Cosley. Pensieve: supporting everyday reminiscence. In *Proceedings of CHI '10*. ACM, 2010.
23. A. Perer, B. Shneiderman, and D. W. Oard. Using rhythms of relationships to understand e-mail archives. *J. Am. Soc. Inf. Sci. Technol.*, 57(14):1936–1948, 2006.
24. D. Petrelli, S. Whittaker, and J. Brockmeier. Autotypography: what can physical mementos tell us about digital memories? In *Proceedings of CHI '08*. ACM, 2008.
25. T. J. Purtell, D. MacLean, S. K. Teh, S. Hangal, M. S. Lam, and J. Heer. An algorithm and analysis of social topologies from email and photo tags. In *Proceedings of the Fifth ACM Workshop on Social Network Mining and Analysis (SNAKDD)*. ACM, 2011.
26. Radicati Group Inc. Email statistics report, 2010-2014. `http://www.radicati.com/?p=5282`.
27. D. Reisberg and P. Hertel. *Memory and Emotion*. Oxford University Press, 2004.
28. J. Schwarz, J. Mankoff, and H. S. Matthews. Reflections of everyday activities in spending data. In *Proceedings of CHI '09*. ACM, 2009.
29. A. J. Sellen and S. Whittaker. Beyond total capture: a constructive critique of lifelogging. *CACM*, 53:70–77, May 2010.
30. J. Stasko, C. Gorg, and Z. Liu. Jigsaw: supporting investigative analysis through interactive visualization. *Information Visualization*, 7:118–132, 2008.
31. A. C. Surendran, J. C. Platt, and E. Renshaw. Automatic discovery of personal topics to organize email. In *Proceedings of CEAS '05*, 2005.
32. E. Tulving. *Elements of Episodic Memory*. Oxford University Press, 1983.
33. J. R. Tyler and J. C. Tang. When can I expect an email response? A study of rhythms in email usage. In *Proceedings of ECSCW'03*. Kluwer Academic Publishers, 2003.
34. F. B. Viégas, D. Boyd, D. H. Nguyen, J. Potter, and J. Donath. Digital artifacts for remembering and storytelling: Posthistory and social network fragments. In *Proceedings of HICSS '04*. IEEE Computer Society, 2004.
35. F. B. Viégas, S. Golder, and J. Donath. Visualizing email content: portraying relationships from conversational histories. In *Proceedings of CHI '06*. ACM, 2006.
36. S. Whittaker, Q. Jones, B. A. Nardi, M. Creech, L. Terveen, E. Isaacs, and J. Hainsworth. ContactMap: Organizing communication in a social desktop. *ACM TOCHI*, 11(4):445–471, 2004.
37. World Wide Web Consortium. W3c contacts api working draft. `http://www.w3.org/TR/contacts-api`.
38. K.-P. Yee, K. Swearingen, K. Li, and M. Hearst. Faceted metadata for image search and browsing. In *Proceedings of CHI '03*. ACM, 2003.
39. J. Zalinger. *Gmail as storyworld: How technology shapes your life narrative*. Unpublished dissertation, Rensselaer Polytechnic Institute, 2011.

A Design Space Analysis of Availability-Sharing Systems

Juan David Hincapié-Ramos
IT University of Copenhagen
Copenhagen DK-2300 Denmark
jdhr@itu.dk

Stephen Voida, Gloria Mark
University of California, Irvine
Irvine, CA 92697–3440 USA
{svoida, gmark}@uci.edu

ABSTRACT

Workplace collaboration often requires interruptions, which can happen at inopportune times. Designing a successful availability-sharing system requires finding the right balance to optimize the benefits and reduce costs for both the interrupter and interruptee. In this paper, we examine the design space of availability-sharing systems and identify six relevant design dimensions: abstraction, presentation, information delivery, symmetry, obtrusiveness and temporal gradient. We describe these dimensions in terms of the tensions between interrupters and interruptees revealed in previous studies of workplace collaboration and deployments of awareness systems. As a demonstration of the utility of our design space, we introduce InterruptMe, a novel availability-sharing system that represents a previously unexplored point in the design space and that balances the tensions between interrupters and interruptees. InterruptMe differs from previous systems in that it displays availability information only when needed by monitoring implicit inputs from the system's users, implements a traceable asymmetry structure, and introduces the notion of per-communications channel availability.

ACM Classification: H5.2 [Information interfaces and presentation]: User Interfaces—graphical user interfaces.

General terms: Design, Human Factors

Keywords: Workplace awareness, availability, interruptibility

INTRODUCTION

Effective collaboration in the workplace requires various modes of interaction. Co-located and remote colleagues may interact face-to-face or over different media such as the telephone, instant messaging, and email. Above all, they must maintain a general awareness of one another. Researchers have explored multiple ways of providing support for this kind of awareness through a class of computational systems that are generally characterized as *awareness systems*. Awareness systems are motivated by the observation that workplace awareness leads to more interactions among colleagues (both remote and collocated) and a general improvement in performance [30]. However, while increased collaboration is often considered beneficial, it also incurs costs: people can interrupt their collaborators at inappropriate times, leading to increased task switching, redundancy in work, and stress [27, 28].

Guided by the premise that better timing of interruptions decreases their disruptiveness [5], a subset of awareness systems focus on communicating the *availability* of others with whom one collaborates. The goal of these systems is to help collaborators identify the most appropriate (and least costly) times to initiate interactions. Availability-sharing systems provide this kind of awareness by directly communicating the other person's activity (e.g., high-fidelity video and audio links [9, 40] or raw sensor values [12]), generating and sharing a more abstract representation of a person's interruptibility drawn from multiple cues (e.g., sensor data [25]), and/or by providing a visualization of historical patterns of activity.

The goal of our research is to examine the design space of availability-sharing systems in terms of the costs and benefits for collaborating partners and to apply this insight to a system design that can optimize the trade-offs. Designing a successful availability-sharing system requires striking the right balance between maximizing the benefit for, and minimizing the costs incurred by, each of the participants in a collaboration (Figure 1). For the *interrupter*—the person who is initiating the interaction—the system should facilitate making a quick, accurate decision about whether, when, and through what communications medium it is appropriate to interrupt the other person. Prior studies of awareness systems suggest that it is beneficial to share more than simple presence information to inform this decision-making process [16], and that it is essential to provide relevant information in a timely fashion [35, 40, 41, 43]. Some of the costs to the interrupter that should be minimized include the effort required to access the availability information, the cognitive overhead needed to correctly

Figure 1: Availability-sharing systems provide information to a potential *interrupter* that facilitates decision making about whether to interrupt a colleague (the *interruptee*), when to do so, and what communications medium to use.

interpret the availability representation(s) [3, 12], and the obtrusiveness of the availability information display [25]. In contrast, the main cost to be minimized for the *interruptee* is the disruptiveness of the communication, which can be achieved by suggesting a communications medium that fits their current activity. Other important costs, such as privacy (i.e., the fidelity of the data [9, 40] and with whom those data are shared [25]), must also be considered.

In this paper, we examine the design space of availability-sharing systems, drawing attention to the inherent design tensions and the pragmatic challenges that others have encountered in attempting to foster collaboration and reduce the intrusiveness of workplace interactions. Based on a review of existing availability-sharing systems, we provide a framework for understanding the different design trade-offs in sharing availability information, highlighting the ways that different implementation and interface decisions provide different degrees of cost and benefit to the participants in these systems. To illustrate how this framework might guide the design of novel awareness systems, we present one example of a system designed specifically to balance the needs of the interrupter and the interruptee.

This research contributes to the literature on availability-sharing systems in three primary ways:

- We present a design space for availability-sharing systems, grounded both in prior theoretical and practical work in this area;
- We discuss how different points in this design space offer different levels of cost and benefit to the different parties in a collaboration; and
- We present the design of InterruptMe, an availability-sharing system that exemplifies an unexplored point in the design space, balancing the needs of interrupters and interruptees, and suggests new directions for research and development in this domain (Figure 2).

RELATED WORK

In this section, we examine the research literature related to the evolution of the notion of availability.

Early Explorations of Availability

Media spaces connect remote locations through audio and video links [9, 40] or slowly updated images [6], aiming to provide remote colleagues with the degree of awareness about presence or current activities that is available to co-located colleagues. One of the key roles for these systems was to enable participants to estimate the availability of remote colleagues before initiating interaction. Fogarty et al. [11] questioned whether video and audio links were good indicators of interruptibility. They carried out a study of office workers' capacity to estimate the availability of another person from snippets of video. Their study revealed that humans are only slightly better than chance in estimating a person's self-reported availability on a 5-point scale.

Figure 2: InterruptMe shows different availability values for each communication medium. Michalina is unavailable for face-to-face and phone interactions (monochrome icons), but is available by instant messaging and email (full-color icons). The system can also provide historical context; in this case, Michalina has been available via IM for 15 minutes, but away from her phone for 30 minutes.

These explorations illustrate several of the challenges faced by availability-sharing systems that are based on the model of continuously transmitting audio and video streams among collaborators. Video and audio links may not provide sufficient information to a potential interrupter to determine their colleagues' availability. Additionally, sharing live video or audio necessarily incurs privacy costs for the interruptee. Finally, displaying the media space video feeds often requires an auxiliary display device or a large dedicated window region on the interrupter's computer, which can be both obtrusive and potentially distracting.

Measuring Availability

The Peepholes [14] system represented a different approach from previous video-based systems, providing awareness without incurring the hardware costs and privacy concerns of media spaces. It provided information about its users' availability by using iconic presence indicators. Peepholes introduced the idea of modeling availability based on users' network connectivity and computer activity levels. This model determined whether a user was working, idle, not logged in, or in an unknown state. The main limitation of this system was that presence, taken alone, communicates little about how busy, and, therefore, how interruptible a person is. Hudson et al. [19] took this approach a step further, and by studying the disruptive effect of interruptions in collaborative work environments suggested modeling personal availability as a function of *interruptibility*.

Different research has measured interruptibility through the use of both manual input and automatic data collection. Manual input was studied in the live addressbook project [35], where users manually entered availability information, which was then distributed to their contacts. A deployment of this system revealed that the costs of maintaining status messages and availability states were unreasonably high, potentially undermining the value of such systems. Automatic data collection has been studied in several systems, such as BlueSpace [24], ConNexus [41], MyVine [12], and SideShow [4]. These systems have all used a combination of computer activity, location, calendar information, and manual user input to model a user's availability. Lilsys [2] and the attentive cellphone [43] used sensor data to infer interruptibility and share availability information with one's colleagues. This approach was generally well received, with some of the studies lasting several months and users continuing to use the system afterwards. However, several problems were identified over the course of these studies. Interruptees reported privacy concerns due to the number of sensors deployed in their office spaces. Interrupters often misinterpreted awareness cues because it was difficult to interpret availability representations; they also often ignored the system due to the high interaction costs of accessing the availability information.

Modeling Availability

Most systems model availability as a single value, often through an icon. Some systems (e.g., MyTeam [24] and MyVine [12]) support gradual refinement of availability information as the user clicks on (or "drills into") specific contacts. These refinements include the raw values collected by sensors deployed in the workspace, a recommended communication channel, the expected time of return, or personal contact information. Other projects, like BlueSpace [24] and Labradoor [36], explored moving availability information off the desktop and into the environment. In doing so, these systems reclaim some of the display real estate required by always-on applications, but raise additional questions about the distractions of desktop and semi-public sharing of availability information.

Some research has questioned the assumption that availability information is one single and comprehensive measure. Horvitz and Apacible [17] investigated how the disruptiveness of an interruption depends on the communication channel, and found considerable differences between different media, such as telephones, pagers, and desktop appliances. In another study, Harr and Wiberg [16] found that *being busy* does not mean *being unavailable* for communications; being busy changes the likelihood of using a particular communication channel and the expected response. They go further to say that availability is also affected by the relationship between the communication partners. Voida et al. [44] and Patil and Kobsa [38] found that users have varying availability preferences, as demonstrated by having different IM accounts for work and for friends.

Gross and Oemig [15] developed the PRIMIFaces system, allowing users to maintain *selective availability*, that is, different indications of availability for different groups of contacts. Users reported that this approach requires a considerable manual effort to keep all of the various status indications up-to-date. In a subsequent study, Fetter et al. [8] instrumented PRIMIFaces to capture sensor data, and performed an experience-sampling experiment to determine the feasibility of *lightweight* selective availability. Their results show that users considered selective availability important, that general availability consistently differs from the one reported in the IM client, and that selective availability strongly relates to the users' locations.

DESIGN SPACE FOR AVAILABILITY-SHARING SYSTEMS

In order to better understand the trade-offs inherent in the design of availability-sharing systems, we undertook an extensive literature review of prior research on interruptions and of systems that communicate availability information among a group of colleagues. In this section, we construct a design space that articulates the axes serving to distinguish among the capabilities of these systems. Our design space seeks to foster research in three important ways: (1) to identify previously unexplored points in the design space, for designing new systems; (2) to introduce techniques that represent new values for a given dimension, as we do later on with traceable asymmetry; and (3) to propose new ways to realize an existing point along an axis that clearly depart from approaches taken in prior systems.

We took a two-stage approach to define our design space for availability-sharing systems. Our first activity was a **top-down review** of the literature aimed at understanding existing taxonomies in the domain of human interruptions. From this activity, we identified MacFarlane's work as the most comprehensive. McFarlane [33] defined a taxonomy of human interruptions with the following dimensions: (1) source of interruption, (2) individual characteristics of a person receiving interruption, (3) method of coordination, (4) meaning of interruption, (5) method of expression, (6) channel of conveyance, (7) human activity changed by interruption, and (8) effect of interruption. McFarlane and Latorella [34] described this taxonomy as an attempt to map the whole space of interruptions and to determine the areas where technology interventions might be helpful.

MacFarlane's *source of interruption* dimension points out places for technological intervention, such as technologies to better deliver system messages to a user (see Jonsson et al. [23] on notification systems) and applications to help users better time their interruptions (availability-sharing systems). However, their general taxonomy provides little guidance for developing each particular kind of system, and especially for availability-sharing systems, it lacks direction on how to help an interrupter make decisions about how and when to initiate interruptions.

Our second activity consisted of a **bottom-up analysis** of existing design spaces in the related areas of *awareness systems*, *ambient displays*, and *notification systems* [13, 29, 31, 39, 42]. In contrast to the theoretically driven models of interruption provided by our top-down analysis, we wanted to understand how these alternative design spaces, derived more from the experience of *building* and *deploying* systems, overlap and extend the design space of availability-sharing systems. Even though availability-sharing systems have a different purpose than these broader classes of systems (as previously discussed in relation to notification systems), the issues involved in designing them are also often present when designing availability-sharing systems.

Combining all of these efforts, we created a more comprehensive set of design space dimensions that relate to availability-sharing systems, identifying resonances among the individual design spaces and collapsing similar axes together. In our final design space, we elected to focus on those aspects of the design that most clearly illustrate design opportunities that affect the cost/benefit trade-offs for the interrupter, the interruptee, or both parties. Our resulting design space, shown in Table 1, is derived from the

Design Dimensions	Types of Values			
Abstraction	Sensor data (e.g., motion sensor values) [2, 3, 41[1]]	Availability (e.g., manual, measured, or predicted) [1, 4, 12, 18, 21, 22, 24[1], 24[2], 24[3], 26, 35, 41[2], 43]	Natural (e.g., audio, video) [6, 9, 40]	Multimedia (e.g., status message annotating a video feed) [32, 36]
Presentation	Continuous (e.g., gradual fade) [12, 36]	Discrete (e.g., icons) [2, 3, 4, 14, 18, 21, 22, 24[1], 24[2], 24[3], 26, 41[1], 41[2], 43]		Literal (e.g., video) [1, 6, 9, 32, 35, 40]
Information Delivery	Always on (e.g., dedicated display) [4, 9, 14, 24[3], 26, 32]	Almost always on (e.g., overlapping window) [2, 3, 6, 12, 22, 21, 41]	On request (e.g., query-based system) [1, 18, 35, 40, 41[2], 43]	Implicit interaction (e.g., situated display) [24[1], 24[2], 36]
Symmetry	Symmetric, Traceable (e.g., contact-based with request history) [9, 18, 22, 40]	Symmetric, Blind (e.g., contact-based) [1, 2, 3, 4, 6, 12, 21, 24[3], 32, 41[1], 41[2], 43]	Asymmetric, Traceable (none)	Asymmetric, Blind (e.g., public display) [14, 24[1], 24[2], 26, 35, 36]
Obtrusiveness	Focal [1, 14, 22, 32, 35, 40, 43]	Selectively focal [2, 3, 4, 6, 12, 18, 21, 41[1], 41[2]]	Secondary appliance [9, 24[3], 26]	Peripheral [24[1], 24[2], 36]
Temporal Gradient	Historical Availability (none)	Recent Availability [2, 18, 41[1], 41[2]]	Current Availability [1, 3, 4, 6, 9, 12, 14, 21, 22, 24[1], 24[2], 24[3], 26, 32, 35, 36, 40, 43]	Predicted Availability (none)

Table 1: Design space dimensions for availability-sharing systems and the position on each axis occupied by 22 existing awareness and notification systems. For systems that could occupy more than one cell on an axis, we categorized them into the cell in which the system would most frequently be used. [24][1] is BlueSpace's office front display, [24][2] is BlueSpace's LED ambient lamp, and [24][3] is the MyTeam component; [41][1] is ConNexus and [41][2] is Awarenex.

concerns of interruptions research, the experiences of systems design, and with the unique constraints and trade-offs of availability-sharing systems in mind.

Although grounded in the taxonomies presented by MacFarlane et al. [33], Matthews et al. [31], and others, our design space differs in multiple ways. MacFarlane et al. aim to map the whole space of interruptions, including non-technical issues like the effect of the interruption, and they attempt to suggest interventions to minimize the impact of interruptions, such as (general) availability sharing, availability modeling, notification delivery systems, etc. In contrast, our design space is specifically geared towards informing technical support in the design of availability-sharing systems. Second, whereas McFarlane et al. focus on the interruptee and Matthews et al. focus on the interrupter (they talk about the "receiver of the information"), our work considers the involvement and interplay of both.

In order to characterize the different values that exist along each of the design space axes, we reviewed the systems-oriented literature and collaboratively coded a wide variety of awareness systems according to each of our dimensions (see Table 1). Based on this classification process, we can more clearly explain the design possibilities along each axis and begin to identify positions in the design space and combinations of system features that are underexplored and may warrant further consideration.

Abstraction

At what granularity (or level of abstraction) are availability data collected and shared with one's colleagues?

A system's positioning along the abstraction axis relates to the types of data that are collected from the interruptee and used to model availability and/or are shared with colleagues. These data are used to calculate how interruptible a person might be, information that can be used by an interrupter to determine whether to carry out an interruption and when and how to do so. A system using *sensor data* abstractions requires interrupters to interpret low-level data directly (e.g., speech level, presence at desk) to determine interruptibility. MyTeam's conversation indicator is an example of this approach [25]. Other systems model *availability* more holistically by aggregating a variety of sensor values. Such systems assume that users can more quickly and unambiguously understand an interpreted measure. Examples of systems adopting this approach include Awarenex [41], BlueSpace's door light system [24], Lilsys [2], the live addressbook [35], and MyVine (at the first level of detail) [12]. A system that presents *natural* cues, like audio and video, relies on the human capacity to read such cues, to determine the interruptibility level, and to identify the best way to interrupt. This is the case in media spaces like Cruiser [9] and Montage [40]. Finally, a system presenting *multimedia* accounts of availability relies on users to read text, images, or videos, and apply contextual knowledge of the situation. Such is the case for online collaborative environments like the one studied by Harr and Wiberg [16] or public embedded displays like the Labradoor [36].

Dimension Values: Sensor data, Availability (manual, measured, predicted), Natural (audio, video), Multimedia.

Presentation

How are availability data presented to the system's users?

In our design space, we associate presentation with Matthews' concept of *abstraction level* and borrow her definition (we use a different name to draw a stronger distinction between this output-related dimension and the previous, input-oriented one):

> Abstraction involves extracting features or reducing the fidelity of information so that it is easier to read "at a glance" than the raw input. Abstraction enables lower attention consumption of information. One reason for this may be that abstract (pictorial) displays aid recall when compared to literal (textual) displays [31].

When no abstraction is performed on the presented data, this dimension takes the value of *literal*. Such is the case for camera-based or text-based systems like media spaces [9, 40], the AwarePhone [1], and the live addressbook [35]. Availability information presented as *discrete* values is the most common approach, and can be seen in systems like ConNexus [41] and Lilsys [2], where availability is shown as a binary value. *Continuous* values can be seen in IMBuddy [18] and MyVine [12], where availability is shown in a range from 0 to 1 (or as a percentage).

Dimension Values: Continuous, Discrete (e.g., icons), Literal.

Information Delivery

When are availability data presented to the system's users?

An *always-on* system constantly presents availability information to the user, minimizing the acquisition cost but potentially creating visual overload. Examples of always-on systems include the dedicated screens of the early media spaces or screen widgets like SideShow [4]. An *almost–always-on* system also continually presents colleagues' availability information, but can be moved into the foreground or background as needed, as in desktop applications like MyVine [12] and Piazza [22]. An *on-request* system has relatively higher overhead, as users must query the system and wait for a response each time, as in AwarePhone [1]. A system designed around *implicit interaction* presents information whenever the user needs it, as he or she moves around the environment or interacts with communication systems. Such systems pose a minimal acquisition cost and create no visual overload, as demonstrated in some components of BlueSpace [24].

Dimension Values: Always on, Almost-always on (e.g., overlapping window), On request, Implicit interaction.

Symmetry

To what extent does the system require or enforce reciprocity in the exchange of availability data? To what extent does the system provide traceability, or accountability, for the dissemination of this information?

Symmetry refers to the broadcast of availability information of users such that it generates mutual knowledge of one another [45]. Symmetry can also be seen as the level of social translucency supported by the system [7]. A *symmetric* system will only share availability data with those individuals from whom availability data is being received. Such is the case in most contact-based systems like MyUnity [3] and MyVine [12]. *Asymmetric* systems do not require disclosure of one's own availability in order to access others' availability information. Such is the case of public displays like BlueSpace's LED door component [24] and Peepholes [14]. The *traceability* sub-dimension characterizes the extent to which users know how others see them, that is, when someone has looked at their availability information and what they saw. This distinction is similar to the idea of accountability in socially translucent systems [7]. Most existing availability-sharing systems are *blind* and do not provide traceability. There are a few notable exceptions—for example, in Cruiser [9], users know when they are being observed because the system automatically establishes a two-way video channel. Traceability can also be subtle, as in IMBuddy [18], where the system accumulates a history of availability requests from other users.

Dimension Values: Symmetric (traceable), Symmetric (blind), Asymmetric (traceable), Asymmetric (blind).

Obtrusiveness

To what degree is availability data presented in the focus?

This dimension relates to whether the availability information is delivered in the focus or the periphery of the interrupter's attention (after [10]). Systems that obtrusively embed their output into the primary display surface (i.e., the computer desktop) make it easy to maintain awareness about others' availability. These systems also emphasize collaboration by prominently displaying the information gleaned from team members. This is the case for desktop collaboration systems like CommunityBar [32] and Piazza [22], for example. Colleagues' availability information can be moved incrementally towards the interrupter's periphery, such that it is made focal only when needed (*selectively focal*), or off-loaded entirely onto a *secondary appliance* or a *peripheral display*. The further into the periphery the information is pushed, the less it interferes with primary work tasks, but the more overhead is required to incorporate availability information into the center of attention when it becomes relevant or is needed.

Dimension Values: Focal, Selectively focal, Secondary appliance, Peripheral.

Temporal Gradient

On what time scale are availability data communicated?

This dimension relates to the use of temporal modifiers on the availability information presented to an interrupter. Temporal modifiers can present historic, recent, current, and/or predictive accounts of availability. *Historic* modifiers represent a sensor value or an availability measure in relation to large-scale previous values (e.g. the last month, days like today). *Recent* modifiers present it in relation to near-range previous values (e.g. the last hour). A *current* modifier presents the actual value. Finally, a *predictive* modifier uses information about past and current availability to estimate future interruptibility. One example of how predictive modifiers might be realized is a machine-generated indication of how long an interruptee's current availability state is likely to last.

Even though a temporal gradient has been previously used in awareness systems, as documented by Tomitsch [5], it has not been widely used in availability-sharing applications. The only exceptions are the *recent* modifiers used by IMBuddy [18], Lilsys [2], ConNexus, and Awarenex [41].

Dimension Values: Historical, Recent, Current, and Predicted availability.

DESIGN GOALS FOR AVAILABILITY-SHARING SYSTEMS

The central tenet of our research is that designing an effective availability-sharing system is primarily a matter of balancing the costs and benefits for each of the system's users. However, accomplishing this goal is not always straightforward, as some design decisions result in a preferable cost/benefit trade-off for one party at the expense of the other. Based on our analysis, we have derived a high-level overview of which positions along each design axis result in the most favorable cost/benefit value for the interrupter, and likewise for the interruptee (Figure 3). These considerations are the result of our analysis of the motivations for and discussions of the implementation and deployment of various availability-sharing systems from the research literature. We paid particular attention to instances where researchers described the shortcomings of their design decisions, feedback from users, and why (in some cases) users stopped using the system. For both the interrupter and interruptee, we found that there are some dimensions for which we could recommend a value; that there are some dimensions for which there is no clear tendency toward any single value; and that there are some dimensions that appear less relevant for a particular role.

Optimizing for the Interrupter

For the interrupter, previous research points toward using the "availability" value along the *abstraction* axis, because sensor data, natural and multimedia values all present several drawbacks. One of the concerns expressed in prior studies is the misinterpretation of information shared by remote users. For example, MyVine [12] assumed speech as an indication of a person being unavailable. However, users interpreted the presence of speech as an indication that the user was present and not engaged in a task demanding quiet attention, thus rendering them available for interaction. This suggests that using higher-level abstractions in availability-sharing systems might be more beneficial than sharing low-level or raw data. Similarly, natural and multimedia abstractions (audio & video) lead to increased mis-

Dimensions	Optimal Values—Interrupter			
Abstraction	Sensor	Avail.	Natural	MM
Presentation	Cont.	Discrete		Literal
Information Delivery	Always	Almost	Request	Implicit
Symmetry	S(T)	S(B)	A(T)	A(B)
Obtrusiveness	Focal	Selective	Appliance	Periph.
Temporal Gradient	Hist.	Recent	Current	Predict.

Dimensions	Optimal Values—Interruptee			
Abstraction	Sensor	Avail.	Natural	MM
Presentation	Cont.	Discrete		Literal
Information Delivery	Always	Almost	Request	Implicit
Symmetry	S(T)	S(B)	A(T)	A(B)
Obtrusiveness	Focal	Selective	Appliance	Periph.
Temporal Gradient	Hist.	Recent	Current	Predict.

Figure 3: The optimal values for each design dimension differ for interrupters and interruptees. (Shaded cells represent more preferable design solutions than un-shaded cells.)

interpretation of colleagues' interruptibility, as discussed by Hudson et al. [19].

The *presentation* used to display availability data to the interrupter impacts the cognitive overhead required to assess the interruptee's availability and the accuracy of these inferences. When literal data are presented to an interrupter, it is up to the interrupter to make sense of the data and draw their own inferences about whether or not it is an appropriate moment to interrupt. At the other extreme, highly abstract presentations of the data can provide a meaningful representation at-a-glance, yet might remove context that can be important in distinguishing nuance. The optimal choice might be a middle ground—clear and relatively unambiguous discrete presentations that make it easier to assess availability at-a-glance, with the ability to "drill down" into more literal data when needed.

Another concern from the interrupter's perspective is that systems often fail at delivering availability information at the appropriate time. Windowed availability-sharing applications have to be explicitly called to focus before they can inform interactions. At the other end of the spectrum, always-visible displays can be distracting and can suffer from the effects of change blindness [20]. The same set of sensors used to determine a user's availability could be used to provide the timely *delivery of information* when a user acts as interrupter by detecting implicit interaction. Similar to the service provided by augmented environments (e.g. BlueSpace [24] and Labradoor [36]) in communicating the presence of an office occupant to potential visitors, availability-sharing systems could provide information about a colleague's availability at the moment that the interrupter begins to compose an email or picks up a telephone handset. As a result, availability information would be delivered in a timely fashion (after the user decided to interrupt, but before the interruption actually occurred) and without incurring the extra cognitive load of explicitly querying the availability-sharing system.

The dimension of *symmetry* defines how the availability-sharing system fits into the interrupter's broader socio-technical context. Although a symmetrical system might help to mitigate power imbalances among collaborators by "implement[ing] some of the basic social rules that surround human face-to-face conversation" [43], asymmetrical systems allow colleagues to retrieve information about one another without requiring reciprocity in hardware deployment or necessitating explicit permission management. As a result, asymmetrical systems may lead to broader adoption and increased access to availability information within groups [45]. However, doing so without also implementing traceability may lead to negative social repercussions (e.g., a feeling that colleagues are "spying" on one another).

The degree of *obtrusiveness* is closely linked to the design decisions made regarding information delivery—"always on" systems generally require that additional hardware or computer display real estate be dedicated to the availability-sharing system. In some environments, this cost might be negligible, but especially for mobile individuals, it might be impractical to assume availability of a purpose-built display or peripheral installation. The optimal value for this axis might also be influenced by the context of the collaboration—tight coupling among colleagues might necessitate a more obtrusive design to foreground the activity of others. While both extremes might offer advantages, designing a system that can either provide output flexibility or a moderate degree of obtrusiveness is probably the best approach for supporting a broad range of information workers.

To assist an interrupter in determining when to initiate an interaction, a system can provide support at a variety of time scales—what we refer to as a *temporal gradient*. For example, an interrupter likely needs to know an interruptee's current availability information just before initiating an interaction. She may need to obtain additional context or a prediction of future availability if she discovers that it not a good time to begin a conversation. Although historical and recent information might provide anecdotal clues about a colleague's availability, the greatest benefit may result from being able to see current availability information or a prediction about the colleague's availability in the future.

Optimizing for the Interruptee

For the interruptee, the dimensions related to the way that the availability information is retrieved by the interrupter, including *information delivery* and *obtrusiveness*, are generally not relevant.

However, the *abstraction* of the interruptee's availability information collected by the system and the *presentation* approach used are perhaps the most important dimensions from the perspective of the interruptee. In general, sharing low-level media streams and sensor data, such as location, triggers a number of privacy concerns. More abstract availability measures have the benefit of mitigating some privacy concerns and reducing misinterpretations. For example, replacing "location" with "presence" or "proximity" to the office could reduce some of the privacy concerns of sharing location data. The presentation approach for this availability could be either abstract or discrete, as both approaches have proved useful in previous research.

Based on the principle of social translucence [7], we argue that *symmetry* is also of importance to the interruptee, since this property allows one to be aware of when and what information is shared and what values are shared with each collaborator. Because availability information may be privacy sensitive, contacts often regard each other at different levels of closeness (see Olson et al. on categories for sharing privacy sensitive information [37]). These varying closeness distinctions suggest that users might like to share availability information at different levels of granularity with different groups or individuals; they might even choose not to reciprocate sharing with a particular interrupter. While this consideration highlights the value of positioning the system to utilize asymmetric availability information exchange, a system that shares this information blindly creates the potential for spying and abuse of users' trust. The solution is to combine asymmetry with traceability, that is, keeping track of what information has been shared with others. These two features—categorized before as the asymmetric–traceable value in our design dimensions—aim at increasing confidence in the system, while also providing support for existing social practices.

Similarly, being able to examine an historical *temporal gradient* of the data captured, stored, and broadcast by the system can help the interruptee to build trust that the system is communicating accurate availability information. Prior awareness systems have placed significant emphasis on allowing users to exert control over the image that they project to others (e.g., [2]). In terms of the *temporal gradient* dimension, having reliable access to both a history of the data collected by availability-sharing systems and the current and predicted values that the system is broadcasting may be critical functionality for systems that rely on the placement of various kinds of sensing technologies in private or semi-private office spaces.

INTERRUPTME

In order to validate our design space as a useful tool for identifying under- or unexplored possibilities for supporting collaboration, we selected a unique combination of

Dimensions	Design Solution—InterruptMe			
Abstraction	Sensor	Avail.	Natural	MM
Presentation	Cont.	Discrete		Literal
Information Delivery	Always	Almost	Request	Implicit
Symmetry	S(T)	S(B)	A(T)	A(B)
Obtrusiveness	Focal	Selective	Appliance	Periph.
Temporal Gradient	Hist.	Recent	Current	Predict.

Figure 4: InterruptMe's design space classification.

Figure 5: InterruptMe user interface. Color icons indicate availability and monochrome icons indicate unavailability. Tiles can be expanded to show availability history (center), and a "followers" list (right) promotes traceability for sharing.

points on each design axis to create a novel availability-sharing system, InterruptMe, guided by the design goals of balancing the needs of interrupters and interruptees (Figure 4). InterruptMe allows availability information to be shared on a per-colleague and per-communications medium basis, implements an asymmetric-traceable approach, and delivers information by means of implicit interaction.

On the interrupter's side, InterruptMe displays availability information about the interrupter's colleagues (Figure 5) using a projector-based display (Figure 6D). On the interruptee side, InterruptMe combines a suite of physical and electronic activity sensors (Figure 6B and C) to determine the interruptee's availability for collaboration over different kinds of communications media and shares this availability information according to the relationship to the interrupter. In this section, we present InterruptMe and its design rationale. Our design choices reflect a suite of hypotheses about the ways that availability-sharing systems are adopted and appropriated in the real world; we plan to evaluate them in depth in a future deployment study of the system.

InterruptMe addresses the *abstraction* dimension by using sensor data and computer activity information to model the availability of a user. The system differs from previous approaches in that it calculates a different availability value for each communications medium. This availability is shown according to a discrete *presentation*, i.e. the interruptee is either available or unavailable on each channel. The upper-left cell in Figure 5 shows the availability information of a user as four different values, one for each communication medium: the user is unavailable for face-to-face and phone interactions (monochrome icons with an optional blue history label), but she is available by instant messaging and email (full-color icons with optional red history label). This approach facilitates data interpretation by sharing an easily interpretable value for each communications medium, but does not disclose raw sensor or computer activity data, leaving little room for alternative or incorrect readings and preserving the interruptee's privacy.

InterruptMe uses a suite of sensors not only as information sources for our availability model, but also to unobtrusively bring the interface to the focus of the user, addressing the *information delivery* and *obtrusiveness* dimensions. InterruptMe avoids information overload and the effects of display blindness [20] by showing the interface only upon request (moving the mouse into the projector-based display) or when the user implicitly prepares to use a communications tool; the rest of the time, InterruptMe keeps the projection blank. The projected interface becomes visible when, for example, the user picks up their telephone hand-

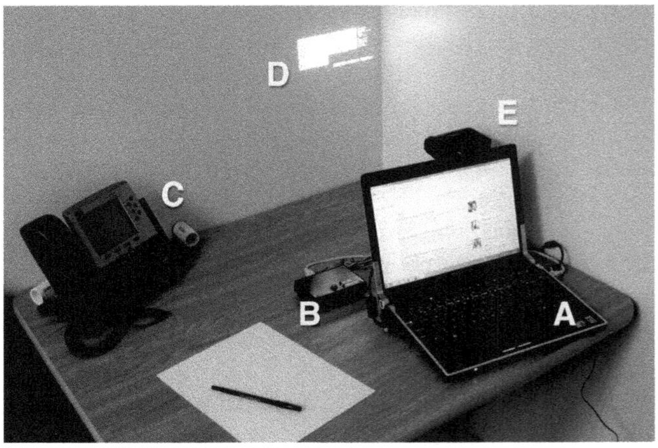

Figure 6: InterruptMe's physical setup. System components include (A) a computer, running the InterruptMe software and capturing electronic activity; (B) a Phidgets InterfaceKit module; (C) several motion, pressure, and contact sensors installed around the office space, and (D) the peripheral availability display, generated by (E) a tripod-mounted pico-projector.

set. InterruptMe detects that the interrupter is about to place a call and grays out those colleagues who are not currently available to receive phone calls. A similar response occurs when the user activates an IM application or email client on their desktop computer. By using implicit interaction, InterruptMe provides interrupters with availability information as an interaction is being initiated. This information helps them to decide whether to carry on with the intended interaction (when the user is available), to delay it, or to try a different communications medium. For example, if the interrupter lifts the telephone handset to call his colleague Michalina and sees the visualization shown in Figure 5 (in the upper-left cell), he might decide to IM or email her instead. However, our system is not proscriptive; the interrupter can always choose to go ahead and place the call.

InterruptMe addresses the symmetry dimension in two ways. First, in calculating the availability for each communications medium, InterruptMe takes into account the type of relationship existing between the users. InterruptMe builds upon Olson et al.'s categories of people for sharing sensitive information: *spouse*, *family*, *boss and trusted colleagues*, *other colleagues*, and *public* [37]. Each user classifies the people he or she shares information with according to these five groups (Figure 7A). The user can configure different levels of privacy for each communications medium and group (Figure 7B), choosing whether or not to share availability information and the level of detail at which to share. For example, the user in Figure 7B shares all availability information with the *spouse* group, and none with users in the *public* group; *family* (indicated by the green checkmarks), *boss and trusted colleagues*, and *colleagues* receive information only in relation to face-to-face and phone availability. When a group is configured not to receive information on a communications medium, the system shows that channel as being unavailable. This set of features position InterruptMe as an asymmetric system and aims at reducing some privacy-related problems by providing interruptees control over how and with whom their information is being shared.

The second way that the system addresses the symmetry dimension is by allowing non-reciprocal relations. User A can start following user B without B having to explicitly approve A's availability information request. In this case, user B will be notified about having a new *follower*. This new follower is placed, by default, in B's *public* group (see the public column of Figure 7A); B can later decide whether to move A to a more appropriate group, leave A in the public group, or block A from receiving further availability updates. B can also choose to reciprocate A's "friendship" and begin following A for access to his or her availability information. Moreover, the system keeps track of the last time A received information about B's availability. These features create a comprehensive traceable–asymmetry relationship between users. It is asymmetric because they do not have to assign the same privileges to one another, and it is traceable because each user is notified that they are being followed—and how often their information is requested.

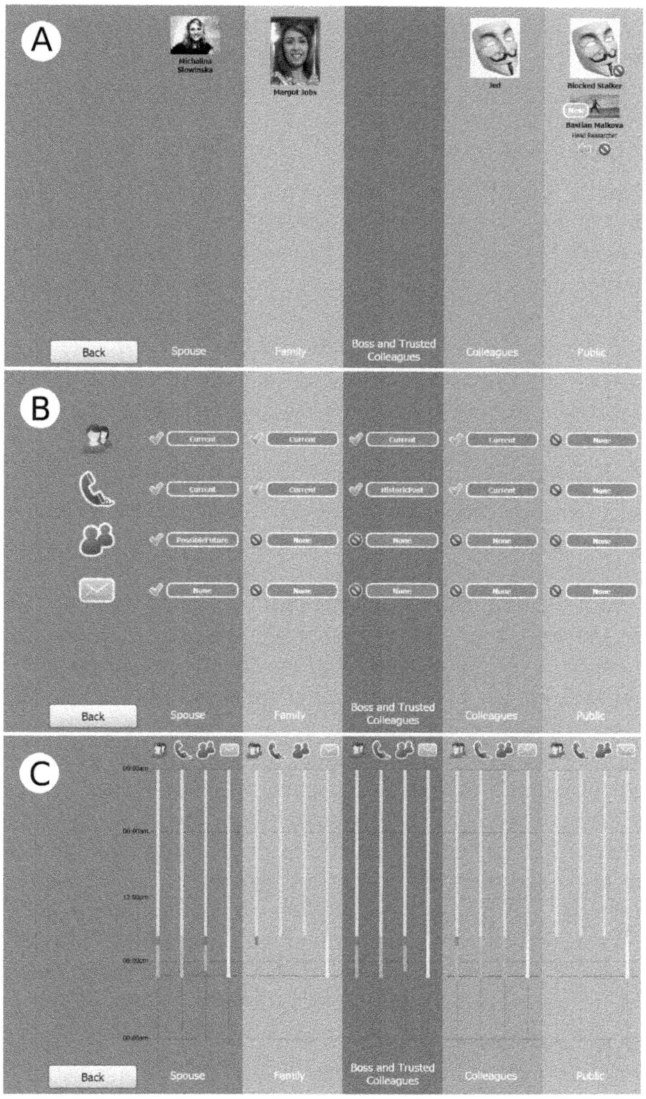

Figure 7: InterruptMe's privacy management interfaces: (A) assigning colleagues to groups, (B) choosing the availability information that each group can see; and (C) a summary of the resulting availability information shared during the current day.

Our system's asymmetry also supports the visibility characteristic of *socially translucent* systems, another of our design goals. To support mutual awareness of the information shared and to foster accountability, InterruptMe keeps track of one's own availability values throughout the day (Figure 7C) and of those received from other users. The third contact in Figure 5 has been expanded to reveal the changes of availability on each communications medium throughout the day. These historical values provide not only an increased level of social translucence, but also allow users to compare the information provided through the system with what they know about their contacts through other means, ideally leading to an increased degree of trust in the system.

InterruptMe is designed to require minimal active engagement from its users. In particular, users interact with the system only when they want to change their privacy settings, add contacts, or modify the relationships with their followers; InterruptMe provides an interface and sensible defaults for these operations (informed by previous systems and studies that we have described), allowing—but not requiring—users to fine-tune their settings.

Finally, building upon Greenberg's Peepholes system [14], InterruptMe allows users to actively monitor one another's availability, facilitating the "ambushing" behavior that is sometimes critical in dynamic workplace environments. Figure 5 shows small *tag* symbols that the local user has placed on the second contact's phone and IM channels. These tag icons indicate that when the contact becomes available through either of these communications media, a notification will be delivered to the local user.

InterruptMe differs from previous availability-sharing systems in three important ways. First, InterruptMe uses implicit interaction for displaying availability information, a characteristic previously seen only in systems that provide "walk-up" indications of availability. Second, InterruptMe implements traceable asymmetry, where interrupters can request availability information about their colleagues without having to be manually "approved" and where the interruptee does not have to symmetrically reciprocate in sharing availability information. Moreover, even though it is not explicit in the design space, InterruptMe introduces the notion of per-channel availability. These three differences set InterruptMe apart from prior availability-sharing systems and illustrate how our design space can be used to identify novel opportunities for designing availability-sharing systems and ameliorate previously identified problems (e.g., privacy, misinterpretation, and timely information delivery) in this class of systems.

CONCLUSION

In this paper, we explored the design space of availability-sharing systems. We used previous research on interruptibility and awareness systems to construct a new design space for availability-sharing systems. For each of the six axes in our design space—*abstraction*, *presentation*, *information delivery*, *symmetry*, *obtrusiveness*, and *temporal gradient*—we determined the range of values that each axis might take on, based on a survey of previous systems, and we discussed which values might be optimal for users with different roles in a collaboration.

We illustrated the utility of our design space in the design and implementation of InterruptMe, an opportunistic media-centered and person-dependent availability-sharing system. InterruptMe illustrates the utility of our design space: it introduces traceable asymmetry as a new point along a design space axis, and illustrates the use of pico-projector extended displays as a new way to realize an existing point in the space (information delivery by implicit interaction). We hope to complete a deployment study of this system in the future to validate its usefulness for supporting collaborations in the workplace.

InterruptMe is one illustration of a system designed specifically to balance between the needs of interrupters and interruptees, countering limitations of existing systems in this genre. The significance of our design space for availability-sharing systems is in enabling system designers to understand the important characteristics that define this class of systems and to think more concretely about how balancing these trade-offs in real-world collaborations.

ACKNOWLEDGEMENTS

This work was supported by the Danish Agency for Science, Technology, and Innovation under project #09-061856 the by the National Science Foundation under awards CNS-0937060 to the Computing Research Association for the Computing Innovation Fellows Project and IIS-0808783. We would also like to thank David Nguyen, Aurélien Tabard, Amy Voida, the STAR research group at UC Irvine, and our anonymous reviewers for their helpful feedback about this research.

REFERENCES

1. Bardram, J.E. and Hansen, T.R. The aware architecture: Supporting context-mediated social awareness in mobile cooperation. In *Proc. CSCW 2004*. ACM Press (2004), 192–201.
2. Begole, J.B., Matsakis, N.E., and Tang, J.C. Lilsys: Sensing unavailability. In *Proc. CSCW 2004*. ACM Press (2004), 511–514.
3. Biehl, J.T., Turner, T., Quarfordt, P., van Melle, B., Dunnigan, T., and Golovchinsky, G. MyUnity: Building awareness and fostering community in the workplace. http://adsabs.harvard.edu/abs/2010arXiv1006.5024B.
4. Cadiz, J.J., Venolia, G., Jancke, G., and Gupta, A. Designing and deploying an information awareness interface. In *Proc. CSCW 2002*. ACM Press (2002), 314–323.
5. Dabbish, L. and Kraut, R.E. Controlling interruptions: Awareness displays and social motivation for coordination. In *Proc. CSCW 2004*. ACM Press (2004), 182–191.
6. Dourish, P. and Bly, S. Portholes: Supporting awareness in a distributed work group. In *Proc. CHI 1992*. ACM Press (1992), 541–547.
7. Erickson, T. and Kellogg, W.A. Social translucence: An approach to designing systems that support social processes. *ACM Trans. Computer–Human Interaction, 7,* 1 (2000), 59–83.
8. Fetter, M., Seifert, J., and Gross, T. Lightweight selective availability in instant messaging. In *Ext. Abstracts CHI 2010*. ACM Press (2010), 3817–3822.
9. Fish, R.S., Kraut, R.E., Root, R.W., and Rice, R.E. Evaluating video as a technology for informal communication. In *Proc. CHI 1992*. ACM Press (1992), 37–48.
10. Fitzpatrick, G. *The Locales Framework: Understanding and Designing for Wicked Problems*. Kluwer, Dordrecht, The Netherlands, 2003.
11. Fogarty, J., Hudson, S.E., Atkeson, C.G., Avrahami, D., Forlizzi, J., Kiesler, S., Lee, J.C., and Yang, J. Predicting human interruptibility with sensors. *ACM Trans. Computer–Human Interaction, 12,* 1 (2005), 119–146.
12. Fogarty, J., Lai, J., and Christensen, J. Presence versus availability: The design and evaluation of a context-aware communication client. *International Journal of Human–Computer Studies, 61,* 3 (2004), 299–317.

13. Garcia Vazquez, J.P., Rodriguez, M.D., and Andrade, A.G. Design dimensions of ambient information systems to assist elderly with their activities of daily living. In *Ext. Abstracts UbiComp 2010*. ACM Press (2010), 461–464.

14. Greenberg, S. Peepholes: Low cost awareness of one's community. In *Ext. Abstracts CHI 1996*. ACM Press (1996), 206–207.

15. Gross, T. and Oemig, C. From PRIMI to PRIMIFaces: Technical concepts for selective information disclosure. In *Proc. SEAA 2006*. IEEE Computer Society (2006), 480–487.

16. Harr, R. and Wiberg, M. Lost in translation: Investigating the ambiguity of availability cues in an online media space. *Behaviour & Information Technology, 27,* 3 (2008), 243–262.

17. Horvitz, E. and Apacible, J. Learning and reasoning about interruption. In *Proc. ICMI 2003*. ACM Press (2003), 20–27.

18. Hsieh, G., Tang, K.P., Low, W.Y., and Hong, J.I. Field deployment of IMBuddy: A study of privacy control and feedback mechanisms for contextual IM. In *Proc. UbiComp 2007*. Springer (2007), 91–108.

19. Hudson, J.M., Christensen, J., Kellogg, W.A., and Erickson, T. "I'd be overwhelmed, but it's just one more thing to do": Availability and interruption in research management. In *Proc. CHI 2002*. ACM Press (2002), 97–104.

20. Intille, S. Change blind information display for ubiquitous computing environments. In *Proc. UbiComp 2002*. Springer (2002), 193–222.

21. Isaacs, E., Walendowski, A., and Ranganthan, D. Hubbub: A sound-enhanced mobile instant messenger that supports awareness and opportunistic interactions. In *Proc. CHI 2002*. ACM Press (2002), 179–186.

22. Isaacs, E.A., Tang, J.C., and Morris, T. Piazza: A desktop environment supporting impromptu and planned interactions. In *Proc. CSCW 1996*. ACM Press (1996), 315–324.

23. Jonsson, M., Jansson, C., Lönnqvist, P., Werle, P., and Kilander, F. Achieving non-intrusive environments for local collaboration. Technical Report 2002-021, Department of Computer and Systems Sciences, Stockholm University/KTH, Stockholm, Sweden (February 2008).

24. Lai, J., Levas, A., Chou, P., Pinhanez, C., and Viveros, M. BlueSpace: Personalizing workspace through awareness and adaptability. *International Journal of Human–Computer Studies, 57,* 5 (2002), 415–428.

25. Lai, J., Yoshihama, S., Bridgman, T., Podlaseck, M., Chou, P., and Wong, D. MyTeam: Availability awareness through the use of sensor data. In *Proc. INTERACT 2003*. IOS Press (2003), 503–510.

26. MacIntyre, B., Mynatt, E.D., Voida, S., Hansen, K.M., Tullio, J., and Corso, G.M. Support for multitasking and background awareness using interactive peripheral displays. In *Proc. UIST 2001*. ACM Press (2001), 41–50.

27. Mark, G., Gonzalez, V.M., and Harris, J. No task left behind?: Examining the nature of fragmented work. In *Proc. CHI 2005*. ACM Press (2005), 321–330.

28. Mark, G., Gudith, D., and Klocke, U. The cost of interrupted work: More speed and stress. In *Proc. CHI 2008*. ACM Press (2008), 107–110.

29. Markopoulos, P. A design framework for awareness systems. In P. Markopoulos, B. de Ruyter, and W. Mackay (Eds.), *Awareness systems: Advances in theory, methodology and design*. Springer, Dordrecht, The Netherlands (2009), 49–72.

30. Markopoulos, P., de Ruyter, B., and Mackay, W. *Awareness systems: Advances in theory, methodology and design*. Springer, Dordrecht, The Netherlands (2009).

31. Matthews, T., Dey, A.K., Mankoff, J., Carter, S., and Rattenbury, T. A toolkit for managing user attention in peripheral displays. In *Proc. UIST 2004*. ACM Press (2004), 247–256.

32. McEwan, G. and Greenberg, S. Supporting social worlds with the community bar. In *Proc. GROUP 2005*. ACM Press (2005), 21–30.

33. McFarlane, D.C. Interruption of people in human-computer interaction: A general unifying definition of human interruption and taxonomy. Technical Report NRL/FR/5510-97-9870, Naval Research Laboratory, Washington, DC (1997).

34. McFarlane, D.C. and Latorella, K.A. The scope and importance of human interruption in human-computer interaction design. *Human–Computer Interaction, 17,* 1 (2002), 1–61.

35. Milewski, A.E. and Smith, T.M. Providing presence cues to telephone users. In *Proc. CSCW 2000*. ACM Press (2000), 89–96.

36. Nichols, J., Wobbrock, J.O., Gergle, D., and Forlizzi, J. Mediator and medium: Doors as interruption gateways and aesthetic displays. In *Proc. DIS 2002*. ACM Press (2002), 379–386.

37. Olson, J.S., Grudin, J., and Horvitz, E. A study of preferences for sharing and privacy. In *Ext. Abstracts CHI 2005*. ACM Press (2005), 1985–1988.

38. Patil, S. and Kobsa, A. Instant messaging and privacy. In *Proc. HCI 2004*. British Computer Society (2004), 85–88.

39. Pousman, Z. and Stasko, J. A taxonomy of ambient information systems: Four patterns of design. In *Proc. AVI 2006*. ACM Press (2006), 67–74.

40. Tang, J.C., Isaacs, E.A., and Rua, M. Supporting distributed groups with a montage of lightweight interactions. In *Proc. CSCW 1994*. ACM Press (1994), 23–34.

41. Tang, J.C., Yankelovich, N., Begole, J., van Kleek, M., Li, F., and Bhalodia, J. ConNexus to Awarenex: Extending awareness to mobile users. In *Proc. CHI 2001*. ACM Press (2001), 221–228.

42. Tomitsch, M., Kappel, K., Lehner, A., and Grechenig, T. Towards a taxonomy for ambient information systems. Position paper presented at the Workshop on the Issues of Designing and Evaluating Ambient Information Systems at PERVASIVE 2007, Toronto, ON (2007).

43. Vertegaal, R., Dickie, C., Sohn, C., and Flickner, M. Designing attentive cell phone using wearable eyecontact sensors. In *Ext. Abstracts CHI 2002*. ACM Press (2002), 646–647.

44. Voida, A., Newstetter, W.C., and Mynatt, E.D. When conventions collide: The tensions of instant messaging attributed. In *Proc. CHI 2002*. ACM Press (2002), 187–194.

45. Voida, A., Voida, S., Greenberg, S., and He, H.A. Asymmetry in media spaces. In *Proc. CSCW 2008*. ACM Press (2008), 313–322.

Injured Person Information Management during Second Triage

Yuki Takahashi, Hiroaki Kojima
Graduate School of Science and Technology
Keio University
3-14-1 Hiyoshi Kohoku-ku
Yokohama Kanagawa, Japan
{takahashi, kojima}@mos.ics.keio.ac.jp

Ken-ichi Okada
Faculty of Science and Technology
Keio University, JST CREST
3-14-1 Hiyoshi Kohoku-ku
Yokohama Kanagawa, Japan
okada@mos.ics.keio.ac.jp

ABSTRACT

In a large-scale disaster in which many persons are injured at the same time, triage has been introduced. Triage is a method that temporarily delays the treatment of people with mild to moderate injuries and symptoms and gives priority to those in a critical condition. In the process of multiple triage, more specific information is needed in the second triage compared to the first to accurately prioritize the persons injuries and state. To solve this problem we proposed and constructed a touch-based interface for managing information inserted during second triage. A touch-based tablet interface is introduced to specify wound areas and gestures for wound types. The information is shared wirelessly with all emergency personnel, giving medics shared, data-centric, visibility of overall triage status for the first time. The evaluation experiment shows that this proposed system enables to reduce input errors, speed up injured person care, and facilitate information sharing between medics efficiently. As a result, we believe that many more injured persons can and will be saved.

ACM Classification: H5.2 [information interfaces and presentation]: user interfaces; graphical user interfaces.

General terms: design, human factors.

Keywords: triage, touch panel, electronic tag, biological information, interface.

INTRODUCTION

In a large-scale disaster, lifesaving emergency activities become difficult as medical resources such as doctors and medical treatment machines are limited. Consequently, a medic first carries out triage. Triage determines the priority of treatment on the basis of degree of severity or urgency of treatment of injured persons. The purpose is to save as many injured persons as possible through the efficient use of limited medical resources. Currently, paper triage tags are often used to indicate the condition of patients and to record information on their injuries. However, there are several problems with this current system. It is difficult for medical staff to obtain information on all injured persons in real time. Secondly, blood and mud may obscure the paper tags. Therefore, We investigated the computerization of triage by Team Type Research (CREST) through a system called "Man Information Sensing System, which supports medical services for those in need" [1][2][3].

In this paper, we propose an interface for an input system whereby medics can enter information of injured persons received during second triage. Touch-based interface for second triage management can reduce input errors, speed patient care, and facilitate information sharing between medics. We introduce a touch-based tablet interface to specify wound areas and gestures for wound types. This information is shared wirelessly with all emergency personnel, giving workers shared, data-centric, visibility of overall triage status for the first time. Consequently, injured persons can be promptly transported to hospitals, and many more lives will be saved.

In Section 2, we provide an outline and discuss issues of the triage system. In Section 3, we explain our proposal for solving issues. Section 4 introduces the implementation of the interface. Section 5 discusses assessment of the system. Section 6 discusses the future work. Finally in Section 7, we present our closing remarks.

RELATED WORK

Medical Services Based on Triage

Triage determines the degree of emergency and severity of the symptoms of injuries persons and is used to decide the level of prioritization. Injured persons are categorized as follows: Red →Yellow →Green→ Black [4].

- [Red] Immediate treatment required. E.g., massive bleeding or shock.
- [Yellow] Life is not endangered when treatment is delayed; stable vital signs.
- [Green] Treatment not required by a specialist because wounds are easy to treat.
- [Black] Fatal case; or one with no chance of survival, despite cardiopulmonary resuscitation.

Figure 1 shows a triage tag. The level of priority of each person is presented by removing unmatched colors when

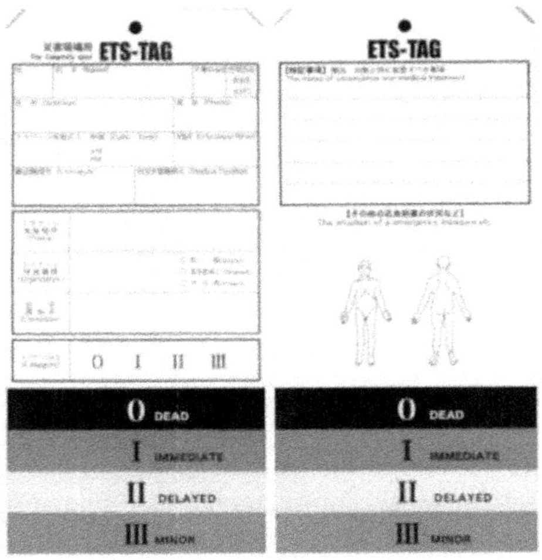

Figure 1. Triage Paper Tag

attaching the tag. In addition, the following information must be completed in the appropriate cell: anatomical abnormality, circumstance of injury, vulnerable person category, name, age, blood type, transportation, organization, and name of the medic in charge.

Current State of Second Triage

In Japan, the first triage at the triage post diagnoses the injured person using the Simple Triage and Rapid Treatment Method (START), which determines the level of priority according to physiological opinions of vital signs such as respiratory rate and pulse. The START method assesses medical situations and abnormalities in the following order: walking ability → spontaneous respiration → respiratory rate → pulse rate → consciousness [5][6]. The purpose of the first triage is to classify the injured according to the above signs, but not to treat them.

However, because symptoms change over time, and because more information is required, triage is insufficient when performed only once. Consequently, second and third triage stages are performed. Second triage is executed in a tent for one of the colors allocated at first triage. When details of the classification change as a result of second triage, they are recorded on the tags. For such matters, the injured are not moved between tents.

Issues

There are a number of issues regarding the use of paper tags. For example, rewriting on the tags is difficult when symptoms change after filling in the results of the previous triage. Moreover, medics other than those who carried out the triage must obtain information on the injured by going directly to each person to check the tag. In addition, words written in haste are often messy and not easily readable. In recent years, and in different parts of the world, systems based on radio frequency identification (RFID) tags and sensors to be used for emergency lifesaving in disasters have been researched [7][8]. In the CodeBlue Project [9], [10], vital signs obtained from watch-type sensors are collected through *ad hoc* wireless networks. In the Tech Specs Project, a new type of network for disaster areas called WIISARD [11] has been developed. Furthermore, a study which displays information collected through a wireless sensor network to a personal digital assistant has been conducted [12]. By carrying an information terminal that display details of the injured, medical staff are able to obtain information quickly and efficiently.

However, some problems remain for the above research; for example, sufficient time is required to input the vast amount of information, and only selected people are able to interpret such input information. Moreover, there is no particular type of interface for each stage of triage. Various input interfaces have been developed in research of the care card [13][14][15]. However, triage in which medics aim to input limited information rapidly differs from that in which the clinical record presents detailed and clear information. In addition, triage is used to diagnose many injured persons at the same time, and changing information is expected to be instantly disseminated among the medics. The triage user interfaces should not be treated the same way as the clinical records' UI in such circumstances. For these reasons, research that overcomes such problems has so far not been introduced.

INJURED PERSON INFORMATION MANAGEMENT DURING SECOND TRIAGE

The merits of computerizing the current paper tag are effectiveness of input and information sharing. Currently, collaboration between medics who have never previously worked together is difficult, and promptness and accuracy must also be re-evaluated. The importance of a computerized system, therefore, is necessary to minimize lost information between medics. It is important for medics to input information on injured persons at a disaster scene promptly and to transmit the information accurately. Therefore, when information is input, only necessary information is collected. As a result, the time for the information to be input is shortened, the volume of information is decreased, and the load of transmission is reduced. Consequently, interfaces specially adapted for each triage stage are necessary.

We proposed and constructed an interface for the second triage. Our proposed system presents injured person information collected at the first triage and inputs anatomic abnormality, circumstances of injury, and vulnerable person category as new information at the second triage. The input information is then easily transmitted.

Assumption Environment

In the present system, the first triage allows injured persons to stay in the tent of the color for which they were first classified. Similarly, it is assumed that second triage is practiced in the tent of the corresponding color and that the injured person is transported to a medical facility. The scale of disaster for which this system is suitable is from small-to-medium, such as the Fukuchiyama JR line derailment and the Akihabara bloodshed incident.

Vital Signs

Vital signs such as respiratory rate, pulse, and SpO2 (oxygen density in blood) are acquired. It is abnormal if the respiratory rate falls below 10 breaths per minute or exceeds 30. Moreover, it is abnormal if the number of pulses exceeds 120 beats per minute. If the Spo2 is less than 95%, some abnormalities will be discovered. If vital signs deteriorate considerably, the color of the triage will change.

Input Items of Second Triage

The purpose of the second triage is to add the following three items: "Anatomical abnormality", "Circumstances of injury", and "Vulnerable person category" (Table 1), in addition to the information collected at the first triage. For Anatomic abnormality, options include "Open Skull Fracture" and "Pelvic Fracture", with an especially high severity of symptoms. For instance, it is possible to add information on low-risk injuries, such as a wrist fracture or a nosebleed as an option. However, in order to reduce the amount of information, options with low priority are excluded in the emergency. Next, we indicate certain injuries that often worsen over time. For example, a fall from height needs to be classified as yellow. Vulnerable person category is also classified as yellow.

Table 1. Input items of second triage

	Input item (examples)	Classification
Anatomical Abnormality	Depression of the skull Abdominal protuberance Fractured pelvis Paralyzed extremity Penetrating trauma etc.	Red
Circumstance of Injury	Pressure of the trunk Fall from height etc.	Yellow
Vulnerable Person category	Child Pregnant woman Geriatric Ill person	

The second triage is completed when the above three factors are input and the tag color has been decided from the result of the first triage and the second triage according to priority. The items of input, the content of input, and classification of the triage division were decided in discussions with the staff of Juntendo University, which is attached to Urayasu Hospital.

Display Items of Injured Person Information

After the Fukuchiyama JR line derailment, many medics from various medical institutions were concentrated at the disaster scene. However, in the confusion, medics from different organizations were not able to communicate productively. For example, problems such as inaccessible information on whether triage was finished for certain patients, or which medics had conducted triage on which person, was not shared successfully and resulted in a situation where some medics were not able to be actively involved in lifesaving duties.

Therefore, collecting injured person information from the first triage and the second triage and displaying it clearly and promptly will support the lifesaving activities of all medics at the disaster scene. The information displayed by this interface comprises the following: the number of injured persons in each color tent, the number of patients that can be accommodated, current accommodation status, and the second triage execution record. In addition, color of the triage tag for the accommodated person, respiratory rate, pulse, SpO2, age, sex, name, anatomic abnormality, circumstance of injury, vulnerable person category, and record of second triage are displayed.

IMPLEMENTATION

Implementation Environment

Figure 2 shows the configuration of the system of our study. To start with, the first triage (START method) is executed at the triage post. The input terminal of the first triage uses an Apple iPod Touch. At this time, a wireless sensor network device, a SunSpot, is attached to the injured person to acquire vital signs. Next, the injured person is transported to the tent of his tag color after completing first triage. In this tent, second triage is executed. The SunSpot always transmits vital signs to the database, and highlights an LED on the sensor with the appropriate color of priority. This study proposes and constructs the interface used in the tent of each tag color (Figure 2, right panel). "Sending and receiving of vital signs using SunSpot" and "Input of the first triage using an iPod touch"(Figure 2, left panel) were added to the results of our previous work. Now, both systems are

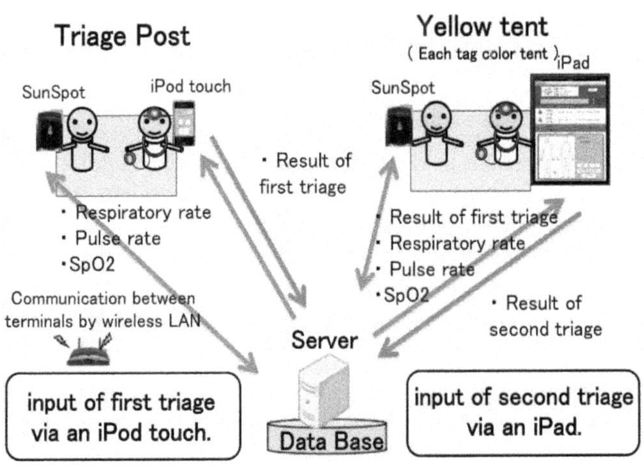

Figure 2. System Configuration

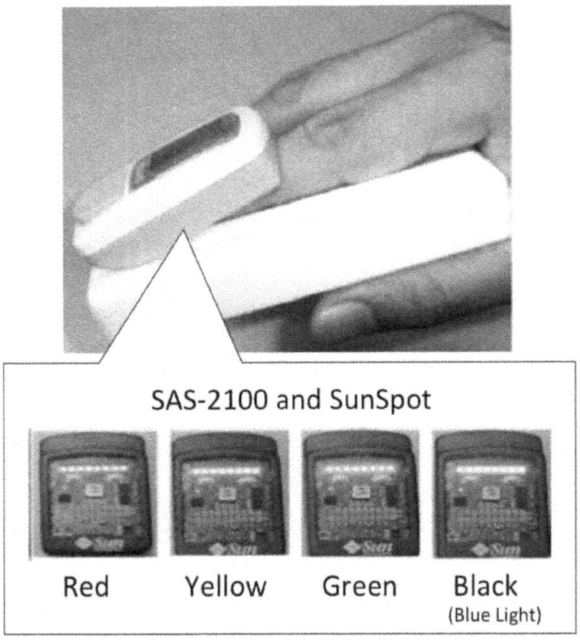

Figure 3. LED by triage color

combined; the injured person information management interface which is used to input and transmit information obtained at the second triage has been implemented. Moreover, an Apple iPad is used as the information terminal. All interfaces described in this paper are operated via an iPad. Furthermore, it has been confirmed that an iPad can be operated while wearing latex gloves.

Electronic Triage Tag

Figure 3 shows an example of LED colors after triage. SunSpot is a wireless sensor network device based on the ZigBee protocol. A SAS-2100 continuously collects data measuring the respiratory rate, pulse rate, and SpO2 via sensors. SunSpot receives the data collected from the SAS-2100 and transmits it to a server at constant intervals. The SunSpot LED lights will change accordingly to the injured person's state. In addition, each SunSpot has a unique number. Attaching a SunSpot to each injured person will prevent information misplacement and confusion by confirming the device number on the tablet.

Input Interface of Second Triage

The environment in which triage medics work is not a controlled environment where operation is orderly and smooth. In contrast, they are thrown into a disaster scene where chaos and confusion are prevalent. Therefore, our research is based not on an idealistic view of what could be done, but rather on the real-life people who work and criticize the current response system.

The proposal for a new user interface (UI) was made to not only improve the speed, but also the efficiency and accuracy of information of an injured person. In the second triage, it is necessary that information can be input promptly, even in confused situations, and all data must be input via the

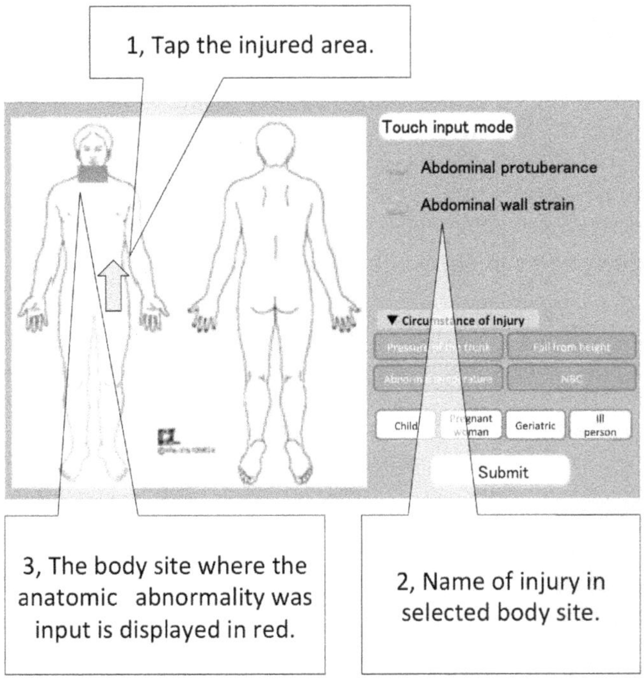

Figure 4. Touch Input Mode

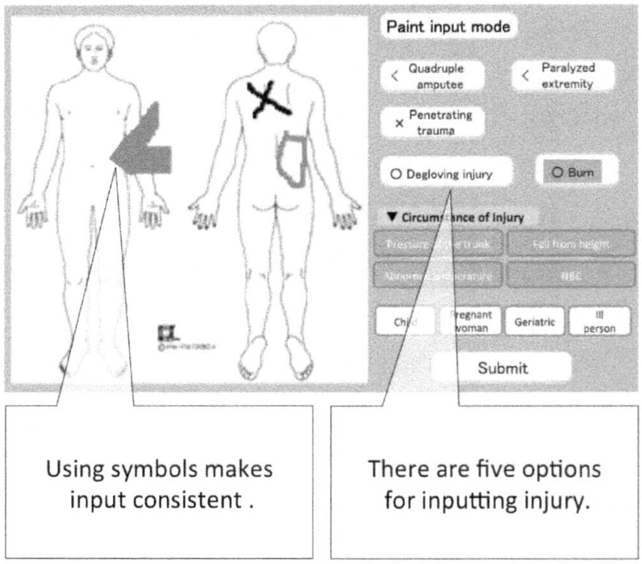

Figure 5. Paint Input Mode

same form. The process of input by the proposed technique is shown in Figures 4 and 5.

At a disaster site, it has become clear that choosing from only a few predetermined options and selecting by touch screen is the most user-friendly method. This became apparent following comparisons with options such as pull-down menus and keyboard input, among others. Here, the focus is on the anatomical abnormality, which has the most diverse input options in second triage (Table 1). Such options were classified by the number of body sites where wounds had developed. For example in the case of an open skull fracture, the appearance is shown only in the brainpan. However, a number of degloving injuries can happen to unspecified parts of the body. Therefore, we have classified injuries based on whether or not the area of injury can be specified. Table 2 shows the results of the classification.

Table 2. List of input actions

Injury	Location	Action
Depression of the skull Abdominal protuberance Fractured pelvis etc.	Head Abdomen Pelvis	Touch
Quadruple amputee Paralyzed extremity	Limbs Somewhere	Paint (<)
Penetrating trauma	Whole body Somewhere	Paint (×)
Degloving injury Burn	Whole body Somewhere	Paint (○)

Input of wound information is completed by tapping the corresponding body site on the illustration. The input appearance of the affected part is displayed in red. On the other hand, injuries that correspond to two or more types of appearances are classified in more detail, according to the kind of injury received; for example: injured only in the limbs, injured by a point (e.g., stab/pierce/puncture) and line (e.g., incision), or injured across a wide area (e.g., burn). The above categories are indicated by "Scissors (<)", "Christcross (×)", and "Round (○)" symbols, respectively. When the same symbol is drawn for multiple injuries, the color for each one is changed accordingly.

Unique cases exist where specific detail on the location and range of a symptom are necessary. In such cases, a UI enables handwritten illustrations similar to clinical records, which is familiar and easy for medics to understand. However, the chaos of handwritten illustrations is not desirable, thus the system provides an outline of a human body (front and back views) where the medic can choose from a list of injuries. Once a type of injury is selected, medics can make simple marks on the displayed human outline that can be easily associated with a type of injury.

Next, the process of inputting the circumstance of injury and vulnerable person category are shown in Figure 7. Input options for circumstance of injury and vulnerable person category are less than that for anatomical abnormality. Therefore, the options are input by touch. Moreover, a notice will appear to inform you what you have input and then change in style or color. In addition, some option categories are exclusive; for example when a child has been selected in the vulnerable person category, a pregnant woman cannot be selected.

When this input interface was designed, input for second triage was possible through only four commands. There are four distinguishable shapes to rely on when labeling injuries so that errors will be limited. Everyone understands the result with the rule more than the result without rule. The readability and display of the UI offers not only flexibility but also simplicity at the same time. The medic at the site has the option to input via an illustration or by a word or phrase for complex situations. The convenience of both functions ensures that clarity is established (i.e., location of injury: illustration; how the victim was injured: word or phrase). Sometimes, text can reveal more than illustrations.

Finally, the second triage can be input on a single screen, and a complex input is solved by using the screen of an iPad (1024px×768px). Input can be performed as text or illustration, according to the situation. When triage of multiple people is continuously executed, input can be performed for each person on the same screen, as shown in Figure 7. As a result, triage of more than one person can be executed without page transitions. We believe this design will prevent input mistakes and reduce the time for inputting information.

Injured Person Information Display Screen

A key discussion for project members was how quickly a medic could determine the situation at a disaster site; for example, what are the doctors doing, who are they attending to, and how many injured patients are in a tent, within a single page view.

Figure 6 shows the list of injured persons. The way in which information is displayed is important for understanding the situation in the tent. In this interface, the following three factors are displayed on the same screen: list of injured persons in the tent, accommodation status, and status of the second triage executed in the tent. In the injured person's list, status is displayed by using an icon to promptly identify the triage results. The icon displays the triage color; red, yellow, green, or black. Red is for an anatomical abnormality, and yellow is for problems related to circumstance of injury as well as for vulnerable person category. An additional mark is added for children or pregnant women. Information can be understood clearly and easily by using illustrations in addition to words.

Figure 6 shows information displayed in the yellow tent, and it is clear that there is one injured person classified as red in the second triage. Details on the injured person's vital signs, anatomical abnormality, circumstance of injury, vulnerable person category, name, sex, and age are displayed simply in words. Arranging all information on the same screen enables easy and rapid comparison. Moreover, the number of accommodating tents and the accommodation situation of other tents are presented by a graph. Finally, the triage history regarding time of triage transportation are also displayed. Recent history is displayed first. Communication between medics is supported by preserving the

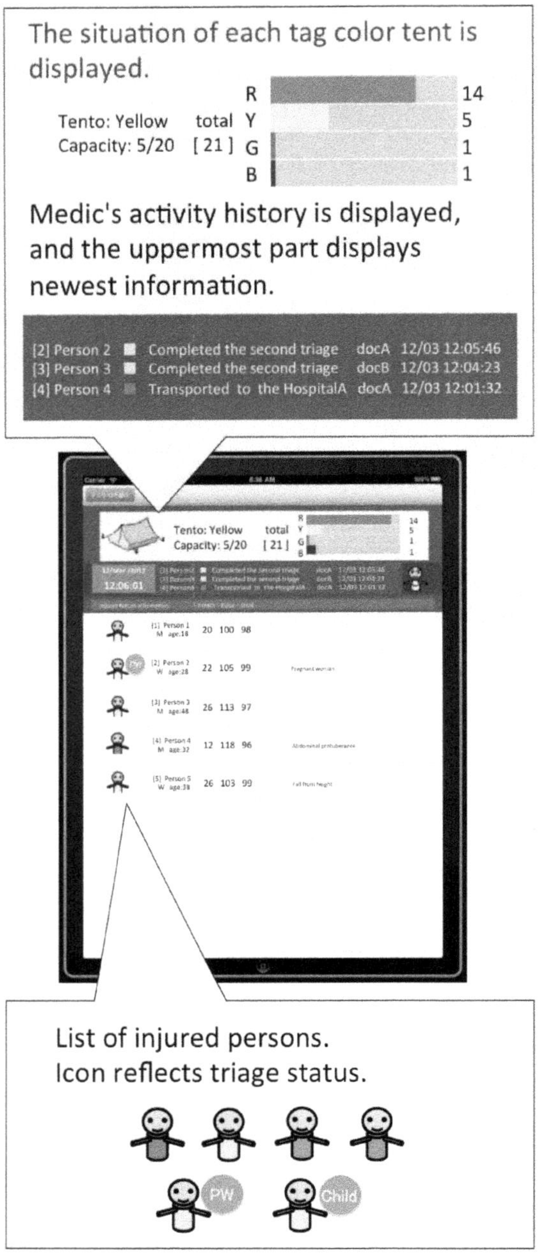

Figure 6. List of Injured Person Information

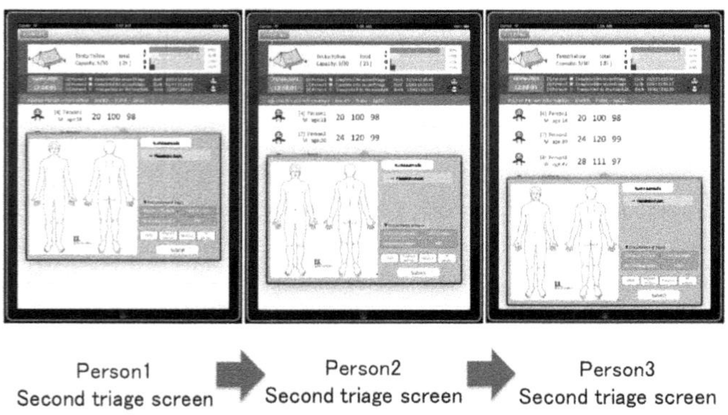

Figure 7. Pop Up Display

history of medic activities and sharing the information. As a result, medical services are performed efficiently.

The second triage input screen is accessed by selecting the record of the respective injured person, as shown in Figure 7. It is a pop up display that doesn't require page transition even when the following person is in triage. As seen in Figure 7, the user can look at the injured persons profile, without confusing one injured person to another, with one touch on the populated injured persons list.

EVALUATION

Two assessment experiments were performed. In the first evaluation, the utility of the second triage input terminal and that of the paper tags were compared. In the second evaluation, efficient assessment of injured person information in the tent by each method was compared.

The size, number of people, and the state of the JR Fukuchiyama line accident, was used as the setup condition for the 2 experiments. For the present study, testers were 15 students because this proposal is still a prototype. However, in the future, medics will be the testers, which will enable a more realistic field setting.

Experimental Procedure

Experiment: I. The tester executed the second triage in each tent by looking at the information on 15 injured persons, as written on paper and as shown by color tags. The time required for the input was measured. Figure 8 shows an example of the paper with the information of the injured person. This was used in the electronic triage training and the assessment experiment done under the CREST Project (September, 2010). Next, the same operation was done for the proposed system.

Experiment: II. The tags of injured persons were randomly placed on a desk (0.7 m x 0.9 m) and read, and the priority level of all injured persons was decided in accordance with their symptoms, wound classification, and special notes. This work was done using both paper tags and the second triage input terminal. The triage tag was attached to the body of the injured person, whereas, the proposed system did not carry out categorization of injured persons in the

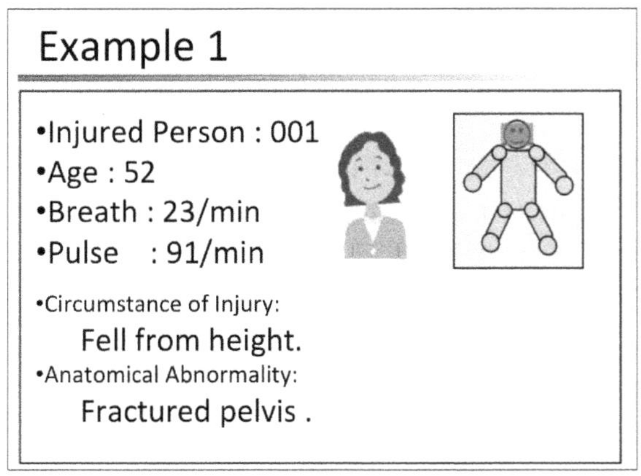

Figure 8. Example of a paper tag

tent, so the tags were detached. Therefore, neither the positions of injured persons in the tent nor their tags should be rearranged or removed. Because a tag is always attached to the injured person, acts such as rearranging the tags or misplacing them cannot be done. However, because there weren't any people to act out the injured person in this assessment experiment, the tags could move freely so rearrangement and misplacement could easily occure. Therefore, to reproduce a more realistic disaster site, "sorting tags on the desk" and "walking with multiple tags in hand" are prohibited.

Results

Experiment: I. Table 3 shows the results. The average input time shows the time necessary for the execution of the second triage. The proposed system reduced input time by around 30 s. When using paper tags, a column must be completed by hand. This is time consuming and Chinese characters with many strokes require time and thought to ensure correct usage and to describe the situation accurately. On the other hand, the triage input terminal selects only the second triage injuries and conditions. Although the input time is slightly increased when symbols are drawn, it is still a lot faster than using paper tags.

Secondly, we focused on the "wrong data rate". The wrong answer is considered an inputting error, an input omission, and inputs that cannot be comprehended. With the paper tag, written characters were often messy and/or impossible to read, and sentences were too simplified to understand and be transmitted properly to others. Therefore, the ratio of the number of wrong data increased. On the other hand, the proposed system avoids ambiguity because items are selected. However, there were a few mistakes when options were entered in a hurry. Consequently, the proposed system was found to be quicker and more accurate than the conventional paper tag method.

Table 3. Result of Experiment I

	Required Time	Wrong Answer Rate
Paper Tag	47.9	16.3%
Proposed System	8.8	0.6%

Thirdly, Table 4 shows the results of a questionnaire on the usability of the second triage input. Observers answered each question on a scale of one to five (5 was rated the highest and 1 the lowest).

- Question 1: Could you input injured person information easily?
- Question 2: Did you often feel exhausted after completing the input task?

The proposed system received a high score for all items. This shows that usability of the proposed system for inputting injured person information is more successful than using paper tags.

Table 4. Result of the Questionnaire of Experiment I

	Paper Tag	Proposed System
Question 1	1.7	4.7
Question 2	2.3	4.3

Experiment: II. The required time was the time necessary for deciding the level of priority for nine injured persons. The results show that the required time was greatly reduced in the proposed system compared to the paper tag method. When using paper tags, information on all injured person is memorized, and the priority list is decided through memory. As a result, the work becomes very difficult and a lot of time is required. Moreover, there is always a limit to one's memory. Thus it becomes necessary for one to read the tags repeatedly until they are fully memorized. On the other hand, the proposed system orderly displays the information and allows the medics to compare it efficiently to decide the best order of priority. In such a case, the required time for making decisions is greatly reduced.

Next we compared incorrect answers between the paper and proposed systems. When using paper tags, there were many wrong answers for the following reasons: the decision methods for deciding the order of priority were forgotten, information for all persons could not be memorized at the same time and was confusing, and tags were difficult to read obliquely. With the proposed system, decisions for prioritizing were easily made because information on injured persons was displayed and compared on one screen.

Moreover, the number of wrong answers decreased. In the case of paper tags, the tester sometimes did not notice the mistakes. This means that the identification of injured persons at the highest priority would vary between medics. Even with nine injured persons, there were mistakes, resulting in a situation where information on the injured was not fully understood. However, such problems improved the proposed technique, and promptness and accuracy of information transmission were realized. The results of the experiments demonstrated that it was easy to confirm the personal information of the injured.

Table 5. Result of Experiment II

	Required Time	Number of Incorrect Answers
Paper Tag	105.8	1.9
Proposed System	19.6	0

Finally, we focused on the usability of received injured person information (Table 6).

- Question 1: Could you see the contents of the screen easily?
- Question 2: Could you decide the priority of the injured person?
- Question 3: Did you feel tired after deciding?

Table 6. Result of the Questionnaire of Experiment II

	Paper Tag	Proposed System
Question 1	3.1	4.4
Question 2	1.5	4.7
Question 3	2.8	4.5

The proposed system obtained the highest reputation value in all items. Therefore, the usability of received injured person information on the proposed system is more successful than that of using paper tags.

FUTURE WORK

In medical fields, many UIs for care cards exist. However, the care card inputs detailed symptoms of an injured person and is intended for collecting a large amount of information. Our system automatically observes vital signs, reflects diagnostic outcomes of some medics in real time, and offers a UI that promptly enables a dynamic care card.

In addition, it is applicable to not only disaster scenes, but also to emergency medical treatment hospitals and waiting rooms in hospitals. Triage is performed in a crowded waiting room, and priority is assigned in order of emergency degree, and not on a first-come-first-served basis. Thus, one can become proficient in triage and operation of the system by using it in a medical context on a daily basis. However, in a non-disaster scene, the number of simultaneously injured persons is a lot less, and therefore, more time is available. Therefore adding content and diagnosis in the future is a possibility, as well as inputting injuries that are minor which can be helpful in a non-disaster situation. An electronic triage system for daily use would probably be effective if two UIs are developed; one for the disaster scene mode and one for the non-disaster scene mode.

The present study showed that drawing or selecting options by touch is effective for confused situations. The UI decreases input time in an accurate manner. A function should be considered that allows the user to begin drawing a symbol and the interface to recognize the shape without the user having to complete it. Therefore, a UI that supports handwritten input will also be developed.

CONCLUSION

Recently medics have conducted triage of injured persons who are in need of immediate care at disaster scenes. Triage enables medics to care for, attend to, and send the injured to hospitals as quickly and efficiently as possible. However, there are some limitations with the current triage system. When paper tags are used, medics have trouble efficiently processing information on the injured persons.

Here we proposed a UI for inputting information of injured persons received at triage. First, we developed the technology for collecting vital signs. Next, we developed the technology for adding information via a portable terminal, and we limited the interface to control input volume, and intelligence sharing between medics was also facilitated.

To confirm the effectiveness of the proposed system, we evaluated it through a mock-up experiment. As a result, we confirmed the effectiveness of the proposed input system and confirmed that medics were able to input information of injured persons collectively and rapidly. Their burden was also decreased.

With this new system, medics in a disaster scene can input and transmit information of injured persons more efficiently than using the conventional paper tag-based system. Consequently, patients can be promptly transported to hospitals, and many more lives will be saved.

ACKNOWLEDGEMENTS

This research was supported in part by JST, CREST.

REFEREMCES

1. Japan Science and Technology Agency (JST), http://www.jst.go.jp/
2. JST News "More Sophisticated Triage", http://www.jst.go.jp/pr/jstnews/2009/200912/page08.html
3. Higashino Lab, Designing Advanced Electronic Triage System for Efficient Rescue Operations, http://www.higashi.ist.osaka-u.ac.jp/research/etriage.html
4. Critical Illness and Trauma Foundation, Inc., THE TRIAGE TAG, http://www.citmt.org/start/tag.htm
5. Association of doctorin Osaka Prefecture emergency and disaster medical treatment part, "Standard of behavior for medical facilities at disaster (the first edition) ", http://portal.osaka-bousai.net/
6. Association of doctor of corporation Nagaoka City, "Medical treatment support activity manual when natural disaster occurs", Surveillance study on correspondence and system in medical treatment for health that bases Mid Niigata Prefecture Earthquake, http://www.nagaoka-med.or.jp/
7. A.Sonoda, S.Inoue and K.Oka, Experiment of Large Scale Triage with RFID, Transactions of Information Proceeding Society of Japan, 48(2):802-810, 2007.

8. A.Sonoda and S.Inoue, Effective Use of Individual Information in the Emergency Activity, Proceedings of the 18th Data Engineering Workshop, 2007

9. D.Malan, T.Fulfordjones, M.Welsh and S.Moulton, Codeblue:An ad hoc sensor network infrastructure for emergency medical care, Proceedings of International Workshop on Wearable and Implantable Body sensor Networks, 203-216,2004.

10. V.Shnayder, B.Chen, K.Lorincz, T.R.F.Fulford Jones and M.Welsh, Sensor Networks for Medical Care, Harvard University Technical report, 2005.

11. L.A, Lenert, D.A.Palmer, T.C.Chan and R.Rao, An intelligent 802.11 triage tag for medical response to disasters, Proceedings of American Medical Informatics Association 2005 Symposium, 440-444, 2005.

12. Tio Gao and David White, A Next Generation Electronic Triage to Aid Mass Caualty Emergency Medical Response, AMIA Symposium Proceedings, 2006.

13. R. Marti, S. Robles, A. Martin-Campillo, J. Cucurull," Providing early resource allocation during emergencies: The mobile triage tag ", Journal of Network and Computer Applications ELSEVIER ,2009.

14. Pamela B. Andreatta, EdD, Eric Maslowski, Sean Petty, Woojin Shim, Michael Marsh, MS, Theodore Hall, Susan Stern, MD, and Jen Frankel, MD, " Virtual Reality Triage Training Provides a Viable Solution for Disaster-preparedness ", SCIENCE OF SIMULATION IN EMERGENCY MEDICINE,2008.

15. National Cerebral and Cardiovascular Center, http://www.ncvc.go.jp/res/divisions/biomedicalsystem/bms002.html

Yelling In the Hall: Using Sidetone to Address a Problem with Mobile Remote Presence Systems

Andreas Paepcke, Bianca Soto, Leila Takayama
Willow Garage
68 Willow Road
Menlo Park, CA 94025
paepcke,sotob,takayama@willowgarage.com

Frank Koenig
1944 Tasso St.
Palo Alto, CA
94301
frank@dunmovin.com

Blaise Gassend
Willow Garage
68 Willow Road
Menlo Park, CA, 94025
blaise@willowgarage.com

ABSTRACT

In our field deployments of mobile remote presence (MRP) systems in offices, we observed that remote operators of MRPs often unintentionally spoke too loudly. This disrupted their local co-workers, who happened to be within earshot of the MRP system. To address this issue, we prototyped and empirically evaluated the effect of sidetone to help operators self regulate their speaking loudness. Sidetone is the intentional, attenuated feedback of speakers' voices to their ears while they are using a telecommunication device. In a 3-level (no sidetone vs. low sidetone vs. high sidetone) within-participants pair of experiments, people interacted with a confederate through an MRP system. The first experiment involved MRP operators using headsets with boom microphones (N=20). The second experiment involved MRP operators using loudspeakers and desktop microphones (N=14). While we detected the effects of the sidetone manipulation in our audio-visual context, the effect was attenuated in comparison to earlier audio-only studies. We hypothesize that the strong visual component of our MRP system interferes with the sidetone effect. We also found that engaging in more social tasks (e.g., a getting-to-know-you activity) and more intellectually demanding tasks (e.g., a creativity exercise) influenced how loudly people spoke. This suggests that testing such sidetone effects in the typical read-aloud setting is insufficient for generalizing to more interactive, communication tasks. We conclude that MRP application support must reach beyond the time honored audio-only technologies to solve the problem of excessive speaker loudness.

ACM Classification: H.5.5 [Information Interfaces and Presentation]: Sound and Music Computing. H.5.2 [Information Interfaces and Presentation]: User Interfaces - Auditory (non-speech) feedback.

General terms: Design, Human Factors

Keywords: Telepresence, sidetone, computer mediated communication, loudness regulation, experiment

Figure 1: Remote *pilot* (left) interacts with a *local* (right) via an Internet-connected mobile remote presence (MRP) system, which is the pilot's physical 'avatar.' Problem: The pilots tend to speak too loudly, which threatens acceptance of the technology.

INTRODUCTION

Mobile remote presence systems (MRPs) have reached the cusp of commercial viability. An MRP system represents a remote operator, who uses the system to interact with others at a distance. Remote operators can drive the system around a physical environment, conversing with people at the MRP's location. A typical environment for MRP systems is a company's headquarters, in which a few workers are located elsewhere around the world (aka: hub-and-satellite teams [24]). MRPs are available at the central office for roaming around the office space. Remote employees 'inhabit' one of these MRPs via Internet connection (Figure 1). They remotely drive the machine around the premises, visiting co-workers in their offices, conversing in the hallway (e.g., Figure 2), or attending meetings.

Figure 1 depicts one example, an MRP system constructed and used at several companies for field testing. It is used for supporting communication between geographically distributed co-workers. This MRP is 1.57 meters tall (5' 2") and has a rolling base that holds a vertical rod. At the top, a pan-tilt web camera, 48.26 cm (19") LCD display, microphone and loudspeakers provide live duplex video and audio. In our discussion, we call an MRP's controller the *pilot*; we call people at the MRP's location *locals*. The locals who engage in conversations with the pilots are called *participants*, whereas locals who are near the MRP systems, but do not interact with them, are called *bystanders* [4].

Of course, a work environment is just one example scenario for telepresence. Others include remote family visits, remote

Figure 2: *Local participant* (left) in California chats with remote *pilot* (right) in Colorado after a project meeting at a field site, standing in a shared workspace near an open office door.

medical consultations [13], or supporting independence for older adults [3].

Most mobile remote presence systems today share the basic design that is exemplified in Figure 1, including the personal roving presence (PRoP) [15], the Geminoid (android telepresence robot) [17], and BiReality [9], as well as commercially available products such as the Giraffe, Anybots QB, TiLR, and vGo. Interactions between people through these devices are quite lively, and can quickly become second nature. Considering findings in the computers-as-social-actors paradigm, [16] such ease is not surprising. While this comfortable interaction is desirable, MRP system designers encounter pitfalls that stem precisely from the resulting semi-transparency of the mediation. The root of these pitfalls is that locals transfer social norms they internalized in their lifetime of unmediated interaction onto the MRP. These norms include deeply seated and sometimes subconscious elements, like social distance [7, 2, 20, 11], politeness in yielding the way when meeting in a narrow hallway [26, 27], and turn-taking in conversation [22]. Consistent with [23], we have found that when people using MRP systems break these social norms surrounding appropriate speaking volumes in the workplace, locals react with consternation and anger. This has been observed across four of our field sites. We do not yet know the full list of norms that this technology must respect to ensure wide acceptance although we have concrete evidence for parts of this list (e.g., [11]).

Problem Statement

In this work we focus on a deal-breaking item on the list of behavioral norms that locals insist on seeing respected: Pilots must modulate the loudness of their voices through the MRP in accordance with convention. We hush our voices when in the halls of a workplace, a hospital, or in an elevator. In meetings, we use the loudness of our voice with consideration to our organizational status, the personalities of other attendees, and the intention behind our statements.

From field deployments of our MRP prototypes, we know that pilots very frequently speak inappropriately loudly, even when this behavior is pointed out to them (e.g., Figure 3). These findings are consistent with field studies conducted by

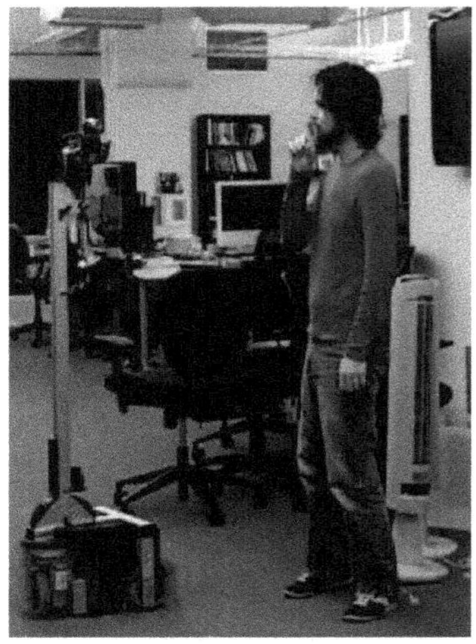

Figure 3: *Local participant* (right) in California shushes a remote *pilot* (left) in New York, who was disrupting the nearby standing meeting by speaking too loudly at a field site.

Tsui, et al. [23], who used the QB and vGo systems. At an office, where these MRP systems are used every day, we have observed co-workers slamming their office doors shut when a hallway conversations with MRP pilots become too loud. Even when local participants, who are engaged in conversation through an MRP system, often hesitate to tell pilots that they are being too loud. Possibly because of politeness norms, they seem to find it to be easier to tell pilots when they are being too quiet than when they are being too loud. In fact, what often happens is that local participants end up aligning to the loudness levels of the remote pilots so both the pilots and the locals end up speaking too loudly, exacerbating the problem of disrupting other local bystanders.

A physical volume control is available on the MRP. Locals could thus moderate the MRP system loudness themselves. Yet they rarely avail themselves of this power, even when they are annoyed by how loudly the MRP system is projecting the pilot's voice. Operating the volume control not only requires penetration into the pilot's (virtual) personal space, but even manipulation of the pilot's 'body.' Thus, locals suffer the uncouth behavior (disruptively loud conversations), which is, of course, purely a breakdown in mediation, and not an indicator of pilot intent or rudeness.

One reason why pilots speak too loudly may be that they operate in a much more complex environment than when using a more commonplace remote presence tool, the telephone. Pilots are very engaged and busy attending to views from the MRP system cameras (e.g., pointing the pan-tilt head camera) and navigating (e.g., driving the MRP system around the office space) on top of talking and listening. Another issue is that reproduction of MRP environment sound levels at the pilot side are not necessarily faithful; therefore, pilots cannot properly compare their voice loudness levels to that of locals.

Previous Attempts at Solutions

As a first measure, we tried graphical Sound Pressure Level (SPL) meters in the pilot's graphical user interface. The meters communicated sound levels measured at the MRP to the pilot, similar to a stereo sound system gain monitor. Unfortunately, pilots quickly forgot to observe the meter. Such meters present additional work for pilots, who have to learn how to interpret the meters and continuously check them.

Another solution we tried was audio compressors. These digital signal processing modules automatically reduce the gain of an incoming signal processing chain without clipping, once the input level exceeds a threshold. A related technology is ambient noise compensation, which similarly adjusts gain, but in this case to compensate for fluctuating noise levels in the surroundings at the receiving end. While a well known and readily available technology, these devices must be adjusted so that they react quickly to sudden increases in loudness, while also letting go of control within a reasonable time.

In an MRP's frequently changing environment it is difficult to keep these adjustments properly tuned. For example, predicting the duration of noises is easy for humans, but not for these loudness regulators. A sneeze, for instance, is known to a human as a brief burst that does not warrant a subsequent increase in voice amplification. In contrast, the onset of a drill or printer noise is expected to last for a while. These fluctuations in appropriate thresholds, attack, and decay times compromised our success with compressors.

While more sophisticated solutions can be attempted, we decided to try a telephony feature: the *sidetone* [12]. This technology consists of letting human speakers hear an attenuated stream of their own voices. When we speak into the mouthpiece microphone of a traditional landline telephone, our voice is in fact played into our own handset receiver's earpiece at an attenuated level. The level is just enough to induce in us a subconscious tendency towards appropriate adjustment of our voice loudness. Too little feedback, and the effect is lost. Too much, and we might be self conscious or distracted. Many cell phones today do not include sidetone; this lack of auditory feedback is one of the reasons why cell phone users often yell into their phones [14]. Determining the appropriate levels of sidetone for the current study was an involved process, which is discussed in the Experiment Manipulation section.

Sidetone cannot easily be applied in the context of speaker phones, because microphone and speakers are close together. That proximity easily causes screeching acoustic feedback. The question is whether the technology can be employed for MRP pilots, who sometimes use a headset/microphone combination, other times a loudspeaker to listen to their MRP's environment.

If usable, sidetone would be beautifully simple to implement. Two advantages over more complex solutions would be that no loudness level information would need to be transmitted across the Internet, and that the human sources of sound themselves would accomplish the loudness control through mostly subconscious self regulation.

We conducted an experiment to test whether sidetone can help pilots overcome this serious problem of inadvertent yelling when using MRP systems. After reporting on related work, we describe the experimental setup and results. These sections are followed by a discussion of our findings, and concluding remarks.

RELATED WORK

The loudness of speakers and singers is impacted by two components: the noise level that surrounds the speaker, and the level and clarity at which speakers can hear their own voices (sidetone) [12]. Lane et al. [10] have shown that when confronted with changes in either surrounding noise or sidetone level, speakers will produce their compensatory reaction at one half the size of those changes. For example, when sidetone level is quadrupled, speakers will cut their loudness in half. That is, they determined that the slope of the sidetone reaction on a decibel/decibel scale is -0.5.

Siegel and Pick [18] showed that the loudness moderating effect of sidetone interacts with surrounding noise levels. When surrounding noise levels are higher, the effect of varying sidetone levels is amplified. This finding did not bode well for our experiment. Our remote pilots were most annoying in quiet environments, where according to Siegel and Pick's study the effect of sidetone is least powerful (albeit significant).

Goodman and Johnston describe a variation of sidetone injection in which sidetone level is varied in response to the loudness of the speaker [5]. The authors did not report upon any experimental results.

In human-computer interaction, the use of sidetone has been explored in the domain of driver user interfaces. A controlled experiment found that the addition of sidetones increased conversational engagement (e.g., verbosity of spoken responses), but also increased the cognitive load that drivers experienced [21]. Sidetone can be a mixed blessing.

Sidetone is also used at concerts to help singers stay in tune. In that context, loudspeakers are sometimes used instead of headphones, and special care must be taken to avoid acoustic feedback [8]. To our knowledge, no formal studies have examined the efficacy of sidetone for speaker loudness self control when visual as well as aural communication is involved. In contrast to earlier studies, our exploration also included engaging and challenging creativity questions, which varied the tasks' intellectual demands and carried the potential of triggering raised speaking loudness in the participants.

Despite the widespread use of sidetone for telephones and live musical performances, it is rarely used at all in computer-mediated communication contexts. Norman raised this issue six years ago [14] and it has yet to hit the mainstream mobile phone or videoconferencing systems on the market. Providing auditory feedback in the form of sidetones improves the user experience for landline telephones [14] and holds the promise for being useful in these new computer-mediated communication contexts such as mobile remote presence.

The current work differs from previous uses of side tone in two major ways: (1) the addition of the video channel and (2) the addition of a mobile system that can wander around very diverse acoustic environments.

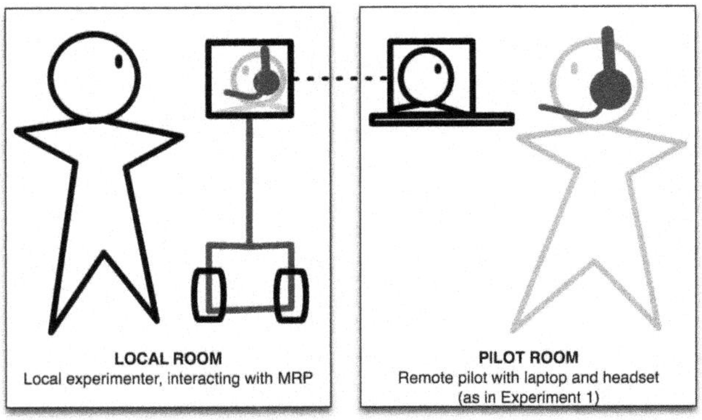

Figure 4: Local vs. pilot rooms.

EXPERIMENT

We conducted two experiments in which participants interacted remotely with the experimenter. Sidetone level was a within-participants independent variable in both studies. In Experiment 1, participants used a headset with a boom microphone. In Experiment 2, participants used a loudspeaker and desktop microphone.

Experiment Manipulation

In both experiments we mixed each of three sidetone levels into the audio that participants heard when they were speaking. We call these levels S_{no}, S_{low}, and S_{high}. These values were measured in decibels comparing the pressure levels of the generated sidetone with those of the participant's voice. For example, a headset condition sidetone level of $-3dB$ resulted from attenuating a participant's voice by $3dB$ and mixing that signal into the participant's headset while they spoke.

S_{no} is zero; the absolute values of S_{low} and S_{high} differed between the loudspeaker and the headphone conditions (see below in the respective subsections). All participants experienced all three sidetone levels one after the other, albeit in random order.

Participants

The first experiment, which used headsets, included 20 adult volunteer participants (9 female, 11 male), ranging from 20 to 69 years of age, *M*=39.7, *SE*=3.7. The second experiment, which used loudspeakers, included 14 adult volunteer participants (8 female, 6 male), ranging from 24 to 68 years of age, *M*=32.1, *SE*=3.1.

Experiment Protocol

Study participants played the role of the MRP pilot, using a laptop to communicate through the MRP system. The experimenter sat in a separate room, playing the role of a local, interacting with the pilot through the MRP system. See Figure 4. Table 1 shows a summary of this experimental procedure.

To simulate a quiet office environment, we mixed an approximately $45dB$ background typing noise into the signal that participants heard. This background noise varied in volume over time.

	Example Participant 1		*Example Participant 2*	
Round1	*Low sidetone*	*wordlist*	*No sidetone*	*wordlist*
		warmup		*warmup*
		creativity		*creativity*
Round 2	*High sidetone*	*wordlist*	*Low sidetone*	*wordlist*
		warmup		*warmup*
		creativity		*creativity*
Round 3	*No sidetone*	*wordlist*	*High sidetone*	*wordlist*
		warmup		*warmup*
		creativity		*creativity*

Table 1: Summary of experimental procedure for two sample participants.

For each sidetone level, participants went through a round of three exercises—nine exercises in all. Participants filled out a questionnaire about their experience between each of the three rounds.

For the first exercise, the experimenter asked the participant to read a list of words from the Modified Rhyme Test (MRT) collection [1] (*wordlist* exercise). These were semi-scripted interactions in that the experimenter read instructions and worked from a script.

For the second exercise, the experimenter asked the participant to answer five questions that were designed to free participants from excessive attention to their environment. Two sample questions were, "If you were an animal, what would it be, and why?" and, "When did you last write a handwritten letter?" (*warmup* exercise). These questions were designed to be more conversational in nature; thus, they were modified from a set of coffee table cards that are typically used to start conversations.

For the final exercise of each round, the experimenter named an object, and asked the participant to list as many non-standard uses for this object within 60 seconds. We repeated this question for the objects "shoe" "key" and "bed sheet" (*creativity* exercise). This approach is adapted from the Alternate Uses Creativity Task [6].

The order of exercises within each round was fixed, and no variables other than sidetone were modified for any one participant. These three tasks were used to cover a variety of interaction scenarios. The word list was reading aloud without time constraints. The warm up was revealing information about oneself and was very personal in nature. The creativity task was about generating divergent thinking ideas and had hard time constraints.

From the perspective of a participant in this study, he or she would sit at a desk in a relatively quiet office space. An open laptop sat upon the desk, displaying the user interface for controlling the MRP system, which included a live video feed to the Local Room. The participant would then fill out a study agreement form. The experimenter explained the procedures for the study, then left the Pilot Room to sit in the Local Room. The participant then saw and heard the experimenter through the laptop. The participant did each of the three tasks (word list, warm up, and creativity), filled out a paper questionnaire, and repeated those two steps two more times. Upon completing the study, the experimenter debriefed the participant and answered the participant's questions.

As we will describe, we recorded all speech. From the recordings, we extracted the portions where participants were speaking—as opposed to thinking about answers or listening to the experimenter. On these extracts, we then computationally compared each participant's speech pressure levels in sidetone conditions with their levels without sidetone.

The following three subsections describe the acoustics and psychoacoustic terms that are necessary for understanding the experiment set-ups, the headset experiment conditions, and the loudspeaker conditions.

Defining Terms

The ultimate goal of this study is to decrease inadvertent loudness of MRP pilots, who are projecting their voices too loudly through the MRP systems. "Loudness" is a term that applies to the subjective psychological experience of sound. In order to decrease the experience of MRP pilots being too loud, the current experiments explored ways to get MRP pilots to self-regulate their loudness, but we chose to use an objective measure rather than a subjective one.

We needed to measure how much each participant's sound pressure level changed across the experiment conditions so we chose to use the objective measure of "sound pressure level." This is a logarithmic measure of sound pressure (averaged over time, using root mean square) relative to some reference level (typically 20μPa in air, a standard set by the American National Standards Institute). Sound pressure levels are often measured in decibels ($dB(SPL)$). dB is an abbreviated term for $dB(SPL)$. L is an abbreviated term for "sound level." Frequency weighting is a process of scaling loudness measurements to match the human perception of sound, which is frequency dependent.

When you record the sound pressure levels in a room, you get a combination of many different sources, including atmospheric pressure, sidetones (in the case of Experiment 2), and the voice of the participant. To isolate the sound pressure levels of only the sidetones or only the voice of the participant, we had to measured the sources of extraneous sound pressure. The following sections explain the experiment set ups that we created to (1) create the sidetones, (2) measure the sound pressure levels of the sidetones, and (3) to record and calculate the participant voice sound pressure levels, isolating it from the other sources of sound pressure.

Experiment 1 Set Up: Headset

Figure 5 shows a block diagram of the headset condition. The participant's voice was captured in two digital recorders. Recorder 1 (R_1) was placed about 1m away from the participant, so that limited movement of the participant's head would not significantly impact the captured voice loudness. We used the R_1 recordings for our analysis.

Additionally, we captured the signal from the boom microphone in Recorder 2 (R_2) so that we could monitor the source from which sidetone was generated. The switch allowed us to choose between sidetone levels (S), which for the head-

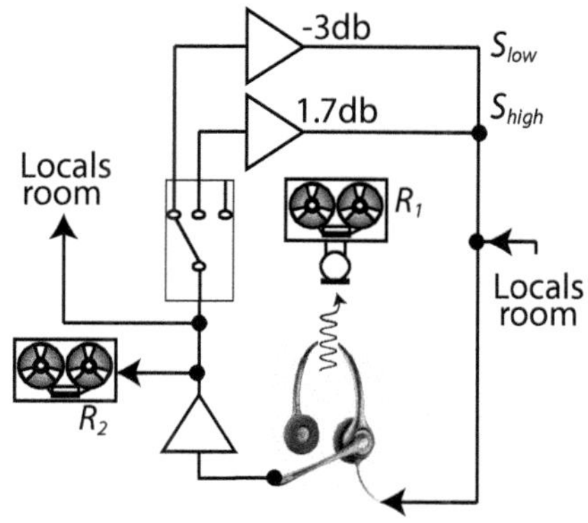

Figure 5: Experiment 1: Block diagram of the headset experiment set up.

set experiment were set to $S_{low} = -3db$ of the participant's voice level, and $S_{high} = 1.7db$. We chose these levels such that the low setting was just barely audible in the headset, while the high setting was clearly present. Sidetone was mixed with the voice from the experimenter seated in the locals room.

Headset Data Preparation Procedure In order to analyze the impact of sidetone on participant voice levels we needed to extract from R_1 the relative loudness of each participant when sidetone was administered, versus when they heard no sidetone. We generated these ratios as follows.

From R_1's *.wav* file recordings we extracted the amplitudes of R_1's stereo channels. We computed the root mean squares *rms* of each channel, and averaged the results to obtain rms_{no}, rms_{low}, and rms_{high} for each of the sidetone levels (no sidetone, low sidetone, and high sidetone). We then computed the sound pressure level ratios (L) in decibels without frequency weighting:

$$L_{high} = 20 * log_{10}(rms_{high}/rms_{no}) \quad (1)$$
$$L_{low} = 20 * log_{10}(rms_{low}/rms_{no})$$

Note that sidetone generation (Figure 5) involved microphones, the switch, amplification, and so on, which are all components that impact audio signals as they pass through. The quantification of sidetone levels that we selected by ear thus needed to be quantified via a calibration process, which we describe next.

Headset Sidetone Level Quantification Figure 6 shows the headset quantification procedure's two stages. First (Figure 6*a*), one of the authors read aloud one of the word lists while wearing the headset. The resulting audio signal was passed through the entire signal chain, with the switch set to generate no sidetone. The output was recorded via cable into R_1.

Next (Figure 6*b*), the recording was transferred to R_2 and replayed three times through the signal chain, once without sidetone, once with the switch set to generate S_{high}, and once to generate S_{low}. Each output was again recorded via cable into R_1. We then computed the *rms* for each recording, and used Equation 1 to quantify the sidetone levels. The results

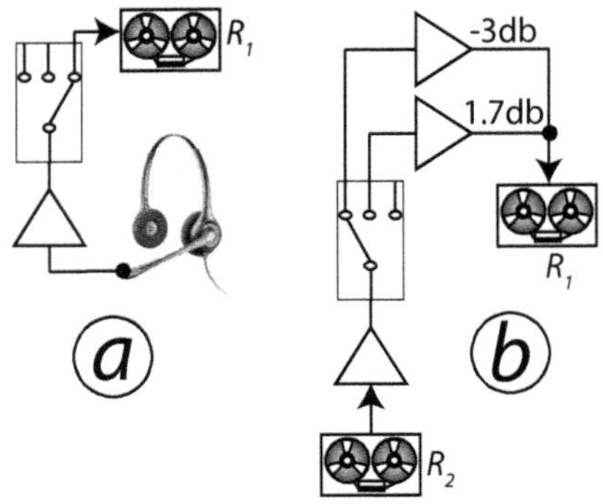

Figure 6: Experiment 1: Block diagram of the headset sidetone quantification procedure.

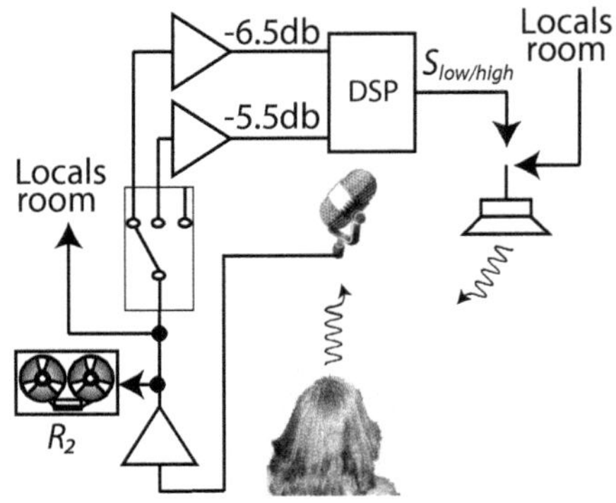

Figure 7: Experiment 2: Block diagram of the loudspeaker experiment set up.

were $S_{low} = -3db$, and $S_{high} = 1.7db$, a difference of approximately $5dB$.

Experiment 2 Set Up: Loudspeaker

Figure 7 shows our arrangement of the loudspeaker setting. The participant was again seated about 1m from the microphone, which in this setup was not R_1's microphone, but a table microphone. In contrast to the headset experiment, the sidetone signal passed through a digital signal processing (DSP) stage consisting of notch filters that eliminated some frequencies that caused audio feedback ringing. The loudspeaker was placed about 2m away from the participant, to the right and below a table on which the microphone rested. The table surface thus prevented point-to-point travel of the audio signal between the sidetone source and the microphone.

This separation served two purposes. First, it helped avoid acoustic feedback problems, and second, the audio signal's multi-path travel ensured that the participant's voice and their sidetone arrived at the microphone incoherently. This incoherence assured that we could use power addition in our signal analysis.

Loudspeaker Data Preparation Procedure The procedure for extracting the treatment effect in the loudspeaker condition was more complex than in the headset case. Note that the microphone in Figure 7 was exposed to both the participant's voice, and any sidetone signal that managed to travel via echo paths from the loudspeaker to the microphone; (the direct path was blocked by a table). This sidetone component needed to be separated from the participant's voice.

For clarity, we describe the math using low sidetone. High sidetone is analogous. Recall that S_{low} is a decibel value comparing sidetone with the signal from which the sidetone was generated. Let L_{voice} be the unknown participant voice sound pressure level in decibel relative to the standard 20μPa. L_Σ is the combination of the (incoherent) participant's voice and the sidetone. At the microphone, the (incoherent) participant's voice and sidetone combine as follows:

$$L_\Sigma = 10 * log_{10}(10^{(L_{voice}/10)} + 10^{(S_{low}/10)})$$

$$Therefore:$$

$$L_{voice} = 10 * log_{10}(10^{(L_\Sigma/10)} - 10^{(S_{low}/10)}) \quad (2)$$

We computed L_Σ as usual:

$$L_\Sigma = 20 * log_{10}(rms_{low}/rms_{no})$$

We used Equation 2 for our analysis. It provides the sound pressure level of the participant's speaking voice, excluding the sound pressure level of the sidetone manipulation.

Loudspeaker Sidetone Level Quantification Sidetone levels S_{low} and S_{high} were more constrained in the loudspeaker experiment than for the headset setup, because audio feedback leads to whistling when sidetone is too high. We adjusted S_{high} to be the highest possible in the room.

Figure 8 shows our procedure, which is analogous to the headset quantification. We recorded a reference wordlist recitation into R_2 without sidetone (not illustrated in the Figure). We then injected the resulting recording electronically into the signal chain from R_2. The recording was played three times, once without sidetone, and once with each of S_{low} and S_{high}. No acoustic signal other than the room's natural background noise were present. The desk microphone recorded the sidetone into R_1. We then again computed sidetone levels from the files' *rms* values. The results were $S_{low} = -6.5dB$ and $S_{high} = -5.5dB$.

Note that while these values lead to accurate ratio calculations for our eventual data analysis, they are not good indicators of sidetone levels that participants actually heard at their location. In an effort to provide a better intuition for their experience we performed acoustic measurements in parallel to the above described procedure.

While playing just sidetone through the loudspeaker, we used a commercial grade sound pressure level meter to measure pressure levels where the participants' heads would be during the actual experiments. Those levels came to $43dBA$ at low sidetone, and $45dBA$ at high sidetone setting. The room's noise floor was $37dBA$ at the time. Sidetone was thus clearly audible to participants.

Equipment and Implementation

The switch and all amplifiers in Figure 5 and Figure 7 were implemented with a Tascam M-164UF (*Mixer1*) and a Behringer Eurorack M802A *Mixer2* mixing board. These devices were daisy chained for the experiment. The pilot room mi-

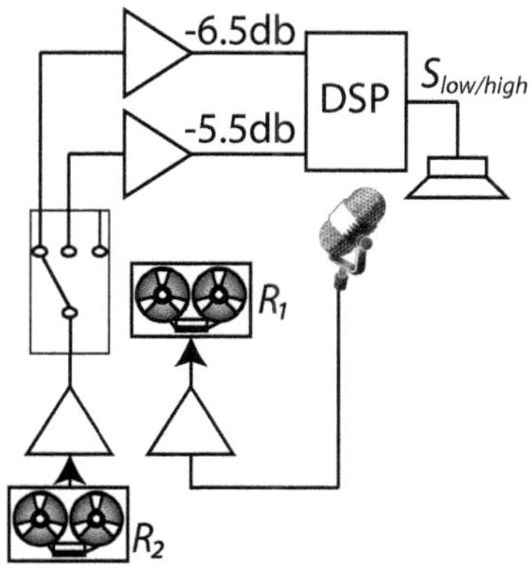

Figure 8: Experiment 2: Block diagram of the loudspeaker sidetone quantification procedure.

crophone were connected to *Mixer1*. That signal was routed to the locals room for communication with the experimenter.

Depending on the sidetone condition, the microphone signal was also routed channel 1, 2, or 3 of *Mixer2*. These channels were pre-adjusted to generate S_{no}, S_{low}, or S_{high}, respectively. When changing condition the experimenter would visit the pilot room and replug the patch cable that connected *Mixer1* to *Mixer2*. This reduced the chance of making mistakes in adjusting a single potentiometer.

In addition to the microphone signal from *Mixer1*, *Mixer2* received audio from the locals room (i.e. the experimenter's voice and the typing loop). The resulting mix of sidetone and the incoming locals signal drove the headset or loudspeaker in the participants' (pilot) room.

The pilot headset/boom microphone was an inexpensive Plantronics set with boom electret microphone. The desktop microphone used for the loudspeaker experiment was an AKG 414. R_1 was a Zoom model H4 digital recorder, R_2 was a Zoom model H4n recorder.

A Behringer 31 band Ultragraph FBQ-Pro 3102 graphic equalizer and Behringer Feedback Destroyer Pro provided acoustic feedback control in the loudspeaker experiment. These devices correspond to the DSP box in Figure 7. The sound pressure level meter used during the loudspeaker sidetone quantification procedure was a class 2 CEM model DT-8851.

RESULTS

Experiment 1: Headset

We ran repeated measures ANOVA, using the three sidetone levels (none, low, and high), and three task type levels (word list, warm up, and creativity) as within-participant independent variables. We introduced participant gender (two levels: female and male) as a between-participant factor. The dependent variable was sound pressure level in $dB(SPL)$ level.

Figure 9 shows our measurement results as we varied sidetone. The vertical axis indicates the $dB(SPL)$ of participants' speech, averaged over all participants and all tasks. Figure 10 shows our results by task, averaged across participants and sidetone levels.

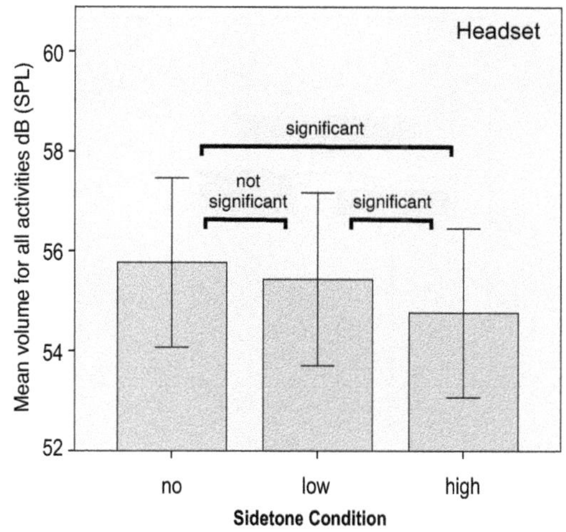

Figure 9: Speaking level averaged over participants across all sidetone settings in Experiment 1: Means and 95% confidence intervals.

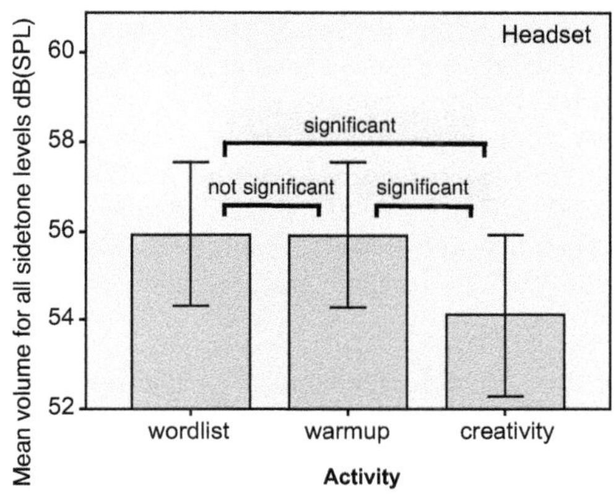

Figure 10: Speaking level averaged over participants across all tasks in Experiment 1: Means and 95% confidence intervals.

We found that sidetone level affected people's vocal sound pressure levels, $F(2,36) = 7.21$, $p<.01$. Planned contrasts identified (*i*) a significant difference between the high sidetone condition and the no sidetone condition, $F(1,18) = 13.25$, $p<.01$, (*ii*) a significant difference between the high sidetone condition and the low sidetone condition, $F(1,18) = 6.59$, $p<.05$, and (*iii*) a non-significant difference between the low sidetone condition and the no sidetone condition. That is, people spoke more quietly in the high sidetone situation.

We also found that task type affected people's vocal sound pressure levels: $F(2,36) = 5.61$, $p<.05$, Greenhouse-Geisser corrected to account for a violation of the ANOVA sphericity assumption. Planned contrasts revealed a significant difference between the creativity task and the other two task types, warmup ($F(1,18) = 23.40$, $p<.001$), and word list ($F(1,18) = 5.06$, $p<.05$). That is, people spoke most quietly when doing the creativity task. See Figure 10.

Gender and the interaction effects between task and sidetone were not found to be significant predictors of vocal sound pressure levels.

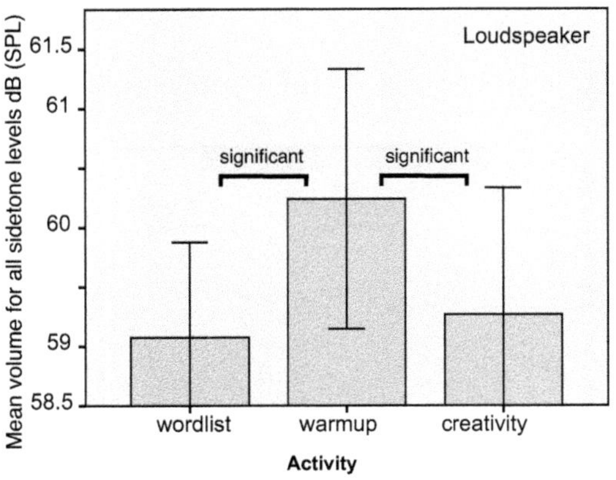

Figure 11: Speaking sound pressure level averaged over participants across all tasks in Experiment 2: Means and 95% confidence intervals.

Experiment 2: Loudspeaker

We performed the same ANOVA analysis on our loudspeaker data that we applied to the headset data. We found that task type affected people's vocal sound pressure levels, $F(2,24) = 3.63$, $p<.05$. Planned contrasts revealed a significant difference between the warmup task and the other two task types, creativity ($F(1,12) = 5.86$, $p<.05$) and word list ($F(1,12) = 5.76$, $p<.05$). That is, people produced higher sound pressure levels when doing the warmup task, which was relatively more socially oriented than the other two tasks. See Figure 11.

Sidetone level, gender, and interaction effects were not found to be significant predictors of people's vocal sound pressure levels.

DISCUSSION

For the headset condition we can compare our results against prior literature. The most striking aspect of our findings is that while we detected the expected statistically significant volume reducing impact of sidetone, the effect was smaller than was found in previous studies. Lane et al. [10] summarized ten sidetone experiments that mostly yielded slopes of around -0.5 for the linear function that describes the relationship between sidetone and speaker volume. Our observed slope is -0.1, a much reduced response. Only two of the ten studies found slopes as low as -0.25, and -0.3, respectively. Those studies administered sidetone monaurally, and they did not include any two-way communication tasks. Participants only read prepared passages.

In addition to the metastudy, Lane et al. conducted their own sidetone experiments [10]. We manually reproduced the sidetone portion of Lane's Figure 1, applied their x-axis shift to our sidetone levels, and reconstructed their original sidetone volume levels from their graph[1]. We then superimposed Lane's results with our mobile remote presence results.

Figure 12 shows Lane's results as squares against the right-hand side vertical axis. The current studies' results are the

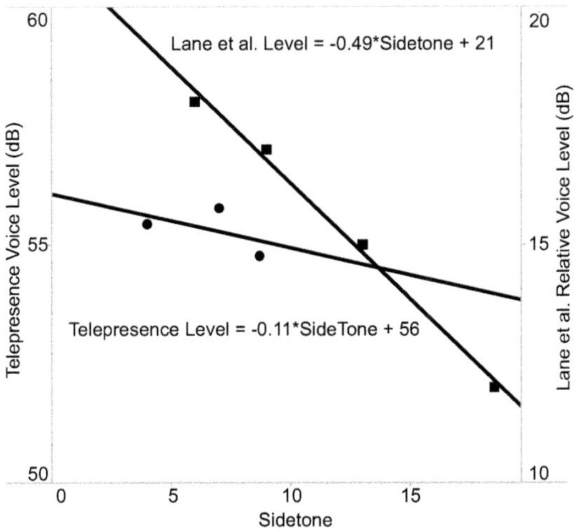

Figure 12: Comparison Lane et al. with this study's mobile remote presence sidetone effect.

circles, and correspond to the left-hand side vertical axis. The vertical shift of the graphs is immaterial for two reasons. First, Lane added a base noise level to their audio. Second, the differences in microphone distance from all the different participants' mouths cannot easily be controlled in any of the experiments because it is very difficult to control without forcing study participants into very artificially constraining physical configurations. These distance variations will cause corresponding variations in absolute speaker volumes. All sidetone studies examine the *relative* variations produced by each individual in response to the sidetone manipulation, so the differences in absolute level are unimportant.

An implication of the shallow slope in our results is that even for high sidetone, which in contrast to levels used in telephones was clearly noticeable, the attenuation effect was $1dB$. That difference is (by definition of the decibel unit) the smallest difference still noticeable through the human ear.

At $2dB$, the effect of task type was stronger. The effect supports Lane's claim that actual communication tasks (as opposed to read-aloud tasks) will strengthen sidetone effects. In computer-mediated communication settings such as this one, we care about actual communication tasks.

In the loudspeaker experiment, only the task effect was significant, although the warmup task traded places with creativity. In addition, the effect was reduced from $2dB$ to $1dB$. We hypothesize that the sidetone effect is weaker with loudspeakers than headsets because (1) sidetone might be interpreted as ambient noise when it is heard through loudspeakers, (2) the speaker's own voice might sound dissimilar enough from his or her in-head experience, and/or (3) acoustic feedback limits the amount of sidetone that one can generate via loudspeakers.

The tasks may have been different for several reasons. We noticed that people seemed to be quietly thinking aloud to themselves in the creativity task, which was different from trying to speak loud enough to communicate in the first two tasks. The creativity task seemed to be the most cognitively

[1] This reconstruction was simply the reversal of Lane's complementing their sidetone vs. volume function, which they had undertaken to facilitate slope comparisons with manipulations other than sidetone.

demanding and engaging. We hypothesize that the task type results changed between Experiment 1 and Experiment 2 because people may be more sensitive to the sidetone manipulations during the first task out; it may have felt more strange to hear sidetone from a loudspeaker rather than a headset.

The main difference between our study and the prior work is that we introduced visual contact between the participants and the experimenter. The majority of earlier sidetone studies limited contact to binaural or monaural communication channels, like telephones or pilot-ground communication links. One study that did include a visual component was Siegel et al. [19], which worked with three and four year old children (with caretakers present), who were spoke about picture books they knew well. This situation is quite different from the current adult telepresence scenario.

We suspect that the high fidelity, almost head size screen presence of conversation partners in our application interferes with the sidetone effect. Thus, our hypothesis is that visual clues weaken the influence of sidetone.

LIMITATIONS AND FUTURE WORK

The two experiments presented explored a focused set of independent variables in the task domain of mobile remote presence. We chose the independent variables of sidetone levels and sound device (headset vs. loudspeaker) because previous literature suggested that they would influence how loud people would speak through the MRP system. Other levels of sidetones with other sound devices should also be explored if we are to rely upon the model presented in Figure 12, which requires more data points before we can have more confidence in its regression model.

To test the hypothesis that the presence of the video display influences the strength of the sidetone effect, a follow-up experiment could manipulate the video display presence vs. absence as an independent variable. To test the generalizability of these findings, other potentially useful independent variables would include the types of local MRP acoustic environments, ambient noise levels, degrees of experience with using MRP systems, and the types of conversational settings.

For any given user experience issue, there are a wide variety of design directions that one could choose from. Other design directions that could be explored include: more proactive visual displays to indicate when a user is speaking too loudly, ambient auditory feedback (e.g., alerts), less invasive interfaces for locals to decrease MRP volume levels, more directional audio outputs on the MRP systems, etc. Other effects to measure include the speaking volume of the locals, not just the pilots; we have noticed that locals align their speaking volumes to match those of the pilots, often without realizing it. This exacerbates the problem of annoying local bystanders and is an issue that also needs to be addressed.

A very different approach to controlling speaking volume is to override the user's volume, using digital signal processing (DSP). DSPs use limiters and compressors [25], which are algorithms—implemented in hardware or software—that control the volume at which a sound signal will be reproduced through a loudspeaker or headphones. A compressor is set to a particular threshold, ensuring that an input signal does not excessively rise above that limit. Several parameters may be tuned to accommodate different types of sound materials. The most important is the *attack*, the speed with which the compressor will gain reduce an overly loud input signal. Another is the *release*, which is the amount of time the compressor will subsequently exert control over the signal. The third is the compression *ratio*, which is the amount of gain reduction the compressor will impose. A limiter is an extreme form of compression, in which a signal is guaranteed not to exceed the threshold at all. Many variations exist for these DSP approaches. As described in the introduction, all suffer from shortcomings when they are placed in acoustically highly unpredictable environments, but there is potential for exploration in this direction.

CONCLUSION

We set out to address the problem of mobile remote presence operators speaking too loudly through their MRP systems, which frustrated locals near the MRP. Using lessons from the telephone industry, we explored the effectiveness of using sidetones to provide auditory feedback to remote operators to subtly moderate their speaking volume levels. Prior studies examined sidetone under headset conditions, often using one-way read-aloud tasks. Our MRP scenario is more complex in that the roaming nature of the *ersatzperson* precludes the use of headphones for locals who interact with the remote pilots. In addition, the depth of conversational engagement through MRP systems is nearly comparable to face-to-face interactions so we used a set of more interactive tasks.

In the first experiment, we used headsets to check if sidetone effects would work at all through our MRP system. Indeed, it did. Remote pilots spoke more quietly when they heard high sidetones as opposed to low or no sidetones. Because many pilots actually do use headsets when operating MRP systems, this is a promising result for aiding those pilots in speaking at more appropriate volume levels through the MRP systems.

In the second experiment, we used loudspeakers instead of headsets because some remote pilots use loudspeakers when piloting MRPs. This is very different from prior work with telephone headsets. It was clear from the start that providing sidetone via loudspeakers would introduce audio feedback problems that would require significant engineering effort. Indeed, we had to change the sidetone levels to avoid screeching audio feedback problems. In this second experiment, we did not find evidence that these sidetones were helpful for aiding remote pilots (who use loudspeakers) in self-regulating their speaking loudness.

In both experiments we found that the task type influenced how loudly people spoke. This suggests that exploring a wider variety of communicative tasks could provide insight into the ways that mediating communication influences how people talk with one another.

In MRP and similar systems (e.g., video conferencing), the current studies provide support for the notion that sidetones could help with self-regulation of loudness by remote operators, who use headsets. However, we did not find evidence that sidetones would help remote operators, who use loudspeakers. This work presents the first test of sidetones in the mobile remote presence task domain.

Despite the widespread use of sidetones in landline telephones, it is rarely used in computer mediated communication settings. These prototypes and studies point us in the direction of reviving historically effective (though often forgotten) technologies for new application domains. Of course, these technologies will not necessarily work exactly the same way in the context of these new technological settings so it is important to evaluate these solutions in the new contexts before re-adopting them.

ACKNOWLEDGMENTS

Thanks go to the MRP project team and the participants in studies. Thanks also to Bill Smart for his writing guidance.

REFERENCES

1. American National Standards of the Acoustical Society of America. American National Standard method for measuring the intelligibility of speech over communication systems, May 2009.
2. M. Argyle. *Bodily Communication*. Methuen, New York, NY, 1975.
3. J. M. Beer and L. Takayama. Mobile remote presence systems for older adults: Acceptance, benefits, and concern. In *Proceedings of Human Robot Interaction: HRI*, pages 19–26, 2011.
4. H. Clark. *Using Language*. Cambridge University Press, Cambridge, UK, 1996.
5. D. Goodman and J. Johnston. Sidetone expansion for the regulation of talker loudness. *Electronics Letters*, 15(16):492 – 493, 1979.
6. J. Guilford, P. Christensen, P. Merrifield, and R. Wilson. Alternate uses task manual, 1978.
7. E. Hall. *The Hidden Dimension*. Doubleday, New York, NY, 1966.
8. E. S. Jones. Providing Foldback with Out-Of-Phase Loudspeakers. *Journal of the Audio Engineering Society*, 19(4):306–&, 1971.
9. N. P. Jouppi. First steps toward mutually-immersive mobile telepresence. In *Proceedings of Computer Supported Cooperative Work: CSCW*, pages 354–363, 2002.
10. H. Lane, B. Tranel, and C. Sisson. Regulation of voice communication by sensory dynamics. *Journal of the Acoustical Society of America*, 47:618 – 624, 1970.
11. M.-K. Lee and L. Takayama. "Now, I Have a Body": Uses and social norms for mobile remote presence in the workplace. In *Proceedings of Human Factors in Computing Systems: CHI*, 2011.
12. E. Lombard. Le signe de l'elevation de la voix. *Ann. maladies oreille larynx nez pharynx*, 37:109–119, 1911.
13. D. Nestel, P. Sains, C. Wetzel, C. Nolan, A. Tay, R. Kneebone, and A. Darzi. Communication skills for mobile remote presence technology in clinical interactions. *Journal of Telemed Telecare*, 13(2):100–104, 2007.
14. D. A. Norman. Minimizing the annoyance of the mobile phone, 2005.
15. E. Paulos and J. Canny. PRoP: Personal roving presence. In *Proceedings of Human Factors in Computing Systems: CHI*, pages 296–303, 1998.
16. B. Reeves and C. Nass. *The media equation: How people treat computers, television, and new media like real people and places*. Cambridge University Press, 1996.
17. D. Sakamoto, T. Kanda, T. Ono, H. Ishiguro, and N. Hagita. Android as a telecommunication medium with a human-like presence. In *Proceedings of Human Robot Interaction: HRI*, pages 193–200, 2007.
18. G. Siegel and H. Pick Jr. Auditory feedback in the regulation of voice. *Journal of the Acoustical Society of America*, 56(5):1618 – 1624, 1974.
19. G. M. Siegel, H. L. Pick, M. G. Olsen, and L. Sawin. Auditory feedback in the regulation of vocal intensity of preschool children. *Developmental Psychology*, 12(3):255–261, 1976.
20. L. Takayama and C. Pantofaru. Influences on proxemic behaviors in human-robot interaction. In *Proceedings of Intelligent Robotic Systems: IROS*, pages 5495–5502, St. Louis, MO, USA, 2009.
21. L. Takayama, J. G. Sison, B. Lathrop, N. Wolfe, A. Chiang, A. Nielsen, and C. Nass. Bringing design considerations to the mobile phone and driving debate. In *Proceedings of Human Factors in Computing Systems: CHI*, pages 1643–1646, 2009.
22. D. Tannen. *You Just Don't Understand: Women and Men in Conversation*. Harper Paperbacks, 2001.
23. K. Tsui, M. Desai, H. A. Yanco, and C. Uhlik. Exploring use cases for telepresence robots. In *Proceedings of Human Robot Interaction: HRI*, pages 11–18, 2011.
24. G. Venolia, J. Tang, R. Cervantes, S. Bly, G. Robertson, B. Lee, and K. Inkpen. Embodied social proxy: Mediating interpersonal connection in hub-and-satellite teams. In *Proceedings of Human Factors in Computing Systems: CHI*, pages 1049–1058, 2010.
25. Wikipedia. Dynamic range compression.
26. M. Wolff. *Peoples In Places: The Sociology Of The Familiar*, chapter Notes On The Behaviour Of Pedestrians, pages 35–48. Praeger, 1975.
27. N. Wolfinger. Notes on the behaviour of pedestrians. *Journal of Contemporary Ethnography*, 24:323–340, 1995.

A Tongue Input Device for Creating Conversations

Ronit Slyper, Jill Lehman, Jodi Forlizzi, Jessica Hodgins
Disney Research Pittsburgh and Carnegie Mellon University
Pittsburgh, PA
{rys,jef,forlizzi,jkh}@cs.cmu.edu

Figure 1: Our tongue joystick allows an actor to invisibly select prerecorded audio clips, letting the articulated-head dragon converse with children in its own voice.

ABSTRACT

We present a new tongue input device, the tongue joystick, for use by an actor inside an articulated-head character costume. Using our device, the actor can maneuver through a dialogue tree, selecting clips of prerecorded audio to hold a conversation in the voice of the character. The device is constructed of silicone sewn with conductive thread, a unique method for creating rugged, soft, low-actuation force devices. This method has application for entertainment and assistive technology. We compare our device against other portable mouth input devices, showing it to be the fastest and most accurate in tasks mimicking our target application. Finally, we show early results of an actor inside an articulated-head costume using the tongue joystick to interact with a child.

ACM Classification: H5.2 [Information interfaces and presentation]: User Interfaces. - Input devices and strategies.

General terms: Design, Human Factors

Keywords: mouth, interface, dialogue tree, turn-taking.

INTRODUCTION

Theme parks have the goal of bringing characters to life by having them act out and describe their stories. Many of the costumed characters, however, cannot converse with guests. Actors in these costumes wear large fur or plastic head pieces that prevent them from talking. Several of the characters also have highly recognizable accents and speech patterns, which actors cannot replicate accurately. These characters are reduced to using body language and gestures to communicate.

Articulation abilities have recently been added to some of these costumes. Motors in the eyes and mouth let them open and shut, as shown in Figure 1. This technology is currently used in shows in the Disney parks, where the mouth moves in sync with prerecorded audio coming out of loudspeakers.

We would like to use this articulation technology to allow these characters to converse directly with guests. Because these characters have such distinct voices, the actors inside the costumes will need to trigger context-appropriate prerecorded audio snippets. This situation suggests using a dialogue tree and a heads-up display inside the costume to show the current location in the tree. Although a dialogue tree cannot cover the full scope of conversation, the theme parks present a constrained situation. Actors for the current talking characters in the park (e.g., princesses) tell us that conversations with guests tend to be character-driven: children frequently turn shy and let the actor lead the conversation; and when children actively interact, they ask the same questions (e.g., princesses are always asked where their prince is).

In this paper, we are primarily concerned with the input device that the actor inside the costume will use to navigate a dialogue tree with a branching factor of four. We consider four to be the minimum number of responses to hold a reasonable conversation: if a character asks a question, the guest's response can be categorized as 1) affirmative, 2) negative, 3) other (question-dependent), or 4) uncooperative; the character should have a response ready for any of these four cases.

Common input devices are not usable in this selection task, because they rely on the hands. A character's hands are visible at all times, waving, gesturing, and signing autographs. Instead, we seek an input method using the mouth. We need a device that has a low error rate and is fast enough to enable smooth conversations.

We compare three mouth input devices, using breath, teeth, and tongue. For breath, we use the leading portable mouth input device for people with quadriplegia, the sip/puff switch.

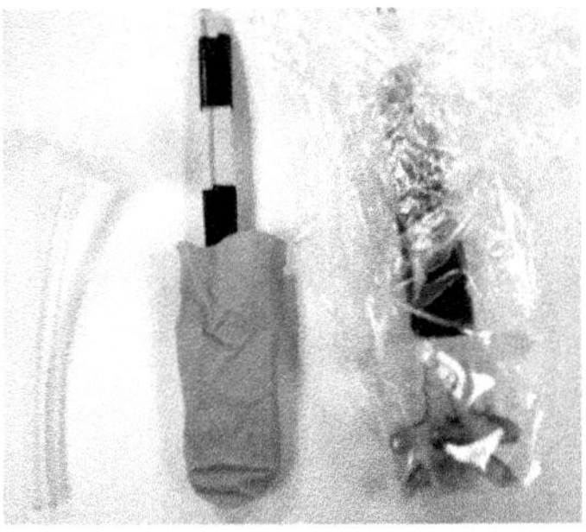

Device	Direction			
	Left	Right	Up	Down
Sip/puff switch	soft puff	hard puff	soft sip	hard sip
Bite senor	two short bites	short long	long short	long long
Tongue joystick	press left	press right	press up	press down

Figure 2: All three devices, ready for testing. From left to right: sip/puff mouthpiece, bite sensor, and tongue joystick. Four-direction selection is accomplished using the actions in the table.

For the teeth, we built a binary bite sensor. For the tongue, we built a new device. Its construction demonstrates using rapid prototyping and an unconventional combination of silicone and conductive thread as a flexible method for creating cheap, low-actuation-force devices.

We tested these devices with a user study that mimics aspects of our target application. The study included a speed test and a conversational interaction using a four-branch dialogue tree. Figure 2 summarizes how each device was used to select among the four directions. We found the tongue joystick to be both the fastest and most accurate. Dialogue latencies when using the tongue joystick ranged from 3 to 4 seconds, which is fast enough to hold a conversation with a child [6]. No significant difference was found between the bite sensor and the sip/puff switch.

Our results have implications for the study of physical and situational impairments [27]. We show that the tongue is agile enough to select among multiple discrete locations, and thus should be further explored as an input device for people with quadriplegia or who otherwise cannot use their hands. Although preliminary work has been done in the area of capturing tongue gestures [26, 12], we are the first to test a form factor that requires no customization or attachment to the user.

In the following section, we describe less common input methods, and show why we converged on the *mouth* as the best high-degree-of-freedom input modality for this situation. Next we describe the three mouth devices. We detail the protocol of our user study to compare them, and show the results of the study. Based on the results, we select the tongue joystick to incorporate in a functional prototype system for an articulated character head. We conclude with possibilities for future work, both in our application and in assistive technology.

RELATED WORK

Nearly all of our computer interfaces today – keyboard, mouse, touchscreen, driving wheel, button pad, gamepad – rely on fine dexterity in the hands. In our application, however, the hands cannot be used for input. An actor's hands must be free to interact with guests.

The human voice also has incredible degrees of freedom. Unfortunately, we found that sound transmits easily through our character head, ruling out standard voice recognition or nonverbal command inputs such as vowel [3] or duration of sound [13]. Whisper recognition or throat-microphone input would be possible, but to achieve high levels of accuracy, command phrases would need to be several syllables in length and easily differentiable, e.g. "show me A", "select option B", inducing a confusing lack of parallelism as well as slowing down the system.

Interfaces developed for people with physical disabilities show that other parts of the body can be used to communicate with computers. Any feature that can be tracked in two dimensions can serve as a substitute for the mouse. Head tracking can be done with an infrared camera [21] or with an inexpensive webcam [2, 18]. Eye tracking, using infrared reflection [8] or electrooculography [17, 7], requires less movement, but any type of eye-based input will monopolize the actor's attention. This compromise is acceptable for assistive technology, but not for our application, where the actor must attend to the child.

Any high-level voluntary movements that can be captured can be used for switch input. Examples include foot switches, eyebrow switches, and blink switches. These would be awkward or tiring to accomplish in costume.

Low-level signals from the body also present interesting opportunities. Electromyography (EMG) has been used to control artificial limbs [16]; attempts have been made to use it for mouse input [14] and wheelchair control [10]. Electrical skin potential has been tested as a switch input, but provides low accuracy [19, 20]. Brain-computer interfaces continue to make progress, although they lack the speed and accuracy required for our application. Current research efforts involve techniques such as fMRI, electroencephalography (EEG), and electrocorticography (ECoG); see [11] and [29] for good overviews.

The mouth provides numerous methods of input; some of these can even provide direct spatial mapping. Sip/puff interfaces provide a single degree of freedom, but are portable and easy to use. BLUI [24] is an interface that extends the idea of using blowing as a means of input, but adds a spatial dimension, using a microphone to plot the location of a puff on a laptop screen. Breath can also be spatio-located using thermotransducers [9] and piezo film sensors [15]; the latter work adds selection using tooth-touch recognition with a bone-conduction microphone.

Non-portable mouth devices commonly in use include joysticks, manipulated with the chin, lips, or tongue [5], and mouth sticks, held in the mouth and used to tap directly on a keyboard or touch screen.

Our work was inspired by Huo and Ghovanloo's Tongue Drive System [12]. The system consists of headgear containing magnetic sensors, and a small magnet affixed to the user's tongue. Voluntary motions of the tongue are classified and translated into powered-wheelchair control commands. We were drawn to this system for several reasons. First, as Huo and Ghovanloo point out, tongue muscle is similar to heart muscle, not tiring easily. In our application, we must be wary of repetitive stress injuries. Second, the tongue is very fast. In a similar setup, Struijk [1] constructed a retainer with embedded coils inductively triggered by the proximity of a magnet attached to the tongue. Due to the stringent safety requirements of our application, we sought a self-contained device without the risk of swallowing a magnet.

Recent work by Saponas et al. [26] uses optical infrared sensors to recognize four tongue gestures. The proximity sensors are placed in the right, left, front, and back of a dental retainer. Simple heuristics based on the pattern and timing of triggering are used to recognize one of four tongue gestures: left swipe, right swipe, tap up, and hold up. The 92% accuracy subjects achieved shows this approach to be promising. The Tongue-touch keypad [22], a custom-molded dental plate containing nine buttons, was briefly on the market. The Tonguepoint [25], a mouthpiece containing an isometric joystick, showed that tongue dexterity improves with practice. These devices all require a custom retainer to achieve a low profile, but still present reasonable alternatives to our device.

DEVICES

Our target application, real-time conversational interaction, created a set of requirements for our input device:

Speed: The device must be fast and impose low cognitive load, as the actor will be simultaneously acting and conversing.

Accuracy: Wrong selections would either trigger non sequiters or slow down a conversation as the actor navigates backwards in the dialogue tree; the device must have near-perfect accuracy.

Portability: The device must be self-contained and fit inside the costume.

User independence: For convenient and low-cost testing and replacement, the device will preferably not be customized to fit a particular actor.

Ruggedness and safety: Character costumes are in use day in and day out; the device must be designed without weak points.

We explore which of the three input modalities of the mouth – the breath, teeth, and tongue – can be used to best meet these requirements. We represent these three modalities by portable input devices that attempt to make optimal use of their affordances: a sip/puff switch (breath), bite sensor (teeth), and tongue joystick (tongue). We present details of the devices in the following three sections.

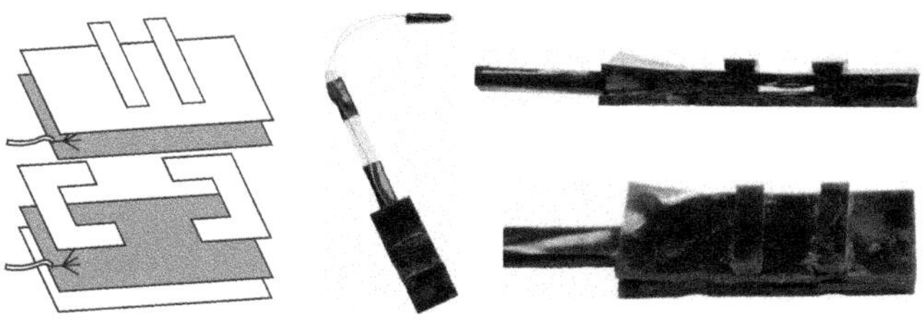

Figure 3: *Left*, an exploded view of the bite sensor's construction; white layers are insulating rubber, grey layers are conductive tape with attached wires. *Center*, the finished bite sensor with mounting stick. *Right*, side and top view.

Sip/puff switch

We used an off-the-shelf USB sip/puff switch from Origin Instruments Corporation [23]. Each subject in our study was given a new filtered mouthpiece when testing the device.

Four-direction selection with the device was done using soft puff, hard puff, soft sip, and hard sip to represent left, right, up, and down, respectively. This combination of breath force and direction is a common way to get four commands. Only the maximum (or minimum) value of the force signal was relevant, not the duration. Softness and hardness were assigned using pre-determined thresholds. Signals less than 80 milliseconds long were dropped as transient.

Bite sensor

Commercial binary bite switches are used for skydiving photography and in cases of severe disability, e.g. ventilator dependence. These switches cost around $100 [4]. Figure 3 shows the construction of our lower-cost switch. We use $\frac{1}{16}$"-thick polyurethane rubber, Shore 60A, and conductive adhesive tape. Thin top rectangles let the user locate the bite area by feel. For each study participant, the bite sensor was covered in a new piece of thin nitrile (a finger cut off an examination glove).

For four-direction control on this one-bit device, we used bite duration to add a second bit. The four directions were represented by the four combinations of short ($<$ 200ms) or long ($\geq$ 200ms) bite followed quickly (in $<$ 500ms) by another short or long bite.

Tongue joystick

We designed a new device for the tongue that captures our goals of portability and user independence. Although we could have used any number of sensing technologies, e.g. camera-based tracking, or the magnetic or infrared sensors from previous tongue work, we chose binary switches because they require minimal processing time and encourage the user to be speedy by providing a tactile "click" as soon as a gesture has been accomplished.

For the form factor, we looked for inspiration to other objects that we manipulate in our mouths: we chew on gum, lick lollipops, bite pencil erasers and worry pen clips; and, as babies,

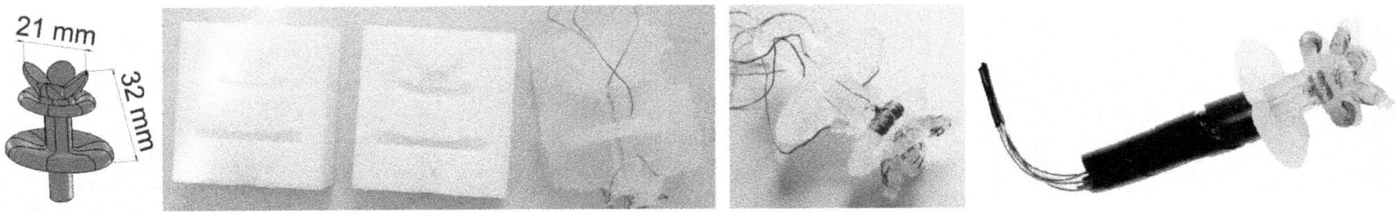

Figure 4: The tongue joystick molding process. From left to right: 3D model; tongue joystick coming out of the printed mold; contact pads being sewn out of the embedded conductive thread; the finished product.

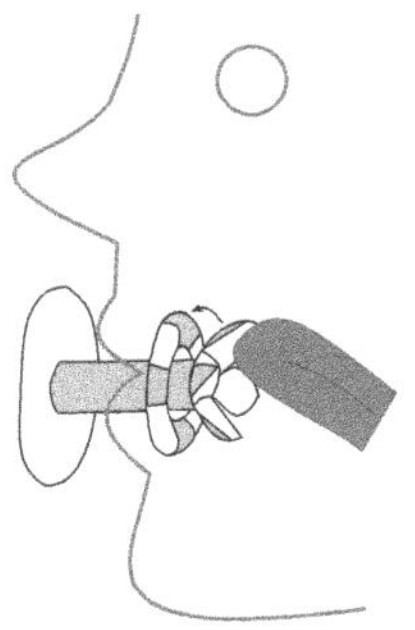

Figure 5: The user bites on the stem (grey), then pushes one of the petals with his tongue (red). The petal contains a contact pad (cyan) which touches the ring beneath, also containing a contact pad (cyan).

we suck on pacifiers. The pacifier turned out to be the perfect inspirational form factor – it is designed to lodge itself securely in a baby's mouth, with the baby's cheeks and gums braced in the stem between the bulbous tip and cheek guard.

Our device is shaped like a pacifier, but with the bulbous tip turned into a flower shape with a ring and four "petals". The tongue can easily align itself perpendicularly to a petal to push on it, as shown in Figure 5. (An early test using a four-directional joystick inserted in a pacifier had shown that though the tongue is dexterous, it actually cannot exert much sideways force.)

Figure 4 shows the steps in the construction of the tongue joystick. We designed the device in a 3D modeling program, and 3D-printed a plastic mold. To build the device, we fixed four strands of conductive thread to the inside edges of the mold, and one going through the center. We then poured Shore 40A RTV silicone into the mold. The device was cured and demolded. Then for each strand protruding from the silicone, we threaded it onto a needle, and "sewed" contact pads using the silicone as "fabric". The central conductive thread was sewn to the undersides of the top petals, forming the ground layer for the contact switches. The four outside threads were each sewn to a segment of ring beneath a petal, creating the signal layer.

This combination of materials – silicone and e-textile's conductive thread – creates a device which is completely soft and basically unbreakable. The silicone switches close with a low enough actuation pressure that they can be comfortably pressed by the tongue. Typical low-actuation pushbutton components close around 150 gram force; our switches close around 50 gram force.

Four-direction control is achieved through direct spatial mapping. In the study, signals less than 50 milliseconds long were dropped as transient. We covered the device in a new piece of plastic wrap for each subject in the user study; in production, the device would have a removable thin stretchy silicone skin in the shape of its convex hull.

USER STUDY

We evaluate these three devices with tasks involving four-directional selection. In this setting, these devices represent different tradeoffs between cognitive load and motor complexity.

The tongue joystick has a direct spatial layout and thus the lowest cognitive load. While this spatial layout inherently biases our study in favor of the tongue joystick, it is the goal of the study to test whether the tongue has enough accuracy and agility to allow this lower cognitive load to dominate its performance.

The sip/puff switch, inversely, has the highest cognitive load. Its two-word prompts (e.g. "hard sip") must be combined along two dimensions (soft vs. hard, puff vs. sip) to produce a motor action.

The bite sensor also uses a combination prompt (e.g. "long short"), but each word maps to an independent motor action modulated only by time (short vs. long). Thus the bite sensor should have a slightly lower cognitive load. The bite sensor also has the simplest motor action, a bite, requiring little physical agility.

We have the following hypotheses:

1. The joystick will be the fastest, as it has a direct mapping from prompt to motor action.

2. The bite sensor, with a smaller cognitive load, will start out faster than the sip/puff switch. After a learning period where the sip/puff prompts are internalized, the results should flip, as sip/puff signals are shorter.

Experimental Design

The sip/puff switch, bite sensor, and tongue joystick were compared using a within-subjects design, counterbalanced for device order. Twenty-four users (11 women and 13 men, ranging in age from 18 to 58) participated. Users were recruited from an on-campus behavioral research subject pool and were paid $15 for the one hour study.

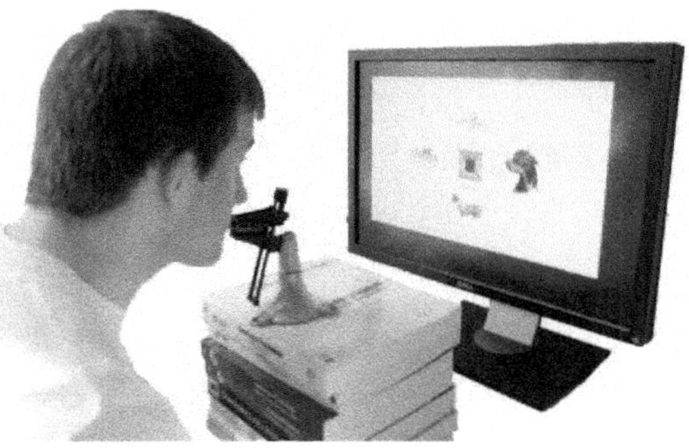

Figure 6: A subject performs a forced-choice four-direction speed test of the tongue joystick.

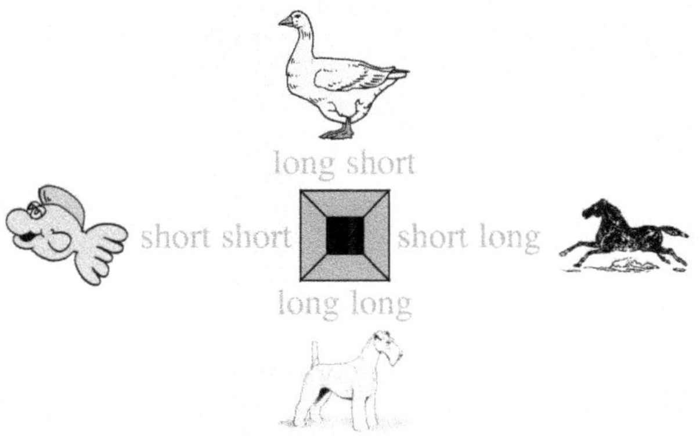

Figure 7: The Animals task with prompts for the bite sensor.

Figure 6 shows the experimental setup. Devices were clamped at mouth height. Stimuli were presented on screen and consisted of four choices encircling a segmented central square with text reminders of the selection method. When a direction was chosen, feedback was provided by temporarily changing the color of the associated segment.

For each device in turn, subjects performed a Spelling and an Animal selection task. In the Spelling task, the device was explained and demonstrated to the subject, who then used it to spell six four-letter words. The correct letter occurred equally often in each of the four positions. Subjects were required to correct mistakes, thus ensuring a basic level of mastery of the device.

In the Animals task, we tested the response time of the device in combination with an audio prompt and changing selections, thus mimicking our target application. Subjects saw four new black and white animal pictures in each trial (Figure 7) and were given an audio prompt, 250ms later, of "bird", "horse", "dog", or "fish". Although subjects were asked to do as many trials as possible in ten minutes, all subjects received fifteen blocks of four trials, with a four second rest period between blocks.

After performing both tasks, subjects filled out a device questionnaire with a seven point scale for each of speed (slow/fast), accuracy (inaccurate/accurate), lack of fatigue (tiring/not tiring), and ease of use (confusing/easy to understand).

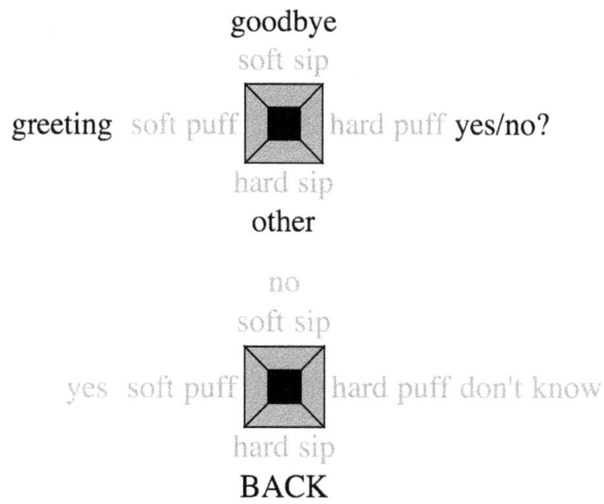

Figure 8: The two-level dialogue tree: category selection is shown at top; response selection for the category "yes/no?" is shown at bottom.

After testing each device, subjects performed a Dialogue task. Subjects were asked to choose one device to use for holding three conversations with a computer agent named Katie. Katie took four turns. For each of Katie's turns, the subject first assigned Katie's speech to one of the categories "greeting", "yes/no question", "goodbye", or "other" (Figure 8, *top*). Subjects then saw three within-category options for their response and the "back" option in case they wished to re-categorize Katie's speech (Figure 8, *bottom*). When one of the response options was chosen, an audio file with that meaning was played aloud, and the screen reset to the category level.

A final questionnaire asked for ranked comparisons of the three devices using the superlative of the four scales (fastest, most accurate, least tiring, and easiest to understand). Subjects also provided general comments about their experiences and preferences.

RESULTS

We give results of the Animals and Dialogue tasks, followed by summaries of the surveys.

Animals Task

The tongue joystick proved the fastest and most accurate in the Animals task. Means and standard deviations for reaction time, measured from the onset of the visual prompt, are reported in Table 1. A repeated measures ANOVA showed

Device	N	Reaction Time (ms)		Error Rate
		Mean	Std Dev	
Sip/puff	24	3186	1721	23%
Bite sensor	24	3016	1258	20%
Tongue joystick	24	2065	880	10%

Table 1: Reaction times for the Animals task for all subjects.

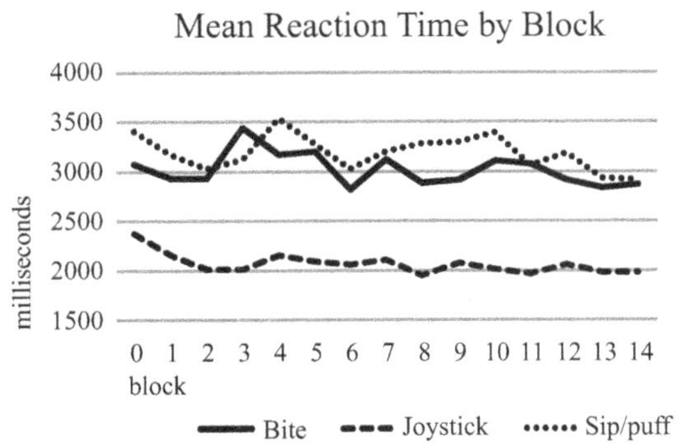

Figure 9: Average reaction times of the twenty-four subjects across the fifteen blocks of the Animals task.

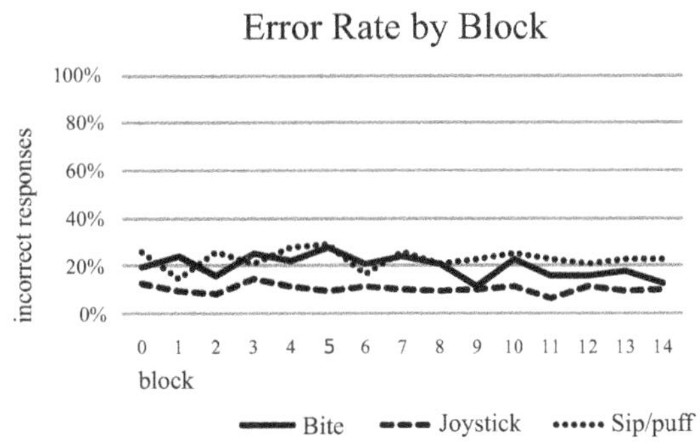

Figure 10: Average error rates of the twenty-four subjects across the fifteen blocks of the Animals task.

that device significantly affected reaction time ($F(2, 22) = 42.27$, $p < .001$). Bonferroni-corrected pairwise comparisons showed the joystick to be significantly faster than the bite sensor ($p < .001$) and the sip/puff switch ($p < .001$). No significant difference was found between the latter two devices. Thus only the first of our hypotheses, not the second, was borne out. We conjecture that subjects were still mastering the bite sensor and the sip/puff switch during the fifteen blocks; the variability in reaction times for these two devices, seen in Figure 9, supports this view. In contrast, subjects learned the tongue joystick quickly and had consistently less variability. In future work, we plan to extend our study, looking for trends over a longer time period.

The joystick was the most accurate (Bonferroni-corrected, $p = .024$ vs. bite, $p = .001$ vs. sip/puff); no significant difference in error rates was found between the other two devices. Error rates by block are given in Figure 10. An analysis of the confusion matrices revealed that subjects had the most trouble with the "short long" and "long short" prompts for the bite sensor, and with thresholding soft versus hard for the sip/puff switch. This result supports our conjecture that subjects were still in transition for the two devices.

Dialogue Task

The Dialogue task recreates a language understanding component closer to our target application. For this task, 17 (71%) of the subjects chose to use the joystick, 5 (21%) chose the sip/puff switch, and 2 (8%) chose the bite sensor.

	Category (action)	Response Latency (ms) Mean	Std Dev	Error
Social	greeting (left)	3552	1832	0%
	bye (up)	3412	1582	6%
Content	yes/no (right)	4129	2695	14%
	other (down)	4198	2494	20%

Table 2: Average milliseconds taken by the twelve joystick subjects to navigate through the two-level tree, grouped by top level (category) and type of response (social vs. content).

Error rates were computed based only on category selection; Katie would reply cooperatively to any second-level response. Several of the subjects simply did not understand the task; because our interest is the viability of the device when used by a skilled performer, we eliminated from our analysis any subject whose error rate was above 25%. This elimination left 12 joystick users, 1 sip/puff user, and 2 bite sensor users. With such small numbers for two devices, we analyze only the tongue joystick results.

Table 2 shows mean response latencies and error rates for the tongue joystick, grouped by category. Latency is defined as the time from the end of Katie's speech, through category selection, to final response selection.

The difference in response latency between social and content categories was not significant. Error rates were significantly different between social and content categories ($F(1, 11) = 12.78$, $p = .004$). This significance is not attributable to direction, which showed no comparable pattern in the Animals task.

Overall, subjects took about 3.8 seconds to compose a response (two selections at about 2 seconds per selection), with 90% accuracy, roughly in line with their Animals task results.

User Surveys

Figure 11 shows the mean ratings for the individual surveys. On every dimension, the joystick was rated significantly better than the bite sensor (Bonferroni-corrected, $p < .05$ for each) and comparable to or significantly better than the sip/puff switch ($p < .05$ for accuracy only). Users did not rate the joystick significantly faster than the sip/puff switch, despite the better joystick timings.

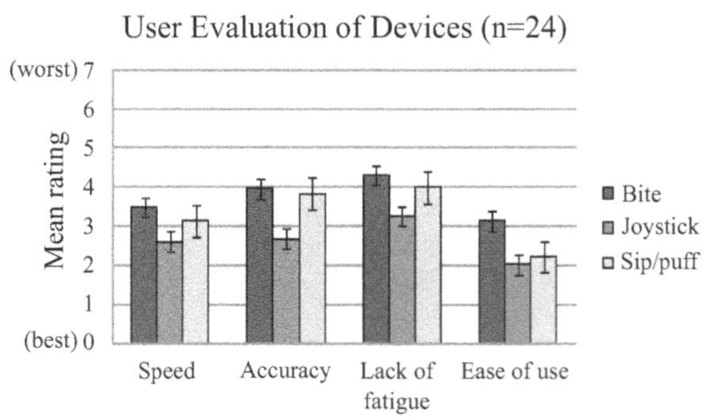

Figure 11: Average ratings given by subjects to each device after testing it in the Animals task.

Ordering	Fastest	Most accurate	Least tiring	Easiest
joy > bite > sip	8	10	4	9
joy > sip > bite	2	4	2	4
bite > joy > sip	2		2	1
bite > sip > joy		1		
sip > joy > bite	3	2	7	
sip > bite > joy	3	1	3	4

Table 3: Frequencies of the six device orderings for each category in the final comparative rankings (18 subjects completed the survey correctly).

After the Dialogue task, users provided a set of comparative rankings, tabulated in Table 3. Preferences at the end of the study mirror earlier judgments. The joystick was ranked better than the bite sensor for all characteristics (Wilcoxon Signed Rank, $p < .05$ for all), but was ranked significantly higher than the sip/puff device only for accuracy ($p < .01$). No comparisons between the bite sensor and sip/puff switch were significant.

ARTICULATED CHARACTER HEAD PROTOTYPE SYSTEM

We incorporated the tongue joystick into a system prototype using the custom articulated-head dragon shown in Figure 1. We built a heads-up display that lodges in the character's snout, and designed a dialogue tree appropriate for interacting with a young child (Figure 12). The actor holds the tongue joystick in her mouth while donning the dragon head. When she presses one of the petals in the tongue joystick, feedback is shown on the heads-up display; if a line of audio is triggered, it plays out of a speaker while the mouth moves automatically to prerecorded puppeteering. All hardware is connected through an external laptop.

As shown in the accompanying video, where the dragon meets a 6-year-old girl, the actor is able to use the tongue joystick quickly enough to engage in smooth, natural turntaking using prerecorded audio. The dialogue-tree system excels at constrained situations where responses are predictable, such as knock-knock jokes and simple questions such as "What's your favorite color?" We thus optimized the tree for taking the initiative to control the conversation and guide it down one of these paths. This situation mirrors that of our target application, where conversations with characters in the theme parks are usually character driven. The tree also had a branch containing responses such as yes, no, and thanks.

From our trial sessions, we learned that we need to more thoroughly examine the dynamic of conversation with children. We rapidly learned that one often needs to repeat a phrase until they focus enough to hear. Also, having a supply of giggles and other phatic expressions that could be inserted into a dialogue path without interrupting it would cover most awkwardnesses.

DISCUSSION AND CONCLUSION

We presented a new tongue input device, the tongue joystick, for maneuvering within a dialogue tree to select pieces of prerecorded audio. The device has a pacifier form factor which makes it both user-independent and firmly grippable for speed and accuracy. In building the tongue joystick, we developed a new method of constructing rugged, soft, low-actuation force devices by using both molding and sewing techniques to combine soft silicone and flexible conductive thread. Our hope is that this method will be useful to the assistive technology community in designing new devices.

The form factor and manufacturing method of our tongue joystick are amenable to easily incorporating other sensors: a bite switch could be located in the stem, for example, or a sip/puff tube embedded in the middle. Airflow and weight must be considered in any design, however. The device fit inside the dragon head, but the wires reduced the head mobility of the actor; we plan to build our next prototype with a wireless chip and small battery embedded in the cheek guard.

Our study design attempted to balance speed and accuracy. We urged subjects to work quickly, but did not penalize them for wrong answers. The error rate for the tongue joystick, 10%, was thus very high. In future work, we will run studies that isolate reaction time and error rate, giving a better lower bound for each while helping us better understand learning and fatigue effects. Future studies will also train users longer so that they will be closer to the "expert" user expected in our application.

The current user study showed that subjects were able to use the tongue joystick to respond to conversational turns with pauses around 3-4 seconds. Our articulated character head prototype system showed that a skilled actor could control conversational turns even faster. The maximum amount of latency that avoids conversational awkwardness is situation dependent; for instance, while cross-cultural analysis has shown that adults minimize the silence between turns [28], at least one study has demonstrated that 7-10 year olds will converse cooperatively with an animated character with a 3-4 second response latency. Our application has more resilience than standard conversation, as the actor can cover pauses with physical acting. In our prototype testing, a case arose where the actor did not have audio for a particular situation; she switched from dialogue to solely physical acting for several minutes without the child noticing the transitions. Thus with a combination of lively acting, expressive costumes, and our tongue joystick, we hope to bring a new set of characters to life.

REFERENCES

1. L. Andreasen Struijk. An inductive tongue computer interface for control of computers and assistive devices. *IEEE Transactions on Biomedical Engineering*, 53(12):2594–2597, 2006.

2. M. Betke, J. Gips, and P. Fleming. The camera mouse: visual tracking of body features to provide computer access for people with severe disabilities. *IEEE Transactions on Neural Systems and Rehabilitation Engineering*, 10:1–10, 2002.

3. J. Bilmes, X. Li, J. Malkin, K. Kilanski, R. Wright, K. Kirchhoff, A. Subramanya, S. Harada, J. Landay, P. Dowden, and H. Chizeck. The vocal joystick: a voice-based human-computer interface for individuals with motor impairments. In *Conference on Human*

```
3 (chcknjoke) "I have a joke. Do you want to hear it?"
  1 (Yes:Xroad?) "Why did the dragon cross the road?"
    1 (punch) "Because...chickens weren't invented yet!"
    2 (answr:hey) "Hey, how did you know that?"
    3 (nope:punch) "Nope! 'Cause chickens weren't invented yet!"
  2 (No:Sad) "No? But it's such a funny joke. I'm sad."
```

Figure 12: A snippet of dialogue tree, shown on the heads-up display normally lodged in the dragon's snout. The display contains a collimating lens so that the actor's eyes do not need to refocus between the screen and child.

Language Technology and Empirical Methods in Natural Language Processing, pages 995–1002. Association for Computational Linguistics, 2005.

4. Broadened Horizons. Bite Switch, 2011. broadenedhorizons.com.
5. Broadened Horizons. QuadMouse, 2011. broadenedhorizons.com.
6. C. Darves and S. Oviatt. Adaptation of users' spoken dialogue patterns in a conversational interface. In *International Conference on Spoken Language Processing*, pages 561–564, 2002.
7. P. DiMattia and J. Gips. Eagleeyes: Technologies for non-verbal persons. In K. Thies and J. Travers, editors, *Handbook of Human Development for Health Care Professionals*, pages 429–448. Jones and Bartlett, 2005.
8. EnableMart. EyeTech TM2, 2009. enablemart.com.
9. G. Evreinov and T. Evreinova. "Breath-joystick" – graphical manipulator for physically disabled users. In *International Conference on Computers Helping People with Special Needs*, pages 193–200, 2000.
10. T. Felzer and B. Freisleben. Hawcos: the "hands-free" wheelchair control system. In *ACM Conference on Assistive Technologies*, pages 127–134, 2002.
11. L. Hochberg and J. Donoghue. Sensors for brain-computer interfaces. *IEEE Engineering in Medicine and Biology Magazine*, 25(5):32–38, Sept.-Oct. 2006.
12. X. Huo and M. Ghovanloo. Using constrained tongue motion as an alternative control surface for wheeled mobility. *IEEE Transactions on Biomedical Engineering*, 56(6):1719–1726, 2009.
13. T. Igarashi and J. Hughes. Voice as sound: using non-verbal voice input for interactive control. In *ACM Symposium on User Interface Software and Technology*, pages 155–156, 2001.
14. J. S. Kim, H. Jeong, and W. Son. A new means of HCI: EMG-MOUSE. In *IEEE Conference on Systems, Man and Cybernetics*, volume 1, pages 100–104, 2004.
15. K. Koichi. Input device for disabled persons using expiration and tooth-touch sound signals. In *ACM Symposium on Applied Computing*, pages 1159–1164, 2010.
16. T. Kuiken, G. Li, B. Lock, R. Lipschutz, L. Miller, K. Stubblefield, and K. Englehart. Targeted muscle reinnervation for real-time myoelectric control of multifunction artificial arms. *Journal of the American Medical Association*, 301(6):619–628, 2009.
17. J. LaCourse and F. Hludik. An eye movement communication-control system for the disabled. *IEEE Transactions on Biomedical Engineering*, 37(12):1215 –1220, 1990.
18. F. Loewenich and F. Maire. Hands-free mouse-pointer manipulation using motion-tracking and speech recognition. In *ACM Australasian Conference on Computer-Human Interaction: Entertaining User Interfaces*, pages 295–302, 2007.
19. F. Masuda and C. Wada. Effects of visual stimuli on a communication assistive method using sympathetic skin response. In *International Conference on Computers Helping People with Special Needs*, pages 189–192. Springer-Verlag, 2010.
20. M. Moore and U. Dua. A galvanic skin response interface for people with severe motor disabilities. In *ACM Conference on Computers and Accessibility*, pages 48–54, 2004.
21. Natural Point. SmartNav, 2011. naturalpoint.com.
22. New Abilities. Toungue-touch keypad, 2009. newabilities.com.
23. Origin Instruments Corporation. Sip/puff Breeze, 2011. orin.com.
24. S. Patel and G. Abowd. BLUI: low-cost localized blowable user interfaces. In *ACM Symposium on User Interface Software and Technology*, pages 217–220, 2007.
25. C. Salem and S. Zhai. An isometric tongue pointing device. In *ACM Conference on Human Factors in Computing Systems*, pages 538–539, 1997.

26. T. S. Saponas, D. Kelly, B. Parviz, and D. Tan. Optically sensing tongue gestures for computer input. In *ACM Symposium on User Interface Software and Technology*, pages 177–180, 2009.

27. A. Sears, M. Young, and J. Feng. Physical disabilities and computing technologies: An analysis of impairments. In A. Sears and J. Jacko, editors, *The Human-Computer Interaction Handbook*, pages 829–852. 2008.

28. T. Stivers, N. Enfield, P. Brown, C. Englert, M. Hayashi, T. Heinemann, G. Hoymann, F. Rossano, J. Peter de Ruiter, K. E. Yoon, and S. Levinson. Universals and cultural variation in turn-taking in conversation. *Proceedings of the National Academy of Sciences*, 106(26):10587–10592, 2009.

29. J. Wolpaw, N. Birbaumer, D. McFarland, G. Pfurtscheller, and T. Vaughan. Brain-computer interfaces for communication and control. *Clinical Neurophysiology*, 113(6):767–791, 2002.

ShowMeHow: Translating User Interface Instructions Between Similar Applications

Vidya Ramesh, Charlie Hsu, Maneesh Agrawala, Björn Hartmann
University of California,Berkeley — Computer Science Division
533 Soda Hall, Mailcode 1776, Berkeley, CA 94720
{vidyaramesh,cphsu}@berkeley.edu,{maneesh,bjoern}@cs.berkeley.edu

ABSTRACT
Many people learn how to use complex authoring applications through tutorials. However, user interfaces for authoring tools differ between versions, platforms, and competing products, limiting the utility of tutorials. Our goal is to make tutorials more useful by enabling users to repurpose tutorials between similar applications. We introduce *UI translation interfaces* which enable users to locate commands in one application using the interface language of another application. Our end-user tool, *ShowMeHow*, demonstrates two interaction techniques to accomplish translations: 1) direct manipulation of interface façades and 2) text search for commands using the vocabulary of another application. We discuss tools needed to construct the translation maps that enable these techniques. An initial study (n=12) shows that users can locate unfamiliar commands twice as fast with interface façades. A second study shows that ShowMeHow enables users to work through tutorials written for one application in another application.

ACM Classification: H5.2 [Information interfaces and presentation]: User Interfaces. - Graphical user interfaces.

General terms: Design, Human Factors, Documentation

Keywords: tutorials, instructions, mapping, translation

INTRODUCTION
Over the last two decades, we have witnessed a proliferation of software for creating and editing digital content – images, audio, video, animation, diagrams, illustrations, and 3D models. The interfaces of such applications can be dauntingly difficult to learn and use effectively. Often, the more powerful an application is, the more complex its user interface becomes. As a result, many users rely on tutorials to learn how to execute procedural tasks in the applications.

Tutorials describe a sequence of steps users must perform to reach a desired goal. The most effective tutorials contain screenshots and use interface-specific operation names to visually depict the GUI elements that must be manipulated in each step [10]. Creating high-quality tutorials and other documentation materials is often time consuming and requires expertise in the underlying application. As a result, the tutorial space is fragmented — a tutorial in one application often does not have equivalent counterparts for other, similar applications or other versions of the same application.

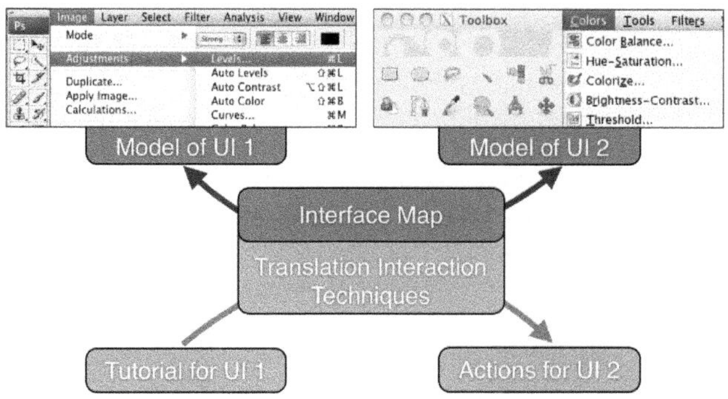

Figure 1: ShowMeHow helps users to translate instructions between applications that offer similar functionality, e.g., the image editing applications Photoshop and GIMP.

Consider a tutorial on red-eye correction in an image manipulation program. Many applications, including Photoshop, GIMP, Darkroom, and Aperture, support correction of red-eye. However, their interfaces are different enough that a tutorial written for one application is not immediately applicable to another. Even for the same application, the user interface often evolves between versions and may be inconsistent across different operating systems (e.g., Office 2003 vs 2007, Office on OS X vs Windows). This variety of interfaces limits the reach of online tutorials.

In this paper we present *UI translation interfaces* that enable users to translate commands in one application to a different version of the application or to another applications in the same domain (Figure 1). We focus on the domain of image manipulation applications, as such applications are complex and their user interfaces differ widely. Our end-user tool, *ShowMeHow*, allows users to to locate commands in GIMP using the interface language of Photoshop.

ShowMeHow introduces two novel *query interactions*: First, users can search for interface commands in one application through *direct manipulation of an interface façade* of another application. Interface façades replicate the look of an application (i.e., its menus, toolbars, dialogs) and allow users to leverage their visual memory. We implement façades using screen capture images. Second, users can perform *text searches for interface commands* in one application using command names and keyboard shortcuts in another application. These techniques are based on *interface translation maps*: data structures that relate semantically equivalent actions in different user interfaces. Maps are based on correspondences between pairs of *interface models* which capture the hierarchical structure, visual appearance, and names of UI elements. Maps are currently authored manually; we discuss strategies for automating and crowdsourcing the map construction process.

We conduct two studies showing that ShowMeHow increases success in locating commands across different applications. In the first study, twelve users see 20 Photoshop commands and locate equivalent commands in GIMP, with and without the use of ShowMeHow. When using ShowMeHow UI façades, participants are twice as fast ($\mu = 26$ seconds vs $\mu = 52$ seconds, $p < 0.0001$). However, text search is not significantly faster than the control condition ($\mu = 49$ seconds). Twelve additional participants, all GIMP novices, apply tutorials written for Photoshop within GIMP, with and without ShowMeHow. Participants complete more subtasks with ShowMeHow and rate the tool highly for ease of use, speed and utility as a learning aid.

While our focus is on increasing the utility of tutorials, UI translation techniques have broader applicability: they may effectively scaffold the learning of new, unfamiliar applications by providing access to the interface of a familiar application as necessary. We conclude with a discussion of directions for future work.

RELATED WORK

A sizable body of work exists on the design of application documentation [2], online help [19, 13, 28], software tutorials [17, 10], and application learnability [11].

Early work pointed out the failures of lengthy manuals – users don't read them – and argued for task-centered learning [4]. Tutorials are effective because they teach techniques in the context of a concrete task. While most tutorials are created manually, it is possible to automatically generate visual step-by-step instructions by recording actions users take in a UI [10]. Graphical histories for image editing show operation histories so users can understand how images came to be, and reapply these histories in new contexts [21, 12, 23].

Noting that readers have trouble interpreting and following tutorials, researchers have proposed interfaces that walk users through operations step-by-step [3], highlight relevant operations with stencils [17], or programmatically interpret and execute how-to instructions [22].

At a lower level, users need to locate and understand individual commands. Various query mechanisms have been proposed to do so, e.g., a natural language interface for UNIX commands [30]. Mac OS X 10.5 introduced a menu search that programmatically opens menu trees and shows the user where a command is located in the tree. But these techniques cannot translate between different interfaces.

Little work has addressed the problem of transferring knowledge between user interfaces. Davis et al. [6] studied behavioral differences between *initial* and *subsequent* users of an application, but do not explore the design space of tools to enable transfer learning. One solution is to change interface appearance: the open-source *GIMPShop* project modifies the GIMP menu structure and application vocabulary to mirror Photoshop's UI [1]. GIMPShop required editing the application source code. ShowMeHow enables users to translate commands without modifying the applications.

The ShowMeHow approach is most closely related to the site-to-service map and introduced by d.mix [14]. In both approaches, a correspondence map between semantically equivalent actions in two different interfaces is used. d.mix enables programmers to use direct manipulation on web pages to synthesize equivalent web service API calls. ShowMeHow uses direct manipulation actions in one graphical interface as query input to retrieve equivalent actions in a second direct manipulation interface.

UI translation maps also enable retargeting. Bricolage [20] identifies equivalent DOM elements in web pages to apply the look and feel of existing pages to new content. UNIFORM can adapt user interfaces to match other interfaces a user is already familiar with [24]. While Bricolage employs machine learning to identify matches, UNIFORM uses string and variable type matching combined with manual editing. ShowMeHow follows UNIFORM's semi-automated approach.

Figure 2: The ShowMeHow user interface offers a UI façade that enables users to locate commands with direct manipulation. Translated commands are shown in the left panel.

SCENARIO: TRANSLATING WITH SHOWMEHOW

Kyle's company is cutting its software budget and migrating from Photoshop to the free GIMP application. He is creating a donation web site for tsunami victims and consults an online tutorial for creating text embedded in the crest of a wave. He starts by creating text with a drop shadow. In Photoshop, this command can be invoked through the LAYER–STYLE–DROPSHADOW menu. Kyle pulls up the ShowMeHow façade and navigates to the submenu (Figure 2, 3A). The ShowMeHow sidebar indicates that the equivalent GIMP command is FILTERS–LIGHTANDSHADOW–DROPSHADOW menu, under the LIGHT AND SHADOW submenu (Figure 3B).

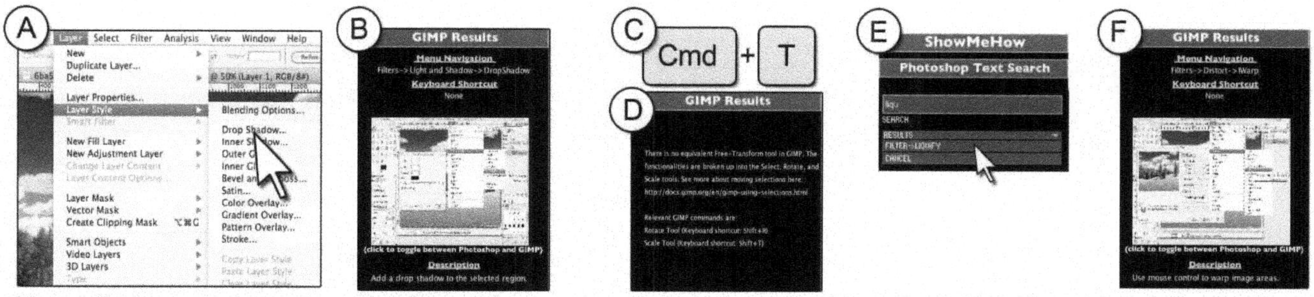

Users selects menu command in the Photoshop UI Facade.

Result panel shows equivalent GIMP command.

Users enters keyboard shortcut and sees list of alternative actions.

Users searches for commands by name.

Result panel shows equivalent GIMP command.

Figure 3: Users locate corresponding commands through manipulation of an interface façade (A,B); keyboard shortcuts (C,D); or text search for command names (E,F).

Kyle switches to GIMP and performs this action. Since Kyle is an accomplished Photoshop user, he performs many operations through keyboard shortcuts. To rotate and translate the text he created, he presses Cmd+T in ShowMeHow (Figure 3C) – this is the keyboard shortcut to perform a free transform operation in Photoshop. ShowMeHow indicates that there is no direct match for this command in GIMP but it lists multiple possible alternatives that can be used to achieve individual aspects of free transform (Figure 3D). Kyle next wants to distort the text. He types in "Liquid" into the ShowMeHow search box as he does not remember the precise name or location of the filter he wants to use. As he types, search results update incrementally and he discovers the FILTER-LIQUIFY command (Figure 3E). Clicking on the result yields the GIMP command FILTERS–DISTORT–IWARP (Figure 3F). With a couple of clicks, Kyle has successfully performed his tasks in GIMP with the help of ShowMeHow.

IMPLEMENTATION

Translating between different user interface actions requires the following fundamental building blocks:

- An *interface model* that describes the structure of the user interface for each application.
- A *translation map* that describes correspondences between elements of two models.
- A *query interaction* in which users select actions from the source interface to find corresponding actions in the target interface.

Interface Models

In order to translate commands, a tool must first have a list of available commands. ShowMeHow captures this information in an interface model. Users invoke commands through different interface widgets: menus, toolbars, palettes, and dialogs. Widgets can be referenced in different ways: by name, by picture, or by keyboard shortcuts. In addition, widgets may not be visible on screen at all times (e.g., submenus, palettes). Therefore, a description of the path required to make an action visible may be needed. Our model uses a tree representation: each node is an action, described by name, image, and optional accelerators. The model does not encode command semantics (what commands mean, or what code they execute).

Many interfaces today are built using declarative specifications (e.g., HTML, XAML) — these source files can be used to build interface models. In *model-based UI systems*, designers author an abstract model, and the system generates a concrete UI (e.g., [9, 26, 25]). Such systems can also provide the interface model for free. However, at least some of the applications we wish to support are closed source and not model-based. Given a concrete application, how might we derive a suitable descriptive model of it?

Much of the needed information is available programmatically — through accessibility APIs, UI framework inspection methods, or interface functions. In our example, both Photoshop and GIMP can generate complete command lists (through EDIT–KEYBOARD SHORTCUTS–SUMMARIZE and HELP–PROCEDURE BROWSER, respectively). For Photoshop, we read these lists with a custom parser, then manually augment them with images of command widgets.

Translation Maps

The translation map relates pairs of interface models. Our maps support three types of entries: $1:1$ correspondences between commands, *alternatives* where one command has multiple matches, and *workarounds* that use plain text to capture instructions if no direct match is available. Mappings are expressed in an XML file format that relates model elements (Figure 4). Correspondences where one command is equivalent to a sequence of steps can be expressed in the map format, but are not yet supported in the ShowMeHow interface.

Correspondences express semantic equivalence of actions. Establishing equivalence may require human judgment. Thus fully automatic map construction may not be possible. We create maps manually but also examine automatic and crowdsourcing techniques to accelerate map creation.

Automation through String Matching Automatic techniques can be used to seed a map and to aid users in establishing additional correspondences manually, e.g., through suggestion interfaces. Matching command names is a promising first step [24], as commands with similar functionality are likely to have similar names. For different versions of the

```
<map-direct ps_key="menu_image_rotate_arbitrary"
  gimp_key="toolbar_rotate" />
<map-many ps_key="edit_freetransform"
  xtra_desc="There is no equivalent Free-Transform tool.
  See more about moving selections here: http://...">
    <gimp_key id="gimp_toolbar_rotate.jpg"/>
    <gimp_key id="gimp_toolbar_scale"/>
</map-many>
<map-missing ps_key="layer_style"
  info="There is no layer styling in GIMP.
  Some effects can be achieved through filters." />
```

Figure 4: Examples of map entries.

	Matches Found	% of PS commands	False Positives	Accuracy
String matching	133	19.9%	17	87.2%
MTurk, ≥ 2 workers in agreement	93	13.9%	25	73.1%
Not found by string matching	66	9.9%	24	63.6%
MTurk, single confident worker	99	14.8%	48	51.5%
Not found by string matching	72	10.7%	41	43.0%

Figure 5: Results from constructing mapping tables automatically and through crowdsourcing on Mechanical Turk.

	Photoshop CS3	GIMP 2.6
Correct string match	Image,Adjustments, Color Balance...	Colors, Color Balance...
Incorrect string match	View,Show,Grid	Filters,Render,Pattern,Grid...
Correct manual match	Filter,Last Filter	Filters,Repeat Last
Incorrect manual match	Filter,Sketch,Torn Edges...	Filters,Edge-Detect,Edge...

Figure 6: Example map entries generated through string matching, and on Mechanical Turk.

same application, many commands and their position in the interface hierarchy will remain identical. To understand how interfaces change across versions, we ran Chawathe's change detection algorithm [5] on XML trees of two Photoshop versions – CS and CS3. 72% of commands remained identical.

When translating between different applications in the same genre (e.g., Photoshop and GIMP), different naming schemes and UI organization reduce the number of tree correspondences. To find matches across applications, our string matching algorithm performs a case-insensitive search over leaf command names, ignoring ancestors and omitting special characters. As a benchmark, we compared menus and tools in Photoshop CS3 (670 entries) and GIMP 2.6 (502 entries). 19.9% of Photoshop command names matched GIMP names, with 12.8% false positives (see Figure 5 for statistics and Figure 6 for examples of correct and incorrect matches).

Crowdsourcing the Map Semantically identical commands can be described in syntactically different ways, so string matching has limited reach. To find additional equivalences, we investigated whether non-expert users can match commands. This process lends itself to crowdsourcing as it is *embarrassingly parallel*: map entries are independent of each other and can be provided by different users. ShowMeHow's Web-based authoring tool presents users with a single command in a source application and asks them to identify a match in a target application (Figure 7). We deployed this tool on Amazon's Mechanical Turk labor market, paying $0.11 each for 1000 mappings from Photoshop to GIMP. A total of 941 jobs for 513 distinct Photoshop commands were completed by 45 workers. We analyzed mappings where

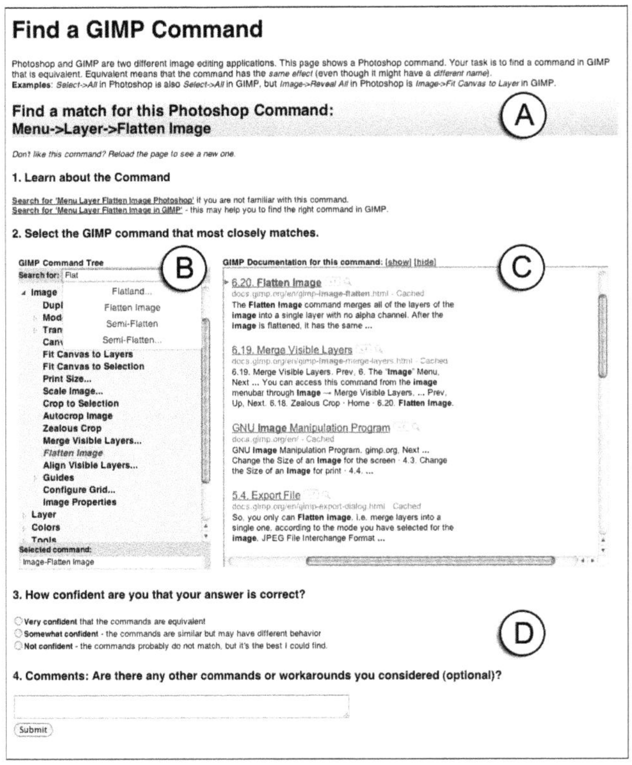

Figure 7: Users author correspondences in a Web interface. The UI shows a source command (A) and asks users to find an equivalent target command (B). Incremental auto-completion shows potential matches. Automatic search over application documentation helps users to verify chosen commands (C). Users also indicate their confidence (D) and workaround information if no match exists.

multiple workers agreed on the target command and mappings where workers indicated high confidence in their answer (see Figure 5). The results suggest that non-expert workers can add a significant number of useful entries not found by string matching, but that additional verification (e.g., voting) is necessary to limit false positives.

To quantify the cost of building a map by experts, we also hired three freelancers with Photoshop experience on oDesk. At $5-$15 per hour, these workers created 31-41 mappings per hour, leading to a price per map entry of $0.12-$0.41. The best worker had 94% accuracy on mappings where she indicated high confidence in her answer.

Query Interaction

Query interaction techniques have two phases: query specification, and translation result display. Queries can be specified through interface façades and text search.

Building Interface Façades Façades enable users to leverage visual memory; this is especially valuable for commands invoked through tool icons. Interface façades should let users explore the user interface as if the façade were the real application — to the extent necessary so the user can locate commands. This implies that menus should unroll; toolbar buttons should expand; dialogs should appear at the appropriate times.

To achieve these goals, we execute each command and screen capture the entire application. To add interactivity, different images have to be hyperlinked to each other — specifically, nodes in the UI model have to link to their children. We use image maps to express these links: polygons in image coordinates that describe both the location of *hot spot* areas and the a target state in the UI model (i.e., the identifier of an XML node). We created a tool to generate these image maps: the tool presents the user with a captured application image, and prompts the user to draw a bounding box for a given child command.

At runtime, façades implement a variation of *event bubbling*: the façade keeps track of the last active node. When the user clicks, the façade hit-tests cursor locations against all hot spots on the current node. If a hot spot is hit, the façade navigates to the correct child node in the interface tree. If no hot spot is hit, the façade bubbles the event upwards in the tree, repeating hit tests on each parent until the root. This algorithm allow users to jump between different tree levels.

Text Search: Commands and Shortcuts ShowMeHow provides a text search box with incremental search. As characters are entered, ShowMeHow searches the source application's UI model and shows all matches in a result list. ShowMeHow currently uses regular expression matching to find results. Clicking on any of the results is equivalent to selecting a command in the façade — it updates the façade view appropriately.

Expert users commonly rely on keyboard shortcuts for frequently used commands. To handle keyboard shortcuts, ShowMeHow intercepts keystrokes outside the search box and finds equivalent accelerators in the UI model. Again, to provide appropriate feedback, the façade view is updated to the corresponding model state whenever keyboard shortcuts are received.

Presenting Translated Commands ShowMeHow provides realtime translation correspondence back to the user. The result panel displays how to achieve the equivalent command in GIMP. It provides menu traversal instructions, a keyboard shortcut, a description of the current state, and a thumbnail of a GIMP screenshot corresponding to the current façade state. To see results in more detail, the thumbnail can be clicked to toggle the main display between the Photoshop façade and a full-size version of the GIMP screenshot.

USER EXPERIENCES WITH SHOWMEHOW

Our evaluation of ShowMeHow seeks to answer the following questions:

- *Utility:* Given instructions for a source application, are users able to operate a target application effectively with the aid of ShowMeHow?
- *Productivity:* Can we quantify the productivity gain of using ShowMeHow?
- *Usability:* What are the unique benefits and shortcomings of the different interaction techniques to access the translation map?

We conducted two user studies with 12 participants each, all recruited from UC Berkeley. Participants were required to have some expertise in Photoshop, but little or no expertise with GIMP. Participants self-rated their Photoshop proficiency on a scale from 1 (Novice) to 5 (Expert). For study 1, $\mu = 3.2$, $\sigma = 0.7$; for study 2, $\mu = 3.0$, $\sigma = 0.7$.

Study 1: Measuring Performance

In the first study, 12 participants were asked to translate individual commands from Photoshop to GIMP. Participants saw the name of the command and a screenshot of it. In our within-subjects design, participants completed half of the translations with ShowMeHow, and half without. Participants performed 20 translations of commands in Photoshop that existed in different UI locations in GIMP. For example, the FILE–OPEN action is the same in both interfaces, and thus was *not* used. Chosen commands included the MAGNETIC LASSO (maps to INTELLIGENT SCISSORS) and IMAGE– ADJUSTMENTS–LEVELS (maps to COLORS–LEVELS).

In each task we gave participants a Photoshop command and asked them to identify and execute the equivalent command in GIMP. Users alternated between using ShowMeHow and the control (no ShowMeHow) every 5 tasks. Start conditions were counterbalanced. We measured the time taken to successfully identify the command in GIMP and, for ShowMeHow trials, the type of query mechanism used (façade, text or shortcut). Time was measured from the moment of viewing the command to the moment when the user located the command in GIMP and hovered. The experimenter did not suggest which interaction method to use. If a participant had not identified the correct command after 90 seconds, the task was terminated and counted as a failure. Incorrect command choices were counted as false attempts.

Performance Results

Users identified GIMP commands more quickly when using ShowMeHow (see Figure 8). Without ShowMeHow, users took $\mu = 52$ seconds to successfully identify a command in GIMP. With ShowMeHow's Photoshop UI façade, users were twice as fast, taking $\mu = 26$ seconds to find a task. (two-sample $t(216) = 6.64$, $p < 0.0001$). When using ShowMeHow's text search, users averaged 49.7 seconds to find a task (not significant, two-sample $t(137) = 0.31$, $p > 0.05$). We hypothesize that the slower time for text search was due to engineering issues; some users remarked that the text search was slow and only searched for exact substring matches.

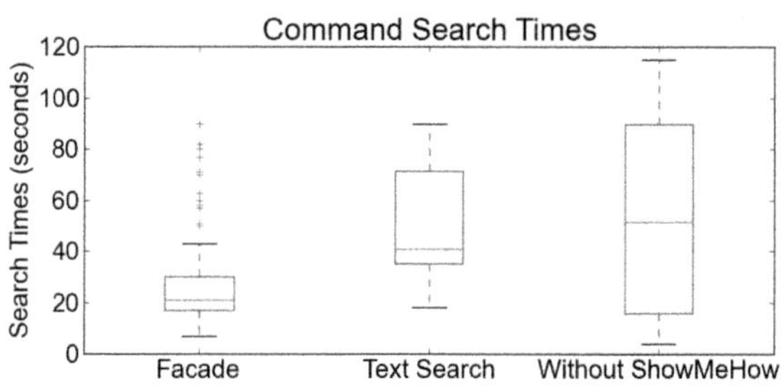

Figure 8: UI façades are significantly faster than text search and aid users in finding commands faster.

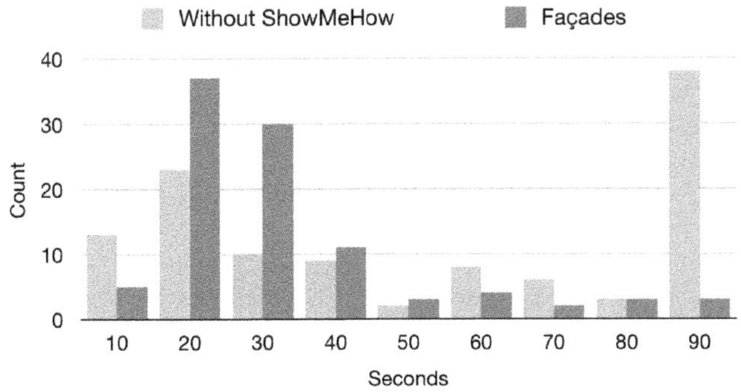

Figure 9: Histogram of task times in the control and façade conditions. Façades have a greater minimum cost; but without Façades, users are often lost.

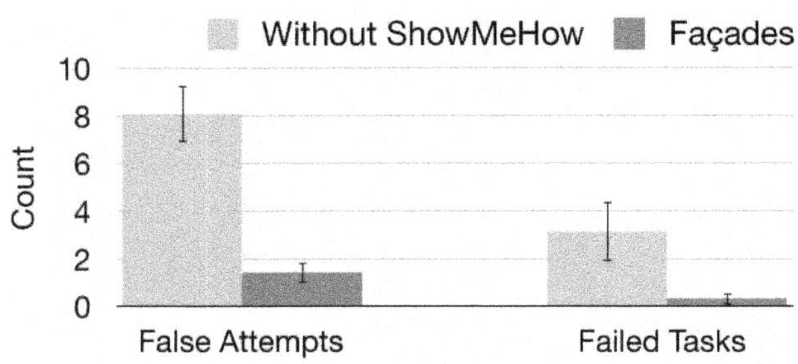

Figure 10: Participants had more false attempts and misses without ShowMeHow. Error bars show 95% CI.

Figure 9 compares search time histograms for ShowMeHow façades and the control condition. ShowMeHow has a larger minimum task time, because of the extra interaction steps and application switching. Without ShowMeHow, some commands are found quickly, but users are often lost if they cannot find the command right away.

ShowMeHow also led to fewer false attempts ($\mu = 1.4$ vs 8.1, two-tailed $t(22) = 3.40$, $p < 0.01$) and fewer failed tasks ($\mu = 0.3$ vs 3.2 per participant, two-tailed $t(22) = 4.19$, $p < 0.001$, see Figure 10). For example, when attempting to replace a range of colors in an image with another (Photoshop: IMAGE–ADJUSTMENTS–REPLACE COLOR, GIMP: COLORS–MAP–ROTATE COLORS), users without ShowMeHow would tend to incorrectly identify commands such as COLORIZE or COLORIFY as equivalents. Participants still made some false attempts with ShowMeHow; we believe these are due to participants forgetting query results while switching between ShowMeHow and GIMP.

Study 2: Translating Entire Tutorials

In the second study, participants completed a multi-step image manipulation tutorial written for a familiar interface (Photoshop) within an unfamiliar interface (GIMP). Participants performed this task twice, with two different tutorials: once with the aid of ShowMeHow and once without. Condition order and assignment of tutorial to condition were counterbalanced. Tutorials were taken from public web sites. Afterwards, participants completed a survey with Likert-scale and free-response questions.

Experimenters gave participants a brief overview of GIMP that introduced major tools and fundamental differences from Photoshop. Participants had 20 minutes for each tutorial and were stopped if the tutorial was not completed at this point. The tutorials comprised 9 and 12 steps; each step had 2 to 3 subtasks. Participants were encouraged to move on to the next subtask if they were unable to complete a subtask.

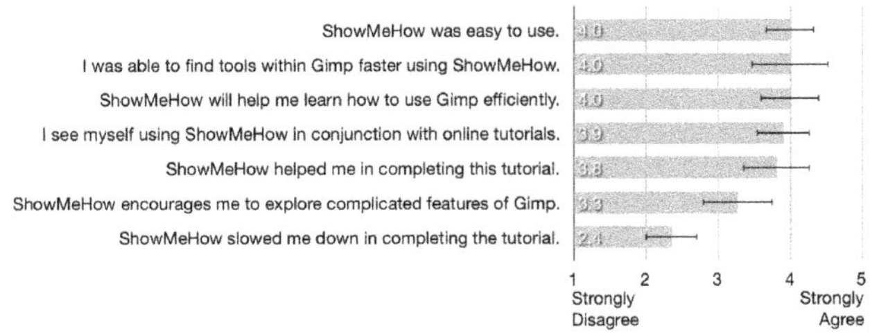

Figure 11: Likert scale ratings for ShowMeHow in study 2 Ratings range from 1:Strongly disagree to 5:Strongly agree. Error bars show 95% CI.

Participants were able to accomplish 3.6 more subtasks with ShowMeHow than without for the first tutorial. However, we observed that participants used ShowMeHow to find only the most difficult commands; many opted to directly struggle with the GIMP UI for commands they perceived as easier to find. Actively encouraging use of ShowMeHow by detecting when users "fumble" is an area for future work. On average, a participant looked up 6.74 commands in ShowMeHow. We also noticed that participants tended to strongly prefer one query technique — though there was no clear favorite across users. Only 2 participants preferred using keyboard shortcuts over the other methods while 5 participants each favored either the mock interface or text search.

In our post-test survey Likert questions, participants gave the highest marks to ShowMeHow for three dimensions: ease of use, speedup, and helping them learn how to use GIMP (Figure 11). Users felt that ShowMeHow helped them and made it easier to accomplish tasks in GIMP, even though our quantitative analysis did not show a statistically significant difference in time. One user remarked that "it was quite clear what I had to do in order to make something work in GIMP" and another that "ShowMeHow was really helpful for quick [lookups]". Participants were less enthusiastic about using ShowMeHow as a tool to openly explore how the two interfaces differed: it's main benefit is to quickly look up commands on demand, then disappear.

Participants also suggested usability improvements: search should cover keywords and related words, as web search engines do; our implementation only searched for exact command names. This limitation was partially ameliorated by the display of incremental results, which allowed participants to refine their search as they saw possible results.

We found that differences in parameters and parameter presets caused the biggest amount of confusion for our participants once they located the correct command. This suggests mapping command parameters in future work.

LIMITATIONS

There are several limitations of our approach that we plan to address in future work.

Multi-Step Translations Not Supported

Our current approach only handles single-step correspondences: one command in the source interface corresponds to one command (or a set of alternative commands) in the target interface. This limitation is primarily due to the chosen query interaction techniques. It is straightforward to describe multi-step sequences in the translation map. However, the current query interactions do not lend themselves to expressing multi-step queries: because the façade is not a functional interface, it is awkward to perform multiple steps in a row as the user cannot see the result of any one step.

Command Parameters Not Supported

ShowMeHow matches high-level commands, but does not handle parameters for those commands. However, most commands are parameterized. For example, the Rotate Canvas dialog takes an angle parameter It is possible to extend the current map syntax to cover parameters, but this would significantly increase the effort needed to capture correspondences. When parameters do not map directly onto each other, human expertise will be needed. We also observed that participants in our study tended to copy values from the tutorials directly into the application. If parameters do not match between programs, this practice yielded unexpected results.

User Must Switch Applications Frequently

Once a user has found a translated action, she still has to switch to the target application and perform the command displayed by ShowMeHow. This leaves a sizable *gulf of execution* [15]: the user may forget the precise menu path or shortcut during the application switch, especially if both applications cannot be shown side-by-side. Such short-term memory problems occurred repeatedly in our evaluation. They stem from the decision to implement ShowMeHow as an independent application. Integrating ShowMeHow into a target application could enable directly showing and executing actions in context. However, some authoring tools do not permit extensions to receive UI events. Accessibility APIs can, but many complex UIs do not use platform widgets. Pixel-based reverse engineering techniques like Prefab [7] might be able to extract event data at the appropriate level.

Façades Only Offer Partial Functionality

Users expect façades to act like the real application. Our Photoshop façade implements basic interactions with menus and toolbars. However, interactions that depend on application state are not yet supported. For example, users might try to add a new layer and then access layer-specific commands in context menus. Since our façade does not model application state, we are unable to translate such actions.

Users May Not Learn Target Interface

One unintended side-effect observed in our evaluations is that once users have located the appropriate command in the target application, they often proceeded to take the shortest possible path to execute that action — copying the keyboard shortcut. However, the shortcut does not help users understand how to locate the action inside the UI. Users who take advantage of the menu traversal instructions reap additional learning benefits. Unintended side-effects caused by assistive interfaces have been observed elsewhere and termed the "paradox of the assisted user" [29].

FUTURE WORK

Future work should investigate alternative approaches to generating user interface translation maps as well as additional interaction techniques.

Automate Map Construction

Two avenues for automation appear feasible. First, it may be possible to learn correspondences from pairs of demonstrations of the same task in different UIs. Application instrumentation can be be used to record what users do; in fact, some applications already have recording facilities for user-defined macros. Second, it may be possible to mine Web pages for correspondences. Command names appear on official documentation sites, blogs and forums. Correspondences be established from pages with similar features. Query-feature graphs [8] which relate application functions to search queries are a first step in this direction.

Further inspiration for automating map creation can be taken from analogous problems in *multi-version program analysis* in software engineering [18] and *schema matching* in database systems [27]. In particular, Potluck shows that better interaction techniques can reduce the cost of authoring equivalences [16].

New Query Interactions: Translate Tutorials

If ShowMeHow is predominantly used to translate tutorials found on the Web, the translation functionality could be built directly into the Web browser. We envision that ShowMeHow could automatically parse a loaded tutorial in the browser, find command names contained in the tutorial, and annotate these commands with possible translations. Such an annotated tutorial would obviate the need for an extra translation application, but poses the additional challenge of robustly identifying commands in unstructured text.

CONCLUSION

This paper introduced *UI translation interfaces*. These interfaces can help users adapt tutorials from one application version to another, and between different applications within the same genre. Translation interfaces can also help users leverage existing knowledge when users change software versions. UI translation interfaces are based on interface models and maps which relate pairs of models. We introduced *interface façades* which model the appearance, but not the functionality, of an application. Façades require more effort to construct, but yield larger gains. In our study, façades effectively reduced the time it took users to locate commands in an unfamiliar interface and eased the frustration of dealing with complicated, foreign interfaces. ShowMeHow is a first step in studying the translation of user interface actions between applications in a similar genre.

ACKNOWLEDGMENTS

We thank Intel and Google for their support. This research was supported by NSF grant CCF-0643552

REFERENCES

1. GIMPshop. http://www.gimpshop.com/. Retrieved 4/2011.
2. Ron Baecker. Showing instead of telling. In *Proceedings of the 20th annual international conference on Computer documentation*, SIGDOC '02, pages 10–16, New York, NY, USA, 2002. ACM.

3. Lawrence Bergman, Vittorio Castelli, Tessa Lau, and Daniel Oblinger. Docwizards: a system for authoring follow-me documentation wizards. In *Proceedings of the 18th annual ACM symposium on User interface software and technology*, UIST '05, pages 191–200, New York, NY, USA, 2005. ACM.
4. John M. Carroll. *The Nurnberg funnel: designing minimalist instruction for practical computer skill.* MIT Press, Cambridge, MA, USA, 1990.
5. Sudarshan S. Chawathe, Anand Rajaraman, Hector Garcia-Molina, and Jennifer Widom. Change detection in hierarchically structured information. *SIGMOD Record*, 25:493–504, June 1996.
6. Sid Davis and Susan Wiedenbeck. The mediating effects of intrinsic motivation, ease of use and usefulness perceptions on performance in first-time and subsequent computer users. *Interacting with Computers*, 13(5):549 – 580, 2001.
7. Morgan Dixon and James Fogarty. Prefab: implementing advanced behaviors using pixel-based reverse engineering of interface structure. In *Proceedings of the 28th international conference on Human factors in computing systems*, CHI '10, pages 1525–1534, New York, NY, USA, 2010. ACM.
8. Adam Fourney, Richard Mann, and Michael Terry. Queryfeature graphs:bridging user vocabulary and system functionality. In *Proceedings of the 24th annual ACM symposium on User interface software and technology*, UIST '11, New York, NY, USA, 2011. ACM.
9. Krzysztof Z. Gajos, Daniel S. Weld, and Jacob O. Wobbrock. Automatically generating personalized user interfaces with supple. *Artificial Intelligence*, 174(12-13):910–950, 2010.
10. Floraine Grabler, Maneesh Agrawala, Wilmot Li, Mira Dontcheva, and Takeo Igarashi. Generating photo manipulation tutorials by demonstration. *ACM Transactions on Graphics*, 28:66:1–66:9, July 2009.
11. Tovi Grossman, George Fitzmaurice, and Ramtin Attar. A survey of software learnability: metrics, methodologies and guidelines. In *Proceedings of the 27th international conference on Human factors in computing systems*, CHI '09, pages 649–658, New York, NY, USA, 2009. ACM.
12. Tovi Grossman, Justin Matejka, and George Fitzmaurice. Chronicle: capture, exploration, and playback of document workflow histories. In *Proceedings of the 23nd annual ACM symposium on User interface software and technology*, UIST '10, pages 143–152, New York, NY, USA, 2010. ACM.
13. Susan M. Harrison. A comparison of still, animated, or nonillustrated on-line help with written or spoken instructions in a graphical user interface. In *Proceedings of the SIGCHI conference on Human factors in computing systems*, CHI '95, pages 82–89, New York, NY, USA, 1995. ACM Press/Addison-Wesley Publishing Co.
14. Björn Hartmann, Leslie Wu, Kevin Collins, and Scott R. Klemmer. Programming by a sample: rapidly creating web applications with d.mix. In *Proceedings of the 20th annual ACM symposium on User interface software and technology*, UIST '07, pages 241–250, New York, NY, USA, 2007. ACM.
15. Edwin L. Hutchins, James D. Hollan, and Donald A. Norman. Direct manipulation interfaces. *Human-Computer Interaction*, 1:311–338, 1985.
16. David F. Huynh, Robert C. Miller, and David R. Karger. Potluck: semi-ontology alignment for casual users. In *Proceedings of the 6th international The semantic web and 2nd Asian conference on Asian semantic web conference*, ISWC'07/ASWC'07, pages 903–910, Berlin, Heidelberg, 2007. Springer-Verlag.
17. Caitlin Kelleher and Randy Pausch. Stencils-based tutorials: design and evaluation. In *Proceedings of the SIGCHI conference on Human factors in computing systems*, CHI '05, pages 541–550, New York, NY, USA, 2005. ACM.
18. Miryung Kim and David Notkin. Program element matching for multi-version program analyses. In *Proceedings of the 2006 international workshop on Mining software repositories*, MSR '06, pages 58–64, New York, NY, USA, 2006. ACM.
19. Kevin Knabe. Apple guide: a case study in user-aided design of online help. In *Conference companion on Human factors in computing systems*, CHI '95, pages 286–287, New York, NY, USA, 1995. ACM.
20. Ranjitha Kumar, Jerry O. Talton, Salman Ahmad, and Scott R. Klemmer. Bricolage: Example-based retargeting for web design. In *Proceedings of the 29th international conference on Human factors in computing systems*, CHI '11, New York, NY, USA, 2011. ACM.
21. David Kurlander and Steven Feiner. A history-based macro by example system. In *Proceedings of the 5th annual ACM symposium on User interface software and technology*, UIST '92, pages 99–106, New York, NY, USA, 1992. ACM.
22. Tessa Lau, Clemens Drews, and Jeffrey Nichols. Interpreting written how-to instructions. In *Proceedings of the 21st international jont conference on Artifical intelligence*, pages 1433–1438, San Francisco, CA, USA, 2009. Morgan Kaufmann Publishers Inc.
23. Toshio Nakamura and Takeo Igarashi. An application-independent system for visualizing user operation history. In *Proceedings of the 21st annual ACM symposium on User interface software and technology*, UIST '08, pages 23–32, New York, NY, USA, 2008. ACM.
24. Jeffrey Nichols, Brad A. Myers, and Brandon Rothrock. Uniform: automatically generating consistent remote control user interfaces. In *Proceedings of the SIGCHI conference on Human Factors in computing systems*, CHI '06, pages 611–620, New York, NY, USA, 2006. ACM.
25. Fabio Paterno. *Model-Based Design and Evaluation of Interactive Applications.* Springer-Verlag, London, UK, 1st edition, 1999.
26. Angel R. Puerta. A model-based interface development environment. *IEEE Software*, 14:40–47, July 1997.
27. Erhard Rahm and Philip A. Bernstein. A survey of approaches to automatic schema matching. *The VLDB Journal*, 10:334–350, December 2001.
28. Christian Spannagel, Raimund Girwidz, Herbert Löthe, Andreas Zendler, and Ulrik Schroeder. Animated demonstrations and training wheels interfaces in a complex learning environment. *Interacting with Computers*, 20:97–111, January 2008.
29. Christof C. van Nimwegen, Daniel D. Burgos, Herre H. van Oostendorp, and Hermina H. J. M. Schijf. The paradox of the assisted user: guidance can be counterproductive. In *Proceedings of the SIGCHI conference on Human Factors in computing systems*, CHI '06, pages 917–926, New York, NY, USA, 2006. ACM.
30. Robert Wilensky, Yigal Arens, and David Chin. Talking to unix in english: an overview of uc. *Communications of the ACM*, 27:574–593, June 1984.

Pause-and-Play: Automatically Linking Screencast Video Tutorials with Applications

Suporn Pongnumkul[1], *Mira Dontcheva*[2], *Wilmot Li*[2], *Jue Wang*[2], *Lubomir Bourdev*[2], *Shai Avidan*[2], *Michael F. Cohen*[3]

[1]University of Washington
suporn@cs.washington.edu

[2]Adobe Systems
{mirad, wilmotli, juewang, lbourdev, avidan}@adobe.com

[3]Microsoft Research
mcohen@microsoft.com

ABSTRACT
Video tutorials provide a convenient means for novices to learn new software applications. Unfortunately, staying in sync with a video while trying to use the target application at the same time requires users to repeatedly switch from the application to the video to pause or scrub backwards to replay missed steps. We present Pause-and-Play, a system that helps users work along with existing video tutorials. Pause-and-Play detects important events in the video and links them with corresponding events in the target application as the user tries to replicate the depicted procedure. This linking allows our system to automatically pause and play the video to stay in sync with the user. Pause-and-Play also supports convenient video navigation controls that are accessible from within the target application and allow the user to easily replay portions of the video without switching focus out of the application. Finally, since our system uses computer vision to detect events in existing videos and leverages application scripting APIs to obtain real time usage traces, our approach is largely independent of the specific target application and does not require access or modifications to application source code. We have implemented Pause-and-Play for two target applications, Google SketchUp and Adobe Photoshop, and we report on a user study that shows our system improves the user experience of working with video tutorials.

ACM Classification: H5.2 [Information interfaces and presentation]: User Interfaces. - Graphical user interfaces.

General terms: Design, Human Factors

Keywords: video tutorial, screencast, instructions

INTRODUCTION
Screencast video tutorials are becoming increasingly prevalent as a means of helping novice users perform procedural tasks across a variety of software applications. On YouTube, only one of many video sharing sites, there are over 100,000 video tutorials for Adobe Photoshop, over 30,000 video tutorials for Microsoft Word, and over 12,000 video tutorials for Apple's Final Cut Pro. Google reports 1.8 million global monthly queries for "video tutorial(s)." There are several potential reasons for the growing popularity of such tutorials. First, video tutorials are relatively easy to create; typically, the author simply records a demonstration of the procedure (using widely available screen capture software) and then adds some narration explaining the steps in detail. In contrast, creating well-designed step-by-step tutorials (that include static text and images) often requires the author to capture all of the relevant images of the application user interface, add visual annotations to show complex mouse/pen interactions, lay out the appropriate images for each step, and write clear, concise prose describing the procedure. Furthermore, in contrast to static step-by-step tutorials, videos provide time-varying visual and audio information that can help users learn and understand dynamic procedures (e.g., brushing on a canvas). Finally, unlike human tutors, screencast video tutorials are available on demand to a large audience of users via a variety of Internet video sharing channels.

Once the user finds a relevant tutorial, a natural next step is for him to replicate the depicted procedure on a local version of the target application. Typically, users employ what we refer to as a *work along* strategy, where they try to perform

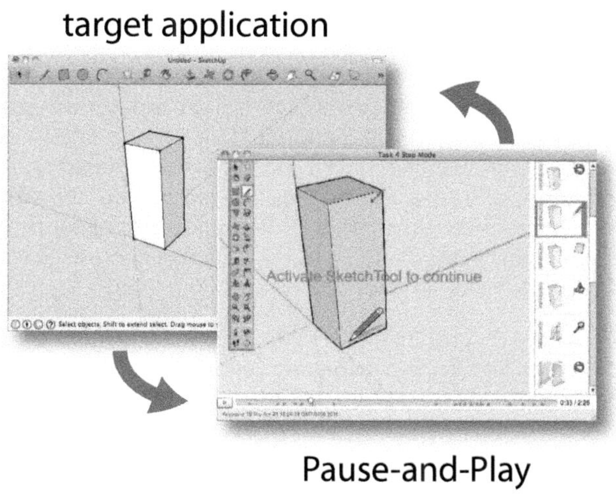

Figure 1: Pause-and-Play links the target application with the progress-aware video player. The video player automatically pauses when the user lags behind the video tutorial, and displays an annotation informing the user how to proceed.

the procedure while simultaneously playing the relevant portions of the video. While this approach allows the user to see the details of each step as he attempts to complete it, working along with a video involves several important difficulties. First, the user has to manage two pieces of software (the video player and the target application) at the same time. Second, since the user typically ends up working at a different pace from the video tutorial, he often has to switch focus from the target application to the video player in order to pause, rewind or fast forward the tutorial. Finally, if the user misses or forgets a step, it can be difficult to find the relevant portion of the video by scrubbing the video timeline.

In this work, we present Pause-and-Play, a video tutorial system that directly addresses these three problems. Our approach takes an existing video tutorial as input, automatically detects important events within the video, and then links these to corresponding events in the target application as the user works along with the tutorial. This linking allows our system to automatically adapt video playback based on the working pace of the user by pausing and playing the video at the appropriate times. In addition, knowing the locations of important events enables video navigation controls that let users quickly skip to relevant portions of the video.

The three key challenges in realizing such a system are 1) developing an effective automatic approach for detecting important events in a screencast video, 2) defining a lightweight method for tracking the progress of the user in the target application, and 3) designing a set of navigation controls that helps the user work along with the video. To detect important events in the video, we use computer vision to extract relevant metadata. This approach allows us to analyze video tutorials in a way that is largely independent of the specific target application, which makes it easier to extend our technique to a broad range of applications. To track user progress in the target application, we leverage its extensibility infrastructure (e.g., the plug-in architectures and/or scripting support provided by many mature, full-featured applications) to detect relevant events without having to do real-time computer vision processing or to modify the target application's source code. Finally, to design effective navigation controls, we identify key user requirements based on an observational study and then develop a set of automated and interactive controls that addresses these requirements.

While we believe our high level approach generalizes to most types of applications, this paper focuses on generating effective video tutorials for design software, such as Adobe Photoshop, GIMP, Google SketchUp, etc. This is an important class of software with many existing video tutorials targeting these applications. Most design applications share a few key characteristics. They typically adopt a tool-based paradigm in which users can activate and then apply a wide variety of tools to create or edit content. In addition, they often have rich graphical user interfaces (GUIs) that provide visual feedback and support many interaction techniques. We leverage these characteristics in the design of our algorithms for automatically detecting important events.

We should note that we are not the first to present work to enhance video tutorials, as in for example, the Chronicle [7] system. However, in contrast to previous work, our methodology does not rely on having access to the application source code. Rather, we perform instrumentation solely via application scripting plug-ins. While some plug-in architectures might expose enough detailed information to support the extensive instrumentation support necessary for a video-based history system, like Chronicle, the plug-in architectures we have encountered are limited and do not give access to dialog interactions or allow major modifications to the application interface. In a related effort that aims to make it easier to use video tutorials, the AmbientHelp [11] system shows how an application plug-in architecture can be used to create a video recommender system. AmbientHelp, just like Pause-and-Play relies on application plug-ins to track user behavior.

Our work makes the following specific contributions:

- We identify and explicitly describe the challenges of working along with a screencast video tutorial.
- We propose an automated technique for detecting and linking important events in a video to corresponding events in the target application.
- We present automatic and interactive navigation controls that help users work along with a video tutorial.
- We demonstrate our approach with two working prototypes: one for Photoshop and one for SketchUp.
- We describe user evaluations that indicate the effectiveness of our video tutorials approach.

RELATED WORK

While previous work [15] has argued for the benefits of expert demonstrations as a learning aid, there is some debate in the research community about the effectiveness of *video* demonstrations (i.e., tutorials) compared to other types of instructional material. Some evaluations of video instruction (e.g., [12, 8, 9]) found little benefit of video tutorials over traditional text tutorials, despite the fact that videos provide more explicit links between user input and system response and show animated depictions of application dynamics. More recent work has shown that short (10-25 second) contextually available videos that provide "a bare minimum demonstration of how to use a specific tool" are more effective in helping users accomplish tasks and retain what they learned than traditional text-based tutorials [6]. In contrast, researchers studying longer (2-3 minute) task-oriented tutorials found that users performed better with text tutorials than videos because users could not work at the same pace as the video and either missed steps or had to pause, rewind and scrub the timeline to stay in sync with the tutorial [5]. Despite the differences between previous findings, almost all research on instructional videos points to a need for segmented videos that emphasize each step of the task because without segmentation one "may not be able to identify and encode specific aspects of the procedure [8]."

To this end, interactive tutorial systems, like Stencils [10] and DocWizards [1], and systems that offer rich visual histories, such as Chronicle [7] and Interactive Storyboards [16], focus specifically on steps and allow the user to interactively step through or query a procedure. These systems may also be able to automate parts or all of the tutorial procedure, similar to application macros. Another type of interactive learning aid is an Intelligent Tutoring System (e.g., [9, 4]), which uses artificial intelligence to provide adaptive, customized feedback to students. Although all of these solutions offer compelling alternatives to static text-based tutorials, they typically require significant instrumentation of the application source code and thus incur a heavy cost for supporting new applications. We focus on a more lightweight, application-independent approach that also works for existing videos.

Our approach for detecting important events in existing video tutorials is inspired by recent vision-based techniques for analyzing screencast images, such as Sikuli [17] and Prefab [3]. Much like those existing systems, we use computer vision to extract useful metadata from images (i.e., video frames) of a user interface. In particular, we use a simple analysis technique that is similar in spirit to the visual matching in Sikuli's screenshot search engine. While our informal experiments suggest that our method works more reliably than Sikuli for many of the low resolution and highly compressed screencast videos typically found on the Web, the main contribution of our work does not lie in the specifics of our vision algorithm. Instead, we focus on understanding the challenges of working along with video tutorials and designing a system that helps users overcome these challenges.

Finally, our work is also related to previous research on content-aware video playback and navigation. For example, Petrovic et al. [13] analyze videos using a statistical scene model that enables automatic fast-forwarding to preferred frames, Cheng et al. [2] modify playback speed based on video content, and Pongnumkul et al. [14] present a content-aware dynamic timeline control. Our approach also uses content analysis to improve video playback and navigation. However, we focus specifically on optimizing how users work along with video tutorials of software applications, whereas the systems mentioned above propose techniques for viewing general-purpose videos. Thus, we propose more targeted playback and navigation features designed to help users stay in sync with videos and quickly skip between tutorial steps. In addition, one key distinguishing characteristic of our system is that it automatically links playback to the state of the target application as the user works along with the video.

UNDERSTANDING THE WORK ALONG TASK

In order to develop effective design goals for our video tutorials system, we first conducted a small observational study to help us identify the specific difficulties users face when working along with instructional videos. We recruited 5 participants (4 men, 1 woman) and brought each one into the lab for a 30 minute session. In each session, we asked the participant to perform two red eye removal tasks (one simple and one more complex) in Adobe Photoshop by following video tutorials we found on YouTube. The participants reported some to no previous experience with the software. We chose red eye removal because it is a common task that many users attempt. The videos were 0:37 and 4:11 minutes long, and both had audio narration in English. The short video showed how to use Photoshop's fairly automated "red eye removal tool," while the longer video showed an alternative technique for situations where the automatic tool is not effective. Participants performed the tasks using a single display setup with a 17" 1680x1050 pixel flat screen monitor, a keyboard, and mouse. In addition to observing participants as they worked along with the videos, we also conducted a short interview at the end of each session to determine what additional information and interactions they would have found useful.

Findings

Our observations led us to several key findings about how users work along with video tutorials.

Syncing. Since users almost always end up working at a different pace than the video, the main challenge they face is staying in sync with the tutorial. Thus, the most common interaction pattern we observed is for users to play the video for a few seconds, pause, switch to the target application to replicate the operations they have just watched in the video, and then continue playing the video. The frequency of the pauses varies across subjects but seems fairly consistent for each user. In general, more novice users tend to pause more frequently in order to keep the state of their target application relatively close to that of the video, while more experienced users often watch longer stretches of video to gain more context about a particular set of steps. In either case, users end up switching back and forth between the application and video several times in order to stay in sync with the tutorial.

Seeking. The second most common behavior is to seek along the video timeline to find important events. For example, users often scrub backward to replay specific parts of the video, such as when a menu dialog opens or how the parameters within a dialog are set. Replaying these events reminds the user how to perform the relevant step in the application and also confirms that he has performed the step correctly. In addition, novice users often scrub backwards to replay brief operations that are hard to see and/or not explicitly described in the narration. While less common, scrubbing forwards seems to occur in two main scenarios. Some users will scrub forwards to skip a long introduction to a tutorial, and more experienced users will occasionally scrub ahead when they think they know what is going to happen in a step and want to confirm their theory. In all of these situations, users typically have to scrub around for a few seconds before they find the desired location along the timeline.

Steps. In the closing interviews, users indicated that having information about the meaningful steps in the video could help them work along with the tutorial. Consistent with previous findings [8, 12], knowledge about steps, or video segments, enables users to make informed pauses at the end of step boundaries. Also, having access to the comparison between before and after images for a given step could be useful in confirming that the each step is executed correctly.

Audio narration. The quality of the audio narration for a video tutorial plays a big part in the overall quality of the video. We observed that the higher the expertise of a participant, the more they relied almost exclusively on the audio to accomplish the task. This may be because they already knew where the tools were located and only needed instruction on how to use them. In contrast, novices rely on the visuals to show them where new tools were located. Additionally, au-

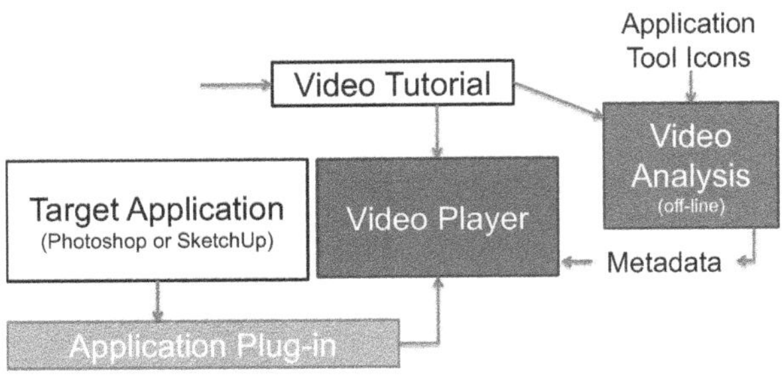

Figure 2: The Pause-and-Play system architecture has three main components: a video analysis module, an application plug-in and a progress-aware video player. It takes in as input the video tutorial.

dio narration allows the instructor to generalize the technique and share how it might be used in other contexts.

Screen management. As is often the case when users attempt to multitask by operating two applications simultaneously, managing screen real estate becomes an issue. Most users make the video player relatively large so that they can clearly see the changes that happen in the video. Some try to arrange the screen so that they can see both the video and application at the same time. Others maximize both the video and application and then bring one or the other to the front.

Design Goals

Based on these findings, we have developed several design goals for our system. We focus on optimizing syncing and seeking interactions, as well as enabling step-based navigation. We leave audio integration and screen management to future work.

1. ***Automate play/pause when possible.*** Since playing and pausing is a very common interaction that takes the attention away from the target application and task, we would like our video player to automatically pause and play the tutorial at the appropriate points. As we observed, the frequency of pausing and playing depends on the expertise of the user; thus, any automated play/pause functionality should adapt to the pace of the user.

2. ***Easy access to important frames.*** To prevent users from spending too much time looking for specific locations within the video, we aim to provide easy access to key events within the tutorial.

3. ***Visual highlights.*** Since some of the operations in a video tutorial may be brief, subtle and thus easily missed (especially by novice users), we aim to detect and visually emphasize such operations.

4. ***Low transaction cost.*** Several of our findings indicate that users frequently switch back and forth between the video and the target application. Thus, we seek to provide an interface where users can focus on the task at hand within the application and still be able to easily navigate the video.

SYSTEM OVERVIEW

Our system, Pause-and-Play, has three main components (see Figure 2): a video analysis module that processes videos and extracts metadata, an application plug-in that generates a trace of user behavior, and the user-aware video player, which automatically pauses and plays a video tutorial as the user interacts with the application and completes each step described in the video.

As noted in the introduction, an important aspect of our work is that it does not rely on access to the application source code. Thus, overall, our approach is largely independent of the specific target application, which means that applying our method to enable smart video playback for new applications is relatively straightforward. That said, we do make some assumptions about the applications we support:

Graphical. We focus on GUI-based applications that are visual in nature, and we assume that all important events have a visual representation in the application. This allows us to take a vision-based approach to detect important events in video tutorials.

Tool-based. Our approach also assumes that the target application adopts a tool-based paradigm in which users activate and then apply various tools to create or edit content. More specifically, we assume that changes in the active tool constitute important events in application usage. While many applications are tool-based (e.g., Microsoft Word and PowerPoint, Adobe Photoshop and Illustrator, Google SketchUp), command-line software (e.g., MATLAB) and form-based applications (e.g., TurboTax) are outside the scope of this work.

Supports extensibility. Many complex applications offer an SDK or scripting API so that third party developers may add new features through plug-ins. We leverage such extensibility capabilities to automatically detect important events in the application while the user works along with a tutorial. In particular, our plug-ins register event listeners and log the stream of user events.

There are a variety of applications that conform to these three criteria, including Microsoft Word, Adobe Photoshop, Google SketchUp, and Autodesk's Maya. Using the overall architecture shown in Figure 2 and the specific techniques described in the remainder of this section, we developed working video tutorial prototypes for two target applications, SketchUp (Figure 3) and Photoshop (Figure 7). The only application-specific components of these two prototypes are the application plug-ins and the tool icons used by the video analysis module.

Interacting with the Pause-And-Play video player

We describe our video player interface in the context of a user task. Julie is learning how to use Google SketchUp, a 3D modeling application, and wants to build a chair. She has found a video tutorial and is following along using the Pause-and-Play video player. The video shows how to select the *rectangle tool* to make a square. At this point, Pause-and-Play automatically pauses (indicated with a transparent red overlay) and instructs Julie to select the *rectangle tool* to continue. Since Julie is not familiar with SketchUp's interface, she looks for the icon that Pause-and-Play emphasizes and highlights in the application toolbar (see Figure 3a). When she selects the rectangle tool the video continues playing. Julie makes a square as instructed by the video instructor.

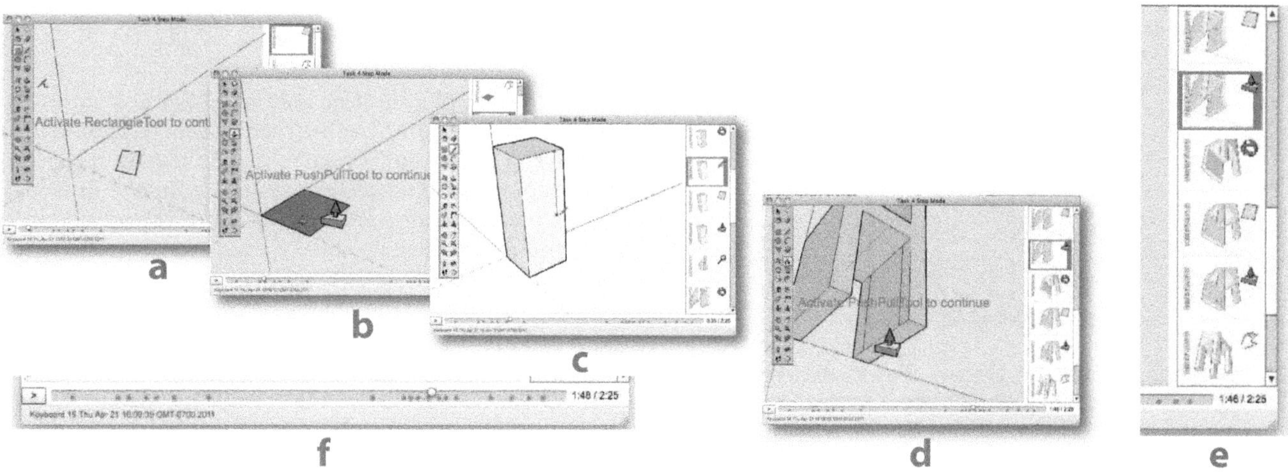

Figure 3: This figure illustrates Pause-and-Play's video player. (a, b, d) The video player automatically pauses and instructs the user to activate the *rectangle tool* or *push-pull tool*. (c) When the user works at the same pace as the video, the video player does not pause. (e) A visual table of contents that shows how the canvas has changed allows the user to jump to different sections of the video more easily. (f) The timeline indicates different segments of the video using red dots. When the cursor hovers over a red dot, the tool name corresponding to that segment is shown.

When the video moves to the next step in the tutorial, the player automatically pauses and instructs Julie to select the *push-pull tool* (see Figure 3b) to continue. Julie wants to see how to use the *push-pull tool*, so she presses the space bar. She doesn't have to leave SketchUp to interact with Pause-and-Play; she interacts with it as though it is the foreground application. The video shows her how to make a cube. Julie is able to make the cube and follow along at the pace of the video. The narrator says that next he will draw the back of the chair with the *pencil tool*. Julie switches to the *pencil tool* at the same time as the video. This time Pause-and-Play does not pause and keeps going since Julie is keeping up (see Figure 3c).

Later, when Julie is working on the legs (Figure 3d) she gets confused. Her chair legs are not the same width. Julie jumps back to the beginning of the chair leg section using the visual table of contents in Pause-and-Play, which shows visualizations of how the model has changed in each step (Figure 3e). Julie realizes her mistake and begins fixing the legs. She presses the left arrow key to rewind a step she wants to see a couple of times. The timeline of Pause-and-Play shows the video steps with dots (Figure 3f). The left and right arrow keys move backwards and forwards one step at a time.

To enable the Pause-and-Play interface we created a system that could segment a video tutorial into steps and track user behavior. Next we describe these two components in detail.

Segmenting video tutorials

There are a number of recent computer vision approaches for analyzing screen captured images including the Sikuli [17] and Prefab [3] systems. These approaches inspired our initial investigations in processing screencast videos. Much like Sikuli and Prefab, our video analysis module performs pixel-based analysis of screencast images (i.e., video frames) to identify user interface elements and detect important changes in application state. The main challenge in applying existing techniques directly is that most video tutorials found on the Web are low resolution and include many compression artifacts, which make it impractical to use the exact pixel-by-pixel matching methods of Prefab. While Sikuli's approach of using SIFT features could theoretically handle compressed, low resolution input, our informal experiments using the Sikuli implementation published online produced unreliable matching results. Our approach uses a robust template matching designed to handle the noise due to resampling and compression.

In designing our video analysis algorithms, we made the following observations:

- tool palettes in SketchUp and Photoshop are made up from a grid of icons,
- the active tool is visually emphasized,
- and there are limited number of icons.

For a given target application, the video analysis module takes as input a tool palette template and the application tool icons and produces a metadata file that lists tool changes with video timecodes. A tool palette template is an image of the tool palette that can be captured from the running application at any resolution. For example, we took a screenshot of Photoshop to get its tool palette template. The tool icons are part of an application's installation and thus are easily accessible.

In each frame of the video, the system first finds the tool palette by comparing to the tool palette template. The comparison is done in greyscale using a blurred version of the template, which adds robustness to noise, color and scale variations. We use the sum of the differences of the grayscale pixel values. As the resolution of the video may be different from our template, we conduct the search in multiple resolution and find the best match.

Next, the system identifies the active tool position by analyzing the frame differences between adjacent frames. The system considers all differences in the tool palette region that are rectangular and grid aligned as tool changes. Notice how

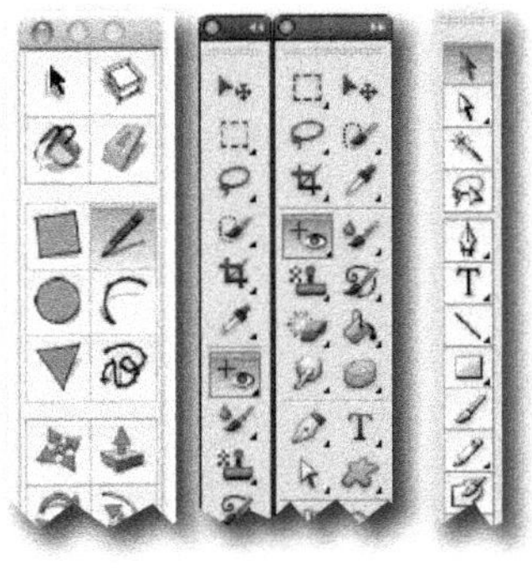

Figure 4: Tool palettes for Google SketchUp, Adobe Photoshop (two versions), and Adobe Illustrator

in Figure 4 the *pencil tool icon* in the Sketchup tool palette appears differently than the rest of the icons. Once the selected tool position is identified, the system searches through the available tool icons to identify the selected tool.

Some applications, such as Photoshop, use very similar icons for different tools, which can make it difficult to identify the correct selected tool in the video. To make our analysis more robust, we associate a preferred tool palette grid position with each tool icon as part of the input, which limits the number of icons the system must match against for a given selected tool position.

Some video tutorials include special effects such as camera cuts, zooms and pans. While we mainly experiment with "static camera" screencast videos, our template matching does not strictly assume a static camera. Since we perform template matching at multiple resolutions, we can handle cases where the camera cuts or zooms/pans to a different portion of the screen, as long as enough of the tool palette is still visible to find a good match. To support a variety of camera effects, we may need to search over a wider range of resolutions, which would slow the performance of our video analysis module.

The video analysis module is implemented in MATLAB. Our current implementation does not process video in real-time but it could be optimized to work in real-time. We expect that each video would be processed off-line once, and its metadata would be available for anyone who wants to use the Pause-and-Play system.

Linking video playback to user behavior

For Pause-and-Play to respond to user interactions it requires a real-time trace of user events such as keyboard use and tool use. While a user trace can be generated through computer vision or application-specific instrumentation, using application plug-ins that register callbacks for application events provides a fairly lightweight alternative that does not require modification of an application's source code, while still providing rich application-specific information.

To allow users to control the video playback from within the target application, we customized application shortcuts to trigger the plug-in to write commands to the user trace. In our studies with Google SketchUp, we used the space bar and arrow keys to control the video player, but a user can customize other keyboard shortcuts to control the Pause-and-Play player.

The application plug-in generates a log file and stores two types of events: the active tool and any keyboard shortcut events. The active tool events are detected by registering to the appropriate callback events. For example, in Google SketchUp we register a callback for the `onActiveToolChanged` event. The log includes each tool or key name and a timestamp. The video player reads from the log file to check for new events every 0.5 seconds. Therefore, it gets real-time updates of application events. As the video plays, the video player checks the metadata associated with the video. When there is a tool change in the video the player checks whether the user's active tool matches the current video tool. If not, the player automatically pauses the video to wait for the user to catch up, as it expects that the user is still working on the previous step. As Figure 3d shows, the player prompts the user with a message asking him to activate the appropriate tool to continue. Once the user activates the tool, the video player automatically plays the video, as this means that the user has caught up and completed the previous step. The user can always override the video player and play or pause the video by pressing the spacebar, clicking on the play/pause button in the video player, or clicking on the video itself.

After experimenting with many videos, we modified the video player to automatically pause not at the exact moment that the instructor changes the tool but two seconds later. We found that often instructors select a tool and then say the tool's name. This two second buffer worked well for most videos, but a more robust approach would be to analyze the audio stream and find appropriate audio boundaries.

Limitations

Although our techniques for segmenting videos and linking them to user behavior work well for many of the SkecthUp and Photoshop video tutorials we found on the Web, our approach does have some limitations:

Other types of important events. Our video analysis module segments videos by detecting active tool changes. However, some tutorials include other types of events that represent important steps for completing the task, such as opening a dialog box or changing the parameters of a tool. Our system currently does not detect such events.

Single tool tasks. A few of the video tutorials we encountered include long sequences of complicated actions that only involve a single tool (e.g., creating a painting in Photoshop using just the brush tool). Since we do not analyze changes in the actual document or 3D model in the video, our system would only extract a single step for such sequences, even if there are several semantically meaningful steps in the procedure. While this is a limitation, we found tool changes to be a reasonable indicator of step boundaries for most SketchUp and Photoshop videos.

Incorrect playback. The fact that our adaptive playback mechanism only considers the currently active tool in the target application and not whether a user has completed a step may result in the video resuming playback at the wrong time. For example, the user might undo a few steps and select the *rectangle tool* in order to redraw a rectangle. Since undo operations are not tracked by our system, the system will proceed playing the video, as it thinks that the user is ready for the next step, while he is in fact a few steps behind.

Work along errors. Finally, our playback design does not detect whether the user makes mistakes when completing a step. Thus, Pause-and-Play will allow users to continue through a tutorial even if they make errors along the way. We leave automatic error detection for future work.

USER STUDY

To evaluate Pause-and-Play we carried out a qualitative user study comparing a traditional video player to our Pause-and-Play video player. Based on feedback from this study we improved the design of the Pause-and-Play video player and gathered a second round of user feedback to assess the effects of the changes. We carried out both studies with Google SketchUp because compared to Adobe Photoshop, fewer people are familiar with this application and 3D modeling, and thus it was easier to control for previous experience.

Our goal was to answer the following questions:

- Is automatic pause and play useful?
- Does Pause-and-Play pause at appropriate times?

Methodology

We recruited 15 participants (11 male, 4 female) ranging in age from 18 to 49 using a university distribution list. We targeted participants with little or no experience with Google SketchUp or other 3D modeling tools. All participants were compensated with a $20 gift card.

We used a within-subjects experimental design. Each participant was asked to complete four tasks: two with a traditional video player (control condition), and two with Pause-and-Play (experimental condition). To minimize the effects of the look and feel of existing commercial video players, we created a basic version of Pause-and-Play that did not include any of the newly proposed features but allows users to pause, play, and scrub, much like most standard video players. We independently varied the order of the interfaces.

For the four tasks, we chose video tutorials that illustrate how to create an object: a dog house (6 minutes), a sphere (1.8 minutes), a house (3.7 minutes), and a chair (2.4 minutes). All of the videos had audio and were available online at YouTube when we did the study. All participants performed the tasks in the same order.

The participants completed the tasks in one-hour sessions, with a moderator leading the session. The participants were told to follow the tutorials as best as possible. At the beginning of each session, the participant filled out a short questionnaire about his or her previous experience with 3D modeling applications. After filling out an introductory questionnaire, the participants were introduced to Google SketchUp through a short (18 seconds) video that shows how to create a box. The participants were asked to replicate the box task. Each of the four subsequent task lasted 5-10 minutes, and the

Figure 5: This figure illustrates the user study set up. One participant is working on the chair task.

participants completed a short questionnaire after each one. No assistance was provided, but if after 20 minutes a participant had not completed the task, he or she was asked to to continue on to the next task. At the end of the four tasks, the participants filled out a final questionnaire comparing the two video player interfaces and provided free-form comments. We asked each user to complete a spatial cognition test at the end of the session to control for variability in 3D spatial cognition.

The laboratory setup included a 2.66GHz Intel Core i7 macbook pro running Mac OS X 10.6, with an external monitor, a standard external keyboard and a standard external mouse, as shown in Figure 5. The video audio played via the laptop speakers. Google SketchUp ran on the external monitor which is set as a main display at 1280x1024, while the video displayed on the laptop monitor at 1280x1024. We chose a two-display setup because we wanted to minimize the effects of limited screen space. Although many users have two displays, those who only use one display face a real challenge in using two applications simultaneously. We don't focus on this challenge in this work.

Results

Overall the participants were very positive about Pause-and-Play. Although we did not see any significant differences in completion time or error rate, 13 out of the 15 participants preferred the Pause-and-Play video player over the traditional player.

We observed a wide variety of behaviors for using video tutorials. With the traditional player 13 of the 15 participants preferred to work at the same time as the video was playing, while the remaining two preferred to watch the entire video before executing any of the steps. In both cases the participants did end up syncing and seeking when they were using the target application. Only one person was not able to complete a task (sphere task). Fourteen participants used the space bar to play and pause the video. Eight participants used the left arrow key to move backward. Only one participant did not use any keyboard shortcuts. And only one of the participants used the visual outline to move to a different segment of the video.

Is automatic pause and play useful? Thirteen participants found the automatic pausing and playing useful for learning new tools. For example P1 said, *"It pauses on the tool* *change–I find this extremely helpful when there is a new tool being introduced that I haven't used before and don't know by name. Pausing and 'unpausing' was also straightforward."*

The participants also mentioned that the automatic pausing made it easier for them to follow the instructions because it made it impossible for them to fall behind. P3 mentioned, *"I liked the automatic stops, because if I got behind I didn't have to stop the video myself."* P9 said *"Basically the step mode automates what I already do in manual mode. Also, the tasks were broken into logical pieces; since the video paused until I chose the correct tools, there was no way to fall behind. There were many times in manual mode when the video played further ahead, but I really wasn't listening because I was too far behind. In fact, the sound of the video continuing made me anxious to catchup and I was less efficient with my activity."*

Even participants who when using the traditional video player would watch the entire video before executing the steps, found Pause-and-Play useful and changed their behavior. For example, P5 said *"I liked [Pause-and-Play] because usually I try to see the whole video once and then try out the tasks. Because if I start on the task, I will miss what is being said in the video. But this step video removed that problem and encouraged me to work on the software side by side."*

On the other hand, this model of work was not favored by everybody. Two of our participants preferred the traditional video player because it was familiar and appeared to provide more control. P12 mentioned *"I prefer this one [traditional] because it is easier to play, pause and rewind at will, I think because it looks similar to other video tools I have previously used. ... I don't think I knew whether I could pause and rewind at will, I felt like I could only rewind/forward from one section to the next/previous one and not in between."* P15 said *"The traditional player is more smooth and easier to follow because I can pause whenever I want. I sometimes find Pause-and-Play disturbing for pausing at unnecessary places (such as selecting a tool that's commonly used) or at weird places (in the middle of a phrase). However, for a more complicated project, Pause-and-Play may be more useful, if it involves using a lot of new tools, but for simple designs like the ones that's done in this study, the traditional player is enough."*

Does Pause-and-Play pause at appropriate times? Given that 13 out of 15 participants found the pausing useful, it seems that even our simple model of keeping track of the active tool helps users stay in sync with the video. However, there is room for improvement. Seven participants mentioned that there were some pauses that were not necessary. For example, pausing for camera tools seemed unnecessary since the camera tools were often used to show different sides of the 3D model and were not specific steps in the procedure. Also for some videos, such as the chair video, the tool changes happen so quickly that the video pauses too often, resulting in choppy short clips of video that don't include a complete step. The study made it clear that the automatic pausing needs to be sensitive to step duration.

Controlling the video from the application. Four participants mentioned that the ability to control the video from Google SketchUp was useful. P7 said *"... the complete integration with the SketchUp program was great. I mean, not having to switch over was nice"* P1 said *"The good thing of Pause-and-Play is that I can start and stop the video with the space key, which makes it easier than having to move the mouse all the way to the video window, find the pause/play button and press it."*

The segmented timeline was also mentioned by five people. One user mentioned that *" [Pause-and-Play] provided convenient 'chapters' so i didn't have to manually scrub to a random point in the video."*

We also looked at whether users complete video tutorials faster and with fewer errors with Pause-and-Play. However, we did not find significant differences in completion time or error rate. We think this may be due to two factors. First, the chosen videos vary significantly in difficulty, teaching style and speed. Second, users struggled with different steps and varied in their attention to detail. While we recruited participants with no experience in 3D software, we found varying levels of expertise from novice to intermediate, perhaps influenced by expertise with GUIs and 3D concepts. Both of these issues and the fact that we did not tell the participants to go ask quickly as possible confound direct comparisons of completion time and errors.

PAUSE-AND-PLAY DESIGN ITERATION

In response to the feedback from our participants, we sought to improve the Pause-and-Play design. We made the following modifications.

- We removed pauses for camera and canvas navigation tools, including the *zoom tool*, *hand tool*, *orbit tool*, and *dolly tool*. These tools do not change the 3D model or image and using them is not required to complete the tutorial.
- Since only one participant used the visual table of contents, we removed it.
- We added a display for the upcoming tool for the users who were able to keep up with the pace of the video (Figure 6a). By selecting the next tool early, users avoid any pauses in the video playback.
- We observed that when the steps were short and the video quickly switched tools, users often got confused. To assist with fast tool changes, we removed automatic pausing for tool changes that were less than five seconds apart. To show the user that the video had now moved on to a new tool, we added a visual list that shows the user the steps he must complete to catch up to the video (Figure 6b). The video player continues playing until the user has fallen behind a maximum of three steps. If the user falls behind three steps, the player automatically pauses and waits for the user to catch up (Figure 6c). As the user accomplishes each of the steps, the player shows his progress in the video display (Figure 6d).

Second round of user feedback

Our goal for the second user study was to understand whether the updated design led to pausing in more appropriate parts of the video. We considered bringing back some of our participants from the first study, but we were concerned that too

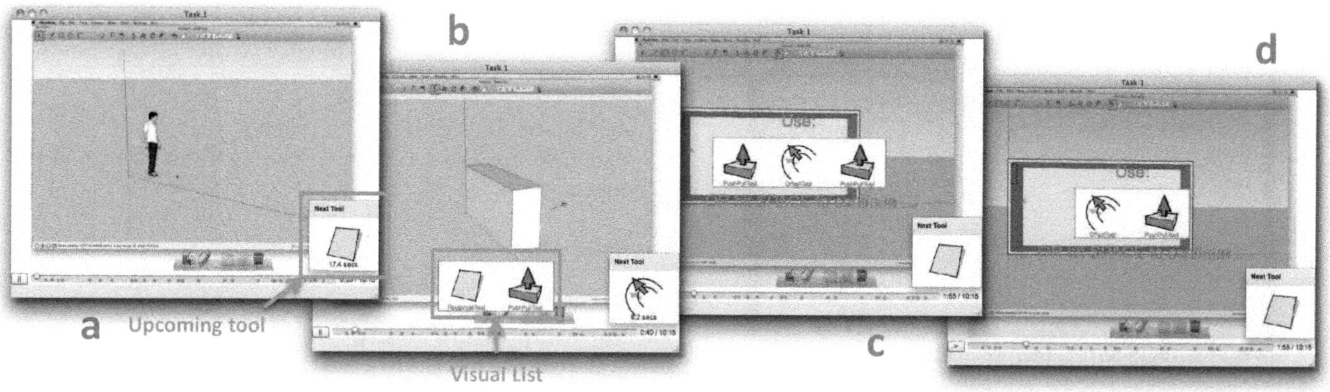

Figure 6: We changed the Pause-and-Play video player interface in response to user feedback. (a) For advanced users we show the next tool in the bottom right corner. (b) We remove pausing for short steps and show the user the steps as a visual list. (c) After a maximum of three missed steps, the video pauses. (d) As the user makes progress, the display updates to show the remaining steps.

much time (a month) had passed since the original study. To get a sense for whether we were on the right track, we carried out a pilot study with the new redesigned Pause-and-Play video interface.

We recruited 4 participants (2 male, 2 female) ranging in age from 18 to 65. The laboratory set up and the recruiting criteria were the same as the first study. Instead of 4 tasks with two video players, we asked them to perform only two tasks (the house and chair tasks) with only one interface (the redesigned Pause-and-Play video player). Again we considered the house task as a practice task. After they accomplished both tasks, we asked users to rate the frequency of the pauses on a scale of 1 (too infrequent) to 5 (too frequent) where 3 is about right and asked for open ended feedback on the video player experience. Each participant session lasted 30 to 50 minutes, and all participants were compensated with a $15 gift card.

All of the participants completed the tasks and used the keyboard shortcuts to play and pause the video. Three of the participants used the left arrow to move back to previous steps. The participants rated the frequency of pauses as 2.8, 3, 2.5 and 2.5 and expressed that there were times when they wished the video has paused when it didn't. S1 mentioned *"One specific place I got lost was in selecting materials. I missed the step of selecting 'bricks' instead of the default 'roofing', and so picked the most likely looking material, which turned out to be some shingles. It might be good to pause until the user picked the correct material. Otherwise, the pauses seemed well placed. Waiting just until I picked the correct tool seemed helpful."* S2 said *"there was one instance where I wished it had paused earlier."* S4 mentioned *'I used Space-bar pausing - so this means that it was not frequent enough for me."*. So although no one mentioned that the video paused too often, three of the four participants felt that perhaps there weren't enough automatic pauses.

The display of the upcoming tool (Figure 6a) was not heavily used, perhaps because the pace of the video was such that the participants were focused on the task and were not looking ahead. Although the display did not seem to prompt users to pick the next tool, at least one of the participants found it useful. S2 mentioned that *"knowing which tool comes up next is good to keep in mind. Mentally helps you know where the tutorial is heading."* S4 found *"the box showing the Next tool was not helpful but not really too distracting either."*

All of the participants observed a list of upcoming tools (Figure 6b) two or more times . While it seemed that the visual list was useful, there were mixed feelings about the lack of an automatic pause between two different steps in the tutorial. S4 expected a pause after each tool and was distracted when *"the 'teacher' would do two things, and the pause would happen after both instead of after each one."*. S4 found the visual list particularly useful when she wanted to go back and fix mistakes. *"When it was waiting - it would list the tools I needed next. This was especially useful when I went back to fix mistakes, and came back - it helped me remember what I had to do next."*

In conclusion, the second round of user feedback showed us that we improved the ability of the video to stay in sync with the user by removing navigational tools, though there is room for improvement in situations when tools are used in quick succession. Since the participants expected that the video player would pause for every tool, they found the aggregation of up to three tools distracting. On the other hand, the visual list was found to be useful when users replay the video, reminding them of the steps.

CONCLUSION AND FUTURE WORK

We have demonstrated an approach for helping users replicate the steps in existing video tutorials. Based on an observational study, we identified key challenges that users currently face when working along with videos, and we designed an interactive video tutorial system, Pause-and-Play, that addresses these problems. Pause-and-Play detects and links important events in existing videos to corresponding events in the target application, which enables progress-aware video playback based on the working pace of the user and convenient navigation controls for skipping directly to relevant portions of the video. Since our method does not require access or modifications to the application source code,

Figure 7: In addition to the core adaptive playback and navigation features described in the System Overview, our Pause-and-Play prototype for Photoshop allows the tutorial author to manually specify additional metadata for each step, including customized text descriptions (as shown here), visual annotations, and zoom locations that focus on specific parts of the interface.

there is a relatively small overhead for supporting new applications.

We see several interesting directions for future work. In order to deploy a system like Pause-and-Play in real world settings for many actual users, we need more investigation. As mentioned earlier, one limitation of our system is that we only detect active tool changes in the input video. Thus, we could extend our vision-based video analysis to detect other events (e.g., menu selection, opening a dialog, drawing operations) and include audio input to avoid placing step boundaries in the middle of a sentence. However, while such techniques would certainly improve our video segmentation, a completely automatic analysis will likely never be perfect. As a result, we plan to enable tutorial authors to improve automatic segmentation by adding, deleting or changing step boundaries, and enhancing the tutorial with additional metadata. For example, the author could add annotations that enable expertise-dependent step boundaries, ease search and navigation, and indicate the most salient regions of the user interface for specific steps. We have experimented with adding some of these manual authoring features to our Pause-and-Play prototype for Photoshop (Figure 7).

One common problem with following a tutorial occurs when there is a mismatch between the user's content and the content used in the tutorial. For example, the method for selecting the red region in a red-eye removal tutorial may not work well if the eye is too small or the image is blurry. In this case an inexperienced user may get stuck, and his only option is to look for another more suitable tutorial. A future extension would allow users to create a discussion thread associated with a video segment in order to share any difficulties they may be experiencing. More expert users could provide alternative solutions, for example, a link to another tutorial that handles "blurred red eye removal".

In conclusion, we believe Pause-and-Play is only a first step in bridging the gap between applications and video tutorials. We are confident there are many other unexplored ways of leveraging video demonstrations to encourage and empower users to learn a wide variety of software applications.

ACKNOWLEDGMENTS

We thank the user study participants for their time and valuable comments.

REFERENCES

1. L. Bergman, V. Castelli, T. Lau, and D. Oblinger. Docwizards: a system for authoring follow-me documentation wizards. In *Proc. ACM UIST*, pages 191–200, 2005.
2. K.-Y. Cheng, S.-J. Luo, B.-Y. Chen, and H.-H. Chu. Smartplayer: user-centric video fast-forwarding. In *Proc. SIGCHI*, pages 789–798, 2009.
3. M. Dixon and J. Fogarty. Prefab: implementing advanced behaviors using pixel-based reverse engineering of interface structure. In *Proc. SIGCHI*, pages 1525–1534, 2010.
4. S. Gilbert, S. B. Blessing, and S. Kodavali. The extensible problem-specific tutor (xpst): Evaluation of an api for tutoring on existing interfaces. In *Proc. the conf. Artificial Intelligence in Education*, pages 707–709, 2009.
5. F. Grabler, M. Agrawala, W. Li, M. Dontcheva, and T. Igarashi. Generating photo manipulation tutorials by demonstration. In *Proc. ACM SIGGRAPH*, pages 1–9, 2009.
6. T. Grossman and G. Fitzmaurice. Toolclips: an investigation of contextual video assistance for functionality understanding. In *Proc. SIGCHI*, pages 1515–1524, 2010.
7. T. Grossman, J. Matejka, and G. Fitzmaurice. Chronicle: capture, exploration, and playback of document workflow histories. In *Proc. ACM UIST*, pages 143–152, 2010.
8. S. M. Harrison. A comparison of still, animated, or nonillustrated on-line help with written or spoken instructions in a graphical user interface. In *Computer Human Interaction*, pages 82–89, 1995.
9. C. Hategekimana, S. Gilbert, and S. Blessing. Effectiveness of using an intelligent tutoring system to train users on off-the-shelf software. In *Proc. Society for Info. Tech. and Teacher Education Intl Conf., AACE*, 2008.
10. C. Kelleher and R. Pausch. Stencils-based tutorials: design and evaluation. In *Proc. SIGCHI*, pages 541–550, 2005.
11. J. Matejka, T. Grossman, and G. Fitzmaurice. Ambient help. In *Proc. SIGCHI*, pages 2751–2760, 2011.
12. S. Palmiter and J. Elkerton. An evaluation of animated demonstrations of learning computer-based tasks. In *Proc SIGCHI*, pages 257–263, 1991.
13. N. Petrovic, N. Jojic, and T. S. Huang. Adaptive video fast forward. *Multimedia Tools Appl.*, 26:327–344, 2005.
14. S. Pongnumkul, J. Wang, G. Ramos, and M. Cohen. Content-aware dynamic timeline for video browsing. In *Proc. ACM UIST*, pages 139–142, 2010.
15. B. Shneiderman. Direct manipulation: A step beyond programming languages. *Computer*, 16(8):57 –69, 1983.
16. S. L. Su. *Enhanced Visual Authoring Using Operation History*. PhD thesis, Massachusetts Institute of Technology, Boston, Massachusetts, 2009.
17. T. Yeh, T.-H. Chang, and R. C. Miller. Sikuli: using gui screenshots for search and automation. In *Proc. ACM UIST*, pages 183–192, 2009.

Creating Contextual Help for GUIs Using Screenshots

Tom Yeh, Tsung-Hsiang Chang[§], Bo Xie[†], Greg Walsh[†], Ivan Watkins[†], Krist Wongsuphasawat, Man Huang[†], Larry S. Davis, and Ben Bederson

Department of Computer Science College of Information Studies[†]
University of Maryland, College Park
College Park, MD
{tomyeh,boxie,gwalsh,iwatkins,kristw,manhuang,lsd,bederson}@umd.edu

MIT CSAIL[§]
Cambridge, MA
vgod@mit.edu

ABSTRACT

Contextual help is effective for learning how to use GUIs by showing instructions and highlights on the actual interface rather than in a separate viewer. However, end-users and third-party tech support typically cannot create contextual help to assist other users because it requires programming skill and source code access. We present a creation tool for contextual help that allows users to apply common computer skills—taking screenshots and writing simple scripts. We perform pixel analysis on screenshots to make this tool applicable to a wide range of applications and platforms without source code access. We evaluated the tool's usability with three groups of participants: developers, instructors, and tech support. We further validated the applicability of our tool with 60 real tasks supported by the tech support of a university campus.

ACM Classification: H5.2 [Information interfaces and presentation]: User Interfaces. - Graphical user interfaces.

General terms: Human Factors; Design

Keywords: Help; Contextual Help; Pixel Analysis

INTRODUCTION

Contextual help has been shown effective for learning graphical user interfaces [3,4,13,16,17,18,25]. Unlike traditional help based on screenshots or screencasts, contextual help allows users to receive help in the actual interface they are interacting with, rather than in another help interface such as in a web browser or a video player. For example, with contextual help, users can see a dropdown box highlighted in the live interface and an instruction such as "select the WEP key" displayed next to it. Users can immediately practice the step as instructed. In contrast, with traditional help, users may see a captured screenshot of that dropdown box on a webpage. In order to practice the step, users need to switch to the live interface and try to locate the dropdown box that matches the screenshot. Also, they need to remember the instruction they read on the webpage regarding which option to select. This process illustrates traditional help's two usability problems—split attention and delayed practice [21] that could be avoided simply by presenting help contextually.

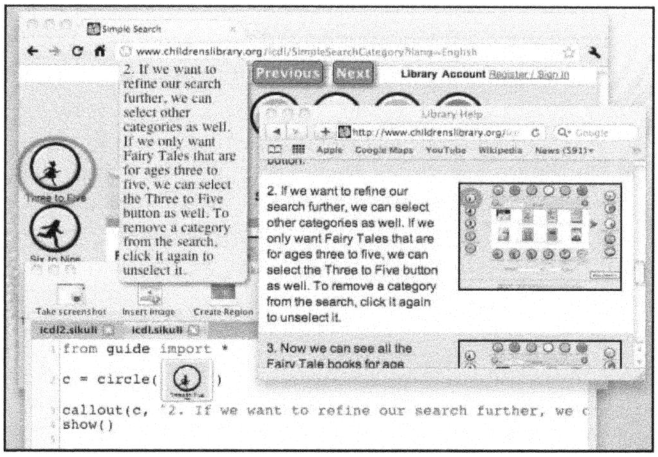

Figure 1. Creating contextual help for a GUI. The window in the far back is the interface of the International Children's Digital Library. A separate window in the front displays existing help content for this interface. Our tool enables help designers to create help content that can be presented contextually in the actual interface (i.e., yellow callout and red circle) by writing a simple script and taking screenshots, as shown in the editor below. (www.childrenslibrary.org)

However, for help designers, it is difficult to create GUI help for other users that can be presented contextually. For instance, to add a contextual highlight to a button, one may need to identify the source code responsible for that button and modify the code to draw highlight on the button [16,17]. Yet, many GUIs are proprietary. Third-party help designers are prevented from making contextual help to support these GUIs. Alternatively, help designers can use the accessibility API to determine that button's screen location and write an external program to draw highlight directly at that location on the screen [3,4]. Yet, for many GUIs, such API is either unavailable or unsupported [15]. Moreover, even if both the source code and the accessibility API are available, using them still requires high-level programming skills, a requirement that alienates many users from creating contextual help to assist other users.

In this work, we aimed to democratize contextual help. Specifically, we developed a tool to empower help designers in the general public (e.g., advanced users, computer instructors, third-party tech support) to create contextual help. Rather than requiring advanced programming skills, our tool allows a help designer to apply basic computer skills including taking screenshots and writing simple markup similar to HTML or Wiki. At design time, a help designer can select an interface component by capturing the component's screenshot (e.g., ) and then specify the type of contextual help to add to that component using a simple visual markup (e.g., highlight()). When the help is presented to a user, the pixels on the user's screen are visually searched to locate the component that matches the screenshot. Once the component is found, contextual help can be drawn near the component. This visual search is performed using the Sikuli library [32], an open-source library for search and automation based on pixel analysis. The generalizability of screen pixels across all applications and platforms, a property already demonstrated by various applications [1,2,7,15,19,20,24,33], allows our method to be applicable to any GUI regardless whether the source code or accessibility APIs are available.

RELATED WORK

Contextual Help

Most GUI help is presented to users outside the GUI in a separate context such as in a web browser for seeing annotated screenshots or in a video player for watching screencasts. This out-of-context poses major usability problems such as split-attention and the lack of support of practice [21]. Contextual help solves these two problems [13] and allows hands-on practice and exploration at the same time, which has been shown to be key ingredients of successful learning of an interface [30].

The most prevalent form of contextual help is the tooltip [9]. Several efforts aimed to improve upon tooltips, such as Side Views that allow users to contextually preview the effect of a command [29], ToolClips that present to users short video clips and other rich help content next to toolbar buttons contextually [13]. In HCI research, contextual help has been applied to initial guidance to new features in the context of a map interface [16], to stencil-based tutorials for young school children in the context of Alice [17], to programming tasks in the context of an Eclipse editor [3], and to practical tasks such as booking flights in the context of a web browser [4]. In the commercial world, contextual help can also be spotted in interfaces that evolve quickly. For example, Google Docs periodically introduces new features and greets returning users with text bubbles to draw their attention to these features. However, in each instance cited above, content creation requires either advanced programming skill or privileged access to the source code, requirements that rule out a large population of help designers such as expert users, computer instructors, and third-party tech support.

Creating GUI Help

The majority of GUI help online today is created manually. Help designers use software such as Camtasia to make screencasts or MWSnap to take screenshots and annotate them with highlights and instructions. Guidelines have been provided for creating effective screencasts [23]. But meeting these guidelines requires significant manual effort. To reduce human effort, automatic methods have been proposed that aim to create tutorials based on knowledge of a UI derived from a UI model [27], UI specification [22] or a UI event log [5]. However, automatic methods have not been reliable enough to be used in practice.

A more practical approach to help creation that seeks to balance convenience and reliability has been the semi-automatic approach based on the notion of Programming by Demonstration (PBD) [3, 11,14]. To create help for a task, help designers simply perform that task. The interaction involved is captured and a descriptive summary of this interaction is automatically generated. Then, designers can manually review this summary and make necessary changes before publishing it as help. Taking this approach, Graphstrack [14] records designers' click actions and captures regional screenshots around each click location to generate minimalist help showing only images of relevant interface targets rather than the entire interface. The tool developed by Grabler et al. seeks to create succinct step-by-step help for a photo manipulation task while an expert demonstrates the task [11]. However, content generated by these two creation tools is intended to be viewed in a traditional manner in a context separate from the actual interface. DocWizard is most closely related to our work in that it also aims to simply the creation process of contextual help [3]. It allows help designers to record an interaction sequence that can be played back in the real interface, drawing a red circle on the relevant interface target in each step of the sequence. However, DocWizard is limited to the Eclipse editor or other interfaces based on the same platform (i.e., Java SWT).

Generalizability of Pixels

Pixels offer a possibility to make interaction techniques generally applicable to a wide range of interfaces [1] by providing interfaces with a general attachment point for these techniques [19]. Early effort exploring this possibility includes Triggers [24], IBOTS [33], and Segman [2]. Recent effort has seen successful applications of pixels to provide general solutions to many practical problems such as note taking [20], GUI automation [32], click target identification [15], and advanced behaviors [7]. In the current work, we seek to leverage the universality of pixels to make the creation of contextual help generally accessible. This idea has been previously suggested [32,8], but it has not been fully explored and only limited proof-of-concept examples have been presented.

CONTEXTUAL HELP USING SCREENSHOTS

We present a tool for creating and presenting contextual help for GUIs using screenshots. At creation time, this tool provides help designers with a set of visual scripting commands to specify which GUI components to provide help for and what help content to present. At presentation time,

Figure 2. Graphics objects (top: circle, rectangle, bracket, bottom: spotlight, arrow) can be contextually rendered on GUIs to draw users' attention.

it uses computer vision to visually track GUI components on users' screen and display help near these components, allowing users to receive help in context.

Scripted Slideshow Metaphor

We surveyed existing GUI help based on screenshots or screencasts (e.g., eHow) and tools for creating them (e.g., MWSnap, Camtasia). We observed four important content characteristics of such help:

1. **Script:** Help tends to follow a particular script.
2. **Length:** Some help was as short as a single step while others were a dozen steps or more.
3. **Visuals:** Help can include a wide combination of text, screen capture, annotated screens and video.
4. **Pacing:** Some help was completely automated along a strict timeline while others may require user action to continue at each step.

Informed by this observation, we chose *scripted slideshow* as the metaphor to conceptualize contextual help. This metaphor adequately captures the characteristics above while remaining simple to promote learnability. First, a script can have steps that map naturally to slides in a slideshow. Second, a slideshow can be of arbitrary length. Third, each slide can include multiple graphics and/or text objects. Fourth, a slideshow can be advanced automatically or by user actions.

Visual Commands

Our tool provides help designers with a rich set of visual commands for creating a scripted slideshow. The Sikuli IDE [32] provides a convenient way for editing these visual commands. These commands include graphics, text, positioning, steps, animated effects, pacing, and support for ambiguity, each of which is described below:

Graphics: To draw a user's attention to an interface target, help designers can write a simple command based on an image of the target. For example, circle(🏠) paints a circle around the icon 🏠 in the actual interface. We support five types of graphical highlights: *circle*, *rectangle*, *bracket*, *arrow*, and *spotlight*, as shown in Figure 2.

Text: After drawing the user's attention to a target, it is also important to explain to the user what the target does. This is typically achieved by adding text objects near the target.

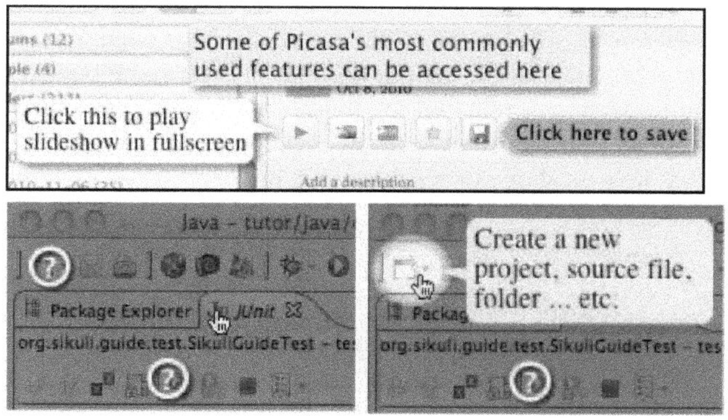

Figure 3. Text objects (top, from left to right: callout, text, flag, bottom: hotspot) can be contextually rendered on GUIs to provide helpful information.

We support three types of simple text objects: *text*, *callout*, and *flag* and one type of mouse-over text object: *hotspot*. Designers can add a new text object to a step by writing a simple function call that takes two arguments. The first argument specifies the target this text object is associated with and the second argument specifies the content to be displayed. Examples of these text objects can be seen in Figure 3.

Positioning: By default, graphics and text objects are automatically placed in the best position relative to the target. For instance, a *callout* is normally displayed to the left of a target but will be positioned to the right if there is not screen space to the left. Also, a *bracket* is placed according to the target's aspect ratio; it is placed above if the target is landscape and to the left if it is portrait. Alternatively, designers can position graphics and text objects themselves using a set of optional positioning parameters. Using positioning parameters designers can place objects in an empty area of the interface without occluding existing interface components. These parameters include the *side* parameter that specifies which side of a target to place contents (e.g., top, left, bottom, right), the *alignment* parameter that specifies how objects should be vertically or horizontally aligned with a target, and the *offset, margin,* and *spacing* parameters to further fine-tune the positions.

Step: Help designers can group graphics and text objects into steps using two methods. The simpler method is to express each step as a sequence of function calls for adding content objects followed by an explicit call to *show()* to mark the end of the step. Below is an example of a two-step contextual help expressed in this way:

Each call to *show()* displays the content objects added since the previous call to *show()*. It also clears the content before advancing to the next step.

```
callout([icon], "Click this to save")
callout([icon], "Click this to print")
show()
callout([icon], "Click this to create a new document")
show()
```

Another method is to represent steps as individual functions. At the end of the script, these functions can be passed as an array to a single call to *show()* to present these steps contextually in the users' interface. Below is the same contextual help as above re-written using this method:

```
def step1():
    callout([icon], "Click this to save")
    callout([icon], "Click this to print")
def step2():
    callout([icon], "Click this to create a new document")
show([step1, step2])
```

The former method offers simplicity, whereas the latter offers more power such as the ability to reorder and reuse content. These two methods can also be mixed to allow even greater flexibility.

Animated Effects: Appropriate uses of animation can enhance contextual help [28] as they help grab users' attention. We enable help designers to add common animated effects such as fly-in, fade, blink, and circling, by supplying an optional animation parameter. For example, rectangle([icon], animation = "flyin") allows rectangle to enter the scene from the edge of the screen and *fly* to the target, and flag([icon], "Here", animation = "circling") makes the flag object moving in a circular motion next to the target.

Pacing: Help designers specify how the presentation of contextual help should be paced in two ways similar to the presentation of a slideshow. The typical way is to give the control to users. Users can decide when to advance to the next step by clicking the Next button. This behavior can be achieved by adding a dialog box to the current step. For example, dialog("Enter Password Here") displays a dialog box like below. This pacing option is preferable for problem-oriented and training-oriented contextual help, since users may spend an arbitrary amount of time to perform the operations related to a step.

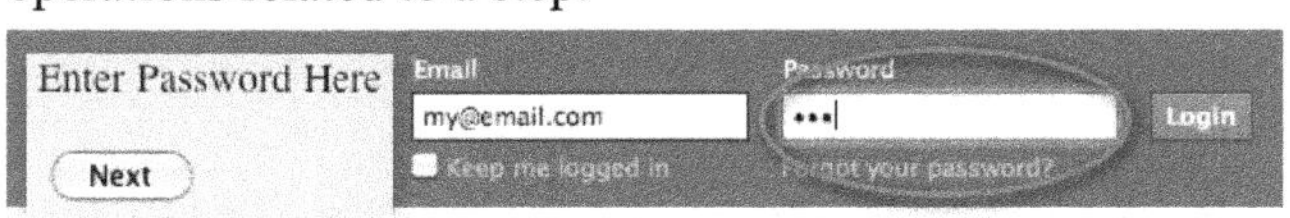

Another way to control pacing is to specify a timeout period explicitly (e.g., *show(3)*). This method is more suitable for demoing new features when fewer actions are required.

Ambiguity: Ambiguity arises when multiple instances of the same or similar-looking targets are visible on the screen (e.g., multiple sliders). Help designers can disambiguate using other distinctive objects nearby (e.g., the slider under the label "Double-Click Speed") using Sikuli Script's built-in spatial operators. For example, a *flag* can be placed next to a specific slider as shown in the figure below by flag(find([Double-Click Speed]).below().find([icon]),"Drag this").

Evaluation of Prototype

We built a prototype and publicly released it in early 2011 as an extension to Sikuli. Based on an earlier survey on traditional GUI help, we identified three distinct scenarios GUI help is often administered:

- **New Features:** Introduces new capabilities to users to aid in future discovery.
- **One-time Solution:** Helps user solve specific problems (e.g., installing a printer). The problem often needs to be solved only once, which implies retention is less important.
- **Training:** Teaches users how to do important and recurring tasks. Retention is important and the training is sometimes scenario based, involving fictional data that can differ significantly from that of the user's real task.

Participants

Informed by the scenarios above, we recruited three distinct groups of help designers to participate in the evaluation of the prototype.

The first group is developers of novel GUI applications. It is crucial for this group to introduce new features to would-be users. We worked with selected members in Sikuli's user community and the researchers of the LifeFlow project [31] as representative users in this group.

The second group is tech support for large institutions. A large body of help content created by this group is to help users with one-time solutions. Participants representing this group were the members of the Office of Information Technology at the University of Maryland. We conducted an hour-long focus group with seven manager-level members overseeing matters related to user support.

The third group is computer instructors for novice computer users. Help created by this group tends to be training oriented. The representative participants we recruited for this group were three researchers who study how older adults learn and use computer technology. They regularly create computer tutorials based on screenshots and screencasts for older adults to learn how to find health information on the Web. Initially, we met with these researchers and demonstrated to them how to write simple scripts to create contextual versions of the same tutorials they previously created. After understanding the basic premise of our contextual help framework, these researchers worked with us to design and run two participatory design sessions (March 4 and 11) with older adults to further understand the framework's potential and limitations.

Findings and Discussion

All participants were impressed by the prototype and were able to create contextual help using our tool to benefit the respective user population they serve. However, they also identified several limitations discussed below:

Lack of robust startup. Before contextual help can begin, the target GUI is assumed to be visible so that the relevant component in the first step can be found on the screen and highlighted. For example, to present contextual help on

Facebook's login page, the page must be visible in order to highlight the relevant input fields. However, our participants reported that this assumption is often violated; users may launch a contextual help script before switching to the target GUI. Since the target GUI is not visible, the script simply fails immediately. This finding motivated us to develop features to improve the robustness of contextual help during startup.

Lack of flexible pacing options. Our participants found the two pacing options provided by the prototype too limiting. The time-based pacing option is impractical when it is not possible to predict how much time the user might need for the current step. The dialog-based pacing option is laborious, since it requires users to always make an extra click on the Next button to advance. These limitations motivated us to develop additional pacing options that are more flexible.

Lack of conditional help. A strict slideshow model follows a predetermined sequence of steps. While this is acceptable for many simple procedural tasks, our participants found it restrictive in certain scenarios where subsequent steps may be conditioned on what users have done and/or what the GUI looks like in the current step. The need to support these scenarios motivated us to develop features to allow contextual help to react to user actions and GUI states.

Lack of area-based selection. Our participants in the developer group informed us that when the purpose of contextual help is to give a feature overview of a GUI, it is often necessary to point at a general area in the GUI rather than individual components, for example, to introduce the toolbar area and the content area. In traditional screenshot help, an area is often marked and explained by a rectangle drawn around it and some text placed in the middle. In screencasts, a commonly used (but not necessarily effective) technique is to move the mouse cursor in a circular motion around an area while talking about it. However, it is often not possible to select an area by a single screenshot, as the size and the location the area can vary widely. For example, the toolbar area often changes as the size of the container window changes. This finding motivated us to develop an area selection method based on multiple visual landmarks.

Lack of cursor support. Our participants in the computer instructor group reported that in addition to receiving the cognitive knowledge of which interface target to interact with and how, some older adult learners would also like to receive assistance to perform the motor movement required to interact with the target. While it is possible to automate this interaction, doing so would deny these learners the chance of hands-on practice, which is crucial for learning [30]. This observation motivated us to implement a number of cursor enhancement techniques help designers can incorporate in contextual help to simplify motor movement.

Lack of tracking. In pixel-based GUI automation, a target's screen location needs to be found only once. As soon as the location is found, interaction commands such as *click* is delivered immediately to that location to simulate the effect of a human user clicking on that target. Similarly, in contextual help, drawing commands such as *circle()* can be applied to the target's location immediately after the location is determined. While the effect of an interaction command (e.g., click) ends as soon as that interaction is carried out, the effect of a drawing command needs to last for as long as users are still viewing the current step. Users may operate the GUI in a way that causes the target to move (e.g., scrolling) or disappear (e.g., switching to another window). However, the prototype did not re-compute the target's location; contextual help remained visible in the old location even though it was no longer relevant to any target nearby. Our participants found this behavior confusing. This observation motivated us to implement a visual tracker to continuously monitor the visual states of targets.

Lack of a WYSIWYG editor. While our participants in the tech support group and GUI developer group found the syntax for writing contextual help scripts easy to learn, our participants in the computer instructor group still preferred a visual editor supporting WYSIWYG. They were more familiar with GUI tools such as PowerPoint and Camtasia. This finding motivated us to develop a visual editor to further simplify the creation of contextual help.

Lack of an effective deployment strategy. To deploy a contextual help script, help designers can saved the script as a Sikuli executable (i.e., a runnable jar) and publish it on a website. Users can download this executable and run it on their own machines to receive contextual help. Our participants in the tech support group informed us that a more desirable deployment strategy would be to publish contextual help scripts alongside the traditional help already hosted on the official support website. The reason is that this website is the default place these users have learned to visit and look for help and the place they would trust. This finding motivated us to consider how contextual help can be seamlessly integrated with existing traditional help for more effective deployment.

ADVANCED FEATURES

We further present eight advanced features developed as a direct response to the limitations identified by our participants during the evaluation of the prototype.

Switching to the Target GUI

We provide two methods for help designers to assist users to switch to the target GUI when contextual help begins.

First, help designers can automate the steps to switch to the target GUI by composing a simple Sikuli automation script, for example, opening the System Preferences window by click(); click(System Preferences...).

Second, help designers can explicitly instruct users how to switch to the target GUI when the GUI is not already visible. This instruction can also be provided in the form of contextual help. For example, many configuration tasks on Mac share a common starting point at the System Preferences window. A help designer can create a common help script for switching to this window. When needed, any other contextual help that begins from this window can invoke this script to help users start in the right place.

Pacing by Visual Triggers and User Clicks

We developed two additional pacing options based on visual triggers and user clicks. To pace by visual triggers, help designers can give a list of visual patterns expected to be visible only in the next step. For example, the statement next(Empty Trash) means the Empty Trash button will be seen next and can be interpreted as a signal that the current step is over. To pace by user clicks, help designers can write a simple statement like clickable(Empty Trash). This statement places a mouse click detector on top the button. When the user clicks on that button, help automatically proceeds to the next step. We implemented this detector in pure Java using an almost transparent window on top of the button to intercept clicks. Once a click is detected, the window is hidden and the click is immediately delivered to the interface underneath the window.

Supporting Conditional Contextual Help

To address the lack of conditional help, we augmented the scripted slideshow model with the ability to present help conditionally. There are two scenarios when conditional contextual help naturally arises. The first scenario is when users need to make a choice in a particular step and the choice may take the users on a different path in subsequent steps. For example, at some point during printer installation it may be necessary to choose whether the printer is shared or not. Subsequent help depends on this choice. If users need to click on one of two buttons to make the choice, help designers can place a *clickable* object on each button. This clickable object can detect users' click on the button. Each clickable object is associated with a unique ID. The ID is returned by *show()* and can be used in a conditional statement to decide which help path to take next. The script below gives an example:

```
clickable( [keyboard] ,"KEYBOARD")
clickable( [mouse] ,"MOUSE")
if (show() == "KEYBOARD"):
    help_keyboard()
else:
    help_mouse()
```

Alternatively, if the actual GUI does not offer the choices explicitly, help designers can place *virtual* buttons on the GUI and assign unique ID's to them to offer conditional contextual help, e.g., button("Do it"). The example shown next combines all of these mechanisms giving the choices to return to the previous step, advance to the next step, quit, or let the computer perform the step automatically.

The second scenario conditional contextual help is useful is when help designers want to account for the different states the system may be in at run time and choose a help path accordingly. For example, a printer installer GUI may display different messages depending on whether or not the printer's driver can be found. Designers can use Sikuli Script's *exists()* function to check whether certain indicative visual pattern exists and choose the appropriate next step, using a conditional statement like below.

```
if exists( [Printer not found.] ):
    help_find_driver()
else:
    help_install_driver()
```

Assisting Target Selection

To address the lack of cursor support, we implemented three cursor enhancement techniques inspired by the state-of-the-art [10, 12] that can be invoked by help designers with simple visual commands. First, the *beam* cursor paints a lighted path from the current cursor location to the target and accelerates the movement toward the target if the user begins to move the cursor in that direction. This technique is suitable for problem-oriented help where each step tends to involve a single target. For example, beam([wrench]) produces the following effect at presentation time:

Second, the *magnet* cursor acts like a magnet that attracts targets to the cursor's vicinity as *virtual* targets. Users can interact with these virtual targets as if interacting with the real targets. Since these virtual targets are closer, less effort is needed to operate the cursor. When users move the cursor over a virtual target, the corresponding real target is highlighted, allowing the users to learn where the target actually is. This cursor technique is especially useful when relevant targets are scattered across the GUI. For example, magnet([[wrench],[home]]) achieves the effect shown below. It brings the two targets from opposite sides of the GUI to where the mouse cursor is; users do not need to move the cursor far across the screen to choose.

Third, the *clickcross* cursor [10] spreads a group of targets along a large orbit. This technique is useful when the targets are closely situated and making precise selection among them is hard for certain users without fine-motor control due to aging or disabilities. By spreading the targets apart, this technique has been shown to significantly reduce the physical demand on fine-motor control. For example, clickcross(, []) spreads a group of targets (2nd argument) when the user clicks on the target area (1st argument), as shown next:

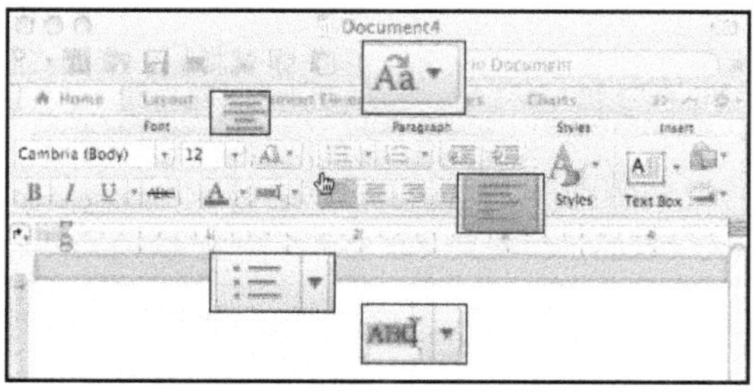

The theoretical capability of pixels to implement cursor enhancement techniques on a wide range of interfaces has been previously demonstrated by Prefab [7]. In this work, we further contribute by enabling designers to deploy these techniques in practice. Also, rather than system-wide application to every interface widget as was done in Prefab, we allow designers to apply these techniques judicially only to the parts of an interface where users need help the most.

Tracking Targets

When changes in a target's location or visibility are detected, the contextual help associated with that target must be repositioned or hidden/shown accordingly, maintaining the relevance of the help content, as exemplified in Figure 4. To detect location changes efficiently, we devised heuristics informed by several observations regarding how targets typically change their location:

1. In practice, users tend *not* to move interface targets when they try to follow contextual help. This implies that the tracker should always look at the target's last location to see if it remains before looking elsewhere to find where it might have moved.
2. When users did move interface targets, one common reason is scrolling such as scrolling a web interface. This implies that when a target is no longer seen in its last location, the first logical place to look for the target again is along the vertical strip and the horizontal strip extending from the target's last location.
3. Another common reason interface targets might move is that the user drags their container window to a different location. This implies that the next logical place to look should be around the same relative location from the target's last location as the relative location of the cursor from where it was dragged.
4. Interface targets in the same interface tend to move in the same way. This implies that after finding the first target's new location relative to its previous location, the search for the other targets should begin from the same relative locations from their previous locations.

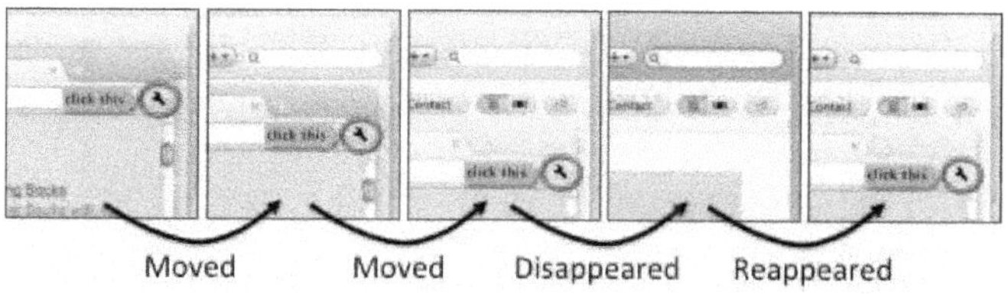

Figure 4. Tracking targets and updating contextual help.

5. Lastly, if none of these heuristics worked, the tracker will fall back to full-screen search to relocate a moved interface target.

To detect visibility changes, we also rely on heuristics informed by how targets typically disappear and re-appear:

1. Common reasons a target may disappear are that the user minimizes the window or switches to another window. After a while, the user may restore the window or bring the window to the front, making that target visible again in its last location. This implies that once a target is no longer found and relevant content hidden, it is necessary to check the target's last location periodically so that the content can be redisplayed as soon as the target reappears there.
2. In some less common scenarios, a temporarily occluded target may reappear in a completely different location from its last location. The only way to detect reappearance of this kind is to conduct full-screen search. Since such scenarios are less common, we can perform full-screen search at lower frequency.

Defining Resizable Areas

To address the lack of area-based selection, we implemented a new visual command *area*() to allow designers to describe an area by a set of salient landmarks. For example, spotlight(area([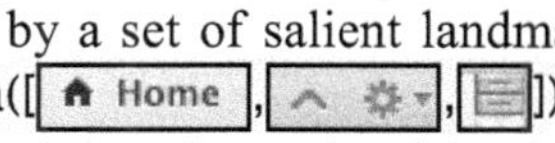])) defines a rectangular area containing three visual landmarks and paints a spotlight on it, like below:

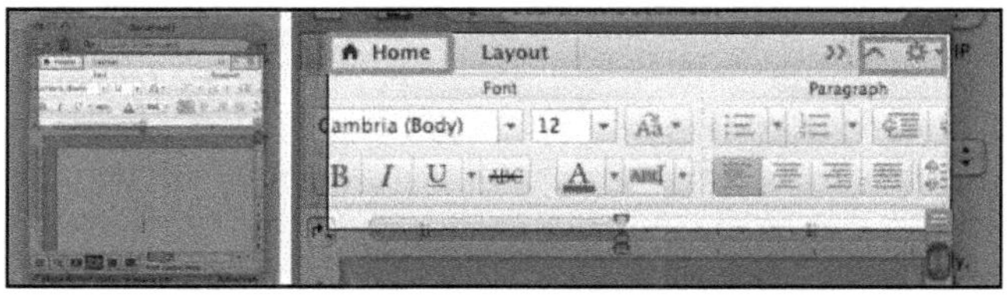

These landmarks will be found and tracked on the user's screen at run time to dynamically update the area.

Another way to specify an area is to describe the landmarks that form the vertical and horizontal bounds. Moreover, an area can also be derived from other areas through set operations such as union and intersection. For example, the script below defines the area shown on the next page,

h = area([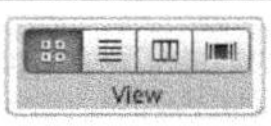, ], range = "horizontal")
v = area([, 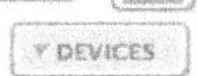], range = "vertical")
spotlight(intersection(h,v))

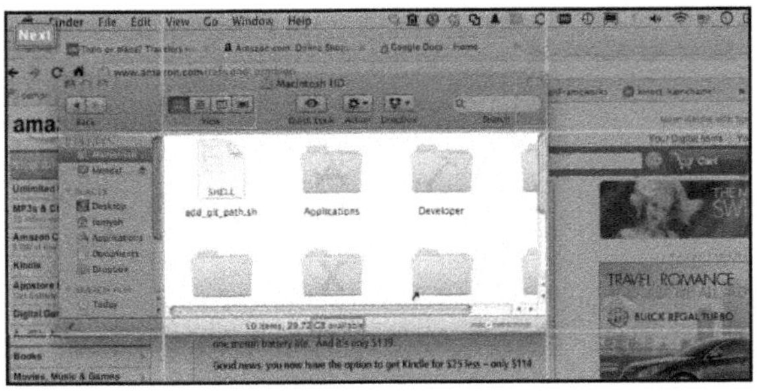

Note that using this method, it is possible to describe an area using landmarks outside the area.

An alternative pixel-based approach would be to analyze the structure of an interface and derive a structural path (e.g., XPath) from the root window to the desired area [8]. But this approach cannot be applied to arbitrary areas that do not correspond to any container widget.

Supporting WYSIWYG

To further lower the skill requirement, we developed a visual editor to complement the script editor. To promote learnability, we borrowed familiar design elements from popular presentation software such as PowerPoint and Keynote. As a result, the editor has a layout that consists of the main editing area, an overview panel, and a toolbar, as shown in Figure 5.

Using the visual editor to create contextual help for a particular interface, a designer first captures the screenshot of the *entire* interface and imports it into the editor. The screenshot is placed on a slide in the editing area. The designer then can choose from the toolbar a type of content object (e.g., callout), select a location on the slide to insert the object (e.g., 20 pixels to the left of the OK button), and edit the properties of the object (e.g., set the text to Click Here). The above process is similar to annotating a screenshot using typical presentation software. The only difference is that the designer needs to explicitly mark the target (e.g., the OK button) and link relevant content objects to the target. This marking is achieved by placing a special *anchor* object on the target. An anchor object is a rectangle that can be resized by the designer to fit the target. At presentation time, pixels within this rectangle will be used to form a template to search the screen for the target's actual location. Once the target is found, content objects linked to the target will be displayed on the screen in the same relative locations to the target as indicated in the slide.

As in typical presentation software, our visual editor allows the designer to preview the content while they are developing it. In the preview mode, the editor is hidden temporarily so that the screenshot in the editing area would not be mistaken for the real interface. The designer can then bring the real interface to view, see whether content objects are rendered correctly with respect to the targets, and return to the editor to continue editing. Once the content is ready, it can be converted to equivalent script commands and exported to an executable to be distributed to users.

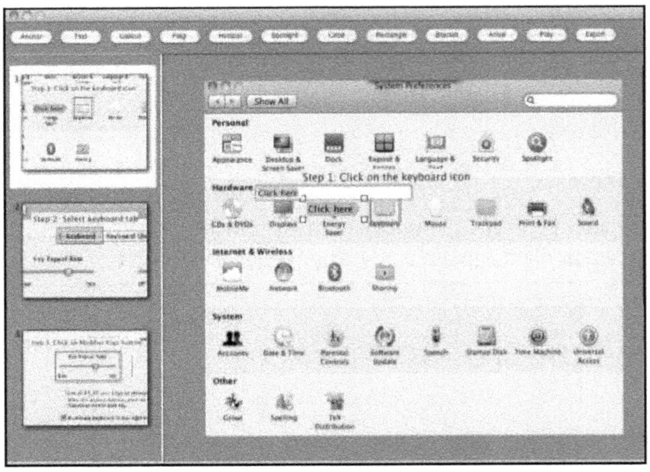

Figure 5. Visual editor for creating contextual help.

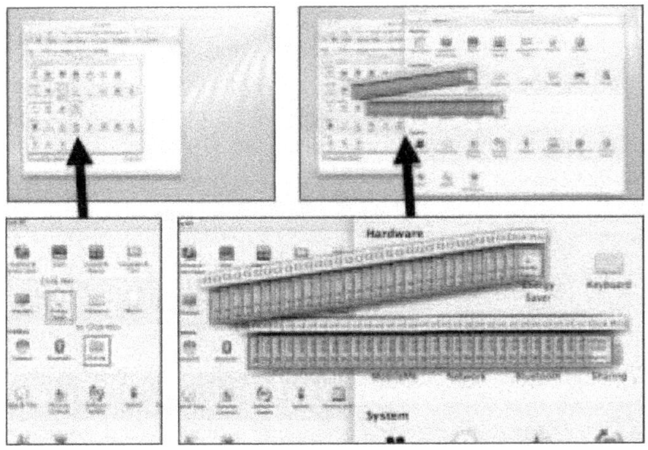

Figure 6. *Popout & Connect* for visualizing the mapping from static annotations on a screenshot to contextual help in a live interface.

Integrating with Existing Screenshot Help

To integrate contextual help more seamlessly with traditional screenshot-based help, we introduced the *Popout & Connect* feature to provide a clear transition from static screenshots in a web browser to contextual help on a live interface. When users click on an interface screenshot with some components annotated, they will see these components *popping out* from the screenshot along with the annotations. Once users switch to the live interface, these popped out virtual components then fly across the screen and land on top of the corresponding components on the live interface, carrying with them the annotations. This animated effect helps users visualize the *connection* between the static screenshot and the live interface. For example, in Figure 6, a screenshot in a web browser contains two annotated components. They popped out and flew across to the live interface on the right side of the screen.

Given a contextual help script and a static screenshot on a webpage, the *Popout & Connect* feature is implemented by first running the script only on that screenshot to locate the annotated elements so that we know where to render the *popout* effect. Since the screenshot may have been resized,

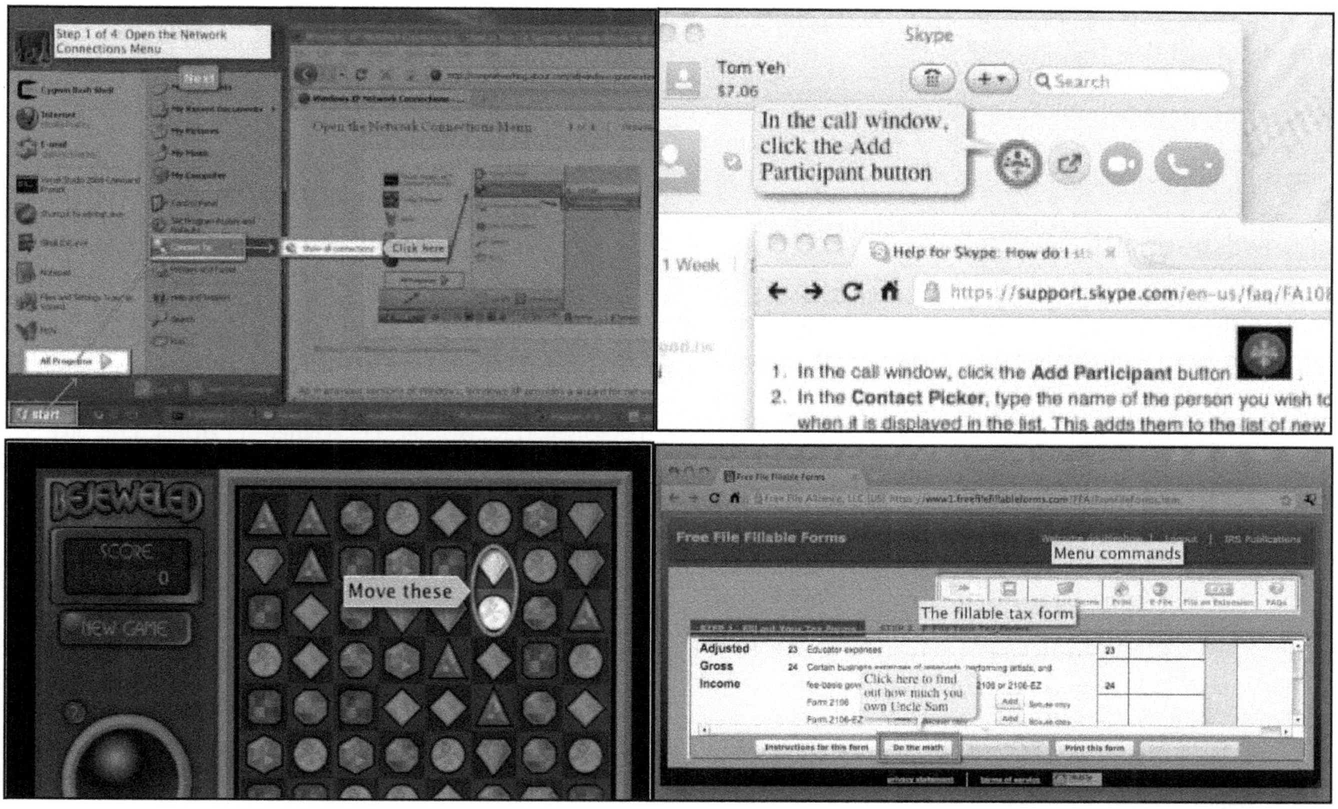

Figure 7. Examples of contextual help created by our tool. These examples demonstrate our tool's wide applicability to many applications (Skype, Flash), platforms (Windows, Mac, Web browser), and tasks (setup, chat, game, filing tax).

pattern matching needs to be performed across multiple scales in order to find the right scale. Afterward, the same script is run on the whole screen on regular intervals until the live interface becomes visible. Once the locations of relevant components are known on the live interface, it is possible to render the animation of these components flying across the screen to achieve the *connect* effect.

VALIDATION THROUGH APPLICATIONS

Our primary goal for this research is to enable a large population of help designers to generate contextual help for a broad range of interfaces and interactive tasks. As validation, Figure 7 shows a set of four representative examples of real-world applications of our tool.

To more systematically understand how broadly our technique can work, we attempted to create contextual help for a real life set of static help currently offered by University of Maryland's help desk website. We picked what we were told by our participants was one of the most visited topics: configuring Exchange Calendars. We sampled 60 of the 110 topics currently available related to this task on the site. There are a total of 376 steps in this sample. The average length of each topic is 6.26 step-long. We found 173 of 376 steps (46%) were already illustrated by screenshots. Out of these, 167 (96.5%) can be converted to contextual help using our tool. The problems we did find were due to three reasons:

1. The content is specific to time and date, for example, a dropdown menu prepopulated with dates corresponding to the day before and after.
2. The content is specific to the user, for example, a profile screen showing personal information.
3. The content is specific to a particular example, such as the name of a fictional meeting entered in a text box.

IMPLEMENTATION

The ability to locate widgets based on screenshots is provided by the Sikuli Library, an open-source cross-platform library for automating graphical user interfaces based on screenshots [32]. Rendering of contextual help on an interface is achieved by painting on a full screen transparent window that always stays on top. This transparent window is implemented based on Java Swing's JWindow class. The algorithm for tracking the movement of a target and repositioning relevant help content dynamically is implemented in Java. The WISIWYG editor is implemented in Java.

LIMITATIONS AND FUTURE WORK

By taking the pixel approach to generalizability, our tool inevitably suffers from the same limitations faced by any pixel-based technique such as scale changes and theme variations. In our particular case, the severity of these limitations varies depending on the user population. According to our participants in the tech support group, many institutional users they support share a standard issued computing environment and thus less susceptible to these limitations. On the other hand, older adult computer users often enlarge the font sizes for better readability, making scale invariance an important issue. A possible solution worth pursing in the future is to include multiple versions of the same pattern at different scales.

ACKNOWLEDGEMENT

This research is supported by the Intelligence Advanced Research Projects Activity (IARPA) via Department of Interior National Business Center contract number D11PC20071[1]. We thank the HCIL, Raimund Hocke, Chip Denman, Linda Rossi, and our older adult participants for their ideas, feedback and support.

REFERENCES

1. St. Amant, R., Lieberman, H., Potter, R., and Zettlemoyer, L. Programming by example: visual generalization in programming by example. *Communications of the ACM 43*, 3 (2000), 107-114.
2. St. Amant, R., Rey, M., Riedl, M.O., Ritter, F.E., and Reifers, A. Image Processing in Cognitive Models with SegMan Image processing in SegMan. In *Proc. of HCI*, 2001.
3. Bergman, L., Castelli, V., Lau, T., and Oblinger, D. DocWizards: A System for Authoring Follow-me Documentation Wizards. In *Proc. of UIST,* 2005.
4. Bigham, J.P., Lau, T., and Nichols, J. TrailBlazer: Enabling Blind Users to Blaze Trails Through the Web. In *Proc. of IUI,* 2009.
5. Chakravarthi, Y.A., Lutteroth, C., and Weber, G. AIMHelp: Generating Help for GUI Applications Automatically. In *Proc. of CHINZ,* 2009.
6. Chapuis, O. and Roussel, N. UIMarks: Quick Graphical Interaction with Specific Targets. In *Proc. of UIST,* 2010.
7. Dixon, M. and Fogarty, J. Prefab: Implementing Advanced Behaviors Using Pixel-Based Reverse Engineering of Interface Structure. In *Proc. of CHI,* 2010.
8. Dixon, M., Leventhal, D. and Fogarty, J. Content and Hierarchy in Pixel-Based Methods for Reverse Engineering Interface Structure. In *Proc. of CHI 2011.*
9. Farkas, D.K. The role of balloon help. *ACM SIGDOC Asterisk Journal of Computer Documentation 17*, 2 (1993), 3-19.
10. Findlater, L., Jansen, A., Shinohara, K., et al. Enhanced Area Cursors: Reducing Fine Pointing Demands for People with Motor Impairments. In *Proc. of UIST,* 2010.
11. Grabler, F., Agrawala, M., Li, W., Dontcheva, M., and Igarashi, T. Generating photo manipulation tutorials by demonstration. *ACM Transactions on Graphics 28*, 3 (2009), 1.
12. Grossman, T. and Balakrishnan, R. The Bubble Cursor: Enhancing Target Acquisition by Dynamic Resizing of the Cursor's Activation Area. In *Proc. of CHI,* 2005.
13. Grossman, T. and Fitzmaurice, G. ToolClips: An Investigation of Contextual Video Assistance for Functionality Understanding. In *Proc. of CHI,* 2010.

[1] The U.S. Government is authorized to reproduce and distribute reprints for Government purposes notwithstanding any copyright annotation thereon. Disclaimer: The views and conclusions contained herein are those of the authors and should not be interpreted as necessarily representing the official policies or endorsements, either expressed or implied, of IARPA, DoI/NBC, or the U.S. Government.

14. Huang, J. and B. Twidale, M.B. Graphstract: Minimal Graphical Help for Computers. In *Proc. of UIST,* 2007.
15. Hurst, A., Hudson, S.E., and Mankoff, J. Automatically identifying targets users interact with during real world tasks. In *Proc. of IUI,* 2010.
16. Kang, H. and Plaisant, C. New approaches to help users get started with visual interfaces: multi-layered interfaces and integrated initial guidance. In *Proc. of the 2003 annual national conference on Digital government research*, (2003).
17. Kelleher, C. and Pausch, R. Stencils-Based Tutorials: Design and Evaluation. In *Proc. of CHI,* 2005.
18. Lau, T., Bergman, L., Castelli, V., and Oblinger, D. Sheepdog: Learning Procedures for Technical Support. In *Proc. of IUI,* 2004.
19. Olsen, D.R., Hudson, S.E., Verratti, T., Heiner, J.M., and Phelps, M. Implementing interface attachments based on surface representations. In *Proc. of CHI,* 1999.
20. Olsen, D.R., Taufer, T., and Fails, J.A. ScreenCrayons: Annotating Anything. In *Proc. of UIST,* 2004.
21. Palaigeorgiou, G. and Despotakis, T. Known and Unknown Weaknesses in Software Animated Demonstrations (Screencasts): A Study in Self-Paced Learning Settings. *Journal of Information Technology Education 9*, (2010).
22. Pangoli, S. and Paternó, F. *Automatic generation of task-oriented help.* ACM Press, 1995.
23. Plaisant, C. and Shneiderman, B. Show Me! Guidelines for Producing Recorded Demonstrations. In *Proc. of VL/HCC,* 2005.
24. Potter, R.L.-S. Pixel data access: interprocess communication in the user interface for end-user programming and graphical macros. (1999).
25. Prabaker, M., Bergman, L., and Castelli, V. *An evaluation of using programming by demonstration and guided walkthrough techniques for authoring and utilizing documentation.* ACM Press, New York, New York, USA, 2006.
26. Riedl, M.O. and St. Amant, R. Toward automated exploration of interactive systems. *Proceedings of the 7th international conference on Intelligent user interfaces - IUI '02*, ACM Press (2002), 135.
27. Sukaviriya, P. and Foley, J.D. *Coupling a UI framework with automatic generation of context-sensitive animated help.* ACM Press, New York, New York, USA, 1990.
28. Sukaviriya, P. *Dynamic construction of animated help from application context.* ACM Press.
29. Terry, M. and Mynatt, E.D. Side Views: Persistent, On-Demand Previews for Open-Ended Tasks. In *Proc. of UIST,* 2002.
30. Wiedenbeck, S. and Zila, P.L. Hands-on practice in learning to use software: a comparison of exercise, exploration, and combined formats. *ACM Transactions on Computer-Human Interaction 4*, 2 (1997), 169-196.
31. Wongsuphasawat, K., Guerra Gómez, J., Plaisant, C., Wang, T., Taieb-Maimon, M., Shneiderman, B. LifeFlow: Visualizing an Overview of Event Sequences. In *Proc. of CHI 2011.*
32. Yeh, T., Chang, T.-H., and Miller, R.C. Sikuli: Using GUI Screenshots for Search and Automation. In *Proc. of UIST, 2009.*
33. Zettlemoyer, L.S., St. Amant, R., and Dulberg, M.S. IBOTS: Agent Control Through the User Interface. In *Proc. of IUI,* 1999.

Real-Time Collaborative Coding in a Web IDE

Max Goldman, Greg Little, and Robert C. Miller
MIT CSAIL
32 Vassar St.
Cambridge, MA 02139
{maxg, glittle, rcm}@mit.edu

ABSTRACT

This paper describes *Collabode*, a web-based Java integrated development environment designed to support close, synchronous collaboration between programmers. We examine the problem of collaborative coding in the face of program compilation errors introduced by other users which make collaboration more difficult, and describe an algorithm for error-mediated integration of program code. Concurrent editors see the text of changes made by collaborators, but the errors reported in their view are based only on their own changes. Editors may run the program at any time, using only error-free edits supplied so far, and ignoring incomplete or otherwise error-generating changes. We evaluate this algorithm and interface on recorded data from previous pilot experiments with Collabode, and via a user study with student and professional programmers. We conclude that it offers appreciable benefits over naive continuous synchronization without regard to errors and over manual version control.

ACM Classification: D.2.6 [Software Engineering]: Programming Environments

General terms: Human Factors

Keywords: Collaboration, collaborative editing, pair programming

INTRODUCTION

In the current state of the art, software developers collaborate almost exclusively using one of two strategies: working together on a single copy of the code, using a single integrated development environment (IDE); or working in parallel on separate copies, integrating their efforts using a source code version control system. Neither approach, however, is ideal for close synchronous collaboration where both programmers actively contribute to the same piece of code. Using a single IDE (e.g. pair programming) means only the programmer who controls the keyboard and mouse can navigate, search, and write code. And using version control requires programmers to manually push and pull changes, while striving to avoid conflicts that require further manual resolution.

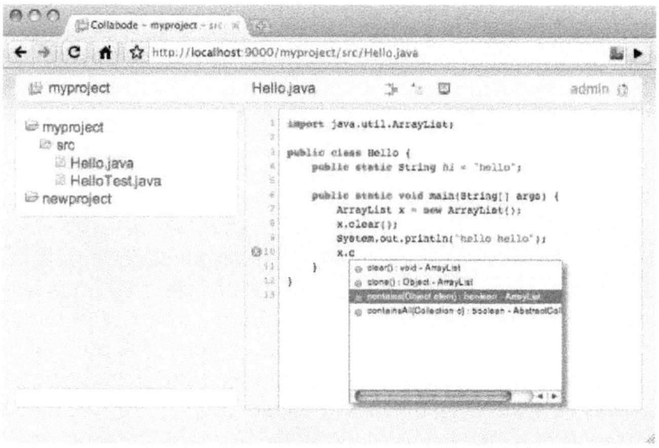

Figure 1: The Collabode web-based IDE allows multiple simultaneous editors to work together.

We have built a collaborative web-based IDE for Java, called *Collabode* (Figure 1), to study how a programming environment built to support close collaboration can improve the quality both of the collaboration and of the software produced [10]. In Collabode, changes by multiple programmers can be shared immediately, without the overhead of version control. This allows for more than one active contributor to the same module of code. Moreover, each programmer can use a different interface that supports their role in the collaborative effort, unlike the use of a single IDE where collaborators must share a single view.

Pilot studies with two to ten programmers working together simultaneously suggest that real-time shared editing can be effective and fun, and that it offers novel opportunities for collaborative software development [9]. However, a persistent problem has repeatedly bothered the collaborators: when one programmer introduces a bug, everyone has to live with that bug until someone fixes it. In particular, a compilation error created by one programmer's work-in-progress might prevent others from seeing less catastrophic compiler errors of their own, or might prevent them from running the program to test their code.

For example, suppose Alice and Bob are working together on the same Java class. Both are adding new methods, and Alice, working nearer the top of the file, begins (as any good programmer) by adding a comment to document her new method: she types /**, and suddenly Bob, working on his own method right below, is surprised to see his error markers and syntax highlighting disappear. To the compiler, his code has temporarily become part of Alice's comment, until she resolves the incomplete syntax with */. Such interference will be a constant drag on their collaboration.

In this paper, we examine an algorithm and user interface for addressing this issue of breaking the collaborative build, without introducing the latency and manual overhead of version control, and without unduly restricting the ability of both programmers to actively contribute. While programmers continuously and immediately see the text of one other's edits, the algorithm maintains separate working copies for each collaborator, compiling those copies separately to generate and display to each editor only their own errors. Once any subset of a programmer's edits can be applied to the on-disk version of the code without generating errors, those edits are applied and propagated to others' working copies.

In a study of how the algorithm behaves on recordings of collaborative programming sessions conducted without it, we found that it was able to integrate contributions that were originally copied manually into a master integration project. In another study where 14 student and professional programmers used Collabode with this synchronization algorithm to work in pairs on a realistic programming task, we found that developers were generally positive about the experience of collaborative coding and about the automatic error-mediated integration. Participants in the study were able to work without interference from their partner's unfinished code, and code was shared between participants approximately twice as often as it would have if participants had manually shared their code every single time it was error-free.

The contributions of this paper are (1) the Collabode web-based IDE for collaborative software development, (2) an algorithm for automatic error-aware integration that allows collaborating programmers to work in parallel, and (3) an evaluation of that algorithm as implemented in Collabode that demonstrates its efficacy for pairs of programmers working together in one source file.

After reviewing related work, we describe Collabode and the variety of collaborative programming scenarios it was designed to study; we discuss the algorithm, its implementation, and user interface; we describe and report the results of our evaluations; and then we conclude after some discussion.

RELATED WORK

Programming Methodologies

In *pair programming*, two developers work together on the same code in a single development environment, with the goals of improved communication and team knowledge sharing, increased productivity, and better software quality [2]. *Side-by-side programming* is a more flexible variant in which programmers sit together at separate machines [6]. This same style of interaction has also been studied with remote collaborators [7], and could be supported using a tool such as Collabode.

Collaborative Editing

Operational transform (reviewed in [25]) is the technique for maintaining a consistent view of the shared document that underlies most real-time collaborative editing systems, including Collabode.

Previous work in collaborative editing systems has examined the problem of maintaining semantic consistency, for example in graphic design [4] and hierarchical documents [15].

In the context of software development, *change impact analysis* computes the set of unit tests impacted by a collection of code changes [19] and was implemented in Chianti [18]; and *safe-commit analysis* determines code changes that can safely be committed to version control without breaking tests [29]. Most closely-related is the use of data dependencies and program slicing to perform *semantic interference detection* between changes made in parallel [24].

Development Tools

There exist a variety of commercial and open source systems for web-based collaborative programming. EtherPad enables real-time text editing collaboration and is used by Studio SketchPad (`sketchpad.cc`) for collaborative graphics programming. Ace (`ace.ajax.org`, formerly Skywriter, formerly Bespin), CodeMirror (`codemirror.net`), and Ymacs (`ymacs.org`) are web-based text editing components designed to be embedded in an IDE or other application. Kodingen (`kodingen.com`) is one such IDE for web programming, as are jsFiddle (`jsfiddle.net`) and CodeRun Studio (`coderun.com`). All three offer collaboration mediated by copying or version control – multiple programmers cannot edit the same files simultaneously. The Palm Ares environment (`ares.palm.com`) demonstrates an online graphical application development environment. Current research projects include Adinda [27], a web-based editor backed by Eclipse.

Flesce was one early implementation of a shared IDE to support authoring, testing, and debugging code [8]. The Jazz project [5] brought collaboration tools to Eclipse to support both awareness (e.g. via annotated avatar and project item icons) and joint work (e.g. with instant messaging and screen sharing). Different features of Jazz provide developer support throughout the software development process [26].

The CollabVS tool for ad-hoc collaboration shares similar awareness and collaboration goals [12], and the Sangam system was developed to support distributed pair programming [13]. Many other systems have focused on awareness features to keep loosely-collaborating software developers aware of others' work, e.g.: Palantír [22], Syde [11], Saros [21], CASI [23], and YooHoo [14].

COLLABODE: COLLABORATIVE CODING

Collabode is our web-based collaborative integrated development environment designed for experimenting with how programmers can write code in close collaboration with one another. Since the editor is a web application, programmers use a standard web browser to connect to a Collabode server that hosts their projects. The user interface is implemented in standard HTML and JavaScript and runs entirely in the browser.

New programmers can join a project and immediately start working together simply by visiting the same URL. There is no need to check out code or set up a local development environment. This feature enables some of the new collaborative models discussed in the next section, and motivates the implementation of Collabode as a web application.

Collabode uses EtherPad (`etherpad.org`) to support collaboration between multiple simultaneous editors. Any number of programmers can open the same file simultaneously, and their concurrent changes are shared in near real-time to enable smooth collaboration whether they are working together remotely or at the same desk.

On the server side, Collabode uses Eclipse (`eclipse.org`) to manage projects and power standard IDE services: syntax highlighting, continuous compilation, compiler errors and warnings, code formatting and refactoring, and execution. The system also supports continuous test execution [20]. Collabode currently supports Java editing, and any Eclipse Java project can be compiled and modified using the system (including Collabode itself), with an interface familiar to anyone who has used Eclipse (Figure 1). Project code is executed on the server and clients can view console output, so Collabode is not currently suited for developing programs with desktop graphical user interfaces. As with source code, all collaborators can observe program output or open the console to view it after the fact, to support collaborative debugging.

The development of Collabode is ongoing work, and we are currently working on improvements to the user interface (especially project navigation and awareness of other editors) and expanding language support (console input, and supporting languages other than Java).

MODELS FOR CLOSE SYNCHRONOUS COLLABORATION

An immediate and obvious application of the Collabode editor is pair programming, whether remote or co-located, as well as the similar practice of side-by-side programming. Indeed, we believe that the pair or side-by-side programming experience in a collaborative system such as Collabode is substantially different from the experience of using a single editor, or two editors linked only via version control, and will offer some evidence of this in later sections.

A primary goal of this project, however, is to examine models of collaboration that go beyond pair and side-by-side programming. These models might take advantage of specific user interface support built into the collaborative development environment, and can allow programmers to take on distinct roles in the collaboration. We have previously proposed three interesting models to explore in this space: *test-driven pair programming* [10], *micro-outsourcing* [9], and *mobile instructor*.

In order to motivate our work on Collabode, we describe these models briefly below. In all of them, however, as well as in the straightforward pair or side-by-side programming model, and in the many other collaboration models one might imagine, experience piloting collaborative programming with both students and professional programmers leads us to anticipate a common problem: naive continuous synchronization of unfinished code makes it difficult for individual collaborators to make progress. Errors introduced by one programmer make it hard for others to understand the status of their own work, or to run or debug the project. Motivated by the exciting possibilities of the models below, the remainder of this paper will focus on that issue.

Test-Driven Pair Programming

This model combines the practices of pair programming with test-driven development. In test-driven development, developers follow two rules: "write new code only if an automated test has failed," and "eliminate duplication" [3], with short, rapid development cycles as a result.

In our test-driven pair programming model, the process of test-driven development is parallelized, with one member of the pair working primarily on tests, while the other works primarily on implementation. To begin work on a particular feature or module, the tester might write a black-box test, which the implementer will then satisfy. The tester can then investigate the implementation and write glass-box tests to weed out errors. These further tests will be addressed by the implementer, and the testing and implementing continues. Rapid collaboration in this model will rely on interface support for visualizing passing and failing test cases and who in the collaboration is responsible for taking the next step to address any failures, and for navigating between test cases and code.

Micro-Outsourcing

In this model, one programmer draws on the distributed expertise of a crowd of other programmers who make small contributions to the project. Micro-outsourcing allows the original programmer to remain "in the flow" at one level of abstraction or in one critical part of the code, while a crowd of assistants fill in the details or "glue" code elsewhere in the module or project.

In contrast to traditional outsourcing, which typically operates at the granularity of a whole module or project, micro-outsourcing requires a highly collaborative development environment and specific user interface support to make the collaboration effective. For workers, the interface must strike a balance between focusing on their limited task and allowing them to navigate and understand necessary dependencies or useful contributions from others. And for the original programmer, the system must make visible and understandable the small contributions of many others, allowing the programmer to easily integrate work or redirect the efforts of the contributors.

Mobile Instructor

Finally, we envision a Collabode-based system for students and instructors in a computer lab setting. Instructors and students work together to achieve educational goals, but their roles are highly asymmetric: the expert instructor structures the learning process, and the novice student participates in it. This asymmetry should be mirrored by a programming system designed for computer science education that goes beyond screen sharing tools such as iTALC (`italc.sf.net`).

While students continue to use the familiar IDE user interface, teachers utilize a mobile device interface that leaves them free to move around the classroom and work one-on-

one with students. This mobile view will summarize student progress and offer remote control of students' environments. Such a use case highlights the flexibility of a web-based IDE. Since the Collabode server has centralized up-to-the-second knowledge of every student's code, it can provide powerful tools to analyze or summarize student progress without interrupting their work or requiring student action.

COLLABORATIVE EDITING WITH SEMANTICS

Collaborative editing of source code files presents the particular problem that program errors introduced by one collaborator may disrupt the progress of their colleagues. Source files must conform to a particular programming language syntax and semantics, but it is impossible to expect users to maintain semantic validity throughout the coding process: almost any partially written expression, statement, block, method, class, or program is likely to contain errors according to the parser or compiler. Structured editors [17] address this problem only at the significant cost of requiring convoluted steps to make certain simple changes [28], and most programmers do not use them.

To see how errors introduced by one user can make it more difficult for another user to continue, consider the following simple program:

```
class Hello {
    int x;
    void a() { x = true; }
}
```

This contains an error, since the integer field x cannot be assigned a boolean value. However, suppose another user begins defining a new method:

```
class Hello {
    void b() {
    int x;
    void a() { x = true; }
}
```

At this point the Eclipse compiler will report instead that "x cannot be resolved to a variable," masking the true error because x now appears to be a local variable of method b. The particular set of failure cases and their likelihood and severity will depend on the compiler. Eclipse attempts to prevent common problems such as unbalanced braces from generating opaque errors elsewhere, but it cannot always succeed.

The problem is much worse in the case of running the program: although Eclipse will allow the programmer to launch an error-containing program, any attempt to execute an error-containing line will result in failure. This has the potential to prevent collaborating programmers from writing and testing their code incrementally, and we have observed this problem during pilot studies with both Python and Java programmers. Rather than constrain collaborating programmers to agree on and reach points at which the program is sufficiently error-free for them to run it and test code in progress, we instead account for the semantic content automatically in our synchronizing behavior.

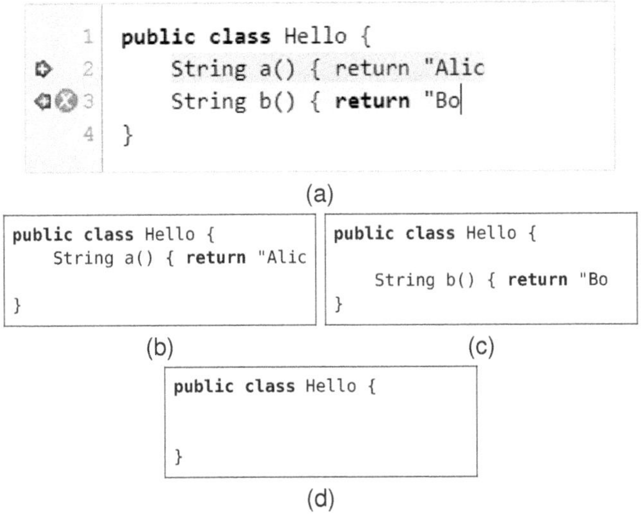

Figure 2: Alice and Bob are working concurrently to define methods a and b. (a) The *union* of their changes is displayed in the editor, shown here from Bob's perspective: his un-integrated change is in yellow, with an outgoing arrow; Alice's is in gray, with an incoming arrow. (b) Alice's *working copy* and (c) Bob's working copy contain only their own changes. (d) The *disk* does not reflect their work-in-progress, since both of their changes still contain errors.

Overview

Collabode addresses this issue by first giving each programmer a separate, persistent *working copy* of the program, and then maintaining two versions that integrate programmers' changes from their working copies: a *disk* version and a *union* version. The union version is the text that users see and manipulate, and it contains all edits applied by all users, with highlighting and icons to indicate provenance. So if Alice has begun defining method a and Bob is writing method b, the union version contains both in-progress methods, and both methods appear in the user interface (Figure 2a). As long as their methods contain compilation errors, the working copies of Alice and Bob will each contain only their own method (2b-c) and the *disk* will contain neither (2d). Once their methods compile, their edits will be shared both with their collaborator's working copy, and with the *disk* version, which corresponds to the content on disk. It is this disk version that is run when either programmer elects to run the program. This version is always free of compilation errors.

Algorithm

We define an *edit* as the replacement of a single contiguous span of text with a new content string. Conventional additions and deletions are both special cases: an addition replaces a zero-length span with content, and a deletion replaces a span with zero-length content.

Given n users, the algorithm operates on several initially-identical (or empty) error-free documents $union$, $disk$, and wc_1, ..., wc_n. It also maintains the set E of edits that have not yet been applied to $disk$. This set is initially empty.

- Each new incoming edit e_i from editor i is applied both to $union$, for displaying the content of the edit to all editors, and to wc_i, for computing the compilation errors to display to editor i.

- e_i is then merged with E. If e_i overlaps, adjoins, contains, or is contained by edits in E, the relevant (parts of those) edits will be removed.
- We then find a largest subset S of E such that when S are applied to $disk$, the resulting document is error-free. This set may be empty, and need not be a contiguous sequence.
- If S is nonempty, we apply each $s \in S$ to $disk$ and to all working copies where s was not already applied, and remove them from E.
- Finally, if it was changed, we write $disk$ to disk.

The result is that after each edit, we attempt to find a largest set of outstanding un-integrated edits that can be applied cleanly to the shared version on disk, and apply those edits if any. Since edits will frequently occur in rapid sequence, we need only merge them into E as they occur, and could delay subsequent searching for subset S until users are quiescent. We did not find it necessary to implement such a delay.

Implementation

The EtherPad component of Collabode implements simultaneous editing (using operational transform) so that other components, including the error-mediated integration, see only a sequence of edits as defined above. We have implemented the algorithm by further reducing incoming edits to contiguous *regions* of text that either exist only in $disk$, because they were deleted from $union$ but that deletion cannot yet be integrated without error; or exist only in $union$, because they were inserted but also cannot yet be integrated. The system maintains similar sets of regions correlating each working copy with $union$.

One limitation of this particular implementation is that the un-integrated edits in E from different authors must be non-overlapping; that is, if one author has inserted error-inducing text, no other editor can delete or modify that text. This limitation would become increasingly untenable as the number of authors in close proximity increases, but made it possible to implement and evaluate the idea more rapidly. It is not a limitation of the algorithm, only our current implementation.

More inherent to the approach is the limitation that, since deletions by one author are seen by all authors, they can no longer modify the text that was deleted, even if their working copy still contains that text because the deletion induces an error and is waiting in E. If we assume, however, that the authors have coordinated at some level regarding the deletion, in many cases there should be little need to modify code that they have already decided to remove.

A crucial assumption required by this algorithm is that the set E of edits not yet applied to disk is small, since we examine a number of possible combinations of those edits that grows exponentially. We evaluate this assumption below, but believe it is justified by two assumptions about programmer behavior:

- We assume that a programmer's own edits tend to be consecutive or overlapping. In this case, the edits can be merged and E remains small. Refactorings, which may require a large number of widely distributed small edits, break this assumption and would be better handled as single multi-location edits to be integrated whole.
- We assume that programmers tend to fulfill error-eliminating obligations actively rather than allowing large blocks of code to accrue with simple errors. Examples include balancing braces before working on their contents, and fixing minor syntax errors as they write rather than in a later proofreading step.

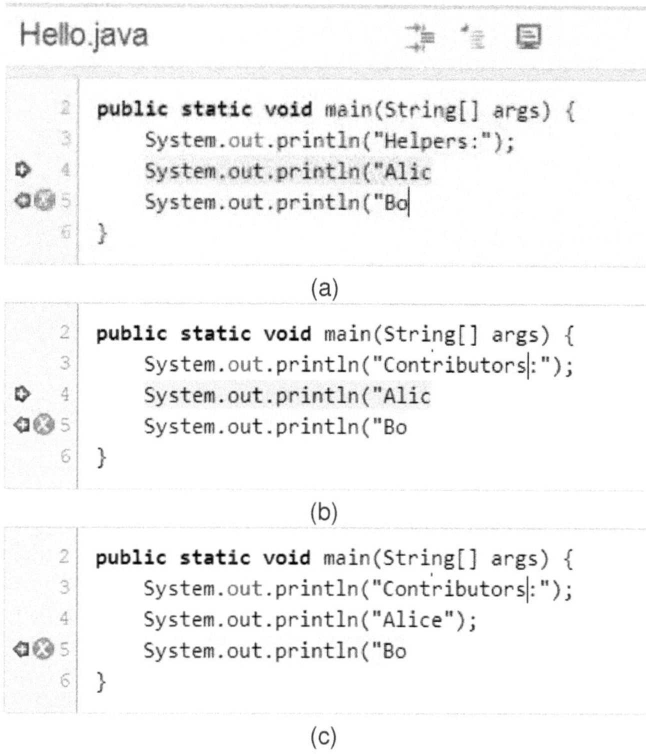

Figure 3: Bob's view of a collaboration with Alice: (a) `Hello.java` as both he and Alice begin adding to the `main` method; (b) after he improves the initial `println`, and his change is immediately integrated; (c) and after Alice completes her contribution, which is also automatically integrated.

Evidence for both patterns of editing exists in the case of Java programmers performing software maintenance [16]. The second assumption will be especially impacted by the details of compiler feedback. A tool such as DuctileJ [1], which allows programmers to temporarily relax static typing requirements and still run the program to see feedback, may reduce the scope of this assumption by giving the programmer flexibility to ignore what would otherwise be an error.

Interface

The result of applying this algorithm is shown in Figure 3. First Alice and then Bob begin making changes that do not compile (3a). Each of them sees only their own errors, and in-progress code is highlighted according to its origin. The figure shows Bob's view of their collaboration, so his un-integrated edits are highlighted in yellow, while Alice's are shown in gray. Arrows in the margin indicate Bob's 'outgoing' changes by pointing out of the text, while Alice's 'incoming' work is marked with inward-pointing arrows.

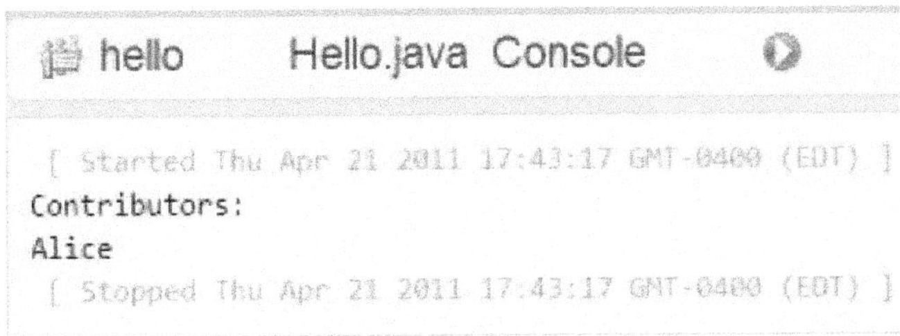

Figure 4: The output from running the program after Alice and Bob's collaboration: changes on lines 3 and 4 are integrated, but the unfinished line 5 exists only in Bob's working copy.

Once each of them completes edits that can be introduced to the project error-free (3b-c), those edits are applied to the version on disk. Then, even though one of Bob's changes still has errors, this does not affect either programmer's ability to run the project and debug their code (Figure 4). In this case, even though Bob began working first on line 5 and abandoned that work in progress to make a critical change on line 3, that completed change is not held back by his incomplete earlier work, and he needs to take no extra steps to share only the working contribution.

That the interface displays the work of both contributors is a crucial feature of the system. Each programmer has specific awareness about what other users are working on, and can shift attention to their code at any time. Both the clear benefits as well as some drawbacks to the interface were identified by participants in the user study discussed below.

EVALUATION: WILL IT BLEND?

In order to evaluate whether error-aware integration would be useful in practice, we first examined how the algorithm would perform in comparison to manual integration performed by programmers. We reviewed edit logs from pilot experiments conducted in Collabode without automatic integration and replayed them against a version of the system with the algorithm. In the original experiments, participants were research lab members engaged in *micro-outsourcing* as described previously. The original programmer (OP) directed co-located workers to complete various tasks (e.g. perform research, implement a method, design a representation), and then was required to manually copy the output of those workers into the original program.

Across three pilot sessions, we identified 18 instances where the OP copied worker code into the original project. In 14 of these instances (78%), the error-aware integration algorithm also would have automatically integrated the identical block of code into the project.

All four cases where the algorithm did not match manual integration were instances where the OP chose to integrate error-containing code. In two of those cases, the worker's contribution could reasonably be judged to satisfy the OP's specification: the OP requested that workers create a number of methods with correct signatures but empty bodies, yielding compilation errors in a number of places. In the other two cases, workers failed to meet the OP's specific instruction to "get rid of compile errors" in the initially broken code he provided them. It is therefore unclear whether the failure of the algorithm to integrate these contributions would have violated the OP's expectations.

The 78% of manually-integrated contributions that were also automatically integrated is a measure of the *recall* of this approach: what fraction of contributions judged "good" by humans are also selected algorithmically. We cannot use the same data to estimate the *precision* (that is, what fraction of algorithmically-selected contributions are "good") because in all of the pilot experiment sessions, there were large amounts of working code that OPs failed to integrate due to insufficient time or attention, not because the code was unacceptable.

This result gives us confidence that the algorithm can operate in a collaborative programming scenario without requiring programmers to change their behavior to meet its requirements. In fact, there were several instances where the OP incorrectly copied too little or too much code from the worker's project and had to correct the mistake. This effort would have been eliminated by the automatic approach.

EVALUATION: SIDE-BY-SIDE PROGRAMMING

To more fully evaluate the error-aware integration and the entire Collabode collaborative programming system, we conducted a user study in which pairs of programmers worked for approximately 30 to 40 minutes to complete a coding task, working together in a single source code file.

Four student participants were recruited from the authors' institution, and ten professional participants were recruited from local offices of two large technology companies. The average self-reported age of participants was 36, two of the 14 participants were female, and five were studying for or held a bachelor's degree while the other nine were studying for or held a master's degree. Participants were asked to rate their proficiency in Java on a 7-point Likert scale (min = 2, max = 7, mode = 6) and their experience with pair programming (min = 1, max = 5, mode = 1).

Pairs were *not* randomly assigned, and pair familiarity ranged from students who had never met prior to the study to co-workers who are also good friends. For this reason, and because of the wide variance in behavior and ability between programmers, we make no attempt here to compare the performance of different pairs; results are broken down by session only to illuminate this variance. This is also the reason we did not undertake a controlled experiment to compare Collabode to other collaborative editing approaches at this stage of the system's development.

In each one-hour session, participants:

- gave informed consent to participate and completed a demographic questionnaire;
- received a brief tour of the Collabode interface and the operation of the automatic integration algorithm, with the opportunity to ask questions;
- worked together on a programming task;
- completed a post-task questionnaire to give written feedback regarding their experience;

- and discussed the experience with the experimenter and their partner based on questions from the experimenter.

Tour

This experiment was not designed to test the learnability of Collabode, since it is by its nature a system for expert users who invest time to learn the complex tools of their trade. Participants were shown how to edit and run the project, and the experimenter demonstrated how multiple editors would see each other's changes. Participants took part in the demonstration but could not make edits, in order to keep idle experimentation to a minimum in the limited time.

Task

Participant pairs were first explicitly instructed that they could use "any web resources" in order to complete the task and that they could organize their work any way they liked. All pairs used Google to conduct searches and referenced the Java API documentation at some point. Pairs were initially seated at a 90° angle at the corner of a rectangular table or at a small circular table, and the majority moved to sit side-by-side during the session. This move enabled easier sharing of documentation or other web pages, and also allowed those pairs to see one another's focus or cursor location (not currently a feature of Collabode). Pairs were also informed that they could only edit a single shared source code file; this restriction was designed to maximize opportunities to exercise the synchronization algorithm and UI.

The task was:

> Using the `nytimes.com` RSS feeds, display a list of recent headlines from the New York Times "Science" category. Use regular expressions or other string processing, not an RSS or XML processing library. Don't worry about converting XML entities or other encoding issues.

Participants were also given several hints in the initially-provided source code: pointers to the Times' directory of RSS feeds; to a class and a method relevant to retrieving the contents of a URL; and to the reference for Java regular expressions. While interesting, the research and API understanding stages were not the focus of this study, so we attempted to equip participants as well as possible to get to work quickly. Nevertheless, understanding the minutia of, variously, URL retrieval in Java, regular expressions in Java, and RSS consumed significant participant time.

Does the Set of Un-Integrated Regions Remain Small?

The efficiency of the automatic integration depends strongly on the assumption that there are few outstanding un-integrated regions. Considering all 4,543 edits performed in the course of the study, the average number of un-integrated regions for the algorithm to consider has a mean of 2.2 and a median of 2. The mode is 1, and since an edit has just occurred, the number is zero only when that edit precisely eliminates the only current region (this occurs 23 times). As shown in Table 1, pairs 6 and 7 tended to have about twice as many un-integrated regions, on average, as pairs 1 through 4 (up to the observed maximum of 15). Both of the these pairs experienced bugs in Collabode that prevented the shared code file from updating correctly, leading to invisible unresolved errors participants could not correct until they reverted to an earlier version.

These results validate our assumption that the set of such regions remains small, at least in the case of two programmers. Since we might expect this number to grow in proportion to the number of concurrent contributors, the efficiency of this algorithm beyond pair programming remains to be seen.

Is the Algorithm an Improvement Over Integrating Only Error-Free Code?

For each edit recorded during the study, we can ask whether that edit resulted (a) in an error-free source file and (b) in an automatic integration. Since sequences of edits where participants wrote inside comments or string literals result in rapid sequences of commits to the project that are not useful to count as separate instances, we collapse consecutive edits into blocks for which the answers to (a) and (b) remain constant.

In Table 1 we see a mean number of commit blocks per minute of 1.8, compared to a mean number of error-free blocks per minute of 0.7. This gives an average increase in the rate of commits by 2.8 times over a scheme that commits only when error-free (the result is an equivalent 2.6 times if we consider all edits without blocking). If we asked developers to integrate code manually using version control, this frequency of error-free states is likely an upper bound on the frequency with which they could reasonably go through the overhead of committing it.

A different way to view this result is to observe that 63% of commit blocks occurred with other error-containing regions still outstanding; that is, only some of the available edits were integrated into the project (this number falls to 58% when we examine edits individually, due to the effect of e.g. comments and strings noted above). We conclude that this algorithm is significantly different from integrating only error-free versions. More frequent integration means less opportunity for programmers' code to diverge and reduced lag between authorship by one programmer and use by another.

Can Developers Work Concurrently?

Table 1 also shows the proportion of edits attributed to the member of each pair who contributed the least. We see that in the most unequal case, that person still contributed more than one quarter of the edits (this is not necessarily a measure of how much code that participant wrote if, e.g., they copied an example from the web, or they tended to add but then delete). And on average, over one third of the edits occur in a state where both participants have an error, from which we might infer that they are actively working on or thinking about some part of the task. Based on experimenter observation, in every session, the two programmers were at some point actively working on incomplete code at the same time.

We argued earlier that, in addition to allowing participants to write independently and see appropriate IDE feedback, error-aware integration also allows programmers to run the program more often without worrying about their collaborators' errors. As shown in the last column of Table 1, the results from this study do not support such a hypothesis. Pairs ran

Session	Unintegrated regions	Commit block rate	Error-free block rate	Commit block ratio	Commit blocks with unintegrated regions	Edits by lower contributor	Edits where both editors have errors	Program runs with errors
1	1.6 per edit	3.0 per minute	1.3 per minute	2.3 per error-free block	59 %	41 %	14 %	0 %
2	1.7	2.3	1.0	2.3	58	38	20	20
3	1.6	0.9	0.7	1.4	52	43	41	0
4	1.4	1.1	0.8	1.4	49	38	19	0
5	2.4	2.3	0.5	5.1	80	48	65	0
6	3.2	1.5	0.4	3.6	72	31	43	100
7	3.2	1.3	0.4	3.3	72	26	50	25
Mean	**2.2** per edit	**1.8** per minute	**0.7** per minute	**2.8** per error-free block	**63** %	**38** %	**36** %	**21** %

Table 1: Per-session and mean statistics from the side-by-side programming user study.

the project only 5.7 times on average (4.7 times excluding consecutive runs with no intervening edits), and did so almost exclusively when the project had no outstanding error-causing code (with the exception of session 6). This is in contrast to statements made by participants during the post-task interview, which we discuss below.

Overall, participants made many edits where the errors reported were computed without regard to error-containing code concurrently introduced by their partner, and this offers strong support for our claim that developers are able to make concurrent progress using the system.

Feedback: Collaborative Coding

Study participants were largely positive about the experience of working together collaboratively, making statements such as "I found it really useful," "I thought it was a lot of fun," and "that was pretty cool."

In many instances, developers began to brainstorm different use cases for the system:

- "You could essentially be real-time debugging each other's code"
- "If you laid out an entire class with methods that needed to be implemented, [...] it would be pretty cool to see how that would work, if you were implementing one method, I was implementing another method" (cp. micro-outsourcing)
- From an operations engineer, "we have a lot of time-critical stuff, I could see this being occasionally useful" for "crisis programming"

Participants also suggested that the system could improve communication between collaborators, who can easily reference one another's code, and would be useful for learning. One participant said during the discussion, "I [...] gained an insight into how you [my partner] think, how you problem solve."

While pair programming works well for many developers, several participants reported that Collabode would work better for them than the traditional approach. One summarized the sentiments of many:

> "It always seemed that if you had one or two people looking over your shoulder, you became a puppet, and you just are doing what they're telling you to do. But when we each had a keyboard, it didn't feel that way. I was thinking one step ahead, and whether it was just going to the Java API documentation to see what's the next little thing that we can do to push this forward, [or working in parallel,] it was both of us trying to actually program this thing, instead of just one person."

Some participants were more ambivalent:

- "I think it boils down to, if you buy into pair programming, then this is a very good way to do it"
- "Once your task is well-defined, the module is well-defined, I wanted to go into a separate page"

One participant stated flatly, "overall, I wasn't a huge fan of it," and continued: "no, I don't like other people touching my stuff." While this is certainly a disappointing attitude from the perspective of collaborative software development, it is only one point along a spectrum of reasonable concern developers must have for their ability to think and code independently.

Feedback: Automatic Integration

Asked whether they thought the automatic error-aware integration was "useful" or perhaps "confusing," developers were generally positive:

- "I found it really useful, I liked the fact that you can see what they're doing, but that it doesn't interfere with the functionality"
- "I think that it's hugely useful"
- Without it, "I would have been totally hung up on, 'oh, what the heck is my stupid syntax error there,' and [...] that would have just stopped me in my tracks;" this participant's partner replied: "right, and we have an alternative, which was, you try your way, and I'll try my way," which they did during the session
- "I can picture myself spending ten minutes writing a method, [...] and if it doesn't compile, then [...] I don't want you to wait [on me], or me to wait on you"
- "I think you definitely don't want it to commit with errors, because then you can't test things as you're [...] making small changes that you want to be able to just test immediately"

- "I really like the idea that essentially whatever's in the system, whatever that is, will always run"

No developer reported being confused by the system as designed, although several reported being confused when bugs in Collabode were exposed. Nevertheless, some comments made by participants lead us to suspect that some participants had incorrect or incomplete mental models of the system, in particular with respect to what version of the program would run in the console.

Developers who thought error-mediated synchronization was less important tended to focus on running the program. One developer suggested that holding back changes with errors was unnecessary for a task of this size, although this participant's partner responded that they should have tried to run the code sooner, and that "we should have tested running the program with just my changes [and] when there was a compilation error with his changes, I should have tested running it." Another participant's statement that "I don't mind about the compilation errors because, when we cooperate, I think, 'I do not mind, if it's not ready, I just do not run'" also seems more closely aligned with the data presented above. We hypothesize that two factors combined to limit participants' use of this feature:

- First, the notion of a console that runs only the working parts of the code is novel, and participants may have preferred to synchronize rather than consider what would be run.
- Second, because the console output was shared, participants may have thought of running the program as a shared activity best done together when both were ready.

Feedback: Missing Pieces

Hitting on two of the limitations of the current system, several participants wanted to be able to see their partner's errors and to be able to edit their partner's un-integrated changes. One participant described how the incoming and outgoing change icons in the margin could provide an affordance for taking ownership of a change, which might help clarify for the change's originator why their code was now being edited. Several participants articulated how the ability to see collaborators' errors (perhaps with indicators to differentiate them from their own) was crucial for collaborative debugging. Some developers also mentioned wanting a changelog, and rightly pointed out that the current user interface becomes confusing with more than two collaborators because the specific owners of changes other than one's own are not displayed.

Several participants also made the case for when manual integration might be preferable in place of or in combination with automatic integration:

- "I like this as a default, but I think, it would be nice if you could hit a button that says, 'stop committing what I'm going to write,' [...] if I know I'm going to be working on a large chunk of code"
- "One place I see [manual] coming in really useful is, if you're working with someone, and you're pounding through the problem really quickly, and you solve it really inefficiently... and, say [...] I decided to go back and try to make some early part more efficient, I don't want to just delete the inefficient part, because then she can't test any more" if the intermediate state ever compiles

This is a particularly insightful observation from only half an hour of experience with the system: while error-aware integration is helpful, it might be straightforward to produce error-free programs that nevertheless impede the progress of collaborators. Improving the automatic integration algorithm and adding both language-specific and language-agnostic heuristics to detect "good" and "bad" changes is ongoing work.

DISCUSSION AND FUTURE WORK

Overall, we were pleased to hear from several participants statements such as "I want it" and questions about when the system would be production-ready for their own programming. Despite their enthusiasm, bugs in the concurrent interaction between the EtherPad shared editor and the automatic integration algorithm driving compilation in Eclipse caused Collabode to fail periodically, which frustrated programmers during the user study and often led them to treat the system warily rather than push its boundaries.

That participants in the study did not often run the program while it had errors means we can only speculate on whether having the program as it appears on disk be different than how it appears in the editor is a problem. Although they did not say so, users may have avoided running the program until it was error-free for precisely this reason. This question will require further evaluation.

Finally, it may be that resolving the issue of compiler errors impeding programmers' collaborative work will allow a different problem to dominate – changes that compile but produce runtime errors for other programmers. One approach we can apply to this problem is test-mediated integration, as in tools such as JUnitMX [30]. New collaboration structures and user interfaces may mitigate this problem without requiring test suites.

CONCLUSION

In this paper we have demonstrated the efficacy and usability of an algorithm and user interface for addressing the issue of errors in collaboratively-edited source code. We integrate only contributions that can be applied error-free, without introducing the latency and manual overhead of version control, and without restricting the ability of both programmers to actively contribute. This algorithm is implemented in Collabode, our browser-based collaborative programming system, which we are using to investigate how different models and user interfaces for close collaboration between programmers can yield novel and effective strategies for collaboration.

Why build a web-based IDE? Is this not merely a return to the days of terminals and mainframes, with VT100 replaced by shiny new HTML5 – now with animation! We believe otherwise. The collaborative opportunities offered by a browser-based IDE are too exciting to pass up: instant participation by anyone with a URL, collaboration with zero setup cost, and a development server that can serve appropriate user interfaces for collaborators using a variety of interfaces and devices.

ACKNOWLEDGEMENTS

We thank all the user study participants; Jay Goldman for helping to organize the study; and all the User Interface Design Group members who have contributed to this work, especially Patrick Yamane and Angela Chang. This work is supported in part by National Science Foundation award IIS-0447800 and by Quanta Computer as part of the T-Party project. Opinions, findings, conclusions, or recommendations expressed herein are those of the authors and do not necessarily reflect the views of the sponsors.

REFERENCES

1. M. Bayne, R. Cook, and M. D. Ernst. Always-available static and dynamic feedback. In *ICSE*, page 521, 2011.
2. K. Beck. *Extreme Programming Explained: Embrace Change*. Addison-Wesley, 1999.
3. K. Beck. *Test-Driven Development: By Example*. Addison-Wesley, 2003.
4. J. Bo, B. Jiajun, C. Chun, and W. Bo. Semantic consistency maintenance in collaborative graphics design systems. In *Proc. Computer Supported Cooperative Work in Design*, pages 35–40. IEEE, Apr. 2008.
5. L.-T. Cheng, S. Hupfer, S. Ross, and J. Patterson. Jazzing up Eclipse with collaborative tools. In *OOPSLA workshop on eclipse technology eXchange*, 2003.
6. A. Cockburn. *Crystal Clear: A Human-Powered Methodology for Small Teams*. Addison-Wesley, 2004.
7. P. Dewan, P. Agarwal, G. Shroff, and R. Hegde. Distributed side-by-side programming. In *CHASE*, page 7, 2009.
8. P. Dewan and J. Riedl. Toward Computer-Supported Concurrent Software Engineering. *IEEE Computer*, 26:17–27, 1993.
9. M. Goldman, G. Little, and R. C. Miller. Collabode: Collaborative Coding in the Browser. In *CHASE*, page 65, May 2011.
10. M. Goldman and R. C. Miller. Test-Driven Roles for Pair Programmming. In *CHASE*, pages 515–516, 2010.
11. L. Hattori and M. Lanza. Syde: a tool for collaborative software development. In *ICSE*, pages 235–238, 2010.
12. R. Hegde and P. Dewan. Connecting Programming Environments to Support Ad-Hoc Collaboration. In *ASE*, pages 178–187. IEEE, Sept. 2008.
13. C.-W. Ho, S. Raha, E. Gehringer, and L. Williams. Sangam: a distributed pair programming plug-in for Eclipse. In *OOPSLA workshop on Eclipse Technology eXchange*, page 73, 2004.
14. R. Holmes and R. J. Walker. Customized awareness: recommending relevant external change events. In *ICSE*, pages 465–474, 2010.
15. C.-L. Ignat and M. C. Norrie. Handling Conflicts through Multi-level Editing in Peer-to-peer Environments. In *Proc. CSCW Workshop on Collaborative Editing Systems*, 2006.
16. A. J. Ko, H. H. Aung, and B. A. Myers. Design requirements for more flexible structured editors from a study of programmers' text editing. In *CHI Extended Abstracts*, CHI EA '05, page 1557, 2005.
17. S. Minor. Interacting with structure-oriented editors. *International Journal of Man-Machine Studies*, 37(4):399–418, Oct. 1992.
18. X. Ren, F. Shah, F. Tip, B. G. Ryder, and O. Chesley. Chianti: a tool for change impact analysis of java programs. In *Proc. OOPSLA*, volume 39, 2004.
19. B. G. Ryder and F. Tip. Change impact analysis for object-oriented programs. In *Workshop on Program Analysis for Software Tools and Engineering*, 2001.
20. D. Saff and M. D. Ernst. Reducing wasted development time via continuous testing. In *International Symposium on Software Reliability Engineering*, pages 281–292. IEEE, 2003.
21. S. Salinger, C. Oezbek, K. Beecher, and J. Schenk. Saros: an Eclipse plug-in for distributed party programming. In *CHASE*, pages 48–55, 2010.
22. A. Sarma, Z. Noroozi, and A. van Der Hoek. Palantír: raising awareness among configuration management workspaces. In *ICSE*, pages 444–454, 2003.
23. F. Servant, J. A. Jones, and A. V. D. Hoek. CASI: preventing indirect conflicts through a live visualization. In *CHASE*, pages 39–46, 2010.
24. D. Shao, S. Khurshid, and D. E. Perry. Evaluation of Semantic Interference Detection in Parallel Changes: an Exploratory Experiment. In *International Conference on Software Maintenance*, pages 74–83. IEEE, Oct. 2007.
25. C. Sun and C. Ellis. Operational transformation in real-time group editors. In *Proc. Computer Supported Cooperative Work*, pages 59–68, 1998.
26. C. Treude and M.-A. Storey. Awareness 2.0: staying aware of projects, developers and tasks using dashboards and feeds. In *ICSE*, pages 365–374, 2010.
27. A. van Deursen, A. Mesbah, B. Cornelissen, A. Zaidman, M. Pinzger, and A. Guzzi. Adinda: a knowledgeable, browser-based IDE. In *ICSE*, pages 203–206, 2010.
28. R. C. Waters. Program editors should not abandon text oriented commands. *ACM SIGPLAN Notices*, 17(7):39, July 1982.
29. J. Wloka, B. Ryder, F. Tip, and X. Ren. Safe-commit analysis to facilitate team software development. In *International Conference on Software Engineering*, pages 507–517, 2009.
30. J. Wloka, B. G. Ryder, and F. Tip. JUnitMX - A change-aware unit testing tool. In *International Conference on Software Engineering*, pages 567–570, 2009.

d.tour: Style-based Exploration of Design Example Galleries

Daniel Ritchie, Ankita Arvind Kejriwal, Scott R. Klemmer
Stanford University HCI Group
Department of Computer Science
Stanford, CA, USA
(dritchie, ankitak, srk)@cs.stanford.edu

ABSTRACT
In design, people often seek examples for inspiration. However, current example-finding practices suffer many drawbacks: templates present designs without a usage context; search engines can only examine the text on a page. This paper introduces exploratory techniques for finding relevant and inspiring design examples. These novel techniques include searching by stylistic similarity to a known example design and searching by stylistic keyword. These interactions are manifest in d.tour, a style-based design exploration tool. d.tour presents a curated database of Web pages as an explorable design gallery. It extracts and analyzes design features of these pages, allowing it to process style-based queries and recommend designs to the user. d.tour's gallery interface decreases the gulfs of execution and evaluation for design example-finding.

ACM Classification: H5.2 [Information interfaces and presentation]: User Interfaces - Graphical user interfaces.

General terms: Design, Human Factors

Keywords: Design, examples, search

INTRODUCTION
People often begin design work by referring to, copying, or adapting existing designs [19, 12]. Prior work has provided techniques to adapt the content [13] and the style [18] of example pages to designs.

However, finding relevant design examples remains a challenge. People commonly query search engines for pages with similar content to their own. However, search engines demand keywords, which can be hard to articulate [12]. This is especially true for design novices, as they often engage in exploratory search without clear stylistic goals. Furthermore, current search engines offer little help because they index and present only the *contents* of a page, not its *design style*. Another common approach is to browse design template repositories. But templates present designs without showing them in use, so it can be hard to gauge their value [19].

Figure 1: d.tour enables search for designs by style. The "Show more like" interaction supports search by stylistic similarity, using examples as queries (design outlined in green). The results (second set of designs) incorporate features from these examples.

How can tools enable people to explore designs for inspiration? Prior work has introduced two main strategies for design search. One strategy is to retrieve designs given a rough layout sketch [10]. However, this requires people to have concrete layout ideas before they can begin exploring examples. They also cannot explore along non-layout design dimensions. The second strategy is a browsable design gallery [19, 21]. Existing gallery strategies have been limited to browsing. We employ a gallery approach, introducing techniques for search, recommendation, filtering and style-based exploration.

This paper introduces techniques for finding design examples by style, which are manifest in d.tour—an exploratory search tool for Web design. In many domains, it is difficult to specify what one wants, but easy to provide positive and negative examples. Recommender systems leverage this insight [3], and d.tour extends it to the design domain. It can be easier to specify design goals by visual example than with language, so d.tour allows people to search its gallery for designs that are stylistically similar/dissimilar to an example design. People can also search by high-level style terms such as 'minimal' and 'clean.' To support such queries, d.tour automatically extracts style-related features from a curated database of designs. The d.tour project investigates example-finding techniques for visual design; the prototype presented in this paper focuses on Web design.

d.tour contributes the following:

- An interface and interaction techniques for style-based gallery exploration.
- A curated database of Web pages for people to search.
- Methods for extracting stylistic and structural features from Web pages; these features make our novel search modalities possible.
- A recommender system that processes queries and returns relevant pages from the database.

The d.tour Web interface is located at http://bricolage.stanford.edu/search.

We believe that style-based exploration of a design gallery can help people of all skill levels find relevant and inspiring design examples more effectively. To get an initial sense of the utility of this direction, an online study asked participants to find inspirational design examples using either the d.tour prototype or keyword Web search. Participants who used d.tour reported a positive example-finding experience compared to those who used Web search. The current d.tour prototype uses a 300-page corpus of designs selected from design blogs, award lists, and the Alexa Top 100. In future work, it will be important to investigate the effect of corpus size on user experience.

The remainder of this paper is organized as follows: first, we describe the d.tour interface and the search interactions it supports. We then identify a set of design features and describe algorithms to extract them from Web pages and use them to answer search queries. We describe the online study and our experimental results, and conclude with discussion and directions for future work.

USER INTERFACE

The d.tour interface comprises five components (Figure 2):

(a) *Search Results*: Presents search results as interactive thumbnails.

(b) *Search box*: Supports query by text, color, and style. Allows users to add their own pages via URL.

Figure 2: The d.tour Web interface: (a) Search Results, (b) Search box, (c) Current Query, (d) Ambient Style Display, and (e) Bookmarks. In (c), the user has searched for 'design' and has given a positive rating to one page and a negative rating to another. The Search Results (a) displays pages matching this query.

(c) *Current Query*: Displays all keywords and Web pages currently influencing the search results.
(d) *Ambient Style Display*: Helps people understand why pages are recommended.
(e) *Bookmarks*: Keeps track of interesting pages.

d.tour initially presents a random sample of pages from the system's database. The user can search by querying for designs similar/dissimilar to design examples or by entering keywords into the search box.

Search Results

d.tour enables people to use design examples as a query interface by providing 'Show more like' (▲) and 'Show less like' (▼) controls that update the design gallery accordingly (Figure 1). These controls become visible when hovering over a page, as seen in the first result in Figure 2a. Other interactions include clicking a page thumbnail to expand the page to full size, ↗ to open it in a new tab, and ☆ to bookmark and add notes to the page.

Search box

With d.tour's search box, people can search with keyword queries and URLs. First, the user can search for documents that contain a particular *text* string. The user can also search by *color* keywords, *style* terms, or any combination of the three. For example, searching for 'colorful image-heavy' retrieves colorful pages that make heavy use of images (Figure 3). The d.tour prototype supports style keywords that arose frequently in our discussions with potential users; this set could of course be expanded. The user can query for designs similar to any page on the Web by entering its URL into the search box.

Figure 3: Performing style keyword search with d.tour. Searching for 'colorful image-heavy' retrieves colorful pages that make heavy use of images.

Current Query

This right-hand pane displays the keyword and page queries that specify the current state of the design gallery. The user can freely modify this state by changing or removing items.

Pilot studies indicated that people often like only *some* attributes of design examples; example-based querying could be more efficient if users provided information about their rationale for liking a page. Building simple interfaces for users to convey rationale is an important open issue in recommender systems [30]. After experimenting with several alternatives, we found that checkboxes for *Color* and *Layout* work well.

Ambient Style Display

Explaining recommendations can improve user experience, build trust, and support evaluation of system conclusions [28, 25, 9]. d.tour provides the Ambient Style Display to help explain search results. This bar chart visualizes the aggregate stylistic attributes of the current example queries. When a user hovers over a page, the display provides instant feedback by showing stylistic attributes for that particular page (Figures 2d and 4).

The Ambient Style Display also makes the supported style search terms transparent to the user. Instead of typing style keywords into the search box, the user can click on any style term displayed here to search for pages that are strong in that style.

Bookmarks

The 'Bookmarks' tab allows people to review the pages they have bookmarked, edit their notes, and delete bookmarks. Bookmarks persist when a user resets the Current Query; this allows the user to maintain a collection of interesting pages across several search sessions.

IMPLEMENTATION

This section describes the current prototype system behind the d.tour interface.

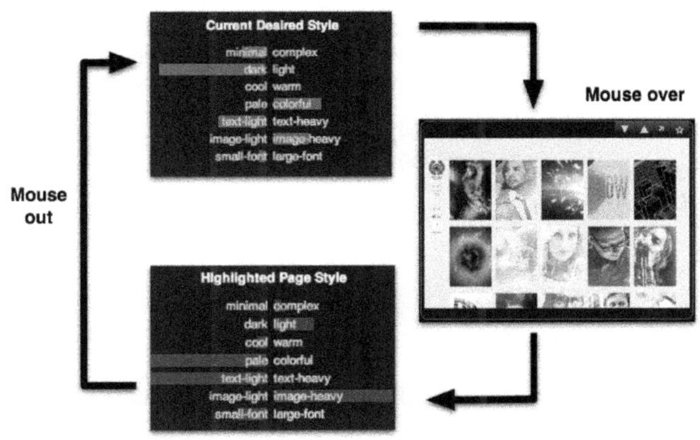

Figure 4: The Ambient Style Display shows the aggregate style attributes of the current example queries. When the user mouses over a page thumbnail, it instead shows that page's stylistic attributes.

Database

The current prototype includes around 300 Web pages listed on sites such as webbyawards.com, designmeltdown.com, ilovetypography.com, sixrevisions.com, and the Alexa Top 100. The complete contents of the database can be found at bricolage.stanford.edu/database. As d.tour automatically extracts features, the database could easily expand by crawling the Web. Techniques such as Website rating prediction [15] could help automatically pick out good designs. People can already add pages to d.tour's database with the search box; given enough users, the database could expand by crowdsourcing. Social moderation techniques [20] could help maintain quality as the corpus grows organically.

System Architecture

All utilities for processing pages and extracting features are implemented in C++ with the Qt framework; we use the QtWebKit API to interface with the WebKit browser engine.

The d.tour search interface is written in HTML, JavaScript, and CSS; it supports HTML5-compliant browsers such as Firefox, Safari, and Chrome. The Web server is also written in JavaScript using node.js [1].

FEATURE EXTRACTION

To support interactive search, d.tour precomputes style features for every page in its database and any new page added during runtime. d.tour focuses on global features that describe a design's use of space, color, text, and images (Figure 5). Our choice of these features was informed by interviews with designers and principles from the design literature [27]. From our observations, these features compose to predict higher-level stylistic attributes. For example, a shallow DOM tree, large foreground-to-background ratio, and few colors form a good predictor of a 'minimalist' style. Many of these features are derived from the page's Document Object Model (DOM) tree. Features such as "number of fonts" can be directly read from the DOM tree. Other features require segmentation. d.tour applies the Bento page segmentation algorithm [18] to ensure that the DOM tree accurately reflects the page's visual layout. The system also computes a color histogram of the rendered page, quantizing the image into 216 colors that evenly sample the RGB color cube. After extraction, the system standardizes all features, so that those with typically large values (such as the size of image elements) do not unduly dominate the others.

Use of Space	DOM tree depth (min, max, mean, stddev), # of DOM leaf nodes, document width/height, amount of separation between content blocks, foreground/background ratio, overlapping element area, connected components in rendered image (#, minarea, maxarea, meanarea)
Use of Color	Color (mean, stddev), saturation (min, max, mean, stddev), value (min, max, mean, stddev), # of colors (in DOM, in rendered page), most dominant color, most dominant text color, # of dominant colors, text-to-background contrast (min, max, mean, stddev), histogram
Use of Text	# of words in page, # of words per block (min, max, mean, stddev), # of fonts, font size (min, max, mode, mean)
Use of Images	# of images, aspectRatio (min, max, mean, stddev), area (min, max, mean, stddev), complexity (min, max, mean, stddev)

Figure 5: d.tour leverages these global page features, which were selected based on discussions with designers and principles from the design literature.

d.tour computes additional features for the local structure of Web pages. The Bricolage algorithm [18] transfers the contents of a source page into the style of a target page by computing a mapping between the two pages' DOM trees. It uses an optimization framework, so each mapping has an associated cost. Mapping between two design-similar pages induces a low cost, whereas mapping between dissimilar ones induces high cost. This cost can be viewed as a 'stylistic distance' between Web pages, and d.tour exploits this by precomputing mapping costs between all pairs of pages in the database. The Bricolage mapping costs are computed offline.

All the features for each page are concatenated into one combined vector. This is d.tour's final representation of a page.

We could have treated Web pages purely as images and used content-based image retrieval (CBIR) to answer queries [24, 7, 4]. However, the low-level pixel features used in CBIR were developed with natural images in mind; when applied to Web pages, they capture little information about design style. Recent work in GUI automation and reverse engineering computes patch-based image features to identify interface components [32, 5]. While this strategy works well for exactly matching individual components in designs, local patches do not capture the gestalt style and structure of designs themselves.

QUERY PROCESSING

d.tour uses the text contents of its pages and the combined feature vectors described above to respond to different types of queries.

'Show More/Less Like'

To represent the user's overall preferences according to the current query, the system takes a weighted average q of all feature vectors for pages rated via 'show more/less like.' Let M be the set of feature vectors for all 'show more like' pages and L be the set of vectors for all 'show less like' pages. Then:

$$q = \frac{1}{(|M| + |L|)}(\sum_{\mathbf{m} \in M} \mathbf{m} - \sum_{\mathbf{l} \in L} \mathbf{l})$$

If the user has turned off the *Color* toggle for a particular page, all color-related features are set to zero in that page's feature vector. If the *Layout* toggle is off, all other features are set to zero. The system then ranks each page in the database by its feature vector's cosine distance to the query vector q and returns the ranked list.

Text Keyword Search

For each page in the database, the system computes a TF-IDF score for each word in the page's document text [26]. It returns a ranked list of the pages whose combined scores for the query terms are greater than zero.

Color Keyword Search

The system converts each color keyword into an RGB color c^* for that word using a hard-coded lookup table; the current prototype supports twelve common color words. To determine how well a page matches the query color, it computes a score s based on the page's histogram h. h is a set of pairs (c_i, f_i), where c_i is an RGB color and f_i is the fraction of pixels in the page whose nearest histogram color is c_i. Then:

$$s = \sum_{i=1}^{|h|} s_i$$

where, for each histogram pair (c_i, f_i)

$$d_i = ||c^* - c_i||_2 \quad \text{and} \quad s_i = \begin{cases} \frac{f_i}{1+d_i^2} & \text{if } d_i < \epsilon, \\ 0 & \text{otherwise} \end{cases}$$

Intuitively, frequently-occurring colors that are close to the query color should have a high score contribution s_i. We clamp the contribution to zero if the color is not sufficiently close; this prevents extremely frequent but only marginally similar colors from skewing the score. We use a value of $\frac{\sqrt{3}}{3}$—one-third the diagonal length of the RGB color cube—for the threshold ϵ, which works well in practice. The system returns as search results only the pages with s greater than a heuristically determined threshold.

Style Keyword Search

We informally asked participants to tag Web pages with stylistic descriptor words. Some words occurred much more frequently than others. Our next step was to operationalize these keywords as compositions of style features. For instance, *minimal* pages have few DOM leaf nodes and few image connected components. Style keyword search works by consulting a rule for each query term, scoring pages that closely conform to the rule higher than those that do not. The system multiplies a page's scores for each query term and heuristically thresholds the search results. The current prototype supports 35 terms—including synonyms—that map to 14 unique rules (Figure 6). Terms corresponding to these unique rules also drive the Ambient Style Display interface component described in the User Interface section.

Minimal, Minimalistic, Clean, Simple, Plain, Sparse Few DOM leaves; few image connected components	↔	**Complex, Complicated, Busy, Dense, Intricate** Many DOM leaves; many image connected components
Dark Low mean color value	↔	**Light, Bright** High mean color value
Cool, Cold Mean color close to pale blue	↔	**Warm** Mean color close to orange
Pale, Monochrome, Faded Low mean saturation	↔	**Colorful, Saturated, Vivid** High mean saturation; high number of colors
Text-light, Text-sparse Few words on the page	↔	**Text-heavy, Text-centric, Text-focused** Many words on the page
Image-light, Image-sparse Low total image area	↔	**Image-heavy, Image-centric, Image-focused** High total image area
Small-font Small mean font size; small mode font size	↔	**Large-font** Large mean font size; large mode font size

Figure 6: The current d.tour prototype invokes these rules when the user searches for the bold terms. All the features in any single rule are weighted equally.

Supporting a larger vocabulary would almost certainly improve the search experience. However, many style terms have complex, subjective meanings and resist d.tour's current heuristic strategy. For instance, it is not clear how 'professional' or 'fun' map onto our feature set. Employing crowdsourcing and machine learning to expand the keyword set is an important direction for future work.

EVALUATION

Method

An online study instructed participants to find a set of inspirational design examples—*Inspiration Boards*—for redesigning a Website. Participants were randomly assigned to use either d.tour or a Web search engine to find examples. Afterwards, they provided feedback about their search strategies and experience.

Participants We recruited 40 participants: 20 through student email lists at our university and 20 more via Amazon Mechanical Turk. Participants answered two questions about their prior Web design experience: "How many Web pages have you designed?" and "Of these, how many were paid, professional assignments?" Participants of different expertise levels were distributed across using either d.tour or a Web search engine by random assignment.

Study Design All participants searched for inspirational design examples for the same client: The Science Bus, an after-school science education program [2]. We chose this group because we believed that most participants could sympathize with its mission, care about the study task, and fully apply themselves [11]. Also, the Website to be redesigned was not heavily styled; we believed that such a raw starting point would help participants avoid design fixation [16].

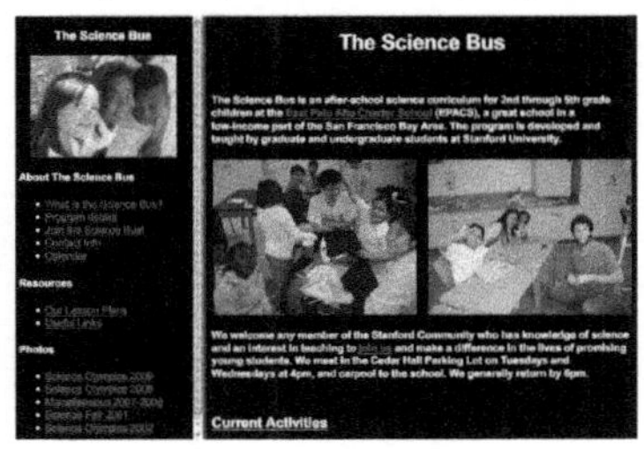

The online system randomly assigned each participant to use either d.tour or a Web search engine to search for examples. Each participant submitted URLs for four inspirational design examples and provided reasons for choosing each page. Participants were free to spend as long as they wanted on the tasks; average completion time was around 25 minutes.

Procedure Participants began by reading a written design brief describing the client and their assigned task; see the

Appendix for the full text. Participants using d.tour also received a link to the d.tour Web interface.

Participants using d.tour watched a four-minute video tutorial which launched automatically when participants first viewed the tool and was available for repeat viewing at any time. For participants using search engines, we assumed familiarity with Google or a similar search engine.

Participants then searched for design examples. Upon finishing their search, they responded to a questionnaire. They first provided URLs and explanations for their chosen examples. They then answered survey questions about their search strategies and overall experience.

Results

Participants using search engines mainly reported querying with keywords such as 'science,' 'kids,' and 'education.' They also retrieved pages from their own mental search history, recalling well-designed, potentially relevant sites they had seen recently.

Several of these participants cited the lack of style-based search or the insufficiency of searching by page content as serious roadblocks. One participant wished for a search function that "rated sites by mood or feel." Another observed that "Google is only really useful for searching for actual page content, not page style. Google was less useful than I imagined it would be."

Feedback from participants using d.tour was generally positive. One participant described d.tour as a "really good tool to find quick examples." Every search technique was used by some participant, the most heavily used being 'show more like'. A participant mentioned that different query types proved useful at different stages of his search: "It was hard for me to describe what I liked . . . But once I had some examples . . . it made it easy to find common ground and then make the search more explicit." This account aligns well with the 'orienteering' theory of search described in [22].

Participants also singled out specific interface features as useful. One found value in having the 'Current Query' always present on the side of the screen as reminder of search history. Another reported using "a very zoomed-out view" to compare many designs simultaneously. The 'Ambient Style Display' received mixed feedback, as a few participants reported difficulty interpreting and operationalizing the information it provided.

Some participants also cited low corpus size as a limitation for d.tour; potential remedies for this issue were discussed earlier in the Implementation section.

Summary

Compared to those who used search engines, participants who used d.tour reported a positive example-finding experience. They identified key search features and interface components as specifically helpful in their exploration. These

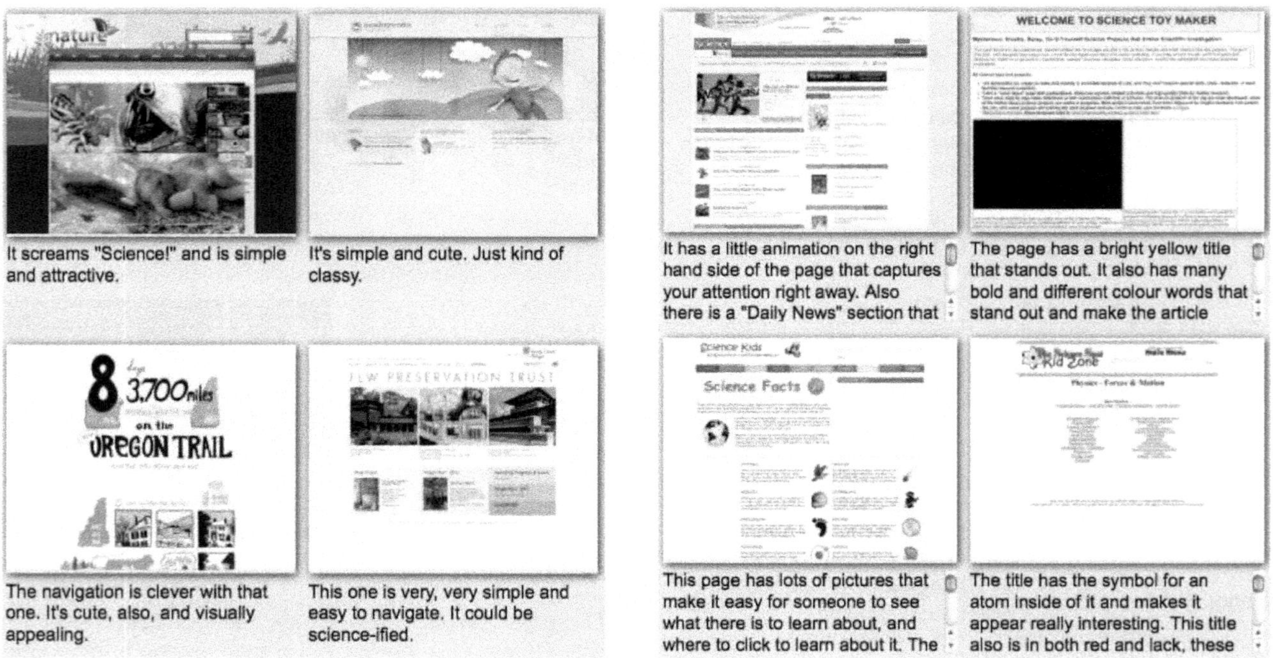

Produced using *d.tour* **Produced using a *search engine***

Figure 7: Inspiration Boards (examples and rationales) produced by participants. (Right) Many participants using search engines chose pages on a topic relevant to the design task. (Left) Participants using d.tour focused on the style and presentation of their chosen designs.

initial results suggest that style-based exploration of a design gallery can improve the example-finding process.

Further research is needed to isolate the factors that make d.tour effective. Specifically, it will be important to build a theory of how corpus size and interaction style affect user experience.

DISCUSSION

We showed the participants' Inspiration boards to two professional Web designers and two members of the Science Bus. Both groups strongly preferred pages that specifically addressed the Science Bus's content presentation needs—how to showcase recent work, for instance. This suggests that design search tools should support search by function in addition to style. Design pattern galleries, such as patterntap.com and designofsites.com/designpatterns, provide organized collections of functional Web page elements (navigation bars, slideshows, etc.) Unifying d.tour's high-level style search with pattern galleries' more bottom-up approach could markedly improve the search experience. To achieve this, 'show more like' could be refined to operate on individual page *components*; automatically classifying Web page components might provide a starting point [17].

One participant who used d.tour wished she could insert the Science Bus's content into candidate example pages to see how well it fit. While the examples found in our experiment were used for inspiration as-is, one could imagine integrating d.tour with the Bricolage Web page retargeting algorithm [18]. Seeing example pages adapted to the desired content could help non-experts look past surface dissimilarities and overcome conformity bias.

Participants who used d.tour produced more domain-diverse examples than those who used search engines. d.tour's currently small corpus makes focusing on a particular domain difficult, but even given a larger corpus, style-based search could still encourage this behavior more than keyword search. Search engines are optimized for topic-based search, so people often use them to find designs by domain. When searchers exhaust the good designs in one domain, however, finding a new one to explore can be challenging. Searchers often navigate between 'patches' of relevant content, continually trading off the cost of further examining one patch with the cost of locating a new one [23]. With keyword search, patches are topically organized, and textually-presented search results lack a scent/preview of the design. With d.tour, design patches are style-based, and 'show more like' makes jumping between domains easier. For example, when asked to show more like apple.com. d.tour retrieves onlynylives.com and clubjoomla.com amongst others—these design-similar pages come from three very disparate domains (Figure 1).

Style-based gallery exploration may have an advantage over search engines simply by presenting results in a design gallery. For design finding, visual display of search results provides stronger information scent [23] than the textual document surrogates [11] typically presented by Web search engines. This helps the searcher decide which results are worth clicking through. It also shrinks the gulf of evaluation [14], providing more immediate feedback on query usefulness. Though commercial search engines rely primarily on textual display, several research systems have explored visual result presentation [6, 31]. Some search engines such as Bing and Google provide optional visual previews, increasing their usefulness as design search tools. Gallery presentations are common for Web image search. For search tasks that are exploratory, low precision, or difficult to specify, galleries are highly effective.

CONCLUSION AND FUTURE WORK

This paper presented a new approach for style-based design example-finding. It described d.tour, a prototype gallery exploration tool that supports several novel search interactions by extracting and analyzing design features from a curated corpus of Web pages. In an initial evaluation, d.tour received positive feedback from participants performing a design-example finding task.

There are several opportunities for future work. First, some stylistic properties likely influence human similarity judgments more than others. However, d.tour currently standardizes all page features, effectively giving them all the same weight. One could potentially learn the appropriate weights from human paired comparisons of Web pages; [29] proposes a related method for learning the perceptual distance between glossy materials.

Second, expanding the stylistic vocabulary is critical to supporting robust, language-based design search. As mentioned previously, one could apply machine learning techniques to a large corpus of stylistically-tagged Web pages to learn which design features predict frequently-occurring tags. Research is required to design a task environment in which crowds can produce high-quality style labels.

Third, an expanded style vocabulary will require more advanced design features. Many of d.tour's features rely on the HTML DOM, which simplifies a page to a hierarchy of rectangles. In the page shown in Figure 8, the wine bottles and some of the type overlap, breaking the strong grid lines specified by the DOM. d.tour's current features cannot detect 'organic' layouts where perceptually-coherent chunks span DOM elements. Combining DOM analysis with more

Figure 8: The wine bottles and the type on this page overlap and span multiple DOM nodes (outlined in blue). d.tour's current feature set cannot support queries about 'organic' page layouts such as this.

sophisticated computer vision algorithms could address this limitation.

Fourth, d.tour does not attempt to capture non-static aspects of design such as animation or interaction. Future work could address searching for designs by such elements.

Fifth, a full-fledged system should scale to much large page databases—perhaps even the entire Web. Such a system could use standard Web search indexing techniques to accelerate keyword queries. Locality Sensitive Hashing has been successfully applied to the nearest neighbor problem with large amounts of high-dimensional data [8]; it could help pick similar designs out of a large database.

Finally, and perhaps most exciting, is the possibility of embedding d.tour into real Web design software and observing how it affects the creative process.

ACKNOWLEDGMENTS

We would like to thank Martin Hunt for his help implementing the Web interface, Steven Dow for helping with study design, and the Stanford HCI group for valuable discussion. We would also like to thank Mira Dontcheva, Ranjitha Kumar, and the reviewers for their helpful feedback on earlier drafts of this paper. This work was supported by a Stanford Graduate Fellowship, the Stanford Computer Forum, and NSF Grant IIS-0745320.

REFERENCES

1. node.js. http://nodejs.org, 2011. Retrieved March 17, 2011.
2. The Science Bus. http://www.stanford.edu/group/sciencebus, 2011. Retrieved March 17, 2011.
3. G. Adomavicius and A. Tuzhilin. Toward the next generation of recommender systems: A survey of the state-of-the-art and possible extensions. *IEEE Transactions on Knowledge and Data Engineering*, 17, June 2005.
4. J. Cui, F. Wen, and X. Tang. Intentsearch: interactive on-line image search re-ranking. In *Proceedings of MM: ACM Conference on Multimedia*. ACM, 2008.
5. M. Dixon and J. Fogarty. Prefab: implementing advanced behaviors using pixel-based reverse engineering of interface structure. In *Proceedings of CHI: ACM Conference on Human Factors in Computing Systems*. ACM, 2010.
6. S. Dziadosz and R. Chandrasekar. Do thumbnail previews help users make better relevance decisions about web search results? In *Proceedings of SIGIR: ACM Conference on Research and Development in Information Retrieval*. ACM, 2002.
7. G. Giacinto and F. Roli. Bayesian relevance feedback for content-based image retrieval. *Pattern Recognition*, 2004.
8. A. Gionis, P. Indyk, and R. Motwani. Similarity search in high dimensions via hashing. In *Proceedings of VLDB: International Conference on Very Large Data Bases*, pages 518–529. Morgan Kaufmann Publishers Inc., 1999.
9. S. Gregor and I. Benbasat. Explanations from intelligent systems: theoretical foundations and implications for practice. *MIS Quarterly*, 23, December 1999.
10. Y. Hashimoto and T. Igarashi. Retrieving web page layouts using sketches to support example-based web design. *2nd Eurographics Workshop on Sketch- Based Interfaces and Modeling*, 2005.
11. M. A. Hearst. *Search User Interfaces*. Cambridge Univesity Press, 2009.
12. S. R. Herring, C. Chang, J. Krantzler, and B. P. Bailey. Getting inspired!: understanding how and why examples are used in creative design practice. In *Proceedings of CHI: ACM Conference on Human Factors in Computing Systems*. ACM, 2009.
13. V. Hollink, M. van Someren, and V. de Boer. Capturing the needs of amateur web designers by means of examples. In *Proceedings of the 16th Workshop on Adaptivity and User Modeling in Interactive Systems*, 2008.
14. E. L. Hutchins, J. D. Hollan, and D. A. Norman. Direct manipulation interfaces. *Human-Computer Interaction*, 1(4), Dec 1985.
15. M. Y. Ivory and M. A. Hearst. Statistical profiles of highly-rated web sites. In *Proceedings of CHI: ACM Conference on Human Factors in Computing Systems*. ACM, 2002.
16. D. G. Jansson and S. M. Smith. Design fixation. *Design Studies*, 12(1), 1991.
17. C. Kulkarni and S. R. Klemmer. Automatically adapting web pages to heterogeneous devices. In *Proceedings of CHI: ACM Conference on Human Factors in Computing Systems Extended Abstracts*. ACM, 2011.
18. R. Kumar, J. O. Talton, S. Ahmad, and S. R. Klemmer. Bricolage: Example-based retargeting for web design. In *Proceedings of CHI: ACM Conference on Human Factors in Computing Systems*. ACM, 2011.
19. B. Lee, S. Srivastava, R. Kumar, R. Brafman, and S. R. Klemmer. Designing with interactive example galleries. In *Proceedings of CHI: ACM Conference on Human Factors in Computing Systems*. ACM, 2010.
20. J. Lou, K. Chen, and C. Lei. A collusion-resistant automation scheme for social moderation systems. In *Proceedings of CCNC: IEEE Conference on Consumer Communications and Networking*. IEEE Press, 2009.
21. J. Marks et al. Design galleries: a general approach to setting parameters for computer graphics and animation. In *Proceedings of SIGGRAPH: ACM Conference on Computer Graphics and Interactive Techniques*. ACM, 1997.
22. V. L. O'Day and R. Jeffries. Orienteering in an information landscape: how information seekers get from here to there. In *Proceedings of CHI: ACM Conference on Human Factors in Computing Systems*. ACM, 1993.
23. P. Pirolli. *Information Foraging Theory: Adaptive Interaction with information*. Oxford University Press, 2007.
24. K. Porkaew and K. Chakrabarti. Query refinement for multimedia similarity retrieval in mars. In *Proceedings of MM: ACM Conference on Multimedia*. ACM, 1999.
25. P. Pu and L. Chen. Trust building with explanation interfaces. In *Proceedings of IUI: ACM Conference on Intelligent User Interfaces*. ACM, 2006.
26. J. A. Ramos. Using TF-IDF to determine word relevance in document queries. In *Proceedings of ICML: International Conference on Machine Learning*, 2003.
27. T. Samara. *Design Elements: A Graphic Style Manual*. Rockport Publishers, 2007.
28. N. Tintarev. Explanations of recommendations. In *Proceedings of RecSys: ACM Conference on Recommender Systems*. ACM, 2007.

29. J. Wills, S. Agarwal, D. Kriegman, and S. Belongie. Toward a perceptual space for gloss. *ACM Transactions on Graphics*, 28, September 2009.
30. W. Wong, I. Oberst, S. Das, T. Moore, S. Stumpf, K. McIntosh, and M. Burnett. End-user feature labeling: a locally-weighted regression approach. In *Proceedings of IUI: ACM Conference on Intelligent User Interfaces*. ACM, 2011.
31. A. Woodruff, A. Faulring, R. Rosenholtz, J. Morrsion, and P. Pirolli. Using thumbnails to search the web. In *Proceedings of CHI: ACM Conference on Human Factors in Computing Systems*. ACM, 2001.
32. T. Yeh, T. Chang, and R. C. Miller. Sikuli: using GUI screenshots for search and automation. In *Proceedings of UIST: ACM Conference on User Interfaces Software and Technologies*. ACM, 2009.

APPENDIX: Experimental Design Brief

Introduction

The Science Bus is an after-school science curriculum for 2nd through 5th grade children at the East Palo Alto Charter School (EPACS), a great school in a low-income part of the San Francisco Bay Area. The program is developed and taught by graduate and undergraduate students at Stanford University.

The leaders of The Science Bus program are not satisfied with their current Web site; they think it's kind of ugly and want to make it a lot nicer and more design-oriented. They want their new design to serve three purposes:

- Be a recruitment tool for Stanford students
- Present their awesome work to anyone who's interested
- Be a resource for similar science education programs across the country

Stylistically, they want the new page to scream "Science!" They're also fans of simplicity, so the new page shouldn't be too cluttered.

Your Task: Find inspiring design examples

Your task is to provide URLs for *four (4) Web pages* that are good design examples for The Science Bus. The Science Bus should be able to build a well-designed page that meets their needs by referring to your examples for inspiration.

For each example page that you provide, you'll also be asked to *explain what makes that page a good example.* In your explanations, you might want to refer to color scheme, layout, typography, or other elements of style. This is by no means an exhaustive list; feel free to discuss anything about the pages you select.

The pages you provide don't have to be perfect in all aspects. Each page being excellent in just one–color scheme, for instance–can make for a great set of design examples.

IP-QAT: In-Product Questions, Answers & Tips

Justin Matejka, Tovi Grossman, and *George Fitzmaurice*
Autodesk Research
firstname.lastname@Autodesk.com

ABSTRACT

We present IP-QAT, a new community-based question and answer system for software users. Unlike most community forums, IP-QAT is integrated into the actual software application, allowing users to easily post questions, answers and tips without having to leave the application. Our in-product implementation is context-aware and shows relevant posts based on a user's recent activity. It is also designed with minimal transaction costs to encourage users to easily post, include annotated images and file attachments, as well as tag their posts with relevant UI components. We describe a robust cloud-based system implementation, which allowed us to release IP-QAT to 37 users for a 2 week field study. Our study showed that IP-QAT increased user contributions, and subjectively, users found our system more useful and easier to use, in comparison to the existing commercial discussion board.

ACM Classification: H5.2 [Information interfaces and presentation]: User Interfaces. - Graphical user interfaces.

General terms: Design, Human Factors

Keywords: Q&A, Community, Help, In-Product Learning

INTRODUCTION

Despite years of HCI research, learnability continues to be a challenge for software applications [9]. This is especially true for complex and feature rich programs which have been shown to continuously grow in their number of features with each release [15]. However, new trends and technologies are available for providing assistance to learning, which were not prevalent in the earlier days of HCI research.

In particular, the world-wide-web has the power to create online communities, allowing users to share their knowledge with one another. For popular software applications, one can find dozens of discussion boards, where community members can discuss topics about the software, including learning challenges. However, we would argue that such forums are not optimized for allowing users to get help with specific learnability challenges, and we highlight two particular problems and associated opportunities.

First, discussion forums are accessed and presented outside of the context of the software application, which can impair a user's awareness and access of relevant material [18]. Furthermore, once out of the application, it can be difficult and cumbersome for question askers to express their questions, using proper terminology and necessary images or attachments. Some online systems, such as Intuit's TurboTax, have community Q&A services integrated into their websites [20]. We believe there is an opportunity to build upon such work to also improve community help for desktop software applications.

Second, threads in traditional discussion forums often turn into true "discussions" making it difficult for a user to find a concise answer for a specific problem or question. Outside of the software domain, many *question and answer* (*Q&A*) sites, such as Yahoo! Answers [2] and Stack Overflow [16], have become popular, and have shown to be a fast and effective way to learn from the community. Users are encouraged to ask short, concise questions, answerers are motivate to provide high quality responses, and the presentation and layout of the content makes it easy for subsequent users to see questions and their associated answers. We believe that there is an opportunity for developing integrated Q&A systems to target the learning of complicated software applications.

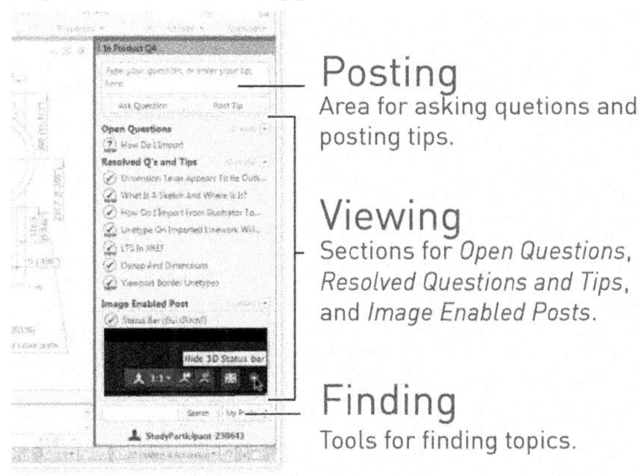

Figure 1. IP-QAT system interface overview.

In this paper, we investigate both of these opportunities, by presenting IP-QAT: "In-Product Questions, Answers & Tips", a community-based question and answer system that is provided as a palette within the target application (Figure 1). IP-QAT was developed for AutoCAD, a popular but difficult to learn application for 2D and 3D architectural design. IP-QAT allows users to: post questions, answers, and tips; include annotated images and attachments with their posts; and tag their posts with relevant UI components. All interactions are accomplished with a low transaction cost compared to traditional out-of-product community forums. Particular effort was made to provide an image-rich experience, to facilitate shared understanding between users referring to spatial data within complex software [5]. IP-QAT also supports opportunistic learning, by displaying answered questions and tips relevant to a user's current context of usage.

Our main contribution is a fully-functional implementation of a community Q&A system integrated into a graphical desktop application. We also contribute an investigation and discussion of the challenges and opportunities related to the development of such a system. Finally, we contribute a 2-week user study, comparing our system to an online software discussion board. Our study shows that IP-QAT increased user contributions, and subjectively, users found our system more useful, easier to use, in comparison to the existing commercial discussion board, and provided numerous enthusiastic and encouraging comments which we summarize and discuss.

RELATED WORK

Discussion Forums and Q&A Sites

Usenet newsgroups [7], pre-dating even the internet, and more recently web-based discussion forums, have been a popular method for people to communicate online. Singh et al. explored discussion forums of 8 open source software applications [21,22] and by qualitatively analyzing the threads was able to identify a number of problematic interactions encountered during the help-seeking process.

As opposed to general purpose discussion forums, which as the name implies are generally designed to promote discussion, Q&A sites have distinctive characteristics designed to promote the specific tasks of asking and answering questions. An early example of a Q&A based knowledge system is Ackerman's Answer Garden [1] which maintained an organically growing database of questions and expert answers for a single domain.

A sizable body of work focuses on the analysis of general purpose Q&A sites such as Yahoo Answers [2,3,6,11], Windows Live QnA [24], and a popular Korean Q&A site, Naver [12,19]. Mamykina et al's detailed analysis of Stack Overflow [16] looks to understand the factors behind the site's success and attributes it, in part, to the daily involvement of the design team with the community of users it serves. The Q&A site Aardvark [14] differs from most others in that it routes questions directly to individual users who are known to be online to elicit faster responses.

These explorations into Q&A sites provide useful guidance towards designing our system, however, none of the existing systems examine the implications of integrating the Q&A system directly into the target application.

TurboTax Live Community

Intuit's TurboTax[1] has an integrated Q&A service alongside the main window [20]. As a highly structured, form-filling application, the context of the user's activity can be determined by which page or field they are working on, which is used to select contextually relevant questions. Only textual questions and answers are supported, which is natural given the text-only nature of the system.

The IP-QAT system builds upon the Live Community concept, to create a system that works with non-linear, graphically intensive applications. Since these programs are not form-based, the user's context cannot be trivially determined, so we infer context based on recent command usage. Additionally, the increased complexity and visual nature of content-authoring applications creates more difficult problems for users to express simply using text [5], which motivates the IP-QAT system to promote and make extensive use of imagery.

Software Learning

To address the prevalent problem of software learnability [9], several research projects have focused on in-product learning techniques.

With Blueprint [4], Brandt et al. embedded a task specific search engine into a programming integrated development environment (IDE) to help users locate appropriate sample code. Hartman et al.'s HelpMeOut [13] is also integrated into an IDE and uses a recommender system to match build and debugging errors the user is having to solutions which have worked for other users in similar situations. While integrated into the target application, these systems are designed for a single discipline (coding), where our system could be used in multiple application domains.

CommunityCommands [15,17] leverages the power of the user community by using collaborative filtering algorithms to generate personal, contextual command recommendations. The AmbientHelp system [18] uses the context of recently used commands to find and automatically display relevant existing help content. Several systems present tool-specific animated help within the application including ToolClips and Google SketchUp's "Instructor" panel [10]. These systems use application context to present useful commands and existing help content, while our system selects relevant discussion topics. Additionally, none of these system support direct communication between users.

Researchers have also looked at ways outside of online forums that users can help each other. Twidale [23] studied "over the shoulder learning": informal help shared between colleagues in a workplace. This work serves as an important reference; however, it focuses on collocated assistance, as opposed to remote, online assistance.

DESIGN PRINCIPLES

We created a set of five design principles to guide the development of IP-QAT. The names in parenthesis after each heading indicate how each principle will be referred to in the system description.

Promote Rich Visuals (*visuals*)

Discussion boards and Q&A sites are typically dominated by text-based posts. Most sites provide support for

[1] http://turbotax.intuit.com/best-tax-software/why-choose-turbotax/help-live-community.jsp

attaching files or images; however, the process is often less than straightforward. Users are generally required to take and edit a screenshot using 3rd party software, and then manually find and upload it as an attachment to their post.

In Chilana et al's research into product support [5], support specialists described screenshots as being the most useful attachment type for diagnosing software problems, with over 90% agreeing they were useful. Despite their usefulness, less than 8% of support issues initially included screenshots, and often the specialists would need to explicitly request them.

Besides promoting the inclusion of visual attachments, increasing the prominence of such images while browsing the system is also desired. In current systems you need to click on a post, and often an "attachment" link before you are able to see an image. In other cases only registered users are able to see images associated with a post. Additionally, images can be a useful way to quickly "scan" and find interesting topics [25], so we would like to promote visual information to the top level of the system.

Make Use of Contextual Information (*context*)

There are many posts in modern discussion and Q&A sites where a potential question answerer begins by requesting additional information from the asker such as *"What version of the program are you using?"*, or *"What plug-ins do you have installed?"* Answers to these and other similar questions could have easily been included in the original question, but the asker either didn't think it was relevant, or perhaps thought it might be, but didn't want to bog the question down with potentially irrelevant details.

Some help systems are able to make use of the user's context to recommend commands [15,17] or pull up potentially relevant pre-existing help content [18] by looking at aspects of a user's context such as which commands have recently been used. Similarly, it would be useful for a community help system to be able to call up relevant community discussions based on the user's history.

Present Content Within the Application (*in-app*)

Current discussion and Q&A sites are accessible through a web browser, separate from the primary application the user is working with. In order to access these communities, the user must switch out of their primary application and search for help or interact with the community in this secondary program. If the content is presented in the primary application we gain several benefits:

Increased Awareness. Users are more likely to be aware of the community help system if it is an integrated feature of their program as opposed to an independent website they must leave to find and access.

Supports Opportunistic Learning. With content hosted in an external application, users will only switch to that program when they explicitly want to learn something. While working, users often have many short periods of down-time [17], and if the community help content is being displayed within the application the user will have a chance to glance over during this time. Additionally, since new material is being "pushed" to the user as opposed to the traditional "pull" model of help, the user has the chance to learn things they never would have considered looking for.

Minimize Transaction Costs (*min-cost*)

A primary consideration of our system is to minimize the transactions costs associated with both authoring content, and consuming content. For authors, we don't want the feeling of *"it's too much work"* to prevent anyone from contributing content. It should also be easy to include images and document source files. For those viewing the content, it should be easy to quickly browse through many topics to see if any are of interest. Topics should load immediately without any additional delay caused by waiting for the content to be downloaded from a server.

Small reductions in the transaction cost may individually not seem to make a huge difference, but previous work has shown that small improvements in interactions can cause categorical behavior changes that far exceed the benefits of the resulting decrease in task times [4,8,18].

Create a Positive Initial Experience (*initial*)

The first experience for a user at most traditional discussion and Q&A sites can be quite overwhelming. There are many different groups, boards, sub-boards, and forums to look at and it is not obvious which ones are appropriate to the user's interests. If the user decides they want to ask a quick question, or even propose an answer, they may first be inundated by login screens, registration procedures, confirmation emails, etc. Creating a good first experience with the system makes it more likely that user's will continue to work with it and both find help for themselves, and eventually contribute to the community.

SYSTEM DESCRIPTION

Based on the above mentioned design principles, we created the In-Product Questions, Answers & Tips (IP-QAT) system, a fully functional implementation of a community help system integrated into a graphical desktop application (Figure 1). In this section, as features relate back to the guiding design principles they will be noted in parenthesis (e.g., *initial, in-app*)

Overview

The IP-QAT system resides in a dockable panel within the host application. The system automatically creates a unique user-id when upon first being launched. There is no requirement to create a new account, which contributes to creating a positive initial experience (*initial, in-app*).

Main Interface

The view of the system consists of three main sections, one each for: *posting*, *viewing*, and *finding*.

The interface is designed to accommodate screens of varying sizes and resolutions and will gracefully reduce the exposed functionality as the window height is decreased (Figure 2). The panel can also be "rolled-up" into a narrow 15px wide bar which is restored when the cursor moves over it (Figure 2E). Even at very small sizes the system remains usable, and allows the user to customize the display to fit their preferred workspace (*initial*).

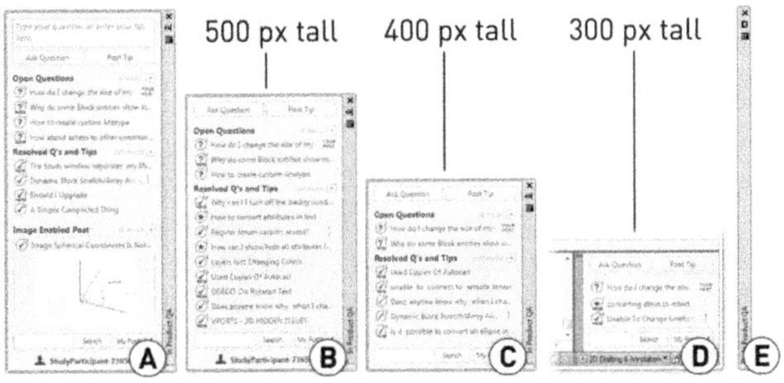

Figure 2. Progression of the interface from the full experience (A), to a very small compressed version (D). The rolled-up version is shown in (E).

Posting

The top part of the interface contains a text field for the user to enter their question or tip. The text field is relatively small to encourage conciseness, and is visible at the top level of the interface to encourage frequent use. On many discussion forums you will see minimally helpful "titles" such as *"I need help"* or *"What am I doing wrong?"* Non-descriptive titles like these may make it difficult for users to browse the topics; they will need to open up the thread to see what it is about. We omitted an explicit "title" field to encourage users to maximize the fraction of useful content in their posts (*min-cost*).

Questions and Tips

In addition to providing support for traditional question and answer type threads, the IP-QAT system creates a top-level mechanism for users to generate "tips". The main interface includes two buttons: "Ask Question" and "Post Tip". Tips give users a way to contribute to the system even if they are unable to answer any currently open questions. Also, tips provide a way for expert users to share their knowledge about smaller features, or "tricks" that they use which might not be something that a user would ever think to explicitly ask about. An example of a tip in a desktop setting might be *"Press F2 to rename a file"*; most people already know how to rename a file in some way, but this tip might let them do it more efficiently.

Supporting Information and Materials

Once the user has clicked on either of the "Ask Question" or "Post Tip" buttons, they are brought to the second-level posting dialog (Figure 3). If no additional information is needed, pressing *Enter* will post the question or tip with only the text entered in the main interface (Figure 3A). However, if additional supporting information is required, it can be added with this top-level modeless dialog.

Clicking on the "Add Description" button (Figure 3D) expands the window to include a second, larger text area to include a more detailed account of the issue. Figure 3B contains a list of tools and commands which the user feels are relevant to this question or tip. Rather than including command names as free-form tags or choosing commands from a long, exhaustive list, the user adds relevant commands to the post by clicking on them in the main interface of the application (*min-cost, in-app*). Since the dialog is modeless, a convenient workflow for asking a question involves launching the post dialog, and then attempting the task you have a question with. In doing this, the commands you use in your attempt will be automatically captured in the relevant tools list (*context*).

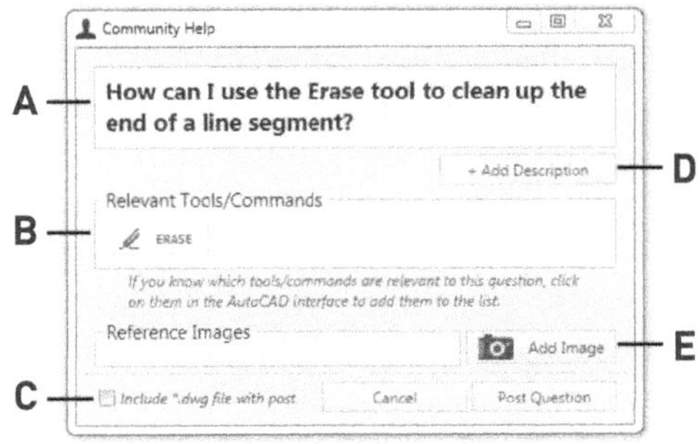

Figure 3. Dialog for posting a question or tip.

The "Add Image" button (Figure 3E) launches the built-in screen-shot utility (*visual*). Similar to the "rectangular snip" mode of the Windows 7 Snipping Tool or TechSmith's SnagIt, the function puts a semi-transparent white overlay over the entire desktop and allows the user to drag a box over the area of interest. The image is inserted directly into the dialog and the user is able to create red "ink" markups on the image to highlight important areas (Figure 4).

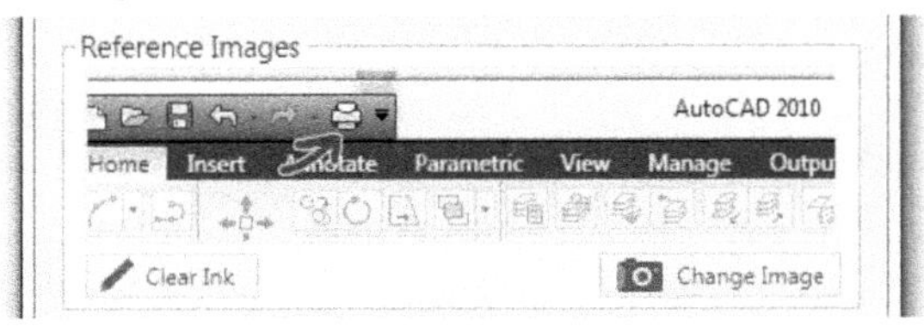

Figure 4. Image portion of the posting dialog box.

Including the active document as an attachment to the post in typical systems involves saving a copy of the document and then finding it through a file system dialog. Since the IP-QAT system has access to the application data, simply selecting a check box (Figure 3C) saves a copy of your document and uploads it with the post (*min-cost, visuals*).

Viewing

The majority of the IP-QAT interface is dedicated to displaying questions and tips, and is divided into three subgroups: *Open Questions*, *Answered Q's and Tips*, and *Image Enabled Posts* (Figure 1). Each section contains a specific selection of topics: *Open Questions* are questions which are still looking for an answer; *Answered Q's and Tips* contains a mixture of questions which have already been answered and contributed tips; and *Image Enabled Posts* selects one or more posts with an image component and displays the topic and image at the top level of the interface (*visual*). Promoting visual posts to an additional dedicated portion of the interface serves as an advertisement to other users that image-based posts are encouraged, and promote them to include images in their posts.

Selecting Topics to Display

Typical discussion boards order topics in chronological order based on the most recent post; all of the threads which were most recently updated are at the top. This helps in finding the newest posts, but potentially interesting threads without any recent activity quickly slip past the first page of results and become more difficult to find.

The IP-QAT system selects which topics to display by running two separate algorithms and then combining the results into one list. The first algorithm sorts all topics in the category by date of last activity; this ensures that the threads with recent activity (including newly created topics) are shown. The second algorithm looks at the context of the application (*context*) and gives each topic a relevance score, $\{S\}$. The algorithm takes the topic $\{t\}$, the user, $\{u\}$, and the ten most recently used commands $\{C\}$. and weights topics using those commands more highly. The particular algorithm used also considers if the user has seen all of the posts in the topic already or is the author of the topic, if they and other users have marked the thread as "interesting", and how many views the thread has:

$$\begin{aligned} S(t,u,C) = &\ u.hasNotSeen(\forall t) * 11 \\ &+ u.author(t) * 25 \\ &+ u.foundInteresting(t) * 17 \\ &+ \textstyle\sum_C (t.uses(c_i) * 3) \\ &+ \textstyle\sum_{\forall u} (u_i.hasSeen(t) * 1.1) \\ &+ \textstyle\sum_{\forall u} (u_i.foundInteresting(t) * 4.1) \end{aligned}$$

This is just one possible scheme, which we found worked well in our pilot studies, but has not been formally tuned. The results from the two algorithms are interleaved to generate the list of topics presented to the user.

The system checks for new posts on the server, and to minimize potential distractions, the list of topics will update at most once per minute if new posts are created or the user's context has changed. To guard against the list re-ordering while the user is interacting with the system, changes are queued up while the cursor is over the IP-QAT window and will take affect once the cursor has been away from the window for three seconds.

Displaying Individual Topics

The individual topic rows in the main view are marked up with various informative icons (Figure 5). The main icon on the left indicates the type of post (either a tip or a question), and, if a question, whether it has been answered or not. Additional graphical badges on the left indicate if there are posts in this thread that you have not read, and a counter of how many users have found the topic interesting.

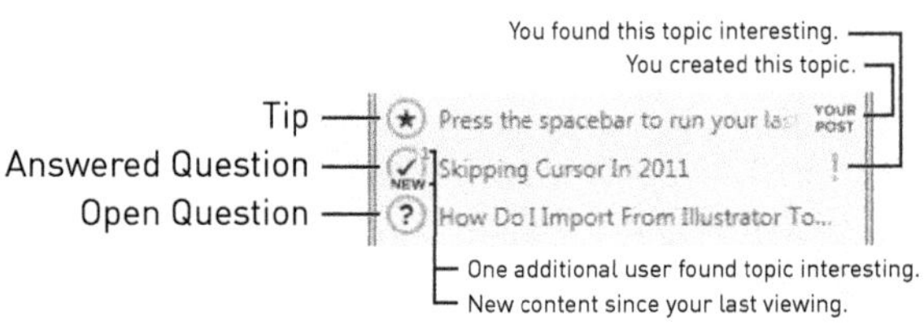

Figure 5. Interface elements for individual topics.

To mark a post as interesting, users click on the '!' icon on the right side of the display bar. These topics receive a higher weighting in the selection algorithms; that is, if a topic you are interested has a new response that you have not seen, it will be promoted to the top of your display list. Additionally, there is a "Your Post" graphic to indicate which topics were created by this user.

When placing the cursor over an individual topic display, the user is presented with a detailed tooltip showing the thread of posts (Figure 6). If any of the posts have images associated with them, they are also displayed (*visuals*). All posts and images are downloaded in a background process and stored locally so there is no loading delay when activating the topic tooltips (*min-cost*) making it possible and convenient for a user to quickly run over many topics and essentially "flip through" them to see if any are of interest. The detailed tooltip also contains the poster's name and when the post was submitted for each post.

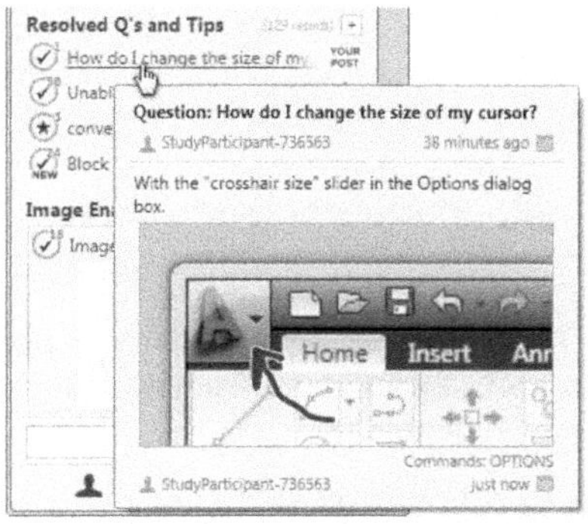

Figure 6. Tooltip interface for quick browsing of topics. When available, images are also displayed.

Clicking on a topic brings up the modeless view/reply dialog (Figure 7). The bottom portion of this window is similar to the posting dialog (Figure 3), while the top portion displays the content of the posts which make up the thread. This view not only shows the commands and tools relevant to each post, but also additional contextual information about which version of the software the author was using (e.x., *AutoCAD Electrical 2011*).

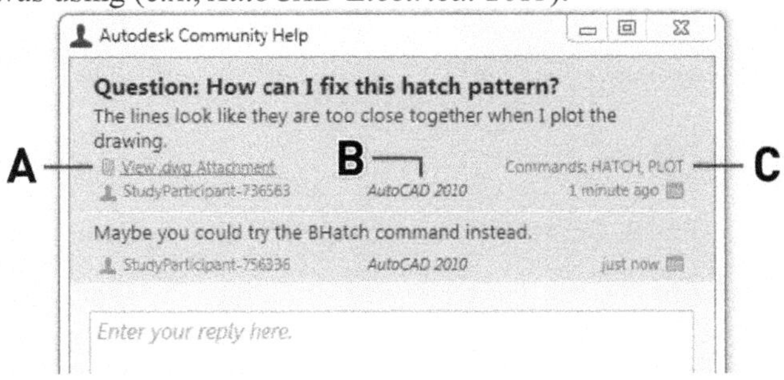

Figure 7. The view/reply window showing the textual post content as well as a link to open the source file (A), the version of the program the post originated from (B) and the relevant commands (C).

Combining the thread viewing and responding functions into a single window streamlines the interface for the user, reducing the number of clicks required to contribute to the community, reducing overall transaction cost (*min-cost*). Once an open question has been replied to, it becomes an "answered" question. If the original asker does not feel the question has been adequately answered, when they reply to the topic they are given the option to select whether or not this question should be marked as answered. If they choose "no", then the question becomes open again.

Finding

While the collection of posts in the interface dynamically updates to display the newest and most relevant topics, there will still be times where the user wants to search for specific content. The search box at the bottom of the interface allows searching for keywords, commands and user names over the entire collection of postings. As characters are entered in the text field, the main display updates in real time to show all matches (*min-cost*).

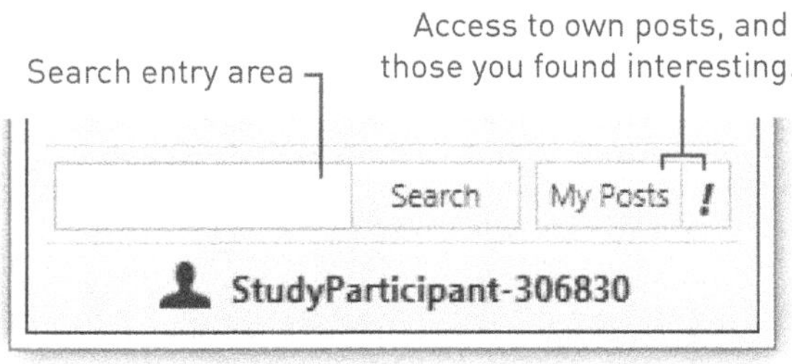

Figure 8. Interface elements for finding posts; by keyword search, those you have authored, or those you marked as interesting.

The "My Posts" button gives users the ability to find all of the content they have contributed, and it is possible for a user to see all topics which they have marked as interesting by clicking on the '!' button.

Context Menu Access

To permit access to the system even if the main interface panel is closed, we implemented a context-menu augmentation which adds IP-QAT specific items into the application's exiting context menu (Figure 9).

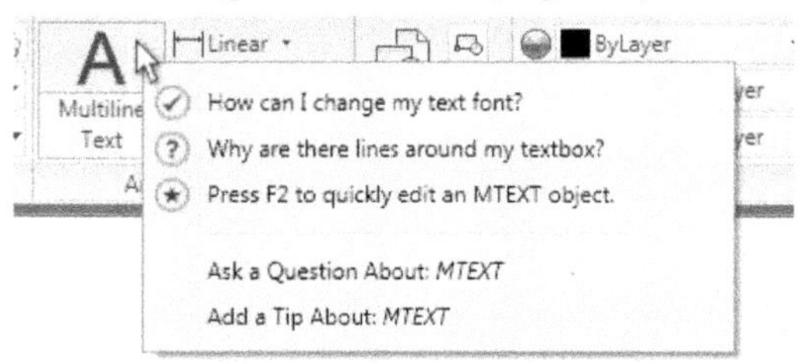

Figure 9. Context menu access of IP-QAT system.

These options can be accessed from either the right click menu of the application, or by right-clicking directly on a tool icon (*in-app*). When accessed from an individual tool, the most highly rated topics related to that particular tool are presented. The tool-button context menu also includes items to ask a question or post a tip about the selected tool. When selected, these options launch the posting dialog (Figure 3) with the current tool preloaded into the relevant tools/commands list (*context*).

SYSTEM IMPLEMENTATION

To perform our intended field study, the implementation of the IP-QAT system needed to be fully functional and robust enough to distribute to users and have them use it for an extended time on their primary workstations while performing their regular jobs.

A significant technical challenge was determining how to reasonably communicate and synchronize the posts, images, and attachment files across all the users of the system. A conventional approach is to run a web-server and database on the back-end for communicating with the clients and storing the data. However, configuring and running this type of system requires specialized expertise, dedicated hardware, and involves a significant overhead cost for setup and maintenance.

As an alternative, we chose to use the Amazon Simple Storage Service (Amazon S3) as our back-end. Locally, each post is stored as a folder, with simple text and image files containing the post data. When the user creates a new post, the folder is created locally, and then uploaded to the S3 server. At regular intervals, each client queries the S3 server and downloads any new posts on a background thread, saving them into folders in the file system. Once downloaded, the posts are loaded into the system. As a benefit of having the data downloaded and stored locally, the user is still able to view existing topics while off-line, and they are also able to post new content which gets updated next time they connect to the internet.

The connection with the S3 server also allows the easy and automatic collection of usage data and statistics, which is a significant convenience when performing distributed, remote, user studies.

AutoCAD Plug-in

The system was implemented as a plug-in to AutoCAD using the ObjectArx framework. The logic of the system was coded in C# and the interface was developed using Microsoft's WPF. The entire system was bundled into a single installer which added the necessary registry keys so the plug-in would start automatically when any of the 21 supported versions of AutoCAD 2010 or 2011 were run. It is possible to have more than one version of AutoCAD running on a machine at one time, and the system implementation includes redundancies ensuring that the system continues to work in these cases.

EVALUATION

To understand how the IP-QAT system would work with a community of users, and compare it to traditional software discussion boards, we performed a two week user study.

Participants

We recruited 48 professional AutoCAD users (ages 22-47: μ=36, 12 female) for the two week study. To qualify, the paid volunteers were required to use AutoCAD for at least 10 hours/week. An initial survey asked how often they typically looked at, and/or contributed to, online AutoCAD discussion forums (Figure 10) and to rate their AutoCAD expertise level. In general, most users looked at discussions somewhat regularly, but were far less likely to contribute.

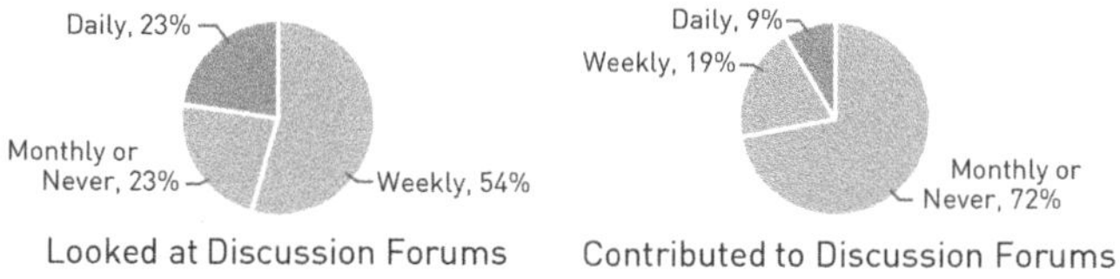

Figure 10. Distribution of user's pre-existing habits of looking at, and contributing to, online forums.

A number of participants dropped out part way though the study, or did not meet the minimum time requirements, leaving us with 37 valid participants.

Design

The participants were split into two groups with the most prolific forum users being evenly divided between the groups, and the rest of the users divided to equally distribute the level of AutoCAD expertise.

Community Help Systems

As an alternative to the IP-QAT help system described in this paper, the *forum* condition consisted of a private discussion forum accessible only to study participants. This private forum was hosted on the existing Autodesk Community site which draws over 200,000 visitors daily. The Autodesk forums typically require users to create an account, but we provided pre-activated accounts for the study to simplify the process. The presentation order of the community help systems were counterbalanced between the two user groups and after one week the groups switched to the alternate system.

Procedure

The participants installed an AutoCAD plug-in which contained both the IP-QAT help system, and the ability to launch a web-browser for directly accessing the private discussion forum of the *forum* condition. When AutoCAD launched, the assigned help system for that week would be automatically loaded (i.e., the IP-QAT panel would open, or a browser would open with the *forum* page loaded). Users were not required to keep the help system open, however, after 6 hours the active system would re-open as a gentle reminder that the study was going on. Participants were told that the automatic opening of both community help systems was a property of the study, and not the standard behavior of either system.

A collection of 140 questions and associated answers were collected from the existing public discussion forum and used to seed each of the communities with content. This allowed users to experience the viewing/consuming aspects of the systems immediately without needing to wait for their fellow participants to contribute topics. 70 topics were used for the first week (the same ones for each community help system), and the remaining 70 were used as the seed questions for the second week. Between conditions the content contributed from the previous group was removed.

Users were encouraged to use the provided community help systems during the course of the study, but were not prevented from looking for help from other sources. At a minimum, participants were asked to contribute three posts in each condition. To better simulate a larger and more active user community, bonus prizes ranging from \$100 to \$25 were awarded to the top five contributors in each condition for each group, on top of the \$50 base amount given to each user for participating. At the end of the study user's filled out a web-based questionnaire.

Results

Volume and Rate of Posting

Over the duration of the study the IP-QAT system generated 316 new posts compared to 252 in the *forum*. Repeated measure analysis of variance showed a main effect for posts per user ($F_{1,36} = 5.17, p < .05$) with means of 8.54 and 6.81 for *IP-QAT* and *forum* respectively (Figure 11). This amounts to a 25% increase in the volume of posts for the *IP-QAT* system over the *forum*. We can consider the first three posts to be "mandatory" since that was the minimum requirement to participate in the study and look at posts beyond that to be "voluntary". That breakdown results in means of 5.81 for *IP-QAT* and 3.94 for *forum,* for a 47% increase in the amount of voluntary posting activity ($F_{1,36} = 6.81, p < .05$).

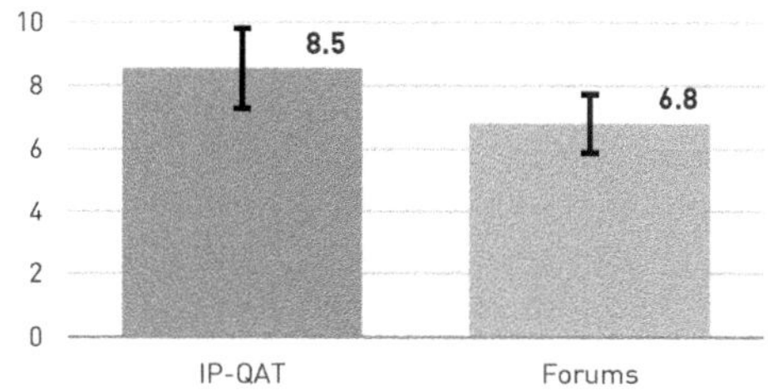

Figure 11. Mean number of posts contributed per user. (Note: error bars report standard error)

The IP-QAT system also led to the creation of more new topics overall (103 for *IP-QAT*, 82 for *forum*), however the effects per user did not reach significance ($F_{1,36} = 1.7$, ns).

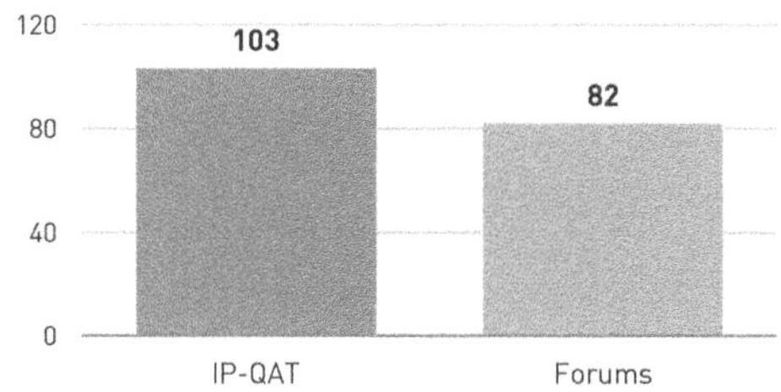

Figure 12. Number of new topics created.

The additional monetary motivation used for the study likely contributed to higher post volumes than a natural scenario. However, since the rewards were paid out for both conditions, we feel the overall trends would translate to a real deployment. Anecdotally, the monetary rewards did not seem to be the main driving factor for any of the participants; for example, there were no instances of users "gaming" the system by creating many posts of limited value. It was clear that the participants were using the system to ask detailed and technical questions that they genuinely had about AutoCAD, and were making an effort to provide accurate answers when responding. Questions that were asked and resolved during the study included topics such as: creating custom hatch patterns, scaling multiple MTEXT objects at once, and temporarily hiding objects to see what is being obscured.

We manually tagged newly created topics from the *forum* as questions or tips. Of the new 185 total new topics created over both conditions, 40 were tips, and 35 of those came during the *IP-QAT* condition. In the questionnaire, users were asked to rate a series of questions on a 5-point Likert scale, including if they found tips useful, to which 28 of the 37 users responded with agreement compared to only 2 who viewed tips negatively (Figure 13).

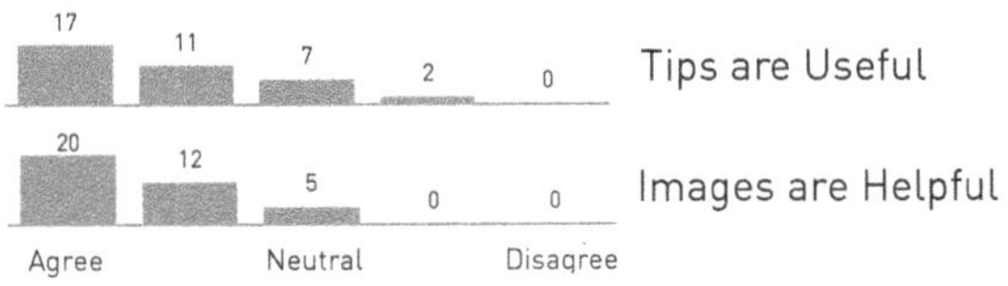

Figure 13. Subjective results for *"It is useful when people post tips, as opposed to only questions and answers."* and *"I find images helpful for explaining and answering questions."*

Another metric to look at is how long it takes for a question to receive an answer, which can be correlated with the size of the community [16]. On StackOverflow the 300,000 users are able to deliver a median time-to-first-answer (TTFA) of ~11 minutes [16]. In our study with 18 and 19 users in each group the median TTFAs were 61 minutes for *forum* and 38 minutes for *IP-QAT* (Figure 14). This result did not reach significance (Mann-Whitney, $p > .05$).

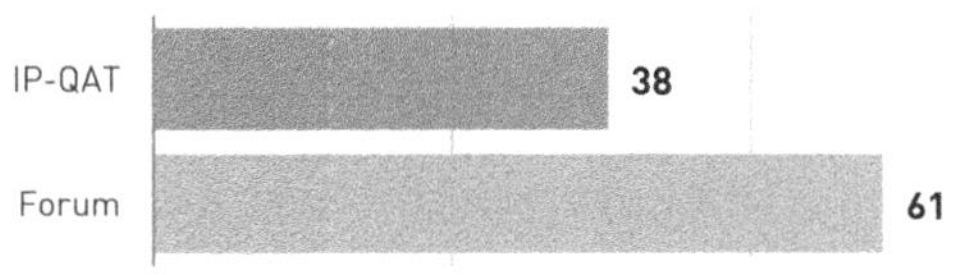

Figure 14. Median Time-to-First-Answer (Minutes).

Use of Images

Overall, 38 images were associated with posts in the *IP-QAT* condition compared to 9 in the *forum* (Figure 15). This amounts to 12.2% of *IP-QAT* posts, and 4.2% of *forum* posts containing images. In contrast the image attachment rate on the public Autodesk discussion boards is approximately 2%.

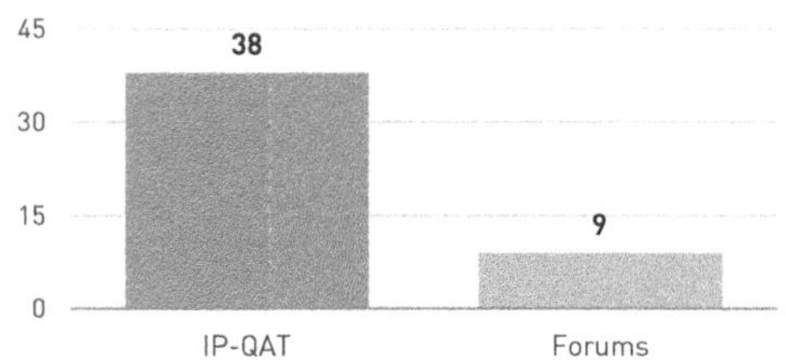

Figure 15. Total number of images used.

Users were also asked to rate the usefulness of images. As found in the product support domain [5], the majority of users consider images useful (Figure 13). Besides simply making images easier to include in a post, the IP-QAT system also simplifies the process of adding pen-type markups to the images. Of the 38 images from the IP-QAT system 8 contained overlaid markups, compared to only 1 from the *forum* condition.

Subjective Comparison

At the end of the exit survey participants were asked to score the statements *"I found this system easier to use"*, *"I found this system more useful"*, and *"I would prefer to use this system"* on a 5-point scale ranging from *IP-QAT* on one end to *Forum* on the other (Figure 16). Valuing the answers on a scale from 2 to -2, all questions reached significance on a one sample t-test: *Easier to Use* ($t(36) = 0.76$, $p < .005$), *More Useful* ($t(36) = 0.78$, $p < .0005$), *Would Prefer to Use* ($t(36) = 0.89$, $p < .0001$).

While the IP-QAT system was the dominant response for these questions, the forum was preferred by some users and several users suggested that it would be useful to have the content from each system available on the other. Likewise, we do not see these systems as alternatives to one another, but rather as systems that could work together to create a more complete community experience.

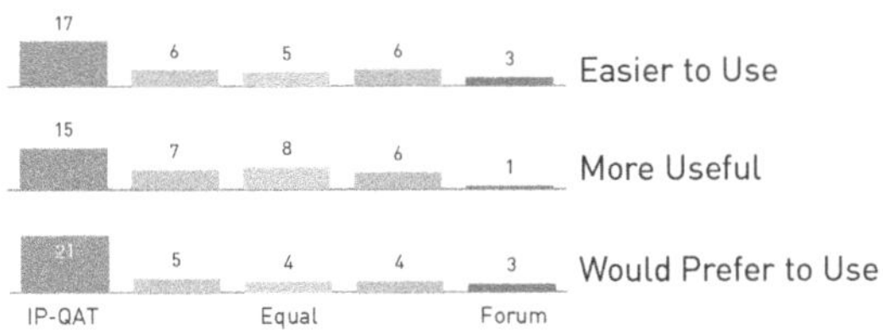

Figure 16. Subjective results comparing the *IP-QAT* and *forum* community help conditions.

Visualization of Activity

With so many topics and posts being created, it is difficult to get an overall feel for how individual threads are evolving. To get a sense of the activities occurring in the community, we created visualizations of each thread and grouped them by week and condition (Figure 17).

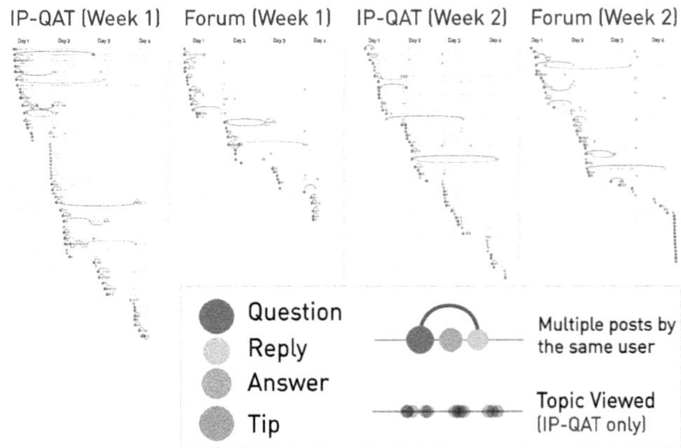

Figure 17. Visualization of all topics created during the study. (Note: this is a vector graphic, zoom in to see in more detail)

To generate the visualization, all posts entered during the study were manually classified into one of four categories:

Questions: Posts of a problem looking for an answer.
Answers: Attempts at answering a question.
Tips: Helpful statements not answering a question.
Replies: Responses not providing answer.

Posting activity was then organized by thread and displayed in chronological order as color coded dots from left to right on the timeline. When a single user made multiple posts in one thread, arcs were drawn connecting all of the user's posts. For example, in Figure 18A we can see that there were 7 total posts, but by looking at the arcs connecting the nodes, we see that the first user made posts #1, 3, 5, and 7, while a second user made posts #2, 4, and 6. This thread is an example of a common pattern where there is one question asker, and one answerer going back-and-forth trying to figure out the solution to the problem.

Another pattern we see and recognized by Singh [10] is where one user asks a question, and many others jump in with replies; more or less saying "me too". Figure 18B shows an example of this type of thread, with 10 total posts, and 7 unique authors.

Figure 18. Two example conversations. Between two users (A), and many unique users (B).

Besides posting information, the IP-QAT system is also implemented to know when users viewed the topic. These events are represented on the timeline as small grey dots, and in Figure 19 we see an example where the views had trailed off for a particular thread, and then once a new post was made, the views picked up again.

Figure 19. "Topic Viewed" dots showing a resurgence of interest in a thread after a new post is made.

It is interesting to note how the group who used the forums in the first week posted zero tips, while the group in the forums for the second week (who had used IP-QAT the first week) contributed 15 tips; once they became used to tips in the IP-QAT system they decided to try them in the *forums* condition even though the forums contained no explicit support for publishing tips. We are hopeful that going forward, as the community grows, visualizations like this may expose longer term trends.

User Feedback

Numerous positive comments were obtained in the questionnaire. In particular, several users commented favorably about the quick access IP-QAT provides:

I preferred the in product version much better than having to access a separate forum. It seemed much easier to access and in general just more convenient!

Users also mentioned the ease of attaching images:

I liked that it was always on, and I could take a peek at any time, but that it could be rolled up out of the way to save space. I liked that it was easy to attach a snapshot of the portion of the drawing.

In contrast, images were found to be difficult to attach in the *forum* condition:

I found that I needed another program to be able to add an image to my post, and that slowed me down versus the in product system which had the imaging software included.

Users also had a particular appreciation for the instant feel that the IP-QAT system provided:

It gave me a feel that the questions would be more immediately answered. It almost gave me the feel of a blackberry messenger app. or texting in general. I really think if this system is modeled after a platform like that it will be a success. Who doesn't text anymore? Overall, it kinds of creates an environment that allows users to more readily "text" a question. I think for the newer users or younger generation of users, this system will be quite attractive.

Another user provided a similar comment:

A nice idea of bringing experienced users together with those experiencing issues. Easy to throw a question out there at the moment you experience it, while in the program, and easy to check to see if there are any answers.

We were encouraged to see such enthusiastic comments from real-world end-users, giving us confidence that IP-QAT would be welcomed by user communities at large.

DISCUSSION AND FUTURE WORK

A main contribution of our work is a study demonstrating behavioral differences between using an in-product, and out of product community help system. Our study has shown some clear values of integrating the community help system within the application. The study also provided us with future topics of research.

Several of the study participants found it difficult when looking at a question with more than once answer to determine which one the asker found useful. Creating a way for both the author and others to mark which responses were helpful, as well as configurable ways to order the list of available posts, are among our future directions.

While we used the user's command history to determine context, it would be interesting to use other cues such as which GUI elements are active (e.g., ribbon tab, tool pallets, dialog boxes) or gathering semantic information from the active document. Additionally, many questions and tips centered around dialog box elements, so the ability to mark posts with such elements (in addition to commands) will be useful.

Fostering a community of active users is an important aspect of any community helps system, which we did not address in this paper. Established Q&A sites such as Stack Overflow have effective mechanisms for motivating users [16] such as badges, awards and leaderboards which would be useful to integrate into our system in the future.

We would like to deploy the IP-QAT system in the wild for a wider scale deployment, and to do this we will need to address privacy and confidentiality issues related to employees sharing company data. Some possibilities include automatically or manually blurring sensitive areas of screenshots, site controls for managers to block the uploading of files, or the ability to transform a confidential source file into a sharable one which exhibits the same problem as the original.

A wide-scale deployment may also require us to reconsider the system architecture. Besides being easy to setup and use, the Amazon S3 service was extremely cost effective; even with over 1.2 million PUT, GET, and LIST requests and more than 10 GB of data transferred over the course of the study, the web services cost came to only $3.78. As such, we see this is a scalable solution.

CONCLUSION

To conclude, we have investigated a community-based question-answer system within the context of a desktop software application. We discussed a number of relevant design principles, and presented our new system, IP-QAT. Particular attention was given to providing an image-rich experience, and reducing the transaction cost of posting and browsing content on the system. Furthermore, we contribute a robust and cheap architecture that allowed us to deploy the system to 37 users for a 2 week filed study. The evaluation identified a number of quantitative and qualitative benefits on our system, which we hope will serve as inspiration for future research.

ACKNOWLEDGMENTS

The authors thank Eric Wright for his assistance with the Autodesk discussion forums.

REFERENCES

1. Ackerman, M.S., and Malone, T.W. (1990). Answer Garden: a tool for growing organizational memory. *ACM SIGOIS and IEEE CS TC-OA,* 31-39.
2. Adamic L.A., Zhang, J., Bakshy, E., Ackerman, M.S. (2008). Knowledge sharing and yahoo answers: everyone knows something. *ACM WWW*, 665-674.
3. Bouguessa, M., Dumoulin, B., and Wang, S. (2008). Identifying authoritative actors in question-answering forums: the case of Yahoo! Answers. *SIGKDD,* 866-874.
4. Brandt, J., Dontcheva, M., Weskamp, M., Klemmer, S.R. (2010). Example-centric programming: integrating web search into the development environment. *ACM CHI,* 513-522.
5. Chilana, P., Grossman, T., and Fitzmaurice, G. (2011) Modern Software Product Support Processes and the Usage of Multimedia Formats. *ACM CHI*, 3093-3102.
6. Dearman D and Truong KN. (2010). Why users of yahoo!: answers do not answer questions. *CHI,* 329-332.
7. Fiore, A.T., Tiernan, S.L., Smith, M.A. (2002). Observed behavior and perceived value of authors in usenet newsgroups: bridging the gap. *CHI*, 323-330.
8. Gray, W. D. and Boehm-Davis, D. A. (2000). Milliseconds Matter: An Introduction to Microstrategies and to Their Use in Describing and Predicting Interactive Behavior. *Journal of Experimental Psychology: Applied*, 6 (4), 322-335.
9. Grossman, T., Fitzmaurice, G., and Attar, R. (2009). A survey of software learnability: metrics, methodologies and guidelines. *ACM CHI*, 649-658.
10. Grossman, T. and Fitzmaurice, G. (2010). ToolClips: an investigation of contextual video assistance for functionality understanding. *ACM CHI*, 1515-1524.
11. Harper, F.M., Moy, D., and Konstan, J.A. (2009). Facts or friends?: distinguishing informational and conversational questions in social Q&A sites. *CHI,* 759-768.
12. Harper, F.M., Raban, D., Rafaeli, S., and Konstan, J.A. (2008). Predictors of answer quality in online Q&A sites. *ACM CHI* , 865-874.
13. Hartmann, B., MacDougall, D., Brandt, J., Klemmer, S.R. (2010). What would other programmers do: suggesting solutions to error messages. *CHI,* 1019-1028.
14. Horowitz, D., and Kamvar, S.D. (2010). The anatomy of a large-scale social search engine. *WWW,* 431-440.
15. Li, W., Matejka, J., Gossman, T., Konstan, J.A., and Fitzmaurice, G. (2011 – in press). Design and Evaluation of a Command Recommendation System for Software Applications. *ACM TOCHI.*
16. Mamykina, L., Manoim, B., Mittal, M., Hripcsak, G., and Hartmann, B. (2011). Design Lessons from the Fastest Q&A Site in the West. *ACM CHI,* 2857-2866.
17. Matejka, J., Li, W., Grossman, T., and Fitzmaurice, G. (2009). CommunityCommands: command recommendations for software applications. *ACM UIST,* 193-202.
18. Matejka, J., Li, W., Grossman, T., and Fitzmaurice, G. (2011). Ambient Help. *ACM CHI,* 2751-2760.
19. Nam, K.K., Ackerman, M.S., and Adamic, L.A. (2009). Questions in, knowledge in?: a study of naver's question answering community. *ACM CHI,* 779-788.
20. Pal, A., and Konstan, J.A. (2010). Expert Identification in Community Question Answering: Exploring Question Selection Bias. *ACM CIKM,* 1505-1508.
21. Singh V and Twidale MB. (2008). The confusion of crowds: non-dyadic help interactions. *CSCW*, 699-702.
22. Singh V, Twidale MB, and Rathi D. (2006). Open Source Technical Support: A Look at Peer Help-Giving. *IEEE HICSS,* 6, 118c-118c.
23. Twidale, M. B. (2005). Over the Shoulder Learning: Supporting Brief Informal Learning. *CSCW,* 505-547.
24. Welser, H.T., Gleave, E., Barash, V., Smith, M., and Meckes, J. (2009). Whither the Experts? Social Affordances and the Cultivation of Experts in Community Q&A Systems. *IEEE ICCSIT*, 4, 450-455.
25. Yeh, T., Chang, T., and Miller, R.C. (2009). Sikuli: using GUI screenshots for search and automation. *UIST*, 183-192.

TwitApp: In-product Micro-Blogging for Design Sharing

Wei Li, Tovi Grossman, Justin Matejka, George Fitzmaurice
Autodesk Research
210 King St. E., Toronto, Ontario, Canada
{firstname.lastname@autodesk.com}

ABSTRACT
We describe TwitApp, an enhanced micro-blogging system integrated within AutoCAD for design sharing. TwitApp integrates rich content and still keeps the sharing transaction cost low. In TwitApp, tweets are organized by their project, and users can follow or unfollow each individual project. We introduce the concept of automatic tweet drafting and other novel features such as enhanced real-time search and integrated live video streaming. The TwitApp system leverages the existing Twitter micro-blogging system. We also contribute a study which provides insights on these concepts and associated designs, and demonstrates potential user excitement of such tools.

ACM Classification: H5.2 [Information interfaces and presentation]: User Interfaces. - Graphical user interfaces.

General terms: Design, Human Factors

Keywords: Micro-blogging, Design, Twitter, Sharing

INTRODUCTION

Social media and networking systems have been rapidly evolving over the last 10 years. The information streams of web 2.0 feeds provide a popular means for information awareness [6]. In particular, micro-blogging systems, such as Twitter, have become extremely popular for keeping community members aware of each other's activities. For example, Twitter has approximately 200 million users, who send 140 million tweets daily – about one billion a week[1,2].

Given its prevalence, there has been a recent surge of research in the HCI community studying numerous aspects and potential uses of micro-blogging sites, and in particular, Twitter, ranging from friend network analysis [14], workplace applications [28], to content visualizations [19]. However, one unexplored area which we see as having a rich potential, is the use of micro-blogging systems for sharing design activities within software applications.

[1]http://www.bbc.co.uk/news/technology-12805216
[2]http://en.wikipedia.org/wiki/Twitter

The emergence of the World Wide Web has indeed made sharing design activities and workflows quite popular. It is common to see discussion forums with specific threads for users to share their work, with step by step instructions of how they proceeded. Many designers also maintain personal blogs, where they can post information about their current projects on a day to day basis.

While technologies such as blogs and discussion forums are effective ways to share designs and software application activities, they have several limitations. First, these sites are typically external to the actual software application. As such, the content must be manually created which can be laborious. Second, because of the high authoring cost and low feedback ratio, blog users do not update their blogs as frequently as micro-blogging [20]. On discussion forums and tutorial sites, posts are typically only made once a project is completed, preventing the community of users from following along with the author's progress.

Micro-blogging provides a different sharing experience for designers. In one potential usage scenario, Adam, a young architect, shares his personal design portfolios to his followers using micro-blogging. His current design may get comments or critiques while he is still working on it. His colleagues discuss and collaborate with him at work. And he learns new skills by following senior architects' designs. Sometimes, he also receives notification of live software tutorials in real-time.

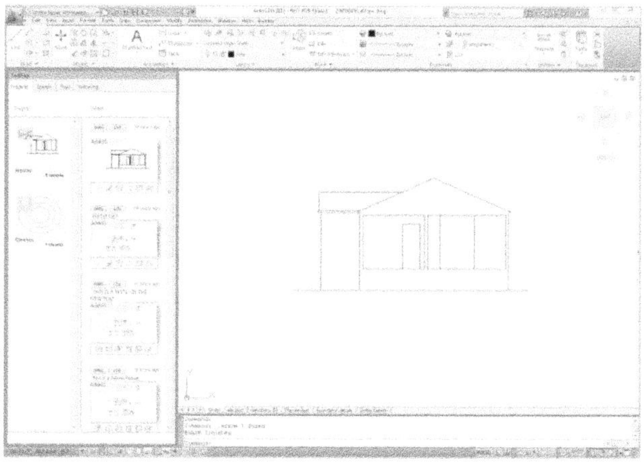

Figure 1. The TwitApp plug-in is displayed as a palette within AutoCAD.

In this paper we introduce TwitApp, an in-product micro-blogging system that allows users to both author and follow information about software design activities (Figure 1). We developed TwitApp within AutoCAD, a popular computer-aided design application used by over 10 million users worldwide. Using Twitter's existing back-end architecture

TwitApp allows an author to easily and frequently post messages about their current design work: authors can add useful metadata to their posts such as screenshots, application drawing files, and command logs; and draft posts can be automatically authored based on time or command triggers. TwitApp also provides a mechanism for users to search for and follow specific designers or projects of interest, communicate in real time with the content authors, and even view a live video stream of an author's work.

The benefits of TwitApp are two-fold. First, by placing the micro-blogging client within product, the transaction cost for authoring and sharing content becomes extremely low, and as mentioned, can even be done automatically. Second, by leveraging existing micro-blogging technologies, authors can relay information about their design work on a frequent basis, while followers can keep a close eye on a project of interest, with an opportunity to engage the author if specific workflows of interest are viewed.

After reviewing related work, we provide a thorough description of the TwitApp system and its implementation details. We then present an evaluation, where we invited users to try out the features of the system, to gather usage observations and user feedback. The results of the study showed that TwitApp possesses a number of features that excite potential users, and indicated the general approach of supporting in-product micro-blogging is a promising one. We conclude by discussing potential usage scenarios, limitations of our work, and possible future research topics.

RELATED RESEARCH

Micro-blogging

Micro-blogging is proving extremely useful for the fast exchanges of thoughts, ideas and information sharing [10]. It has been widely used in sharing information and exchanging thoughts [13, 16], tracking conferences and events [9, 24, 25], facilitating live broadcasting [26], training and learning [2, 10], and updating one's status to family and friends [20].

Some specialized social network sites are targeted towards specific user groups, such as professionals in medicine, finance and advertising industries [7, 27]. This indicates that micro-blogging can provide value to a wide spectrum of users and professional domains.

The research thus far on micro-blogging has been focused on four aspects: network analysis [13, 14], content [6, 21, 25], motivations [11, 28, 29], and beneficial applications. Very little research has been published on improving the existing designs of micro-blogging systems.

Design Sharing

The focus of this paper is on design sharing, which can span many different domains, including architecture, landscape and urban design, media and entertainment, digital photography, animation, and many more. Amongst all of these domains, there are some unique aspects of sharing. For example, most designers share very rich visual content with colleagues, customers, friends, or the public, and they use design applications to create their work.

Previous research in design sharing focuses on collaborative design, which supports design teams operating on a project in the same location [4], or in physically independent locations, simultaneously or asynchronously [15, 18]. Some research has been done for sharing informal ideas in the workplace [22, 29]. However, the idea of sharing design using micro-blogging has not been explored.

In-Product Micro-Blogging

Low sharing cost is one major reason why people like micro-blogging. The 140-character limitation on text messages helps reduce the cost of sharing [29]. However, current micro-blogging platforms are not ideal for designers to share their work with others. As an example, Twitter users need to go though several steps to locate and attach an image as a shortened URL link in a tweet. Furthermore, the brief text updates plus URLs are not optimized to provide a visual presentation that a designer may desire.

To minimize the switching cost, we propose an in-product micro-blogging system. The only related example we are aware of, is a command line based Twitter client within Eclipse [23]. While this client is provided in-product, it was not developed to support rich content sharing, and only supports short text messages.

With TwitApp we also explore the use of live video broadcasting to share design workflows in real-time. In order to share videos with Twitter users, a previous approach is to post the video description and a link to Twitter for all followers to see [3]. Our approach is similar, except it updates the author's live streaming status in real time.

In summary, previous research has been focused on the application and analysis of general micro-blogging systems. The problem of redesigning a micro-blogging system for a specific user group has not been explored. In our work, we introduce TwitApp, a new micro-blogging system that has been specifically developed to support in-product design sharing with low transaction cost, and places a particular emphasis on creating a rich visual experience.

DESIGN GOALS AND METHODOLOGY

Design Goals

Based on the requirement of design sharing, we indentified three design goals when developing our new system.

Sharing Rich Design Content. In addition to a short message, the system should support sharing rich design content.

Maintaining a Low Transaction Cost. We should minimize switching cost, so that designers can generate tweets using their design data automatically without interrupting their workflow.

Supporting Real-time Awareness. When a new tweet matches the follower's interest, the system should provide unobtrusive real-time notifications.

Design Methodology and Considerations

To achieve an appropriate design that achieved the above outlined goals, we explored multiple system designs. We explored both stand-alone and in-product clients, and both command-based and graphical interfaces. We also considered tweets containing pure text and tweets embedded with multimedia content. The text-based messages prevented us from easily embedding multimedia data, such as images and videos. Although we could put URLs in messages, it would require a browser to view the content.

We also explored different presentation layouts, from a simple tweet list to an automatically generated magazine layout for mobile devices. Our final design, which will be presented in the next section, evolved through a process of several iterations. For example, one of our original prototypes used a command line interface.

TWITAPP SYSTEM

TwitApp was implemented within AutoCAD, a 2D and 3D design and drafting software program used by over 10 million users. We choose AutoCAD for developing TwitApp because of the large user base, the large number of design domains supported, and the ease of extending the program with customized plug-ins via the ObjectArx programming API. However, we believe it is straightforward to generalize this concept and the prototype to design software in other domains.

Enhancements to Twitter

We chose Twitter because it is probably the most well-known micro-blogging platform currently available on the web. Although TwitApp leverages the existing Twitter platform and back-end API, the functionality of TwitApp goes beyond traditional Twitter clients in the following ways:

Rich Tweet Content: In addition to a short text message, TwitApp also integrates high resolution images, design data, user command history and video streaming within each tweet.

Project Organization: TwitApp extends the traditional way of displaying every tweet you received from friends in the temporal order as a timeline and introduces the concept of a *project*. In TwitApp, tweets are organized by both users *and* projects. Thus, each user can have multiple projects and each one can be individually followed or unfollowed.

Tweet Drafting: TwitApp also introduces the concept of automatically drafting tweets, triggered by user configured application events. This further helps reduce the sharing cost, allowing designers to create new tweets while maintaining focus on their work and workflow.

Enhanced Search: TwitApp also extends the notion of the "real time search" that is largely synonymous with searching tweets [5]. In TwitApp, the real time search is enhanced to not just search across the text messages within the tweet, but also the meta data attached with tweets, such as the users' command steam. This allows users to find relevant projects to follow.

System Overview

The TwitApp client manifests as a palette in the user interface of AutoCAD (Figure 1). The credentials for the Twitter account are saved in the AutoCAD system preferences for each designer. The user does not need to leave the working environment to send or receive messages, as the functionality is all presented within-product.

The functions of TwitApp are organized by four tabs in the palette: *Projects*, *Search*, *Post*, and *Following* (Figure 2). In the *Projects* tab, design projects which the user is following are displayed on the left side of the window and individual tweet messages for the selected project are shown in the right side of the panel. The *Search* tab allows users to find designers and projects to follow. The *Post* tab is used to send tweets, and the *Following* tab is used to select projects and users to follow or un-follow.

Viewing Followed Projects

Following a designer on TwitApp means that a user is subscribing to some or all of his/her Project Tweets as a *follower* and those tweets will appear in the user's stream of updates when he/she logs in. When the user initially follows the designer, he/she may select from a list of known projects to follow. When one unfollows someone, all of that designer's projects are automatically unfollowed.

One contribution of TwitApp is the ability to select a specific project to follow. We define *a project* as a sequence of tweets which provide updates on the same design file. This concept allows us to organize tweets into a set of projects.

Figure 2. The TwitApp palette is organized into four tabs: Projects, Search, Post, and Following.

Projects

The *Project* tab in TwitApp shows a list of all projects the user is currently following on the left (Figure 2). Users can scroll through the list and select a project to view its details. The projects are displayed as thumbnail images that are associated with that project (Figure 3 Left). A thumbnail image in the upper left corner represents the author of that project. Below the project image, we display the name of the project, as well as the number of new tweets and the total number of tweets. If the author is currently broadcasting their work, a "live" icon will be displayed. When a user hovers over a project thumbnail, a Reply button is made visible for the user to quickly send a tweet to the project.

Tweets

When a project is selected, each of its associated tweets are displayed in a scrollable list, sorted by time, on the right side of the panel. On the right side, Figure 3 illustrates how individual tweets are displayed in TwitApp.

The top portion of the tweet contains buttons to access attached data and a message showing when the tweet was sent (see Figure 3 B and C). If the current design file is attached to the tweet a *DWG* button is displayed. If a log of the user's commands is attached a *LOG* button is displayed. Clicking the *DWG* button loads that file into the user's application while clicking the *LOG* button displays a text file, showing a log of commands used since the previous tweet.

Below this, the tweet contains the content of the user's textual message. Next, a large thumbnail is displayed in the center of the tweet. Clicking on it opens a high resolution screen capture image of the drawing in the user's default image viewer. The user name is overlaid on the top-left of the thumbnail image.

A row of command icons, which represent commands used by the author, but which have not been used by the current user, are displayed under the thumbnail (Figure 3E). This serves as a potential learning aid.

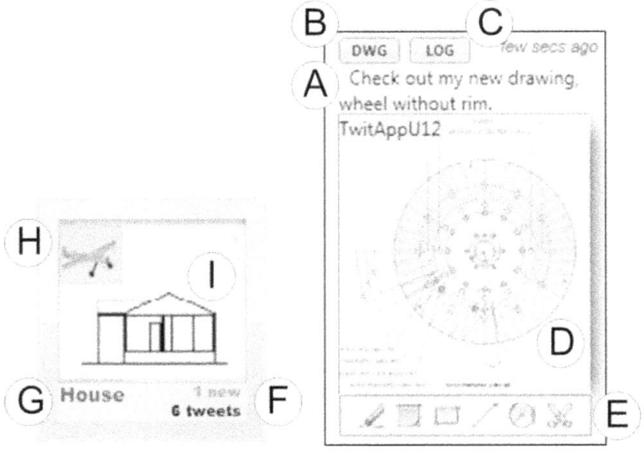

Figure 3. A project (left) and a rich content tweet in TwitApp A) Text message, B) Drawing data file, C) User command history, D) Thumbnail screen image, E) Command icons, F) New tweet and total tweet count, G) Project name, H) User screen image, and I) Screen image

Managing Followed Projects

Within the *Following* tab, users can see the collection of users (i.e. designers) they are currently following in a scroll list ordered from most-to-least recently added (Figure 4 A). Each designer has their personal thumbnail, name, and two control buttons. For each designer being followed, the user can click a check mark to temporarily un-follow that user. By clicking the *Follow Projects* button, a user can view all the projects created by that designer and add or remove projects to follow (Figure 4 B). Modifications to the projects being followed will update which projects are displayed in the *Projects* tab.

Searching

Users can find new users and projects to follow by using the *Search* tab. There are three options in the search window: *View All Latest Tweets*, *Keyword Search*, and *User Search*. Regardless of which search options are used, the search results are updated in near real-time. Whenever a new hit that satisfies the current search criteria is received, the search results are updated. The number of new hits since the search was performed is shown in brackets in the *Search* tab, for example, "Search (1)". See Figure 5.

Figure 4. A) Following Tab, B) Project dialog window for a given designer.

The default *View All Latest Tweets* option, shows all of the latest tweets produced by all TwitApp users (in the results list, sorted by time). This allows users to browse the TwitApp community for new projects or users. The *Keyword search* option allows users to specify a search phrase and presents matches to those tweets whose text message or command log contains the search phrase, ordered by date. This feature, in combination with the real time search, is useful for when a user is interested in a specific command. For example, if a user searches for the *HATCH* command in TwitApp, when a designer later uses the *HATCH* command and subsequently posts a tweet, the *Search* tab title will change and notify the user that there is a new tweet satisfying the search query.

The *User search* option returns user names that match a given search phrase. The result list shows matched user profile images and all the projects created by that user. From the search results, users can follow a user, or a specific project of that user. Thus a user can explore and find new tweets, projects, and users.

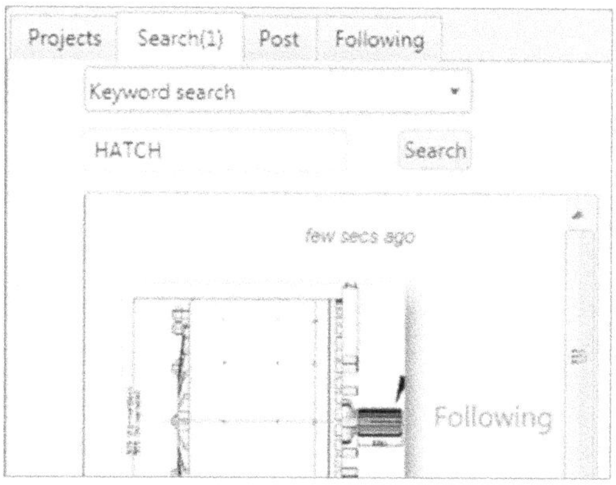

Figure 5.Real time search find a new tweet, which used command HATCH.

Tweet Authoring

Like regular Twitter clients, TwitApp users can create text messages and post new tweets. However, as a benefit from the in-product design, TwitApp also allows users to attach multiple data formats with their tweets. To create a new tweet, the user clicks on the *Post* tab and opens the Post New Tweet dialog (Figure 7) by clicking the *New* button shown in Figure 6.

The Post New Tweet dialog allows users to enter their message using a text field at the top of the dialog. A screen capture image is automatically displayed below. Clicking on the drop-down menu presents four options to alter the attached image. They can also specify if they wish to attach the current *DWG* file and command LOG file.

Users can also quickly author tweets by replying to existing projects in the *Project* tab. When the cursor hovers over a project, a reply button is displayed. Clicking that button will also display the Post New Tweet dialogue.

Figure 6. The Post Tab.

Tweet Drafts

A main contribution of our system is the ability to automatically create tweet drafts. This allows the system maintain a low transaction cost. Designers are able to maintain updates without explicitly breaking from their primary task. A tweet draft is a tweet which has editable attachments and has not been posted yet. Tweet drafts that are created are added to the "Automatically Generated Drafts" section of the *Post* tab (Figure 6). Hovering over a tweet draft, the user has the option to click on the *Delete* or *Preview* button. Clicking the *Delete* button will remove the draft from the collection. Clicking on the *Preview* button will bring up and populate the Post New Tweet dialog (Figure 7) with the project information, draft image and a timestamp message of when the draft was originally produced. The system also defaults to attaching a snapshot of the DWG file and command log reflecting the moment in time when the draft was originally captured. The user can adjust any of the information before posting the tweet.

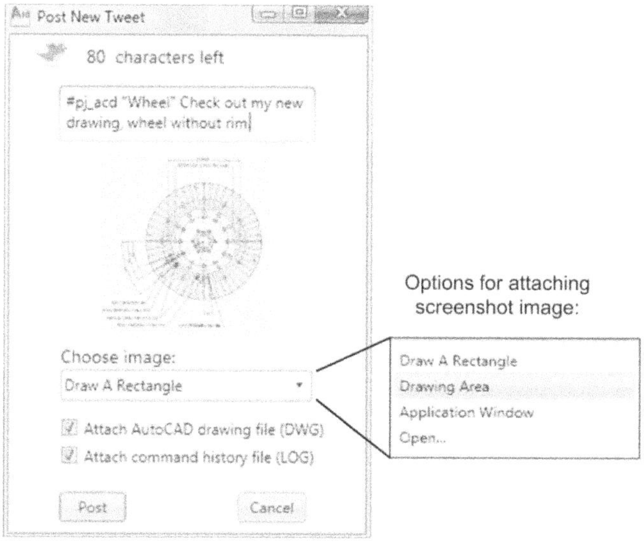

Figure 7. Post new tweet window

TwitApp provides two mechanisms for triggering the automatic creation of tweet drafts: time triggers and command triggers. These triggers are configured in a settings dialog (Figure 8).

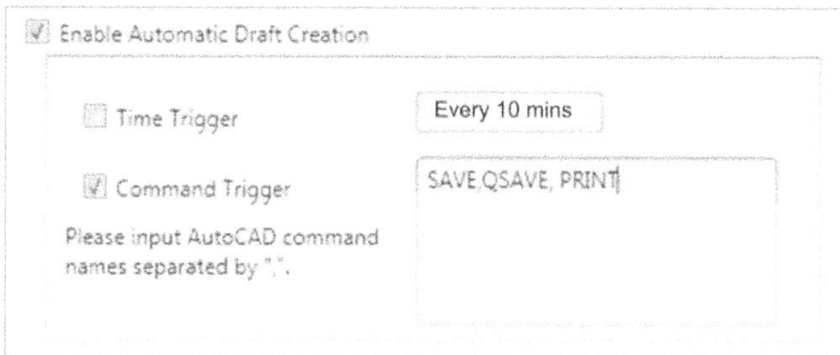

Figure 8.The setting dialog provides UI controls to setup the time trigger and the command triggers.

Time Triggers

The time trigger is used to create tweets in a periodic time interval. Users can select from 1 minute, 5 minutes, and up to an hour. Figure 9 shows three tweet drafts created by the time trigger with the time interval set to one minute.

Command Triggers

In the situation when the user does not need to change the current drawing or has simply left his desk, the time trigger will repeatedly create the exact same tweet drafts. To avoid a large number of duplicate during this idle time, and to allow for more flexibility, TwitApp provides a command trigger. This allows users to specify a set of AutoCAD commands to control the automatic creation of drafts. To specify a command trigger, the user types the command name in a text box within the settings dialog (Figure 8). Multiple commands can be separated by comas. Drafts will be triggered if *any* of the commands are used.

We noticed that several commands are good indicators of when the project has been significantly updated. For example, AutoCAD users often use the SAVE command after some meaningful design or drafting work has been done. However, some users may frequently save their projects, even nothing been changed. In this case, the combination of a time trigger and command trigger can be useful. In these configurations, drafts will only be created when both the time *and* command triggers have been satisfied.

Figure 9.Automatically generated tweet drafts.

Live Video Streaming and Following

While the micro-blogging that TwitApp provides give users the chance to follow snapshots of a designer's work in near real-time, they cannot see firsthand how authors carry out their work. To support true design workflow sharing, we implemented a live broadcast feature within TwitApp.

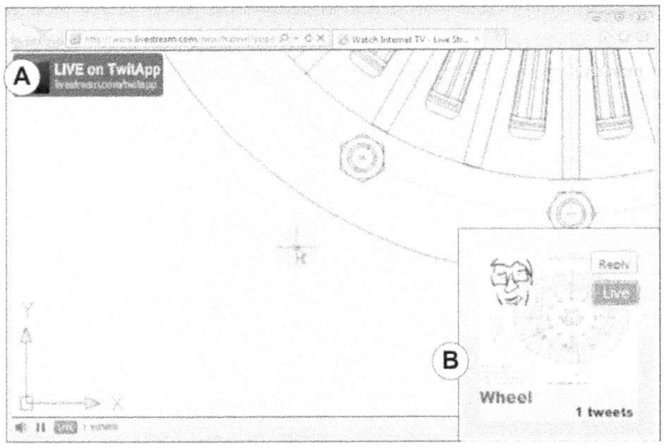

Figure 10.A) Live video player window lauched by TwitApp, B) A live broadcasting button (red) displayed over a project control.

As a proof of concept, we used the LiveStream[3] web service to enable video streaming (Figure 10 A). Additionally, TwitApp recognizes when the LiveStream service has started and displays a *Live* broadcasting button on the associated project in the *Project* tab (Figure 10 B). Followers of that project can click on it to open a live video window. While watching the live stream, the user can post comments and questions using the reply button.

IMPLEMENTATION

Our system consists of the TwitApp client and several backend services (Figure 11). The client communicates with the servers using web-based APIs.

TwitApp leverages the existing micro-blogging system and the user community. The content delivered with each tweet is stored and managed using multiple web services. Tweets sent from TwitApp are compatible with the existing system, and, as such, clients can view the message and images on the Twitter website or mobile devices. The cost of building and maintaining this system is extremely low. As such, this architecture serves as a good approach for experimenting with micro-blogging research systems and techniques.

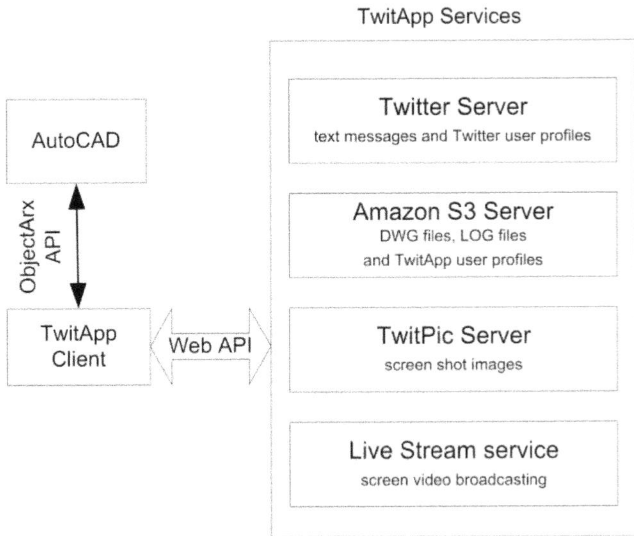

Figure 11. TwitApp architecture.

Project and Verification

Twitter hashtags are a simple way of grouping messages with a "#" sign followed by a name or a special code which will form a unique tag for a specific purpose. TwitApp uses the hashtag "#pj_acd" to label every tweet sent from a TwitApp client. This label is followed by the name of the specific project, such as "House". Once the TwitApp client receives a tweet with the "#pj_acd" in its text message, TwitApp starts to verify this tweet with data distributed in other websites. After confirmation that the tweet is in the valid TwitApp format, the data will be downloaded from multiple services and displayed in the client.

It may be desirable to allow users to check regular tweets in the design software. In our current design, TwitApp does not display tweets without the "#pj_acd" tag.

TwitApp Web Service

We implemented the TwitApp web services using: the web API provided by Twitter, the Amazon Simple Storage Service, TwitPic and LiveStream. The integrated data is decomposed for each tweet and distributed on the appropriate servers in the required format.

The Twitter web service provides user account and credential management, text message storage, and user profile

[3] http://www.livestream.com/

storage (including user's ID, screen name, following and follower lists). Once the user successfully logs into Twitter, a unique key is generated for each tweet. The Amazon S3 server was created to organize and store the TwitApp customized data, such as drawing files and command log files. Also, TwitApp maintains a list of TwitApp users who have communicated with this server. Finally, TwitPic and Live Stream are used to store and access images and videos.

TwitApp generates a unique key number for each tweet and uses this key to name files stored in S3, TwitPic and Live Stream servers. Using the key and TwitPic API, the client can easily map the user data with the user account stored on the Twitter server.

TwitApp Client

The TwitApp client integrates within AutoCAD as a plug-in. The user interface of the TwitApp client was developed with Visual Studio C#, Windows Presentation Foundation and ObjectArx (an API to access AutoCAD's functions). For users who want to broadcast live screen video, a video broadcast client is also installed.

Twitter Rate Limiting

To protect its service from overloading, Twitter only allows clients to make a limited number of calls in a given hour, in our case 350 per hour[4]. Although it is important to reduce the frequency of calls made, TwitApp clients must remain responsive and useful despite the rate limitation.

We implemented a Twitter request planning component which checks the current rate limit of a user account and determines when to send requests directly to Twitter, and when to send requests to a queue maintained by our client. If the queue is not empty and the rate limit has not been reached, a request will be made, and the results will be passed to other components of the client asynchronously.

A caching system was also implemented for lowering the operating cost of the system. Before downloading an image or a data file from a server, the client checks its cache first. This way, we improve the download speed and overall system performance. During our user study, the user's experience was not affected by the rate limiting.

EVALUATION

To evaluate the concepts and features of TwitApp, we conducted a qualitative user study. The main goal of the study was to generate initial observations and to assess which features would be most welcomed, and identify any features that may need to be revised or rethought.

Participants

We recruited eight external users, aged 26-40, from an online posting. Because we wanted to get observations from potential end users, participants had to be familiar with both AutoCAD and Twitter. Three participants use AutoCAD daily, three of them used AutoCAD at least once a month, and the rest used AutoCAD occasionally. All participants were familiar with Twitter, and five of them had active Twitter accounts. Participants were paired to bring a more personal feeling to the evaluation, and so users could experience the real-time sharing features.

Apparatus

The study was run on two Xeon 3.0Ghz Windows 7 workstations with a broadband internet connection. Participants were sitting in the same room but on opposite sides of a table so were not able to watch each other's screen.

Procedure

The whole evaluation lasted approximate 1 hour, and was divided into 4 parts. Participants were first given a 5 minute introduction to the system. This was followed with a 35 minute full walkthrough of the system. During this walkthrough, the participants were shown every feature of TwitApp, and asked to accomplish 49 "atomic" tasks, such as "find the project called 'wheel design'" and "create a command trigger using the HATCH command".

After the walkthrough, participants completed two tasks together. In the first task, one participant acted as the author, and was asked to modify an AutoCAD drawing of a house, and post tweets using the tools that they were introduced to. The other user "followed" the author, and viewed and replied to the tweets which were received. After 5 minutes, the participants switched roles.

In the second task, one user again acted as an author and worked on the design of a house. This time, the author enabled the live broadcast. The other user watched the broadcast and posted comments to the author using TwitApp. The participants switched roles after 5 minutes.

After completing all 4 parts, users filled out a questionnaire about the individual features in the system. For each feature the questionnaire asked them to rate, on a 7-point Likert scale, the statements "I found it easy to use" and "I think it would be useful", on a scale from 1 (poor) to 7 (excellent).

Results

The observations from the study were very encouraging. Users were impressed with the features of TwitApp, and were enthusiastic about the idea of sending out tweets from within the application.

The system seemed easy to use for all users. Users completed every "atomic task" independently after the brief introduction, and were able to complete the final 2 tasks in both the "author role" and "follower role".

The results from the questionnaire were generally positive. Average response for the overall system were 6.4 for *easy to use* (all scores out of 7) and 6 for *would be useful*.

The features users found most useful were:

- Ability to quickly send out tweet inside AutoCAD (6.8)
- Video broadcasting (6.6)
- Including screen shot images in a tweet (6.6)
- Organizing and viewing the tweets by projects (6.3)
- Send/Receive/View AutoCAD drawings in tweets (6.3)

[4] http://dev.twitter.com/pages/rate-limiting

The features users found easiest to use were:

- Real time search of commands and keywords (6.9)
- Including screen shot images in a tweet (6.9)
- Following and unfollowing projects (6.8)
- Browsing and following the latest tweets (6.8)

Only 3 features got less than 5 for *would be useful*:

- Attaching a command log in a tweet (4.1)
- Viewing the command log attached to a tweet (4.1)
- Viewing icons of commands used by others (4.3)

The exact same 3 features were the only features that got less than 5 for *easy to use.* Their scores are 4.5, 4.8 and 4.9. This data makes it clear that features related to logging and displaying command histories were not as well-accepted as the other features of the system.

Many positive comments were made by the participants in the questionnaire. Five of the participants provided comments indicating that they would recommend TwitApp as a learning tool. One user, who is an architect and uses AutoCAD every day, wrote "I think this is a terrific idea, especially for AutoCad training, [other] technical training or project sharing, also for video conferencing." Another user wrote "In a learning environment, TwitApp could be [a] useful tool to accelerate learning the software." These types of comments indicate that TwitApp could provide a new medium to support community-based learning.

Four of the participants indicated they would like to use the system for the purpose of sharing. An AutoCAD instructor commented "it is very easy to share my project in real time." A senior AutoCAD user wrote "it is excellent for teaching and sharing modifications of DWG", and another user commented "it is a really useful application for users to share their design".

Participants mentioned several potential limitations about TwitApp. Almost every user had concerns about the privacy and confidentiality. For example, a user commented that it could be useful in many situations, but sharing a drawing file with outside people is against his company policy. Another user wrote "this application should be used in professional social networks, not in general social networks." These comments are important to consider, and a commercial deployment would need to be careful about allowing users to send files and commands logs to the public.

Three users also wrote comments about using TwitApp inside the office environment. Another user, who works in an architecture firm, wrote "TwitApp could be an alternative tool for the (internal) email system, I can see it will reduce emails". He also commented "TwitApp is also a good tool for project managers for revising, coordinating, [and] integrating documents. I see this tool as a collaboration tool between members of the same team and even companies."

Overall, we are very encouraged by the observations from our study, as well as the feedback questionnaire results.

MOTIVATING SCENARIOS FOR TWITAPP

We see a number of potential scenarios of usage where micro-blogging could be a welcomed feature within design software applications. Some of these scenarios are directly related to comments received from our evaluation, while others are based on our own intuitions and experiences.

Design Sharing

Most notably, TwitApp reduces the transaction cost to support design sharing within user communities. Users who want to share their work, or show off their skills, either to the broad user community, or to specific followers, can use TwitApp to easily share their designs.

Micro-Critique

By supporting micro blogging, TwitApp also supports micro-critiquing. Designers who use TwitApp can receive close to real-time feedback on their designs. Again, this feedback can be received from the public user community, or from work colleagues or managers. Micro-critiquing will allow designers to consider feedback as they work, rather than waiting for feedback after a draft is completed.

Online Tutoring

TwitApp gives instructors a new medium to provide live, interactive, tutorials. For example, instead of posting a video tutorial to a website, instructors can advertise a tutorial session that they will be carrying out at a specific time, so members of the user community can follow the tutorial in real-time, with an opportunity to interact with the instructor.

Learning

TwitApp can also support learning, by allowing users to follow projects that demonstrate relevant workflows of interest. Users can look at any project of interest, and view its history of posts, to get a sense of the workflows that were used. If further information is needed, users could send messages to the originating author.

Workplace Co-operation

TwipApp can be used as a mechanism for members of a workplace to maintain an awareness of the status of each other's work. It allows users to receive notifications when projects are updated, or to look at a project of interest that a colleague is working on, to see its current status. This may also help colleagues share design ideas among one another.

Personal Journal

TwitApp can also be used for completely personal reasons, allowing a user to keep a journal of their own workflow activates. This may be useful for users to review or remember what they have done, or to simply have a record of it – with an indifference to community members viewing it. This type of behavior is common among bloggers, who wish to "document their life". TwitApp allows users to document their designs.

DISCUSSIONS

Application Dependence

Most features in TwitApp leverage contextual information in the application. For example, tweets are organized using the current design file, tweet drafts are generated based on application commands, and command streams are used to search for relevant tweets. Although TwitApp was developed for AutoCAD, our vision is that its main features could be integrated into any application used for design. From an implementation and architecture standpoint, there should be no real barriers in doing so in other applications.

Privacy

One of the main concerns expressed by our participants was the issue of privacy. Privacy is indeed a concern for social network sites in general [1, 7, 8]. Although Twitter offers basic privacy settings, which allow users to control who can read their updates, users still need to monitor their followers' list to block suspicious following. Of course, when messages involve confidential architecture drawing files, privacy is a much more serious concern.

A typical practice adopted by many social network sites is to design an access control policy. For example, to control who sees what content, users can limit the visibility of their sensitive data files to their immediate connections or they can choose to allow any followers to see their content. Because TwitApp was implemented to store and manage different types of data distributed over separate web servers, TwitApp's architecture can support numerous policies for access control. In this way, TwitApp could support users who want to use the system to exchange design data with their close colleagues, as well as support users reaching out to the entire community.

TwitApp in The Workplace

We can see many useful applications if TwitApp can be served as a coordination and communication tool inside design companies. Combined with version control applications, TwitApp could provide a very cost efficient cooperative solution.

For privacy issues at work, TwitApp could be setup behind the enterprise firewall. Previous research shows that privacy is less of a concern within the enterprise [7]. Because of this, we see no need for more extensive privacy controls for intranet environments compared with the internet environment. Furthermore, open sharing across the enterprise specifically could enable connecting with colleagues, showcasing one's designs, building up one's profile and personality, developing one's career and facilitate campaigning.

From Twitter to TwitApp

Our implementation, which uses the existing twitter framework, allowed us to quickly and inexpensively develop a new and robust micro blogging system. We believe this implementation, in itself, is a contribution and hope other researchers will be able to learn from our experiences. However, another reason we used the existing Twitter backend, is that it allows users to follow designers without running TwitApp, but instead from a traditional Twitter client. Tweets sent from TwitApp will have additional hash tags, but otherwise, view quite well on standard Twitter clients, and could also be viewed on mobile devices, potentially by a design manger during a commute (Figure 12).

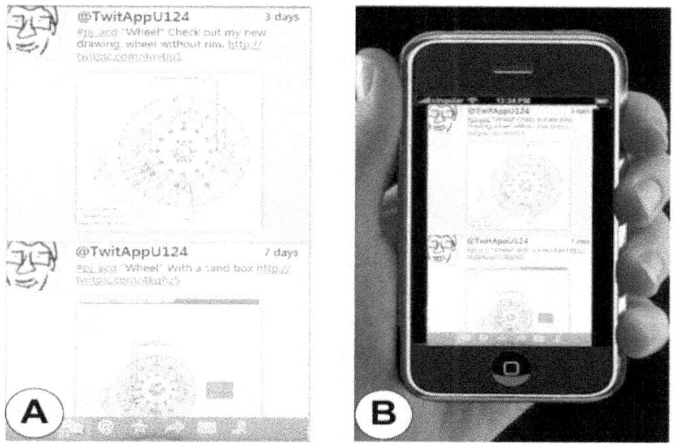

Figure 12. a) Layout of actual TwipApp tweets displayed by an existing Twitter client. b) Mockup of the same client within a mobile device.

Visualized Command History

Attaching and viewing command data was the least popular feature in our evaluation. A common concern was one of privacy. For instance, an employee may not want to update their managers with time stamped command streams. One option would be to investigate alternative ways to visualize command usage, or alternatively, this feature could be removed. However, even if command logs were not visible to users, they could still be used to index and search projects.

FUTURE WORK

We have implemented TwitApp and conducted a qualitative user study. We believe this research opens up new future topics of research, related to in-application micro-blogging, and using micro-blogging for sharing designs.

Our evaluation did show that TwitApp, and in-app micro-blogging in general, is a worthwhile concept to pursue. However this study did not formally validate our design. One area of future work we will be hoping to do is to carry out a more comprehensive field study to evaluate our current design and implementation in a larger deployment. This would allow us to analyze adoption and usage metrics in real scenarios, and potentially compare TwitApp with both discussion forums and personal blogs.

In addition to sharing design data, future work could explore real-time sharing of a designer's workflow. This would be similar to Li [17], who explored the idea of sharing users' browsing history using social networks. This could allow designers to repeat someone else's workflow.

In the mobile environment, micro-blogging is a mainstream communication approach. The integration of a rich content micro-blogging client and mobile data also creates many open questions for both HCI research and design.

In our user study, participants gave positive feedback to the automatic tweet drafting feature. We would like to advance upon our command and time triggers, and further consider more advanced methods for triggering automatic drafts. For example, Grabler [12] proposed to use the application state to help aggregate the user's input events into higher level event clusters. By exploring the application's contextual information, the modification history, and the user's action history, a more optimized and intelligent approach of automatically generating tweets could be possible. Furthermore, we believe it may be possible to define content-based triggers for users to register portions of the application data that they want to be notified by a tweet if it is changed.

CONCLUSION

In this paper, we introduced a system design and architecture of TwitApp, an enhanced Twitter system integrated within AutoCAD for design sharing. The system introduces numerous novel features that could be utilized by practitioners. We also contribute a study which provides insights on these concepts and associated designs, and demonstrates potential user-excitement of such tools. Initial user reaction is very positive and supports our belief in providing within-application, data rich, micro-blogging capabilities for flexible and enhanced design sharing.

REFERENCES

1. Acquisti, A. and R. Gross (2006). Imagined communities: awareness, information sharing, and privacy on the Facebook. *6th Workshop on Privacy Enhancing Technologies*. 36-58.
2. Borau, K., C. Ullrich, et al. (2009). Microblogging for language learning: using Twitter to train communicative and cultural competence. *8th International Conference on Advances in Web Based Learning*. 78-87.
3. Bornoe, N. and L. Barkhuus (2010). Video microblogging: your 12 seconds of fame. *ACM CHI-10*. 3325-3330.
4. Buxton, W., G. Fitzmaurice, et al. (2000). "Large displays in automotive design." *IEEE Computer Graphics and Applications,* 20(4): 68-75.
5. Chen, C., F. Li, et al. (2011). TI: An efficient indexing mechanism for real-time search on tweets. *SIGMOD'11*. 648-660.
6. Chen, J., R. Nairn, et al. (2010). Short and tweet: experiments on recommending content from information streams. *ACM CHI-10*. 1185-1194.
7. DiMicco, J., D. R. Millen, et al. (2008). Motivations for social networking at work. *ACM CSCW-08*. 711-720.
8. Dwyer, C. and S. R. Hiltz (2007). Trust and privacy concern within social networking sites : a comparison of Facebook and MySpace. *AMCIS 2007*.
9. Ebner, M., H. Mühlburger, et al. (2010). Getting cranular on Twitter : tweets from a conference and their limited usefulness for non-participants. *WCC 2010*, 102-113.
10. Ebner, M. and M. Schiefner (2008). Microblogging-more than fun. *IADIS Mobile Learning Conference 2008*. 155-159.
11. Ehrlich, K. and N. S. Shami (2010). Microblogging inside and outside the workplace. *ICWSM-10*.
12. Grabler, F., M. Agrawala, et al. (2009). Generating photo manipulation tutorials by demonstration. *ACM SIGGRAPH 2009*. 1-9.
13. Java, A., X. Song, et al. (2007). Why we twitter: understanding microblogging usage and communities. *9th WebKDD and 1st SNA-KDD 2007 workshop on Web mining and social network analysis*. 56-65.
14. Kivran-Swaine, F., P. Govindan, et al. (2011). The impact of network structure on breaking ties in online social networks: unfollowing on Twitter. *ACM CHI-11*. 1101-1104.
15. Kvan, T. (2000). "Collaborative design: what is it?" *Automation in Construction* 9: 409-415.
16. Kwak, H., C. Lee, et al. (2010). What is Twitter, a social network or a news media? *WWW-10*. 591-600.
17. Li, I., J. Nichols, et al. (2010). Here's what I did: Sharing and reusing web activity with ActionShot. *ACM CHI-10*. 723-732.
18. Li, W. D., W. F. Lu, et al. (2005). "Collaborative computer-aided design—research and development status." *Computer-Aided Design* 37(9): 931-940.
19. Marcus, A., M. S. Bernstein, et al. (2011). TwitInfo: aggregating and visualizing microblogs for event exploration. *ACM CHI-11*. 227-236.
20. McFedries, P. (2007) All a-Twitter. *IEEE Spectrum*
21. Naaman, M., J. Boase, et al. (2010). *Is it really* about me?: message content in social awareness streams. *ACM CSCW-10*. 189-192.
22. Pederson, E., K. McCall, et al. *(1993). T*ivoli: An electronic whiteboard for informal workgroup meetings. *ACM CHI-93*. 391-398.
23. Reinhardt, W. (2009). Communication is the key - support durable knowledge sharing in software engineering by microblogging. *Software Engineering Workshops 2009*
24. Reinhardt, W., M. Ebner, et al. (2009). How people are using Twitter during conferences. *5th EduMedia Conference*.
25. Shamma, D. A. and E. F. Churchill (2010). Tweetgeist: can the Twitter timeline reveal the structure of broadcast events? *ACM CSCW 2010*.
26. Shamma, D. A., L. Kennedy, et al. (2009). Tweet the debates: understanding community annotation of uncollected sources. 1st *SIGMM Workshop on Social Media*. 3-10.
27. VASCELLARO, J. E. (2007) Social networking goes professional *Wall Street Journal*
28. Zhang, J., Y. Qu, et al. (2010). A case study of micro-blogging in the enterprise: use, value, and related issues. *ACM CHI-10*. 123-132.
29. Zhao, D. and M. B. Rosson (2009). How and why people Twitter: the role that micro-blogging plays in informal communication at work. *ACM Group-09*. 243-252.

Searching for Software Learning Resources Using Application Context

Michael Ekstrand[1,2], *Wei Li*[1], *Tovi Grossman*[1], *Justin Matejka*[1], *and George Fitzmaurice*[1]

[1]Autodesk Research
210 King St. East
Toronto, Ontario, Canada, M5A 1J7
{firstname.lastname@autodesk.com}

[2]GroupLens Research
CS&E Dept., University of Minnesota
4-192 Keller Hall, 200 Union St.
Minneapolis, MN, USA 55455
ekstrand@cs.umn.edu

ABSTRACT

Users of complex software applications frequently need to consult documentation, tutorials, and support resources to learn how to use the software and further their understanding of its capabilities. Existing online help systems provide limited context awareness through "what's this?" and similar techniques. We examine the possibility of making more use of the user's current context in a particular application to provide useful help resources. We provide an analysis and taxonomy of various aspects of application context and how they may be used in retrieving software help artifacts with web browsers, present the design of a context-aware augmented web search system, and describe a prototype implementation and initial user study of this system. We conclude with a discussion of open issues and an agenda for further research.

Author Keywords

Help search, context-based search, software learning.

ACM Classification Keywords

H.5.2 [**Information Interfaces and Presentation**]: User Interfaces---training, help, and documentation; H.3.3 [**Information Storage and Retrieval**]: Information Search and Retrieval---search process

General Terms

Algorithms, Experimentation, Human Factors

INTRODUCTION

For about as long as there has been software, there have been help resources for using it. These have come in the form of reference manuals, vendor-provided training and consultancy, third-party books, integrated electronic documentation, in-program assistance (tooltips, agents, etc.), and more recently, Internet-based documentation from software vendors, professional third parties, and other users.

UIST '11, October 16-19, 2011, Santa Barbara, CA, USA.

Users typically access computerized help resources via text queries issued web search engines or the search facility of a program's help browser [12], or via in-program help interfaces and agents [10,22]. Search queries allow users to express nuanced questions about their needs, such as "How do I draw a circle in Illustrator?". Search engines, however, are largely unaware of the specifics of particular applications or of the user's context (the contents of their document, what dialogs they have open, etc.). Context-sensitive, in-program help, on the other hand, is generally restricted to answering descriptive questions about user interface elements.

We attempt to combine the strengths of these two approaches – the context-awareness of in-program help and the expressiveness of text searches – by using the user's context to improve results when they search for help artifacts on the Internet.

The user's interaction with the program contains a wealth of information related to their needs: what menu items they have tried, what types of objects they are trying to manipulate, what panels and dialogs they have seen, etc. It seems that it should be possible to use this information to retrieve help artifacts that are more closely targeted to the user's current situation, particularly when they may not know the correct terms to find the resources they need. We focus on help queries that are issued within they user's workflow – while they are using an application – as context is most readily available in that situation. It may be possible to extend the ideas we present to support search use cases, such as general queries for ideas or tutorial material.

In this paper, we first present a taxonomy for understanding context as it relates to user help needs. This framework serves as a basis for understanding how context can be harnessed to help locate help artifacts. We then describe the design of a help retrieval system that takes some elements of user context into account, a prototype implementation of this system, and a preliminary user study. We conclude with a discussion of open issues and directions for future work on this topic.

BACKGROUND AND RELATED WORK

Our present work sits at the intersection of two lines of research. We connect work on software documentation and learning with developments in context-aware search and user-oriented information retrieval.

Context-Sensitive Software Help and Documentation

The computer science community has long been interested in the nature and use of software documentation resources. As early as 1981, EMACS was using the term "self-documenting" to advertise itself [26]. O'Malley et al. wrote of the need to organize documentation around user needs, with varying types of documentation aimed at meeting different software learning or reference goals [25].

Context-sensitive help systems use contextual information from the user's current interaction with a particular application to drive or aid the access for help. Frequently this takes the form of a button or command the user can use to request documentation for the currently-open dialog or a particular widget on the screen; Lee's "?" [22] and the "What's This" help in Microsoft Windows both take this approach. Balloon help [10] and tooltips integrate short help descriptions into an application in the form of small panels shown when the user hovers the mouse pointer over an interface element. Recently, ToolClips has extended this to include short videos showing the particular tool in action [13].

Myers et al. extended the notion of contextual help to allow the user to ask more sophisticated questions about interface elements or application behaviors with Crystal [24]. Crystal allows users to ask "why did this happen?" and other types of why/why not questions while using a program.

The Lumière [18] and EUROHELP [28] projects built complex models of user goals, needs, and knowledge to provide customized instruction or assistance. Lumière integrated with Excel, attempting to infer the user's likely goals from their interactions with the software and provide goal-based, context-sensitive guidance.

Simple contextual help is limited by only allowing the user to contextually retrieve descriptive information about the user interface elements on their screen, while the full user modeling approaches of Lumière and EUROHELP require complex models that are difficult to design and apply. Our context retrieval lies in the gap between these extremes: we use more sophisticated observations of user behavior and application context to disambiguate and clarify user help requests, but do not attempt to build comprehensive user models or provide automated intervention. Beyond improving help searches, strengthening the connection between learning resources and the software environment may also improve software learnability [14].

Context and User Needs in Search

In its early days, web search operated under the traditional text information retrieval model: users would provide queries in the form of keyword lists, phrases, and Boolean expressions, and the system would respond with a list of relevant documents. Researchers have since sought to use context in web search [21]; IntelliZap [11] enabled users to form queries by selecting words in web pages, using the page content combined with a semantic network to augment those queries with additional context. Yahoo! implemented a web-scale system along similar lines, with Y!Q allowing the user to type free-text queries which would be augmented with contextual information from the page from which the query was initiated [19]. Watson [5] took a different approach, extracting text from a user's active word processor document to aid in refining web search for document-related research tasks. The work of Brandt et al. uses source code snippets to aid searches for example code [3].

Bringing contextual search closer to our domain, Wen et al. describe a model for incorporating information about a user's computing environment as context to refine searches related to PC troubleshooting [27]; our work is similar but more general, using information from the user's interaction to aid in help searches. Heckerman and Horvitz probabilistically related terms in user search queries to an engineered help database to match results to the user's information needs [16]. Our taxonomy can serve as a theoretical basis for further development of such systems and the system we present is both simpler and applies to non-engineered sources of help information.

Meeting a user's information need does not end with providing a list of relevant documents. The user must also be able to recognize which documents meet their particular need and make use of its content. The recommender systems field has seen significant work on providing users with explanations of their recommendations [17]; Coyle and Smyth argue that this should be done in search as well [7]. Chi et al. present "information scent" as a paradigm for understanding how users decide whether a particular link is likely to result in useful information [6]. Explanations can be viewed as deliberate scent markers leading the user to a particular resource.

We extend previous work to locate software help by augmenting search queries with contextual data from a user's software application. We also use this contextual data to provide additional information in the search interface so the user can more easily relate retrieved documents back to the application and their context.

UNDERSTANDING CONTEXT

In order to understand how we might use context to aid software help search, it is first necessary to examine what context is and how we understand it. Lieberman and Selker [23] provide a useful functional definition of context as "everything that affects a computation except the explicit input and output". To apply this understanding to the design of an information retrieval system, we can say that context is everything that a perfect information retrieval system would need to know about the user, their situation, the domain, and anything else in order to return exactly the results relevant to the user's stated query.

Dourish [8] further argues that context cannot be understood only as a static set of facts providing the background for an action such as a web search. Context and action have a cyclical relationship as context induces actions which give rise to further context; context is therefore dynamic and relational, changing and arising in relationship to actions. Anand and Mobasher [2] provide a useful approach to computationally managing this view of context: rather than trying to entirely model context, their approach looks for definable, observable *contextual cues* that can be incorporated into the context-sensitive retrieval process.

There are many factors which may help determine the intent of a help query and the relevance of particular artifacts to that query. In the remainder of this section, we describe a framework for understanding contextual factors and how they relate to each other and to the user's information need. This framework provides two major benefits. First, it gives us a way to reason about what information we may want to incorporate into the search process and what cues might yield that information. Second, it allows us to understand how particular cues relate to the broader picture of the user's context. Our framework describes contextual factors in terms of their visibility, type, and scope; Figure 1 provides a graphical summary of these dimensions (dimensions in bold are used by our prototype implementation).

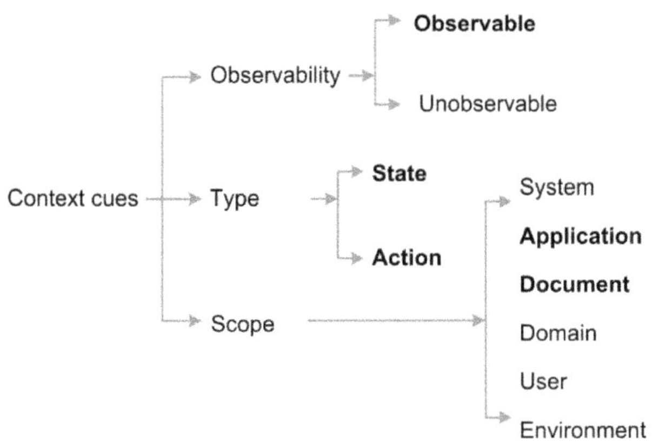

Figure 1: Context factors in help needs

Context Observability

Not all contextual factors are immediately visible to the system. Some things, such as the software settings and the user's recent actions, are directly observable by the application and help system. Others, such as the user's high-level goal (e.g. "draw a basement remodeling plan") or whether they prefer text or video tutorials are not directly observable, at least in any meaningful fashion, and must be inferred, approximated, or ignored.

While it is difficult to make direct use of unobservable contextual factors, recognizing and identifying them allows us to better understand how observable context relates to the user's entire information need, identify strengths and weaknesses in a particular context-aware system, and look for ways to infer or approximate the unobservable factors.

Context Factor Type

Many obvious contextual factors can be described as *state*, or a snapshot of a portion of the system at a particular time. The currently open windows, document, screen resolution, and available hardware are all elements of the current state.

If we only considered state, we would be left with the static background understanding of the context. We therefore approximate the cyclical relationship of context and action by allowing actions themselves to be considered context. This results in our second context type: *action*.

Actions can be performed by the user, the system, or some external agent. Drawing a square, deleting text, and plugging in a graphics tablet are all actions. Actions result in new states; states and actions can therefore be thought of as nodes and edges, respectively, in a graph representing the user's changing context.

We make this distinction to allow states and the means by which those states were reached to be treated separately. If the user's document contains a single square, the user could have created that state by drawing a square on an empty document or by deleting circle from a document containing two shapes. It is conceivable that some information needs depend only on the current state, while others are influenced by the actions which produced the state.

Context Scopes

Finally, we define a number of scopes for contextual factors. *System-level context* pertains to the user's computer system as a whole, independent of any particular application: the operating system and version, configured hardware, installed applications, etc. *Application-level context* is related to the particular application the user is using. This includes the current display state and application modes, open palettes and dialogs, the currently selected tool, etc.

The next two scopes, *document* and *domain*, are related to the work the user is currently doing. The work as it is represented in the application, the objects making up the user's data file and the actions taken on them, makes up the document-level context. Domain-level context relates to the meaning of the system and its components in the context of the user's work domain. If a document contains a circle and a rectangle, that is a document-level contextual factor; the fact that the user is drawing a conference room with a circular table is domain-level. There can be substantial overlap between document cues and domain-level factors or none at all; bitmap image editors typically have a low-level representation of the user's work, while tools such as CASE software and Autodesk's Revit suite store high-level domain information in the document data model.

The next scope is *user-level context*: user states and actions which affect their information needs. This can include their current knowledge of the program, their goals, and other factors. Some observable cues may help in assessing elements of this scope, such as using browsing behavior to identify what types of documents a user finds most helpful.

Finally, there is *environmental context*. A good deal of attention is devoted to this aspect of context in some areas of research, such as ubiquitous computing, but for application help it seems to be less important. There may, however, be elements of the environment that are relevant, such as a physical source object the user is trying to model, or whether there are others in the area who would be distracted by playing a tutorial video.

USING CONTEXT IN HELP SEARCH: SYSTEM DESIGN

We see three primary places in the search process where this additional data can be incorporated. The first is in the normal information retrieval process of generating results for a user's query. Information about the user's context can be considered as an additional component of the query. How exactly this is done may vary across applications and context elements: for applications, it may be appropriate to restrict the scope of the search engine to only return results for that application; for other elements, such as the document contents, it may be more appropriate to simply favor documents mentioning portions of the user's context in the ranking process.

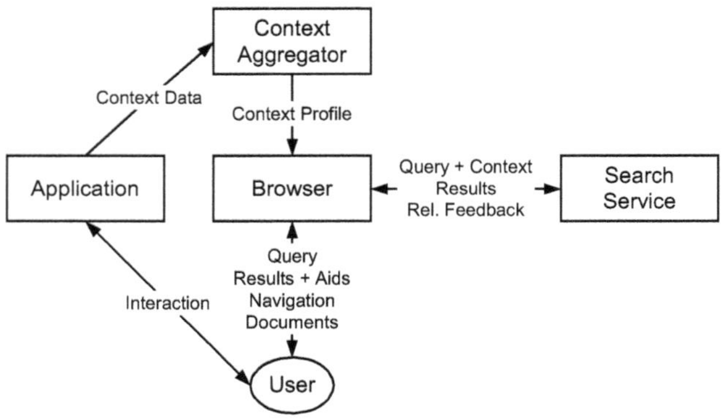

Figure 2: Architecture of contextual search system

The second point where contextual information can be introduced is in presenting the search results. Information scent theory [6] says that users look for markers or cues to indicate whether a particular link is likely to be useful or relevant. A search system aware of the user's context has the ability to provide deliberate cues in the search results to help the user determine which result is most likely to meet their needs.

Finally, the system can use context to provide navigational assistance when viewing the help artifact itself. Visual cues can be helpful to users when trying to find the location of on-screen elements [9]. It may be possible to help users more efficiently use help resources by showing how those resources relate to their context. Indicating what sections of a web page discuss particular tools or objects could help the user more quickly identify the content they are looking for. Calling out mentions of tools with explanations of how to activate them may help users more effectively apply what they learn from a particular resource.

Our proposed architecture, shown in Figure 2, contains several components to support these uses of context. Specific implementations may combine two or more of these components into a single subsystem.

Application Instrumentation

The application(s) for which contextual help search is to be supported must record information about the user's interaction so that it is available in the search process. This can be done internally by modifying the application and its underlying libraries to record this information or by using the operating system or widget toolkit's external inspection and instrumentation facilities. The application instrumentation reports user activities, such as button clicks or tool activations, as well as document-level events and actions to the context aggregator. It may also record other application- or document-level cues.

Context Aggregator

The context aggregator collects contextual information from applications and makes it available to the search service. It maintains a context profile to be used when the user searches for help, possibly aggregating from multiple applications and allowing multiple help browsers to all have access to context information. The context aggregator can also collect system and environmental cues.

Help Browser

The help browser takes context profiles from the aggregator, submits them to the search service along with the user's query, and uses them to augment the search results display and help the user browse help resources. When the user interacts with results, it can also send information back to the search service for relevance feedback and augment displayed resources with further contextual navigation aids. This component can be a dedicated help search and browsing application or an extension for a standard web browser.

Search Service

The search service takes queries and contextual information and provides search results. It can be a standard search engine, in which case the help browser would generate queries incorporating the context data and post-process the results, or a specific context- and application-aware service.

PROTOTYPE IMPLEMENTATION

We prototyped a context-aware search interface to search the Web for help related to the Inkscape vector drawing application[1]. We chose Inkscape because it is open source, allowing us to easily instrument it, and because its docu-

[1] http://www.inkscape.org

ment model contains somewhat structured data (high-level graphical shapes), allowing us to observe meaningful document-level cues.

We instrumented Inkscape to collect user actions and application state changes. Some instrumentation was done in GTK+[2], the widget toolkit used by Inkscape, to log actions such as windows opening and closing. Inkscape and GTK+ report the collected information to the context aggregator over a socket with a simple binary protocol.

We implemented the context aggregator and help browser as a single application using the Qt[3] toolkit. The browser injects custom JavaScript code into each web page after it loads to rewrite search results and augment page content with context-derived hints; context query results and information about pages' references to UI elements are cached to speed up subsequent searches. The browser also provides a navigational panel to allow the user to quickly jump to mentions of various Inkscape user interface elements.

We used Google as the search service, augmenting queries with contextual information and rewriting search results with JavaScript.

Collected Context

Many of the contextual factors discussed earlier are impossible to observe directly, and inferring them can be difficult. In our system, we will need to use context cues that can be observed. Because of little prior work in this area, it is unknown at present what cues are useful and practical to consider in a help system. Further, without an existing set of context, search, and relevance data, it is not possible to learn a model for result relevance to queries and cues. Therefore, from the large set of potential cues, we chose what we thought to be a reasonable selection of context cues at the application and document scopes for our prototype and experiment, preferring cues that can easily be converted into textual queries; the categories from which our cues are taken are indicated in bold in Figure 1. Each context profile contains:

- Last 5 active tools (application scope, state)
- Last 5 editing actions, such as "draw an ellipse", as reported by Inkscape's undo/redo framework (document scope, action)
- Titles of all open palettes, such as "Fill and Stroke" (application scope, state)
- Types of the currently selected drawing objects (document scope, state)

Search Augmentation

Kraft et al. [20] describe a variety of methods for integrating context into search. Since we built our implementation on top of an existing search system we do not control, we used *iterative filtering meta-search* to integrate context with the user's query. For each cue, our system creates a new query by concatenating a query relevant to that particular context element (such as "select tool" when the user has selected the Select tool). Each generated query also contains "inkscape"; this is prepended to the query if the user did not specify "inkscape" in their query. The injected JavaScript runs each of these queries in the background and merges results with the results returned for the user's initial query. 100 results are requested for each query. The final results are displayed in pages of 10.

The weighting and scoring method we describe represents our attempt to devise a mechanism that is reasonably well-principled. The methods employed and their parameters evolved iteratively but have not been empirically tuned.

Weighting Queries

Each query q_i is assigned a weight w_i. If the query entered by the user, denoted q_u, contains the word "inkscape", then its weight $w_u = 0.5$. Otherwise, $w_u = 0.2$ and a new query with weight 0.3 is generated by prefixing q_u with "inkscape". Thus the total weight for the user's initial query, adjusted to prefer results about Inkscape, is 0.5.

Table 1 describes the weights given to each context-generated query. Before blending with the user's query, these weights are normalized to sum to 0.5, resulting in a 50-50 blend of the user's query and contextually-generated queries when the final search results are determined.

Component	Weight
Event contexts	$\frac{1}{2^i}$ for the ith most recent context ($i = 1$ for the current context)
Editing actions	Same as event contexts
Open palettes	1
Selected object types	$\sum_{i=0}^{n-1} \frac{1}{2^i}$ where n is the number of objects of that type selected.

Table 1: Weights of context queries

Ranking Merged Results

In order to rank the merged result list, each resource c is assigned a score $s_i(c)$ for each query q_i. If c is not included in the first 100 results for q_i, then $s_i(c) = 0$; if c appears at position j, s_i is computed using the following formula:

$$s_i(c) = \frac{1}{2^{\frac{j-1}{\alpha-1}}}$$

This equation is derived from the half-life utility metric used by Breese et al. [4]. Using an exponential decay rather than simple rank as used by Kraft et al. works around a problem we observed in early testing where pages that matched multiple queries but only appeared deep in result lists would out-rank more relevant pages that scored very

[2] http://www.gtk.org
[3] http://qt.nokia.com

highly for one or two queries. We use $\alpha = 10$, the length of the default Google search results listing; this causes an article at position 10 to have a score of 0.5 and causes the scoring function to be nearly linear over the first page of results. Each article's cumulative score $s(c)$ is computed as the weighted sum $s(c) = \sum_i w_i s_i(c)$ of its per-list scores. The merged result list is then ranked in decreasing order of article score.

Search Result Presentation

To help the user assess the relevance of search results, our injected JavaScript also augments the search result display with information about the Inkscape tools, palettes, and menu commands mentioned in the page (see Figure 3). This display was designed to show this information in a manner which fits into the existing search results display, providing a context-aware augmentation of the document surrogate [15]. The displayed items are detected by searching the page text for the names of the interface elements along with some synonyms (such as "line tool" for the line and curve tool). Currently-open palettes are indicated in bold face and the current tool's icon is surrounded with a black box. Each item in each of these lists is also a hyperlink to the first mention of that item in the target page.

Figure 3: Search result presentation

In-Page Aids

To aid the user in making use of particular web pages, our browser displays a summary panel containing the Inkscape elements mentioned in that page as in the search results list. This is to help the user quickly jump to portions of the page that discuss tools or commands they are trying to use. All mentions of Inkscape elements are also highlighted in yellow, and hovering over a mention yields a pop-up item describing that command or palette and where to find it in the interface (see Figure 4).

If the user clicks an item in the summary panel, that item is selected: all of its mentions are highlighted green, and the browser jumps to the next mention. The "Jump to Next" and "Jump to Previous" buttons jump to the next and previous mention of a selected interface element. This allows the user to quickly navigate to portions of the page which talk about portions of the interface they have seen or think might be relevant to their task.

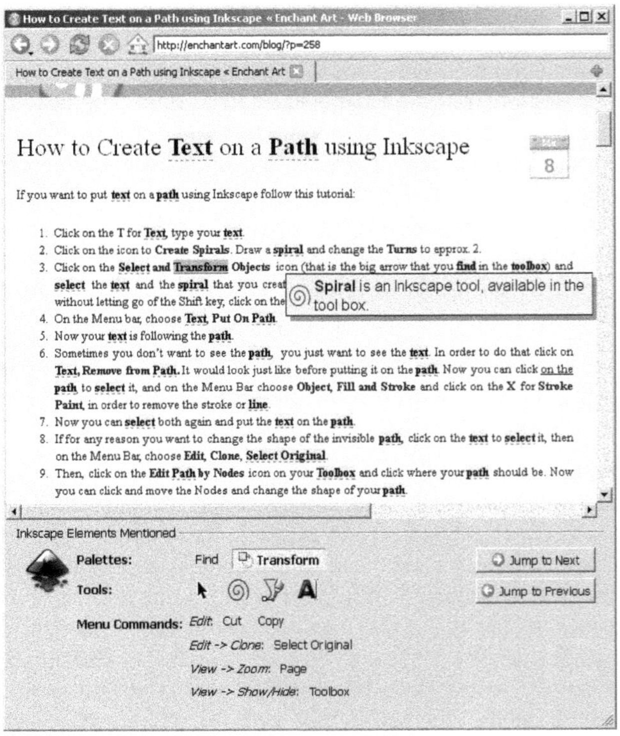

Figure 4: Summary panel and in-page aids; Transform has been clicked in the navigational controls.

USER STUDY

We conducted a user study to see how users interact with and respond to our enhancements. The purpose of this study is not to conclusively validate the benefits of contextual search; rather, it is intended to provide insights into the benefits and challenges inherent in both building and evaluating contextual software help interfaces, and gather user impressions and observations on both the general concept of context-aware search and our system prototype.

Experiment Setup

The study consisted of 4 image construction tasks. These tasks are intentionally arranged from a simple to line drawing using basic tools, to a complicated 3D effect where a sphere had to be drawn and shaded:

1. Draw shapes with the line/curve tool
2. Create text objects and effects
3. Manipulate shapes with Boolean operations
4. Draw and shade a 3D sphere

Users were instructed to work through each task, searching for help as they needed. They were also instructed to avoid hunting through the interface by trial-and-error but rather to search when they did not know how to do something. The task instructions and completion criteria did not focus on details, as our primary interest was in the search behavior and document relevance. The instructions were primarily graphical to minimize the impact of task instructions on query vocabulary; only the first task specifically named any tool, technique, or menu item.

Each user used either our *enhanced* search system or the standard *stock* Google search for the first 2 tasks and the other interface for the remaining tasks. The standard Google search was performed via our browser with the navigation panel disabled to keep the interface consistent and facilitate logging. To keep response times consistent across conditions, we delayed stock Google results by performing the context-dependent queries but only showing the unenhanced results; this was to prevent users from preferring stock Google searches solely because they were faster. Each user started with empty query and info caches.

Prior to tasks 1 and 3 the observer briefly explained the search interface that they would be using, with a search for "inkscape" as the example results page. For the unmodified condition, the observer explained that it was a standard Google search results page. For the modified case, they explained the search result presentation and demonstrated the summary panel with the Wikipedia article on Inkscape. They also explained the basic browser controls with the first interface used. The observer monitoring the experiment session took notes for further analysis. In particular, the observer recorded which search results they found helpful. Results were considered helpful if the user was able to move forward with the task after referring to it; if uncertain, the observer asked the user whether they found the result useful or if it answered their question.

Users were limited to 20 minutes for each task, at which point they were instructed to move on to the next task. During the experiment, only clarifying questions about the requirements of the tasks were answered – no hints on how to carry them out were provided.

For the study, we posted an ad on Craigslist to recruit users with some experience using graphics software such as Photoshop, Illustrator, or Paint.NET but little to no experience with Inkscape. Fifteen paid participants between the age of 21 and 47 participated in the study.

Experiment Results

Most users did not complete more than 1 or 2 of the tasks; no one completed all tasks correctly. Of the 60 task attempts, 19 were completed (with varying degrees of attention to detail and correctness), 35 timed out, and 6 were stopped early due to user frustration. Search interface had negligible impact on task completion rates.After removing searches occurring too late in the task to be of any use and searches which were immediately corrected by the user, users performed a total of 263 searches with an average of 4.38 searches per task. 98 of the 263 searches were successful, leading directly or indirectly to a page that helped the user with the task. shows the search counts by task and search mode; there are no significant effects of task or mode, although users who used the enhanced search first performed more searches ($p < 0.01$).

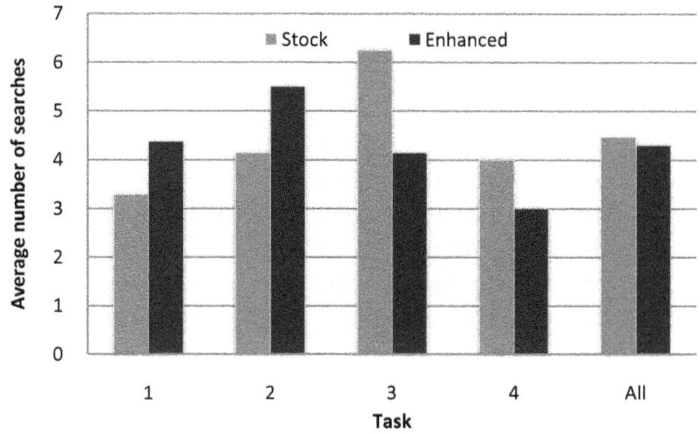

Figure 5: Searches per task by task and mode.

Search Results

To gain insights on the impact of the contextual search system, we looked at the utility achieved by the search results provided by each system. We computed achieved utility by having helpful pages accrue utility for the searches that led to them. Helpful pages (pages enabling the user to move forward) listed directly in the search results produced a utility score of 1; helpful pages linked indirectly by pages in the search results produced a score of 0.75. Only one search query generated multiple helpful pages (in this case, we only considered the higher-ranked of the two), and no search queries generated useful pages more than 1 link removed from the search results.

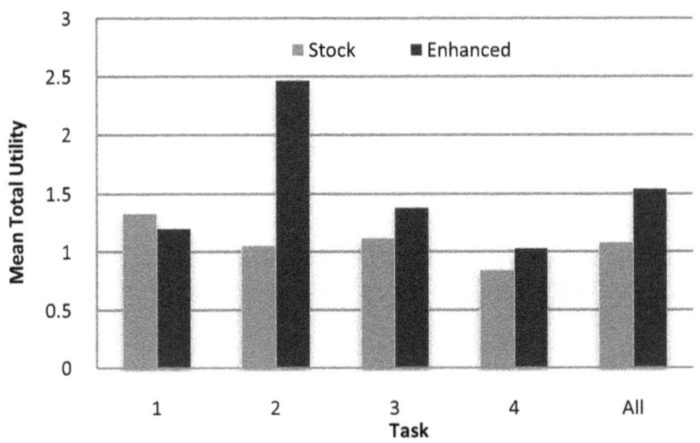

Figure 6: Average total utility per task.

The utility for each search results listing was then computed using the half-life utility metric with $\alpha = 5$ [4]; α was selected based on the empirical analysis of search behavior by Agichtein et al. [1]. If the user found the search results page itself helpful – something in a page summary or list of menu items met their information need – that was recorded as a utility of 1 and a rank of 0. Half-life utility is similar to the commonly-used *discounted cumulative gain* metric, with the added benefit of being based on a probabilistic model of user behavior.

shows average total utility for each task attempt (the utility of each user's searches during a task is summed, and the sums are averaged over all users for a particular task and interface). Two-way ANOVA shows a marginally significant main effect of search mode on total utility ($p = 0.074$) and no effect of task or task-mode interaction.

Users achieved grater utility with the enhanced search than the stock search in all tasks but the first. One potential reason for this is the nature of the tasks: task 1 was the easiest and exercised a single tool in various ways, while the other tasks were more workflow-oriented where users had to combine several tools or operations to achieve the desired effect. Most searches in task 1 were for things such as "inkscape line tool"; it seems that such queries may already be sufficiently specified that additional context information only introduces noise into the search process. If we exclude task 1 from our analysis, the effect of search mode on total utility becomes significant ($p = 0.031$). This is an early, but encouraging, result.

We also found that the impact of different context sources in providing results varied across tasks – in task 3, edit actions were the most powerful source of useful links, while users found links located by open palettes or active tools more useful in other tasks. This suggests that the utility of various types of contextual cues varies by context – not all information needs will be met equally well by the same classes of contextual information.

User Behavior

Users exhibited some noteworthy behavior while browsing. The first is their use of information on the search results page itself. Sometimes users did not even need to click a link to have their question answered – the text snippet Google extracted from some page contained the information they needed (such as a keyboard shortcut). Two users commented explicitly on this in discussion after the study, saying they appreciated immediate information related to their query. Additionally, help documents sometimes provided keywords that the user used in a subsequent search.

Users also frequently scanned a page quickly to find things that looked relevant, particularly images of effects or screenshots that they could recognize as related to the task. We had intended the highlighting and summary panel navigation to help with this, but users did not make substantial use of the summary panel's navigational capabilities and rarely consulted the pop-ups on UI element references. This was quite possibly due to lack of familiarity. The highlighted references also did not seem to help users skim the page. Our browser highlighted all detected references; a more selective approach may make this feature more useful.

User Receptiveness

Users were divided on whether they found the enhanced results useful. Of the 14 users who told us their preference, 9 preferred the enhanced search to some degree. User response to the augmentation of the search results display was mixed; some users thought it was too distracting, while others found it helpful. One user commented that "the pictorial element helps a lot, just for visually honing in on something". Users were similarly mixed in their response to the summary panel; some found it useful for providing an overview, while others found it goes in the way.

Difficulties and Limitations

We encountered a number of difficulties in conducting this study. Users had difficulty adjusting to Inkscape's user interface and mode errors were common. The nature and quality of available documentation also caused problems. Inkscape tutorials and guides vary greatly in format as well as both technical and presentational quality. Further, much of the documentation is in the form of tutorials and other blog posts that seem good for showing users what kinds of things they can do and satisfying needs in a browse-for-options surfing mode, but are less suited to answering questions about the interface or particular drawing tasks. Many resources, including some of the best tutorials and manuals, were also broad in scope; since our system is currently limited to only retrieving entire documents, it had difficulty locating focused material on specific tools.

There were two areas in which terminology mismatches caused experimental issues. The first occurred in the first task, where we instructed the users to use the "line tool" to draw some simple shapes. The official name for this tool within Inkscape is the "pen tool", but documentation is inconsistent in referring to it and often calls it either the "line" or "curve" tool. With further refinement, context or at least application awareness could make it much easier to resolve these searches. The other mismatch was that many sites call Inkscape's node editor the "node tool", while our UI element detection code only looked for "node editor". Two users noticed that the tool was not detected when it should have been. The effect of these problems on our results is unknown.

LESSONS LEARNED

Our study yielded several promising observations and certain beneficial trends seemed to emerge. In light of previous work showing local context to be useful in search tasks [9], our experiences provide insight into some of the outstanding difficulties in using context to locate help resources. First, the relationship between context and page content must be carefully designed. When context is used to generate additional query terms, as it is in our implementation, the queries need to be appropriate and well-constructed. A combination of expert knowledge of the application and empirical testing should produce query expansions that produce useful results; the difficulties we had with the line tool demonstrate the consequences of errors in this process.

Contextual data is not all positive signal – spurious contextual information also introduces noise. Further, the utility of various contextual factors is not necessarily constant – it may vary based on query or difficult-to-observe factors such as user task. When the contextual data raises the rank of less-useful results, it can cause user confusion; in one of our experiment sessions, the user adjusted their queries (adding quotation marks, additional keywords, and other query refinement techniques) because they did not think the contextually-retrieved results were relevant and were looking for a query that excluded them in favor of more relevant resources. It would be useful to understand not only what factors were improving results, but what factors were introducing noise. More detailed future studies will hopefully shed more light on which types and scopes of context are most effective for providing useful results. Showing the context-generated queries and allowing users to adjust them may also be beneficial.

The utility of contextual search also depends on the existence of diverse, high-quality content. Without diverse content, it becomes less relevant to include context in the query, since results are already limited. Without quality content, the results will not be useful to the user, even if they accurately match the user's current context of use.

We limited our prototype and experiment to simple document- and application-level contextual cues in the current prototype, but have limited data on their efficacy. It may be that we need more sophistication either in the cues we collect or the way we use them (e.g. using more inferred factors, perhaps at the domain scope, or building better ways of incorporating the contextual data into search) in order to see significant impact. More detailed studies will hopefully shed light on how to improve or reenvision incorporating contextual data into the search process.

We have found that information retrieval does not end with presenting a list if results. The benefit users derived from information contained within the search results page itself is noteworthy: if users can have their need met without having to select and browse to a page, it seems that they will be able to continue with their work more quickly. One user specifically suggested overview or disambiguation pages – for example, including a survey of what ellipses are and some of the basic operations that can be performed on them when the user searches for "ellipse". Search engines currently incorporate some of this; besides the snippets extracted from pages, Google answers common queries such as arithmetic, ticker symbols, or currency conversions with immediate answers, and also provides its "I'm Feeling Lucky" to immediately take the user to the first result. The search engine Duck Duck Go[4] takes this a step further, providing "Zero-Click Info" from Wikipedia, Stack Overflow, and other informational sites in a box at the top of the search results page. This seems like a promising direction both for software help search and for general web searches.

[4] http://duckduckgo.com

CONCLUSION AND FUTURE DIRECTIONS

There is a good deal of work left to be done to make context-aware help search a practical reality. We have identified a number of types of contextual information, but have only used a few of them in the present work. How best to incorporate other types of information remains to be explored; in doing so, greater consideration needs to be given to how help and search systems can select and use appropriate contextual data. The relevant algorithms may well need to be adaptive, adjusting what context is used or how it is incorporated into the search process based on context and the user's search queries. The feature selection and search augmentation methods also need to be tuned, and indexing document passages as well as whole documents may help future systems identify more focused material.

Context could also be incorporated in places beyond the search process itself. More nuanced relationships between context and help artifacts could feasibly be defined as artifacts are created; if a tutorial contains a machine-readable description of the menu commands used, for example, then that could be matched against the user's context to find examples for recently-reverted user commands with high accuracy. Q&A services could similarly capture the context of the question-asker, allowing other users to later find that question when encountering similar problems.

Contextual search further has the potential to help address the information retrieval issues of polysemy and synonymy. Including search terms from the user's context can help guide the search engine to the user's intent. More sophisticated approaches may be able to explicitly use context to resolve identified ambiguities in query or document terms.

It appears particularly promising to use context in a manner more similar to collaborative filtering or relevance feedback: if the system stores contextual "fingerprints" of users that found each resource to be useful, those could be used to help later users find resources which helped others in similar contexts.

User context provides a wealth of information that can be used to improve the ability for search services to meet users' information needs. There are many opportunities in applying context to software help, particularly as the types and sources of that help diversify. We have presented a framework for understanding context with respect to help needs and the contextual cues which may be mined to improve the help retrieval process. We have also prototyped such a help system, studied users' interaction with it, and laid several outstanding challenges in making help systems more sensitive to the nuances of users' particular needs.

REFERENCES

1. Agichtein, E., Brill, E., Dumais, S., and Ragno, R. Learning user interaction models for predicting web search result preferences. In *Proc. SIGIR '06*, ACM (2006), 3-10.
2. Anand, S.S. and Mobasher, B. Contextual Recommendation. In B. Berendt, A. Hotho, D. Mladenic and G. Semeraro, eds., *From Web to Social Web: Discovering and Deploying User and Content Profiles*. Springer Berlin Heidelberg, Berlin, Heidelberg, 2007, 142-160.
3. Brandt, J., Dontcheva, M., Weskamp, M., and Klemmer, S.R. Example-centric programming: integrating web search into the development environment. In *Proc. CHI '10*, ACM (2010), 513-522.
4. Breese, J.S., Heckerman, D., and Kadie, C. Empirical Analysis of Predictive Algorithms for Collaborative Filtering. In *Proc. UAI '98*, (1998), 43-52.
5. Budzik, J. and Hammond, K.J. User interactions with everyday applications as context for just-in-time information access. In *Proc. IUI '00*, ACM (2000), 44-51.
6. Chi, E.H., Pirolli, P., Chen, K., and Pitkow, J. Using information scent to model user information needs and actions and the Web. In *Proc. CHI '01*, ACM (2001), 490-497.
7. Coyle, M. and Smyth, B. Supporting intelligent Web search. *ACM Trans. Internet Technol. 7*, 4 (2007), 20.
8. Dourish, P. What we talk about when we talk about context. *Personal Ubiquitous Comput. 8*, 1 (2004), 19-30.
9. Ehret, B.D. Learning where to look: location learning in graphical user interfaces. In *Proc. CHI '02*, ACM (2002), 211-218.
10. Farkas, D.K. The role of balloon help. *SIGDOC Asterisk J. Comput. Doc. 17*, 2 (1993), 3-19.
11. Finkelstein, L., Gabrilovich, E., Matias, Y., et al. Placing search in context: the concept revisited. *ACM Trans. Inf. Syst. 20*, 1 (2002), 116-131.
12. Goodall, S.D. Online help: a part of documentation. In *Proc. SIGDOC '92*, ACM (1992), 169-174.
13. Grossman, T. and Fitzmaurice, G. ToolClips: an investigation of contextual video assistance for functionality understanding. In *Proc. CHI '10*, ACM (2010), 1515-1524.
14. Grossman, T., Fitzmaurice, G., and Attar, R. A survey of software learnability: metrics, methodologies and guidelines. In *Proc. CHI '09*, ACM (2009), 649-658.
15. Hearst, M.A. Presentation of Search Results. In *Search User Interfaces*. Cambridge University Press, 2009.
16. Heckerman, D. and Horvitz, E. Inferring Informational Goals from Free-Text Queries: A Bayesian Approach. In *Proc. UAI '98*, Morgan Kaufmann (1998), 230--237.
17. Herlocker, J.L., Konstan, J.A., and Riedl, J. Explaining collaborative filtering recommendations. In *Proc. CSCW '00*, ACM (2000), 241-250.
18. Horvitz, E., Breese, J., Heckerman, D., Hovel, D., and Rommelse, K. The Lumière project: Bayesian user modeling for inferring the goals and needs of software users. In *Proc. UAI '98*, Morgan Kaufmann (1998), 256--265.
19. Kraft, R., Maghoul, F., and Chang, C.C. Y!Q: contextual search at the point of inspiration. In *Proc. CIKM '05*, ACM (2005), 816-823.
20. Kraft, R., Chang, C.C., Maghoul, F., and Kumar, R. Searching with context. In *Proc. WWW '06*, ACM (2006), 477-486.
21. Lawrence, S. Context in web search. *Bulletin of the Tech. Comm. on Data Eng.*, (2000).
22. Lee, W. "?": a context-sensitive help system based on hypertext. In *Proc. ACM/IEEE DAC 1987*, ACM (1987), 429-435.
23. Lieberman, H. and Selker, T. Out of context: computer systems that adapt to, and learn from, context. *IBM Syst. J. 39*, 3-4 (2000), 617-632.
24. Myers, B.A., Weitzman, D.A., Ko, A.J., and Chau, D.H. Answering why and why not questions in user interfaces. In *Proc. CHI '06*, ACM (2006), 397-406.
25. O'Malley, C., Smolensky, P., Bannon, L., et al. A proposal for user centered system documentation. In *Proc. CHI '83*, ACM (1983), 282-285.
26. Stallman, R.M. EMACS the extensible, customizable self-documenting display editor. In *Proc. Text Manip. '81*, ACM (1981), 147-156.
27. Wen, J., Lao, N., and Ma, W. Probabilistic model for contextual retrieval. In *Proc. SIGIR '04*, ACM (2004), 57-63.
28. Winkels, R. User modelling in help systems. In *Proc. CAL '90*, Springer (1990), 184-193.

Keynote Talk

Breaking Barriers with Sound

Ge Wang
ge@ccrma.stanford.edu

Abstract
The computer, in its many shapes and sizes, is evolving rapidly and pervading our everyday lives like never before. Mobile computing devices have become much more than simply "mobile", increasingly serving as personal and "natural" extensions of us. Therein lies immense potential to reshape the way we think and interact, and especially in how we engage one another creatively, expressively, and socially. This talk explores interaction and social design for music through the computer, told through laptop orchestras, mobile phone orchestras, an audio programming language, designing the iPhone's Ocarina, ecosystems for crowd-sourcing musical creation, and an emerging social dimension where computer, music, and people interact.

Author Keywords: computer, music, mobile, social, interaction design, ocarina, laptop orchestra

ACM Classification Keywords: J.5 Arts and Humantities: Music.

General Terms: Design, Human Factors, Experimentation, Languages

Bio
Ge Wang is an Assistant Professor at Stanford University in the Center for Computer Research in Music and Acoustics (CCRMA), and researches interactive software systems and programming languages for computer music, mobile and social music, musical interaction design, sound synthesis and visualization, new performance ensembles, and education at the intersection of computer science and music. Ge is the author of the ChucK audio programming language, the founding director of the Stanford Laptop Orchestra (SLOrk) and of the Stanford Mobile Phone Orchestra (MoPhO). Concurrently, Ge is the Co-founder, CTO, and Chief Creative Officer of Smule, and the designer of the iPhone's *Ocarina*, *Leaf Trombone: World Stage*, and the iPad's *Magic Piano* and *Magic Fiddle*.

UIST'11, October 16–19, 2011, Santa Barbara, California, USA.
ACM 978-1-4503-1014-7/11/10.

Query-Feature Graphs: Bridging User Vocabulary and System Functionality

Adam Fourney
afourney@cs.uwaterloo.ca

Richard Mann
mannr@uwaterloo.ca

Michael Terry
mterry@cs.uwaterloo.ca

Cheriton School of Computer Science
University of Waterloo

ABSTRACT

This paper introduces query-feature graphs, or QF-graphs. QF-graphs encode associations between high-level descriptions of user goals (articulated as natural language search queries) and the specific features of an interactive system relevant to achieving those goals. For example, a QF-graph for the GIMP graphics manipulation software links the query "GIMP black and white" to the commands "desaturate" and "grayscale." We demonstrate how QF-graphs can be constructed using search query logs, search engine results, web page content, and localization data from interactive systems. An analysis of QF-graphs shows that the associations produced by our approach exhibit levels of accuracy that make them eminently usable in a range of real-world applications. Finally, we present three hypothetical user interface mechanisms that illustrate the potential of QF-graphs: search-driven interaction, dynamic tooltips, and app-to-app analogy search.

ACM Classification: H5.2 [Information interfaces and presentation]: User Interfaces. - Graphical user interfaces.

General terms: Design, Human Factors

Keywords: Query-feature Graph, Search-driven Interaction, Dynamic Tooltips, Analogy Search

INTRODUCTION

When faced with a new task to accomplish, users of interactive systems must often navigate a *gulf of execution* [17]: They have a goal, they are able to succinctly express their goal, but they are unsure of how to accomplish the goal using the interactive system.

One of the hurdles in overcoming this knowledge gap is a difference in terminology. More specifically, the way users conceptualize and articulate their needs does not always match the (rather terse) vocabulary of the interactive system. In the research described in this paper, we are interested in creating a bridge between the user's vocabulary and the vocabulary

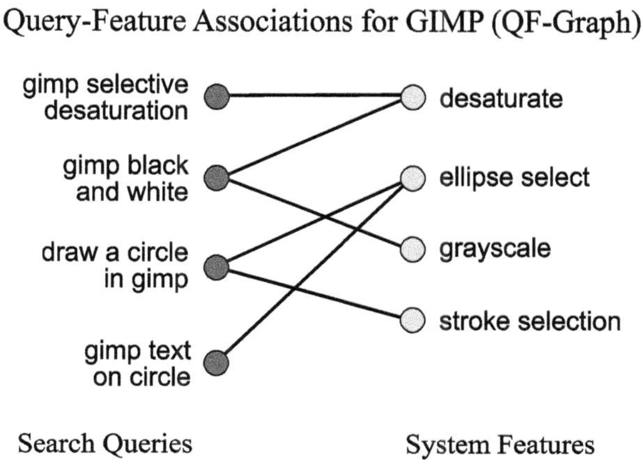

Figure 1: The query-feature graph pairs tasks, as naturally expressed in user search queries, with relevant system features.

of the system. Additionally, we wish to be able to automatically construct and update this bridge as a system's user base grows and as people's use of the system evolves.

Currently, users often bridge gulfs of execution by turning to Internet search engines. In the ideal case, a search engine returns links to web pages that describe how to achieve the desired goal. As an example, consider the search "GIMP black and white," a commonly executed query used to learn how to simulate the effect of black and white film using the GIMP raster graphics editor [8]. Since GIMP has no command named "black and white," users who wish to achieve this effect must learn that commands such as "desaturate," "grayscale," or "channel mixer" will yield the desired effect. Indeed, searching for the phrase "GIMP black and white" returns web pages describing the use of these very commands.

There are several notable aspects of this existing, manual process. First, the user articulates their goal in their own words, typically by expressing the desired outcome, rather than by using the low-level language of the interface and its commands. Second, the search engine (ideally) directs users to relevant web pages. Third, the web pages most likely to assist the user in achieving their goal combine natural language descriptions of the task with the *specific names* of the commands, tools, and preferences necessary to accomplish the task. In essence, the web pages serve as "Rosetta Stones" between users' conceptualizations of tasks and the actual tools necessary to accomplish those tasks.

Inspired by this manual process, this paper presents a system that automatically uncovers these relationships between users' vocabularies and the relevant system components. These pairings are represented in what we call a *query-feature* graph (Figure 1), or *QF-graph* (where "feature" in this context refers to elements in an interactive system).

The QF-graph is a weighted bipartite graph with nodes representing queries on one side, and nodes representing system terminology on the other. Edges express an association between a query and an interface component. The strength of these associations are encoded as edge weights. While a QF-graph can conceivably be assembled in a variety of ways, this paper describes how to construct QF-graphs using search query logs, search engine results, web page content, and localization data from interactive systems. As we will later argue, this mode of construction confers with it a number of advantages.

Once formed, a QF-graph can provide the foundation for a range of novel interaction techniques. In this paper, we illustrate its potential by outlining three possible interaction techniques:

- a search-driven interface in which users type the task they wish to accomplish, and the interface assembles a list of the most relevant commands for the task
- dynamic and ever-evolving tooltips that display tasks which reflect how the user community uses a given command
- app-to-app analogy search, which provides a mapping between the tools necessary to perform a task in one interface and the equivalent tools in a second interface

Collectively, the QF-graph, its mode of construction, our validation of the technique using real-world data, and the example uses of the QF-graph constitute the primary contributions of this paper.

In the remainder of this paper, we first contextualize this research with respect to prior work, then describe the query-feature graph and its automated construction in more detail. We then present results from our analysis of the technique in order to validate the quality of the query-feature associations expressed in the QF-graph. We describe three novel interaction techniques enabled by a QF-graph and conclude with a discussion of the approach's limitations and directions for future research.

RELATED WORK

The overall vision guiding this work is to create a system that can connect users' articulations of their goals with the actual system functionality necessary to achieve these goals. In this section, we describe existing mechanisms and past research that aim to help users make these connections, then discuss previous work that informed our approach of using search queries and their related web pages to construct the QF-graph.

Software commonly includes built-in help that can be searched. However, current offerings represent static collections of documents developed by the software creators. As a result, application-provided help may not always match the vocabulary of the users, nor evolve to mirror how the software is actually used in practice. Recognizing this deficiency, many software applications now augment built-in help with the capability to execute the help query on web-based knowledge bases. For example, Microsoft Word for Windows allows users to perform a help search on Microsoft's web servers if none of the local results meet their needs. While these facilities offer a useful dynamic extension to traditional static built-in help, searches are typically limited to the software producer's web properties and still require the user to manually link results with the actual functionality in the application.

This process of manually linking web-based information to the task at hand was observed by Brandt et al. in a study of software developers [5]. For example, it was noticed that developers often incorporate example code found on the web into their own code projects. These findings led the researchers to develop Blueprint, a system that more deeply integrates search-based practices into an IDE. Using Blueprint, programmers can search for, navigate, and import code examples from the web by simply typing a few keywords in the source code editor and pressing a hotkey. This mode of interaction resembles the familiar auto-completion features of modern IDEs, but greatly extends their capabilities to include knowledge culled from the web. Our work developing QF-graphs shares similar motivations to this prior research, though our focus is on explicitly linking user vocabularies with system vocabularies.

In recent years, search-like interfaces for finding and issuing commands in a user interface have grown in popularity. For example, in all modern operating systems, users are able to enter a few keywords into a search field to launch applications and load documents. Mac OS X takes this idea further, and offers a search field in the system-wide help menu that provides users with a means of searching and executing commands found in the top few levels of any application's menuing system. Similarly, programs like Quicksilver [4], Enso [11], and Ubiquity [15] allow keyword search to be used to both issue commands and specify command parameters.

This "search line" style of interaction has also been explored in the research community. Notably, Inky provides "command line functionality for the web," allowing users to send emails, book flights, and reserve conference rooms, all by entering a few keywords in a text field [14]. Inky provides some tolerance of user input by recognizing a limited set of synonyms, correcting spelling, and offering "sloppy syntax." In our own work, we are similarly motivated to allow users to express their intentions without needing to know complex syntax or specialized terminology.

The GEKA project by Jeff Hendy et al. [10], achieves search-driven interaction in the form of "graphically enhanced keyboard accelerators." These enhanced keyboard accelerators make heavy use of query auto-completion to quickly search through menus, toolbars and dialogs for commands. Users can also specify command parameters within their input.

While Inky, GEKA, and kin optimize the execution of commands, they cater to users who already know what commands they would like to issue. For users unfamiliar with a task or interface, these tools will be less useful. Our work building the QF-graph is intended to help this latter class of users by providing a bridge between high-level descriptions of tasks and the actual system features necessary to complete those tasks.

From this user-centric view of QF-graphs, we turn now to work related to the construction of a QF-graph.

The query-feature graph is similar in spirit to the query-document bipartite graph discussed by Beeferman and Berger in [2]. The graph described by Beeferman associates search queries with web documents, and is constructed by recording "click-through" patterns: As people perform web searches and visit resultant pages, their transactions serve to associate queries with documents. A similar query-document graph was described by Baeza-Yates and Tiberi in [1]. In contrast, we build a bipartite graph between queries and system functionality using question-answering techniques. Specifically, we use the question answering passage retrieval algorithm (QAP) described in [6] to form query-feature associations (again, where "features" in this context refer to the commands, tools, preferences, and other elements of an interactive system). Since click-through data is not made available to the public, our approach is arguably more accessible and actionable in generating QF-graphs.

In sum, given a high-level objective to accomplish with an interactive system, a number of mechanisms exist to assist users in translating that goal to actual system functionality. However, at present, users must manually find and establish these connections between tasks and system features. In the section that follows, we describe how we automatically establish these associations via query-feature graphs.

THE QUERY-FEATURE GRAPH

The query-feature graph directly associates user search queries with relevant system features (commands, menu items, dialogs, preferences, etc.) via an undirected weighted bipartite graph. Formally, the query-feature graph, $G = (\{Q, F\}, E)$, is composed of the following components:

- **Graph Vertices:**

  $Q = \{q_i \,; 1 \leq i \leq N\}$

  Where Q is a set of distinct search queries pertaining to the use of a given interactive system.

  $F = \{f_j \,; 1 \leq j \leq M\}$

  Where F is a set of features, commands, menu items or other interface components present in the system.

- **Graph Edges:**

  $E = \{(q_i, f_j, w_{ij}) \,; q_i \in Q, f_j \in F, w_{ij} \in \mathbb{R}\}$

  Where E is a set of 3-tuples, each representing a weighted edge from a query vertex to a feature vertex. Each weight, w_{ij}, expresses the strength of the association.

System	Description of Feature Vertex Set F
Kindle	**210 commands** discovered through manual exploration of the interface.
GIMP	**830 commands** enumerated by the ingimp [21] project.
Inkscape	**1785 strings** extracted from Inkscape's primary en-US string table.
Firefox	**583 strings** extracted from Firefox's primary en-US string table.
Chrome (Chromium)	**3088 strings** extracted from Chrome's primary en-US string table.

Table 1: The five interactive systems for which we generated QF-graphs, along with a description of the data source used to popular each graph's feature vertex set.

We create a QF-graph by first enumerating the relevant search queries and system features that populate the vertex sets Q and F, respectively. We then establish associations between queries and features using techniques from question-answering research. We describe each of these steps in detail below.

Enumerating relevant search queries (Populating Q)

Assembling a meaningful set of queries, Q, is the first challenge in creating a QF-graph. While any string of characters is a valid search query, it is desirable that Q contain queries that best reflect common tasks and user vocabularies. An obvious way to populate this set, then, is to sample the search query logs of web search providers, looking for queries mentioning the interactive system. However, search query logs are not made publicly available.

To approximate search query logs, we build upon our previous research by employing the *CUTS* procedure described in [8]. CUTS leverages query auto-completion services (e.g., "Google Suggest") to sample popular queries from the logs of top-tier search engines. For publicly available software applications, this technique has been demonstrated to reveal tens or hundreds of thousands of queries for a given system.

Enumerating system features (Populating F)

To enumerate the features, F, of a system, we extract all strings contained within the system's internal string tables. String tables are used for language localization, and contain the text of all commands, error messages, and other user interface elements used by the application. As such, there are typically hundreds or thousands of strings in a string table.

Table 1 lists the five interactive systems we use as examples throughout the rest of this paper. With the exception of the Amazon Kindle, the listed applications are open source, and the string tables are distributed along with each project's source code. In order to obtain a list of features for the Amazon Kindle, we systematically crawled the Kindle interface and manually transcribed the UI components encountered.

Associating Queries with Features (Populating E)

Associating queries with features is the final step in constructing a QF-graph. In this section, we present the specific challenges inherent in this final step, then describe our use of the question-answering approach, *QAP*, to establish query-feature relationships.

Challenges

The goal of a QF-graph is to associate the text of queries with the text representing software features. However, both queries [12] and software features typically consist of only a few words, limiting the range of approaches that can be used to establish associations. More specifically, simplistic term-matching approaches such as the vector space model of information retrieval [18] cannot be readily applied: In the vector space model, the similarity of two phrases depends on the set of terms that the two phrases have in common. If the phrases share few words, then their similarity score is low. In our case, the use of term overlap is further confounded by the fact that many queries are task or goal-related and tend to have few words in common with any particular feature of the system.

In order to address the issue of term sparsity, one can simply emulate existing search practices: Each search query can be submitted to a search engine, the relevant web pages can be retrieved, and the commands, actions or tools mentioned within the web pages can be identified. This process enables us to create associations between search queries and related system functionality.

The strategy of using document retrieval to expand the set of terms associated with a short phrase is not new. Specifically, Bernstein et al. employed document retrieval to help cluster short Twitter messages [3], and Shen et al. used document retrieval to help classify search queries [19]. However, while this approach has been found to be very effective in these latter contexts, in the context of pairing search queries with specific elements of an interface, this technique breaks down when the resulting documents are multi-topical. For example, a query to learn how to perform a particular task with an application can yield web pages on user forums, frequently asked question (FAQ) pages, or blogs, all of which are inherently multi-topical documents that can reference a wide range of system features in the same document. The challenge, then, is to determine which portion of a document is most relevant to a given search query.

To address this problem of multi-topical documents, one can repeat the basic search process *within* each document, identifying and retrieving short passages that are most relevant to the original query. These passages can then be processed to identify what system features they mention.

This pipeline of retrieving relevant documents, retrieving relevant passages, then identifying a set of relevant system components, is essentially the same as that employed by many question answering (QA) services (e.g., see [20]). As such, we employed the QAP (Question Answering Passage) algorithm originally described by Clarke et al. [6] to discover associations between queries and system functionality. We briefly describe QAP in the next section. Interested readers are directed to [6] and [7] for a more thorough treatment of the QAP algorithm.

An Overview of QAP

QAP proceeds in three distinct steps: 1) retrieve short document passages relevant to the user's question or query, 2) identify potential answers in those passages, and 3) rank or otherwise validate potential answers so that a final summary can be presented to the user.

STEP 1: PASSAGE RETRIEVAL

The first step of QAP is to retrieve passages relevant to the user's query. QAP employs a cover-density ranking approach that treats all document substrings that both begin and end with a query keyword as potential passages. The details of this cover-density ranking are beyond the scope of this paper, but the ranking weighs the number of query keywords contained within each substring against the substring's length. Favourable ranks are assigned to short substrings that contain many query keywords. Once substrings are scored, longer fixed-length passages are extracted by expanding each substring about its midpoint. We elected to extract passages consisting of 300 words after early experiments suggested that this value was effective for the types of web pages and documents we were analyzing (forums, blogs, etc.). The original QAP paper, [6], utilized passages consisting of 200 words.

The original QAP papers employed cover-density ranking over all documents in the corpus. In the QA literature, it is more common to first limit the search space by creating a short list of documents that are potentially relevant to the original question or search query [20]. Passage retrieval is then employed over this smaller set of documents. To approximate this first step, we simply used Google's public search API [9] to retrieve the top 8 documents for each query. Whether using the original QAP formulation, or our modification, each document contributes only its highest scoring passage to the next step of the process.

STEP 2: ANSWER EXTRACTION

The second step of QAP is to identify potential answers mentioned within the top k scoring passages. In our case $k = 8$. In general, k can be any integer not exceeding the total number of passages (and documents, since each contributes only its top passage). In the original QAP work, each query was analyzed to determine the form of its expected answer. Depending on the question, answers might take the form of dates, proper names, cities, numbers etc. Such answers can be detected using regular expressions, or by matching a passage's phrases against lists of potential answers. In the context of our problem, document phrases are matched against the features enumerated in the QF-graph's vertex set F.

STEP 3: RANKING ANSWERS

The final step of QAP is to rank the potential answers that were identified in passages. To do this, QAP exploits the built-in redundancy of the web: The web is a large corpus, and the answer to any question is likely to be found in many documents. As such, QAP ranks answers using the following measure:

$$\text{score}(q, f) = n_{q,f} \times log\left(\frac{|D|}{d_f}\right) \quad (1)$$

Here, $n_{q,f} \leq k$ represents the number of passages returned for query q in which the feature f is mentioned. Similarly, d_f is the number of distinct documents in the corpus in which the feature's corresponding phrase f occurs, and $|D|$ is the number of documents in the corpus overall. The term $|D|/d_f$ is just the familiar inverse-document frequency (*idf*) of the phrase/system feature f. Since we do not have access to the full Google document corpus, we estimate the *idf* statistic from our smaller corpus of web pages relating to the interactive system under investigation. Depending on the interactive system, this corpus consists of tens or hundreds of thousands of web documents collected using standard web crawling practices.

Using QAP to generate edges

At the heart of the QAP question answering algorithm is the function $score(q, f)$, given by equation 1 above. This function assigns a numeric score to the tuple (q, f), expressing the strength of the association between the query q and system feature f. This score provides a means for weighting the edges in the QF-graph. Specifically, G's edges are defined as follows:

$$\begin{aligned} E \ = \{ \ & (q_i, f_j, w_{ij});\ q_i \in Q,\ f_j \in F, \\ & w_{ij} = \text{score}(q_i, f_j) \ \ \} \end{aligned} \quad (2)$$

Additionally, notice that QAP accepts any sequence of words as input. As such, the QF-graph can be actively updated as new searches are performed. This is accomplished by simply appending new queries to the query vertex set Q, and executing QAP to establish each new query's associations with the fixed set of system features F.

In theory, this method should establish reasonable connections between user queries and specific elements in the user interface. The next section presents results from our analysis examining the quality of these connections.

EVALUATION

To evaluate the quality of a QF-graph, we employed a variety of metrics. Some of these metrics are standardized and are used throughout information retrieval literature. Another was developed by us for this particular problem domain. Since results are often difficult to interpret on their own, we compare QAP results to those achieved when using a more basic term-matching approach for associating queries with features (specifically, the standard vector space model [18]).

Experiment Setup

The QF-graphs produced by our technique were evaluated using the following high-level steps. First, a set of test queries is chosen. Second, for each test query, QAP's results are recorded. Finally, the relevance of each result is judged by an expert. Since we have already covered how we construct the QF-graph, we describe the first and last steps of this process.

Selecting test queries

For this experiment, we randomly selected 20 queries from the query-feature graphs pertaining to each of the five interactive systems listed in Table 1. Because queries were selected from the query-feature graphs (which itself was built using queries harvested via CUTS), the queries represent real-world user searches.

Judging relevance

Many queries describe a goal or a task that the user would like to perform. We would like to know which system features are relevant to the query, but we would also like to know which sets of features are sufficient for completing the task implied by the search. To accommodate both needs, we manually crafted *solutions* for each test query. A solution is a collection of relevant commands or system features that "solves" or accomplishes the goal implied by the query. As an example, there are two solution sets for the query "firefox how to clear cookies":

1. Clear Recent History, Cookies, Clear Now
2. Preferences, Privacy, Show Cookies, Remove All Cookies

A system feature is said to be relevant to a query if the feature appears in any of the query's solutions. Similarly, we say that a set of features, S, *covers a solution* when S contains references to all system features required to implement that solution. By this definition, the full set of features F covers all solutions, and the empty set $\emptyset$ covers no solutions.

Given a selection of test queries and their associated solutions, it is possible to employ a number of metrics to measure the quality of the QAP query-feature associations. We describe these metrics next.

Performance Metrics

We employed four search-quality metrics to assess our QF-graphs: Mean precision at 1, percent correct at 10, mean average precision, and mean precision at *. Each of these metrics is described below.

- **Mean precision at 1**
  Mean precision at 1, denoted $\overline{P_{@1}}$, is a standard information retrieval metric [22] that measures the proportion of test queries whose top-ranking QAP result is judged to be relevant.
- **Percent correct at 10**
  The *percent correct at 10* measure (%C@10) is another simple metric that measures the proportion of test queries for which at least one correct solution is covered by the query's top-10 QAP results.
- **Mean average precision**
  Mean average precision (MAP) is a widely used information retrieval metric that averages the precision of a set of

search results, measured at various levels of recall (see [22] for more details). It is generally described as a measure of the area underneath the precision-recall (or, receiver operating characteristic) curve. MAP scores range from 0 to 1, with higher scores indicating better results.

- **Mean precision at ***
  In question answering literature, one standard measure of performance is *mean reciprocal rank* (MRR) [20]. A query's reciprocal rank is simply the multiplicative inverse of the rank corresponding to the first correct answer in the queries' list of results. The mean reciprocal rank metric is the average of the reciprocal ranks of all test queries.

  In our domain, many queries cannot be "answered" by a single result, but rather are "covered" by a set of results that combine to form a correct solution. As such, we developed a metric similar in spirit to MRR, described below, which we refer to as *mean precision at **.

  For each query q, let r^* be the smallest integer such that q's top r^* ranking QAP results cover one complete solution for the query. Precision at r^*, denoted $Prec_*(q)$, is the proportion of the top r^* results that are judged to be relevant to the query. $\overline{P_*}$ is the arithmetic mean of these $Prec_*(q)$ scores across all test queries.

  Importantly, the $\overline{P_*}$ measure is equivalent to MRR in cases where the query's solution is covered by a single command or system feature.

Experiment Results

Results from applying these four metrics to the experimental QF-graphs are listed in Table 2. On average, 77% percent of the test queries were "answered" (or covered) by the top-10 results returned by QAP. Moreover, the first QAP result was relevant to the query in 63% of test cases.

Regarding individual applications, results for GIMP are quite good in part because we were able to obtain a very accurate list of GIMP's commands, but also because GIMP command names are sufficiently technical to not conflict with everyday language, making it easier to identify commands mentioned in web pages. Similarly, results for Firefox are superior to those of Chrome because Firefox's localization format allowed us to easily identify strings associated with menu items, buttons and other command-related UI components. Conversely, Chrome's localization database does not provide this information. As a result, Chrome's QF graph contains a much broader set of strings (which explains why table 1 lists nearly six times as many strings from Chrome as it does for Firefox). While most of these spurious strings rarely occur in search queries or web documents, some strings (e.g., Chrome's "And then click") are sufficiently common to introduce errors.

To provide further context for interpreting these results, and to measure the impact of QAP, we repeated the experiment using a typical implementation of the vector space model to match query phrases to system features. This approach is

System	$\overline{P_{@1}}$	$\overline{P_*}$	MAP	%C@10
GIMP	0.800	0.725	0.467	90%
Firefox	0.750	0.601	0.496	75%
Chrome	0.500	0.598	0.382	75%
Inkscape	0.500	0.536	0.264	70%
Kindle	0.600	0.633	0.458	75%
Overall	0.630	0.619	0.413	77%

Table 2: Performance when using QAP for discovering query-feature associations for five different interactive systems.

System	$\overline{P_{@1}}$	$\overline{P_*}$	MAP	%C@10
GIMP	0.450	0.302	0.132	30%
Firefox	0.500	0.501	0.264	70%
Chrome	0.050	0.197	0.074	45%
Inkscape	0.150	0.160	0.081	35%
Kindle	0.400	0.384	0.124	50%
Overall	0.310	0.309	0.135	46%

Table 3: Performance when using the vector space model for discovering query-feature associations.

similar to those employed in existing interface search tools (e.g., Mac OS X's help menu search), and ranks query-feature associations by averaging the importance weights of the words that both the query and system feature have in common. A word's importance weight is simply its inverse document frequency, described previously. Results from these trials are listed in Table 3.

In all cases, with all metrics, QAP's results are superior to those obtained when using simple term matching (the standard vector space model).

From these experiments we conclude that, for a given query, the top-10 query-feature associations discovered by QAP are reasonable, and, in every case, the results obtained using QAP are better than those produced by more typical implementations of interface search. Finally, these experiments establish a baseline with which future research can be compared, and improvements measured.

APPLICATIONS

QF-graphs can serve as the computational back-end for a number of novel interface mechanisms. In this section, we describe how the QF-graph can improve search-driven interaction, support dynamic tooltips, and enable application-to-application analogy search. We use example data from actual QF-graphs to illustrate the utility of QF-graphs in these hypothetical interface mechanisms.

Search-driven Interaction

The concept of search-driven interaction is simple: The user types in a few keywords and the system returns a ranked list of relevant system commands and interface components. This style of interaction can be useful when an application's features number in the hundreds or thousands [16].

QF-graphs provide a direct means of supporting search-driven interaction. When the user enters a query, the QF-graph is consulted to retrieve relevant system features. If the QF-graph does not contain an entry for the query, QAP can be used to provide this information on demand.

To illustrate the potential of this approach, the following examples demonstrate search results obtained using QF-graphs for three different interactive systems. For each example, we provide the top five results returned from querying the QF-graph. The queries themselves were drawn from the corpora of queries produced by CUTS, and thus represent frequently issued queries by users.

Query: *"gimp convert to black and white"*
As noted in the Introduction, this query is issued by users who would like to convert color digital images to images that consists only of shades of gray. This effect is most easily achieved using GIMP's, *grayscale* or *desaturate* commands, but can also be accomplished by selecting a "monochrome" option in the *channel mixer* tool, or by *decomposing* the image in order to extract its Luminosity channel (in HSL color space).

QF-graph search results:
- Channel mixer
- Grayscale
- Desaturate
- Channels
- Decompose

Query: *"how to get the kindle to read to you"*
In this case, the user would like to enable the text-to-speech feature of the Amazon Kindle. This is accomplished by pressing the *Aa* hardware button, then navigating to the *Text-to-speech* section of the dialog, and finally selecting the *turn on* command.

QF-graph search results:
- Aa
- Text to speech
- Turn on
- Web browser
- Down (directional keypad)

Query: *"change download location firefox"*
Here, a user of the Firefox web browser would like to change the location to which Firefox saves downloaded files. This can be achieved by opening Firefox's general preferences and entering a different value in a text field titled "Save files to." Alternatively, the user can check the radio button titled "Always ask me where to save files."

QF-graph search results:
- Save files to
- Always ask me where to save files
- Always ask
- Location
- Save

Importantly, each of these three queries are task-related and do not mention any system commands by name. Nevertheless, the QF-graph returns results directly relevant to the goals implied by the queries, demonstrating the utility and robustness of the approach.

Rank	Query
1	gimp draw circle
2	draw a circle in gimp
3	drawing a circle in gimp
4	gimp drawing circle
5	gimp tutorial circle
6	draw ellipse gimp
7	gimp ellipse draw
...	

Table 4: A partial list of queries neighbouring GIMP's "ellipse select" command.

Dynamic tooltips

The features represented in a QF-graph can also be "queried" to determine the set of search queries associated with a given feature. This capability motivates *dynamic tooltips*.

Dynamic tooltips extend standard tooltips or balloon help by proactively describing the range of tasks that utilize the command or interface component currently in focus. These task descriptions are derived from QF-graphs, which are themselves derived from real-world user search queries and from web content, such as FAQs, forums, tutorials, and blog posts. As a result, these tooltips dynamically track and reflect current use of the software by the community. Figure 2 provides an example of the contents such a dynamic tooltip could display for GIMP's "ellipse select" command (where the contents are derived from GIMP's actual QF-graph).

To generate the contents of a dynamic tooltip, the system first determines which queries are associated with a given system feature f. The set of related queries Q_f is simply the set of vertices neighbouring f in the QF-graph. As an example, Table 4 provides a partial list of the queries neighbouring the "ellipse select" command in GIMP's query-feature graph.

An exhaustive examination of these queries (in this case, numbering over 750), reveals references to a variety of tasks other than drawing circles or ellipses (e.g., writing text along a circle, or correcting red eye). However, while there may exist numerous queries, many of these queries refer to the same topic, as can be seen in the partial list of queries associated with "ellipse select" shown in Table 4. In other words, there is considerable redundancy in Q_f.

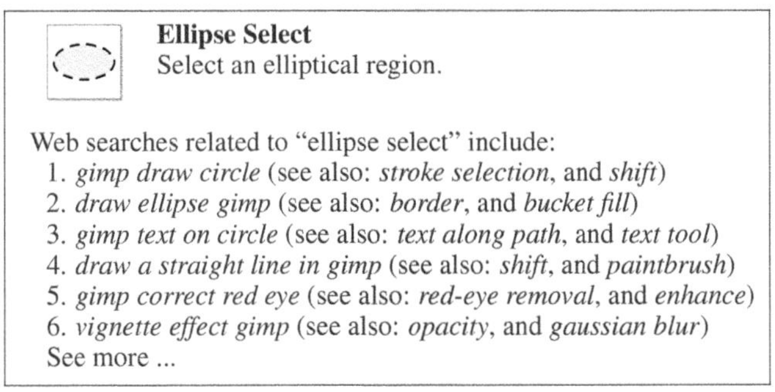

Figure 2: The dynamic tooltip for GIMP's "ellipse select" command. The list of related searches is derived from GIMP's QF-graph, as are the pairs of commands associated with each search query.

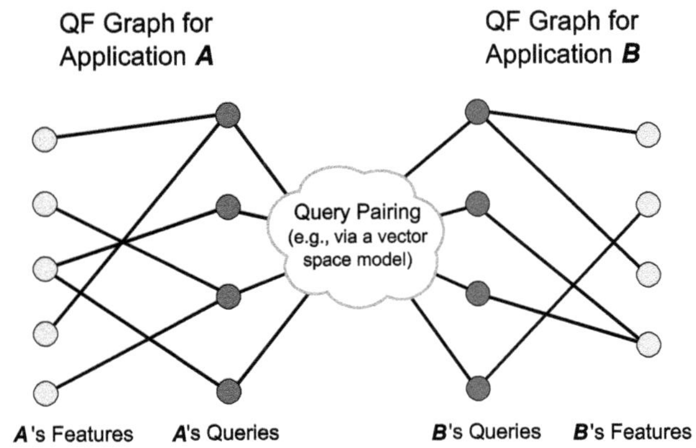

Figure 3: App-to-app analogy search relates features found in one application to similar features found in other applications. To accomplish this, the QF-graphs of two applications are essentially joined together by using the standard vector space model to identify similar queries.

By removing redundancy in the set Q_f, one can more concisely express the variety of tasks in which the command f is involved. In order to remove redundancy in Q_f, we can repeatedly remove queries q whose query-feature edge weight is less than that of some *equivalent query*, $p \in Q_f$. We consider two queries, q and p, equivalent if they share 4 of their top-5 search results. Applying this procedure to the set of queries related to GIMP's "ellipse select" tool yields the queries listed previously in Figure 2.

The queries listed in a dynamic tooltip can also be augmented with an additional list of related commands. More specifically, the top two features associated with each query (excluding the command for which the tooltip is generated) can be displayed to provide more context about the tools necessary to complete the task represented by the query. As an example, the dynamic tooltip for the "ellipse select" tool in Figure 2 lists an example query, "gimp text on circle", along with two additional commands: "text along path" and the "text tool". Both of these latter commands can be used in conjunction with "ellipse select" to print text along the circumference of a circle. In some cases, these additional commands may be sufficient to describe the set of commands necessary to accomplish a task, thus aiding the user in learning how to use the interface. This specific use of QF-graphs is similar in spirit to the user and item-based command recommendations discussed by Matejka et al. in [13]. However, the recommendations generated from QF-graphs are likely to be more task-specific and task-focused since they derive from web pages and tutorials describing specific tasks.

App-to-App Analogy Search

Within a given domain, competing applications often provide similar functionality, but use different naming conventions or vocabularies for those features. As an example, in the domain of web browsers, Firefox's "private browsing" feature is equivalent to Chrome's "Incognito" mode (both modes limit the amount of information tracked and exchanged when browsing the web). Despite these different system names, users issue similar queries when searching for these capabilities (since queries typically express a high-level goal). These similarities in user queries make it possible to associate queries in one application to queries in a second, comparable application.

Linking queries from two different applications serves to connect the QF-graphs of the two applications (Figure 3). Once connected, the paired graphs enable *analogy* search, or the ability to directly relate the commands of one application to similar commands in the second application.

As a demonstration of this concept, the results of applying analogy search to the aforementioned private browsing example are listed below. As can be seen, analogy search is able to correctly associate Firefox's "start private browsing" command to Chrome's "new incognito window" command.

Analogy: *Chrome commands similar to Firefox's "Start Private Browsing" command:*

Results:
- New incognito window
- Incognito
- Session
- And then click

In this example, analogy search begins by identifying the top 10 queries in Firefox's QF-graph related to the "Start Private Browsing" command. For each query, a term frequency inverse document frequency (tf-idf) vector is created, as is standard in the vector space model of information retrieval [18]. A weighted sum of the 10 query vectors is then computed in order to synthesize a single feature vector for the "Start Private Browsing" command. Weights in the summation correspond to the query-feature edge weights in the QF graph. This amalgamation of queries into a communal feature vector helps to mitigate the term sparsity problem, which was previously discussed in the section entitled "Associating Queries with Features." Once the feature vector is computed, an identical process is performed for each of Chrome's commands. The similarity between pairs of commands is then computed as the dot product of the two vectors, and the highest scoring Chrome commands are listed in the search results.

As a further example of the effectiveness of app-to-app analogy search, consider two somewhat different applications: GIMP and Inkscape. GIMP is a raster graphics editor, while Inkscape is a vector graphics editor. Importantly, GIMP and Inkscape both edit images, but do so using vastly different metaphors and data (namely, pixels vs. vectors).

As an example of how these applications differ, GIMP allows users to crop an image using a "crop" tool. To achieve a similar effect in Inkscape, users must first select objects of interest, then either set the "clipping region," or "fit the page to the selection." Despite these marked differences, app-to-app analogy search is able to correctly associate GIMP's crop tool with the appropriate Inkscape commands.

Analogy: *Inkscape commands similar to GIMP's "crop" command:*

Results:
- Crop marks
- Select all in all layers
- Select
- Fit page to selection

Finally, it is also possible to use analogy search to identify related commands *within the same* application. The following example illustrates this point:

Analogy: *GIMP commands similar to GIMP's "stretch contrast" command:*

Results:
- White Balance
- Auto (Levels)
- Stretch Contrast
- Colors

In the above example, analogy search correctly inferred that GIMP's "stretch contrast", "white balance" and "auto levels" commands are related in that they are often used in conjunction (or in place of) one another, in order to enhance a digital photograph. (In this case, each of these commands is used to manipulate an image's histogram.)

DISCUSSION

We conclude our discussion of QF-graphs by considering some of their limitations, challenges in automatically creating query-feature associations, and directions for future work.

"Feature" ambiguity in web documents

In this paper, we identified system features referenced within web pages by simply searching those web pages for instances of phrases matching the names of commands, menus, and other interface components. This approach works rather well for commands with technical names (e.g., "unsharp mask"), or for longer phrases ("Always check to see if Firefox is the default browser on startup"). Such phrases are unlikely to appear accidentally in documents. However, for short commands (e.g., "Delete", "Save"), there is considerable ambiguity, and it is difficult to decide if the document is referencing a command, or if the phrase is simply part of the document's prose. In this paper, the QAP scoring function (equation 1) addresses the problem by exploiting the redundancy afforded by multiple relevant passages, all the while using inverse document frequency to reduce the impact of common phrases. In other words, the scoring function requires that a feature with a common name appear in many relevant passages in order to achieve a high score.

In future research, we would like to explore more sophisticated means of identifying references to system features. In examining tutorials and forum postings, we have noticed that people often specify the full paths of commands in their text. As an example, rather than simply writing "grayscale", many authors write "Image→Mode→Grayscale" when referring to GIMP's grayscale command. In the latter case, it is clear that the terms "Image", "Mode" and "Grayscale" are references to interface components. Identifying these types of patterns could increase the confidence that the use of a word actually refers to an element in the system. Matching the phrase to the known hierarchical organization of commands within an interface could further increase confidence measures.

Exploiting temporal associations

Additionally, just as search queries are often task-related, so too are the documents they retrieve. As such, many documents specify sequences of commands that must be executed in a particular order to achieve a desired outcome. These command sequences are not reflected in the current QF-graph, nor in the search results returned by QAP. This can be disconcerting when the order of commands returned does not match the order in which those commands should be executed. As an example, consider the query "how to draw a circle in gimp". Depending on the strengths of the query-feature associations, our system may return a ranked list of commands where "stroke selection" appears before "ellipse select" (where both commands must be used to draw a circle in GIMP since it provides no tools for drawing geometric primitives).

In the future, we would like to extract command sequences from documents, and use this sequencing information to improve the range of possible applications of QF-graphs. As an example, it would be beneficial if search-driven interaction could return sequences of actions rather than individual commands. Similarly, the availability of sequencing information could allow the recommendations made by dynamic tooltips to automatically update as the user progresses through a given task.

CONCLUSION

In this paper, we have presented QF-graphs, and demonstrated how they can be constructed automatically from logs of search queries, web pages, and localization data. While it is conceivable that QF-graphs can be constructed using alternative means or data sources, the approach outlined in this paper confers a number of advantages. Specifically, by drawing from query logs and web pages, we ensure that QF-graphs graph can be continuously updated as system usage patterns change. Moreover, a completely automated approach ensures that data from thousands of users can be considered when associating queries with system features.

This paper also outlined how QF-graphs can be used to advance search-driven interaction, while paving the way for new interaction techniques such as dynamic tooltips and application-to-application analogy search. Collectively, these mechanisms help to bridge the gulf of execution in cases where users are able to articulate their goals as search queries, but are unsure of how to accomplish those goals in an interactive system.

ACKNOWLEDGEMENTS

We would like to thank Charles Clarke for discussions which helped to clarify various details regarding the QAP passage retrieval algorithm.

REFERENCES

1. Ricardo Baeza-Yates and Alessandro Tiberi. Extracting semantic relations from query logs. In *Proceedings of the 13th ACM SIGKDD international conference on Knowledge discovery and data mining*, KDD '07, pages 76–85, New York, NY, USA, 2007. ACM.
2. Doug Beeferman and Adam Berger. Agglomerative clustering of a search engine query log. In *Proceedings of the sixth ACM SIGKDD international conference on Knowledge discovery and data mining*, KDD '00, pages 407–416, New York, NY, USA, 2000. ACM.
3. Michael S. Bernstein, Bongwon Suh, Lichan Hong, Jilin Chen, Sanjay Kairam, and Ed H. Chi. Eddi: interactive topic-based browsing of social status streams. In *Proceedings of the 23nd annual ACM symposium on User interface software and technology*, UIST '10, pages 303–312, New York, NY, USA, 2010. ACM.
4. Blacktree Software. Quicksilver: OS X at your fingertips. `http://qsapp.com/`, Retrieved April, 2011.
5. Joel Brandt, Mira Dontcheva, Marcos Weskamp, and Scott R. Klemmer. Example-centric programming: integrating web search into the development environment. In *Proceedings of the 28th international conference on Human factors in computing systems*, CHI '10, pages 513–522, New York, NY, USA, 2010. ACM.
6. Charles L. A. Clarke, Gordon V. Cormack, and Thomas R. Lynam. Exploiting redundancy in question answering. In *Proceedings of the 24th annual international ACM SIGIR conference on Research and development in information retrieval*, SIGIR '01, pages 358–365, New York, NY, USA, 2001. ACM.
7. Charles L. A. Clarke, Gordon V. Cormack, and Elizabeth A. Tudhope. Relevance ranking for one to three term queries. *Information Processing and Management*, 36(2):291 – 311, 2000.
8. Adam Fourney, Richard Mann, and Michael Terry. Characterizing the usability of interactive applications through query log analysis. In *Proceedings of the 2011 annual conference on Human factors in computing systems*, CHI '11, pages 1817–1826, New York, NY, USA, 2011. ACM.
9. Google Corperation. Google custom search APIs and tools. `http://code.google.com/apis/customsearch/`, Retrieved April, 2011.
10. Jeff Hendy, Kellogg S. Booth, and Joanna McGrenere. Graphically enhanced keyboard accelerators for GUIs. In *Proceedings of Graphics Interface 2010*, GI '10, pages 3–10, Toronto, Ont., Canada, 2010. Canadian Information Processing Society.
11. Humanized Inc. Enso. `http://www.humanized.com/enso/`, Retrieved April, 2011.
12. Melanie Kellar, Carolyn Watters, and Michael Shepherd. A field study characterizing web-based information-seeking tasks. *J. Am. Soc. Inf. Sci. Technol.*, 58(7):999–1018, 2007.
13. Justin Matejka, Wei Li, Tovi Grossman, and George Fitzmaurice. Communitycommands: command recommendations for software applications. In *Proceedings of the 22nd annual ACM symposium on User interface software and technology*, UIST '09, pages 193–202, New York, NY, USA, 2009. ACM.
14. Robert C. Miller, Victoria H. Chou, Michael Bernstein, Greg Little, Max Van Kleek, David Karger, and mc schraefel. Inky: a sloppy command line for the web with rich visual feedback. In *Proceedings of the 21st annual ACM symposium on User interface software and technology*, UIST '08, pages 131–140, New York, NY, USA, 2008. ACM.
15. Mozilla Labs. Ubiquity: An experimental interface based on natural language input. `https://mozillalabs.com/ubiquity/`, Retrieved April, 2011.
16. Don Norman. The next UI breakthrough: command lines. *interactions*, 14:44–45, May 2007.
17. Donald A. Norman. *Cognitive Engineering*, chapter 3. User Centered System Design: New Perspectives on Human-computer Interaction. Lawrence Erlbaum Associates, 1986.
18. G. Salton, A. Wong, and C. S. Yang. A vector space model for automatic indexing. *Commun. ACM*, 18:613–620, November 1975.
19. Dou Shen, Rong Pan, Jian-Tao Sun, Jeffrey Junfeng Pan, Kangheng Wu, Jie Yin, and Qiang Yang. Q2C@UST: our winning solution to query classification in KDDCUP 2005. *SIGKDD Explor. Newsl.*, 7:100–110, December 2005.
20. Stefanie Tellex, Boris Katz, Jimmy Lin, Aaron Fernandes, and Gregory Marton. Quantitative evaluation of passage retrieval algorithms for question answering. In *Proceedings of the 26th annual international ACM SIGIR conference on Research and development in informaion retrieval*, SIGIR '03, pages 41–47, New York, NY, USA, 2003. ACM.
21. Michael Terry, Matthew Kay, Brad Van Vugt, Brandon Slack, and Terry Park. ingimp: introducing instrumentation to an end-user open source application. In *Proceeding of the twenty-sixth annual SIGCHI conference on Human factors in computing systems*, CHI '08, pages 607–616, New York, NY, USA, 2008. ACM.
22. Andrew Turpin and Falk Scholer. User performance versus precision measures for simple search tasks. In *Proceedings of the 29th annual international ACM SIGIR conference on Research and development in information retrieval*, SIGIR '06, pages 11–18, New York, NY, USA, 2006. ACM.

Stacksplorer: Call Graph Navigation Helps Increasing Code Maintenance Efficiency

Thorsten Karrer† *Jan-Peter Krämer*† *Jonathan Diehl*† *Björn Hartmann*‡ *Jan Borchers*†

†RWTH Aachen University
52062 Aachen, Germany
{karrer, kraemer, diehl, borchers
@cs.rwth-aachen.de

‡Computer Science Division
University of California
Berkeley, CA 94720
bjoern@cs.berkeley.edu

ABSTRACT
We present Stacksplorer, a new tool to support source code navigation and comprehension. Stacksplorer computes the call graph of a given piece of code, visualizes relevant parts of it, and allows developers to interactively traverse it. This augments the traditional code editor by offering an additional layer of navigation. Stacksplorer is particularly useful to understand and edit unknown source code because branches of the call graph can be explored and backtracked easily. Visualizing the callers of a method reduces the risk of introducing unintended side effects. In a quantitative study, programmers using Stacksplorer performed three of four software maintenance tasks significantly faster and with higher success rates, and Stacksplorer received a System Usability Scale rating of 85.4 from participants.

ACM Classification: H5.2 [Information interfaces and presentation]: User Interfaces. - Graphical user interfaces.

General terms: Design, Human Factors

Keywords: Development Tools / Toolkits / Programming Environments, Visualization.

INTRODUCTION

A large part of a software developer's work is maintaining existing code bases. This includes adding new features, fixing bugs, and refactoring code after the software has been shipped. Maintenance has been shown to make up as much as 70% of the total expenses of a software project [19]. Because of this, analyzing and improving how programmers maintain code has recently become an active area of research.

Maintenance often comprises reading and understanding an unfamiliar piece of source code and identifying problematic sections. The developer then has to modify these sections while being aware of potential side effects [15]. To do this, the developer spends a large part of his time navigating through the code [20]. Navigating source code includes file-based navigation, such as switching between classes that are usually implemented in separate files, and navigating the semantics of the code, e.g., locating a variable definition or exploring the callers and callees of a certain method. Navigating the call graph has been shown to be particularly important to understand code, to find out where to modify it, and to assess the scope and side effects of any changes [13].

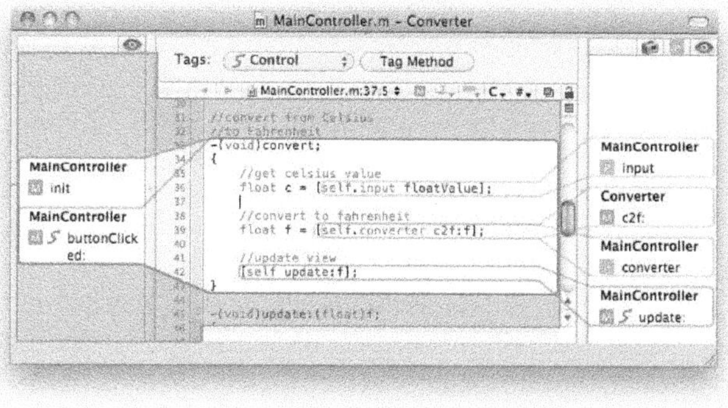

Figure 1: Stacksplorer visualizes and allows browsing the call graph of an application's source code. For the current *focus method*, it shows callers in the left column and methods called in the right.

We present Stacksplorer, a plug-in that modifies the user interface of the Xcode[1] integrated development environment (IDE) to visualize and navigate the neighborhood of any given method in the call graph (Fig. 1). Stacksplorer lets developers see and access the callers "upstream" of a method, reducing the risk of introducing unintended side effects. They can also navigate downstream to understand how operations are implemented in an unknown piece of code. The call graph visualization helps developers retain the context of a method and simplifies exploring and backtracking along interesting branches of the call graph.

In a controlled experiment, developers solved code maintenance tasks using Xcode with and without Stacksplorer. Our results show that Stacksplorer helps developers to solve more tasks correctly in less time, with a heightened awareness of possible side effects.

[1]http://developer.apple.com/technologies/tools/xcode.html

RELATED WORK

Navigation Behavior

Today, most IDEs offer only limited tools for call graph related code navigation. Moreover, these tools are often difficult to find and invoke. By observing programmers working with Eclipse on five change tasks in a 500SLOC[2] Java application, Ko et al. [11] found that about a quarter of the developers' time was spent navigating, either by following dependencies or by searching for names. Between code segments related through structural relationships, users navigated using scroll bars and the package browser (14% of the test period) or using the find and replace tool, although more suitable and effective tools are available in Eclipse (see also [18]). To perform comparisons, developers navigated back and forth between code segments because by default, Eclipse uses a single editing window.

Lawrance and Burnett [16] presented PFIS (Programmer Flow by Information Scent), a model based on information foraging theory to predict a programmer's navigation. In information foraging theory, each link between two pieces of information has a certain scent that determines how likely a user will follow this link on her search for relevant information. In PFIS, a link is defined as any navigation possible with one click; scent is determined by comparing words used in the source code with those used in a bug report, which verbally describes the users task. In an experiment, PFIS was capable of predicting the navigation behavior of professional software developers in a bug fixing task.

Recommender Systems

Recommender systems for software development aim at determining automatically which information is relevant to the developer's current task. Most systems first calculate a 'degree of interest' depending on the source file that is being edited, for all files in the project. They then recommend files with a degree of interest exceeding a threshold. Recommender systems may take into account: a programmer's navigation history [23]; the navigation history of all programmers in the same code [6]; the history of editing activities in addition to navigation [10]; and non-code resources such as version control systems [24].

For small tasks, user studies of these tools consistently found that the total effort spent on navigating through a project could be reduced significantly, and that users considered automated guidance in software projects helpful, especially when they were new to the project. For more complex projects, however, the effect recommender tools have may be minor compared to task and strategy specific effects [4]. In contrast to Stacksplorer, the recommender systems presented reduce the amount of information shown in the IDE, but they do not introduce new ways to visualize the structural relationships that led to the recommendations.

Call Graph Utilization

The Whyline [12] allows asking "Why did" or "Why didn't" questions about the textual and graphical output of an application. For example, a line drawn in a painting application may, after execution stopped, be queried "Why did this line's color = blue". Using a trace of the actual program execution, the Whyline computes a dynamic slice, i.e., it determines which method executions influenced the relevant property. Novice programmers using the Whyline could solve a bug fixing task significantly faster than expert developers without the Whyline. Stacksplorer is, in contrast to the Whyline, not a debugging but a navigation tool; it does not allow users to formulate an explicit question about a trace from a single execution but facilitates exploration of the call graph during code editing.

LaToza and Myers [14] scope searches in source code by restricting them to branches of the call graph originating in or leading to a certain method. The search results are visualized in a graph, revealing the paths leading from the starting point of the search to each result. Unlike Stacksplorer, this visualization is a feature of the search tool and not integrated with the source code editor as a means for navigation.

Commercial IDEs such as Visual Studio, Eclipse, or Xcode offer various tools for exploring the call graph. Eclipse, for example, is able to show multiple levels of callers and callees of a method in a tree view; Visual Studio offers similar functionality. These tools can be used for navigation, but they do not update automatically when the user navigates through the source code, and they are not part of, or visually connected to, the code editor. For navigation inside the source code editor, most IDEs provide functionality to directly jump to the definition of a method from where it is called, and some support jumping to callers; these tools, however, lack a permanent visualization that could provide additional information scent and help the user stay oriented.

Code Layout

Other tools focus solely on laying out relevant source code elements visually in order to help developers navigating and keeping track of source code. DeLine et al. [5] use the graphically scaled down source code text file as an overview map for navigation. While being too small to be readable, it allows discerning the structure of the source code, thus supporting inter- and intra-file navigation.

In Code Bubbles [2], code is viewed and edited in bubbles, which can be arranged freely on a 2D plane. The bubbles are connected with arrows representing existing relationships between them. Users can use a number of tools, e.g., "Open Declaration", to find exactly the bubbles they need. Code Bubbles is based on single methods as the basic navigational unit, thus breaking the prevalent paradigm of regular IDEs, which are based on a class-file dualism. In a qualitative study, programmers solved one of two maintenance tasks significantly faster with Code Bubbles than with Eclipse. The need for back-and-forth navigation was also reduced significantly. To combine the benefits of Code Bubbles and traditional IDEs, Stacksplorer offers the familiar file- (or class-)based navigation extended by a method-based navigation along the call graph.

[2]source lines of code (number of non-comment, non-empty lines of source code)

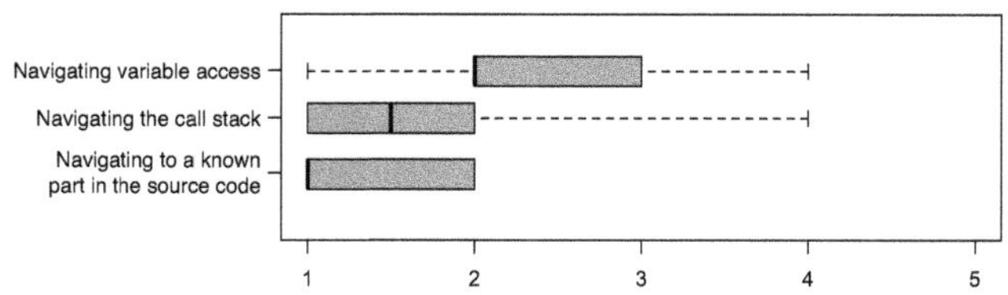

Figure 2: The boxplot diagrams above show how frequently (from 1=frequently to 4=seldom, 5=never) developers think they perform navigation of different types when working on bug fixing tasks.

FORMATIVE STUDY: HOW DEVELOPERS NAVIGATE IN XCODE

We conducted a small formative study to understand how developers navigate source code in different situations when using Xcode. To build on the findings of the aforementioned studies, which used Java and Eclipse, we first had to confirm that developers using Objective-C and Xcode navigate code in ways similar to Java developers.

Six Objective-C developers who worked on maintenance tasks at the time agreed to participate. Through a contextual inquiry, we analyzed the set of navigation actions our participants used during their work. For each navigation action we noted the goal (e.g., "find first definition of variable") motivating the action and the tool used to perform it (e.g., "jump to definition tool from contextual menu"). Afterwards, we asked the participants to estimate the importance of the different goals, and to rate the support the IDE provided for their navigation needs.

The most important goal when navigating source code was to edit sections of code that were well-known to the developers both in location and content (see Fig. 2). This kind of navigation happened mostly by switching between files and scrolling through the source, and it was perceived to be well supported by the IDE. When the developers' knowledge of the code was not sufficient to solve a task, and parts of the source code had to be analyzed and understood, they mainly followed structural relationships in the source code; most importantly, the call graph was explored, and they investigated which parts of the source code accessed an important variable. Since variable access usually happened through accessor methods, this also required an analysis of the call graph.

These findings confirmed our assumption that Xcode developers and Eclipse developers navigate through source code similarly. Interestingly, the developers not only navigated along edges of the call graph often, but they did so consciously, and regarded it as important. They also actively expressed that better tools for call graph navigation were needed.

NAVIGATING WITH STACKSPLORER

These results motivated the main idea of Stacksplorer's design: analyzing the code's *call graph* [21] to offer relevant information related to the user's *focus method*, i.e., the method she is currently working on or trying to understand. The call graph is a finite, directed graph in which each node corresponds to one method in the source code. For any pair (A, B) of methods, there exists an edge from A to B if (and only if) method B is called from the implementation of method A.

At any time, Stacksplorer shows the neighborhood of the focus method in the call graph, thus giving the user access to the callers of and methods called from the focus method. This is closely related to the way Herman *et al.* [8] suggest incremental exploration of graphs by placing a window on top of the graph, so that one *logical frame* is shown at a time. Huang *et al.* [9] coined the term *focus node* for the logical frame's central node, which defines which other nodes will belong to the logical frame. In our case, the focus method corresponds to the focus node, and, together with the information from its neighborhood in the call graph, forms the logical frame.

Stacksplorer directly integrates with Xcode, adding two interactive views alongside the code editor (Fig. 1). These three views together display the current logical frame, basically acting as a fisheye view [7] for the call graph. In the central source code editor, the focus method is displayed in the usual way. The side views show the names and classes of the neighboring methods in the call graph. The left view shows methods calling the focus method, the right shows methods called from the focus method.

The items in the side columns are always positioned to minimize the on-screen distance to the related code in the editor. This simplifies grasping the context of the focus method. Since the items in the right column reflect the order they appear in the code, this also provides a rough overview of what the focus method does. For densely written code, e.g., nested method calls, the assignment of items in the columns to code locations can become unclear. To address this, Stacksplorer optionally displays graphical overlays that connect the method call in the source code to the corresponding item in the side column (Fig. 1).

Most importantly, Stacksplorer adds a new 'axis' for navigation through a project's source code; in addition to navigating through a single class by scrolling vertically in the editor, Stacksplorer allows navigating horizontally by clicking on a method in one of the side columns. This shifts the logical frame inside the call graph and makes that method the focus method. For example, navigating to a method that calls the focus method by clicking on it in the left column will cause the contents of all three columns to shift to the right (Fig. 3). The method that was selected moves to the center and opens in the central editor, and the side columns are updated accordingly. The previous focus method becomes an entry in the list of called methods to the right. While this functionality is similar to the *go to definition* and *find all references* commands of most IDEs, it differs in the way that it continually displays information scent and navigation affordances that update dynamically.

Developers often find that existing means of documentation are either hard to maintain or do not convey enough information to fully understand how a given feature of an application is implemented [15]. Comments in the source code, for example, are tied to one location, making it difficult to communicate which paths in the call graph constitute a fea-

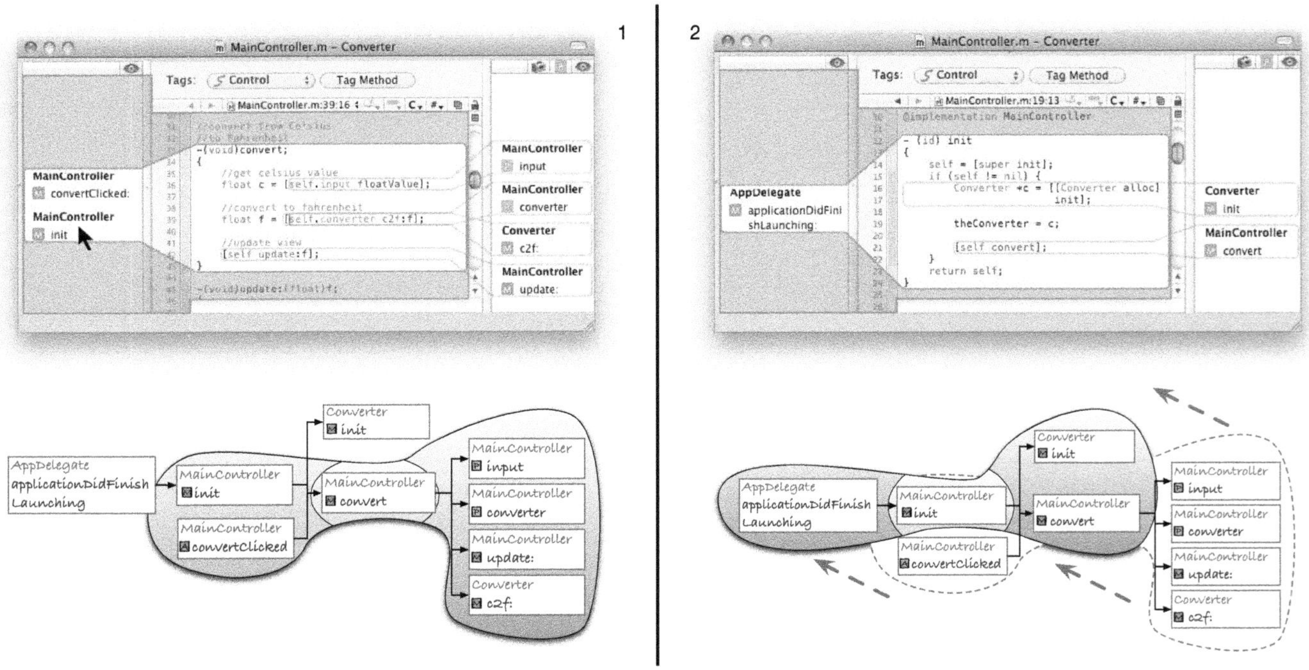

Figure 3: The focus method that is being edited in the IDE (top) corresponds to the focus node in the call graph (bottom). Clicking on a method in the left column of the Stacksplorer UI (1) shifts the logical frame inside the call graph and makes the clicked method the focus method (2).

ture and how the methods involved work together. To this end, Stacksplorer supports assigning *tags* to methods as a lightweight form of documentation; important paths through the call graph can be bookmarked for later reference by tagging their methods. Tags can be named, and they are visualized by colored frame overlays in the source code, such as the red frames in Fig. 1. This way, tags can communicate what purpose a certain method serves, or which features of the application use a specific method. For example, the methods that are involved with screen redraws could be assigned a common tag "redrawing" to clearly delineate this section of the source code.

One of the limitations of call graph navigation (and, therefore, of Stacksplorer) is that we cannot accurately determine all call stacks that may be executed during a real program execution; in other words, it is impossible to correctly and completely determine the call graph. In general, the question if a path is reachable at runtime is undecidable [17]. For example, static analysis is not able to detect if methods are dynamically dispatched to a different object or a different implementation at runtime. For these cases, tracing an execution of the application would be needed. Despite these limitations, we still decided to base Stacksplorer on static analysis: the list of callees is populated with all methods that match the name of the Objective-C selector and whose class or ancestor class matches the class of the receiver. Thus, we also get all possible overrides of a method, which is acceptable in Objective-C with its typically fairly flat inheritance structures. In terms of robustness against syntax errors, we rely on Xcode's parser. This approach yields a result more quickly than runtime traces, and it works even if the source code does not compile because of a bug. While providing live updates to the visualization on every keystroke is possible, we currently limit updates to every save operation for performance reasons.

EVALUATION

We tested the effectiveness of Stacksplorer's call graph visualization and navigation in an experiment with 16 experienced programmers performing code maintenance tasks with and without Stacksplorer support. Our main goals for this study were to better understand how practitioners use Stacksplorer's features when working with unknown code, and to quantitatively compare task performance and success rates. For the latter, we formulated the following hypotheses:

H1 More programmers can successfully solve a time-constrained task that requires browsing and understanding previously unknown source code when using Stacksplorer than when using a default Xcode installation.

H2 Programmers can solve tasks that require browsing and understanding previously unknown source code more quickly when using Stacksplorer than when using a default Xcode installation.

H3 Programmers can identify side effects of changes made to unknown code more quickly when using Stacksplorer than when using a default Xcode installation.

As a code base for the study, we used the open source project BibDesk[3], a bibliography manager for Mac OS X. We selected this project because it is sufficiently complex with

[3]http://bibdesk.sourceforge.net

about 88.000 lines of code in over 400 classes, it is stable, and it is written entirely in Objective-C.

The experiment was conducted on a Mac Pro computer with a 23" screen at a resolution of 1920x1200. Xcode was opened with the test project in a maximized window, and the screen was recorded for the entire session.

Methodology

In the experiment, we compared two conditions: in the *experimental condition* participants could make use of Stacksplorer's features; in the *control condition* Stacksplorer was not available. Participants had to solve two similarly difficult programming tasks, each consisting of two subtasks as explained below. We counterbalanced task order and task to condition assignment.

At the beginning of each user test, we demonstrated Stacksplorer using an unrelated code base from one of our own projects. We explained how to use the interactive visualization of the call graph neighborhood and the tagging feature. To mitigate possible learning effects between the two trials for each participant, we allowed them to then familiarize themselves with the BibDesk source code for 10 minutes.

The participants did not know all tasks beforehand; we always introduced only the task they should work on next. The time to complete each task was limited to 25 minutes for the first subtask and 15 minutes for the second subtask to limit the effects of fatigue. Additionally, participants were allowed to take breaks between the tasks. While solving a task, speed was the priority of the participants but it was made clear that they should arrive at a working solution. To be consistent with [2, 20], participants were allowed to use all of Xcode's code navigation features, except for runtime analysis tools such as the debugger. The participants were, however, allowed to examine the run-time behavior of the BibDesk software using a precompiled version of BibDesk as a reference.

For each task and subtask, we measured the time until the participant considered the task complete, and we checked whether the task was solved correctly. We also encouraged users to think aloud and tell us their motivation for using certain navigation techniques when working on the tasks. An experimenter was supervising each trial and took notes; additionally, the trials were videotaped for further analysis.

After the test, we asked our participants to fill out a questionnaire with the questions of the System Usability Scale (SUS) [3] and six additional questions (see Fig. 5) specifically addressing the usefulness of the extra features introduced by Stacksplorer. Finally, we conducted an open interview with each participant to gain more insights into their behavior.

Participants

Our group of participants consisted of 14 students (6 graduate, 8 undergraduate) and 2 professional software developers. By employing mostly students, we aimed to reduce the impact of different levels of programming expertise on the study, in accordance with [2]. Age ranged from 22 to 34 ($M = 27.7$), and there were no female participants (although this was not intended by design). All participants were familiar with Xcode; their experience with the IDE ranged between 3 months and 6 years ($M = 2$ years), and they reported to do programming work between less than an hour and 40 hours a week ($M = 13.1$ hours). Ten participants were already familiar with the BibDesk application, but none of them had seen the source code before.

Tasks

The tasks should include searching for a specific location in the code and identifying side-effects of a specific change of the code. Therefore, we designed two different task types: (1) identifying where a certain functionality is implemented and change it; (2) identifying what side effects a change of a certain functionality has. Tasks of type (1) were considered solved if the suggested modification by the participant would have achieved the intended effect. This was determined by the experimenter who was familiar with the code. For tasks of type (2), we considered any functional change in the behavior of the application (other than the one requested in the task) that was caused by the modifications applied to the code a side effect. For each type, we defined two separate tasks to allow testing both conditions with every participant.

The first task concerned BibDesk's *Autofile* feature, which automatically sorts PDF documents of publications into dedicated folders and renames them according to a user-definable naming scheme. In the first subtask (1.1), participants were asked to prepend the string "TRIAL" to every generated PDF file name. In the second subtask (1.2), we asked the participants to identify side effects that would occur if the change from the first subtask was implemented in a specific method.

The second task was to modify the behavior of BibDesk when generating BibTeX output. In the first subtask (2.1), participants were asked to prepend the string "TRIAL" to every publication's notes entry. The second subtask (2.2) concerned the search command from BibDesk's AppleScript API. Participants were asked to change the behavior of the search command to also match the search string against a publication's journal name. Furthermore, the participants had to identify what side effects this change had.

Both tasks were similar in complexity, because the subtasks of type 1 required navigating along at least three edges of the call graph to solve them, and the subtasks of type 2 likewise required at least two edges. A task was considered to be completed successfully if both subtasks were solved correctly.

Quantitative Results

Task Success. Only four participants were able to solve both tasks. All tasks except for task 2.1 were solved correctly more often by participants in the experimental condition. However, the difference in success rates was only significant for task 1 (Fisher's test, $p = 0.041$). Hence, the results are not conclusive enough to prove H1.

We assume that the non-significant results for task 2 were caused by two factors: firstly, in task 2.1 the participants could benefit from knowledge in standard APIs more than in task 1.1 because task 2.1 was concerned with document saving, which uses a standardized API. Secondly, task 2.2 was probably the easiest of all tasks; independent of the condition, it was completed successfully most often.

Task Completion Times. Average times are shown in Table 1. Developers solved task 1 in the experimental condition significantly faster than in the control condition ($t(14) = -2.32$, $p = 0.018$, $d = 1.16$, one-tailed). A comparison for task 2 did not yield a statistically significant result ($t(14) = 0.20$, $p = 0.84$, $d = 0.10$, two-tailed). Further analysis revealed that task 2.2, like task 1, was solved significantly faster in the experimental condition ($t(14) = -2.37$, $p = 0.016$, $d = 1.18$, one-tailed). The results for task 2.1 were inconclusive ($t(14) = 1.17$, $p = 0.26$, $d = 0.58$, two-tailed). Apart from subtask 2.1 these results support H2.

We specifically designed subtasks 1.2 and 2.2 to require finding and understanding the side effects that would arise from changes to the code. The comparison for subtask 2.2 clearly supports H3; the analysis of subtask 1.2 also indicated that developers could identify side effects better using Stacksplorer, but the results were not significant ($t(14) = -1.25$, $p = 0.12$, $d = 0.62$, one-tailed).

	experiment		control	
	M	SD	M	SD
Task 1	**20m 43s**	**6m 49s**	**28m 45s**	**7m 4s**
Task 1.1	14m 45s	5m 54s	19m 39s	6m 16s
Task 1.2	5m 58s	4m 5s	9m 5s	5m 49s
Task 2	**22m 55s**	**9m 22s**	**22m 0s**	**8m 34s**
Task 2.1	17m 14s	7m 46s	13m 3s	6m 29s
Task 2.2	5m 42s	2m 13s	8m 58s	3m 12s

Table 1: Average task completion times for the different tasks and subtasks in the experiment and control conditions.

Qualitative Results

We observed that all participants used a similar high level strategy for finding the correct location to implement a change. When searching for a location for a change, participants usually started with an *exploration phase*, in which they searched for an *anchor point*. These anchor points correspond to what Sillito et al. [22] called *focus points*. Ko et al. [11] also observed similar behavior and referred to the exploration phase as *search phase*. Once the users found an anchor point, a *traversal phase* followed, in which they traversed the call graph until they either found the correct location for a change or noticed that they got lost and had to start again with a new exploration phase. During the traversal phase, participants often navigated along an outgoing path in the call graph and came back to the previously viewed method or to the anchor point if they decided to discard the path. This simple model is depicted in Fig. 4.

In tasks 1.1 and 2.1, all users started with some exploration phase, the length of which varied substantially. In task 1.2 and 2.2, the starting point for participants was indicated clearly, so the exploration phase was much shorter and had much less influence on success and completion time for these tasks. During the exploration phases, the participants used different techniques: Most performed a project-wide search for a term probably related to the task. Another popular technique was to find the UI related to the task and to look up which methods were called by the controls in the interface.

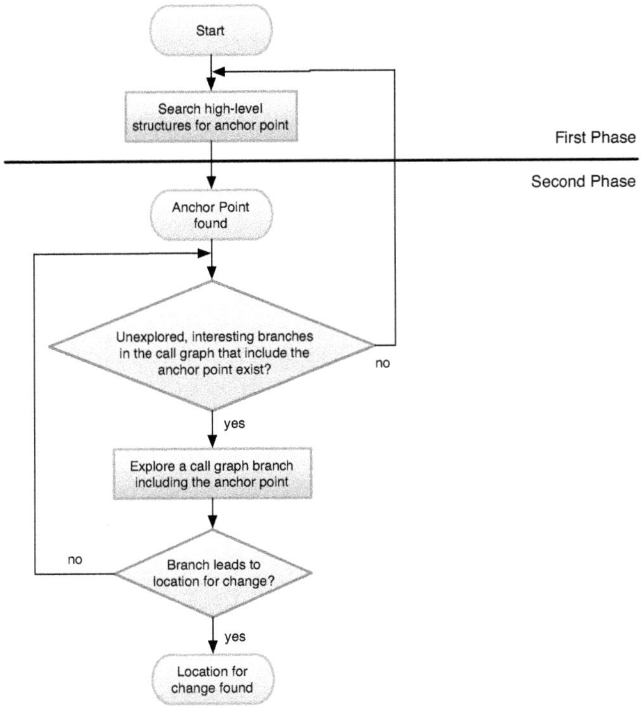

Figure 4: A simple model of programmers' navigation behavior splitting exploration of source code into two phases: developers first search for a place to start their investigation from, then they use the call graph to navigate through the source code.

Stacksplorer is not designed specifically to support the initial exploration phase, as it does not provide a high-level overview of the project and does not facilitate searching or opportunistic browsing [20]. It is much more useful during the traversal phase. Two techniques participants employed to utilize the plug-in could be differentiated clearly: Most participants read a part of the source code and tried to understand (at varying levels of detail) its purpose. When they had identified the relevant section of the source code for the task at hand, they enabled Stacksplorer's overlays to see which methods were called from this section and then navigated there. In contrast, another group of participants read the methods presented by Stacksplorer in the right column as a summary of the method. In the extreme case, these participants did not inspect the source code at all; instead, they only browsed through the called methods and navigated to whatever they found interesting. Once Stacksplorer no longer revealed interesting called methods, the participants read the focus method's source code to decide if they had found the correct location for the requested change. The latter technique is of course much more prone to error, but it can be very fast.

Using Stacksplorer resulted in a significantly increased use of Xcode's forward and back navigation buttons. They work like the forward and back buttons in a web browser to navigate through a history stack of visited locations in the source code. In the preliminary study, these buttons were only used on very rare occasions. Stacksplorer tempted participants to explore a path to see where it brought them and to discard it if they found themselves getting stuck. When a path was discarded, the participants used the back button to navigate back to a previous anchor point and started exploring another path from there. In a refined version of Stacksplorer we now accommodate for this behavior by showing the five most recently visited methods in the side columns with a colored background, the saturation of which is lower the further away the method's position in the history stack is.

All participants highly appreciated Stacksplorer's ability to help identify side effects. To determine the side effects of a change in a method, it is generally required to analyze all paths in the call graph that lead to the changed method. In Xcode, this requires searching for the changed method's name in the project; some other IDEs provide a dedicated tool to reveal callers of a method. Using Stacksplorer for this analysis was faster and more robust against errors in comparison to the project-wide search that otherwise was required in Xcode. Participants often missed Stacksplorer in the second task if they had already used it in the first task ("Can I get the plug-in for that [task 2.2] again?").

We observed that users analyzing side effects of a change tended to only inspect the direct predecessors of the changed method in the call graph. For example, in task 2.2 the changed method is only called once. Side effects exist only because this single caller of the changed method is used in a different context than the one described in the task. When using Stacksplorer, participants navigated back once from the starting point and then found the relevant information in the left side column. In the control condition, users performed a search to find callers of a method, but they often hesitated to explore higher degree neighborhoods in the same way, in some cases causing them to fail the task.

Postsession Questionnaire

The combined score from the SUS questions was 85.4 on average ($SD = 7.4$). According to Bangor *et al.* [1], this score can be considered "excellent". This result is quite promising given that Stacksplorer is still a research prototype with some performance issues and minor bugs.

Nearly all participants strongly agreed that Stacksplorer makes it easier to understand source code compared to Xcode without the plug-in (Fig. 5, Q12). However, quite a few participants still found understanding source code challenging even when using Stacksplorer. This comes as no surprise since a large, feature-rich software project is a complex artifact and hard to understand without prior knowledge.

More than half of the participants strongly agreed that navigation with Stacksplorer is faster than without it. We think that this is primarily due to Stacksplorer's support for navigation to callers of a method. This type of navigation seems to be important for programmers: Stacksplorer improved their overall impression of how quickly they can navigate through source code solely by improving call graph navigation.

More than half of the participants did not feel lost in the source code when using Stacksplorer (Fig. 5, Q16). Compared to Xcode, users found that Stacksplorer supports orientation in the source code considerably better (Fig. 5, Q15).

SUMMARY AND FUTURE WORK

We presented Stacksplorer, a new tool to support source code navigation and comprehension. Stacksplorer visualizes the call graph neighborhood of a method in an application and supports navigating through it. Thus, Stacksplorer exploits a semantic aspect of source code to suggest relevant methods for exploration. Information displayed in Stacksplorer is visually linked to the source code. A prototype of Stacksplorer was implemented as a functional IDE plug-in.

Our user study showed that software maintenance tasks in a large open-source application could be completed significantly faster with Stacksplorer support. Participants reported that they were very satisfied with the plug-in and would like to use it for real world projects.

Two aspects present themselves as promising directions for future work: Firstly, having found that structural relationships in source code are of particular value for developers to better comprehend source code, more of theses relationships besides the call graph could be visualized and made accessible in IDEs. Secondly, we found that in some situations an additional, higher-level overview of the source code than what is provided by Stacksplorer would have been beneficial to get a first idea of the application's structure. This visualization could support transitioning fluently between a Stacksplorer-like view, which shows much source code with some context, and a new kind of visualization, showing less source code but a greater part of the application's structure.

ACKNOWLEDGEMENTS

This work was funded in part by the German B-IT Foundation and by the German Government through its UMIC Excellence Cluster for Ultra-High Speed Mobile Information and Communication at RWTH Aachen University.

REFERENCES

1. A. Bangor, P. Kortum, and J. Miller. An Empirical Evaluation of the System Usability Scale. *Intl. Journal of Human-Computer Interaction*, 24(6):574–594, Aug. 2008.

2. A. Bragdon, R. Zeleznik, S. P. Reiss, S. Karumuri, W. Cheung, J. Kaplan, C. Coleman, F. Adeputra, and J. J. LaViola. Code Bubbles: A Working Set-based Interface for Code Understanding and Maintenance. In *Proc. CHI '10*. ACM, 2010.

3. J. Brooke. *SUS-A quick and dirty usability scale.* Taylor and Francis, London, 1996.

4. B. de Alwis, G. C. Murphy, and M. P. Robillard. A Comparative Study of Three Program Exploration Tools. In *Proc. ICPC '07*, pages 103–112. IEEE, 2007.

5. R. Deline, M. Czerwinski, B. Myers, G. Venolia, S. Drucker, and G. Robertson. Code Thumbnails: Using Spatial Memory to Navigate Source Code. In *Proc. Visual Languages and Human-Centric Computing 2006*. IEEE, 2006.

6. R. DeLine, M. Czerwinski, and G. Robertson. Easing Program Comprehension by Sharing Navigation Data.

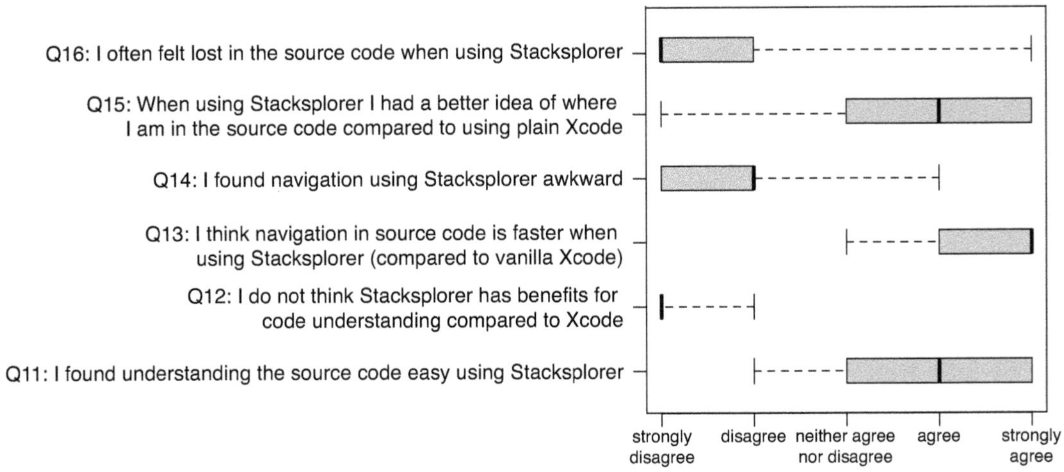

Figure 5: The boxplot diagrams show how the participants of our study responded to the six questions of the post-session questionnaire that did not belong to the SUS.

In *Proc. Visual Languages and Human-Centric Computing 2005*. IEEE, 2005.

7. G. Furnas. Generalized Fisheye Views. In *Proc. CHI '86*. ACM, 1986.
8. I. Herman, G. Melancon, and M. Marshall. Graph Visualization and Navigation in Information Visualization: A Survey. *IEEE Transactions on Visualization and Computer Graphics*, 6(1):24–43, 2000.
9. M. Huang, P. Eades, J. Wang, and P. R. China. Online Animated Graph Drawing Using a Modified Spring Algorithm. *Journal of Visual Languages and Computing*, 9(6), 1998.
10. M. Kersten and G. C. Murphy. Mylar: A Degree-of-Interest Model for IDEs. In *Proc. Aspect-oriented Software Development*, pages 159–168. ACM, 2005.
11. A. Ko, B. Myers, M. Coblenz, and H. Aung. An Exploratory Study of How Developers Seek, Relate, and Collect Relevant Information during Software Maintenance Tasks. *IEEE Transactions on Software Engineering*, 32(12):971–987, 2006.
12. A. J. Ko and B. A. Myers. Debugging Reinvented: Asking and Answering Why and Why Not Questions about Program Behavior. In *Proc. ICSE '08*, pages 301–310. IEEE, 2008.
13. T. D. LaToza and B. A. Myers. Developers Ask Reachability Questions. In *Proc. ICSE '10*, pages 185–194. ACM, 2010.
14. T. D. LaToza and B. A. Myers. Searching Across Paths. In *2nd Intl. Workshop on Search-driven development: Users, Infrastructure, Tools and Evaluation*, 2010.
15. T. D. LaToza, G. Venolia, and R. DeLine. Maintaining Mental Models: A Study of Developer Work Habits. In *Proc. ICSE '06*, pages 492–501. ACM, 2006.
16. J. Lawrance, R. Bellamy, M. Burnett, and K. Rector. Using information scent to model the dynamic foraging behavior of programmers in maintenance tasks. In *Proc. CHI '08*. ACM Press, 2008.
17. H. R. Lewis and C. H. Papadimitriou. *Elements of the Theory of Computation*. Prentice-Hall, 1981.
18. G. C. Murphy, M. Kersten, and L. Findlater. How Are Java Software Developers Using the Eclipse IDE? *IEEE Software*, 23(4):76–83, 2006.
19. R. S. Pressman. *Software Engineering: A Practitioner's Approach*. McGraw-Hill, 7. edition, 2010.
20. M. P. Robillard, W. Coelho, and G. C. Murphy. How Effective Developers Investigate Source Code:An Exploratory Study. *IEEE Transactions on Software Engineering*, 30(12), 2004.
21. B. G. Ryder. Constructing the Call Graph of a Program. *IEEE Transactions on Software Engineering*, 1979.
22. J. Sillito, G. C. Murphy, and K. D. Volder. Asking and Answering Questions during a Programming Change Task. *IEEE Transactions on Software Engineering*, 34(4):434–451, 2008.
23. J. Singer, R. Elves, and M.-A. Storey. NavTracks: Supporting Navigation in Software Maintenance. In *Proc. IEEE Software Maintenance*. IEEE, 2005.
24. D. Čubranić and G. C. Murphy. Hipikat: Recommending Pertinent Software Development Artifacts. In *Proc. ICSE '03*. IEEE, 2003.

Cracking the Cocoa Nut: User Interface Programming at Runtime

James R. Eagan[1,2]
eaganj@lri.fr

Michel Beaudouin-Lafon[1,2]
mbl@lri.fr

Wendy E. Mackay[2,1]
mackay@lri.fr

[1]LRI (Univ. Paris-Sud & CNRS); [2]INRIA
91405 Orsay Cedex, France

ABSTRACT

This article introduces *runtime toolkit overloading*, a novel approach to help third-party developers modify the interaction and behavior of existing software applications without access to their underlying source code. We describe the abstractions provided by this approach as well as the mechanisms for implementing them in existing environments. We describe Scotty, a prototype implementation for Mac OS X Cocoa that enables developers to modify existing applications at runtime, and we demonstrate a collection of interaction and functional transformations on existing off-the-shelf applications. We show how Scotty helps a developer make sense of unfamiliar software, even without access to its source code. We further discuss what features of future environments would facilitate this kind of runtime software development.

Keywords: user interfaces, meta-toolkits, runtime software development, runtime toolkit overloading

ACM Classification: H.5.m Information interfaces and presentation (HCI): Misc.

General terms: Human Factors

INTRODUCTION

Software designers create software with a particular model in mind of how it will be used. Even in the most thoughtfully designed systems, however, these assumptions may break in the face of users' own constraints and demands. Assumptions made by a designer, based on a deep understanding of hardware, software, and human constraints, may change. As these constraints evolve, so too must the software, often in ways not easily reconcilable with its original design.

Even when these constraints do not evolve, users frequently push their software in ways not anticipated by its designers [20]. A user's interaction is strongly situated in a particular context, with particular needs that may arise and disappear spontaneously and in unforeseeable ways [22], even with the best design practices. As such, there is a gap between the designers' conception of how software will be used and its actual use. These gulfs are likely to continue to grow as software is used in an increasingly rich, ubiquitous, and distributed environment.

Different approaches have been taken to bridge these gulfs by making software more flexible, including giving users more control over their software's configuration [16], runtime behaviors [18, 8] and interfaces [21, 9], or by giving programmers more control over their language [15]. These approaches all build on the notion that, although the designer may have a good understanding of how to create software that supports the most common use cases, users will push their software in unintended ways.

Our goal is to bridge the gap between the designed use and actual needs of software by enabling runtime software development. Runtime software developers are third-party developers who can modify the behavior and/or interface of software that nearly satisfies the user's needs. Runtime development is concerned with taking the existing behavior of an application and changing it in some way, without requiring access to the application source code.

In this paper, we show how to facilitate this kind of runtime software development in existing applications, we show how it can facilitate new interactions, and we argue for changes to better support it. In particular:

- We present *runtime toolkit overloading*, a novel approach that provides high-level abstractions to make the redefinition of program behaviors a first-class operation, without access to the the application's source code;
- We describe how to implement this approach using a set of deep hooks into existing toolkits and runtime systems, taking advantage of modern programming languages;
- We present *Scotty*, an implementation of runtime toolkit overloading in the Mac OS X Cocoa environment, and illustrate its use to modify a set of off-the-shelf applications;
- We provide recommendations to improve support for runtime development in future user interface toolkits.

RELATED WORK

Some applications are designed with modification as an explicit design concern and thus offer some kind of plugin, scripting, or extension mechanism. Most applications, however, are not designed for such extensibility. For these kinds of applications, other methods are necessary. In this section, we examine different approaches to black-box modification of programs (Figure 1). These approaches are black-box in the sense that they do not assume that the runtime developer has any access to the program source code or to its internal structures.

Scripting, Plugins, and Extensions

Many applications support some degree of extensibility by users through scripting interfaces and/or plugin and extension mechanisms. Almost all Mac OS applications, for example, offer a scripting interface (through AppleScript) that gives control over standard functionality such as launching, quitting, and moving windows [3]. Many web browsers, including Safari, Firefox, and Chrome, offer plugin and extension interfaces, allowing one to write modifications to the way the browser loads and displays web pages. Scripting and plugin interfaces can provide varying degrees of control, depending on what internal structures of the application they expose and what, if any, sandboxing they perform to insulate the plugin code from the rest of the application. For example, the Firefox browser is open enough to enable the Chickenfoot [7] plugin to provide a domain-specific scripting language with deep access to web pages. Similarly, Google's Chrome Frame[1] uses Internet Explorer's plugin system to replace the rendering engine with that of the Chrome browser.

These interfaces can potentially offer a high degree of power, but only if the application developer has included explicit support for them. Moreover, for complex changes to the program behavior, it is typically necessary to create *ad hoc* modifications on a per-application basis. Thus, they may be of limited utility for defining new behaviors for all applications. In order to support runtime software development, we want a general mechanism to write plugins for any application, regardless of whether it was designed with such support in mind.

Changing Program Behavior

When the application does not provide explicit support for runtime modifications, other approaches are necessary. The most basic of these approaches is to operate on the surface representation of a window. The surface representation is the part of the application directly exposed to the user, such as the collection of pixels on the screen, but it could also include auditory, haptic, or other modalities.

Surface Representations A typical example of this approach is VNC [19], which teleports the pixels of an entire desktop from one machine to another, allowing the user to remotely use the entire desktop. While such remote-use capabilities have long been embedded in the design of some windowing systems (*e. g.* X Windows), this approach grafts runtime capabilities into the desktop environment, allowing arbitrary applications to be used remotely. WinCuts [23] uses a similar approach to allow the user to create proxy windows based on just a relevant region of a window. Both of these approaches provide a user with the means to change the display of existing applications at runtime. They rely on the fact that the modification environment does not need to know about the deeper semantics of the application. It suffices to simply transport or transform the display and let the user make sense of it. Because no semantic information is available, however, the transformations are therefore limited.

[1]www.google.com/chromeframe, 20 April 2011.

	WinCuts	Façade	Prefab	SubArctic	Scotty
Access to Surface Rep	√	√	√	√	√
Can change surface rep.		√	√	√	√
Access to widgets		√	√	√	√
Can change widgets		(via I/O redirection)	(via I/O redirection)	√	√
Access to program model				(only parts that touch toolkit)	√
Can change program model				(only parts that touch toolkit)	√
Works with multiple platforms	√		√		
Modifications are typically "safe/ robust"	√	√	√		

Figure 1: Summary of the capabilities and characteristics of different approaches to runtime modification.

Augmented Surface Representations It is possible, though, to augment the surface representation with supplemental semantic information. Façade [21], for example, integrates with the X Windows system to gather information about the widget hierarchy. With this additional information, Façade is able to operate at a finer granularity than WinCuts and can even change the behavior of individual widgets.

Prefab [9, 10] takes a different approach to augmenting its understanding of the surface representation of widgets: it uses a vision-based system to recognize widgets using their visual appearance and to create visual stand-ins for them. This has the advantage of being able to operate in a multi-platform environment, simultaneously operating on, *e. g.*, native Windows widgets, Mac OS and X Windows widgets via a VNC connection, and Flash widgets embedded in a web page. Nonetheless, it can only handle widgets it has been trained to recognize.

All of these approaches face the same limitation: Even with supplemental information about, *e. g.*, the widget hierarchy, widgets are still opaque objects. The system may know, for example, that a collection of pixels on the screen corresponds to a pull-down menu with n items, but it cannot know that widget's relation to other program objects beyond what can be inferred from its surface representation.

Toolkit Integration Integrating with the underlying toolkit can provide deeper access to interactive software. Because this approach works at the toolkit level, it has access to program objects that interact with the toolkit interfaces. Modifying the toolkit can thus allow all applications built using that toolkit to use those changes. However, those changes will only apply to applications that were built using that toolkit. Thus, changes made to Java's Swing will not apply to Mac OS or web applications and *vice versa*.

SubArctic [11] uses this approach to add output modification hooks to Java's AWT. It uses a combination of subclassing and wrapping to make the graphics capabilities of SubArctic applications extensible. With these hooks, developers can write new modules that transform the way objects are drawn. The design of the toolkit allows these new modules to be added without explicit support by the application developer.

JAMM [5] uses a clever approach that alters Java's serialization mechanism to swap out certain classes in the serialization stream with collaboration-aware subclasses. This approach makes it possible to completely or partially replace the behavior of existing classes as long as they support serialization and have not previously been serialized. It does not, however, support the replacement of non-serializable classes or the dynamic modification of classes after serialization, since the remote end would have already received a previous version of the object's class name.

In a different area, Chromium [14] replaces the OpenGL backend of an application to automatically distribute rendering to a cluster of graphics cards and displays without recompilation. Mercator [12] uses a similar approach to infer semantic information about user interfaces in order to create auditory interfaces for blind users. The first part of this approach, like Façade, involves monitoring the communications between the application and the window server. The second part involves modifying the low-level toolkit libraries so that they communicate additional accessibility-related semantic information. While this does not require modifying the source code, it does require relinking the application.

If a toolkit is available as a shared library, however, it may be possible to avoid relinking by creating a binary-compatible stand-in for that library. This approach has been used by the WINE project[2] to create a reverse-engineered implementation of the Windows APIs for Linux. Besacier and Vernier [6] have also combined this technique with the wrapping technique used by SubArctic to create dynamic library stand-ins that partially override the behavior of a toolkit, such as replacing check boxes with crossing-enabled [1] variants.

The World Wide Web Web-based applications are built upon a combination of the HTML document object model (DOM), Javascript, and the HTTP client-server protocol. The open nature of this model lends itself to runtime modifications of web pages, in particular through browser extensions such as Greasemonkey.[3] However, any computation performed on the server remains opaque. Additionally, many programmers have taken to obfuscating their Javascript code, either to prevent human comprehension or to support code compression.

RUNTIME TOOLKIT OVERLOADING

In order to create a general solution for runtime software development, we need the power of an unrestricted plugin architecture, the generality of toolkit integration, and the ability of surface representation approaches to operate without access to a program's source code. To accomplish this, we propose a technique called *runtime toolkit overloading* that relies on dynamically loading code into an existing application. Since we do not want to require a runtime developer to reverse engineer the internal structure of every program, we provide a set of high-level abstractions that runtime developers can use to create a rich variety of modifications to an application's existing behavior. Together with the existing underlying toolkit, these abstractions form an extensible toolkit that allows a runtime developer to build on the interface and functionality already present in the application.

[2] www.winehq.org, 20 April 2011.
[3] www.greasespot.net. 20 April 2011.

Hook	Description	Cocoa Method Overridden
windowCreated	Gives access to window after it has been created but *before* it appears on screen.	NSWindow -init..:
windowDidAppear	Called *after* window appears on screen.	(built-in)
windowIsUpdating	Gives access to previous window contents, just *before* redraw.	NSWindow -flushWindow
windowDidUpdate	Called *during* the rendering loop, just *after* actual drawing occurs.	NSWindow -flushWindow
windowWillHide	Gives access to window just *before* it is removed from the screen.	NSWindow -orderOut:
windowDidHide	Called with the ID of a window after it has been removed from the screen.	(built-in)

Figure 2: Window hooks available in our Scotty demonstrator. Widget hooks are similar.

Runtime toolkit overloading uses a model in which developers create *plugins* that integrate into existing applications, modifying their interface and/or behavior in arbitrary ways. These plugins use the abstractions described below to modify program behavior without having to inspect the underlying program implementation unless necessary. They are different from the plugin interfaces in many applications in that they have full, unrestricted access to the application's program space. We now describe the six abstractions that we have found useful to support runtime development.

Window and Widget Hooks In order to transform how windows and widgets appear on the screen, we need to be able to intercept and modify windows *before* they appear on the screen, such as by adding or removing widgets, changing their layout, or changing attributes such as having a title bar or being minimizable. We have defined a set of window hooks (Figure 2) that go beyond standard notifications to tap into the window creation and drawing systems. Unlike SubArctic [11], which uses subclasses to wrap the native drawing system, our approach incorporates its hooks directly into the native drawing system. In other words, rather than deriving an extensible toolkit, we transform a non-extensible toolkit into an extensible one.

Window notifications are a standard part of most UI toolkits that allow a programmer to react to window creation, update, and dismissal. These notifications, however, are not designed with program modification in mind and do not provide the necessary hooks. For example, window creation notifications are typically posted after a window has been exposed to the screen. Any changes made to that window, then, will appear only after the window has already been drawn once, creating an undesirable flashing effect. By contrast, our window hooks are also called *before* the window appears or disappears from the screen (Figure 2).

Similarly, window update notifications are often posted *after* a window has already been updated. These events thus occur after any window redrawing operations have been completed, precluding operations that need to be performed within an active drawing state such as those that alter the graphics context. Additionally, if these notifications are posted after redrawing has already been completed, any modification that depends on the previous state of the window will need to cache the previous contents of the window. With our hooks, however, a plugin can query and even alter the window graphics state just before the repaint is posted to the screen.

In the Web environment, applications do not have access to low-level drawing of elements. Instead, the content of the DOM tree, together with the style sheet, define how elements are drawn. Window update events therefore do not make sense. However standard DOM events track the changes to the DOM structure and therefore can be used to implement the widget appearance and disappearance hooks.

Event Funnels Many toolkits, including Java Swing, Mac OS Cocoa, and the DOM, use an event model in which interaction events are delivered through an application, window, and widget hierarchy to a callback appropriate to the event. In Cocoa, for example, a mouse press event on a widget is dispatched to its `-mouseDown:` method[4] and a mouse release event to its `-mouseUp:` method. We want to be able to intercept *all* events sent to a widget, window, or application, regardless of event type. In Cocoa and Swing, there is a single method to capture all events sent to an application, but not for all events sent to a particular window or widget.

An event funnel is a *metaclass* that intercepts any standard event (*e. g.* mouse, keyboard, tablet, cursor) and dispatches it to a single general-purpose event handler. This handler provides a way to selectively intercept all events sent to an object while maintaining the context of the object, eliminating the need for plugin developers to re-write each callback by hand and decreasing the likelihood that they might accidentally omit a stray event (*e. g.*, a tablet event). Furthermore, they relieve the programmer from having to replicate the complex event dispatch chain when redirecting events.

Glass Sheets Glass sheets are transparent layers drawn on top of whatever the software has already drawn. These sheets can be affixed to a given widget, a window, or the screen as a whole. When attached to a widget or window, the sheet will automatically reposition and resize itself as expected with its widget or window. Transparent overlays are a standard feature of the Java Swing toolkit but are not present in other common toolkits such as Mac OS Cocoa or the DOM.

Glass sheets allow the developer to create a drawing surface that is tied to a widget but independent of the widget's drawing methods. Thus, a developer can create, *e. g.*, an overlay above a video player where the overlay only redraws when it needs to change. (If the overlay does need to synchronize with drawing of the underlying view, it can use the aforementioned window hooks.) Additionally, a glass sheet that is attached to the screen instead of a particular window or widget can be used for displaying content that is independent of any widget or window's position on the screen.

```
1 @scotty.replaceMethod(NSWindow.flushWindow)
2 def scottyFlushWindow(self):
3     try:
4         # ... trigger window pre-draw hooks here ...
5     finally:
6         # This next line invokes the original flushWindow code
7         self.scottyFlushWindow()
```

Figure 3: Replacing the implementation of `NSWindow`'s `-flushWindow` method. The decorator on line 1 adds a new method, `scottyFlushWindow`, to the `NSWindow` class's method table, containing the code in lines 2–7. It then swaps the two implementations, such that when `scottyFlushWindow` is later called (line 7), it invokes the original Cocoa implementation.

Dynamic Code Support Runtime software development fundamentally relies on being able to dynamically load code into the program space of an existing program and on being able to change the implementation of its objects. First, we automate this code loading process using a plugin model. As described in the next section, a programmer simply writes a plugin. Loading it is handled automatically by our toolkit.

Second, we need to be able to override and overload method implementations in existing classes. Even in languages such as Objective-C that provide explicit support for doing so, this support may be cumbersome to use. We provide explicit support to simplify this process. The example in Figure 3 is used to implement some of the window hooks described earlier. Beyond Objective-C, we have implemented proof-of-concept versions of such method-swapping (also called method swizzling) that work on public methods in Java and on their equivalent in Javascript.

Object Proxies When adapting existing user interfaces it is common to need to modify a single instance object. For example, one might wish to change what happens when the user hovers over one particular button but not others. Object proxies provide a way of performing such an operation.

An object proxy is a metaclass that allows a developer to override, overload, or add new methods to a particular instance object. It uses an existing instance object to dynamically create a subclass of that instance's class. Any methods in the resulting proxy class invoke their equivalent in the proxied object, yielding its result if any. In this way, a developer can effectively replace a method's implementation at the object level rather than the class level. Object proxies thus permit the runtime wrapping of existing program objects.

While object proxies rely on the capabilities of the underlying object model and are used, for example, in some distributed environments, we use them to transform behavior

[4]Objective-C purists who object to our use of the term "method" should read "message handler" in its place.

rather than to merely distribute it. To the best of our knowledge their use in the context of user interface toolkits is novel.

Code Inspection For some modifications, such as the Scribbler example below, it may be sufficient to be familiar with the programming toolkit used (*e. g.* Cocoa on Mac OS X, Swing for Java, jQuery or other Javascipt frameworks for Web applications) and the toolkit's inherent design patterns. For deeper modifications, however, a strong understanding of the toolkit is not sufficient. A third-party programmer must be able to discover certain aspects of the organization of the underlying code. For example, to modify the behavior of a particular button, it is necessary to know what method is invoked when it is clicked. While DOM inspection tools exist in some browsers, *e. g.* Safari and Firefox, to help debug web applications, they are not found in traditional toolkits.

To aid this discovery process, we provide several run-time inspection tools: a *hierarchy browser* to explore the application's window and widget hierarchy (Figure 7); an *object inspector* to list the class and methods of an arbitrary object; a *widget picker* that maps a click in the interface to the code object backing the clicked widget; and an *interactive interpreter* (Python) that runs inside the program, allowing interactive probing and inspection of the application, much in the same way as the original Smalltalk environment supported code inspection [13].

Together, these tools help decrease the complexity of making sense of an existing application. To the extent possible, our goal is to reduce the task of writing a third-party modification to that of writing a small program in the underlying programming environment.

Summary

The six abstractions described above can be grouped into two classes: those that let third-party developers create modifications to existing programs without deep understanding of their internal structures, and those that help them to make sense of and deeply integrate with the underlying implementation of the program. Event funnels, window hooks, and glass sheets fall into the former category, permitting developers to "bolt on" new behaviors. Dynamic code support, object proxies, and code inspection tools fall into the latter category, helping developers to figure out what parts of an existing program need to be modified and providing ways to do so in minimally-invasive ways.

THE SCOTTY DEMONSTRATOR

Scotty[5] is our reference implementation of runtime toolkit overloading. Its goal is to demonstrate the viability and utility of this approach in creating deep modifications to software applications *without access to their source code*. Scotty adds a plugin architecture to existing, unmodified Cocoa applications on Mac OS X. Runtime developers can use this toolkit to write plugins that augment, enhance, or otherwise modify the application at runtime. End users can then use these plugins to transform their interaction with the original application.

[5]Scotty is named after the miracle-working engineer on Star Trek and is available from `insitu.lri.fr/Projects/Scotty`.

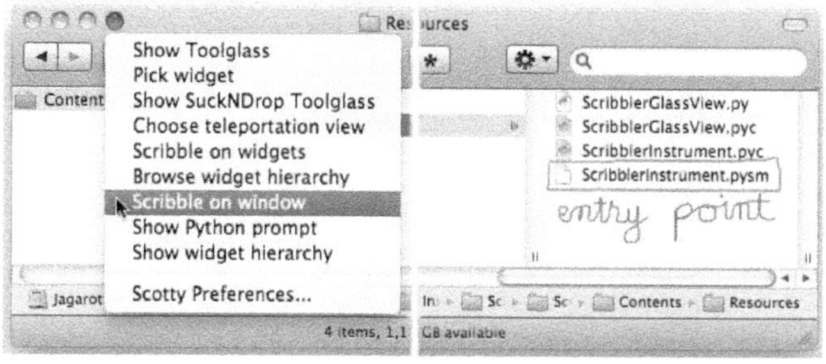

Figure 4: The Scribbler plugin running in the Mac OS Finder. The user activates the Scribbler instrument (left), and uses it to draw an annotation (right).

When a Cocoa application launches, Scotty bootstraps itself into the existing application environment. We describe how this bootstrap works in more detail in the Implementation section below. The first step of this bootstrap process is to confirm with the user that she wishes to activate Scotty, along with an option to remember that choice for the specified application. If the user chooses to activate Scotty, the available plugins will be looked up in the user's `Library` folder.

Scotty plugins are based on a model of instrumental interaction [4], where plugins define interactive instruments that augment the capabilities of the underlying application. A predefined plugin adds the Scotty button (the fourth button from the left in the titlebar in Figure 4) to the application windows. Clicking this button activates the current instrument, while pressing and holding it shows the Scotty menu, which lists the available instruments.

In the remainder of this section, we present a selection of plugins created using Scotty. We created these plugins out of real-world needs that have arisen in our own use, and also to show a breadth of the capabilities of these abstractions.

Creating a Plugin: Scribbler Plugins are simply folders that contain a description of the plugin, the plugin code, and any plugin resources. To give an idea of what it is like to create such a plugin, we describe how to create a simple *Scribbler* plugin that allows the user to draw annotations on a window. These annotations will be attached to the window, so that they move as the window moves. First, we create a folder, `Scribbler.instrument`, containing an `Info.plist` file. This file uses an XML structure to describe meta-data about the plugin, such as its name, associated code files, *etc.*

When a plugin loads, Scotty loads the code specified in the `Info.plist`. It then looks for any `Instrument` subclasses defined in the loaded code. For each new instrument (a plugin may define many), it invokes the `registerInstrument` class method, which, among other things, registers the instrument with the Scotty menu.

To create a Scribbler instrument, then, involves creating a Python file that defines an `Instrument` subclass, such as shown in Figure 5. When the user selects the instrument from the pulldown menu (Figure 4, left), Scotty queries the instrument to see if it needs a glass window (line 9). If it does, then it automatically creates one or reuses an exist-

```
1  class ScribblerInstrument(Instrument):
2      @classmethod
3      def registerInstrument(cls, instrumentID):
4          # ... register for notifications if needed ...
5          super(ScribblerInstrument, cls).registerInstrument(...)
6      def __init__(self):
7          # ... setup scribbler data ...
8          self.stateMachine = self
9      def wantsGlassWindow(self):
10         return True
11     def newGlassViewForGlassWindow(self, glassWindow):
12         parent = glassWindow.parent()
13         view = ScribblerGlassView(parent.frame(), self)
14         return view
```

Figure 5: Scribbler instrument. The class method `registerInstrument` (lines 2–5) is called when the instrument plugin is first loaded to, *e. g.*, register for window creation notifications. In the constructor, the instrument registers itself as a state machine (line 8). This state machine (not shown) describes how the instrument translates input events into drawing on its glass view. Line 9 registers that the instrument will draw to a glass window, which will automatically be created. Line 14 returns a view (not shown) that will be added to that window to handle all drawing.

ing one. It then asks the instrument for a view to add to the glass window (lines 11–14). This view is responsible for any drawing that will be overlaid. Glass windows are themselves event funnels, redirecting all input events sent to the glass window to the associated instrument's state machine (set on line 8). The state machine describes which events are intercepted and how to handle each event. For brevity, we do not show the state machine itself. It describes a simple click-and-drag interaction to draw arbitrary shapes and remembers these shapes to redraw them when the window refreshes its content. The description of state machines uses a technique inspired by the Swing States library for Java [2].

Teleporting Windows to a High-Resolution Wall Display
When the user activates the window teleportation instrument, clicking on the Scotty button toggles a window's teleportation state (Figure 6). When a teleported window repaints, it must send a raster or vector representation of its content to a remote host, depending on which mode is active. Sending a raster representation is easily achieved by accessing the backing of the window. But in order to take advantage of the size and resolution of a wall display, we need a vector representation of the teleported window.

A vector representation describes a window's objects such as fonts, lines, primitive shapes, and more complex bezier paths in a resolution-independent way. SubArctic's graphics object wrapping approach works well in Java, where all drawing goes through an instance of a `Graphics` object that defines how each graphical object is drawn to the screen. On Mac OS X, however, there are several different kinds of drawing contexts: high-level Cocoa drawing contexts that use an object-oriented API, low-level Carbon contexts that use a C API, and OpenGL contexts. Because toolkit overloading operates on the object-oriented runtime layer, it cannot overload the lower-level C drawing operations; it only has access to the Cocoa-based drawing contexts. As such, we cannot easily

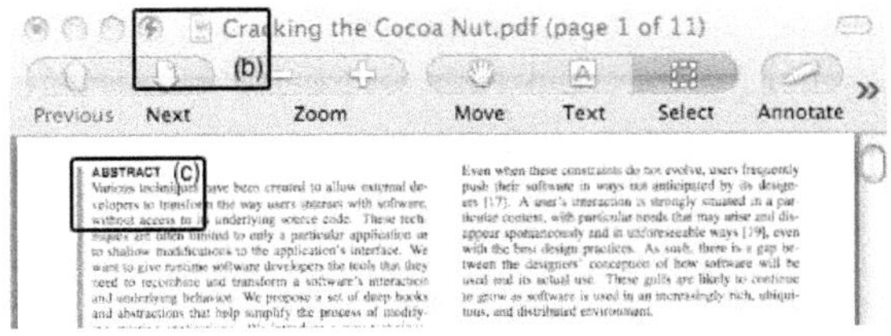

(a) Teleporting Preview, the Mac OS PDF viewer

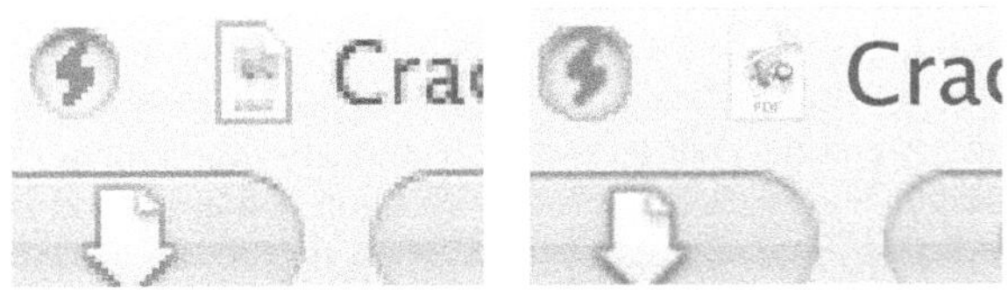

(b) Close-up of the title bar in raster and vector mode

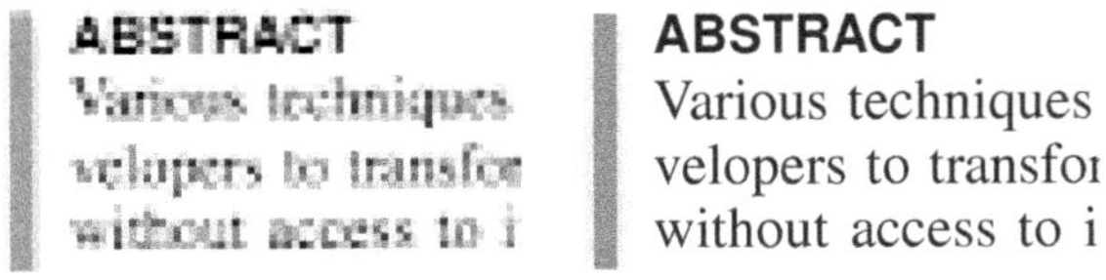

(c) Close-up of some text in raster and vector mode

Figure 6: (a) Teleporting the Preview PDF viewer. Enlarged detail regions are typeset directly from their window backings. (b) Bitmap data is scaled up as chunky pixels, but the icon remains crisp because it is backed by a higher-resolution image. (b) Rasterized text that would otherwise be difficult to read remains clear.

create a wrapped version of the drawing contexts that saves the vector data of objects drawn to the screen. Instead, we need another approach.

Fortunately, Cocoa includes printing hooks that access the lower-level vector representation of the contents of a window suitable for printing.[6] A programmer can thus use Scotty's window repaint notification to trigger the appropriate calls to this printing system, yielding a PDF representation of the window that can then be sent to a remote client (Figure 6).

This example illustrates two of the challenges involved in runtime software development. First, the programmer must be able to make sense of an existing program or, in this case, toolkit. For many kinds of modifications, as in this case, it is sufficient to know the toolkit used to build the application.

Second, access to the underlying program objects may sometimes be insufficient: Pragmatic choices made at design time or during the evolution of the software may restrict the operations that can be readily performed. As a result, it is sometimes easier to operate at a lower level of abstraction. For example, to transmit only the raster representations of windows or even widgets, surface representation-based approaches may be more appropriate. Indeed, when teleporting raster representations, Scotty uses a similar approach by accessing the window backings. When deeper access to the underlying program components is necessary, however, those methods fall short, and higher-level access is required.

[6]In practice, the printing system is much slower than drawing to the screen, but we have still been able to maintain interactive local frame rates on a 5-year-old 2 GHz Intel Core Duo laptop.

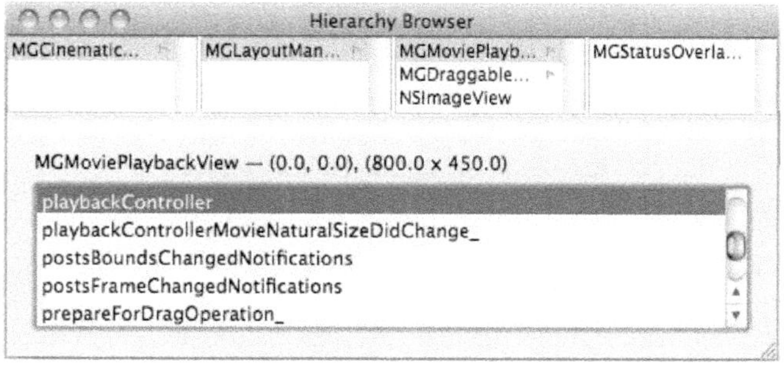

Figure 7: The hierarchy browser revealing the structure of the QuickTime Player window on the top and the methods available to the selected view below. Selected views in the browser are highlighted in the running application (not shown).

Adding Subtitles to DRM-encumbered Movies We want to integrate external subtitles into the standard Mac OS Quicktime Player, which is capable of playing the DRM-locked videos purchased from the iTunes Store. In order to properly handle the subtitles, the text must be properly laid out on the screen, even if the user resizes the window. The subtitles must also stay synchronized with the video, even if the user skips around in the video.

A solution to this problem must solve two challenges: to display subtitles on top of Quicktime Player's video playback view, and to keep them synchronized with the video playback as the user plays, pauses, and scrubs through the video. A programmer will thus not only have to figure out how to solve the tasks of his problem domain, *i. e.*, fetching the subtitles, but also how to integrate with an unfamiliar codebase.

The first part of this problem is easy to solve by attaching a glass window to the video playback widget. Glass windows automatically register for resize notifications on their parent. By tracking these notifications, the glass window will automatically resize with the parent, keeping its contents (in this case, the subtitles) in a consistent location on the screen, even as the user resizes the window or enters and exits fullscreen mode. The programmer need only determine to which widget to attach the glass window, in this case using the widget hierarchy browser (Figure 7).

The second challenge is in keeping the subtitles synchronized with the video playback. Using the hierarchy browser, the developer identifies the method of the playback view (`MGMoviePlaybackView`) that gives access to the video controller object (`MGMoviePlaybackController`). With access to the underlying video controller, the developer can directly handle changes to the video playback properties, regardless of whether the user presses a button on the screen, uses a keyboard shortcut, or a remote control to play, pause, or skip around in the video. The key is that instead of reacting to input events, we interact with their associated logical operations at the controller level, *e. g.* play or skip.

Adding New Toolbar Commands Most video players offer the ability to make playback windows float on top, with the notable exception of the Quicktime Player in recent versions of Mac OS. For this and other applications, it would be useful to be able to add a new window button that toggles this floating property. More generally, we want to be able to dynamically create new buttons for windows and toolbars and even to redefine the behaviors of existing buttons.

Scotty integrates an interactive Python interpreter into existing Cocoa applications. Using this interpreter, the runtime developer can interactively enter code, define new classes and even add or replace methods on existing classes. She can interactively develop and test a new feature, such as making a window float above others using an `NSWindow`'s `-setLevel:` method, a standard method in the Cocoa API, but one that few applications make available in their interface. Once refined, she can add a new window button for that function. She can first test the button by writing the code that creates it interactively in the code window, and then integrate it into the plugin code. Once part of the plugin, that button will be added to all new windows with title bars via a window creation hook. In some sense, this is akin to creating Buttons [17], but within the application.

In addition to adding new buttons to a window, we can also redefine button actions. For example, when sending a message in Apple's Mail program, we would like to inspect the contents of the message to verify that the user has not forgotten to attach a referenced document. We do not want to merely intercept pressing the Send button, but also its equivalent interactions such as a menu item or keyboard shortcut.

Cocoa uses a target-action pattern for callbacks. In a well-written program, the action associated with a button is written in a generic action handler that is shared across each of these different triggers. The runtime developer therefore first needs to find the callback invoked when the button is pressed. She then needs to perform her domain-specific modification to access the email body and attachments.

To find the callback associated with the send button, she could use the hierarchy browser to find the button. Alternatively, she could activate the widget picker instrument, which maps a click to a widget, giving access to its target and action. Thus, the programmer can simply click on the Send button using the widget picker instrument to reveal that she needs to modify the `-send:` method of the `MailDocumentEditor` class. Further exploration of the methods listed in this class reveals how to access the message body and attachments in the associated message. Using the interactive interpreter, the programmer can confirm that these methods do indeed yield the anticipated results. After refining her code, she then saves the modifications so that they will be applied in subsequent program invocations.

SCOTTY IMPLEMENTATION

Runtime toolkit overloading relies on two primary elements: the ability to dynamically replace method implementations at the object-oriented dispatch level and a well-defined object-oriented toolkit built on that object system. Object-oriented programming languages such as Python, Java, Smalltalk, Objective-C, Javascript, and even C++[7] all use dynamic dispatch in method invocation. This dynamic dispatch is governed by

[7] when the `virtual` keyword is used

a small runtime component that maps the name of a method to the code that implements it, usually based on the type of the object invoked. It is this runtime component that ensures that the code `widget.trigger(sender)` will invoke the appropriate `trigger` code regardless of whether the widget is a button, a menu item, or a text field. By dynamically redefining these mappings, we can change the behavior of a class.

We implemented Scotty on Mac OS X using Cocoa, which implies the use of Objective-C. One feature of this language is that it provides access to this runtime component in the language. In other languages, the difficulty of this task depends on how well-defined the runtime component is, whether it is standardized across compilers, and whether the language provides hooks to access it. We have successfully implemented method swizzling in both Java (for Swing) and in Javascript (for web applications). In Java we use the introspection API to change the implementation of any public method. In Javascript, we use the delegation model to achieve the same effect.

Scotty is implemented in Python using the Python/Objective-C bridge, PyObjC[8]. Although one is interpreted and the other is compiled, Python and Objective-C have a very compatible runtime object system. PyObjC provides a two-way dynamic bridge, allowing classes in either language to subclass those defined in the other. As such, we can take advantage of Python's introspective capabilities to interact with the Objective-C environment.

Bootstrapping

In order to use our runtime modifications in existing programs, we need a way to be able to *dynamically* modify the object-oriented method and class tables. We need to be able to run our modifications in the same program space as an arbitrary Cocoa application. We use an old feature of the Cocoa runtime, called Input Managers, that enables applications to change the way that Cocoa handles user input. Through this mechanism, another process can gain access to the underlying Objective-C runtime of the host application.[9]

A similar result can be achieved in other environments. One solution is to take advantage of the dynamic loading of shared libraries, an approach used by Besacier and Vernier in the Windows environment [6]. In the web environment, Greasemonkey, among others, uses the extension capabilities of modern browsers such as Firefox and Safari to inject code into any loaded page. We have successfully used a modified class loader in Java and browser extensions in Javascript to demonstrate that bootstrapping works for both Swing applications and web applications.

Once loaded inside of the program space, Scotty first creates a `ScottyController`, a singleton manager that governs the loading of Scotty plugins, preferences, *etc.* This manager then grafts itself into the Cocoa environment, overloading the implementations for `NSWindow`'s `-flushWindow` method (Figure 3) and the windows' initializers (not shown). These methods provide access to Cocoa's window creation and rendering operations. It also taps into the event dispatch system to intercept UI events sent to the application but not associated with a particular window, such as mouse motion events over the desktop when the application is active.

Obviously, replacing methods of an existing application is dangerous. The replacement method will be called in place of the original one, so it must not break any of the implicit or explicit assumptions made by the application designers. It is, therefore, a brittle operation that requires care and defensive coding practices. To reduce the risk of breaking applications, we minimize the number of methods that are replaced and we provide developers with higher-level abstractions and wrappers that are safer than directly replacing methods.

DISCUSSION

The examples we have developed with Scotty illustrate how runtime toolkit overloading can help a runtime developer to alter the behavior and interface of existing applications, building on the interface and functionality that are already present in the application. The Scribbler example shows how to add a new capability without deep understanding of the toolkit. The teleportation example shows how to make deeper modifications on the toolkit level. In both cases, the user need only be familiar with the standard toolkit API and the Scotty abstractions. Sometimes, however, deeper integration with a particular application is necessary, as shown in the *ad hoc* modifications to Quicktime Player and Mail.

In both the Quicktime and Mail examples, the developer must figure out what parts of code to interact with without having a published API to help. In both cases, the fact that the user interface provides a human-interpretable interface to the underlying program objects gives the programmer a tractable starting point. Using either the window hierarchy browser or the widget picker, she can get a handle on the program object associated with an arbitrary widget. She can then browse the list of that object's methods similarly to an (undocumented) API summary listing. In this way, when a developer does need to deeply integrate with the core of an application, Scotty helps guide that search based on the externally visible parts of the software, that is, the interface.

The various examples show a cross-section of the kinds of modifications that runtime toolkit overloading makes possible. Augmented surface representation approaches could potentially support some of these modifications. Façade, for example, could modify a window's position in the window hierarchy to have it float over all other windows. Sikuli's visual scripting interface [24] could be used to create automated tasks. For window teleportation, however, surface representation methods do not have access to the underlying structures to send an alternative vector representation.

Interacting with the underlying application logic is simply not possible with surface representation approaches. Checking for missing Mail attachments and properly synchronizing subtitles in the Quicktime video player requires inspecting the underlying application models. While such deep integration may be more challenging than surface modifications, it enables modifications that were previously impossible.

[8]PyObjC: pyobjc.sourceforge.net, 20 April 2011.

[9]SIMBL, the Smart Input Manager Bundle Loader, uses this same process. www.culater.net/software/SIMBL/SIMBL.php, 20 April 2011.

Runtime Program Modification

More generally, approaches to runtime program modification can be characterized along two dimensions: *depth of integration* with the underlying application and *generality* of the approach. Depth of integration refers to how much access the technique provides to a program's underlying objects. The generality of the approach describes how well the technique applies to all applications or to specific ones. The work presented in this paper offers both deep integration and generality across a toolkit.

Approaches such as scripting and extension interfaces can be deeply integrated with the application and can offer a rich degree of modification. These interfaces allow a third-party programmer to create rich modifications to the underlying behavior of the program, but with the risk that those modifications could cause instability, data corruption, or unexpected interactions with the program. They are powerful, but with this power comes a higher risk. To mitigate this risk, the abstractions we have used reduce the surface area of the underlying application requiring modification.

At the other end of the spectrum are shallow integration techniques, including surface representation approaches and their augmented variants. Their lower integration footprint helps make them less fragile, but they are still not without risk. For example, if a bug in a surface level modification sends multiple mouse release events without an intervening mouse press event, the application may crash. Furthermore, these approaches often cannot completely graft a new behavior into an existing application or toolkit. They may be able to create close approximations, but they lack the tight integration necessary to handle edge cases, and they cannot handle cases that require deeper semantic understanding of program objects.

Surface level approaches, however, are typically more general across applications built with different toolkits. Façade can handle any X Windows applications, regardless of what toolkit it uses, because it integrates with the underlying windows on which those toolkits are built. Prefab can handle any widget it has been previously trained to recognize, regardless of whether it is running locally, inside of a remote VNC connection, a virtual machine, embedded in a Flash application, or just simply in a screenshot. As such, they can potentially offer more general, toolkit-independent solutions, but with a limited understanding of the underlying program.

Deciding which approach to use involves weighing the needs of the particular modification against the risk involved in modifying an application's behavior. One of the advantages of the abstractions we have developed is that they support a similar degree of input/output hijacking as existing surface representation approaches. Runtime program modification using our abstractions therefore faces a risk similar to surface-level approaches, with the important difference that it runs inside the application. This approach may therefore offer the best of both worlds when using a single toolkit.

FACILITATING RUNTIME SOFTWARE DEVELOPMENT

Runtime software development relies on the ability to examine and modify live objects in program space, and the ability for the runtime developer to make sense of those objects. The first of these relies on three technical abilities: to run arbitrary code in program space, to modify class and method tables at runtime, and to intercept and redirect input events before delivery. While our demonstrator is implemented in Cocoa, we have implemented proofs of concept in both Java and Javascript, demonstrating the generality of the approach.

In all three cases however, we rely on specific and sometimes obscure features of each environment. A much better approach would be for the UI toolkit itself to directly support the type of extensibility we have described. Window Hooks, Event Funnels, and Glass Sheets can easily be natively supported by new toolkits. Dynamic Code Support and Object Proxies require proper runtime support at the programming language level, but could be explicitly supported by the toolkit for its own objects and methods. The bootstrapping process could use the same approach as applications that support plugins, *i. e.* to load the content of a well-known directory at start-up.

Finally, Code Inspection is mostly a human issue: how to help a runtime developer make sense of someone else's program. Even with access to source code, the task is difficult. The inspection tools in Scotty go some way to helping make sense of the code, but could be improved. This task is simpler than general code comprehension because it only involves methods and objects connected to elements of the user interface. Since the user interface is intended to be human understandable, it should support the exploration process, as we have done with the simple widget picker.

CONCLUSIONS & FUTURE WORK

The goal of runtime software development is to support the extension and adaptation of existing software applications without access to their source code. While some tools exist, they are usually somewhat limited, and programming extensions and adaptations proves difficult.

We have presented *runtime toolkit overloading*, an approach that makes it possible to perform powerful adaptations on existing applications without modifying to their source code. Specifically, we have shown how Window Hooks, Event Funnels, Glass Sheets, Dynamic Code Loading, Object Proxies, and Code Inspection help to augment or replace behaviors of existing program objects. We have demonstrated Scotty, a prototype system that implements these abstractions in existing Cocoa applications in Mac OS X. We have shown how Scotty can be used to implemented a variety of modifications, including teleporting vector or raster representations of windows, adding subtitles to a video player, and dynamically adding or redefining toolbar buttons.

We have shown how to create and use runtime toolkit overloading in the Cocoa environment and have created proofs of concept in two other application environments: Java/Swing and web applications. We further argue that new toolkits can better support runtime development by directly incorporating these abstractions into their design.

In future work, we will study how this approach can better foster adaptation as a core design concept, facilitating the development of applications that not only support users at altering their interaction and behavior, but also by incorporating runtime adpatation as an explicit design element.

ACKNOWLEDGEMENTS

This work was supported in part by the French ANR grant "iStar" (#2007-TLOG-009-03) and by the Digiteo/Région Île-de-France grant "WILD" (#2008-25D).

REFERENCES

1. J. Accot and S. Zhai. More than dotting the i's — foundations for crossing-based interfaces. In *CHI '02: Proceedings of the SIGCHI conference on Human factors in computing systems*, 73–80, New York, NY, USA, 2002. ACM.
2. C. Appert and M. Beaudouin-Lafon. SwingStates: adding state machines to Java and the Swing toolkit. *Softw. Pract. Exper.*, 38(11):1149–1182, 2008.
3. Apple Computer Inc. *AppleScript Language Guide*. Addison-Wesley Longman Publishing Co., Inc., Boston, MA, USA, 1994.
4. M. Beaudouin-Lafon. Instrumental interaction: an interaction model for designing post-wimp user interfaces. In *CHI '00: Proceedings of the SIGCHI conference on Human factors in computing systems*, 446–453, New York, NY, USA, 2000. ACM.
5. J. M. A. Begole. *Flexible collaboration transparency: supporting worker independence in replicated application-sharing systems*. PhD thesis, Virginia Polytechnic Institute and State University, Blacksburg, VA, 1998.
6. G. Besacier and F. Vernier. Toward user interface virtualization: legacy applications and innovative interaction systems. In *EICS '09: Proceedings of the 1st ACM SIGCHI symposium on Engineering interactive computing systems*, 157–166, New York, NY, USA, 2009. ACM.
7. M. Bolin, M. Webber, P. Rha, T. Wilson, and R. C. Miller. Automation and customization of rendered web pages. In *UIST '05: Proceedings of the 18th annual ACM symposium on User interface software and technology*, 163–172, New York, NY, USA, 2005. ACM Press.
8. A. Cypher, D. C. Halbert, D. Kurlander, H. Lieberman, D. Maulsby, B. A. Myers, and A. Turransky, editors. *Watch what I do: programming by demonstration*. MIT Press, 1993.
9. M. Dixon and J. Fogarty. Prefab: implementing advanced behaviors using pixel-based reverse engineering of interface structure. In *CHI '10: Proceedings of the 28th international conference on Human factors in computing systems*, 1525–1534, New York, NY, USA, 2010. ACM.
10. M. Dixon, D. Leventhal, and J. Fogarty. Content and hierarchy in pixel-based methods for reverse engineering interface structure. In *Proceedings of the 2011 annual conference on Human factors in computing systems*, CHI '11, 969–978, New York, NY, USA, 2011. ACM.
11. W. K. Edwards, S. E. Hudson, J. Marinacci, R. Rodenstein, T. Rodriguez, and I. Smith. Systematic output modification in a 2d user interface toolkit. In *UIST '97: Proceedings of the 10th annual ACM symposium on User interface software and technology*, 151–158, New York, NY, USA, 1997. ACM.
12. W. K. Edwards, E. D. Mynatt, and K. Stockton. Providing access to graphical user interfaces—not graphical screens. In *Assets '94: Proceedings of the first annual ACM conference on Assistive technologies*, 47–54, New York, NY, USA, 1994. ACM.
13. A. Goldberg and D. Robson. *Smalltalk-80: the language and its implementation*. Addison-Wesley Longman Publishing Co., Boston, MA, USA, 1983.
14. G. Humphreys, M. Houston, R. Ng, R. Frank, S. Ahern, P. D. Kirchner, and J. T. Klosowski. Chromium: a stream-processing framework for interactive rendering on clusters. In *SIGGRAPH '02: Proceedings of the 29th annual conference on Computer graphics and interactive techniques*, 693–702, New York, NY, USA, 2002. ACM.
15. G. Kiczales, J. des Rivières, and D. G. Bobrow. *The Art of the Metaobject Protocol*. MIT Press, 1991.
16. W. E. Mackay. Triggers and barriers to customizing software. In *CHI '91: Proceedings of the SIGCHI conference on Human factors in computing systems*, 153–160. ACM Press, 1991.
17. A. MacLean, K. Carter, L. Lövstrand, and T. Moran. User-tailorable systems: pressing the issues with buttons. In *CHI '90: Proceedings of the SIGCHI conference on Human factors in computing systems*, 175–182, New York, NY, USA, 1990. ACM Press.
18. B. A. Nardi. *A small matter of programming: perspectives on end user computing*. MIT Press, 1993.
19. T. Richardson, Q. Stafford-Fraser, K. R. Wood, and A. Hopper. Virtual network computing. *IEEE Internet Computing*, 2(1):33–38, Jan/Feb 1998.
20. M. Robinson. Design for unanticipated use... In *ECSCW '93: Proceedings of the third conference on European Conference on Computer-Supported Cooperative Work*, 187–202, Norwell, MA, USA, 1993. Kluwer Academic Publishers.
21. W. Stuerzlinger, O. Chapuis, D. Phillips, and N. Roussel. User interface façades: towards fully adaptable user interfaces. In *UIST '06: Proceedings of the 19th annual ACM symposium on User interface software and technology*, 309–318, New York, NY, USA, 2006. ACM.
22. L. A. Suchman. *Plans and Situated Actions: The Problem of Human-Machine Communication*. Cambridge University Press, December 1987.
23. D. S. Tan, B. Meyers, and M. Czerwinski. Wincuts: manipulating arbitrary window regions for more effective use of screen space. In *CHI '04 extended abstracts on Human factors in computing systems*, 1525–1528, New York, NY, USA, 2004. ACM.
24. T. Yeh, T.-H. Chang, and R. C. Miller. Sikuli: using gui screenshots for search and automation. In *UIST '09: Proceedings of the 22nd annual ACM symposium on User interface software and technology*, 183–192, New York, NY, USA, 2009. ACM.

Monte Carlo Methods for Managing Interactive State, Action and Feedback Under Uncertainty

Julia Schwarz[1] *Jennifer Mankoff*[1] *Scott E. Hudson*[1,2]
[1]Human-Computer Interaction Institute & [2]Heinz College Center for the Future of Work
Carnegie Mellon University, 5000 Forbes Avenue, Pittsburgh, PA 15213
{julia.schwarz, jmankoff, scott.hudson}@cs.cmu.edu

ABSTRACT
Current input handling systems provide effective techniques for modeling, tracking, interpreting, and acting on user input. However, new interaction technologies violate the standard assumption that input is *certain*. Touch, speech recognition, gestural input, and sensors for context often produce uncertain estimates of user inputs. Current systems tend to remove uncertainty early on. However, information available in the user interface and application can help to resolve uncertainty more appropriately for the end user.

This paper presents a set of techniques for tracking the state of interactive objects in the presence of uncertain inputs. These techniques use a Monte Carlo approach to maintain a probabilistically accurate description of the user interface that can be used to make informed choices about actions. Samples are used to approximate the distribution of possible inputs, possible interactor states that result from inputs, and possible actions (callbacks and feedback) interactors may execute. Because each sample is certain, the developer can specify most of the behavior of interactors in a familiar, non-probabilistic fashion. This approach retains all the advantages of maintaining information about uncertainty while minimizing the need for the developer to work in probabilistic terms. We present a working implementation of our framework and illustrate the power of these techniques within a paint program that includes three different kinds of uncertain input.

ACM Classification: H.5.2 [Information interfaces and presentation]: User Interfaces - Graphical user interfaces.
General terms: Human Factors
Keywords: Probabilistic Modeling, Uncertain Input, Dialog Specification, Finite State Machines.

INTRODUCTION
Advances in input methods such as touch, pen gestures, in-air interaction and speech recognition have begun to turn the promise of natural user interfaces into reality. Unfortunately, these input modalities are inherently uncertain. Most interface toolkits assume that input occurred *exactly as reported*. As a result, any uncertainty in input must be resolved quickly and often simplistically. For example, traditional input systems often treat touch input as a single point (the centroid of the touch region) instead of a touch area. Because the center of the touch area may not be over the user's intended target, small differences in position can lead to big errors and a stunted user experience.

UIST'11, October 16–19, 2011, Santa Barbara, CA, USA.

Handling uncertain input is a multifaceted problem that includes mechanisms for modeling uncertain input, deciding which interactive element(s) an input gets dispatched to, interpreting input with respect to interactive state, and mediating between alternative interpretations to decide which actions to execute and/or feedback to show. Past work has focused on mechanisms for modeling and dispatching uncertain input [18] and resolving uncertainty [11]. In this paper, we focus on how to interpret uncertain input with respect to interactor state and on giving appropriate feedback to accurately reflect this uncertainty.

Because user input takes place over the course of a sequence of events, interactors must be able maintain internal state across the delivery of events. State machines are a convenient mechanism for modeling state that many interactors use implicitly, if not explicitly.

We show how to automate the process of tracking uncertain state for each interactor, while requiring developers to only provide a deterministic state machine description. A developer also specifies when an interactor should provide feedback or invoke callbacks, but must encapsulate these actions in *action requests* rather than executing them directly. These small changes allow the framework to automatically track the probabilities of multiple alternative interactive states as inputs arrive, and correctly update state as decisions are made about alternative actions.

MONTE CARLO APPROACH
Our approach uses Monte Carlo methods [13]. Monte Carlo methods span a range of specific techniques but share the property that probability distributions are approximated by a set of samples over that distribution. This allows operations on the distributions to be approximated by carrying out the operations on each sample, without an analytical characterization of the operations. We use this property to transform the operations of conventional event

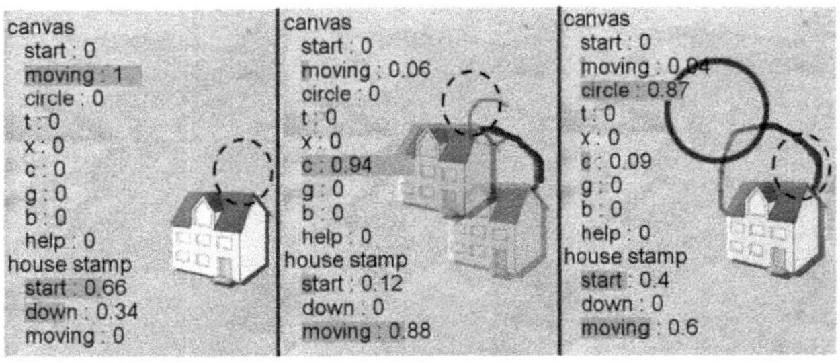

Figure 1: Screenshots from application built using our system. (left) User starts a circle gesture over a moveable icon (dotted circle indicates touch location). (middle) User begins the circle gesture. The system indicates a possible drag and a possible C gesture as equally likely. (right) User completes circle gesture. The system recognizes the circle as the most likely interpretation. Note: The state probability information at the left is for illustration and is not part of the interface.

handling from a definite computation into the equivalent operations working on probability distributions. Our system uses samples to approximate uncertain probability distributions in three places: input events, interactor state, and potential actions. When we combine (definite) event samples with (definite) state samples, we can compute (definite) action samples representing potential actions the interface may take. All of this is handled by applying conventional event handling operations to individual (definite) samples. Uncertainty only needs to be considered where specialized feedback of ambiguity is desired or a decision between alternative actions must be made. Note that unlike some Monte Carlo techniques, our approach is not performing simulation. Rather, live user input is used to track the probabilities associated with ongoing interactions. Additionally, our implementation does not use knowledge about prior distributions of input, state, or action, though our framework does not preclude this.

MOTIVATING EXAMPLE

To concretely illustrate our contribution, consider the gesture-based painting program shown in Figure 1 and implemented using our framework. In the scenario depicted here, the user executes a circle gesture on a paintable canvas, but happens to starts the gesture over a moveable icon (a 'house stamp'). The canvas in this example responds to seven different gestures, each represented as a state in its state machine. These are listed in Figure 1 as 'circle', which creates a new stamp, through 'help' (see Figure 8 for a full list of gestures and their resulting actions). The canvas' state machine also tracks whether the user is painting on the canvas (the 'moving' state). The moveable icon in Figure 1 (the 'house stamp') can either be moved ('moving' state, see Figure 2) or clicked on, which copies an image of the stamp to the canvas ('down' state). When the stamp is dragged, it updates its position (which can be modeled as a *state variable*) after each move event. As the user is executing the circle gesture, the framework simultaneously tracks the possibility that the house stamp is 'moving' (indicating a possible drag), that the user is

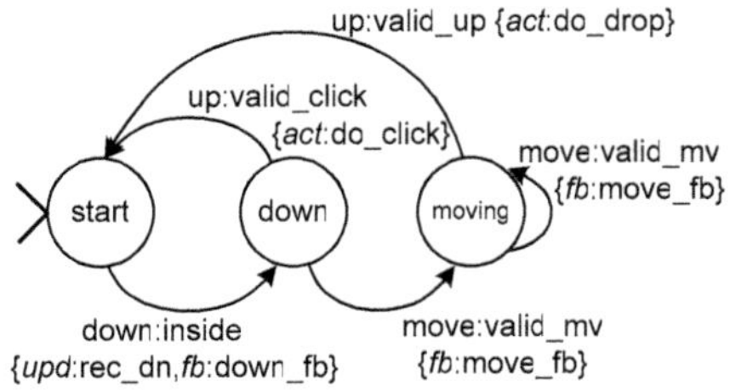

Figure 2: The state machine used by the house stamp. Each transition is annotated with **type:predicate {optional parameters}**. Type is the event the transition fires on, the predicate checks for any additional requirements. Optional parameters include *upd* (an update method for updating state variables), *fb* (a feedback method for displaying feedback to the user), and *act* (an action method).

drawing on the canvas, and that the canvas is receiving a gesture. No irreversible changes are made because it is unclear which state is correct. Initially, the likelihood that the icon is in the moving state is high (Figure 1, left). As the user continues, the likelihood of executing a 'c' gesture, and moving the house stamp are approximately the same, and this uncertainty is reflected in the feedback (Figure 1, middle). As the user finishes the gesture, the likelihood that the icon is in the moving state decreases and the likelihood that the user is making a circle gesture increases to 0.87 (Figure 1, right), causing the circle feedback to be most salient, and the stamp drag feedback to disappear. Our tool automatically tracks these probabilities for the developer, allowing her to focus on other aspects of interaction.

RELATED WORK

Past tools for managing uncertainty fall into two categories. One set of tools has sophisticated support for merging input from multiple uncertain modalities. Bourguet developed a tool for visually specifying how multimodal input should be interpreted using state machines [2] while xml-based languages have been used to specify the relationship between incoming event triggers and outgoing actions [5]. In each case, the specification focuses on the flow of interaction through an overall dialog with the user, as opposed to the details of how each individual interactor operates (*e.g.*, [4]). By combining modalities, it has been shown in multiple domains that it is possible to gain new evidence for disambiguating the interpretation of uncertain input (*e.g.*, text input [7], speech [15], and multimodal input [17]). This research typically assumes that all of the uncertainty will be resolved before any input reaches a specific interactor (or the application proper). As a result, the uncertainty does not integrate smoothly with our well evolved and familiar GUI interaction techniques.

Another approach (the one taken here) attempts to manage uncertain input within a general model which is based on mainstream approaches for input handling. In prior work we have explored several of the sub problems of modeling and dispatching uncertain events (input modeling, dispatch, action, feedback and mediation) [18]. Mankoff *et al.* outline basic aspects of modeling input and provide a mechanism

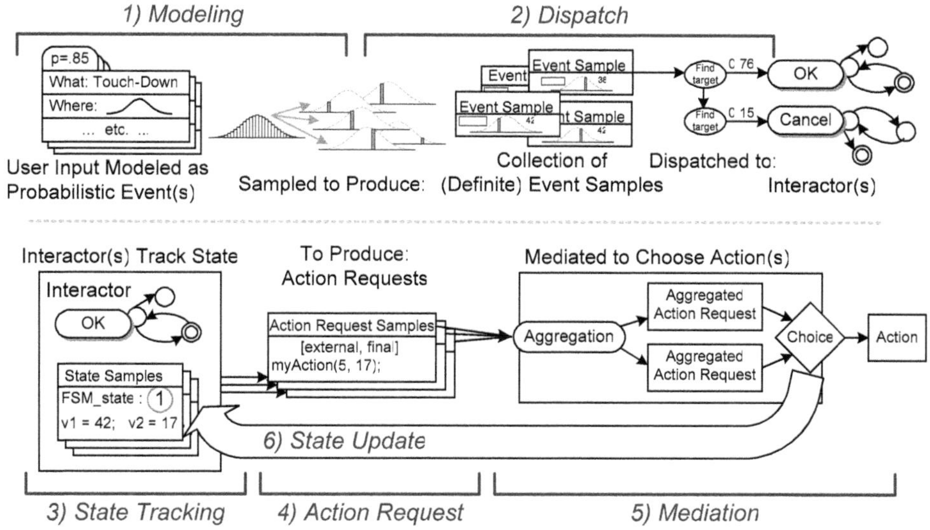

Figure 3: Overview of processing steps within the input framework.

for dispatching and mediating ambiguous input [10, 11]. However, little work has explored managing interactive state. Hudson and Newell address this problem in [8], outlining a theoretical approach for tracking interactive state given uncertain input. However, this approach is not fully integrated with other aspects of input handling and has not been implemented. Moreover, the approach discussed in [8] restricts computational power to strict regular languages and thus may present difficulties in practical use. This paper builds directly on ideas in [8, 10, 11, 18].

In the next section we present an overview of our framework, focusing on the main contributions in this paper: our approach to tracking and managing uncertain state within interactors, without requiring interactor developers to think probabilistically. The framework we've designed uses the concepts introduced in [18] as a starting point and expands on issues concerning state maintenance. As validation we then briefly describe our implementation and a set of sample interactors we built using probabilistic state machines. Our examples illustrate the power of our framework, which brings us one step closer to developing an end-to-end system for handling uncertain input.

FRAMEWORK OVERVIEW

As illustrated in Figure 3 the overall framework we operate in has six components, each of which includes multiple steps. (1) First is *modeling* uncertain input (which produces many event samples). (2) As shown at top of Figure 3, these samples are *dispatched* to interactors. (3) Next, the framework *tracks* the internal state of interactors (Figure 3, bottom left). (4) This produces *action/feedback* requests. (5) *Mediation* aggregates and selects among these requests (bottom right). (6) Finally, a *state update* process ensures that interactor state correctly reflects the fact that certain actions were selected over others.

Modeling: As with conventional input, uncertain input is modeled using events. However, these events may be probabilistic in nature, and may contain probabilistic properties. In the example in Figure 1, the user's input is modeled as a set of alternative events (including gesture and touch events). The gesture events are represented as a distribution over possible gestures (circle, t, x, c, g, b, and help) and the location of touch events is represented as a distribution over possible x, y positions (in this case derived from the touch centroid using a 2d Gaussian function).

Dispatch: Given a representation of uncertain input, the framework needs to deliver, or *dispatch*, that input to interested interactors. Details about user input such as its type and location are traditionally used during dispatch to make decisions about which interactors should receive each event. Since this information may be uncertain, our dispatch process must be probabilistic in nature. To reflect uncertainty about which interactor will consume an event sample, the system splits each event sample into several based on the set of interactors that want to consume it. Each split sample is weighted based on the probability that it is consumed. For example, in Figure 1, the user's input is modeled using a number of samples (representing possible locations and gestures). Each of these samples is split in two (one delivered to the canvas and one to the house stamp, each weighted with the probability of that dispatch).

Maintaining State: As event samples are delivered, each interactor needs to maintain its own interactive state. Since the interactor's state is based on multiple uncertain prior inputs, it is probabilistic. The distribution across possible interactor states is represented as a collection of samples. Each *state sample* includes a current state (such as "start" or "moving") and values for any variables associated with the state machine. Operation of a *probabilistic state machine* based on these samples is a central focus of this paper and is described in detail in later sections. Figure 2 shows the state machine for the house stamp in Figure 1.

Action Request: Each state machine transition may have an associated action. When an input event sample causes a transition with an associated action, an *action request* *sample* is generated to request that some action be taken. Action request samples are conceptually related to command objects [14] and contain information about the action, such as a method to carry it out as well as its likelihood. For example, when the user lifts his finger, the canvas interactor will transition to a state indicating a completed circle gesture. This in turn causes an action request sample to be generated that will create a new stamp if invoked. Because interactors are uncertain about their actual state, many possible action samples may be generated for each uncertain input event that is dispatched. This collection of action samples represents a probability distribution across possible actions the system might take.

Actions may have permanent consequences and/or effect future interactors, or may only produce feedback and not affect future interactions. We call these two forms of actions *final* and *feedback actions* respectively. For example in Figure 1, the user's stroke is shown as feedback, as is a circle and a semi-transparent indication of the house's potential new location. When the user lifts her finger, both the canvas and stamp send final action samples to create a house stamp and copy an image to the canvas, respectively.

Mediation and Action: Mediation is a decision process that determines which action request samples (if any) to invoke (accept) and which to reject. In addition to a probability estimate for each action sample, the system tracks which requests are compatible with each other, and which are mutually exclusive, to aid in mediation. Mediation processes are considered in detail in [11] and we borrow those approaches as a starting point for the work here.

Our default mediator permits all feedback requests. For action requests, the mediator selects the most probable action, which (in the case of Figure 1) creates a new stamp.

State Update: When a final action request is accepted, this implies that the system has decided to act based on one interpretation of the inputs. Other interpretations may not be compatible with this action. The process of *state update* removes any state samples which are incompatible with an accepted action, leaving each interactor's state machine in a less ambiguous state. For example, when the circle gesture is completed and acted upon in Figure 1, all state samples representing other possible gestures will be removed.

To summarize, our framework takes a probabilistic event, generates *event samples*, and dispatches each sample to various interactors which might receive the input. These interactors track their state using *state samples* and generate potential *action samples*. The mediation system decides which (if any) *action samples* to execute, and interactive state is updated accordingly. Collectively, these samples represent a distribution across input events, interactive state, and action. However, individually these samples can be treated by developers as deterministic since they each encapsulate a set of specific values.

MONTE CARLO METHODS FOR MANAGING STATE AND ACTION UNDER UNCERTAINTY

In this section we discuss the details of the framework described above. We show how our framework manages sampled input, state, and actions to accurately track uncertainty throughout the input handling process.

Modeling Events

As with conventional input, probabilistic input is modeled using event records. Roughly following the approach in [8], a distribution across alternative events is indicated by assigning a weight to each event alternative, reflecting the probability that this alternative is the true input. Extending [8] (and following [18]), however, we also allow properties of each event alternative to be uncertain. These properties are modeled using a probability mass function (PMF).

By default, separate probabilistic events are assumed not to be compatible, meaning they are part of a distribution of possible alternative interpretations of the user's input. For example a "move" and a "gesture" resulting from the same underlying touch would be incompatible with each other (only one interpretation is correct). However, certain events represent parallel but independent (compatible) actions by the user. An example is simultaneous touches by two different fingers in a multi-touch system.

Dispatching Probabilistic Input

Figure 3 illustrates our system's sample-based dispatch process. Instead of dispatching an uncertain event directly as in [18] (and thus forcing interactor developers to directly handle uncertain events), our dispatch method samples the probabilistic event. Each *event sample* is weighted according to the estimated probability that this sample represents a correct interpretation of the user's actual intent. The dispatch mechanism then dispatches each (definite) event sample to each appropriate interactor in an interface. The events are dispatched in a dispatch order defined by the normal interactor structure (*e.g.*, by performing hit tests, using the current input focus, "bubbling" events, etc.).

To reflect the uncertainty about which interactor should consume each event sample, we break each event sample into multiple samples representing a distribution across the interactors they might be delivered to as follows: when each event sample is dispatched to an interactor, *i,* it is split into two new samples. One split sample represents the possibility that the original sample should be dispatched to *i* (with probability p_i). The other split sample represents the possibility that the original sample should not be dispatched to *i* (weighted with probability ($1- p_i$). The value of p_i, represents the probability that the event sample is consumed by the interactor *i*. This *consumption probability* is the sum of the probabilities of all action requests made by *i*. The second split sample is dispatched to the next interactor in the dispatch order and split again using the same algorithm. This continues until all interactors have seen the sample, or the sample probability reaches zero.

State Machine Description

State machines are a convenient mechanism for modeling interactive state. Prior tools have introduced augmentations to make state machines more practical and easy to use (*e.g.*, [9, 16, 19]). In our system, interactor developers specify interactor behavior with a simple XML description. This description encodes an augmented form of a familiar *deterministic finite state machine*. We have added a small set of state variables and corresponding transition predicates. These variables can be used along with event properties in the transition predicates to help decide whether a transition should be taken. For instance, in a multi touch interface, the current pointer ID can be modeled as a state variable. A transition predicate can then ensure that an interaction starts and ends with the same pointer ID by comparing the current event sample's touch ID to the touch ID stored in the pointer ID state variable at the start of the interaction.

By definition, every state machine has a start state. Our framework extends this notion by allowing multiple states to be designated as *stable* states (always including the start state). Stable states may represent the start of a new interaction. For example, a conventional check box might have two stable states, one for its checked state and one for its unchecked state. This allows our framework to roll the state machine back to the last sensible (stable) state when a possible interaction is rejected. For each stable state, the developer can optionally provide code for initializing or resetting the variables of the machine to correspond to that state.

Figure 2 illustrates a state machine in a graphical notation. Each node represents a state, while directed edges between nodes represent transitions. Edges (transitions) are annotated with the notation **type:predicate {optional parameters}** to describe the type of input to transition on, a predicate function which must be satisfied to take the transition, an optional update function which updates state variables when a transition is taken, and optional feedback or actions functions to execute when taking the transition.

Feedback and action functions are encapsulated as feedback and final action request samples to be executed if/when the requests get accepted. An action request sample encapsulates a method to carry out the action, along with a likelihood score, links to the event and state samples that led to that action being created. This gives the action's method access to state variables and event properties that may be needed to carry out the action.

Neither predicate nor state update functions may have side effects in the application. The update function may modify state variables only. Note that this state machine specification is deterministic: It could be used unchanged in a standard non-probabilistic input handling framework.

State Machine Operation

When an interactor receives an input event during the dispatch process, it must correctly update its internal state and produce actions based on this input. In a deterministic setting, as each event arrives, an interactor's state would be updated to a new (deterministic) state based on the type of the input event. In the case of our augmented state machine, the predicate function would also need to return true for a transition to be taken. Additionally, all of the methods associated with the selected transition (feedback, state variable update, and action) would be executed.

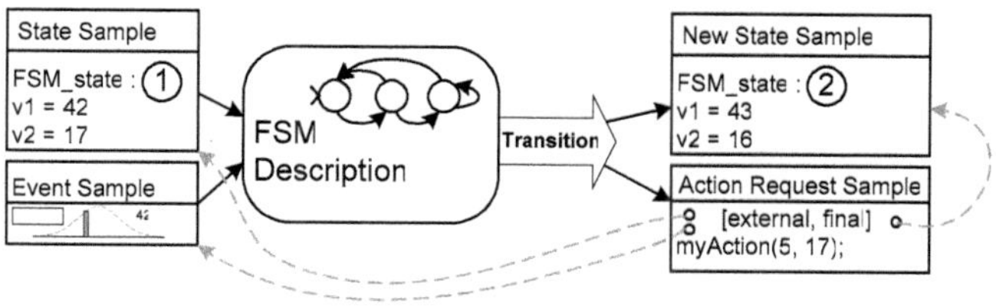

Figure 4: Our framework takes a state machine description, a state sample, and an event sample, and executes the appropriate transition of the state machine. The result is a new state sample and (in some cases) a final and/or feedback action request sample.

In the case of probabilistic input, interactor state is a probability distribution over multiple possible states rather than a single current state. Our framework uses a collection of weighted *state samples* to track this state distribution. Each *state sample* contains a current state and a collection of values for the state machine variables. Together, these characterize a (deterministic) sample "state" of the state machine. When a (deterministic) event sample arrives, the state sample contains sufficient information to transition to a new state. As illustrated in Figure 4, this process produces a new state sample containing the new machine state and a new set of state variable values (as produced by the developer specified *update function* for the transition). If the developer has specified a *feedback function* or an *action function* for the transition, one or more *action samples* are produced. Each action sample is assigned a probability (weight) defined as $p_{es} * p_{ss}$, where p_{es} is the probability associated with the event sample (a combination of occurrence and dispatch likelihood) and p_{ss} is the probability that the state machine is actually in the state indicated by the state sample.

Each *event sample* is combined with every *state sample* in a given interactor to determine its probabilistic transitions. The set of new *state samples* produced after all event samples are processed represents the new distribution of interactor state. Action samples are accumulated across all transitions resulting from samples of a given probabilistic event. The set of action samples produced by each interactor represents the distribution across potential actions that interactor could invoke (as implied by the transition from the old state distribution to the new state distribution).

Mediation – Choosing Between Alternate Actions

Once dispatch of all the samples generated from a set of compatible probabilistic events is complete, we will have produced a set of one or more competing action samples.

The *mediation* process decides which action samples to accept and invoke.

As mentioned in the overview, there are two types of action samples: *feedback actions and final actions.* Feedback actions are assumed to be transient and reversible. They provide information to the user, but do not change the future behavior of the system. An example is showing visually how a gesture is being interpreted. Final actions are assumed to have irreversible consequences which may change external objects in the application or the way the system acts in the future. An example is adding or removing an application component as a result of a completed gesture.

Since feedback actions are reversible and do not change the future behavior of the system, they are by default assumed to be compatible with each other (meaning that more than one of them can safely be invoked together). This has the benefit of indicating to the end user that ambiguity is present, as in Figure 1 where a circle and a faded second house are both visible. In the case of the faded house, the feedback action has translated its likelihood (weight) into an alpha value for the feedback image being drawn. The assumption that all feedback actions are compatible with one another is useful but does not always hold. For example, in the case of a pannable, paintable canvas, the feedback for panning may cause the feedback for the paint to be distorted or to disappear. Feedback independence is an assumption of the default feedback currently provided, but is not a fundamental limitation of our approach. We plan to build more sophisticated feedback aggregation mechanisms that combine conflicting feedback in future work.

Final actions on the other hand would normally be incompatible with other actions. However, they may be compatible if they represent interpretations of the user input and resulting state that do not conflict with each other. An example of this is input coming from two different users, two different devices, or even just two different fingers acting independently on a multi-touch device. In that case the resulting actions do not conflict and may be executed together. To handle this more general case, action requests each have an *isCompatible*() method which by default returns true only if the action requests come from different interactors and the probabilistic events which cause the action are compatible (as indicated by their *isCompatible*() methods). This allows inputs involving e.g., multiple devices or users to be handled correctly with minimal developer intervention. Additionally, the developer may override *isCompatible()* to handle more complex situations.

Before mediation can begin, *action aggregation* must take place. The event sampling, dispatch, and state tracking processes will often produce a number of action samples that invoke the same feedback or final action method. These samples, however, may vary in the sampled values found within the particular state and event samples they depend on. For example, two actions associated with the same gesture may contain different samplings of the user's touch location. However, these action samples might logically be considered equivalent. Our framework aggregates such samples into one aggregated action request.

Although this can be overridden by the developer, our current implementation of action aggregation provides a default aggregation strategy that combines equivalent actions. Equivalent actions both encapsulate the same method (meaning they execute the same operation if invoked), and are associated with transitions within the same interactor's state machine. The combined action is assigned a weight that is the sum of all of the individual actions it is based on. More sophisticated custom strategies might, for example, only consider actions to be similar enough if certain state variables are within a limited variation of each other or might even perform a simple clustering of action samples based on state variable values.

The result of action aggregation is a collection of aggregated action request samples (each of which links back to the full set of action samples they aggregate over so that no information is lost). The next step in mediation is to form sets of incompatible action requests. These are requests that cannot logically be executed together because they each represent a decision to commit to different interpretations of input and resulting state that are in conflict with each other.

Since these aggregated actions cannot all be executed, the mediation system must decide to *accept* zero or more aggregated actions in each set of incompatible action requests. All remaining actions in the set are either *rejected*, or if the system cannot yet make a final decision *deferred*. When an action is deferred, the mediator typically seeks more information from the user.

Although algorithms for deciding between actions are not the main focus of this work (and of course many options exist [10]), we will briefly describe the default mediation algorithm used in our examples. Each incompatibility group is handled separately as follows: First, the algorithm rejects requests below some developer-specified minimum probability. Next, if there are only feedback requests left, all feedback actions are accepted. Otherwise, the algorithm selects a threshold equal to the most probable final action in the current incompatible group. It then considers all final actions requests with likelihood within a developer-specified delta of that threshold. If there is one final action within delta of the threshold, that action is accepted and all other actions are rejected. If there are multiple final actions within delta of the threshold, the interaction is considered "too close to call". In this case, the mediator rejects all actions below the delta, defers the final actions within the delta, and rejects any feedback actions within the delta. For deferral it invokes a developer specified mediation method. The default version of this method displays an "N-best list" choice dialog to the user (a common approach as described in [10]). Alternatively, the developer can specify a different method. Once the user designates a choice, the other possibilities are rejected and the chosen action is accepted.

Carrying Out Actions

The result of mediation is a list of action requests to be accepted and a list to be rejected. All accepted final action requests are executed as indicated in the action request. At present, feedback actions are treated the same way. As shown in Figure 1, small changes in how an interactor is drawn (transparency, shadow, *etc.*) or simple indicators (such as the current most likely gesture) are easily distinguishable and work well even in a complex application. In future work we envision a feedback merger step which might use negotiation techniques, related to those developed for fluid documents [3], to produce more sophisticated, flexible feedback of ambiguity. This would allow feedback to scale up to even more complex situations.

When an accepted feedback or final action request is invoked, it is passed a copy of the aggregated action request object as a parameter. This aggregated request contains links to all of the original action requests it was aggregated from, which in turn link to the set of event and state samples (including state variables and event properties) causing the transitions which led to those actions. The system provides an extensible library of *value aggregators* such as *average*, *median*, and *most-probable*, which allow the action method to quickly establish definite values for all the values it needs to carry out its function.

State Update and Resampling

Once actions have been executed, we update interactive state to reflect the logical consequences that this implies. Acceptance and execution of a set of feedback actions does not require any state adjustment. However, acceptance and execution of a final action represents a decision to commit to a particular interpretation of input, associated with a particular state machine state. As a result, we need to adjust the state distributions to reflect this decision. For each interactor executing one or more accepted final actions, the mediator ensures that its state is consistent with those actions. Since each action arises from a transition, the target states of those transitions are consistent with the interpretation of the user's input that has been selected. All state samples not matching one of the target states of the aggregated accepted actions are deleted.

For interactors which have rejected actions but no accepted actions it is necessary to reset the interactor state to one that would be consistent with rejecting all current interpretations. This is done by *resetting* each state sample in the machine – specifically by restoring it to the last stable state it passed through during its execution history (each sample maintains a record of this state). Resetting sets the state sample state number to the stable state and executes a reset method to establish consistent state variable values. Restoring the state samples makes the state distribution compatible with where the state distribution would have been if the rejected input sequence had never happened.

The final step that must be taken is *resampling* to reduce the total sample count. If left unchecked, over time the number of state samples will grow exponentially. This increase occurs each time multiple event samples arrive and are combined with each transitioning state sample. However, state distributions can generally be adequately approximated by a limited number of samples. We resample and renormalize the state distribution based on a developer specified limit of total samples.

In our current implementation (on a memory and CPU limited mobile phone) we enforce a fairly small sample budget. To stay within this budget, we use an aggregation process to combine similar samples. In systems allowing a more generous sample budget an alternative approach would be to employ importance sampling as is commonly used with particle filters [6, 12] (which have the same state expansion issues). Once resampling is complete we renormalize the weights of the states in each interactor's state machine so that they again sum to 1.0.

IMPLEMENTATION

We implemented a proof of concept system that uses the sampling techniques described above to accurately track interactive state. Our system is built for the Windows Phone OS on top of the XNA game framework, which has a primitive input handling system supporting only polling for input but not events. We chose the phone because touch input is a widely-used medium that contains a large amount of uncertainty (i.e., the intended location of the touch event is uncertain). The phone also illustrates that our approach works on systems with relatively low amounts of memory and processing power. We support touch, gesture, and accelerometer-based shake events. The framework has about 2,000 lines of C# code, and the 10 demos we wrote (some of which are described below) totaled about 1,000 lines of C# code. Our development and testing has been done on a phone with 512MB of RAM and a 1GHz processor, which compared to typical modern desktop or laptop machines is quite limited. Due to these limitations, our example application implementation employed a very limited sample budget: using at most 50 samples per event and resampling to 10 state samples per interactor. These values can of course be changed by the developer depending on the interface/application. In practice we ran into no problems using these low sample numbers because of the small state machine size that most interactors have. Fortunately, even for unusual cases needing very large state machines, our approach is highly parallelizable, offering plenty of room for future optimizations.

Once details such as the number of samples are specified, developers rarely have to think probabilistically when they are developing interactors and applications that use these interactors. Aside from feedback methods that make use of likelihood, neither the interactor code nor the application code we developed involves explicit consideration of multiple possible interpretations of the user's input.

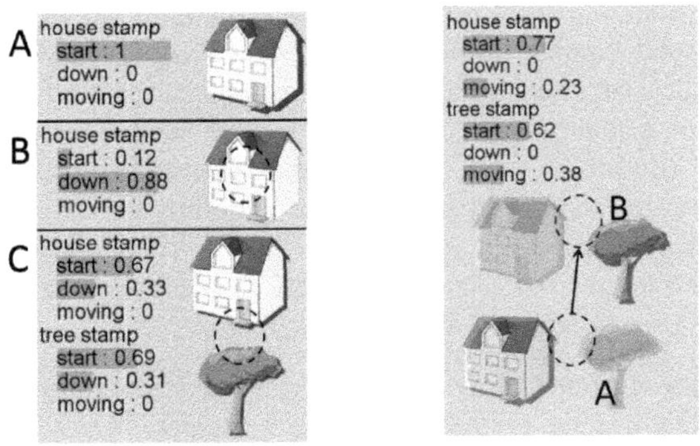

Figure 5: Screenshots of feedback provided by stamp interactors. The dotted circles have been added to indicate the position of the user's finger. **(left)** Press feedback: A: Stamp unpressed. B: Stamp depressed completely when press is unambiguous. C: Stamp depressed partially when press is ambiguous. **(right)** Move feedback. A: User pressed in between the house and tree when beginning their drag, overlapping the tree more than the house. B: Both the house and tree are shown, with the tree being less transparent than the house reflecting overlap difference.

EXAMPLE USES

To test the effectiveness of our approach and demonstrate its applicability to a wide range of problems, we developed six interactors of varying complexity. We combined them in a gesture-based paint application. Please refer to the accompanying video figure to see the application in action.

Below we briefly highlight the implementation of several interactors we built to show what developers should expect when writing interactors. Although developers have access to probabilistic data (aggregated action requests and their associated events and state samples), they rarely need to concern themselves with this information. All of our example interactors were written largely without regard to probabilistic events (an exception is feedback designed to indicate the probability of a specific potential action). The paint application using the interactors is written entirely without regard to uncertain events, and is a relatively simple application consisting of roughly 400 lines of code with the same setup code and logic as any standard paint application.

Stamps: Moveable Buttons

Our paint application allows users to stamp images onto their painting. To support this we developed an interactor which can be both moved and pressed. The stamp interactor uses three states to accomplish this. Figure 2 illustrates the state machine description used for stamps. The state machine has two state variables – the drag start position and the touch ID (to support multitouch). Stamps provide feedback to indicate the likelihood that they are being pressed *vs.* moved. Stamps provide press feedback by manipulating the shadow to make the interactor appear depressed in proportion to the likelihood that they are pressed (Figure 5, left). To provide feedback about moving, stamps show a 'ghost' version of the moved stamp. The

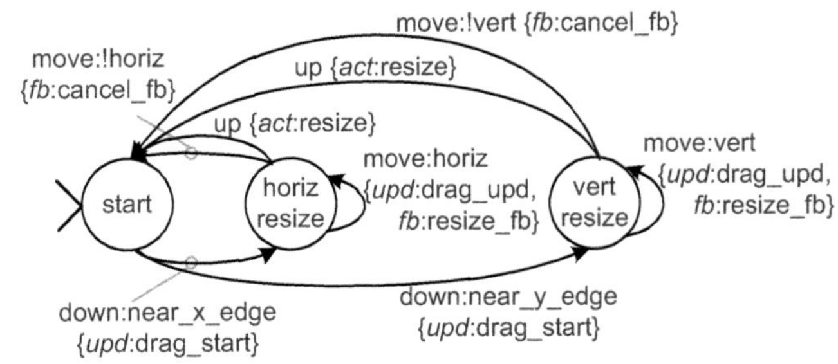

Figure 6: State machine for resizeable interactor.

transparency of the ghost stamp is based on the stamp's move likelihood (Figure 5, right). Sometimes multiple stamps might be selected or moved ambiguously (because the initial touch overlapped both interactors). To accommodate this, each stamp uses an alpha value corresponding to its move likelihood, which helps the user to see what the system thinks is happening (Figure 5, right). This has the advantage that the user can back out of an incorrect interpretation before any final actions are invoked (by moving the stamp away from and then back to its original position). Importantly, we do not explicitly support this escape mechanism: it is a natural solution that arises from an understanding that dragging and pressing are both possible. Move far enough and a drag is more likely, move back and you can let go without fear of an incorrect stamp.

The specific feedback used by the stamp class is different for different transitions. However, all of them use likelihood as a drawing parameter (for shadow size, transparency, etc.). Outside of this parameter, the stamp has no other code that uses probabilities.

Resizable Box: Context-Dependent Interaction

Our system allows developers to create resizeable interactors that use direction of motion to differentiate between a resize action and other input such as a gesture or moving another interactor which may be underneath. To facilitate such interactions in previous work [18] required manually tracking the probability in each state. Our framework simplifies this drastically. The developer simply writes two predicates – one to check whether the current event is horizontally related to the original touch down (stored as a state variable), and the other to check whether the current event is vertically related to the original touch down. Once these predicates are associated with the appropriate transitions (from the middle and right state in Figure 6, respectively), the interactor will behave properly. As with stamps, feedback depicts probability using transparency in a 'ghost' view of the resize result.

Canvas: Handling Paint and Gesture Simultaneously

Stamps and resizable boxes demonstrate the impact of uncertainty about which exact screen location the user intends to touch, what direction the user is moving, what interactor is being targeted, and so on. In these examples uncertainty arises directly from the properties of individual input events. Another source of uncertainty is recognized input, as in the case of gesture recognition. This uncertainty

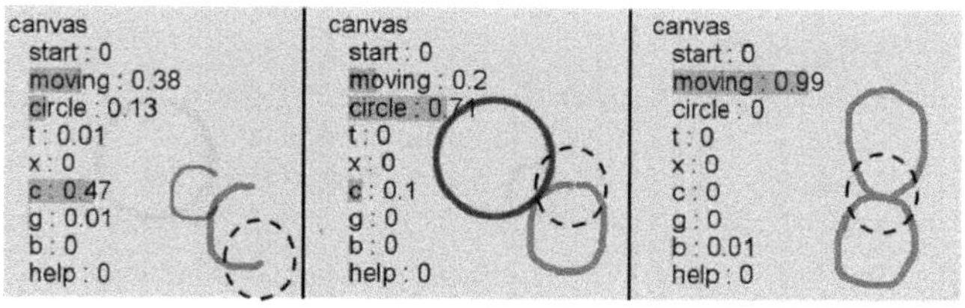

Figure 7: Screenshots of the canvas interactor as user draws a figure 8. Dotted line indicates finger location. **(left)** Initially a 'c' gesture is most likely (probability 0.47). Feedback indicates that c is the most likely interpretation, though a circle is possible. **(middle)** The system becomes confident that the gesture is a circle, reflecting this in feedback (also evident in state distribution). **(right)** As the user completes the figure 8, the canvas believes the user is painting and removes all gesture feedback.

can be especially problematic when the recognizer is inaccurate or the gesture set is large.

Gestures that are prefixes of one another (such as 'c', 'g' and circle gestures) are especially problematic. Many applications are designed to avoid common prefixes or provide sophisticated feedback (as in the OctoPocus system [1]) because of the resulting high degree of ambiguity.

Our framework handles this sort of uncertainty without requiring any special effort by the developer. By default, the recognizer is called repeatedly after each new input event (*e.g.*, **touch_move**) arrives. Each time, it generates a probabilistic gesture event which contains a distribution specifying the probability that each possible gesture is the correct interpretation. During event sampling, this event is divided into event samples for individual gestures (*i.e.*, a circle gesture, a 'c' gesture, etc.), weighted by likelihood.

We developed a canvas interactor for our paint application that handles both 'moving' (for painting) and gesture events. Figure 8 shows the gestures the canvas recognizes. The canvas interactor has 9 states (one for each recognized gesture as well as a start and moving state), and 37 transitions. Figure 9 illustrates a partial state machine for this interactor, which includes only a 'c' gesture and painting. The rest of the state machine is similar in form to what is in Figure 9. The canvas provides feedback about the canvas state (paint and interpreted gestures) using transparency. Figure 7 illustrates what happens when the user paints an 8 shape on the canvas. Because 8 shares a common prefix with 'c' and 'circle', the top hypothesis shifts from 'c' to 'circle' to painting on the canvas as the user draws.

Because the canvas provides visual feedback about the top recognized gestures, the user can change her gesture in real time to disambiguate. The feedback also allows the user to know when her gesture is 'good enough' to be interpreted, or (if she intends to paint something that looks like a gesture) the user can "cancel" recognition without affecting the intended drawing by reversing direction and retracing part of the drawing before lifting the finger.

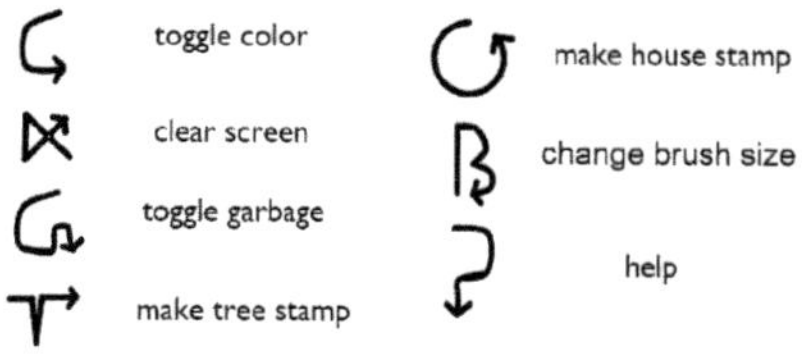

Figure 8: Gestures recognized by the canvas.

Developers working in a conventional input handling framework could certainly implement this canvas, however they would need to track not only the gesture probabilities, but also would need to include logic to determine when to decide whether the user is painting or gesturing. In our framework, the developer handles all of this simply by including both gestures and raw down/move/up events on transitions in the canvas's state machine. The underlying system handles all logic relating to tracking probabilities and deciding between paint and gesture events.

Beyond Touch: Accelerometer-based interaction

Although all of the input discussed so far is based on touch, our framework is not limited to touch. Any probabilistic event can be handled using the same mechanisms. For example, a shake event can be modeled with probability based on the vigor of the shake. We have built a recognizer that generates probabilistic shake events from accelerometer readings. We built a shake interactor which takes these shake events, provides feedback about the shake vigor and executes actions when shake events are above a developer-specified threshold.

Putting it all together

Each of these interactors is interesting individually, but the interactions become even more interesting when the interactors are combined in an application.

In addition to ambiguity about touch location and gesture, for any user action it is always unclear whether a user intends to paint on the canvas, execute a gesture, click on a button, or move a stamp. The success of the paint application hinges on its ability to manage multiple alternative interpretations *across multiple interactors* for as long as possible (*i.e.*, until the user lifts his/her finger). The framework we developed ensures that the application gives appropriate feedback about each possible action to the user. When the user lifts her finger, the framework acts appropriately (either resolving input when the resulting action is clear or prompting the user to disambiguate). No changes are required to the interactors described above for this to happen: Thanks to our framework, this complex application simply works.

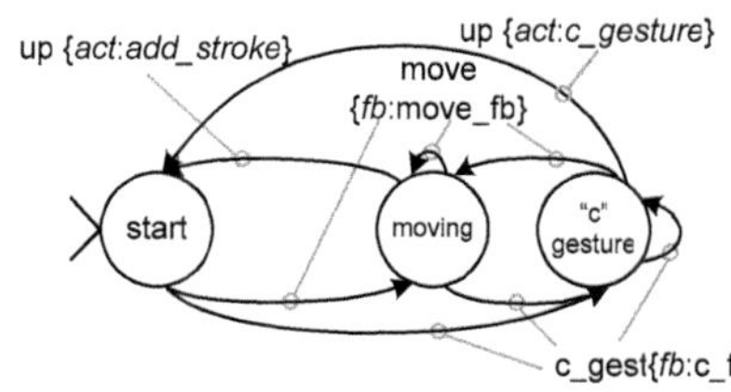

Figure 9: Partial state machine for the canvas interactor.

Consider the situation when the user intends to do a circle gesture but accidentally selects a stamp (Figure 1). This demonstrates uncertainty about the touch target (canvas or stamp), type (gesture or drag) and location. Since both possible targets process the input during dispatch, both the canvas and stamp will show feedback based on how likely each corresponding action is. The user continues the circle gesture and releases when she sees that the system will correctly interpret her results. If instead the user accidentally draws a circle when she intends to move the stamp, she could simply move her finger back and forth so that the circle gesture is no longer recognized.

The framework's support for tracking the *compatibility of* actions easily supports multitouch. As with any multi-touch interface, each interactor must include logic to make sure that it responds only to touch events that have the correct touch ID. For example, in our implementation, multiple stamps may be moved simultaneously, and any number of simultaneous fingers may be painting on the canvas. Because touch events with different IDs are considered compatible, our framework handles all logic for accepting and canceling events correctly.

The power of our framework is clear when all of these interactors are combined together. While it might be feasible to write these interactors individually using a conventional input framework, writing an application that correctly handles uncertainty *across* interactors would be extremely difficult, and not reusable. Our framework provides a general method for handling uncertain input, tracking interactive state and resolving ambiguous actions.

CONCLUSIONS AND FUTURE WORK

The arrival of new recognition-based input technologies requires that applications handle input with uncertainty. This presents new challenges for developers. Our framework supports managing interactive state, feedback and action without requiring developers to think probabilistically. Our contribution greatly simplifies the task of developing interactors that handle uncertain input, and brings us one step closer to developing an end-to-end toolkit for handling uncertain input.

The examples in the previous sections represent illustrations of the complex interactors that our system can accurately support including touch, gesture, and accelerometer input. In the future we hope to expand this library of interactors to make use of additional forms of uncertain inputs. Although our example feedback methods (*e.g.*, changing the transparency of various drawn objects) are effective, they only begin to explore the space of possible feedback for ambiguity. Future work will also consider more complex approaches to feedback.

ACKNOWLEDGEMENTS

This work was funded in part by grants IIS-0713509, IIS-0803733, and IIS-0840766 and a Graduate Research Fellowship from the National Science Foundation, by a grant from the Center for Future Work at Heinz College, CMU, a grant from the Intel Research Council, and an ARCS Foundation Fellowship.

REFERENCES

1. Arulampalam, M., Maskell, S., Gordon, N., Clapp, T. "A tutorial on particle filters for on-line nonlinear/non-Gaussian Bayesian tracking," *IEEE Trans. on Signal Proc.* **50**(2), 16-17, 2002.
2. Bau, O., Mackay, W. "OctoPocus: a dynamic guide for learning gesture-based command sets." in *Proc. UIST 2008*, 37-46.
3. Bourguet, M. L. "A Toolkit for Creating and Testing Multimodal Interface Designs." Posters and Demos from UIST'02, Paris, Oct. 2002, 29-30.
4. Chang, B.-W., Mackinlay, J.D., Zellweger,P.T., and Igarashi, T. A negotiation architecture for fluid documents. in *Proc. UIST '98*, 123-132.
5. Dumas, B., Lalannel, D., Guinard, D., Koenig, R., and Ingold, R. "Strengths and weaknesses of software architectures for the rapid creation of tangible and multimodal interfaces." in *Proc. TEI 2008*, 47-54.
6. Dumas, B., Lalannel, D., Oviatt, S. "Multimodal Interfaces: A Survey of Principles, Models and Frameworks." *Human Machine Interaction.* vol. 5440, 3–26, 2009.
7. Gordon, N. J., Salmond, D. J., Smith, A. F. M. "Novel approach to nonlinear/non-Gaussian Bayesian state estimation". *IEEE Proc. F on Radar and Signal Proc.* **140**(2):107–113.
8. Grover, D., King, M., Kushler, C., "Reduced keyboard disambiguating computer." U.S. Patent 5818437, Oct. 6, 1998.
9. Hudson, S. E., Newell, G. L. "Probabilistic state machines: dialog management for inputs with uncertainty." in *Proc. UIST 1992*, 199-208.
10. Jacob, R., Deligiannidis, L, Morrison, S. "A software model and specification language for non-WIMP user interfaces." *TOCHI* **6**(1):1-46, 1999.
11. Mankoff, J., Hudson, S. E., Abowd, G. D. "Interaction techniques for ambiguity resolution in recognition-based interfaces." in *Proc. UIST 2000*, 11 – 20.
12. Mankoff, J., Hudson, S. E., Abowd, G. D. "Providing integrated toolkit-level support for ambiguity in recognition-based interfaces." in *Proc. CHI 2000*, 368-375.
13. Metropolis, N., Ulam, S. "The Monte Carlo Method". *J. of the American Statistical Association* **44**(247):335–341, 1949.
14. Myers, B., and Kosbie, and Kosbie, D. "Reusable hierarchical command objects." in *Proc. CHI 1996*, 260-267.
15. Odell, J. "The use of context in large vocabulary speech recognition." PhD thesis, Univ. of Cambridge, England, 1995.
16. Olsen, D. "Propositional production systems for dialog description." in *Proc. CHI 1990,* 57-64.
17. Oviatt, S. "Ten myths of multimodal interaction." *CACM* **42**(11):74–81, 1999.
18. Schwarz, J., Hudson, S., Mankoff, J. "A Framework for Robust and Flexible Handling of Inputs with Uncertainty." in *Proc. UIST 2010*, 47-56.
19. Wasserman, A.I. "Extending State Transition Diagrams for the Specification of Human-Computer Interaction." *IEEE Trans. Software Engineering.* **11**(8):699-713, 1985.

Associating the Visual Representation of User Interfaces with their Internal Structures and Metadata

Tsung-Hsiang Chang
MIT CSAIL
32 Vassar St.
Cambridge, MA 02139
vgod@mit.edu

Tom Yeh
University of Maryland
College Park, MD 20742, USA
tomyeh@umd.edu

Rob Miller
MIT CSAIL
32 Vassar St.
Cambridge, MA 02139
rcm@mit.edu

ABSTRACT

Pixel-based methods are emerging as a new and promising way to develop new interaction techniques on top of existing user interfaces. However, in order to maintain platform independence, other available low-level information about GUI widgets, such as accessibility metadata, was neglected intentionally. In this paper, we present a hybrid framework, PAX, which associates the visual representation of user interfaces (i.e. the pixels) and their internal hierarchical metadata (i.e. the content, role, and value). We identify challenges to building such a framework. We also develop and evaluate two new algorithms for detecting text at arbitrary places on the screen, and for segmenting a text image into individual word blobs. Finally, we validate our framework in implementations of three applications. We enhance an existing pixel-based system, Sikuli Script, and preserve the readability of its script code at the same time. Further, we create two novel applications, Screen Search and Screen Copy, to demonstrate how PAX can be applied to development of desktop-level interactive systems.

ACM Classification: H5.2. Information interfaces and presentation: User Interfaces.

General terms: Human Factors, Design

Keywords: Pixel, accessibility API, text detection, text segmentation, graphical user interfaces

INTRODUCTION

Pixels are the most common characteristic and the ultimate elements produced by every application with a graphical user interface (GUI). In late 90's, researchers proposed using pixel-based methods for end-user programming and programming by example on existing user interfaces [9,10,17]. More recent work explores different possibilities with pixel-level interpretation for GUI automation, testing, and customization [3,4,5,16].

However, pixel-based methods have room for improvement in terms of speed and accuracy. For example, Sikuli Script [16] is not very fast, because it searches the screenshots of GUI elements across the whole screen and does not know how to narrow down the search space. Furthermore, it is hard to detect and extract the text content from pixel data.

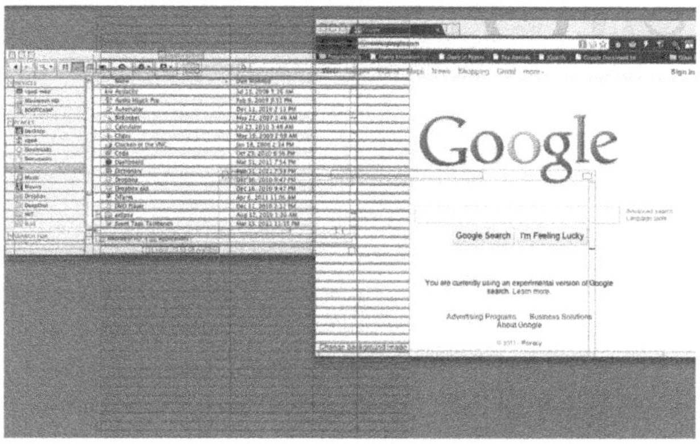

Figure 1 The internal structure of a GUI given by Accessibility APIs (AX) may not necessarily correspond to the actual visual representation of the GUI. Boxes above indicate the windows and widgets returned by AX even though they are not visible to users.

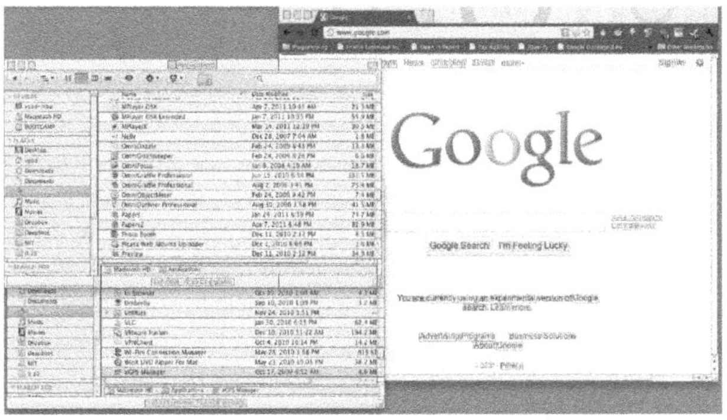

Figure 2 PAX combines pixels and Accessibility APIs for more accurate association between the visual representation and internal structure of a GUI. It filters accessibility information for only visible objects (red boxes) and also provides role, content, location, and size of objects detected by pixel-based methods (green boxes).

Current Optical Character Recognition (OCR) algorithms are designed for scanned documents, which are high-resolution with white background and simple column-based layouts, but not for on-screen text, which is low-resolution with colored background and could be randomly placed on the screen. Using current OCR algorithms on screen text would generate poor results [14,15].

Current pixel-based systems focus on using pixels as the sole source of input from the interfaces they operate. In order to maintain platform independence, these systems have intentionally neglected the other information that can be obtained from window managers or accessibility APIs. Unlike pixels, these extra sources of information are not necessarily available. For example, accessibility APIs are the standard hooks for exposing the internal structured metadata of a GUI to third-party assistive programs, such as screen readers, but to support such APIs requires engineering effort from individual software developers. As a result, accessibility hooks may be omitted or added later as the software matures. Fortunately, many popular commercial applications and built-in software on modern operating systems are accessibility-enabled. Therefore, why not leverage the accessibility metadata if the target applications provide them?

This paper introduces *PAX*, a hybrid framework combining *Pixels and Accessibility APIs*. PAX enhances the capabilities of current pixel-based systems and enables new interactive applications on top of existing interfaces. The key insight is that accessibility and pixel interpretations complement each other. Thus, both of these sources of information should be used together if possible.

PAX combines pixels with other information sources provided by GUIs, including accessibility metadata and low-level rendering data from the window manager, and associates the pixels with their internal hierarchical and structured attributes. As a result, PAX not only knows what is visible to the user on the screen but also understands the content and structures behind the pixels. We use accessibility metadata as a convenient and accurate source of widgets' information. If the accessibility metadata is not available, PAX automatically switches to pixel-level interpretation and still returns useful data. Furthermore, we use pixel-level methods to optimize the accessibility metadata. For instance, when accessibility APIs are not fine-grained enough to return the position of each word in a paragraph of text, we use a pixel-based segmentation algorithm, along with the known text for the whole paragraph obtained from the accessibility API, to locate the words with high precision.

The potential impact of PAX lies in its ability to improve existing pixel-based systems and to enable implementation of novel interaction techniques on top of existing interfaces. We validate this claim with concrete examples: the enhancement of pixel-based GUI automation (i.e., Sikuli Script [16]) and the implementation of two novel applications: *Screen Search* and *Screen Copy*. Screen Search is an attempt to allow users to conduct text-based search across multiple applications over the entire desktop rather than being limited to a particular window. It is applicable to any GUI components with text on the screen (e.g. on a title bar or in a tooltip of a button), even if it is occluded by other windows. Screen Copy is an attempt to allow users to copy the text content of a GUI component as well as the component itself. Users can paste the copied text into a text editor or reuse the copied component in a GUI designer application. The tool can be applied even when the text is not selectable or when the source code of the GUI is not available.

We make the following contributions in this paper:

- A hybrid framework that demonstrates how pixel analysis and accessibility metadata can be used together and complement each other.
- A text detection algorithm that finds text in screenshots, even with colorful backgrounds.
- A text segmentation algorithm that segments an image of a paragraph of text into individual word images, given known text.
- Validation of the framework in two novel applications and one enhancement of an existing system.

RELATED WORK

The idea of pixel-based interface interpretation and interaction emerged in the late 90's. Potter [9] developed a system, Triggers, to support application-independent end-user programming purely based on direct pixel access. Zettlemoyer and St. Amant [17] developed VisMap and VisScript to interpret pixels as high-level and structured representation of user interface objects, and then provided a set of mouse and keyboard commands (e.g. *mouse-move, single-click,* and *double-click*) to operate on the interpreted objects. WinCuts allowed users to cut a sub-region of an existing window and create an independent live view of the source, but did not interpret its content [12].

Recently, more pixel-based work has emerged. ScreenCrayons allows annotation on screen pixels [8]. Mnemonic Rendering determines the visibility of applications and shows motion trails of the changes when the hidden parts of windows are being revealed [1]. Sikuli Search allows users to search documents using the screen shot of GUI widgets [16]. Sikuli Script allows users to script user interfaces by taking screen shots of the targets the user wants to control [16]. Sikuli Test uses computer vision algorithms to analyze the pixels to generate testing scripts automatically [3]. Prefab interprets the pixels of a GUI and generates a high-level model of the widgets and their hierarchy [4,5]. The characteristic common to all this prior work is that it is completely focused on the pixel level. Instead of pure pixel methods, our work uses a hybrid approach that leverages pixels, the accessibility API, and the other useful information from the operating system to boost the robustness and performance of existing work and to enable new applications.

Most modern operating systems and GUI toolkits support Accessibility APIs, which were originally designed to be a standard hook for assistive technology applications, such as screen readers, or for GUI automation tools to communicate with a user interface programmatically. In addition to the assistive use of accessibility information, Stuerzlinger *et al.*'s User Interface Façades uses such information to allow users to customize an interface with copy-and-paste [11].

However, accessibility APIs are not widely available in every application and GUI widget. Hurst et al. reported that the Microsoft accessibility API can only correctly identify 74% of targets in eight popular applications on Windows [7]. Thus, they developed a hybrid approach that leverages the visual representation (i.e. the pixels) of a user interface to improve the accuracy of accessibility APIs for target identification. However, their approach does not deal with content; it is mainly for post-analysis of interaction logs to identify what targets the users might have clicked. In contrast, our approach is designed for real-time use to associate GUI widgets' internal metadata and their pixel representation. Chang *et al.*'s Deep Shot was a framework and an interaction technique that mixed pixel-based methods and accessibility APIs [2]. Deep Shot used visual features to identify which portion of the screen the user is looking at through a camera, and then found the application in that area using accessibility APIs. In addition, accessibility information was a backup channel if the target application of interest did not support the Deep Shot framework. Our work is a new abstraction layer that provides extra accessibility information to pixel-based systems and also expands the coverage for accessibility-based applications by providing the pixel interpretation of an interface with the same API.

PIXEL ANALYSIS VERSUS ACCESSIBILITY API

In this section, we describe the advantages and disadvantages of pixel-based methods and how we can use accessibility APIs to enhance the capabilities and performance of those methods.

Pixel Analysis

Pixels are the most common output medium of current computing devices. Every GUI application is eventually rendered as pixels on a screen. Unlike the pixels perceived from the real world and generated by a digital camera, the pixels generated by a computer itself have no noise, no distortion, and no other source of interference. Thus, early systems were able to use naïve bitmap matching to find targets on a screen [9,17]. Furthermore, Prefab has demonstrated that a UI model can be built from pixels in real-time so that researchers can build new interaction techniques on top of existing interfaces [4,5].

In contrast to understanding the UI model behind pixels, Sikuli Script takes a different approach to automate existing interfaces. In order to let users use loosely-bounded screenshots of automation targets, Sikuli uses template matching to fuzzily find the screenshots on the whole screen.

While they hold promise, the effectiveness of pixel-based methods can be challenged by four factors:

1. **Visibility constraints.** Invisible information, such as the items out of the current scrolling area or even the targets that are occluded by other windows, cannot be detected by pixel-based methods.
2. **Visual variations.** The accuracy of pixel analysis depends heavily on the look of target interfaces. If the user makes dramatic changes to the color scheme or the application theme, neither Prefab's trained prototypes nor Sikuli Script's fuzzy template matching screenshots can deal with the visual variations that result from such changes.
3. **Exhaustive screen search**. Pixel analysis is a potentially expensive operation, especially in high-resolution and multiple monitor environments with many millions of pixels. However, existing pixel-based methods such as Sikuli and Prefab often need to consider every pixel on the screen indiscriminately in order to locate certain targets, unless there is an external mechanism to direct their attention to specific regions on the screen.
4. **Low-resolution text.** The text content of an interface is hard to extract purely from pixels. Existing OCR engines are designed for high-resolution (150 to 300 DPI) scanned documents with white background and simple column-based layouts, but not for low-resolution screens (72 or 96 DPI) with colorful backgrounds and arbitrary layout. Simply plugging an existing OCR engine into a pixel-based system does not immediately work.

Accessibility API

Accessibility APIs are the standard interfaces built in modern desktop operating systems for assistive applications, such as screen readers, to access the low-level information of a user interface. Accessibility metadata is hierarchical, structured, and precise. For example, for an "OK" button in a confirmation dialog, we can get its role (AXButton), role description for humans, title, help message (the tooltip), enabled or disabled state, parent component, parent window, position, size, etc.

Accessibility APIs provide a convenient way to access many low-level attributes of existing software. However, to support such an API, application developers have to put in extra engineering effort to correctly expose the internal data. As a result, not every application and GUI widget supports accessibility APIs.

Fortunately, there are many applications that already accessibility-enabled. Hurst *et al.* reported that 74% of the widgets in eight popular applications were correctly identified by the accessibility API [7].

We conducted our own investigation into the current accessibility APIs for Mac OS X and Microsoft Windows (Microsoft Active Accessibility) regarding their capabilities and application compliance. We identified five challenges:

1. **Indifference to visibility.** Accessibility APIs does not know if a window or a GUI component is visible or not (see Figure 1). The location and the size of a minimized window would be returned as its original place and size before minimizing. If items are out of a scrolling area, they still can be reached by the accessibility API, and there is no way to tell which of them are visible to the user. This can lead to excessive and incorrect information when the developer just wants information about those the visible objects.
2. **Point-based object access.** Accessibility APIs support hit testing to gain access to an interface object shown on the screen. However, this ability is point-based and is limited to a single object; it is not possible to access a group of objects in a given region.
3. **Incomplete support.** Even applications that support accessibility APIs may not do so completely. An application may include new or complicated widgets that do not provide any accessibility metadata because they are not in the standard widget set.
4. **Coarse granularity.** The granularity of accessibility metadata may not fulfill the developer's needs. For example, the text content of a document may be returned as a block of text, where an novel interface technique may need the location of each individual word.
5. **Inconsistent text.** The text shown on an interface is not necessary consistent with the accessibility metadata, as it can be reformatted in an unknown way. For example, a date in accessibility metadata is "Friday, April 15, 2011 10:48:27 PM ET" but could be displayed as "Today, 10:48PM" on the screen.

Recognizing the respective strengths and weaknesses of pixels and accessibility APIs, we believe it would be ideal to combine them in a complementary manner, offering both generality from pixels and precision from accessibility metadata at the same time.

PAX: A HYBRID FRAMEWORK

We propose PAX, a Pixel+Accessibility hybrid framework that associates the high-level visual representation of GUI widgets with their low-level structured and hierarchical information. PAX has three sources of input: pixels, accessibility APIs, and window managers. PAX consolidates the information from these three sources into a new API that allows developers to easily access not only the pixels of the GUI widgets on the screen but also their internal information.

PAX associates the pixel representation of each GUI element on the screen with its underlying attributes, such as its role (which could be a button, a text field, etc.) and its text content or value. The underlying attributes are retrieved from the accessibility API if available. If not, PAX attempts to infer the role of the element from its pixel representation using template matching and uses pixel-based algorithms to detect and recognize the text (see Figure 3).

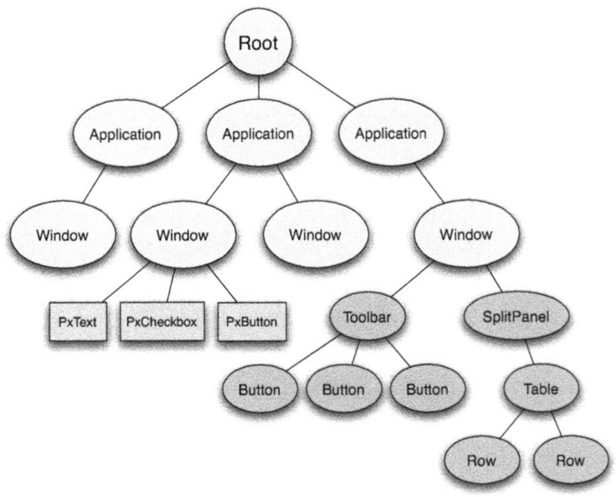

Figure 3 The tree of PAX UI elements. The yellow nodes, created using accessibility and window manager information, do not require any support from application developers. The red nodes are the elements exposed using accessibility APIs, while the green ones are reverse engineered from pixels.

PAX can improve the effectiveness of existing systems that are based purely on accessibility APIs or on pixels. On the one hand, systems based on accessibility APIs can benefit from the knowledge of the GUI's apparent visual representation to resolve certain ambiguities. On the other hand, pixel-based systems can use PAX to improve speed and accuracy. For example, PAX enables identification of a particular UI element using an XPath. Sikuli Script can store the XPath to a target UI component when taking the screen shot of it along with the screen shot image (e.g. in the header of the PNG file) and later use that path to locate the component without running template matching on the whole screen, or to constrain the search in a smaller region. Furthermore, PAX enables Sikuli Script to accept simple commands, e.g. `find(` 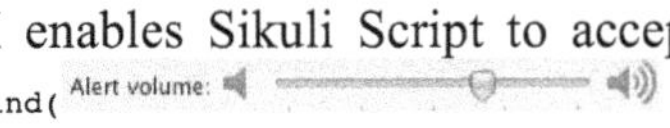

`).value()`, to easily retrieve the value of a slider without calculating the position of the thumb to infer it.

Designing PAX

There are three design goals for PAX:

1. The framework should enable existing pixel-based systems to easily access internal widget information given a region or a point on the screen.
2. The framework should simplify the difficulty and complexity in implementing novel interaction techniques on existing interfaces.
3. The framework should automatically give the most accurate results from available resources (either from accessibility metadata or pixel reverse engineering).

PAX maintains a tree of *UIElement* objects shown on the screen. The root of this tree is a virtual node, which does not represent any physical GUI elements. The root returns all running applications as its children and can be obtained by calling a global function `getUIElementRoot()`. Each application is also a UI element, which returns its opened windows. Each window recursively contains the same hierarchical structure of its title bar, tool bar, and all the other UI elements.

PAX distinguishes three different visibility levels for a UI element:

- **Visible.** This element can be seen on the screen.
- **Virtually visible.** This element is meant to be visible on the screen but is partially or entirely occluded by other windows in front of it because of limited screen space; if the screen was infinitely large and no windows needed to overlap, this element would be visible.
- **Invisible**. This element is not meant to be seen by users because it is scrolled out of view, in a minimized window, or hidden by design.

Therefore, each UI element has three different methods to get its children according to their visibility: *getVisibleChildren(), getVirtuallyVisibleChildren(), getChildren(),* where they return the visible children, virtually visible children, and all children, respectively. Because a UI element may be partially invisible, PAX also provides two methods, *getVisibleBounds*(), which returns the bounds of the visible part of a UI element, and *getBounds*(), which returns the original bounds.

Like accessibility APIs, PAX provides *getRole*(), *getText*(), and *getValue*(), for getting the role, the text, and the value of a UI element, respectively. A role represents the type of a component, e.g. a button or a list item. Text can be the label or the string value of a component. A value is a number that is only meaningful for some components, e.g. a slider or a check box. These values are retrieved from accessibility APIs if they are available; otherwise pixel reverse engineering techniques are used. Further, PAX also provides *getVisibleText*(), which returns the text actually shown to the user.

In addition to the standard accessibility attributes, each UI element has a *getScreenshot*() method for getting the screen shot of the element even it is only virtually visible, and *getXPath*(), which returns an XPath to the element, such as /Application[name="Word"]/Window[1]/TabGroup[1]/Group[text="Paragraph"]/MenuButton[text="Bulleted List"]. The *name* attribute in an XPath is only valid for Applications nodes, whereas *text* and *value* can be used in the remaining nodes. Developers can save the path and locate the same element quickly with a global function `locateUIElement(xpath)`.

To find particular elements, two methods can be used, by screen location or by content. PAX supports single-point hit testing with `getUIElementAtPoint(x, y)`, which returns the element at the given point, and `getUIElementsInRect(rectangle)`, which returns all the visible elements in the given rectangle on the screen. To find by content, each UI element has the three methods *findChildren(pattern), findVisibleChildren(pattern)* and *findVirtuallyVisibleChildren(pattern),* which return all, visible, and virtually visible children whose text content matches the given regular expression pattern.

Finally, to better support advanced interaction techniques, each UI element has a method *focus*(), which sets the keyboard focus to that element and also brings its parent window to the front at the same time. This is particularly useful when the developers need to perform further interaction on a UI element.

Bridging between Accessibility APIs and Pixels

One of this framework's goals is to automatically give the most accurate results from the available resources. Therefore, PAX constructs the UI element tree from all running applications and their corresponding accessibility handles. If an application has exposed all necessary accessibility hooks, its descendants in the PAX tree are simply copied from the accessibility tree and wrapped up with a *UIElement* interface. Sometimes a few widgets or even the entire application do not support accessibility APIs, and in this case, each of these widgets or windows looks like a black hole, with only a single node in the accessibility tree to record its boundaries.

When PAX walks down the accessibility tree and reaches a leaf node, it determines if there is a need to reverse engineer the pixel contents of the node with three simple rules: (1) if the node is a text component (e.g. a text label, a text field, or a text area), run our text segmentation algorithm to breaks the text into word component pieces; (2) if the node's role is not a container and not a text component (e.g. it is a check box, a radio button, etc.), do nothing; (3) otherwise run pixel reverse engineering methods on the node's screenshot. The text segmentation algorithm is useful for higher-granularity information about text components, and will be described later in this section.

With pixel reverse engineering methods, such as Prefab, we still can provide similar information to the accessibility metadata even if we reach a dead end in the accessibility tree. In our current prototype, we did not attempt to completely build the hierarchy of UI widgets from pixels using Prefab's method, but we used Sikuli's template matching to find a small set of GUI widgets (e.g. radio buttons, check boxes, sliders) instead. Furthermore, we developed a new algorithm for locating arbitrary text content in a complicated component, e.g. a web view.

A PAX tree is lazily generated on demand. Once parts of it are generated, the results are cached for fast response. The developer can explicitly request the cache to be updated. With proper event hooks that monitor the updates of the corresponding UI, the cache can be updated automatically after the UI is changed. For the reverse-engineered components, the tree can be automatically updated by comparing the consecutive screen shots. Comparing two 1680x1050 screenshots takes only 30ms on a modern PC; therefore, it is feasible to use this technique to continuously monitor the changes of a UI.

In the last parts of this section, we discuss how we have dealt with the challenges mentioned above as well as the text segmentation and detection algorithms.

Determining the Visibility of UI Elements

With only accessibility APIs, we cannot tell if a window or a component is visible or not. To address this problem, our solution is to request the *z-order* of each window from the *window manager*, and create "masks" to cover the occupied areas of each window from top to bottom. Thus, if a component is not fully covered by the masks and also intersects with its parent's visible bounds, it is visible from the user's point of view.

For virtually visible elements, we only care if a UI element intersects with its parent's bounds. If so, it is virtually visible; otherwise it is invisible.

Region-based Hit Testing

Accessibility APIs usually support hit testing, which is used for getting the accessibility information on a particular point on the screen. Unfortunately, this feature is limited to a single point and a single object.

To get multiple elements in a region, a naïve method is to run the single-point hit testing on each point in that region. However, this is inefficient because a region could have millions of points. Another method is to traverse the component tree and find all visible elements that intersect with the given region. But this is not possible with pure accessibility APIs, because they do not know if a component is visible or not.

Fortunately, PAX already has precise information about the visibility of each UI element. Therefore, PAX provides a function that enables developers to get the internal information of multiple objects in a given region on the screen.

Text Detection and Extraction From Pixels

Current pixel reverse engineering techniques, such as Prefab, can locate common GUI widgets and extract their textual content. However, Prefab's method requires text be located over predictable backgrounds that Prefab can model based on provided examples. If the text is on a background for which Prefab has not been trained, or a complicated background that Prefab cannot model (e.g., a photographic wallpaper), it will not find the text. Recently, computer vision researchers have conducted research on segmentation and recognition methods for small screen-rendered text and reported accuracy achieved of 99.2346% [13,14,15]. However, they assumed the position of the text is known and did not address the problem of text detection. To complement these pixel reverse engineering techniques, we have developed a text detection algorithm that locates text in arbitrary position in a screen image.

Given a screen image, the algorithm for converting it to words has three major steps: (A1) segment the image into disjoint blobs of pixels, (A2) merge character blobs into word blobs, and finally apply OCR to extract words.

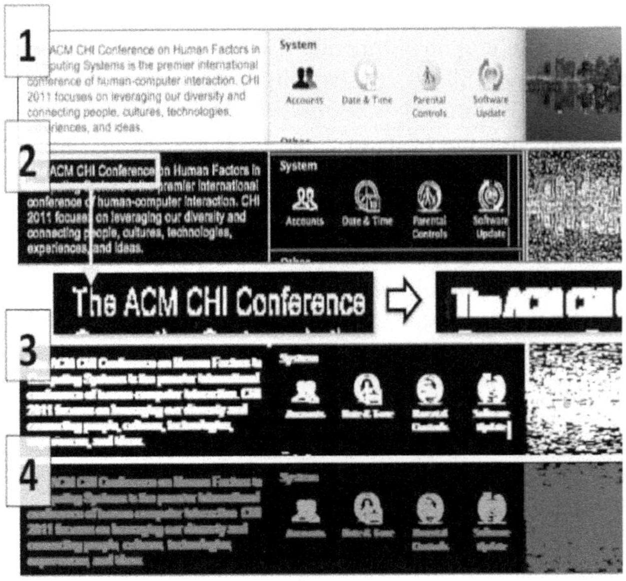

Figure 4 Text Detection process. (1) Given an image, (2) foreground pixels are extracted as small blobs. (3) Blobs are connected to form larger blobs, (4) which are classified into text (red), icon (green), or photo blobs (blue).

A1. Salient Component Detection

The goal of this step is to decompose a screen image into a set of salient components, each of which is composed of a blob of foreground pixels. Given a screen image as input, we first convert the image from color to grayscale. We apply an adaptive threshold to filter out low-contrast pixels. Figure 4-2 gives an example of the image after this process. Many container widgets such as panels have large areas of plain background pixels that can be easily filtered out in this way. From the high-contrast foreground pixels that are left, we detect long lines that might be window borders or grouping cues. These long lines are then removed so that components close to those lines would not be mistakenly interpreted as being connected by the lines. After this process, text elements turn into a set of blobs, each of which correspond to a character, whereas image elements turn into a set of disjoint parts.

A2. Text Extraction

Next, we merge blobs of individual characters into larger blobs of words and use OCR to extract text from each word blob. To merge blobs, we apply a dilation operator to expand the extent of each blob horizontally. If a blob is a character, horizontal dilation will connect it with the characters before and after, as long as the amount of dilation exceeds the amount of character spacing. This spacing depends on the font size, which can be estimated from the height of the blob. Figure 4-3 shows the output of this merging process. Then, given a string of connected blobs, we check two properties to decide whether it is likely to be text. First, we check if these blobs share a common height and baseline. Next, we check if the color variation among the foreground pixels is low, since GUI text tends to be rendered in a single, solid color to improve readability. Blobs satisfying both conditions are considered to be text blobs (red pixels in Figure 4-4) and passed to the OCR engine to extract words from them.

We did not implement Wachenfeld's screen text recognition algorithms [13,14,15], but used the Tesseract OCR engine (http://code.google.com/p/tesseract-ocr/) in our current prototype instead. If it were given the whole screen image as input, the Tesseract OCR engine would perform poorly because it assumes the text is in a single column. If we segment screen images into blocks of words that are processed individually by the OCR engine, the overall performance is better.

Text Image Segmentation Given the Text

The minimum granularity returned by accessibility APIs is one UI component. This may be not enough if developers need the location and the bounds of each individual word or even each character in a text component. Therefore, we have developed an algorithm that segments the image of a text component into individual word blobs. Unlike other text segmentation algorithms, the text string is known from the accessibility API, so we have additional clues to locate each word more accurately. Furthermore, since this algorithm runs on the leaf nodes in accessibility trees, we can assume the text is on a GUI widget with a simple or gradient background for the sake of readability. If the text has a complicated background, our algorithm would not work.

Given that the text is already known (except for some inconsistent cases, e.g. reformatted dates), this problem is not as hard as the original text segmentation problem in OCR. We describe this algorithm in two steps: (B1) segment images into N blobs, where N is the number of words in the given text; (B2) sort and match each blob to its corresponding word in the text.

B1. Text Segmentation

By assuming the background of the text is a solid or gradient color, we look for a vertical or horizontal line for which each pixel is the same color, in a descendent or an ascendant order in the given region. Once we have found such a line, we create a background by repeating this line to fill the size of the image, and then subtract the original image with this background to get an image with pure text pixels.

We use a top-down approach that is modified from recursive X-Y cut [6] to break a text image into word blobs. We assume the text could be split into multiple lines, but no single word is broken with hyphens. The idea of this algorithm is to calculate the sum of the pixels in each horizontal and vertical line to produce a density graph of white space. This graph shows several peaks that define horizontal or vertical gaps between lines or words, which are also the cut points we need to segment the image into smaller pieces. Our algorithm finds the largest gap, defined by its number of pixels, in the image, and cuts the image horizontally or vertically until the number of pieces remaining equals the number of expected words.

Figure 5 Text segmentation algorithm. Each number represents the order of the cut. (blue is vertical, red is horizontal)

B2. Matching each word with a blob

After the first step, we have N small blobs, each of which corresponds to a word. Next, we sort these blobs vertically and group them into lines with similar baselines. Blobs in a line group are then sorted horizontally to match the writing order of western text.

Matching Accessibility Metadata with What Users See

The *getVisibleText*() method of a *UIElement* should return the text that users see on the screen. One goal of PAX is to deliver the most accurate results. Therefore, we should use the text from the accessibility API if possible. However, the text shown on the screen is not necessary consistent with the one returned by the accessibility API.

A common example is automatic truncation when a string is too long. For example, "a very very very long file name.txt" may appear on the screen as "a very very...name.txt". Another example is time and date formation. For instance, "Friday, April 15, 2011 10:48:27 PM ET" could be shown as "Today, 10:48PM" on the screen.

To address this inconsistency, we compare the text from the accessibility API and the text from OCR. If the edit distance between these two strings is smaller than a threshold that is proportional to the length of the OCR string, we infer that no inconsistency exists and return the accessibility string as the visible text. Otherwise, when the strings are inconsistent, the OCR text is returned. Note the developer does not necessarily need the visible text, which is why we provide *getVisibleText*() and *getText*() for developers to choose according to their scenario.

EVALUATION OF TEXT ALGORITHMS

In this section, we describe the evaluation of our text detection and segmentation algorithms in PAX.

Text Detection Algorithm

To test the performance of our text detection algorithm, we constructed a dataset that consists of six high-resolution screenshots downloaded from the Internet. This dataset covers a variety of GUI widgets and text content on three major platforms (Mac OSX, Ubuntu Linux, and Windows 7). Each word in the screenshots was located and labeled manually as ground truth. The total number of visible words in this dataset is 1141. The number of visible windows is 16. This dataset was held back while we were developing the text detection algorithm; we used screenshots of our own computers for training purpose and preserved this collection only for testing.

During testing, we manually cropped the images of the 16 windows (since window bounds are available in PAX) and applied our text detection algorithm to each image. Our algorithm made 1236 detections. We compared the results to the ground truth and found our algorithm was able to achieve a precision of 84.39% (1043/1236) and a recall of 91.41% (1043/1141). The most common errors were isolated digits that were too small and were repeatedly mistaken by the algorithm as noise for 32 times (2.81%).

Text Segmentation Algorithm

To evaluate the performance of our text segmentation algorithm, we built a dataset of 331 images each of which is a tightly bound block of text. This dataset was split into training and test sets to prevent overfitting when developing the algorithm. The former has 546 words in 57 images and the latter has 2046 words in 274 images. Each image block has at least two words. These images were collected from our own Mac computers and covered popular desktop applications and web sites (e.g., Microsoft Word, twitter.com, cnn.com). We applied the text segmentation algorithm to each image and manually verified the results. We found only 30 words out of 2046 words were incorrectly segmented, which represents an accuracy of 98.55%.

VALIDATION THROUGH EXAMPLE APPLICATIONS

To validate the usefulness of PAX, we present three novel applications enabled by PAX: enhanced Sikuli Script, Screen Search and Screen Copy.

Sikuli Script

Sikuli Script, developed by Yeh et al., is a pixel-based approach to GUI automation that lets users take a screenshot of a target to direct mouse or keyboard inputs to that target [16]. It was deployed in early 2010 and a sizable user community has grown since. The discussions on its user forum suggest some difficulties of using Sikuli in practice. First, full-screen matching leads to ambiguity and slow performance. Users need an efficient way to constrain the search space to a certain application. Second, screen matching fails if the target window is occluded by other windows. It would be better if the matching worked even when the target window is only virtually visible. Finally, users need a reliable method to read the text from applications and can accept poor OCR results as better than nothing.

To demonstrate the validity of PAX, we enhanced Sikuli Script by addressing the above issues using the system. First, we added a new *App class,* which manages the information about an application and its window. App provides methods to open, close, and switch focus to a certain application by giving its name or a disk path. Once an application has opened, the corresponding App instance saves a reference to the *UIElement* of that application. Thus, a user may call *app.window(n)* to get the *n*th window as a Sikuli region and then all subsequent pixel computation can be constrained to this region for improved efficiency. This App class uses applications' accessibility information provided by PAX to enable Sikuli Script to constrain the matching area within an application window dynamically instead of using a fixed region on the screen, and also addresses the performance and ambiguity problem.

Figure 6 As the cursor moves, the boundaries of the target can be identified automatically in Sikuli Script. After the user clicks to capture a screenshot, the XPath to this target is also stored with the screenshot image for future use.

Second, we enhanced Sikuli's screen capture interface and searching algorithm with PAX. In the screen capture interface, we use PAX's hit testing to automatically identify the target's boundaries as the mouse cursor moves (see Figure 6). A user can simply click on a target to take its screenshot, or use the original method of dragging out a rectangle around the target. When a screenshot is taken, the XPath to the target's UIElement is also saved along with the screenshot (as metadata of the PNG file). Later, when the script is executed, Sikuli Script attempts to find the target with its XPath using PAX first, and then uses the original template matching method if the XPath fails or is unavailable.

Unlike the first enhancement that requires explicit use, this implicitly speeds up the time spent searching for a target and removes the ambiguity. If the complete XPath is not available, because the target widget does not support accessibility APIs, the enhancement still helps because we can at least know which application the target belongs to and constrain the search within the region of that application. This enhancement also addresses the second issue to allow Sikuli to search virtually visible windows, whose screen content can be seen from PAX even when they are overlapped by others.

Finally, we enhanced Sikuli's region-based operation by linking each region with the corresponding UIElements and propagating the value and text from leaf components to their logical group. This allows a script to read text from a region or get the value of a component. For example, *find(* 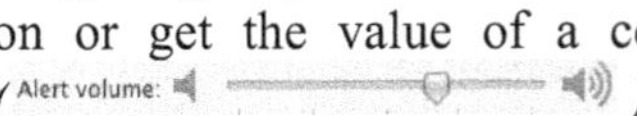

).value() can be used to read the value of a slider. Similarly, text also can be read by *region.text()*. Although PAX tries to unify pixels and accessibility metadata so that Sikuli users can be unaware of PAX, there are some notable differences when using different source of underlying information together. In the slider example we just mentioned, if the slider exists in the accessibility tree, PAX simply returns its absolute value. How-

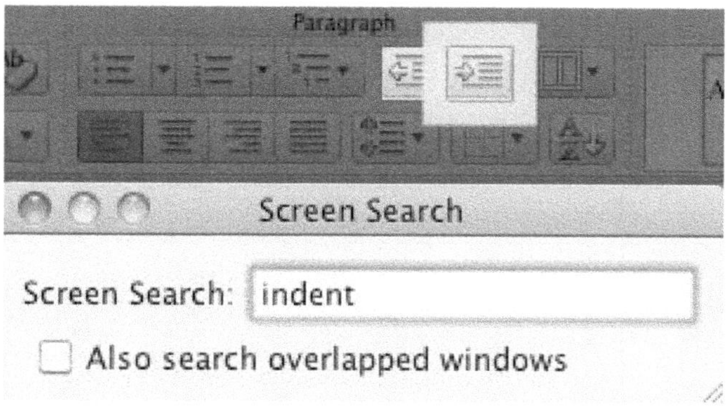

Figure 7 The two buttons with only image icons "Decrease Indent" and "Increase Indent" can be searched with Screen Search.

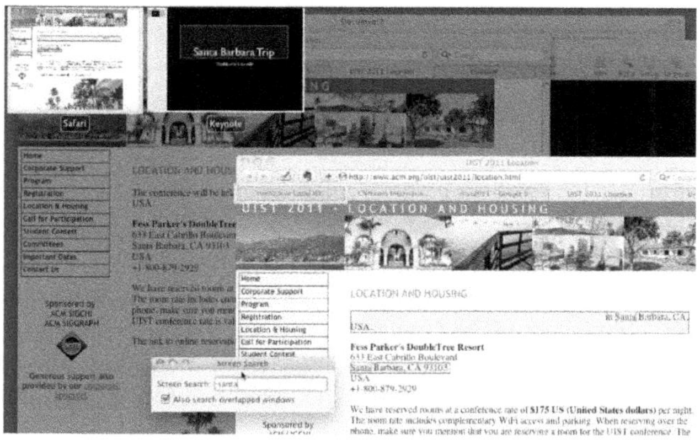

Figure 8 Screen Search finds the given keyword in multiple applications and shows the matched components and their windows at the same time.

ever, if it does not exist, there is no way to read its absolute value from the pixels. In this case, PAX returns a value between 0 and 1 by measuring the distance from the thumb to the two ends of the slider.

Our enhancements have addressed several practical issues in Sikuli Script. At the same time, the readability and the learnability of Sikuli code are preserved.

Screen Search

Search is a common and important feature in almost every application. However, it is usually limited to the application's text content. There is no general method to search the GUI components in a user interface. For example, the text in a text field or in a text area is searchable, but the buttons on a toolbar or the text label on a check box are not. As GUI applications become large and complicated, searching GUI components is especially useful for the users who are not familiar with an interface. For instance, toolbars are widely used in many applications, but the image icons on them are not necessarily easy to understand. In these cases, a user must move the mouse cursor to hover over each button and wait for the tooltip to learn its meaning. The ability

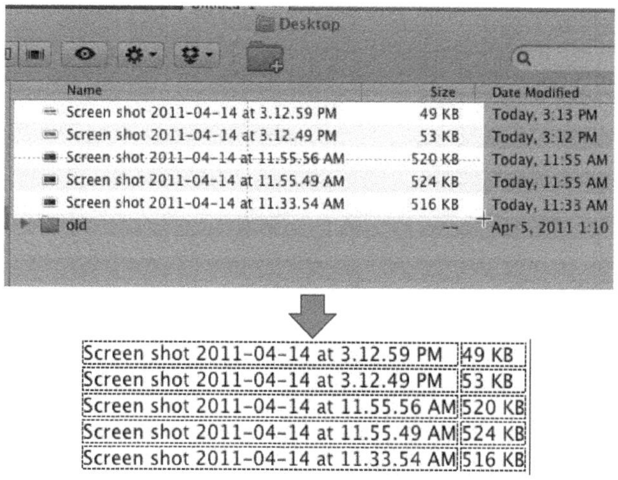

Figure 9 Screen Copy can be used to select and copy columns of a table or a list view.

to search components by their label or description would be a solution for this problem.

We have created Screen Search as a sample application to demonstrate how PAX can support building new interaction techniques on existing user interfaces. Screen Search enables a user to search not only text but also all GUI components on the screen by keywords.

Unlike the usual search bound to a single application, Screen Search is a global function that searches the content and UI of multiple applications at the same time. Furthermore, it allows a user to quickly navigate or switch the keyboard focus to any components found by Screen Search. In other words, this feature enables the use of a keyboard to navigate a user interface in a non-sequential order. For example, a user can search for "indent" to locate the "Increase Indent" and the "Decrease Indent" buttons on a toolbar, and hit the Enter key to select the highlighted one (Figure 7).

Screen Search has two modes: searching only the visible objects (the ones that can be seen on the screen), or virtually visible objects (the ones can be seen or are just overlapped by other windows). Each mode has a different way to present matched objects. Because the matched objects in the first mode are visible on the screen, we simply highlight them using a yellow box. In the second mode, matched objects are not necessarily visible, so we cannot just draw a box at each position. Instead, we draw a thumbnail of each window that has matched objects in a row and a big preview window with the current selected object. The user can press the Tab key to switch the focus among all matched objects and also bring their parent window to the preview position.

With PAX, the implementation of Screen Search is straightforward because PAX has decided the best source for obtaining the metadata of a component. A naïve implementation is calling *findVisibleChildren* or *findVirtuallyVisibleChildren* of the root of the *UIElement* tree, de-

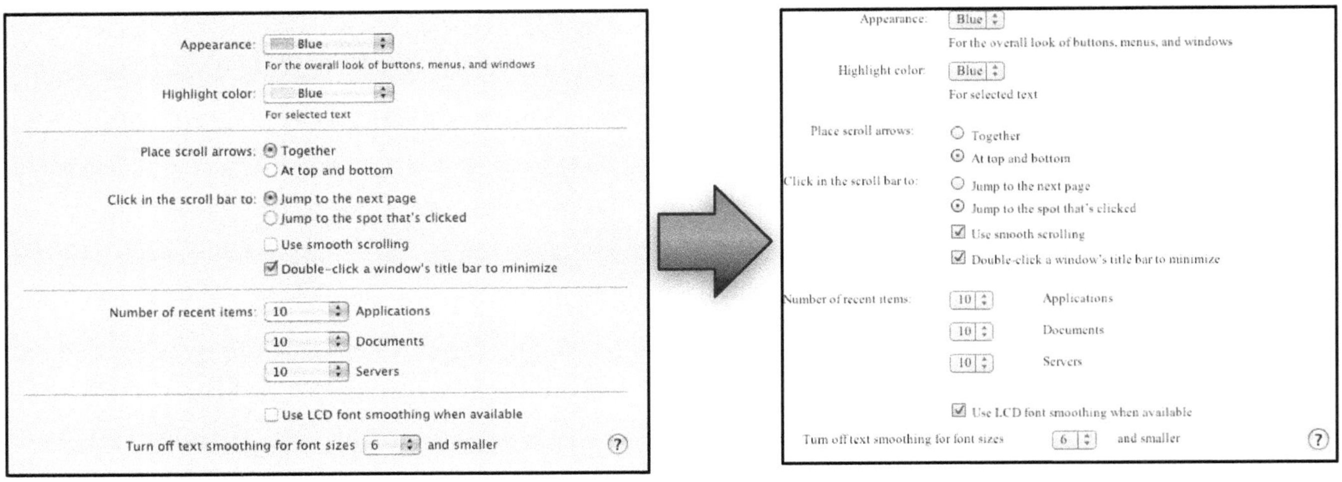

Figure 10 With Screen Copy, one can copy a Mac OS X user interface and paste it into a WYSIWYG HTML editor to create an HTML version of the same interface.

pending on the search mode, to retrieve the matched components in each window. However, to support incremental search, we traverse all nodes in the *UIElement* tree and build an index of the text in each node in a background thread periodically. This requires more complexity but provides a better interface that suggests how many and which objects are matched as a user types.

Screen Copy

Screen Copy is a novel application we have built using PAX. Screen Copy allows a user to select a rectangular area on the screen and copies not only the text but also the GUI widgets within that area into the system clipboard. Figure 10 shows an example where the interface for setting the appearance on Mac OS X can be copied and pasted into a WYSIWYG HTML editor.

Screen Copy does not simply copy GUI widgets independently, but preserves the hierarchy of widgets and their logical grouping. In the example shown in Figure 10, the two sets of radio buttons are correctly grouped together. Thus, only one button in each group can be selected at a time.

Screen Copy is useful for copying an existing interface without its source code and converting it into another format of representation. For example, we could train a library of Flex/Flash widgets using template matching or methods based on machine learning such as Prefab, and then use Screen Copy to convert a Flex/Flash interface to HTML.

Screen Copy also provides a rectangular selection model to existing programs that only have the common text selection implementation. For example, in a web browser, it is very hard to select and copy any non-text objects, such as a table or a form with pictures. The selection is constrained by the flow of text and the underlying structure of HTML. Thus, one can not easily select only one column of a table or two objects across their different containers. However, these can be achieved with the rectangular selection model provided by Screen Copy (see Figure 9).

Screen Copy is straightforward to implement with PAX. Using PAX's rectangular hit testing, the corresponding UIElements within the selected area can be retrieved easily. With the selected objects, Screen Copy transforms each UIElement to HTML tags according to its role and content. Finally, the HTML is copied into the system clipboard and a proper MIME type of the data is set so other applications can then convert it into their own format.

Screen Copy only copies the static interface of an application. It does not copy the dynamic behavior or animated effect on the interface. Additionally, some items that require more interactions to see (such as a drop-down box or a context menu) cannot be copied, so the drop-down boxes in Figure 9 were populated with only the one item that was visible at that time. Currently, as a tool implemented to demonstrate PAX, it does not copy widgets that cannot be represented in standard HTML tags. However, in the future, more complex transformations can be implemented to support non-standard widgets.

CONCLUSION AND FUTURE WORK

We have described PAX, a hybrid framework that uses pixels and accessibility metadata to complement each other. We proposed and evaluated two new algorithms for detecting text on screen and segmenting a text image into word blobs assuming the text is known. We validated our framework by implementing three applications: improving Sikuli Script, Screen Search, and Screen Copy. While promising, PAX has several limitations for future work:

First, in our prototype system, we used template matching to identify GUI widgets from pixels as a proof of concept. The modular design of our framework makes it possible to integrate other powerful pixel reverse engineering methods such as Prefab in the future.

Second, the developers who use PAX need to be aware of the uncertainty due to OCR errors. As future work, more robust OCR algorithms can be integrated with PAX to minimize this uncertainty.

Third, PAX currently uses the accessibility APIs provided by each OS. However, other sources of hierarchical UI representation, such as DOM, can also be integrated nicely with PAX to further improve coverage. For example, on Mac OS X, the built-in browser Safari has implemented a transformation that converts a DOM to an accessibility tree, making this integration possible.

Lastly, PAX currently uses the most common set of accessibility metadata for maximum compatibility on each platform. If more platform-specific metadata and APIs can be used, this opens the door for a diverse body of research. For example, we can add more actions, such as push buttons, or open a drop down menu, to each UIElement, so PAX could be a UI automation framework that automatically uses accessibility APIs or Sikuli Script as its backend. PAX could also support UI customization that provides set methods on each UIElement and draw a customized UI on top of the existing one to show different layout or effects.

ACKNOWLEDGMENTS

We thank the anonymous reviewers and UID group for great suggestions and feedback. This work was supported in part by by the National Science Foundation under award number IIS-0447800 and by Quanta Computer as part of the TParty project. Any opinions, findings, conclusions or recommendations expressed in this publication are those of the authors and do not necessarily reflect the views of the sponsors.

REFERENCES

[1] Bezerianos, A. and Dragicevic, P. Mnemonic Rendering. *UIST 2006.*

[2] Chang, T. and Li, Y. Deep Shot: A Framework for Migrating Tasks Across Devices Using Mobile Phone Cameras. *CHI 2011.*

[3] Chang, T., Yeh, T. and Miller, R. GUI Testing Using Computer Vision. *CHI 2010.*

[4] Dixon, M. and Fogarty, J. 2010. Prefab: Implementing Advanced Behaviors using Pixel-based Reverse Engineering of Interface Structure. *CHI 2010.*

[5] Dixon, M., Leventhal, D. and Fogarty, J. Content and Hierarchy in Pixel-Based Methods for Reverse Engineering Interface Structure. *CHI 2011.*

[6] Ha, J. and Haralick, R. Recursive XY Cut using Bounding Boxes of Connected Components. *ICDAR 1995.*

[7] Hurst, A. and et al. Automatically Identifying Targets Users Interact with during Real World Tasks. *IUI 2010.*

[8] Olsen, D.R., Jr, Taufer, T. and Fails, J.A. ScreenCrayons: Annotating Anything. *UIST 2004.*

[9] Potter, R.L. Pixel Data Access: Interprocess Communication in the User Interface for End-User Programming and Graphical Macros. Ph.D. Thesis, University of Maryland at College Park. 1999.

[10] St Amant, R., Lieberman, H., Potter, R. and Zettlemoyer, L. Visual Generalization in Programming by Example. *Communications of the ACM.* 43, 3 (2000), 107-114.

[11] Stuerzlinger, W., Chapuis, O., Phillips, D. and Roussel, N. User Interface Façades: Towards Fully Adaptable User Interfaces. *UIST 2006.*

[12] Tan, D.S. WinCuts: Manipulating Arbitrary Window Regions for More Effective Use of Screen Space. *CHI 2004.*

[13] Wachenfeld, S. and Fleischer, S. A Multiple Classifier Approach for the Recognition of Screen-Rendered Text. *Computer Analysis of Images and Patterns*, Vol 4673, 921-928, 2007.

[14] Wachenfeld, S., Fleischer, S. and Klein, H. Segmentation of Very Low Resolution Screen-Rendered Text. *ICDAR* 2007.

[15] Wachenfeld, S., Klein, H.-. and Jiang, X. Recognition of Screen-Rendered Text. *ICPR 2006.*

[16] Yeh, T., Chang, T. and Miller, R. Sikuli: Using GUI Screenshots for Search and Automation. *UIST 2009.*

[17] Zettlemoyer, L. A Visual Medium for Programmatic Control of Interactive Applications. *CHI 1999.*

Gliimpse: Animating from Markup Code to Rendered Documents and Vice Versa

Pierre Dragicevic[1]
[1]INRIA
F-91405 Orsay, France
dragice@lri.fr

Stéphane Huot[2,1]
[2]LRI - Univ. Paris-Sud & CNRS
F-91405 Orsay, France
huot@lri.fr

Fanny Chevalier
OCAD University
Toronto, Canada
fchevalier@ocad.ca

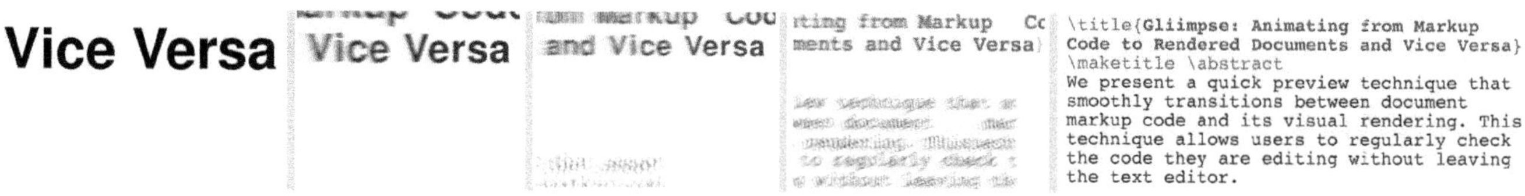

Figure 1: Detail of an animation between this article and its source code.

ABSTRACT
We present a quick preview technique that smoothly transitions between document markup code and its visual rendering. This technique allows users to regularly check the code they are editing in-place, without leaving the text editor. This method can complement classical preview windows by offering rapid overviews of code-to-document mappings and leaving more screen real-estate. We discuss the design and implementation of our technique.

ACM Classification: H5.2 [Information interfaces and presentation]: User Interfaces. - Graphical user interfaces.

General terms: Design, Human Factors.

Keywords: Document editing, Animation, Markup code.

INTRODUCTION

Despite the popularity of WYSIWYG editors, authoring and editing styled documents using markup languages such as LaTeX and HTML is a widespread practice among computer literates and has recently been democratized by Wikis. Markup languages are widely used and advocated because they provide a clean separation between content and form, with benefits in terms of maintenability, portability, visual consistency, predictability, expressive power and expert user performance [9]. Some users also find it easier to focus on the content without having to deal with the form — or even without having to *see* the form, as exemplified by the recent popularity of "dark room" word processors [4].

One difficulty with markup code is that, although it is human-readable, users cannot always predict the results with accuracy and need to regularly check if it is correct and produces expected results. This typically requires a series of actions to re-render the document and display it in a separate environment from the text editor. This causes disruptions of the editing flow that can be daunting to beginners who need to continuously check their code and sometimes search for commands by trial-and-error. Even the most experienced users occasionally need to check commands they are unsure about and having to switch from the domain object (e.g., an article being written) to the tools (a markup interpreter or document viewer) [3] may cause them to lose their train of thought.

A great deal of effort has been spent in text editing environments to address these issues. Markup editors help users write correct code from the start by providing tools such as syntax highlighting and auto-completion. Since these tools will never eliminate the need for checking the final document, many efforts have also been spent at improving the document preview workflow. Most editing environments now provide shortcuts for re-rendering and refreshing the document into the viewer. Some of them further support rendering on-the-fly, and sometimes WYSIWYG selection and/or editing. Although these tools dramatically improved the usability of document markup languages, they still require users to deal with two separate windows.

In this article, we present an alternative, in-place document preview approach called Gliimpse. This technique lets users quickly "glimpse" into the rendered document by having the markup code smoothly transition to the rendered document upon a hot key press. It is based on the observation that markup code bears visual similarities with the document it produces, making it a good candidate for animated transitions [16, 7, 8]. Animated transitions have unique features that can potentially make them a useful complement to existing document markup editing tools. They are:

- *Implicit.* Users do not have to explicitly select the pieces of code or regions in the document they are interested in as in synchronized views: they only have to follow them visually during animated transitions.
- *Contextual.* Animated transitions provide context on regions that are not of immediate interest to users, and thus can possibly help them by giving quick overviews of where things go from the code to the document and providing opportunities for incidental discoveries (e.g., spotting a mistake elsewhere). The explanatory power of animations might further help beginners learn a new markup language.
- *Concise.* When the animation is invoked as a quasi-mode like in Gliimpse (using a hot key), users can quickly check the results of a formatting command they are unsure about and immediately come back to the code (the only bottleneck being rendering time). Our animations are fast but smooth enough to let users follow objects of interest and/or build a quick mental map of where pieces of code end up in the final document.
- *In-place.* The document is shown within the text editor itself, which saves screen real-estate and makes it possible to display more content relevant to the writing task. Gliimpse additionally uses a visual stabilization algorithm that tries to have the region of code currently edited stay in place.

After providing a brief overview of related work, we describe the basic features of Gliimpse. We then go into more details on the design and implementation issues behind our technique and finally discuss possible future work.

RELATED WORK

Gliimpse is related to two bodies of work: document editing and animated transitions. We briefly review them here.

Document Editing

Document markup languages and WYSIWYG systems are two approaches for editing documents, each with their own advantages and drawbacks. There has been a lot of effort in developing tools that combine the benefits of the two.

Examples of such efforts are integrated editing environments that combine a markup language editor with a WYSIWYG view. This idea was first introduced with the Lilac document editor [5]. Current examples include Dreamweaver and Firebug for HTML, and Instant Preview and Whizzy-TeX for TeX. These tools typically support synchronized highlighting (hovering an element in one view highlights the corresponding element in the other) and in some cases synchronized editing (changes in one view are reflected in the other). Such tools have been proved very valuable but since the use of two windows might sometimes come with disadvantages — for one thing, two windows take more screen real-estate than one — single-view approaches have also been explored.

Single-view preview approaches are either markup-oriented or WYSIWYG-oriented. Markup-oriented ones include text editors with WYSIWYG display features like WikEd, LyX and X-Symbol [12]. These pre-render symbol commands (e.g., displaying `\int` as $\int$) or use rich font attributes in their syntax highlighting that resemble the final document. Preview-latex [12] pushes the concept further by rendering code regions such as math formulaes in-place. As for WYSIWYG input features, toolbars and menus for inserting markup commands into the code are common in advanced code editors like emacs. Conversely, WYSIWYG-oriented editors exist that let users type markup code that is either inserted in the document and interpreted later like in Wikispaces or interpreted on-the-fly like in TeXmacs [17]. To further explore this rich design space, we propose an alternative in-place preview approach that uses animated transitions.

Figure 2: Animation of an HTML form.

Animated Transitions

Animated transitions are a type of animation that consist in showing a visual change in a smooth rather than an abrupt way. Their use in user interfaces has been advocated [7, 16] and studies have shown that they can help understand the spatial relationship between views and help users track changes in a variety of tasks (for a brief review, see [8]).

Animated transitions can however be hard to design and to implement. Animated text, in particular, has been used for various purposes such as expressing ideas and emotions [14] but there has been little work on when and how to support animated text transitions. Two exceptions are Chang et al's system for showing and hiding annotations in documents [6] and more recently Diffamation, a system for showing document edits over time [8]. The latter work has shown that animating text between revisions rather than abruptly flipping pages helps users navigate in edit histories.

Gliimpse targets a different application domain and also differs from the design and implementation standpoints. Chang et al's system merely animates the scale and position of text paragraphs. The Diffamation system introduces a richer animation language involving text insertions and deletions and paragraph reflow. Gliimpse goes a step further by supporting animation between documents having a different layout, different fonts, and possibly involving complex transitions such as a markup command changing into an image.

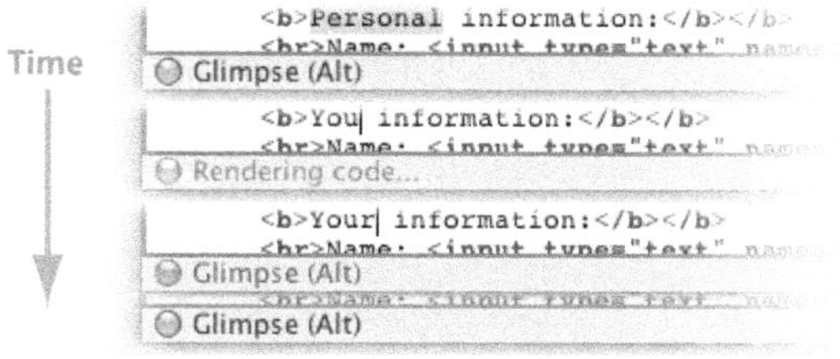

Figure 4: Gliimpse's status bar.

GLIIMPSE OVERVIEW

Gliimpse has been designed to be a quick, in-place preview tool for document markup languages. With Gliimpse, users stay in their text editing environment and can focus on their code, but are still able to check its rendering whenever they need. Whenever the user presses a hot key (we use Alt), the text editor switches to a document view with a fluid 1-second animation (Figures 1, 2). When she releases the hot key, the reverse animation is performed and she is back in her code.

The use of smooth animated transitions rather than abrupt view switches is motivated by previous work showing their benefits for navigating across text revisions [8]. Although fast and visually rich animated transitions can initially intimidate users, specific portions of text are easy to follow [8].

Gliimpse always transitions to the document region corresponding to the code currently in focus. The code focus is the area immediately surrounding the caret when it is visible, or the whole viewport content otherwise. The result is that the piece of code being edited will not move while the animation is performed, unless the document viewer has reached its scrolling limits. When the user moves the caret outside the viewport by scrolling elsewhere in the text editor and uses Gliimpse, the overall motion of the viewport is stabilized.

Since an actual document viewer is displayed upon completion of the animation, the user can scroll the rendered document while holding the hotkey. The viewport motion is then stabilized in the opposite direction at key release and Gliimpse animates back to a possibly new region of the code. Gliimpse can therefore be used as a navigation aid: the user just has to zoom the document out then gliimpse whenever she wants to jump to a different part of the document.

Because the layout of documents and markup code do not always match (e.g., with table cells and floating figures), visual objects can cross each other. To address this, Gliimpse has an option where objects that move with respect to the current focus follow curved paths. Figure 3a on the next page shows an example where a table (green square) is being edited. While gliimpsing, a larger table defined below in the code jumps above but goes around the focus (purple arrow). The user sees that the large table went to the wrong place and edits its placement options, which changes the focus to the large table and stabilizes it during the next gliimpse (Figure 3b).

This scenario illustrates how the overview and context provided by animations can help users make incidental discoveries and quickly build a mental map of where things go from the code to the document and vice versa. This didactic aspect of code / document animation can be exploited to help users learn a markup language, for example in Web tutorials.

Finally, when the code is edited, a background process re-renders the document and the animation. In our current prototype, this can last from 1/10 sec to more than a minute depending on document size (see the implementation section). A gray light in the Gliimpse status bar indicates that the process is working (Figure 4). After the user stops editing and once the animation is ready, the light switches to green, meaning that Gliimpse can be used. After a few seconds the light then switches to blue, meaning that a higher-quality, visually smooth version of the animation is ready to play.

DESIGN AND IMPLEMENTATION

We implemented the Gliimpse prototype in Java, with basic support for LaTeX, HTML, MediaWiki and RTF documents. We describe how we animate between these markup languages and the rendered documents.

Mapping the Code View with the Document View

To be able to compute animations, one needs to first generate a *code view* (i.e., a visual representation of the code as shown by the text editor), a *document view*, and retrieve a precise (character-level) mapping between the two views.

Figure 5 illustrates the problem and introduces notations that will be used in the rest of this section. It shows relationships between the markup text (T_0, bottom left of the Figure), the code view (V_0, top left), the document view (V_1, top right) and the document in raw text format (T_1, bottom right). We use the notation $X_A Y_B$ to denote a function that maps subsets of X_A to subsets of Y_B (thick black lines in the Figure):

- V_0V_1 (top) is the mapping between the two views. We assume V_0 and V_1 to be collections of glyphs and other graphical objects (possibly structured as a scene graph) with all information needed to render them individually (bounds, font, etc.). The mapping function V_0V_1 is the information we need in order to compute animations, which virtually no programming library or API directly provides.
- T_0V_0 (bottom left) is the mapping between the source code and its rendering in the text editor, which we assume to be a function that maps subsets of T_0 (i.e., collections of character indices) to subsets of V_0. This information is typically provided by the text editor's inspection methods or accessibility API.

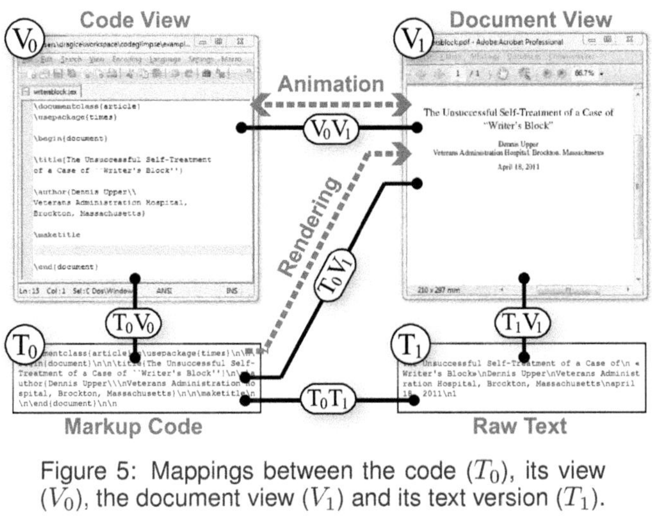

Figure 5: Mappings between the code (T_0), its view (V_0), the document view (V_1) and its text version (T_1).

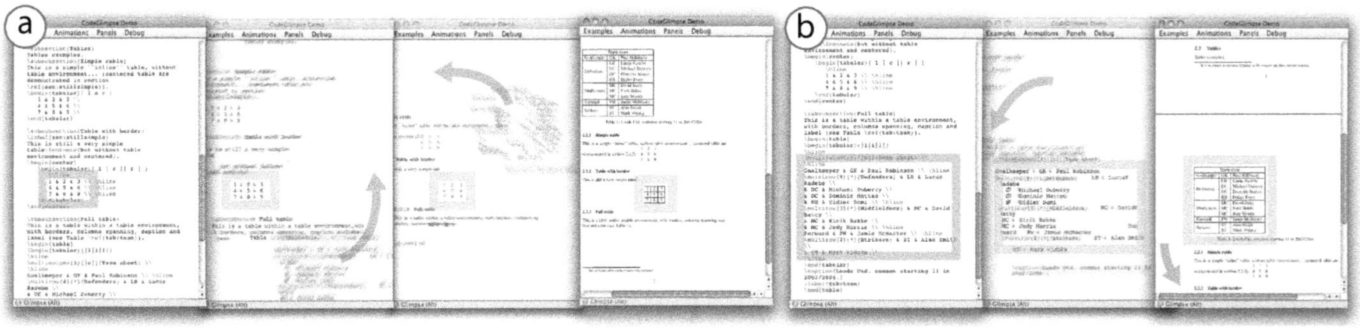

Figure 3: a) Motion of a large table (arrows) while another table is in focus (rectangle) ; b) The large table is now the focus.

- T_0V_1 (diagonal line) is the mapping between the source code and the document view. Markup language interpreters and renderers rarely maintain this information and when they do, it is often at a too coarse level of granularity to allow for precise animations. For example, TEX Source Specials and SyncTEX only provide mappings at the line level due to limitations of the TEX engine [13].
- T_1V_1 (bottom line) is the mapping between a raw text version of the document and the document view. This information is typically maintainted by document viewers to allow for text selection or to provide accessibility support.

The best way to reconstruct V_0V_1 is by computing $V_0V_1 = T_0V_0^{-1} \circ T_0V_1$. However, since getting T_0V_1 at the character level is hard in practice and because we initially just wanted to build a prototype, we chose to reconstruct V_0V_1 by computing $V_0V_1 = T_0V_0^{-1} \circ T_0T_1 \circ T_1V_1$. This approach is less robust but more flexible and makes it easier to plug Gliimpse into any interpreter and renderer available in Java.

In our current prototype, we obtain V_0 and T_0V_0 from the Java's text component (`JEditorPane`) inspection methods. The same Java component is used to render HTML, MediaWiki and RTF documents, and also provides V_1, T_1 and T_1V_1. LATEX source code is interpreted through a native call to `pdflatex` and the generated PDF file is rendered with a custom Java component based on the Sun PDF Renderer. We use the fonts from this renderer and the Apache PDFBox library to extract V_1, T_1 and T_1V_1. In all formats, non-character elements are mapped to white spaces in T_1.

The mapping T_0T_1 is built by cleaning up T_0 and T_1 and computing a diff between the two strings. We use Myer's diff algorithm [15], which supports deletions, insertions and moves. The cleaning up of T_0 essentially consists in stripping out markup elements and replacing non-character elements such as `<img*/>` with custom tags. The white spaces in T_1 that are mapped to non-character glyphs are replaced with the same tags. All string operations maintain a mapping with the original character indices. T_0T_1 can therefore be obtained by computing $T_0T_1 = T_0T_0^{\star} \circ T_0^{\star}T_1^{\star} \circ T_1T_1^{\star-1}$, with $T_0^{\star}$ and $T_1^{\star}$ being the processed texts and $T_0^{\star}T_1^{\star}$ their diff.

For the formats we support, this method accurately rebuilds character mappings between markup code and the raw text version of simple documents. It is however not robust enough for a final product: duplicate text regions and complex mappings can defeat the diff algorithm and cause document regions to be either wrongly animated or not animated at all. We implemented a T_0T_1 mapping editor and used it to author the LATEX math tutorial scenario shown in the accompanying video. Fully automated approaches are arguably preferable and we hope that in-place preview techniques like Gliimpse will inspire the implementation of accurate, robust and usable APIs for mapping code views with rendered views.

Animating Between Fonts

In contrast with text animation techniques described in previous work [6, 14, 8], we need to animate between different fonts. Parametric typefaces [1] can linearly interpolate between glyphs but only if they share the exact same structure by design. Morphing between arbitrary shapes is a hard problem for which methods have been proposed [2] but they are computationally expensive.

For the purposes of animated transitions, we found that simply using alpha-blending to produce a dissolve effect yields excellent visual results. However, for this effect to work glyphs need to be properly aligned. Glyphs from different fonts can significantly differ in size even when the same font point size is used (Figure 6a). Aligning those glyphs based on their logical or geometrical bounds (Figure 6b,c) does not fully solve the problem. We therefore chose to refine glyph alignment using a pixel-based approach (Figure 6d).

We first collect all pairs of glyphs that need to be animated. For each pair, we draw one of the two glyphs off-screen with a fixed size (we use a point size of 30) and draw the other one on top using the method from Figure 6c. We compute the pixel color difference then vary the geometry of the second glyph (x, y, $width$, $height$ and x-$shear$ for italics) using a gradient descent scheme until a local minimum is reached. The result is cached and generalized to fonts of different sizes using linear interpolation. This method works best for within-character animations but can also polish animations such as changes in title capitalization.

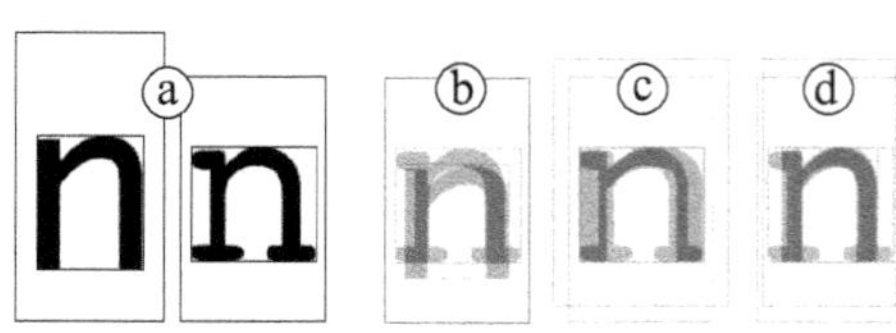

Figure 6: Alignment of two glyphs with the same font size (a), based on logical bounds (b), geometrical bounds (c) and pixels (d).

Animating the Document

Gliimpse's animation scheme is similar to the Diffamation system [8], with a few notable differences we outline here.

Object Interpolation. Like Diffamation, Gliimpse builds a parametric scenegraph that displays the initial document when rendered at $t = 0$ and the final document when rendered at $t = 1$. For $t \in]0, 1[$, the scenegraph essentially performs a linear interpolation of its nodes' bounding boxes.

We support 3 basic node types: *glyph transitions*, *non-glyph transitions* and *paragraph transitions*. Non-glyph transitions include transitions from a glyph to an image and between glyph groups. They are rendered by linearly interpolating the bounding boxes of the initial and final objects and alpha-blending them. Glyph transitions are computed the same way in addition to the alignment transformation previously described. Non-glyph objects are currently rendered as rectangles (see Figure 2). Paragraphs will be described later on.

When an object in V_0 or V_1 maps to nothing, we rapidly fade it in or out, in-place (as opposed to [8] where objects grow or shrink). Furthermore, we found that animating between groups of glyphs produces visual clutter or very wide characters (e.g., when animating from `\ref{fig:teaser}` to 1), both of which are visually unpleasant. We therefore occlude those transitions at the middle of the animation by overlaying a rectangle with opacity $1 - 2 \cdot |t - 1/2|$ (see Figure 2). Finally, the scenegraph's root is animated by interpolating its background color and its position in the two viewports.

Paragraph Extraction. Like in [8], we group scenegraph nodes in paragraphs to be able to animate text reflow. However, we cannot rely on well-formed paragraph structures because some formats such as PDF produce V_1 content that merely consists in flat collections of glyphs. We therefore extract paragraphs from individual glyphs as follows:

We iterate over characters t^i of T_0 and at each step we compute the bounding box B^i of the object $T_0V_1(t^i)$ in V_1 and append it to the bounding box L^i of the current text line in V_1. At each step we test the following cases (for all our formats we use $vspace_{T0} = 2$ and $vspace_{V1} = 2$):

- If $\{t^{i-k}, \ldots, t^i\}$ contains only whitespaces among which $vspace_{T0}$ carriage returns, a new paragraph is created,
- if $T_0V_1(t^i) = \varnothing$ we proceed to the next index $i + 1$,
- if $B^i_{y0} > L^{i-1}_{y0} + vspace_{V1} \cdot L^{i-1}_{height}$ a new paragraph is created,
- if $B^i_{x0} < B^{i-1}_{x0}$ and $B^i_{y0} > L^{i-1}_{y0}$ a new line is started, in which case L^i is initialized to B^i,
- if $B^i_{x0} > B^{i-1}_{x0}$ and $B^i_{y1} > L^{i-1}_{y0}$ and $B^i_{y0} < L^{i-1}_{y1}$ the line continues and L^i is updated to $L^{i-1} \cup B^i$.
- otherwise, a new paragraph is created.

Once a paragraph is created for the indices i to j, we iterate over all subsets of $\{t^i, \ldots t^j\}$ of cardinality > 1 that map to content in V_1 and add them to the paragraph if their content lies within the paragraph bounds in V_1.

Text Reflow. Gliimpse animates text reflow within paragraphs in a way similar to [8]: depending on which path is shorter, a character can either follow a direct path or be "modulo-animated", i.e., move along its line and reach the edge to re-appear on the other side. In our algorithm, each character is animated independently and modulo-interpolations are limited to a full paragraph width. The visual effect on a paragraph with growing width would be that words on the second line move slowly to the left, those on the third line move similarly but faster, and so on until a line breaks in two pieces, one going quickly to the left and the other one slowly going up. Finally, our modulo metrics accounts for the fact that our paragraphs can have lines of different heights and these heights are linearly interpolated during the animation.

Scrolling stabilization. We stabilize horizontal and vertical scrolling between the code and the document viewports by minimizing the average motion of objects that are visible in the source viewport, as described in [8]. In addition, when the caret is visible, we use its position as the region of interest and stabilize the nearest object rather than the entire viewport. Stabilization is recomputed every time the user scrolls into the code, moves the caret, or scrolls into the document.

Curved Trajectories. In contrast with [8], we support diff move operations and chunks of text can therefore cross on the screen. To make these motions easier to understand and limit occlusions of the region of interest, an option allows objects to follow curved trajectories (see Figure 3). Our method, inspired from link drawing techniques in graphs [11], consists in having objects follow an arc and those moving in the opposite direction follow an arc oriented to the opposite side. More specifically, after scrolling stabilization we add to the absolute trajectory $P^{(t)}$ of each object (paragraph or isolated node) the vector $sin(\pi t)^k \cdot [r_x(P^{(1)}_y - P^{(0)}_y), r_y(P^{(1)}_x - P^{(0)}_x)]$. We use $k = 0.5$, $r_x = -0.5$ and $r_y = 0.05$.

Since arc radii are proportional to object motion, animations with no crossings will have close-to-straight trajectories (since they have been stabilized) but crossing objects will deviate from their path as if they tried to avoid each other. Even if this method does not guarantee the absence of overlaps, it presents the advantage of being context-free (every object ignores the position of others), which makes it simple and guarantees motion coherence (objects which are normally close will remain close). The asymmetry between the values we chose for r_x and r_y stems from fact that documents are structured in lines.

Playing Back and Recomputing Animations

The animated scenegraph is parented to a Java layered container that also contains the document viewer and the text editor. When the hot key is pressed, the scenegraph is set to $t = 0$, brought to the top and the animation starts. When the scenegraph shows the final document at $t = 1$ the actual document viewer is brought to the top. This transition is shown with a quick dissolve effect because the document view occasionally shows decorations that are not inspectable and hence not visible during the animation. The reverse sequence of operations is performed when the hot key is released.

We animate between $t = 0$ and 1 with a duration of 1 second, which has been shown to be appropriate for reasonably complex visual transitions and with a slow-in slow-out pacing, which has been shown to facilitate object tracking [10].

		Task a (s)	b (s)	c (s)	d (s)	e (s)	FPS (Hz)
HTML	1st	0.21	0.12	0.04	0.03	0.29	75
	2nd	0.21	0.07	0.02	0.01	0.01	89
LaTeX 1	1st	1.90	0.28	0.41	0.06	0.64	36
	2nd	0.97	0.26	0.28	0.04	0.02	40
LaTeX 2	1st	3.72	37.0	8.68	10.5	19.5	12
	2nd	2.68	41.3	8.53	10.5	0.62	13

Table 1: Task execution times for three documents.

Animations are updated on-the-fly by a scheduler that runs in a separate thread and skips unnecessary computations. For example, modifying the source code requires a) re-rendering the document, b) computing the T_0T_1 mapping, c) inspecting the views for T_0V_0 and T_1V_1, d) building the scenegraph, e) aligning new glyphs and f) stabilizing the views. However, when a view is resized only tasks c) to f) are performed, and when it is scrolled only task f) is done. After the animation is ready the scheduler runs an off-screen rendering task after which complex animations play back more fluidly with an optional motion blur effect (visible in the Figures).

Table 1 shows computation times on a PC with a 2.40GHz Intel Xeon processor for the tasks mentioned above (task f is negligible), as well as the animation frame rate. Figures are given for the first run (1st) and after inserting a character in the code (2nd). The first two examples are a short HTML file (700 characters) and LaTeX file (1900 characters, about 1 page). These computation times are adequate for interactive use but the third example, a 5-page LaTeX draft of this article (30,000 characters), shows that our current prototype does not scale up. The most expensive task is the code/document mapping task, which uses heavy regexp searches and hashtables. This operation can be optimized or avoided altogether with an API that provides T_0V_0 as previously discussed.

CONCLUSION AND FUTURE WORK

We presented Gliimpse, a quick in-place preview technique that smoothly transitions between markup code and its visual rendering. This technique is an alternative to classical preview tools that takes less screen real-estate and offers rapid overviews of code-to-document mappings.

More work is needed to identify the actual benefits of animations over well-established approaches such as synchronized views. We hypothesize that animations can save users time and effort because they involve *attentional* rather than *explicit* selection of regions of interest. This is however only a conjecture that needs to be put to the test. And even in case animation helps, it is likely that synchronized views are more suited for some tasks and that both need to be supported.

Possible future extensions include local animated previews, integration with synchronized highlighting and editing, animation of series of code transformations (e.g., XSLT) and animation of non-textual markup documents like music sheets or vector graphics. Furthermore, Gliimpse is currently only a prototype and a more robust version is necessary for users to be able to try it on real writing tasks.

ACKNOWLEDGEMENTS

We thank Jean-Daniel Fekete for insightful discussions.

REFERENCES

1. Adobe. Designing multiple master typefaces, 1995. `http://partners.adobe.com/public/developer/en/font/5091.Design_MM_Fonts.pdf.`
2. M. Alexa, D. Cohen-or, and D. Levin. As-rigid-as-possible shape interpolation. In *Annual Conference on Computer Graphics*, 157–164, 2000.
3. M. Beaudouin-Lafon. Instrumental interaction: an interaction model for designing post-wimp user interfaces. In *Proc. CHI '00*, 446–453. ACM.
4. S. bin Ali. 20 fantastic full screen text editor for distraction free writing, 2009. `http://www.techmalaya.com/2009/02/07/full-screen-text-editor-blogger/.`
5. K. Brooks. Lilac: a two-view document editor. *Computer*, 24(6):7 –19, jun 1991.
6. B.-W. Chang, J. D. Mackinlay, P. T. Zellweger, and T. Igarashi. A negotiation architecture for fluid documents. In *Proc. UIST '98*, 123–132. ACM.
7. B.-W. Chang and D. Ungar. Animation: from cartoons to the user interface. In *Proc. UIST '93*, 45–55. ACM.
8. F. Chevalier, P. Dragicevic, A. Bezerianos, and J.-D. Fekete. Using text animated transitions to support navigation in document histories. In *Proc. CHI '10*, 683–692. ACM.
9. J. H. Coombs, A. H. Renear, and S. J. DeRose. Markup systems and the future of scholarly text processing. *Commun. ACM*, 30:933–947, Nov. 1987.
10. P. Dragicevic, A. Bezerianos, W. Javed, N. Elmqvist, and J.-D. Fekete. Temporal distortion for animated transitions. In *Proc. CHI '11*, 2009–2018. ACM.
11. J.-D. Fekete, D. Wang, N. Dang, and C. Plaisant. Overlaying graph links on treemaps. In *Proc. Infovis '03 (demo)*, 2003.
12. D. Kastrup. Revisiting WYSIWYG paradigms for authoring latex, 2002. `http://www.tug.org/TUGboat/tb23-1/kastrup.pdf.`
13. J. Laurens. Direct and reverse synchronization with synctex. *TUGboat*, 29(3), 2008.
14. J. C. Lee, J. Forlizzi, and S. E. Hudson. The kinetic typography engine: an extensible system for animating expressive text. In *Proc. UIST '02*, 81–90. ACM.
15. E. Myers. An $o(nd)$ difference algorithm and its variations. *Algorithmica*, 1(2):251–266, 1986.
16. G. G. Robertson, J. D. Mackinlay, and S. K. Card. Cone trees: animated 3d visualizations of hierarchical information. In *Proc. CHI '91*, 189–194. ACM.
17. J. van der Hoeven. Gnu texmacs: A free, structured, wysiwyg and technical text editor. In *Actes du Congres GUTenberg*, volume 39-40, 39–50, 2001.

RhythmLink: Securely Pairing I/O-Constrained Devices by Tapping

Felix Xiaozhu Lin
Department of Computer Science
Rice University
Houston, TX 77005 USA
xzl@rice.edu

Daniel Ashbrook, Sean White
Nokia Research Center
2400 Broadway
Santa Monica, CA 90404 USA
{daniel.ashbrook,sean.white}@nokia.com

ABSTRACT
We present RhythmLink, a system that improves the wireless pairing user experience. Users can link devices such as phones and headsets together by tapping a known rhythm on each device. In contrast to current solutions, RhythmLink does not require user interaction with the host device during the pairing process; and it only requires binary input on the peripheral, making it appropriate for small devices with minimal physical affordances. We describe the challenges in enabling this user experience and our solution, an algorithm that allows two devices to compare imprecisely-entered tap sequences while maintaining the secrecy of those sequences. We also discuss our prototype implementation of RhythmLink and review the results of initial user tests.

ACM Classification: H5.2 [Information interfaces and presentation]: User Interfaces—Haptic I/O, Input Devices and Strategies

General terms: Design, Human Factors, Security

Keywords: Device pairing, mobile devices, input, rhythm, security, taps

INTRODUCTION
As technology shrinks, the user interface for mobile devices is becoming the largest physical part of the device. Some input devices now consist solely of sensors [13, 14] or physical affordances [1]. As devices get smaller and cheaper, Weiser's vision of "'scrap computers'... that can be grabbed and used anywhere" [23] may extend to general input and output peripherals that can be connected on the fly to laptops, mobile phones, watches, and other personal, mobile devices.

User interaction with such peripherals has been explored, but a remaining challenge is the way in which these tiny, wireless devices are connected together or "paired". Consider a set of Bluetooth headphones: most have just a few buttons and no visual interface at all. In order to connect the headphones to a phone, the user must follow a multi-step procedure: retrieving the phone from wherever it is stored (pocket, bag, or purse, for example), scanning for devices and selecting the headphones, typing in the headphone's security code, and placing the phone back into the pocket or bag.

While these steps are familiar to many users of wireless technology, research indicates that this pairing process is often slow [10] and confusing [22]. Our research addresses the usability of device pairing, while at the same time maintaining security.

In this paper, we introduce our system "RhythmLink" which improves on prior pairing methods. RhythmLink allows users to securely pair a peripheral with a host device such as a mobile phone via rhythmic taps, entirely bypasses the usual discovery phase, needs just a single button or other binary input device to work, and does not even require the user to be in physical possession of the intended host device.

RhythmLink Use Example
The following example illustrates the fundamental ideas of our system. Alice has just purchased a new RhythmLink-enabled phone. As part of the setup procedure, the phone asks her to input a new pairing tap password. After considering for a moment, she taps out the rhythm of the chorus from "Let It Be" by The Beatles.

A few weeks later, Alice is at a friend's party. Her friend has some new RhythmLink-enabled wireless speakers, and invites Alice to play some tunes. She taps out "Let It Be" on the pairing button on the back of one of the speakers. In just a few seconds, the speakers have securely paired with Alice's phone—still sitting at the bottom of her purse—and started to play her music.

Contributions
Our research makes two major contributions. First, RhythmLink improves the *usability* of mobile device pairing, from both a speed and a user experience standpoint. It does so by a) removing the need to search for devices with which to pair; and b) allowing pairing to be initiated and completed from the peripheral, without having to hold, touch, or be physically near the phone.

Secondly, RhythmLink accomplishes the above while maintaining the *security* of mobile device pairing. As we will discuss, this is not a trivial problem: RhythmLink must compare a tapped sequence with the stored tapped password on surrounding devices, but without any of the devices revealing their tap data.

Design Challenges

For clarity, in the rest of this paper, we will use *phone* to indicate the host device—whether it be phone, music player, computer or television—and *peripheral* to identify the device that is to be connected to the host. In the example above, we would refer to the wireless speakers as the peripheral.

Because both usability and security are important features of wireless pairing, we have identified the following as desiderata for an improved pairing procedure:

Security Undesired peripherals must not be able to be paired without the phone owner's knowledge or consent. Likewise, the peripheral should only be paired to the intended phone.

Fast selection Selecting which of a number of peripherals to pair with should be fast and natural.

Fast authentication Authentication—the user verifying that indeed two devices should be paired—should be fast and natural.

Variety of input mechanisms No particular kind of input device such as keypads should be required: peripherals come in all shapes and sizes, so the pairing process should work with a wide variety of input mechanisms such as buttons or accelerometers.

Variety of output mechanisms Similarly, no particular kind of rich output should be assumed for either peripherals or phones.

Low power Some tiny devices may be very computationally- and battery-constrained: pairing shouldn't be slow or drain too much power.

As we discuss in the rest of the paper, RhythmLink attempts to fulfill each of these desiderata.

RELATED WORK

Wireless Pairing

In order to understand RhythmLink, it is helpful to have a basic understanding of wireless pairing and how it works. The essential goal of a pairing procedure is to establish trust between two devices that have no pre-existing information about each other. Because peripherals can expose private data (e.g., a GPS receiver) or control the host device (e.g., a phone headset), it is important to verify that the two device should really be connected. That is, the user should have confidence that only her phone can connect to her GPS, and that nobody else will be able to connect their headset to her phone.

Because wireless devices must operate over untrusted channels, their communication is susceptible to compromise by methods such as the *man-in-the-middle* (MITM) attack, during which an attacker is inserted in between the two devices, making them believe that they are securely communicating, whereas in fact the attacker is relaying—and possibly modifying—the messages.

In order to be secure against MITM attacks, the two devices should have a *shared secret*: some information that they each know, that is used to verify that the two devices are directly communicating. *It is vital that this shared secret is not given away to anyone*—that is, it is not sent over wireless either in the clear (because a third party could find it out) or sent encrypted to another device (because a MITM attack could already be underway). The only way the shared secret can work is if both devices *independently* know it.

The shared secret is often communicated between devices using *out-of-band* (OOB) information sent by a different channel than the primary wireless connection. Frequently, the OOB channel is human-perceptible: when the communication can be directly perceived by the user, an attacker cannot modify messages without being detected. Various OOB channels have been explored. Bluetooth, for example, can display a number on one device that is typed in on the other device. In this case, the human is the OOB channel.

The next sections discuss various authentication and pairing methodologies in more detail, and the advantages and drawbacks of each.

Rhythm-Based Authentication

RhythmLink's tap input is inspired by two rhythm-based approaches to authentication found in the literature. Westeyn and Starner's Prescott [24] uses song-based rhythmic eye-blinking patterns to authenticate a user. The system detects blinks using a camera and computer vision and compares them to a database using dynamic time warping. Due to the eye/camera line of sight, Prescott is intrinsically secure for fixed installation (the authors give the example of a door at an airport).

Wobbrock's TapSongs [25] extends the rhythm-based concept to any binary sensor such as a button. With a wired connection between the sensor and the computer, TapSongs compares the input rhythm to a database of taps using non-dynamic linear warping.

By showing that rhythmic input through sensors such as button or cameras is a feasible method for entering password information, Prescott and TapSongs provide a way to minimize the I/O requirements of peripheral devices. However, there are two reasons that neither system is suitable for wireless pairing. First, they both feature a database of stored passwords to which the candidate input is directly compared. Direct comparisons are not desirable in a wireless pairing scenario: until a trusted connection is established, neither party will want to reveal their passwords. Secondly, in Prescott and TapSongs, the system is trusted end-to-end: the input (camera or button) is coupled to the database of rhythms, so there is little possibility that someone will steal a password. On the other hand, wireless connections are susceptible to eavesdropping, so directly transmitting the blinked or tapped password would be insecure; even cryptographic techniques such as public key exchange still allow MITM attacks.

Bluetooth Pairing

The current state of the art for connecting wireless peripherals and hosts is Bluetooth, so any new pairing procedure should improve upon its operation. From the user's perspective, there are several steps to successfully completing pairing with Bluetooth:

1. (Optional for some peripherals) The user sets the peripheral to "discoverable" mode.
2. On the phone, the user initiates the pairing process.
3. The phone searches for discoverable peripherals and displays a list; the user selects the desired peripheral.
4. The user completes one of several security procedures [11] including: entering a Personal Identification Number (PIN), possibly hardcoded to a default such as "0000"; comparing a number on two displays; or using an *out-of-band* (OOB), non-Bluetooth-based mechanism such as RFID to communicate security information.
5. The devices are paired and ready to use.

There are a number of usability issues with the Bluetooth pairing process: discovery of available devices is often slow, and the found devices can have similar ("iPhone") or confusing ("1USA24881") names; both devices must be physically available to the user to confirm the pairing procedure (except with a special "just works" security protocol [11], which offers no MITM protection); and there is little support for truly secure pairing with I/O-constrained devices such as headsets.

Bluetooth's security is not adaptable to rhythm-based input. Bluetooth avoids revealing PINs by performing cryptographic calculations on each bit of the PIN; only if the results exactly match on each end do both devices know that they have matching codes. However, because of the variability of human rhythm input, this technique cannot work for RhythmLink: even a millisecond of difference between two taps will yield very different calculations on the two devices.

Pairing Research

Some of Bluetooth's usability issues with respect to pairing have been addressed in prior research. For an overview of many of these efforts, including evaluation of their usability, see the work of Kumar *et al.* [10]. Similar to our work, the aim of prior research is frequently to simplify pairing by removing discovery and/or simplifying authentication.

Some such systems use the proximity of two devices as OOB information [5, 12, 16, 20]; however, this approach requires that the devices be able to get near to each other, which prevents, for example, pairing a phone with a remote large-screen display or pairing a headset with a phone in a bag across the room.

Another solution is to use simultaneous input through shaking the devices together [7, 12] or concurrent button presses [15, 19] or gestures [4]. These solutions require proximity as well—either to hold both devices in one hand, or to access buttons on both devices at the same time. If one device is too large to hold, is remote (e.g., the aforementioned large-screen display), or is simply inaccessible in a bag or pocket, these methods will not work.

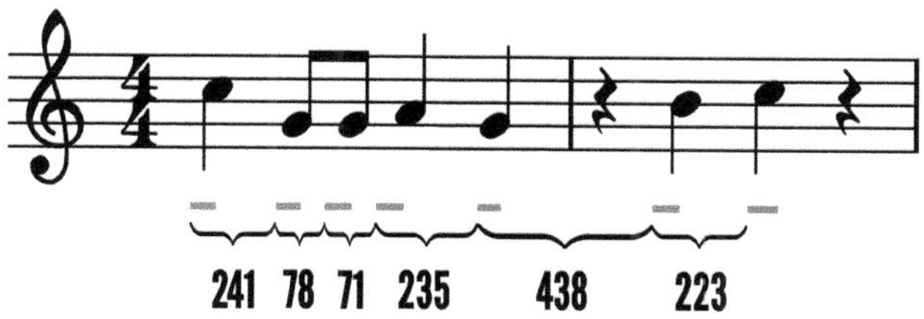

Figure 1: The tune "Shave and a Haircut, Two Bits". ♩ and ♪ represent one beat each, ♫ is a double beat, and each 𝄽 is a one-beat rest. The red lines represent the taps input for the same tune by one user. The numbers indicate the length of each interval between tap starts, in milliseconds.

RHYTHMLINK

RhythmLink builds on Prescott [24] and TapSongs [25] by using rhythm-based passwords for authentication. The idea is simple: the user starts by entering a tapped password—or "tapword" (a representation distinct from the TapSongs method in terms of model and comparison algorithm)—on the phone. This tapword is defined once per phone (or other host device) and does not need to be changed unless the user desires. When the user wants to connect a peripheral to the phone, she taps out the same tapword on the peripheral. The peripheral then—without revealing the tapword—queries all of the phones in the vicinity to see if any possess a similar tapword. If one does, that phone pairs with the peripheral.

RhythmLink uses tap-based input in order to require a minimum of I/O capability on the peripheral. A button is the simplest way to put in a tapword, but any sensor that can be binarized could be used: a microphone, accelerometer, capacitive or resistive touch sensor, or pressure sensor all provide miniature, "tappable" input.

Similar to Prescott and TapSongs, RhythmLink's tapwords are rhythmic. This is not due to any algorithmic constraint, but simply because—as Wobbrock points out in his TapSongs paper—people are rhythmic by nature. A simple example of a tapword is the rhythm from "Shave and a Haircut", illustrated in Figure 1.

RhythmLink addresses many of the usability problems encountered in earlier research:

- The difficulty of discovering and identifying the peripheral with which to pair: RhythmLink starts at the peripheral, and the tapword identifies and authenticates the phone.
- The necessity of having both the phone and peripheral in hand: RhythmLink only requires the peripheral to be held by the user; the phone can be anywhere within radio range.
- The need for rich input and/or output: in contrast to schemes requiring screens [3], keyboards [3], extra sensors [17], or even lasers [12], RhythmLink requires only a button or other binary sensor.

By design, RhythmLink is very simple from the user's perspective. However, comparing two tapwords in a secure way—without revealing a tapword to an untrusted device—is more complex.

Security Challenges

Using taps rather than alphanumerics for password input means having to do more complex comparisons in order to determine if the user has provided the right password. For normal textual passwords, there is a one-to-one mapping between a correct password and its stored analogue: "`pickle`" is the same every time a user enters it, and if it's not, it's not the right password—"`picklE`" is still incorrect.

Taps are more ambiguous, however, because they depend on timing. Humans cannot exactly reproduce timing, so each time a tapword is entered, there will some amount of error in the relative timing between notes. In fact, as Wobbrock [25] points out, Weber's law indicates that the longer the interval between taps, the more variable a person's timing will be [21]. This is why pattern matching techniques were used in Prescott and TapSongs: a candidate sequence is compared in turn to each stored sequence—yielding a closeness score, or distance—until a sufficiently close match is found. One challenge for wireless pairing therefore, is how to do a distance comparison in the vein of Prescott or TapSongs, but without revealing the devices' tapwords.

Another challenge is the limited computational power and battery available on tiny devices. A peripheral such as a pair of headphones will be very limited in its ability to compute and communicate, so any security algorithm must be lightweight. Computation is not only a concern from a battery life perspective. If the pairing process is so computationally intense that it takes many seconds to complete, it will be frustrating to the user.

Finally, tapwords share some weaknesses with text-based passwords. The shorter a tapword is, the more susceptible it will be to brute-force attacks (where an attacker tries to guess every possible combination). An ideal text password will contain a high degree of randomness (e.g., "`kS!U;jL%rq`"), whereas by their very nature tapwords are less random. Although Wobbrock found that rhythmic variation between individuals usually prevents an attacker from logging in with a stolen password, it would be ideal to provide the user an estimate of the strength of their password.

Comparing Tapwords

In order to calculate the similarity between two tapwords, RhythmLink needs a numeric representation of each. Although information such as pitch (the vertical location of each note in Figure 1) or pressure or acceleration (depending on the sensor) could be used as part of the tapword, RhythmLink currently uses only the interval between the starts of two tap events (rather than intervals, TapSongs [25] uses the time of down and up events, but we found no advantage with this approach). Therefore, the tapword "Shave and a Haircut, Two Bits" might be represented by RhythmLink as shown at the bottom of Figure 1.

As illustrated in Figure 2, a user will not tap in exactly the same way every time; so to enable non-precise matching, we want to capture some of this variability. We do this similarly to TapSongs: by having the user input their personal tapword multiple (5–10) times on the phone, and building a model based on the mean (μ) and standard deviation (σ) of the length of each interval. We then store, on the phone, a model of the n interval-long tapword: $(\mu_1, \sigma_1), \ldots, (\mu_n, \sigma_n)$.

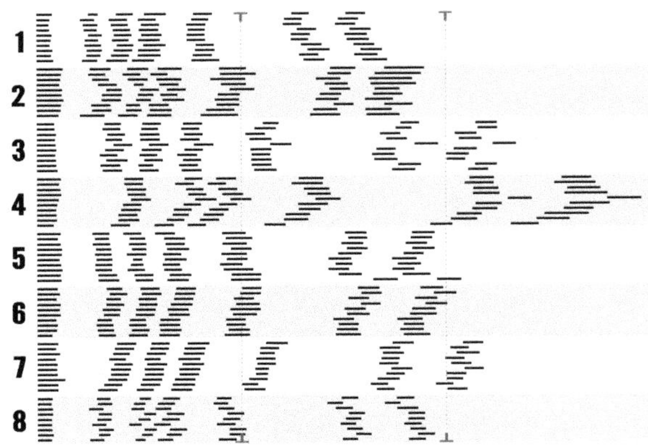

Figure 2: "Shave and a Haircut, Two Bits" for all eight participants in the pilot study. Each shaded band represents one user; within each band, the black lines show the duration of each press for ten repetitions of the sequence. The horizontal axis is three seconds long; the dotted blue vertical lines indicate one-second intervals.

As discussed earlier, the requirement for secrecy in pairing means that—unlike Prescott [24] and TapSongs [25]—RhythmLink cannot directly compare sequences. However, due to the properties of our encryption system (discussed in the next section), RhythmLink can calculate the Euclidean distance between two tapwords without revealing the tapwords themselves. This distance is defined, for a tapword x and model (μ, σ):

$$dist = \sqrt{\sum_i \left(\frac{\mu_i - x_i}{\sigma_i}\right)^2} \qquad (1)$$

For each interval i, we divide the difference between its length x_i and the model's mean length μ_i by the standard deviation for that interval σ_i. Dividing by σ makes it easier to match with longer intervals, which—in accordance with Weber's law [21]—will have a higher standard deviation.

When tapword is entered on the peripheral, it communicates with each of the surrounding phones. Using the Euclidean distance, it compares its tapword with each phone's model; if the distance is less than some threshold, then the two devices know their tapwords match, and connect.

Security

In order to securely pair, neither device should reveal its tapword to the other. The challenge is how the Euclidean distance calculation can be performed without either client being able to directly interact with the other's tapword.

Terminology and Preliminaries Encryption of x with key K is denoted $E_K(x)$, while decryption of the same is $D_K(x)$. We therefore might have $D_K(E_K(x)) = x$.

RhythmLink uses elliptic curve cryptography (ECC) [8], a cryptographic scheme that is often used for embedded devices. ECC is *asymmetric*; that is, each party has a public key (K) and a private key ($\tilde{K}$). Anyone can use a public key to encrypt a message: $E_K(m) = \hat{m}$, but the public key cannot be used to decrypt $\hat{m}$. Only the private key can be used: $D_{\bar{K}}(\hat{m}) = m$. When a number is encrypted, it looks like a random number; for example, the value "5" might encrypt to $E_K(5) =$ `1dcca23355272056f04fe8bf20edfce0`.

One of the interesting properties of ECC is that two encrypted numbers can be added to each other without decrypting them first, and an encrypted number can be multiplied by an unencrypted number without decrypting it first. So, for a given numeric constant j, $E_K(j)+E_K(x) = E_K(j+x)$ and $j \cdot E_K(x) = E_K(jx)$. In RhythmLink, these two properties allow the phone and peripheral to *collaboratively* perform the Euclidean distance calculation on their tapwords without actually revealing the tapwords to each other.

Distance Calculation As described earlier, the user trains the phone for their tapword, yielding a model $(\mu_1, \sigma_1), \ldots, (\mu_n, \sigma_n)$. When pairing, the user inputs a tapword—a single time—on the peripheral. This tapword is represented as a set of intervals $x_1, \ldots, x_n$ (later we will discuss the situation where the tapword and the model are of unequal lengths). The goal of the peripheral is to find a phone with a matching model; so it communicates with each visible phone in turn. During this communication, the goal of the two devices is to determine if the Euclidean distance between the peripheral's tapword and the phone's model is under some threshold t: $dist <? \ t$. To collaboratively calculate the distance, Equation 1 can be squared and expanded:

$$dist = \sqrt{\sum_i \left(\frac{\mu_i - x_i}{\sigma_i}\right)^2}$$

$$\begin{aligned} dist^2 &= \textstyle\sum_i \left(\frac{\mu_i - x_i}{\sigma_i}\right)^2 \\ &= \textstyle\sum_i \frac{\mu_i^2 - 2\mu_i x_i + x_i^2}{\sigma_i^2} \\ &= \textstyle\sum_i \frac{\mu_i^2}{\sigma_i^2} + \sum_i \left(\frac{-2\mu_i}{\sigma_i^2} \cdot x_i\right) + \sum_i \frac{x_i^2}{\sigma_i^2} \\ &= \underbrace{\textstyle\sum_i \frac{\mu_i^2}{\sigma_i^2}}_{ⓐ} + \Big(\underbrace{\frac{-2\mu_1}{\sigma_1^2}}_{ⓑ} \cdot x_1 + \ldots + \underbrace{\frac{-2\mu_n}{\sigma_n^2}}_{ⓑ} \cdot x_n\Big) + \textstyle\sum_i \Big(\underbrace{\frac{1}{\sigma_i^2}}_{ⓒ} x_i^2\Big) \end{aligned}$$

This equation requires input from both sides to compute: the intervals x_i from the peripheral and the model (μ_i, σ_i) from the phone. However, because the phone and peripheral don't trust each other yet, they don't want to reveal this information. Therefore, they use encryption to hide the values, collaboratively computing the result of the distance equation.

The phone generates a public key *PH* and sends it to the peripheral. Using its key, the phone also encrypts the sum of its squared intervals ⓐ $E_{PH}(\Sigma\mu_i^2/\sigma_i^2)$ and, for each individual interval i, $E_{PH}(-2\mu_i/\sigma_i^2)$ (the ⓑs) and $E_{PH}(1/\sigma_i^2)$ (the ⓒs), and sends these to the peripheral.

The peripheral's goal is to generate $dist^2$. Recalling that, using ECC, we can multiply and add encrypted values and they will remain encrypted, the peripheral calculates the third term, using the encrypted ⓒs and its own x_is:

$$\begin{aligned} \textstyle\sum_i \left(\frac{1}{\sigma_i^2} x_i^2\right) &= \frac{1}{\sigma_1^2} x_1^2 + \cdots + \frac{1}{\sigma_i^2} x_i^2 \\ &= E_{PH}\left(\frac{1}{\sigma_1^2}\right) x_1^2 + \ldots + E_{PH}\left(\frac{1}{\sigma_n^2}\right) x_n^2 \\ &= E_{PH}\left(\frac{1}{\sigma_1^2} x_1^2\right) + \ldots + E_{PH}\left(\frac{1}{\sigma_n^2} x_n^2\right) \\ &= E_{PH}\left(\textstyle\sum_i \frac{x_i^2}{\sigma_i^2}\right) \end{aligned}$$

In a similar fashion, provided with n $E_{PH}(-2\mu_i/\sigma_i^2)$s (the ⓑs), the peripheral can compute the center term, yielding

$$E_{PH}\left(\textstyle\sum_i \frac{-2\mu_i x_i}{\sigma_i^2}\right)$$

Now the peripheral has, encrypted, all of the pieces of the equation, which it can add together:

$$\begin{aligned} E_{PH}\left(\textstyle\sum_i \frac{\mu_i^2}{\sigma_i^2}\right) + E_{PH}\left(\textstyle\sum_i \frac{-2\mu_i x_i}{\sigma_i^2}\right) + E_{PH}\left(\textstyle\sum_i \frac{x^2}{\sigma_i^2}\right) &= \\ E_{PH}\left(\textstyle\sum_i \frac{\mu_i^2 - 2\mu_i x_i + x^2}{\sigma_i^2}\right) &= \\ E_{PH}\left(\textstyle\sum_i \left(\frac{\mu_i - x_i}{\sigma_i}\right)^2\right) &= E_{PH}(dist^2) \end{aligned}$$

Now the peripheral can send $E_{PH}(dist^2)$ to the phone, which can decrypt it $D_{\bar{PH}}(E_{PH}(dist^2)) = dist^2$ and compare it with the threshold: $dist^2 <? \ t^2$.

Assuming that the result is under the threshold, the phone now trusts the peripheral. However, the peripheral still does not trust the phone, so the phone must prove that its model is compatible. Since the phone trusts the peripheral, it can simply send its model to the peripheral, which can compare it directly. However, there is still the possibility of an ongoing MITM attack. To encrypt both the model and further communication, the two devices must establish a session key in a way resistant to MITM attacks. Using Password-Authenticated Key Exchange (PAKE) [2], such a key can be created using simple information known to both devices. In our case, the number of intervals (known *a priori* to each device) can be used to bootstrap secure key generation. Using this session key, the phone can encrypt its model and send it to the peripheral, which decrypts it and computes the Euclidean distance directly with its x_is. If there is a match, the peripheral knows it can trust the phone.

Unequal Tapword Lengths An issue is how to compare tapwords that are unequal lengths. The problem is twofold: first, the Euclidean distance works only on sequences of equal length, and second, to remain completely secure, neither the phone nor the peripheral should know whether or not their tapwords have the same number of intervals.

Our solution for this is to work with a standard length: we pick some average number of intervals n, and any tapword that is longer than n gets truncated. Any tapword shorter than n gets padded to n intervals with a pre-determined set of large filler values f_i. (In order to prevent guessing the number of filler values, each has a tiny random amount added to it, thus changing the encrypted value.) The values are universally agreed upon by RhythmLink-compliant systems, so that two tapwords of length m (where $m < n$) compare correctly with the Euclidean distance: the remaining f_i values will calculate as having (nearly) 0 distance, and only the m differing values will have any affect on the final calculation of $dist$. Tapwords of differing lengths will have $x_i - f_i$ included in the distance, yielding a large value that will not fall under the threshold.

Further Securing the Calculation A remaining issue is that the phone gains some information—$dist$—about how its sequence compares against the peripheral's, and could potentially use this to guess at its sequence. Ideally, either device would find out whether its sequence matches or not without ever learning $dist$. We can accomplish this goal through the use of a so-called "black box" function, which will allow the peripheral to perform the comparison $dist <? \ t$ without revealing $dist$.

Recall that, at the end of its calculations, the peripheral is in possession of $E_{PH}(dist^2)$. It generates a random value r and adds it: $E_{PH}(dist^2 + r) = E_{PH}(v)$ and sends the result to the phone. The phone can use its key and decrypt this message: $D_{\tilde{PH}}(E_{PH}(v)) = v$. Because the phone doesn't know r, it can't calculate $dist^2$ from v.

To compare $dist^2$ with t^2, the peripheral creates an encrypted, or "garbled", function [9]; similar to arithmetic computation with ECC, this function allows efficient *comparison* of two values without revealing the values to either device. The peripheral constructs and sends this function to the phone.

To make the comparison, the garbled function takes v and t^2 as input, internally performing the computation

$$\begin{aligned} f(v, t^2) &= v - r <? \ t^2 \\ &= (dist^2 + r) - r <? \ t^2 \\ &= dist^2 <? \ t^2 \end{aligned}$$

returning a one-bit Boolean value T to the phone. Because the garbled function is constructed by the peripheral, it can be confident that the phone is not trying to find out what $dist^2$ is. If T is true, the phone knows it can trust the peripheral. As above, it then sends the peripheral its model, which compares it with its intervals and determines that it can trust the phone, and they set up secure communications.

Choosing the Threshold Because a phone will be owned by a single user, but peripherals may pass between people, the phone should be the device that determines the threshold for matching. The threshold can be dynamically generated on the phone when the tapword is initially input by the user. Taking each of the N repetitions of the tapword, and finding the Euclidean distance to each of the other inputs will give us a mean μ and standard deviation σ; we can then set the threshold to $\mu \pm k\sigma$. We can pick k to be more or less restrictive; assuming a normal distribution, $k = 3$ will encompass 99.7% of the variation in a user's taps.

Efficiency

As discussed earlier, RhythmLink is intended to work with I/O-constrained devices. In a phone/peripheral pairing situation, it is possible that at least the peripheral will have a small battery and a low-power embedded processor. To maintain an acceptable user experience, delays in pairing should be minimized; thus, it is important that RhythmLink be efficiently executable on low-end CPUs and microprocessors.

The major power drain in RhythmLink comes from the computation involved in ECC. Therefore, if we can avoid doing cryptographic operations unless they are absolutely necessary, we can save both power and time. In an ideal situation, the entire tapword comparison process described above will only take place once: between the peripheral and the intended phone. However, the real world is rarely ideal—in a room full of phones, we want to avoid the peripheral having to attempt to authenticate with each one!

In order to encourage a closer-to-ideal situation, RhythmLink uses a *selector*, consisting of a minimal set of information about the tapword, to attempt to narrow down the number of potential matches between a peripheral and the surrounding phones. Each phone allows unencrypted viewing of its selector, and so a peripheral will only try to pair with a phone that has the same selector as itself.

The rationale behind the selector is twofold: first, it reduces the computational overhead of pairing by orders of magnitude. Without the selector, the peripheral must attempt secure authentication with every phone in the vicinity until it finds one that matches, incurring not only a significant power drain, but increased latency. Secondly, using a selector reduces the information about the tapword that is leaked during the course of normal usage: each failed authentication eliminates a possibility, making the tapword less secret. The selector eliminates most failed authentications; additionally, it allows the peripheral to treat phones that claim to have a matching selector but fail authentication as suspicious.

The challenge in choosing a selector is that it should disclose *just enough* information about the tapword to determine whether two devices should attempt authentication—but no more, to prevent guessing of the tapword (for example, using the number of intervals in the tapword would reveal information useful to an attacker). Additionally, the selector generation needs to work with the random timing errors present during human tapword input.

Currently, RhythmLink uses the first two intervals of a tapword as the selector. Before any authentication attempt, the phone reveals the mean (μ_i) and standard deviation (σ_i) of the lengths of the first two intervals of its tapword to the peripheral. The peripheral tries to match its first two intervals (x_i), and only proceeds if there is a reasonably close match. Because it has direct access to both devices' selectors, RhythmLink uses part of TapSongs' [25] matching process to determine whether there is a match or not:

$$|x_i - \mu_i| \leq? \ 3\sigma_i$$

We chose the selector this way for three reasons. First, the selector must be based on pattern matching, like the full authentication, because human timing errors make statistics based on the tapword as a whole unreliable. Secondly, by generating a selector based on the start of the tapword, a peripheral can determine whether each phone is a potential match before performing encrypted computations. Finally, after experimentation (see "Preliminary Experiments" section), we chose to use two intervals as a balance between keeping the tapword secret and efficiently pre-emptively rejecting non-matching phones.

Tapword Strength

Another important consideration in RhythmLink is how to encourage users to choose good tapwords. One way is to give feedback to the user on how "strong" a given tapword is. Similar to systems using text-based passwords that indicate whether a password will be resistant to guessing—for example, setting a password for online banking—we likewise want to assign a given tapword a strength score. There are a number of metrics we can use to indicate the strength of a tapword; most either assign or take away points from the total score:

length Is the tapword long enough? A minimum length can be required, or points can be deducted for shorter tapwords, or points assigned for longer ones.

speed A shorter—in terms of time, rather than number of taps—tapword might be harder for another party to overhear, and so may be more secure.

commonality Similar to how "`password`" is a common, and poor, password, "Shave and a Haircut, Two Bits" may likewise become a common and poor tapword. Given a built-in list of common rhythms, RhythmLink can use the Euclidean distance to prevent such tapwords from being chosen.

interval sizes Having a mix of long and short intervals will make a tapword harder to guess; therefore, counting the number of intervals larger or shorter than some percentage of the overall length (i.e., if the tapword is 1000 milliseconds long, counting intervals under 5%—50 ms—or over 60%—600 ms) can contribute to the score.

consecutive intervals The more heterogeneous the interval lengths are, the more secure the password will be. We can look at each set of two consecutive intervals, and assign a score based on the difference between them as compared to the overall length. For example, if the tapword is 1000 ms long, and we have two tap intervals at 100 and 110 ms, we can assign a score of $-(1000/(110-100)) = -100$.

specific rhythms Specific sub-rhythms can be looked for. For example, a (desirable) fast double-tap can be defined as an interval shorter than some fixed value (rather than a percentage of the total length) such as 50 ms, or a long interval can be similarly defined (e.g. 250 ms).

RHYTHMLINK IMPLEMENTATION

To evaluate the RhythmLink security protocol, we employed TASTY [6], a protocol compiler for performing secure cryptographic computation. We provide a high-level description of the RhythmLink protocol, and use TASTY to automatically generate programs that simulate the phone and peripheral. Once invoked, these programs execute RhythmLink over the network, and log the protocol overhead during execution.

We created a prototype RhythmLink system with three Nokia N900 mobile phones, where one phone (N900-P) acts the part of "peripheral" and the other two (N900-X and N900-Y) act as "phones". In our prototype, we used the touchscreen as input to RhythmLink. In an ideal RhythmLink implementation, devices would perform authentication over a low-level protocol, like Bluetooth; however, in the interests of rapid prototyping, our N900-based system communicates over a local 802.11 network.

To use our prototype, a user enters their tapword by tapping on the touchscreen of N900-P. N900-P then generates its selector according to the mechanism described in the Efficiency section, and requests selectors from all visible phones. N900-X and -Y respond with their selectors; if either is a match, N900-P will launch the TASTY-generated "peripheral" program to perform secure RhythmLink authentication with the "phone" program on the other device.

PRELIMINARY EXPERIMENTS

Data Collection

In order to test our algorithms, we asked eight volunteers to input tapwords. Participants were drawn from our lab, ranged in age from 24–40, and two were female. Using our Nokia N900 RhythmLink prototype to record the taps on the resistive touchscreen, we asked each volunteer to tap in a tapword of their own devising ten times. Then participants were requested to tap "Shave and a Haircut, Two Bits" (Figure 1) ten times. We recorded timestamps for tap down and release events. Figure 3 illustrates each volunteer's personally-chosen tapword, and Figure 2 shows "Shave and a Haircut" for each participant.

We asked the volunteers what rhythm they chose for a personal tapword; from 1–8, they used: "Day Glow" by Tow Head, "On" by Aphex Twin, a song from a Chinese movie, Mozart's "Requiem in D Minor", "Row Your Boat", "Mary Had a Little Lamb", "Jingle Bells", and an impromptu rhythm.

Selector Performance

As described earlier, the purpose of the selector is to prevent devices from having to authenticate if it is unlikely that they will have a match. To investigate the performance of the selector, we perform leave-one-out validation: we remove one instance of an initial tapword from the list of tapwords, and then build a model with those remaining. We then use the remaining tapword, and all other users' tapwords, to create selectors, and compare them with the model.

We tested using one, two, and three intervals for the selector. For each test, we recorded the true positive rate (how often the selector correctly indicated the two devices should connect) and the false positive rate (how often there would have been an unnecessary authentication attempt).

Using two intervals for the selector, the average rate of true positives for the users' custom rhythms was 98%: just two

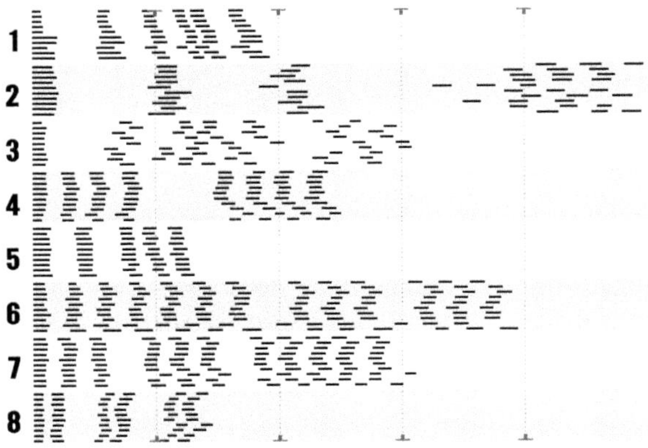

Figure 3: The custom tapword for all eight participants in the pilot study. Each shaded band represents one user; within each band, the black lines show the duration of each press. The horizontal axis is five seconds long; the dotted blue vertical lines indicate one-second intervals.

users had one out of ten tested selectors fail to indicate an authentication attempt should be made. The false positive rate was 9%. For "Shave and a Haircut", the average true positive rate was 94%, while the false positive rate was naturally higher at 32%.

For using the first three intervals to make up the selector, the average true positive rate for custom rhythms was 92%—lower than for two intervals! The false positive rate was just 3%. For "Shave and a Haircut", the true positive rate was still high at 93%, while the false positive rate was 14%.

These results highlight the impact of human error on the system. That is, the more taps the user makes, the more likely she is to make an error. Therefore, to err on the side of a satisfactory user experience—a successful connection on the first try—we use two intervals for the selector.

Tapword Distinguishability

One of the most important aspects of RhythmLink, of course, is that the tapwords themselves are secure; that is, that someone can't accidentally perform a successful authentication with the wrong tapword. To investigate this issue, we used RhythmLink to perform leave-one-out validation on our users' tapwords.

First, we compare the custom tapwords from each user. On average, the Euclidean distance between tapwords from the same user was 26.40, with a standard deviation of 5.10. Because only two users had tapwords with the same number of taps, differing tapwords were easily rejected. Truncating every user's tapword to the shortest number of intervals—four—the average distance between users' own tapwords was 1.27, while the mean distance between different users' tapwords was 20.52, a sufficiently large difference to easily reject wrong attempts.

Following Wobbrock in TapSongs [25], we next compare all users on the same rhythm. With the "Shave and a Haircut" tapword, the average distance within a single user was 18.45, with a standard deviation of 7.35. Between users, the average distance was 79.50, with the average minimum distance between two users' tapwords being 25.59. This is a promising result, showing us a very low probability of accidental overlap between two users with the same tapword. Indeed, Wobbrock addressed purposeful attempts to break security, and discovered that users found it very difficult to tap exactly the same rhythm as another user.

Tapword Reproducibility

In order to determine how well people can remember their tapwords, we re-collected data from each user after between five and twelve days after the initial test. We asked each volunteer to do the same thing as the initial study—to tap in their custom tapword, and then "Shave and a Haircut". For each user, we then created a model based off of their first day's tap input, and used each individual second day tap as input to RhythmLink.

We found that—with one exception—for their custom tapwords, users were in general able to remember and re-tap their rhythms. One user could not remember his rhythm. For the other users, there was an average difference of 6.72 between taps entered on the initial day and on the latter day.

Efficiency

Our N900-based prototype executed the RhythmLink protocol extremely quickly, with no user-perceivable delay. However, the N900 possesses a 600MHz processor—standard for a modern smartphone, but unrealistic for a peripheral device such as a headset or wristwatch. To validate RhythmLink on lower-capability devices, we measured the performance of ECC on an NXP LPC1343[1], a low-power embedded CPU. Processors of this type are commonly found in devices such as headsets, medical devices, and appliances.

For the LPC1343 running at 72MHz, optimized ECC takes .139 seconds per mathematical operation. On the peripheral, RhythmLink has an overhead of two operations per tap interval. Thus, each interval costs us .278 seconds. If our maximum tapword length is 12 taps, we have 11 intervals. Taking off two for the selector, we have 9 intervals involved in computation. So for this processor and maximum tapword length, we can expect a pairing time of around 2.5 seconds. Note that because the selector generation and communication takes place after the first three taps (two intervals), during the remaining taps, it takes no user-perceptible time.

With optimized hardware, RhythmLink can be made even more efficient. ECC encryptions, which dominate the computational overhead of RhythmLink, can be accelerated by several orders of magnitude with lightweight, inexpensive dedicated hardware. For example, an ECC engine based on a 9.9MHz FPGA [18] reduces the computational latency to 56μs per operation, representing a 100,000-times improvement over the general-purpose LPC1343 processor that we measured. Such hardware cryptography accelerators are becoming common in embedded chips, such as the AES (a standard for encryption) engine in many Bluetooth chips. Therefore, we envision that RhythmLink will greatly benefit from

[1] http://ics.nxp.com/products/lpc1000/lpc13xx/~LPC1343/

hardware ECC acceleration as it becomes available in off-the shelf components and devices.

Pairing Speed

RhythmLink requires much less pairing time than existing pairing methods, as it is bounded by computation rather than the speed of user input. As discussed above, with a maximum of nine intervals in a tapword, a RhythmLink pairing procedure will take under three seconds. This pairing time is shorter than almost all of the pairing methods described in the literature. Compare RhythmLink with, for example, the widely-used number-matching pairing method, which takes 8.6 seconds on average [10]. As hardware speed improves, RhythmLink's performance will likewise improve.

CONCLUSIONS

RhythmLink enables secure device pairing while improving usability: it is fast to execute, intuitive for the user, and does not require that both devices be physically co-present. By using rhythmic tap input, RhythmLink allows peripheral devices to have little to no visible input mechanism for pairing: just a button will do. The technique only requires input output sufficient to inform the user whether pairing worked, obviating the need for more complex displays.

In an informal post-study survey, user response to RhythmLink was generally positive, with pilot study participants indicating they would enjoy using such a system to pair their devices.

Compared to other methods, RhythmLink shifts the overhead in pairing from the user to the computational device. That is, the user interaction is less involved, but there is more computation involved. This is a decided advantage, as computing power continues to increase, while human capability remains relatively constant.

Our next steps are to implement RhythmLink on embedded hardware and test it during longer-term use. We are also interested in the impact of using different input modalities: does using a button lead to different rhythmic variability than the touchscreen, and does using a button on one device and a microphone on the other make the tapwords harder to match?

REFERENCES

1. D Ashbrook, P Baudisch, and S White, *Nenya: Subtle and eyes-free mobile input with a magnetically-tracked finger ring*, Proc. CHI, 2011, pp. 2043–2046.
2. S Bellovin and M Merritt, *Encrypted key exchange: password-based protocols secure against dictionary attacks*, Proceedings of IEEE Symposium on Research in Security and Privacy, 1992, pp. 72–84.
3. Bluetooth SIG, *Bluetooth core specifications*, `http://www.bluetooth.org`, April 2011.
4. MK Chong, G Marsden, and H Gellersen, *GesturePIN: Using discrete gestures for associating mobile devices*, Proc. MobileHCI, 2010, pp. 261–264.
5. T Falck, H Baldus, J Espina, and K Klabunde, *Plug 'n play simplicity for wireless medical body sensors*, Mobile Network Applications **12** (2007), no. 2-3, 143–153.
6. W Henecka, S Kögl, AR Sadeghi, T Schneider, and I Wehrenberg, *TASTY: tool for automating secure two-party computations*, Proc. ACM Conf. on Computer and communications security, 2010, pp. 451–462.
7. LE Holmquist, F Mattern, B Schiele, P Alahuhta, M Beigl, and HW Gellersen, *Smart-its friends: A technique for users to easily establish connections between smart artefacts*, Proc. Ubicomp, 2001, pp. 116–122.
8. N Koblitz, *Elliptic curve cryptosystems*, Mathematics of Computation **48** (1987), no. 177, 203–209.
9. V Kolesnikov, AR Sadeghi, and T Schneider, *From dust to dawn: Practically efficient two-party secure function evaluation protocols and their modular design*, Cryptology ePrint Archive, Report 2010/079, 2010, `http://eprint.iacr.org/`.
10. A Kumar, N Saxena, G Tsudik, and E Uzun, *A comparative study of secure device pairing methods*, Pervasive and Mobile Computing **5** (2009), no. 6, 734–749.
11. J Linsky, *Simple pairing whitepaper*, `http://mclean-linsky.net/joel/cv/Simple%20Pairing_WP_V10r00.pdf`, April 2011.
12. R Mayrhofer and H Gellersen, *Spontaneous mobile device authentication based on sensor data*, Information Security Technical Report **13** (2008), no. 3, 136–150.
13. C Metzger, M Anderson, and T Starner, *Freedigiter: a contact-free device for gesture control*, Proc. ISWC, 2004, pp. 18–21.
14. T Ni and P Baudisch, *Disappearing mobile devices*, Proc. UIST, 2009, pp. 101–110.
15. J Rekimoto, *Synctap: synchronous user operation for spontaneous network connection*, Personal and Ubiquitous Computing **8** (2004), no. 2, 126–134.
16. J Rekimoto, T Miyaki, and M Kohno, *Proxnet: Secure dynamic wireless connection by proximity sensing*, Proc. Pervasive, 2004, pp. 213–218.
17. R Roman and J Lopez, *KeyLED—transmitting sensitive data over out-of-band channels in wireless sensor networks*, Proc. MASS, 2008, pp. 796–801.
18. N Saqib, F Rodriguez-Henriquez, and A Diaz-Perez, *A parallel architecture for fast computation of elliptic curve scalar multiplication over gf(2m)*, Proc. Parallel and Distributed Processing Symp., 2004, pp. 144–152.
19. C Soriente, Gene Tsudik, and E Uzun, *Secure pairing of interface constrained devices*, International Journal of Security and Networks **4** (2009), no. 1/2, 17–26.
20. A Spahić, M Kreutzer, M Kahmer, and S Chandratilleke, *Pre-authentication using infrared*, Proc. Workshop on Privacy, Security and Trust within the Context of Pervasive Computing, 2005, pp. 1–7.
21. D Sternad, WJ Dean, and K M Newell, *Force and timing variability in rhythmic unimanual tapping*, Journal of Motor Behavior **32** (2000), no. 3, 249–267.
22. E Uzun, K Karvonen, and N Asokan, *Usability analysis of secure pairing methods*, Financial Cryptography and Data Security, 2007, pp. 307–324.
23. M Weiser, *The computer for the 21st century*, Scientific American (2002), 94–104.
24. T Westeyn and T Starner, *Recognizing song–based blink patterns: Applications for restricted and universal access*, Proc. Automatic Face and Gesture Recog., 2004, pp. 717–722.
25. JO Wobbrock, *Tapsongs: tapping rhythm-based passwords on a single binary sensor*, Proc. UIST, 2009, pp. 93–96.

Access Overlays: Improving Non-Visual Access to Large Touch Screens for Blind Users

Shaun K. Kane[1,6], Meredith Ringel Morris[2], Annuska Z. Perkins[3], Daniel Wigdor[4], Richard E. Ladner[5], Jacob O. Wobbrock[6]

[1]Information Systems, UMBC
Baltimore, MD, 21250 USA
skane@umbc.edu

[2]Microsoft Research
Redmond, WA, 98052 USA
merrie@microsoft.com

[3]Microsoft Research
Redmond, WA, 98052 USA
annuskap@microsoft.com

[4]Computer Science
University of Toronto
Toronto, ON, Canada
dwigdor@dgp.toronto.edu

[5]Computer Science & Engineering
University of Washington
Seattle, WA 98195 USA
ladner@cs.washington.edu

[6]Information School | DUB Group
University of Washington
Seattle, WA 98195 USA
wobbrock@uw.edu

ABSTRACT
Many touch screens remain inaccessible to blind users, and those approaches to providing access that do exist offer minimal support for interacting with large touch screens or spatial data. In this paper, we introduce a set of three software-based *access overlays* intended to improve the accessibility of large touch screen interfaces, specifically interactive tabletops. Our access overlays are called *edge projection, neighborhood browsing,* and *touch-and-speak.* In a user study, 14 blind users compared access overlays to an implementation of Apple's VoiceOver screen reader. Our results show that two of our techniques were faster than VoiceOver, that participants correctly answered more questions about the screen's layout using our techniques, and that participants overwhelmingly preferred our techniques. We developed several applications demonstrating the use of access overlays, including an accessible map kiosk and an accessible board game.

Author Keywords
Accessibility, touch screens, blindness, visual impairments.

ACM Classification Keywords
H.5.2. Information interfaces and presentation: User Interfaces–*input devices and strategies.* K.4.2. Computers and Society: Social issues–*assistive technologies for persons with disabilities.*

General Terms
Design, Experimentation, Human Factors.

INTRODUCTION
For blind people, accessing touch screen interfaces remains a significant challenge, as most touch screens rely on visual interaction and are not usable by touch and audio alone.

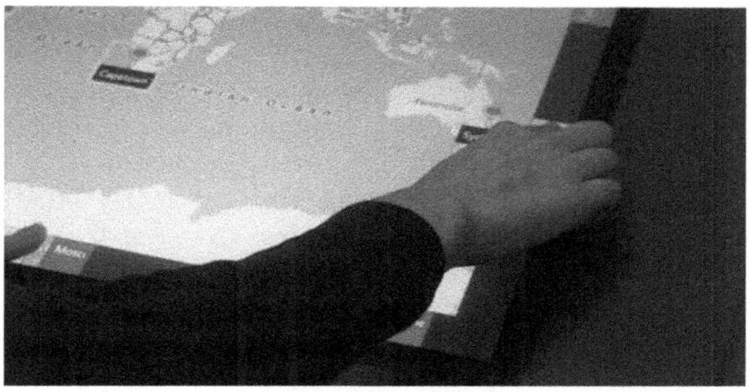

Figure 1. Access overlays allow a blind user to accurately locate items on a 2-D touch screen map.

Despite this significant problem, touch screens are increasingly found in consumer technologies such as mobile devices, home electronics, and computers in public spaces (*e.g.*, ATMs, airport ticket kiosks, and interactive maps). The inaccessibility of touch screens can have profound effects, preventing otherwise independent blind people from performing routine tasks without help, which can lead to feelings of embarrassment [17]. Blind consumers have responded to the spread of inaccessible technologies through press events [7], and have organized lawsuits and boycotts [23]. Furthermore, inaccessible touch screens not only impact millions of blind people (more than 1.3 million in the U.S. alone[1]), but also seniors and others with low vision, as well as other people who use touch screens eyes-free, such as while multitasking.

Fortunately, some touch screen devices now provide accessibility features for blind people. Many touch screen ATMs provide an alternative button-based interface and a headphone jack for blind users. In recent years, several research projects (*e.g.*, [10,16]) and commercial tools such as Apple's VoiceOver for iOS[2] and Google's Eyes-Free

[1] http://www.nfb.org/nfb/blindness_statistics.asp
[2] http://www.apple.com/accessibility/iphone

Shell for Android[3] have introduced accessible touch interfaces that combine gesture input with speech output.

While techniques such as VoiceOver demonstrate that touch screens can be made at least somewhat accessible, it is not at all clear that such interfaces are optimal, as performance comparisons of accessible touch screen interfaces are rare. Furthermore, as larger touch screen devices become more common, additional interaction challenges emerge. In particular, increased screen size may result in increased search time to find on-screen targets, and many interactions with large touch screens may require a blind user to understand the spatial layout of the screen, such as when exploring a map or working collaboratively with a sighted partner. Most current touch screen accessibility tools are designed for small, mobile phone-sized devices, and may not address the challenges of interacting with larger touch screens, such as interacting with two hands and working with spatial data.

In this paper, we introduce *access overlays* (Figure 1), a set of new techniques that enable blind people to explore and interact with applications on interactive tabletops. We describe our formative work in developing these techniques, and introduce three access overlays. We then describe a study in which 14 blind computer users compared access overlays to VoiceOver. Our results show that access overlays enable users to perform tasks faster than VoiceOver, improve users' ability to answer questions about the screen's spatial layout, and are preferred.

RELATED WORK

Our work extends prior access techniques for small touch screens by introducing techniques for spatial exploration of larger touch screens, and is inspired by prior approaches to increase the accessibility of virtual maps and diagrams.

Touch Screen Accessibility

Touch screen interfaces have been popular for over 20 years [5], and concerns about touch screen accessibility have remained active throughout this time [4]. Touch screen accessibility research has considered various device form factors. Early research explored accessibility for devices such as information kiosks [29] and drawing tablets [19]. These techniques relied upon hardware modifications, such as augmenting a touch screen with physical buttons or placing a physical overlay atop the screen. Such approaches may be expensive to install, may limit the flexibility of the underlying software (by imposing physical structures), and may interfere with use by sighted people; unsurprisingly, such techniques have not been widely adopted.

More recent efforts have focused on using gestures to provide blind users with access to touch screens without modifying the underlying hardware. For example, Slide Rule [16] used multi-touch gestures to allow blind users to browse and explore content on a touch screen-based smartphone. Similar interfaces now appear in consumer devices such as Apple's iPhone[2] and Android-based smartphones[3]. Researchers have also explored techniques to address specific aspects of blind touch screen interaction, such as text entry [3,10,36] and gesture selection [18]. However, these techniques have often focused on small, mobile phone-sized screens. Furthermore, many of these techniques change the fundamental layout of the screen to improve accessibility. Thus, our current work addresses interaction with larger touch screens, and explores methods to preserve users' understanding of the screen layout.

Accessible Maps and Diagrams

While some touch screen accessibility techniques rely on changing the screen layout to improve usability, researchers have also explored methods to improve the accessibility of spatial information such as maps [20], walking directions [25,26], and diagrams [6,22,30]. However, these techniques have typically targeted specific domains, and are not generalizable to all touch screen interfaces. Furthermore, many of these techniques require haptic controllers or other specialized hardware. Our present work explores methods to access spatial layouts on unmodified multi-touch screens.

DESIGN GOALS FOR LARGE TOUCH SCREENS

When designing new touch screen interfaces for blind people, it is important to consider the criteria for success. Prior approaches have often considered performance metrics such as speed and error rate (*e.g.*, [3,16]). However, large touch screens such as tablets, kiosks, and interactive tabletops may introduce additional interaction challenges related to navigating spatial layouts, collaborating with others, and using unfamiliar devices in public spaces. Among those issues, our current work focuses on concerns related to *preserving spatial layout, leveraging bimanual interaction, reducing search space,* and maintaining usability in *walk-up-and-use scenarios.*

Preserving spatial layout. Access techniques that distort or remove spatial information may reduce users' spatial understanding and memory, making it more difficult for a blind person to understand maps and diagrams or to collaborate with sighted peers. Thus, blind users should be able to interact with the original spatial layout of an application when desired.

Leveraging bimanual interaction. Most accessible touch screen interfaces do not support bimanual interaction, even on larger touch screens. Accessible touch screen interfaces should leverage bimanual interactions on devices that support them to improve performance.

Reducing search space. Since blind people must search a touch screen using their hands, rather than glancing at the screen, the user interface should minimize the distance that a user needs to cover in order to search on-screen content.

Walk-up-and-use. Because touch screens are increasingly found in public spaces, touch screen interfaces for blind users should be usable in walk-up-and-use scenarios, and

[3] http://code.google.com/p/eyes-free

should not require users to memorize complex gestures or screen locations, or to recognize auditory icons.

In addition to the above criteria, there are additional challenges that are specific to larger touch screens, such as multi-user interaction and interacting with physical objects. Although our formal evaluation did not specifically address these issues, our techniques and applications were influenced by these concerns, and can be extended to address these concerns in the future.

FORMATIVE INTERVIEWS

We began our research by investigating how blind people organize their workspaces, to uncover organization strategies that could potentially be used to inform the design of touch screen user interfaces for blind people. We interviewed 8 blind people (4 female, 4 male, aged 31-66) in their place of work. The interview began with a guided tour of the participant's workspace, followed by a discussion of strategies used to organize and search that space. Finally, the participant was presented with a collection of souvenirs provided by the researcher (*e.g.*, postcards, figurines, and coins) and asked how he or she would organize those items to show them to a friend.

Organization strategies varied across participants. We inquired whether participants had received vocational training to help organize their workspace, but none had received any such training. Some participants had very rigorous organization structures, such as one person who "put everything in quadrants," while others were much less formal. However, participants' workspaces were typically organized from an egocentric viewpoint, such that objects were arrayed around the participant's chair. Frequently used objects were placed near the resting places of participants' hands, while less frequently used objects were moved to the corners of the workspace to keep them out of the way. Most participants noted the importance of keeping items in a consistent location so that they could be relocated later.

Search strategies also varied across participants. Most participants remembered the approximate location of an item, or the drawer it was in, but not its precise location. Participants would relocate the object by feeling around a general area for an item until they recognized it by touch. Because it was possible to accidentally bump or knock over an object while searching, participants were very careful to keep fragile objects in a consistent, out-of-the-way location, such as tucking a water cup behind a computer screen.

Our present design work was inspired primarily by our participants' use of structured spatial layouts in their workspaces, their use of edges and corners to organize space, and their use of local search to find items.

ACCESS OVERLAYS

Access overlays are accessible interaction techniques that improve touch screen usability while preserving an application's original spatial layout. Access overlays are implemented as semi-transparent windows that reside above a standard application. When activated, an access overlay gathers information about the location and content of all on-screen targets, and provides access to these targets through a combination of speech and audio feedback, alternative gesture input, and additional user interface controls. Access overlays are entirely software-based, and do not require alterations to the underlying touch screen hardware. While blind touch screen users would likely benefit from the additional haptic feedback provided by physical touch screen overlays, or by new technologies such as TeslaTouch [1], these technologies are not yet widely available. In contrast, access overlays are designed to improve the accessibility of existing touch screen hardware.

We developed a number of access overlays, and after iterative design and testing, refined three of the most promising overlays, which we now describe.

Edge Projection

One strategy used by prior touch screen access techniques (*e.g.*, [16,29]) is to convert a two-dimensional interface to a linear list of targets, which we call *linearization*. Linearization enables blind users to quickly scan a list of on-screen items without the need to search the entire screen, but removes information about the screen's original layout.

The *edge projection overlay* (Figure 2) provides the benefits of linearization while maintaining the original spatial layout of the screen. When edge projection is active, touching any on-screen target reads that target's name. In addition, the edge projection overlay displays an *edge menu* that surrounds the screen. Each on-screen target has a corresponding *edge proxy* along each edge of the screen. Touching the edge proxy highlights the corresponding on-screen target and reads its name. Blind users can quickly browse through the list of targets by sliding their finger across the edge menu. Furthermore, because the position of the edge proxy corresponds to the *x*- or *y*-position of the target, users can drag their fingers from an edge proxy toward the interior of the screen to locate the desired target.

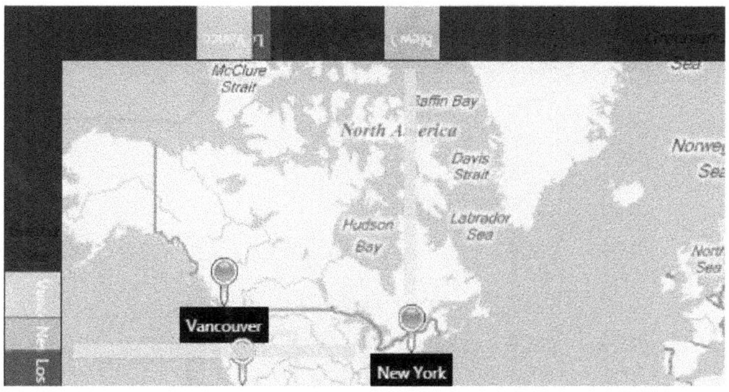

Figure 2. Edge projection. Targets are projected to the edge of the screen. Lines illustrate the correspondence between an edge proxy and its associated target.

Edge projection leverages bimanual interaction by allowing users to locate on-screen targets using two hands. For example, the user may locate a target on the bottom edge with one hand, locate the same target on the right edge with another hand, and move their hands together toward the interior of the screen to locate the target. Our prototype also supports a *bimanual context menu* that allows the user to locate a target along one edge, and then browse a list of actions that can be performed on that target by touching a second edge. In another mode, the second edge can be used to select from a group of closely clustered targets: touching a cluster of targets along one edge causes the corresponding edge proxies to spread out along the second edge, allowing users to more easily select the desired proxy.

Edge projection was inspired by our interview participants' tendency to place objects in the edges and corners of their workspaces. Edge projection preserves the original layout of on-screen content, reduces search space, and leverages bimanual interaction. Edge projection also supports collaboration by allowing users to explore the screen using the edge closest to them, avoiding conflict with other users.

Neighborhood Browsing

A major difficulty in exploring a touch screen without sight is actually finding targets on the screen. Most visual interfaces use empty space to separate and group targets. Without appropriately designed feedback, a blind person touching an empty area of a touch screen might not know where they are touching, or even if the system has registered their touch. Locating targets on the screen likewise requires navigating through that empty space.

The *neighborhood browsing overlay* (Figure 3) addresses the problem of searching a large touch screen by increasing the size of targets and reclaiming empty space. Neighborhood browsing uses a Voronoi tessellation [8] to define a neighborhood around each on-screen target. Touching anywhere on the screen speaks the name of the nearest target. Users can precisely locate a target by touching within a target's neighborhood and performing a second-finger tap gesture [16]. The system then provides *guided directions* to the nearest target, as described in the *Additional Features* subsection below.

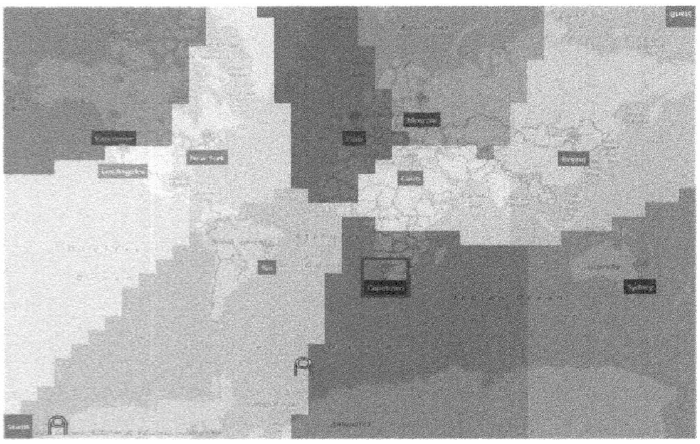

Figure 3. Neighborhood browsing uses a Voronoi tessellation to increase target size. Aliasing of the regions is a visual artifact, and did not affect functionality.

Neighborhood browsing was inspired by our participants' tendency to remember the approximate location of items in their workspace, and to search locally in that approximate location to find the item, and is also inspired by the bubble cursor [9]. Neighborhood browsing preserves spatial layout and reduces search space.

Touch-and-Speak

Blind PC users often rely on keyboard shortcuts that can be performed without sight. Because many touch screen-based devices do not have keyboards, blind touch screen users must enter commands by browsing through a speech menu, which may be slow and tedious. The *touch-and-speak overlay* allows users to perform actions much more quickly by combining touch interaction with spoken commands. Users initiate a voice command by performing a second-finger tap gesture on the screen and speaking a command.

Currently, three commands are supported: (1) saying *"list"* reads all on-screen targets from left to right; (2) saying *"nearby"* reads all targets in the same quadrant of the screen as the user's touch; and (3) speaking the name of a target provides guided directions from the user's finger to the named target. Because speech commands begin with a touch gesture, commands can be bound to the touch location, and recognition accuracy can be improved by only considering options relevant to the current location [27].

Touch-and-speak was inspired by our formative interviews and by prior work that used speech commands to improve pointing precision [27]. Touch-and-speak preserves spatial layout, and reduces search space by allowing users to find any target from any screen location. The simple voice commands also support walk-up-and-use scenarios.

Additional Access Overlays

We prototyped several other access overlays, including several types of area cursors [35], a *grid overlay* that divided the screen into a regular grid, and a *world-in-miniature overlay* that presented an overview of the entire screen in one corner. Pilot participants had difficulty using these overlays, and so we omitted them from our user study.

Additional Features

In addition to the access overlays described above, our prototype provides several other accessibility features.

Auditory Touch Feedback

Some touch screen applications present visual feedback to let users know that a touch event has been recognized [32]. Our techniques provide audible feedback of touch events, emitting a low beep whenever a touch is detected. This feedback helps to prevent errors in which the user touches the screen too lightly to be detected.

Audio Dividers

One advantage of using a large touch screen is the ability to divide the screen into sub-regions. In a visual interface, these regions are typically denoted by drawing borders or assigning different backgrounds. Our techniques use soft, looping background sounds to differentiate regions of the screen. This allows users to identify when they have moved between regions, and to identify the boundaries of a region.

Our current prototype uses white noise loops, filtered at different frequencies, to differentiate regions.

Guided Directions

Both neighborhood browsing and touch-and-speak offer guided directions from the user's current touch location to an on-screen target. Directions are created by an algorithm that generates straight line paths between the user's finger (x_u, y_u) and the on-screen target (x_t, y_t) as follows:

1. If $y_t < y_u$, move *down* to point (x_u, y_t);
2. If $x_t \neq x_u$, move *left* or *right* to x_t;
3. If $y_t > y_u$, move *up* to y_t.

Generated paths first move down (*i.e.,* toward the user) if possible, in order to keep the majority of movement close to the user, reducing the need to stretch and the likelihood of colliding with physical objects on the surface. Diagonal movements are avoided because pilot subjects found it difficult to accurately follow diagonal paths; however, participants were capable of following horizontal and vertical paths. If a physical object is present along the path, the system identifies its bounding box and uses $A*$ [12] to route around the object. Figure 4 shows an example path.

Figure 4. Path from the user's finger to an on-screen target. Directions are provided via speech feedback at each segment of the path, *e.g.*, "Right 8 inches."

Audio feedback is provided as spoken directions (up, down, left, and right), and distances (in inches). While some prior systems have used mappings between tone and direction to guide users (*e.g.,* [15,22]), spoken directions are usable without training, and are thus ideal for walk-up-and-use scenarios. The system first reads the direction to and distance of the next point in the path, *e.g.*, "Right 4 inches." As a user continues on the path, he or she receives continuous feedback to continue in that direction, *e.g.*, "Right, right, right, …" When the path changes direction, the system speaks the direction and distance to the next path point. If the user diverges from the path beyond a certain threshold, the system guides the user back onto the original path. All pilot testers and study participants were able to follow these directions effectively, and some participants could easily estimate distance, moving their finger to the next path point in one fluid movement, rather than relying upon continuous audio feedback.

EVALUATION

We conducted a user study of the three access overlays described above. The access overlays were compared to an implementation of Apple's VoiceOver, which is used by as many as 100,000 blind people [28]. The study examined both overall performance when using the interface, as well as participants' spatial understanding of the screen layout.

Participants

We recruited 14 blind computer users (7 male, 7 female), with an average age of 46.4 (SD=12.6). All participants used a screen reader. Five participants were current VoiceOver users, and two other participants had previously tried VoiceOver but did not regularly use a touch screen. No other participants regularly used a touch screen.

Apparatus

The study was conducted using a Microsoft Surface tabletop computer with a 24-inch by 18-inch multi-touch screen, running Windows Vista. Because the Microsoft Surface's touch screen was surrounded by a bezel that felt identical to the touch screen itself, we added electrical tape around the screen to make it easier for participants to find the edge. We also added an external microphone and speakers. No other hardware modifications were made.

Participants tested each technique using a custom application, referred to here as *grid-map* (Figure 5). This application presented a grid-aligned map containing random points of interest. Each grid cell was 2 inches square, and 5 items were shown on the map at any time. Of the 108 cells, 44 cells were excluded as they overlapped portions of the access overlays' user interfaces. To avoid confounds, points of interest were randomly placed, and used randomly generated names consisting of a place type ("Bar," "Café," "Hotel," or "Store") and a letter (*e.g.*, "Café Z").

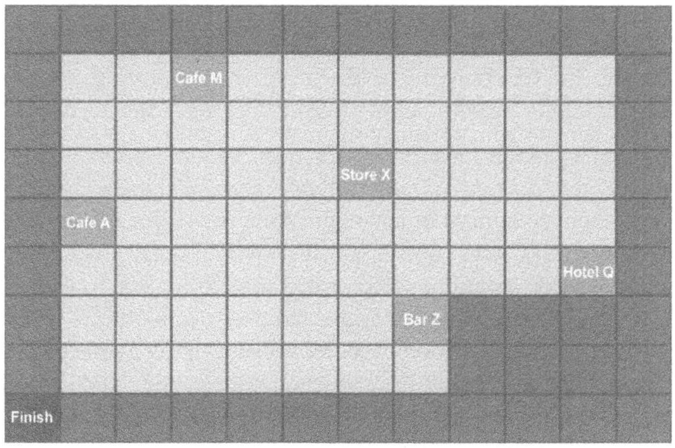

Figure 5. Grid-map application used in the experiment. Highlighted squares indicate points of interest on the map.

The study software recorded the start and end of each study trial, as well as the start time, end time, and position of each touch on the screen, calculated using the Surface SDK. Study data was saved to a log file. Participant feedback was recorded by the experimenter in a separate text file.

Procedure

Participants used each of the techniques to perform five distinct tasks using the grid-map application. To address both traditional performance metrics and spatial understanding, tasks involved both selecting targets and answering questions about the map's layout. The following tasks were used:

- *Locate.* Given the name of a target, the participant was required to touch the grid cell containing that target.
- *Count.* The participant was asked to report the number of targets on screen of a specified type (*e.g.*, hotels).
- *Relate.* The participant was given the names of two on-screen targets, and was asked to name the topmost or leftmost of the two targets (randomly chosen).
- *Select.* The participant selected a target, either by directly touching it or by some other method, such as by touching its edge proxy. When a target was selected, the system spoke the target name and a randomly selected "opening time." The participant was asked to report the opening time.
- *Relocate.* This task consisted of two steps. Five targets were randomly placed on the map. During the first step, the participant located each target, as in the *locate* task. During the second step, the participant located each target a second time.

These tasks covered traditional target acquisition (*select*), browsing speed (*count*), spatial understanding (*locate* and *relate*), and spatial memory (*relocate*).

Participants performed the study tasks using the following techniques: *edge projection, neighborhood browsing, touch-and-speak,* and *VoiceOver*. To reduce learning time, *bimanual context menus* were excluded from edge projection and the *nearby* command was excluded from touch-and-speak. We adapted Apple's VoiceOver technique to the Microsoft Surface. VoiceOver enables users to select targets by touching them directly, or by moving an on-screen cursor through a list of targets using swipe gestures.

Each participant performed five trials of each task for each technique. *Locate*, *count*, *relate*, and *select* tasks were presented in random order within each technique block. The *relocate* task was presented last within each technique block. Map locations were randomized for each *locate*, *count*, *relate*, and *select* trial, and were randomized once per each technique block for the *relocate* task. Trials began when the participant first touched the screen, and ended when the participant tapped a *Finish Task* button in the lower left corner of the screen.

Following each technique block, participants rated the technique using Likert-type scales (described below). After all techniques had been tested, participants ranked the techniques in order of preference and provided general feedback. Questionnaires were administered verbally, and the experimenter recorded the answers in a text file. The experiment took between 1.5 and 2 hours to complete.

Results

We present performance results for each of the techniques, participants' ratings for each of the techniques, and our observations of common interaction styles and challenges.

Data Collection

Each participant performed 5 trials of the 5 tasks for each of the 4 techniques. Because the *relocate* task featured two steps, two trials were recorded for that task. One participant was unable to test VoiceOver due to time constraints. A total of 1650 trials were recorded. For each trial, we recorded the start time, end time, all touch events, and participant responses for the *count*, *relate*, and *select* tasks.

Completion Time

Because trial completion time was not normally distributed (Shapiro-Wilk W=0.75, p<.01), we used the nonparametric Aligned Rank Transform (ART) [13,24,33] on completion time. The ART enables parametric F-tests to be used on nonparametric data, while preserving the correctness of interaction effects. After using the ART, the resulting data was analyzed using a mixed-effects REML model, which preserves large denominator degrees-of-freedom but compensates with wider confidence intervals. Pairwise comparisons used Holm-Bonferroni correction [14].

We found significant effects of *technique* ($F_{3,1591}$=43.47, p<.0001) and *task* ($F_{5,1589}$=133.95, p<.0001) on completion time, as well as an interaction between *technique* and *task* ($F_{15,1589}$=15.55, p<.0001). The average completion time for each technique is shown in Figure 6. Pairwise comparisons revealed that touch-and-speak was faster than VoiceOver and neighborhood browsing ($F_{1,1592.66}$=26.05, p<.01; $F_{1,1589.05}$=91.32, p<.01) and that edge projection was faster than VoiceOver and neighborhood browsing ($F_{1,1592.66}$=27.96, p<.01; $F_{1,1589.05}$=94.96, p<.01).

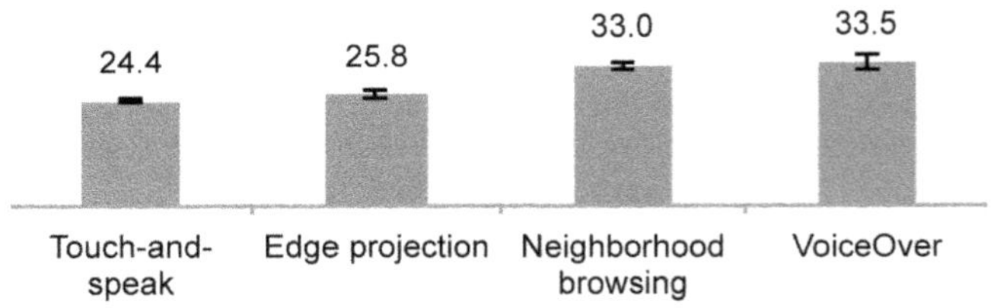

Figure 6. Task completion time across all tasks in seconds. Lower is better. Error bars show ±1 SE.

We also computed pairwise differences for each task:

- Touch-and-speak was faster than VoiceOver for the *locate, count,* and *select* tasks ($F_{1,267}$=21.07, p<.05; $F_{1,267}$=10.04, p<.05; $F_{1,267}$=8.05, p<.05).
- Touch-and-speak was faster than neighborhood browsing for the *count* and *select* tasks ($F_{1,267}$=145.95, p<.05; $F_{1,267}$=8.67, p<.01).
- Touch-and-speak was faster than edge projection for the *count* task ($F_{1,267}$=10.08, p<.01).
- Edge projection was faster than VoiceOver for the *locate* and *relate* tasks ($F_{1,267}$=12.75, p<.01; $F_{1,267}$=8.77, p<.01).
- Edge projection was faster than neighborhood browsing for the *count* task ($F_{1,267}$=79.32, p<.01).
- Neighborhood browsing was faster than VoiceOver for the *locate* task ($F_{1,267}$=11.38, p<.01).
- VoiceOver was faster than neighborhood browsing for the *count* task ($F_{1,267}$=75.37, p<.01).

There was a marginal time difference between the two steps of the *relocate* task ($F_{1,510}$=3.68, p=0.056). For the first step, touch-and-speak, edge projection, and neighborhood browsing were all significantly faster than VoiceOver ($F_{1,267}$=8.94, p<.01; $F_{1,267}$=8.10, p<.01; $F_{1,267}$=10.10, p<.01). On the second step, there was no significant effect of *technique* on task time ($F_{3,267}$=1.01, p=.38, *n.s.*). Note that while VoiceOver was significantly slower than the other techniques at first, it approached the speed of the other techniques for the second step. Figure 7 shows the average task completion time for the *relocate* task.

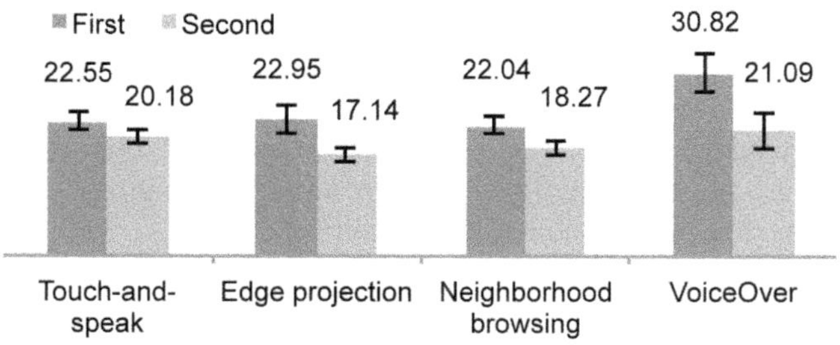

Figure 7. Task completion times in seconds for the two steps of *relocate*. Lower is better. Error bars show ±1 SE.

Correct Answer

Each trial was marked as correct or incorrect. For *locate* and *relocate* tasks, a trial was correct if the participant touched the specified target on the screen. For other tasks, a trial was correct if the participant provided the correct response to the question. As with completion time, we performed an ART procedure and analyzed the results using a mixed-effects REML model. There was a significant difference in correct answers by *technique* ($F_{3,1596}$=131.34, p<.0001) and *task* ($F_{5,1589}$=77.70, p<.0001), as well as a significant interaction between *technique* and *task* ($F_{15,1589}$=23.11, p<.0001). Pairwise comparison showed that there were significantly more incorrect answers when using VoiceOver than when using touch-and-speak, edge projection, or neighborhood browsing ($F_{1,1601.33}$=7.31, p<.05; $F_{1,1601.33}$=235.20, p<.05; $F_{1,1601.33}$=27.70, p<.05). Figure 8 shows the overall correct percentage by technique.

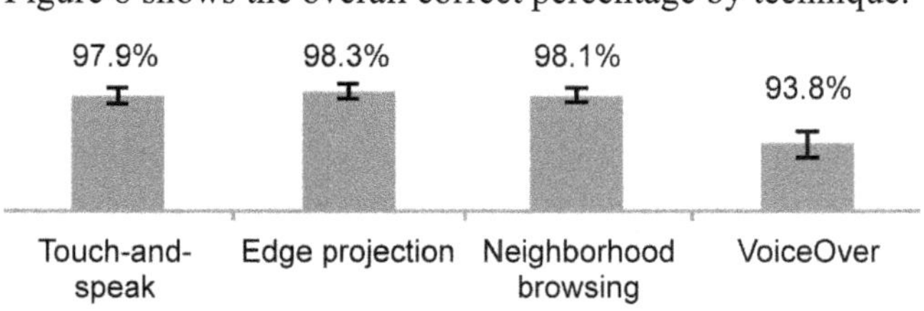

Figure 8. Correct answer percentage by technique. Higher is better. Error bars show ± 1 SE.

Subjective Ratings

Participants rated each technique by indicating their agreement with a series of statements using a 7-point Likert-type scale (*1=strongly disagree, 7=strongly agree*). The following statements were used: this technique was *enjoyable*; this technique was *fast*; this technique was *accurate*; this technique was *frustrating*; this technique was *useful*; this technique was *easy to understand*; this technique *helped me to understand the map*.

Likert ratings were analyzed using a Friedman nonparametric test, with Wilcoxon signed-rank tests for pairwise comparisons. Because one participant did not complete all four techniques, that participant's data was excluded from this analysis. Significant results were found for the following measures: *enjoyable, fast, useful,* and *easy to understand* ($\chi^2_{3,N=13}$=15.27, p<.01; $\chi^2_{3,N=13}$=13.53, p<.01; $\chi^2_{3,N=13}$=8.74, p<.05; $\chi^2_{3,N=13}$=8.31, p<.05). Pairwise comparison found the following significant differences: touch-and speak was significantly more enjoyable than VoiceOver (Z=2.85, N=13, p<.05), and touch-and-speak was perceived as faster than VoiceOver (Z=2.85, N=13, p<.05). No other pairwise differences were found.

Participants also ranked each of the techniques that they tested from most to least favorite. A Friedman test revealed a significant effect of *technique* on rank ($\chi^2_{3,N=13}$=15.92, p<.001). Pairwise comparison showed that touch-and-speak and edge projection were ranked significantly better than VoiceOver (Z=3.00, N=13, p<.05; Z=3.25, N=13, p<.05). Figure 9 shows the number of first and second choice picks per each technique.

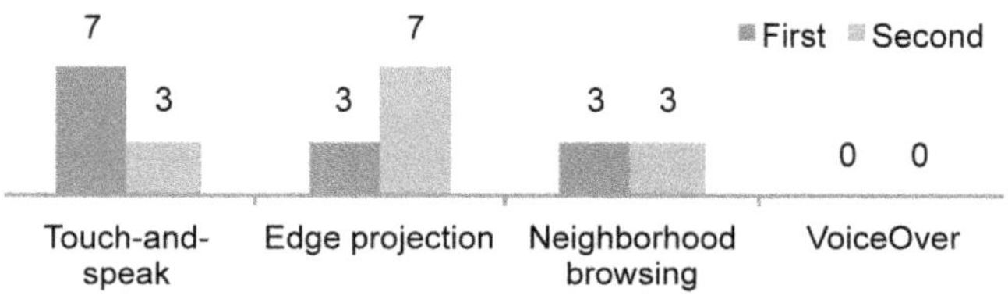

Figure 9. Number of participants who chose each technique as their first or second preferred choice.

General Observations and Participant Feedback

In general, participants varied widely in their search strategies. However, we noticed a number of challenges that were commonly experienced when using the touch screen interfaces. Regardless of the technique used, searching the entire screen to find an item was difficult, time-consuming, and often appeared to frustrate participants. Interestingly, many participants seemed to adopt and adhere to suboptimal search strategies. Most participants explored the screen in an unsystematic, random fashion, causing them to revisit places that they had already explored. More than half of the participants explored the screen by tapping repeatedly, rather than dragging their finger over the screen, which sometimes caused them to pass over and miss a target while their finger was raised. These strategies may have been adopted due to participants' lack of familiarity with touch screens, or may have matched their strategies for searching a physical space (*i.e.,* by "feeling around").

Participants also varied considerably in the speed with which they moved their hands. In some cases, moving too quickly could be confusing, such as when users moved their hands quickly across the screen and through a target, but had moved past it by the time its name had been read. Users then sometimes struggled to locate the target again.

Although participants were told that they could use one or two hands, most used only one hand at a time. However, some participants used their non-dominant hand to tap the *Finish Task* button, while others used their non-dominant hand to "measure" the distance between targets during the *relate* task. In other cases, participants rested their non-dominant hand at the edge of the screen, but sometimes were confused when they accidentally touched the screen and performed some unintended action.

Edge projection overlay. Participants often commented positively about this technique while using it. Most participants relied primarily on the bottom edge closest to themselves, which seems reasonable, as it required them to stretch the least, although one left-handed participant primarily used the left edge. Participants sometimes "missed" an item when browsing along the edge because they started their search from an arbitrary point along the edge rather than from the corner. One reason for this behavior may have been to avoid accidentally activating the *Finish Task* button, although participants were told that nothing "bad" would happen if they did accidentally press the button. Very few participants used two hands to triangulate on-screen targets. Furthermore, although it was possible to use the position of the edge proxies to quickly find the leftmost or topmost target in the *relate* task, most participants did not discover this advanced strategy, and instead located each target separately on the screen.

Neighborhood browsing overlay. Although neighborhood browsing was popular with participants (three chose it as their favorite technique, and another three chose it as their second favorite), participants often were slow in using this technique. Neighborhood browsing was especially slow for *count* tasks, as the participant needed to explore the entire screen to count all of the items. One possible explanation is that participants had difficulty creating the proper mental model for the screen layout. Also, participants often used more than one finger or their whole hand to search the screen (consistent with prior research [34]), and in so doing accidentally activated the guided directions feature. Despite these difficulties, the guided directions were extremely popular, and participants were overall quite effective in following them. Many participants commented positively about this feature; for example, one participant stated, "I just love the coaching to find things on screen."

Touch-and-speak overlay. This technique was popular, and participants could use this technique quickly. As with neighborhood browsing, participants enjoyed following the guided directions. Some participants unsuccessfully tried to invent additional commands, such as saying "list hotels" to list only the hotels on the map, or performed natural language queries such as, "What time does Store 'X' open?" However, these problems were quickly resolved. Many participants noted that they liked this technique, but would not use it in all situations, such as in noisy environments, or in public places (due to privacy concerns).

VoiceOver. Participants experienced several problems when using VoiceOver. Participants found the two selection modes (swiping to move through the list of targets, and directly touching a target to select it) to be particularly confusing, and were often unsure which of the two actions they had taken. Often participants would perform a swipe gesture, hear the name of a target that they had selected, and then be puzzled about how to actually locate that target on the screen. Swipe gestures were also performed with considerable variation, and thus were sometimes misrecognized. Although the list of targets was ordered from left to right, and thus participants could swipe through the list to quickly answer *relate* questions, few did so.

In general, because VoiceOver provided no additional support for locating targets, tasks that required participants to locate on-screen targets (*e.g., locate* and *relocate*) were particularly challenging. Participants described this as "a pain," and one participant was forced to give up on a *locate* task after being unable to find the target.

DISCUSSION

As mentioned previously, using touch screen interfaces remains a significant and sometimes intimidating challenge for blind people. At the start of the study session, numerous participants mentioned their lack of skill with touch screens, and one participant stated that she was "terrified of touch screens." Improving the usability, accessibility, and approachability of touch screens could therefore significantly help this currently excluded population.

Our current research began with our assertion that touch screen interfaces *can* be made more effective for blind people. We introduced three new accessible touch screen interaction techniques that improve upon current techniques in several ways: two of the three techniques performed significantly faster than a popular commercial technique, all three techniques resulted in greater spatial understanding of the screen layout, and all three techniques were preferred to the commercial technique for interacting with a large touch screen application.

In spite of this general success, it is difficult to declare a clear winner from our current evaluation. While touch-and-speak was preferred by participants and performed faster overall, many participants stated that they would not be comfortable using that technique in some contexts. In addition, edge projection was marginally faster for the *relate* task. It is possible that there is no "best" solution, and that different access overlays may be appropriate for specific scenarios, much as PC-based screen readers have multiple modes. When asked to choose their preferred technique, multiple participants said that they would most prefer the ability to combine or to switch among techniques.

Design Recommendations

We designed access overlays to support the criteria of *preserving spatial layout*, *leveraging bimanual interaction*, and *reducing search space* in *walk-up-and-use scenarios*. Our study results reaffirm the importance of these criteria for developing usable touch screen interfaces for blind

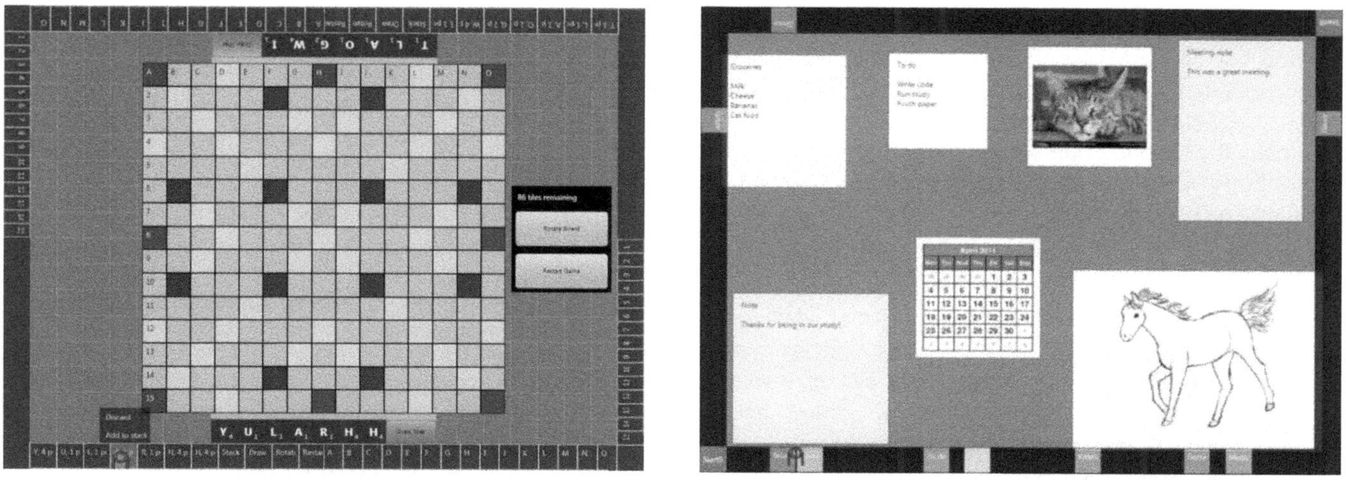

Figure 10. Board game (left) and bulletin board (right) applications, made accessible using an edge projection overlay.

people. In addition to supporting these criteria, our study results and observations suggest additional design guidelines for accessible touch screens:

- *Allow users to quickly switch between linearized and two-dimensional navigation.* Neighborhood browsing was especially slow for tasks such as *count* because it provided no easy way to scan through on-screen targets.
- *Avoid implicit mode switching.* Switching between modes should be clear and deliberate. In VoiceOver, which used both direct touch and swipe gestures, participants sometimes accidentally performed one or the other, and were confused by the result.
- *Avoid distinctions based on the number of fingers used.* Participants often used multiple fingers to explore the screen or inadvertently brushed the side of their hand against the screen. Multi-finger gestures such as split-tap should not be used to change modes, or should require some type of confirmation to avoid accidental activation.

New Accessible Touch Screen Applications

As access overlays offer new opportunities for blind people to interact spatially with touch screens, we are developing a number of applications to demonstrate these techniques. We describe three such applications, two of which are illustrated in Figure 10.

Map. We developed an interactive map that allows users to explore cities, countries, and points of interest using each of the access overlays. In the city view, users may request walking directions to local points of interest and send these directions to their phone via SMS. This prototype was recently demonstrated at the 2011 *CSUN International Technology and Persons with Disabilities Conference,* where it was tested by approximately a dozen blind people.

Board game. We have added access overlays to a prototype board game application, specifically the Scrabble crossword game. Currently, blind game players are often restricted to specialized Braille versions of board games, and many of our study participants were excited about the possibility of using a touch screen to play games.

Bulletin board. The bulletin board application allows users to explore notes, calendars, and images on a virtual bulletin board. This interface, built using a modified version of the Microsoft Surface's scatter view control, could be used in the future to organize and share other types of documents.

FUTURE WORK

The results of our study suggest several opportunities to refine our existing access overlays. Neighborhood browsing might benefit from a more robust layout algorithm (*e.g.,* Starburst [2]). Touch-and-speak might benefit from additional commands, such as searching within a user-defined region or searching for items of a specific type.

In addition to extending existing overlays, the system of access overlays could also be extended to utilize additional feedback channels, such as multiple synthesized voices, individualized audio feeds [11,21], or physical add-ons such as SLAP widgets [31]. Combining well-designed audio feedback with additional feedback modalities could significantly improve overall performance.

Current access overlays support limited bimanual input, but do not provide appropriate output when the user is touching the screen with both hands. Some study participants used both hands to search the screen, but were unsure which hand (or part of the hand) touched an item. Following such an encounter, one participant stated, "I touched it, but I don't know where I touched it." This problem may be resolved by providing richer feedback about where items are on the screen when they are touched.

Currently, access overlays assume that on-screen targets remain in place while the user explores the screen. The user is not notified when on-screen items move. Future versions could enable users to track the movement of on-screen objects over time, enabling access to dynamic content.

While large touch screens are often used collaboratively by multiple users, access overlays are currently designed for a single user. In the future, access overlays may be extended to support collaborative use, either between multiple blind users or between blind and sighted collaborators.

Finally, access overlays may be extended to general applications on the Microsoft Surface or other touch screen devices. Although the applications presented in this study were specially constructed, future versions could automatically capture on-screen targets using existing accessibility APIs, and thus could provide access to many standard touch applications.

CONCLUSION

While current touch screen accessibility techniques provide basic access to touch screens, we suggest that an ideal touch screen interface must also address issues such as spatial understanding, especially on large touch screen displays. We have introduced three techniques, called access overlays, which are optimized for exploring spatial interfaces on large touch screens. Our evaluation showed that access overlays enabled users to locate on-screen targets faster than traditional techniques, improved spatial understanding, and were preferred. This work introduces new approaches for improving touch screen accessibility.

REFERENCES

1. Bau, O., Poupyrev, I., Israr, A., and Harrison, C. TeslaTouch: electrovibration for touch surfaces. *UIST '10*, 283-292.
2. Baudisch, P., Zotov, A., Cutrell, E., and Hinckley, K. Starburst: a target expansion algorithm for non-uniform target distributions. *AVI '08*, 129-137.
3. Bonner, M., Brudvik, J., Abowd, G., and Edwards, W.K. No-Look Notes: accessible eyes-free multi-touch text entry. *Pervasive '10*, 409-427.
4. Buxton, W., Foulds, R., Rosen, M., Scadden, L., and Shein, F. Human interface design and the handicapped user. *SIGCHI Bulletin 17*, 4 (1986), 291-297.
5. Buxton, W., Hill, R., and Rowley, P. Issues and techniques in touch-sensitive tablet input. *SIGGRAPH '85*, 215-224.
6. Calder, M., Cohen, R.F., Lanzoni, J., and Xu, Y. PLUMB: an interface for users who are blind to display, create, and modify graphs. *ASSETS '06*, 263-264.
7. Carew, S. Touch-screen gadgets alienate blind. *Reuters* (2009). http://reut.rs/gHji5X
8. Fortune, S. A sweepline algorithm for Voronoi diagrams. *Algorithmica 2*, 1 (1987), 153-174.
9. Grossman, T. and Balakrishnan, R. The bubble cursor: enhancing target acquisition by dynamic resizing of the cursor's activation area. *CHI '05*, 281-290.
10. Guerreiro, T., Lagoa, P., Nicolau, H., Gonalves, D., and Jorge, J. From tapping to touching: making touch screens accessible to blind users. *IEEE Multimedia 15*, 4 (2008), 48-50.
11. Hancock, M.S., Shen, C., Forlines, C., and Ryall, K. Exploring non-speech auditory feedback at an interactive multi-user tabletop. *GI '05*, 41-50.
12. Hart, P.E., Nilsson, N.J., and Raphael, B. A formal basis for the heuristic determination of minimum cost paths. *IEEE Transactions on Systems Science and Cybernetics 4*, 2 (1968), 100-107.
13. Higgins, J.J. and Tashtoush, S. An aligned rank transform test for interaction. *Nonlinear World 1*, 2 (1994), 201-211.
14. Holm, S. A simple sequentially rejective Bonferroni test procedure. *Scandinavian Journal of Statistics 6*, (1979), 65-70.
15. Jagdish, D., Sawhney, R., Gupta, M., and Nangia, S. Sonic Grid: an auditory interface for the visually impaired to navigate GUI-based environments. *IUI '08*, 337-340.
16. Kane, S.K., Bigham, J.P., and Wobbrock, J.O. Slide Rule: making mobile touch screens accessible to blind people using multi-touch interaction techniques. *ASSETS '08*, 73-80.
17. Kane, S.K., Jayant, C., Wobbrock, J.O., and Ladner, R.E. Freedom to roam: a study of mobile device adoption and accessibility for people with visual and motor disabilities. *ASSETS '09*, 115-122.
18. Kane, S.K., Wobbrock, J.O., and Ladner, R.E. Usable gestures for blind people: understanding preference and performance. *CHI '11*, 413-422.
19. Landau, S. and Wells, L. Merging tactile sensory input and audio data by means of the Talking Tactile Tablet. *Eurohaptics '03*, 414-418.
20. Loomis, J.M., Golledge, R.G., and Klatzky, R.L. Navigation system for the blind: auditory display modes and guidance. *Presence 7*, 2 (1998), 193-203.
21. Morris, M.R., Morris, D., and Winograd, T. Individual audio channels with single display groupware: effects on communication and task strategy. *CSCW '04*, 242-251.
22. Plimmer, B., Crossan, A., Brewster, S.A., and Blagojevic, R. Multimodal collaborative handwriting training for visually-impaired people. *CHI '08*, 393-402.
23. Reisinger, D. Universities reject Kindle over inaccessibility for the blind. *CNET* (2009). http://cnet.co/gSjyv9
24. Salter, K.C. and Fawcett, R.F. The ART test of interaction: a robust and powerful rank test of interaction in factorial models. *Communications in Statistics-Simulation and Computation 22*, 1 (1993), 137-153.
25. Su, J., Rosenzweig, A., Goel, A., de Lara, E., and Truong, K.N. Timbremap: enabling the visually-impaired to use maps on touch-enabled devices. *MobileHCI '10*, 17-26.
26. Talbot, M. and Cowan, W. On the audio representation of distance for blind users. *CHI '09*, 1839-1848.
27. Tse, E., Hancock, M., and Greenberg, S. Speech-filtered bubble ray: improving target acquisition on display walls. *ICMI '07*, 307-314.
28. U.S. Bureau of Engraving and Printing. EyeNote. (2011). http://moneyfactory.gov/images/ EyeNote_Press_Release_4_4-19_2_4.pdf
29. Vanderheiden, G.C. Use of audio-haptic interface techniques to allow nonvisual access to touchscreen appliances. *HFES 40*, (1996), 1266.
30. Wall, S. and Brewster, S. Feeling what you hear: tactile feedback for navigation of audio graphs. *CHI '06*, 1123-1132.
31. Weiss, M., Wagner, J., Jansen, Y., Jennings, R., Khoshabeh, R., Hollan, J.D., and Borchers, J. SLAP widgets: bridging the gap between virtual and physical controls on tabletops. *CHI '09*, 481-490.
32. Wigdor, D., Williams, S., Cronin, M., Levy, R., White, K., Mazeev, M., and Benko, H. Ripples: utilizing per-contact visualizations to improve user interaction with touch displays. *UIST '09*, 3-12.
33. Wobbrock, J.O., Findlater, L., Gergle, D., and Higgins, J.J. The Aligned Rank Transform for nonparametric factorial analyses using only ANOVA procedures. *CHI '11*, 143-146.
34. Wobbrock, J.O., Morris, M.R., and Wilson, A.D. User-defined gestures for surface computing. *CHI '09*, 1083-1092.
35. Worden, A., Walker, N., Bharat, K., and Hudson, S. Making computers easier for older adults to use: area cursors and sticky icons. *CHI '97*, 266-271.
36. Yfantidis, G. and Evreinov, G. Adaptive blind interaction technique for touchscreens. *Universal Access in the Information Society 4*, 4 (2006), 328-337.

Imaginary Phone: Learning Imaginary Interfaces by Transferring Spatial Memory from a Familiar Device

Sean Gustafson, Christian Holz and Patrick Baudisch
Hasso Plattner Institute
Potsdam, Germany
{sean.gustafson, christian.holz, patrick.baudisch} @ hpi.uni-potsdam.de

ABSTRACT
We propose a method for learning how to use an imaginary interface (i.e., a spatial non-visual interface) that we call "transfer learning". By using a physical device (e.g. an iPhone) a user inadvertently learns the interface and can then transfer that knowledge to an imaginary interface. We illustrate this concept with our *Imaginary Phone* prototype. With it users interact by mimicking the use of a physical iPhone by tapping and sliding on their empty non-dominant hand without visual feedback. Pointing on the hand is tracked using a depth camera and touch events are sent wirelessly to an actual iPhone, where they invoke the corresponding actions. Our prototype allows the user to perform everyday task such as picking up a phone call or launching the timer app and setting an alarm. Imaginary Phone thereby serves as a shortcut that frees users from the necessity of retrieving the actual physical device.

We present two user studies that validate the three assumptions underlying the transfer learning method. (1) Users build up spatial memory automatically while using a physical device: participants knew the correct location of 68% of their own iPhone home screen apps by heart. (2) Spatial memory transfers from a physical to an imaginary interface: participants recalled 61% of their home screen apps when recalling app location on the palm of their hand. (3) Palm interaction is precise enough to operate a typical mobile phone: Participants could reliably acquire 0.95cm wide iPhone targets on their palm—sufficiently large to operate any iPhone standard widget.

Author Keywords
Imaginary interface, mobile, wearable, spatial memory, screen-less, memory, non-visual, touch.

ACM Classification
H5.2 [Information interfaces and presentation]: User Interfaces. - Graphical user interfaces.

General Terms
Design, Human Factors, Experimentation.

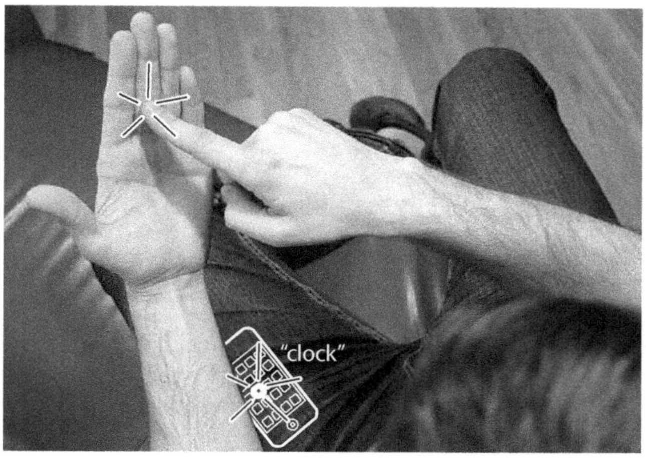

Figure 1: This user operates his mobile phone in his pocket by *mimicking* the interaction on the palm of his non-dominant hand. The palm becomes an *Imaginary Phone* that can be used in place of the actual phone. The interaction is tracked and sent to the actual physical device where it triggers the corresponding function. The user thus leverages spatial memory built up while using the screen device. We call this *transfer learning*.

INTRODUCTION
Imaginary interfaces were proposed as a means for enabling pointing input on screen-less mobile devices [5]. With their hands tracked by a chest-worn camera, users of imaginary interfaces point and draw in the *empty space* in front of them. Their non-dominant hand, held up in an "L-gesture", forms the origin of a 2D coordinate system. This visual reference allows users to acquire targets using coordinates of the style "two thumbs up and three index fingers to the right". This allowed for reliable acquisition of targets measuring 4.8 × 4.3cm.

However, if we try to transfer this approach to *multi-widget* imaginary interfaces, we obtain an interaction style reminiscent of a voice menu: the system would have to read out choices such as "For mail, select one thumb right, two index fingers up. For weather…" Having to listen to such a list makes interaction slow and frustrating [26]. Extended use would eventually allow users to select widgets without listening to the choices anymore (to *dial ahead* [18]), but since real-world interfaces can hold dozens of widgets, learning all the widget locations can take a long time, leaving users stuck with the voice-menu style of interaction.

Transfer learning

We propose an alternative approach which we call *transfer learning*. By designing imaginary interfaces that mimic the layout of a mobile device that users are already familiar with, users are able to operate an imaginary interface by *mimicking* their use of the corresponding real-world screen interface (Figure 1). As we demonstrate in this paper, this allows users to apply the spatial knowledge gathered on the physical device to an imaginary interface. We will refer to this by saying that the spatial knowledge *transfers* from the physical device to the imaginary interface.

CONTRIBUTION

This paper has two main contributions: (1) the concept of learning imaginary interfaces by *transfer* and as an example of that concept (2) our *Imaginary Phone* prototype. We also present two users studies that serve to validate the underlying principles of transfer learning and the Imaginary Phone prototype.

THE IMAGINARY PHONE

We start by illustrating the concept with a prototype we call Imaginary Phone: an imaginary interface that offers a shortcut interface for an iPhone (Figure 2). Instead of retrieving and operating the physical phone, users *mimic* the interaction by pointing and dragging on their empty hand. Our prototype tracks the pointing interaction between the two hands (see *Prototype and Tracking Hardware*) and sends the touch position to a physical mobile device, here an iPhone located in the user's pocket. The physical device supplies feedback to operations via the built-in speaker or a wireless headset worn by the user.

Walkthrough

Users can choose, either because it is necessary or just convenient, to use their Imaginary Phone for various quick tasks instead of retrieving the physical device from their pocket. Here is an example scenario:

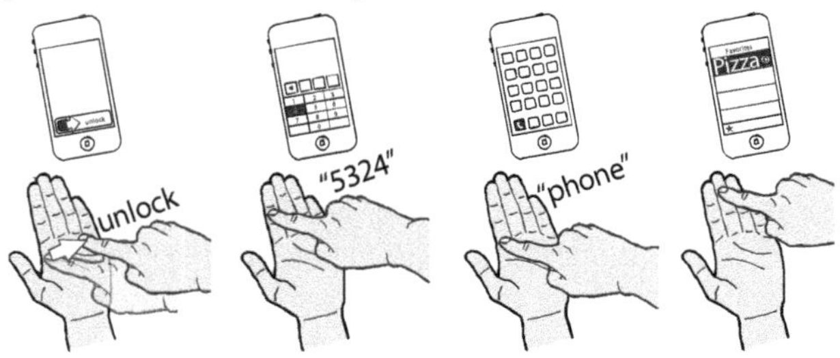

Figure 2: Walkthrough of making a call with the Imaginary Phone: (a) unlock with a swipe, (b) enter your pin, (c) select the 'phone' function and (d) select the first entry from the speed dial list.

Karl is cleaning up the dishes and receives a phone call. Since his hands are wet, he cannot take the call on his physical phone and uses the Imaginary Phone instead. He answers the call by swiping on his hand, which is the same interaction he would have performed on the physical phone. The call is from a friend that wants to go jogging tomorrow morning. Karl ends the call by touching the location of the 'End' button on this wet palm then launches the 'Clock' application. From here he selects the location for "Alarms" and enables his early morning alarm to ensure he gets up in time.

Later, while watching TV, Karl wants to order food but cannot find his phone in his pockets. Not wanting to get up from the couch and search, he chooses the Imaginary Phone to place a call as shown in Figure 2.

RESULTING INTERACTION MODEL AND BENEFITS

Interaction with an imaginary interface that is learned by transfer, such as by Karl in the previous scenario, is possible only because the user has been using the physical screen device over a period of time and has learned the spatial locations of the necessary user interface elements. This happened inadvertently—without extra effort users become increasingly familiar with the locations of such widgets over time. The spatial knowledge they gained from using the physical device can be *transferred* to an imaginary interface.

At some point, the user has performed an operation often enough to know the locations and sequence of touches needed to execute it and he can begin to perform that operation on the imaginary version of the interface. This will occur one operation at a time, with the simpler and more common operations being transferred earlier. Therefore, microinteractions [3] will generally be the first to transition to an imaginary interface.

As a result, this transfer model essentially turns the screen device into a *training mode* for the imaginary interface—or, depending on your perspective, the imaginary interface into an *expert mode* for the screen device. Accordingly, the benefit of the transfer model depends on the use case:

For users of physical devices, the main benefit of the transfer model is that it allows mobile phone users to instead perform their interactions on an imaginary interface. This saves these users the effort of retrieving the physical device, because the shorter the interaction, the greater the relative speedup. The latter makes the transfer model particularly valuable for microinteractions, such as dismissing an alarm dialog. Since the transfer model allows users to leverage their experience with the physical device, users can redeem these benefits right away, without the need for a separate training period.

For users of imaginary interfaces (i.e., users that only have access to the imaginary interface), the transfer model replaces the voice menu-style training period. Offloading the learning phase to a screen device, (1) allows learning to take place in a visual and inherently parallel way and, (2) unlike when using a voice menu-style interface, interaction is fast during training, lowering the entrance barrier to learning imaginary interfaces.

PROTOTYPE AND TRACKING HARDWARE

Our prototype senses touch using a depth camera and, after processing, injects touch events into a standard iPhone.

Sensing hardware

While imaginary interfaces as originally proposed required an infrared camera [5], interaction on the palm opens up other sensing options, such as gloves [11], Skinput [6] or depth cameras. We chose to use a time-of-flight depth camera, because unlike other approaches, it supports interaction with empty hands and allows for dragging interaction. Although currently mounted on a tripod and looking over the user's shoulder, we imagine future depth cameras to be small enough to be mounted on the chest as originally proposed for imaginary interfaces [5].

Our choice to use a time-of-flight camera can lead to occlusion issues (e.g., back of the hand occluding the pointing finger), but it does enable our prototype to work in all lighting conditions, including outside in direct sunlight (as shown in Figure 3b-c), unlike standard infrared cameras or Kinect [14]. Our depth camera is a PMD[vision] CamCube that provides frames at 40Hz with 200 × 200px resolution.

Figure 3: (a) We track input using a time-of-flight depth camera (PMD[vision] CamCube), which allows our Imaginary Phone prototype to also work in direct sunlight (b-c).

Algorithm

In order to extract the two hands from the input image, we pre-process the raw depth image as shown in Figure 4. We first find the closest pixels in the depth image (a), remove all pixels with relative depth values of more than 30cm, and smooth all remaining values. To determine the number of visible hands, we create a depth histogram of the masked image (c) and calculate the number of strong peaks (indicated by green squares in Figure 4c). Based on the two distributions in the histogram, we classify pixels in the depth image (d) to obtain the masks for the pointing hand (e) and the reference hand's palm (f).

To determine if and where the user is touching the palm, we pick a location inside the pointing hand (Figure 4e) and fill using a small tolerance value, eventually walking "down" the finger towards the reference hand (f). If the fill does not reach a depth value that belongs to the reference hand while staying within the tolerance value, we infer no touch. If it does, we infer that the finger is touching.

Due to the limited resolution of the depth camera, we cannot find the precise end of the touching finger. Instead, we determine the touch location from the end of the point mask offset by a small vector in the direction of the finger (green square in Figure 4g).

The width of the reference frame for touch events is set to the width of the fingers excluding the thumb (see *Design Discussion* for other possibilities). We first calculate the width from the top 3cm of the hand to exclude the thumb (the depth values allow translating this into pixels measurements) and draw a frame around those values. We then set the height of this reference frame to match an aspect ratio of 1.5. The final frame is shown in Figure 4f and g. As this reference frame is subject to noise if the pointing hand is present, we update the reference frame only if one hand is visible and, upon sensing both hands, adapt it by tracking the reference hand.

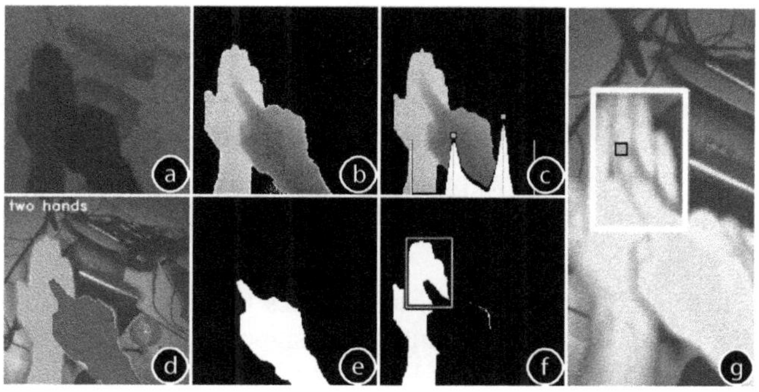

Figure 4: In processing the (a) raw depth image, our system (b) thresholds and (c) calculates a depth histogram to (d) segment the image into two masks: (e) pointing hand and (f) reference hand. From that we calculate (g) the final touch position and reference frame.

As the computed raw locations are subject to strong noise, we use hysteresis to maintain touch states (touch/no touch) and smooth input coordinates, which enables smooth dragging or even free-form drawing. This also prevents processing inadvertent input, such as a hand waving by the camera. Our system supports all of the same single-touch interactions that are possible on the phone: swiping, scrolling, tapping, dragging, drawing, etc.

After determining touch position on the palm, our prototype relays touch input to the iPhone. A custom-written input daemon on the iPhone receives the smoothed events via TUIO over WiFi and injects them into the event stream of the iPhone. The VoiceOver [1] accessibility mode (built into Apple iOS 4.0 and greater) provides auditory confirmation of actions. The unlock gesture on the iPhone to prevent inadvertent touch input additionally helps our system to disregard spurious input through gestures that happen naturally when not using the system.

RELATED WORK

Imaginary Phone draws on several areas of related work: wearable and mobile computing, microinteractions, sensing approaches for using the hand as an input surface and imaginary interfaces.

Wearable and mobile computing

Like Imaginary Phone there is a wide range of wearable and mobile computing systems that allow the user to interact without holding a device in their hands. Notably,

BodySpace [20] assigns functions to position on the body, Abracadabra [7] senses movement of a magnet placed on the finger tip from a wrist-mounted display and GesturePad [19] provides a touch sensitive pad embedded into clothing.

Microinteractions

Imaginary Phone is particularly well suited for supporting microinteractions—the quick mobile device interactions that characterize the dominant interaction mode for mobile phones [3]. Ashbrook et al. [2] showed that it takes over 4.5 seconds on average just to begin an interaction with a mobile phone stored in your pocket. This is a substantial overhead for an interaction that overall only lasts a few seconds [17].

Using the hand as input surface

Unlike the original imaginary interfaces, this paper proposes using the palm of the non-dominant hand as an interaction surface. Several projects, such as Haptic Hand [10], Sixth Sense [15] and Brainy Hand [21], also propose using the palm.

There are a few technical approaches to sensing touch on the surface of the hand. First, a designer could place sensing material on the palm. For example, KITTY [11] covers parts of the hand with electrical contacts that, when touched with another contact, register a touch event at a specific location. Although this method could produce highly reliable and perhaps high-resolution input, the fact that the user must wear something over their hand prohibits the general use of this approach.

Second, a system could observe the physical manifestations of touch from afar. For example, GestureWrist [19] senses hand postures by observing the changes in the shape of the wrist and Skinput [6] senses taps on the hand and forearm by measuring the different patterns of vibrations that travel up the arm.

Finally, computer vision has been used for a wide range of hand sensing [23] but we are unaware of any computer vision based approach that allows the user to use their uninstrumented finger to select a position on their bare hand. This, perhaps, has not been done previously because of the difficulties of separating the two hands. Using a depth camera allowed us to segment both hands and sense touch on the surface of the palm.

Imaginary interfaces

Imaginary interfaces are spatial, non-visual interfaces [5]. They were originally proposed as free-hand interface based on a finger and thumb coordinate system as shown in Figure 5.

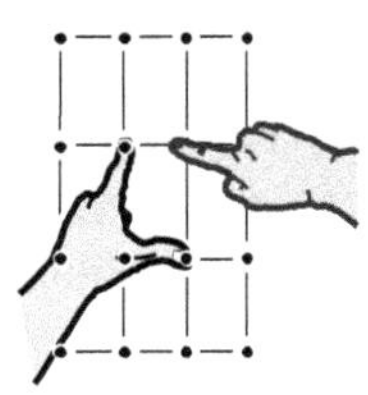

Figure 5: The finger and thumb coordinate system for the original imaginary interfaces [5].

Other researchers have proposed interfaces that are non-visual for controlling input (e.g., Mouse-less [16], Virtual Shelves [12]) or describing shapes and objects (e.g., Spatial Sketch [25], Data Miming [9]).

MAKING IT WORK: THE THREE REQUIREMENTS

The Imaginary Phone is based on the concept of transfer learning that can be broken down into a chain of three logical steps (Figure 6), each of which depends on one assumption:

1) Spatial memory: while using a screen device, users inadvertently learn where user interface elements are located.

2) Transfer: with an appropriate mapping, spatial memory acquired on a physical device can be recalled on an imaginary interface.

3) Accuracy: the imaginary interface allows users to point with sufficient accuracy to provide the pointing accuracy required by the associated physical device.

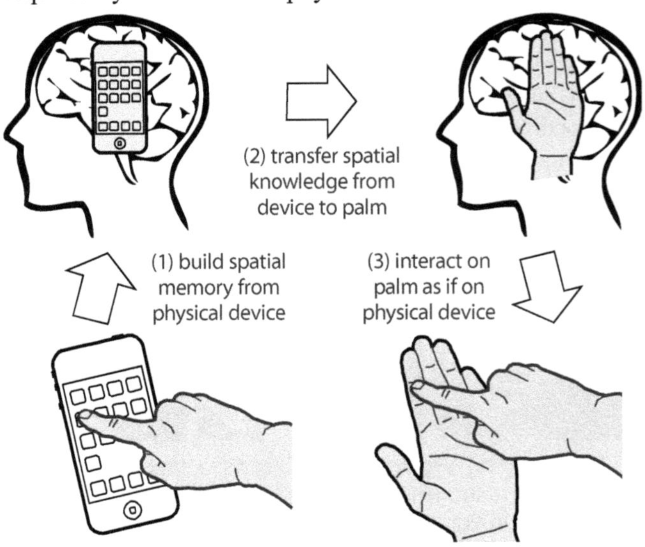

Figure 6: Our design is based on three assumptions: (1) using a physical device builds spatial memory, (2) the spatial memory transfers to the imaginary interface and (3) users can operate the imaginary interface with the accuracy required by the physical device.

These three assumptions inform the design of transfer-based imaginary interfaces and in particular Imaginary Phone. Next, we support these assumptions with a design discussion and empirical results from two studies.

DESIGN DISCUSSION

Assumption 2 (transfer) and 3 (accuracy) depend heavily on the design of the imaginary interface. Here we present the design alternatives we explored and explain the rationale for our choices.

Pointing in empty space vs. on the palm

The original imaginary interface lets users point in empty space, framed by an L-gesture (Figure 7a). When designing Imaginary Phone, we moved the interaction to the palm of the non-dominant hand (Figure 7b).

While the original imaginary interfaces concept, based on empty space, offered a much larger interaction area, the palm-based version offers a benefit we consider essential for transfer learning: *memorable landmarks*. The findings in [5] indicate that proximity to landmarks—in that case the tip of index finger and thumb—helps acquire targets; yet, the empty space design is all but void of landmarks. The palm, in contrast, is full of landmarks, many of which even have commonly known names, allowing users to create symbolic associations. The obvious match between four fingers and four-column layouts in, for example, the home screen, made it clear that the palm was the better platform for Imaginary Phone.

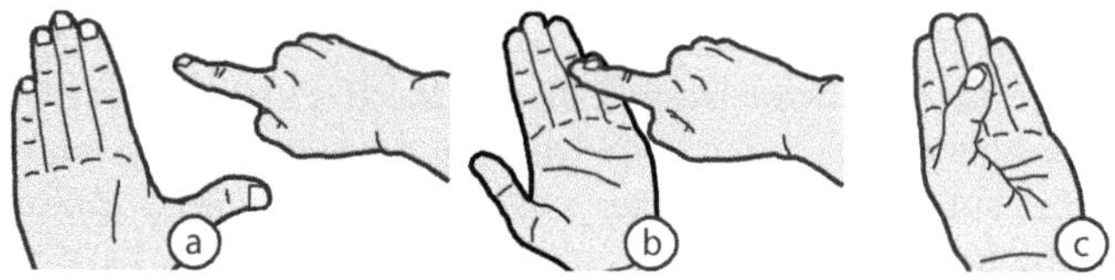

Figure 7: (a) The original Imaginary Interface had users interact in empty space framed by the L-gesture. (b) In this paper, we moved the interaction onto the non-dominant hand, which conceptually also allows (c) one-hand interaction.

As a side effect, on the palm, a tap is established by the physical contact, very much like on any touch screen. This results in four additional benefits:

1. *Stabilize finger:* physical contact between hands stabilizes the finger during pointing.

2. *Eliminate pinching:* most users are more experienced and thus skilled with tapping than with the pinching gesture required by the original empty space version.

3. *Spatial haptic feedback:* during tapping, the sensation on the non-dominant hand reflects the acquired location, providing an additional cue for target location.

4. *Eliminate parallax:* when targeting in empty space, the finger is free to move in 3D and is thus often outside the 2D interaction plane of the imaginary interface. Mapping the finger position to the desired 2D point on the plane, however, is subject to ambiguity and pointing error because we cannot know how the user conceptualizes this projection: orthogonal projection, line-of-sight, etc. Pointing on the palm avoids this problem.

While it is hard to compare the overall number of addressable locations in empty space to the palm (with empty space, pointing resolution decreases with distance from the reference hand [5]) the combination of the four factors listed above increases the pointing resolution on the palm to the point where it provides the resolution required to address widgets on an iPhone (see User Study 2). Also, the size of the palm matched the physical device much better than the large low-resolution empty space, whose large size could prove to be socially awkward.

Finally, interaction on the palm also allows for a one-handed version (as in PinchWatch [13]), illustrated in Figure 7c. This would allow for even more immediate use, albeit with less interaction space.

Defining the mapping from palm to physical screen

Palm and device screen generally do not have the same size and shape, requiring us to define a *mapping*.

Our prototype uses a simple regular grid mapping as illustrated by Figure 8b. This layout allows users to simply imagine the bounding rectangle of their hand and use that to find the position. Even more importantly, the layout is generic, thus applies to any interface including free form input, such as sketching and handwriting.

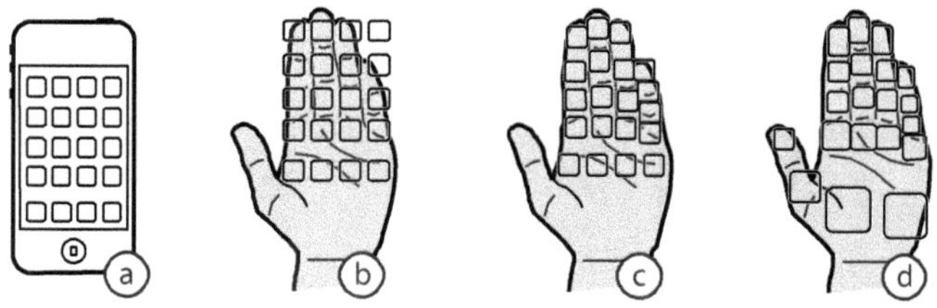

Figure 8: Mapping (a) the iPhone home screen mapped to (b) a regular grid, (c) a semi-regular grid where the columns are mapped to fingers and (d) arbitrary mapping to the best landmarks.

The more specific layouts (Figure 8c and d) should allow for increased pointing accuracy by making even better use of landmarks, but could cause confusion when trying to operate controls that assumed a rectilinear screen (Figure 9). Highly specialized layouts (Figure 8d) are impractical, as they require users to relearn mappings on a per-application basis.

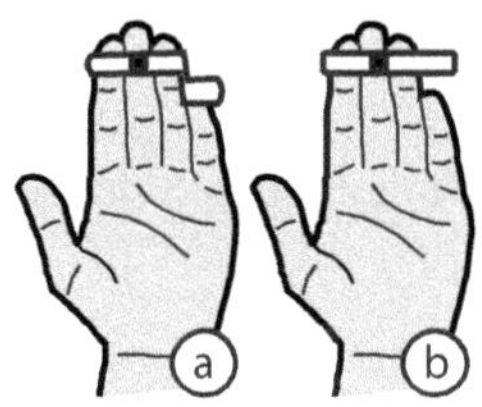

Figure 9: (a) Non-regular mappings fail when placing sliders and list items that span the width of the screen. (b) The regular grid works fine.

Our Imaginary Phone prototype uses the "4-finger scale" as shown in Figure 10c. This maps input from the larger palm to a smaller screen size, resulting in a scale factor of approximately 1.86. Unlike the more obvious 1:1 mapping (Figure 10b) the scaling allows us to include additional landmarks and thus increase the effective pointing accuracy on the mobile device. We could continue this logic by increasing the scale to include the whole hand but at the expense of leaving a large amount of the interaction space off the surface of the hand—a space devoid of landmarks.

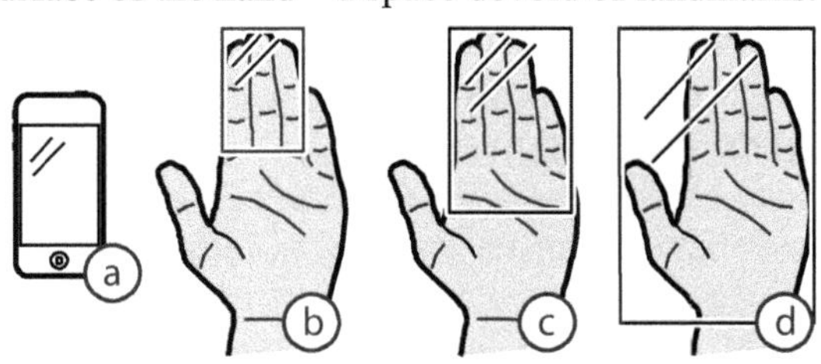

Figure 10: (a) The screen on a current 5 × 7cm mobile devices (b) maps to approximately three fingers of an adult male hand. (c) Using a scaled mapping allows us to map to four finger or (d) the whole hand. The iPhone and hands are to scale.

The four-finger scale works best with interfaces laid out in four column layouts, such as the iPhone home screen (Figure 11a). Other layouts, such as a seven-column month calendar (Figure 11b) could be mapped by assigning every other day to the space between two fingers, which also make good landmarks. Similarly, we could map three-column layouts (Figure 11c) to only the spaces between fingers.

Figure 11: iOS screens laid out in (a) four, (b) seven, (c) and three column grids.

Some mappings, such as the semi-regular grid (Figure 8c) are simple enough to communicate with a diagram (as we did in Study 1) but with others, such as the regular grid (Figure 8b), it is not clear how user interface elements map to specific features on the user's hand. Figure 12 shows an approach we explored to teach users the regular grid mapping. If we have access to the device's wallpaper, we display a photo of the user's hand as wallpaper. During use users now learn not only target locations but also the mapping from a widget to its location on the user's palm. This design allowed us to minimize learning time in Study 2.

Figure 12: A photo of the user's hand as wallpaper helps learn the association between widget and location on the user's palm.

The arguments just presented form logical support for the three assumptions that transfer learning is based on. The following two studies complement this discussion with empirical results.

STUDY 1: RECALL YOUR HOME SCREEN LAYOUT AND TRANSFER IT TO YOUR HAND

This first study investigated the first two of the three assumptions behind transfer learning as illustrated in Figure 6. First, we wanted to know how much spatial memory users build up through the regular use of a touch-screen mobile device. Second, we wanted to know how much of that knowledge transfers to the hand. Together, these numbers would tell us *how useful* an Imaginary Phone could be. We did not test a specific hypothesis in this study. We were purely interested in participants' recall abilities.

To investigate this we asked daily iPhone users to recall the locations of the (up to) twenty home screen app icons of their own iPhone from memory and without feedback. In a between-subjects design, half of the participants recalled and communicated their choice by pointing to a non-functional iPhone prop (*phone prop* condition Figure 13a) while the other half recalled locations by pointing to the palm of their own non-dominant hand, using a predefined scheme of how buttons on their iPhone would map to locations on their palm (*palm* condition, Figure 13b).

Research questions

The goal of this study was to determine how many app locations had been learned as a side effect of regular use and how much of that knowledge would successfully transfer, using the supplied mapping, to the participants' palm. Participants in the *palm* condition would not only have to recall, but also map locations onto their hand. The difference between the two conditions would serve as an indication for how much information is lost in transfer. We also expected the frequency of use to correlate with the user's ability to recall.

Task and procedure

After we seated participants, they unlocked their phone and, without looking at the screen, handed it over to us. Participants in the *palm* condition were now taught the semi-regular-grid mapping scheme (see Figure 8c in the Design Discussion). This preparation took less than a minute for all participants.

The experimenter then conducted a series of trials, one for each app on the participant's home screen. For each trial, the experimenter picked a different app and cued the participant with the app's name and a description of the app icon's visual appearance.

Participants responded by pointing to the app's presumed location within the 4 × 5 icon home screen. Participants in the *phone prop* condition pointed to cells displayed on a printed prop of an iPhone (unlabeled all-white icons in Figure 13a). Participants in the *palm* condition instead pointed to a location on their own non-dominant hand (Figure 13b).

In both conditions, the experimenter determined what location the participant was pointing to by observing them point. While we did not measure pointing accuracy directly (we investigated that in Study 2), the experimenter had no difficulty identifying which targets participants referred to.

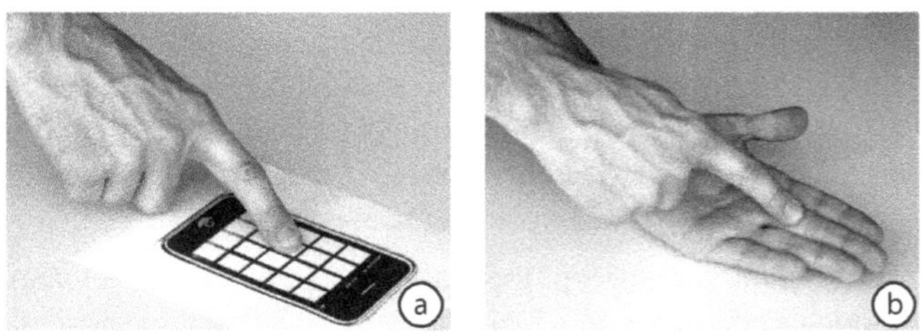

Figure 13: Study 1 task: (a) participants in the *phone prop* condition recalled app locations by pointing to an empty iPhone prop, (b) participants in the *palm* condition pointed on their own non dominant hand.

After completing all trials, participants classified each of their home screen apps as used either *daily* (at least once a day), *weekly* (at least once a week) or *rarely* (less than once per week).

Finally, participants filled out a demographic questionnaire. All participants completed the study in 15 minutes or less.

Participants

We recruited 12 participants (5 female) in the cafeteria of our institution. Participants were on average 23.6 years old (SD=4.2) and two were left-handed. All participants were daily iPhone users and carried it with them. They were given a small gift for their time.

Results

The twelve participants had on average 18.4 apps on their home screens and recalled each only once, for a total of 221 app recall trials. No outliers were removed but three trials were discarded (leaving 218 for analysis) because of errors by the experimenter. Figure 14 shows the responses from all participants.

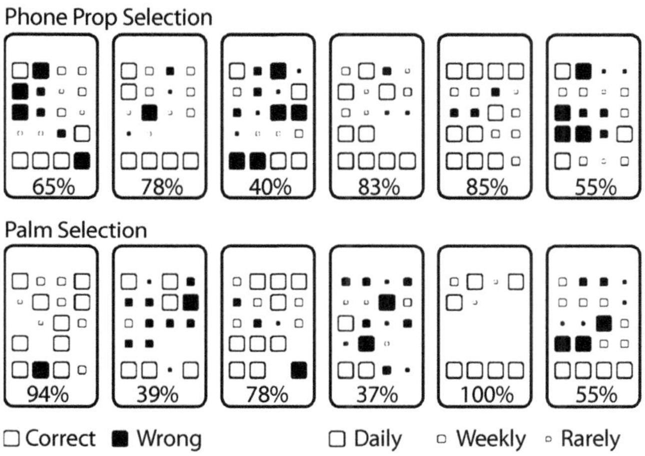

Figure 14: Study 1 raw results: each of the 12 rounded rectangles represents one participant's phone home screen. Each black (wrong) or white (correct) square represents a specific home screen app. Percentages indicate the participant's recall rate.

Our main finding was that participants, on average, correctly positioned 64% of the apps on their phone (68% for *phone prop*, 61% for *palm*). The success rate was higher for apps used daily (71% for *phone prop*, 80% for *palm*). T-tests did not show any significant differences. When they were wrong, 45% of guesses were only a single cell off, suggesting that participants had some spatial knowledge. Figure 15 shows these aggregated statistics.

Overall the frequency of use of an application correlated with percentage correct (Pearson's r_3=0.998, p=0.043) but we found no trends relating performance to age, gender or duration of phone ownership.

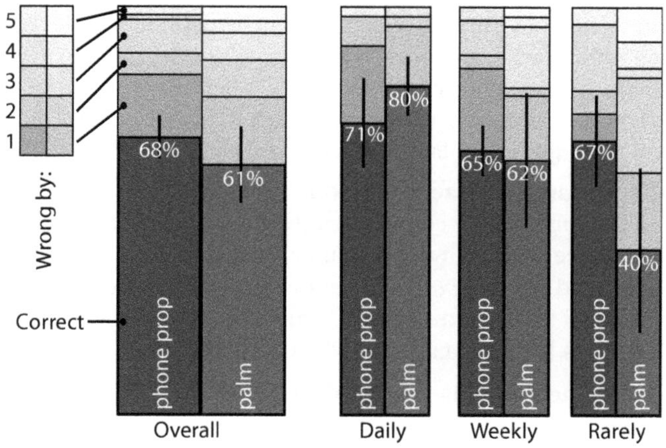

Figure 15: Study 1 aggregated results: percentage correct by use frequency (+/- std. error of the mean). The chart is stacked with mean percentages for incorrect responses separated by how far (in Manhattan distance) they were wrong by.

Discussion

Since none of the participants were aware of the task or project before the study, a mean recall rate of 64% of their home screen apps can only be explained as a side effect of regular phone use. This supports the first of our three main assumptions behind the transfer learning approach.

Note that the recall rates observed with these untrained users effectively form a lower bound as actual users of an Imaginary Phone would have an incentive to actively learn locations.

We did not find a significant difference between recall on *phone prop* and *palm* conditions. However, while the lack of significance is expected given the small number of participants and high variation, the fact that both numbers are in the same range suggests that the loss of spatial knowledge during transfer cannot be too large. This is also supported by our observations—participants seemed to recall on their hands almost as easily as on a phone. This supports the second of our three main assumptions: spatial knowledge can indeed transfer to the hand.

STUDY 2: TARGETING ON ARBITRARY LAYOUTS

Our goal of this study was to verify our design's third main assumption—that a palm-based imaginary interface, such as Imaginary Phone, supports sufficient pointing accuracy to operate the typical functions of a mobile phone. In particular, we wanted to know whether this interaction style would allow users to operate the widget sizes common to today's touch devices. If so, imaginary interfaces that mimic touch devices would become viable. To be able to compare palm interaction to previous work [5] (that used a different sensing mechanism) we included the traditional empty space imaginary interface (Figure 16a) as a control.

In order to evaluate the *concept* rather than the current condition of our Imaginary Phone prototype (whose touch resolution is limited by the depth camera's 200 × 200px resolution) we conducted this study using "perfect" tracking, i.e., post-hoc analysis of high resolution photos.

In contrast to Study 1, where targets were directly associated with hand landmarks, we chose to conduct this experiment with randomly placed targets. Therefore these results show performance worse than with a layout designed to align widgets with landmarks on the hand.

(Imaginary) interfaces tested in this study

In the *empty space* control condition participants targeted in the space framed by their thumb and index finger (Figure 16a) and in the *palm* condition participants targeted on palm of their hand (Figure 16b). The size of the tracked area was kept constant for both conditions.

To shorten training, we used the *wallpaper* approach described earlier in the design section (see Figure 12) where participants' own hand was displayed behind the targets. With this approach, they were able to readily associate the arbitrary target locations with landmarks on their own hand.

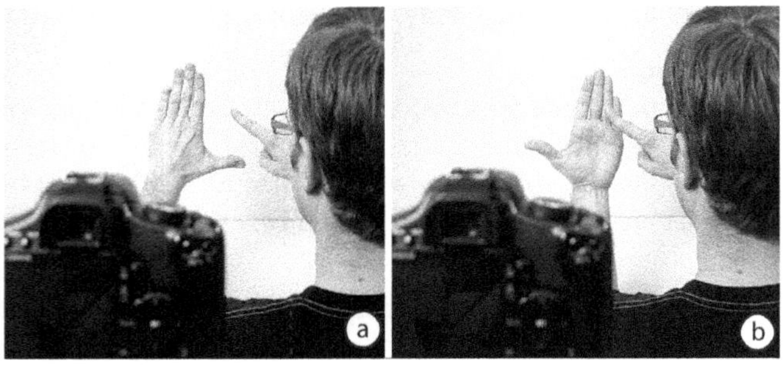

Figure 16: Study 2 apparatus: (a) *empty space* condition and (b) *palm* condition.

Task and procedure

During each trial, participants targeted three locations at a time (in pilots we determined participants were able to remember three locations easily). Participants learned the three target locations by repeatedly targeting them on a screen device (here an iPod Touch) until they were able to reliably target with at least 5mm accuracy on the touch screen. Participants were then prompted repeatedly with a target number and responded by recalling the respective position in *empty space* or on their *palm* depending on the condition.

There were two independent variables: Target Location (4 groups of 3 locations) and Interface (*empty space* vs. *palm*). As a within-subjects design, half of the blocks used the *empty space* interface and the other half the *palm* interface. The order of interfaces was counterbalanced across participants. Participants recalled and touched each target five times in random order; each participant completed four such blocks (two for each interface) with each block featuring a different set of 3 targets. Together, the experiment consisted of 12 participants × 2 interfaces × 2 blocks × 3 targets × 5 reps = 720 trials. Each participant completed the experiment session within 30 minutes.

Apparatus

We used a DSLR camera to record participants' touch interactions (Figure 16). We extracted touch locations from the high-resolution photos on a millimeter level, which kept tracking errors to a minimum.

Participants

12 participants (1 female) were recruited at our institution. They were between the ages of 19 and 28 (M=21.8, SD=2.56). All participants were right-handed. They were given a small gift for their time.

Research question and hypothesis

The main purpose of this study was to determine the accuracy of the *palm* interface. If we should find that the minimum button size of the hand interface is comparable to studies of conventional touch (such as the 15mm buttons from [8]) that would indicate that the transfer concept was viable.

Reflecting our earlier discussion on the properties of the palm interface, we hypothesized that the *palm* interface would allow participants to target with higher accuracy than in the *empty space* condition.

Results

We discarded 7 bad trials where no data was recorded and 15 outlier trials where the touch location was greater than 3 standard deviations away from the centroid. This left us with 720-7-15=698 trials in our analysis. To allow for comparison between participants, we normalized all hand sizes so that the index finger was 7.25cm long (the population's average index finger length [4]). This length corresponds to 3.90cm in the iPhone, leaving us with a scaling factor of 1.86.

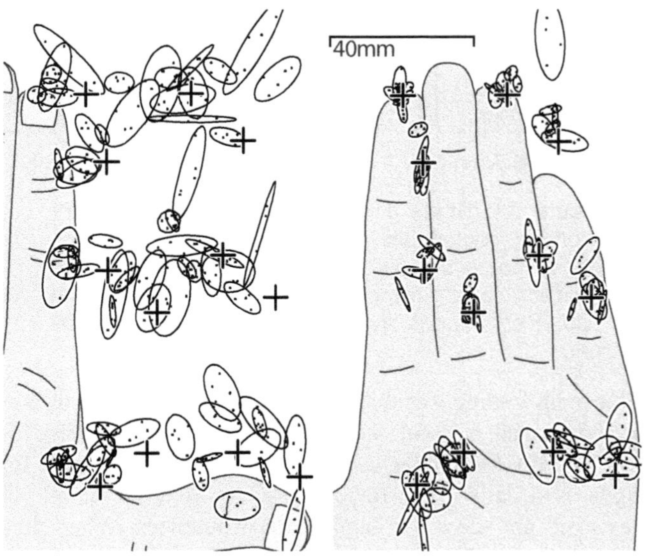

Figure 17: Study 2 results: all touches from all participants for (left) the *empty space* condition and (right) the *palm* condition. Plus signs indicate actual target positions. Ovals represent the bivariate normal distribution of selections per participant per target.

Figure 17 shows the raw data where each ellipse contains the 5 trials from one participant for one target. For the remaining analysis, we decomposed the targeting error (distance between target and acquired location) into systematic error (*offset*) and noise (*minimum button size*), as suggested by [8]. We assume one overall offset, instead of per user offsets. This is a more liberal estimate of touch accuracy, because it is not calibrated per user.

On average, the diameter of a circular minimum button on the *empty space* interface is 27.9mm (SD=0.32) and 17.7mm (SD=0.22) on the *palm* interface. This difference is statistically significant (t_{11}=2.912, p=0.014, Cohen's d=0.84).

When input is mapped back to the iPhone screen, all interactions are scaled down by a factor of 1.86 (the ratio of hand size to screen size). This in turn affects minimum button sizes—they now shrink to 15mm for the *empty space* condition and 9.5mm with the *palm* condition.

Discussion

As hypothesized, the *palm* interface was more accurate than the traditional *empty space* interface. This supports the reasoning presented earlier (see *Design Discussion*) and also confirms our choice to build the Imaginary Phone with a palm-based interface.

Also unsurprisingly (because we offered no feedback), the raw accuracy (i.e., before scaling down) obtained with the two imaginary interfaces is worse than the accuracy values obtained by other researchers with modern touchscreens. They report, using different study conditions, minimum button sizes of 15.0mm [8], 11.5mm [24] and 10.5mm [22]. The touch distributions we measured in this study indicate minimum button sizes of 9.5mm when scaled to fit the phone, which are comparable to a touch device. This, of course, is due to the palm offering a bigger input surface than the actual device, such that input errors shrink as input locations are mapped back to the device. In particular, this provides the necessary accuracy to acquire standard widgets on current touch devices, such as the iPhone, therefore making the transfer concept viable.

That said, these results were obtained with a tracking mechanism more accurate than what our current prototype can deliver. Consequently, these results could be considered a theoretical minimum for feedback-less targeting on the palm.

SUMMARY OF THE TWO STUDIES

Summarizing the two studies reported above, we find that all three of the assumptions of the transfer learning model stated earlier have support.

(1) Users indeed build up spatial memory automatically while using a physical device: participating iPhone users knew the correct location of 68% of their own iPhone home screen apps by heart.

(2) Spatial memory indeed transfers from physical to imaginary interfaces: participants recalled the location of home screen apps with 61% accuracy when pointing on the palm of their hand.

(3) Pointing on the palm is precise enough to allow operating the device: using accurate tracking, participants can reliably acquire targets less than 17.7mm in diameter on their palm. Mapping these back to the smaller iPhone increases precision to 9.5mm button sizes. This is sufficient to operate standard widgets on today's mobile touch devices.

We conclude that the transfer model is viable, even though full accuracy will not be redeemed until higher resolution tracking equipment becomes available.

CONCLUSIONS

In this paper, we presented a method of learning imaginary interfaces based on transfer and illustrated the concept with our Imaginary Phone prototype.

From the perspective of a mobile device user, the main benefit of imaginary interfaces based on transfer learning is that it saves users the effort for retrieving the device.

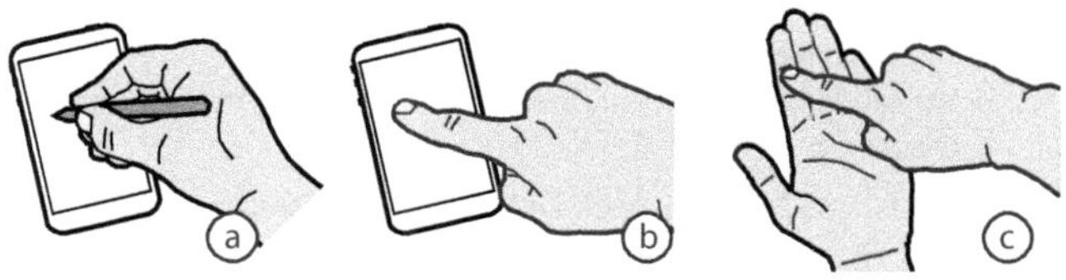

Figure 18: (a) Early mobile devices required users to retrieve a stylus and the device. (b) Current touch devices require retrieving only the device. (c) Imaginary interfaces do not require retrieving anything.

What is promising is that a similar transition has happened before, as illustrated by Figure 18. While early devices required users to retrieve device and stylus (e.g., PalmPilot), usage eventually transitioned to touchscreen-based devices. This move took place even though stylus input is in many ways superior to touch input—it offers higher precision (no fat finger problem [22, 8]).

At the expense of losing even more precision and essentially limiting interaction to microinteractions, systems like the Imaginary Phone have the potential to offer even more convenience, namely there is no need to retrieve the device anymore. While hardly viable on its own, we argue that the combination of an imaginary interface and a physical mobile device is an intriguing form factor.

As future work, transfer learning could be applied to a broader range of devices, such as remote controls and instrument panels. In particular, it would be interesting to investigate if the transfer learning principle can be applied to such devices (that have a strong tactile component) rather than the visual interface as we have shown here.

ACKNOWLEDGEMENTS

Sincere thank you to the members of our lab, in particular Anne Roudaut, Christian Loclair and Henning Pohl for help generating ideas, proofreading and unending support. Special thanks to Matthias Ringwald for his lib-hidsupport that enabled touch event injection on the iPhone.

REFERENCES

1. Apple VoiceOver, http://www.apple.com/accessibility/iphone/vision.html
2. Ashbrook, D.L., Clawson, J.R., Lyons, K., Starner, T.E. and Patel, N. Quickdraw: the impact of mobility and on-body placement on device access time. In *Proc. CHI*, (2008), 219–222.
3. Ashbrook, D. *Enabling Mobile Microinteractions*. PhD Thesis. (2010).
4. Greiner, T.M. *Hand Anthropometry of U.S. Army Personnel*. U.S. Army Report ADA244533, (1991).
5. Gustafson, S. Bierwirth, D. and Baudisch, P. Imaginary Interfaces: spatial interaction with empty hands and without visual feedback. In *Proc. UIST*, (2010), 3–12.
6. Harrison, C., Tan, D. and Morris, D. Skinput: appropriating the body as an input surface. In *Proc. CHI*, (2010), 453–462.
7. Harrison, C. and Hudson, S.E. Abracadabra: wireless, high-precision, and unpowered finger input for very small mobile devices. In *Proc. UIST*, (2009), 121–124.
8. Holz, C. and Baudisch, P. The generalized perceived input point model and how to double touch accuracy by extracting fingerprints. In *Proc. CHI*, (2010), 581–590
9. Holz, C. and Wilson, A.D. Data Miming: inferring spatial object descriptions from human gesture. In *Proc. CHI*, (2011), 2501–2510
10. Kohli, L. and Whitton, M. The Haptic Hand: providing user interface feedback with the non-dominant hand in virtual environments. In *Proc. GI*, (2005), 1–8.
11. Kuester, F., Chen, M., Phair, M.E. and Mehring, C. Towards keyboard independent touch typing in VR. In *Proc. VRST*, (2005), 86–95.
12. Li, F.C.Y., Dearman, D. and Truong, K.N. Virtual Shelves: interactions with orientation aware devices. In *Proc. UIST*, (2009), 125–128.
13. Loclair, C., Gustafson, S. and Baudisch, P. PinchWatch: a wearable device for one-handed microinteractions. In *Proc. MobileHCI Workshop on Ensembles of On-Body Devices*, (2010), 4 pages.
14. Microsoft Kinect, http://www.xbox.com/kinect
15. Mistry, P., Maes, P., and Chang, L. WUW - wear Ur world: a wearable gestural interface. In *CHI Extended Abstracts*, (2009), 4111–4116.
16. Mistry, P. and Maes, P. Mouseless. In *Adjunct Proc. UIST*, (2010), 441–442.
17. Oulasvirta, A., Tamminen, S., Roto, V. and Kuorelahti, J. Interaction in 4-second bursts: the fragmented nature of attentional resources in mobile HCI. In *Proc. CHI*, (2005), 919–928
18. Perugini, S., Anderson, T.J. and Moroney, W.F. A study of out-of-turn interaction in menu-based, IVR, voicemail systems. In *Proc. CHI*, (2007), 961–970.
19. Rekimoto, J. GestureWrist and GesturePad: unobtrusive wearable interaction devices. In *Proc. ISWC*, (2001), 21–27.
20. Strachan, S., Murray-Smith, R. and O'Modhrain, S. BodySpace: inferring body pose for natural control of a music player. In *CHI Extended Abstracts*, (2007), 2001–2006.
21. Tamaki, E., Miyaki, T. and Rekimoto, J. Brainy Hand: an ear-worn hand gesture interaction device. In *CHI Extended Abstracts*, (2009), 4255–4260.
22. Vogel, D. and Baudisch, P. Shift: a technique for operating pen-based interfaces using touch. In *Proc. CHI*, (2007), 657–666.
23. Wachs, J.P., Kölsch, M., Stern, H. and Edan, Y. Vision-based hand-gesture applications. *CACM 54*, 2 (2011), 60–71.
24. Wang, F. and Ren, X. Empirical evaluation for finger input properties in multi-touch interaction. In *Proc. CHI*, (2009), 1063–1072.
25. Willis, K.D., Lin, J., Mitani, J. Igarashi, T. Spatial Sketch: bridging between movement & fabrication. In *Proc. TEI*, (2010), 5–12.
26. Yin, M. and Zhai, S. The benefits of augmenting telephone voice menu navigation with visual browsing and search. In *Proc. CHI*, (2006), 319–328.

NaviRadar: A Tactile Information Display for Pedestrian Navigation

Sonja Rümelin[1], *Enrico Rukzio*[2/3], *Robert Hardy*[3]
[1] University of Munich, Germany, sonja.ruemelin@ifi.lmu.de
[2] paluno, University of Duisburg-Essen, Germany, enrico.rukzio@uni-due.de
[3] School of Computing and Communications, Lancaster University, UK, hardyr@comp.lancs.ac.uk

ABSTRACT

We introduce NaviRadar: an interaction technique for mobile phones that uses a radar metaphor in order to communicate the user's correct direction for crossings along a desired route. A radar sweep rotates clockwise and tactile feedback is provided where each sweep distinctly conveys the user's current direction and the direction in which the user must travel. In a first study, we evaluated the overall concept and tested five different tactile patterns to communicate the two different directions via a single tactor. The results show that people are able to easily understand the NaviRadar concept and can identify the correct direction with a mean deviation of 37° out of the full 360° provided. A second study shows that NaviRadar achieves similar results in terms of perceived usability and navigation performance when compared with spoken instructions. By using only tactile feedback, NaviRadar provides distinct advantages over current systems. In particular, no visual attention is required to navigate; thus, it can be spent on providing greater awareness of one's surroundings. Moreover, the lack of audio attention enables it to be used in noisy environments or this attention can be better spent on talking with others during navigation.

ACM Classification: H.5.2 [Information Interfaces and Presentation]: User Interfaces – Input devices and strategies; Prototyping. H.1.2 [Models and Principles]: User/Machine Systems – Human Factors.

General terms: Design, Human Factors, Experimentation.

Keywords: Pedestrian navigation, tactile feedback, radar.

INTRODUCTION

Mobile navigation, which has become very popular in the last decade, started with availability of affordable satnavs and is now widely used on mobile phones for pedestrian navigation, for example, Nokia's Ovi Maps and Google Maps. The communication of navigational information when walking via visual information or spoken instructions provide certain, self-evident, disadvantages when it comes to the user's attention (awareness of the traffic and the user's ability to focus on the walking task itself) and the user's environment (information clarity in noisy environments and obtrusiveness in a social context).

We present a navigation technique using only tactile feedback, provided by a single vibrator on a mobile device, to communicate directional information using a radar metaphor. Distinct tactile feedback is provided when the constantly rotating radar sweep crosses the current direction (D_C) and the direction in which to travel (or desired direction, D_D) as illustrated in the Figure 1.

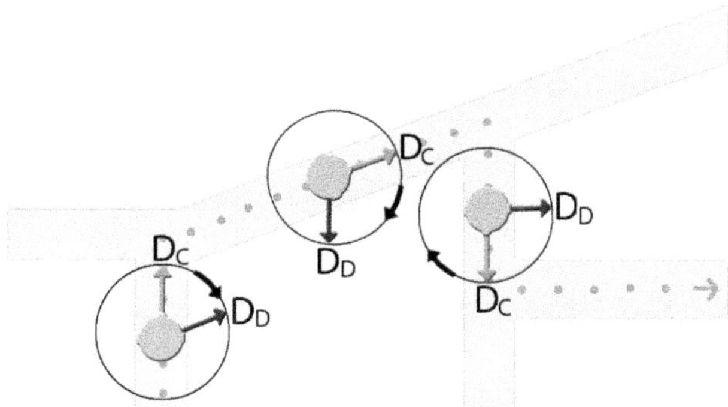

Figure 1. NaviRadar concept illustrating a path where the user has to turn right, right again and left (D_C – current direction, D_D – desired direction)

The user is able to differentiate between the two directions as they are communicated via different tactile patterns called tactons [3]. Our user studies showed that the participants quickly learned the correspondence between the radar sweep time and the angle difference between D_C and D_D. The mobile phone screen could provide a radar visualization; however, the intended use is that the user walks without looking at the screen, rather using predominantly the tactile feedback to navigate. Therefore, NaviRadar provides unobtrusive navigation, which enables the user to focus on the walking task, pay attention to the traffic, and to talk with others.

This paper reports two different studies. Firstly, the overall concept and different vibration patterns are evaluated. Secondly, NaviRadar is compared with the provision of navigational information via spoken instructions and PocketNavigator – another approach providing navigational information via tactile feedback. The first study showed that all participants easily understood the NaviRadar concept. It also demonstrated that communicating the current direction with one vibration and the desired direction with two vibrations in close succession is the most accurate and preferable approach. Furthermore, it was shown that changing the intensity of the vibrations can effectively be used to communicate the distance to the next crossing. The second study was performed outdoors and participants were required to navigate along predefined routes. The results show that NaviRadar achieves a similar navigation performance in a realistic setting when compared with spoken navigation information. A comparison with PocketNavigator shows advantages of NaviRadar with regard to navigation performance.

BACKGROUND

Route instructions provided by mobile devices are typically communicated via: spoken instructions, text, 2D route sketches, routes on 2D or 3D maps, and combinations of the previously mentioned possibilities [8]. A large amount of information can be communicated via the screen of the mobile device, but it is rather impractical to look at the screen while walking. This is due to the fact that it is difficult to read text and recognize visual route instructions due to the constant movement of hand, head and body [19]. Furthermore, it becomes difficult to concentrate on the walking task itself while in "heads-down" mode as this affects the awareness of other pedestrians, lamp posts or the traffic [2]. This leads to the fact that users immersed in the usage of their mobile phones are more likely to walk into other people or objects, or to stumble [12].

The usage of spoken instructions provides several advantages as the visual channel is not required to communicate route instructions. Therefore, visual attention can be solely dedicated to observing the environment. However, spoken instructions could have a high level of intrusion for others nearby as the feedback delivery time cannot be controlled. Furthermore, spoken instructions may not be received in noisy environments, such as a busy crossing or during a conversion [6].

The usage of tactile feedback for the provision of navigation information has been widely investigated in recent years. One such reason for this fact is that this feedback channel does not disturb the user's primary tasks (walking, talking or awareness of traffic, other pedestrians and objects) as much as visual and auditory information do. Therefore, tactile user interfaces are, in general, less distracting in terms of divided attention and disturbance than visual and auditory interfaces [3,18]. A range of different parameters, such as frequency, amplitude (intensity), duration, timing and rhythm, can be changed in order to create different tactile patterns [3]. With multiple vibrators, further parameters, such as location of vibration [2], movements or speed [6], could be manipulated.

Several projects used two vibrators to communicate "left" and "right" to the users. In previous work, such vibrators were attached to the left and right hand [2], thumb and forefinger [5] or left and right shoulder [14]. Other prototypes involved several vibrators attached to a belt [18] or vest [17] to communicate directional information via the location of the vibrators. Those approaches provide a very efficient, simple, and easy to understand way to communicate directional information, but they require special wearable equipment. Sahami at al. present a mobile device with 6 different vibration motors that could be used to communicate different directions. Such work demonstrated that is possible to communicate directional movements via patterns such as Top-to-down or Right-to-left [16]. We decided to use only one vibrator to communicate the NaviRadar patterns so standard mobile phones which have just one vibrator can be supported.

Another approach is to provide concrete navigation information via tactile feedback from one single mobile device with built-in vibrator. Here, directional information must be encoded via distinguishable tactons. The approach presented by Lin et al. uses three different rhythms to communicate *Turn Right, Turn Left* and *Stop* [9]. The rhythms were also played in two different tempos in order to communicate the distance to the next crossing. The PocketNavigator is a similar approach, that uses the different tactons shown in Figure 2 to indicate the user to go straight on (two short pulses), to turn around (three short pulses), to turn left (long vibration followed by short vibration), and to turn right (short vibration followed by long vibration) [11]. This system also supports the communication of different angles. For each side, three different angle areas can be indicated by adjusting the length of the longer vibration.

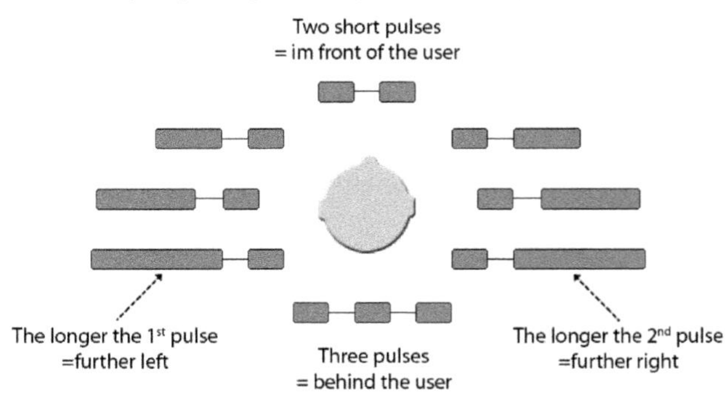

Figure 2. PocketNavigator tactons communicate direction [11].

The advantage of NaviRadar when compared with the previous two systems is the possibility to communicate arbitrary directions in the full range of 360°, rather than only left and right as in Lin at al.'s system, or the three angles areas per side as in the PocketNavigator. Moreover, only one pattern is used to indicate the desired direction (cf. PocketNavigator uses different patterns for indicating go ahead and turn around).

Robinson et al. presented an approach where the user receives tactile feedback if they point in the direction of the destination [13]. The system does not provide turn-by-turn instructions, though it does help the user to travel in the correct direction. However, it is an interesting option for tourists who wish to travel to a specific place in addition to exploring the area along the way.

The Rotating Compass [15] provides navigation instructions via the combined use of a public display and a mobile device. It uses a public display that constantly iterates over available direction options, indicating them publicly to all bystanders. It is the user's mobile phone that notifies each user their individual direction via a short vibration when the correct direction is indicated. However, it does require a public display to be installed at every crossing – an assumption that is currently impractical.

COMPARISION OF TACTILE PATTERNS

The goal of the first experiment was to analyze whether the NaviRadar concept could be easily understood by users and which tactile patterns offer the best performance when communicating distinct directions (current and desired) and distances (close and far).

Introducing the Compared Tactile Patterns

We conducted preliminary tests to analyze which tactons could potentially be used to communicate the direction to go at the next crossing and the distance to it. From these tests, we concluded that changing the duration, intensity, rhythm and roughness of the vibration are good candidates and should be tested in our study.

Table 1 shows the five different vibration patterns compared in the study. The icons in the table visualize a situation where the user is currently going straight and has to turn right at the next crossing. The circle represents the radar metaphor, the arrow the direction of the rotational sweep and the thin rectangle facing ahead the current direction. The height of the rectangle shows how strong the vibration is and the width shows the duration of the vibration. We decided to always use a short (50ms) and strong vibration to communicate the current direction as this is the most simple and easy to perceive tacton.

The first row of Table 1 shows three different patterns which communicate the difference between the current direction (D_C) and desired direction (D_D) via the different duration of the two tactons (D_C: 50ms, D_D: 200ms). Within this first row, there are three different ways in which distance can be indicated. *DurInt* communicates the distance to the next crossing using intensity (intense when close and weak when distant). *DurRhy* uses two different rhythms (close: two pulses, distant: one pulse). *DurRou* uses roughness (close: rough, distant: normal).

The second row shows *IntInt* where direction is indicated using a buildup of vibration intensity from D_C where this intensity finishes at D_D (vice versa when communicating a direction on the left hand side). The final strength of the vibration is also used to indicate the distance. The third row shows *RhyInt* where the current direction is communicated via a single vibration and the desired one via two vibrations in quick succession.

		Distance		
		Intensity	Rhythm	Roughness
Direction	Duration	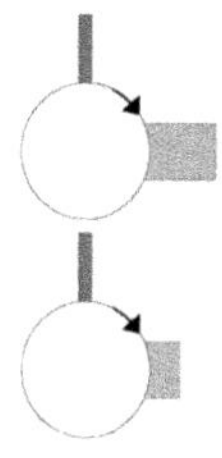 DurInt	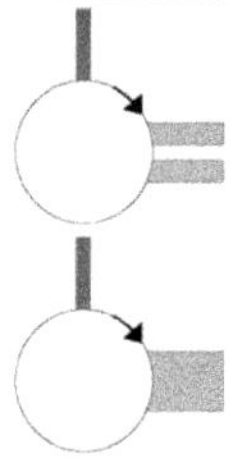 DurRhy	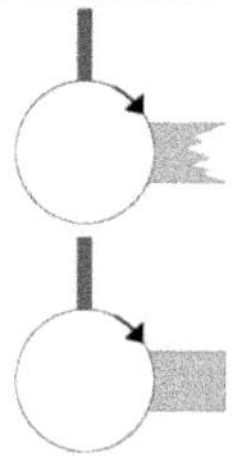 DurRou
	Intensity	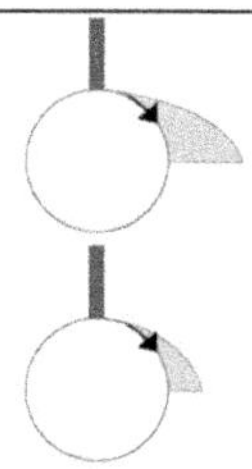 IntInt		
	Rhythm	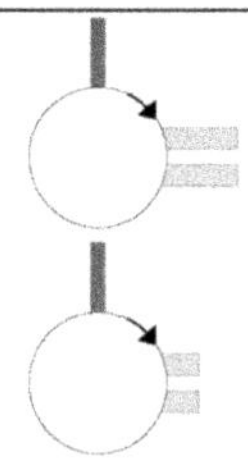 RhyInt		

Table 1. Tactile patterns (upper ones: close to crossing, lower ones: distant)

When using intensity and rhythm to communicate the direction, it is not practical to use rhythm or roughness to communicate the distance. Those missing combinations have been studied in our earlier informal tests and were not seen as good candidates. As one example, it is very difficult to feel a change in intensity when applying a rhythm or roughness simultaneously.

Participants

12 paid participants, 6 female and 6 male, took part in the first user study. All of them were either students or employees of Lancaster University, were aged between 19 and 32 (mean = 21.3) years, and are not involved in the presented research. On average, they rated themselves with a high experience with computers and medium-high experience with mobile phones (scale used: 1=none, 2=poor, 3=medium, 4=high, 5=expert). All of them had used a satnav before, though only 4 had used a map application on a mobile phone.

Apparatus

One EAI C2 tactor [1] was attached on the backside of a Motorola Milestone as show in Figure 3. The C2 tactor is a small and light tactile actuator that provides a strong, localized sensation on the skin and has been widely used in previous research [7]. It is able to provide richer feedback when compared with the built-in vibrator of the Motorola Milestone and parameters such as roughness and intensity can be controlled easily. Figure 3 shows the positioning of the tactor on the phone and where fingers are placed during the study. The C2 actuator was connected to a FiiO E5 headphone amplifier. This was, in turn, connected to the audio out port of a Sony Vaio NR11Z controlling the C2 tactor with a 250 Hz signal. The intensity of the vibration was controlled via the amplitude of the audio signal and roughness was generated by amplitude modulation.

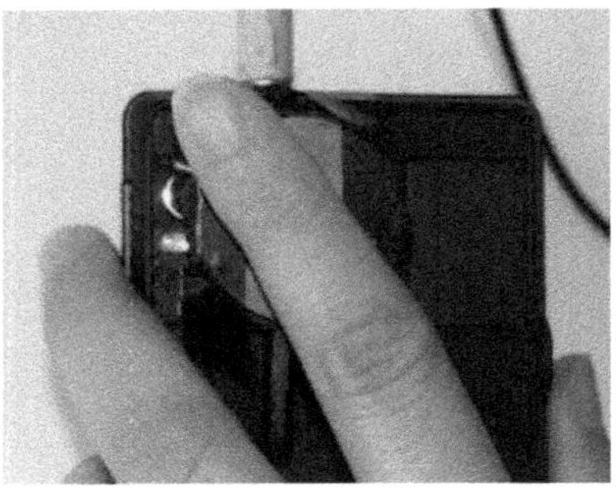

Figure 3. Motorola Milestone with C2 tactor.

Experimental Design

The experiment used a within-subjects design with three independent variables: **tactile pattern** containing the five levels from Table 1 *(DurInt, DurRhy, DurRou, IntInt, RhyInt)*, **direction** (30°, 60°, 90°, 135°, 180°, 225°, 270°, 300°, 330°) and **distance** containing two levels: *close* (to a crossing) and *distant*. The measured dependent variables were their reported direction and distance.

The Study Procedure

The participants took part in the study individually and the study was performed in a laboratory setting. The study procedure began with a demonstration of the hardware used and how they should hold the mobile phone. Afterwards, they took the position indicated in Figure 4 in which they held the mobile phone in their left hand and controlled the study application (running on the laptop) with the mouse in their right hand.

One important aim of the study was to analyze how accurate participants could recognize the indicated direction. Their task was to select an orientation on a circle which can be executed much more accurately with a mouse when compared with finger-based input on a mobile phone, so the test application (implemented in Android) was running on an emulator on the laptop instead of on the phone. The test application automatically presented the different test conditions to the user and logged all user input for further analysis.

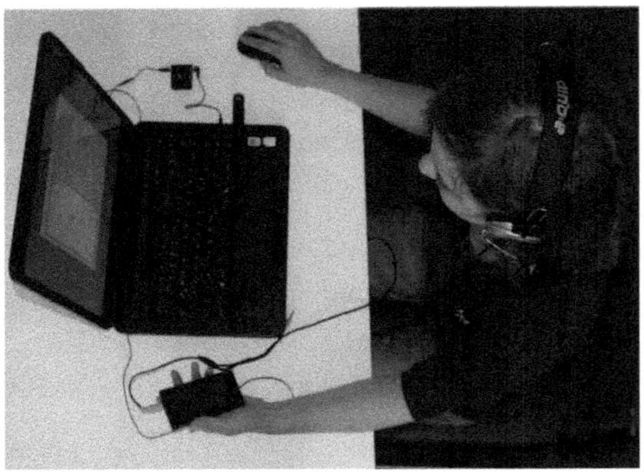

Figure 4. Study setting and participant interaction position

Initially, the participants were presented with a training application using a few animations to explain the overall concept of NaviRadar (Figure 5a&b). Following this, several directions were communicated and the participant was required to indicate the desired direction D_D with a mouse click on the circle (marked with a turquoise arrow). In response, the system provided them feedback regarding how correct the estimation was (red arrow in Figure 5c). They were also trained how to report a close (touch point on inner circle, Figure 5d) and distant crossings (touch point outer circle). During tasks, participants were able to ask the instigator questions.

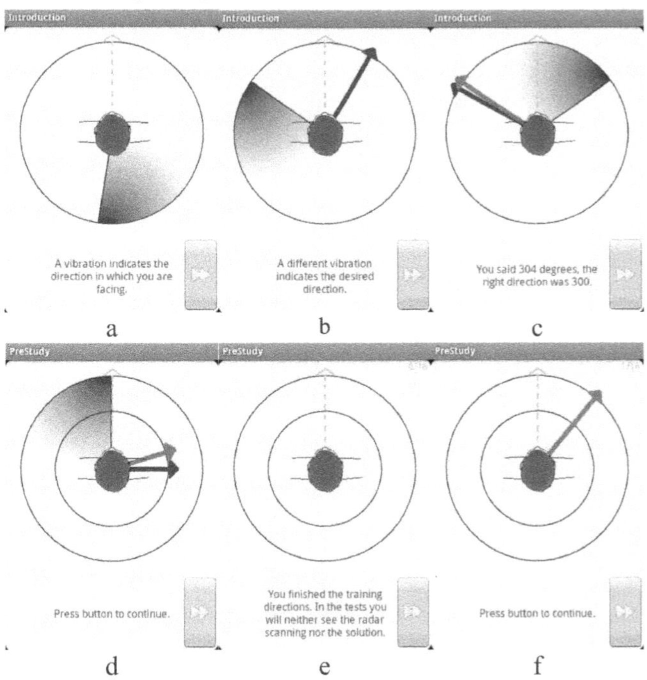

Figure 5. Test application running on a laptop.

Following the training stage, the participants were asked to wear headphones playing a mixture of white noise and typical street noise [4]. These were used to block any sounds generated by the C2 tactors. Then, they were presented with one of the five tested patterns. This started with an introduction into the pattern being based on textual information and an illustration. Then, they were presented with two close and two distant crossings where they selected distance (select inner or outer circle) and direction (location on circle) and received feedback regarding the accuracy of their selection. Once the training for this pattern was completed, they were required to define direction and distance for 18 different settings (2 distances x 9 directions) for this particular pattern. Here, no radar sweep was shown (Figure 5e) and they did not receive any feedback from the application regarding the correctness of their selection (Figure 5f). Then, they were asked 7 questions regarding this particular pattern pertaining to understandability, clearness, intuitiveness, mental effort and their personal rating. Next, the training for the following pattern started. The sequence of presented tactile patterns was counterbalanced using a Latin square, and the sequence of directions and distances was randomized for each test.

Results

The results of the study were analyzed in order to see whether the NaviRadar concept can be efficiently used to communicate direction and distance. Moreover, the results were used to see which tactile pattern leads to the best results. Unless otherwise stated, all effects will be reported at a .05 level of significance.

Recognition of Direction

The most important aspect of a navigation system is that it shows the user the correct direction. Figure 6 shows a strong relationship between the angle that has been communicated (outside of the circle) via the tactons and the mean angles recognized by the participants in the study (inside of the circle). It considers all tactile patterns, distances and participants. For instance, participants reported on average an angle of 22° when an angle of 30° was communicated by the system. Interestingly though, the participants always perceived the communicated angle to be closer to the current direction as it actually is.

When investigating the deviation of the reported angles, a relatively high variance can be seen. Table 2 shows that the mean deviation from the correct angle ranged from 37.5° to 50.5° when comparing the different tactile patterns. Mauchly's test violated the assumption of sphericity for the main effect of *pattern* ($\chi^2(9) = 17.53$); therefore, degrees of freedom were corrected using the Greenhouse-Geisser correction ($\varepsilon = 0.50$). The main effect of *pattern* was significant ($F_{1.99, 21.94} = 5.49$). Bonferroni post-hoc tests revealed a significant difference between patterns *IntInt* and *RhyInt* showing that when *RhyInt* is used, input values are perceived more accurately.

The participants needed on average 8.6s to 12.7s to report the direction and distance. This implies that they needed circa 3 to 4 rotations to make a decision as the time of circulation was 3 seconds. Mauchly's test indicated that the assumption of sphericity had been violated ($\chi^2(9) = 42.69$). Applying a Greenhouse-Geisser correction ($\varepsilon = 0.50$), the ANOVA revealed that input time was significantly affected by the main effect of *pattern* ($F_{1.42, 15.82} = 4.64$). More time was needed using *IntInt* than when patterns *DurInt*, *DurRhy* or *DurRou* were used.

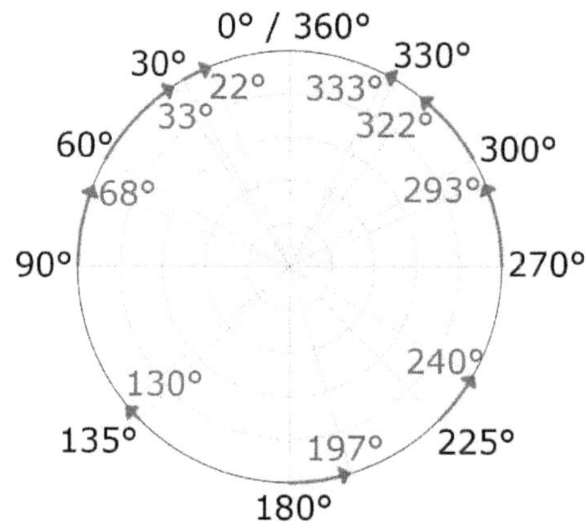

Figure 6. Relationship between communicated angle to go and mean reported angle.

The participants were also asked how clear, understandable and intuitive the representations of direction for the different tactile patterns were. The corresponding results can be seen in Table 2 as well. Friedman's ANOVA showed that ratings for clearness were significantly affected by the pattern used ($\chi^2(4) = 16.89$). Post-hoc tests revealed that using *IntInt* affected the rating negatively compared to *DurInt*, *DurRhy* and *RhyInt*. Differences regarding intuitiveness were not significant.

	DurInt	DurRhy	DurRou	IntInt	RhyInt
Mean deviation (SE) (in degree)	50.5 (5.1)	41.9 (4.3)	39.1 (4.5)	54.2 (5.5)	37.5 (4.8)
Mean input time (SE) (in s)	8.6 (1.0)	7.9 (0.7)	8.9 (0.8)	12.7 (2.2)	8.8 (0.8)
Clear and under-standable (SD)	4.0 (0.8)	3.9 (0.8)	3.6 (0.8)	2.6 (0.9)	4.1 (0.8)
Intuitive (SD)	4.0 (0.5)	3.8 (1.0)	3.6 (0.7)	3.2 (1.1)	3.9 (0.7)

Table 2. Recognition of angle, input time, subjective ratings (scale from 1 – strongly disagree to 5 – strongly agree).

When analyzing the results, one can see that the pattern responsible for communicating direction via rhythm and distance via intensity (*RhyInt*) had the lowest mean deviation from the given angle. In addition, it had the second lowest mean input time, was considered as the most clear and understandable one, and was rated second best with respect to intuitiveness.

Recognition of Distance

Table 3 shows the percentage of correctly recognized distances and subjective ratings of distance representations. *DurInt* and *DurRhy* performed excellent as more than 90%

of all distances were correctly recognized. *RhyInt* provided even better results with a recognition rate above 95%. The assumption of sphericity had not been met ($\chi^2(9) = 19.21$), so a Greenhouse-Geisser correction was applied ($\varepsilon = 0.69$). The ANOVA shows that the main effect of *pattern* significantly affected these differences ($F_{2.75, 30.26} = 11.07$, $p < 0.001$). Bonferroni-corrected post-hoc tests reveal that *DurInt* and *RhyInt* cause significantly less errors concerning distance than *DurRou* and *IntInt*. Looking at the mean ratings, *RhyInt* placed second best when considering how clear and understandable distance was perceived and placed second when considering the intuitiveness of the direction indication.

	DurInt	DurRhy	DurRou	IntInt	RhyInt
Correct distance	90,3%	90,3%	59,7%	69,0%	95,8%
Clear and understandable (SD)	3.8 (0.9)	4.6 (0.5)	3.1 (1.1)	3.4 (0.9)	4.1 (0.8)
Intuitive (SD)	4.0 (0.6)	4.3 (0.5)	3.2 (1.2)	3.6 (0.8)	4.0 (0.8)

Table 3. Recognition of distance and subjective ratings (scale from 1 – strongly disagree to 5 – strongly agree) for distance.

Mental effort

Participants were also asked to rate the mental effort required in order to understand the encoded direction and distance for a recently completed test. Mental effort should be as low as possible to allow one to understand the presented information – especially as walking and taking care of other pedestrians, traffic and objects is the main task. The results as shown in Figure 7 indicate that *DurRou* and *IntInt* require a relatively high mental effort where *DurInt*, *DurRhy* and *RhyInt* performed best. These ratings differ significantly regarding the pattern they describe ($\chi^2(4) = 27.21$, $p << 0.01$). Post-hoc tests show that *IntInt* causes a significantly higher effort to interpret the presented information than *DurRhy* and *RhyInt*, the last performed significantly better than *DurRou* also.

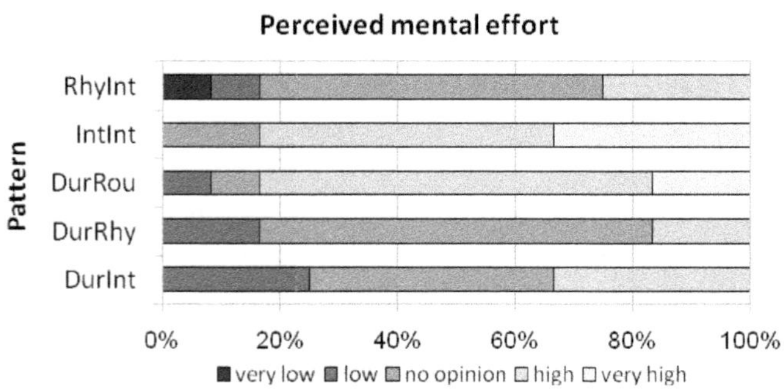

Figure 7. Ratings of perceived mental effort.

Subjective Preferences

At the end of every post-questionnaire, participants were asked to rate each pattern on a scale from very bad to very good. *RhyInt* received the best rating for 8 out of 12 participants. *DurRhy* and *DurInt* were perceived best by 7 and 4 participants, respectively. The other patterns achieved one or zero "very good" votes. As worst, 9 of the 12 participants rated *IntInt*. *DurRou* received 5 votes. The other patterns never achieved the worst result.

Training effect

The importance to not only analyze experimental conditions such as vibrotactile parameters but also training effects for vibrational feedback on results has been mentioned in [10]. Hoggan and Brewster [7] show the results of training runs where participants were presented 18 different tactons twice per run. On average, it took three training sessions before participants were able to identify the tactons with recognition rates of 90% or higher.

Taking these findings into consideration, we analyzed how the average deviation regarding the difference between indicated and reported direction to travel changed over the 6 different runs. Figure 8 shows that the average deviation improved from 55.9° in the first run to 36.7° in the last run. This is a reduction of more than 30%. Pearson r for the correlation between order and deviation is -0.14. This indicates that the more participants became familiar with the vibrations, the smaller the error became.

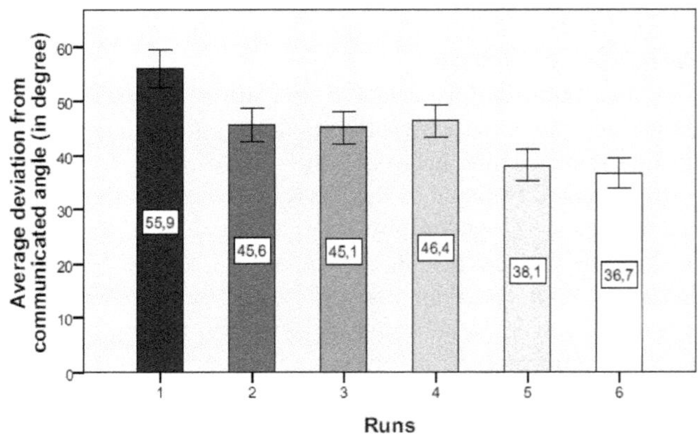

Figure 8. Effect of training on average deviation of reported from given angle (Error bars: +/- 1 SE).

No statistical effects were measurable regarding improvement of recognition of distance and input time due to repeated usage.

Participants' Comments

The participants generally liked the concept of encoding the distance via the intensity of the vibration as they linked it to the model of sound that gets louder the closer it is (*DurInt*). Similarly, they liked the idea of using rhythm for the encoding of the distance (*DurRhy*) and often said that the double pulse feels like a warning that they have to turn shortly. The perceived intensity of a tacton is also increased by an increased roughness of the signal and, therefore, the increase of the roughness when nearing a crossing was also well-perceived (*DurRou*).

Communicating the direction via a change in intensity was disliked by the participants as they found it difficult to recognize the communicated direction. Reason for this is that they were required to constantly pay attention when the vibration has its peak and stops (*IntInt*). *RhyInt* was also well-perceived and performed best overall. Therefore, it was selected for the second study.

Results for RhyInt

Our results show that rhythm is the most effective way to create distinct vibrations for both distance and direction. Therefore, this parameter should be used to communicate the most important information – namely direction – whereas for distance, intensity proved to be most efficient. Consequently, we will discuss further results for *RhyInt,* which performed best in the first study. Figure 9 shows the locations of the reported angles through color coding and shows the mean deviation of the reported angles through the central angle and radius of the pie slice.

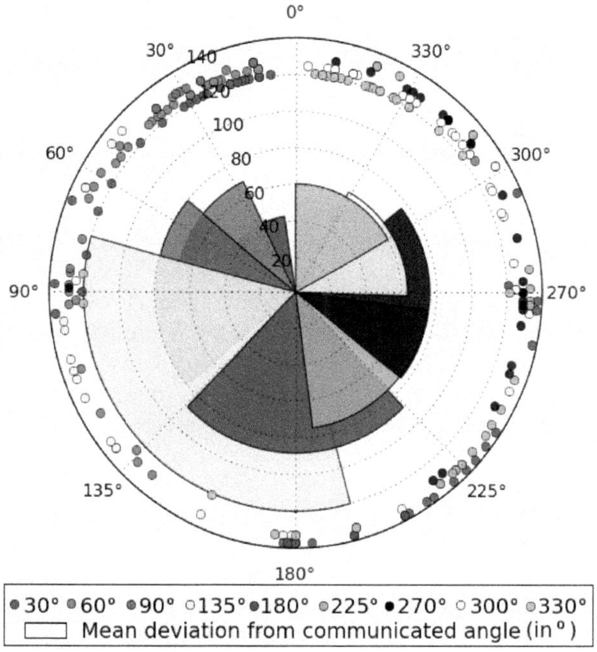

Figure 9. Location of reported angles and mean deviation of reported angles from indicated angles for *RhyInt*.

For instance, the mean deviation of the angle 30° was 21.4°. This implies the high likeliness that the users perceive this angle in the interval 30° ± 21.4°. Therefore, the corresponding pie in Figure 9 has a radius of 42.8 (2 x 21.4°) and a central angle of 42.8°. The reported angles for 30°, 60°, 300° and 330° are clustered around those angles, indicating that participants recognized the directions accurately with only slight deviations, which in turn leads to small pies. In contrast, reported directions for 135°, 180° or 225° are spread over greater intervals and corresponding pie slices are of a bigger size.

Figure 9 shows that directions around the back of the user (ranging from 135° to 225°) are recognized worse than directions in front. We expect this to be due to the fact that there are longer interval durations between D_C and D_D for the directions behind the user. Consequently, they are harder to estimate. A solution could be to increase the rotation speed; thus, decreasing the duration between signals.

Figure 10a-c shows different scenarios where NaviRadar provides sufficient accuracy. The red pie slices indicate the mean deviation for a given angle. Figure 10d shows a scenario where an error could occur easily, because pies for different directions overlap indicating that the user could consider an indication to show a wrong direction. However, as soon as the user turns towards the rough direction, the situation changes, and instead of three left turns, a straight as well as slight turns to the left and right are available (see Figure 10e). This leads to greater separation of the deviation areas as the direction "straight on" is distinctly indicated by a single pulse because the two directions D_C and D_D coincide, and deviation areas of the slight turns do not overlap. A method to prevent errors emerging from overlapping areas could be to indicate the ambiguity with a special vibration signal; in this case, the user would have to view the phone screen. But this would not occur frequently as, in practice, there are not that many crossings where several paths point in a similar direction.

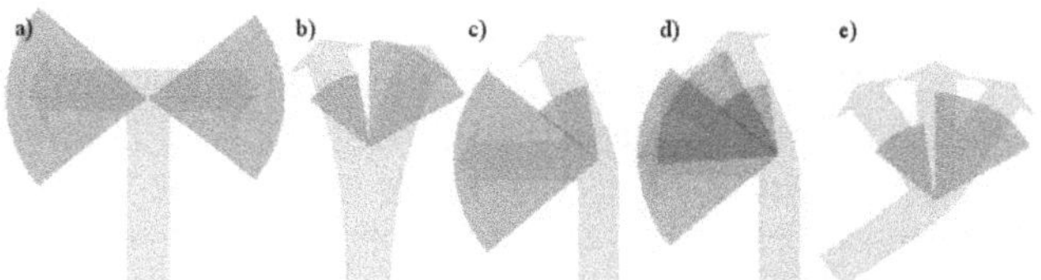

Figure 10. Practical implications of deviations of *RhyInt*.

COMPARISION IN CONTEXT

An outdoor study was conducted in order to test the concept of NaviRadar in a realistic setting where it would be compared with two other navigation systems. The navigation with all three systems relied solely on nonvisual information provided via either tactile or audio feedback. This allows the user to easily chat with others and to concentrate on traffic, other pedestrians and objects (such a lamp posts, which could be easily walked into when looking at the mobile phone screen).

Compared Systems

There were choices for comparison with NaviRadar. We omitted the work by Lin et al. as it supports only the communication of left and right [9]. We also omitted the work by Robinson et al. as it requires active scanning of the desired direction and its obtrusiveness as the user has to explicitly point at several directions [13]. We decided to compare NaviRadar using the *RhyInt* tacton with PocketNavigator as it also can communicate several different directions unobtrusively via tactile feedback. We also compared it with a system offering spoken instructions known from commercial navigation systems.

We did not compare NaviRadar with a system offering visual feedback as it is clear that the participants can navigate proficiently with it (e.g. in terms of task completion time and error rate). However, the user must divide their visual attention between mobile device and environment. The latter is a significant and inherent disadvantage as the user cannot always concentrate visually on the environment, traffic and other pedestrians.

PocketNavigator

PocketNavigator is a map-based pedestrian navigation application available in the Android market that also offers hands free navigation via tactile feedback [11]. It does provide turn-by-turn instructions but these are provided only when the user reaches the next turn. Duration of the pulses is used to indicate direction as shown in Figure 2.

There are several conceptual differences between NaviRadar and PocketNavigator. Firstly, PocketNavigator uses different patterns for the different directions. This might make it more difficult to learn. Consequently, one could assume that NaviRadar can communicate different directions (e.g. 60° vs. 90°) more accurately as they are communicated via the time difference between the two vibrations, not by the duration of one single vibration as used by PocketNavigator.

Spoken Instructions

NaviRadar has been compared to the approach used in Ovi Maps and Google's pedestrian navigation, which offers visual, tactile and spoken instructions to guide the users. It can be used easily while walking and without using the visual information provided. Therefore, the user holds the phone in one hand while walking and is informed via a short vibration that spoken audio instructions (e.g. "turn left in 50 meters") will follow soon. In response, the user can then bring the phone to their ear in order to hear the spoken instructions more clearly.

For the study, the timing and vocabulary used in Ovi Maps are taken. It is widely used and preinstalled on many Symbian phones. Google Navigation for pedestrians had not been released when the study was conducted; however, the principle of combined feedback is the same.

Apparatus

A Motorola Milestone running Android 2.1 was used to re-implement the features of PocketNavigator and Ovi Maps required for the study. As the mobile phone screen was not used during the study, none of the visual aspects of those systems have been implemented.

The decision for reimplementation was done because of health and safety considerations and a risk assessment. Because of this, we had to perform the study in a pedestrian area without any traffic on our University campus. The streets of this area are not included in any available mobile navigation system. Therefore, we had to re-implement PocketNavigator and Ovi Maps as it is not possible to add our own map of the University campus. We analyzed PocketNavigator and Ovi Maps very carefully to make sure that our re-implementations are as similar as possible when compared with the original implementations.

As our first study identified the optimal tactons using the C2 tactor, we used it once more for the comparative study using NaviRadar. Unfortunately, the C2 tactor that was attached to the backside of the phone heavily influenced the built-in compass. Accordingly, we had to place an external compass 32 cm from the tactor using an extension mounted to the phone. This external compass communicated via Bluetooth with the mobile phone and offered accuracy comparable to the built-in compass.

Participants

12 participants, 6 female and 6 male, took part in the study. None of them had been participating in the previously reported study. Their age ranged from 19 to 51 (mean = 28.3) years and are not involved in the presented research. Participants rated themselves as highly experienced with computers and mobile phones (scale used: 1=none, 2=poor, 3=medium, 4=high, 5=expert). Only 4 out of 12 indicated a high experience with car navigation systems.

All of them had experience with pedestrian navigation in terms of using paper maps or tourist guides and half of them had used electronic devices for pedestrian navigation before. Two participants had never been to the area of the study before, three had been there a few times, and the others had been living there for some time. However, since the routes were not shown on a map and participants did not know their destination, but only received instructions on where to travel before they actually had to turn, there was no advantage in being familiar with the area.

Experimental Design

The experiment used a within-subjects design with one independent variable: navigation technique, with three levels: *NaviRadar*, *PocketNavigator* and *Spoken Instructions*. Three different routes were selected in an area within the campus of Lancaster University which is occupied by many 5-floor student houses. Within a small area, it offers a high number of crossings (see Figure 11).

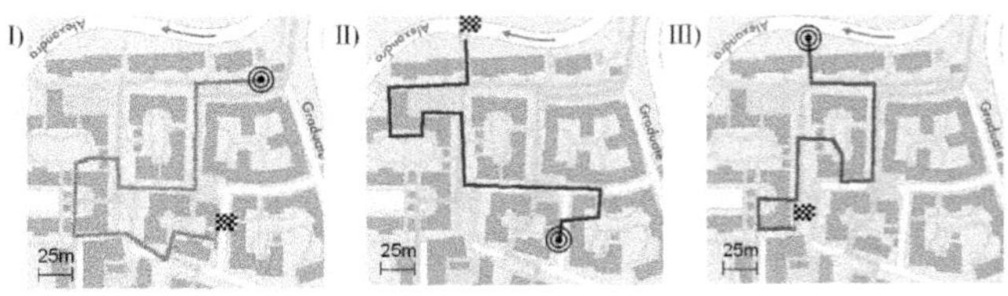

Figure 11. Routes I-III on Lancaster University campus.

Table 4 shows the number of left and right turns per route, the number of crossings where the participants had to go straight on, and the overall length of the routes. The participants experienced the three different navigation techniques in counterbalanced sequences using a 3x3 Latin square and all of them experienced the routes in the sequence I → II → III. Using this approach, every navigation technique was used four times per route.

Route	Left turns	Right turns	Overall turns (+ crossings without turns)	Overall length
I	6	4	10 (+5)	360 m
II	5	5	10 (+4)	410 m
II	6	4	10 (+3)	370 m

Table 4. Characteristics of tested routes.

Procedure

Participants took part in the study individually. In the beginning, they were introduced in the purpose of the study. The researcher then led them to the starting point of the first route. There, they were introduced into the first navigation technique. In the case of the spoken instructions, they were presented with some sample instructions. For the tactile approaches, a more sophisticated training was needed. Here, the concept was explained to the participants and then 18 directions were presented (similar to the first study, see Figure 5f) where they had to indicate where they would travel using a circle on the phone. Participants were allowed to ask questions throughout the experiment. The next stage was to instruct the participants to navigate the first route using the given navigation system. They were instructed to walk with their normal walking speed while two experimenters accompanied them. One experimenter was responsible for the user's safety, answered questions if needed, and led the user back to the route if they walked in the incorrect direction for more than 5 meters. The other experimenter filmed the study. After each route, participants were asked to answer questions about their subjective impression of the most recently tested navigation technique and could provide additional comments. After all three routes had been completed, a further questionnaire was filled in that contained questions about participant demographics, as well as a comparison and ranking of all three systems.

Limitations of the Study

An important issue during the user study was the inaccuracy of GPS measurements which have been negatively influenced by the proximity of nearby buildings. Several tests had been run before the study to decide on the best placement of waypoints so that instructions are provided at the correct time. Unfortunately, traces from the tests are widely spread around the defined route. This led to problems with the timing of commands and even incorrect indications. Incorrect indications were logged during walking and by analyzing the videos taken during the study, the behavior of the participants at these turns are not included in the following count of errors or disorientations. 26 out of 120 crossings have been removed for NaviRadar, 27 for PocketNavigator and 13 for spoken instructions. Another problem was the compasses used (external for the NaviRadar and internal for PocketNavigator). They were calibrated between the tests, however, measurements showed incorrect results on three occasions. When this occurred, the compasses required recalibration. Moreover, task completion times were not examined since these are distorted by GPS/compasses issues and environment obstacles, such as passing cars. It was anyway not expected that the task completion time between the three navigation techniques varies significantly as the most important contributing factor is the time needed for walking and the time needed for navigation is almost negligible as already shown in [15].

Results

The study results show that all three navigation techniques could be effectively used for navigation. Figure 12 shows the overall number of disorientation events and navigation errors that were observed during the study. An error occurred when a participant travelled in the incorrect direction for more than 5 meters. When this occurred, the participant was stopped by the experimenter and was redirected back to the correct route. A disorientation event was recorded when the participant stopped for more than 2 seconds.

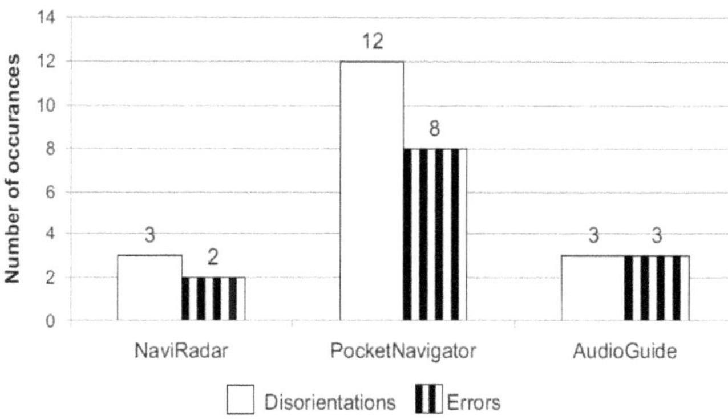

Figure 12. Overall count of errors and disorientation events for all participants.

NaviRadar and spoken instructions both had a very low number of errors (only 3 times each for all participants). Participants using PocketNavigator travelled in the incorrect direction 8 times. When using NaviRadar and PocketNavigator, the errors occurred when a signal was misunderstood, while errors with the spoken instructions occurred when several turns to one side were available and participants took the incorrect one because they misjudged the provided distance, for instance, they turned left after 25 meters when the instruction "In 45 meters, turn left" had been given. Disorientation events occurred four times more often, overall at 13% of crossings, when using the PocketNavigator when compared with the other two systems (both 3%) and additionally participants estimated their walking speed slower when compared to the other two. This is due to the concept that a new direction is only shown when the last waypoint had been reached. Participants slowed down when coming to a turn waiting for the new direction to be indicated or stopped walking for scanning the new direction.

Perceived usability satisfaction of the three navigation techniques was measured using the IBM Computer Usability Satisfaction questionnaire; this showed positive results for all three approaches. Spoken instructions had the highest average usability satisfaction followed by NaviRadar and PocketNavigator. No significant differences in the ratings of NaviRadar and spoken instructions could be detected. This suggests that our tactile interface did not affect the ratings negatively compared to the (commonly used) audio feedback. In contrast, PocketNavigator was rated significantly worse than spoken instructions in terms of ease of use, learnability, completion time and satisfaction level ($p < .05$). An analysis of the perceived task load using the NASA Task Load Index showed a low to very low task load for spoken instructions and a neutral to low task load for the other approaches. In terms of mental demand and effort, the advantage of spoken instructions is statistically significant ($p < .05$). However, there is no significant difference regarding the frustration level of NaviRadar and spoken instructions. This indicates that even raised effort (at least in the beginning) in order to understand the tactile feedback does not affect experienced frustration. Furthermore, we asked the participants to state their first, second and third preference towards the three navigation techniques. Spoken instructions received on average place 1.33, NaviRadar 2.25 and PocketNavigator 2.42.

CONCLUSION

This paper introduced NaviRadar, a novel approach for pedestrian navigation that uses a single vibrator and distinct tactile patterns to communicate the distance to the next crossing (where the user has to turn) and the direction in which to travel. The first study was conducted in the laboratory and showed the feasibility of the NaviRadar concept as the participants were able to identify communicated directions with a mean deviation of 37°. The second study showed that NaviRadar worked in a realistic outdoor setting. What's more, it had a similar performance regarding usability and errors when compared with spoken instructions (with which most participants were very familiar with) and performed better – especially in terms of errors and disorientation events – when compared with the PocketNavigator approach.

In our future work, we will evaluate the effect of a shorter circulation time of the radar sweep from which we expect a higher accuracy in terms of the perceived direction. Furthermore, we will investigate approaches to handle incorrect GPS and compass readings through more sophisticated filtering algorithms. Moreover, we plan to test how the directional accuracy improves through prolonged usage of NaviRadar and how NaviRadar could efficiently be added as a feature to current solutions such as Ovi or Google maps.

ACKNOWLEDGEMENT

The presented research was partially conducted within the Emmy Noether research group Mobile Interaction with Pervasive User Interfaces funded by the DFG.

REFERENCES

1. Engineering Acoustics, INC. *Tactile System Products.* http://www.eaiinfo.com/Tactor%20Products.htm.
2. Bosman, S. et al. GentleGuide: An Exploration of Haptic Output for Indoors Pedestrian Guidance. *In Proc. Mobile HCI 2003*, 358-362.
3. Brewster, S. and Brown, L.M. Tactons: structured tactile messages for non-visual information display. *In Proc. of AUIC 2004*, 15-23.
4. Freitas, N. Busy Lhasa Street. www.freesound.org/samplesViewSingle.php?id=1127.
5. Ghiani, G., Leporini, B., and Paternò, F. Vibrotactile feedback as an orientation aid for blind users of mobile guides. *In Proc. Mobile HCI 2008*, 431-434.
6. Hoggan, E., Anwar, S., and Brewster, S.A. Mobile multi-actuator tactile displays. *In Proc. of HAID 2007*, 22-33.
7. Hoggan, E. and Brewster, S. Designing audio and tactile crossmodal icons for mobile devices. *In Proc. ICMI 2007*, 162–169.
8. Kray, C., Elting, C., Laakso, K., and Coors, V. Presenting route instructions on mobile devices. *In Proc. IUI 2003*, 117-124.
9. Lin, M., Cheng, Y., Yu, W., and Sandnes, F.E. Investigation into the feasibility of using tactons to provide navigation cues in pedestrian situations. *OZCHI 2008*, 299-302.
10. Mortimer, B.J.P., Zets, G.A., and Cholewiak, R.W. Vibrotactile transduction and transducers. *The Journal of the Acoustical Society of America 121*, 5 (2007), 2970-2977.
11. Pielot, M., Poppinga, B., and Boll, S. PocketNavigator: Vibro-Tactile Waypoint Navigation for Everyday Mobile Devices. *In Proc. Mobile HCI 2010*, 423-426.
12. Richtel, M. Forget Gum. Walking and Using Phone Is Risky. *The New York Times*, 17.01.2010.
13. Robinson, S., Eslambolchilar, P., and Jones, M. Evaluating haptics for information discovery while walking. *In Proc. British HCI 2009*, 93-102.
14. Ross, D.A. and Blasch, B.B. Wearable interfaces for orientation and wayfinding. *ASSETS 2000*, 193-200.
15. Rukzio, E., Müller, M., and Hardy, R. Design, implementation and evaluation of a novel public display for pedestrian navigation: the rotating compass. *In Proc. CHI 2009*, 113-122.
16. Sahami, A., Holleis, P., Schmidt, A., and Häkkilä, J. Rich Tactile Output on Mobile Devices. *In Proc. of AmI-08*, 210-221.
17. Smets, N.J.J.M., Brake, G.M.T., Neerincx, M.A., and Lindenberg, J. Effects of mobile map orientation and tactile feedback on navigation speed and situation awareness. *In Proc. Mobile HCI 2008*, 73-80.
18. Tsukada, K. and Yasumura, M. ActiveBelt: Belt-Type Wearable Tactile Display for Directional Navigation. *In Proc. Ubicomp 2004*, 384-399.
19. Vadas, K., Patel, N., Lyons, K., Starner, T., and Jacko, J. Reading on-the-go: a comparison of audio and hand-held displays. *In Proc. Mobile HCI 2006*, 219-226

PocketTouch: Through-Fabric Capacitive Touch Input

T. Scott Saponas[1] *Chris Harrison*[1,2] *Hrvoje Benko*[1]

[1]Microsoft Research
One Microsoft Way
Redmond, WA 98052
{ssaponas, benko}@microsoft.com

[2]Human-Computer Interaction Institute
Carnegie Mellon University
5000 Forbes Avenue, Pittsburgh, PA 15213
chris.harrison@cs.cmu.edu

ABSTRACT
PocketTouch is a capacitive sensing prototype that enables eyes-free multitouch input on a handheld device without having to remove the device from the pocket of one's pants, shirt, bag, or purse. *PocketTouch* enables a rich set of gesture interactions, ranging from simple touch strokes to full alphanumeric text entry. Our prototype device consists of a custom multitouch capacitive sensor mounted on the back of a smartphone. Similar capabilities could be enabled on most existing capacitive touchscreens through low-level access to the capacitive sensor. We demonstrate how touch strokes can be used to initialize the device for interaction and how strokes can be processed to enable text recognition of characters written over the same physical area. We also contribute a comparative study that empirically measures how different fabrics attenuate touch inputs, providing insight for future investigations. Our results suggest that *PocketTouch* will work reliably with a wide variety of fabrics used in today's garments, and is a viable input method for quick eyes-free operation of devices in pockets.

ACM Classification: H.5.2 [Information interfaces and presentation]: User Interfaces - Graphical user interfaces; Input devices and strategies.

General terms: Algorithms, Design, Human Factors

Keywords: Touch, gestures, eyes-free, touch-stroke text entry, always-available input, wearable computing.

INTRODUCTION
Modern mobile devices are sophisticated computing platforms, enabling people to handle phone calls, listen to music, surf the web, reply to emails, compose text messages, and much more. These devices are often stored in pockets or bags, requiring users to remove them in order to access even basic functionality. This demands a high level of attention - both cognitively and visually - and is often socially disruptive. Further, physically retrieving the device incurs a non-trivial time cost, and can constitute a significant fraction of a simple operation's total time [2].

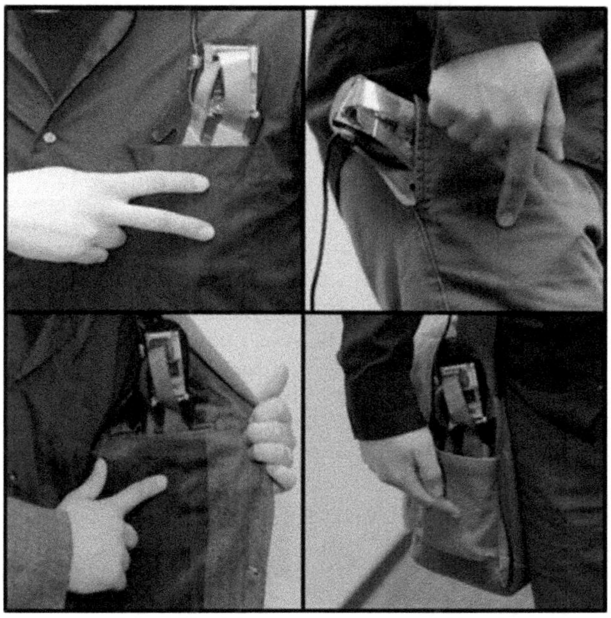

Figure 1. PocketTouch can sense multitouch finger input through a variety of garments.

To address these issues, several techniques have been implemented or proposed. Many consumer mobile devices already include one mechanism for quick, through-pocket interaction: a physical button. For example, one can use a physical switch to quickly silence an incoming phone call. Although simple, this feature is extremely valuable. However, supporting in-pocket operation using physical buttons is limiting, since one can only support a few discrete actions. In response, several research projects have sought to expand the interaction space by taking advantage of richer input channels. Of note are Tap Input [11] and Whack Gestures [7]. Both of these techniques support a small vocabulary of through-pocket gestures using a device's accelerometer (directional taps and coarse whacks, respectively). An entirely different approach is to embed sensing for interaction directly into textiles [8,9]. However, this requires wearing custom garments equipped with sensing.

In this work, we present a novel method for through-pocket interaction, called *PocketTouch*. Our approach utilizes capacitive sensing to detect finger-strokes through fabric (Figure 1). Sensing strokes through pockets enables a wide variety of interaction possibilities in situations where taking

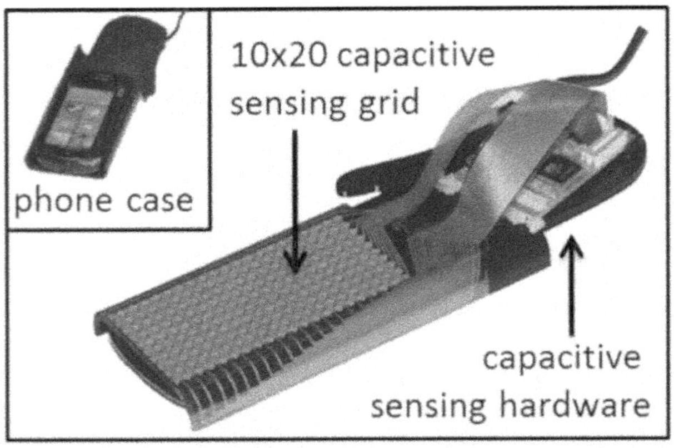

Figure 2. PocketTouch prototype. Inset shows PocketTouch mounted on the back of a smartphone.

out a device is inconvenient or impossible. Our technique contributes to the domain of eyes-free and always-available interfaces [12]. In this paper, we demonstrate two uses of through-pocket stroke detection. First, we show that single and multi-stroke gestures can be used to issue commands to mobile devices such as —next song" or —new message." Second, we illustrate how through-pocket strokes can be used for eyes-free text input on an enclosed device.

The core contribution of this paper is demonstrating the feasibility of using finger-strokes to control a mobile device equipped with capacitive sensing *through* a pocket‘s enclosing material. In our prototype, we built a custom capacitive sensor that fits on the back of a mobile phone. However, we envision future mobile devices having capacitive-sensing ability on both sides, enabling *PocketTouch* interaction regardless of a device‘s in-pocket orientation.

Finally, for brevity, we use the term —pocket." However, we consider this to encompass a variety of possible storage locations, including pants, shirts, jackets, purses, outside pockets on backpacks, and many other garment placements.

PROTOTYPE HARDWARE

Enabling through-pocket use of capacitive touch screens requires adaptively adjusting the low-level sensitivity settings of the sensor not typically exposed by a capacitive touch controller‘s APIs. Our custom unit allowed us full programmability of the sensor (Cypress Semiconductor CY8CTMA3), but similar capabilities can be enabled on many existing capacitive touchscreens through low-level access to the sensor. Our input area measures 46x97mm.

We mounted our touch sensitive surface to a 3D-printed base 11.5mm thick, with a flat top, simulating a smart phone form factor (see Figure 2). The touch controller board is also attached to the base. The controller is tethered over USB to a host machine and all touch processing described in this paper is performed on a PC host. To further explore interactions in the mobile domain, our form supports being mounted on the back of an existing smartphone (Figure 2, inset). This configuration is for mockup purposes at present; exploration of through-pocket smartphone interactions remains future work.

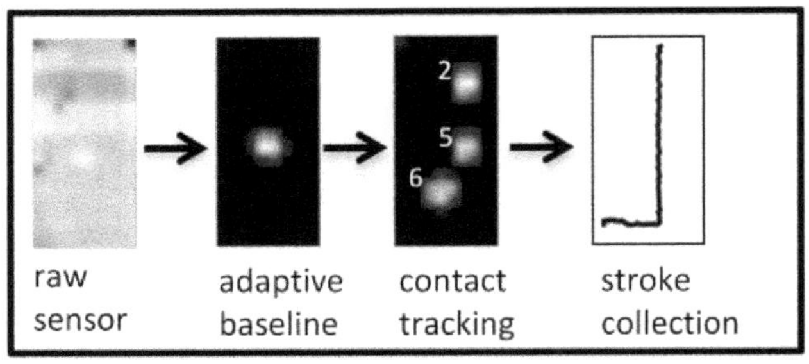

Figure 3. PocketTouch processing pipeline.

TOUCH PROCESSING

To enable touch gesture detection in the pocket, it is important to understand the underlying touch processing that extracts and tracks individual contacts. Our capacitive system samples a 10x20 grid of electrodes at approximately 100 Hz. For simplicity, it is easier to consider this matrix as a 10x20 image of capacitive pixels where the intensity of each pixel corresponds to the capacitive signal at that location. In each frame, we segment finger contacts by subtracting the current signal from a baseline image. We then search for connected components, labeling each connected component as a contact, and track each contact over time thus producing strokes. This touch tracking process is similar to many camera-based sensing prototypes (e.g., [10]) or other capacitive sensing devices [13,14].

What is different about our approach is that inserting the device into a pocket dramatically changes the operating conditions of the senor. Most touch sensors are calibrated to work in a direct-contact manner and to reject signal that is weaker than the baseline. However, with *PocketTouch*, the touch signal is attenuated by the fabric requiring the software to continuously calibrate the sensor, thus effectively normalizing the signal and adapting it to the current conditions. Our baseline is created by sampling each pixel at startup and continuously adapting the baseline by adding 0.05% of the current value at each pixel to 99.95% of the baseline value. This acts as a slow high-pass filter to adapt to changing conditions.

To avoid including noise or inadvertent touches as strokes, we first discard any contacts that are only visible for a short period of time or do not move far during their existence. We also smooth strokes with gaps or that eclipse the boundary of the sensor by merging together strokes where the end of one stroke is temporally and spatially near the beginning of the next stroke.

GESTURE AND TEXT RECOGNITION

One very useful application of stroke detection through a pocket is stroke-based gesture input. This style of input can be quick, expressive, and eyes-free. In our prototype system, we detect single and multi-stroke gestures using an implementation of the $N gesture recognizer [1].

To demonstrate the expressivity of *PocketTouch*, we built a text entry recognizer. This is more complex than gesture recognition given the small size of mobile device screens.

Figure 4. A sequence of strokes (top) can be formed into characters, words, and ultimately sentences (bottom). A '>' character acts like a space bar (blue highlight). Strokes from multistroke characters (t, k, f, x) are spatially merged (red highlight).

Indeed, it is near impossible to accurately stroke an average word in the confines of a small handheld screen. However, an individual character can easily be drawn in the space of a mobile phone. We utilize this ability to implement a through-pocket text entry system.

When characters are drawn in sequence they are written on top of one another. To address this, we use an additional stage of stroke processing. To separate words, we use the > gesture, which acts like a space bar. Single stroke letters are easily segmented, and can be arranged in temporal order to form words. To handle lowercase letters composed of two strokes (k, t, f and x), we take advantage of the fact that the second stroke is unique. Specifically, if a < — \ or / gesture is encountered, we simply merge the stroke with the previously entered character (Figure 4). Our approach makes it impossible to enter these reserved characters, but we feel that the brief ad hoc operation in pocket will not be impeded much by missing these few characters.

Once an entire word is entered, followed by a > gesture, we lay out the character strokes in 2D (Figure 4). We then pass this composite stroke collection to the Microsoft Ink API, which uses a language model for word recognition. Importantly, this step also resolves ambiguities between characters such as i and l (e.g., —llt" is recognized as —ilt").

The main benefit of our approach is that it does not require the user to learn a new gesture alphabet, but simply to draw characters on top of the device. However, other stroke-based text entry approaches are also possible (e.g. Palm OS' Graffiti). Additionally, if the touch sensitive area incorporated a physical border, EdgeWrite offers several advantages including physical stability and tactility [15].

EXAMPLE USES

An always-available input mechanism for mobile phones that does not require removing the phone from the pocket is useful in many scenarios. For example, using strokes as the basis for simple gestures, a user could send commands to an application running on their phone through their pocket. Some simple examples are dismissing an incoming call, switching among alert modes, or controlling a music application. A more complex application of through-pocket gestures is playing an audio-based trivia game where a user might respond with a multiple choice answer of 1, 2, or 3. Alphanumeric text entry combined with gesture can also enable scenarios such as following a dismissed phone call with a short text message reply to the caller. *PocketTouch* also enables lightweight querying. For example, a user could search for unread text messages, emails, or voice mails. Feedback could be provided through a Bluetooth headset, headphones, audio from the device [3], near-eye display, or through a vibrotactile actuator [4].

FABRIC ATTENUATION OF CAPACTIVE TOUCH

An obvious concern (and perhaps the most important challenge) for *PocketTouch* is under what circumstances can strokes be reliably detected through fabric. If there is sufficient signal to reliably segment strokes, applications such as gesture recognition and text entry are easily achieved. However, if the signal is too faint, there will be significant gaps in strokes (i.e., tracking loss). Consequently, the system will not be able to disambiguate purposeful strokes from inadvertent touches or noise.

To explore this issue, we collected through-fabric sensor data using 25 different materials. We chose fabrics from typical apparel and purposefully included a range of thicknesses, natural and synthetic fibers, men's and women's garments, types of garments, and pocket location (see Appendix for photos and fabric composition). For each fabric, we measured the relative signal strength of a finger contact. Our method for calculating signal strength was to measure the total capacitance signal from baseline for a contact at four predefined locations on the sensor surface. We gathered 500 samples (approximately five seconds) of data from each location and took the average sum of signal for the contact. To ensure we were touching the same four locations, we used an acrylic guide with four holes that magnetically aligned to our sensor through the fabric (Figure 5). Further, to ensure a consistent signal source, we used a solid metal cylinder with a similar capacitance to a finger.

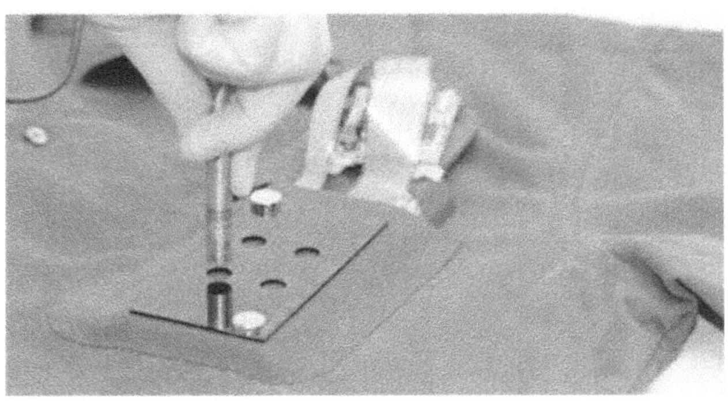

Figure 5. Experimental setup for material attenuation study.

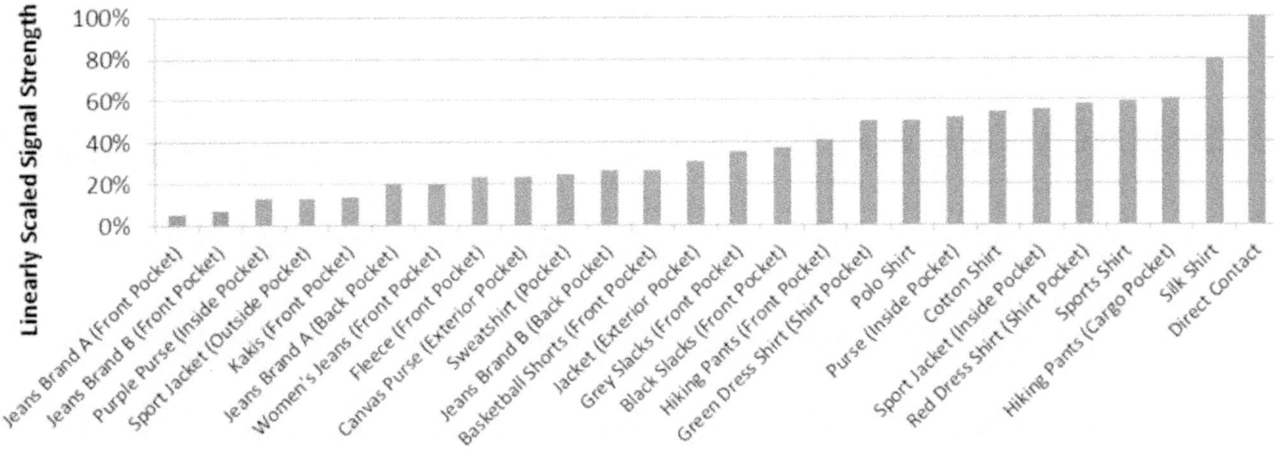

Figure 6. Capacitive signal strength through common fabrics. Signal strength is normalized relative to direct contact. Materials in red failed our text entry test.

This data collection provides a relative ordering of fabrics and a linearly scaled value of signal strength for each fabric (Figure 6). To relate these values to the viability of our prototype, we attempted to enter text through different fabrics. We purposely selected text entry as it is a high bar for evaluation - if such a complex operation can be achieved, a wide variety of applications are possible. Encouragingly, our investigation shows that text entry is robust on all fabrics with signal strength of at least 12.95% - 23 of our 25 test fabrics. On all these fabrics, text entry looks similar to that seen in Figure 4.

Two fabrics proved unreliable for text entry: the front pockets of two pairs of jeans. We were surprised these pockets performed poorly when the back pockets of jeans and much thicker materials (e.g., fleece) performed well. One possible explanation is that the air between the pocket lining and the outer denim fabric attenuates the capacitive signal more than the thickness or the composition of the fabric itself. This serves to demonstrate that the capacitive behaviors of fabrics are a complex interplay of material, thickness, density, layering, and many other factors.

DISCUSSION

Enabling *PocketTouch* on consumer devices will require several considerations. Foremost, it will be necessary to vary the sensitivity of the screen given the physical context (e.g., default sensitivity when operating —out of pocket" and increased sensitivity when operating —in pocket"). There are several mechanisms that could be employed to detect whether a device is in-pocket including ambient light level, proximity detection, material detection [6], and self-capacitance measurements on the sensor itself, which could be tuned to detect proximity.

Another important consideration is being able to —unlock" a device for operation in any orientation. The concerns here are that the system needs to be robust to inadvertent touch contact as well as be able to correctly interpret strokes for hand writing recognition. We suggest that this can be addressed by a single *orientation-defining unlock gesture*. For examples, a single stroke _L' is unlikely to be generated by inadvertent contact [5] and also implicitly indicates the device's orientation. This enables recognition of orientation dependent strokes (e.g. the characters -d" and -p").

CONCLUSION

PocketTouch enables capacitive touch-based gesture control and text input on a mobile device *through* fabric enclosing the device (e.g., a pocket or bag). Our results demonstrate that with many of the textiles used in today's garments, *PocketTouch* is a viable input method for quick eyes-free operation of devices in your pocket.

REFERENCES

1. Anthony, L. & Wobbrock, J.O. 2010. A lightweight multistroke recognizer for user interface prototypes. In *Proc. Graphics Interface 2010* (GI '10). 245-252.
2. Ashbrook, D.L., Clawson, J.R., Lyons, K., Starner, T.E., & Patel, N. 2008. Quickdraw: the impact of mobility and on-body placement on device access time. In *Proc. CHI '08.* 219-222.
3. Blattner, M., Sumikawa, D. & Greenberg, R. 1989. Earcons and icons: Their structure and common design principles. *Human Comp. Interaction* 4, 1 (1989), 11-44.
4. Brewster, S. & Brown, L.M. 2004. Tactons: structured tactile messages for non-visual information display. In *Proc. AUIC '04.* 15-23.
5. Grossman, T., Hinckley, K., Baudisch, P., Agrawala, M., Balakrishnan, R. 2006. Hover widgets: using the tracking state to extend the capabilities of pen-operated devices. In *Proc. CHI '06.* 861-870.
6. Harrison, C. & Hudson, S.E. 2008. Lightweight Material Detection for Placement-Aware Mobile Computing. In *Proc. UIST '08.* 279-282.
7. Hudson, S.E., Harrison, C., Harrison, B.L., & LaMarca, A. 2010. Whack gestures: inexact and inattentive interaction with mobile devices. In *Proc. TEI '10.* 109-112.
8. Karrer, T., Wittenhagen, M., Lichtschlag, L., Heller, F., & Borchers, J. 2011. Pinstripe: eyes-free continuous input on interactive clothing. In *Proc. CHI '11.* 1313-1322.

9. Orth, M., Post, R., & Cooper, E. 1998. Fabric computing interfaces. In *Proc. CHI '98*. 331-332.
10. Rekimoto, J. 2002. SmartSkin: An Infrastructure for Free-hand Manipulation on Interactive Surfaces. In *Proc. CHI '02*. 113-120.
11. Ronkainen, S., Häkkilä, J., Kaleva, S., Colley, A., and Linjama, J. Tap input as an embedded interaction method for mobile devices. In *Proc. TEI '07*. 263-270.
12. Saponas, T. S., Tan, D. S., Morris, D., Balakrishnan, R., Turner, J., and Landay, J. A. Enabling always-available input with muscle-computer interfaces. In *Proc. UIST '09*. 167-176.
13. Song, H., Benko, H., Guimbretiere, F., Izadi, S., Cao, X., and Hinckley, K. Grips and Gestures on a Multi-Touch Pen. In *Proc. CHI '11*. 1323-1332.
14. Villar, N., Izadi, S., Rosenfeld, D., Benko, H., Helmes, J., Westhues, J., Hodges, S., Butler, A., Ofek, E., Cao, X., and Chen, B. 2009. "Mouse 2.0: Multi-touch Meets the Mouse". In *Proc. UIST '09*. 33-42.
15. Wobbrock, J.O., Myers, B.A. and Kembel, J.A. 2003. EdgeWrite: A stylus-based text entry method designed for high accuracy and stability of motion. In *Proc. UIST '03*. 61-70.

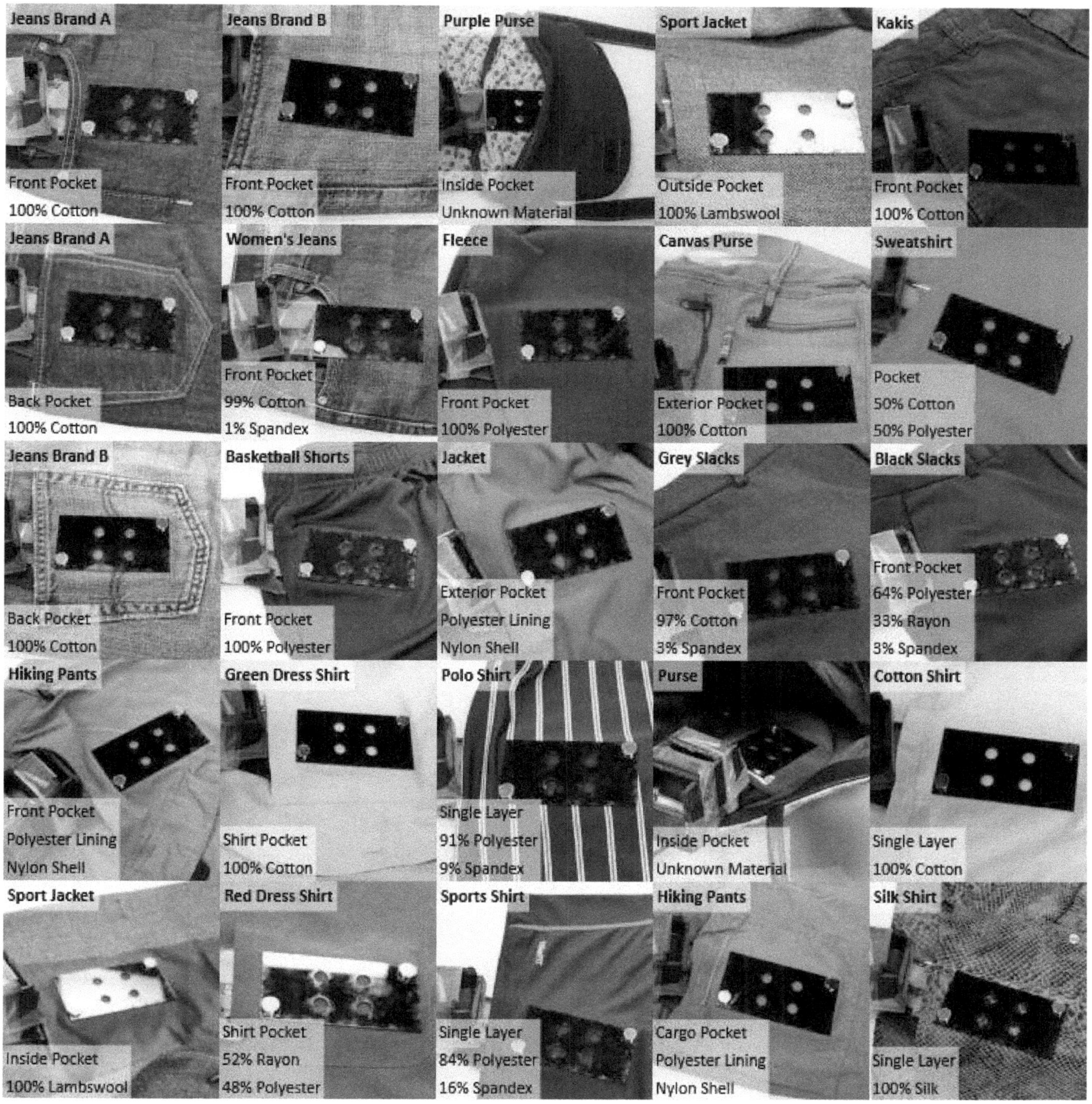

Appendix: The 25 materials from our fabric attenuation comparison, including test location and material composition.

Tap Control for Headphones without Sensors

Hiroyuki Manabe, Masaaki Fukumoto
Research Laboratories, NTT docomo
3-6, Hikarino-oka, Yokosuka, Kanagawa, JAPAN
manabeh@rd.nttdocomo.co.jp, fukumoto@acm.org

ABSTRACT
A tap control technique for headphones is proposed. A simple circuit is used to detect tapping of the headphone shell by using the speaker unit in the headphone as a tap sensor. No additional devices are required in the headphone shell and cable, so the user can use their favorite headphones as a controller while listening music. A prototype is implemented with several calibration processes to compensate the differences in headphones and users' tapping actions. Tests confirm that the user can control a music player by tapping regular headphones.

ACM Classification: H5.2 [Information interfaces and presentation]: User Interfaces. - Input devices and strategies.

General terms: Design, Human Factors, Experimentation

Keywords: Headphones, tap, input device, wearable.

INTRODUCTION
Music is indispensable to our everyday life, and we can tune-in anytime and anywhere by wearing headphones. However, most headphones are just output devices and we have to use another input devices to control the music player, such as remote control pods. Since headphones are placed where the user can access them easily, commands could be entered quickly if they provide basic input functions. Some headphones already provide input functions by using special sensors. However, headphones selection is a huge concern for most users; for example sound quality, wearability, portability, cost as well as shape and color for fashion. Therefore, the user will resist giving up their favorite headphones even though some special headphones can provide input functionality.

Our proposal allows regular headphones to become an input-and-output device without adding sensor devices in the headphone shell or cable, so the user can use his favorite headphones as a controller. It uses a simple circuit to detect tapping of the headphone shell by using the speaker unit in the headphone as a tap sensor, set tapping patterns are recognized and used to control the music player. In this paper, we describe the principle, experiments conducted, and also calibration methods needed to compensate the differences in headphones and users' tapping actions. A test of the implemented prototype that confirms its performance is also reported.

RELATED WORKS

Various methods have been used to provide headphones with input functionality. A button switch is the major method because it is simple and low cost. Touch sensors can be used to minimize the operating force [1], they are also used to detect contact with the ear [2]. Sony Ericsson's headphones, MH907, detects ear insertion to control a mobile phone along with the music player [3]. Headsets, which pair headphones with a microphone, provide the user with voice control. While most microphones are placed near the mouth, some headphones have microphones inside their shells to detect the speech which leaks via the ear canal. Gestures have applied as an input method for headphones. For example, Brewster et al. use head gestures such as nods [4]. Taniguchi et al. detect the movements of the ear canal by a optical reflective sensor implemented in ear canal headphones [5]. Manabe et al. attach electrodes to the headphones to detect electrooculogram (EOG) and eye movements can be used to control a music player [6]. Though these headphones offer some level of input, they require additional sensors, which means the user may have to dispose of his current favorite.

Since it is well known that a speaker can work as a microphone, using the speaker unit inside the headphone as a sensor requires no additional sensors. For example, some intercoms use only a speaker to provide half duplex communication. This approach is quite simple, but switching of direction is required. Powerful echo and noise canceling techniques enable full duplex communication without microphones [7]. Unfortunately, they are complex and consume a lot of electric power.

Considering that just a few commands are needed to control a music player (a typical application of headphones), voice control is overkill and more simple input functions are preferred. Tap control, on which many researchers have worked, is one possible approach for the headphones. For example, "Whisper" which is a wristwatch style handset recognizes rhythmical tapping actions [8], "TapSongs" uses taps for password input [9], and "Skinput" detects where the arm is being tapped [10].

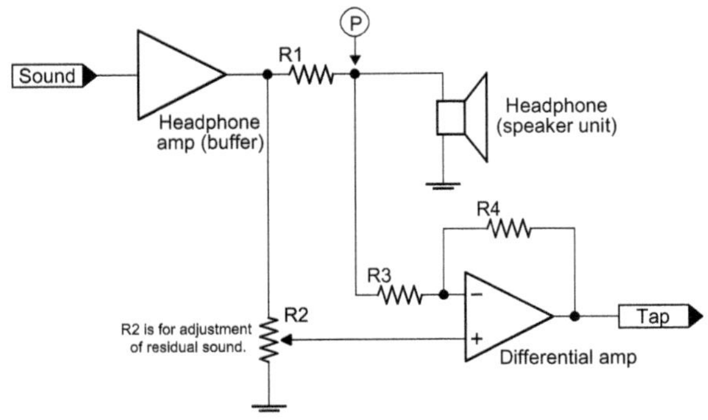

Figure 1: Basic circuit schematic for tap detection.

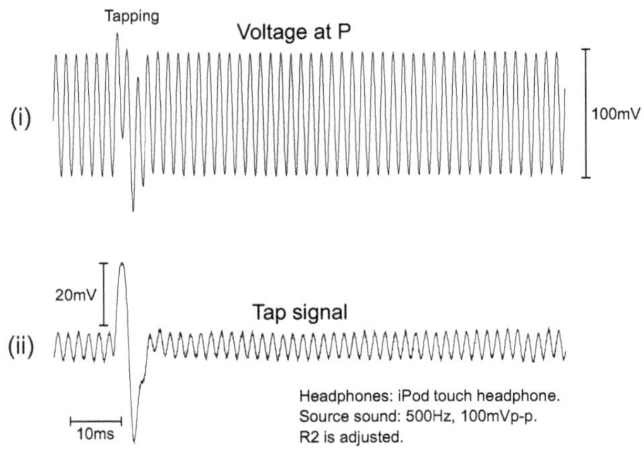

Figure 2: Voltages when tapping headphone.

TAP CONTROL WITH HEADPHONES

The proposed technique uses the speaker unit inside the headphone for tap capture as well as sound output. Since no additional sensors are needed, the user can retain his favorite headphones. While conventional headphones that use the speaker unit as a microphone focus on speech, our technique detects only tapping action which triggers a larger change than speech, taps can be detected while playing music by a simple circuit with low power consumption.

Detection of headphone tapping

Fig.1 shows the basic circuit schematic used to detect taps. The buffer and resistor R1 constitute a usual headphone amplifier (R1 is normally used to limit the current and prevent oscillation), resistors R2, R3, R4 and a differential amp (op-amp) are added to detect taps. When the headphone shell is tapped, current is generated by the speaker unit of the headphone and the voltage at point P is changed. If R2 is adjusted properly, most of the sound signal is canceled by the differential amplifier, and the signal corresponding to the tap remains in the output of the differential amp, which we call the tap signal. Since the impedance of the headphone has reactance components and the phase is shifted, the sound signal is not fully canceled even if R2 is carefully adjusted. Some approaches could be used to further suppress the music, i.e. by applying phase compensation, but complicated circuits or high computing power would be required.

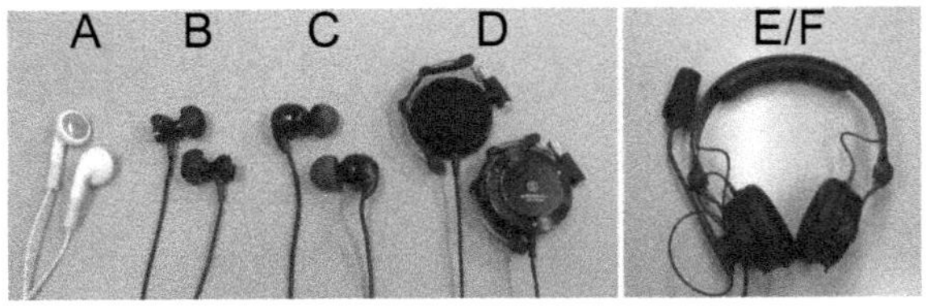

	Headphones	Shape	Type	Impedance
A	Apple iPod touch headphone	intra-concha	dynamic	32Ω
B	Victor HA-FXC71	canal	dynamic	16Ω
C	Shure SE110	canal	BA	27Ω
D	Audio technica ATH-EM700	clip	dynamic	32Ω
E	Sennheiser HD25-1	overhead	dynamic	70Ω
F	Sennheiser HMD25-1	overhead	dynamic	600Ω

Figure 3: Headphones examined.

Using 100Ω as R1 and a stock iPod touch headphone as the headphone, Fig.2 (i) shows an example of the voltage at P in Fig.1 when the headphone shell is tapped. The sound is a sine wave of 500Hz adjusted to 100mVp-p across the headphone. Tapping the headphone disorders the sine wave. When R2 is adjusted to minimize the sound on the tap signal, the voltage change caused by tapping is clearly observed, see Fig.2 (ii).

Differences among headphones

Headphones come in various sizes, shapes, types, and electrical characteristics. Some headphones have a headband and large earpads (labeled "overhead" in Fig.3), some are placed outside the ear canal ("intra-concha"), some are inserted into the ear canal ("canal"), and some have clips to attach to the ear ("clip"). The headphone configuration changes the ease of tapping, tap strength, tap direction, and feeling.

Transducer type is a key factor in choosing headphones. "dynamic" is the most common and some small headphones use balanced armatures ("BA"). There are other types of transducer, such as piezoelectric and electrostatic, however they are seldom used in everyday life.

Each headphone has different electric characteristics, for example impedance and sensitivity. The typical impedance values are, as shown in the specification sheets, 16 to 32Ω for small headphones (earphones) and 32Ω or higher for full-size headphones. Not only the absolute value of impedance but also the phase shift impacts the sound cancellation step and thus tap detection performance.

We examined 6 headphones with 4 shapes and 2 types of transducer, see Fig.3. For each headphone, a 500Hz sine wave of 100mVp-p was injected after R2 was adjusted to minimize the residual sound in the tap signal. When the headphone shell is tapped, a positive peak is observed on the tap signal for all headphones (a negative peak often follows), which is shown in Fig.4. It is because the speaker unit of the headphone is basically connected in the same polarity. This graph indicates that the peak can be easily extracted for various headphones when R2 is correctly adjusted. It is also important that the sound is canceled well enough in all headphones to allow peak detection. In addition, some properties

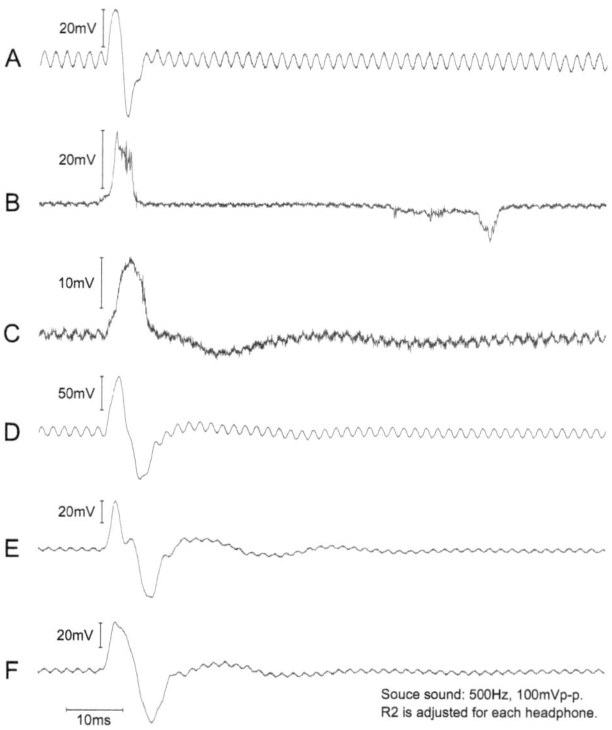

Figure 4: Tap signals of various headphones.

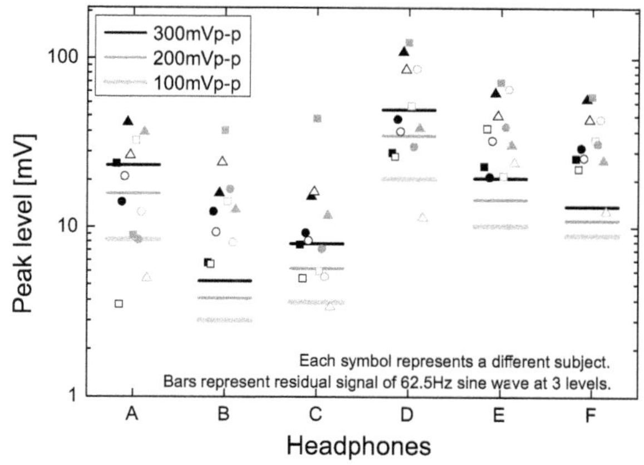

Figure 5: Different peak level of taps compared to typical music levels.

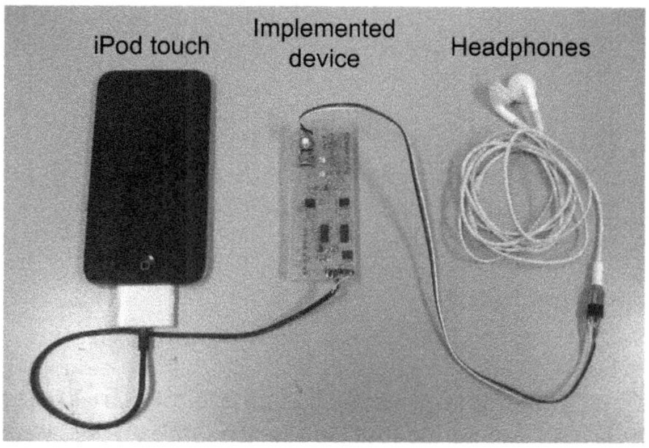

Figure 6: Implemented prototype.

of the signal, such as amplitude, the number of peaks, and time duration of them, differ with the headphone.

Since the peaks corresponding to the tap have several low frequency (about 50-200Hz) components, we injected a 62.5Hz sine wave as a reference sound while adjusting R2.

Differences among users

The peaks created by tapping are altered by the strength, direction, and point of tapping. Some users tap well and big peaks are observed, while some users generate only minor peaks. To investigate the differences, 12 subjects (9 males and 3 females, 33 years old on average, all were right-handed) were asked to tap headphones. They wore the headphones and tapped the right-side-headphone shell ten times. Special directions, for example the point to be tapped, were not given and no feedback was given other than a flash of light at 1 second intervals as a guide for tap timing.

Fig.5 shows the average level of the positive peaks (peak height) when tapping. Each symbol corresponds to a different subject. It is noted that no peak was observed for one subject with headphone [B]. The amplitudes (peak-to-peak) of the residual sound corresponding to reference sounds (62.5Hz at 100mVp-p, 200mVp-p, and 300mVp-p across the headphones) are also shown as bars in the figure; these are to simulate the maximum residual signal level when music is present. If the peak level of tapping is higher than the bars, the taps will be recognized properly, otherwise it becomes difficult. The peak level differs with the subject, so tap detection should be adjusted for each user.

IMPLEMENTATION

A prototype was implemented as an external adapter for a portable music player (Apple's iPod touch), see Fig.6. Digital potentiometers were used for R2 and a PIC microcomputer ran the adjustment processes. R1 was set at 100Ω. The gain of differential amplification was set to 10. The power of 3.3V was supplied from the iPod. The tap signal was captured after low pass filtering (cut-off frequency was 230Hz) and the PIC calculated whether the signal contained a peak corresponding to tapping. When a series of taps was matched to a template (Fig.7), the corresponding control command was issued to the player.

Calibration processes

Calibration is needed because there are differences in headphones and users. Two calibration processes were implemented to cover different headphones and/or different users.

For different headphones, the first process adjusts R2 to minimize the residual sound. After the user triggers calibration, the device searches for the minimum point while it drives the headphone with a reference sound. R2 is set to the minimum point and the amplitude of residual sound is recorded.

For different users, the second process sets the threshold used to detect taps. This calibration requires the user to tap the

Both-hand mode	One-hand mode	Command
Single tap (R or L)	♩	Play / Pause
Double tap (RR)	♪♩	Volume up
Double tap (LL)	♩ ♩	Volume down
Double tap (RL)	♪♪♩	Next track
Double tap (LR)	♩ ♪♩	Previous track

Figure 7: An example of command assignment.

headphones several times to calculate the threshold. The threshold affects the rates of false negatives and false positives. When it is set to be small, false negatives will not occur with weak taps however false positives caused by head motions or residual sound will increase. In the prototype, the threshold was set to be one third of the minimum amplitude of the above mentioned reference taps to prevent false negatives.

False positives caused by the residual sound can be prevented by setting an allowable maximum volume which is calculated from the residual sound level in the first calibration step and the threshold for tap detection.

Issuing commands

In order to control the device, such as a music player, taps must be translated as commands. Two kinds of taps, right-side and left-side tap, can be detected with stereo headphones, and tap sequences or tap rhythm can be used for issuing commands. Fig.7 shows the command assignment implemented in the prototype for controlling a music player. There are two modes, both-hand mode and one-hand mode. The former allows commands to be issued quickly, however it is difficult to use when one hand is occupied such as carrying luggage. The command assignment is arbitrary and so can match the user's demand, and it can be used in various applications, for example music games.

Evaluation

The threshold for detecting taps sets a trade-off relation between false negatives and false positives, and so must be set properly. Evaluation experiments with 6 subjects were performed. Each subject was asked to remember the command assignment in both-hand mode shown in Fig.7 and operate the music player by tap control with headphones [A] and [D] in a period of about ten minutes. In this training period, each subject jumped and shook his head to check whether false positives occurred. After becoming familiar with the prototype, he input commands 50 times (5 commands x 10 trials) following random instructions in a resting state (all subjects sat except one who stood). After that, he input commands 30 times (5 x 6 trials) while walking and going up/down stairs.

Fig.8 shows the accuracy captured in the experiments. Many subjects could achieve a control accuracy of over 95% even while walking, however the accuracy decreased in same cases.

For example, subject i complained that headphone [A] was hard to tap while walking, subject iii mentioned that headphone [A] tended to move away from the ear when tapped. However both subjects had no problem with headphone [D]. In the experiments with subjects i to v, no false positive occurred and almost all the errors were caused by false negatives, which allowed double taps to be detected as a single tap. On the other hand, subject vi tapped very weakly because he disliked applying force to his ears, and he tapped not only the headphones but the surrounding area with multiple fingers to decrease the pressure. Some false positives occurred in his trials, which were considered as multiple finger tap with time lag and his "intentional" single tap was recognized as multiple taps. It occurred once also when he jumped. False negatives were frequent which degraded his accuracy.

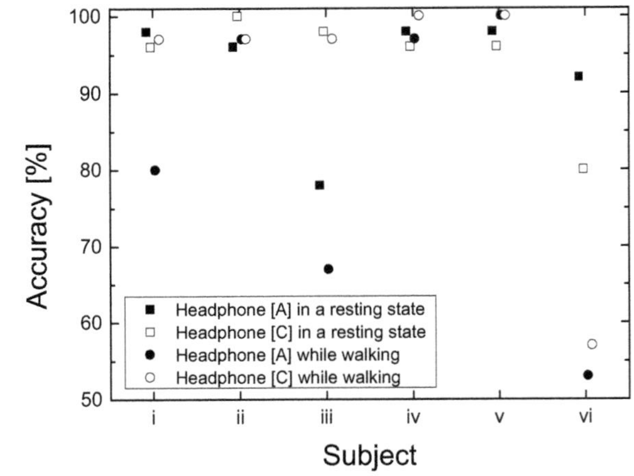

Figure 8: Accuracy of command input.

False positives also occurred in some cases when the headphones hit the desk or headphones were pinched while being mounted or demounted. The allowable maximum volume was set to be low enough to prevent false positives in these experiments. Though some subjects complained the volume was too small for listening, no false positive were caused by residual sound.

More than 10 headphones including the 6 headphones shown in Fig.3 were tested. This prototype worked well with many headphones, however it could not work well with some headphones, such as Ultimate Ears 700 (balanced armature), because the tap peak was as weak as the residual sound (minimum volume) which meant that false positives often occured.

DISCUSSION

The performance depended on both the headphones and the user. In the evaluation, the prototype did not always work well. Various solutions are possible. Using a high-performance peak detector may be the interesting. For example, the negative peaks that follow the first positive ones can be used (the prototype used only the positive peaks). The frequency of the peak of tapping depends on the headphone (it may be affected by the resonant frequency of the shell f_0), so applying a sharp band-pass filter will extract the peak clearly. If the tap peak can be more robustly and accurately detected, not only will false negatives be decreased but also the maximum volume can be increased.

Since the speaker unit inside the headphone works as an accelerometer of one axis, the tap peak changes with the point and the direction of tapping even if the user taps with the same force. Some audio feedback about the amplitude of the tap may help the user to tap efficiently and improve performance.

In the experiment, some subjects reported that tapping the headphones caused discomfort. Though the experiment demanded more frequent tapping than would be expected in real life, it is certain that tapping the headphones creates discomfort [11]. Audio feedback will also reduce the discomfort by achieving accurate taps with small force.

CONCLUSION

A simple technique that changes regular headphones into input-and-output devices was proposed. It detects tapping of the headphone shell by using the internal speaker unit as a sensor, so no additional sensor is required. Our calibration processes enable stable tap detection for various headphones and users. A test confirmed that the prototype works well in most cases. Music players and other systems can be controlled by tapping without replacement of the user's favorite headphones.

REFERENCES

1. Buil, V., Hollemans, G., Wijdeven, S., Headphones with touch control. *Proc. MobileHCI '05*, 2005, pp. 377–378.
2. Dietz, P., Yerazunis, W., Real-time audio buffering for telephone applications. *Proc. UIST '01*, 2001, pp. 193–194.
3. Sony Ericsson Mobile Communications, MH907, http://www.sonyericsson.com/cws/products/accessories/compatiblephones/mh907?cc=gb&lc=en
4. Brewster, S., Lumsden, J., Bell, M., Hall, M., Tasker, S., Multimodal 'eyes-free' interaction techniques for wearable devices. *Proc. CHI '03*, 2003, pp. 473–480.
5. Taniguchi, K., Nishikawa, A., Kobayashi, E., Miyazaki, F., Sakuma, I., Me-Me Switch: a wearable input device using movement of ears. *Proc. interaction '10*, 2010. (in Japanese).
6. Manabe, H., Fukumoto, M., Full-time wearable headphone-type gaze detector. *Extended abstracts of CHI '06*, 2006, pp. 1073–1078.
7. Nittetsu Elex, e-mimi kun, http://www.ns-elex.co.jp/solution/security/factory/factory02.html (in Japanese).
8. Fukumoto, M., Tonomura, Y., Whisper: a wristwatch style wearable handset. *Proc. CHI '99*, 1999, pp. 112–119.
9. Wobbrock, J. O., TapSongs: tapping rhythm-based passwords on a single binary sensor. *Proc. UIST '09*, 2009, pp. 93–96.
10. Harrison, C., Tan, D., Morris, D., Skinput: appropriating the body as an input surface. *Proc. CHI '10*, 2010, pp. 453–462.
11. Buil, V., Hollemans, G., Acceptable operating force for buttons on in-ear type headphones. *Proc. ISWC '05*, 2005, pp. 186–189.

The Proximity Toolkit: Prototyping Proxemic Interactions in Ubiquitous Computing Ecologies

Nicolai Marquardt[1], Robert Diaz-Marino[2], Sebastian Boring[1], Saul Greenberg[1]

[1] Department of Computer Science
University of Calgary, 2500 University Drive NW
Calgary, AB, T2N 1N4, Canada
[nicolai.marquardt, sebastian.boring, saul.greenberg]@ucalgary.ca

[2] SMART Technologies
3636 Research Road NW
Calgary, AB, T2L 1Y1, Canada
robdiaz-marino@smarttech.com

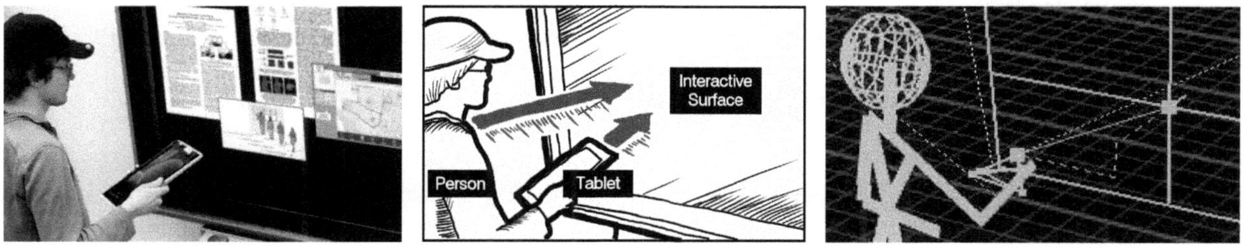

Figure 1. Left: three entities – person, tablet and vertical surface; **Center**: proxemic relationships between entities, e.g., orientation, distance, pointing rays; **Right**: visualizing these relationships in the *Proximity Toolkit*'s visual monitoring tool.

ABSTRACT

People naturally understand and use *proxemic relationships* (e.g., their distance and orientation towards others) in everyday situations. However, only few ubiquitous computing (ubicomp) systems interpret such proxemic relationships to mediate interaction (*proxemic interaction*). A technical problem is that developers find it challenging and tedious to access proxemic information from sensors. Our *Proximity Toolkit* solves this problem. It simplifies the exploration of interaction techniques by supplying fine-grained proxemic information between people, portable devices, large interactive surfaces, and other non-digital objects in a room-sized environment. The toolkit offers three key features. 1) It facilitates rapid prototyping of proxemic-aware systems by supplying developers with the orientation, distance, motion, identity, and location information between entities. 2) It includes various tools, such as a visual monitoring tool, that allows developers to visually observe, record and explore proxemic relationships in 3D space. (3) Its flexible architecture separates sensing hardware from the proxemic data model derived from these sensors, which means that a variety of sensing technologies can be substituted or combined to derive proxemic information. We illustrate the versatility of the toolkit with proxemic-aware systems built by students.

ACM Classification: H5.2 [Information interfaces]: User Interfaces – input devices and strategies, prototyping.

General terms: Design, Human Factors

Keywords: Proximity, proxemics, proxemic interactions, toolkit, development, ubiquitous computing, prototyping.

INTRODUCTION

Ubicomp ecologies are now common, where people's access to digital information increasingly involves near-simultaneous interaction with multiple nearby digital devices of varying size, e.g., personal mobile phones, tablet and desktop computers, information appliances, and large interactive surfaces (Figure 1). This is why a major theme in ubiquitous computing is to explore novel forms of interaction not just between a person and a device, but also between a person and their set of devices [32]. *Proxemic interaction* is one strategy to mediate people's interaction in room-sized ubicomp ecologies [2,9]. It is inspired by Hall's Proxemic theory [11] about people's understanding and use of interpersonal distances to mediate their interactions with others. In proxemic interaction, the belief is that we can design systems that will let people exploit a similar understanding of their proxemic relations with their nearby digital devices, thus facilitating more seamless and natural interactions.

A handful of researchers have already explored proxemic-aware interactive systems. These range from spatially aware mobile devices [17], office whiteboards [15], public art installations [28], home media players [2], to large public ambient displays [31]. All developed novel interaction techniques as a function of proxemic relationships between people and devices.

Building proxemic-aware systems, however, is difficult. Even if sensing hardware is available, translating low-level sensing information into proxemic information is hard (e.g., calibration, managing noise, calculations such as 3D math). This introduces a high threshold for those wishing to develop proxemic interaction systems. As a result, most do not bother. Of the few that do, they spend most of their time with low-level implementation details to actually access and process proxemic information *vs.* refining the interaction concepts and techniques of interest.

To alleviate this problem, we built the *Proximity Toolkit*. Our goal was to facilitate rapid exploration of proxemic interaction techniques. To meet this goal, the Proximity Toolkit transforms raw tracking data gathered from various hardware sensors (e.g., infra-red motion capturing systems, depth sensing cameras) into rich high-level proxemic information accessible via an event-driven object-oriented API. The toolkit includes a *visual monitoring tool* that displays the physical environment as a live 3D scene and shows the proxemic relationships between entities within that scene. It also provides other tools: one to record events generated by entities for later playback during testing; another to quickly calibrate hardware and software. Thus our work offers three contributions:

1. The design of a toolkit architecture, which fundamentally simplifies access to proxemic information.
2. Interpretation and representations of higher-level proxemic concepts (e.g., relationships, fixed/semi-fixed features) from low-level information.
3. The design of complementary visual tools that allow developers to explore proxemic relationships between entities in space without coding.

The remainder of the paper is structured as follows: we recap the concepts of proxemic interaction and derive challenges for developers. We then introduce the design of our toolkit; we include a running example, which we use to illustrate all steps involved in prototyping a proxemic interaction system. Subsequently, we introduce our visual monitor and other tools, and explain the toolkit's API. Next, we discuss the flexible toolkit architecture and implementation. This is followed by an overview of applications built by others using our toolkit. Finally, we discuss related toolkit work in HCI.

BACKGROUND: PROXEMIC INTERACTION

Proxemics – as introduced by anthropologist Edward Hall in 1966 [11] – is a theory about people's understanding and use of interpersonal distances to mediate their interactions with other people. Hall's theory correlates people's physical distance to social distance. He noticed zones that suggest certain types of interaction: from intimate (6-18"), to private (1.5-4'), social (4-12'), and public (12-25'). The theory further describes how the spatial layout of rooms and immovable objects (*fixed features*) and movable objects such as chairs (*semi-fixed features*) influence people's perception and use of personal space when they interact [11].

Research in the field of *proxemic interaction* [2,9,31] introduces concepts of how to apply this theory to ubicomp interaction within a small area such as a room. In particular, such ubicomp ecologies mediate interaction by exploiting fine-grained proxemic relationships between people, objects, and digital devices. The design intent is to leverage people's natural understanding of their proxemic relationships to manage the entities that surround them.

Proxemic theories suggest that a variety of physical, social, and cultural factors influence and regulate interpersonal interaction. Not all can be (or needs to be) directly applied to a proxemic ubicomp ecology. Thus the question is: what information is critical for ubicomp proxemics? Greenberg et al. [9] identified and operationalized five essential dimensions as a first-order approximation of key proxemic measures that should be considered in ubicomp.

1. *Orientation*: the relative angles between entities; such as if two people are facing towards one another.
2. *Distance*: the distance between people, objects, and digital devices; such as the distance between a person and a large interactive wall display.
3. *Motion*: changes of distance and orientation over time; such as a person approaching a large digital surface to interact with it directly.
4. *Identity*: knowledge about the identity of a person, or a particular device.
5. *Location*: the setup of environmental features; such as the fixed-feature location of walls and doors, and the semi-fixed features including movable furniture.

Previous researchers have used a subset of these five dimensions to build proxemic-aware interfaces that react more naturally and seamlessly to people's expectations of proxemics. *Hello Wall* [29] introduced the notion of 'distance-dependent semantics', where the distance of a person to the display defined the possible interactions and the information shown on the display. Similarly, Vogel's public ambient display [31] relates people's presence in four discrete zones around the display to how they can interact with the digital content. Snibbe [28] investigated people's use of proxemics in the *Boundary Functions* public interactive art installation, where they also noticed cultural differences in people's implicit use of proxemics (similar to Hall's observations). Ju [15] explored transitions between implicit and explicit interaction with a proxemic-aware office whiteboard: interaction from afar is public and implicit, but becomes more explicit and private when closer. Ballendat et al. [2] developed a variety of proxemic-aware interaction techniques, illustrated through the example of a home media player application. Their system exploits almost all of the 5 dimensions: it activates when the first person enters, reveals more content when approaching and looking at the screen, switches to full screen view when a person sits down, and pauses the video when the person is distracted (e.g., receiving a phone call). If a second person enters, the way that the information displays is altered to account for two viewers in the room [2].

This previous research in proxemic interaction opened up a promising direction of how to mediate people's interaction with ubicomp technology based on proxemic relationships. The caveat is that they are really just starting points of how we can integrate proxemic measures into interaction design. Further explorative research – including the development and evaluation of actual proxemic-aware systems – will help to refine our understanding of how proxemic theories apply to ubicomp.

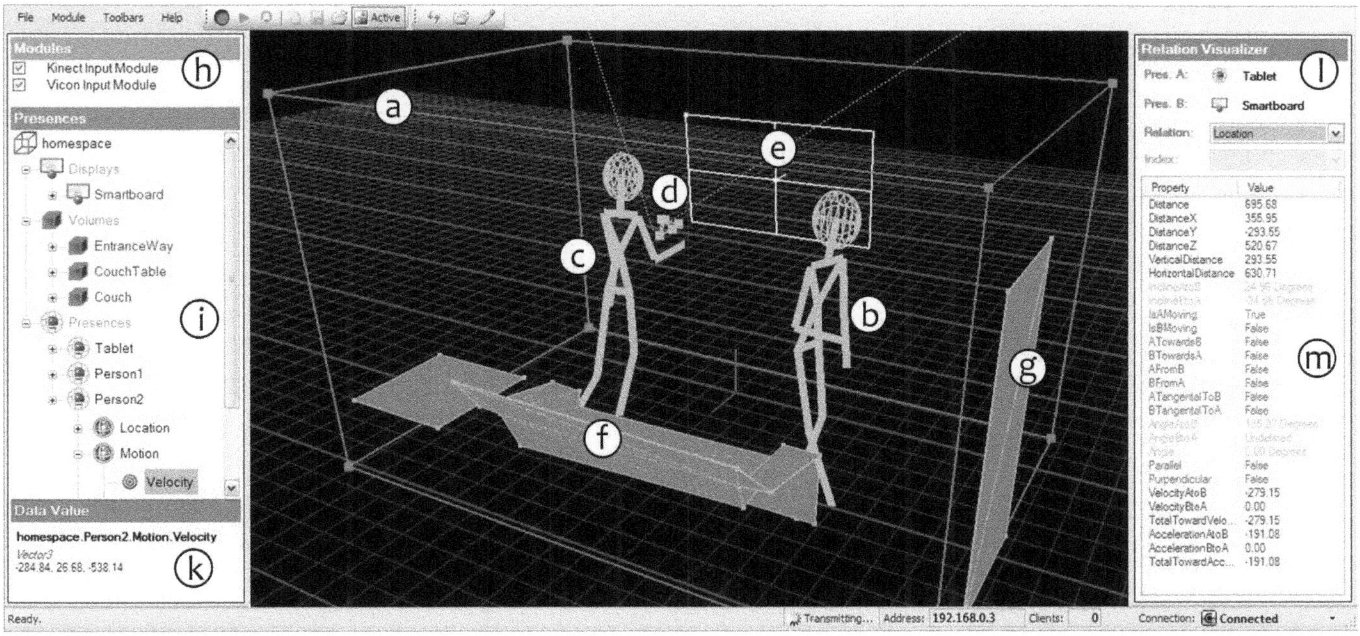

Figure 2. Proximity toolkit monitoring tool. (a) tracked ubicomp environment; (b-g) visual representation of tracked entities in Figure 3; (h) list of available input modules; (i,k) list of all tracked entities; and (l,m) relation visualizer.

DERIVED CHALLENGES FOR DEVELOPERS

Building proxemic-aware systems such as the ones described previously is difficult and tedious. This is mostly due to the serious technical challenges that developers face when integrating proxemic information into their application designs. Several challenges are listed below.

1. *Exploring and observing proxemic measures between entities in the ecology.* Developers need to do this to decide which measures are important in their scenario.
2. *Accessing proxemic measurements* from within software that is developed to control the ubicomp system. Developers currently do this through very low-level programming against a particular tracking technology, requiring complex 3D transformations and calculations, and often resulting in brittleness.
3. *Support for proxemic concepts* is created from scratch by developers, e.g., when considering distance of spatial zones or the properties of fixed and semi-fixed features (e.g., the spatial arrangement) in applications.
4. *Debugging and testing* of such systems is difficult due to a lack of sensing and/or matching monitoring tools.

THE PROXIMITY TOOLKIT

The Proximity Toolkit directly addresses these challenges. It facilitates programmers' access to proxemic information between people, objects and devices in a small ubicomp environment, such as the room shown in Figure 3 and visualized in Figure 2. It contains four main components.

a) **Proximity Toolkit server** is the central component in the distributed client-server architecture, allowing multiple client devices to access the captured proxemic information.

b) **Tracking plug-in modules** connect different tracking / sensing systems with the toolkit and stream raw input data of tracked entities to the server.

c) **Visual monitoring tool** visualizes tracked entities and their proxemic relationships.

d) **Application programming interface (API)** is an event-driven programming library used to easily access all the available proxemic information from within developed ubicomp applications.

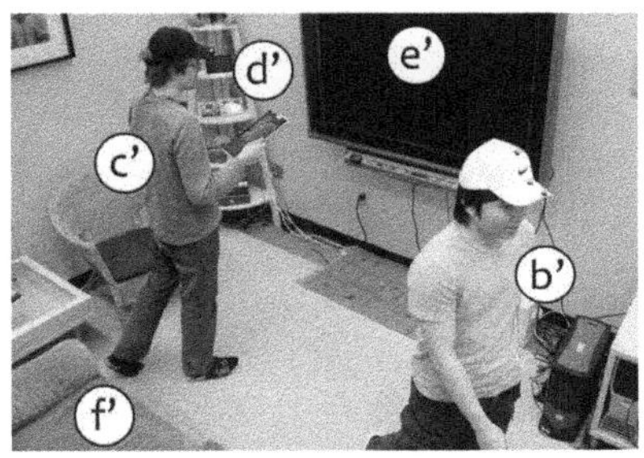

Figure 3. The Proximity Toolkit captures proxemic relationships between: people (b' and c'), devices (d' and e'), and fixed- and semi-fixed features (f').

We explain each of these components in more detail below, including how each lowers the threshold for rapidly prototyping proxemic-aware systems. Also see the video figure.

However, we first introduce a scenario of a developer creating a proxemic interaction system (also in video figure). Through this scenario, we will illustrate how the Proximity Toolkit is used in a real programming task to create a prototype of a proxemic-aware ubicomp application. The example is deliberately trivial, as we see it akin to a *Hello World* illustrating basic programming of proxemic interaction. Still, it shares many similarities with more comprehensive systems built for explorations in earlier research, e.g., [2,15,31].

Scenario. Developer Steve is prototyping an interactive announcement board for the lounge of his company. In particular, Steve envisions a system where employees passing by the display are: attracted to important announcements as large visuals from afar; see and read more content as they move closer; and post their own announcements (typed into their mobile phones) by touching the phone against the screen. To create a seamless experience for interacting with the large ambient display, Steve plans to recognize nearby people and their mobile devices. Steve builds his prototype to match the room shown in Figure 3.

Proximity Toolkit Server

The Proximity Toolkit Server is the central component managing proxemic information. It maintains a hierarchical data model of all fixed features (e.g., walls, entranceways), semi-fixed features (e.g., furniture, large displays), and mobile entities (e.g., people or portable devices). This model contains basic information including identification, position in 3D coordinates, and orientation. The server and toolkit API then perform all necessary 3D calculations on this data required for modeling information about higher-level proxemic relationships between entities.

The server is designed to obtain raw data from various attached tracking systems. For flexibility, each of the tracking systems is connected through a separate plugin module loaded during the server's start-up. These plugins access the captured raw input data and transfer it to the server's data model. The current version of our toolkit contains two plugins: the marker-based VICON motion capturing system, which allows for sub-millimeter tracking accuracy [www.vicon.com], and the KINECT sensor, which allows tracking of skeletal bodies [www.kinect.com]. In a later section we discuss the implementation, integration, and combination of these tracking technologies, and how to setup the server to match the environment. Importantly, the server's unified data model is the basis for a *distributed Model-View-Controller* architecture [3], which in turn is used by the toolkit client API, the monitoring tool, and to calculate proxemic relationships between entities.

Scenario. Developer Steve begins by starting the server. The server automatically loads all present tracking plugins. Based on the information gathered from these plugins, it populates and updates the unified data model in real-time. By default, our toolkit already includes a large pre-configured set of tracked entities with attached markers (such as hats, gloves, portable devices) and definitions of fixed and semi-fixed features (large interactive surface, surrounding furniture). To add a new tracked object, Steve attaches markers to it and registers the marker configuration as a new tracked entity. This process takes minutes.

Visual Monitoring Tool: Tracked Entities

The visual monitoring tool helps developers to see and understand what entities are being tracked and how the data model represents their individual properties. Figure 2 is a screenshot of this tool: the visualized entities in (b-f) correspond to real-world entities captured in Figure 3 (b'-f').

Specifically, the visual monitoring tool connects to the server (through TCP) and presents a 3D visualization of the data model (Figure 2 centre). This view is updated in real-time and always shows:

- the approximate volume of the tracked space as a rectangular outline box (Fig. 2a)
- position and orientation of people (Fig. 2bc)
- portable digital devices, such as a tablet pc (Fig. 2d)
- digital surfaces, such as the large wall display (Fig. 2e)
- fixed and semi-fixed features, such as a table, couch (Fig. 2f), and entranceway (Fig. 2g).

The left side of the monitoring window shows a list of the activated input tracking plugins (Figure 2h) and another list with an overview of all currently tracked entities (Figure 2i). Clicking on any of the items in this list opens a hierar-

		Property name	Description	Data type	Distance	Orientation	Movement	Identity	Location
A Individual entity	I1	**Name**	Identifier of the tracked entity	string				■	
	I2	**IsVisible**	True if entity is visible to the tracking system	bool				■	
	I3	**Location**	Position in world coordinates	Point3D					■
	I4	**Velocity**	Current velocity of the entity's movement	double			■		
	I5	**Acceleration**	Acceleration	double			■		
	I6	**RotationAngle**	Orientation in the horizontal plane (parallel to the ground) of the space	double		■			
	I7	**[Roll/Azimuth/Incline]Angle**	The orientation angles (roll, azimuth, incline)	double		■			
	I8	**Pointers**	Access to all pointing rays (e.g., forward, backward)	Array [ ]		■			
	I9	**Markers/Joints**	Access individual tracked markers or joints	Array [ ]					■
B Relationships between two entities A and B	R1	**Distance**	Distance between entities A and B	double	■				
	R2	**ATowardsB, BTowardsA**	Whether entity A is facing B, or B is facing A	bool		■			
	R3	**Angle, HorizontalAngle, ...**	Angle between front normal vectors (or angle between horizontal planes)	double		■			
	R4	**Parallel, ATangentalToB, ...**	Geometric relationships between entities A and B	bool		■			
	R5	**[Incline/Azimuth/Roll]Difference**	Difference in incline, azimuth, or roll of A and B	double		■			
	R6	**VelocityDifference**	Difference of A's and B's velocity	double			■		
	R7	**AccelerationDifference**	Difference of A's and B's acceleration	double			■		
	R8	**[X/Y/Z]VelocityAgrees**	True if X/Y/Z velocity is similar between A and B	bool			■		
	R9	**[X/Y/Z]AccelerationAgrees**	True if X/Y/Z acceleration is similar	bool			■		
	R10	**Collides, Contains**	True if the two volumes collide, or if volume A contains volume of B	bool	■				■
	R11	**Nearest**	The nearest point of A's volume relative to B	Point3D	■				■
C Pointing Relationships between A and B	P1	**PointsAt**	Pointing ray of A intersects with volume of B	bool		■			
	P2	**PointsToward**	A points in the direction of B (w/ or w/o intersection)	bool		■			
	P3	**IntersectionDegree**	Angle between ray and front facing surface of B	double		■			
	P4	**DisplayPoint**	Intersection point in screen/pixel coordinates	Point2D	■	■			
	P5	**Intersection**	Intersection point in world coordinates	Point3D	■				■
	P6	**Distance**	Length of the pointing ray	double	■				
	P7	**IsTouching**	A is touching B (pointing ray length ~ 0)	bool	■				

Table 1. Accessible proxemic information in the Proximity Toolkit: individual entities, relationships between two entities, and pointing relationships. This information is accessible through the toolkit API and the toolkit monitor visualization.

chical list of properties showing the item's current status (e.g., its location, or orientation). When Steve selects any of these properties, the monitoring window shows the corresponding value (e.g., the current position as a 3D Vector, or the velocity; Fig 2k). Part A of Table 1 shows an overview of the most important available properties.

Scenario. Before Steve starts to program, he explores all available proxemic information through the visual monitoring tool. He inspects the currently tracked entities (Figure 2 left, also displayed in the center), as well as which entity properties are available for him to use. Steve finds this visual overview particularly important to his initial design, as he is still investigating the possible mappings of proxemic relationship to system behaviour. In later stages, he will also use this monitoring tool to test and debug his program.

Visual Monitoring Tool: Relationships

Another major feature of the visual monitoring tool is to let people set and observe particular *proxemic relationships* between entities, where developers will use these relationships to define particular proxemic interaction behaviours. Specifically, the *Relation Visualizer* panel (Fig. 2, l-m) allows a developer to select a type of relationship between entities, and then to observe the values of all related properties. The complete list of proxemic relationships that are available to observe are summarized in part B/C of Table 1.

Scenario. Steve wants to observe a relationship between *Person1* (representing the first person entering the space) and the *Smartboard* display. Steve drags the two entries from the list of tracked entities (Fig. 2i) to the top of the *Relation Visualizer* panel (Fig. 2l). Next, Steve selects one of the following relationship categories from a drop down menu.

- **Orientation** (e.g., angles between entities)
- **Location** (e.g., changes in distance between the person and the smartboard)
- **Direction** (e.g., if the front of the person's body faces towards the screen)
- **Movement** (e.g., acceleration or velocity)
- **Pointing** (e.g., the display intersection point of the right arm pointer of the person)
- **Collision** (e.g., if the volumes of two tracked entities are so close that they collide)

Steve can now observe how those entities relate to each other. The panel in Fig. 2m shows the numeric values of any properties belonging to this category. The categories plus the properties within them operationalize the five essential elements of proximity mentioned previously.

With his public announcement application in mind, Steve is interested in knowing when a person is in close distance to the display. He selects the *Location* category, and looks at the values of the *Distance* property, which – in this case – measures the distance of the person's body to the board (Fig. 2m). Next, he wants to know when the person is facing towards the screen. He selects the *Direction* category from the menu, and immediately sees the related proxemic properties with their current values and their graphical appearance in the visualization. He is particularly interested in the *ATowardsB* property, which is *true* if the person [A] is facing towards the smartboard [B]. He decides to use the information about direction and distance to adapt the content shown on the announcement board.

Steve continues exploring other proxemic relationship categories and makes note of the types of relationships that he will integrate into his application. As he selects these other categories (Fig. 2l), the 3D visual representation changes accordingly. Figure 4 illustrates three other visualizations of proxemic relationships that Steve explored: the distance between the person and the display (Fig. 4a), the forward pointer of the left arm and its intersection point with the smartboard (Fig. 4b), and the collision volumes (Fig. 4c).

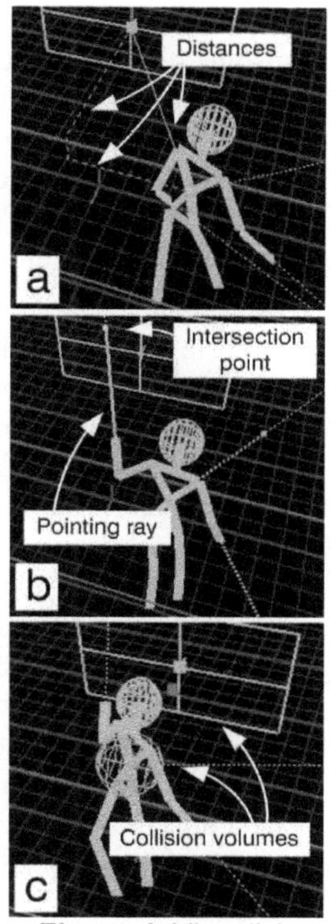

Figure 4. Visualizing proxemic relationships: (a) distance, (b) pointing and (c) collision.

SIMPLIFIED API ACCESS TO PROXEMIC INFORMATION

We now take a closer look at the development API, offered via an *object-oriented C# .NET development library.* We designed it to be fairly easy to learn and use (1) by taking care of and hiding low-level infrastructure details and (2) by using a conventional object-oriented and event-driven programming pattern. Essentially, the API lets a developer programmatically access the proxemic data previously observed in the monitoring tool. We explain how this works by continuing our scenario.

Scenario. Steve adds the Proximity Toolkit API library to his own PC-based software project. The only criterion is that his PC needs network access to the proximity server. Steve begins by initializing his software. To set up his software to use the server, he adds three lines of code (lines 1-3 in Figure 5). First, he creates a new client connection object, then starts the connection to the server (at the given IP address and port), and finally creates a `ProximitySpace` object, which provides a high-level framework for monitoring the interaction of tracked presences, such as people and objects. The `ProximitySpace` object maintains a list of all available tracked entities, and is used to create instances of entities or for initializing event handlers to monitor relationships. Next, Steve initializes three of the entities he is interested in (lines 4-6): the `person` representing the first person entering the space, the `smartboard`, and a `tablet` (`PresenceBase` is a special object that represents individual tracked or static objects).

The following describes how Steve then monitors the relationships *between* these entities. We go through each of the five proxemic dimensions introduced earlier (albeit in a slightly different order), explaining how Steve writes his application to monitor changes in each of these dimensions, and how he uses that information to mediate interaction with his interactive announcement board.

1. Orientation

Monitoring orientation changes allows (1) accessing the exact angle of orientation between two entities and/or (2) determining whether two entities are facing each other. Steve is mostly interested in the relationship between a person and the smartboard display. He adds line 7, which creates a relationship between these two as indicated by their parameters. The system is now tracking both entities relative to each other. Steve is also interested in knowing when the orientation and location between these two changes. For orientation, he initializes an event handler to receive updates of the *Direction* relationship between the person and the smartboard (line 8). The `OnDirectionUpdated` method is invoked when the system recognizes any changes in orientation between the person and the smartboard (line 10). While Steve could access each entity's precise orientation values (e.g., angles of orientation), he is only really interested in knowing whether a person is facing towards the smartboard. Consequently, he writes the event handler callback method (lines 10-12) to access the `ATowardsB` property in the event arguments: it is `true` if the person is facing the smartboard (line 11).

Entries R2-R5 and P1-P3 in Table 1 give an overview of further orientation relationships that can be monitored. As well, the programmer can access the absolute orientation of an individual entity at any time (see entries I6 – I7 in Table 1). For example, the following property returns the current yaw angle of the tablet: `tablet.Orientation.Yaw;`

2. Distance, including Location, Pointing and Touching

Similarly, Steve can monitor changes of distance between entities. We illustrate how Steve can receive updates about distance changes by adding another event callback for `OnLocationUpdated` events (line 9). This callback method (line 13-15) is invoked whenever the location of at least one of the two entities changes. In line 14 Steve accesses the current distance between the person and the smartboard, and uses this distance value to make the visual content on the announcement board vary as a function of the distance between the person and the display. The closer the person, the more content is revealed.

Other available properties relate to distance. First, the actual location property of each entity, i.e, its position within the space, is accessible at any time. For example Steve can access the current coordinates of the person by accessing `this.person.Location`. Second, *pointing relationships* monitor orientation *and* distance simultaneously. Pointing is similar to ray-casting. Each entity can have one or multiple pointers. Each pointer has a pointing direction, and the callback returns the intersection of that direction with the other entity. It also returns the length of the pointing ray between entities, which may not be exactly the same as distance. To illustrate, Steve tracks not only the close distance of a tablet computer to the smartboard, but where that tablet raycasts onto the smartboard. He initializes a second `RelationPair` between the `tablet` and the `smartboard` (line 16). He subscribes for `OnPointingUpdated` events that are triggered whenever any of the pointers of the tablet changes relative to the board (line 17). In the event callback method (lines 18 to 22) Steve first checks if the tablet's forward pointer faces the display (`PointsTowards`) and if the ray length between tablet and board is smaller than 50 cm (line 19). If this is the case, he shows an icon on the ray's intersection point (line 20) on the smartboard to let the person know they can touch the surface to initiate a transfer.

Third, Steve checks if the tablet is touching the surface - (`IsTouching`, line 21) – a distance of ~0. If so, he initiates transfer of the content on the tablet to the large display. By using the intersection point of the tablet with the screen Steve can show the transferred content at the exact position where the tablet touches the board.

```
01 ProximityClientConnection client = new ProximityClientConnection();
02 client.Start("192.168.0.11", 888);
03 ProximitySpace space      = client.GetSpace();
04 PresenceBase person       = space.GetPresence("Person1");
05 PresenceBase smartboard   = space.GetDisplay("SmartBoard");
06 PresenceBase tablet       = space.GetDisplay("Tablet");
07 RelationPair relation     = space.GetRelationPair(person, smartboard);
08 relation.OnDirectionUpdated += new DirectionRelationHandler(OnDirectionUpdated);
09 relation.OnLocationUpdated  += new LocationRelationHandler(OnLocationUpdated);
10 void OnDirectionUpdated(ProximitySpace space, DirectionEventArgs args) {
11     if (args.ATowardsB) { [... person is facing the display, show content ...] } else { [...hide...] }
12 }
13 void OnLocationUpdated(ProximitySpace space, LocationEventArgs args) {
14     double distance = args.Distance; [... change visual content as a function of distance ...]
15 }
16 RelationPair relationTablet = space.GetRelationPair(tablet, smartboard);
17 relationTablet.OnPointingUpdated += new PointingRelationHandler(OnPointingUpdated);
18 void OnPointingUpdated(ProximitySpace space, PointingEventArgs args) {
19     if (args["forward"].PointsToward && (args["forward"].Distance < 500.0)) {
20         Point intersection = args["forward"].DisplayPoint;
           [... show awareness icon on smartboard display ...]
21         if (args["forward"].IsTouching) {
               [... transfer content from the tablet to the large display ...]
22 }}}
```

Figure 5. Partial source code for the proxemic-aware announcement board application.

3. Identity

The toolkit allows access to the identity information of all tracked entities. The `Name` property provides the identifier string of each entity, and `IsVisible` is true if the entity is currently tracked by the system. A developer can subscribe to events notifying about any new tracked entities that enter the ubicomp space through the `space.OnPresenceFound` event. In the associated event callback method, the event arguments give information about the type and name of the detected entity. For example, Steve could have his system track and greet a previously unseen person with a splash screen on first appearance, and dynamically initialize any necessary event callbacks relating that person to other entities in a scene.

4. Motion

Motion events describe the changes of distance and orientation over time, e.g., to receive updates of changes in acceleration and velocity of any entity. For example, Steve can have his application ignore people moving quickly by the display, as he thinks they may be annoyed by any attempts to attract their attention. To receive such velocity updates, Steve would add an event handler (similar to lines 8 and 9) through `OnMotionUpdated` and then simply access the value of the `args.Velocity` property. Based on that value, he would activate the display only if the velocity was less than a certain threshold. Of course, Steve could have determined a reasonable threshold value by observing the velocity value of a person rushing by the display in the visual monitoring tool.

5. Location: Setup of Environment

Using location, the toolkit lets one track the relationships of people and devices to the semi-fixed and fixed features in the physical environment. For example, the model may contain the fixed-feature position of the entranceway to a room, allowing one to know if someone has crossed that threshold and entered the room. It may also contain the location of semi-fixed features, such as the chairs and table seen in Figure 3. Monitoring event handlers for fixed and semi-fixed features can be initialized similarly to the ones we defined earlier.

Steve sets up several fixed feature entities – the smartboard and the entrance-way – through several initial configuration steps. This only has to be done once. Using a physical pointer (the stick in Figure 6a), he defines each entity's volume by physically outlining them in space. Under the covers, the toolkit tracks the 3D tip location of this stick and builds a 3D model of that entity. Each location point of the model is confirmed by pressing a button (e.g., of a wirelessly connected mouse). Figure 6 illustrates how Steve defines the smartboard. After placing the pointer in the four corners of the display plane (Fig. 6a), the coordinates appear in the visualization (6b), and a control panel allows fine adjustments. He saves this to the Proximity Toolkit server as a model. Similarly, Steve defines the entrance-way by outlining the door (Fig. 2g), and the couch by outlining its shape (Fig. 2f). Steve can now monitor proxemic relationships between all moving entities and these new defined features. For example, he can create an event handler to receive notifications when a person passes through the entrance-way (by using the `OnCollisionUpdated` event) and when a person sits on the couch (using the `Distance` property of the `OnLocationUpdated`).

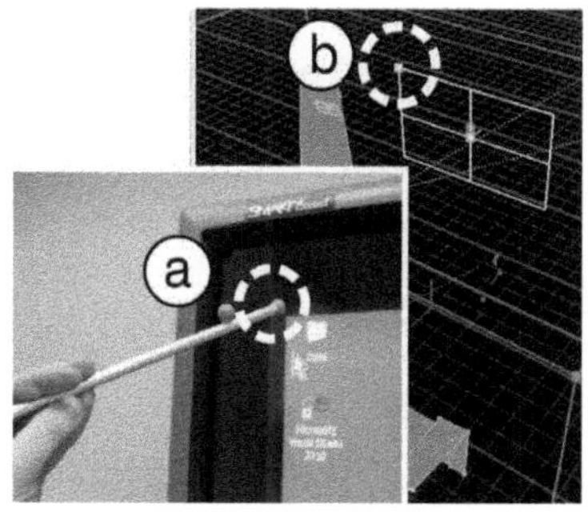

Figure 6. Defining new fixed and semi-fixed features (e.g., display) using a tracked physical pointer (a) and visual feedback (b).

Semi-fixed features differ. While they are part of the environment, they are also movable. As with fixed features, a developer would model a shape by outlining it with the stick. Unlike fixed features, he would also add markers to that entity. The toolkit tracks those markers, and repositions the entity accordingly. For example, Steve could have modeled a chair, tracked where it is in the room, and adjusted the presentation if a person was sitting on it.

We should also mention that we believe location should also include further contextual information about this particular environment, e.g., the meaning of that place. Such contextual information is not yet included in the toolkit, but could be easily added as metadata.

Scenario – next steps. Our walkthrough example illustrated the easy-to-use mechanisms of integrating proxemic measurements into a ubicomp system. While simple, this starting point allows Steve to further extend the system functionality exploring proxemic interactions. Examples include: (1) subscribing to events of a second person to let the system react to both persons' movement to the display. (2) Monitoring additional tablet computers, and enabling content-sharing between them as a function of the device's distance. Overall, the toolkit minimizes the effort necessary for such extensions, and allows rapid exploration and alteration of interaction techniques.

Additional Tools Facilitating Prototyping Process

The toolkit is more than an API, as it offers additional tools to lower the threshold for developing proxemic-aware systems. The already-discussed visual monitoring tool is one of these. Several others are described below.

Recording and playback of proxemic sequences. To test applications, developers would need actors to perform the proxemic movements between entities every time.

This is problematic for many reasons: it is tedious; the sensing equipment may not be available; and it is difficult to repeat particular test sequences. To alleviate this, the toolkit provides a record/playback tool within the visual monitoring tool. With the click of a button, developers can record events generated by entities moving in the environment. They can later play back these sequences for testing. Under the covers, each individual sequence is recorded as an XML file, where the toolkit uses that record to recreate all events. Because the tracking hardware is not needed during playback, testing can be done anywhere, e.g., a desktop workstation located elsewhere. For example, Steve could have recorded test sequences such as: a person passing by the screen, a person approaching the display, or a device pointing towards the display. He would then replay these sequences while developing and testing his software at his desk.

Component library, templates, and examples. We leverage developers' existing practices by seamlessly integrating the toolkit into the familiar capabilities of a popular IDE, Microsoft *Visual Studio* (but our ideas are generalizable to other IDEs). First, the toolkit includes a library of *drag-and-drop* components (compatible with both *WPF* and *Windows Forms*), where the programmer can view and set all their properties and generate event handlers for all available events via direct manipulation rather than coding. This not only reduces tedium and coding errors, but also reduces the threshold for inexperienced developers (such as students) as all properties and events are seen. Second, we reduce start-up effort by including a set of templates containing the minimum required code. Third, to ease learning, we provide a large set of teaching applications illustrating standard programming patterns. Using a very simple example, each of them illustrates the code required to implement a particular proxemic relationship.

FLEXIBLE AND EXTENSIBLE ARCHITECTURE

Our first version of the toolkit [5] was tightly linked to a particular tracking technology. This means that other technologies could not be exploited. The toolkit's current version decouples the API from underlying tracking technologies.

Plugin architecture. The data providers of raw tracking input data are implemented as separate plugin modules, which are dynamically loaded into the proximity server at start-up. We currently have plugins for two different tracking technologies – the VICON motion capturing system that tracks infrared reflective markers, and the Microsoft KINECT depth camera). We anticipate a variety of further plugins for tracking systems (e.g., other IR tracking).

Templates, base classes, interfaces, and utility classes facilitate plugin development. Programmers begin with the plugin template, derived from the `Plugin` base class. This base class provides a set of utility methods, such as one for affine transformations from the tracking system's local coordinate system to the Proximity Toolkit's unified coordinate system. This affine matrix is calculated through a simple one time calibration process. Next, developers implement several mandatory methods, including `OnStartup` (to start and initialize tracking hardware) and `OnClose` (to stop tracking hardware). In our two plugin implementations, the `OnStartup` method causes the VICON plugin to initialize the underlying NEXUS software [30], and the KINECT plugin to initialize the OPENNI [24] software. Once initialized, plugins receive raw data of tracked people, objects, and/or devices in 3D space. The `OnUpdate` method of each plugin module is responsible to stream raw tracking data into the toolkit.

Diverse tracking capabilities. In order to allow the integration of hardware with different tracking capabilities, the plugins specify the kinds of proxemic information they support. For example, a tracking system might gather information about the position of an entity, but *not* its orientation. Following the *decorator pattern* [7], each plugin can specify exactly what kind of input data a particular tracking hardware provides. The decorator pattern describes a mechanism to extend the functionality of objects at run-time. In our case, the plugin creates decorator objects for *each* proxemic dimension of input data it supports and calls the update method on these decorators. For example, the `LocationDecorator` updates location of an entity and the `OrientationDecorator` its orientation (plugins can add custom decorators for any proxemic information not yet supported by available decorators). During each update cycle (i.e., when `OnUpdate` is called), the decorator objects update the proxemic information in the server's unified data model as proxemic information of each entity. No high-level calculations on raw input data are required for the plugin implementation, as these are performed by the proximity server or API.

The available dimensions of input data for each tracked entity are directly visible in the monitoring tool: a list view and 3D view give direct feedback about the available proxemic dimensions. These dimensions can be also checked from the client API by using the `IsVisible` properties for each available input dimension.

Distributed data model. The server's unified data model is a collection of hierarchical key-value pairs representing all currently tracked entities. The keys are structured according to the following pattern:

```
/[space]/[presence]/[proxemic-dimension]/[identifier]
```

For example, the following key-value pairs are part of the data model of a tracked person (i.e., location, motion, and orientation):

```
/home/person/locationdecorator/location      = [12.4,3.7,8.2]
/home/person/motiondecorator/velocity        = [0.1,0.6,20.5]
/home/person/orientationdecorator/rollangle  = -95.5
```

This data model is implemented through a shared hash table that is accessible through TCP connections [3]. Thus, the data model is accessible from all computers linked in the same network. Usually the underlying data model is hidden from developers (though they can access and modify it if desired). The server and the toolkit API calculate necessary proxemic relationships for the entities present in the data model. To reduce computational overhead, the necessary 3D calculations are done only on demand, i.e., when a client subscribes to events for a particular relationship between two entities.

Substitution. Tracking systems/plugins can be *substituted*, providing that their hardware gathers similar tracking information. For example, instead of using the depth camera for tracking people's positions and postures, a programmer can use the IR motion capture system instead by attaching IR reflective markers to a person's body. Due to the separation of tracking hardware and API, a programmer's access to this proxemic information via the toolkit API remains unchanged, regardless of the underlying tracking mechanism used.

Uncertainty. All 3D tracking systems provide input with some kind of uncertainty. As tracking systems differ in precision of tracking data they provide, plugins are required to provide additional information about this uncertainty of tracking information. In particular, two values describe tracking uncertainty in our toolkit. First, the `Precision` value specifies how accurate the system tracks entities (normalized between 0.0 and 1.0). `Precision` is defined as *1 / [minimum resolution]*, where the minimum resolution is measured in mm (e.g., minimum resolution is 1mm for the VICON system, and 20mm for KINECT). Thus, the lower the resolution, the higher the precision value is. Second, the `Confidence` value indicates the estimated accuracy of the provided tracking information. It ranges from 0.0-1.0, where 0 is 0% confidence (i.e., lost tracking), and 1 is 100% confidence. In our plugins, the VICON motion capturing system provides estimated accuracy information for all tracked markers, and this value is mapped directly to our `Confidence` value. In contrast, the `Confidence` value of a person tracked by the OPENNI depth cameras is calculated by dividing the recognized parts of the body (e.g., arms, legs) to the total number of possible parts to recognize (i.e., the `Confidence` is 1.0 if the full body of a person is tracked). These confidence and precision values are applied to each individually tracked entity. Furthermore, the precision value can differ depending on where in the 3D space an entity is tracked (e.g., precision is higher when a person stands closer to the depth sensing camera).

A developer can monitor the quality of input data with the visual monitor tool. A table view lists confidence and precision values, and the 3D view gives direct feedback of the precision (or absence) of tracking. Similarly, the API exposes the `Confidence` and `Precision` values of each entity. It also includes the `IsVisible` (false if lost tracking) and `LastUpdated` (timestamp of the last update) properties.

Combination. In cases where different plugins provide *complementary* tracking information of a single entity, the information can be combined in the proximity server's data model. For example, the KINECT and VICON systems could both track a single person simultaneously: the KINECT system provides information about the person's body position in 3D space, and the VICON system tracks a glove the person is wearing in order to retrieve fine-grained information of the person's finger movements. Both plugins then update the entity's data model in the server with their tracked information. If two systems provide *overlapping/conflicting* tracking data (e.g., two systems provide information about an entity's location), the information will be merged in the server's data model. To do so, the server calculates a weighted average (taking the `Confidence` and `Precision` values) of all values received in a certain time frame (i.e., one update cycle) and updates the proxemic data model of that entity. This means, that the higher the confidence and precision value of a given entry, the more it affects the final merged value of that entity.

Alternatively, other algorithms for tracking data fusion (e.g., [33]) could be seamlessly implemented on the server level (thus not requiring any changes to the plugins or the API). We could also extend the toolkit's uncertainty information via Schwarz et al.'s [27] framework for handling ambiguous input, where this could track ambiguous information simultaneously and delay event triggers.

Availability. Our toolkit including software and documentation facilitating development of custom plugins (or other possible extensions to the toolkit) are available as open source on the *GroupLab Proximity Toolkit* website [10].

APPLICATIONS OF PROXEMIC INTERACTION

The Proximity Toolkit allowed our colleagues – most who were *not* involved in the toolkit design and coding – to rapidly design a large variety of proxemic-aware ubicomp systems. The toolkit was invaluable. Instead of struggling with the underlying low-level implementation details, colleagues and students focused on the design of novel interaction techniques and applications that considered people's use of space. This includes comprehensive systems such as the proxemic media player by Ballendat et al. [2], and other applications presented in Greenberg et al. [9].

Application	*Monitored relationships*	*LOC*	*LOC proximity*
Attention demanding advertisements	2 people, 1 large surface, 1 tablet	284	32
Spatial music experience	2 people, 4 objects	181	64
Proxemic-aware pong game	2 people, 1 large surface	209	47
Proxemic presenter	1 person, 1 large surface	92	18
ProxemiCanvas workspaces	2 people, 2 notebook computer	393	58

Table 2. Overview of built proxemic-aware applications, the proxemic relationships they monitor, the total lines of code (LOC), and the code for accessing proxemic information (LOC proximity). LOC are approximate.

To stress the ease of learning and developing with our toolkit, we summarize a few projects built by students in a graduate ubicomp class in Fall 2010. They received a one-hour tutorial presentation and a demonstration of two programming examples. The students' assignment was simply to create a proxemic interface of their choosing, where they had to demonstrate it in the next class. Thus all examples (listed in Table 2 and briefly explained below) were built and demonstrated by the students within a week of the tutorial.

Attention-Demanding Advertisements (Miaosen Wang) explores how future advertisement displays might try to grab and keep a person's attention. A digital advertisement board:

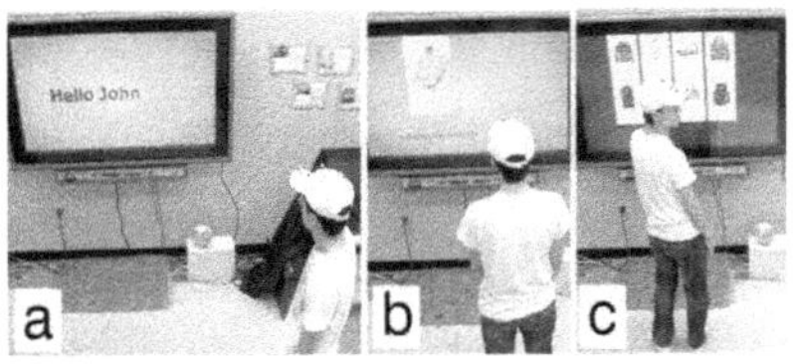

(a) attracts the attention of a passer-by by welcoming them by calling out their name; (b) shows items of interest to them as they look; (c) and persistently tries to regain the attention of that person if they look or move away by playing sounds and flashing the background color.

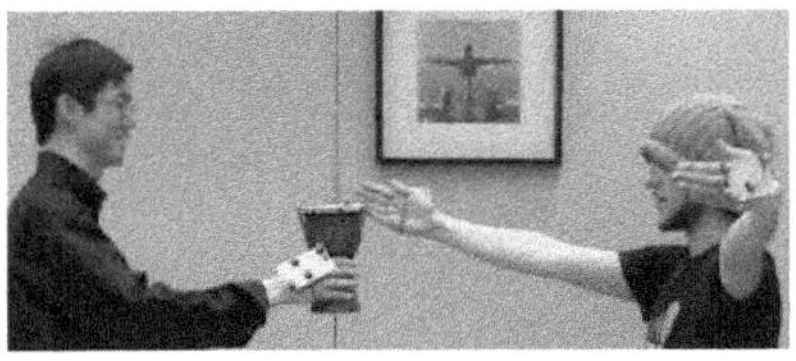

Spatial Music Experience (Matthew Dunlap) is an interactive music installation. The kinds of sounds generated and their volume is determined by the proxemic relationships of *people* and *physical objects* in the space. Generated sounds react fluently as people move and perform gestures in the space, and when they grab and move physical objects.

Proxemic-aware Pong (Till Ballendat) is inspired by Atari's Pong game. A person controls the paddle for bouncing the ball by physically moving left and right in front of a large screen. The game recognizes when a second person enters, and creates a second paddle for multiplayer play. To increase the game play difficulty over time, it increases the required physical distance to move the paddles. When players move close to the screen, they can adjust the paddle size through direct touch. When both sit down on the couch, the game pauses.

Proxemic Presenter (Miaosen Wang) is a presentation controller that reacts to the presenter's position relative to a large display [9]. Presentation slides are displayed full screen on the large display. When the presenter stands at the side and turns his head towards the display, a small panel appears next to him, showing speaker notes, a timer, and buttons to navigate the slides. If he switches sides, the panel follows him. When facing back to the audience, the panel disappears immediately. When he moves directly in front of facing towards the display, the system shows an overview of all slides as touch-selectable thumbnails. When he turns back to the audience, the presentation reappears.

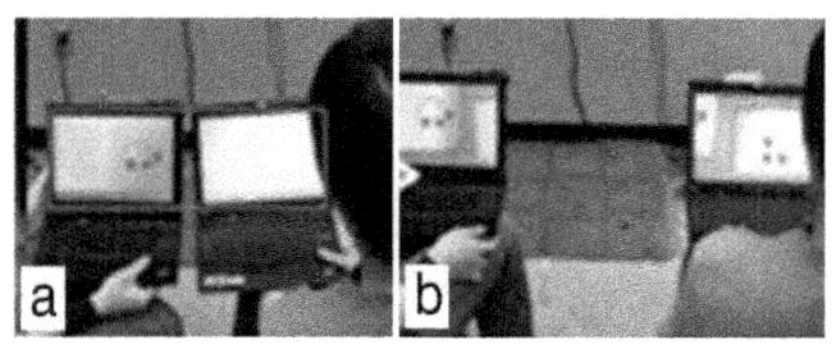

ProxemiCanvas (Xiang Anthony Chen) is an interactive drawing application in which drawing canvases displayed on people's portable computers gradually merge as a function of proxemic relationships between people and devices. For instance, from close to far distance, this ranges from: (a) merged workspaces when very close, (b) awareness of other people's work when sitting nearby, to no shared information when turning away (e.g., when people are sitting back to back).

What is important in these examples is how the Proximity Toolkit lowered the threshold for these students to begin their exploration of proxemics in the ubicomp context (Table 2). Easy access to proxemic information through the toolkit and API allowed them to rapidly prototype alternative system designs, all leading towards exploring the design space of future proxemic-aware ubicomp systems.

RELATED WORK

Our research is inspired by earlier toolkits enabling the rapid prototyping of ubicomp interactions. We sample and review related work in three areas: toolkit support in HCI, ubicomp development architectures, and 3D spatial tracking.

Post-GUI Toolkits

Several development toolkits facilitate the prototyping of physical and tangible user interfaces that bridge the connection between the digital and physical world [14]. Many of these toolkits focus on a low *threshold*, but simultaneously aim for maintain a relatively high *ceiling* [23]. For example, *Phidgets* [8] and the *iStuff* toolkit [1] provide physical building blocks (buttons, sensors) that programmers can easily address from within their software. *Shared Phidgets* took this concept further by simplifying the prototyping of distributed (i.e. remote located) physical user interfaces [21]. Hartmann's visual authoring environment in *dTools* [12] brought similar concepts to interaction designers. Other toolkits simplified the integration of computer vision techniques into novel user interfaces, such as Klemmer's *PapierMache* [16].

Ubicomp Development Architectures

On a somewhat higher level of abstraction, Dey introduced an architecture to compose context-aware ubicomp systems with the *Context Toolkit* [4]. They provide *context widgets* as encapsulated building blocks, working in conjunction with *generators*, *interpreters*, or *aggregators*. The context toolkit allows the composition of new applications through a concatenation of the basic components – and thus facilitates scaffolding approaches. Matthews applied similar concepts to the programming of peripheral ambient displays [22].

Other systems facilitate access to location information of devices in ubicomp environments. For example, Hightower's *Location Stack* [13] fuses the input data from various sources to a coherent location data model. Krumm and Hinckley's *NearMe* wireless proximity server [18] derives the position of devices from their 802.11 network connections (without requiring calibration), and thus informs devices about any other devices nearby. Li's *Topiary* [19] introduced prototyping tools for location-enhanced applications.

3D Spatial Tracking

Few development toolkits support the exploration of novel interfaces considering the presence, movements, and orientation of people, objects, and devices in 3D space. For example, some toolkits allow development of augmented reality (AR) applications. To illustrate, Feiner's prototyping system allows exploration of novel mobile augmented reality experiences (e.g., with a head mounted 3D display, or a mobile tablet like device) [6]. This was developed further in Mac-

Intyre's *DART* [20], *Open Tracker* [25], and Sandor's prototyping environment [26] for handheld-based AR applications. These toolkits mostly focus on supporting augmented reality applications running on mobile devices, and not on ubicomp ecologies in small rooms. Some commercial systems track 3D data of objects. For example, the VICON Nexus software gives access to 3D spatial information of tracked objects. This information, however, only includes low level position data, which developers need to process manually in order to gain insights into proxemic relationships.

Our Proximity Toolkit builds on this prior work. Like post-GUI toolkits, it bridges the connection between the virtual and real world, but in this case by tracking proxemic information. Similarly, it extends ubicomp architectures and 3D spatial tracking by capturing and providing fine-grained information about 3D proxemic relationships in small ubicomp spaces (i.e., not only location, but also orientation, pointing, identity, etc.). Like the best of these, it supplies an API that, in our case, makes the *five essential proxemic dimensions* [9] easily accessible to developers. Like the more advanced tools, it also provide additional development tools, such as a monitoring tool for visualizing proxemic relationships, a record/playback tool to simplify testing; templates, documentation, examples, and so on.

CONCLUSION

The Proximity Toolkit enables rapid prototyping and exploration of novel interfaces that incorporate the notion of proxemic relationships. Through hiding most of the underlying access to tracking hardware and complex 3D calculations, our toolkit lets developers concentrate on the actual design and exploration of novel proxemic interaction.

We invite other researchers to use it. The Proximity Toolkit is available as open source [10].

ACKNOWLEDGMENTS

This research is partially funded by the iCORE/NSERC/SMART Chair in Interactive Technologies, Alberta Innovates Technology Futures, NSERC, and SMART Technologies Inc.

REFERENCES

1. Ballagas, R., Ringel, M., Stone, M., and Borchers, J. iStuff: a physical user interface toolkit for ubiquitous computing environments. *Proc. of CHI'03*, ACM (2003).
2. Ballendat, T., Marquardt, N., and Greenberg, S. Proxemic Interaction: Designing for a Proximity and Orientation-Aware Environment. *Proc. of ITS'10*, ACM (2010).
3. Boyle, M. and Greenberg, S. Rapidly prototyping multimedia groupware. *Proc. of DMS, Knowl. Sys. Institute*, (2005).
4. Dey, A.K., et al. A conceptual framework and a toolkit for supporting the rapid prototyping of context-aware applications. *Hum.-Comp. Int. 16*, 2, L. Erlbaum (2001), 97-166.
5. Diaz-Marino, R. and Greenberg, S. The proximity toolkit and ViconFace: the video. *Ext. Abst. CHI '10*, ACM (2010).
6. Feiner, S., et al. A touring machine: Prototyping 3D mobile augmented reality systems for exploring the urban environment. *Personal Technologies 1*, 4 (1997), 208-217.
7. Gamma, E., et al. *Design Patterns: Elements of Reusable Object-Oriented Software*. Addison-Wesley, 1994.
8. Greenberg, S. and Fitchett, C. Phidgets: Easy Development of Physical Interfaces Through Physical Widgets. *Proc. of UIST'01*, ACM (2001), 209–218.
9. Greenberg, S., Marquardt, N., et al. Proxemic interactions: the new ubicomp? *interactions 18*, ACM (2011), 42–50.
10. GroupLab. *Proximity Toolkit website, http://grouplab.cpsc.ucalgary.ca/proximitytoolkit,* Retrieved July 5, 2011.
11. Hall, E.T. *The Hidden Dimension*. Doubleday, N.Y, 1966.
12. Hartmann, B., et al. Reflective physical prototyping through integrated design, test, and analysis. *Proc. UIST*, ACM (2006).
13. Hightower, J., et al. The location stack: A layered model for location in ubiquitous computing. *Proc. of WMCSA'02*, (2002).
14. Ishii, H. and Ullmer, B. Tangible Bits: Towards Seamless Interfaces Between People, Bits and Atoms. *Proc. of CHI'97*, ACM (1997), 234–241.
15. Ju, W., et al. Range: exploring implicit interaction through electronic whiteboard design. *Proc. of CSCW'08*, ACM (2008).
16. Klemmer, S.R., et al. Papier-Mache: Toolkit Support for Tangible Input. *Proc. of CHI'04*, ACM (2004), 399–406.
17. Kortuem, G., et al. Sensing and visualizing spatial relations of mobile devices. *Proc. of UIST'05*, ACM (2005), 93-102.
18. Krumm, J. and Hinckley, K. The NearMe wireless proximity server. *Lecture notes in computer science*, (2004), 283-300.
19. Li, Y., et al. Topiary: a tool for prototyping location-enhanced applications. *Proc. of UIST '04*, ACM (2004).
20. MacIntyre, B., et al. DART: a toolkit for rapid design exploration of augmented reality experiences. *Proc. of UIST'04*, ACM (2004).
21. Marquardt, N. and Greenberg, S. Distributed Physical Interfaces with Shared Phidgets. *Proc. of TEI'07*, ACM (2007).
22. Matthews, T., et al. A toolkit for managing user attention in peripheral displays. *Proc. of UIST '04*, ACM (2004).
23. Myers, B.A., et al. Past, Present, and Future of User Interface Software Tools. *TOCHI 7*, 1, ACM (2000), 3–28.
24. PrimeSense. *OpenNI SDK, http://www.openni.org,* Accessed July 5, 2011.
25. Reitmayr, G. et al. OpenTracker: A flexible software design for three-dimensional interaction. *Virt. Reality 9*, (2005).
26. Sandor, C. and Klinker, G. A rapid prototyping software infrastructure for user interfaces in ubiquitous augmented reality. *Pers. and Ubiq. Comp. 9*, (2005).
27. Schwarz, J., et al. A framework for robust and flexible handling of inputs with uncertainty. *Proc of UIST*, ACM (2010).
28. Snibbe, S.S. et al. Social immersive media: pursuing best practices for multi-user interactive camera/projector exhibits. *Proc. of CHI '09*, ACM (2009), 1447–1456.
29. Streitz, N., et al. Ambient displays and mobile devices for the creation of social architectural spaces. In *Public and Situated Displays*. Kluwer, 2003, 387-410.
30. Vicon Motion Systems. *Nexus software, http://www.vicon.com/products/nexus.html,* Retrieved July 5, 2011.
31. Vogel, D. et al. Interactive public ambient displays: transitioning from implicit to explicit, public to personal, interaction with multiple users. *Proc. of UIST'04*, ACM (2004).
32. Weiser, M. The Computer for the 21st Century. *Scientific American 265*, (1991), 94.
33. Zhao, T., Aggarwal, M., Kumar, R., and Sawhney, H. Real-Time Wide Area Multi-Camera Stereo Tracking. *Proc. of CVPR'05*, IEEE (2005), 976–983.

ZeroN: Mid-Air Tangible Interaction Enabled by Computer Controlled Magnetic Levitation

Jinha Lee[1], *Rehmi Post*[2], *Hiroshi Ishii*[1]

[1]MIT Media Laboratory
75 Amherst St.
Cambridge, MA, 02139
{jinhalee, ishii}@media.mit.edu

[2]MIT Center for Bits and Atoms
20 Ames St.
Cambridge, MA, 02139
rehmi.post@cba.mit.edu

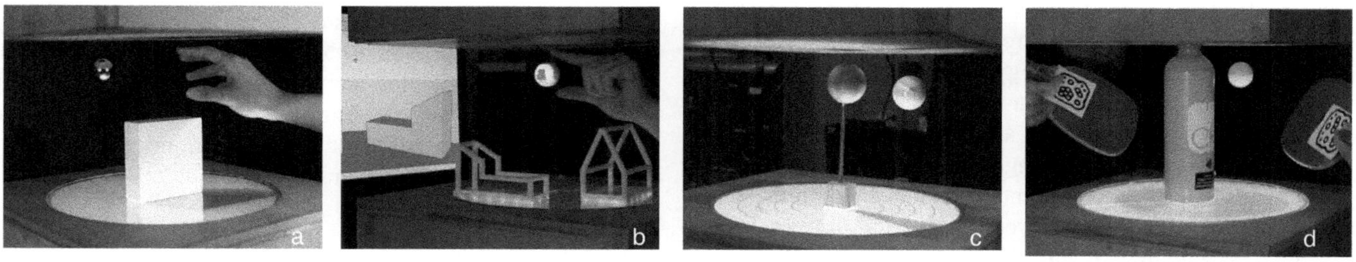

Figure 1. What if users could take a physical object off the surface and place it in the air? ZeroN enables such mid-air tangible interaction with computer controlled magnetic levitation. Various 3D applications can be redesigned with this interaction modality: a),b) architectural simulation, c) physics simulation, d) entertainment: tangible 3D pong-game.

ABSTRACT

This paper presents ZeroN, a new tangible interface element that can be levitated and moved freely by computer in a three dimensional space. ZeroN serves as a tangible representation of a 3D coordinate of the virtual world through which users can see, feel, and control computation. To accomplish this we developed a magnetic control system that can levitate and actuate a permanent magnet in a predefined 3D volume. This is combined with an optical tracking and display system that projects images on the levitating object. We present applications that explore this new interaction modality. Users are invited to place or move the ZeroN object just as they can place objects on surfaces. For example, users can place the sun above physical objects to cast digital shadows, or place a planet that will start revolving based on simulated physical conditions. We describe the technology, interaction scenarios and challenges, discuss initial observations, and outline future development.

ACM Classification: H5.2 [Information interfaces and presentation]: User Interfaces.

General terms: Design, Human Factors

Keywords: Tangible Interfaces, 3D UI.

INTRODUCTION

Tangible interfaces attempt to bridge the gap between virtual and physical spaces by embodying the digital in the physical world [7]. Tabletop tangible interfaces have demonstrated a wide range of interaction possibilities and utilities. Despite their compelling qualities, tabletop tangible interfaces share a common constraint. Interaction with physical objects is inherently constrained to 2D planar surfaces due to gravity. This limitation might not appear to be a constraint for many tabletop interfaces, when content is mapped to surface components, but we argue that there are exciting possibilities enabled by supporting true 3D manipulation. There has been some movement in this direction already; researchers are starting to explore interactions with three-dimensional content using space above the tabletop surfaces [5][4]. In these scenarios input can be sensed in the 3D physical space, but the objects and rendered graphics are still bound to the surfaces.

Imagine a physical object that can float, seemingly unconstrained by gravity, and move freely in the air. What would it be like to leave this physical object at a spot in the air, representing a light that casts the virtual shadow of an architectural model, or a planet which will start orbiting. Our motivation is to create such a 3D space, where the computer can control the 3D position and movement of gravitationally unconstrained physical objects that represent digital information.

In this paper, we present a system for tangible interaction in mid-air 3D space. At its core, our goal is to allow users to take physical components of tabletop tangible interfaces off

Figure 2. ZeroN can represent a 3D coordinate of the virtual world. Ex. displaying an orbit of a planet.

the surface and place them in the air. To investigate these interaction techniques, we created our first prototype with magnetic levitation technology. We call this new tangible interaction element ZeroN, a magnetically actuated object that can hover and move in an open volume, representing digital objects moving through 3D coordinates of the virtual world. Users can place or move this object in the air to simulate or affect the 3D computational process represented as actuation of the object as well as accompanied graphical projection.

We contribute a technical implementation of magnetic levitation. The technology includes stable long-range magnetic levitation combined with interactive projection, optical and magnetic sensing, and mechanical actuation that realizes a small 'anti-gravity space'. In the following sections, we describe our engineering approach and the current limitations as well as a road map of development necessary to scale the current interface.

We investigate novel interaction techniques through a set of applications we developed with ZeroN. Based on reflection from our user observation, we identify design issues and technical challenges unique to interaction with this untethered levitated object. In the following discussion, we will refer to the levitated object simply as *ZeroN* and the entire ensemble as the *ZeroN system*.

RELATED WORK

Our work draws upon the literature of Tangible Interfaces, 3D display and interaction techniques. As we touch upon the evolution of tabletop tangible interfaces, we review movements towards employing actuation and 3D space in human computer interaction.

Tabletop Tangible Interfaces

Underkoffler [22] and Patten [12] have shown how the collaborative manipulation of tangible input elements by multiple users can enhance task performance and creativity in spatial applications, such as architecture simulation and supply chain optimization. Reactable [9], AudioPad [13], or Datatiles [19] show compelling qualities of bimanual interaction in dynamically arranging visual and audio information.

In previous tabletop tangible interfaces, while users can provide input by manipulating physical objects, output occurs only through graphical projection. This can cause inconsistency between physical objects and digital information when the state of the underlying digital system changes. Adding actuation to an interface, such that states of physical objects are coupled with dynamically changing digital states will allow the computer to maintain consistency between the physical and digital states of objects.

In Actuated Workbench [11], an array of computer-controlled electromagnets actuates physical objects on the surface, which represent the dynamic status of computation. Planar Manipulator [20] or Augmented Coliseum [21] achieved similar technical capabilities using robotic modules. Recent examples of such actuated tabletop interfaces include madget, a system that has the capability of actuating complex tangibles composed of multiple parts [23]. Patten's PICO [14] has demonstrated how physical actuation can enable users to improvise mechanical constraints to add computational constraint in the system.

Going Higher

One approach to the transition of 2D modalities to 3D has been using deformable surfaces as input and output. Illuminating Clay employs deformable physical material as a medium of input where users can directly manipulate the state of the system [15]. In Lumino, stackable tangible pucks are used to express discrete height as another input modality [1].

While in this system the computer cannot modify physical representation, there has been research in adding height as another output component to RGB pixels using computer-controlled actuation. Poupyrev, et.al provide an excellent overview of shape displays [18]. To actuate deformable surfaces, Lumen [17] and FEELEX [8] employ an array of motorized sticks that can be raised. Art+com's kinetic sculpture actuates multiple spheres tethered with string to create the silhouette of cars [24]. Despite their compelling qualities as shape display, they share two common limitations as interfaces. First, input is limited by the push and pull of objects, whereas more degrees of freedom of input may be desired in many applications; users might also want to push or drag the displayed object laterally. More importantly, because the objects are physically tethered, it is difficult for users to reach under or above the deformable surface in the interactive space.

Using Space above the Tabletop surface

Hilliges and et al. show that 3D mid-air input can be used to manipulate virtual objects on a tabletop surface using the second-light infrastructure [5]. Grossman et.al introduced interaction techniques with 3D volumetric display [3]. While they demonstrate a potential approach of exploiting real 3D space as an input area, the separation of a user's input from the rendered graphics does not afford direct control as in the physical world, and may lead to ambiguities in the interface. A remedy for this issue of I/O inconsistency may come from technologies that display free-standing volumetric images, such as digital holography. However these technologies are not yet mature, and even when they can be fully implemented, direct manipulation of these media would be challenging due to lack of a persistent tangible representation.

Haptic and Magnetic Technologies for 3D Interaction

Studies with haptic devices, such as Phantom, have shown that accurate force feedback can increase task performance in the context of medical training and 3D modeling [10]. While most of these systems were used with a single monitor or head-mounted display, Plesniak's system lets users directly touch a 3D holographic display to obtain input and output coincidences [16]. Despite their compelling practical qualities, tethered devices constrain the degree of freedom in user input. In addition, constraining the view angle often isolates the user from real world context and restricts multi-user scenarios.

Magnetic levitation has been researched in the realms of haptic interfaces [2] and robotics [6] to achieve increased degrees of freedom. Berkelman and et al. developed a high-performance magnetic levitation haptic interfaces to enable the user to better interact with simulated virtual environments [2]. Since their system was designed to be used as a haptic controller of graphical displays, the emphasis was on creating accurate force feedback with a stable magnetic field in a semi-enclosed hemispherical space. On the other hand, our focus was on achieving a collocated I/O by actuating an I/O object along the 3D paths through absolute coordinates of the physical space. Consequently, more engineering efforts were made to actuate a levitated object in an open 3D space in a reasonably stable manner.

3D and Tangible Interaction

Grossman and Wigdor present an excellent taxonomy and framework of 3D tabletop interfaces based on the dimensions of display and input space [4]. Our work aims to explore a realm where both display and input occur in 3D space, mediated by a computer-controlled tangible object, and therefore enabling users' direct manipulation. In the taxonomy [4], physical proxy was considered an important 2D I/O element that defines user interaction. However, our work employs a tangible proxy as an active display component to convey 3D information. Therefore, to fully understand the implication of the work, it is necessary to create a new framework based on spatial properties of physical proxies in tabletop interfaces. We plotted existing tabletop interfaces in figure 3 based on the dimension of the I/O space and whether the tangible elements can be actuated.

Our paper explores this novel design space of tangible interaction in the mid-air space above the surface. While currently limited in resolution and practical quality, we look to study what is possible by using mid-air 3D space for tangible interaction. We aim to create a system where users can interact with 3D information through manipulating computationally controlled physical objects, without physical tethering by mechanical armatures or requiring users to wear an optical device such as a head-mounted display.

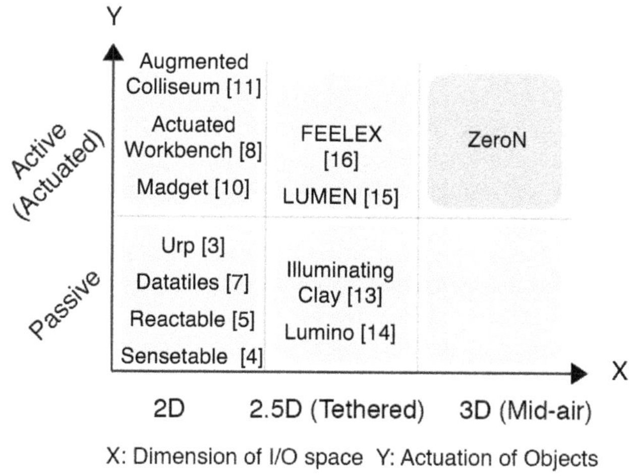

Figure 1. A framework for tabletop tangible interfaces based on the dimension of I/O space and actuation

OVERVIEW

Our system operates over a volume of 38cm x 38cm x 9cm, in which it can levitate, sense, and control the 3D position of the ZeroN, a spherical magnet with a 3.17cm diameter covered with plastic shell onto which digital imagery can be projected. As a result, the digital information bound with a physical object can be seen, felt, and manipulated in the operating volume without requiring users to be tethered by mechanical armatures or to wear optical devices. Due to the current limitation of the levitation range, we made the entire interactive space is larger than this 'anti-gravity' space, such that users can interact with ZeroN with reasonable freedom of movement.

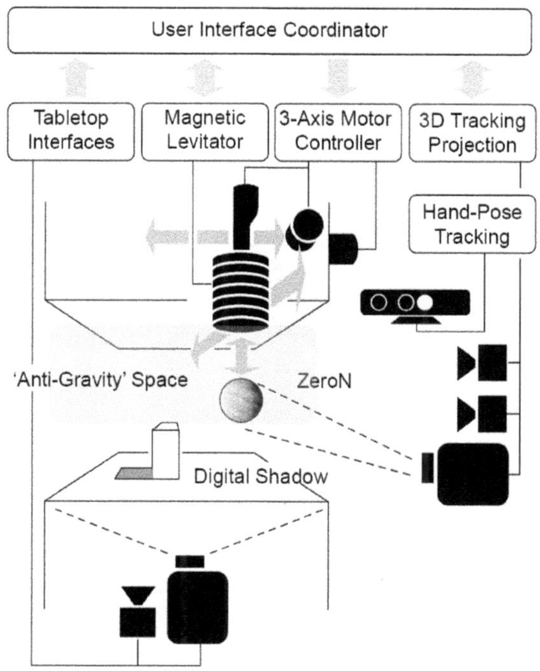

Figure 4. Overview of the ZeroN System

TECHNICAL IMPLEMENTATION

The current prototype comprises five key elements as illustrated in figure 4.

- A magnetic levitator (a coil driven by PWM signals) that suspends a magnetic object and is capable of changing the object's vertical suspension distance on command.
- A 2-axis linear actuation stage that laterally positions the magnetic levitator and one additional linear actuator for moving the coil vertically.
- Stereo cameras that track ZeroN's 3D position.
- A depth camera to detect users' hand poses.
- A tabletop interface displaying a scene coordinated with the position of the suspended object and other objects placed on the table.

Untethered 3D Actuation

The ZeroN system implements untethered 3D actuation of a physical object with magnetic control and mechanical actuation. Vertical motion was achieved by combining magnetic position control which can levitate and move a magnet relative to the coil, and mechanical actuation that can move the entire coil relative to the entire system. Two approaches complement each other. Although the magnetic approach can control the position with lower latency and implies promising direction for scalable magnetic propulsion technology, the prototype with pure magnetic controls demonstrated limits in its range: when the permanent magnet gets too close to the coil it becomes attached to the coil even when the coil is not energized. 2D lateral motion was achieved with a plotter using two stepper motors. Given a 3D path as input, the system first projects the path on each dimension, and linearly interpolates the dots to create a smooth trajectory. Then the system calculates velocity and acceleration of each axis of actuation as a function of time. With this data, the system can actuate the object along a 3D path approximately identical to the input path.

Magnetic Levitation and Vertical Control

We have developed a custom electromagnetic suspension system to provide robust sensing, levitation, and vertical control. It includes a microcontroller implementing a proportional-integral-derivative (PID) control loop with parameters that can be set through a serial interface. In particular, ZeroN's suspension distance is set through this interface by the UI coordinator. The PID controller drives the electromagnet through a coil driver using pulse-width modulation (PWM). The field generated by the electromagnet imposes an attractive (or repulsive) force on the suspended magnetic object. By dynamically canceling gravity by exerting a magnetic force on ZeroN, the control loop keeps it suspended at a given distance from the electromagnet. This distance is determined by measuring the magnetic field immediately beneath the solenoid.

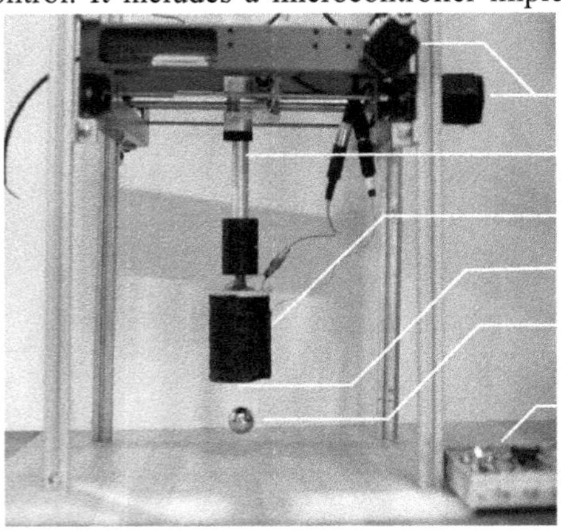

Figure 5. Mechanical actuation combined with magnetic vertical control enables 3D untethered actuation of an object.

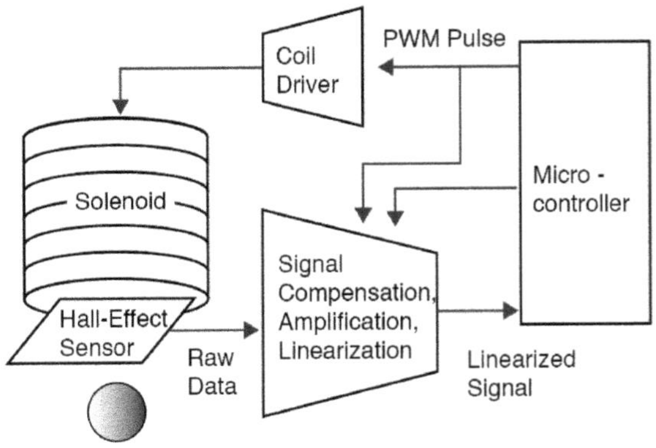

Figure 6. A simplified version of the magnetic range sensing and levitation circuits.

Magnetic Range Sensing with Hall-effect sensor

Properly measuring the distance of a magnet is the key component in stable levitation and vertical control. Since the magnetic field drops off as the cube of the distance from the source, it is challenging to convert the strength of the magnetic field to the vertical position of a magnet. To linearize signals sensed by the hall-effect sensor, we developed the two-step gain logarithmic amplifier. It logarithmically amplifies the signal with two different gains, based on whether the signal exceeded a threshold voltage value.

Designing ZeroN Object

We used a spherical dipole magnet as a levitating object. Due to the geometry of magnetic field, users can move the spherical dipole magnet while still keeping it suspended, but it falls when they tilt it. To enable input of a user's desired orientation, a loose plastic layer is added to cover the magnet as illustrated in figure 7.

Stereo Tracking of 3D position and 1D orientation

We used two modified Sony PS3Eyecams[1] to track the 3D position of ZeroN using computer vision techniques with a pair of infrared images as in figure 8. To measure orientation, we applied a stripe of retro-reflective tape to the surface of ZeroN. We chose this approach because it was both technically simple and robust, and didn't add significant weight to ZeroN: an important factor in a levitating object.

[1] http://codelaboratories.com/products/eye/sdk/

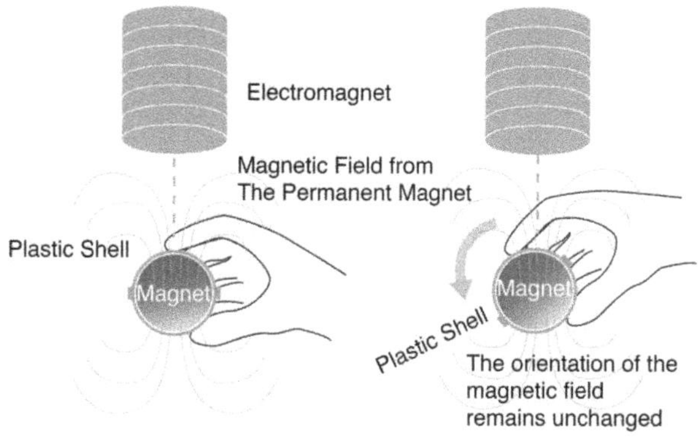

Figure 7. ZeroN Object comprises a permanent magnet loosely covered with a plastic shell. Users can tilt the shell without changing the orientation of the levitated magnet.

Determining Modes

A challenge in emulating the 'anti-gravity space' is to determine if ZeroN is being moved by a user, or is naturally wobbling. Currently, ZeroN sways laterally when actuated, and the system can misinterpret this movement for user input and continue to update a new stable point of suspension. This causes ZeroN to drift around. To resolve this issue, we classify three modes of operation (idle, grabbed, grabbed for long) based on whether, and for how long, the user is holding the object. In the idle mode, when ZeroN is not grabbed by the user, the control system acts to keep the position or trajectory of the levitating object as programmed by the computer. When grabbed by the user, the system updates the stable position based on the current position specified by the users, such that the users can release their hands without dropping the object. If the user is grabbing the object for longer than 2.5s, it starts specific functions such as record and play back.

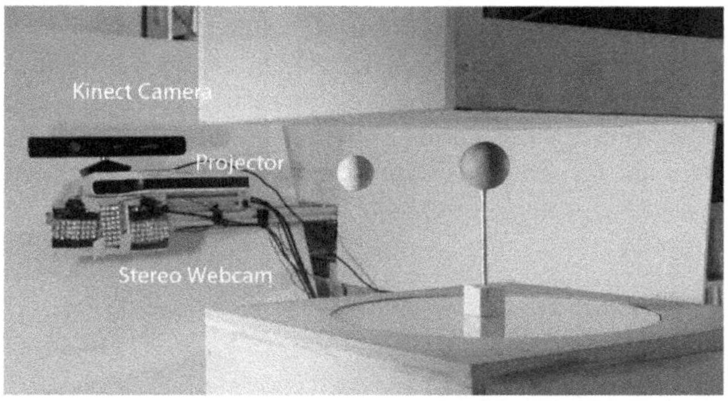

Figure 8. Tracking and Projection System of ZeroN.

While stereo IR cameras were useful in obtaining the accurate position and orientation of the object using retro-reflective tape, it was challenging to distinguish users' hands from background or objects. We chose to use an additional depth camera Microsoft Kinect to detect the user's hand pose with computer vision techniques built on top of

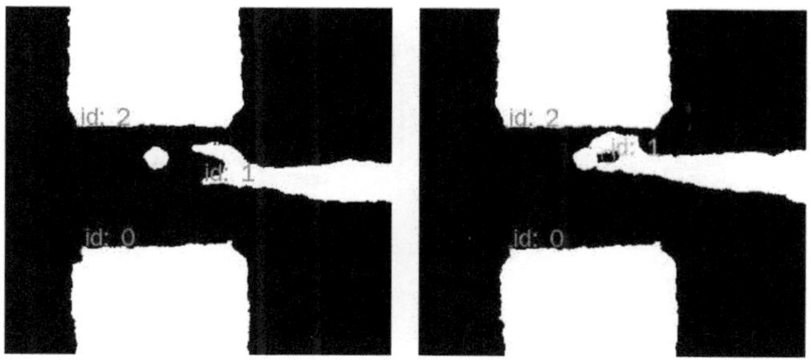

Figure 9. Kinect camera can be used to sense if the user is holding the levitated object or not.

open-source libraries[2]. Our software extracts binary contours of objects at a predefined depth range and finds the blob created between the user's hands and the levitated object.

Calibration of 3D Sensing, Projection, and Actuation

To ensure real time interaction, careful calibration between cameras, projectors and 3D actuation system is essential in our implementation. After finding correspondence between two cameras with checkerboard patterns, we register cameras with the coordinate of interactive space. We position the ZeroN object at each of these fixed four non-coplanar points. Similarly, to register each projector to real-world coordinates, we match the ZeroN positioned at the four non-coplanar calibration points and move a projected image of a circle towards the ZeroN. When the circular image is overlaid on the ZeroN, we increase or decrease the size of the circle image so that it matches the size of ZeroN. This data is used to find two homogenous matrices that transform raw camera coordinates to real world coordinates of the interactive space, and the real coordinates to x, y position and the diameter of the circle. We have not made much effort to optimally determine the focal plane of the projected image - focusing the projectors roughly in the middle of the interactive space is sufficient.

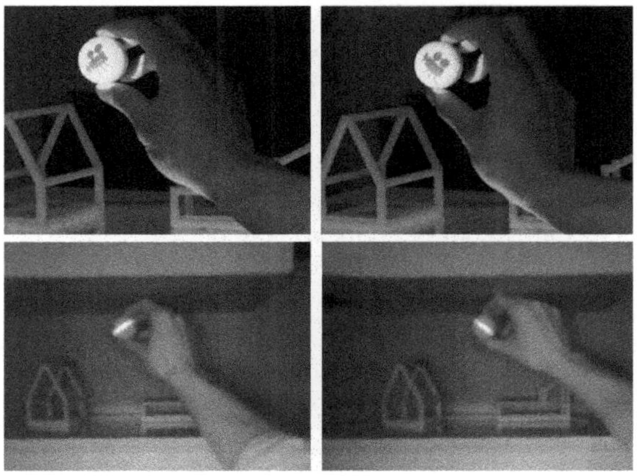

Figure 10. As the user tilts the outer plastic layer, the system senses the orientation and updates the projected images, while the spherical magnet stays in the same orientation.

[2] https://github.com/ofTheo/ofxKinect

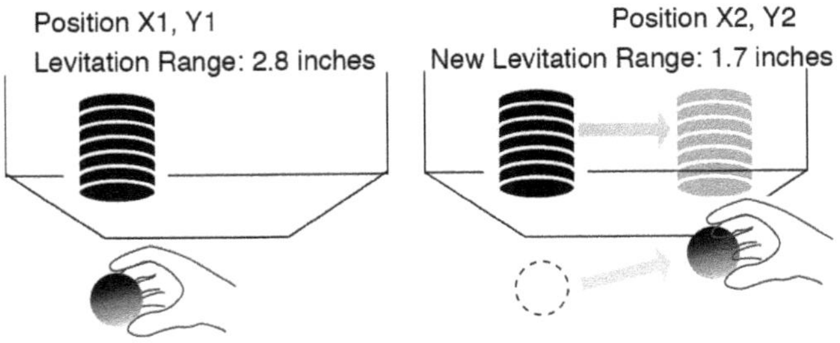

Figure 11. The system can update the stable point of suspension when the user moves the ZeroN to another position.

Engineering 'Anti-Gravity' Space

These various sensing and actuation techniques coordinate to create a seamless 'anti-gravity' I/O space. When the user grabs the ZeroN and places it within the defined space of the system, the system tracks the 3D position of the object, and determines if the user's hand is grabbing ZeroN. The electromagnet is then carried to the 2D position of ZeroN by the 2-axis actuators, and is programmed to reset a new stable point of suspension at a sensed vertical position. As a result, this system creates what we will call a small 'anti-gravity' space, wherein people can place an object in a volume seemingly unconstrained by gravity. The user's hands and other non-magnetic materials do not affect levitation.

Since the levitation controller acts to keep the floating object at a given height, users experience the sensation of an invisible but very tangible mechanical connection between the levitated magnet and a fixed point in space that can be continually updated.

3D POINT AND PATH DISPLAY

ZeroN serves as a dynamic tangible representation of a 3D coordinate, without being tethered by mechanical armature. 3D Position of ZeroN may be updated upon computer commands to present dynamic movements or curved lines in the 3D space such as flight paths of the airplane or orbits of planets. Graphical images or icons may be projected upon the white surface of ZeroN levitating, such as a camera or the pattern of a planet. These graphical images can be animated or 'tilted' to display change of orientation. This complements the limitation of current magnetic actuation system that can only control the 3D position of a magnet, but has little control on its orientation.

INTERACTION

We have developed a 3D, tangible interaction language that closely resembles how people interact with physical objects on a 2D surface – put, move, rotate, and drag, which now serves as a standard metaphor, widely used in many interaction design domains including GUIs and tabletop interfaces. We list the vocabulary of our interaction language (figure 12).

Place

One can place ZeroN in the air, suspending it at an arbitrary 3D position within the interactive space.

Translate

Users can also move ZeroN to another position in the anti-gravity space, without disturbing its ability to levitate.

Rotate

When users rotate the plastic shell covering the spherical magnet, digital images projected on the ZeroN will rotate accordingly.

Hold

Users can hold or block ZeroN to impede computer actuation. This can be interpreted as computational constraint as also shown in PICO [14].

Long Hold

We implemented a long-hold gesture that can be used to initiate a specific function. For example, in a video recording application, we might have an interaction where users could hold the ZeroN for longer than 2.5 seconds to initiate recording, and release to enter "play-back" mode.

Attaching / Detaching Digital Information to the ZeroN

We borrowed a gesture for attaching / detaching digital items to tabletop interfaces [12] It is challenging to interact with multiple information clusters, since the current system can only levitate one object. For instance, in the application of urban planning simulation [22], users might first want to use ZeroN as the Sun to control lighting, and then as a camera to render the scene. Users can attach ZeroN to a digital item projected on the tabletop surface on the ground, just by moving the ZeroN close to the digital item to be bind with. To unbind a digital item from a ZeroN, users can use shaking gestures or remove the ZeroN from the interactive space.

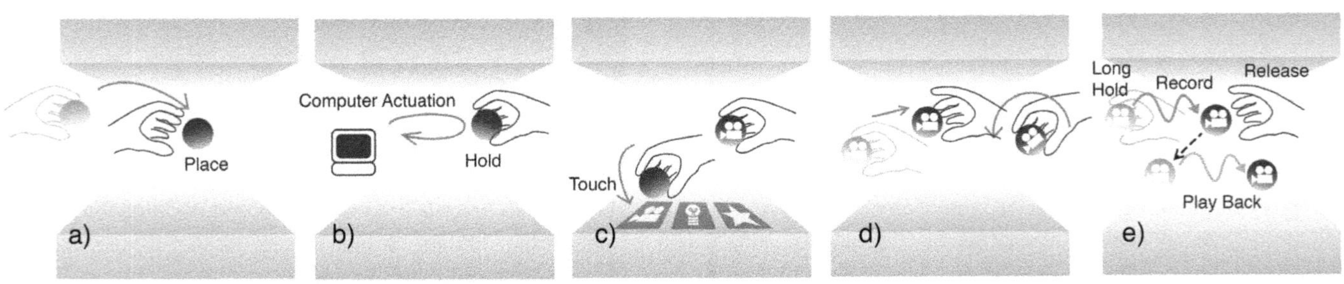

Figure 12: ZeroN introduces a novel interaction language: (a) Users places ZeroN in the air; (b) the computer actuates ZeroN and users intervene with the movement of ZeroN; (c) digital item attached to ZeroN; (d) ZeroN translated and rotated in the air; (e) long hold used to record and play back.

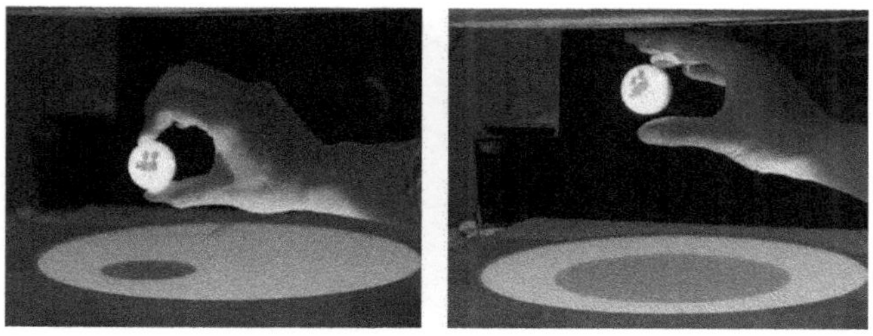

Figure 13. The size of digital shadow is mapped to the height of ZeroN.

Interaction with Digital Shadows

We aim to seamlessly incorporate ZeroN into existing tabletop tangible interfaces. One of the challenges is to provide users with a semantic link between the levitated object and tabletop tangible interfaces on the 2D surface. Since ZeroN is not physically in contact with the tabletop system, it is hard to recognize the relative position of the ZeroN to the other objects placed on the ground. We designed an interactive digital shadow to provide users with visible links between ZeroN and other part of the tabletop tangible interfaces. For instance, levitating ZeroN itself can cast its digital shadow whose size is mapped to the height of the object (see figure 13). For the time being, however, this feature is not yet incorporated in the application scenarios.

APPLICATIONS AND USER REFLECTION

We explore the previously described interaction techniques in context of several categories of applications described below. While the physics and architecture simulation allows users to begin using ZeroN to address a practical problem, the prototyping animation and Zero-pong applications are proof of concepts to demonstrate the interactions one might have with ZeroN.

Physics Simulation and Education

ZeroN can serve as a tangible physics simulator by displaying and actuating physical objects under computationally controlled physical conditions. As a result, dynamic computer simulation can turn into tangible reality, which had previously been possible only in the virtual world. More importantly, users can interrupt or affect the simulation process by blocking actuation with their hands or by introducing other physical objects in the ZeroN space.

Understanding Kepler's Law

In this application, users can simulate a planet's movement in the solar system by placing at the simulation's center, a static object that represents the center of mass as the Sun,

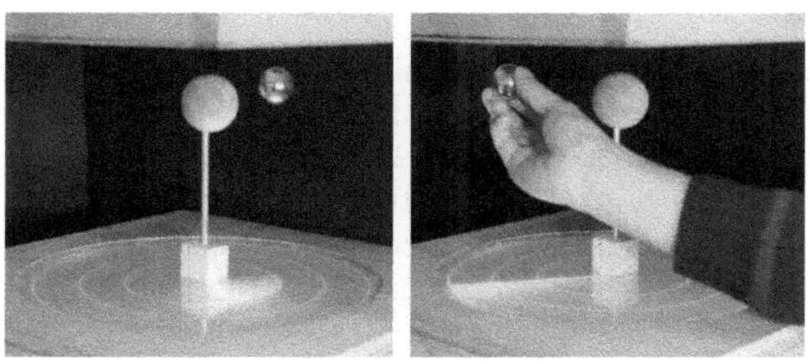

Figure 14. A user is changing the orbit of the ZeroN.

around which the ZeroN will revolve like a planet. Users can change the distance between the Sun and the planet, which will make the ZeroN snap to another orbit. Resulting changes can be observed and felt in motion and speed. Digital projection shows the area that a line joining a ZeroN and the Sun sweeps out during a certain period of time, confirming Kepler's 2nd law (see figure 15).

Three-Body Problem

In this application, users can generate a gravity field by introducing multiple passive objects that represent fixed centers of gravity. A placed ZeroN next to the object will orbit around based on the result of the 3–body simulation. Users can add or change the gravitational field by simply placing more passive objects, which can be identified by a tabletop interface setup (see figure 15).

Figure 15. Visualizing 3-body problem.

Architectural Planning

While there has been much research exploring tangible interfaces in the space of architectural planning, some of the essential components, such as lights or cameras, cannot be represented as a tangible object that can be directly manipulated. For instance, Urp system [22] allows users to directly control the arrangement of physical buildings, but lighting can only be controlled by rotating a separate time-dial. While it is not our goal to stress that direct manipulation outperforms indirect manipulation, there are certainly various scenarios where having direct manipulation of tangible representation is important. We developed two applications for gathering users' feedback.

Lighting Control

We developed an application for controlling external architectural lighting in which users can grab and place a Sun in the air to control the digital shadow cast by physical models

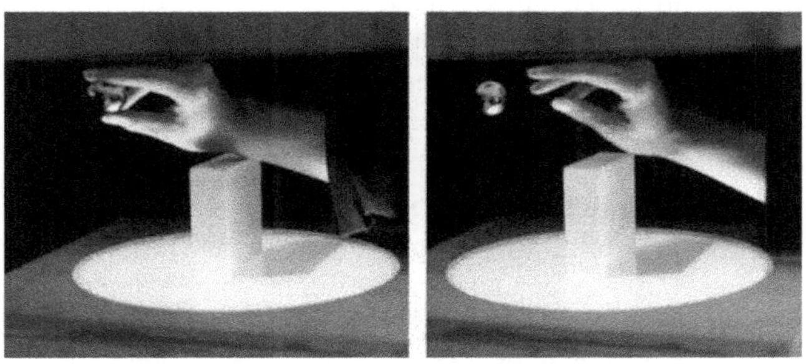

Figure 16. Users can place the Sun above physical models to cast its digital shadow.

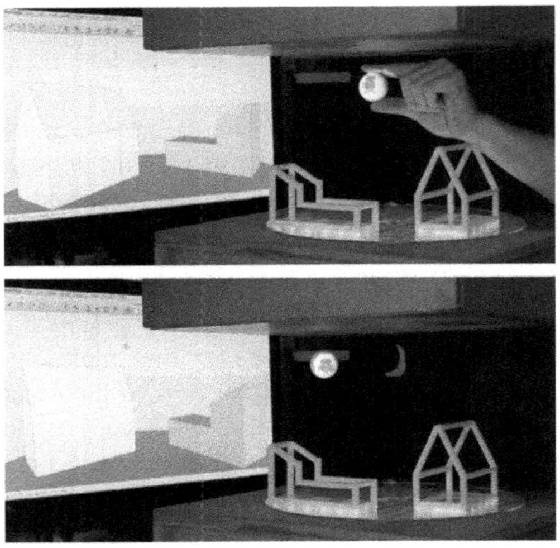

Figure 17. The user can create and edit 3D camera paths above the physical model and see the camera flying along the path.

on the tabletop surface. The computer can simulate changes in the position of the lighting, such as chances over the day, and the representative Sun will be actuated to reflect these changes.

Camera Path Control

Users can create 3D camera paths for rendering virtual scenes using ZeroN as a camera. Attaching ZeroN to the camera icon displayed on the surface turns the sun into a camera object. Users can then hold the ZeroN for a number of seconds in one position to initiate a recording interaction. When users draw a 3D path in the air and release the ZeroN, the camera is sent back to initial position and then moved along the previously recorded 3D trajectory. On an additional screen, users can see the virtual scene of their model taken by the camera's perspective in real time. If the user wants to edit this path, they can intervene with the camera's path and start from the exact current position of the camera to redraw another path.

3D Motion Prototyping

Creating and editing 3D motion for animation is a long and complex process with conventional interfaces, requiring expert knowledge of the software, even for simple prototyping. With record and play-back interaction, users can easily prototype the 3D movement of an object and watch it playing back in the real world. The motion can possibly be mapped to a 3D digital character moving accordingly on the screen with dynamic virtual environments. As a result, users can not only see, but also feel the 3D motion of the object they created. They can go through this interaction through a simple series of gestures; long-hold and release.

Entertainment: Tangible 3D Pong in the physical space

Being able to arbitrarily program the movement of a physical object, ZeroN can be used for digital entertainment. We partially implemented and demonstrated a Tangible 3D Pong application with ZeroN as a pingpong ball. In this scenario, users can play computer-enhanced pong game with a floating ball whose physical behavior is computationally programmed. Users can hit or block the movement of ZeroN to change the trajectory of the ping-pong ball. They can add computational constraints in this game by placing a physical object in this interactive space as in figure 18. While this partially implemented application demonstrates interesting challenges, it suggests a new potential infrastructure for computer entertainment, where human and computation embodied in the motion of physical objects are in the tight loop of interaction.

Figure 18. Tangible Pong in the physical space.

INITIAL REFLECTION AND DISCUSSION

We demonstrated our prototype to users to gather initial feedback and recruited several participants to try out each application. The purpose of this study was to evaluate our design, rather than to exemplify the practicality of each application. We further discuss several interesting unique issues that we discovered through this observation.

Leaving a Physical Object in the Air

In the camera path control application, users appreciated the fact that they could leave a physical camera object in the air and review and edit the trajectory in a tangible way. There were commented that latency in the electromagnet's stability update (between users' displacement and the electromagnet's update of the stable position) creates confusion. In the lighting control application, a user commented that they could better discuss with a collaborator using a system that enables the object to be held in a position in the air. Many of participants also pointed out the issue of lateral oscillation, which we are working to improve.

Interaction Legibility

In the physics education application, a several users commented that not being able to see physical relationship between 'planets' make them harder to expect how to interact with this system, or what would happen if they touch and move the parts. Being able to actuate an object without mechanical linkages in free space allows a more degrees of freedom of movements and allows access from all orientations. On the other hand, this decreases the legibility of interaction by making the mechanical linkages invisible. In contrast a historical orrery (figure 19) machine where the movement of 'planets' are constrained by its mechanical connections, users can immediately understand the freedom of movement that the mechanical structure affords.

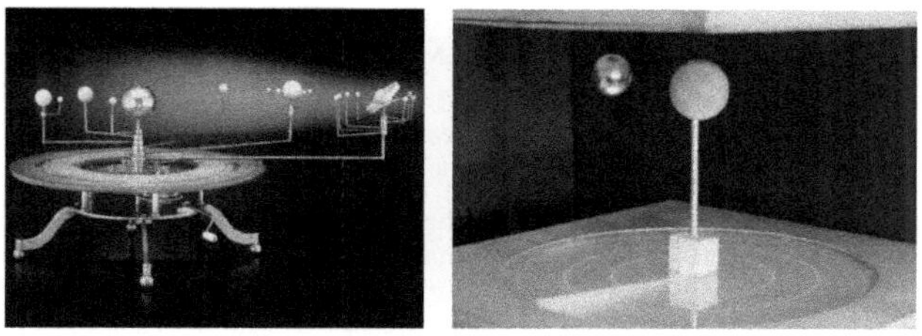

Figure 19. Physical orrery and ZeroN: hiding mechanical structures increases degrees of freedom, but decreases legibility of interaction.

One of the possible solutions to compensate this loss of legibility is to rely on graphical projection or subtle movements of the objects to indicate the constraints of the movement. Carefully choosing an application where the gain of freedom outweighs the loss of legibility was our criteria for choosing application scenarios.

TECHNICAL EVALUATION

Maximum Levitation Range

The maximum range of magnetic levitation is limited by several factors. While our circuits can handle higher currents than currently used, an increased maximum range is limited by the heat generated in the coils. We used a 24V power supply, from which we drew 2A. Above that power, the heat generated by the electromagnet begins to melt its form core. The current prototype can levitate up to 7.4 cm measured from the bottom of the hall-effect sensor to the center of our spherical magnet. To scale up the system, a cooling system needs to be added on top of the coil.

Speed of actuation

The motor used in the system can carry the electromagnet with a maximum velocity of 30.5cm/s and top acceleration of $6.1 m/s^2$. The dynamic response of ZeroN's inertia is the main limit on acceleration. Because of the response properties of this second-order system (e.g. the electromagnet and ZeroN), larger accelerations fail to overcome ZeroN's inertia and would lead to ZeroN being dropped. The result of experiments measuring maximum intertia shows $3.9 m/s^2$ of the lateral acceleration can drop the ZeroN.

Resolution and Oscillation

If we frame our system as a 3D volumetric (physical) display in which only one cluster of voxels can be turned on at a time, we need to define the resolution of the system. Our 2D linear actuators can position the electromagnet at 250,000 different positions on each axis, and there is also no theoretical limit to the resolution of vertical control. However, vertical and horizontal oscillation of the levitated object makes it difficult to define this as the true system resolution. In the current prototype, ZeroN oscillates within 1.4 cm horizontally and 0.2 cm vertically around the set position when moved. We call the regions swept by oscillation "blurry" with "focused" area at its center.

Robustness of Magnetic Levitation

Robust levitation is a key factor for providing users with the sensation of an invisible mechanical connection with a fixed point in the air. We have conducted a series of experiments to measure how much strength can be posed on ZeroN without displacing it from a stable point of suspension. For these experiments, we attached the levitated magnet to a linear spring scale that can measure up to 1.2N of weight and pulled it towards the direction of 0° (horizontal), 15° 30°, 45°, 60°, 75°, and 90° (vertical). The average of 5 times' measurements is plotted in figure 20.

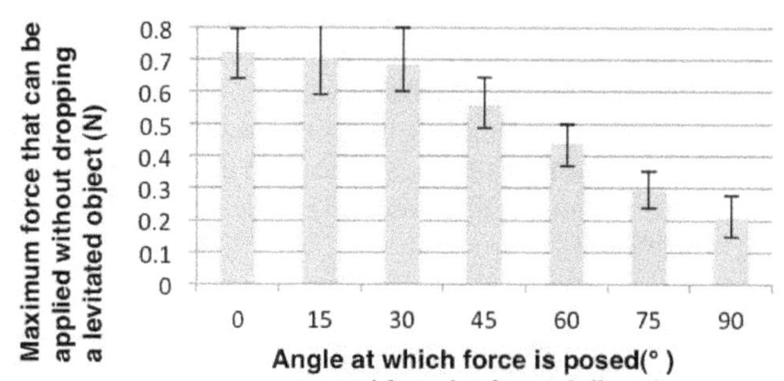

Figure 20. The system can update the stable point of suspension when users move the ZeroN to another position.

TECHNICAL LIMITATION AND FUTURE WORK

Lateral oscillation was reported as the biggest issue to correct in our application scenarios. We plan to implement satellite coils around the main electromagnet that can impose a magnetic force in a lateral direction to eliminate lateral wiggling and provide better haptic feedback. Another limitation with the current prototype is the limited vertical actuation range. This can be addressed by carefully designing the magnetic controller with better range sensing capabilities and choosing a geometry for the electromagnet that increases the range without overheating the coil.

A desirable extension is to use magnetic sensing technology with an array of hall-effect sensors in 3D tracking which would have provided more robust and low-latency object tracking without occlusion. We encountered difficulties using hall-effect sensor arrays in conjunction with our magnetic levitation system because of the strong magnetic field distortions caused by our electromagnets. We believe that this problem can be overcome in the future by subtracting magnetic field generated by electromagnets through precise calibration of dynamic magnetic field. But to avoid these difficulties in the short term, we added a vision tracking to our system prototype despite that this limits the hand input to areas that do not occlude the view of the camera.

Levitating Multiple Objects

While the current research was focused on identifying challenges in interacting with one levitated object, it is natural to imagine interaction with multiple objects in mid-air. A scalable solution will be using an array of solenoids. Under such setup, a magnet can be positioned at or moved to an arbitrary position between the centers of two or more solenoids by passing the necessary amount of current to each solenoid. It is analogous to pulling and hanging a ball with multiple invisible magnetic strings connected to the center of solenoids. However, it will be challenging to position two or more magnets within a small proximity due to magnetic field interference, or to position them on similar x, y coordinates. One approach to tackle this issue might come from levitating switchable magnets, turning them on and off to time-multiplex the influence that each object receives from the solenoids. We would like to leave this concept for future research.

CONCLUSION

This paper presents the concept of 3D mid-air tangible interaction. To explore this concept, we developed a magnetic control system that can levitate and actuate a permanent magnet in a three dimensional space, combined with an optical tracking and display system that projects images on the levitating object. We extend interaction scenarios that were constrained to 2D tabletop interaction to mid-air space, and developed novel interaction techniques. Raising tabletop tangible interfaces to 3D space above the surface opens up many opportunities and leaves many interaction design challenges. The focus of the paper is to explore these interaction modalities and although the current applications demonstrate many challenges, we are encouraged by what is enabled by the current system and will continue to develop scalable mid-air tangible interfaces.

We also envision that ZeroN could be extended for the manipulation of holographic displays. When 3D display technologies mature in the future, levitated objects can be directly coupled with holographic images projected in the air. We believe that ZeroN is the beginning of an exploration of this space within the larger field of future interaction design. One could imagine interfaces where discrete objects become like 3D pixels, allowing users to create and manipulate forms with their hands.

ACKNOWLEDGMENTS

The authors would like to thank the reviewers for their helpful critiques. We would also like to thank Robert Jacob, Joseph Paradiso, V. Michael Bove Jr., Pattie Maes, and students in the MIT Media Lab, Tangible Media Group for valuable discussions regarding the work. We also thank Surat Teerapittayanon, Bee Vang, Ilan Moyer and Max Lobovsky for their assistance in technical implementation. This work was supported by the Things that Think Consortia of the MIT Media Lab, MIT Center for Bits and Atoms, MIT Art Council and Samsung Scholarship Foundation.

REFERENCE

1. Baudisch, P., Becker, T., and Rudeck, F. 2010. Lumino: tangible building blocks based on glass fiber bundles. In ACM SIGGRAPH 2010 Emerging Technologies (SIGGRAPH '10). ACM, New York, NY, USA, , Article 16 , 1 pages.
2. Berkelman, P. J., Butler, Z. J., and Hollis, R. L., "Design of a Hemispherical Magnetic Levitation Haptic Interface Device," 1996 ASME IMECE, Atlanta, DSC-Vol. 58, pp. 483-488.
3. Grossman, T. and Balakrishnan, R. 2006. The design and evaluation of selection techniques for 3D volumetric displays. In ACM UIST '06. 3-12.
4. Grossman, T. and Wigdor, D. Going deeper: a taxonomy of 3D on the tabletop. In IEEE Tabletop '07. 2007. p. 137-144.
5. Hilliges, O., Izadi, S., Wilson, A. D., Hodges, S., Garcia-Mendoza, A., and Butz., A., 2009. Interactions in the air: adding further depth to interactive tabletops. In Proceedings of the 22nd annual ACM symposium on User interface software and technology (UIST '09). ACM, New York, NY 139-148.
6. Hollis, R. L. and Salcudean, S. E. 1993. Lorentz levitation technology: a new approach to fine motion robotics, teleoperation, haptic interfaces, and vibration isolation, In Proc. 6th Int'l Symposium on Robotics Research, October 2-5 1993.
7. Ishii, H. and Ullmer, B. 1997. Tangible bits: towards seamless interfaces between people, bits and atoms. In *Proceedings of the CHI'97*. ACM, New York, NY, 234-241.
8. Iwata, H., Yano, H., Nakaizumi, F., and Kawamura, R. 2001. Project FEELEX: adding haptic surface to graphics. In Proceedings of the 28th annual conference on Computer graphics and interactive techniques (SIGGRAPH '01). ACM, New York, NY, USA, 469-476.
9. Jorda, S. 2010. The reactable: tangible and tabletop music performance. InProceedings of the 28th of the international conference extended abstracts on Human factors in computing systems (CHI EA '10). ACM, New York, NY, USA, 2989-2994.
10. Massie, T. H. and Salisbury, K. "The PHANTOM Haptic Interface: A Device for Probing Virtual Objects." Proceedings of the ASME Winter Annual Meeting, Symposium on Haptic Interfaces for Virtual Environment and Teleoperator Systems,1994.
11. Pangaro, G., Maynes-Aminzade, D., and Ishii, H. 2002. The actuated workbench: computer-controlled actuation in tabletop tangible interfaces. In Proceedings of the 15th annual ACM symposium on User interface software and technology (UIST '02). ACM, New York, NY, USA, 181-190.
12. Patten, J., Ishii, H., Hines, J., and Pangaro, G. 2001. Sensetable: a wireless object tracking platform for tangible user interfaces. In CHI '01. ACM, New York, NY, 253-260.
13. Patten, J., Recht, B., and Ishii, H. 2006. Interaction techniques for musical performance with tabletop tangible interfaces. In Proceedings of the 2006 ACM SIGCHI international conference on Advances in computer entertainment technology (ACE '06). ACM, New York, NY, USA,Article 27.
14. Patten, J. and Ishii, H. 2007. Mechanical constraints as computational constraints in tabletop tangible interfaces. In Proceedings of the SIGCHI conference on Human factors in computing systems (CHI '07). ACM, New York, NY, USA, 809-818.
15. Piper, B., Ratti, C., and Ishii, H., Illuminating Clay: A 3-D Tangible Interface for Landscape Analysis, Proceedings of CHI 2002, 355-364.
16. Plesniak, W. J., "Haptic holography: an early computational plastic", Ph.D. Thesis, Program in Media Arts and Sciences, Massachusetts Institute of Technology, June 2001.
17. Poupyrev, I., Nashida, T., Maruyama, S., Rekimoto, J., and Yamaji, Y. 2004. Lumen: interactive visual and shape display for calm computing. In ACM SIGGRAPH 2004 Emerging technologies (SIGGRAPH '04), Heather Elliott-Famularo (Ed.). ACM, New York, NY, USA, 17.
18. Poupyrev, I., Nashida, T., and Okabe, M. 2007. Actuation and tangible user interfaces: the Vaucanson duck, robots, and shape displays. In Proceedings of the 1st international conference on Tangible and embedded interaction (TEI '07). ACM, New York, NY.
19. Rekimoto, J., Ullmer, B., and Oba, H. 2001. DataTiles: a modular platform for mixed physical and graphical interactions. In Proceedings of the SIGCHI conference on Human factors in computing systems (CHI '01). ACM, New York, NY, USA, 269-276.
20. Rosenfeld, D., Zawadzki, M., Sudol, J., and Perlin, K. Physical objects as bidirectional user interface elements. IEEE Computer Graphics and Applications, 24(1):44–49, 2004.
21. Sugimoto, M., Kagotani, G., Kojima, M., Nii, H., Nakamura, A., and Inami, M. 2005. Augmented coliseum: display-based computing for augmented reality inspiration computing robot. In ACM SIGGRAPH 2005 Emerging technologies (SIGGRAPH '05), Donna Cox (Ed.). ACM, New York, NY, USA, Article 1.
22. Underkoffler, J. and Ishii, H. 1999. Urp: a luminous-tangible workbench for urban planning and design. In CHI '99. ACM, New York, NY, 386-393.
23. Weiss, M., Schwarz, F., Jakubowski, S., and Borchers, J. 2010. Madgets: actuating widgets on interactive tabletops. In Proceedings of the 23nd annual ACM symposium on User interface software and technology (UIST '10). ACM, New York, NY, 293-302.
24. Art+com' Kinetic Sculpture:

http://www.artcom.de/en/projects/project/detail/kinetic-sculpture/

Medusa: A Proximity-Aware Multi-touch Tabletop

Michelle Annett [1,2], *Tovi Grossman* [1], *Daniel Wigdor* [3], *George Fitzmaurice* [1]

[1] User Interface Group
Autodesk Research
{firstname.lastname}@autodesk.com

[2] Department of Computing Science
University of Alberta
mkannett@ualberta.ca

[3] Department of Computer Science
University of Toronto
dwigdor@dgp.toronto.edu

ABSTRACT
We present Medusa, a proximity-aware multi-touch tabletop. Medusa uses 138 inexpensive proximity sensors to: detect a user's presence and location, determine body and arm locations, distinguish between the right and left arms, and map touch point to specific users and specific hands. Our tracking algorithms and hardware designs are described. Exploring this unique design, we develop and report on a collection of interactions enabled by Medusa in support of multi-user collaborative design, specifically within the context of Proxi-Sketch, a multi-user UI prototyping tool. We discuss design issues, system implementation, limitations, and generalizable concepts throughout the paper.

ACM Classification: H5.2 Information interfaces and presentation: Input, User Interfaces.

General terms: Design, Human Factors

Keywords: tabletop, context-aware, gestures, touch, bimanual, multi-touch, proxemics, proximity, hover

INTRODUCTION
Multi-touch tabletop displays, which combine large display and input surfaces on a horizontal plane, offer opportunities for new applications and interfaces. Advances in technology have made such devices the focus of considerable research [22] and have given rise to numerous prototype and commercial platforms. Multi-touch tabletops offer numerous potential benefits, such as the ability to support a more "natural" user experience [36], and allow for casual and collaborative interactions [25].

Despite these benefits, many tabletops still have several limitations. In particular, the majority of touch-based technologies are only capable of sensing touch interaction *on* the display surface. As a direct result, tabletop user interfaces cannot rely on a "tracking state" which is one of three essential input states of traditional GUI's [7]. Furthermore, by limiting their sensing to touch, tabletop devices have no inherent knowledge of where users are situated which users are interacting, or the number of users (if any) that are present. Given the clear relevance of tabletops to collaborative environments, these can be real limitations, and indeed, many research projects have developed software solutions that provide tabletops with this additional information. For example, a tabletop display may attempt to deduce a user's location based on the orientation and footprint of the user's touch points [8,32].

While software solutions are a worthwhile approach, there are also new technologies that allow tabletop devices to sense not only contact with a tabletop's surface, but also above and around the tabletop. For example, depth cameras have enabled interactions between and around display devices [35]. Similarly, the use of proximity sensors has enabled new gestures above and around a device [19].

As these sensing technologies have only recently become commercially available, little research has explored how their additional input channels can be leveraged to augment and improve multi-touch tabletops. We see the integration of tabletop and proximity sensing technologies as opening a range of possibilities to enhance existing multi-touch and collaborative interactions, and enable new ones. In particular, context-aware and proxemic interactions can be enabled [2,29], and existing challenges, such as mapping touch points to users, and users to locations, can be addressed.

Our work provides two primary contributions in this space. First, we present an integrated hardware solution, *Medusa*, which allows a traditional multi-touch tabletop to sense a user around its perimeter, as well as the user's interaction above the surface. Medusa is a Microsoft Surface that has been instrumented with 138 proximity sensors. These proximity sensors enable the Surface to sense the users around it, as well as the hands and arms above its display (Figure 1). Not only are these sensors inexpensive and simple to configure, but also they enable an integrated

Figure 1: A user waving her arms above Medusa, a proximity-aware multi-touch tabletop.

hardware solution, without requiring any markers, cameras, or other sensing devices external to the display platform itself. Our second contribution is a thorough exploration of the design space that results from the use of these additional information channels. As Medusa has an awareness of users' locations, it can for example, identify touch points by user, and disambiguate between touches made with left or right hands. Our exploration of new user interface paradigms and interaction techniques is facilitated by the development of Proxi-Sketch, a UI prototyping application.

RELATED WORK

In this section, we review previous efforts at sensing gestures around touch devices, responding to user location, and alternative sensing technologies.

Sensing Gestures around Touch Devices

There is a long line of research examining the use of explicit mid-air gestures, in particular, in VR research (we refer the reader to two surveys [13,23]). Freehand gestures have also been used as a means to interact with miniature devices [15,20,26]. While such work has relevance to Medusa, the focus of the present work is on the augmentation of traditional 2D touch device interactions with additional sensing channels, rather than on the development of replacement 3D gestures. Significant work, which relies on detecting the hover of a stylus, has also been done. Vogel provides a thorough review of this research [30], which we omit due to the reliance on a tracked object.

Adding a Tracking State for Touch

In modern user interface parlance, *hover* has come to describe the tracking state of an input device, whether or not that state is achieved by physically hovering over anything [7]. Multiple projects have introduced a *tracking* state to a touch device without actually detecting physical hover. These include differentiation of posture of the touching finger [4,10,11] through differentiation based on the number or choice of fingers [21], through the use of physical proxies [32], through sensing the height of the hand above the device while touching with a finger [24], and through EMG-sensed differentiation of posture [3]. While relevant to the current work, the ability to detect physical hover can provide a broader range of capabilities than the straightforward addition of a tracking state.

Physical Hover Detection

The detection of physical hover has been achieved through vision techniques, using either above-device cameras (as with Smart's DVIT device, (smart.com/dvit), and LucidTouch [33]), or beneath-surface cameras [16, 27]. Sensing of induced capacitance has also been used to detect hands above a device [24]. While these approaches can extend the capabilities of touch devices by supporting in-air gestures [16], the physical mounting locations limit the interaction volume. To address this, Wilson and Benko proposed the use of multiple depth-cameras in a LightSpace [35]. As with the earlier approaches, the interaction volume was limited to the viewing area of the cameras. By mounting three rings of proximity sensors directly onto the table, Medusa ensures that the table itself does not occlude the sensors' view of the surrounding area.

Responding to User Location

Medusa is an interactive tabletop able to detect, track, and differentiate between multiple users. Previously, the DiamondSpin project demonstrated the use of user differentiation to augment interaction [25] by relying on capacitive coupling to provide user-differentiation for each contact [9]. While robust for the differentiation of users, user location is based on an assumption of static positions of receiver pads, and requires the user to remain in contact with their pad while interacting with the device. Vision techniques applied to touch input have demonstrated the ability to distinguish between contacts made with the right or left hand [8], but have not provided a mechanism to label hands from multiple users, cannot sense users before they touch the display, nor sense orientation information for each contact.

Multiple projects have demonstrated promising interaction techniques given user tracking, such as in public ambient displays [29], and proxemic interactions [2]. Both of these projected relied on the use of commercial motion trackers to observe fiducial markers worn by the user. Multitoe provided user tracking, but relied on an instrumented floor [1]. Medusa builds on the interactions provided by these systems, while contributing a commercially viable method for achieving user tracking. Also relevant to Medusa is the Range project, which explored the use of proximity sensing of implicit interactions [18]. While our focus is the enabling of explicit interactions, this work has informed some of our designs.

Sensing Technologies

Three rings of proximity sensors provide Medusa's additional information channels. Earlier projects have used these devices to enhance sensing. In Hoverflow, an array of proximity sensors enables the detection of 'coarse gestures' above a worn device [19]. Similarly, SideSight used two arrays of comparable sensors, pointed outwards from the sides of a mobile phone, to detect gestures made on the surface on which the phone was resting [6].

Furthermore, Tanase et al. used an array of 12 proximity sensors to coarsely detect the presence of users around a tabletop [28]. Unlike Tanase et al.'s implementation, Medusa has a much higher spatial resolution, is able to sense user presence around and above a tabletop, and fully explores the design space surrounding proximity-aware multi-touch tabletops.

Summary

While there have been a large number of projects that have informed the design of Medusa, little to no work has previously examined how the information about users around a device can be used in tandem with information about gestures above and touching the device. Further, no device has previously been able to sense the various user parameters without additional external sensors. Finally, the previous explorations have focused on explicit gestures that engage the external sensors, rather than using the sensors to implicitly enhance existing surface-constrained interactions.

HARDWARE IMPLEMENTATION

Medusa is an augmented Microsoft Surface multi-touch tabletop, elevated to a height of 86 cm. To sense a user's body, arm, and hands, 138 low-cost, IR-based proximity sensors are affixed to the top and side panels of the Surface. A combination of Sharp 2Y0A21 long-range (10-80 cm) and 2D120X short-range (4-30 cm) sensors are used.

The proximity sensors are arranged in three rings: an outward ring, an outer ring, and an inner ring (Figure 2). Although the sensors in our prototype protrude from the Surface, in the future they could be embed directly into the bezel or base of any multi-touch tabletop or display. The sensors were connected to the Microsoft Surface via 18 Phidget Interface 8/8/8 Kits. No additional data acquisition devices or hardware upgrades were added to the Surface.

The outward facing ring is composed of 34 long-range sensors, spaced 3.3 cm apart, and mounted at the top of each side of the table. Because the sensors point outwards, they create a horizontal sensing plane that projects 80 cm from the side panels of the Surface, along all sides. When a user walks up to, or near the Surface, their legs engage the sensing plane. Forty-six long-range sensors, spaced 3.3 cm apart and pointed upwards, make up the outer ring of sensors, creating a vertical sensing plane wrapped around the perimeter of the tabletop. Long-range sensors were used to allow users of various heights to interact with the system. Fifty-eight short-range sensors, spaced 0.8 cm apart, are located around the perimeter of the Surface's touch area. Similar to the outer ring, these sensors point upwards to form an inner vertical sensing plane. Shorter-range sensors were used to provide greater sensing resolution. When a user reaches towards the touch area of the tabletop, their arm first engages the outer and then inner sensing planes.

The three rings of sensors allow Medusa to track users, arms and hands, and to identify which *user* and which *hand* generated each touch event detected by the Surface.

SENSING

Multiple proximity sensors have been used in combination before [6,28,31], but to our knowledge, not to the extent of our 138-sensor implementation. As such, special attention

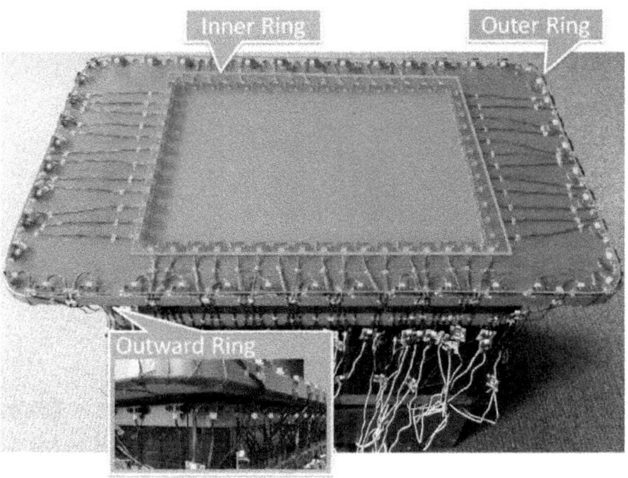

Figure 2: Medusa's sensors are arranged in three rings. An outward-facing ring of 34 sensors is mounted beneath the lip. Two upward facing rings atop the table are made-up of 46 sensors (on the outer) and 58 sensors (on the inner).

is paid to the aggregation, processing, and filtering of the data. Furthermore, reconstructing body, arm, and hand positions is non-trivial. In particular, the sensing resolution is magnitudes lower than what a 3D depth camera provides [35]. Here, we describe the techniques we used to translate the simple proximity data from of our three sensor rings into the 3D location of users, arms, and hands.

Using C# and the Phidget SDK, the signals from each sensor are sampled at 63 Hz and filtered using a median filter with a window size of 17 (for the outward-facing sensors) or 11 (for the upward facing sensors) to remove noise. Different window sizes were used because it is important to have a steady body position (rather than a responsive, more error-prone position), while responsiveness is required for position of the arms. To remove any noise that results from sporadically firing sensors, a uniform-weighted low pass filter with a window size of eight is applied to the result of the median filter.

To speed up processing and prevent the misidentification of arms in touch events, Medusa processes the sensors using a cascading logic approach. On each frame, the sensors in the outward ring are processed. If engagement with sensors in the outward-facing ring is detected, the sensors located in the outer upper-facing ring along the same side of the table are processed. If there is then a disruption in the outer ring, only those sensors in the inner ring, which are located along the same side, are processed. Using this approach prevents unnecessary processing while also preventing users from interfering with the sensing of other users (e.g., reaching over to their side, reaching across them, etc.).

Body Tracking Algorithm

Medusa uses the sensors' known physical locations and reported depth values to determine each user's body position around the Surface. Medusa first looks at all of the sensors in the outward ring to determine which ones are firing. If groups of consecutive sensors that are firing, they are placed into a 'sensor chain'.

Once all firing sensors have been identified, each sensor chain is analyzed. Medusa first discards all chains with a length less than 2 and then computes a Gaussian weighted average of each chain's sensor position and proximity values. This weighted value is used as an estimate of the user's body position (Figure 3). The distances between each body found in the current frame is compared to each previously computed body position. Bodies are mapped to the closest positions in the previous frames. If a new body is more than 50 cm from any previous body position, it is marked as a new body. Body positions are smoothed using a uniform low pass filter with a window size of 13. If a previously detected body has not been updated for 500 ms then that body is no longer considered present. Using this technique, we can robustly track two people along each long side of the table and one person along each short side of the table.

Arm Tracking

Similar to the body tracking method, Medusa looks at the outer and inner ring of sensors to find chains of sensors that

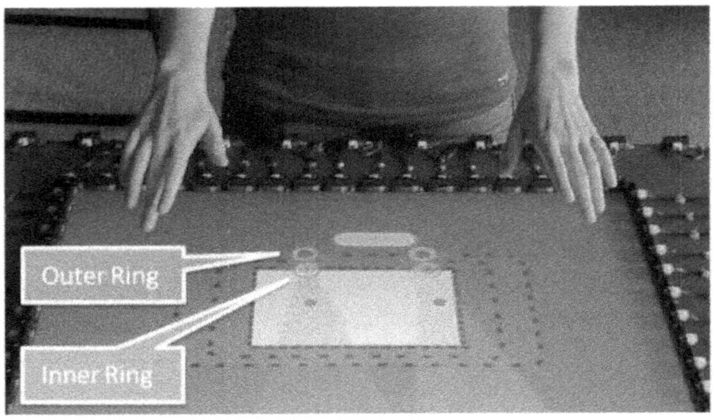

Figure 3: Visualization of tracking output. The location of the user's body is represented by the blue paddle. Right and left arm locations (with respect to the outer ring) are represented by orange and purple circles, respectively. The locations of the user's arms within the inner ring are represented by yellow and pink circles, respectively. The orange and purple cones represent the 'arm projections' of the user.

are firing. Unlike the body tracking, it is possible to disrupt only one sensor with the arm, so all chains are considered.

To find if an arm is present above the outer ring, a weighted average of the positions of each sensor in the chain is computed. Arms are matched across frames with the closest previously detected arm. If the current arm position is more than 20 cm from any previous arm, it is marked as a new arm, and right/left is determined. Arm position is smoothed using a low pass filter with a window size of 13. If an arm position has not been matched or updated for 500 ms, we then consider it as being removed.

To label an arm as right or left, each arm is compared to all body positions that are on the same side of the Surface, and is assigned to the closest one. If the arm is located to the right of the assigned body, it is classified as the right arm, else, the left. The side of the body an arm belongs to is always assigned when the outer ring of sensors is engaged.

The same heuristics are used to track arms above the inner ring of sensors: chains of disrupting sensors are found, and a weighted average of the sensor position is computed and matched against previous arm positions. When a new arm is identified above the inner ring, it is associated with the closest arm position currently sensed above the outer ring, and inherits the right/left arm classification.

When an arm engages both rings of sensors, the reported depth values, along with their known positions, can be used to provide a rough estimate of the horizontal and vertical arm angles (Figure 3).

Mapping Touch Points to Users and Hands

To map the touch points detected by the Surface to a specific user and hand, Medusa considers the orientation of the arms that are currently being tracked. For each arm that is engaging both the inner and outer rings, Medusa computes an 'arm projection', which is the vector that extends from the 3D line segment between the arm's estimated positions above the inner and outer rings. When a new touch point is sensed, Medusa determines the minimum distance that exists between the touch point and each of the arm projections. If the minimum distance to the closest projection is less than 15 cm, the touch point is matched to that arm and user. If no projection passes within that threshold, Medusa determines which arm is engaging the inner ring closest to the touch point. If two or more arms are within 20 cm of the touch point (20 cm), Medusa matches the touch point based on the minimum distance between the touch point and the body positions of the users, and associates the touch point with the arm of the user to which it is closest.

Tracking Accuracy

While we have not formally evaluated the tracking accuracy or robustness of Medusa, our initial experiences are quite encouraging, although there are some problem cases where contact points or arms are incorrectly tagged. In our discussion section, we outline some of the limitations of both our tracking heuristics and of the sensors themselves. Tracking is certainly sufficiently robust to enable our exploration and implementation of the new interaction techniques that are unique to Medusa's enhanced sensing capabilities. This exploration takes place within the context of Proxi-Sketch, our UI layout application.

PROXI-SKETCH

Application Scope and Motivation

To explore the new types of interactions that our additional sensing affords, Proxi-Sketch was created. Proxi-Sketch is an application that enables users to create and edit prototypes of graphical user interfaces (Figure 4), inspired by desktop applications such as Balsamiq (Balsamiq.com). This seemed like a reasonable application domain that would provide us with a sandbox for exploring numerous functions and features. Our contribution is not focused on the application domain itself, but rather how Medusa's sensing information can improve multi-user, multi-touch tabletop applications in general.

Figure 4. A user building a user interface prototype using Proxi-Sketch, running on Medusa.

While Medusa has the ability to sense explicit freehand 3D gestures, we focus instead on how implicit engagement of the sensors can be used to augment traditional 2D interactions. We organize our discussion of Proxi-Sketch based on the properties sensed by Medusa:

- User Position Tracking
- Bimanual Input Distinction
- Pre-Touch Functionality
- Touch + Depth Gestures
- User Differentiation

User Position Tracking

An important aspect of Medusa is that it can detect when users are present, how far away they are from the table , and where around the table they are situated. In this section, we discuss how we leverage this information.

User Presence and Representation

When no users are present, an attract application is displayed. As with any input device that is proximity- or context-aware, it is important to convey to users that the system recognizes their presence and behaviour [29]. We indicate the identification of a user's presence by displaying a persistent visual representation of the user via a glowing orb (Figure 5). When a user first enters the *idle* state (by walking up to the tabletop), they will see a blurry, blue glowing orb (which represents an unknown user). The location of the orb moves with the user as they walk toward, around, and away from the tabletop. If a user chooses to move closer to the tabletop, their orb comes into focus and invites the user to login. If the user exits the *idle* state (by walking beyond sensing range), the orb disappears.

User Login/Logout

Users login to the system by touching the orb, rotating through a carousel of user ID's, and selecting their profile picture (Figure 5). Once logged-in, the blue glowing orb changes to a user-specific colour, displays the user's name, and minimizes to the corner of the screen, allowing immediate visual identification by all users without being intrusive or distracting. If the user moves to another side of the tabletop, the orb moves with them and becomes anchored in a corner of the new side. If the user walks away from the table at any time, the orb changes to gray and then gradually fade out, visualizing a timeout until the user is logged-out.

Once a user has logged-in, the orb acts as a personal gesture dashboard for context-specific gestures. One of the subtle benefits of Medusa is that after logging-in, a user's gesture dashboard remains associated with them, even as they walk around the table. There are five gestures that are supported by the dashboard: *logout, open file, save file, group*, and *do not disturb*. The logout gesture is a 3 finger tap, and allows users to manually logout, instead of automatically logging out by walking away. Opening and saving files is accomplished with a swipe of a finger to the left and right, respectively. Saved content is associated with the user's profile, and the open gesture evokes a carousel of documents associated with their account. The remaining gestures are discussed in the sections that follow.

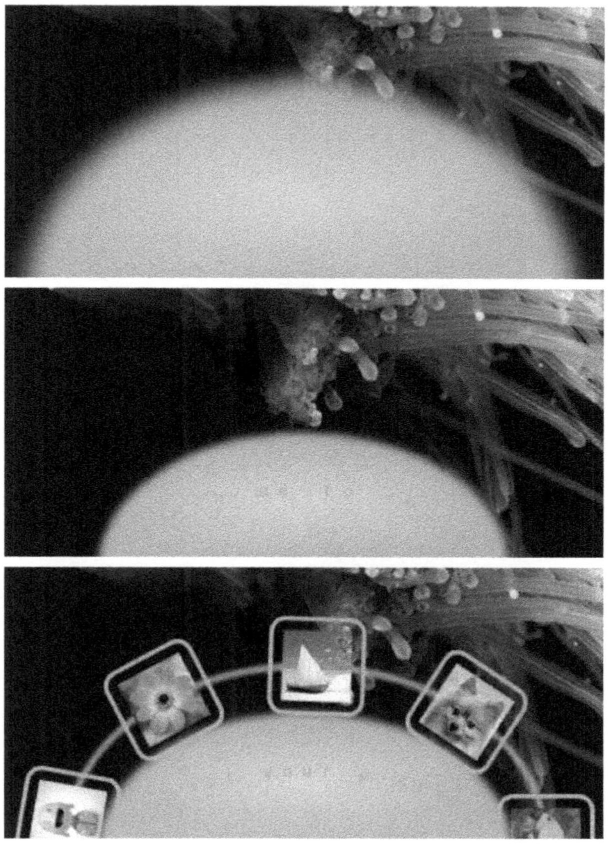

Figure 5: Initially, each user is represented by a blurry, glowing blue orb (Top). After moving closer to the tabletop, the orb comes into focus and encourages the user to login (Center). If a user taps on their orb, it will bring up a rotating carousel of available user accounts (Bottom).

Different Sides / Different Functions

Since Medusa provides knowledge pertaining to a users' location, Proxi-Sketch can assign specific modes, tools, or functionalities to different sides of the tabletop. To explore this possibility, we assigned different sides of the tabletop to different fidelities of the current prototype. By default, prototypes are rendered in a 'sketchy' style. If the user wishes to see their prototype from a fresh point of view, in a higher fidelity, they can walk over to an adjacent side of the tabletop (Figure 6). Not only will the visual style of the interface change, but also the canvas appropriately reorients to face the user's new location. When a user moves to another adjacent side of the tabletop, the interface switches back to the 'sketchy' style and reorient to face the user.

Standing at the Corner

When a user stands at one of the corners of the tabletop, the presence of the user's body is identified but not their arms, arm movements, or touch points. The corners of a tabletop are perfect locations for users who have restricted permissions but are allowed to observe the collaboration process. Within Proxi-Sketch, blue orbs appear for users who are standing at the corners of the Surface to indicate that they are recognized, but are not given the opportunity to login or manipulate any content.

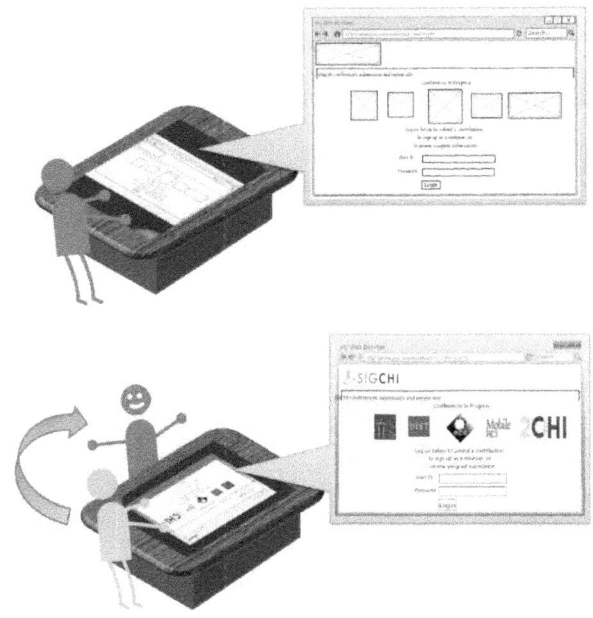

Figure 6: By default, a low-fidelity rendering of each UI component is generated (Top). Once a user walks to an adjacent side of the table, a high fidelity rendering of each component becomes visible (Bottom).

Bimanual Input Distinction

While bimanual input is commonly used in tabletop applications, Medusa is able to distinguish between the user's left and right hands. This distinction is particularly important, as interactions should support a non-symmetric division of labour [14]. This section describes the interactions we explored to leverage this information.

Content Creation and Removal

We use the notion of dominant and non-dominant hands to assign appropriate functionality for adding and removing content. Content is added by tapping on the canvas with the dominant hand. A marker coloured with the identified user's orb colour appears on the canvas. When touched, a hierarchal radial menu opens, oriented towards the user. This menu adds UI components, such as browser windows, media players, and scroll bars to the canvas.

If a user wishes to clear the canvas, she user can touch the canvas with their non-dominant hand, displaying a 'clear canvas' icon, oriented to that user. If the clear icon is touched, all user interface components are removed from the canvas. Assigning removal to the non-dominant hand reduces the risk of users accidentally removing content.

Translation, Rotation, Scaling

On a multi-touch tabletop, it can be difficult to perform controlled manipulations, because a single gesture typically activates rotation, scale, and translation all at the same time. Proxi-Sketch addresses this problem by taking advantage of hand identification. To translate a component, the user can touch the component with one finger and drag it. If a user wishes to rotate the component, they can touch the component with two fingers from the *same* hand. If a user wishes to scale a component, the user touches it with one finger from *each* hand. This differentiation allows for increased precision through transform isolation.

Manipulations with Groups of Content

Proxi-Sketch uses bimanual input distinction to quickly differentiate manipulation gestures as applying to the whole group, or to an individual item.

If a user wishes to manipulate a whole group of components, they can do so by touching any component in the group with their non-dominant hand. Conversely, if the user wishes to manipulate only a single component within a group, thus leaving the rest of the group in place, they touch the desired component with their dominant hand. All of the components belonging to the group become highlighted (to ensure that the user knows that the component is part of a group), but the desired component is the only one that will be manipulated. Our design rationale when making this bimanual separation is in keeping with research in bimanual interaction, which advocates assigning coarser actions (moving all the components in a whole) to the non-dominant hand [14].

Content is grouped by tapping one finger on the gesture dashboard, enabling 'group mode'. Once in this mode, any components touched by the user become highlighted with the user's orb colour. After all desired components are selected, the user can again tap the dashboard with one finger to create the group and exit the mode.

Pre-Touch Functionality

In addition to sensing the proxemic state of users, Medusa can also sense the proxemic states of a user's hands. In particular, Medusa knows if a hand has crossed the bezel or display area, but not come into contact with the display area. This allows us to explore *pre-touch* functionality, discussed below.

Global Gesture Guide

Similar to many other multi-touch tabletop applications, there are a number of gestures that can be performed within Proxi-Sketch. Previous efforts have used on-demand guides to illustrate available gestures [12]. An open problem has been how to display this guide without having to reserve a "help" gesture. Medusa provides an obvious mechanism: guides are displayed when the user's hand hovers over the table, demonstrating hesitation. A global gesture guide (Figure 7) is shown when the user's hand hovers over the bezel of the table. We chose this interaction as it implicitly indicates that the user intends to interact with the system, but may be unsure how to proceed. The guide remains anchored near the user, in the center of the screen, until the user removes their arm or reaches towards the touch area.

Dashboard Gesture Guide

Similar to the global gesture guide, each user has an on-demand, gesture dashboard guide available (Figure 8). The guide becomes visible when the user's hand hovers above their orb, and disappears whenever the user touches their orb or moves their hand away. This extends the notion of traditional gesture guides, allowing users to view context-specific gestures.

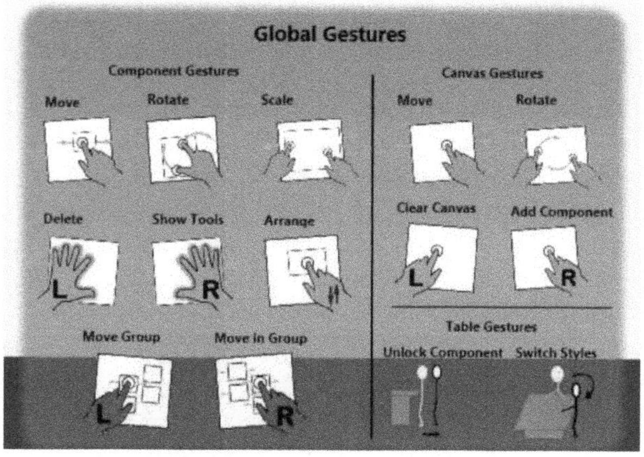

Figure 7: Global Gesture Guide. This guide appears whenever a user's hand dwells over the outer ring of sensors. It assists users in remembering which gestures are permissible in Proxi-Sketch.

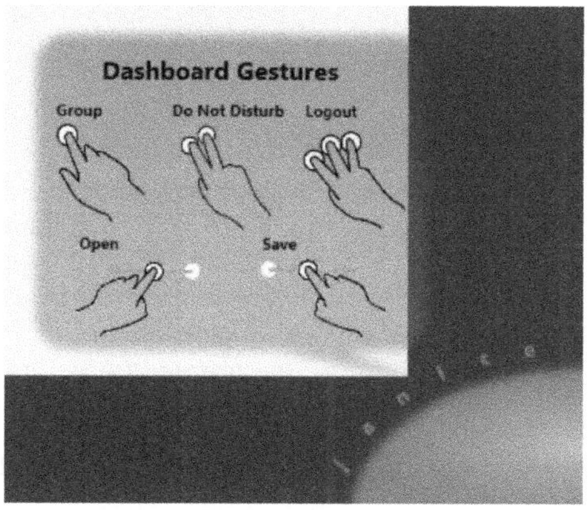

Figure 8: Dashboard Gesture Guide. This guide illustrates gestures that can be performed on an orb. It appears when a user's hand dwells over their orb.

Just-in-Time Widgets

Pre-touch functionality can also be combined with bimanual input distinction. Similar to the addition and removal of canvas content, the actions required to delete or edit a specific user interface components have been divided bimanually. If users wish to edit the colour, text, or other properties of a specific component, they can hover their dominant hand above it, thus causing a coloured marker to appear (Figure 9). This type of "just-in-time" widget is made possible by our 3D arm location sensing. Once touched, a radial marking menu displays available options (Figure 9).

The marking menu is located such that it is not occluded by the user's arm, is oriented towards the user, and its options are located in a convenient position for the dominant hand to access. The selection of an element in this marking menu causes a dialog to appear, allowing the user to make their desired modifications.

If a user wishes to remove a component from the canvas, they hover their non-dominant hand above the desired component. This results in a red 'X' icon being placed on the component's left side (Figure 10). Touching the 'X' icon deletes the component.

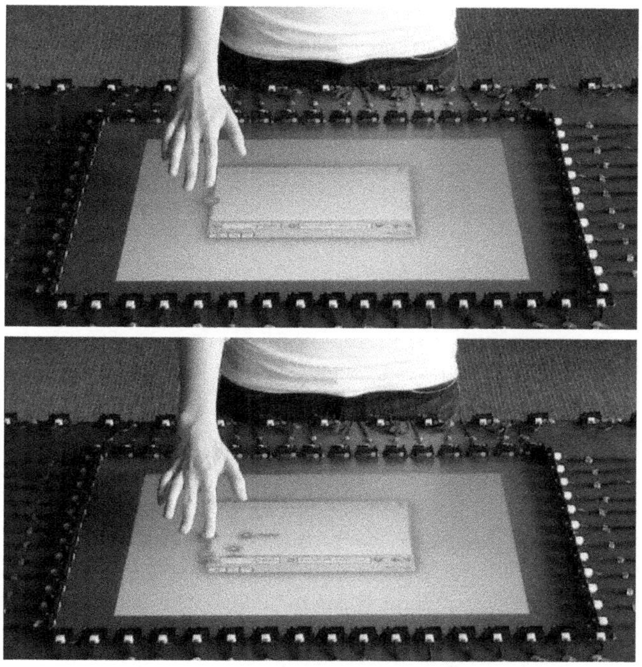

Figure 9: When the right arm is moved over a component, a marker appears below the hand. (Top). Touching this marker displays a component-specific marking menu (Bottom).

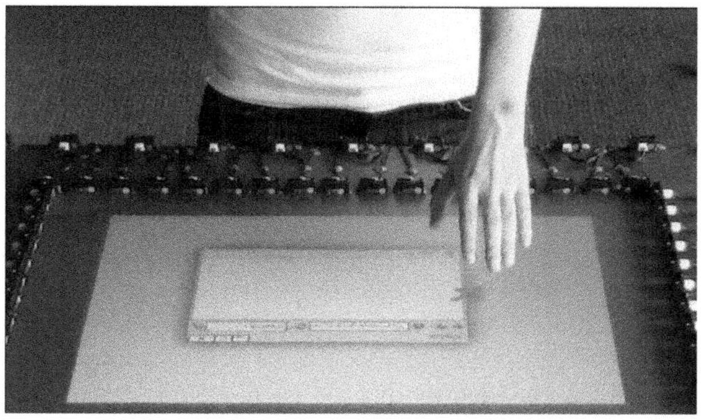

Figure 10: Moving one's left arm over a component brings a red 'X' icon into view. Touching this 'X' icon deletes the component from the canvas.

These just-in-time widgets allow users to preview possible actions with specific application components, and keep the working area clear of user interface clutter.

Touch + Depth Gestures

An important feature when producing UI prototypes is the ability to change the z-order of components of the UI. We developed a new type of gesture that Medusa enables, which *combines touch and 3D sensing* to control item arrangement. To send a component back in *z*, behind all other components, the user touches the component and moves their arm/elbow towards the Surface. To bring a component to the front, the user can touch the component and pick it up (i.e., move their arm upwards, away from the Surface). This new method of arranging components enables users to employ a direct manipulation metaphor to perform a task that is often obfuscated by icons or hidden menus.

User Differentiation

Issues in sharing and territoriality in tabletop collaboration have long been studied [22]. As Medusa provides information regarding user location and touch identity, new elements of facilitated collaboration are possible.

Content Control

In multi-user scenarios, control of content on a multi-touch tabletop has been a long-standing problem, especially when a system is uncertain who is interacting with content [22].

If a user walks up to the tabletop and does not login, all of their interactions with the tabletop are automatically blocked. This is only possible because Medusa associates touch points to users. This allows casual observers to point to content, without accidently changing it.

When multiple users are logged in, Proxi-Sketch makes use of its user-identification to assign ownership of components to users. To prevent users from accessing content from another user or interfering with someone else's work, Proxi-Sketch employs a 'one component per user, one user per component' rule. With this rule, each user has control over one component at a time, and at most one user can own each component at a time. Each 'owned' component is highlighted with its owner's colour and cannot be manipulated, edited, or deleted by anyone but the owner.

To take control of a component, a user simply touches it. As soon as a user begins working with a new component, they automatically give up control of their previously owned component. If a user wishes to give up control of a component, they can take a small step away from the Surface. The user's orb colour changes to grey and the component is free for other users to manipulate.

This approach to content control does not rely on explicit interaction with the tabletop, but rather uses a subtle and intuitive interaction to manage ownership. While devices such as the DiamondTouch could enforce a similar ownership scheme, the identity of the owners would not be robust to movement around the table, nor could a step back from the table be sensed to cede control [9].

Do Not Disturb

Brignull and Rogers identified the *Honeypot Effect* of digital surfaces, which has been amply confirmed by the authors' own experiences. It is quite common when working with a multi-touch tabletop to be interrupted frequently, or bothered by strangers or coworkers who are curious about what the surface is, want to know what is being worked on, and even start touching the surface without invitation [5]. As Medusa is able to identify when users are approaching, would-be users can now be *discouraged* from interacting with the Surface by enacting a new table mode: *Do Not Disturb* (DND), shown in Figure 11.

DND provides users who are currently interacting with the system with a method of discouraging others from approaching, without having to personally acknowledge them or be disrupted. A user working with Proxi-Sketch can evoke DND mode by tapping two fingers on their orb. Once in this mode, any potential user who walks near the tabletop is presented with a bright red 'prohibited' glowing orb (Figure 11). If seen from a distance, this red orb subtly but kindly informs any passersby or potential users that the individuals currently using the tabletop do not wish to be disturbed. If an uninvited user moves closer to the Surface, their orb will not shrink, nor will it let them login or touch any part of the canvas. Once users are ready to allow others to collaborate, they can tap two fingers on their orb to return the tabletop back to its normal state.

Figure 11: If the tabletop has been placed in the 'Do Not Disturb' mode, all logged out and potential users will be greeted with a 'prohibited' glowing red orb, encouraging them to walk away from the table and not bother those currently engaging with it.

Summary

Taken as a whole, Proxi-Sketch builds atop the sensing capabilities included in Medusa to provide a set of unique interactions. User position sensing is used to encourage (or discourage) use of the table, and to provide visual feedback of detected presence. Bimanual input distinction has been used to reduce the likelihood and cost of errors, and to provide improved precision for direct manipulation. Pre-touch functionality provides a new state for interaction, which we have used to explore a solution to gesture learning and to enable just-in-time widgets. Finally, we have demonstrated the utility of user and touch identification to enhance collaboration, and to provide mechanisms, both implicit and explicit, to manage content control and privacy. This has been accomplished while maintaining a viewpoint that Medusa's additional sensing is meant to *enhance* the touch sensing of the underlying Microsoft Surface, rather than to supplant or replace touch-based interaction.

DISCUSSION

We have presented Medusa, a novel system that uses proximity sensors to capture a rich set of user-proximity information, and Proxi-Sketch. In this section, we discuss other sensing solutions, the limitations of proximity sensors, and the generalizability of our interaction techniques.

Sensing: Proximity Sensors and Depth Cameras

The use of proximity sensors has a number of benefits. As proximity sensors are small, it would be plausible to integrate them into the bezels of touch displays, similar to their current usage in mobile phones. The sensors are also inexpensive and do not require any calibration. Most importantly, no external cameras or tracking markers are required, making Medusa a wholly integrated hardware solution.

The data we receive is of a much lower fidelity than what could be obtained from other sensing possibilities. For example, using a Microsoft Kinect depth camera could potentially provide full skeletal tracking, allowing a richer set of body-based gestures and techniques to be explored. However, it is unlikely that a single *integrated* Kinect device could replace the aggregate effect of our distributed sensing solution. Most likely, a Kinect device would need to be mounted externally, such as on the ceiling [35]. Associated technical challenges would thus include occlusions by users, possible interference between the IR emitters and receivers in the depth cameras and Surface devices, and the need to recalibrate each time the Surface is moved. Our solution could be embedded into existing hardware, overcomes issues of occlusion, and requires no calibration.

Another option would be the use of IR cameras mounted below the surface of the display, as demonstrated in SecondLight [16,17]. This however would only provide a restricted field of view, in comparison to the full proximity information our implementation enabled. Medusa is able to sense the location of users around the Surface, identify if the right or left hand is present, and detect which user each arm/hand belongs to. This information is also used to match touch points to specific users. Behind surface cameras may have knowledge of the position, orientation, and depth of the hand, but none of the additional user-based information is available for use. It is also important to note that our approach can be used to retrofit all existing tabletop systems (e.g., capacitive, resistive, FTIR, diffuse illumination, etc.), whereas many current and future multi-touch tabletops will not have a form factor that could support a beneath-surface camera and switching diffuser.

Limitations of Proximity Sensors

There are some limitations of the sensors that should be highlighted. To our surprise, there was little issue with sensors interfering with one another. However, we initially found that sensors would frequently report false positives, (ghost objects), due to IR reflections from reflective material in our lab (e.g. bicycles, exposed ceiling pipes). Once diagnosed, the problem was addressed using strategically placed mirrors, to ensure light was not reflected back towards the sensors. More advanced filtering may reduce or alleviate this issue.

We demonstrated that with some simple tracking algorithms, our arrangement of proximity sensors could track users, arms, hand locations, arm orientations, and could associated arm and touch points to users, as well as identify hands. Certain tracking information was accurate (such as detecting where users arms engaged the sensing planes), whereas other information was more coarse (such as estimating the 3-D location of a user's hand when hovering above the input area). While the tracking performance was robust enough to explore the interaction design space, there were some limitations. For example, if two users cross paths, our body tracking algorithm could mislabel users once they separate, or if two users' hands hover over the exact same area, and only one hand touches the Surface, the touch point may be associated with the wrong user.

Generalization of Interaction Techniques

While Medusa's hardware arrangement and tracking algorithms constitute a contribution of this work, many of the interaction techniques presented would also be suitable for devices built using other sensing modalities. In particular, a technical implementation using Kinect devices would be able to utilize all of the interaction techniques we have explored. An implementation using below-surface cameras would be able to utilize only those techniques that do not require knowledge of users or their locations – such as the hover-based, just-in-time widgets.

FUTURE WORK

Our work opens up new opportunities for future research, with respect to the tracking and the interaction designs.

The tracking algorithms we used were simple, but sufficient in most cases. Future work could formally evaluate the accuracy of our baseline sensing solution and potentially introduce more advanced techniques to match arms and touch points to users. For example, when matching touch points to arms, one could consider the timing correspondence between when the arm entered the touch area, and then the occurrence of the touch. Future work could also look at extending the tracking algorithms to support tabletops with different physical properties (i.e., height, number of sides, length of sides, etc.). More attention could also be given to potential sensing inaccuracies in the interaction design. Important or frequent system features should be mapped to gestures that have the highest accuracy rates, and error recovery techniques should be provided when misclassifications occur.

With respect to our design exploration, there are a number of interesting ideas that could be explored further. We introduced some new gestures enabled by Medusa, but there are many more possibilities. An implementation using a Kinect device may support new types of gestures and techniques that we did not explore. For example, full-skeletal tracking could support the detection of body postures for application control, such as leaning in and out to control zoom levels, or showing private information when other users turn their backs on the table.

New types of widgets could be explored using the sensing information. For example, widgets could become fatigue-aware, as the system could measure the amount of reaching a user was performing. Like previous explorations with the pen, widgets could also become occlusion-aware, based on the position of the user's hand and angle of their arm [30].

Finally, there is a clear need to explore affordances and feedback to help users understand the parameters being sensed, and how to manipulate them, similar to earlier explorations with direct touch input [34].

REFERENCES

1. Augsten, T., Kaefer, K., Meusel, R., Fetzer, C., Kanitz, D., Stoff, T., Becker, T., Holz, C., and Baudisch, P. Multitoe: high-precision interaction with back-projected floors based on high-resolution multi-touch input. *UIST '10*, 209-218.
2. Ballendat, T., Marquardt, N., and Greenberg, S. Proxemic interaction: Designing for a proximity and orientation-aware environment. *ITS '10*, 121-130.
3. Benko, H., Saponas, T.S., Morris, D., and Tan, D. Enhancing input on and above the interactive surface with muscle sensing. *ITS '09*, 93-100.
4. Benko, H., Wilson, A.D., and Baudisch, P. Precise selection techniques for multi-touch screens. *CHI* '06, 1263-1272.
5. Brignull, H. and Rogers, Y. Enticing people to interact with large public displays in public spaces. *INTERACT '03*, 17-24.
6. Butler, A., Izadi, S., and Hodges, S. SideSight: multi-touch interaction around small devices. *UIST '08*, 201-204.
7. Buxton, W. A three-state model of graphical input. *IFIP TC13 '90*, 449-456.
8. Dang, C.T., Straud, M., and Andre, E. Hand distinction for multi-touch tabletop interaction. *ITS* '09, 101-108.
9. Dietz, P. and Leigh, D. DiamondTouch: a multi-user touch technology. *UIST '01*, 219-226.
10. Esenther, A. and Ryall, K. Fluid DTMouse: better mouse support for touch-based interactions. *AVI '06*, 112-115.
11. Forlines, C. and Shen, C. DTLens: Multi-user tabletop spatial data exploration. *UIST '05*, 119-122.
12. Freeman, D., Benko, H., Morris, M.R., and Wigdor, D. Shadow Guides: Visualizations for In-Situ Learning of Multi-Touch and Whole-Hand Gestures. *ITS '09*, 165-172.
13. Grossman, T. and Wigdor, D. Going Deeper: A Taxonomy of 3-D on the Tabletop. *ITS '07*, 137-144.
14. Guiard, Y. Asymmetric division of labor in human skilled bimanual action: The kinematic chain as a model. *Journal of Motor Behavior*, 1987, 9(4), pp. 486-517.
15. Harrison, C. and Hudson, S.E. Abracadabra: Wireless, High-Precision, and Unpowered Finger Input for Very Small Mobile Devices. *UIST '09*, 121-124.
16. Hilliges, O., Izadi, S., Wilson, A.D., Hodges, S., Garcia-Mendoza, A., and Butz, A. Interactions in the air: adding further depth to interactive tabletops. *UIST '09*, 139-148.
17. Izadi, S., Hodges, S., Taylor, S., Rosenfeld, D., Villar, N., Butler, A., and Westhues, J. Going Beyond the Display: A Surface Technology with an Electronically Switchable Diffuser. *UIST '08*, 268-278.
18. Ju, W., Lee, B.A., and Klemmer, S.R. Range: exploring implicit interaction through electronic whiteboard design. *CSCW '08*, 17-26.
19. Kratz, S. and Rohs, M. HoverFlow: expanding the design space of around-device interaction. *MobileHCI '09*, 1-8.
20. Loclair, C., Gustafson, S., and Baudisch, P. PinchWatch: A Wearable Device for One-Handed Microinteractions. *MobileHCI '10*.
21. Matejka, J., Grossman, T., Lo, J., and Fitzmaurice, G. The design and evaluation of multi-finger mouse emulation techniques. *CHI '09*, 1073-1082.
22. Mueller-Tomfelde, C. Tabletops - Horizontal Interactive Displays. Springer. ISBN: 978-1-84996-112-7.
23. Pierce, J. *Expanding the Interaction Lexicon for 3D Graphics*. Ph.D. Thesis, Carnegie Mellon University, 2001.
24. Rekimoto, J. SmartSkin: An Infrastructure for Freehand Manipulation on Interactive Surfaces. *CHI '02*, 113-120.
25. Shen, C., Vernier, F.D., Forliens, C., and Ringel M. DiamondSpin: an extensible toolkit for around-the-table interaction. *CHI '04*, 167-174.
26. Starner, T., Auzier, J., Ashbrook, D., and Gandy, M. The gesture pendant: A self-illuminating, wearable, infrared computer vision system for home automation control and medical monitoring. *ISWC '00*, 87-94.
27. Takeoka, Y., Miyaki, T., and Rekimoto, J. Z-touch: an infrastructure for 3D gesture interaction in the proximity of tabletop surfaces. *UIST '10*, 91-94.
28. Tanase, C.A, Vatavu, R.D., Pentiuc, S.G., and Graur, A. Detecting and Tracking Multiple Users in the Proximity of Interactive Tabletops. *Advances in Electrical and Computer Engineering*, 2010, 61-64.
29. Vogel, D. and Balakrishnan, R. Interactive public ambient displays: transitioning from implicit to explicit, public to personal, interaction with multiple users. *UIST '04*, 137-146.
30. Vogel, D. *Direct Pen Input and Hand Occlusion*. PhD. Thesis, University of Toronto, 2010.
31. Walther-Franks, B. Schwarten, L., Teichert, J., Krause, M., and Herrlich, M. User detection for a multi-touch table via proximity sensors. *ITS '08 Posters*.
32. Wang, F., Cao, X., Ren, X., and Irani, P. Detecting and Leveraging Finger Orientation for Interaction with Direct-Touch Surfaces. *UIST '09*, 23-32.
33. Wigdor, D., Forlines, C., Baudisch, P., Barnwell, J., and Shen, C. LucidTouch: a see-through mobile device. *UIST '07*, 269-278.
34. Wigdor, D., Williams, S., Cronin, M., Levy, R., White, K., Mazeev, M., and Benko, H. Ripples: utilizing per-contact visualizations to improve user interaction with touch displays. *UIST '09*, 3-12.
35. Wilson, A.D. and Benko, H. Combining multiple depth cameras and projectors for interactions on, above and between surfaces. *UIST '10*, 273-282.
36. Wilson, A.D., Izadi, S., Hilliges, O., Garcia-Mendoza, A., and Kirk, D. Bringing physics to the surface. *UIST '08*, 67-76.

Portico: Tangible Interaction on and around a Tablet

Daniel Avrahami[1,2], *Jacob O. Wobbrock*[2] *and Shahram Izadi*[3]

[1]Intel
2200 Mission College Blvd.
Santa Clara, CA 95054-1549

[2]The Information School | DUB Group
University of Washington
Seattle, WA 98195-2840

[3]Microsoft Research
7 J J Thomson Avenue
Cambridge, UK

daniel.avrahami@intel.com, wobbrock@uw.edu, shahrami@microsoft.com

ABSTRACT

We present *Portico*, a portable system for enabling tangible interaction on and around tablet computers. Two cameras on small foldable arms are positioned above the display to recognize a variety of physical objects placed on or around the tablet. These cameras have a larger field-of-view than the screen, allowing Portico to extend interaction significantly beyond the tablet itself. Our prototype, which uses a 12" tablet, delivers an interaction space six times the size of the tablet screen. Portico thus allows tablets to extend both their sensing capabilities and interaction space without sacrificing portability. We describe the design of our system and present a number of applications that demonstrate Portico's unique capability to track objects. We focus on a number of fun applications that demonstrate how such a device can be used as a low-cost way to create personal surface computing experiences. Finally, we discuss the challenges in supporting tangible interaction beyond the screen and describe possible mechanisms for overcoming them.

ACM Classification: H5.2 [Information interfaces and presentation]: User Interfaces—*graphical user interfaces*.

General terms: Design, Human Factors.

Keywords: Tangible, TUI, surface, tablet, portable.

INTRODUCTION

Surface and tabletop computing has been an important area in HCI research for over two decades. Interacting with surface computers allows users to directly manipulate digital elements through touch, and often allows interaction with and through physical objects set directly on the display. Surface computers, however, are typically large, expensive, and neither ―personal" nor portable. In this paper we present *Portico*, a system that enables tangible interaction in a new inexpensive portable form-factor, while still delivering a large interaction space to support physical interaction with objects, touch, and gesture. Portico presents a possibility of enabling low-cost personal surface computers for many users.

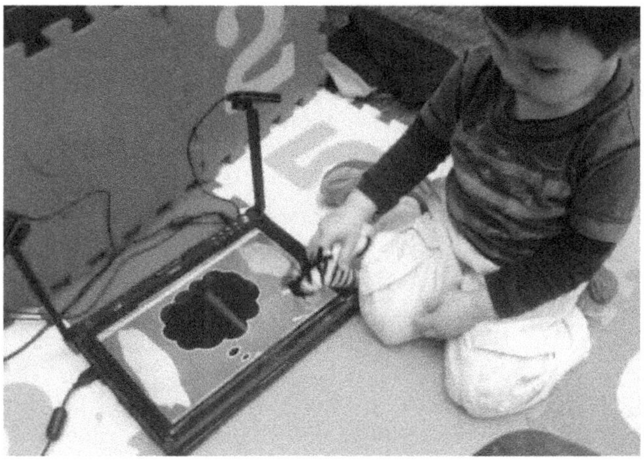

Figure 1. The Portico system in use. Two cameras track objects on the screen and surrounding surface. In this application, a toy zebra is tracked.

The majority of tabletop research and development has focused on the use of surface computing to support co-located groups, a natural outcome of existing tabletop computers resembling everyday tables. However, tangible interaction for personal or individual use is not yet widespread, largely due to the size and cost of today's tabletop computers. As presented by Beckwith *et al.* [3], affordable personal tangible interaction may have particular promise for education. Recent products such as Apple's iPad have started a convergence of portable tablet computers with tabletop computing through the introduction of multi-touch technology to tablets. Tablet computers, being portable and flat and supporting touch input, are prime candidates for enabling personal tangible interaction. However, with the exception of ThinSight [8], which, through the use of sensors embedded in the back of the display is able to recognize hands and objects placed on the screen, current tablet computers lack support for interaction with physical objects. A key challenge is overcoming the constraints imposed by the boundaries of the tablet screen, since, for many tangible applications, small screen real-estate proves prohibitive.

Portico overcomes the challenge of a limited interaction space by using two cameras on small foldable arms that provide a large field-of-view. Portico is thus able to recognize and react to objects manipulated not only on the tablet screen, but also on the surface beyond the tablet screen. In our prototype, Portico provides an interactive space six times the size of a 12" tablet screen, equivalent to the surface area of a 28" screen—a considerable interaction space for a small, lightweight, low-cost device. Designed to be *portable* rather than *mobile*, we envision that Portico will be carried around like a regular tablet but used for tangible interaction when it is on a tabletop, countertop, classroom desk, or the even the living room floor.

In the remainder of this paper, we describe related work, our system's hardware and software, and a number of example applications that take advantage of Portico's capabilities. We then discuss the benefits and limitations of Portico's design.

RELATED WORK

Connecting the physical and virtual has been a long sought-after goal in computing research. The earliest major work in this area was the DigitalDesk by Wellner in 1993 [23]. Ulmer and Ishii [10,22] carried this vision forward, inspiring a long and creative line of research. Much of the work on tangible interaction focused on the manipulation of tangible objects as controls for digital elements, often referred to as Tangible User Interfaces, or TUIs. A nice review of work on TUIs is provided in the literature [18]. With its strong link to the physical world, tangible interaction is typically done in the context of a tabletop or other surface computer that is large, often expensive, and fixed in its environment.

With Portico, we demonstrate how tangible computing can be supported in an affordable and portable form-factor without severely limiting the space available for physical interaction. This vision of a simple, portable device that can be carried around and that can quickly turn into a surface computer is similar to PlayAnywhere [24] and Bonfire [12], both of which create portable tabletop systems with the use of standalone projectors and embedded projectors. While Bonfire allows the laptop to ―spill over" to the tabletop through the use of a projector, Portico achieves much of the same benefits but without requiring a projector, making it substantially cheaper, and requiring significantly less power. Portico can also use the tablet's touch-screen for touch and gesture, which is more robust than vision. Also, with Portico, the primary display is horizontal in the same plane as the tangible objects, whereas Bonfire's primary display was vertical and above its peripheral interactive surfaces. This difference allows Portico to take advantage of physical objects interacting with high-resolution output for the user's primary tasks.

While the key characteristic of Portico—a large interaction space in a portable form-factor—is a novel contribution of our work, the basic use of a tablet as a horizontal display for interaction with objects on top of the screen has been demonstrated by prior work. Edge and Blackwell [5], for example, used a tablet computer on which users could interact with objects as a fixed peripheral display to a workstation. As they point out, however, in their case, the tablet easily could have been replaced with a screen embedded in the desk on which the workstation is located.

The Collaborative Slate (C-Slate) from Izadi *et al.* [11] was designed to support remote collaboration. Not designed to be portable, C-slate uses a horizontally mounted 21" tablet combined with a down-facing stereo camera, a vertical display and webcam, and supports tangible and multi-touch interaction on the tablet screen. C-Slate does, however, include abilities to view a collaborator's face on the vertical display, and to view the collaborator's hands on the tablet screen.

Finally, Hodges *et al.*'s ThinSight [8] uses optical IR sensors embedded behind an LCD to detect fingers and hands on the surface. Although the authors mention it primarily as a future possibility, their system can also detect the base of objects placed on the screen, with potential uses for tangible interaction. Although ThinSight does not go beyond the confines of its screen and sees objects only from underneath, our work was nonetheless inspired by ThinSight and its exploration of tangible interaction on small form-factor screens.

Interacting Beyond the Screen

A primary goal of Portico is to provide a large interaction space despite the limited screen area provided by a tablet computer. The physical design of our system with two cameras enables it to view and respond to users' interactions with objects on the surface *surrounding* the tablet. Thus, our system's input space (what the system sees) is significantly larger than its output space (limited to the screen boundaries). Prior work on mobile interaction explored the ability to manipulate on-screen (digital) content by interacting in the space around the screen. With mobile devices, screen real-estate often makes it impossible to accommodate a user's hands or even fingers without obstructing the digital content on the screen. SideSight [4] was designed for mobile devices and uses infrared (IR) proximity sensors embedded on each side of a mobile device that detect the position of fingers on the surface around the device. Abracadabra [7] was designed to allow finger interaction with graphical interfaces on very small displays using a combination of a magnetometer in the device and a magnet on a ring worn by the user to detect the finger's position. Portico relates to these prior efforts and uses vision to track objects and users' hands outside the device screen area.

THE DESIGN OF PORTICO

Our system comprises both hardware and software components: a custom designed hardware attachment, a vision system used for object detection, and an output system allowing Portico to visualize objects that are on the screen or on the table around it.

Hardware Design

Portico comprises a tablet computer and a pair of standard cameras that are attached to the tablet via custom designed fixtures. These cameras look down at the tablet screen and its surrounding surface. We modeled the fixtures in CAD such that they clasp the sides of the tablet screen (rather than the base, so they do not block any ports). For our

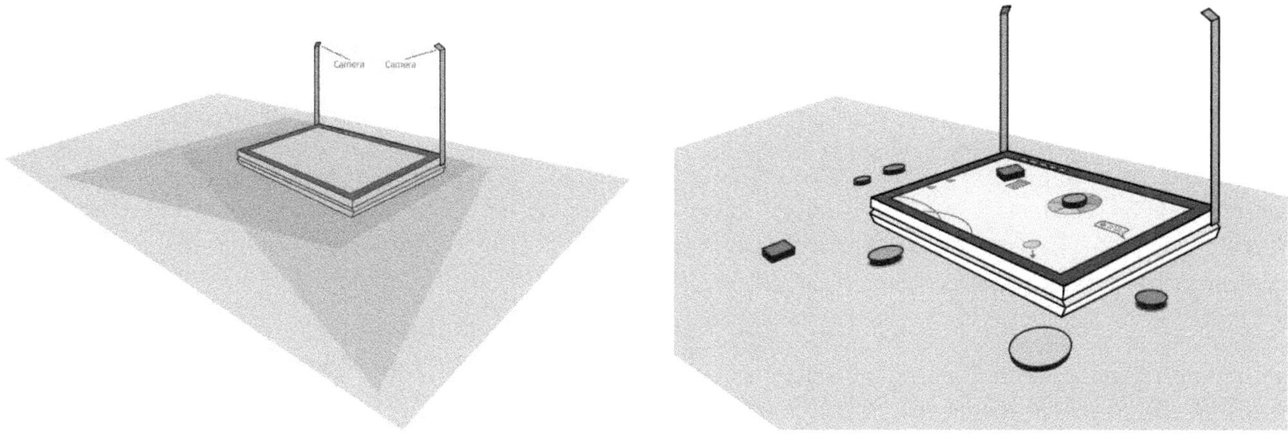

Figure 2. Portico system illustrations: The unified area viewable by the two cameras (left), and the system reacting to object on and around the tablet (right).

prototype, we printed the fixtures out of plastic using a Dimension Elite 3D printer. While printed plastic was satisfactory for prototyping the fixtures, we believe that stronger plastic or even aluminum is preferred. To provide additional robustness to breaking, flexible hinges similar to those used in eye glasses could allow Portico's arms to be bent outwards. Such a design is particularly important when Portico is used on the floor, or used by children playing a game, *e.g.*, our Penalty Shootout application (described below). For our prototype, we used a 12" Dell Latitude XT convertible tablet that supports both pen and finger multi-touch input. We also used a pair of Logitech Webcam Pro 9000 cameras extracted from their original housings. As shown in Figure 1, each camera is mounted at the end of a foldable arm attached to each side of the screen. We designed our system such that when folded down, the arms and cameras are flush against the tablet and do not interfere with normal use.

When the arms are raised, the cameras are bent down using a single rotation hinge to allow them to see the tablet screen and the tabletop. Figure 2a shows an illustration of the unified area viewable by the two cameras. Figure 2b illustrates the system reacting to objects on and around the screen. Finally, to avoid the system confusing digital elements drawn on the screen with physical objects, we applied linear polarizing filters to the screen and cameras. (Note that while LCDs are linearly polarized, in many tablets the touch-sensitive element diffuses the light, requiring another polarizing layer.)

Computer Vision System

We implemented a computer vision system to allow applications to support interactions with objects on the tablet and the surface around it. The vision system was written predominantly in Python and uses Intel's OpenCV library. We now describe the vision system in some detail to enable readers to replicate our system.

As shown in Figure 3 (next page), the vision system was implemented in a threaded, hierarchical structure. At the core of the vision system is the *Camera* Module, which is responsible for retrieving frames from a single camera, performing an optional background subtraction step, and gathering detected objects from different *View* Modules. Each View Module is responsible for manipulating raw camera frames to produce a specific simulated view, and contains a set of object recognition classifiers that operate on the simulated view. These views are useful since, as can be seen in Figure 4a, in order for the camera to see the tablet screen and the surrounding surface (and still be folded down when not in use), the cameras must view the world from a very oblique angle. Our system uses two Camera Modules, one for each camera. Both Camera Modules and all View Modules are threaded to allow the vision system elements to operate concurrently.

A single pass of the vision system consists of these steps:

1. *Grabbing camera frames*. Each Camera Module is connected to a single camera device. Upon request from the Perception Manager, a Camera Module retrieves a new frame from the camera and passes it to each of its View Modules.

2. *Optional background-subtraction*. Portico provides a background subtraction capability and offers it as an optional step in the perception process prior to view generation and object recognition. We use a Gaussian Mixture Models approach for background subtraction [20], with a dedicated model for each camera. When applied, a background/foreground mask is produced and is passed to each View Module along with the raw camera frame.

3. *Producing simulated camera views*. Using calibration homography computed during system setup, a View Module can produce one of a set of simulated views to be used for object detection. Each Camera Module also contains a Raw View Module responsible for object recognition done on the raw camera view (see Figure 4a-b). We have implemented support for a number of simulated views. Our proof-of-concept applications, described below, make use of the following two simulated views. The *Screen and Bezel View* (Figure 4c) produces a rectified view of the tablet screen and bezel and is useful for performing more precise detection of objects placed on the tablet. The *Table View* (Figure 4d-e) produces a rectified view of the tablet

screen and surrounding surface and is computed such that the tablet screen occupies one of the top quadrants of the rectified view depending on whether the left or right camera is used. Finally, a *Screen View* is also available, producing a rectified view of the tablet screen only. If background subtraction is used, a View Module will distort the background/foreground mask received with the raw camera frame such that it matches the simulated view.

We implemented the View Module class such that the resolution of each of the views (Raw, Screen and Bezel, Table, and Screen) is independent and can be changed depending primarily on the details of objects that need to be detected. Note that while the resolution of a rectified view has performance implications in our prototype (rectification is a pixel-wise multiplication operation), such operations can be accelerated in hardware to reduce this performance hit.

4. *Object classification*. Each View Module contains a list of classifiers responsible for vision-based object recognition. After its view is produced, a View Module gives its simulated view to each of these classifiers. Since some classifiers (*e.g.*, Color-Histogram) make use of foreground/background segmentation, while other classifiers do not (*e.g.*, HaarCascade or Template Matching), our implementation allows each classifier to request that images are returned as-is, or that background subtraction operations take place first. Each classifier then returns a list of detected objects, which can be empty.

Our system supports an extensible set of classifiers. Each classifier must implement a set of basic functions, including `classify()`, `trainNegative()`, `trainPositive()`, and `reset()`. Our system already includes a small set of implemented classifiers such as Template Matching, Compound Template Matching, HaarCascade, and a Color-Histogram. We plan to add a 2D marker classifier as well as a SIFT-based classifier, which is robust to rotation and scaling, in the future.

5. *Aligning object coordinates*. Since different views have different resolutions and coordinate systems in relation to the tablet screen, the coordinates of each object must be transformed into a uniform coordinate system prior to passing the objects to the Camera Module. We chose to transform the coordinates of each detected object to conform to the tablets' coordinate system, such that an object placed at the top-left of the tablet screen will have a coordinate of (0,0), and an object placed at the bottom-right corner of the tablet screen will have a coordinate of (1280, 800) in our prototype. At the end of this step, objects to the left of the tablet have negative x-coordinates, objects in front of the tablet have y-coordinates greater than 800, and objects to the right of the tablet have x-coordinates greater than 1280. Converging on this single coordinate system allows our output system to easily tell whether an object is on or off the screen, and choose one or more visualizations appropriately. The list of objects with updated coordinates is passed to the Camera Module.

6. *Removing redundant objects across views*. When entering this step, a Camera Module may hold more than one set of objects classified on different views with potential redundancies. However, each object must be reported at most *once* to the output system. We thus iterate over the lists returned from the different views and remove duplicates of objects that occur in multiple lists. We consider two objects with the same name and an overlap greater than 75% to be duplicates. The single list of objects is then passed from each Camera Module to the Perception Manager for processing.

7. *Unifying objects across cameras*. Similar to the previous step, the final step in the process is to merge objects returned from the two cameras, which is a step relevant to objects within the overlapping area between the two cameras. Unlike merging objects from different views of the same camera, however, we cannot assume that a single object detected by both cameras will have perfect overlap between the views. In fact, for any 3D object, we can assume that this will *not* be the case. Our system uses the overlapping area for an object seen by both cameras as the possible base of the object. For overlapping objects, only the intersecting area is thus reported to the output subsystem to approximate an object's touch point with the

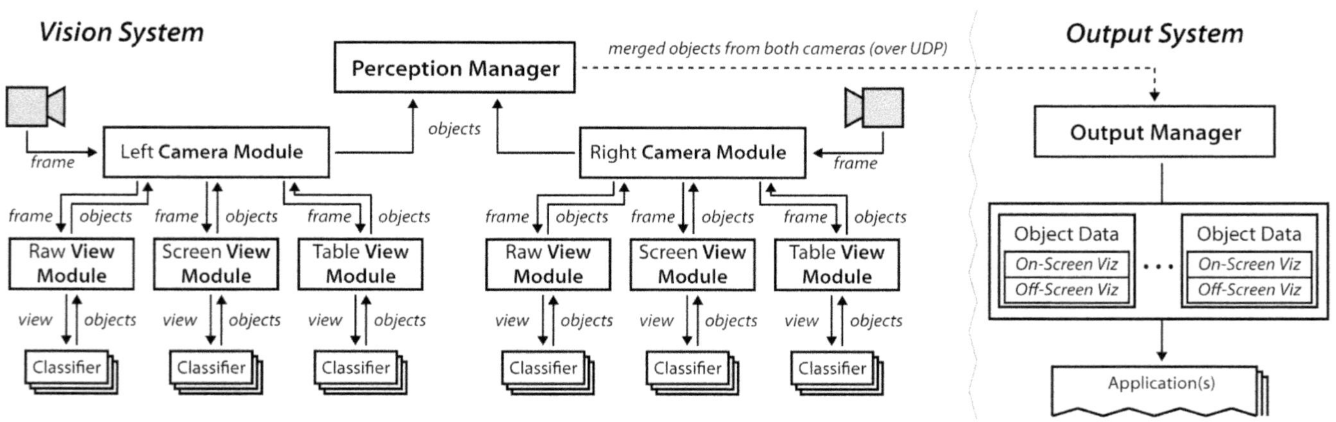

Figure 3. System diagram. Vision system with two camera feeds communicates detected objects to the output system over UDP sockets. Digital representations for each object are created and passed to subscribed applications.

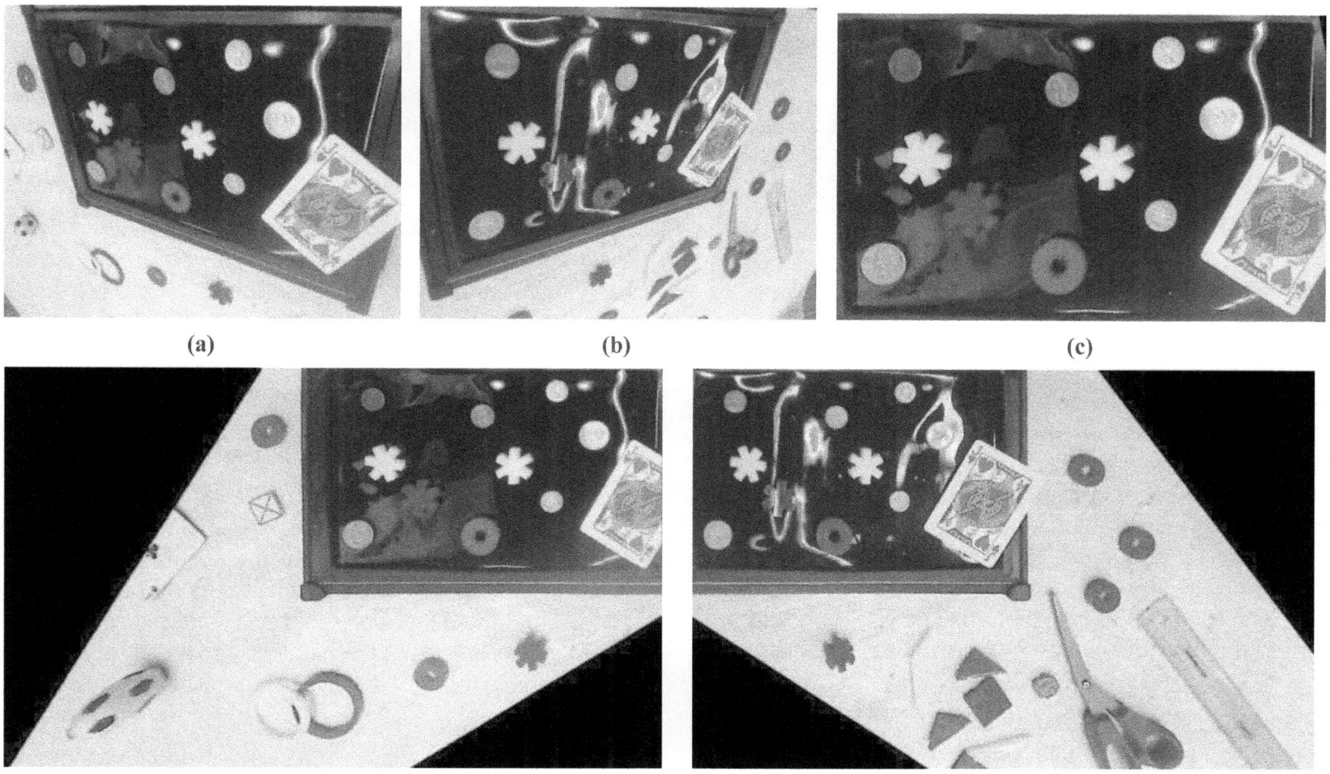

Figure 4. Multiple camera views: The raw camera view of (a) the right, and (b) the left cameras. (c) A rectified view of the screen and bezel (from the left camera), and the rectified view of screen and tabletop surface from (d) the right and (e) the left cameras.

surface and provide feedback at the appropriate position.

8. *Passing Objects to the Output System*. Finally, the unified list of objects from both cameras is passed over UDP sockets to the output system.

System Calibration

Prior to first use ("in the factory"), the system is calibrated to generate the different camera views and to deliver correct object positions. System calibration consists of three steps. Note that because the camera and screen are orthogonally polarized, these steps cannot use virtual on-screen markers. In the first step, the four corners of the screens are located, once per camera. The transformation homographies are stored on file and are loaded whenever the system starts. In our prototype, the corners are manually selected with the stylus; however, in the future, this step should be performed automatically, *e.g.,* by embedding permanent physical markers at the screen corners.

At this point, an object placed on the screen will correctly receive the same coordinates from both cameras. However, because the plane of the tablet screen is elevated *above* the plane of the table, an object placed on the table surface will receive different coordinates from each camera. Thus, to correct for the difference in planes between the screen and tabletop, in the second calibration step, a single physical marker is placed on the table at the overlap between the two cameras (at this point, the system will report seeing two markers on the table). The system computes an offset that aligns the marker's coordinates, stores it, and later applies it to the coordinates of all off-screen objects. Since the thickness of the tablet is fixed, this step needs to be performed only once.

Finally, in order for physical objects to correspond to meaningful coordinates in application space, the calibration marker is placed at the four corners of a calibration application and a transformation is computed based on the coordinates returned by the vision system. This transform is stored, and later used by our various applications.

Output System

Our output system is responsible for listening for objects delivered over UDP from the vision system, and for providing mechanisms to allow an application to visualize and represent physical objects. By using sockets for the communication between the vision system and output system, we were able to support applications written in different languages. Currently we have implemented two versions of the output system, one for writing applications in C# using .NET 2.0 and the other for Java.

As shown in Figure 3 (right side), the output system contains a UDP client that parses incoming messages for physical objects. Our system contains a basic representation of a physical object (the VisionObject class) which can be subclassed to support specific objects. Each VisionObject (or subclass) possesses the knowledge of how to draw itself when it represents an object on the tablet or when that object lies beyond the tablet's boundaries. The output system uses an object's coordinates to determine whether

Figure 5. Some of the off-screen visualizations: arrows, icons, and halos.

the object is on- or off-screen, and objects know how to draw themselves based on where they are found in relation to the screen. An Output Manager then passes the parsed objects to any subscribed application, which allows more than one running application to interact with physical objects simultaneously.

For easier application development, we created a Vision Simulator in C# that allows for using simple drag-and-drop operations to send simulated on-screen and off-screen objects to any application. It has been our experience that this decoupling of an application's computer vision requirements and output capabilities greatly increases the ability to iterate and debug applications.

Optional Feedback for Off-Screen Objects

With an input area larger than the screen, conveying to users the system's perception of objects outside its output space could be useful. For example, in Bonfire [12], information about coffee consumption is presented next to the user's coffee cup. However, a user is unlikely to want to place a beverage on their tablet. Similarly, in Classmate Assist [3], a student is guided through a sequence of actions with math manipulatives. Because of the screen size, in Portico, many of the objects will necessarily be off the tablet. In *Halo* [2], Baudisch and Rosenholtz presented a technique for visualizing off-screen objects using contorted partial ellipses. Originally designed for PDAs and phones, Halo demonstrated the ability to convey the location of landmarks on a large virtual map that are off the current display. In Wedge [6], Gustafson *et al.* modified Halo to convey distance and direction, while reducing screen clutter. Inspired by this work, Portico enables application developers to provide users with optional feedback about objects that are off the screen using a library of visualizations that can be easily modified and extended. Figure 5 shows a number of the off-screen visualizations in action. This library includes visualizations for reflecting the presence of an off-screen object and manipulators that can be applied for conveying the distance of the object from the tablet. The following visualizations are implemented:

Line. A line, or ray, is drawn from the center of the tablet screen in the direction of the object that is on the table. The line can be used with thickness or an alpha-blend to indicate an object's distance from the tablet.

Icon. An icon representing the object is drawn at the edge of the screen. The position of the icon is computed such that the icon is placed at the edge of the screen on the imaginary line connecting the object's and screen's centers.

Arrow. Similar to the icon, an arrow is drawn at the edge of the screen pointing in the direction of the object. Arrows have stems by default, but those can be turned off. In our prototype, thinner, longer arrows are used for objects that are farther away from the tablet screen.

Callout. A callout looks similar to a speech bubble with the tail pointing towards the off-screen object. A callout includes a label and an optional icon. It can be sized and alpha-blended to reflect an object's distance.

Halo. Inspired by Baudisch and Rosenholtz's [2] technique for visualizing virtual off-screen elements, we support halos to visualize physical elements off the tablet screen. Halos are arcs at the screen edge that are part of a virtual circle centered at the physical object. Thus, a halo with a larger radius conveys that an object is further away from the screen.

Alpha Blend. This visualization manipulator changes the alpha value of a visualization based on the object's distance from the screen. When the object is touching the screen, the alpha value is 100%. We set the alpha value for an object at the edge of the outer interaction space to 20%.

Size. This manipulator changes the size of the visualization. By default, greater size indicates that objects are further away; however, this can be easily reversed by altering options in a settings file.

Length. For some elements, a longer representation can be useful to conveying that the object is further away. In our system, the stem of an arrow becomes longer the farther away an object is.

Figure 6. Using physical tokens to play *Tic Tac Toe* on the tablet. The game is supervised by Portico and any illegal moves are flagged (and audibly "buzzed").

Figure 7. *Penalty Shootout.* The player rolls the soccer ball on the table or floor towards the screen. After the toy ball hits the tablet chassis, a virtual ball continues the physical ball's trajectory and speed towards the goal.

Line-Thickness. Portico can change the line thickness used by some visualizations, for example, making lines thicker for objects nearer to the screen.

PORTICO'S PROOF-OF-CONCEPT APPLICATIONS

To put Portico through its paces, we created a number of fully functional applications designed to highlight Portico's capabilities to respond to objects on and off the screen. Our examples highlight some playful uses of Portico.

Tic Tac Toe: Tracking On-Screen Objects

Tic Tac Toe is a basic demonstration of our system's ability to detect objects on the tablet, and to make use of the tablet's screen and touch capabilities. In this application, physical tokens are used by one or two players to play the classic game (Figure 6). Portico recognizes tokens' positions on the screen to determine the state of the game-board and highlight tokens from underneath.

After placing a piece, a player touches the NEXT button on the screen to indicate the completion of their turn. At this point, the application checks the state of the game board to ensure that no —mistakes" or —cheats" were made. If one is found, the application plays an audible buzzer, and visually flags the illegal pieces. Although simple, Tic Tac Toe conveys Portico's ability to oversee physical transactions and augment the experience, in this case, by providing a referee or, if desired, a computer opponent.

Penalty Shootout: Dynamic Off-Screen Interaction

Our second application is called *Penalty Shootout*. In this application, designed to be played on the floor or carpet, the tablet screen shows a soccer goal and goalie. The player physically rolls a small soccer ball-shaped foosball on the carpet toward the virtual goal on the screen. When the physical ball hits the tablet's chassis, a virtual ball appears and flies toward the goal along the same trajectory as the incoming physical ball (Figure 7) and the goalie tries to block the shot.

Penalty Shootout takes advantage of the tablet being raised from the table so that the physical ball can impact the tablet and then return, more or less, to the user. Velocity and acceleration in the physical world are converted directly into virtual motion on the screen. The velocity of the physical ball is translated into the height of the virtual soccer ball on the screen. Thus, if the physical ball is rolled too fast, the shot will appear to travel over the goal.

The direction of the physical ball is computed by performing linear regression on the observed locations of the incoming ball samples. The centroid of the template-matched ball is used. For recognition purposes, the vision system was trained on —blurry" images of a ball being rolled at the tablet as well as stationary soccer balls. Linear regression provided some robustness to noisy samples.

Penalty Shootout highlights our system's ability to detect objects off the tablet, track their velocity and trajectory, and react to them on the screen. Our use of physics calculations was inspired by Wilson *et al.*'s [25] work on bringing physics to interactions with virtual objects on a Microsoft Surface. Penalty Shootout is just one in a large class of possible games that make use of the trajectory and velocity of tracked physical objects around the surface. Others include —eagle-eye" golf, bowling, or marbles.

Portico Arcade: Off-Screen Physical Controls

Portico Arcade pays tribute to Atari's classic 1979 arcade game *Asteroids*. In Portico Arcade, physical interaction with a custom toy we've created takes place entirely off the tablet screen. Similar to SideSight [4], user's actions do not block their view of the screen. In this game, the angle of a plastic spaceship on the table is used to control the rotation of a virtual spaceship on the screen and aim its lasers (Figure 8). As in the original Asteroids game, the player's goal is to shoot floating asteroids while avoiding being hit by them. We also created physical add-on weapons that can be snapped onto the plastic ship for added firepower. In our example, snap-on cannons enable the player to fire three lasers at a time instead of just one. To determine the angle of the spaceship, two circular visual tags, one on each wing, are tracked and the angle between them is calculated. Other visual tags are used to detect the presence of add-on

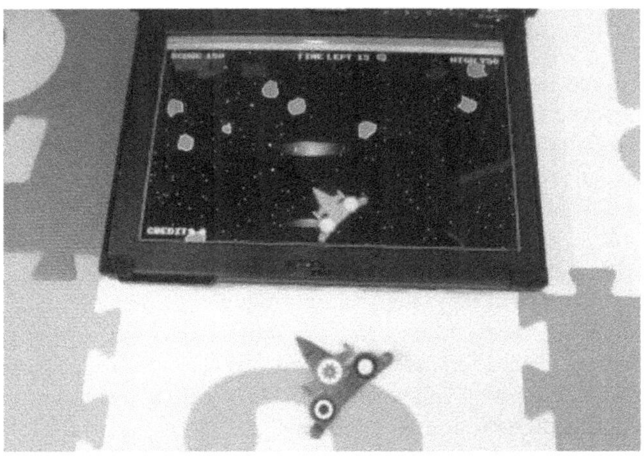

Figure 8. *Portico Arcade* uses a physical spaceship on the table to control the angle of an on-screen virtual spaceship. Physical add-on weapons provide increased firepower.

weapons. If a tag on either wing is not detected, an indicator on the corresponding wing of the on-screen virtual spaceship turns from orange to gray, and the ship does not rotate. This feedback is meant to help the user realize that the system's view of the ship is obstructed, or that the ship is outside the system's interactive area.

Tabletgotchi: Virtual Worlds for Physical Pets

Our fourth proof-of-concept application, *Tabletgotchi*, allows a child to play with an uninstrumented physical toy pet (*e.g.*, a plush zebra), and have the system react to the toy's state on, or around, the tablet (see Figures 1 and 9). Tabletgotchi was inspired by Webkinz[1] and the original Tamagotchi Japanese virtual pets. With Webkinz, a child links a physical plush pet with its virtual instantiation in the digital world on the Webkinz's web site. The child can then play with the virtual toy in its virtual world or with the physical toy in the physical world. However, the physical and virtual remain disconnected. With Tabletgotchi, we establish a link to bring the two worlds directly together.

In Tabletgotchi, a physical toy zebra can "eat" food shown on the screen, or "drink" from a virtual pool of water. (A timer periodically replenishes the supply.) A sand area provides a place for the zebra to use the "potty." The physical orientation of the zebra is also relevant in Tabletgotchi. Specifically, the zebra can "nap," as our system distinguishes between a standing zebra and a zebra lying down. For example, laying the zebra on its side below the tablet triggers a "dream" where a nature video of zebras in the wild plays above the zebra's head on the screen. If the zebra stands up mid-dream, the state change is immediately recognized and the dream promptly stops. Future versions could add 3D gesture tracking to enable actions such as "petting" to be recognized and rewarded.

We believe that allowing the physical toy to participate in play, rather than substituting it as with Webkinz, will encourage young children to interact with objects around them, and reduce the extent to which they focus their attention entirely on digital content.

DISCUSSION

Over the course of this work, we obtained insights into the capabilities and limitations of Portico. We believe that Portico represents a new approach to enabling personal and portable tangible surface interaction. We also believe that the interaction area provided by Portico, larger than the screen of the tablet, is necessary for meaningful and extensible portable tangible applications, and we consider this to be a primary contribution of Portico. Furthermore, with the vision and output systems in place, developing applications is easy. For example, *Tabletgotchi* and *Pentaly Shootout* were 600 and 552 lines of C# code respectively, and each used template matching of prototypical views of the objects with approximately 20 negative examples to train the classifier threshold.

[1] Webkinz: http://www.webkinz.com/

Figure 9. *Tabletgotchi* uses an uninstrumented zebra that "eats" carrots, "drinks" water (right side), uses the sand area (left side), or lays below the tablet and dreams (above). If the zebra stands up, the dream video stops, responding to the change in the zebra's physical state.

Beyond interaction with physical objects for tangible manipulation, prior work, such as DigitalDesk 23] and Bonfire [12], proposed incorporating everyday objects to enrich a person's computing interaction. In the work on Bonfire, for example, a coffee cup is tracked for personal logging. In order to support such interaction with a personal tabletop system, however, a large class of objects (*e.g.*, liquids and other consumables) must be recognized without the need for the user to place them on the screen. Our system provides a natural extension to these systems in its ability to recognize objects around the tablet. A cup placed next to (rather than on) the tablet would be detected and tracked. While the absence of a projector makes it impossible to provide labels right next to objects, off-screen visualizations can be used instead.

System-in-Use

We informally tested our system with one 4 year-old and two 3-year old boys. Our applications clearly targeted a young crowd and the use of familiar physical objects was very appealing to them. The children were keen to use the system and the objects right away and greatly enjoyed their experiences. In one case, one of the 3-year old children showed that he personally identified with the zebra's actions and drew analogies to his own experiences. ("He [the zebra] uses the potty like I use the potty!")

One noteworthy behavior that we did not expect was that, once the children were done using an application as we intended, they attempted to use objects with applications not designed for those objects. For example, one child tried using the tic-tac-toe pieces in the Tabletgotchi application and was confused when the system did not react to these objects. This observation suggests that our classifiers should support the option to recognize the presence of unknown objects, and suggests that applications still act on these unknown objects in some possibly playful or meaningful way.

System Performance

To give a sense of Portico's performance, we examined the number of frames-per-second (fps) under different conditions. As a baseline, with both cameras set to a resolution of 800×600 and without any additional processing, the vision system runs at 30 fps. Next, the system yields 24 fps for rectification of each camera once (*e.g.*, to generate the Table view) and 18 fps to rectify each camera twice (*e.g.*, to generate both the Table and Bezel views). Such frequent matrix manipulations for rectification could take advantage of hardware acceleration. The compute time required for classification is dependent on the type of classifiers used and the number of objects possible in the scene. In Portico Arcade and Tabletgotchi, for example, the system runs at 14 fps, which we found sufficient for our explorations.

System Constraints

Contour of the Interaction Space

One possible limitation of our system mentioned earlier is that the cameras' coverage to the right and left of the tablet screen is angled. As a result, the contour of the area viewed by the cameras resembles a wedge rather than a rectangle, which may make perceiving the bounds of the interaction space more difficult for users. The shape of the interaction space (see Figures 4d-e) is determined by the type of cameras used and their placement. In designing our prototype, for example, we limited the height of the cameras (specifically, the arms on which the cameras are mounted) to the depth of the screen such that, when folded, the cameras are flush with the screen and allow the tablet to be used normally. We also opted to utilize cheap web cameras, as they provide the benefits of being lightweight, low-cost, and widely available. While the current shape of the interaction space does not pose a limitation for all applications, for other applications, growing or widening the interaction space may be desirable. Fish-eye lens cameras, for example, could provide a wider view of the tabletop around the screen than our current cameras, although they would sacrifice image fidelity at the periphery. Similarly, different placements of the cameras, likely with different mounting arms, will produce different interaction spaces. Finally, on-screen visualizations, for example, a ―radar" view of the interaction space that, at a glance, can highlight all objects recognized by the system and convey the extent of the interaction space, may also help.

Sensitivity to Illumination Changes and Obstruction

Like any top-view camera-based system, Portico is sensitive to changes in illumination and obstruction. IR-based sensing, especially when done from behind the screen, can robustly detect the placement of objects on the screen. Top-down camera systems, however, can observe more of the object's shape than merely its contact points with the surface, as well as see objects from the user's point of view. While Portico's top-down cameras were adequate for a proof-of-concept, a system that combines our design with the optical sensors used in ThinSight [4] could benefit from both approaches. IR-based *depth sensing* cameras can provide robustness to illumination, together with added 3D capabilities; however, many of the objects used in tangible educational and playful applications (*e.g.*, coins, Cuisenaire rods, Tangram and jigsaw puzzle pieces) are thinner than the depth resolution provided by current 3D cameras. Another constraint of our system is that cameras may fail to see objects that are very close to or touching the tablet if the tablet is thick. As new tablets are made thinner (the recent iPad's thickness is 8.8 mm compared to our prototype's 35 mm), this problem will be significantly reduced.

Potential for Use in Education

Tangible and surface computing can present significant benefits to education. The use of manipulatives in mathematics education dates back to the 19th century with Swiss educator Johann Heinrich Pestalozzi [16]. Manipulatives are concrete objects that can be viewed and physically handled by students in order to demonstrate or model abstract concepts. In a meta-analysis of 60 studies, Sowell [19] affirms the effectiveness of manipulative material for students' achievement and attitudes in math education, particularly over long-term use. Studying the use of tangible computing for education, Antle *et al.* [1] compared how children solve a digital puzzle using a mouse, a tangible augmented puzzle, and a standard physical puzzle. Their results show that children were more successful and faster at solving puzzles using a tangible-based approach. Related results by Tuddenham *et al.* [21] suggest that when using tangibles, users are both quicker to acquire, and more accurate in manipulating, interface control objects, compared to using multi-touch or mouse-and-puck. Patten *et al.* [15] proposed using Sensetable for chemistry and system dynamics simulation applications. Zuckerman *et al.* [26] presented a system that uses computationally enhanced manipulatives. They show that their manipulatives are accessible to young children and encourage learning of abstract concepts through an iterative hands-on process. Scarlatos [17] used multimedia and visually tagged tangible objects to guide children in collaborative problem solving with the TICLE system. Horn *et al.* [9] demonstrated the use of tangible interaction for instruction of computer programming concepts.

As this prior research shows, the promise of tangible interaction to improve the learning experience is great. Similar to [3], we believe, however, that in order for this promise to be realized at a large scale, tangible interaction must be supported by personal systems, not only by traditional fixed tabletop computers. With Portico, we seek to deliver the benefits of tangible interaction to children in the classroom, in their home, or even on the living room carpet, all in a low-cost portable and personal form.

FUTURE WORK

As mentioned above, our system currently includes only a handful of object classifiers and we intend to extend this set to support a greater range of objects. We also intend to support tracking of objects across frames, as shown in [24]. The use of IR-based cameras could mitigate the sensitivity to illumination changes, while higher resolution cameras will allow for scanning of physical objects, similar to [13].

Our current prototype, which used a 12" tablet, was able to produce an interaction space six times larger. In our desire to support our system's use for education, we have since created a prototype using a small 10" tablet, a platform more suitable for use within schools. We plan to explore the use of our system to support math-manipulative activities in the future.

CONCLUSION

This paper presents Portico, a low-cost surface computing system that supports tangible interaction. Using its mounted cameras, Portico greatly extends a tablet's interaction space to include objects manipulated on the tabletop surface around it. We presented four proof-of-concept applications—*Tic Tac Toe*, *Penalty Shootout*, *Portico Arcade*, and *Tabletgotchi*—each of which highlights an important aspect of Portico's capabilities. Unlike most prior surface computing systems, Portico is based on a *personal* and *portable* form factor, namely a tablet computer, and as such, Portico brings surface computing one step closer to everyday use.

ACKNOWLEDGEMENTS

We thank Shaun K. Kane, Anthony LaMarca, Matthai Philipose, Richard Beckwith, Noam Avrahami, Caelan D. Wobbrock, and Malcolm Greenstein.

REFERENCES

1. Antle, A. N., Droumeva, M., and Ha, D. 2009. Hands on what?: Comparing children's mouse-based and tangible-based interaction. In *Proc. IDC '09*, 80-88.
2. Baudisch, P. and Rosenholtz, R. 2003. Halo: A technique for visualizing off-screen objects. In *Proc. CHI'03*, ACM Press, 481-488.
3. Beckwith, R., Theocharous, G., Avrahami, D. and Philipose M. 2010. Tabletop ESP: Everyday sensing and perception in the classroom. Intel Technology Journal *14* (1), 16-31.
4. Butler, A., Izadi, S., and Hodges, S. 2008. SideSight: Multi-"touch" interaction around small devices. In *Proc UIST '08*, ACM Press, 201-204.
5. Edge, D. and Blackwell, A.F. 2009. Peripheral tangible interaction by analytic design. In *Proc. TEI '09*, 69-76.
6. Gustafson, S., Baudisch, P., Gutwin, C., and Irani, P. 2008. Wedge: Clutter-free visualization of off-screen locations. In *Proc. CHI'08*, ACM Press, 787-796.
7. Harrison, C. and Hudson, S. E. 2009. Abracadabra: Wireless, high-precision, and unpowered finger input for very small mobile devices. In *Proc. UIST'09*. 121-124.
8. Hodges, S., Izadi, S., Butler, A., Rrustemi, A., and Buxton, B. 2007. ThinSight: Versatile multi-touch sensing for thin form-factor displays. In *Proc. UIST'07*, ACM Press, 259-268.
9. Horn, M.S., Solovey, E.T., Jacob, R.J.K. 2008. Tangible programming and informal science learning: Making TUIs work for museums. In *Proc. IDC'08*, 194-201.
10. Ishii , H. and Ullmer, B. 1997. Tangible Bits: Towards seamless interfaces between people, bits and atoms. In *Proc. CHI'97*, ACM Press, 234-241.
11. Izadi, S., Agarwal, A., Criminisi, A., Winn, J., Blake, A., & Fitzgibbon, A. 2007. C-Slate: A multi-touch and object recognition system for remote collaboration using horizontal surfaces. In *Proc. Tabletop'07*. 3-10.
12. Kane, S. K., Avrahami, D., Wobbrock, J. O., Harrison, B., Rea, A. D., Philipose, M., and LaMarca, A. 2009. Bonfire: a nomadic system for hybrid laptop-tabletop interaction. In *Proc. UIST'09*, ACM Press, 129-138.
13. Kirk, D., Izadi, S., Sellen, A., Taylor, S., Banks, R. & Hilliges, O. 2010. Opening up the family archive. In *Proc. CSCW'10*, ACM Press, 261-270.
14. Kratz, S. and Rohs, M. 2009. HoverFlow: Expanding the design space of around-device interaction. In *Proc. MobileHCI '09*, ACM Press, 1-8.
15. Patten, J., Ishii, H., Hines, J., and Pangaro, G. 2001. Sensetable: A wireless object tracking platform for tangible user interfaces. In *Proc. CHI'01*, 253-260.
16. Saettler, P. *A History of Instructional Technology*. New York: McGraw-Hill, 1968.
17. Scarlatos L.L. 2002. TICLE: Using multimedia multimodal guidance to enhance learning. *Information Sciences 140* (1-2), 85-103.
18. Shaer, O. and Hornecker, E. 2009. Tangible user interfaces: Past, present and future directions. *Foundations and Trends in Human-Computer Interaction 3* (1-2), 1-137.
19. Sowell, E. 1989. Effects of manipulative materials in mathematics instruction. *Journal for Research in Mathematics Education*, 20: 498–505.
20. Stauffer, C., and Grimson, W. 1999. Adaptive background mixture models for real time tracking. In *Proc. CVPR'99*, IEEE, 246-252.
21. Tuddenham, P., Kirk, D., and Izadi, S. 2010. Graspables Revisited: multi-touch vs. tangible input for tabletop displays in acquisition and manipulation tasks. In *Proc. CHI '10*, ACM Press, 2223-2232.
22. Ullmer, B. and Ishii, H. 1997. The metaDESK: Models and prototypes for tangible user interfaces. In *Proc. UIST'97*, ACM Press, 223-232.
23. Wellner, P. 1991. The DigitalDesk calculator: Tangible manipulation on a desk top display. In *Proc. UIST'91*, ACM Press, 27 - 33.
24. Wilson, A. 2005. PlayAnywhere: A compact interactive tabletop projection-vision system. In *Proc. UIST'05*, ACM Press, 83-92.
25. Wilson, A. D., Izadi, S., Hilliges, O., Garcia-Mendoza, A., and Kirk, D. 2008. Bringing physics to the surface. In *Proc. UIST'08*, ACM Press, 67-76.
26. Zuckerman O., Arida S., and Resnick M. 2005. Extending tangible interfaces for education: Digital Montessori-inspired manipulatives. In *Proc. CHI'05*, ACM Press, 859-868.

Conté: Multimodal Input Inspired by an Artist's Crayon

Daniel Vogel[1,2] *and Géry Casiez*[1]

[1]LIFL & INRIA Lille
University of Lille, FRANCE
gery.casiez@lifl.fr

[2]Cheriton School of Computer Science
University of Waterloo, CANADA
dvogel@uwaterloo.ca

ABSTRACT

Conté is a small input device inspired by the way artists manipulate a real Conté crayon. By changing which corner, edge, end, or side is contacting the display, the operator can switch interaction modes using a single hand. Conté's rectangular prism shape enables both precise pen-like input and tangible handle interaction. Conté also has a natural compatibility with multi-touch input: it can be tucked in the palm to interleave same-hand touch input, or used to expand the vocabulary of bimanual touch. Inspired by informal interviews with artists, we catalogue Conté's characteristics, and use these to outline a design space. We describe a prototype device using common materials and simple electronics. With this device, we demonstrate interaction techniques in a test-bed drawing application. Finally, we discuss alternate hardware designs and future human factors research to study this new class of input.

ACM Classification: H.5.2 Information Interfaces and Presentation: Input; Interaction styles

General terms: Human Factors

Keywords: pen, touch, gestures, tabletop, multimodal

INTRODUCTION

Touch interaction is arguably more immediate and natural in many situations, but fingers are imprecise [27] and difficult to write with [3,15]. Alternatively, using a pen (or stylus) makes writing more natural and pointing more precise [29]. Luckily, this does not need to be a unilateral choice; pen and touch can be used simultaneously [3,15,29,30]. However, without non-dominant hand coordination or graphical buttons, the pen *itself* supports few modes. This makes single-handed mobile usage difficult and reduces the number of combined touch and pen modes. When frequently switching between pen-oriented modes, such as drawing, handwriting, gestures, and lasso selection [29], this can hurt performance [18]. Inferring modes is difficult, and most users prefer explicit control [7]. Schemes for squeezing multiple *explicit* modes from a pen include adding barrel buttons and classifying pressure [22], tilt [26], barrel rotation [3], or grip [25]. But these can be error-prone and ambiguous. A simple way to add a second mode is by adding an "eraser," a second *contact* point. The pencil analogy lends intuition and users have explicit control.

Our work extends this idea of switching modes using contact points by referencing how artists use a *real* Conté crayon, a square prism-shaped drawing stick. Its faceted shape creates a variety of marks according to how it contacts paper: corner, edge, end, or side (Figure 1). A *digital* Conté crayon could even sense *which* corner, *which* edge, or *which* side. Thus, Conté builds on ToolStone [23], but with notable differences: ToolStone is a larger block shape, uses only side contacts, and is designed for non-dominant hand usage on an indirect tablet. Conté can function single-handed, yet span multiple precise pen-like input modes and modes similar to tangible handles [16]. For example: one corner for drawing and another for handwriting recognition; one end edge for stroke-based gestures and another for lasso selection; one side to reveal a tool palette and another to create guidelines. Artists blend real Conté drawings with their fingers, so combining digital Conté with multi-touch input is natural. By tucking Conté in the palm, same-hand touch may be interleaved and, similar to Manual Deskterity [15], a Conté-enabled mode may be further manipulated with bimanual touch. For example: rotating a guideline with Conté while selecting angle snap with touch.

Inspired by informal interviews with artists, we catalogue digital Conté's characteristics, and use these to outline a design space. A principal challenge is the creation of a functional device. We describe the hardware and software for our digital Conté stick which is compatible with diffuse infrared illumination tabletops. Our solution uses common materials, basic tools, and simple electronics, making it possible for others to build their own Conté. As future work, we discuss alternate device implementations.

With our prototype Conté device, we implemented several compatible interaction techniques in a test-bed drawing application. These specific examples taken from the larger design space demonstrate the feasibility and highlight practical aspects of Conté techniques. A user evaluation would be premature for this nascent device [13], but we close with a discussion of avenues for formal evaluation with an emphasis on fundamental human factors questions raised by this new class of input.

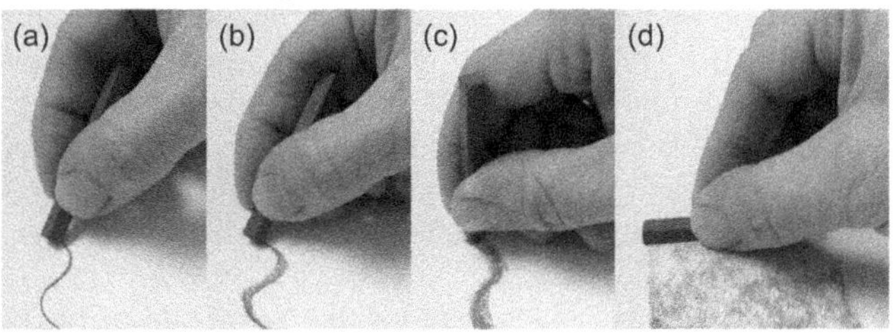

Figure 1. Drawing marks left by an artist's Conté crayon when using: (a) corner; (b) edge; (c) end; and (d) side.

RELATED WORK

Elegantly switching between multiple modes has been a challenge since the first pen input systems. The reader may recall the classic Sketchpad demonstration [31] where the operator is constantly "tickling" toggle switches. Later, DENIM [19] and Tivoli [20] state the problem clearly, and experiment with various techniques. In a study of "ink vs. gesturing" mode selection, Li et al. [18] found that pressing a hardware button with the non-dominant hand was fastest. However, each mode needs a button, and more than two modes may be necessary: Wu et al. [29] suggest 3 pen modes ("...write, annotate and sketch"); Brandl et al. add precise selection [4]; and Song et al. introduce 4 more [25].

Bimanual Touch and Pen Mode Selection. By combining a *single-touch* screen with a pen sensor Yee [30] demonstrates how non-dominant button touches, similar to Li et al.'s hardware button, can select among different pen tools. Wu et al. [29] and Brandl et al. [4] refine this further, by combining a pen with a *multi-touch* surface. Now modes may be selected according to the type of non-dominant hand contact. For example, touching two fingers changes from pen selection to pen inking [29], or a flat palm contact changes from free-form to poly-line pen drawing [4]. These combined touch and pen systems enable a broad continuum of interaction. On one extreme, pen and touch can act independently, like Yee's [30] and Brandl at al.'s [4] use of touch to pan the drawing surface while the pen writes. At the other end, pen and touch can coordinate very closely, such as Yee's [30] combined pen and touch zoom.

Hinckley et al.'s Manual Deskterity system [15] refines bimanual pen and touch coordination by considering the contextual relationship with direct manipulation objects (e.g. notes in a sketchbook application). When used alone, the pen always draws and the hand always manipulates, but when used in the context of an object, an implicit mode is entered. For example, depending on how an object is held with non-dominant touches and the object-relative motion of the pen, a pen stroke may cut like a knife, draw a straight line along an edge, or create a copy of the object. This greatly increases the number of modes in an elegant way, but various hand postures need to be recalled and performed unambiguously [2], and not all modes seem to have obvious bimanual contextual mappings. Consider how Hinckley et al. resort to a toolbar button to change the pen to a highlighter. Finally, along with Yee, Brandl et al., and Wu et al., two hands are required. Hinckley et al. do include redundant pen-only command access via radial menus, but acknowledge this adds syntactical complexity.

Unimanual Pen Mode Selection. Commercial pen input systems, such as the Wacom 6D Art Pen, provide multiple input dimensions which can be used for one-handed mode switching. Among one-handed techniques, Li et al. [18] find pressure and barrel button fastest, but with higher error rates (only beating conventional press-and-hold which was also slowest). Flipping an "eraser"-equipped pen is also slow, but with the lowest one-handed error rate. Li et al. only test binary mode selection, but by classifying continuous parameters like pressure [22], tilt [26], barrel roll [3], or even barrel grip [25], up to 6 modes can be supported. However, these can be ambiguous and error-prone due to interference from normal pen movements.

Mode Selection by Contact. Expanding on Fitzmaurice et al.'s flipbrick idea [8], Rekimoto and Sciammarella's ToolStone [23] is a block which is flipped and rotated to select between as many as 48 different modes. Although designed for non-dominant hand input on an indirect tablet, it illustrates how sensing the device-to-surface *contact* can be harnessed for mode selection. ToolStone focuses on face contacts; edge sensing is mentioned, but not explored. At $25 \times 40 \times 50$ mm, ToolStone is much larger than a pen but, in an elicitation study, Frisch et al. [10] observe some users using the side of a pen in a similar manner.

Summary. Conté builds on the ToolStone concept, but with notable differences. Conté has a much smaller form factor and is capable of detecting a more diverse set of contacts such as corners, short and long edges, sides, and ends. Although not a pen per se, when a corner or end edge contact is used, Conté approaches pen-like manipulation and precision. Thus, with an ability to switch modes based on contact, it directly addresses the unimanual pen mode selection problem. Compared to flipping an eraser-equipped pen, Conté has contact point adjacencies — clusters of different contact points at one end — with much shorter transition times compared to flipping a pen.

Also, unlike ToolStone, Conté is designed to work with multi-touch on a direct input display, a natural combination given how artists blend real Conté strokes with their finger. Dominant single-hand touch input can be interleaved by tucking Conté in the palm or setting Conté down. Bimanual pen and touch like Yee [30], Wu et al. [29], Brandl et al. [3], and Manual Deskterity [15] can also be achieved due to Conté's pen-like form factor. But, with Conté's multimodal capability, the design space is expanded.

EXPLORATORY INTERVIEWS

We conducted interviews with two practicing artists to gain a better understanding of real Conté and its potential digital counterpart. The specific questions and tasks were:

1. *How are real Conté sticks used?* Participants create simple Conté drawings on paper;
2. *How might digital Conté perform fundamental tasks?* Participants write, draw, tap, and trace paths;
3. *How might digital Conté perform basic manipulations?* Participants change contact points, set the stick down and pick it up, and "tuck" it in their palm.

For question 1, participants used a real Conté stick. For questions 2 - 4, they used solid acrylic mock-ups of different sticks with display-like feedback enabled by a "Magic Drawing Slate" novelty toy (Figure 2b). This is a grey sheet of film loosely laid over a black waxy under-layer. Pressing against the film creates a blackish mark and the marks are erased by lifting the film. We found this basic feedback essential to feel how digital Conté may work for mark-making. We tested three different Conté mock-ups (Figure 2a): 6 × 6 × 64 mm (same as artist's Conté crayons), 8 × 8 × 81 mm (same as another type of square prism shaped artist's crayon), 8 × 11 × 81 mm (an extruded rectangle profile we thought might be advantageous). A tablet pen and the short pen from the toy slate were available for comparison.

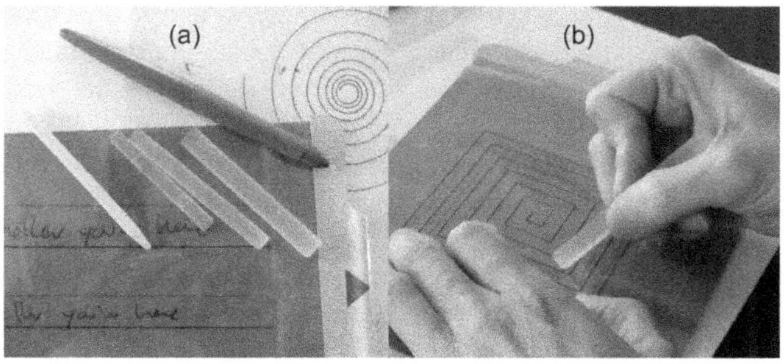

Figure 2. Interviews: (a) Conté mock-ups; (b) simulating fundamental tasks with the Magic Drawing Slate.

Primary observations are below (i.e. **1**a references task **1**):

1a. They use the corner, the end edge, and the side, and they blend with both non-dominant fingers and their dominant hand (by tucking the stick in their palm).

1b. Two different grips are used: a precise dynamic tripod grip, and a finger and thumb grip. The latter enables more contact surfaces to be accessed quickly.

1c. The tip becomes rounded with use, but artists can "find a corner" by feel as they rotate the shaft.

2a. Writing and tracing with a corner was similar to a pen, but the longer 81 mm mock-ups were preferred. Writing with Conté was less comfortable than a pen, but not especially uncomfortable either.

2b. The extruded rectangle profile could be held more securely, and did not reduce manipulative capability.

3a. "Tucking" Conté in the palm was easier than the tablet pen and up to three fingers could be used for touch.

3b. Transitioning contacts was fine, but took longer if the grip also had to be changed or re-adjusted. For example, changing from corner to side, or end to end.

3c. The most difficult contact to hold was a long side edge.

While clearly not a formal design study, these are useful general observations which we refer to later. Moreover, the open structure may have revealed aspects otherwise missed, and participants actually said it was fun.

CONTÉ CHARACTERISTICS AND DESIGN SPACE

In spite of its simple form factor, digital Conté has the potential to quickly switch between expressive input modes while providing additional parameters such as azimuth angle (barrel rotation), elevation angle (tilt), and pressure. After discussing the characteristics and capabilities of Conté, we outline a design space with includes using Conté alone and in combination with multi-touch.

Characteristics

The discussion here stems from our own observations supported by the artist interviews. Conducting formal quantitative experiments would be premature; we will discuss potential human factors studies as future work. To ground our discussion, we focus on the extruded rectangle Conté shape. The shape is pen-like given its crayon heritage, though compared to a pen it is shorter, faceted, and without a well-defined nib. Of course there will be some reduction in comfort and precision as the form factor deviates from a standard pen, and likewise a reduction in the number of stable contacts as the shape deviates from a ToolStone block. Our intention was to optimize this trade-off and we note that even efforts to establish an ideal pen shape are conflicted due to influences of individual preference and task [10,28]. The extruded rectangle shape was favoured by our interview participants and the slight irregularity should help users (and software) distinguish end edges and side faces. This form factor potentially supports 26 *different* contacts, classified into 7 *types* (Figure 3): 8 corners, 4 short end edges, 4 medium end edges, 4 long side edges, 2 end faces, 2 thick side faces, and 2 thin side faces.

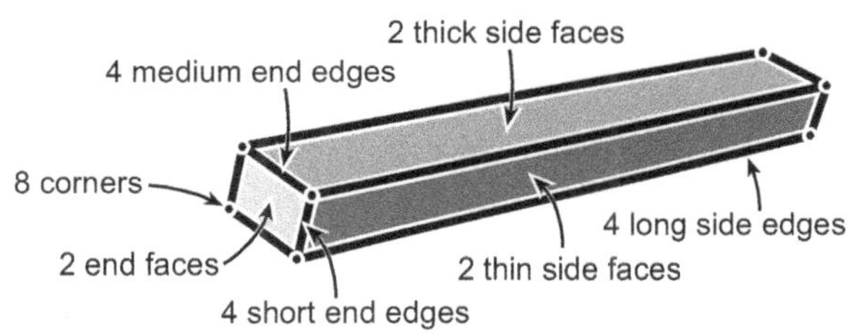

Figure 3. Seven types of contacts.

Contact Point Characteristics. For each type of contact, the combination of hand grip, contact shape, and equilibrium resulting from operating position dictate the availability of additional input parameters, level of precision, manipulation capability, and ability to maintain state when released (Figure 4). Song et al.'s [25] observation that people adopt different grips motivates a pen design which changes mode by sensing the current grip. With Conté, adopting different grips is a natural part of changing the desired contact.

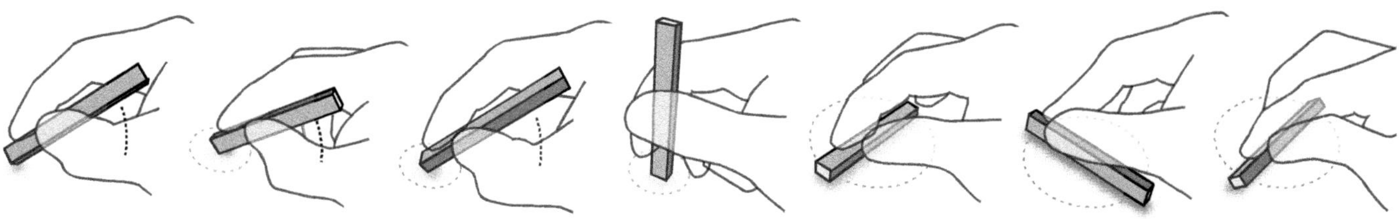

Figure 4. Typical hand grips used for different Conté contacts.

When contacting a corner, Conté is held like a pen using a precision grip, typically a dynamic tripod. The stick must be held at an angle to clearly disambiguate between adjacent contact points, so it has an unstable equilibrium (it must be supported to maintain a corner contact). Depending on the device thresholds for detecting adjacent contacts, usable elevation angles are less than a pen (well within 0 to 90°, clustered near 45°). There is no azimuth angle sensing limit, but in practice this is limited by wrist and elbow range-of-motion to about a 180° arc.

When contacting a short or medium edge, a slightly modified dynamic tripod grip [21] may be used and the increased contact area of the edge adds stability, though it must be held to maintain state. These factors reduce fine manipulation capability compared to the corner (or a pen), but the range of azimuth and elevation angles are similar.

In the exploratory interviews, we found that the long edge required a difficult thumb and index finger pinch grip. The small tolerance between the adjacent side faces reduces usable elevation angles to those near 45°. The instability of the grip and wrist and elbow range of motion reduce azimuth angles to approximately 180°, but rotating is difficult given the challenging grip.

The thick and thin side faces have a large contact surface area and low centre of gravity creating a very stable equilibrium: the grip can be loosened, or the stick set down, and the state maintained. The required pinch grip is much easier compared to the long edge. Also, the stability means azimuth angle covers the full 360° by manipulating with a clutching action. Elevation angle is invariant.

Contacting an end face suggests a further modified dynamic tripod grip which is moving towards a power grip [21]. Due to the high centre of gravity, the equilibrium is unstable and must be held to maintain state. Rolling the stick along the thumb enables 180° of azimuth rotation (like pen barrel rotation). Elevation angle is invariant.

Manipulation Characteristics. In our exploratory interview, participants commented on the extra time required to flip Conté end-over-end. This is similar to a pen nib-to-eraser transition, which takes 1.3 s on average [18]. With Conté, not all contact points are polar opposites; many nearby transitions should be quite fast: moving from a corner to an adjacent edge in a "rolling" adjacency *phrase* [5] for example. Hinckley et al. [15] also observed people "tucking" the pen in their palm to interleave dominant hand touch input. Based on our interviews, Conté's small size should make this even easier. The stable equilibrium of the side contacts also enable Conté to be set down and released (or grip partially loosened) yet maintain the same mode similar to ToolStone [23].

Cognitive Attributes. An open question is whether a user could recall command mappings for 26 different contact points, especially when coupled with rolling adjacency phrases and other parameter contexts such as azimuth angle. Similar strategies to those discussed by ToolStone's authors would increase usability, such as labelling faces for novices and adding tactile patterns for eye-free manipulation [23]. We have not explored this yet, but unlike ToolStone, Conté's greater variety of different contact points have diverse affordances which should assist recall. For example: the small corner size and tripod grip suggests drawing or writing; a medium edge is reminiscent of a highlighter and when oriented vertically, a text insertion point; a long side edge has a sharpness like a cutting blade; the flat ends act like stamps; and when laid on its side, Conté creates a tangible handle [16]. Also, unlike ToolStone, when Conté is used in the dominant hand on a direct input display it is the natural focus of attention. Thus, we can leverage proximal visual feedback to confirm the current mode. We display a rectangular "shadow" outlining the current contact and most activated modes have characteristic visual feedback such as displaying a guideline or rendering a dashed trail for lasso selection.

Design Space

The design space enabled by Conté is a super-set of the spaces demonstrated by commercial tablet pens, ToolStone [23], and Manual Deskterity [15]. At a base level, Conté can function like a pen, but also utilize the affordances and characteristics of different contacts to switch between modes (e.g. corner for drawing, end edge for highlighting).

Touch input can also be interleaved or coordinated with Conté input. For example, Conté could be used like ToolStone [14] in the non-dominant hand to set the mode for dominant hand touch – though contacts which use pen-like grips may be less effective [17]. Perhaps more interesting is *same-hand* touch input enabled by tucking Conté in the palm, setting it down on a stable side, or loosening the grip to free up a finger or thumb. The latter enables a hybrid style of "touch + handle" interaction, in which nearby touch input fine-tunes a mode enabled by Conté.

Conté can also realize the "pen + touch = new tools" design philosophy of Manual Deskterity. In addition to *touch context* techniques where the pen mode is inferred by the object context created by touch, Conté can be used for *pen context* techniques where the mode enabled by Conté contact creates the context for touch. Manual Deskterity's Tape Curve provides one example of this strategy where touch pins a pen stroke down to enter tape drawing mode. Since "the pen always writes" when used alone in Manual Deskterity, there are few possible *pen context* techniques — the only pen context is the stroke. This restrictive design rule makes sense with conventional pens. In contrast, Conté can enable multiple *"pen" context* techniques.

Below are primary qualities which define the total Conté design space covering these different functional styles:

- *Mode Mapping*. Consider precision and physical affordance when assigning contact point to mode (e.g. short edge is a highlighter, long side a ruler, end a stamp).
- *Group Modes*. Keep contact points of task related modes near each other (e.g. creation and revision at each end).
- *Use Adjacency Phrases*. Fast transitions among contacts can enable specialized modes (e.g. edge to corner roll).

- *Parameters for Direct Manipulation.* X-Y position and angle can be used for direct manipulation (e.g. position a guideline), to fine-tune a mode (e.g. pick default option), or to enable multiple modes per face like ToolStone.
- *Parameters at Invocation.* X-Y position and angle can fine-tune modes (e.g. object under contact to form context, angle on contact to pick sub mode).
- *Set It Down.* For stable sides, Conté will maintain the mode while freeing the hand for touch. Including nearby widgets revealed by the mode can further exploit this.
- *Use "Touch + Handle".* By loosening the grip on Conté, a finger or thumb can manipulate nearby widgets.
- *Leverage "Tucking."* Design techniques that interleave touch and Conté with one hand.
- *Set Context for Touch.* As discussed above, Conté's multimodal ability can enable "pen" context modes.
- *Non-Dominant Hand Usage.* Use more stable Conté contacts to set the mode for dominant hand touch.

In a later section, we demonstrate interaction techniques which encompass many of these qualities.

CONTÉ DEVICE PROTOTYPE

Creating a Conté device was challenging for multiple reasons. It was essential to make the device small, which ruled out some approaches. But we also added two more constraints: it must work with an unaltered multi-touch table, and it must be simple enough that researchers and tabletop hobbyists could create their own Conté sticks (we wanted to avoid complex electronics such as MTPen [25]). These constraints ruled out embedding multiple Anoto Pen sensors [4] or using magneto-electric coils like Toolstone [23] since they require too much space and tabletop alterations. Even if advanced magneto-electric pens such as the Wacom 6D Art Pen were compatible with direct touch input, two would have to be combined to support a two-ended Conté stick – and there is still the issue of altering the pressure-activated nib to work on corners, the limited range of elevation angles, and the size of the internal electronics. Instead, Conté emits and reflects infrared (IR) light which is captured by tabletop cameras, and translated by image processing algorithms into Conté input events. Emitting IR light uses simple and small electronics, and any diffuse infrared illumination multi-touch tabletop, such as the Microsoft Surface, can capture reflected IR patterns.

The simplicity of our design does make concessions: we detect and identify 10 out of the 26 possible contacts and we do not sense elevation angle. We detect a corner contact, but not *which* corner; likewise for short, medium, and long edges. Given the tiny surface area of corners and edges, there is little room to create a distinguishing ID pattern for image-based detection (consider that Surface ID tags are 19 × 19 mm). Since digital pens detect only one (or maybe two) contacts, this is still a significant increase and provides enough functionality to test Conté and begin exploring its potential. At the end of this paper, we discuss implementation ideas to detect all 26 contacts, but with added hardware complexity.

Hardware

Our prototype device is 9 × 11.5 × 84 mm and fits comfortably in the palm (Figure 5). It works by emitting IR light from each corner and reflecting IR light from paper labels affixed to the sides. Conceptually simple, we arrived at this design after much experimentation with materials and construction techniques. Two Osram SFH485 LEDs generate 880 nm near-IR light, matching the Surface IR pass band filter. Each LED is partially embedded in a highly polished 9 × 11.5 × 8 mm acrylic block using an open flame (Figure 5d). The acrylic block and LED are wrapped with foil tape to reflect IR light internally. Later, we cut small openings into each corner to let IR light escape (Figure 5c).

To house the electronics and fix the LED-embedded acrylic blocks at the tips, we cast everything in urethane resin using a custom mould (Figure 5b). This method creates a very solid feeling and durable stick, and since our mould was adjustable, it enabled fast prototyping of different shapes and versions. An alternative approach would be to mill a housing out of plastic, or print one using a solid printer, but these require more set up and would require high tolerances for the LED-embedded acrylic blocks.

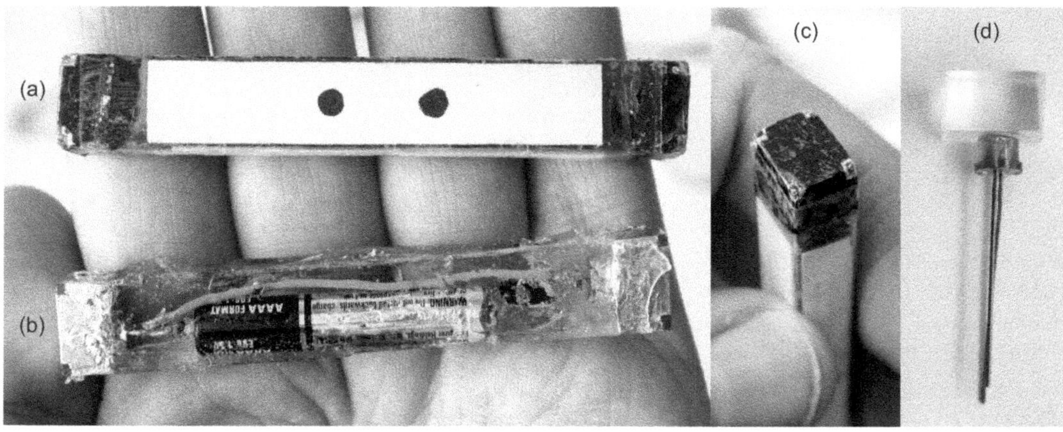

Figure 5. Infrared Conté prototype (shown actual size): (a) completed device; (b) after casting, showing battery and circuit inside; (c) end showing IR "windows"; (d) IR LED embedded in acrylic block; (e) circuit diagram.

After casting, the stick is sanded to fine-tune dimensions and painted matte black to increase the contrast of IR light. Then, small 2 × 2 mm openings are cut into each corner to emit IR light from the LEDs (Figure 5c). On one end, we paint a 3 mm white dot for identification. Finally, we glue foil-backed white paper labels to the side faces, and wrap everything in thin matte transparent tape. The foil backing increases IR reflectivity, and the tape prevents rubbing the paint off as well as protecting the Surface diffuser from scratches. Each label has 3 mm black dots: using the number of dots and size of the label, we can identify the side.

Our basic prototypes are powered by two external batteries supplying 3 V. In spite of being tethered by a thin wire, we found we could manipulate them surprisingly well. However, the protruding wire makes one side face unusable and does reduce manipulative capability somewhat. We found the Osram LEDs require a minimum voltage of 1.4 V, so they can be powered using a single alkaline AAAA battery. At just over 8 mm in diameter, we could embed one and keep a small form factor. With the LEDs wired in parallel and a 3.6 Ω resistor (Figure 5e), enough IR is emitted for tracking. But, compared to the 3 V tethered version, the emitted IR is lower making tracking high velocity movements less reliable (due to camera exposure blurring which we discuss in the next section). Our battery powered Contés operate for about 25 hours. The circuit draws 20 mA (due to battery voltage-current characteristics and LED forward current characteristics) and alkaline AAAA batteries are rated for 500 mAh. Rechargeable NiMH or NiCd AAAA batteries are only rated 1.2 V, so they would require an LED driver (such as the Zetex ZXSC300). We continue to investigate this rechargeable solution.

Unlike Hinckley et al.'s IR pen [15], we do not use tip switches to only activate the LEDs when touching the display. Attaching miniature switches to all contact points would be very difficult. Instead, we found that the combination of pinpoint IR light from the corners, and the Surface's high quality diffuser (Evonik ACRYLITE 7D006), resulted in only slight hover artefacts.

Software

Our software translates the IR light patterns of Conté into events describing the current contact point, position, and, if available, azimuth angle. It is written in C# using the Emgu 2.2.1 (www.emgu.com) OpenCV wrapper. Figure 6 illustrates the following image processing steps.

Pre-Processing. Using the Microsoft Surface SDK 1.0 SP1, we access the 768 × 576 px, 8 bit greyscale image taken by the internal IR cameras. A Top Hat morphological operation is applied using 3 iterations of a 3 × 3 structuring element. This brightens Conté's sharp, bright shapes and darkens the duller smooth contacts of fingers and palms. We found this initial operation to be extremely important.

Position Detection. Next, we locate the approximate size and position of the Conté contact. The pre-processed image is binarized using a *variable* threshold value and then 20 iterations of the Dilate morphological operation is applied, creating large connected blobs. The variable threshold is computed from the velocity of the Conté contact in the previous frame. Specifically, we linearly interpolate between a threshold of 20 when Conté is moving faster than 5 mm/s, and a threshold of 66 when Conté is moving slower than 1 mm/s. When at rest or moving slowly, the high threshold isolates Conté from everything else. With fast movements, the camera exposure blurs the image of the corners or sides, and the threshold must be reduced. Of course, as the threshold is reduced, the intensity of other types of surface contacts will be above the threshold. To address this, we use the binarized image blob closest to the last Conté position — a surprisingly effective and simple rule. Using this approximate contact position, we can update the velocity (which is low-pass filtered with a 0.03 Hz cut off). If the velocity is above 1.4 mm/s, we stop processing and the approximate contact position, together with the last known Conté contact point and azimuth angle, are used to construct a Conté movement event.

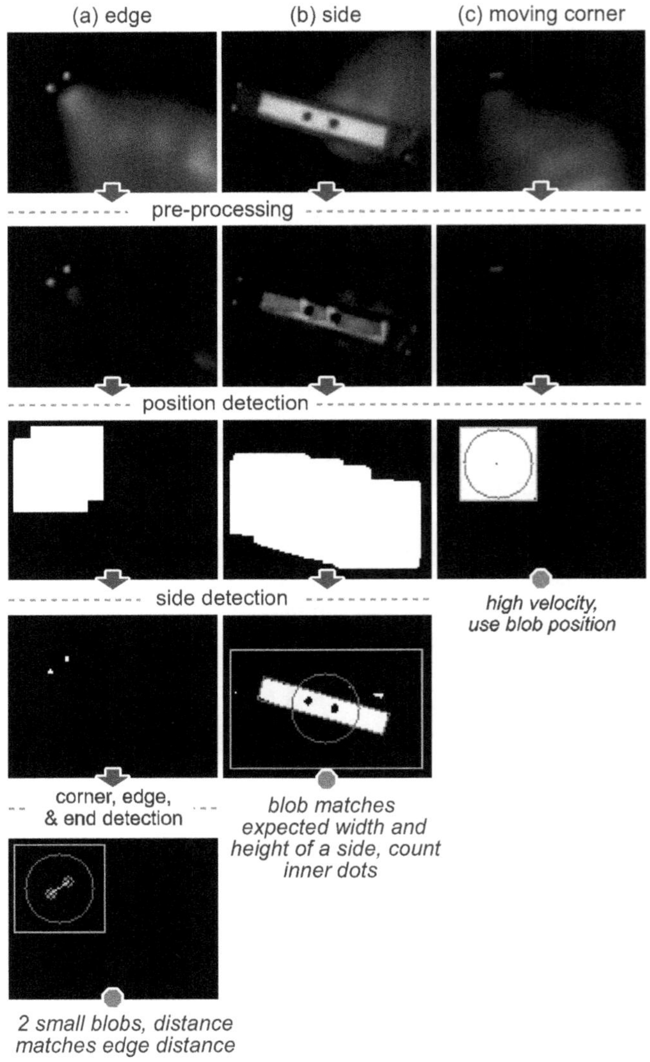

Figure 6. Image processing examples: (a) edge; (b) side; (c) moving corner. Rows show results of an image processing step: capture; pre-processing; position detection; side detection; corner, edge, and end detection.

Side Detection. If the velocity is lower, we continue processing and check whether a side face is touching. The pre-processed image is first binarized using a threshold of 66. Then, the minimum area rectangles of white outer connected component blobs are found (using Emgu `FindContours` and `GetMinAreaRect`). These are compared to the expected width and height of the thick or thin side face labels. If a match is found, the number of black connected component blobs within the matched blob is used to identify *which* side is touching. The minimum area rectangle also provides the azimuth angle of the side.

Corner, Edge, and End Detection. If no matching blobs were found in the side detection step, we search for corners. First, the pre-processed image is binarized using a threshold of 75. Any connected component blobs with an area greater than 16 pixels are removed. The number of remaining blobs and their relative distance determines the contact point: 1 blob is a corner; 2 blobs are an edge if their distance is ± 3 px of 9.5 px for short, 14 px for medium, 100 px for long; and 4 blobs is an end. Any other number of blobs is considered ambiguous and flagged as such. If an end is detected, we apply a lower threshold of 55 to the area between LEDs and determine if there is a white dot which identifies which end is contacting. An improved strategy would be to find the *best* match to all known contacts. For example, 3 blobs are either a corner with the stick held high, or an end with a slight tilt. These could be identified using intra-blob distances, rather than labelled ambiguous.

Performance. The main optimization we made was to restrict the processing area in the *Side Detection* and *Corner, Edge, and End Detection* steps to the contact blob bounding rectangle found in the *Rough Position Detection* step. Our algorithm runs at 45 Hz on a standard Microsoft Surface (Vista, 2.13 GHz dual core CPU, 2 GB RAM).

INTERACTION TECHNIQUE TEST-BED

An obvious application of digital Conté is an artist's sketching application which mimics how a real Conté crayon creates different line thicknesses. We go beyond this direct analogy and demonstrate the potential of Conté more fully in a sketching and drafting inspired application built using C#, WPF, and the Microsoft Surface SDK. Our application has enough complexity to force techniques to be mutually compatible and useful. It includes sketch-based drawing annotation like Manual Deskterity [15], but also demonstrates additional types of precise pen-like input and modal tools like guidelines. Earlier we discussed how Conté can support Manual Deskterity's *touch context* interactions, but we focus on techniques which set Conté apart: unimanual multi-modal input leveraging the characteristics of different contact points and *pen context* techniques where Conté sets the context for touch.

Pen-Like Input

The level of precision and affordance when contacting the corner or end edges suggest one-handed pen-like interactions. The corner is used for freehand drawing, since this is arguably the most precise pen-like contact (Figure 7a). Strokes made with the short end edge are interpreted as shape gestures, a simple solution enabled by Conté for the "ink vs. gesturing" problem [18]. These shape strokes are analyzed with the .NET 4 ink recognizer and replaced by a beautified version (Figure 7b). For example, a circular shape is recognized and replaced with a perfect circle; likewise for ellipses, rectangles, squares, triangles, etc. We use a dashed stroke pattern in the current stroke colour for visual feedback. The medium end edge performs a lasso selection (Figure 7d), a third pen-like input mode. Lasso selections are less precise than drawing and writing, but still require control over shape. A thick black dashed stroke provides visual feedback.

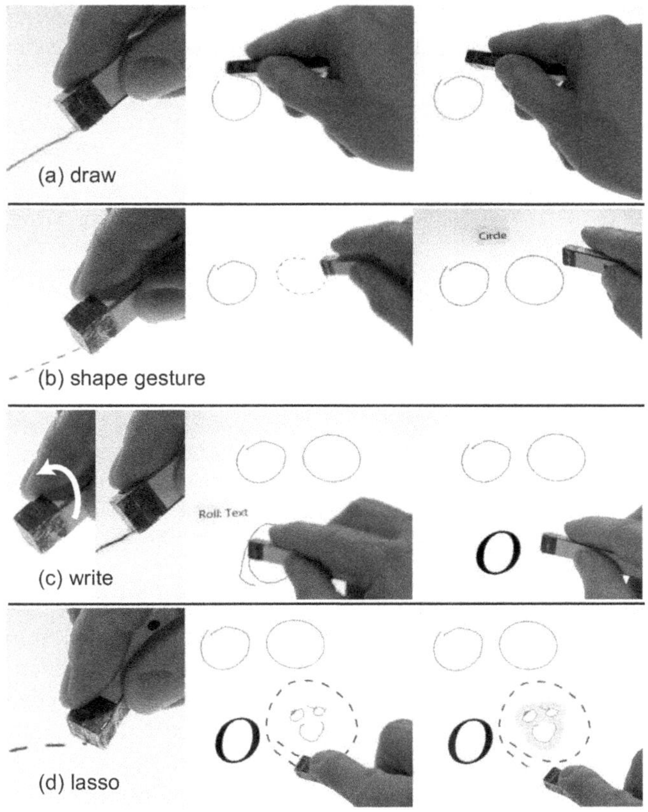

Figure 7. One handed pen-like input modes using corner and end edges: (a) freehand drawing and annotating with the corner; (b) making shape recognition gestures with the short edge; (c) a "roll" from short edge to corner changes corner mode to writing with text recognition; (d) medium edge for lasso selection.

In support of our drafting application scenario, users can enter typographic text by writing with Conté. Like drawing, writing is a precise task requiring fine grain manipulation, so a corner contact is most appropriate. Automatically distinguishing between drawing and writing is unreliable due to many ambiguous strokes (consider strokes resembling an 'O', 'l', or 'L' for example). With Conté, the user explicitly switches between writing and drawing mode. If our prototype Conté device could distinguish between corners, two different corners could be used. Instead, we exploit contact point adjacencies, and use a "roll" from a short end edge to a corner to enter a corner writing mode. A roll is recognized when there is a change to a corner contact less than 1 s after a short end edge contact. We provide visual feedback with a little notification tab which says "Roll: Text" and the stroke colour changes to the current font colour. Corner strokes return to freehand drawing after a subsequent mode change, or when the user explicitly exits with another short end edge to a corner "roll."

Contextual Commands

Contextual commands are common in most applications. In Windows, these are accessed with a right-click on an object and selecting from a context menu (such as 'copy'). In Deskterity, copying is performed by dragging the pen off an object held by a finger. This is an elegant solution, but requires two hands and makes multiple and distant duplication difficult. Moreover, adding more contextual commands means adding more "touch + pen" gestures.

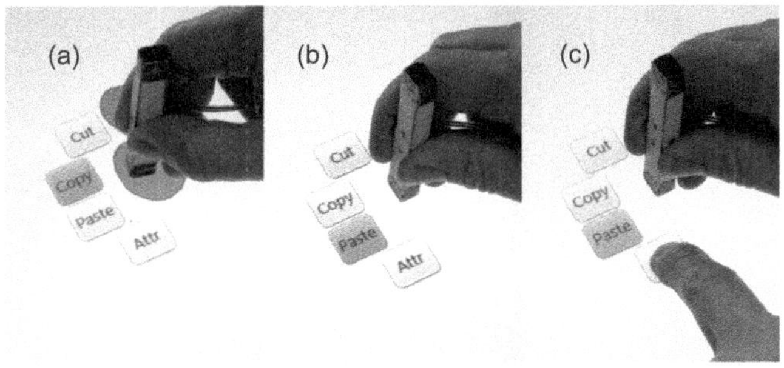

Figure 8. Contextual commands using the end contact: (a) a menu appears with 'copy' as default action since the thick side faces up-down; (b) 'paste' is default when the thick side faces left-right; (c) finger selects other commands which also become the new default for the current thick side orientation.

With Conté, an end contact on an object opens a contextual menu (Figure 8c) showing 'cut', 'copy', 'paste', and 'attr' (paste clipboard object *attributes* only, such as colours, typeface, etc.). The end stamping motion affordance seems to match these actions. To support one-handed operation, we use azimuth angle to *pre-select* a default command when the stick is immediately lifted. For example, when the thick side faces left-right, 'paste' is pre-selected, but when facing up-down, 'copy' (Figure 8a,b). The menu is only revealed after 200 ms, encouraging expert users to quickly access these default commands without visual clutter and enabling novice-to-expert transition. As a further refinement, when a command is selected by a non-dominant finger, it is used as the new default action for the current Conté azimuth orientation. Thus, 'attr' could become the new default when the thick side faces left-right, allowing the user to rapidly paste attributes to multiple drawing objects. Although not implemented, a different context menu could be associated with each end of the stick.

Attribute Palettes

Laying Conté down on one thick side opens one of four attribute palettes (fill colour, stroke colour, font colour, font properties). Since this a very stable contact, Conté can be released (Figure 9c) and an attribute selected with the same hand, or held as the non-dominant hand selects. We placed two touch sensitive buttons just above the stick to cycle through different palettes. With this placement, single-handed, simultaneous Conté and touch manipulation is possible by loosening the grip and using the middle and ring fingers to tap (Figure 9a). By touch-dragging on the palette bezel (Figure 9b), the palette may be "peeled" off Conté to remain visible after Conté is lifted. This can be done with non-dominant fingers or with the dominant hand by loosening the grip, dropping the index finger, and then tucking Conté in the hand. When cycling palettes, peeled palettes are temporarily brought to Conté's location with their peeled location shown as a dashed outline. Palettes are hidden by tapping the same thick side on or near the palette. This has the feeling of "picking up" the palette. We found that with palettes it can be natural to pass Conté to the non-dominant hand similar to ToolStone [23], and the dominant hand is free to touch for attribute selection.

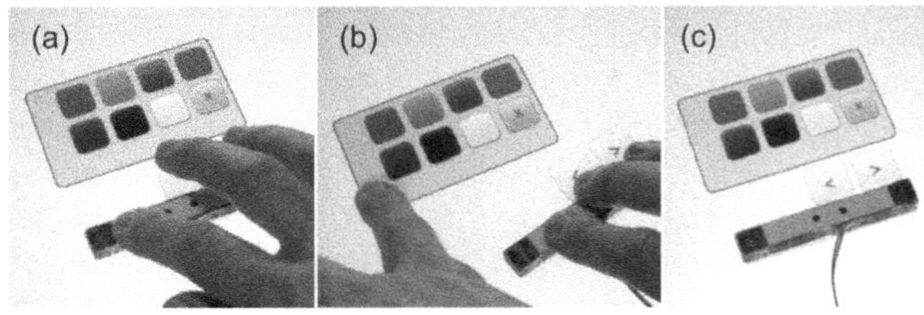

Figure 9. Attribute palettes using a thick side face: (a) one-handed cycling through palettes; (b) "peeling" a palette off to keep it visible; (c) side face is stable, so palette mode is held when Conté is released.

We explored alternate methods of cycling palettes such as using an up or down rolling action from side to adjacent long edge. Theoretically interesting, in practice it was difficult to maintain the necessary grip (partly because of the smooth sides created by wrapping Conté in tape).

Guidelines and Alignment

In commercial applications, guidelines are usually created by dragging off rulers anchored on the edge of the canvas. On a large tabletop this requires reaching, clutters the drawing area, and favours horizontal and vertical guidelines.

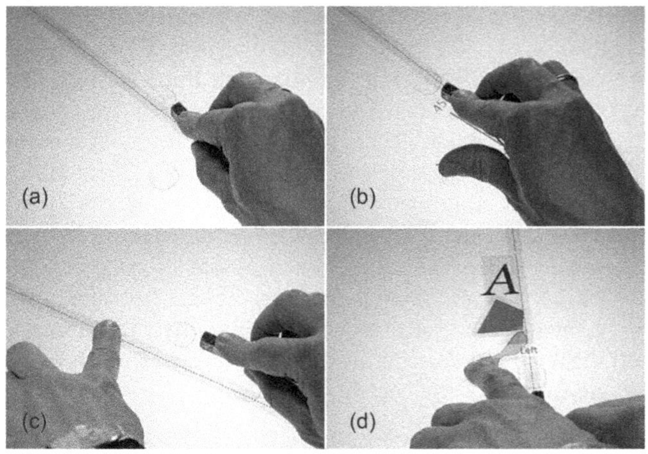

Figure 10. Guidelines using thin side face: (a) revealing and positioning temporary guideline with Conté; (b) adjusting snap angle with thumb; (c) "peeling" temporary guideline to make it permanent; (d) alignment tool, in this case left-aligning objects with a left-swipe.

With Conté, users can create guidelines at any angle by contacting the thin side face (Figure 10a). The stick translates and rotates the guideline, and similar to palettes, they may be peeled off (or perhaps "pinned down") with a dominant or non-dominant touch (Figure 10c). Guidelines are "picked up" by contacting the thin side nearby in the same orientation. Adjusting the guideline snap angle is another example of single-handed, simultaneous Conté and touch manipulation: with a loosened grip, the thumb is free to adjust snap angle by dragging (Figure 10b).

The guideline tool also aligns objects. Tapping or swiping a touch sensitive target just above Conté aligns currently selected objects. Swiping left left-aligns, swiping right right-aligns, and tapping centre-aligns (Figure 10d). While holding Conté, these are most comfortably done with the non-dominant hand, though centre taps are not too difficult with the dominant hand. However, given the stable thin side, the dominant hand can perform a complete alignment task: after positioning a temporary alignment guideline, Conté is released, and still in guideline mode the desired alignment command performed with a tap or swipe, and then the stick picked up to remove the temporary guideline.

Mouse-Like Pointing

Rekimoto and Sciammarella [23] pondered the idea of adding a button to ToolStone to use it as a mouse, and Forlines at al. [9] found that using a conventional mouse on a tabletop can outperform touch for some tasks. Inspired by this, when Conté is laid down on one thick side face it behaves like a standard mouse as it controls an arrow cursor. A stylized image of a mouse is rendered around Conté with its entire surface acting as a single touch sensitive button. This large button accommodates the restricted free finger movements when "clicking," while the remaining fingers continue to grip Conté. With a little practice, we could click and drag objects while maintaining a grip. We create a "mouse-aligned reference frame" [13] by mapping Conté movement vectors in display space to cursor movements. A pointer acceleration function is tuned for aggressive cursor movement with fast movements, but near 1:1 control-display gain when moved slowly. This enables precise selection and minimizes clutching over long distances [6].

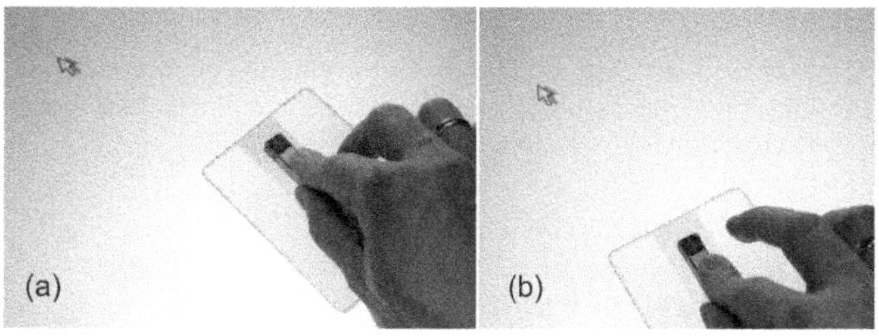

Figure 11. Mouse-like pointing: (a) point; (b) click.

CONCLUSION AND FUTURE WORK

Within the simple idea of recognizing different contacts of a faceted drawing stick lie hardware and software challenges, a new interaction design space, and new human factors questions to investigate. The work discussed in this paper focuses on the first two of these challenges to enable and motivate the third.

Focusing on IR hardware as we have has the advantage of fabrication tractability and tabletop compatibility, but removing these self-imposed constraints enables alternate strategies. One improvement we plan to test is adding a contact microphone to sense movement over the diffuser. If the sound profiles are distinct, this could act like a primitive tip switch. With a switchable diffuser [14] and colour-coded Conté faces, all 26 contacts can be recognized with basic image processing and a model of contact colour patterns. We have already implemented this strategy using a clear tabletop for a future quantitative manipulation experiment. By accepting more hardware complexity, accelerometers and/or a gyroscope could be embedded to accurately measure orientation, and the contact inferred similar to ToolStone. Diffuse or emitted IR light may continue to provide X-Y position information, or for a capacitive touch device, an outer layer of conductive material could be used.

Enabled by a hardware solution, and motivated by demonstrations of an interaction design space, we can turn to human factors. The many characteristics of Conté must be verified and quantified, and we are already planning an investigation of contact-to-contact transitions. Like Conté itself, this appears straightforward, but closer analysis reveals 54 different transitions (accounting for symmetry) which need to be contrasted and compared. This will complement Li et al.'s [18] work and help situate Conté among other mode switching techniques. Other investigations include precision, angular manipulation, grip styles, and recall capability: can people use 26 or more mappings? If not, how many? Related are ergonomic studies to test alternate form factors, construction materials, and tactile patterns.

The interaction techniques described here demonstrate key qualities of the Conté design space, but they may only hint at the potential. For example, some qualities can be pushed farther, such as leveraging "tucking," and others we have not addressed directly like switching Conté between hands. Art historians have argued that the invention of the versatile Conté crayon influenced a new style of art [24]. At the risk of sounding overly enthusiastic, perhaps digital Conté could have a similar effect on human-computer interaction.

ACKNOWLEDGEMENTS

This work was partially supported by the SHIVA project (Interreg IV A –2 seas) and FEDER.

REFERENCES

1. Benko, H., Wilson, A.D., and Baudisch, P. Precise selection techniques for multi-touch screens. *Proc. of the SIGCHI conference on Human Factors in computing systems*, ACM (2006), 1263-1272.
2. Bi, X., Moscovich, T., Ramos, G., Balakrishnan, R., and Hinckley, K. An exploration of pen rolling for pen-based interaction. *Proc. of the 21st annual ACM symposium on User interface software and technology*, ACM (2008), 191-200.
3. Brandl, P., Forlines, C., Wigdor, D., Haller, M., and Shen, C. Combining and measuring the benefits of bimanual pen and direct-touch interaction on horizontal interfaces. *Proc. of the working conference on Advanced visual interfaces*, ACM (2008), 154-161.
4. Buxton, W.A.S. Chunking and phrasing and the design of human-computer dialogues. In *Human-computer interaction: toward the year 2000*. Morgan Kaufmann Publishers Inc, 1995, 494-499.
5. Casiez, G., Vogel, D., Balakrishnan, R., and Cockburn, A. The Impact of Control-Display Gain on User Performance in Pointing Tasks. *Human-Computer Interaction 23*, 3 (2008), 215-250.
6. Deming, K. and Lank, E. *Mode Selection Techniques for Pen Input Systems*. San Francisco State University, 2005.
7. Fitzmaurice, G., Baudel, T., Kurtenbach, G., and Buxton, B. A GUI paradigm using tablets, two-hands and transparency. *CHI '97 extended abstracts on Human factors in computing systems: looking to the future*, ACM (1997), 212–213.
8. Forlines, C., Wigdor, D., Shen, C., and Balakrishnan, R. Direct-touch vs. mouse input for tabletop displays. *Proc. of the SIGCHI conference on Human factors in computing systems*, ACM (2007), 647–656.
9. Frisch, M., Heydekorn, J., and Dachselt, R. Investigating multi-touch and pen gestures for diagram editing on interactive surfaces. *Proc. of the ACM International Conference on Interactive Tabletops and Surfaces*, ACM (2009), 149–156.
10. Goonetilleke, R.S., Hoffmann, E.R., and Luximon, A. Effects of pen design on drawing and writing performance. *Applied Ergonomics 40*, 2 (2009), 292-301.
11. Greenberg, S. and Buxton, B. Usability evaluation considered harmful (some of the time). *Proc. of the twenty-sixth annual SIGCHI conference on Human factors in computing systems*, ACM (2008), 111–120.
12. Guiard, Y. Asymmetric division of labor in human skilled bimanual action: the kinematic chain as a model. *Journal of Motor Behavior 19*, 4 (1987), 486-517.
13. Hartmann, B., Morris, M.R., Benko, H., and Wilson, A.D. Augmenting interactive tables with mice & keyboards. *Proc. of the 22nd annual ACM symposium on User interface software and technology*, ACM (2009), 149–152.
14. Hilliges, O., Izadi, S., Wilson, A.D., Hodges, S., Garcia-Mendoza, A., and Butz, A. Interactions in the air: adding further depth to interactive tabletops. *Proc. of the 22nd annual ACM symposium on User interface software and technology*, ACM (2009), 139-148.
15. Hinckley, K., Yatani, K., Pahud, M., et al. Pen + touch = new tools. *Proc. of the 23nd annual ACM symposium on User interface software and technology*, ACM (2010), 27–36.
16. Jordà, S., Geiger, G., Alonso, M., and Kaltenbrunner, M. The reacTable: exploring the synergy between live music performance and tabletop tangible interfaces. *Proc. of the 1st international conference on Tangible and embedded interaction*, ACM (2007), 139–146.
17. Kabbash, P., MacKenzie, I.S., and Buxton, W. Human performance using computer input devices in the preferred and non-preferred hands. *Proc. of the INTERACT '93 and CHI '93 conference on Human factors in computing systems*, ACM (1993), 474-481.
18. Li, Y., Hinckley, K., Guan, Z., and Landay, J.A. Experimental analysis of mode switching techniques in pen-based user interfaces. *Proc. of the SIGCHI conference on Human factors in computing systems*, ACM (2005), 461-470.
19. Lin, J., Newman, M.W., Hong, J.I., and Landay, J.A. DENIM: finding a tighter fit between tools and practice for Web site design. *Proc. of the SIGCHI conference on Human factors in computing systems*, ACM (2000), 510-517.
20. Moran, T.P., Chiu, P., and Melle, W. van. Pen-based interaction techniques for organizing material on an electronic whiteboard. *Proc. of the 10th annual ACM symposium on User interface software and technology*, ACM (1997), 45-54.
21. Napier, J.R. The prehensile movements of the human hand. *The Journal of Bone and Joint Surgery. British Volume 38-B*, 4 (1956), 902-913.
22. Ramos, G., Boulos, M., and Balakrishnan, R. Pressure widgets. *Proc. of the SIGCHI conference on Human factors in computing systems*, ACM (2004), 487-494.
23. Rekimoto, J. and Sciammarella, E. ToolStone: effective use of the physical manipulation vocabularies of input devices. *Proc. of the 13th annual ACM symposium on User interface software and technology*, ACM (2000), 109-117.
24. Scheyer, E. French Drawings of the Great Revolution and the Napoleonic Era. *The Art Quarterly IV*, 4 (1941), 187-204.
25. Song, H., Benko, H., Guimbretière, F., Izadi, S., and Cao, X. Grips and gestures on a multi-touch pen. *Proc. of the SIGCHI conference on Human factors in computing systems*, ACM (2011).
26. Tian, F., Xu, L., Wang, H., et al. Tilt menu: using the 3D orientation information of pen devices to extend the selection capability of pen-based user interfaces. *Proc. of the twenty-sixth annual SIGCHI conference on Human factors in computing systems*, ACM (2008), 1371-1380.
27. Vogel, D. and Baudisch, P. Shift: a technique for operating pen-based interfaces using touch. *Proc. of the SIGCHI conference on Human factors in computing systems*, ACM (2007), 657-666.
28. Wu, F. G. and Luo, S. Design and evaluation approach for increasing stability and performance of touch pens in screen handwriting tasks. *Applied Ergonomics [Kidlington] 37*, 3 (2006).
29. Wu, M., Shen, C., Ryall, K., Forlines, C., and Balakrishnan, R. Gesture Registration, Relaxation, and Reuse for Multi-Point Direct-Touch Surfaces. *Proc. of the First IEEE International Workshop on Horizontal Interactive Human-Computer Systems*, IEEE Computer Society (2006), 185–192.
30. Yee, K-P. Two-handed interaction on a tablet display. *CHI '04 extended abstracts on Human factors in computing systems*, ACM (2004), 1493-1496.
31. Computer Sketchpad. *Science Reporter (Television Series)*, 1964.

Clip-on Gadgets: Expanding Multi-touch Interaction Area with Unpowered Tactile Controls

Neng-Hao Yu[1], *Sung-Sheng Tsai*[2], *I-Chun Hsiao*[2], *Dian-Je Tsai*[1], *Meng-Han Lee*[2], *Mike Y. Chen*[1,2], *Yi-Ping Hung*[1,2]
[1]Graduate Institute of Networking and Multimedia
[2]Department of Computer Science and Information Engineering
National Taiwan University
jonesyu@ntu.edu.tw

ABSTRACT
Virtual keyboards and controls, commonly used on mobile multi-touch devices, occlude content of interest and do not provide tactile feedback. Clip-on Gadgets solve these issues by extending the interaction area of multi-touch devices with physical controllers. Clip-on Gadgets use only conductive materials to map user input on the controllers to touch points on the edges of screens; therefore, they are battery-free, lightweight, and low-cost. In addition, they can be used in combination with multi-touch gestures. We present several hardware designs and a software toolkit, which enable users to simply attach Clip-on Gadgets to an edge of a device and start interacting with it.

Author Keywords
Tactile input, Tangible, physical controllers, mobile devices, multi-touch, toolkit

ACM Classification Keywords
H5.2 [Information interfaces and presentation]: User Interfaces: Input Devices and Strategies, Interaction Styles.

General Terms
Design, Human Factors

INTRODUCTION
Capacitive multi-touch displays are widely used in mobile devices to enable direct interaction and multi-touch gestures. However, virtual keyboards and virtual controls have several user interaction issues. First, virtual controls and users' "fat fingers" [19] occlude content of interest. Figure 1(a)(b) shows the Street Fighter iPhone game UI with a virtual joystick and four buttons, which obscure 22~40% of the screen. Second, virtual controls provide no tactile feedback and require visual attention.

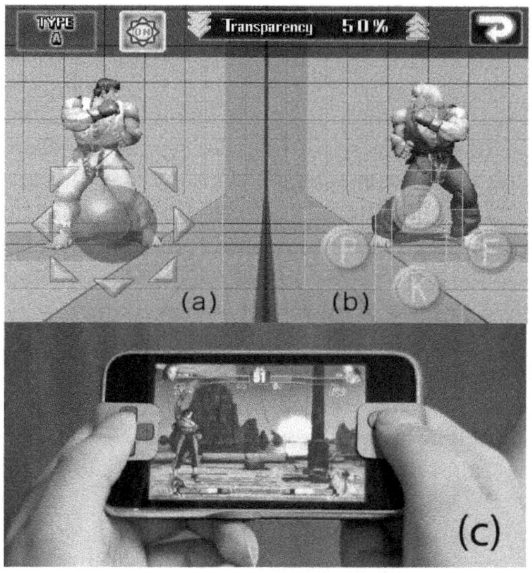

Figure 1: (a) virtual joystick, (b) virtual keypad / buttons (c) Clip-on gadgets map user input to touch points on edges of screens to reduce occlusion

External, tactile controllers have been designed to address these issues. Both wired and wireless controllers eliminate occlusion and provide tactile feedback. However, wireless controllers, typically based on Bluetooth, require batteries to operate and are expensive. In addition, they require pairing to use with a device, and also un-pairing if users would like to control a different device. Wired controllers draw power from the mobile devices themselves. They have to route wires from the devices' connectors to the controls, and are generally more bulky. Another type of controller attaches directly to the screen to provide tactile feedback [22]. It makes the occlusion problem worse by completely obscuring the area occupied by the virtual controls.

In this paper, we present Clip-on gadgets that expand the interaction area to reduce occlusion and to provide tactile feedback. As shown in Figure 1(c), they use conductive material to extend users' touches on the physical controllers to touch points along the edges of the multi-touch screens. Thus, they are battery-free and are easy to construct, and can be freely attached and detached.

RELATED WORK

Mobile input techniques

The fat finger problem [19] is especially noticeable on smaller mobile devices due to the limited screen size. Offset Cursor [15] is designed to avoid finger occlusion on targets and improve selection accuracy. However, the offset between the cursor and the actual touched point makes it difficult to select contents at the bottom. To solve this problem, callout is usually used to display the occluded area. Shift [23] further improves it by avoiding unnecessary callouts, but, still, fingers block part of the touch screen. The backside of the devices has also been used to eliminate occlusion [1, 7, 8, 19, 21].

Several approaches provide tactile feedback, but do not address the occlusion issue. Several actuator solutions have been proposed to generate vibration at the touch position [3, 4, 10, 14, 16]. E-Sense [18] passes an ultra-low current into the pixel to create a small force to fingertips. Tactile Plus [6] pastes transparent haptic buttons on the screen to provide tactile feeling of buttons. Fling game controllers [22] directs stick on the screen with suction cups. Inside of the controller is a spiral that suspends an electrically conductive joystick to match the virtual controls.

Expanding physical interaction on touch devices

FlexiKnob [4] is a set of wireless knobs that enables physical rotary control on computer applications that requires fine-tuning controls, such as audio software. VoodooIO [2] is a system that allows users to construct their own physical control panels to fit their personal preferences and input requirements. DataTiles [17] used tagged transparent tiles to integrate digital and tangible interaction on the sensor-enhanced flat panel display. SLAP widgets [24] introduced transparent tangibles that allow users to get tactile feedback and see displays beneath them. The widgets' footprints are detected and tracked using cameras embedded inside the tabletop.

There are toolkits to alleviate the pain of hardware and software development of developing TUIs, such as Papier-Mache [9]. It is a toolkit for building TUI using computer vision, electronic tags, and barcodes and also uniforms events across multiple input technologies, thus facilitates technology portability and eases application retargeting. TUIC [26] enables object sensing and tracking techniques on the capacitive touch panels. Since most of the mobile touch devices are use capacitive touch display as the input, we can apply this techniques to extend tangible controls.

The aforementioned studies focus on the scale of desktop or tabletop. In this paper, we expand the dynamic tactile controls on mobile devices.

SURVEY OF VIRTUAL CONTROLS

Past studies have reported several typing problems on virtual keys and proposed various solutions [12, 21]. We surveyed the Top 10 arcade games in Apple App Store and found that there are two types of virtual controls (Figure 1 (a) (b)). One is virtual joystick, and another is virtual keypad/buttons. Users move characters around by moving fingers in different directions on the screen. The direction of movement is determined by the relative position of touch point and the center of the controller. Without tactile feedback, the virtual joystick sometimes does not function as expected because users' fingers traverse the center unknowingly. All virtual controls introduce occlusion problem. Not only do virtual controls overlay on top of the content, users' fingers also occlude the display. Base on our calculation, while playing games with thumbs, the occlusion ratio is about 22~40% on iPhone and 12~14% on iPad, respectively.

CLIP-ON GADGET DESIGN

Capacitive multi-touch screens sense changes of capacitance by the capacitive coupling effect [27]. When a conductor is placed on the screen and is connected to human body or ground, it changes the capacitance and the position of the conductor is sensed. We utilize this characteristic to build Clip-on gadgets. Figure 2 shows the design diagram of Clip-on gadgets. While pressing the button, the conductive rubber connects user's finger to the contact points and registers as a touch event on the edge of the touchscreen. We decode the touch events to identify the corresponding buttons.

The Clip-on gadgets are un-powered and are easy to carry . They transform the on-screen touch interactions into off-screen tactile interactions, reducing the occlusion ratio down to 5.8~9.6% on iPhone and 0.7~1.2% on iPad.

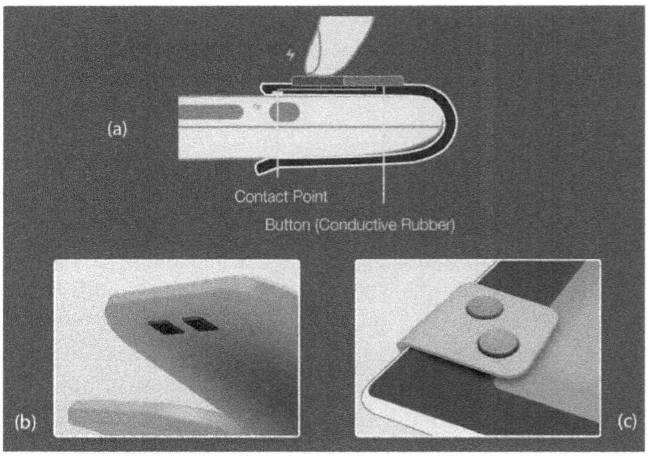

Figure 2: The design of Clip-on gadget (a) the contact points are conductors and connected to the corresponding buttons, (b) the contact points are arranged on the inward side to contact the touch screen and send the status of buttons, (c) the gadget overlays the edge (3~5mm) of the screen to trigger the touch input

Hardware prototyping

Figure 3 shows our clipper-style prototype. In order to provide better tactile feedback, we use physical buttons and switches. We connect one end to the tack, the other to the metal clipper. The tacks are one to one mapping to the buttons and re-arranged linearly to contact the edge of the touch screen. The size of tack is about 5mm to simulate finger touches. We chose median sized clipper as the control holder and attach some foam on the edge to ensure its stability while clipping to the devices. When the user holds the metal clipper, all the ground ends of the buttons are connected to the human body. Once the user presses the button, it causes touch event at the corresponding contact point (tack). In our experiment on iPad, the minimal size of contact points should be at least 3mm in diameter and the minimal gap between each point is 5mm. These values might be applicable to other touch screens with slightly difference.

(a) (b)

Figure 3: The implementation of clipper-style prototype (a) side view, (b) exploded view

SOFTWARE ARCHITECTURE

We developed a toolkit for iOS 4-based devices, written using Objective-C and CocoaTouch APIs included in iOS SDK 4.3. Our prototype devices are Apple iPad 1 and iPad 2 running iOS 4.3. The software architecture consists of three layers and two main components. The three layers works as follows: 1) iOS SDK dispatching touch events to Clip-on toolkit. 2) Clip-on toolkit translating the touch events to the tactile events and dispatches them to the application. 3) The application dispatching the tactile event to the callback functions to perform application-specific logic. The two main components are 1) Clip-on object 2) Detector object.

Clip-on object

The Clip-on object is the abstract object of the tactile controls. It includes two parameters: 1) a set of contact points on the screen, 2) the corresponding tactile events triggered by the contact points. The developer can load a predefined control in their application or customize one.

Predefined controls

Because some controls are commonly used by many applications, we built several predefined controls. For example, a D-pad can be used to control the direction and a knob can be used to control the rotation. Each predefined control maps to a physical Clip-on gadget. For example, a Clip-on D-pad has four buttons: left, right, up, down. So the D-pad object will trigger corresponding events when users click the physical buttons. We designed the four contact points to have different distance ratios between any two points, so that the contact points can be uniquely mapped to each key (Figure 4).

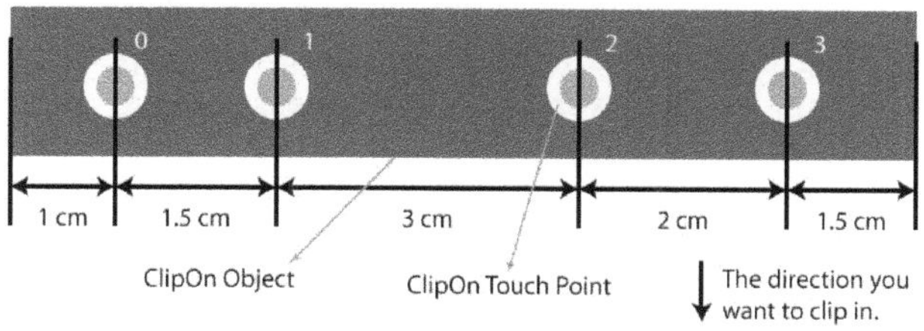

Figure 4: The layout of contact points

Detector object

The detector object contains an event listener, an event dispatcher and a visual UI element (DetectorView). The detector object is used to detect the touch event triggered by the DetectorView and then dispatch the tactile event to the application. The DetectorView shows the sensing area under the contact points and are used to notify the user to attach Clip-on gadget at that position. The width of sensing area on the edge of the screen is about 5mm, the smallest area for which touch events can be reliably detected. The detector object loads the parameter of Clip-on object to assign the height of sensing area.

We also define two modes of the detector object: 1) fixed-position mode, 2) dynamic-position mode. In fixed-position mode, the screen shows a connector symbol on the left side of the iPhone and enforce user to clip the controller at that position (Figure 5(a)). Developers can customize the position of connector symbols for their own application. In dynamic-position mode, the sensing area is any position along the edges of the devices (Figure 5(b)), so users can clip the gadgets anywhere. The toolkit supports a pairing procedure, which provides on-screen visual hints shown on the screen and asks users to press corresponding buttons to trigger each input.

(a) (b)

Figure 5: two modes of Detector object. (a) Fixed-position mode: clip-on gadget has to be attached to specific positions. (b) Dynamic-position mode: clip-on gadget can be attached to arbitrary positions on the edge.

POTENTIAL INTERACTIONS AND FUTURE WORK

In this section, we explore some potential interactions that can be achieved beyond the general-purpose tactile controls such as buttons, sliders or knobs.

Better learning with haptics

Learning with haptic sensation has been shown to improve learning effectiveness [12]. We propose a piano-learning concept as shown in Figure 6(a). We have built a low-cost keyboard that is unpowered and contains only haptic keys. By using our Clip-on approach, each key is mapped to a touch point on the lower edge of the touchscreen.

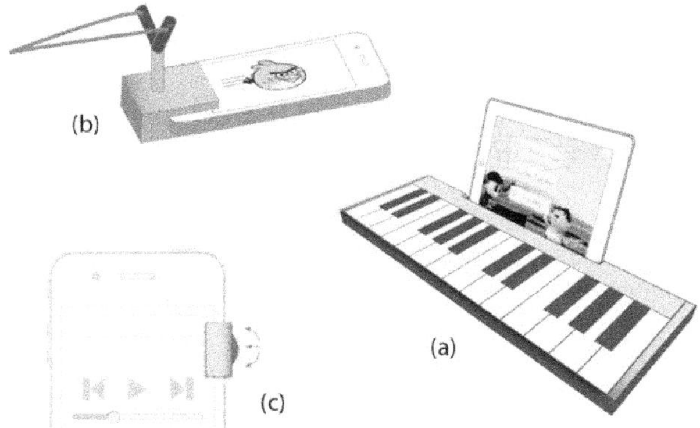

Figure 6: (a) Clip-on piano keyboard, (b) Clip-on Slingshot with force feedback, (c) Clip-on dial

Force feedback

Although software can generate visual effects, they are still virtual. Haptic controls can provide *force feedback* to enhance experience in certain scenarios. As shown in Figure 6(b), a Clip-on slingshot can augment user experience by providing stretching force feedback in Angry Bird-style games. Users can change the weapon on the touch screen by swiping it and pull the slingshot to fire.

Single-hand usage

Mobile phones are often used with one hand, especially while walking or holding items in the other hand. Karlson et al. revealed that the vast majority of users want to use one hand for interacting with mobile devices. However, the touchscreens are not designed to support dedicated single-handed use [5] because some areas are hard to reach by the thumb while holding the phone. We propose a Clip-on dial that can provide up, down and click status. As shown in Figure 6(c), the dial can be used to control e-book reading, music player, and other simple navigation. By combining audio or vibration feedback, it enables users to use the devices eyes free.

Collaboration

Larger touch screens support collaborative work and gaming with multiple people. However, having more fingers on the screen leads to worse occlusion problems. Since the Clip-on gadgets can be easily attached next to the screens, they enhance sharing experience. Figure 7(a) shows four Clip-on gamepads are attached to an iPad to support 2-player games.

Enhancing Productivity

By integrating tactile and multi-touch interactions, we can enhance input efficiency. Figure 7(b) shows a Clip-on Numpad to support number input for accounting. The physical keys can be used with minimal visual attention, which help users to quickly key in numbers.

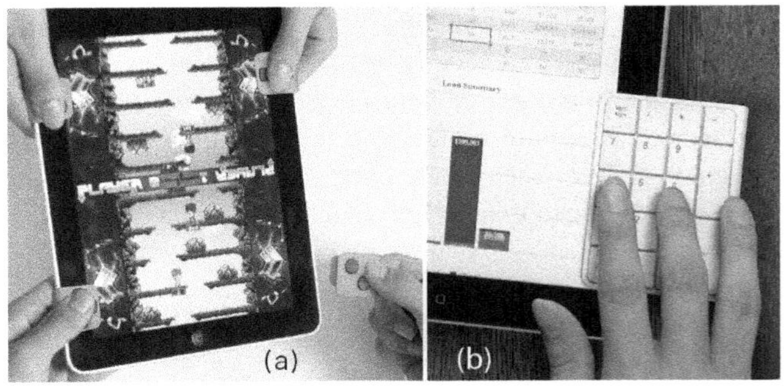

Figure 7. (a) Collaborative gaming. (b) Clip-on Numpad

CONCLUSION

We have presented Clip-on Gadgets for multi-touch mobile devices that expand the interaction area with physical controls. Clip-on Gadgets do not require power, battery, or wireless connections to operate, and the physical controls can be used with minimal visual attention. Users can simply attach the gadgets to the edge of the device and start to interact with it. In addition, tactile and multi-touch input can be combined to support more flexible interactions in the future. Current version of Clip-on gadget uses one-to-one mapping from physical buttons to touch points, and we plan to design touch patterns that can support more types of inputs in the future.

ACKNOWLEDGMENTS

This work was supported in part by the Excellent Research Projects of National Taiwan University, under grants 99R80303,and by the National Science Council, Taiwan, under grant NSC 100-2218-E-002-019-. We would also like to thank Yung-Hsieh Chen, Chung-Ping Lai and Ming-Hong, Yeh for their helps in the hardware prototyping.

REFERENCES

1. Baudisch, P. and Chu, G. Back-of-device interaction allows creating very small touch devices. In *Proc. CHI 2009.* 1923-1932
2. Block, F., Haller, M., Gellersen, H., Gutwin, C., and Billinghurst, M. VoodooSketch -- extending interactive surfaces with adaptable interface palettes. In *Proc. of TEI 2008*, 55-58.
3. Brewster, S. and Chohan, F., and Brown, L. Tactile Feedback for Mobile Interactions, *Ext. Abstracts CHI 2007*, 159-162.

4. Fukumoto, M. and Sugimura, T. Active Click: Tactile Feedback for Touch Panels, *Ext. Abstracts CHI 2001*, 121-122.
5. Gohlke, K., Hlatky, M., Helse, S. and Loviscach, J. FlexiKnobs: bridging the gap between mouse interaction and hardware controllers. In *Proc. TEI 2010*, 241 – 244
6. Hermitage Nouso: Tactile+Plus. http://game.watch.impress.co.jp/docs/series/ggl/20101102_404249.html. .
7. Hiraoka, S., Miyamoto, I. and Tomimatsu, K. Behind Touch, a Text Input Method for Mobile Phones by The Back and Tactile Sense Interface. *Information Processing Society of Japan, Interaction 2003*,131-138.
8. Karlson, A., Bederson, B., Contreras-Vidal, J. (2006) Understanding Single-Handed Mobile Device Interaction. *Tech Report HCIL-2006-02,* Computer Science Dept., University of Maryland
9. Klemmer, R.S., Li, J., Lin, J., and Landay J.A. Papier-Mache: toolkit support for tangible input. In *Proc. CHI 2004*, 399-406
10. Koskinen, E., Kaaresoja, T. and Laitinen, P. Feel-good touch: finding the most pleasant tactile feedback for a mobile touch screen button. In Proc. ICMI 2008.
11. Li, K., Baudisch, P. and Hinckley, K. BlindSight: eyes-free access to mobile phones. In *Proc. CHI 2008*, 1389-1398.
12. MacKenzie, I.S., Soukoreff, R.W. Text entry for mobile computing: Models and methods, theory and practice. *Human-Computer Interaction 17* (2). Lawrence Erlbaum, 2002, 147-198
13. Mangen, A. and Velay J.L. Digitizing Literacy: Reflections on the Haptics of Writing. In Journal of Advances in Haptics (2010), 385-401.
14. Nashel, A. and Razzaque, S. Tactile Virtual Buttons for Mobile Devices, *Ext. Abstracts CHI 2003*, 854-855.
15. Potter, R., Weldon, L. and Shneiderman, B. Improving the accuracy of touch screens: an experimental evaluation of three strategies. In *Proc. CHI 1988*, 27-32.
16. Poupyrev, I. Maruyama, S. and Rekimoto, J. Ambient touch: designing tactile interfaces for handheld devices. In *Proc. UIST 2002*, 51-60
17. Rekimoto, J. Ullmer, B. and Oba, H. DataTiles: a modular platform for mixed physical and graphical interactions. *In Proc. of CHI 2001*, 269–276.
18. Senseg E-Sense® solution. http:// http://senseg.com/.
19. Siek, K.A., Rogers, Y. and Connelly, K.H. Fat Finger Worries: How Older and Younger Users Physically Interact with PDAs. In *Proc. INTERACT 2005*, 267–280.
20. Sugimoto, M. and Hiroki, K.. HybridTouch: an intuitive manipulation technique for PDAs using their front and rear surfaces. In *Proc. MobileHCI 2006*, 137-140.
21. Sun, X., Plocher, T. and Qu, W. An Empirical Study on the Smallest Comfortable Button/Icon Size on Touch Screen. Usability and Internationalization, Part I, HCII 2007, LNCS 4559, 615–621, 2007
22. Ten One Design: Fling analog joystick. http://tenonedesign.com/fling
23. Vogel, D. and Baudisch, P. Shift: A Technique for Operating Pen-Based Interfaces Using Touch. In *Proc. CHI 2007*, 657-666.
24. Weiss, M., Wagner, J., Jennings, R., Jansen, Y., Khoshabeh, R., Hollan, D.J. and Borchers, J. SLAP widgets: bridging the gap between virtual and physical controls on tabletops. In *Proc. of CHI 2009*, 3229-3234.
25. Wobbrock, J.O., Myers, B.A. and Aung, H.H. The performance of hand postures in front- and back-of-device interaction for mobile computing. *International Journal of Human-Computer Studies 2008,* 857-875.
26. Yu, N.H., Chan, L.W., Lau, S.Y., Tsai, S.S., Hsiao, I.C., Tsai, D.J., Cheng, L.P., Hsiao, F.I., Chen, M.Y., Huang, P. and Hung, Y.P. TUIC: Enabling Tangible Interaction on Capacitive Multi-touch Display. To appear in *Proc. CHI 2011*
27. Zimmerman, D.T., Smith, R.J., Paradiso, A.J., Allport, D. and Gershenfeld, N. Applying electric field sensing to human-computer interfaces. In *Proc. of CHI 1995,* 280-287.

Sketch-Sketch Revolution: An Engaging Tutorial System for Guided Sketching and Application Learning

Jennifer Fernquist[1], *Tovi Grossman*[2], *George Fitzmaurice*[2]

Autodesk Research
[1]jen.fernquist@gmail.com, [2]{firstname.lastname}@autodesk.com

ABSTRACT

We describe Sketch-Sketch Revolution, a new tutorial system that allows any user to experience the success of drawing content previously created by an expert artist. Sketch-Sketch Revolution not only guides users through the application user interface, it also provides assistance with the actual sketching. In addition, the system offers an authoring tool that enables artists to create content and then automatically generates a tutorial from their recorded workflow history. Sketch-Sketch Revolution is a unique hybrid tutorial system that combines in-product, content-centric and reactive tutorial methods to provide an engaging learning experience. A qualitative user study showed that our system successfully taught users how to interact with a drawing application user interface, gave users confidence they could recreate expert content, and was uniformly considered useful and easy to use.

ACM Classification: H5.2 [Information interfaces and presentation]: User Interfaces. - Graphical user interfaces.

General terms: Design, Human Factors, Algorithms.

Keywords: Tutorials, Learning, Sketching, Engagement.

INTRODUCTION

Many software applications are difficult and intimidating for new users to learn. As a result, a significant focus of HCI research has been to not only improve the usability of software systems, but also their learnability [15]. One of the most traditional means to addressing software learnability is to provide application tutorials, which can guide users through tasks to obtain specific skills and experience with the system [13, 16, 19, 21].

Tutorials for design software, such as image editing or animation software, are shared among community members to showcase work and associated workflows. These forms of tutorials, which we define as *content-centric tutorials*, seem particularly promising in terms of engaging users. Their prevalence on community websites and discussion boards indicates that there is something compelling about learning by following along with someone else's workflow.

Tutorials for *drawing applications* are particularly interesting to consider because the ability to complete a tutorial not only requires skill with the software *UI*, but may require *domain* artistic skills such as sketching. While sketching is something almost everyone wishes they could do well, the majority of people are not good at it [4]. This presents a challenge for tutorial design for drawing applications—if the challenges presented within these tutorials do not have a good balance with the user's skill level, then the user may not be fully engaged [5, 8, 9]. In particular, it may be difficult for a novice user to get a sense of the holistic, high-level drawing process and to "feel the experience" because they encounter difficulties at individual steps or because it takes an inordinate amount of time to complete a drawing. A more enjoyable experience may be possible if the tutorial could simulate for a new user what a work session would be like if they were already a skilled artist.

In this paper, we present Sketch-Sketch Revolution, an engaging, content-centric tutorial system for drawing applications that allows a user, of any skill level, to experience the success of creating high-quality drawings by providing an adaptable level of *UI*, *domain*, and *content* assistance. The system is built onto SketchBook Pro, an existing application for creating sketches and drawings using digital tools that mimic traditional media. Sketch-Sketch Revolution gives users the opportunity to learn about the application's user interface and its associated workflows and also get exposure to drawing techniques and related foundational concepts. A user study showed that our system taught users how to interact with a drawing application user interface, gave users confidence they could recreate expert content, and was uniformly considered useful and easy to use.

Figure 1. Working with Sketch-Sketch Revolution.

RELATED WORK

Tutorial Systems

Early HCI research quickly recognized the challenge in providing effective help systems for software applications [7]. Help systems quickly evolved, taking into account research proposing minimalist and task-centered documentation [6, 7,28].

More recently, researchers have argued that help systems should be provided within closer context of the actual application [16, 21]. For example, Tooltips [10], and more recently ToolClips [16], provide pop-up help within the application. However, the help which they provide is feature-centric, whereas in our work we hope to provide tutorials for entire high-level tasks.

The Graphstracts help system [19] provides screenshot snippets of the application to help users understand a task sequence. However, Graphstracts were also designed for low-level tasks and were provided outside of the actual application. Some systems, such as Document Wizards provide in-application assistance, but typically this is limited to very simple tasks [27].

Possibly most closely related to our work are the Stencils-Based Tutorials [21]. These tutorials are presented within an application and help users complete an entire task from beginning to end. Furthermore, they provide assistance by forcing a user to perform the correct behavior by overlaying a stencil with a hole to click-through. Google Sketchup's self-paced tutorials [13] also provide a similar experience, but with weaker guidance. These examples serve as important inspiration and, in our work, we explore how such tutorials can be extended to handle more advanced interactions, particularly sketching. We will also explore other new areas of the design space not previously investigated, such as how such tutorials can be configured to match a user's expertise level, how higher level information about the application or domain can be integrated into the tutorials, and how to handle areas of a tutorial that may become redundant or boring for users.

Sketching/Art Assistance

Relevant to our work are systems that have been designed to help users do artistic work. There has been a long line of research on sketch beautification. Examples include the Pegasus [20] and Fluid Sketches [2] systems, which take a user's freehand stroke and beautify it by considering geometric constraints [20]. There are also systems which use predefined geometric templates to aid sketching, such as Digital French Curves [26] and Kinematic templates [12]. We will be presenting a new algorithm to beautify strokes using an author's freehand stroke as a template.

There have also been systems to help users create artistic content. The ILoveSketch [3] and EverybodyLovesSketch [4] systems provide an interface to allow users to create 3D sketches from a 2D perspective viewpoint. Also relevant to our own work are the projector-guided painting [11] and ShadowDraw projects [22]. With these, users are guided by background imagery to recreate an author's artistic content. However, in both systems authors are purely sketching on top of the author's content and are not seeing or experiencing how the author actually created the artwork. In our system, users will be able to experience exactly how authors created content, such as the order and temporal dynamics of their strokes, and how they leveraged software features to obtain their final content.

Capturing and Sharing Workflows

There have been a number of projects that have attempted to automate the process of tutorial creation to mitigate the time required to create tutorial content. Automated Photo Manipulation Tutorials records a user's workflow and automatically creates a static text and image based tutorial [14]. While the work was limited to short tutorials ranging from 4-6 steps, the concept is inspiring and we hope to extend it into full workflow tutorials. In contrast, Chronicle tracks the entire workflow history of a document, including a video screen capture, but does not provide the resulting content as a step-by-step tutorial [17]. Other related projects have looked at recording, visualizing, and navigating software workflows, but not with the intention of using those recordings to create interactive tutorials [23, 24]. Stencils-based tutorials did provide a tool to create tutorials, but authors had to manually enter information about each step. Our work extends these systems by combining the benefits of the automatic tutorial creation of photo manipulation tutorials, the full workflow capture of Chronicle, and the in-application experience of Stencils-based tutorials. Furthermore, our system will assist its users when they try to recreate the actual captured content, in addition to helping with the user interface steps.

Creating Optimal Experiences

One of the goals of our system will be to create a compelling experience so users stay engaged. In psychology, the concept of Flow has been used to describe a state of "optimal experience" [9] (Figure 2). The concept of flow is commonly used to guide HCI research and design [5]. However, we are unaware of research which applies these concepts to the *learning material* presented for user interfaces. Chen et al. [8] identify 3 qualifying factors of the activity itself for reaching the flow state: *perceptions of clear goals*, *immediate feedback*, and *matched skills and challenges*. By designing a tutorial experience that provides these 3 characteristics, users will have the opportunity to achieve an intrinsically rewarding experience [9].

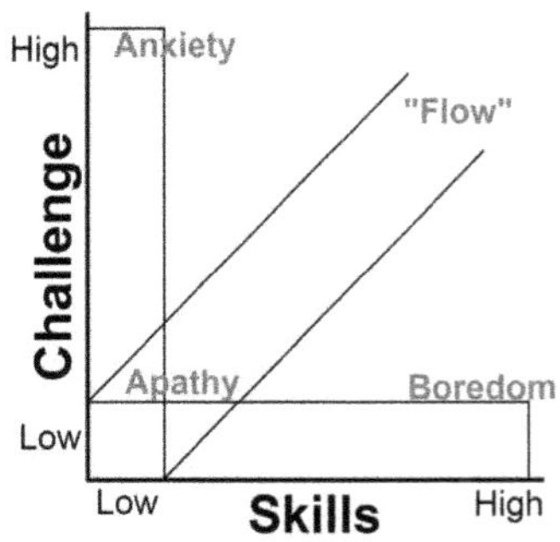

Figure 2. Graphical depiction of Flow [9].

DESIGN SPACE OF INTERACTIVE TUTORIALS

As discussed in our review of related work, there is a wide spectrum of tutorial formats that can be presented to a user. The design space presented below is not meant to provide a full taxonomy of tutorials, but is meant to serve as a summary of the dimensions most relevant to our work and highlight the properties we will be utilizing.

Scope

At the lowest level, tutorials can focus on an individual tool or feature of a system (*feature centric*) [16]. They can also demonstrate how a low-level task can be accomplished (*task-centric*) [14]. At the highest level, tutorials can describe how an entire workflow is used, from beginning to end, to create content (*content-centric*) [21]. We will be focusing on ***content-centric tutorials***.

Interactivity

Traditional tutorials are *passive* if the user only consumes the learning material, such as reading an article or viewing a video [14]. Alternatively, we define tutorials that provide a mechanism to allow users to try out the concepts they are learning as *active* [13]. Lastly, *active* tutorials that are aware of a user's interactions and can respond are considered *reactive* [21]. Our focus will be on ***reactive tutorials***.

Integration

Tutorial materials were initially provided through *physical* books and guides [7]. When the material is available on the computer system, the tutorials are often called *on-line* [19]. At the greatest level of integration, the tutorials can be provided *in-application* [27]. We will be focusing on ***in-application tutorials***.

DESIGN GOALS

In this section we outline the design goals we will adhere to in the design of our tutorials system. These goals are motivated by our high-level effort to create an enjoyable and rich learning experience.

D1. Highly Engaging. Our first goal is to design an experience that will be as compelling as possible. Building from our review of Flow, this will include giving users a perception of *clear goals* and *immediate feedback*.

D2. Provide an Adaptable Experience. Almost all tutorials we have reviewed are rigid; that is, their presentation is fixed regardless of the user's skill level. This reduces the likelihood that the challenge of the tutorial will match the user's skills. Our second design goal is thus to provide an adaptable experience so that the tutorial can be configured to provide a degree of challenge consistent with the user's skill level (Figure 2).

D3. Flexible Time Commitment. Tutorials for creating rewarding content may contain repetitive steps or steps that a user has already mastered. This goal is to provide a mechanism for users to dictate the amount of time they spend on the tutorial or any given step.

D4. Application Learning. A required goal of any application-focused tutorial system is to help users learn about the application. This should include learning where tools are located, how tools are used, and how multiple tools can be used together to perform workflows.

D5. Teach Users About Drawing. It is not the goal of our system to turn any user into a skilled artist. However, we do want to give users exposure to how real artists work. This will be a unique aspect of our system, as software tutorials typically focus on learning the application, not the associated domain knowledge.

D6. Enable Users to Experience Success. Tutorials may be frustrating and difficult to follow when a user lacks the skills required to succeed. In the sketching domain, we want to ensure success with the UI, and have an additional challenge of helping users with the content creation itself. Our final goal is to help users achieve success, to increase their enjoyment of the experience.

FOCUS GROUP MEETINGS

Although the goal for our system is not to provide intense artistic training, we do want to ensure that we adhere to any important fundamentals with respect to learning about drawing. As such, we held two focus group meetings with students and faculty from the Ontario College of Art and Design. During the first we presented the design concept for our system. Feedback received from this meeting confirmed some of the positive aspects of our system, but also resulted in changes to some specifications. The second meeting, in which they piloted a prototype, also elicited feedback resulting in minor modifications. Design decisions affected by these meetings will be highlighted as we describe the system below.

SKETCH-SKETCH REVOLUTION

In this section, we describe our new tutorial system, Sketch-Sketch Revolution.

Target Application and Implementation

SketchBook Pro[1] is a digital drawing application that has marking-menu interface elements and offers drawing tools such as pencils, brushes, and markers, and can be used with pressure-sensitive tablets and tablet PCs. Sketch-Sketch Revolution was implemented by making modifications to the SketchBook Pro source code.

System Overview

Sketch-Sketch Revolution offers two components: an authoring tool and a tutorial system. The authoring tool allows artists to create drawings in SketchBook Pro that are automatically converted into tutorial files, with minimal additional effort required on the author's part. The tutorial system loads an author tutorial file and automatically generates a custom tutorial experience. Users are guided through each step, informed when, where and how to change application settings, as well as when and where to draw, with feedback indicating their success at these tasks.

As we describe the features of the system, we indicate in parentheses the relevant design goals they address.

[1] http://www.autodesk.com/sketchbookpro

Authoring Experience

Similar to previous projects [14, 17], we wanted the authoring experience to be simple so artists could focus on drawing. The only manual input *required* from the author is assigning a tutorial name. All information described below is exported to a custom XML file when capturing is complete.

Capturing Workflows

SketchBook Pro has an existing journaling capability to store all user operations. Sketch-Sketch Revolution utilizes this to automatically record the brush settings, layer manipulations, and colour selections that the author carries out. It also records information for all of their brush strokes, including position, timing, and pressure data.

Author Descriptions

The author has the option to add descriptions to their workflows by entering text into the appropriate text fields in an Author Tool dialog. They can add a label, a description, and additional details. This gives authors the opportunity to describe supplementary information as to the motivation for the step, hints on how to proceed, or relevant domain knowledge (*D5*).

Foundational Concept Overlays

The tutorial author also has the option to choose a *foundational concept overlay* image from a preset list to attach to any step in the tutorial (*D5*). These overlays contain an example image with text briefly describing a fundamental drawing concept, such as lighting, 1- , 2-, or 3-point perspectives, or gauging proportions. We included 9 such concept images—5 created by professional artists specifically for our project, and 4 taken from art text books (Figure 3).

Figure 3. One of nine foundational concept images that authors can associate with tutorial steps.

Tutorial Generation

A tutorial is started by opening an XML file created by the authoring tool. The system automatically parses the data and extracts the workflow information, author descriptions, and fundamental concepts. Regardless of the information authors provide, the tutorial is automatically segmented into steps. Each step consists of a UI phase and a drawing phase, defined by a consecutive set of UI actions followed by a consecutive set of drawing actions (0). Redundant actions (such as changing the brush size twice before drawing) are automatically removed. 'Undo' actions and the strokes they are undoing are also removed. While such actions may be part of the creative process [1], we omitted a mechanism for authors to choose to include undo's in the recorded workflow to simplify the experience for both authors and users.

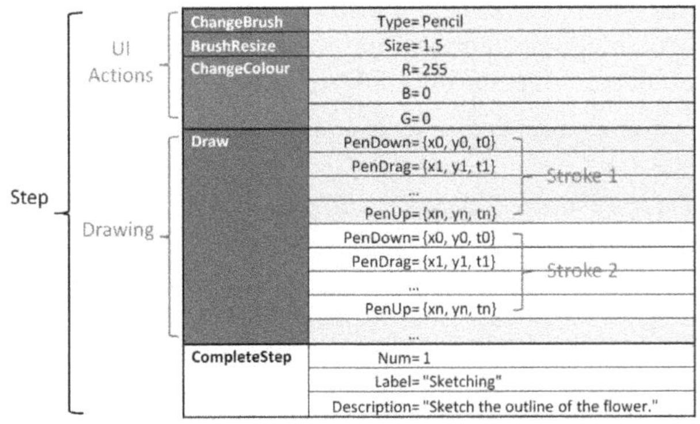

Figure 1. Pseudo code example of parsed XML. A step contains UI actions first, then a drawing action with 1+ strokes, and then a step completion entry.

Tutorial Navigation

Startup Splash Screen

Upon first opening a tutorial, the final author image is shown. Users begin the tutorial by pressing a Start button. The final author image disappears and users are presented with a blank canvas and a Step Navigation dialog.

Step Navigation Dialog

The Step Navigation dialog is used to lead the users through the tutorial (Figure 2). Any information the author added to the tutorial is displayed at the top of this dialog (*D5*). It updates automatically as the user progresses through the tutorial steps. Below, two thumbnail images are shown for reference: the completed step image, and the final image (*D1*). The completed step image is automatically updated as the user progresses through the tutorial, displaying what the author's image looked like upon completion of the current step. At the bottom, the current step instruction is displayed. The Step Navigation dialog also contains several interactive buttons which will be described later.

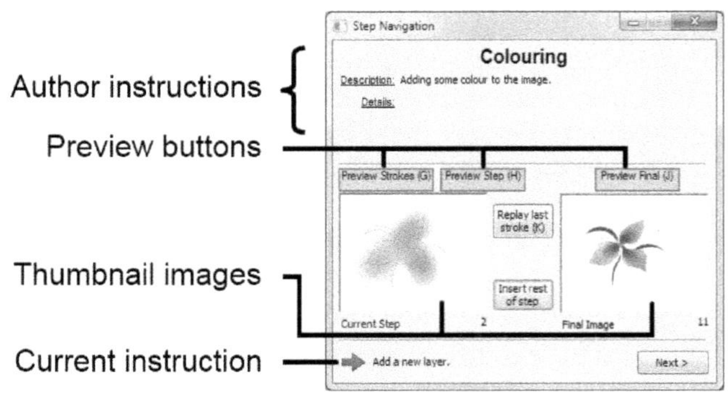

Figure 2. The Step Navigation dialog.

User Interface Phase

Positional Callout Instruction

Step instructions for user interface actions, such as applying appropriate brush settings or manipulating layers, are also displayed in a separate callout dialog that is dynamically positioned next to the associated UI component. For actions involving complex interactions, such as selecting an item in a marking menu, informative images accompany the instruction (Figure 3). The tutorial system dynamically determines if the necessary dialog for a step is not open. If it is not, the callout instruction will first prompt the user to open it. These instructions help teach users where application elements are and how to use them (*D4*).

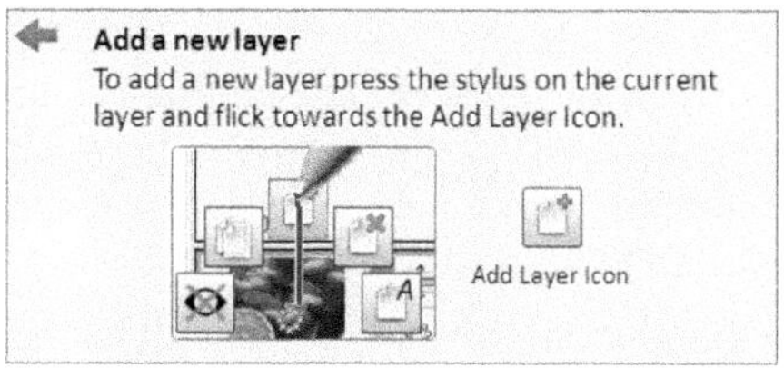

Figure 3. A positional callout instruction informing a user to add a new layer and guiding how.

When the user carries out the appropriate action, a checkmark appears on the screen to give positive feedback to the user and then the callout dialog text and position are updated to the next instruction (*D1 – immediate feedback*).

For steps that require setting a parameter to a continuous value, such as the brush size or colour, the user only needs to set the value within 5% of the target value for the tutorial to progress to the next step.

Sometimes, a user may want to continue to the next step without correctly completing the current one as instructed. This could be useful, for example, if they want to select a slightly different colour than the one the author used. To manually proceed, the user can click the *Next* button in the Step Navigation Dialog.

Drawing Phase

When all UI actions for a step have been carried out, the callout instruction dialog disappears and the Step Navigation instruction text says 'Draw!'

Preview Strokes

To proceed with a drawing action, the user presses the space bar. This causes a preview stroke to play, demonstrating the next stroke that the author drew in the original image. The stroke plays back at the same speed the author drew it. The stroke can be replayed as many times as desired by pressing the hotkey K or clicking the replay button in the Step Navigation dialog. The user can then attempt the stroke and proceed to the next via the space bar. Preview strokes are drawn on a separate layer so users only see authored content while previewing and to prevent synchronization issues between the user and author drawings.

When the user's brush type is a Pencil or Pen, the preview strokes are shown one at a time. When a Pencil/Pen stroke is finished previewing, its opacity decreases (default 50%) so that the user can partially see where they should draw next. The user can overdraw on their own stroke, which automatically removes their previous stroke, until they input a stroke they are happy with.

When the user's brush type is an Airbrush, Paintbrush, Chisel Tip Pen, or Eraser, then at least 3 seconds of preview strokes are shown, even if this spans multiple author strokes. We have found that for these brush types, some author strokes are so brief that it is difficult to discern tiny stylus flicks and too tedious to play them back individually. Opacity of these preview strokes is set to 0 when finished.

The *preview stroke* feature takes the sketching process beyond tracing. This is something we aimed to achieve based on feedback received from our focus group meetings. Tracing only allows users to see the final image they have to achieve. The preview strokes allow users to see, stroke by stroke, how the original image emerged, including the temporal dynamics that the original author used (*D5*). This is useful for users who are overwhelmed by the complexity of a drawing and do not know where to begin. We believe this may increase engagement (*D1*) by providing users with *clear goals*.

Stroke Guidance

One of the challenges with sketching tutorials is not mastering the UI steps, but the actual sketching. Sketch-Sketch Revolution provides *stroke guidance,* so that the content a user creates can resemble the artist's drawing (*D6*). When drawing with the Pen or Pencil, a user's strokes are modified to resemble the artist's original stroke.

We developed a new stroke correction algorithm to accomplish this. In SketchBook Pro, strokes are composed of a series of points and lines are interpolated between them. The algorithm consists of 3 steps. First, it analyses the points of the author's stroke and records the distances between consecutive points, relative to the entire length of the stroke. Second, the algorithm re-samples the user's stroke so that it contains the same number of vertices as the author's stroke, with the same relative distances between consecutive vertices. Third, a new stroke is generated, defined as linear interpolation between each pair of corresponding points of the author and user strokes. The extent of the interpolation is a single parameter in our algorithm that defines the strength of the guidance. When the guidance value is set to 0%, the original user stroke remains. When the guidance is set to 100%, the user's stroke will snap to the author's stroke. By default, our application sets the guidance value to 50% (Figure 4). The stroke guidance enables users to experience success in drawing.

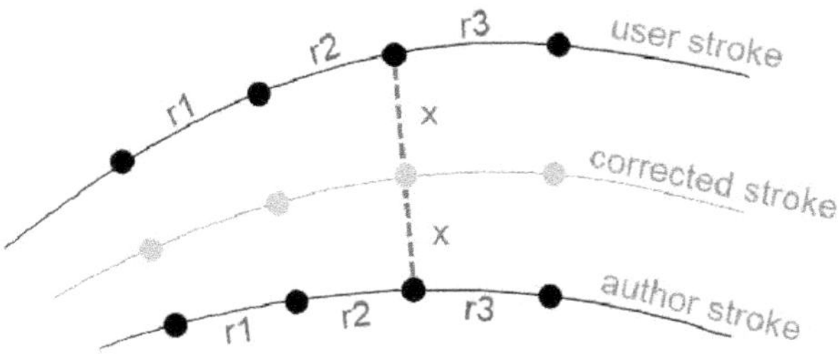

Figure 4. Example of correction applied to a user stroke when the *stroke guidance* value is 50%.

The stroke guidance algorithm resembles the $1 recognizer presented by Wobbrock et al. [29], but the target stroke is not resampled and a non-uniform resampling is used, which preserves the target stroke's original shape. While more advanced techniques could be considered, such as dynamic time warping, our technique is simple to implement and provides good results.

Stroke Feedback

In an effort to better engage users, we provide them with *immediate feedback* after each stroke is drawn (*D1*).

After each Pencil or Pen stroke the user draws, we calculate the average distance between corresponding points in the author's stroke and the re-sampled user stroke. This average pixel distance is subtracted from 100 and presented as a percentage score (e.g. a 90% match corresponds to an average pixel distance of 10). This score is presented to the user when each stroke is completed (Figure 5, left). The average score over the entire drawing is displayed to the user at the end of the tutorial.

We also provide timing feedback. The time difference is deemed to be the difference between the author and user stroke times divided by the author's stroke time. In our focus groups meetings, it was emphasized that drawing strokes faster or slower isn't necessarily an indication of correctness. Thus, we felt it may be useful to visualize the temporal comparison, but not to associate it with any sort of language or score. A range slider indicates the author stroke speed with a blue icon in the center (Figure 5, right). If the user is faster, a green icon appears to the right of center. If they're slower, the icon is to the left of center. The distance between the icons indicates speed difference between strokes, where each slider tick is 10%.

Figure 5. Stroke (left) and timing (right) feedback.

Automatic Step Completion

During a drawing phase, the user can choose to insert the author's strokes for the remainder of the step with the "Insert rest of step" button in the Step Navigation Dialog. The remaining author's strokes are automatically drawn into the current user's image layer. This feature facilitates a rapid walkthrough of a tutorial, allowing users to skip or quickly get through a step they find long and repetitive, without impacting the final content they generate (*D3, D6*).

Preview Images

During the tutorial, a user has the option to preview the author's content. They can preview what the author's content looked like up to the current stroke, to the end of the current step, and to the completion of the tutorial. The previews are overlaid on top of the user's canvas and are shown when the user either presses the preview buttons on the Step Navigation Dialog or hits their associated hotkeys. The previews are spring-loaded, disappearing as soon as the button or hotkey is released. These previews help provide users with *clear goals* (*D1*).

Foundational Concepts

If an author has associated a foundational concept with a step, a button becomes visible in the Step Navigation dialog to indicate its availability. When clicked, the foundational concept image and text is overlaid on top of the user's image. It can be hidden by clicking the button again. This allows users to learn about important drawing concepts as they progresses through the tutorial (*D5*).

Adapting the Tutorial Experience

As set out by our design goal, the tutorial experience is adaptable (*D2*). Novice users can setup the tutorial to provide a heavier level of assistance while more advanced users can opt to work with minimal assistance using the Artistic Assistance Dialog.

The stroke guidance is adjustable via a slider, with the default value set to 50%. The opacities of the preview strokes, author step image, and author final step, are also adjustable via sliders. Users can continually view any combination of these images, at any transparency, to help guide them as they create their drawing.

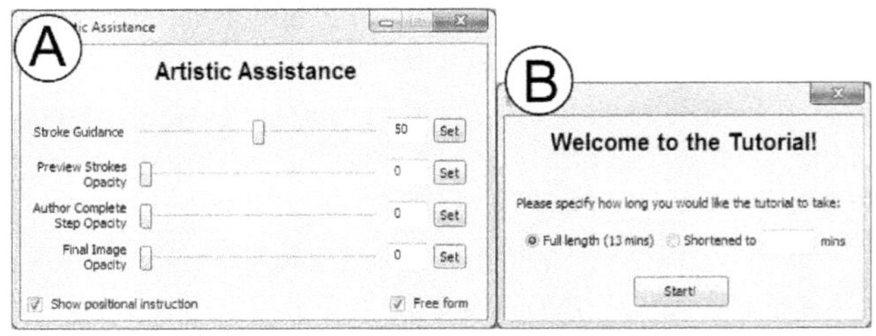

Figure 6. A) The Artistic Assistance dialog and B) the Startup dialog.

The positional callout dialogs can be disabled via a checkbox in the Artistic Assistance dialog. This may be useful to users who are already familiar with the application UI, or to users who want an additional challenge.

A final option from this dialogue is to enter a *freeform mode* where users can draw or perform UI actions without impacting the tutorial. Strokes are not corrected or scored in this mode and steps do not automatically advance.

Users can also customize the amount of time that they want to dedicate to a tutorial using a dialogue shown at the startup splash screen. The user can either take the full, unmodified length, or enter a desired number of minutes in a text field (*D3*). This feature is useful if a user has a limited amount of time to complete a tutorial. When a custom time is set, the system divides the time equally amongst all steps. During the tutorial, once the system detects time has "run out" for a step, it automatically completes the remainder of the step and progresses to the next.

USER STUDY

We conducted a qualitative user study on Sketch-Sketch Revolution. Our goals were to obtain initial observations and feedback from users, understand which features they found most useful or easy to work with, identify any features that may require modification, and gauge users overall enjoyment experienced in drawing with our system.

We tested two versions of Sketch-Sketch Revolution. The first was a full version of our system, as described above. The second was an 'un-guided' version of the tutorial system that lacked stroke guidance, stroke feedback, and previewing. Positional callout instructions were provided, but without the integrated image-based instructions. We tested this version of the system to understand the impact of the most novel features in Sketch-Sketch Revolution in comparison to Stencils-based tutorials [21].

Participants

Eight right-handed participants (4 female) between the ages of 22 and 59 (μ=33.4) with normal colour vision were recruited via online and email postings. No participants had awareness of our project research goals. One participant had significant drawing experience, 3 had minimal experience, and 4 had none. Only one participant had used SketchBook Pro before.

Apparatus

Our user study was conducted with a Wacom Cintiq 21UX tablet, which has an active area of 43.2cm×32.4cm and a resolution of 1600×1200.

For the un-guided tutorial a secondary monitor, with a diagonal of 30" and resolution of 2560×1600, was used to display a 1600×1200 dialog that allowed users to see/toggle between the full sized preview step and final images. This was included to show users what to draw at each step.

Participants sat in front of the tablet, with a stylus in their dominant hand, a keyboard near their non-dominant hand, and the secondary monitor was to the left of the tablet.

Procedure and Design

The study was divided into two trials, lasting about 30 minutes each. In each trial, the user created one drawing with either the fully functioned Sketch-Sketch Revolution system (*Guided*) or the un-guided version (*Un-Guided*). Two sketches and their associated tutorials were created internally by authors with artistic experience – one of a fish, and one of an orchid. The order of the conditions, and the condition to sketch assignments were both fully counterbalanced. Users were briefly trained on the functionality of each system before beginning. Users answered a questionnaire after each trial, and a post-study questionnaire. Participants performed both trials in one session lasting approximately 60 minutes. An experimenter took observations and provided assistance when necessary.

Results and Observations

Questionnaire Results

The questionnaire at the end of each trial contained eight questions about the tutorial system for that trial, which participants were asked to rate on a 1-5 Likert scale (where higher is better) (Figure 7). Reactions to both systems were relatively high. The lowest response across all questions was for drawings being easy to complete, in the un-guided condition (μ=3.63). For guided tutorials, the response to this question was significantly higher (μ=4.5, $F(1,7)=6.24$, $p<.05$). This was the only significant difference in the two conditions, although as Figure 7 shows, responses for the guided system were consistently higher.

Also included on the questionnaire were six TLX-based Likert-style questions [18] (where lower is better) (Figure 8). Responses for the guided system were uniformly better, although no difference reached statistical significance.

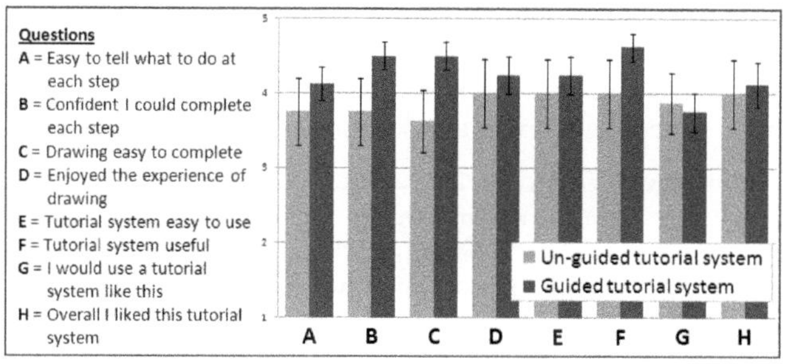

Figure 7. Results from post-trial questionnaires (higher is better). Error bars show standard error.

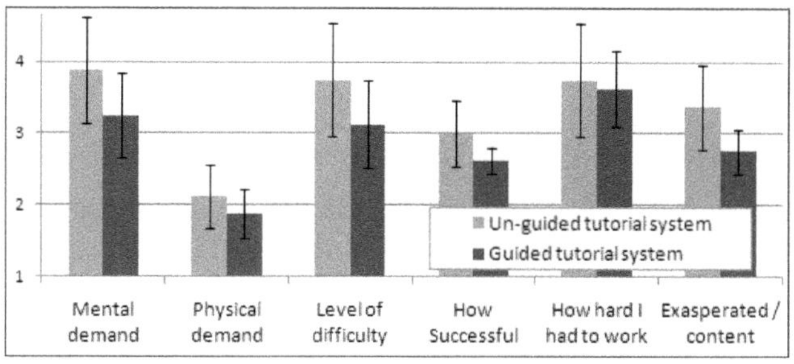

Figure 8. Post-trial questionnaire results from TLX-based questions (lower is better).

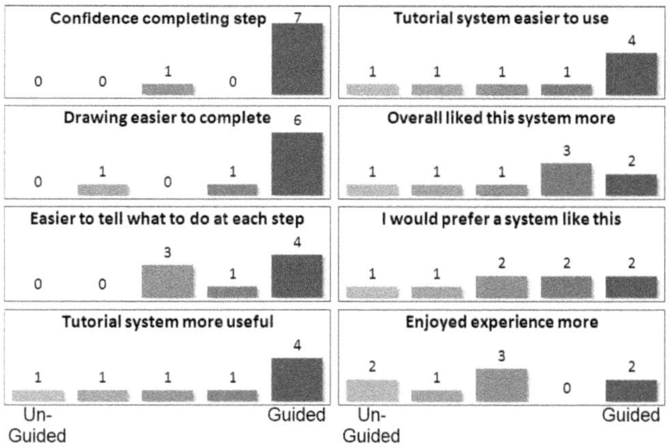

Figure 9. Subjective results comparing the un-guided and guided tutorial systems.

In the post-study questionnaire participants compared the two systems based on the first set of Likert questions. As can be seen in Figure 9, there is an indication that with the guided system, participants: were more confident they could complete each step; found the drawing easier to complete; and found it easier to tell what to do at each step. They also generally found the guided tutorial system more useful and easier to use versus the un-guided system. An interesting result is that users seemed to equally enjoy the experience of both the *guided* and *un-guided* condition. Our hypothesis is that while some users did find that the guided system made things easier, they may have preferred a less guided and more free-form experience. To some extent, this validates our design goal of making the tutorial experience in Sketch-Sketch Revolution adaptable, as it allows users to configure the experience to have less guidance for users who prefer that type of experience.

Observations and User Feedback

Several interesting observations and comments were received from users, which we discuss below. Observations are grouped by the relevant design goal, where applicable.

Engagement (D1): In the un-guided tutorial, users were sometimes unsure of what to draw (P1: "What am I drawing?" P6: "Do I do the outline?") or precisely when they were finished (P1: "Is that all?" P5: "Next, I guess?"). This was more common in erasing and small steps.

Some nuances in steps were also missed in the un-guided tutorial. In particular, in one step in the fish drawing the author used the eraser to make a hard edge on grey shading created with the Airbrush. Three of the four users who drew the fish with the un-guided system did not notice the hard edge and instead used the eraser just to eliminate the excess grey shading outside of the border of the fish.

One participant looked at the author's supplementary text information to determine what to do when he was unsure. Most users repeatedly compared the author's step image on the secondary monitor to their own to determine the action they should carry out.

In the guided tutorial system, users typically knew what to do at each step (because the preview strokes played), and when they were finished (because the strokes for that step would finish). Sometimes they were unsure because they did not notice the preview stroke, and they would replay it.

Overall, users did appear to be engaged with the guided tutorials. For example, P1 began with the un-guided tutorial and (unprompted) verbalized his thought process throughout. During the guided tutorial, he hardly spoke. He was clearly engrossed in the drawing steps, previewing and replicating strokes in the exact manner as the author.

Application Learning (D4): Users who began their session with the un-guided tutorial system had difficulty interacting with the marking menus for layer manipulations, even with the positional callout instructions. In the guided system, where the callouts contained image instructions, three of the four users figured out how to use the marking menu immediately. The one user who did not (P5) confessed he did not "read the instructions" in the callout but, once he read them, he figured it out immediately.

One user (P2), who used the un-guided system first, did not understand how to use the Airbrush. She attempted to add colour to her drawing by tapping but was not getting the same results as in the author's image. It took her numerous attempts before understanding the interaction. Conversely, all users who started with the guided system used the Airbrush correctly since they could see in the preview stroke that the author dragged the pen across the screen.

Regardless of which condition users began with, all users appeared to be comfortable using SketchBook Pro towards the end of their session. Users performed complex interactions, such as layer manipulations and brush resizing, quickly and without assistance, suggesting that we achieved our design goal of providing Application Learning (*D4*).

In their questionnaire comments, 5 users explicitly stated that they thought the guided tutorial was helpful in teaching them how to use SketchBook Pro. (P2: "This tutorial actually had pop-ups describing where and how to use controls, which made it much better than the [un-guided]." P3: "I would use the guided first until I learned the system enough to practice in the un-guided setting." P5: "The guided tutorial moved me through the program quite quickly and has left me with a good base in a program that I was unfamiliar with prior to participating.")

Learning to draw (D5): Participants indicated an appreciation for the artistic guidance and assistance. (P2: "I think this tutorial is really good for beginners, since it shows you the exact moves to make and even auto-corrects. I like that you can control how much help it provides so that you can gradually become more independent.")

P6 began with the un-guided tutorial and had difficulty doing precision erasing. He moved the stylus rapidly back and forth in a scribbling motion, accidentally erasing edges of objects where precision was necessary. The participants who began with the guided tutorial system could see when drawing tasks required, slower, precise movements, and could mimic the speed of the previewed author strokes. So it did appear that users were learning certain drawing strategies from using our system (*D5*).

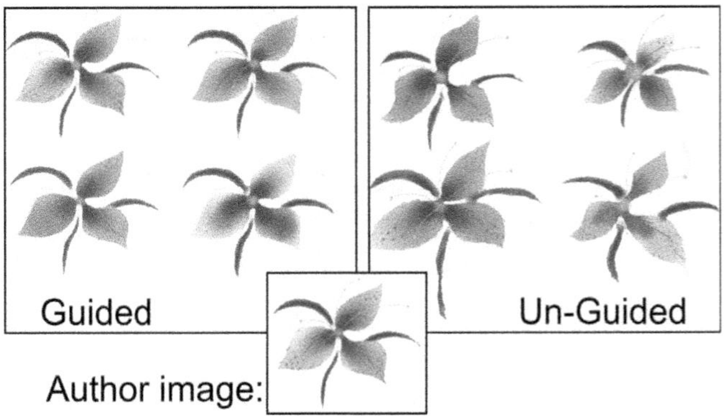

Figure 10. Participants' completed orchid drawing.

Success and Confidence (D6): P2 was not confident in her ability to recreate the drawing with the un-guided system, saying, "It's probably going to look crappy". P6 was also not confident, saying "Oh wow" when presented with a complicated drawing step. P8 sarcastically said "Are you sure this isn't April 1st?" at the start of the same step (drawing details on the orchid petals). These observations indicated that the un-guided tutorial could cause anxiety, possibly preventing a state of Flow (Figure 2).

There was a perceivable difference in the quality of the content generated in the two conditions. Figure 10 shows the results of the orchid, demonstrating that Sketch-Sketch Revolution can help users experience successful content creation (*D6*).

Usage of Features: Most users relied heavily on the previews to see what they should draw next. Some users had to be reminded of the previewing hotkeys during the initial stage guided tutorial when it was clear they were trying to determine what to do in a step.

Almost all users kept their non-dominant hand on the keyboard as they carried out the guided tutorial for quick access to the hotkeys. Users became engrossed in steps that involved many small pencil strokes, resting one hand on the keyboard, the other on the tablet, and quickly alternating between previewing and sketching.

P1 became particularly engaged with the preview strokes. Even when the remainder of an erasing step was obvious, he only erased as much as the author did in any given preview stroke. A few users, on the other hand, got the idea for the erasing steps and erased all excess colour at once without watching each preview stroke.

Several users frequently checked the stroke feedback for each stroke when sketching with the pencil. One user would not progress to the next stroke unless he received a high distance score. Not everyone found the feedback useful. On the system feature questionnaire, P7 said "I can see the results, so 93% seems unnecessary."

Challenges Encountered: At the start of P7's second drawing, even after having added several layers in the guided tutorial, the first instruction said to add a layer and she confessed that she didn't know how. This demonstrates a potential issue with guided tutorials: that users become *too* reliant on guides and do not explicitly learn. This challenge has also been observed with video tutorials [25].

Although preview strokes were one of the most popular features among users, the previews sometimes demonstrate temporal dynamics that the user simply cannot replicate. For example, P6 saw how the author was able to erase very accurately in long ballistic strokes. P6 replicated the author's speed, but not his accuracy, suggesting that this particular author was not his ideal teacher.

A final challenge that appeared exclusively in the unguided system was that errors made earlier in the tutorial could propagate and become more problematic later. For example, P1's drawing was much smaller than the artists and subsequently when he selected the eraser and set its size, it was too large for his drawing and he accidentally erased too much. In the un-guided tutorial, P4 missed one of the three leaves in the original author image. Later in the tutorial, when the leaves were being coloured, she saw that it was missing, remarking "Crap!". While not observed, this type of issue could also occur in the guided tutorial system, and we will discuss it in our future work section.

DISCUSSION

We have presented a new system, Sketch-Sketch Revolution, for automatically creating sketching tutorials that are *in-application*, *content-centric*, and *reactive*. Numerous novel features were implemented to satisfy a set of six design goals, such as providing an engaging and adaptable experience, supporting both application and domain learning, and ensuring the experience is successful.

The results of our qualitative user study were encouraging. Overall the most popular features of our system were the in-depth callouts, stroke assistance, and preview strokes. The in-depth callouts go beyond the "notes" used in Stencils-based tutorials as they provide detailed instructions and images for how to use widgets requiring more involved interactions. This seemed particularly effective for application learning. The stroke assistance was observed to reduce anxiety within users, and also resulted in greater success with the generation of content. The preview strokes were effective as they provided users with clear goals and also helped users learn subtle strategies about the art of drawing.

Our system was developed as an add-on for SketchBook Pro. It is interesting to think about how well our work applies to other application domains. While some specific techniques may not generalize, the higher level design goals which they adhere to should. For example, the stroke guidance algorithm may not be useful in other application domains, but similar application-dependent correction features could be implemented to *enable users to experience success* (D6). The only important distinction would be that the design goal *teach users to draw* would be modified to *teach users the domain*. However, we feel that our work is most relevant to software that requires involved interactions that are prevalent in design software. The actual implementation was facilitated by Sketchbook's existing journaling capabilities. While most of today's software systems have such capabilities, implementation may be more involved if there is no existing journaling mechanism.

FUTURE WORK AND CONCLUSION

There are a number of opportunities for future work.

First, an important follow-up evaluation would study the impact of our system on short- and long-term learning effects for both application and artistic learning. In particular, it would be interesting to formally measure a user's drawing abilities and expertise with SketchBook Pro after extended exposure to our system.

To improve application learning and prevent users from becoming too reliant on the instructional callouts, the amount of assistance could adapt to the user's behaviors and gradually reduce. For example, the system could recognize that a user has become adept at using marking menus, and automatically turn off those instructional callouts. Similarly, the system could detect when a user's sketching is accurate, and gradually reduce the stroke guidance value. The level of adaptation of our system could also be expanded by having the system intelligently choose tutorial content to match a user's skill set.

Our correction algorithm was limited to Pen and Pencil strokes. Some initial attempts to develop correction algorithms for Airbrush and Paintbrush strokes were made, but it turned out to be fairly complex to parameterize and compare two brush patterns. In the future we aim to further investigate possible correction algorithms for additional brushes, such as the Airbrush, Paintbrush and Erasers.

Future implementations of the tutorial system could also contain more infrastructures to support creative freedom. While our system does allow choice between a spectrum of guided and un-guided experiences, the more they diverge from the author's content, the less relevant instructions and preview strokes may become. A future system version could, for example, detect when a user's drawing is out of proportion with the author's and make appropriate brush size suggestions. Regarding content creation, vision algorithms [14] could potentially be used to create preview strokes in the context of the user's drawing, even if it has taken on a much different shape than the author's.

In conclusion, we have created an authoring tool for sketching tutorials that records author actions and automatically generates interactive tutorials. The resulting tutorials were designed to provide an engaging experience for users, teach them how to use SketchBook Pro, assist and provide feedback on the content creation, and allow for customization in terms of assistance level and time commitment. A user study revealed our system to be useful and easy to use.

ACKNOWLEDGEMENTS

The authors thank Mark Davis for providing some of the initial ideas and insights that inspired this work, OCAD University and in particular Martha Ladly and Pedro Bonatto de Castro for their discussions, and Paul Telisman for generating tutorial content.

REFERENCES

1. Akers, D., Simpson, M., Jeffries, R. and Winograd, T. (2009). Undo and erase events as indicators of usability problems. *ACM CHI*. 659-668.
2. Arvo, J. and Novins, K. (2000). Fluid Sketches: Continuous Recognition and Morphing of Simple Hand-Drawn Shapes. *ACM UIST*. 73-80.
3. Bae, S.H., Balakrishnan, R. and Singh, K. (2008). ILoveSketch: As-natural-as-possible sketching system for creating 3D curve models. *ACM UIST*. 151-160.
4. Bae, S.H., Balakrishnan, R. and Singh, K. (2009). EverybodyLovesSketch: 3D Sketching for a Broader Audience. *ACM UIST*. 59-68.
5. Bederson, B.B. (2004). Interfaces for staying in the flow. *Ubiquity*. 5(27).
6. Carroll, J. M. (1990). *The Nurnberg Funnel*. MIT Press.
7. Carroll, J. M. and Rosson, M. B. (1987). *Paradox of the active user. Interfacing thought: cognitive aspects of human-computer interaction*. MIT Press. 80-111.
8. Chen, H., Wigand, R.T. and Nilan, M.S. (1999). Optimal experience of web activities. *Computers in human behavior*. 15(5), 585-608.
9. Csikszentmihalyi, M. (1988). The flow experience and its significance for human psychology. *Optimal Experience: Psychological Studies of Flow in Consciousness*. 15-35.
10. Farkas, D. K. (1993). The role of balloon help. *Journal of Computer Documentation*. 17(2):3-19.
11. Flagg, M. and Rehg, J.M. (2006). Projector-guided painting. *ACM UIST*. 235-244.
12. Fung, R., Lank, E., Terry, M. and Latulipe, C. (2008). Kinematic templates: end-user tools for content-relative cursor manipulations. *ACM UIST*. 47-56.
13. Google SketchUp Training. http://sketchup.google.com/intl/en/training/index.html
14. Grabler, F., Agrawala, M., Li, W., Dontcheva, M. and Igarashi, T. (2009). Generating photo manipulation tutorials by demonstration. *ACM SIGGRAPH*. 28(3):66.
15. Grossman, T., Fitzmaurice, G. and Attar, R. (2009). A survey of software learnability: metrics, methodologies and guidelines. *ACM CHI*. 649-658.
16. Grossman, T. and Fitzmaurice, G. (2010). ToolClips: An investigation of contextual video assistance for functionality understanding. *ACM CHI*. 1515-1524.
17. Grossman, T., Matejka, J. and Fitzmaurice, G. (2010). Chronicle: capture, exploration, and playback of document workflow histories. *ACM UIST*. 143-152.
18. Hart, S. and Staveland, L. (1988). Development of NASA-TLX (Task Load Index): Results of empirical and theoretical research. In P. Hancock & N. Meshkati (Eds.), Human mental workload. 139-183.
19. Huang, J. and Twidale, M.B. (2007). Graphstract: minimal graphical help for computers. *ACM UIST*. 203-212.
20. Igarashi, T., Matsuoka, S., Kawachiya, S. and Tanaka, H. (1997). Interactive beautification: a technique for rapid geometric design. *ACM UIST*. 105-114.
21. Kelleher, C. and Pausch, R. (2005). Stencils-based tutorials: design and evaluation. *ACM CHI*. 541-550.
22. Lee, Y.J., Zitnick, C.L. and Cohen, M. (2011). ShadowDraw: Real-Time User Guidance for Freehand Drawing. *ACM SIGGRAPH*.
23. Li, I., Nichols, J., Lau, T., Drews, C. and Cypher, A. (2010). Here's what I did: sharing and reusing web activity with ActionShot. *ACM CHI*. 723-732.
24. Nakamura, T. and Igarashi, T. (2008). An application-independent system for visualizing user operation history. *ACM UIST*. 23-32.
25. Palmiter, S. and Elkerton, J. (1991). An evaluation of animated demonstrations of learning computer-based tasks. *ACM CHI*. 257-263.
26. Singh, K. (1999). Interactive curve design using digital French curves. *ACM I3D*. 23-30.
27. Sukaviriya, P., Isaacs, E. and Bharat, K. (1992). Multimedia help: a prototype and an experiment. *ACM CHI*. 433-434.
28. Tuck, R. and Olsen, D. R. (1990). Help by guided tasks: utilizing UIMS knowledge. *ACM CHI*. 71-78.
29. Wobbrock, J.O., Wilson, A.D. and Li, Y. (2007). Gestures without libraries, toolkits or training: a $1 recognizer for user interface prototypes. *ACM UIST*. 159-168.

Elasticurves: Exploiting Stroke Dynamics and Inertia for the Real-time Neatening of Sketched 2D Curves

Yannick Thiel, Karan Singh, Ravin Balakrishnan
Department of Computer Science
University of Toronto
{ythiel, karan, ravin}@dgp.toronto.edu

Figure 1: Input strokes are drawn in red, with drawing speed indicated by the spacing of green input points (a). The input stroke in (a) is neatened using Laplacian smoothing with fixed-distance sampling (b), and using elasticurves (c). Note the sharp corners and smooth arcs on the waves and teeth in (c), compared to the featureless smoothing in (b).

ABSTRACT
Elasticurves present a novel approach to neaten sketches in real-time, resulting in curves that combine smoothness with user-intended detail. Inspired by natural variations in stroke speed when drawing quickly or with precision, we exploit stroke dynamics to distinguish intentional fine detail from stroke noise. Combining inertia and stroke dynamics, elasticurves can be imagined as the trace of a pen attached to the user by an oscillation-free elastic band. Sketched quickly, the elasticurve spatially lags behind the stroke, smoothing over stroke detail, but catches up and matches the input stroke at slower speeds. *Connectors*, such as lines or circular-arcs link the evolving elasticurve to the next input point, growing the curve by a *responsiveness* fraction along the connector. Responsiveness is calibrated, to reflect drawing skill or device noise. Elasticurves are theoretically sound and robust to variations in stroke sampling. Practically, they neaten digital strokes in real-time while retaining the modeless and visceral feel of pen on paper.

Author Keywords
Sketching, Stroke-based interfaces, Fair curve design.

ACM Classification Keywords
H.5.2 Graphical User Interfaces, Input Devices, and Strategies;D.2.2User Interfaces;I.3.6 Interaction Techniques

General Terms
Algorithms, Design, Human Factors.

INTRODUCTION
Sketching has been used throughout history as a primitive mode of expression and visual communication. Sketching is also an increasingly viable medium of interaction with devices ranging in size from small tablets to large displays. Sketch strokes are used in a variety of computing scenarios: as curves representing visual content from simple 2D cartoons to complex 3D product designs [4, 15, 16, 23], as motion paths for animation [13, 30] and as general gestural input to invoke commands [3, 17, 22, 24, 25, 34].

An important area of ongoing research deals with attempting to model and eliminate the difference or error between the stroke a user mentally imagines and the one that is drawn using a digital device. In this paper, we refer to this problem as stroke *neatening*.

Stroke neatening can be addressed in two ways: first, by attempting to model the characteristics of the differences between sketched strokes and the resulting curves; second, by using priors that describe desirable properties of curves resulting from user strokes. Perhaps the most common prior is smoothness (Figure 1b) since high-frequency jitter is usually the result of device noise or an unsteady hand and further, smooth or fair [8, 19] curves are generally desirable. Indeed for many applications such as 3D design curves, paths for navigation or spatial curves for visualization, smoothing is sufficient for stroke neatening. There are, however, applications such as 2D cartoon drawing or motion paths for performance-based animation and interactive tracking, where the desired result of a sketch is a mix of smoothness and high-frequency detail in different parts of the neatened output curve (Figure 1c).

In general, the extent to which a user intends the resulting curve to precisely track any portion of a sketched stroke is a directive that must be explicitly defined by the user. While the intended precision along parts of a stroke could be specified after its completion using a variety of interfaces [19, 26], not only would such an approach impede the fluidity of a sketching workflow, it comes too late for real-time applications like drawing or performance animation, where the stroke must be neatened as the user sketches. It would thus be ideal if a user could specify intended precision along the stroke *while* sketching, using an affordance of the drawing tool such as finger pressure or pen tilt [21, 31]. Unfortunately, there is no evidence indicating that there exists a natural relationship between these device affordances and intended precision. We have observed, however, that there is a relationship between drawing speed and intended precision. In accordance with the speed-accuracy trade-off common to human activity [28], users instinctively slow down when drawing parts of a curve where they desire precision and speed up over regions that are smoother or less precise. We note also that drawing speed is a user controlled variable independent of the input device used, be it a finger, mouse, or stylus. Thus, using speed as a mechanism to control precision simply builds on users' inherent sketching behaviour.

A number of approaches that neaten a stroke after its completion [4, 16, 19, 23] typically fit a curve primitive such as a cubic spline [4] or optimize a criterion such as variation of curvature [19], over the entire stroke. Most of these approaches can be further improved by additionally exploiting the precision intent conveyed via stroke speed.

These approaches, however, remain ill-suited to real-time applications, where a neatened curve must be incrementally committed while the user draws. This was especially noted by in-between and clean-up artists sketching over scanned drawings, where the lack of commitment of any part of the neatened curve until a stroke was completed was visually frustrating and often required sketching the same stroke multiple times without guarantee of success. A similar frustration was voiced by animators wishing to lasso-select objects in regions contained within neatened strokes.

To perform real-time neatening, however, the evolving end of a committed curve must differ at times from the current end of the stroke, which we refer to as stroke inertia or spatial lag (see waves in Figure 1c and video). We draw inspiration from the traditional tape drawing technique [5] used by designers where curves are created by rolling out tape with one hand and fastening it with the other. Metaphorically, the hand rolling out the tape defines the stroke and the hand fastening the tape defines the committed curve. The tape in-between the two hands is the spatial lag. In a one-handed sketch-based version of tape drawing [11], the spatial lag has a fixed length and the committed curve can be thought of as being drawn by a pen attached to the user's hand by an invisible rod. The smaller the lag (the shorter the rod), the more closely the committed curve tracks the sketched stroke, and larger lags result in smoother curves with less detail. This is captured in spirit by Dynadraw [12], simulating a pen with mass and friction being physically pulled across the paper. Given that controlling the amount of lag enables the creation of curves with different smoothness and detailed variation characteristics, we propose a novel approach whereby the lag is directly modulated in real-time by the stroke speed. The user can select from different curve primitives such as lines or circular-arcs to model the lag segment, allowing them to generate near perfect lines or arcs despite drawing quickly. At the same time, slowly drawn parts of a curve are tracked precisely without any explicit mode changes.

There exists a continuum of intended curves ranging from completely free-hand to precise geometric primitives like lines and circles [10]. A good real-time stroke neatening algorithm would allow users to move freely within this continuum over the course of a single stroke. We believe elasticurves are the first real-time stroke neatening approach to possess this property.

RELATED WORK

There has been much research in the area of stroke processing. Broadly one branch looks at the symbolic processing of strokes for handwriting and other gestural recognition [3, 17, 22, 24, 25, 34]. Here, the stroke is classified as an instance of a known set of symbols. This is typically done by looking for structure within the stroke in terms of geometric features such as corners or inflections and then by matching these features to corresponding sets of examples for each known symbol. The actual geometry of such strokes serves only to classify and distinguish them.

The second and more relevant branch addresses the neatening of strokes. An essential aspect of stroke neatening is determining which parts of the stroke to neaten. The majority of approaches [4, 19] simply neaten the entire stroke based on the assumption that smooth curves are desirable and that sharp corners or high-frequency detail will explicitly be created by concatenating multiple smooth strokes [4]. While this is perfectly acceptable for many applications, sketches such as that in Figure 1c would be cumbersome to create and require a large number of tiny strokes. Some approaches relax this assumption by breaking the stroke into a number of smooth segments connected at sharp corners [26].

In other approaches users explicitly describe the intended shape of the curve using templates [10] or French curves [27] allowing the creation of very precise curve shapes. The two disadvantages of such approaches are that it is still difficult to transition through different neatening directives within the same stroke, and the external template needs to be invoked explicitly by the user, breaking the desirable flow of pure modeless sketching [14].

There are many different ways of achieving a desired stroke neatening directive. For simple stroke smoothing a variety of techniques exist including Laplacian smoothing [32], cubic spline fitting [4], clothoid fitting [19] and one-handed tape drawing [11]. Piecewise clothoid fitting [19] has been shown to create curves with the most appealing curvature properties but is hard to combine with point, tangent or other precise constraints. Some of these techniques such as Laplacian smoothing and one-handed tape drawing can be used to smooth and commit a stroke as it is drawn, whereas the remainder of the approaches are global in nature, based on optimization or fitting, and require a complete stroke.

Ours is the first approach to propose the principled and explicit use of stroke dynamics as a neatening directive and perform this neatening in real-time as the stroke is sketched. We draw inspiration for this affordance from the kinematics of drawing [18, 28] and research that relates drawing speed to curve features such as cusps and corners [25].

There are a number of other approaches to curve creation and control that are relevant to this work. Fiume [9] introduced arc-length as a control parameter in conjunction with typical Bezier constraints. Using physical forces and dynamics as a control methodology has also been used extensively [6, 12, 29]. Dynadraw [12], aimed at creating calligraphic strokes, indirectly correlates stroke speed and lag by physically simulating a pen pulled across paper. Cords [7] are 3D curves which wrap around scene objects. Cords are procedurally generated from user-defined guide curves and a stiffness parameter that models their pliability. Our elasticurve framework has a similar mathematical formulation.

Variants of the above research exist in commercial software such as Sketchbook-Pro [2], Illustrator [1] and Windows Journal [20]. We discuss these in relation to Elasticurves in the comparisons section.

PROBLEM STATEMENT

Given an input stroke segment Q, compute a neatened curve P that continuously changes from precisely Q to a smooth approximation of Q with increasing drawing speed (Figure 3). The curve construction must also be incremental: i.e. if Q is a sub-stroke of a longer stroke Q', its neatened curve P is the corresponding sub-stroke of the longer neatened curve P' (Figure 2).

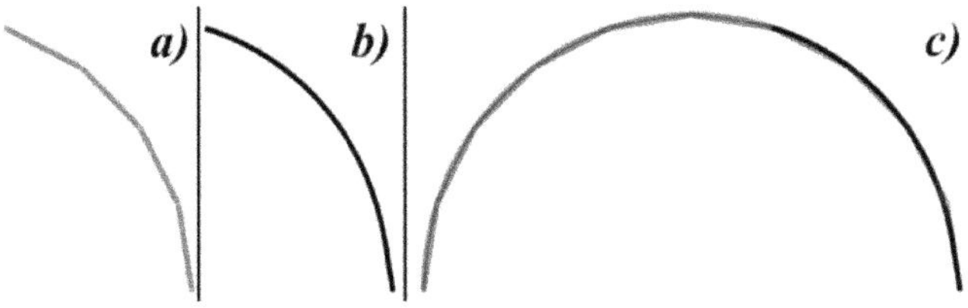

Figure 2: Incremental Elasticurve construction: (a) A partial segment Q of an input stroke. (b) The elasticurve segment P corresponding to Q. (c) The continued stroke Q' and elasticurve P' (in blue). Once commited, P is invariant to subsequent input.

ELASTICURVES ALGORITHM

The elasticurve framework is a "pure" sketching interface, in that all information related to stroke input and neatening is provided by the user in the stroke itself. We describe a minimal number of parameters that allow additional control over the generated curves but in practice users can create their desired curves predictably with the default settings.

Figure 3: The input stroke (left) is parameterized by time: the spacing of the green input points indicates stroke speed. The elasticurve (right) varies with increasing speed from a precise replica to a smooth approximation of the input.

Input Stroke

Input strokes from current sketching devices are typically a sequence of 2D points that are sampled at a small and regular time interval dt ms (see Appendix A). In practice this simply parameterizes the input stroke such that the distance between adjacent point samples is a measure of stroke speed (Figure 3). We denote this input stroke as Q, and the ith point on it as q_i. Elasticurves grow as a fraction (called responsiveness) of the spatial lag between the current elasticurve and stroke. Therefore, in a discrete setting, they only ever get infinitesimally close to the input stroke if subsequent points on the stroke are at the same position. In practice we can replace this converging progression of elasticurve points with an analytic curve segment as long as we can detect such a *paused* stroke state. Note that while the elasticurve will inertially lag and catch-up to the stroke as the user draws, the paused state can be thought of as an explicit catch-up of the elasticurve where the stroke inertia or lag is reset to zero. In practice, the curve often enters the paused state at sharp corners and upon stroke completion. We detect a pause in a stroke at a point where there is no movement for dt_{pause} milliseconds.

Curve Generation

We define an inertial responsiveness parameter r, which controls the mapping from stroke speed to the neatness of the curve. Users typically calibrate r to reflect their drawing skill or the noise and ergonomic inaccuracy of the input device ($0<r<=1$, $r=0.5$ by default). The elasticurve precisely matches the input stroke for $r=1$. Lowering r increases stroke inertia (for $r=0$ the elasticurve is a stationary point) resulting in fairer curves (Figure 6).

We will denote the generated elasticurve as P and its ith point as p_i. While we can use the metaphor of an oscillation-free zero-rest-length elastic band to describe the inertia between p_i and q_i, this is more to describe its visual behaviour than to accurately model its dynamics. Indeed in our case, the points are generated by a generalization of the formulation in [7], subject to $p_0=q_0$.

$$p_{i+1} = p_i + f(r, p_i, q_{i+1}, \dots) \qquad (1)$$

We will refer to the function f as being the *connector* between the evolving elasticurve and the input stroke. The connector locally controls the shape of the elasticurve and thus models prior knowledge of desirable curve shapes (such as lines or circles) that would connect p_i and q_{i+1}. The elasticurve segment between p_i and p_{i+1} is simply the parametric fraction r of this connector (Figure 5). The overall evolution of the elasticurve for linear and circular-arc connectors is shown in Figure 4. We explored various connector shapes and present the mathematical details of lines and circular-arcs in *Appendix A*.

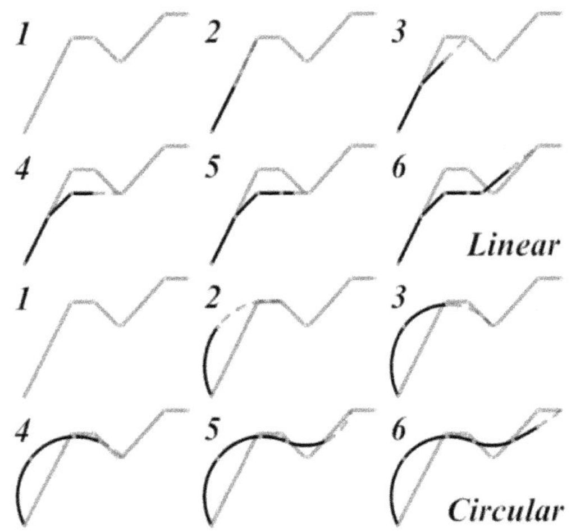

Figure 4: Elasticurve construction for 6 points of an input stroke using linear (top) and circular (bottom) connectors: the elasticurve evolves over six steps. At each step the curve grows by a fraction (r=0.5) along the connector shown by a dashed shape.

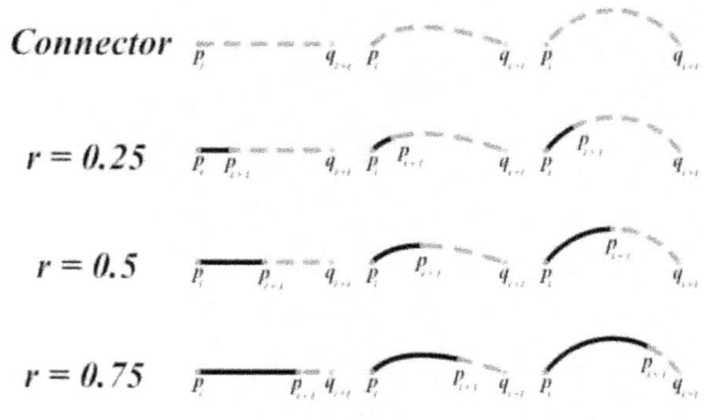

Figure 5: Connector shapes: lines, parabolas, arcs (left to right) with increasing r (top to bottom).

Linear Connectors

Linear elasticurves favour a *linear* interpretation of the input stroke. Intuitively, if the user were to provide input points which were all collinear, the generated curve should be a straight line. Deviations from this linearity in the input stroke result in similar deviations in the elasticurve, albeit dampened by a factor of r. The formulation used is:

$$f(r, p_i, q_{i+1}) = r(q_{i+1} - p_i)$$

Leading to the following recursive formula:

$$p_{i+1} = p_i + r(q_{i+1} - p_i)$$

This allows deviations from linearity in Q to be attenuated in P. As a consequence, P will always be more linear than Q especially when drawn rapidly (Figure 6), making the linear formulation ideal for sketching straight lines quickly. Further, while linear elasticurves seem to be only discrete polylines, they converge with finer sampling of an input stroke to a limit curve with the same degree of continuity as the input stroke (*Appendix A*).

Circular-arc Connectors

Circles are also a common shape prior that can be captured as a connector. Circular-arc connectors are defined by the circle passing through q_{i+1}, p_i with the tangent at p_i being the same as the tangent of P at p_i. Using this circle, we take a fraction r of the smaller-arc between p_i and q_{i+1} to find p_{i+1}. (Figure 5). The first circular-arc connector is defined by the smaller circular-arc connecting q_0,q_1,q_2. Like linear elasticurves, circular-arc elasticurves also converge to a limit curve but are G^1 continuous (a sequence of tangent continuous circular-arcs) even in the discrete setting. Circular-arcs can also represent lines (arcs of infinite radius) and are thus our default choice of connector.

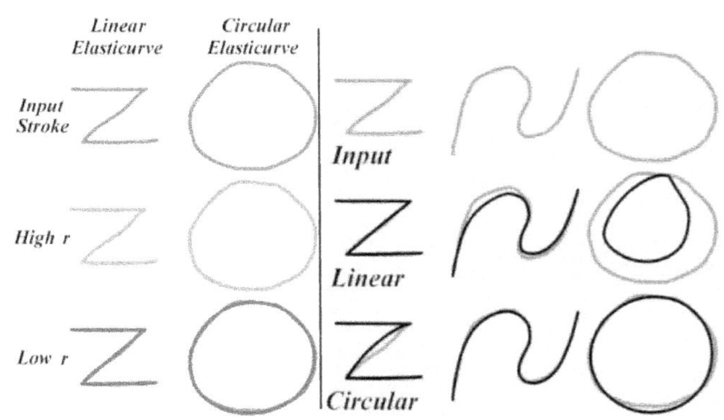

Figure 6: Responsiveness: At high r, elasticurves track the input regardless of connector. The impact of the connector shape is evident at lower r or when drawing quickly (left). A comparison between linear and circular-arcs for the same input at low r shows that circular-arcs handle curved regions better and can also capture line segments (right).

Alternate Connectors

While we present linear and circular connectors in detail, the elasticurve framework can accommodate any parametric connector function f. In particular, cubic Beziers can be used if curvature continuous elasticurves are desired. Curves with desired arc-lengths [9] can also be created using a tangent continuous parabolic connector passing through p_i with an arc length given by $r * \|q_{i+1} - p_i\|$.

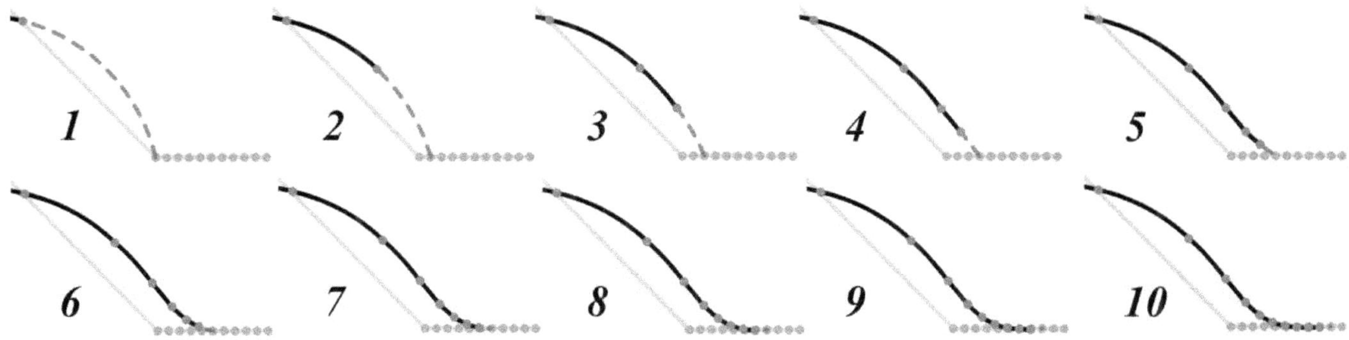

Figure 7: The elasticurve (connector is shown dashed) naturally catches-up to the input in a slowly drawn section.

Elasticurve Properties

Explicit use of drawing speed
An important property of elasticurves is their embodiment of stroke dynamics. Regardless of the connector or the responsiveness, elasticurves *naturally* match the input stroke when the user draws slowly and approximates quickly drawn portions of the stroke, in keeping with the speed-accuracy trade-off seen in human input actions [28].

Figure 7 shows a circular-arc elasticurve approaching a slowly drawn section of the input stroke, indicated by the many input points (sampled at equal time intervals) close to each other. Since the elasticurve grows by a fraction of the connector it gets progressively closer to the input where points are repeated or are close to each other. Within a few such iterations, the elasticurve becomes visually indistinguishable from that of the input stroke until an increase in stroke speed creates visually discernable spatial lag. If multiple points of an elasticurve are built using the same input point repeated over time, the elasticurve converges to the point as an infinite geometric progression of the responsiveness fraction. We identify this condition as a pause in sketching to complete the connector. These pauses occur naturally when drawing sharp corners, cusps and upon stroke completion.

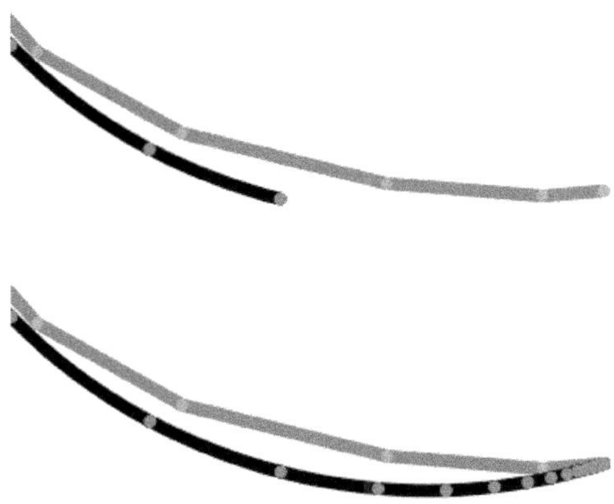

Figure 8: Curve completion: The elasticurve typically lags the end-point of a stroke (top). A paused state causes the curve to grow to the end-point (bottom).

Curve Completion
Once the input stroke is in a *paused* state, which is to say the cursor has not changed position for dt_{pause} ms or the stroke is completed, we complete the curve along its last connector. Conceptually, this is equivalent to creating an infinite number of input points at the given end-point. We implement this by repeating end-points (till the elasticurve is within a distance threshold to the curve) and then snap to the end-point, to keep the point distribution of the generated elasticurves consistent (Figure 8). Using the *paused* state in this manner also allows for the easy creation of cusps and tangent discontinuities, where natural pauses in drawing allow the elasticurve to catch up to the input at corners.

Incremental generation
The incremental construction of elasticurves makes it suitable to real-time curve neatening. In contrast most curve neatening algorithms [4, 19, 26] use a "global" fit to the current stroke, implying that the overall curve is never finalized until the input stroke is completed.

While the "global" fit algorithms can produce curves with nicer mathematical properties such as linear variation in curvature [19], it comes at the cost of losing the immediacy of curve creation, a critical affordance in certain scenarios.

Elasticurve Parameters

Elasticurves have three meaningful parameters: sampling interval (dt), time interval for a pause state to be detected (dt_{pause}), and responsiveness (r). dt is a function of the spatio-temporal resolution of the input device and dt_{pause} a matter of user agility and drawing skill. While we set these manually in our implementation, both are easy to calibrate: dt can be set such that the difference between the user input and the poly-line stroke is below a desired threshold. dt_{pause} can be inferred by asking users to draw a few sharp corners. Responsiveness is the one free parameter that relates to the inertial feel of the curve. While we could attempt to learn a user-specific default setting for r, we find that users grasp its behaviour quickly and adjust it often while sketching.

SPATIAL LAG RELATIONSHIPS

As mentioned above, elasticurves possess an inertial relationship to their input stroke. This spatial lag is a direct consequence of real-time neatening, where the curve can drift from the stroke to smoothen the input but must adhere to it when precision is intended. The spatial lag model used impacts the nature of curves produced. We classify a few existing models: *stick* lag connects the evolving curve and current input by a conceptual stick, akin to one-handed tape drawing [11]. *String* lag models this link as a piece of string. Points are added to the input stroke only when the string is taut, creating curves similar to one-handed tape drawing but allowing sharp corners, by letting the string go slack to abruptly change directions. *Spring* lag, akin to Dynadraw [12], models the link with a zero-rest-length spring, creating physically plausible trajectories that are often pleasing but can have undesirable oscillations. Elasticurves model what can be termed as *speed* lag, where the spatial inertia is directly related to stroke speed. Note that connectors and lag models are complementary and can be arbitrarily paired.

HUMAN ABILITY TO CONTROL SKETCHING SPEED

An obvious question that follows from wanting to use dynamics to indicate stroke precision while drawing is: how naturally and precisely can a user control sketching speed?

Attempting to determine if users had any control over their drawing speed, we asked 5 participants (aged 24-30, 4 right-handed, 1 left-handed), to continuously draw the same shape repeatedly, but with decreasing speed. For example, a participant would begin by drawing a line as fast as they could, and subsequently draw that same line with monotonically decreasing speed. This experiment was performed with lines, Bezier arcs and circles.

The results (Figure 9) illustrate that users do in fact possess reasonable control over their drawing speed, in that they can gradually slow down or speed up. The results, like other sensory controls, tend to follow Weber's law [33], in that a user can more aptly distinguish between slower speeds than fast ones. While a formal investigation of human drawing speed is worthwhile, this experiment suggests that users do possess adequate stroke speed control to utilize elasticurves effectively.

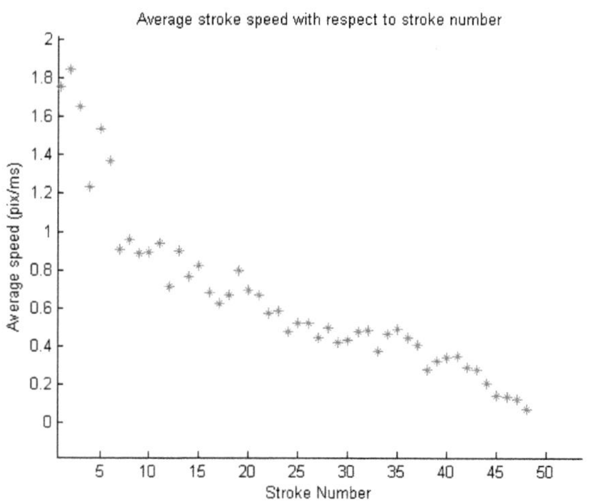

Figure 9: Speed control experiment: plotting average speed (in pix/ms) versus stroke index (decreasing speed).

CURVATURE AND ELASTICURVES

A well-documented perceptual factor affecting sketching speed is curvature. As was noted in [18], stroke speed follows a power law relationship with respect to curvature, namely:

$$v(t) = C * \kappa(t)^{-1/3}$$

Where $v(t)$ is tangential end-point speed, $\kappa(t)$ is the instantaneous curvature of the path, and C is a constant.

This formula entails that sketching speed is lower when attempting to draw areas of high curvature. However, this behaviour arises instinctively; there is no active decision to do so. In other words one might expect that a user intends to draw a curve with the same degree of smoothing but the unconscious drop in speed in regions of high curvature cause them to be drawn more precisely than regions of low curvature. Elasticurves can be modified to compensate for this by computing two speeds: $v_{measured}$, the observed speed of the input stroke, and $v_{expected}$, the speed given by the power law relationship. Discrete curvature is computed at points by looking one input ahead and computing the angle between the neighbours. The difference $v_{actual} = v_{measured} - v_{expected}$ thus captures any conscious variation in stroke speed by the user. We then map v_{actual} to responsiveness.

While the compensation method described above accounts for the perceptual effect curvature has on sketching speed, we found it to have little effect in practice, since the instant visual feedback from the elasticurve lets users compensate for this effect in their drawing directly.

USER FEEDBACK

We evaluated our system by distributing it to 6 users and asking them to try it out and send us their creations. We did not specify which input method they should use; two used a tablet computer, one a trackpad and three a mouse. Each user was aged between 20 and 40, had a familiarity with computers and drawing ability varying from professional to completely inexperienced. Notably, the experienced users used tablets, while the inexperienced ones used a mouse or trackpad as their input device. Their period of usage ranged from one to eight hours. Figures 1 and 10 illustrate sketches created by a user of above-average drawing skill on a pen and tablet interface. Of particular note in these images is how elasticurves satisfactorily handle both precise strokes (such as the arm and book of the character, as well as the fish and shark) and rapid strokes where precision is of no concern (such as the waves, ground, and tree foliage).

Figure 11, on the other hand, illustrates how elasticurves can be used to improve sketching ability. The image was created by a user with no sketching experience using a mouse and a background image to trace over.

The ability of elasticurves to allow users to create desirable primitive shapes (Figures 11-13), with a mouse or trackpad and little drawing experience, is particularly noteworthy.

Figure 10: Elasticurve sketch created using pen and tablet interface. Stroke input (left), overlaid elasticurves (right).

An experienced user also mentioned how she felt she had to draw "extra slow" for it to match her exact movements. We feel this is indicative of how, with experience, skilled artists will become proficient at making precise strokes quickly. While increasing responsiveness easily remedies this problem, it does indicate that parameter calibration is recommended (if not required) before extended use. Yet another user complained that the sampling frequency setting was too coarse for their device, once again hinting that calibration may be required on different input devices. One user also complained that the stroke inertia of elasticurves was distracting. The user felt they had to mentally predict the curve's reaction to their future motion. Given that other users were comfortable with spatial lag, something professional tape-drawing artists live with, we believe that experience with the tool would mitigate such discomfort.

Figure 11: Sketches created by a novice user. Tracing over a background image (top).

Figure 12: Mouse sketches by an intermediate user.

Users described the interface as "cool", "fluid" or "physical" and remarked that the system was different from any sketching applications with which they had prior experience. One user who sketched with a mouse mentioned how when using our tool he "drew in a different way than [he] would using something unassisted" because "with [something else], [he] would try to draw things as straight (or circular) as possible, and probably fail, whereas with [elasticurves], [he] would guide the mouse in the general direction knowing roughly how the program was going to correct it".

Figure 13: Sketches created using a trackpad by an intermediate user. An oversketch (top). Using the trackpad as a virtual skating rink (bottom).

Another user mentioned that it felt like "drawing with hair on bathroom tiles", which we believe is an allusion to the inertial and smooth nature of elasticurves.

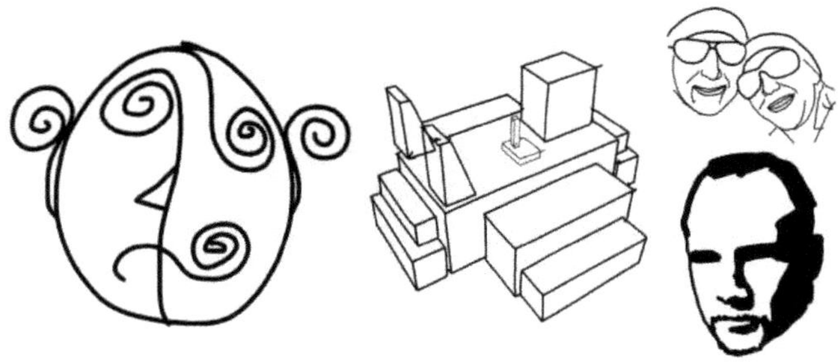

Figure 14: Additional sketches created by various users of intermediate drawing experience.

APPLICATIONS

We believe the affordances provided by an elasticurve sketching system are applicable in many fields. Notable here are: *a front-end to gesture-based interfaces* [3, 17, 22, 24, 25, 34], where the real-time mix of smoothness and sharp corners can provide shape recognizers with improved input; *image tracing for vectorization and cel animation*, where the incremental nature of elasticurves allows visual evaluation of the result while the user draws; *interactive trajectories for performance animation* [30], where in addition to real-time neatening, the timing along the path is encoded in elasticurve parameterization.

In general sketching scenarios, responsiveness provides users a single parameter to control a level of drawing assistance and to compensate for device and motor noise.

Drawing Assistance

Elasticurves were in part developed as a means to assist users lacking the control and practice of a professional artist (Figure 11). Since the responsiveness parameter controls how closely the input stroke is tracked (Figure 6), it provides all users with a manner by which to adjust elasticurves to appropriately augment their personal sketching ability, in particular for drawing near perfect lines or circular arcs.

Device and motor ability compensation

The strong approximations elasticurves with low responsiveness can induce on input strokes make them viable candidates for sketching tasks on commonly used devices that are not designed for drawing such as mice, trackpads, touchscreens and trackballs (Figures 11-13).

Figure 15: An input stroke with jitter is attenuated using a low responsiveness elasticurve.

A similar argument holds for users lacking fine motor control. As shown in Figure 15, by lowering responsiveness to an appropriate level, jitter and noisy input can be attenuated to create visually appealing strokes.

ELASTICURVE COMPARISONS

The neatening of sketches is a long standing problem with a large body of research. To evaluate elasticurves relative to existing research we compare elasticurves to three popular commercial systems: Windows7 Journal [20], Illustrator CS5 [1] and Sketchbook-Pro 2010 [2].

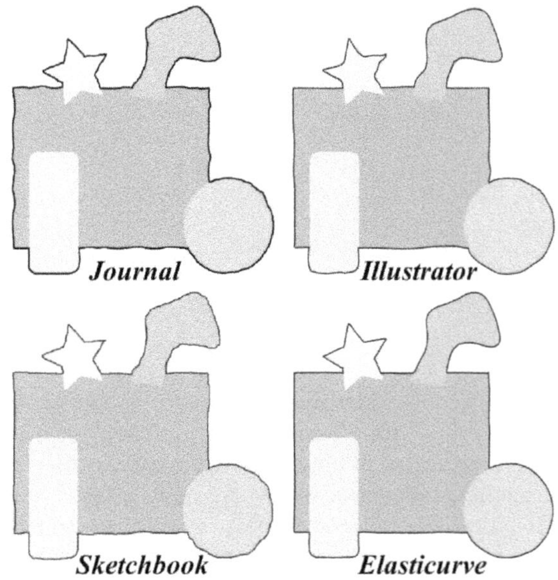

Figure 16: Sketch neatening technique comparison using a trackpad on an image tracing task. The visually neatest result of 7 trials for each technique by an intermediate user are shown.

Sketch neatening in Journal and Illustrator are based on global fitting after stroke completion. Sketchbook-Pro implements a real-time variant of Dynadraw [12]. Theoretically, a fair comparison with elasticurves is difficult. Journal and Illustrator have the advantage of globally optimizing an entire stroke over the real-time local approach of Sketchbook and Elasticurves. Conversely, the latter two use speed as a neatening directive. Elasticurves enable further user control via responsiveness. Despite these issues, to gain some practical insight, we asked an intermediate user to trace the outline of a background image using all four techniques. After a few strokes to gain familiarity with all systems, the user traced over the image with a single stroke. The four techniques were used in turn and repeated overall 7 times. The neatest visual result of each technique using a trackpad is shown in Figure 16. Qualitatively, the neatening in Journal is more localized than Illustrator, resulting in sharp corners but an overall noisier sketch. Illustrator conversely produces a globally smooth but wiggly curve that tends to round subtle corners (the concave corners of the star in Figure 16). Sketchbook is optimized for local real-time neatening and produces noisy results visually similar to Journal. Elasticurves, with low responsiveness, produce the most pleasing result: Corners are precisely created at pauses in the stroke and the circular-arc connector captures lines, arcs and smooth curves with ease. The same task done with a pen produced differences that were subtler but noticeably similar to the trackpad.

Within the genre of elasticurves we further explored viable alternatives to the problem of real-time curve neatening. In both cases we re-parameterized the curve by arc-length and then used stroke speed to modulate a smoothing approach.

Speed modulated Laplacian Smoothing

Simple neighbour averaging is a popular approach to stroke smoothing that is trivial to implement. Conceptually, correlating smoothing strength to stroke speed should result in neatened curves. In practice (Figure 1b), the locality of neighbour averaging can create wiggles or pockets of curvature in curves and varying smoothing strength along the curve can cause irregular spacing of curve points. It also lacks the tangent continuity of circular-arc connectors.

Speed modulated responsiveness

Stroke speed can also be inversely related to the responsiveness of an arc-length parameterized elasticurve. This provides better results than Laplacian smoothing (see Figure 17 and video), but both approaches suffer from re-parameterization artifacts and do not have the convergence guarantees of elasticurves shown in *Appendix A*.

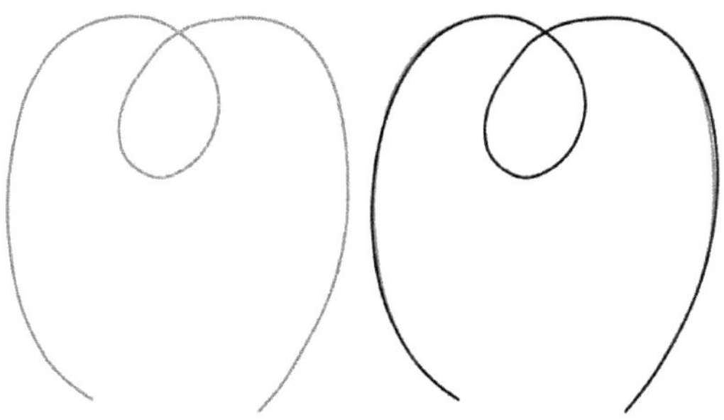

Figure 17: Speed modulated responsiveness built using input points 30 pixels apart. The brightness of the green input points indicates speed.

CONCLUSION

We explored stroke neatening in real-time, and argued that in a general scenario, neatening intent along a stroke should be provided by the user. Motivated by the ergonomics of sketching, we proposed using stroke speed as a neatening directive. An experiment where users drew sequences of strokes while consciously controlling drawing speed led further credence to this choice

We then developed elasticurves, a stroke neatening framework explicitly driven by stroke speed. We capture desirable shapes like lines and circles as connectors along which the elasticurve evolves. We analyzed the geometric properties of elasticurves and showed them to be mathematically stable, robust and convergent with increasing sampling resolution of the input. They are also capable of representing precise shapes like lines and circles.

Our evaluation of elasticurves was two-fold. First a free-form user study with 6 users of varying skills show elasticurves to be an effective and promising solution to the real-time neatening of sketch input. Second, we favourably compared our results with those of three commercial systems for an image tracing task.

Avenues for improvement and future work on elasticurves include the automatic adaption of responsiveness to estimated sketch noise, curvature continuous connectors and an extension of elasticurves to 3D surface modeling.

REFERENCES

1. Adobe Systems Inc. (2010). Adobe Illustrator CS 5. *http://www.adobe.com/products/illustrator.html*
2. Autodesk Inc. (2010). Autodesk Sketchbook Pro 2010. *http://area.autodesk.com/sketchbook*
3. Anderson, D., Bailey, C., & Skubic, M. (2004). Hidden Markov Model Symbol Recognition for Sketch-Based Interfaces. *AAAI Fall Symposium* (pp. 15-21). Menlo Park, CA: AAAI Press.
4. Bae, S.-H., Balakrishnan, R., & Singh, K. (2008). ILoveSketch:As-Natural-As-Possible System for Creating 3D Curve Models. *Proc. UIST*, 151-160.
5. Balakrishnan, R., Fitzmaurice, G., Kurtenbach, G., & Buxton, W. (1999). Digital Tape Drawing. *Proc. UIST*, 161-169.
6. Barzel, R. (1997). Faking Dynamics of Ropes and Strings. *IEEE CGA, 3*, pp. 31-39.
7. Coleman, P., & Singh, K. (2006). Cords: Geometric Curve Primitives for Modeling Contact. *IEEE CGA, 3*, pp. 72-79.
8. Farin, G., Rein, G., Sapidis, N., & Worsey, A. (1987). Fairing Cubic B-Spline Curves. *Computer Aided Geometric Design*, 91-103.
9. Fiume, E. (1995). Isometric Piecewise Polynomial Curves. *Computer Graphics Forum, 1*, pp. 47-58.
10. Fung, R., Lank, E., Terry, M., & Latulipe, C. (2008). Kinematic Templates: End-User Tools for Content-Relative Cursor Manipulations. *Proc. UIST*, 47-56.
11. Grossman, T., Balakrishnan, R., Kurtenbach, G., Fitzmaurice, G., Khan, A., & Buxton, B. (2002). Creating Principal 3D Curves with Digital Tape Drawing. *Proc. CHI*, 121-128.
12. Haeberli, P. (1989). DynaDraw. *Silicon Graphics Corporation*. Mountain View, California, USA. *http://www.graficaobscura.com/dyna/index.html*
13. Igarashi, T., Kadobayashi, R., Mase, K., & Tanaka, H. (1998). Path Drawing for 3D Walkthrough. *Proc. UIST*, (pp. 173-174).
14. Igarashi, T., Kawachiya, S., Matsuoka, S., & Tanaka, H. (1997). In Search for an Ideal Computer-Assisted Drawing System. *INTERACT*, (pp. 104-111).
15. Igarashi, T., Matsuoka, S., & Tanaka, H. (1999). Teddy: A Sketching Interface for 3D Freeform Design. *SIGGRAPH*, (pp. 409-416).
16. Igarashi, T., Matsuoka, S., Kawachiya, S., & Tanaka, H. (1997). Interactive Beautification: A Technique for Rapid Geometric Design. *Proc. UIST*, (pp. 105-114).

17. Labahn, G., MacLean, S., Marzouk, M., Rutherford, I., & Tausky, D. (2006). MathBrush: An Experimental Pen-Based Math System. *Dagstuhl Seminar Proceedings, Challenges in Symbolic Computation.*

18. Lacquaniti, F., Terzuolo, C., & Viviani, P. (1983). The law relating the kinematics and figural aspects of drawing movements. *Acta Psychologica* , pp. 115-130.

19. McCrae, J., & Singh, K. (2008). Sketching Piecewise Clothoid Curves. *SBIM*, pp. 1-8.

20. Microsoft Corporation (2009). Windows 7 Journal.

21. Ramos, G., Boulos, M., & Balakrishnan, R. (2004). Pressure Widgets. *Proc. CHI*, (pp. 487-494).

22. Rubine, D. (1991). Specifying gestures by example. *Proc. SIGGRAPH,* (pp. 329-337).

23. Schmidt, R., Khan, A., Singh, K., & Kurtenbach, G. (2010). Analytic Drawing of 3D Scaffolds. *Proc. SIGGRAPH ASIA (to appear).*

24. Sezgin, T., & Davis, R. (2005). HMM-based efficient sketch recognition. *Proc. IUI* , 281-283.

25. Sezgin, T., Stahovich, T., & Davis, R. (2001). Sketch Based Interfaces: Early Processing for Sketch Understanding. *Proc. PUI* .

26. Shao, L., & Zhou, H. (1996). Curve Fitting with Bezier Cubics. *Graphical Models and Image Processing , 3*, pp. 223-232.

27. Singh, K. (1999). Interactive Curve Design using Digital French Curves. *Proc. I3D*, 23-30.

28. Soukoreff, R., & MacKenzie, I. (2009). An informatic rationale for the speed-accuracy trade-off. *Proc. IEEE SMC*, (pp. 2969-2975).

29. Terzopoulos, D., & Qin, H. (1994). Dynamic NURBS with Geometric Constraints for Interactive Sculpting. *ACM TOG, 2*, pp. 103-136.

30. Thorne, M., Burke, D., & van de Panne, M. (2004). Motion Doodles: An Interface for Sketching Character Motion. *ACM TOG, v.23 n.3.*

31. Tian, F., Ao, X., Hongan, W., Setlur, V., & Dai, G. (2008). Tilt menu: using the 3D orientation information of pen devices to extend the selection capability of pen-based user interfaces. *Proc. CHI*, (pp. 1371-1380).

32. Tsang, S., Balakrishnan, R., Singh, K., & Ranjan, A. (2004). A suggestive interface for image guided 3d sketching. *Proc. CHI*, (pp. 591-598).

33. Weber, E. (1846). Der Tastsinn und das Gemeingefühl. In Wagner, *Handlewörterbuch der Physiologie* (Vol. iii).

34. Wobbrock, J., Wilson, A., & Li., Y. (2007). Gestures without Libraries, Toolkits or Training: a 1$ Recognizer for User Interface Prototypes. *Proc. UIST.* (pp 159-168).

APPENDIX A

We present the computation of linear and circular-arc connectors. We also show convergence to a continuous limit elasticurve with increased sampling frequency

Linear Elasticurves

$$f(r, p_i, q_{i+1}) = r(q_{i+1} - p_i)$$

And substituting back into (1), we get:

$$p_{i+1} = p_i + r(q_{i+1} - p_i)$$

Writing the responsiveness r as $s*dt$, where we fix s to be constant and dt is the sampling interval of time we get:

$$dp/dt = s(q(t) - p(t))$$

which is a linear first order differential equation, whose solution is the elasticurve $p(t)$ as $dt \to 0$.

Circular-arc Elasticurves

Figure 18 shows the circle passing through q_{i+1}, p_i with tangent $\boldsymbol{t}_i$ at p_i, where $\boldsymbol{t}_i$ and $\boldsymbol{n}_i$ are the tangent and normal of the elasticurve at p_i.

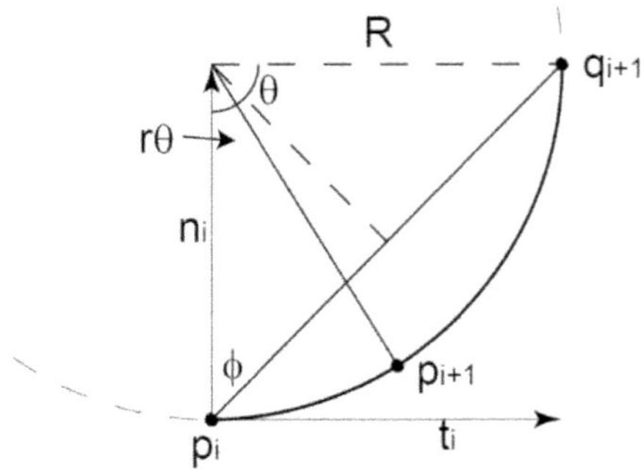

Figure 18: Computing the circular-arc connector.

$$f(r, p_i, q_{i+1}) = R(1 - \cos(r\theta))\boldsymbol{n}_i + R\sin(r\theta)\ \boldsymbol{t}_i$$

The circle radius $R = ||q_{i+1} - p_i||/(2\cos\phi)$ and the connector angle $\theta = \pi - 2\phi$, where

$$\cos\phi = (q_{i+1} - p_i).\boldsymbol{n}_i/||q_{i+1} - p_i||.$$

As before writing r as $s*dt$ we get:

$$dp/dt = R/dt[(1 - \cos(sdt\theta))\boldsymbol{n}_i + \sin(sdt\theta)\ \boldsymbol{t}_i]$$

In the limit as $dt \to 0$, $dp/dt = Rs\theta\boldsymbol{t}_i$

which verifies that the curve is tangent continuous and shows that $p(t)$ converges to the solution of the above equations as $dt \to 0$. It is important to note here that the vectors $\boldsymbol{t}_i$ and $\boldsymbol{n}_i$ are updated by a rotation of $r\theta$.

ReVision: Automated Classification, Analysis and Redesign of Chart Images

*Manolis Savva**, Nicholas Kong†, Arti Chhajta*, Li Fei-Fei*, Maneesh Agrawala†, Jeffrey Heer**

*Stanford University
{msavva, achhajta, feifeili, jheer}@cs.stanford.edu

†University of California, Berkeley
{nkong, maneesh}@eecs.berkeley.edu

ABSTRACT

Poorly designed charts are prevalent in reports, magazines, books and on the Web. Most of these charts are only available as bitmap images; without access to the underlying data it is prohibitively difficult for viewers to create more effective visual representations. In response we present *ReVision*, a system that automatically redesigns visualizations to improve graphical perception. Given a bitmap image of a chart as input, ReVision applies computer vision and machine learning techniques to identify the chart type (e.g., pie chart, bar chart, scatterplot, *etc.*). It then extracts the graphical marks and infers the underlying data. Using a corpus of images drawn from the web, ReVision achieves an image classification accuracy of 96% across ten chart categories. It also accurately extracts marks from 79% of bar charts and 62% of pie charts, and from these charts it successfully extracts the data from 71% of bar charts and 64% of pie charts. ReVision then applies perceptually-based design principles to populate an interactive gallery of redesigned charts. With this interface, users can view alternative chart designs and retarget content to different visual styles.

ACM Classification: H5.2 [Information Interfaces and Presentation]: User Interfaces – Graphical User Interfaces.

Keywords: Visualization, chart understanding, information extraction, redesign, computer vision.

General terms: Algorithms, Design, Experimentation

INTRODUCTION

Over the last 300 years, charts, graphs, and other visual depictions of data have become a primary vehicle for communicating quantitative informationf [28]. However, designers of visualizations must navigate a number of decisions, including choices of visual encoding and styling. These decisions influence the look-and-feel of a graphic and can have a profound effect on graphical perception [6]: the ability of viewers to decode information from a chart. Despite progress in the development of design principles for effective visualization [6, 11, 16, 20, 21, 24, 28], many charts produced today exhibit poor design choices that hamper understanding of the underlying data and lead to unaesthetic displays.

UIST'11, October 16-19, 2011, Santa Barbara, CA, USA.
Copyright 2011 ACM 978-1-4503-0716-1/11/10...$10.00.

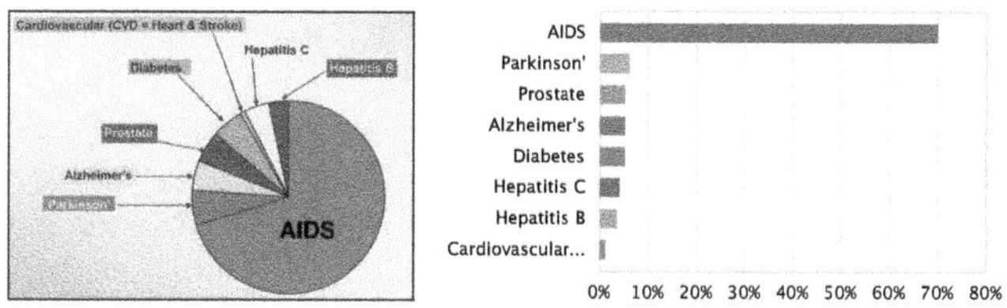

Figure 1: Chart Redesign. Left: A pie chart of NIH expenses per condition-related death. The chart suffers from random sorting, highly saturated colors, and erratic label placement. Right: Plotting the data as a sorted bar chart enables more accurate comparisons of data values [6, 20].

Consider the pie chart in Figure 1 (left), which depicts data concerning the 2005 research budget of the National Institutes of Health (NIH). The design of this chart could be improved in multiple ways: slices are ordered haphazardly, labels are placed erratically, and label text competes with saturated background colors. Moreover, the chart encodes values as angular extents, which are known to result in less accurate value comparisons than position encodings [6, 16, 24]. Figure 1 (right) shows the same data in a redesigned visualization: the bar chart sorts the data, uses a perceptually-motivated color palette [26], and applies a position encoding.

For analysts working with their own data, automated design methods [20, 21] based on visual design principles [6, 11, 16, 28] can lead to more effective visualizations. However, the vast majority of visualizations are only available as bitmap images. Without access to the underlying data it is prohibitively difficult to create alternative visual representations.

We present *ReVision*, a system that takes bitmap images of charts as input and automatically generates redesigned visualizations as output. For example, ReVision produces Figure 1 (right) as a suggested redesign when given Figure 1 (left) as input. Our system identifies the type of chart, extracts the marks (visual elements that encode data) and underlying data, and then uses this information in tandem with a list of guidelines to provide alternate designs. ReVision also supports stylistic redesign; users can change mark types, colors or fonts to adhere to a specific visual aesthetic or brand. We make the following research contributions:

Classification of Chart Images. ReVision determines the type of chart using both low-level image features and extracted text-level features. We propose a novel set of features that achieve an average classification accuracy of 96%. Our image features are more accurate, simpler to compute, and easier to interpret than those used in prior work. While we focus on the task of chart redesign, our classification method is applicable to additional tasks such as indexing and retrieval.

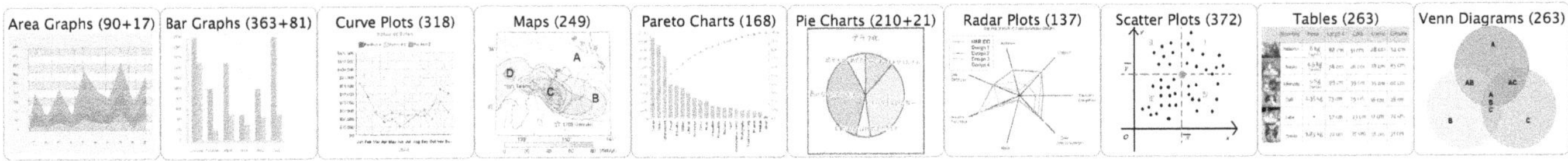

Figure 2: Our 10-category chart image corpus. Numbers in parentheses: (strictly 2D images + images with 3D effects).

Extraction of Chart Data. We present a set of chart-specific techniques for extracting the graphical marks and the data values they represent from a visualization. Our implementation focuses on bar and pie charts. We first locate the bars and pie slices that encode the data. We then apply heuristics to associate the marks with related elements such as axes and labels. Finally, we use this information to extract the table of data values underlying the visualization. We exclude any bar and pie chart images with 3D effects or non-solid shading. We achieve an average accuracy of 71.4% in extracting the marks and an average accuracy of 67.1% in extracting the data after we successfully extract the marks.

Finally, we demonstrate how these contributions can be combined with existing design guidelines to automatically generate redesigned visualizations. We have also compiled a corpus of over 2,500 chart images labeled by chart type. We are making this corpus publicly available in the hope of spurring further research on automated visualization interpretation.

RELATED WORK

Our ReVision system builds on three areas of related work.

Classifying Visualization Images

Classification of natural scenes is a well-studied problem in computer vision [1, 3]. A common approach is to use a "bag of visual words" representation [29] where the "words" are low-level image features such as gradients or local region textures. Each input image is encoded as a feature vector using these words. Machine learning methods then classify the feature vectors and corresponding images into categories.

Researchers have developed specialized techniques for classifying chart images by type: bar chart, pie chart, *etc.* Shao and Futrelle [23] and Huang et al. [17] extract high-level shapes (e.g., line segments) from vector images of charts and then use these shapes as features for classifying six kinds of charts. Their approach relies on an accurate vectorization of charts, which can be difficult to generate from chart images.

Prasad et al. [22] classify bitmap images of charts drawn from five common categories. They apply a series of pre-processing operations to compute global curve saliency and local image segment features. These operations require many input-dependent parameters, complicating generalization to more categories. Additionally, they use Scale Invariant Feature Transform (SIFT) [10] and Histogram of Oriented Gradient (HOG) [9] features to represent higher level properties of image regions. They then compare these features using multi-resolution pyramidal histograms and use the similarity scores to train a multi-class Support Vector Machine (SVM), achieving an average classification accuracy of 84.2%.

The features used by Prasad et al. cannot easily be tied to the presence of specific graphical marks. We are interested in image features at the level of graphical marks because they could be useful in connecting classification to extraction. We desire highly predictive features that (a) are easier to compute, (b) more readily interpreted, and (c) better inform post-classification extraction.

Extracting Marks from Charts

Some researchers have investigated techniques for extracting marks from charts. Zhou and Tan [31] combine boundary tracing with the Hough transform to extract bars from bar charts. Huang et al. [17, 18, 19] generate edge maps, vectorize the edge maps, and use rules to extract marks from bar, pie, line, and low-high charts. Yang et al. [30] built a system incorporating this technique to allow humans to correct automatically generated vector representations of charts. However, their work focuses on extracting the mark geometry rather than the underlying data. Their techniques rely on an accurate edge map, which can be difficult to retrieve from real-world charts, due to large variance in image quality. We designed our techniques to be more robust to such variance.

Automated Visualization Design

Researchers have applied graphical perception principles to automatically produce effective visualizations. Mackinlay's APT [20] generates charts guided by rankings of visual variables for specific data types such as nominal, ordinal, or quantitative data. Stolte et al.'s Polaris [25] is a system for generating small multiples [28] displays based on user queries of a multidimensional data table. Mackinlay et al. [21] extend this work to support a range of automated visualization designs. These systems assist users in producing visualizations directly from data; we seek to first extract data from chart images and then redesign the visualizations. Our current work is complementary to these earlier systems: once we have extracted a data table, we could feed it into any of these systems to generate improved alternative designs.

SYSTEM OVERVIEW

ReVision is comprised of a three stage pipeline: (1) chart classification, (2) mark and data extraction, and (3) redesign. In stage 1, ReVision classifies an input image according to its chart type. This stage uses a corpus of test images to learn distinctive image features and train classifiers. In stage 2, ReVision locates graphical marks, associates them with text labels, and extracts a data table. In stage 3, ReVision uses the extracted data to generate a gallery of alternative designs.

STAGE 1: CLASSIFYING CHART IMAGES

While classification of natural images is a well-studied computer vision problem, chart images are unlike natural images in several important ways. First, marks within data graphics are more discrete and more frequently repeated than textured regions in photographs. Second, there are many areas with constant color, so pixel neighborhoods with low variances are common. Finally, text occurs more frequently and

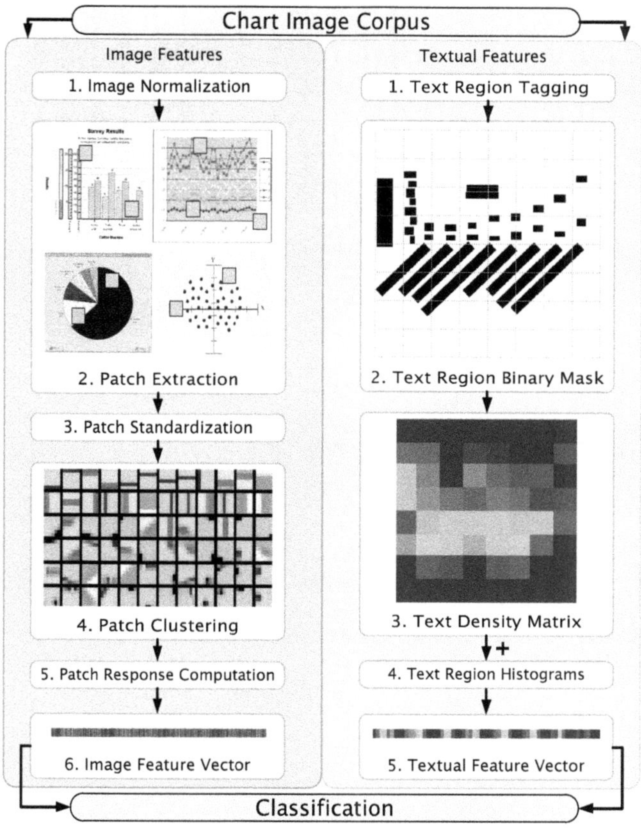

Figure 3: The ReVision classification pipeline, including both image (left) and textual (right) features.

prominently than in natural scenes. The following sections describe how we account for these differences to achieve classification accuracy superior to previous work [22].

Learning Low-Level Image Features

Figure 3 illustrates our classification pipeline. Coates et al. [7] found that random sampling of image patches (small rectangular image regions), followed by K-means clustering of the patches and then classification achieves state of the art performance for classifying natural images. We extend their approach to classifying chart images using a sequence of 7 steps: (1) normalize the input images, (2) extract image patches, (3) standardize the patches, (4) cluster the patches to form a "codebook", (5) compute a "codebook" patch response for each image, (6) formulate a feature vector for each image from the response, and (7) perform classification.

1. Image Normalization. We normalize images to a constant size of $D \times D$ pixels to ensure homogeneous sampling and equivalence of each exemplar in the corpus. We preserve the aspect ratio of the original image by padding with the background color. We convert color images to grayscale, as color is rarely indicative of visualization category. Note that we use the original color images in the mark and data extraction stage of our system. We considered image sizes from $D = 32$ up to $D = 512$ and found that $D = 128$ achieves the best classification accuracy. We believe this is due to the reduction of noise and compression artifacts in the down-sampled images (the average image size is roughly 300×400 pixels).

2. Patch Extraction. We extract square patches from the images by uniform random sampling for 100 locations per image. We tested patch sizes over the range from 2×2 up to 20×20 pixels and found that a patch size of 6×6 pixels gave the best classification performance. The optimal patch size was consistently about 5% of the normalized image dimensions. To filter out frequently occurring constant color regions, we reject sample patches with variance less than 10% of the maximum pixel value.

3. Patch Standardization. For classification, absolute pixel values are not as important as variation within a patch. Thus, we normalize the contrast of each patch by subtracting the mean and dividing by the standard deviation of the pixel values in that patch. This normalization ensures that a single appropriately weighted patch can represent patches with different absolute intensities but similar variations. We perform a "whitening" procedure on the entire patch set which reduces the cross-correlation between patches and improves classification performance [7].

4. Patch Clustering. Given an extracted patch set, we perform K-means clustering to obtain a set of "centroid" patches that correspond to the most frequently occurring patch types. We use a Euclidean L^2 distance metric over the pixel values. In practice we set the number of centroids K to 200 as we found that larger numbers of centroids did not achieve better performance. The centroid patches constitute a feature set, or "codebook", which we can use to describe our image corpus.

These codebook patches capture frequently occurring graphical marks such as lines, points, corners, arcs and gradients. By independently extracting codebooks from each visualization category, we obtain patch sets that reflect the occurrence frequencies of marks characteristic of each category. As an example, in Figure 4 we compare the centroids for 3 categories from the corpus of [22]. We invite the reader to guess which categories are represented.[1]

Using Low-Level Image Features for Classification

To classify an input image, we first normalize it to a 128×128 grayscale image and extract 6×6 sized patches centered on each pixel. We then perform the following steps:

5. Codebook Patch Response. For each extracted patch, we determine the nearest codebook patch by Euclidean distance. We thus obtain a D^2 centroid response map over the entire image, where D (= 128) is the normalized image dimension.

6. Feature Vector Formulation. We reduce the dimensionality of the codebook patch response map by dividing the image into quadrants and summing the activations for each codebook patch in a given quadrant, similar to constructing a histogram of activated patches. We thus obtain a $4K$-length feature vector for each input image. Since we set $K = 200$, we obtain an 800 element image feature vector which is much smaller than the set of all 128×128 patch responses.

7. Classification. We use the feature vectors to perform classification using Support Vector Machines (SVMs) [8] with a quadratic kernel function. We use the SVM implementation provided by the WEKA [14] framework.

Figure 4: Codebook patches for 3 different visualization categories. We invite the reader to guess which categories were sampled.[1]

Using Text-Level Features to Improve Classification

While image features offer powerful cues to determine the category of a chart image, text-level features are also informative. The position and size of text regions in chart images may correlate with the visualization type. We show that textual information can further improve classification accuracy.

We designed a tagging interface to annotate chart images with the position, size, angular orientation and content of text regions. Our tool extracts the text image region and performs OCR using the Tesseract open source OCR engine; the user can correct the OCR output if desired. While manual text annotation is tedious, it is amenable to crowdsourcing and we designed the tagging UI with this scenario in mind. Furthermore, connected components analysis or more sophisticated approaches [4] can extract text region bounding boxes automatically. These methods could allow fully unsupervised textual feature extraction from a visualization corpus.

To capture the distribution and density of text regions in an input image, we construct a binary mask indicating which pixels belong to text regions (step 2 in Figure 3, right). We subdivide the mask into $N \times N$ blocks, calculate the proportion of text region pixels in each block (step 3), and linearize the values into an N^2 element vector. We found that $N = 8$ maximizes classification accuracy. However, at this resolution the exact positions, sizes and relative orientations of text regions are abstracted. To retain this information we compute normalized 10-bin histograms of the distributions of text region length, width, center position, as well as pairwise orientation and pairwise distance between text region centers (step 4). We concatenate these histograms with the text density vector to create a final textual feature vector (step 5).

Classification Performance

We used three collections of chart images to evaluate our system. To compare our classification results with those of Prasad et al. [22], we used their corpus of 667 images drawn from 5 categories: bar charts (125), curve plots (121), pie charts (134), scatter plots (162) and 3D surface plots (125). We also obtained the corpus of Huang et al. [17], which contains 200 images in 4 categories: 2D bar charts (80), 2D pie charts (48), 3D pie charts (12), and line plots (60). Finally, we compiled a new corpus containing 2,601 chart images labeled with 10 categories using a semi-automated tool for querying Google image search. Example images from each category are given in Figure 2. We use this larger corpus to evaluate how our system scales to classifying images from larger sets of visualization categories.

[1]Bar Charts (left), Pie Charts (middle), Scatter Plots (right). Bar corners, pie arcs and scatter points are prevalent within their respective categories.

	Prasad [22]	Image	Text	All	Binary
Bar	90%	85%	57%	89%	95%
Curve	76%	75%	50%	83%	92%
Pie	83%	93%	84%	95%	97%
Scatter	86%	91%	64%	91%	97%
Surface	84%	90%	71%	94%	97%
Average	**84%**	**88%**	**66%**	**90%**	**96%**

Table 1: Classification accuracy for the corpus from Prasad et al. [22]. We compare Prasad et al. to our method using image features (first two columns), text features (1st and 3rd), and both (1st and 4th) in multi-class SVMs. The last column shows results for both features using binary SVMs.

	Multi-Class	**Binary**
Area Graphs	88%	98%
Bar Graphs	78%	95%
Curve Plots	73%	91%
Maps	84%	97%
Pareto Charts	85%	97%
Pie Charts	79%	97%
Radar Plots	88%	93%
Scatter Plots	79%	93%
Tables	86%	97%
Venn Diagrams	75%	97%
Average	**80%**	**96%**

Table 2: Classification accuracy on our 10-category corpus (2,601 images) using only image features.

We first tested the performance of the learned image features for classification by training a multi-class SVM classifier through 5-fold cross-validation on the 5 category image corpus. In each fold, we randomly picked $4/5$ of the images for training and the remainder for testing. We then averaged results over the 5 folds. The first two columns of Table 1 summarize our results in comparison to Prasad et al. [22]. Our average classification accuracy was 88%, compared to Prasad et al.'s 84%. Incorporating text features further increased our accuracy to 90% (the third column of Table 1 uses only text features, while the fourth column uses both text and image features). For the 200 image corpus used by Huang et al. [17] our average accuracy was 94%, exceeding the 90% reported by those authors. We used the same procedure on our larger 10-category corpus where we obtained an average classification accuracy of 80% (see Table 2).

We have found that charts of different categories often include visually similar elements such as axes, grid lines, and legends. Some charts are hybrids of multiple categories (e.g., a combination bar and line chart). The multi-class SVM classifier we have proposed so far enforces disjoint classification (e.g., the image is purely a bar chart or purely a line chart).

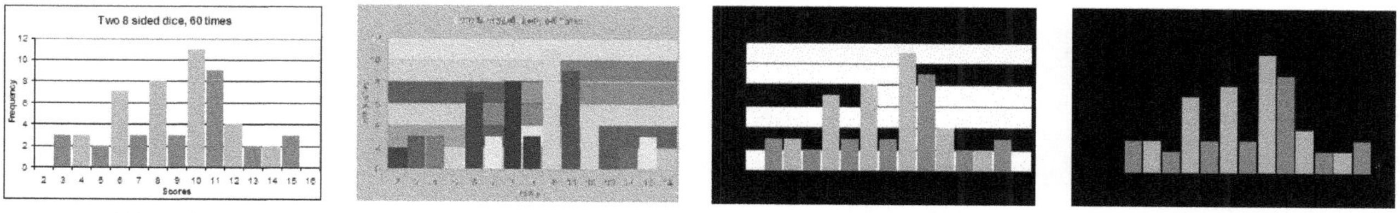

(a) Input chart (b) Connected components (c) Rectangular components (d) Candidate Bars

Figure 5: Bar extraction procedure. We compute connected components (shown false-colored) and discard non-rectangular components. We keep rectangles whose color differs from surrounding colors (see inset figure on this page), that touch the baseline x-axis, and whose height is greater than 2 pixels or whose width is near the average width of the other candidate bars.

The classifier must learn to ignore common elements and cannot handle hybrid charts. A bank of 1–vs–all binary classifiers (1 classifier per class) is more appropriate for a system like ReVision. Each binary classifier computes whether the image contains a visualization of a given class but does not prevent the other classifiers from also labeling the image. A hybrid chart for example might be labeled as both a bar and line chart. We train a binary SVM for each category using in-category images as positive examples and all others as negative examples. Results obtained using this method are given in the rightmost columns of Tables 1 and 2. We achieve an average accuracy of 96% for both our corpus and the Prasad et al. corpus, and 94% for the Huang et al. corpus.

The total time for image feature learning, feature vector extraction and classifier training on the Prasad et al. corpus was 144s on an Intel Xeon E5540 2.53GHz workstation. We classified new images in less than a second.

STAGE 2: MARK AND DATA EXTRACTION

After categorizing charts by type, ReVision proceeds to locate graphical marks and extract data. Our current implementation focuses on mark and data extraction for bar and pie charts, two of the most popular chart types.

We have found that chart images from the web are often heavily compressed and noisy. To reduce such artifacts, we first apply the bilateral filter [27] to each bar or pie chart image given by our classifier. The bilateral filter smooths away small variations in color but retains sharp edges in the image. Next we perform *mark extraction*, which locates graphical marks such as bars and pie slices by fitting models of expected shapes to image regions. Finally, we perform *data extraction*, which infers the mapping between data space and image space, associates labels with marks, and then extracts a data tuple for each mark.

Our algorithms are based on a few simplifying assumptions:

- Charts contain 2D marks and do not contain 3D effects.
- Each mark is solidly shaded using a single color. Marks are not shaded using textures or steep gradients.
- Marks encode a data tuple, where at least one dimension is quantitative and one dimension is nominal. For example, in a bar chart the height of a bar represents a quantitative value, while a nominal label often appears below the bar.
- Bar charts do not contain stacked bars.
- Bar chart axes appear at the left and bottom of the chart.

Based on these assumptions we develop simple, robust data extraction algorithms that apply to a significant number of real-world charts. For example, 42% (52/125) of the bar and 43% (53/125) of the pie charts in the Prasad et al. corpus [22] follow these assumptions.

Mark Extraction

In this step, we locate the marks. For bar charts, we extract the bars and axes. For pie charts, we extract the pie location and slice borders. We discuss each in turn.

Bar Charts

Figure 5 shows the steps of our bar extraction algorithm. We identify bars by looking for rectangular connected components and then use the bar locations to extract the axes.

Find rectangular shapes. We first extract connected components from the filtered image by grouping adjacent pixels of similar color, i.e., those with an L^2 norm less than 0.04 in normalized RGB space (Figure 5b). We then identify rectangular connected components by computing how much each component fills its bounding box. If component pixels fill more than 90% of the bounding box, we classify the component as a rectangle; otherwise, we discard the component. We also discard very small and thin rectangular components (with width or height less than 2 pixels), as such small components are unlikely to represent bars and are often due to image artifacts (Figure 5c). However, some of these components do represent very small bars, and we add them back to our set of candidate bars later in the extraction procedure.

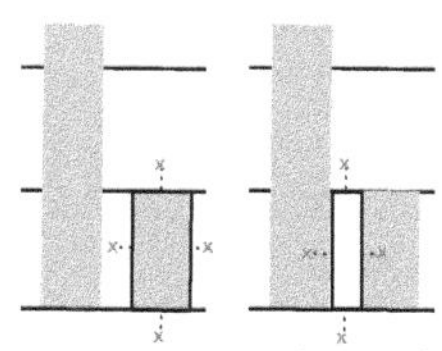

Remove background rectangles. The remaining rectangles are likely to include all data-encoding bars, but may also include background rectangles formed by gridlines. In Figure 5c, the background rectangles are colored white, while the true bars are orange or red. Background rectangles are usually shaded with the same color as adjacent rectangles, since they adjoin other background rectangles. On the other hand, bars tend to be shaded with different colors than adjacent rectangles, due to bars being shaded differently or gaps between bars. We test for background rectangles by comparing each rectangle's color to the color of four points outside the rectangle, as shown in the inset figure. We choose outside points by first finding the color of pixels bordering the rectangle. We then move away from the rectangle until we find a pixel whose color differs from the border pixel, or is 5 pixels away from the rectangle. If any

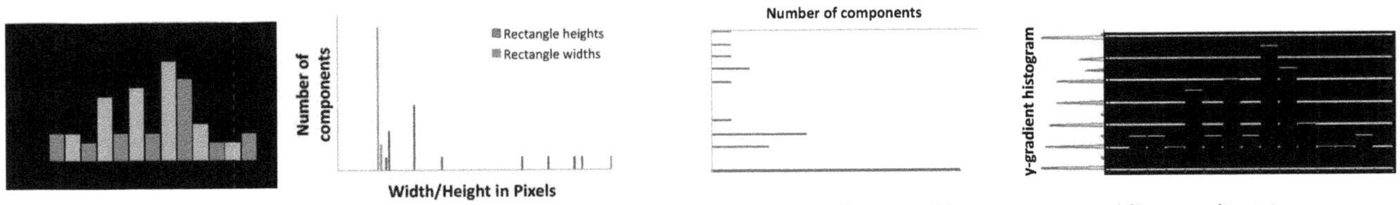

(a) Candidate bars (b) Width and height histograms (c) Histogram of top and bottom y-values of candidate bars (d) y-gradient image

Figure 6: Inferring the orientation of the chart and locating the baseline axis. (a) Candidate bars. (b) Histograms of widths and heights of the bars. Note that the mode of the width histogram (red) is stronger than the mode of the height histogram (blue), indicating that the chart is vertical. (c) To estimate the baseline axis, we build a histogram of the top and bottom y-values of candidate bars and treat the mode of this histogram as our initial estimate of the baseline axis. (d) Many charts draw the baseline axis as a solid line. To refine the axis location, we compute the y-gradient image of the initial chart and then sum the rows to create the y-gradient histogram. We treat the peak of this histogram located nearest our initial estimate as the final baseline axis.

one of the outside points has the same color as the interior of the rectangle, we classify the rectangle as part of the background and discard it; otherwise, we classify it as a candidate bar.

Infer chart orientation. Bar charts may be oriented horizontally or vertically. Since bars encode data using length, they vary in one dimension and remain fixed in the other dimension; e.g., vertical bars vary in height but maintain a fixed width. To identify which dimension varies most we build histograms of the widths and heights of the candidate bars and find the mode of each histogram (Figure 6b). The histogram with the strongest mode represents the constant dimension and gives us the orientation of the chart: vertical if the width histogram has the strongest mode, horizontal if the height histogram has the strongest mode. For brevity, we will describe our algorithms assuming a vertical bar chart, but our system works with horizontal bar charts using analogous analysis techniques.

Baseline axis extraction. For most vertical bar charts the baseline axis is the x-axis that touches the bottom of the bars. However, in some bar charts (e.g., those with negative values), the top of some bars may touch the baseline instead of the bottom of the bars. We therefore build a histogram of the top and bottom y-values of the candidate bars. The mode of this histogram represents the horizontal line that most bars touch, and we use the mode as an initial estimate of the baseline axis (Figure 6c). In practice we have found that noise, antialiasing, and other pixel level artifacts in the charts can sometimes lead to small inaccuracies (e.g., a few pixels) in our estimate of the position of the baseline axis. However, many charts draw the baseline x-axis as a solid line. Thus, we further refine our baseline axis estimate by computing the y-gradient of the original chart and summing the rows of this image to form the y-gradient histogram (Figure 6d). We then treat the peak of this histogram located nearest our estimated baseline axis position as the final baseline position.

We do not extract the y-axis for bar charts. As we will show in the data extraction section, we can extract data values for the bars without knowing the location of the y-axis.

Recovering small bars. Recall that when initially finding rectangular shapes we discard very small rectangles. However, we have found that in a few cases these rectangles may be legitimate bars representing small values. Since bars in a vertical bar chart almost always have the same width, we recover small bars by first computing the average width of the remaining candidate bars and then re-introducing any bars we previously discarded with the same width. Finally, we discard any bar that does not touch the baseline axis. This step leaves us with the final set of candidate bars (Figure 5d).

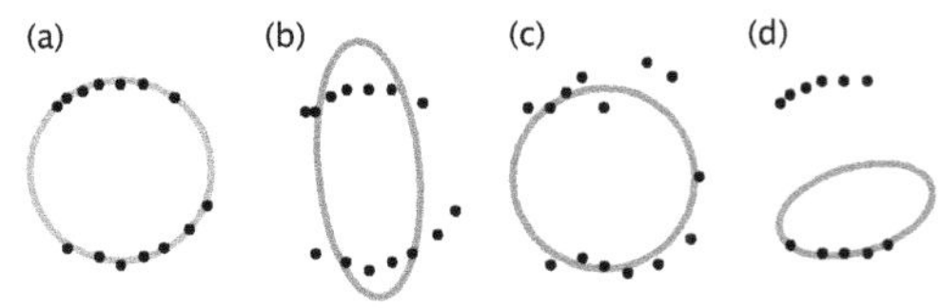

Figure 7: A low scoring ellipse and three high scoring ellipses. (a) A low scoring ellipse maximizes circularity, goodness of fit and coverage. (b) An ellipse with high circularity score, (c) high fit score, and (d) high coverage score.

Pie Charts

Mark extraction in pie charts involves two phases. We first fit an ellipse to the pie. We then unroll the pie and locate strong differences in color to locate the pie sector edges.

Fitting the pie. Although most pie charts are circular, some are elliptical. For greatest generality, we model the pie as an ellipse. Our goal is to fit the ellipse to the set of pixels at the edge of the pie. We start by thresholding the gradient magnitude of the chart to extract gradient pixels (i.e., pixels where the color changes sharply), as these are likely to lie at edges. We set the threshold such that gradient pixels comprise at least $1/30$ of the image pixels, as we empirically found this parameter to be sufficient to fit the ellipse. We use the text region tags to remove gradient pixels due to text.

While the set of gradient pixels is likely to include the pixels at the edge of the pie, it is also likely to include many additional pixels where the color changes sharply. Thus, we adapt the RANSAC [12] algorithm to robustly fit an ellipse to the gradient pixels that are most likely to lie at the edge of the pie while rejecting the other outlier pixels. Our algorithm works as follows: we first randomly select four gradient pixels and compute an ellipse that passes through them using Fitzgibbon et al.'s [13] direct least-squares ellipse fitting method. We then find the set of gradient pixels that are at most 10 pixels away from the ellipse and call them *in-*

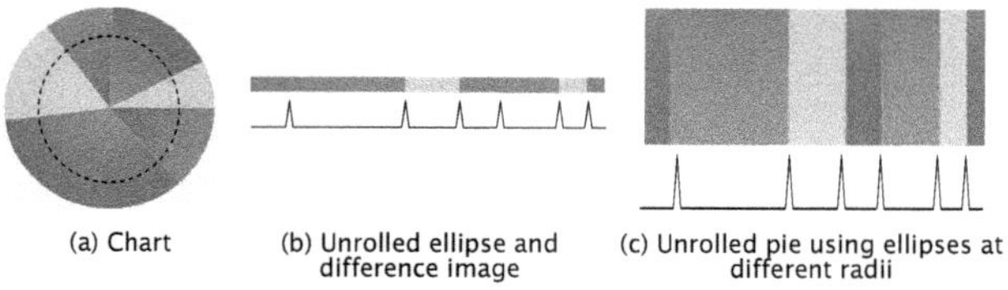

Figure 8: Unrolling the pie. Consider the inner ellipse marked in (a). We unroll the ellipse by sampling points at constant angular intervals (b). Peaks in the horizontal derivative occur at sector edges. To improve edge estimation, we unroll multiple ellipses and sum their horizontal derivatives (c). Peaks in the summed horizontal derivatives occur at sector edges.

liers. Next we check how well the ellipse explains the inliers by computing an ellipse score, which is a weighted sum of three components: the circularity of the ellipse (ratio of the minor to major axis), how tightly it fits the inliers (average distance of an inlier to the ellipse), and coverage (how much of the ellipse is not near inliers). Lower scores indicate better ellipses. Examples of high scoring ellipses are shown in Figure 7. On each iteration, we keep the ellipse if its score is lower than the previous lowest score. We iterate this process 20,000 times, which we experimentally found to work well for the chart images in our corpora.

Locating sector edges. To extract the pie sector edges we first "unroll the pie": we sample an ellipse located inside the pie at constant angular intervals to create a one-dimensional ellipse image (Figure 8a). We then take the horizontal derivative of this ellipse image to identify strong changes in color. Color changes indicate transitions between pie sectors, and so the peaks in the derivative give us estimates for the sector edge locations (Figure 8b). To increase robustness of our estimates, we unroll multiple concentric ellipses and sum their horizontal derivatives (Figure 8c). We identify peaks in the summed derivatives by looking for zero crossings of its first derivative, which we find by convolving the summed derivatives with a derivative of a 3-pixel wide Gaussian. This smoothing handles noise and pixel-level artifacts. Some pies include thin borders between pie slices and the smoothing aggregates the peaks at either edge of the border into a single peak. Finally we retain all peaks that are more than one standard deviation above the mean of the summed derivatives.

Data Extraction

In the data extraction step, our goal is to recover the data encoded by each mark. We assume that a mark encodes a tuple of data, where one dimension is quantitative and one is nominal. We recover these tuples by using the geometry of the extracted marks and the text region tags from the classification stage. The output of our data extraction step is a table that contains an ID and a data tuple for each mark.

Bar Charts

To recover the data from a bar chart, we first infer the mapping between image space and data space. We assume a linear mapping, but we believe our data extraction techniques are amenable to other mappings (e.g., logarithmic). The linear mapping is fully defined by (1) a scaling factor between image space and data space, and (2) the minimum value (usually the value at the x-axis).

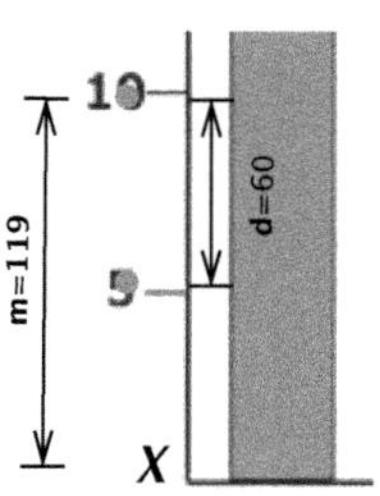

We first recover the scaling factor by considering the y-axis labels. We identify the y-axis labels that encode data values by finding text regions that are equidistant from the leftmost bar and line up vertically. We then estimate the scaling factor using each pair of value labels, as illustrated in the inset figure. We assume the labels were recovered by our text extraction procedure in the classification stage. The pixel distance between labels "5" and "10" is $d = 60$ pixels, and the estimated scaling factor is $60/(10-5) = 12$ pixels/data unit. We compute the scaling factor for each pair of labels and take the median as our final estimate. For this chart, the median scaling factor across all label pairs is 12.5 pixels/data unit.

We then find the minimum value. We begin with the y-axis label vertically closest to the x-axis. If this label is "0", we set the minimum value to 0. Otherwise, we compute the minimum value using a similar procedure to computing the scaling factors. For each label, we estimate a minimum value by using the y-distance (in pixels) from the label's center to the x-axis, and the chart scaling factor. For example, using the location of the "10" label in the inset figure, we find the pixel distance is $m = 119$. Assuming a chart scaling factor of 12.5, we find $X = 119/12.5 - 10 = -0.48$. The actual minimum is 0; our result is not exact, but close. We set the chart's minimum value to the median of these minimum value estimates. For this chart, the median minimum value was -0.2.

Finally, we assign a nominal value to each bar by associating it with the nearest label below the baseline x-axis.

Pie Charts

Each sector of a pie encodes two data values: (1) a quantitative value representing the percentage of the whole pie covered by the sector, and (2) a nominal value representing the label of the sector. We compute the percentage as the angular extent between the edges of the sector. We treat the text label nearest the elliptical arc spanning the sector as the nominal label for the sector.

Extraction Results

To test our extraction algorithms, we used the subset of Prasad et al.'s [22] corpus that met our assumptions, which resulted in 52 bar charts and 53 pie charts. For this test we also assumed the chart type was known a priori, noting that our classification stage provides this information.

To generate ground truth, we manually identified the marks and generated data tuples for each mark based on nearby text labels. We used sector labels (for pie charts) and axis labels under the baseline (for bar charts) as the nominal values. If a quantitative label was located near a mark we treated it as the quantitative value of the mark (e.g., Figure 11 left and Figure 12 left). Otherwise, we did not generate a ground truth quantitative value. For pie charts, we converted quantitative values to percentages. For bar charts, we directly used the labeled values.

Using the ground truth data, we found that ReVision successfully extracted all the marks for 41/52 (79%) of bar charts

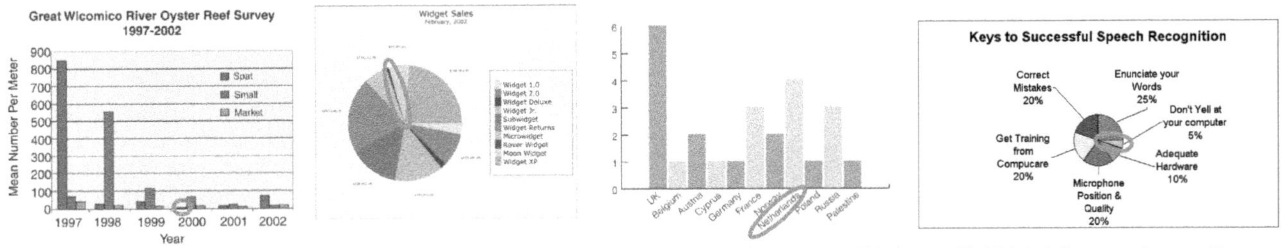

(a) Small bars are missed (b) Small sectors are missed (c) Mislabeled bars due to rotated labels (d) Mislabeled sectors due to callouts

Figure 9: Mark and data extraction failures. If marks are very small, our algorithms fail to extract them. For example, we fail to extract the circled bar in (a) and the circled sector in (b). Data extraction failures occur when marks are mislabeled, e.g., (c) when labels are rotated, or (d) if the chart places labels far from their associated marks, such as the circled marks.

and 33/53 (62%) of pie charts. Most mark extraction failures occurred because we failed to detect small marks (Figure 9a, b). Our algorithms are designed to treat small, thin regions as decorative elements rather than marks that encode data. With relatively small chart images (on average, 342×452 pixels in our corpus) our algorithms can have trouble separating legitimate marks from these decorative elements.

Accurate data extraction depends on accurate mark extraction. Focusing on the charts for which we were able to extract all marks, we accurately extracted data tuples for 29/41 (71%) of the bar charts and 21/33 (64%) of the pie charts. The most common error was incorrect association of a nominal label to a mark. Our simple closest-label heuristic for associating text labels with marks is especially prone to errors when labels are rotated (Figure 9c), or when marks are small and labeled with callouts (Figure 9d).

We could only generate quantitative ground truth for 12 of the bar charts and 17 of the pie charts for which we extracted the data. The remaining 17 bar charts and 4 pie charts did not have quantitative labels. Examining this subset of charts, we found that our extracted quantitative values were on average within 7.7% of the original data for bar charts and within 4.6% of the original data for pie charts. Figures 11 and 12 show examples of successfully processed chart images.

Running times varied widely with chart size. On a 2.4Ghz MacBook Pro with 2Gb of RAM, extracting marks and data from an average sized pie chart took 1,225s. Extracting marks and data from an average sized bar chart took 100s.

STAGE 3: REDESIGN

The output of the data extraction process is a relational data table. ReVision uses this data to populate a gallery of alternative visualizations (Figure 10). We rank visual encodings by *effectiveness* [20] and display a variety of visualizations in a sorted gallery. ReVision chooses different visualizations depending on the input chart type and extracted data. For the input pie chart in Figure 10a, the gallery presents bar charts to support part-to-part comparisons and divided bar, donut, and treemap charts to support part-to-whole judgments [24]. For the input bar chart in Figure 10b, ReVision generates a bar chart and labeled dot plot to support comparison of individual values, and small dot and box plots to enable assessment of the overall distribution. Note that the y-axis of the input chart does not start at zero; ReVision's bar chart correctly incorporates a zero baseline and displays the data range with more appropriate charts (dot and box plots).

In addition, users can select and compare choices of font and color palette. ReVision includes palettes designed for well-spaced, perceptually discriminable colors [15, 26], as well as palettes from popular charting tools and news magazines. We generate charts using Protovis [2]; viewers can export the Protovis definitions for subsequent modification or reuse. Alternatively, users can export the data to create their own charts using tools such as Microsoft Excel or Tableau [21].

LIMITATIONS AND FUTURE WORK

In its current state ReVision is suitable for generating alternative visualizations for many published bar and pie charts. However, more work is needed to overcome limitations of our classification and extraction methods.

With respect to classification, we currently employ a manual approach to annotating text regions. To achieve fully automatic processing of textual features, we would need to employ text identification and extraction algorithms. We do not yet use the text itself for classification; it is possible that such information might further improve classification accuracy.

Our mark and data extraction algorithms are ripe for additional research. Our extraction techniques do not yet handle textured marks or 3D effects (e.g., due to gradient shading or perspective) both of which are common in our corpora. As 3D effects and textural patterns have been shown to hamper graphical perception [5, 11], it would be beneficial to enable redesigns for such charts. We do not yet parse legends. This causes failures on charts where the legend provides necessary labeling information, as in grouped bar or pie charts with categorical color encodings documented in a legend. We also plan to extend our extraction algorithms to additional chart types, such as bubble, line, and donut charts.

Chart design often involves semantic data or connotations beyond the raw data tuples. For example, the y-axis labels in the leftmost chart of Figure 11 are ordered by increasing educational level. By treating labels as nominal data, our redesign does not respect this ordinal relation. Consequently, our design gallery should support sorting data by both value and the initial observed order. Stylistic choices such as color and typography can also shape the message of a chart; our redesigns do not always retain these messages. However, by extracting the underlying data, our system creates an opportunity for redesign (both automatically and by hand) that would otherwise be prohibitively difficult.

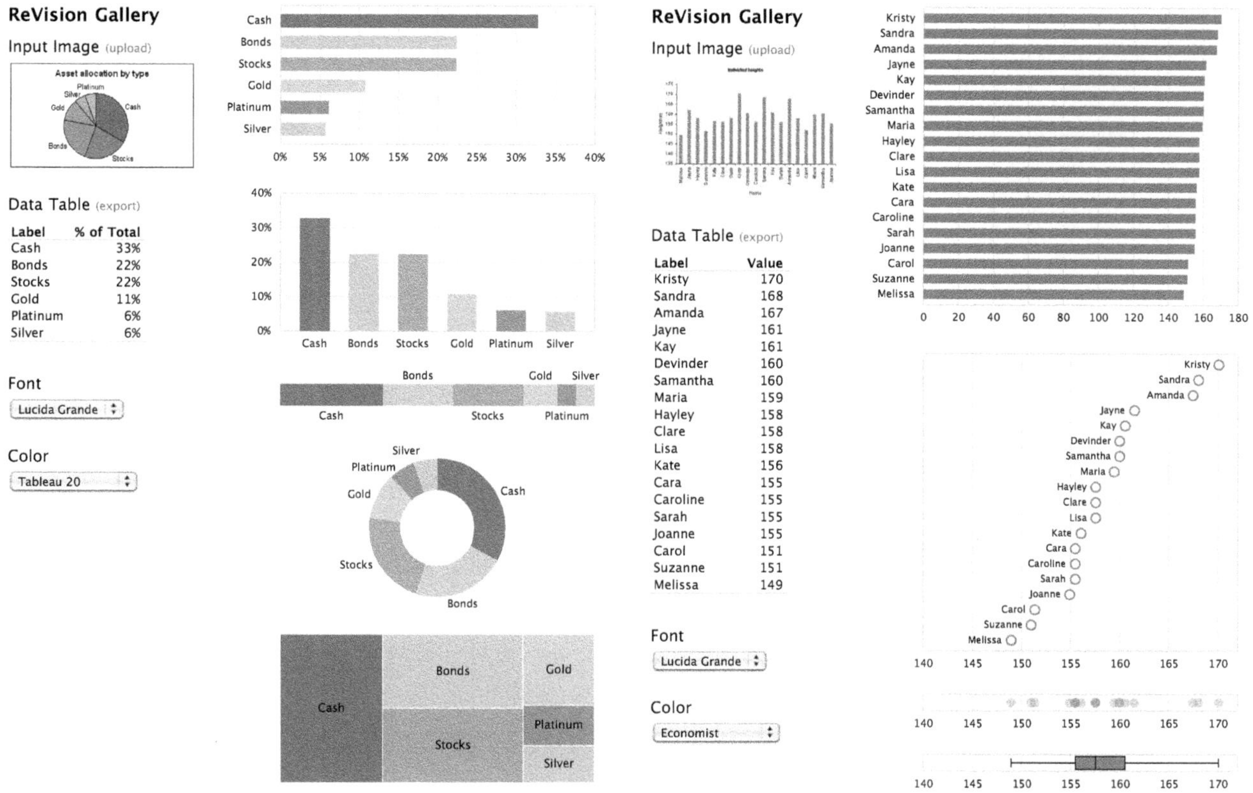

Figure 10: ReVision Design Galleries. Given an extracted data table, the gallery presents a variety of chart types, sorted by proposed perceptual effectiveness rankings [20]. Users can also select and compare color schemes and typefaces.

CONCLUSION

We have presented ReVision, a system that classifies charts, extracts their graphical marks and underlying data table, and then applies perceptually-based design principles to automatically redesign charts. Automated redesign is only one of many possible applications for a system that extracts data from charts. Our techniques could be used to enhance information retrieval systems with chart metadata or to support screen-reading of charts for blind users.

ACKNOWLEDGMENTS

This research has been supported by the Akiko Yamazaki and Jerry Yang Engineering Fellowship Fund, NSF grants IIS-1017745 & IIS-1016920, the Stanford CS Dept., and a gift from Greenplum/EMC.

REFERENCES

1. A. Bosch, A. Zisserman, and X. Munoz. Scene classification via pLSA. *Computer Vision–ECCV*, pages 517–530, 2006.
2. M. Bostock and J. Heer. Protovis: A graphical toolkit for visualization. *IEEE Trans Visualization & Comp Graphics*, 15(6):1121–1128, 2009.
3. M. Boutell, C. Brown, and J. Luo. Review of the state of the art in semantic scene classification. *Rochester, NY, USA, Tech. Rep*, 2002.
4. D. Chen, J. Odobez, and H. Bourlard. Text detection and recognition in images and video frames. *Pattern Recognition*, 37(3):595–608, 2004.
5. W. S. Cleveland. *Visualizing Data.* Hobart Press, 1993.
6. W. S. Cleveland and R. McGill. Graphical perception: Theory, experimentation, and application to the development of graphical methods. *Journal of the American Statistical Association*, 79(387):531–554, 1984.
7. A. Coates, H. Lee, and A. Ng. An Analysis of Single-Layer Networks in Unsupervised Feature Learning. *Advances in Neural Information Processing Systems*, 2010.
8. C. Cortes and V. Vapnik. Support-vector networks. *Machine Learning*, 20:273–297, 1995.
9. N. Dalal and B. Triggs. Histograms of oriented gradients for human detection. In *IEEE CVPR*, pages 886–893, 2005.
10. G. David. Distinctive image features from scale-invariant keypoints. *Intl Journal Comp Vision*, 60(2):91–110, 2004.
11. S. Few. *Show Me the Numbers: Designing Tables and Graphs to Enlighten.* Analytics Press, Berkeley, CA, 2004.
12. M. A. Fischler and R. C. Bolles. Random sample consensus: a paradigm for model fitting with applications to image analysis and automated cartography. *Commun. ACM*, 24:381–395, June 1981.
13. A. Fitzgibbon, M. Pilu, and R. Fisher. Direct least square fitting of ellipses. *IEEE Trans Pattern Analysis & Machine Intelligence*, 21(5):476–480, 1999.
14. S. R. Garner. Weka: The waikato environment for knowledge analysis. In *In Proc. of the New Zealand Computer Science Research Students Conference*, pages 57–64, 1995.
15. M. Harrower and C. Brewer. Colorbrewer.org: an online tool for selecting colour schemes for maps. *The Cartographic Journal*, 40(1):27–37, 2003.
16. J. Heer and M. Bostock. Crowdsourcing graphical perception: Using Mechanical Turk to assess visualization design. In *ACM CHI*, pages 203–212, 2010.
17. W. Huang and C. L. Tan. A system for understanding imaged infographics and its applications. In *Proceedings of the 2007 ACM symposium on Document engineering*, DocEng '07, pages 9–18, New York, NY, USA, 2007. ACM.

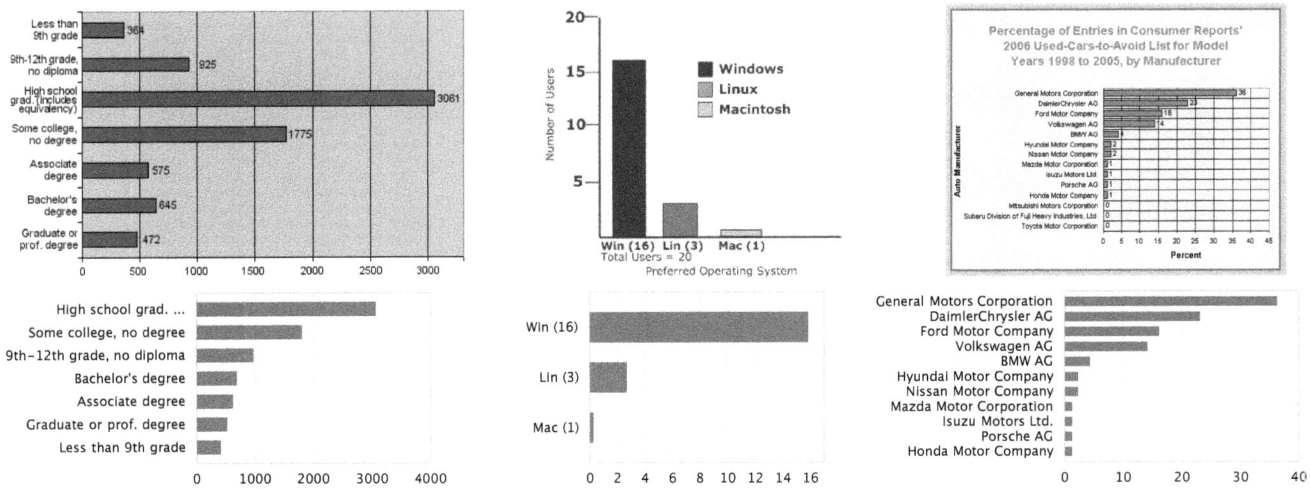

Figure 11: Example ReVision redesigns for input bar charts.

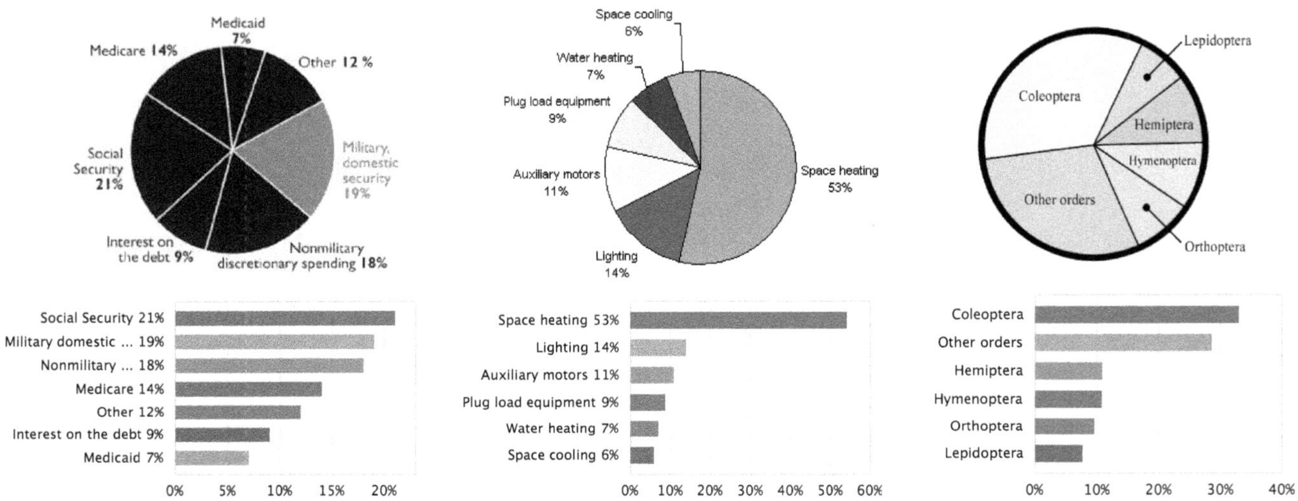

Figure 12: Example ReVision redesigns for input pie charts.

18. W. Huang, C. L. Tan, and W. K. Leow. Model-based chart image recognition. In J. Lladós and Y.-B. Kwon, editors, *Graphics Recognition*, volume 3088 of *Lecture Notes in Computer Science*, pages 87–99. Springer Berlin / Heidelberg, 2004.
19. R. Liu, W. Huang, and C. L. Tan. Extraction of vectorized graphical information from scientific chart images. In *Document Analysis & Recognition (ICDAR)*, pages 521–525, 2007.
20. J. D. Mackinlay. Automating the design of graphical presentations of relational information. *ACM Trans on Graphics*, 5(2):110–141, 1986.
21. J. D. Mackinlay, P. Hanrahan, and C. Stolte. Show me: Automatic presentation for visual analysis. *IEEE Trans Visualization & Comp Graphics*, 13(6):1137 –1144, 2007.
22. V. Prasad, B. Siddiquie, J. Golbeck, and L. Davis. Classifying Computer Generated Charts. In *Content-Based Multimedia Indexing Workshop*, pages 85–92. IEEE, 2007.
23. M. Shao and R. Futrelle. Recognition and classification of figures in pdf documents. In W. Liu and J. Lladós, editors, *Graphics Recognition. Ten Years Review and Future Perspectives*, volume 3926 of *Lecture Notes in Computer Science*, pages 231–242. Springer Berlin / Heidelberg, 2006.
24. D. Simkin and R. Hastie. An information-processing analysis of graph perception. *Journal of the American Statistical Association*, 82(398):454–465, 1987.
25. C. Stolte, D. Tang, and P. Hanrahan. Polaris: a system for query, analysis, and visualization of multidimensional relational databases. *IEEE Trans Visualization & Comp Graphics*, 8(1):52 –65, 2002.
26. M. Stone. *A Field Guide to Digital Color*. A. K. Peters, 2003.
27. C. Tomasi and R. Manduchi. Bilateral filtering for gray and color images. In *ICCV*, pages 839 –846, Jan. 1998.
28. E. R. Tufte. *The Visual Display of Quantitative Information*. Graphics Press, 1983.
29. J. Yang, Y.-G. Jiang, A. G. Hauptmann, and C.-W. Ngo. Evaluating bag-of-visual-words representations in scene classification. In *Workshop on Multimedia Information Retrieval*, pages 197–206, 2007.
30. L. Yang, W. Huang, and C. Tan. Semi-automatic ground truth generation for chart image recognition. In *Document Analysis Systems VII*, volume 3872 of *Lecture Notes in Computer Science*, pages 324–335. 2006.
31. Y. P. Zhou and C. L. Tan. Hough technique for bar charts detection and recognition in document images. In *Intl Conf on Image Processing*, pages 605–608, sept. 2000.

Calibration Games: Making Calibration Tasks Enjoyable by Adding Motivating Game Elements

David R. Flatla[1], *Carl Gutwin*[1], *Lennart E. Nacke*[2], *Scott Bateman*[1], *Regan L. Mandryk*[1]

[1]Department of Computer Science
University of Saskatchewan
Saskatoon, Saskatchewan, Canada

[2]Faculty of Business and Information Technology
University of Ontario Institute of Technology
Oshawa, Ontario, Canada

david.flatla@usask.ca, gutwin@cs.usask.ca, lennart.nacke@acm.org, scott.bateman@usask.ca, regan@cs.usask.ca

ABSTRACT
Interactive systems often require calibration to ensure that input and output are optimally configured. Without calibration, user performance can degrade (e.g., if an input device is not adjusted for the user's abilities), errors can increase (e.g., if color spaces are not matched), and some interactions may not be possible (e.g., use of an eye tracker). The value of calibration is often lost, however, because many calibration processes are tedious and unenjoyable, and many users avoid them altogether. To address this problem, we propose *calibration games* that gather calibration data in an engaging and entertaining manner. To facilitate the creation of calibration games, we present design guidelines that map common types of calibration to core tasks, and then to well-known game mechanics. To evaluate the approach, we developed three calibration games and compared them to standard procedures. Users found the game versions significantly more enjoyable than regular calibration procedures, without compromising the quality of the data. Calibration games are a novel way to motivate users to carry out calibrations, thereby improving the performance and accuracy of many human-computer systems.

Author Keywords: Calibration, computer games, modeling

ACM Classification Keywords: H5.2. Information interfaces and presentation: User Interfaces.

General Terms: Design, Human Factors

INTRODUCTION
Many kinds of interaction with computers require some type of calibration. For example, a user's performance with a new input device may need to be tested in order to choose an optimal control-to-display ratio; a user's ability to see different colors must be established before choosing colors for a visualization; or two representations of a space must be brought into alignment (e.g., a tabletop display and the direct-input device used with it). Calibration, or the lack of it, can have substantial effects on the success of an interaction with a computer system: for example, people may perform poorly with an input device that is incorrectly configured, people may miss important signals if stimuli cannot be detected or differentiated, and selection errors may result from improper alignment of input and output space.

Unfortunately, calibration is often a tedious and dull process, and as a result, many people do not carry out the calibration. Compounding the problem, some situations require that a calibration be carried out multiple times (e.g., as environmental conditions change, or as sensors drift).

Our solution to this problem is to make calibration more enjoyable and less tedious. If calibration is less painful, more people will do it, and more people can gain the benefits of correctly-configured devices and interfaces. To achieve this goal, we create *calibration games* that gather calibration data in an engaging and entertaining manner. To aid in the design of these games, we present a design framework for creating a calibration game from a standard calibration procedure. We identify nine major types of calibration, decompose these types to find the core perceptual and motor tasks that provide the calibration data, match each core task to common game mechanics that can be used as the basis for a calibration game, and specify additional game elements (challenge, theme, reward, and progress) that can be added to improve the quality of the game.

We have developed several calibration games using this framework including a space-invaders-style game to determine color perceptibility, a shooting-gallery game to set optimal C:D ratios, and a launching game that measures the input range for a physiological sensor.

We investigated two main questions with these games: first, whether calibration games are more enjoyable than their standard counterparts, and second, whether the game versions introduced any problems in the quality of the data that was gathered. Our studies showed that users found all three of the game versions to be significantly more enjoyable – suggesting that we can in fact improve the likelihood that users carry out calibrations. In addition, although there were differences in the actual data collected by the game and standard versions, these differences did not reduce the utility of the game data for calibration.

Our work makes four contributions. First, we identify the idea of gamifying calibration as a way to improve motivation to carry out a calibration procedure. Second, we present a framework that simplifies the design of calibration games and shows the broad applicability of the idea. Third, we demonstrate the feasibility of calibration games with three examples. Fourth, we show that calibration games are significantly more enjoyable than standard versions, without compromising data quality.

RELATED WORK

Calibration

Calibration is a necessary task for many different input and output technologies (e.g., [1,5,6,8]). The need for calibration arises out of individual user differences [5,15,22], and environmental and situational changes [5,8,23]. Examples of systems that have addressed calibration include technologies for interactive touch [8,23], 3D sound [15], location-sensing technology [6], eye-tracking [20], heads-up displays [1], glove-based input [10], personalized color displays [5], and physiological sensing – for detecting emotional state [22] or muscle exertion [11].

There is little previous research on improving the enjoyability of calibration – we found only one project that proposed a 'game' for calibration. However, this work did not describe how their activity was a game or why a game for calibration would be desirable (instead, the authors describe the game as a simple task that met the requirements of the calibration) [6]. One other similar project considered the idea of using first-person shooter games for Fitts's Law tasks [9], and found that FPS targeting is well modeled by Fitts's Law. This work suggests that adding game elements to calibration may not unduly alter the core task.

The majority of work on improving calibration has focused on reducing costs: through new mathematical models that reduce sampling requirements [5,15,20], improved calibration protocols that address current inefficiencies [1,10], or dynamic adaptation during the procedure [11]. However, these strategies are not applicable to all types of calibration, and do not address motivation issues.

Gamification

Gamification refers to the use of gameplay mechanics in non-gaming applications to encourage a desired type of behavior [4]. By using techniques such as scoreboards and personalized fast feedback, people feel more ownership and purpose when engaging with tasks [16].

HCI research has previously investigated the use of game elements to engage people in work (e.g., the ESP Game [21] or PSDoom [3]). This research suggests that incorporating game elements into work activities improves motivation [19], but also cautions that it is important to carefully design the integration of game elements with work tasks [21]. In our work, we extend this notion by providing a framework that clearly maps elements of the task to be accomplished (core calibration tasks) to elements of games.

There are several organizations of game elements that have been considered for gamification. First, Malone's early work identified three key concepts of games: challenge (i.e., providing a goal with uncertain attainment), fantasy (i.e., evoking images of non-present and vicarious objects or situations), and curiosity (i.e., motivating users to learn independently) [13]. Reeves et al. [17] list ten ingredients of great games that could be used to improve services and non-game applications: self-representation with avatars, three-dimensional environments, narrative context, feedback and behavior reinforcement, reputations (ranks and levels), marketplace and economies, competition within rules, teams, parallel communication systems, and time pressure. Another set of design elements are Brathwaite and Schreiber's 'game design atoms' [2]: the game state, game view, player representation, game mechanics (i.e., the game rule system), game dynamics (i.e., game mechanics set in motion by players), goals, and game theme. Most of these atoms are built on a formal game framework called MDA (mechanics, dynamics, aesthetics) [7]. This framework distinguishes mechanics as game components on the algorithmic level, dynamics as run-time interaction with the player, and aesthetics as the desired player emotion triggered by mechanics and dynamics.

A DESIGN FRAMEWORK FOR CALIBRATION GAMES

Our framework has four parts, which can be used as a basic design process for building many types of calibration games. The sections below discuss the parts of the framework and cover nine main types of calibration, core tasks that obtain the calibration data, game mechanics that can be built from the core tasks, and additional game elements that improve the subjective aspects of the game.

To develop this framework, we used an iterative process of finding calibration types through literature search, isolating the core task for each calibration type, and identifying the associated game mechanic. Previous literature helped identify the four game design elements [7,13].

Framework Part 1: Calibration Types

There are two main types of calibration in HCI – one addressing human abilities and limitations, and another addressing systems and technologies. First, calibrating for human capabilities determines performance characteristics for perceptual input and motor output.

- *Perceptual thresholds.* These calibrations determine baselines of human perceptual ability, such as the quietest tone that can be heard, or the minimum light level that can be seen in a dark room. Maximum values are used to determine upper limits (e.g., the loudest sound that can be listened to comfortably).
- *Motor thresholds.* These calibrations determine baselines and ranges in human motor ability, including motor skill (e.g., fine motor control or ambidexterity), muscle actuation (e.g., maximum bicep flex), and body measurements (e.g., maximum lung inflation).
- *Just-noticeable differences (JNDs).* These calibrations determine the minimum difference in the value of some attribute (e.g., color, frequency, pressure) such that two stimuli can be differentiated - for example, the minimum difference between two colors necessary for a user to perceive them as different.
- *Perceptual performance.* These calibrations determine a person's abilities to carry out perceptual tasks such as

reacting to a stimulus, visual search, or pattern matching. The performance measures in these tasks are usually response time (e.g., time to find a visual target) and errors (e.g., patterns misidentified in a sequence).

- *Motor performance.* These calibrations determine the details of a person's sensorimotor performance in several areas of HCI: aiming, pointing, steering, and pursuit tracking. The calibration is often used to establish coefficients for a performance model (e.g., Fitts's Law), in order to accurately represent individual differences.
- *Memory performance.* These calibrations determine individual performance in memory tasks including short-term memory (e.g., recall of sets of items), spatial memory (e.g., remembering object locations), or the ability to associate items from one set to another. As with motor performance, calibration can be used to provide coefficients for existing models (e.g., Hick's Law).

A second main class of calibration involves measurement of technology alone, and does not consider human abilities. A common calibration process in human-computer systems is *registration.* Registration is used to bring two spaces into alignment, where the congruence of the spaces is needed to enable subsystems to work together. Three examples of registration involve physical, color, and sound space:

- *Physical space registration.* These calibrations are used to bring two representations of physical space into alignment. A common example is that of registering input and output spaces for direct touch on a digital table.
- *Color space registration.* These calibrations are used to adjust the color output of a device so that it matches some representation of 'ground truth.' Monitor calibration by measuring the maximum output of each RGB channel is an example of color space registration.
- *Auditory registration.* These calibrations are used to match the audio output of different systems (e.g., an orchestra tuning each instrument to the oboe).

Framework Part 2: Core Tasks of Calibration

In moving from calibration to games, the main object of the calibration must be maintained – that is, the game must calibrate the same thing as the standard procedure. However, it is not required that the game use exactly the same presentation as the traditional system.

For example, a standard color JND calibration might present pairs of color swatches and ask the user whether they are the same or different; however, it is not essential that a game version use this same approach. The core task underlying the 'same or different' question is signal discrimination, and so any presentation that implements this core task should be possible for a game version of the calibration. In the color game described below, the signal discrimination task is carried out implicitly, in that the player can only shoot targets that they can see against the background.

Gamification thus requires that we identify tasks that are at the core of calibration procedures, and ensure that these tasks are the basis of game versions. We identify several of these core tasks below (a non-exhaustive list, but one that covers a wide range of possible calibration types):

- *Signal detection:* the minimum level of intensity that a person can perceive for a given stimulus (e.g., light).
- *Signal discrimination:* the minimum amount of difference needed for a person to determine that two stimuli (e.g., two colors, two tones) are different.
- *Maximum / minimum muscle activation:* the maximum and (non-zero) minimum amounts that a person can activate a muscle (e.g., flexing the bicep muscle).
- *Minimum movement:* the minimum amount that a body part can be moved, as a measure of fine motor control.
- *Ambidexterity:* the ability to perform coordinated simultaneous movements with left and right limbs.
- *Reaction time:* the time needed to initiate a response to a perceptual stimulus.
- *Visual search:* the ability to find a visual target in a field of distractors.
- *Pattern matching:* the ability to determine that a given perceptual pattern matches a target pattern.
- *Aiming:* the ability to accurately point a device (e.g., a rifle) at a target, without feedback about the direction.
- *Pointing:* the speed at which a person can move a pointer to a target (with feedback).
- *Steering:* the speed at which a person can move a pointer along a path without going outside the path's borders.
- *Pursuit tracking:* the ability to move a pointer so as to accurately match the location of a moving object.
- *Short-term memory:* a person's ability to memorize and retrieve sets of items, sequences, and mappings.
- *Spatial location memory:* ability to remember locations of items without persistent visual cues.

Framework Part 3: Game Mechanics for Core Tasks

Making games that are based on the core tasks described above can be accomplished because many games are already designed around exactly these building blocks. Figure 1 sets out the ways that core tasks of calibration can be translated into the kinds of game mechanics that are used in many existing games. For example, *signal detection*, which is a core task of perceptual threshold calibration, can be translated to a 'presence of enemies' game mechanic. Similarly, a core task like *visual search*, which underlies some perceptual performance calibrations, can be translated to a 'find treasure' game mechanic.

Although some calibration types use tasks that are currently rare in games, new game mechanics can be designed to fulfill these needs. For example, while some work has looked at using physiological sensors in games [14], the core tasks of muscle activation and minimum movement are not typically used as game mechanics. We explore this area further with one of our example games (BabyLaunch) that demonstrates how non-typical tasks can be gamified.

Framework Part 4: Game Design Elements

The final stage in our process is to add elements from game design that make the calibration procedure more game-like.

We include four basic elements of games, derived from previous taxonomies of game elements [7,13].

Figure 1. Calibration types (left), core tasks (middle), and matching game mechanics (right).

- ***Challenge:*** *providing challenging goal elements tied to rewards.* The system needs to provide clear task goals (e.g., collecting items, shooting objects) that trigger a challenging activity for the player to engage in. The challenge may increase within system boundaries as the game progresses, to keep player interest.
- ***Theme:*** *Vicarious aesthetic representation and theme.* The elements of the calibration system can be cloaked by putting them in a fantasy context (e.g., targets are spaceships, different parts of the game have descriptive names evoking some form of mental imagery), allowing the player to experience a vicarious setting. This applies to the player representation (e.g., the avatar) as well.
- ***Reward:*** *Rewards and behavior reinforcement.* Challenge alone does not provide sufficient motivation to stay engaged in a task, so activities need to be rewarded periodically to provide feedback about player progress and to maintain motivation. Easily-implemented rewards include simple visual animations or pleasant sounds. To trigger curiosity, rewards at random locations can be used to keep the player cognitively engaged.
- ***Progress:*** *Progress units and markers.* Feedback is a central aspect of game design. Providing progress units (e.g., levels, worlds, quests) and achievement markers (e.g., badges, score information) allows players to know how far they have progressed into the game and how well they are doing. Progress units can also serve as reinforcement (e.g., using time pressure to change the speed of an action). In a social context, progress markers such as high scores also enable reputation scores, fostering competition and increasing replay value.

Including these basic elements allows us to design a game scenario around any basic calibration mechanic and thereby increase the engagement and fun in an otherwise dull task. It is important to note that all of these elements need not be present to make a game, and that a single game feature may cover one or more of the elements above.

THREE CALIBRATION GAMES

We developed three games as examples of how calibration can be gamified, using three different types of calibration and three different core tasks.

Calibrating Color Just-Noticeable-Differences (JNDs)

The ability to differentiate color varies between individuals because of many factors, such as environmental lighting, age, fatigue, or the presence of color vision deficiency. To make the best color choices for information visualization, a system can use a model of the color differentiation abilities of the user. In order to generate this model, an in-situ calibration is performed that measures the individual's ability to differentiate between colors [5].

The standard method for calibrating the model asks the user to perform a sequence of signal discrimination tasks. A rectangular field of circles is shown to the user (see Figure 2), with half of the circles one color and half another. The user indicates whether the colors are the same or different. About 10 trials (at one second each) are needed to measure a single differentiation limit, and the model requires 192 of these limits, for a total of 1920 seconds (32 minutes).

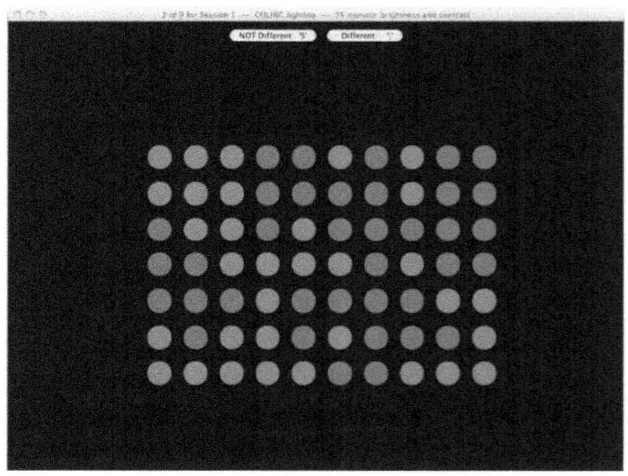

Figure 2. The traditional calibration task. Users respond to each presentation of bicolored circles with 'same' or 'different'. Approximately 1920 of these presentations are used to calibrate the model.

The standard calibration is both lengthy and dull; in addition, it may need to be repeated whenever the environment changes (e.g., lighting levels change). The cost of this procedure quickly outweighs the benefits for users, who are thus hesitant to perform the calibration as often as needed.

To produce a game-based calibration, we built a 'space invaders' style game, which is a 2D side-view shoot-'em-up style game. In the original, the player controls a vehicle at the bottom of the screen from which missiles can be launched. The numerous computer opponents progress in formation from the top of the screen to the bottom. The goal of the game is to shoot every computer opponent with a missile before they reach the bottom of the screen.

The original game relies on the targets being differentiable from the background, and we modified this mechanic to use the 'signal discrimination' core task identified above. By altering the background and target colors, we replicated the 'same or different' task in the game. Instead of the user explicitly indicating whether the colors are the same or different, the game version relied on implicit indication. If the user can see a target (i.e., they see it as a different color than the background), then they shoot it with a missile. The change in presentation from the original calibration procedure meant that we also had to prevent people from differentiating colors based on luminance or movement; therefore, we used a random luminance mask (RLM) over the entire screen, which removes luminance contrast and reduces movement effects, thereby forcing users to differentiate solely based on color [18] (see Figure 3).

In addition, the implicit nature of the signal-discrimination task means that the game version must deal with errors differently. In the original system, there is no way to know whether the user is making an error in judgment, and so the procedure must use repeated trials to obtain a probability measure. In the game version, people may make errors that are based only on the game mechanics (i.e., shooting at a target and missing), and these errors are difficult to interpret in terms of the signal discrimination task. To reduce errors based on simple aiming (which is not our core task of interest), we quantized the horizontal dimension of the game – both the player's vehicle and the invading enemies move discretely across the 20 fixed columns on the screen.

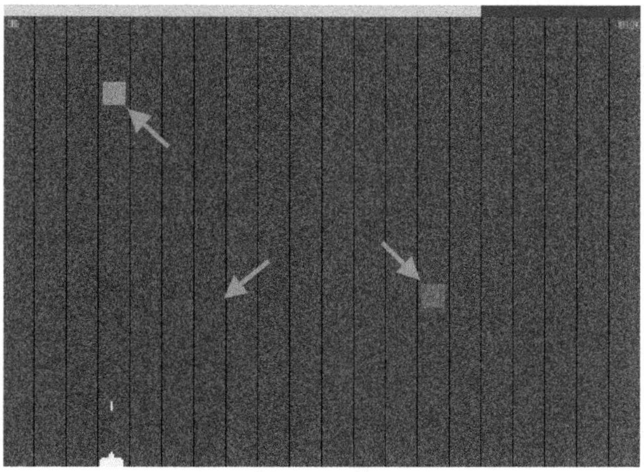

Figure 3. Space invaders color calibration game. The blue arrows (not part of game) highlight a highly visible, less visible and not visible target.

Gamification was enhanced with the following elements:

- *Progress bar, worlds and levels (progress, theme, challenge).* The player is able to track their progress through the current level using the progress bar. There are five levels in each of three worlds (Red, Green, Blue), with each level featuring faster and more numerous targets.
- *Accuracy and score (challenge).* The player is encouraged to keep accuracy near 100%. Firing a bullet that does not hit a target dramatically reduces their score. This helps prevent blanket shooting (which would result in shooting targets that the user cannot see).
- *High score (reward, progress, challenge).* By showing the current high score, the player is encouraged to achieve a higher score by shooting more targets and maintaining a higher accuracy.
- *New items for high accuracy (reward, challenge, theme).* When the player achieves a high accuracy on a level, they are rewarded with a new missile representation and an additional target explosion sound effect.

Calibrating C:D Parameters for Targeting

Many activities in desktop applications involve targeting tasks, and many optimization processes seek to improve targeting by identifying a user's performance characteristics in selection and targeting activities - for example, determining the correct parameters for a model-based interaction technique. In this game we calibrate the control-to-display (C:D) ratio (the relationship between control device movement and on-screen cursor movement [12]).

User performance characteristics are generally determined through repeated-trials calibration sessions, in which the user carries out a number of test tasks. For selection and targeting, calibration typically involves repeated selection of two-dimensional targets on a plain background. In order to stabilize performance, users must often complete a large number of these trials (e.g., 50-100 trials per condition [12]). These repetitions can become tedious and tiring, and it is difficult for users to maintain performance at their peak level - which is an important requirement for some models.

To gamify this calibration, we identified targeting as the core task underlying the calibration, and translated that core task into a pointing-based game mechanic that is common in many computer-based shooting-gallery games (see Figure 1). The shooting game thus used the same presentation as the traditional calibration system; but to this basic platform we added several game-design elements:

- *Plot (theme).* We added a minimal story to the game; the universe is being attacked by 'evil blorgs,' and users must help to defend against the attack. In addition, the different C:D ratios were characterized as different 'worlds' where the cursor would behave differently (e.g., in 'sludge world' a lower C:D ratio was employed).
- *Visible timer (challenge).* The calibration session runs for ten seconds; in the game version of the system, the timer is made visible using a progress bar, encouraging users to shoot as many targets as possible before the bar fills up.
- *Laser gun and explosion effects (theme and reward).* In the game system, the cursor is represented by cross-hairs, and clicking the mouse causes a 'laser beam' effect (see Figure 4). Hitting a target causes it to break into pieces that fall to the bottom of the screen.
- *Sound effects (theme and reward).* The game plays different sound effects for firing, hitting and missing targets, bonuses, and the start and end of a ten-second trial.
- *Bonuses (theme, reward, and progress).* Two kinds of bonus were used (see Figure 4): first, if the user hit five

targets in a row, they received a gold star; second, if the user hit more targets than they had in the previous round, the explosions changed (from broken pieces to bubbles).

The changes made for this game were thus all cosmetic, and there was minimal change in the presentation of the core task. For testing, we designed both a standard calibration version as well as the shooting game. In both systems the goal was to find which of four C:D ratios was optimal for the user's mouse-based input. Both systems tested four C:D ratios, with four 10-second sessions at each ratio.

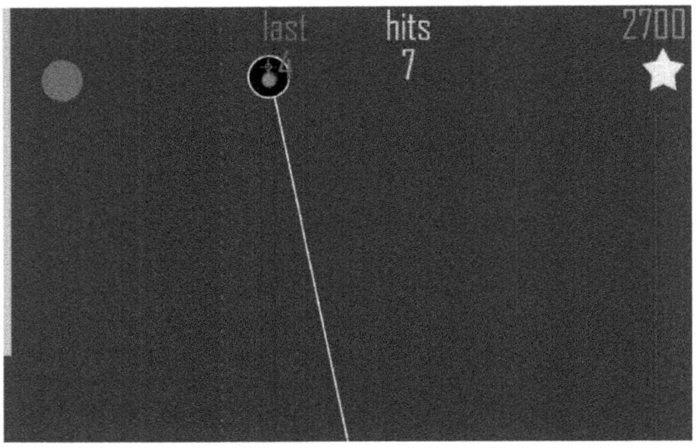

Figure 4. The C:D calibration game. The blue bar on the left marks time passed in the level, and the interface shows last and current hits as well as score. The star in the upper-right corner is a badge for successfully hitting five blorgs in a row.

Calibrating a Physiological Sensor

Some physiological sensors require an individual calibration before they can be used as a direct or indirect control mechanism [10]. An example of this is the respiration chest strain sensor, which senses the changes in chest circumference with breathing. To use it as an interaction device, we need to know the maximum chest circumference. Breathing deeply during the calibration procedure measures this value. To make this procedure more enjoyable, we developed a game called BabyLaunch (see Figure 5).

Figure 5. The BabyLaunch game allows a user to launch a laughing baby out of a picnic basket into a pile of colorful balls, by breathing in deeply.

The standard calibration procedure for chest inhalation sensors is fast (it only requires breathing in deeply a few times), so there is no problem with tedium in this case. We developed BabyLaunch to explore the effects that gamification can have on calibration data for very simple procedures. In particular, we were interested in the effects of rewards (the laughing baby, colorful visuals), challenge (to see how far you can launch the baby), theme (baby playing in the ball pit), and progress (current maximum distance) on people's performance. In addition, we were interested in whether the game elements could detract from performance by distracting the user from the calibration task.

EVALUATION

Our testing of the calibration games involved two main questions: first, whether gamifying a calibration solves the problems identified previously (lack of enjoyment and lack of motivation); and second, whether the addition of game elements reduces the accuracy of the calibration data.

To answer these questions, we compared the gamified (CG) and traditional calibration procedures (SC) in three separate studies. For each study, we recruited 12 people from the local university community, and had them test the two calibration systems in counterbalanced order. We compared the calibration data using paired-samples t-tests to determine whether the game versions produced results that were different from the traditional versions, and we compared people's answers to questions about their enjoyment and effort during the sessions using Wilcoxon Signed Ranks Tests.

Results 1: Subjective Experiences

We measured perceptions of difficulty, frustration, tedium, and enjoyment through a survey given after each session.

Color perception calibration

Survey responses showed three main results. First, people found the game version of the system significantly more enjoyable than the standard system (Table 1, rows 1 and 2). Second, people did not indicate much difference in terms of difficulty or frustration – neither of these survey questions resulted in significant differences (rows 3 and 4, Table 1).

Table 1. Survey responses for color calibration.

	Likert statement (5-point scale)	CG	SC	p
1	I enjoyed completing the task	4.0	2.8	.006
2	Completing the task was fun	4.0	2.9	.016
3	Completing the task was frustrating	2.2	2.0	.763
4	Completing the task was difficult	2.3	2.5	.627
5	The task was physically demanding	2.9	2.1	.088
6	I had to work hard to complete the task	2.7	1.8	.040
7	I felt rushed when completing the task	3.8	1.8	.003
8	The task was mentally demanding	3.3	2.9	.160

Third, the gamification clearly had the effect of *increasing* the perception of effort: people felt that the game version forced them to work harder and rushed them more than the standard version (rows 5-8 of Table 1). This additional effort is not necessarily a problem, however: it could mean that people were trying harder (see discussion below).

C:D-ratio calibration

Survey responses for the C:D calibration showed similar

trends in terms of fun and enjoyment – responses were significantly higher for the game versions (rows 1 and 2, Table 2). Given that the only difference between the two versions of the C:D system was the game elements, it seems that even simple decoration can have an effect on enjoyment (one person commented that "the lack of feedback in the non-game version made it less fun;" another said "it's just more fun when you have a purpose behind it").

Unlike the color calibration, there were no other subjective differences: people ranked the two versions similarly in terms of effort, difficulty, and frustration. The lack of differences here may have to do with the fact that the presentation of the core task was the same in both versions of the C:D game, unlike in the color calibration game.

Table 2. Survey responses for C:D-ratio calibration.

	Likert statement (5-point scale)	CG	SC.	p
1	I enjoyed completing the task	3.8	2.9	.040
2	Completing the task was fun	3.9	2.8	.004
3	Completing the task was difficult	2.3	1.8	.119
4	Completing the task was frustrating	2.0	1.7	.219
5	The task was physically demanding	2.0	2.3	.380
6	I felt rushed when completing the task	3.3	3.2	.527
7	I had to work hard to complete the task	2.1	2.0	.739
8	The task was mentally demanding	2.7	2.1	.161

For the C:D calibration, we also asked participants two additional questions – which system they would prefer if they had to do the calibration once per day, and which they would prefer if they had to do it ten times per day. For the 'once per day' preference, people were evenly divided between the game and the standard calibration. For the 'ten times per day' preference, however, only two people chose the standard system, and ten chose the game version.

Respiration sensor calibration

For the respiration sensor calibration, users again reported significantly higher enjoyment with the game-based version over the standard calibration (row 1, Table 3). However, unlike the other two calibrations, there was no significant difference in fun between the two calibration versions. This suggests that the visual and audio effects provided an entertainment value to the users (thereby increasing their enjoyment), but the input technique (breathing deeply) was too mundane to result in the participants having fun.

Table 3. Survey responses for respiration sensor.

	Likert statement (5-point scale)	CG	SC	p
1	I enjoyed completing the task	4.2	3.3	.007
2	Completing the task was fun	4.2	3.6	.107
3	Completing the task was frustrating	1.7	1.7	1.00
4	Completing the task was difficult	2.0	1.8	.776
5	The task was physically demanding	3.6	2.9	.131
6	I had to work hard to complete the task	2.3	1.8	.167
7	I felt rushed when completing the task	2.5	1.9	.230
8	The task was mentally demanding	2.3	1.9	.157

All other results showed no significant differences between the two versions of calibration. Similar to the C:D calibration, it may be that the core game mechanic of each version (breathing deeply) was so similar that there were no differences in effort, difficulty, or frustration.

Results 2: Calibration Accuracy

Color perception calibration

JNDs can be described mathematically by sigmoid functions. Normalized sigmoid functions transition from a minimum of 0 to a maximum of 1 as the x-axis value increases. For JNDs, this translates into moving from not differentiable to completely differentiable (y-axis) as you increase the difference between two signals (x-axis). In psychophysics, this is called a psychometric function. In Figure 6 six JND psychometric functions (3 RGB channels x 2 calibration techniques) are shown. Each of these functions is the average JND for all participants for a particular RGB channel and calibration type.

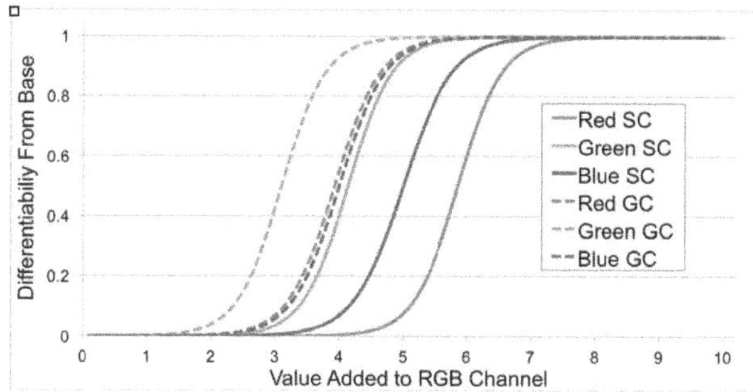

Figure 6. Average red, green, and blue channel JND psychometric functions across all participants.

It is evident from Figure 6 that there are differences between the JND functions for the two types of calibration. We found a significant difference for all ($p<0.05$) but one ($p=0.06$) for the horizontal shift of each function. This suggests that the functions are relatively translated. We also examined the horizontal span of each function as it transitions from 0 to 1 and found no significant differences. This suggests that the functions are not relatively skewed. We will come back to these results in the discussion.

C:D-ratio calibration

The C:D calibration system is designed to determine people's performance at different control-display ratios. Figure 7 shows the mean results from the two systems. Although the relative performance was similar, completion times per target were lower at all ratios for the game system, and this difference was significant ($p<0.05$).

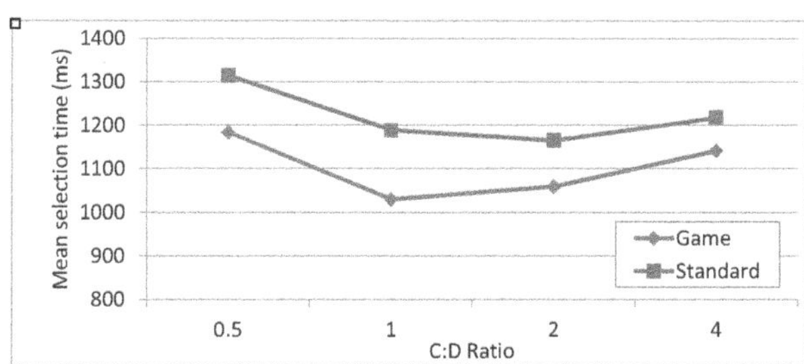

Figure 7. Mean selection time by C:D ratio.

Our observations suggest that the improved performance

may have been caused by people trying harder in the game: that is, it is possible that the game version of the calibration actually produces more accurate data, since it did a better job of encouraging people to try their hardest at the tasks.

We were also interested in whether the game elements would change people's behaviour in ways that would lead to a less accurate calibration. We looked at three issues: selection errors, the gold stars (given after a run of five error-free trials), and the bubble bonus (given if the player beat their previous score). We analysed the actual data, and also asked people if they changed their strategy for any of these elements. There were no significant differences in the number of errors, the number of error-free runs, or the frequency of beating previous scores. In addition, people's responses indicated that only one person made a conscious effort to work toward the stars and the bonus.

Respiration sensor calibration

In contrast to the color and C:D calibrations, no significant difference was found between the maximum respiration reading between the two versions of respiration sensor calibration ($p>0.05$). This may suggest that the lack of a specific reward for higher achievement (the game response was identical no matter how far the baby was launched) caused the participant to not try harder during the game version. It is also possible that the brevity of each calibration version (under one minute each) prevented the user from becoming immersed in the game environment.

DISCUSSION

Our examples and comparisons show five main findings:

- calibration procedures are good candidates for gamification, because they often share core tasks with games;
- calibration games can be successfully built either using the same presentation as the original procedure (the C:D game), or a very different presentation (the color game);
- calibration games were clearly seen as more enjoyable than standard versions, and were strongly preferred;
- some of the game versions did produce significantly different data than the standard calibrations;
- gamification can also change other qualities of the user's experience in addition to enjoyment; the pacing and challenge elements of game versions may lead to experiences that are seen as more effortful and more demanding.

In the following sections we explore several questions including issues of generalizability, feasibility, and cost.

Do game versions solve calibration's motivation problems?

Our evidence suggests that game-based calibrations can solve both motivation problems of standard calibration procedures. The first problem was that people are unlikely to carry out standard calibrations at all, because the procedures are often tedious and unenjoyable. Our studies clearly showed that gamification makes these procedures significantly more fun and more enjoyable.

It is not surprising that people find games more fun; however, it is important to remember that our 'games' were really just dressed-up versions of standard calibration tasks, and so the significant increase in enjoyability represents a confirmation that we can in fact introduce some of the pleasurable experiences of games to tasks like calibration, even without dramatically changing the nature of the task.

The second motivation problem is that people are unmotivated to perform at the level that is needed for many kinds of calibrations. Our evaluations also suggest that the addition of encouragement and reward structures to the calibration procedure can motivate people to try harder.

This conclusion is not unequivocal, since our evidence only shows that people performed differently in the game versions, not why those differences occurred. The changes could also have arisen because of differences in the presentation of the stimuli, or interaction effects with other game elements. However, our observations and comments from participants suggest that there is a motivating effect of the game's rewards and encouragements.

Is game data still usable for calibration?

The risk in changing a calibration procedure is that the data gathered from the game will be inaccurate or biased. Our evaluations show that the data from the game versions is different from that of the standard versions – significantly so – but this difference itself does not mean that the game data is less valuable for calibration.

A problem with all human-based calibrations is that there is no true 'ground truth', and so any calibration procedure is an approximation of the real value – and it may be that the game versions actually provide a more accurate calibration (e.g., by motivating people to try harder). More study is needed to determine why our game-based calibrations differed from the standard versions, but here we consider the potential ramifications of the differences we saw.

If we assume that the standard calibration is correct, we can consider how the game-data differences would affect real-world decisions that might be made from the calibration. In the case of using the C:D calibration to choose the best ratio, the game data would have led us to choose a ratio of 1.0 more often than we should (i.e., since 1.0 was the best ratio for the game, whereas 2.0 was best in the standard system). This difference, however, represents a performance difference of only 25 milliseconds per selection (i.e., the performance difference between a C:D ratio of 1 and 2 for either system); therefore, the results of calibrating with the game version are nearly indistinguishable from that of the standard version. In addition, if we are comparing the game-based calibration to situations where we have no calibration at all (due to a lack of motivation for doing the process), then the game version is a clearly better approach.

This example does raise a related issue, however, that could become a problem for game-based calibration in some settings. If games motivate people to try harder, it is possible that their better performance is dependent on a higher level of effort. In some cases this is not a problem (e.g., when determining relative coefficients); but for other purposes (e.g., choosing the best value to use in a real application), a decision based on game data could lead to a choice that does not accurately reflect the user's mental state or effort level in the situation of use. The generalizability of a calibration task to the real-world situation of interest is an ongoing problem for all human-based calibration, but gamification adds additional issues for designers to consider.

In the case of color calibration, the game version appeared to be more sensitive than the standard calibration. This difference may have arisen through improved motivation, but may also be caused by the difference in presentation (e.g., the addition of random noise in the game may not have removed all perceptual traces of luminance or movement). If the game-based calibration is in fact over-sensitive, it would lead to more false positives in the differentiation predictor (i.e., the predictor would incorrectly state that the user will be able to differentiate some pairs of colors). Again, however, the real-world difference is extremely small and easily solved by using a small fixed-offset value, as proposed in earlier work [5]. This fixed-offset value translates the psychometric functions horizontally, thereby aligning the game-based calibration with the standard calibration.

The color-calibration game shows that changing the presentation of the core calibration task requires an additional step of the system designer – that is, the designer must ensure that any changes in the game version do not make the task different (e.g., easier or harder). This can be accomplished by comparing the standard and new presentations in a non-game context, to control for motivational effects.

It is also worth noting that players of calibration games are likely to be aware of the fact that a calibration process is going on behind the game. The knowledge that there is a larger purpose that benefits the user themselves may help to control any behaviour that would reduce the value of the calibration data. For example, it is unlikely that a user will cheat in order to win the game, when they know that the outcomes of the game are decisions that will affect their performance or satisfaction with the system.

What other calibrations could be gamified?

Figure 1 shows that many calibration types have connections to common game mechanics. The only types listed that do not have strong connections to games are some motor-control thresholds (i.e., minimum movement). As further examples of the range of systems that are possible, we briefly introduce three additional places where calibration could be carried out using gamified versions.

Determining spatial memory abilities. Some interaction techniques work best for users who have good spatial location memory, and calibration can be carried out to assess each person's individual capability. Playing an interactive game based on Concentration (where the user must remember locations in order to match pairs) could provide this assessment; in addition, the presentation could be tuned to the stimuli that are to be used in the interaction technique.

Registering input and output spaces on a table. Projector-based table systems involve representations of space for the input device (e.g., vision-based tracking) and the output (e.g., a projector). These spaces must be aligned, but with some setups a large number of registration points are required (e.g., when nearby metal warps the input space of a magnetic tracker). A targeting or pursuit-tracking game could provide a large number of registration points, even with users such as schoolchildren who are unlikely to carry out traditional calibration. The main design issue in this game would be in determining when the user's input actions were actually on the target (similar to the error issue discussed for the JND game); this could be addressed by making use of varying difficulty levels (e.g., a slower target in a pursuit task is more likely to result in accurate data).

Calibrating a color monitor. Monitor calibration is a task that is rarely if ever carried out by most users, but a properly-calibrated monitor can be extremely useful (e.g., for producing accurate printouts). A game based on visual search and pattern matching (e.g., similar to popular games like Bejeweled) could be used to make monitor calibration less tedious. Printed color swatches could be used as physical tokens in the game, and the player's goal would be to find colors on the screen that match the printed swatches. A staircase approach could be used to deal with errors and home-in on an accurate calibration.

What are the limits to calibration games?

Although calibration games can be widely applied, there are limits to the idea:

- The quality of the calibration data must be the first priority. Although we concluded that the game elements did not compromise the quality of the calibration in our three examples, there are clearly limits to the number and type of game elements that can be added to the system. For example, adding narrative elements or reward structures that dramatically change people's strategy in the game could alter the way they behave, compromising the calibration. Similarly, adding challenge elements to the game could add noise to the data, making it more difficult to interpret the user's behaviour when errors occur.
- If an existing standard calibration procedure is *not* tedious (dull and time-consuming), then there is little need to convert the procedure to a game. For example, ergonomic measurements (e.g., needed to set up a vision-based gestural input system) would only need to be taken once, and would be easy to carry out.
- Games require that the user switch mental contexts, even minimally, to think about the goals and tasks of the game (e.g., the 'invading blorgs' story of the C:D game). In some task situations, this context shift could disrupt a user's work focus (e.g., it could cause them to forget important information for a post-calibration task step).

- Some work settings (e.g., formal offices) may not be appropriate places to play games, and the sound and visual effects of games may disrupt other workers.

What are the added costs of building a game version?
Development costs vary, but in our experience, the added development costs of gamifying calibration are relatively low. All three game implementations required approximately three additional days of design and programming compared to the traditional versions. We estimate that games using the same core task as the original calibration could be developed in as little as two days, although some amount of additional playtesting time will be required to ensure that the game elements work and that the game version actually is more fun than the standard version.

For systems that change the presentation of the core task, development time will necessarily be longer, particularly if testing must be carried out to ensure that the new presentation is providing accurate data. As the idea of game-based calibration sees wider adoption, however, some of these development costs will be reduced through re-use.

CONCLUSIONS AND FUTURE WORK

Calibration is an important part of many human-computer systems, but is often neglected because calibration procedures are tedious and uninteresting. To address this problem, we introduced the idea of calibration games. We presented a design framework that can aid in the development of these games, and demonstrated the process through three example games. Our evaluations showed that the game versions of calibration were much more enjoyable than the standard versions, and were strongly preferred. In addition, although there were differences in the data gathered from the two versions, these differences do not compromise the utility of calibration data obtained from games.

There are several avenues for continued work in this area. First, we plan to develop more calibration games to further test and refine our design framework. Second, we will undertake a more in-depth exploration of the way that data differences actually affect different kinds of decisions, and further investigate the issue of errors raised in the discussion. Third, we plan to package and deploy a set of calibration games, in order to gather additional information about the use of these games in real usage scenarios.

REFERENCES

1. Axholt, M., Peterson, S., Ellis, S. User Boresight Calibration Precision for Large-Format Head-Up Displays. *Proc. VRST 2008*, 141-148.
2. Brathwaite, B., Schreiber, I. *Challenges for Game Designers*. 2008.
3. Chao, D. Doom as an Interface for Process Management. *Proc. CHI 2001*, 152-157.
4. Deterding, S., Dixon, D., Nacke, L., O'Hara, K., Sicart, M. Gamification: Using Game Design Elements in Non-Gaming Contexts. *CHI 2011 Extended Abstracts.*
5. Flatla, D.R., Gutwin, C. Individual Models of Color Differentiation to Improve Interpretability of Information Visualization. *Proc. CHI 2010*, 2563-2572.
6. Hisazumi, K., Fukuda, A. WiPS: Location and Motion Sensing Technique of IEEE 802.11 Devices. *Proc. ICITA 2005*,Volume 2, 346-349.
7. Hunicke, R., LeBlanc, M., Zubek, R. MDA: A Formal Approach to Game Design and Game Research. *Proc. AAAI04 WS on Challenges in Game AI*, 2004, 1-5.
8. Lai, A., Soro, A., Scateni, R. Interactive Calibration of a Multi-Projector System in a Video-Wall Multi-Touch Environment. *Adjunct Proc. UIST 2010*, 437-438.
9. Looser, J., Cockburn, A., Savage, J. On the Validity of Using First-Person Shooters for Fitts' Law Studies. *People and Computers XIX*, 2, 2005, 33-36.
10. Lu, P., Huenerfauth, M. Accessible Motion-Capture Glove Calibration Protocol for Recording Sign Language Data From Deaf Subjects. *Proc. Assets 2009*, 83-90.
11. Lyons, G., Sharma, P., Baker, M., O'Malley, S., Shanahan, A. A Computer Game-Based EMG Biofeedback System for Muscle Rehabilitation. *Proc. 25th Annual International Conf. of the IEEE*, 2, 2003, 1625-1628.
12. MacKenzie, I. Fitts' Law as a Research and Design Tool in Human-Computer Interaction. *JHCI*, 7, 1992, 91-139.
13. Malone, T. Toward a Theory of Intrinsically Motivating Instruction. *Cognitive Science*, 4, 1981, 333-370.
14. Nacke, L.E., Kalyn, M., Lough, C., Mandryk, R.L. Biofeedback Game Design: Using Direct and Indirect Physiological Control to Enhance Game Interaction. *Proc. CHI 2011*.
15. Nishimura, R., Mokhtari, P., Takemoto, H., Kato, H. Headphone Calibration for 3D-Audio Listening. *Proc. IUCS 2009*, 205-210.
16. Pavlus, J. The Game of Life. *Scientific American*, 303, 2010, 43-44.
17. Reeves, B., Leighton Read, J. *Total Engagement*. 2009.
18. Regan, B., Reffin, J., Mollon, J. Luminance Noise and the Rapid Determination of Discrimination Ellipses in Colour Deficiency. *Vis. Res.* 34(10), 1993, 1279-1299.
19. Shneiderman, B. Designing for Fun: How Can We Design User Interfaces to Be More Fun? *Interactions,* 11(5), 2004, 48-50.
20. Villanueva, A., Cabeza, R., Porta, S. Eye Tracking System Model with Easy Calibration. *Proc. ETRA 04*, 55.
21. Von Ahn, L. Dabbish, L. Designing Games With a Purpose. *Comm. ACM*, August 2008, 58-67.
22. Walter, S., Hrabal, D., Scheck, A., Kessler, H., Bertrand, G., Nothdurft, F., Minker, W., Traue, H. Individual Emotional Profiles in Wizard-of-Oz-Experiments. *Proc. PETRA 2010*, 68, 1-2.
23. Wilson, A. PlayAnywhere: a Compact Interactive Tabletop Projection-Vision System. *Proc. UIST 2005*, 83-92.

onNote: Playing Printed Music Scores as a Musical Instrument

Yusuke Yamamoto
Keio University
5322 Endo, Fujisawa-shi, Kanagawa, Japan
usuk@sfc.keio.ac.jp

Hideaki Uchiyama
INRIA Rennes
263 avenue du Gnral Leclerc 35042 Rennes, France
Hideaki.Uchiyama@inria.fr

Yasuaki Kakehi
Keio University
5322 Endo, Fujisawa-shi, Kanagawa, Japan
ykakehi@sfc.keio.ac.jp

ABSTRACT

This paper presents a novel musical performance system named *onNote* that directly utilizes printed music scores as a musical instrument. This system can make users believe that sound is indeed embedded on the music notes in the scores. The users can play music simply by placing, moving and touching the scores under a desk lamp equipped with a camera and a small projector. By varying the movement, the users can control the playing sound and the tempo of the music. To develop this system, we propose an image processing based framework for retrieving music from a music database by capturing printed music scores. From a captured image, we identify the scores by matching them with the reference music scores, and compute the position and pose of the scores with respect to the camera. By using this framework, we can develop novel types of musical interactions.

ACM Classification: H5.2 [Information interfaces and presentation]: User Interfaces. - Interaction styles.; I.4.8 [Image processing and computer vision]: Scene analysis. - Object recognition.

General terms: Algorithms, Design, Human Factors

Keywords: musical instrument, image retrieval, tangible interface

INTRODUCTION

Throughout time, music has played an important role in people's daily life. People usually experience music a part of their everyday life in different forms: listening to music, playing music or composing music. In addition to being a source of entertainment, music is also used in therapy is as an effective tool to heal patients undergoing medical treatment [6]. For seeking further possibilities of the use of music, we investigate novel forms of playing music and music technologies.

Because of the advances in the field of computer technology in recent years, digital musical instruments have been developed for modern musical performances in the field of interactive art [24, 5, 15, 28, 23, 16, 20, 2, 3, 14, 22]. In such instruments, sound can be easily edited and controlled in real-time. For other music-related technologies, digital support using a computer is incorporated into the framework of music composition [10] and music playback systems [13]. However, one of the drawbacks of such digital music media is a lack of semantic relationship between the physical interface and the music generated from those media. If there is no such apparent relationship, it is difficult for users to intuitively understand how to use such media well. For example, we cannot accurately deduce the type of music from the appearance of music records or CD-ROMs. Further, users may need to play music only with their own musical sense if there is no methodology to give a good musical performance. By semantically connecting instruments with music, we can produce a musical performance that is more natural, intuitive and comprehensible than a performance without such a connection.

In this paper, we propose a musical performance system using printed music scores as a musical instrument as illustrated in Figure 1. In this system, the scores do not include any additional fiducial markers. Users can play music easily and intuitively by tracing the music notes on the scores with fingers and composing music by connecting the small pieces of the scores. Compared with traditional systems, the proposed system is more comprehensible because users can visually understand what they are playing from the scores, at least the existence of the sound, and play music as written in the scores.

To develop the abovementioned system, we propose a framework for retrieving music from a music database by capturing printed music scores using a camera to establish a connection between the scores and the digital information. The purpose of our research is similar to [11]. For the database, we first link the scores and their music. When users capture one of

Figure 1: The proposed musical instrument is printed music scores. Users do not need to have any special devices. By putting, moving and touching the scores under a desk lamp, users can play various music performances.

the scores, the captured score is identified by using an image analysis method to retrieve the corresponding music in real-time. This issue can be described as the image retrieval of music scores. Normally, we cannot apply general image retrieval methods [21] to music scores because of a lack of rich texture on the scores. Instead, we modify a method for document image retrieval [19] and apply it to music scores by taking a common point such that both documents and music scores have a binary texture. In our prototype system, a camera is embedded into a desk lamp to capture the scores, as illustrated in Figure 1. By using the proposed framework, we can enhance the functionality of the printed music scores by connecting physical papers with digital information. Moreover, we develop a novel type of interaction that connects human beings with music such that the users can believe that sound is embedded on the music notes in the scores.

The rest of the paper is organized as follows: in the next section, we review traditional digital musical performances and image processing technologies for music scores. Then, we present an overview of the proposed system, a retrieval technique for music scores, and novel musical performances given using the proposed system. In the experimental section, we describe the robustness, performance, and limitations of the proposed system. Finally, we present a summary of the future works.

RELATED WORKS

In this section, we first introduce the related works on digital musical performances and image processing technologies for music scores.

Digital Musical Performances

Mainly in the field of interactive arts, various types of musical performances have already been proposed. We group these into the following categories: tabletop, gesture, and device.

For a tabletop-based musical instrument, Patten et al. developed several interaction techniques using a tangible tabletop interface named Audiopad [24]. In this system, the users move the pucks placed on a tabletop surface according to certain pre-defined manipulations. The motion of the pucks is translated into a command for a musical synthesizer in real-time. D-touch [3] is also a musical instrument that uses tangible tabletop objects. This system utilizes small paper boxes with printed markers as a tangible interface and works as a drum machine or a music sequencer by detecting the positions of the boxes on the tabletop. Jorda et al. discussed the importance of the researches on tabletop-based musical instruments and developed a round-table type of musical instrument named reacTable [15] and scoreTable [14]. They concluded that the development of digital musical instruments could serve as an ideal test-bed for exploring complicated and multi-dimensional interactions.

In the studies of gesture-based musical instruments, the main issues are the selection of a device for gesture acquisition and the design of the musical performance. Wong et al. utilized Wiimote to acquire a 6-degrees-of-freedom movement and designed hand-movement-based manipulation of sound for a virtual drum [28]. Overholt et al. incorporated several sensing technologies such as visual information, audio, and electric fields into a multi-modal music stand system [23]. The real-time audio synthesis and transformation of parameters are performed on the basis of a visual analysis of the motion of a user's body. Ketabdar et al. proposed gestural recognition using a magnetic field sensor equipped with iPhone 3GS [16]. They presented various possibilities of applying a mobile device to musical instruments such as air guitars, harmonicas, and theremins.

As a novel type of digital musical device, Nishibori and Iwai developed TENORI-ON that had a screen consisting of a 16 $\times$ 16 grid of LED switches [20]. In this device sound could be controlled by changing the state of the switches. This system has already been produced as a commercial product. Cassinelli et al. developed a laser-type device that generated sound from the lines of drawings [2]. This device tracks the contours of lines, such as moving silhouettes of human beings, to generate sound from pre-processed data. Sonic Scanner is also an instrument used for musical performance that turns visual information such as drawings and pictures into music by using a handheld scanner-type device [22].

In these researches, the main focus was on the design of musical performances using special devices that were not directly related to music. In contrast, our aim is to develop a novel musical instrument by using the existing music scores. By enhancing the functionality of the existing equipment, we will achieve natural, intuitive, and comprehensible musical interactions.

Image Processing for Music Scores

In the field of image processing and computer vision, the digitization of machine-generated music scores has been achieved through optical music recognition (OMR) [26, 12]. Because it is similar to optical character recognition (OCR) for text documents, OMR can also be called music OCR. In OMR, the essential parts of the scores such as music notes are extracted and recognized by using their positional relationship.

Because musical staffs are inessential, they are removed prior to the recognition [4].

The digitalization of handwritten music scores was also investigated to convert handwritings into a machine readable format [18]. In particular, the digitalization of ancient music scores [25] and the identification of a musical writer [9] were important issues related to the automatic building of a digital library for ancient music as a music heritage.

These traditional methods could be one way to connect printed music scores and digital information for our purpose because these methods can exploit the content of the scores as digital data. However, these are normally performed to clean scanned and well-aligned music scores off-line at a considerable computational cost. In our situation, it is difficult to capture the scores in the same manner because users must be able to freely move, hold, and touch the scores. Moreover, occlusion by fingers may occur during the musical performance. For these reasons, we propose another approach that is based on image retrieval and is carried out performed by matching a captured image with a music score database in real time.

USING PRINTED MUSIC SCORES AS A MUSICAL INSTRUMENT

In this section, we explain the motivation, approach, and setup of the proposed musical instrument called *onNote.*

Research Goal

We started to develop a novel musical performance system using general musical equipment because it would be easier for people to intuitively use such a system as compared to using special devices. In particular, we focused on music scores because the use of paper would not be difficult for people. By considering the advantages of paper, we explored a possibility of using scores as a user-friendly musical instrument.

Normally, printed papers have static information in ink. One strategy to enhance the functionality of the papers is to connect the papers with digital information. In the cases of music, sound can be considered digital information. Therefore, we investigate a way to embed sound into each music note in the printed music scores. Further, we incorporate normal paper manipulations such as touch, move, and fold into our musical performances.

Because our goal is to make users believe that sound is actually embedded on each music note, we have named our instrument *onNote.*

Our Approach

If we select a tablet PC as our device, we can easily embed sound into music notes because both-sound and music notes can be digitally connected. In our case, the main problem is how to connect printed music scores with digital data. An image-processing-based approach can be a solution to this problem because it can extract digital information from the images of physical objects. Moreover, users do not need special devices to use the proposed system because the camera is a non-contact device. To incorporate these advantages into the proposed system, we designed the following configuration.

We used a normal two-dimensional camera to capture images of the printed music scores and users' manipulations. As illustrated in Figure 1, users sat on a chair and placed the scores under a lamp on a table. Inside the lamp, we simply embedded the camera and a projector connected to a computer, as illustrated in Figure 2. We use the projector to provide visual feedback from the proposed system to users.

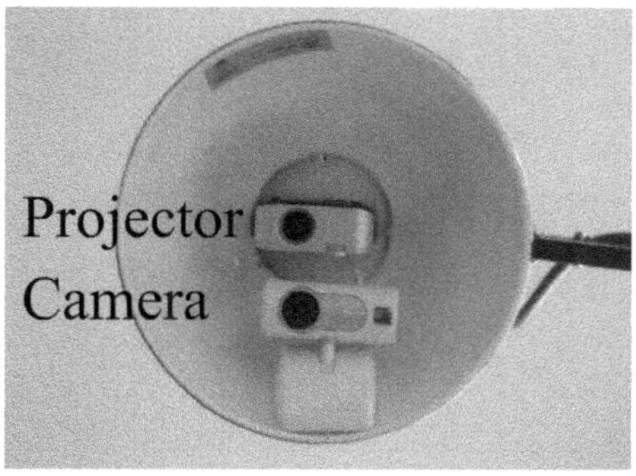

Figure 2: The table lamp in Figure 1 has a camera and a projector. The camera is utilized to capture printed music scores and users' manipulations on the table. Visual feedback is projected on the table by the projector.

Preparation

We prepare the digital images of music scores as references, as illustrated in Figure 3. Each score image is associated with its MIDI data to establish the links between the music notes on the score and their sound. MIDI is a standard digital musical format that includes parameterized signals of sound, pitch, and tempo individually instead of having sound signals directly. We first generate the links between the printed music scores and the music data from MIDI as a database such that sound is manually assigned at a xy coordinate on each score. Further, we store the digital images of the scores as references into a music score database to extract their visual features for the image retrieval of music scores as described in the next section. For our musical instrument, we print the same scores on A4 papers.

RETRIEVAL TECHNIQUE

This section describes the detailed procedure and our implementation of the image retrieval of music scores.

Problem Definition

As described in the previous section, we have reference music scores in a database linked with MIDI data. When the users capture printed music scores, we match them with those in the database to retrieve their MIDI data. In other words, we retrieve the information of the music scores by using a captured image as a query. This problem can be described as the image retrieval of music scores.

Such image retrieval has been investigated actively [21]. A basic and frequently-used approach is a bag-of-visual-words approach that uses local descriptors such as SIFT [17]. How-

Figure 3: We prepare a music score as an image file and print it on a A4 paper. We assign sound data in MIDI to each music note such that a xy coordinate in the score has one of musical scales.

ever, it is difficult to apply this approach to the image retrieval of music scores because local descriptors using local texture work well for rich texture, including a variety of intensities.

In the studies of document image analysis, there is a research issue called document image retrieval in which a captured image, including a document, is utilized as a query to retrieve the information in the document [7]. In this case, a descriptor is composed of a geometrical relationship of keypoints instead of local texture. Because both documents and music scores include a binary texture, we employ the method of document image retrieval and verify its applicability for our purpose.

LLAH [19]

Locally likely arrangement hashing (LLAH) is a fast and scalable method for document image retrieval. We decided to employ LLAH for our purpose because this method works well in real-time with sufficient accuracy. In this section, we briefly explain the procedure to compute the descriptors in LLAH.

Suppose there is a cloud of points as illustrated in Figure 4. For each point, the n nearest neighbor points are first selected. From the n points, m points are selected to compute one descriptor. This implies that each point has ${}_nC_m = \frac{n!}{m!(n-m)!}$ descriptors computed from all combinations. From the m points, four points are selected to compute a ratio of two triangles as an affine invariant as illustrated in Figure 4. The number of combinations (${}_mC_4$) corresponds to the number of dimensions for one descriptor. For fast matching, each ratio is quantized into 2^k levels.

The accuracy of the retrieval depends on the following three parameters: n, m, and k. In the evaluations, we calculate the accuracy of the retrieval results for several combinations of the parameters.

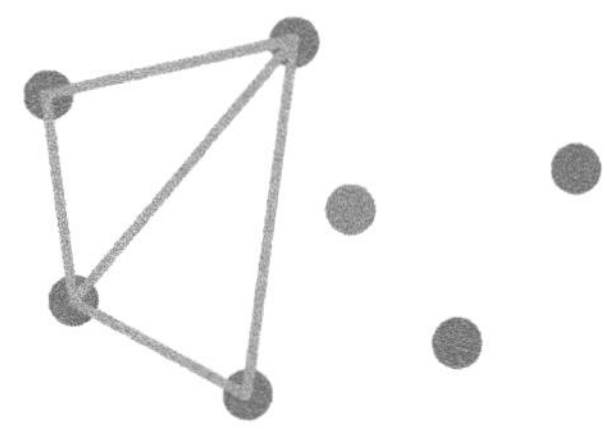

Figure 4: The descriptors in LLAH are composed of the collection of the ratios of two triangles as affine invariants. The ratio is quantized into integer for fast matching.

Algorithm Overview

Here, we introduce the implementation details of image retrieval for music scores. The procedure is basically similar to document image retrieval by LLAH.

In the pre-processing stage, keypoints and their descriptors included in the reference music scores are computed and stored in a music score database. In the on-line retrieval, keypoints are first extracted from a captured image, and their descriptors in LLAH are computed in the same way as in the pre-processing stage. For each keypoint in the captured image, a corresponding keypoint in the database is retrieved by using the descriptors. From a cloud of keypoint correspondences, we have the candidates of music scores included in the captured image. By computing RANSAC-based [8] homography for each music score to verify the geometric consistency of the correspondences, we can obtain the successfully retrieved music scores. Once the scores are retrieved, they are tracked using LLAH based keypoint tracking [27] from the next frame.

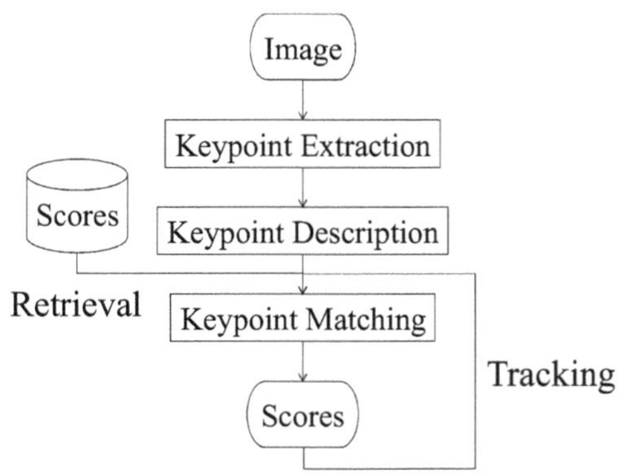

Figure 5: From a captured image, keypoints and their descriptors are computed to match with reference music scores. Once scores are retrieved, they are tracked from the next frame.

Keypoint Extraction

In keypoint extraction of LLAH, an input image is blurred and binarized using an adaptive thresholding with a fixed filter size to extract word regions and compute the center of each region as a keypoint. We utilize the same method to extract keypoints from music scores. The extracted keypoints correspond to the music notes, symbols, and the other parts of the scores, as illustrated in Figure 6. Because the result of the keypoint extraction depends on the distance between the camera and the music scores, we evaluate the robustness of this method according to the viewpoint changes in the evaluations.

Figure 6: An input image (left upper) is blurred and binarized (right upper) using an adaptive thresholding method. Each center of connected regions is extracted as a keypoint (lower).

Retrieval Result

For keypoint description and matching, we follow the original method in LLAH. Keypoint matching is robust to occlusion. If a music score is successfully retrieved, it has correct correspondences between the captured image and the reference music score, as illustrated in Figure 7. Unlike the original LLAH, in the proposed method, we can retrieve multiple music scores simultaneously. When we have the candidates of music scores after keypoint matching, we verify the geometric consistency of the top 10 candidates. If the image includes multiple music scores, we can successfully retrieve and track all of them, as illustrated in Figure 7.

APPLICATIONS OF onNote TO MUSICAL PERFORMANCES

As for applications of the onNote, we think this system is suitable for edutainment. By using our system, users can learn to read music notations or play music while they are having fun. We have implemented four examples of application for music performance and composition using onNote as follows.

Playing Music Like A DJ

A disc jockey (DJ) plays music by quickly moving a vinyl record back and forth on a turntable. In this application, we can use a similar technique using the printed music scores. Users can play a musical composition in various ways, such as backwards and forwards, by a simple movement of the score.

Figure 7: If a music score is successfully retrieved, there are correct correspondences (upper). We can retrieve multiple music scores included in an image simultaneously (lower).

As illustrated in Figure 8, a red circle is projected on a table. This circle is used for pointing on a certain note the score like a phonograph needle on a turntable. When users move the score, the sound of the music note pointed by the red circle is generated. By moving the score toward the right, the users can listen to the music corresponding to the pointed area. Users can easily change the speed of the music by changing the moving speed, and they can play the audio backwards by moving the score in the opposite direction. Using the proposed system, users can play music using several DJ techniques, such as scratching, phase shifting, and back spinning.

Sound Tracing by Fingers

In our second application, the proposed system utilizes the users' fingers as a pointer. For a simple and easy performance, the users can play music by tracing music notes on the score with their fingers. In other words, the users physically touch a music note to play its sound.

In this performance, users have a color marker on their fingers and touch the score as illustrated in Figure 9. From a captured image, we extract the color region and compute the center of the region as a touching position to play the sound corresponding to the position.

In this performance, the users feel that they can actually touch the note's sound with their fingers. Depending on the movement of the finger, the users can play any music they

Figure 8: Users can play music by moving a score such that a DJ rotates a vinyl record. We use a projected red circle as a phonograph needle on a turntable. The sound of the music note in the red circle is played.

want. This implies that a paper music score is equivalent to a tangible user interface. Further, this performance is not limited to a single user. When the system is used by multiple users, a concerto-style performance is achieved.

Music Effector by Moving Scores

The third application is developed for controlling the music effects. We can utilize printed music scores as an interface of a music effector. To control several functions such as volume, pitch and tone, we assign the movement of the scores to the functions for changing the parameters in MIDI. From the image analysis, we obtain the position and pose of the scores with respect to the camera. Using these data, we can control the music effects.

As an example of the control, the volume of the sound is adjusted when users rotate a score as though they were rotating a speaker volume control, as illustrated in Figure 10. Moreover, musical instruments can be switched when the users move the score up and down. For these controls, we utilize the normal manipulations of the papers on the basis of the handle-ability of a score.

Music Composition by Arranging Score Pieces

As our fourth application, we developed several musical performances and compositions using the arrangement of multiple music scores. This is based on our implementation of the image retrieval of music scores that can detect multiple music scores simultaneously.

In the database, we store the pieces of the music scores that are generated by dividing the original music scores. When users compose music, they select music pieces and set them horizontally, as illustrated in Figure 11. The music is placed according to the order of these pieces. Normally, users create high quality music with a digital audio workstation by trimming a sequence of audio data and connecting the pieces. In a similar way, users can easily enjoy music mash-ups by

Figure 9: Users can play music by tracing music notes on a score by fingers. This can provide the feeling such that users actually touch the sound on a music note. By doing with multiple users, it will be a concerto style.

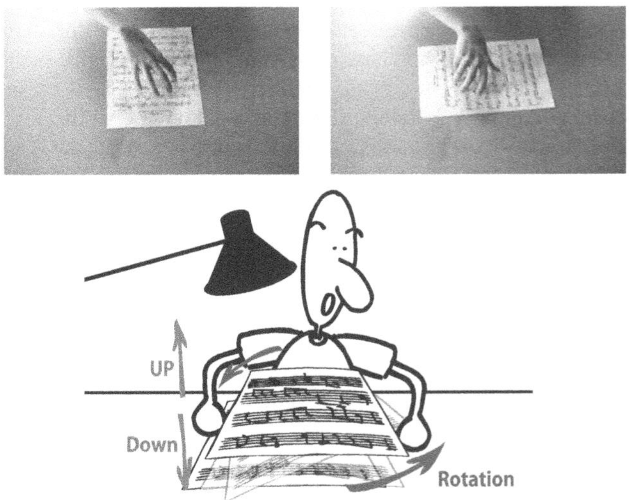

Figure 10: By assigning the movement of the scores to the functions for changing several parameters, these manipulations work as a music effector such that a volume is controlled by the rotation.

connecting and changing the arrangement of music scores in real-time.

We can also develop a music puzzle as an edutainment tool. In this tool, users need to arrange the small pieces of a music score to recover the original one correctly using visual and auditory cues.

Figure 11: Users can intuitively compose music by arranging the pieces of music scores. This can be extended to an edutainment tool such that users correctly arrange the pieces of a music score like a puzzle.

EVALUATIONS

In this section, we evaluate the robustness and the performance of the proposed image retrieval of music scores.

Overview

The accuracy of the retrieval is affected by two aspects: the three parameters (n,m,k) of LLAH and the viewpoint of the camera with respect to the scores. We evaluated these influences and measured the computational costs.

We selected the top 16 piano music pieces, leading to a total of 101 sheets, and downloaded them from [1]. When we stored them into the database, we checked the number of keypoints extracted in each music score as illustrated in Figure 12.

Our experimental set-up was as follows: We used a MacBook with 2.4GHz Intel Core 2 Duo and 2GB RAM. A camera (UCAM-DLU130H) with 640×480 pixels was fixed at a pole and connected to the computer through a USB. All experiments were conducted under indoor lighting conditions. Because the image resolution of the stored music scores affects the retrieval results, we carried out an experiment to find the optimal resolution for our set-up and calculated it to be 452×640 pixels.

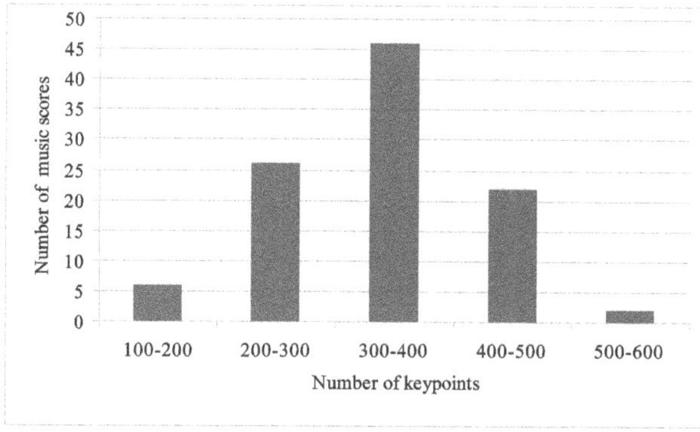

Figure 12: The distribution of the number of music scores with respect to that of keypoints is presented.

Accuracy vs. Parameters

First, we evaluated the influence of the three parameters of LLAH. We tested the following combinations of the parameters to check the influence of each parameter: (n,m,k) = (7,6,4), (7,5,4), (6,5,4), (6,5,3), (6,5,5). We vertically fixed the camera at a distance of 40 cm from the score, as measured by a ruler. From this distance, the printed scores were captured in entirely.

In Table 1, we categorize the retrieved results into four items as follows: Stable indicates that a music score was stably retrieved for many frames. Unstable includes two conditions such that a music score was retrieved only for some frames or only when it was set at specific positions. Duplicate indicates that the retrieved results included incorrect results in addition to the correct result, as illustrated in Figure 13. Failed indicates that a music score was not retrieved even when it was tested at various positions.

For all combinations of parameters, one common and notable result appeared in Duplicate. 28% of the scores resulted in duplicates for the following two combinations: (n,m,k) = (7,5,4), (7,6,4). This is because the music score of a song sometimes include the same structure of notes because of the repetition of beats. Further, if a part of two scores is common, both the scores will be retrieved in the image retrieval. The solution to this problem is to select the music score that has the maximum number of correct correspondences when multiple scores are retrieved in the same region. Moreover, segmented music scores could be stored to avoid storing the same structures. On the other hand, this can be regarded as a useful property for clustering music scores that have the same structures in the duplicate retrieval.

In the case of the influence of the abovementioned three parameters, a remarkable difference was not observed for the retrieval of the 101 music scores in terms of the accuracy. This result is almost the same as that of the original LLAH for text documents described in [19]. If the number of stored music scores is around 100, the influence on the accuracy of the selection of the parameters is small.

Table 1: Retrieval results and their computational costs according to different sets of three parameters in LLAH.

n	m	k	Number of Retrieved Scores				Computational Cost (msec/frame)	
			Stable	Unstable	Duplicate	Failed	Keypoint Extraction	Keypoint Matching
7	6	4	64	8	28	1	20	22.5
7	5	4	66	7	28	0	24	191.5
6	5	4	71	10	17	3	29	42
6	5	3	67	11	21	2	29	168.5
6	5	5	67	7	21	6	25.5	16.5

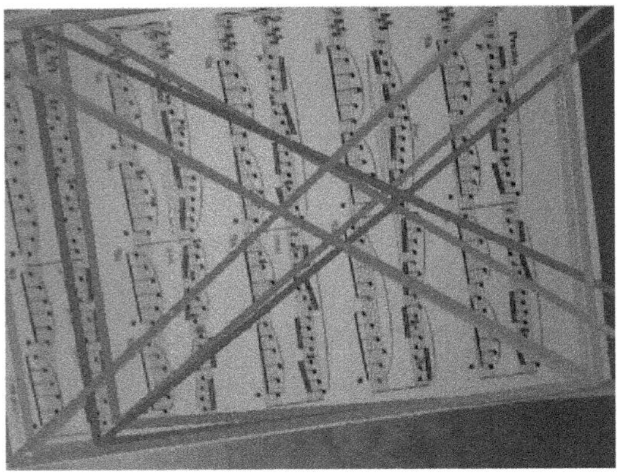

Figure 13: Multiple scores can be retrieved for one score because they sometimes include same structure. This can be avoided by selecting a music score that has maximum number of correct correspondences.

Accuracy vs. Viewpoints

Next, we evaluated the influence of viewpoints. In this experiment, we fixed the parameters as (n,m,k) = (7,5,4). For 66 music scores that were successfully retrieved using this parameter set in the previous experiment, we tested two types of view changes: distant and angular. As described in Table 2, we first set the vertical distance between the camera and the score to a value ranging from 25 cm to 50 cm. Most of the 66 scores were successfully retrieved between 30 cm and 45 cm, whereas many of the scores were not retrieved at 25 cm and 50 cm. This result was obtained by the method of keypoint extraction with a fixed filter size that was valid for a single scale. For the distance between 30 cm and 45 cm, the distribution of the extracted keypoints was almost same. However, the distribution changed drastically at 25 cm and 50 cm because of the change in the scale. As a solution, we can utilize a multi-scale pyramid representation of an input image

Second, we set the angle between the camera and the score to a value ranging from 75° to 45°, as measured by a protractor. An angle of 90° degrees implies that the camera is set vertically with respect to the table. The distance between the camera and the score was fixed at 40 cm to check only the influence of angles. As described in Table 3, the retrieval still worked for an angle of 45° because we utilized affine-invariance-based descriptors. Some scores could not be retrieved because of the specific structure of the scores. For example, the pose of the score was incorrectly recognized, as illustrated in Figure 14, when the structure of the left half of the score was almost the same as that of the right half because of the repetition of the beats.

Table 2: Retrieval results according to different distances.

Distance (cm)	Number of Retrieved Scores		
	Stable	Unstable	Failed
25	24	12	30
30	61	5	0
35	66	0	0
45	66	0	0
50	6	7	53

Table 3: Retrieval results according to different angles.

Angle (degree)	Number of Retrieved Scores		
	Succeed	Unstable	Failure
75	63	1	2
60	59	5	2
45	55	8	3

Computational Costs

We measured the computational costs of the proposed method. For this experiment, we selected one music score with 347 keypoints and captured it in 100 frames while moving it at a vertical distance of 40 cm from the camera. Because the costs depend on the combination of the parameters, we measured the costs for all the combinations used in the previous experiment, as described in Table 1.

The cost of the keypoint extraction was almost the same for all combinations because the extraction was not related to the parameters. On the other hand, the cost of the keypoint matching increased for the following sets of parameters. For (n,m,k) = (7,5,4), the number of descriptors (${}_nC_m$) was three times more than that for the other combinations. For (n,m,k) = (6,5,3), the descriptor was less discriminative such that many collisions occurred and led to searching costs in the descriptor database of the LLAH. Because the parameters affect the computational cost, we need to select appropriate ones depending on the requirement of the application.

PRELIMINARY USER-FEEDBACK

We asked several people to give us comments and suggestions for the improvement of the proposed system as the preliminary user feedback.

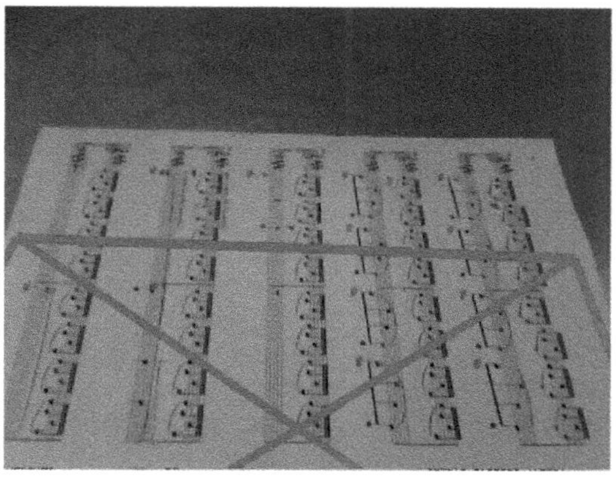

Figure 14: When the structure of the left half of the score was almost same as that of right half by repeats of beats, pose estimation failed.

On the positive side, people said that this system was very interesting because they could easily change the tempo of the music as they wanted in a simple way. They enjoyed playing music by moving the music scores because they felt the sound was coming from the music notes on the scores. The proposed system will be a useful tool for learning music because beginners can simultaneously obtain both visual and audio information of the music notes by touching the notes.

People also pointed out one improvement. It is difficult to continuously play music from one row to the next because the last part of a row (the right edge) is far from the beginning of the next row (the left edge) in the score. For this, we need to design a methodology to seamlessly play all the music on a score.

As a suggestion, it might be interesting if we can use handwritten scores for our musical performances. In this scenario, the users will first have to write music on a score, and then play the music by touching the score. Currently, the scope of our research does not cover such kind of interactions. However, in the future, we would like to achieve this scenario by developing real-time recognition of handwritten music scores. An effective use of the projector is also considered because music scores have only music notes and symbols. As visual feedback, the detailed information of the music such as composers and arrangers can be displayed.

CONCLUSIONS AND FUTURE WORKS

In this paper, we presented a framework to use printed music scores as a musical instrument for novel musical interactions.

To develop this framework, we proposed a technique of image retrieval of music scores using LLAH. For musical interactions, we developed four different examples: playing music like a DJ, sound tracing by fingers, music effector by moving scores and music composition by arranging score pieces. In the experiments, we evaluated the influence of the retrieved results using the parameters of LLAH, and the robustness with respect to the change in viewpoints.

As for the applications, we introduced example uses of the output data (pose of a music score) computed by the proposed our method. In this paper, we mainly indicated the applicability of the proposed method to various interactions. Because these applications were individually developed, we have not developed a method to switch from one interaction mode to another. Such implementations for our applications will be a further research topic.

In addition, according to the user feedback, some issues would still need to be solved for a good musical performance. For example, in the interaction with fingers, it is difficult to continuously play music from one row to the next. In the music effector application, the rotation of scores makes it difficult to read the musical notation printed on them. We plan to develop further applications by taking these issues into consideration.

Moreover, we will incorporate other paper manipulations, such as deformation and overlap of the scores, into the proposed system. For example, users can connect two folded music scores to merge sequences if we can detect the folded regions of the papers. In the future, the proposed system will become a common platform for creative music activity by proposing intuitive music manipulations.

REFERENCES

1. http://www.free-scores.com/.
2. A. Cassinelli, Y. Kuribara, A. Zerroug, M. Ishikawa, and D. Manabe. scoreLight: playing with a humansized laser pickup. In *NIME*, pages 144–149, 2010.
3. E. Costanza, M. Giaccone, O. Kueng, S. Shelley, and J. Huang. Tangible interfaces for download: initial observations from users' everyday environments. In *CHI*, pages 2765–2774, 2010.
4. C. Dalitz, M. Droettboom, B. Pranzas, and I. Fujinaga. A comparative study of staff removal algorithms. *PAMI*, 30(5):753–766, 2008.
5. P. L. Davidson and J. Y. Han. Synthesis and control on large scale multi-touch sensing displays. In *NIME*, pages 216–219, 2006.
6. W. B. Davis, K. E. Gfeller, and M. H. Thaut. *An Introduction to Music Therapy: Theory and Practice. Third Edition.* AMTA, third edition, 2008.
7. D. Doermann. The indexing and retrieval of document images: a survey. *CVIU*, 70:287–298, 1998.
8. M. A. Fischler and R. C. Bolles. Random sample consensus: a paradigm for model fitting with applications to image analysis and automated cartography. *C. of the ACM*, 24:381–395, 1981.
9. A. Fornes, J. Llados, G. Sanchez, and H. Bunke. On the use of textural features for writer identification in old handwritten music scores. In *ICDAR*, pages 996–1000, 2009.
10. A. Forsberg, M. Dieterich, and R. Zeleznik. The music notepad. In *UIST*, pages 203–210, 1998.

11. C. Fremerey, M. Müller, and F. K. M. Clausen. Automatic mapping of scanned sheet music to audio recordings. In *ISMIR*, 2008.

12. I. Fujinaga, B. Alphonce, B. Pennycook, and K. Hogan. Optical music recognition: Progress report. In *ICMC*, pages 66–73, 1991.

13. M. Goto. SmartMusicKIOSK: music listening station with chorus-search function. In *UIST*, pages 31–40, 2003.

14. S. Jordá and M. Alonso. Mary had a little scoretable* or the reactable* goes melodic. In *NIME*, pages 208–211, 2006.

15. S. Jorda, G. Geiger, M. Alonso, and M. Kaltenbrunner. The reacTable: exploring the synergy between live music performance and tabletop tangible interfaces. In *TEI*, pages 139–146, 2007.

16. H. Ketabdar, A. Jahanbekam, K. A. Yuksel, T. Hirsch, and A. Haji Abolhassani. MagiMusic: using embedded compass (magnetic) sensor for touch-less gesture based interaction with digital music instruments in mobile devices. In *TEI*, pages 241–244, 2011.

17. D. G. Lowe. Distinctive image features from scale-invariant keypoints. *IJCV*, 60:91–110, 2004.

18. H. Miyao and M. Maruyama. An online handwritten music symbol recognition system. *IJDAR*, 9(1):49–58, 2007.

19. T. Nakai, K. Kise, and M. Iwamura. Use of affine invariants in locally likely arrangement hashing for camera-based document image retrieval. In *DAS*, pages 541–552, 2006.

20. Y. Nishibori and T. Iwai. TENORI-ON. In *NIME*, pages 172–175, 2006.

21. D. Nister and H. Stewenius. Scalable recognition with a vocabulary tree. In *CVPR*, pages 2161–2168, 2006.

22. D. Overholt. Visually controlled synthesis using the sonic scanner and the graphonic interface. In *AES Convention*, 2004.

23. D. Overholt, J. Thompson, L. Putnam, B. Bell, J. Kleban, B. Sturm, and J. Kuchera-Morin. A multimodal system for gesture recognition in interactive music performance. *CMJ*, 33:69–82, 2009.

24. J. Patten, B. Recht, and H. Ishii. Interaction techniques for musical performance with tabletop tangible interfaces. In *ACE*, 2006.

25. J. C. Pinto, P. Vieira, and J. M. Sousa. A new graph-like classification method applied to ancient handwritten musical symbols. *IJDAR*, 6(1):10–22, 2004.

26. A. Rebelo, G. Capela, and J. S. Cardoso. Optical recognition of music symbols: A comparative study. *IJDAR*, 13:19–31, 2010.

27. H. Uchiyama and H. Saito. Augmenting text document by on-line learning of local arrangement of keypoints. In *ISMAR*, pages 95–98, 2009.

28. E. L. Wong, W. Y. F. Yuen, and C. S. T. Choy. Designing wii controller: a powerful musical instrument in an interactive music performance system. In *MoMM*, pages 82–87, 2008.

Peripheral Paced Respiration: Influencing User Physiology during Information Work

Neema Moraveji, Ben Olson, Truc Nguyen, Mahmoud Saadat, Yaser Khalighi, Roy Pea, Jeffrey Heer
Calming Technology Lab, Stanford University, Palo Alto, CA
neema, benolson, nguyen90, mahmoud, khalighi, roypea@stanford.edu, jheer@cs.stanford.edu

ABSTRACT

We present the design and evaluation of a technique for influencing user respiration by integrating respiration-pacing methods into the desktop operating system in a peripheral manner. *Peripheral paced respiration* differs from prior techniques in that it does not require the user's full attention. We conducted a within-subjects study to evaluate the efficacy of peripheral paced respiration, as compared to no feedback, in an ecologically valid environment. Participant respiration decreased significantly in the pacing condition. Upon further analysis, we attribute this difference to a significant decrease in breath rate while the intermittent pacing feedback is active, rather than a persistent change in respiratory pattern. The results have implications for researchers in physiological computing, biofeedback designers, and human-computer interaction researchers concerned with user stress and affect.

ACM Classification: H5.2 [Information interfaces and presentation]: User Interfaces. - Graphical user interfaces.

General terms: Design.

Keywords: Respiration, peripheral, biofeedback, stress.

MOTIVATION

Voluntary breath regulation is a common, empirically validated technique for reducing stress and anxiety [3, 10, 19], relieving symptoms of asthma [4], reducing blood pressure [5, 16], and focusing the mind for optimal performance [9]. Conversely, patterns in respiration reveal information about one's psychological state [9]; changes in breath may result from frustration, pain, stress, test anxiety [8], and post-traumatic stress disorder (PTSD) [1].

Schliefer and Ley [17] investigated the effect of computer data entry compared to baseline relaxed periods. They found that breath rate increased 26% during data entry and that subjects exhibited decreased heart rate variability (HRV) and increased self-ratings of tension. The differences were comparable to those linking threats of electric shock or anxiety of students before an exam with differences in respiration [17].

For our purposes, the most salient finding from studies investigating breath regulation is that reducing (some claim simply regulating [10, 1]) breath rate activates the parasympathetic nervous system (PNS), the so-called 'rest-and-digest' response, to relax the body, reducing stress and anxiety.

To date, technology-mediated respiration pacing has required the user to stop their current task and focus their full attention on the pacing. However, humans can "regulate their respiration rates in a relatively short time period" [1], making breath regulation a viable treatment for sporadic and subtle stressors such as those that may be encountered during the frequent task switching of information work.

We investigate methods of integrating respiration-pacing techniques into the desktop computing environment to enable *peripheral paced respiration* (PPR). Such a system would allow users to engage in other tasks while regulating breath, increasing its accessibility and frequency. To that end, this paper makes two contributions. The first is a peripheral visual feedback technique to influence respiration of a desktop user. The second is the results of a study evaluating the effects of PPR compared to a control condition lacking visual feedback.

RELATED WORK

Practitioners use various methods to entrain or pace respiration that fall generally into two categories: (1) consciously controlling their respiration or (2) entraining the breath to an external stimulus such as a visual animation [7, 19], a light in binary states for inhalation and exhalation [7], ambient lighting [1], or metronome [16]. In the second category, the choice of stimulus can lead to ambiguity about the length of each inhalation and exhalation. Methods with binary states (*e.g.*, when will the light turn off?) or brightness (*e.g.*, what is maximal brightness?) do not clearly indicate the end point of the current inhalation or exhalation.

Some end-user tools have emerged that aim to complement voluntary breath regulation. Resperate [16] uses auditory tones to guide relaxed breathing to reduce blood pressure. MyBreath [11] infers respiratory pattern from microphone input as the user breathes into their mobile phone. Pranayama [14] guides the user's breath during meditation with both visual animation of a pie chart being filled alongside auditory tones for inhalation and exhalation.

Existing respiration-pacing tools are *modal*: they require the focused attention of the user. Given the demonstrated ease with which users can entrain their breath to visual stimuli, we propose using short but frequent pacing sessions that are *peripheral*, allowing the user to engage in other tasks while concurrently pacing their respiration.

Breath rate (breaths per min, or bpm) is calculated by the number of times the chest rises (inhalations) in a minute. Breath rate, like heart rate, changes frequently even in a resting state [9]. It is affected by arousal, talking, posture, personal health, and other factors. There is no standard resting human breath rate; studies have found it to be between 12-20bpm for adults [9, 18]. There are different perspectives on what an optimal target breath rate should be. Song and Lehrer found a general optimal range of 4-6bpm is correlated with the greatest HRV and that HRV generally increases as breath rate decreases [20]. Stark, *et al.* showed that a target rate too different from one's resting breath rate requires greater attention and effort [1].

Peripheral pacing requires continuous monitoring and a medium for intermittent biofeedback. Only recently has the technology has become available to do continuous ambulatory monitoring (cf. Picard *et al.* [12]). To our knowledge, the work here is the first instance of peripheral respiration pacing being integrated directly into the desktop.

Picard and her colleagues describe *affective computing* as "computing that relates to, arises from, or deliberately influences emotion or other affective phenomena" [12]. Work in this genre attempts to create technology that adapts to, measures, or communicates the user's affective state [15]. Complementing this approach, our research attempts to influence the physiological factors underlying affective response.

A PERIPHERAL PACED RESPIRATION INTERFACE

Our design goal was to evaluate the feasibility of peripherally regulating the respiration of a desktop computer user. Such a system requires two functions: (1) sensing user respiration and (2) feedback to pace the respiration across computing tasks.

Respiration Sensor

There are a number of possible techniques for sensing user respiration (a review is available in [1]). Beyond methods enumerated in that review, researchers have used features extracted from video of a user's face, with [1] or without [13] thermal cameras.

As our focus is on pacing respiration, not non-invasive sensor design, we chose to build a sensor using off-the-shelf components. We measure changes in thoracic circumference, a robust and straightforward measure of respiration

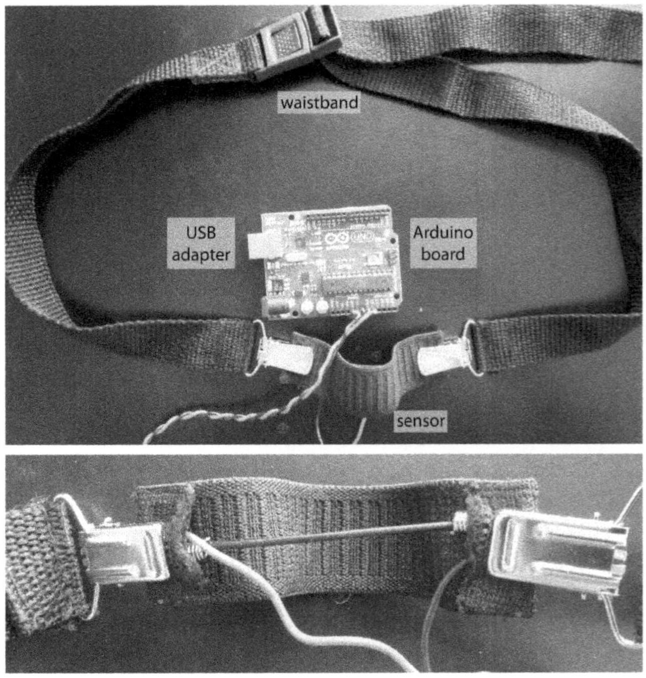

Figure 1: (Top) The adjustable sensor band with the Arduino *Uno* board. (Bottom) Close-up of the stretch sensor held in place by two clips.

for healthy individuals (*i.e.*, those without apnea or obstructed airways) who are not moving a great deal. We use a single strap to sense breath rate. Such a sensor could be built into clothing or undergarments and does not require direct contact with the skin.

Our sensor (shown in Figure 1) uses a standard 2" cylindrical strain gauge attached to a canvas belt whose length can be adjusted with a common clip. The strain gauge works by changing resistance when stretched. Each end of the sensor is connected to an Arduino *Uno*, which in turn is connected to the computer using USB. The sampling frequency is 20Hz (50ms) plus a small variable error from reading serial data (~2ms), making it near-real-time.

Wizard-of-Oz Prototype

We first created a Wizard-of-Oz prototyping tool to assess qualitative reactions to different forms of feedback. The researcher would sit behind the user as they worked at their desk and we would manually observe the user's breathe rate due to chest rises. They would approximate the rate and input it using a slider onto a web form. The pacing prototype installed on the user's computer read this data from the webpage and updated its current user breath rate accordingly.

An important early consideration was whether feedback should be integrated into a specific application (e.g., programming IDE, web browser, or productivity software) or system wide. Because information work involves multiple applications, we opted for the latter.

We used visual pacing because information workers often listen to music and work in social areas. The first prototype used the common method of a pulsing circle atop other windows in the top-right screen corner as pacing stimulus.

Using this prototyping method on ourselves and with several users in our lab, we found two primary issues. First, though seemingly useful, real-time feedback regarding one's breath rate is highly distracting, as users frequently check the accuracy of the detected rate. Second, the rate of the pulsing circle was not noticeable when users were deeply engaged in their work, even when we exaggerated the pulse rate.

User Interface

The final design does not require any mouse- or keyboard-based interaction and does not require researcher interaction. We implemented three pacing techniques and a calibration mode. 'Screen Dim Feedback' sets the pacing stimuli to dim the entire screen from near-black to maximum brightness at the target rate. 'Menu Dim Feedback' does the same but only to the Mac OS menu bar. 'Bounce Feedback' uses an animated horizontal bar to pace respiration (see below). The calibration mode option toggles the display of a gray bar whose y-position is controlled in near real-time by the resistance of the stretch sensor. In calibration mode, the user can determine if the gray bar is indeed moving up and down as they breathe or if the band requires tightening or repositioning.

Pacing Respiration Peripherally

We implemented and tested a pulsing light technique, two dimming techniques (screen and menu bar) and one object animation technique. We chose the animation technique because it is recommended to biofeedback practitioners [7] and performed best in our early tests: users could identify clear end points to inhalation and exhalation in their periphery.

The object animation technique (Figure 2) works by moving a screen-wide, semi-translucent grey bar up and down across the screen, representing inhalation (up) and exhalation (down). The ratio of up to down is 1:1. Slow-in and slow-out animation [6] is used to provide smooth movements and aid tracking. The bar moves across the lower third of the screen to reduce both distraction and distance travelled (using the full screen height would require a fast and distracting animation).

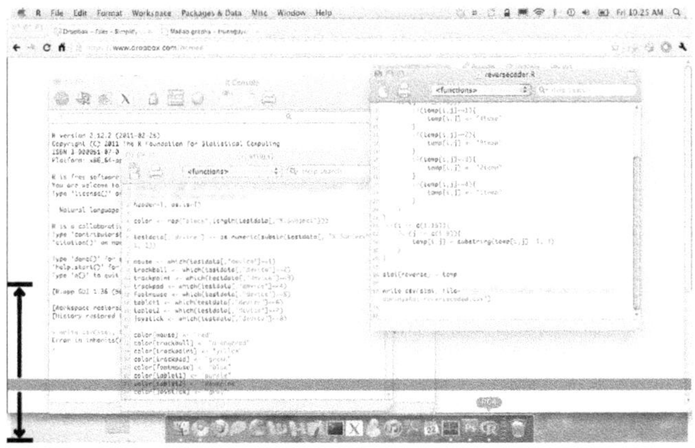

Figure 2: The peripheral paced respiration feedback used an animated, semi-translucent grey bar stretching across the screen. Vertical arrows on the left indicate the full range of motion.

Each user's target breath rate is set relative to an individual resting baseline, rather than a universal target that might require too much effort [1]. The target rate is set to 20% below their baseline to exaggerate the slow rhythm of resting breath.

The software continuously samples sensor data and determines when to display visual feedback. If the user's current breath rate is 20% above their resting rate, pacing is triggered. The software will also automatically trigger pacing at least once every six minutes. Similar to prior studies, we use a 2-minute duration [2, 19]. After each pacing period (during which the user is expected to be able to carry on with existing work), a score is calculated. The score (displayed in the menu bar) is the normalized sum of the percent difference between user and target breath rates over that 2-minute period.

We conducted an experiment to evaluate the efficacy and feasibility of using a PPR system to pace users' respiration to a resting rate while authentically engaged in information work.

EXPERIMENT

Our experiment was designed to determine if PPR influences user respiration across computing tasks in a naturalistic manner. We recruited participants who had existing work to do (e.g. research, programming, writing). We recruited thirteen university students (9 male, 4 female, mean age=25.5 yrs) from computer science and related disciplines to participate. We told them they could conduct their existing work during the experiment. We wanted participants to be genuinely engaged and to work naturally (i.e., switch windows and tasks as they normally do). Participants were not compensated. According to our post-study questionnaire, no participants had existing respiratory conditions.

We conducted a counterbalanced, within-subjects experiment in which participants were exposed to two conditions: (1) no feedback and (2) PPR feedback. As a control, participants wore the respiration sensor in both conditions.

Procedure

Participants first wore the sensor band and the administrator tightened it. They were told that the sensor measures their respiration. A short calibration period ensured the band was positioned accurately. Participants sat in a chair in front of their laptops, working alone and not speaking. Their posture was not controlled, again to ensure a naturalistic testing environment. Hence, they were allowed to lean backwards and forwards in the chair, which can have an effect on respiration rate [19].

Participants first completed a pre-survey and consent form. As in prior studies [8], participants were then asked to close their eyes for 3-minutes and relax. Unbeknownst to participants, baseline data was collected during this relaxation period. Three participants did not take part in the relaxation period; their baseline was recorded as they completed a pre-survey.

After recording the baseline, the experiment began with the participant being told they could start working on their own tasks. They were also told that when the gray bar appeared, it represents their *target* breath rate.

To guarantee that pacing would occur at least three times during the PPR condition (at least once every six minutes), the duration of each condition was 20 minutes. When activated, PPR occurred for 2 minutes.

RESULTS

The raw respiration signal, filtered signal, and detected peaks (i.e., inhalation endpoints) are shown over a period of 30 seconds in Figure 3. Breath rate (bpm) is calculated by counting the number of inhalations in one minute. Due to the presence of high-frequency noise, we smoothed the signal using a Hanning window. The window width is selected based on a reasonable maximum breath rate of 40bpm. The peaks are detected by comparing the value of each data point in the filtered signal to data points taken immediately before and after that point. The breath rate is then calculated based on the number of peaks in a 30sec interval proceeding that time.

Consistent with prior studies, the mean breath rate across conditions was 16.67bpm (SD=4.28) and the breath rate of the relaxation period baseline was 9.33bpm (SD=5.31).

Figure 4 (top) shows the mean for each condition with 95% confidence intervals. We conducted a paired t-test to compare the means of each condition. We found a significant difference between no-feedback (M=17.58, SD=4.18) and PPR (M=15.7, SD=4.49) conditions; $t(12)= 3.83$, $p<0.005$. The mean difference between conditions was 1.8bpm.

Figure 4 (bottom) shows the mean breath rate during the PPR condition when PPR was active or inactive. We conducted a paired t-test to compare the means between when PPR was activated (M=14.96, SD=4.44) and when it was not (M=17.09, SD=5.25); t(12)=t3.5647, $p<0.005$. The mean difference was 2.13bpm. The mean proportion of time that the feedback was activated was 0.60 (SD=0.14).

We also conducted a paired t-test to compare the breath rate in the PPR condition when feedback was unavailable (M=17.09, SD=5.25) and the breath rate during the no-

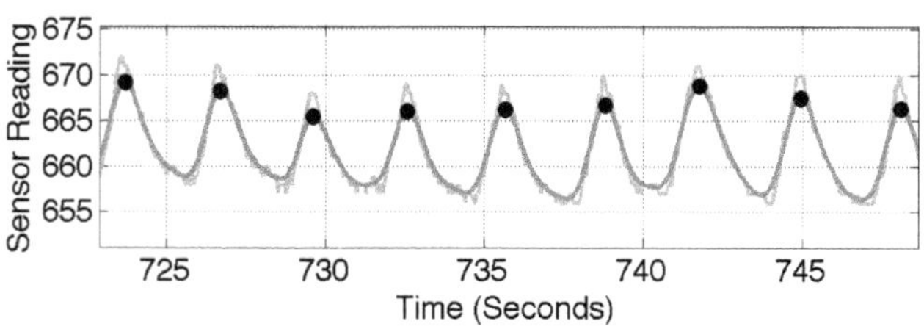

Figure 3: The raw signal (red), shown filtered (blue) and with peaks (black) detected.

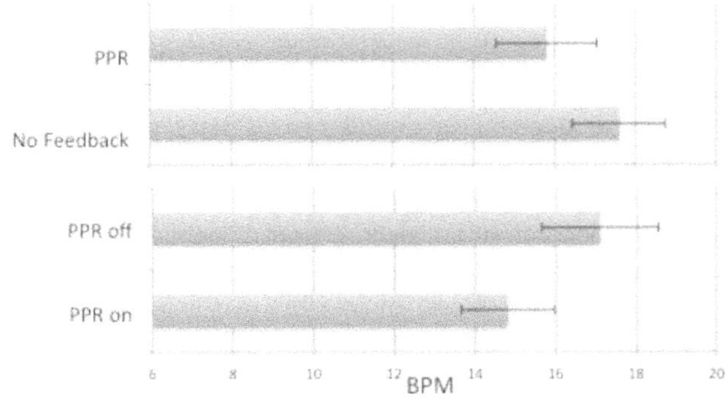

Figure 4: (Top) Mean breath rate for the No Feedback and PPR conditions with standard error bars. (Bottom) Mean breath rate during the PPR condition when PPR was on and off.

feedback condition (M=17.58, SD=4.18); t(12)=0.989, $p>0.05$. When feedback was not present, breath rates returned to their working rates.

To illustrate how the breath rate is impacted by PPR, Figure 5 depicts the breath rate of one participant in each of the conditions. The no-feedback condition (top) shows a relatively consistent, high breath rate. While PPR was active (bottom) the breath rate decreased.

Using Likert scales from 1 to 5, participants rated the 'annoyingness' of PPR 2.0 (SD=0.87). Concerning how much it adversely affected productivity, PPR was rated 2.2 (SD=0.6). Lastly, participants gave a score of 3.7 (SD=1.0) as to how likely they would be to use the software all day long while working, were the sensor non-invasive.

DISCUSSION AND FUTURE WORK

Our hypothesis that PPR influences user respiration while engaged in naturalistic tasks is supported; the peripheral feedback reduced breath rate significantly. The 1.9bpm difference is close to the 2bpm interval changes shown by Song and Lehrer to correspond with significantly higher heart rate variability amplitude [20].

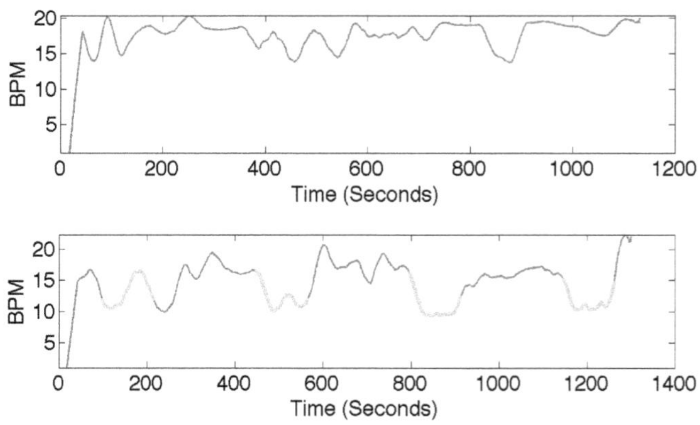

Figure 5: Breath rate for one participant in both no feedback (top) and PPR (bottom) conditions. Bold (orange) areas indicate where PPR occurred.

Breath rates were observed to return to working levels between pacing instances. Hence, there was no evidence of persistent rate change. This is a viable area for future study; cues, social feedback, and game mechanics, among other methods, could help motivate users to maintain low respiratory rates as they work.

Based on self-report data, PPR feedback was not too distracting and participants expressed motivation to use PPR for sustained periods in the future. The results motivate longitudinal research that attempts to motivate, trigger, or incentivize users to pace their respiration even when pacing is not active. This allows for long-term respiration pacing that could complement existing methods of respiratory habit-change. The pacing algorithm could factor in the physiological and work history of the user. Such 'context-sensitive biofeedback' could be used to influence the physiological factors underlying cognition, and affect.

Quantitative measures of the level of distraction caused by PPR (such as working while pacing) were not collected in this study. Further, the PPR method used goes beyond breath rate and implicitly proposes time and duration for inhalation and exhalation, which is beyond our goals and may have required greater effort than is necessary. This presents an opportunity for future work to identify the optimal balance between pacing efficacy and distraction.

As a tertiary contribution, to our knowledge this study is the first to quantify the effect of naturalistic information work on respiration rate. In our case, resting breath rate was almost half the working rate. This result highlights the issue of mild but chronic stress that occurs during information work, and again recommends longitudinal studies.

CONCLUSION

This paper presented the design of a peripheral paced respiration technique and evaluated its efficacy in a naturalistic task environment. We found that peripheral pacing significantly reduces breath rate, but these changes are not sustained for the duration of the tasks. The results motivate further research on incorporating biofeedback and physiological training into the operating system to complement long durations of information work, hopefully reducing users' stress and tension.

REFERENCES

1. Al-Khalidi, F., Saatchi, R., Burke, D., Elphick, H., Tan, S. (2011). Respiration rate monitoring methods: A review. *Pediatric Pulmonology*, Wiley-Liss, Inc.
2. Bloch, S., Lemeignan, M., Aguilera, N. (1991). Specific respiratory patterns distinguish among human basic emotions. *Intl Journal of Psychophysiology*, 11.
3. Clark, M. & Hirschman, R. (1990). Effects of paced respiration on anxiety reduction in a clinical population. *Biofeedback and Self-Regulation*, 15.
4. Cooper S., Oborne J. (2003). Effect of two breathing exercises (Buteyko and pranayama) in asthma: a randomised controlled trial. *Thorax* 58 (8).
5. Grossman, E., Grossman, A., Schein, M., Zimlichman, R., Gavish, B. (2001). Breathing-control lowers blood pressure. *Journal of Human Hypertension.*
6. Lasseter, J. (1987). Principles of Traditional Animation applied to 3D Computer Animation. *ACM SIGGRAPH.*
7. Lehrer, P. M., Vaschillo, E., & Vaschillo, B. (2000). Resonant frequency biofeedback training to increase cardiac variability: Rationale and manual for training. *Appl. Psyc & Biofdbk*, 25.
8. Ley, R., Yelich, G. (1998). End-tidal CO2 as an index of the effects of stress on math performance and verbal memory of test-anxious adolescents. *Biological Psychology*, 49.
9. Ley, R. (1999). The Modification of Breathing Behavior: Pavlovian and Operant Control in Emotion and Cognition. *Behavior Modification.* Vol. 23, No. 3.
10. McCaul, K., Solomon, S., Holmes, D. (1979). Effects of Paced Respiration and Expectations on Physiological and Psychological Responses to Threat. *Journal of Personality and Social Psychology*, Vol. 37, No. 4.
11. MyBreath iPhone app. http://BreathResearch.com
12. Picard, R. Affective computing. http://affect.media.mit.edu
13. Poh, M.Z., McDuff, D.J., Picard, R. (2010). Non-contact, automated cardiac pulse measurements using video imaging and blind source separation. *Optics Express*, Vol. 18, no. 10.
14. Pranayama iPhone application. http://Saagara.com
15. Puri, C., Olson, L., Pavlidis, I., Levine, J., Starren. J. (2005). StressCam: non-contact measurement of users' emotional states through thermal imaging. *ACM CHI EA*, NY, NY.
16. Schein, M., *et al.* (2001). Treating hypertension with a device that slows and regularizes breathing: A randomised, double-blind controlled study. *Journal of Human Hypertension*, 15.
17. Schleifer, L., & Ley, R. (1994). End-tidal pCO2 as an index of psychophysiological activity during data-entry work and relaxation. *Ergonomics*, 37.
18. Sherwood, L. (2006). Fundamentals of Physiology: A Human Perspective, *Thomson Brooks/Cole*, ISBN 0534466974
19. Sisto, S.A., Tapp, W., Drastal, S., Bergen, M., DeMasi, I., Cordero, D., Natelson, B. (1995). Vagal tone is reduced during paced breathing in patients with the chronic fatigue syndrome. *Clinical Autonomic Research* 5.
20. Song, H., Lehrer, P. (2003). The Effects of Specific Respiratory Rates on Heart Rate Variability. *Applied Psychophysiology and Biofeedback.* Vol. 28, No. 1.
21. Stark, R., Schnienle, A., Walter, B., Vatil, D. (2000). Effects of paced respiration on heart period and heart period variability. *Psychophysiology.* 37.
22. Zucker, T., et al. (2009). The Effects of Respiratory Sinus Arrhythmia Biofeedback on Heart Rate Variability and PTSD Symptoms: A Pilot Study. *Appl. Psychophysio Biofeedback.*

Sex, Food, and Words: The Hidden Meanings Behind Everyday Language

Dan Jurafsky
Stanford University
jurafsky@stanford.edu

ABSTRACT
Language is a subtle and powerful tool for communication. But the words we use also provide a rich mine of information for the social scientist. The history of words like *ketchup*, *ceviche*, or *dessert* tells us about the relationships between the superpowers who dominated the globe 500 or 1000 years ago. The words on the back of potato chip packages can demonstrate popular attitudes toward social class. And the names we give ice cream f avors may be an evolutionary ref ex of the attempt by early mammals to appear larger than their competitors. The language of dating is just as informative as the language of food. In experiments with speed dating, work in our lab shows that we can detect f irtation or other stances in men and women on dates, just by looking at linguistic features like their pitch, their use of negative words like *can't* or *don't*, or how often they use hedges like *sort of* or *kind of*. The language of these two popular topics of conversation, food and dating, can teach us a lot about history, culture, and psychology.

General Terms
Human Factors

Author Keywords
Food, dating, language

ACM Classif cation Keywords
J.4 Computer Applications: Social and Behavioral Sciences.

BIOGRAPHY
Dan Jurafsky is Professor of Linguistics and Professor by Courtesy of Computer Science at Stanford University. Dan received a B.A in Linguistics in 1983 and a Ph.D. in Computer Science in 1992, both from the University of California at Berkeley, and also taught at the University of Colorado, Boulder. He is the recipient of a MacArthur Fellowship, and is the co-author with Jim Martin of the widely-used textbook "Speech and Language Processing". His research focuses on language understanding and applications of NLP to the behavioral and social sciences. Other research interests include the linguistics of Chinese and the linguistics of food.

UIST'11, October 16–19, 2011, Santa Barbara, California, USA.
ACM 978-1-4503-1014-7/11/10.

SideBySide: Ad-hoc Multi-user Interaction with Handheld Projectors

Karl D.D. Willis [1,2] *Ivan Poupyrev* [1] *Scott E. Hudson* [3,1] *Moshe Mahler* [1]

[1] Disney Research Pittsburgh
4720 Forbes Avenue
Pittsburgh, PA 15213
{karl, ivan.poupyrev, moshe.mahler}
@disneyresearch.com

[2] Computational Design Lab, [3] HCI Institute &
Heinz College Center for the Future of Work,
Carnegie Mellon University
5000 Forbes Avenue,
Pittsburgh, PA 15213
scott.hudson@cs.cmu.edu

ABSTRACT

We introduce *SideBySide*, a system designed for ad-hoc multi-user interaction with handheld projectors. *SideBySide* uses device-mounted cameras and hybrid visible/infrared light projectors to track multiple independent projected images in relation to one another. This is accomplished by projecting invisible fiducial markers in the near-infrared spectrum. Our system is completely self-contained and can be deployed as a handheld device without instrumentation of the environment. We present the design and implementation of our system including a hybrid handheld projector to project visible and infrared light, and techniques for tracking projected fiducial markers that move and overlap. We introduce a range of example applications that demonstrate the applicability of our system to real-world scenarios such as mobile content exchange, gaming, and education.

ACM Classification: H5.2 [Information interfaces and presentation]: User Interfaces.

General terms: Design, Human Factors, Experimentation

Keywords: Interaction techniques, handheld projector, pico projector, multi-user, ad hoc interaction, games.

INTRODUCTION

Handheld computing devices have become a ubiquitous part of modern life. They allow us to communicate, retrieve, and record information at any time, view digital content on the go, and play games in any location. Interaction with handheld computing devices, however, remains a largely solitary, single user experience. Today's devices do not typically provide interfaces and supporting technologies for co-located multi-user work, learning, and play – crucial elements of human interactions in the real world.

Our research is motivated by the vision of handheld computing devices that allow users to dynamically interact with each other in shared interactive spaces. Handheld projectors are an enabling technology that could realize this vision. They are sufficiently small to be grasped in a single hand, and light enough to be moved from place to place. Multiple users can project digital content directly into the physical environment. The relatively large size of projected images allows them to be easily seen by multiple users, making them a particularly natural fit for co-located multi-user interaction (e.g. Figure 1).

Figure 1: Interacting with the *SideBySide* system.

There has been rapidly growing interest in handheld projectors from both the industry and research communities [17,18], however, most work has focused on single user applications [e.g. 1]. Although there has been some work exploring the potential of handheld projectors for multi-user interaction [2,7], these systems require instrumentation of the surrounding environment with often complex sensing infrastructure. This significantly reduces the usefulness of multi-user handheld projection systems in any real world scenario where user mobility is required. We are unaware of any system allowing multiple handheld projectors to interact together without instrumenting the environment.

We present *SideBySide*, a system designed for ad-hoc multi-user interaction with handheld projectors. *SideBySide* does not require instrumentation of the environment and can be used almost anywhere. It uses a device-mounted infrared (IR) camera and a novel hybrid visible/IR light handheld projector. The *SideBySide* software platform tracks multiple independent projected images in relation to one another using invisible fiducial markers projected in the near-IR spectrum. The resulting system allows a broad range of new interaction scenarios where users are not tied to a fixed location. Exchanging digital content, such as personal contact information or media files, can be initiated without any infrastructure. Multiple users can play projected games together by creating ad-hoc gaming spaces. Interaction scenarios for education allow teachers and students to study together using a shared information space. Most importantly, these interaction scenarios can happen anywhere – in an elevator up to a business meeting, in a child's bedroom after lights out, or in the hallway outside a classroom.

We present the following contributions:

1. We outline the design and implementation of our hardware system, including a hybrid handheld projector unit that projects both visible and IR light.
2. We introduce our software system for tracking multiple projected images in relation to one another with invisible fiducial markers. In particular we present techniques for tracking overlapping fiducial markers and optical communication between devices.
3. We present a range of applications that demonstrate the exciting and engaging multi-user interaction scenarios possible with the *SideBySide* system.

RELATED WORK

Research related to the *SideBySide* system can be divided primarily into three categories: projector-based augmented spaces, multi-user handheld projector systems, and invisible marker tracking.

Projector-Based Augmented Spaces

An important aspect of multi-user interaction is extending interaction beyond a single user's screen and into the environment. Rekimoto's *Pick-and-Drop* system defined interaction techniques to support data transfer between multiple computers and handheld devices [15]. The *Augmented Surfaces* project later established a direct spatial relationship between laptop screen content and content projected onto nearby surfaces [16].

The use of arbitrary surfaces for content projection was explored with the *Everywhere Displays Projector* [14] to augment indoor spaces with projected content at any location using a steerable projector. The *Play Anywhere* system used a portable short-throw projector to create interactive tabletop experiences with handheld devices and tangible objects [27]. The *Bonfire* system also offered a portable form-factor to extend the desktop computing experience onto the tabletop using several handheld projectors mounted on the back of a notebook computer [8].

These projects highlight the potential for projected content to enhance the user experience by operating beyond the bounds of a single display. They are however, designed for use in a stationary position and are not suitable for use when moving between different locations. The recent emergence of handheld projectors offers a lightweight solution for unbounded mobile interaction.

Multi-user Handheld Projector Systems

Early pre-cinema use of handheld projectors stems from the development of the *Magic Lantern* in 17th century Europe and its later adaption in Japan for the *Utsushi-e* performance [25]. This performance involved small wooden slide projectors used from behind a large rice paper screen to act out a story for an audience. Multiple performers would coordinate their movement to change the size and location of projected images. This enabled the creation of relatively complex real-time animation in the pre-cinema era. This important pre-history of handheld projector-based interaction underlines the potential for multiple small projectors to interact together in a seamless way.

The relatively large public displays created by modern handheld projectors make them ideal for multi-user interaction scenarios. Sugimoto et.al. created a mockup system where two overlapping projection screens were used with a PDA touch screen to initialize file transfer between devices [21]. An exhaustive range of multi-user interaction techniques were developed by Cao et.al. using a motion capture system for location tracking [2]. These interactions focus on operations within a virtual workspace, such as content ownership, transfer, viewing, and docking.

Multi-user games have also been developed that allow users to work together to reach a goal. Hosoi et.al. developed a multi-user handheld projector game for guiding a small robot along a projected path [7]. Users line up pieces of track for the robot to follow and reach its goal. Cao et.al. developed a multi-user jigsaw game where users would pick up and place pieces of a puzzle together [3].

To enable interaction between multiple handheld projectors, these systems rely on infrastructure being added to the environment. This ranges from a fixed camera above the interaction area [7], to a professional motion capture system [2]. Relying on fixed infrastructure within the environment severely limits where handheld projectors can be used, substantially limiting their mobility. Our vision is to enable multiple users to interact side-by-side, anywhere, in any space. This is one of the main design considerations for this research, and one that strongly differentiates our technical solution from past work.

Invisible Marker Tracking

Fiducial markers have been used widely for location tracking due to their lightweight, robust performance. A well-known issue with structured, 2D barcode-style fiducial markers is their unnatural appearance that users cannot read or understand. Barcode style markers are difficult to integrate into the design of interactive systems due to their fixed aesthetic and form-factor that is intolerant to changes in color, shape, or material.

To address these concerns numerous systems have been

developed to disguise or hide fiducial markers from the user. Custom marker patterns have been developed that are disguised to look like wallpaper [19], markers have been created with invisible inks for use with IR cameras [13], retro-reflective markers have been used together with IR cameras and lights [11], temporal sequencing of markers has been used with projectors and high speed cameras [6], structured pattern style markers have been projected with IR lasers [9,24], and several systems have been developed using IR projection from a fixed projector in either pure IR [5,20,23] or with hybrid IR/visible light [10].

Natural marker detection techniques have also been developed to detect imagery and objects based on their natural features without any structured marker pattern [12]. However, natural marker detection typically requires time consuming training for each object and is computationally expensive when compared to structured marker detection.

To track the movement of handheld projectors we developed a handheld projector that can project both invisible fiducial markers in the near-IR spectrum as well as content in the visible spectrum. As noted above, this has previously been accomplished using a fixed projector, but we are unaware of any system implementing IR projection in a handheld form-factor. The smaller form-factor and portability of handheld projectors introduces a number of new considerations for IR marker tracking with multiple users, where markers constantly move and can frequently overlap.

SIDEBYSIDE APPROACH

Our approach is guided by the vision of multiple users playing and interacting with each other using handheld projection devices (Figure 2). Key to this vision is interaction that can happen anywhere, at any time, in a fluid, spur-of-the-moment fashion. Users should be able to establish and break off interaction in a natural and transparent manner. Standing side-by-side and projecting images into the same space should be sufficient to establish immediate communication between devices and initiate interaction. Figure 3 shows the fundamental system design and technology solution we propose to realize this vision. Two requirements guide the development of our system: on-device sensing and lightweight communication.

On-device Sensing

We chose to embed all sensing on the projection device itself. Prior instrumentation of the environment, either with passive or active sensing infrastructure, should not be necessary. Each of our projection devices is equipped with a camera, an inertial measurement unit (IMU), a ranging sensor, and a push button (Figure 6).

A key requirement of any projector based multi-user interaction scenario is accurate registration of moving images projected from different devices. Each device must understand what other devices are projecting and where they are projecting it. We use on-board cameras to accurately track the position and orientation of moving projected images relative to each other.

Figure 2: The *SideBySide* concept – a self-contained, full color, handheld projection device allowing multi-user interaction in almost any space.

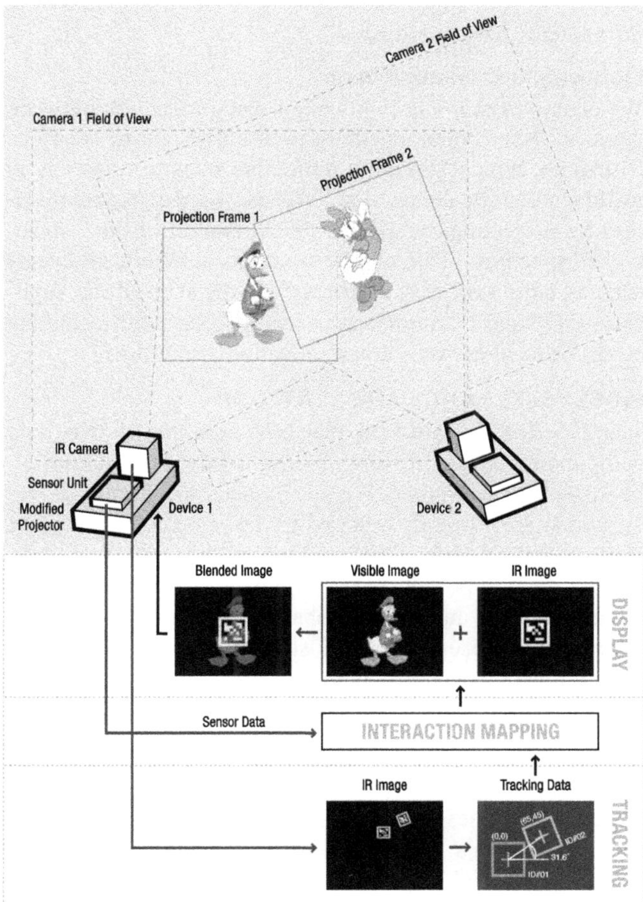

Figure 3: The *SideBySide* system overview.

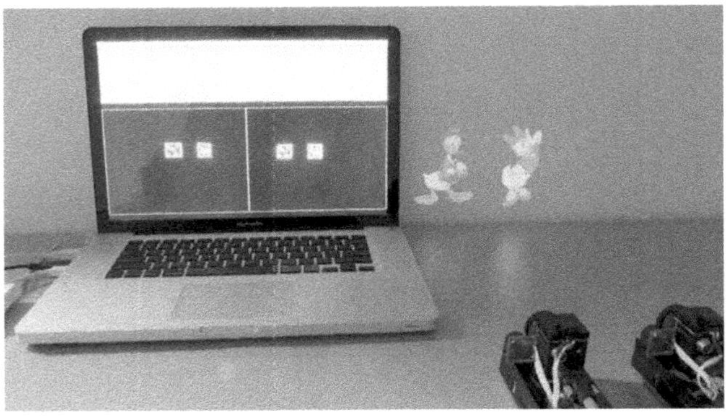

Figure 4: Projecting visible and IR images in a single stream. The characters are visible to the user, and the markers are visible to the IR camera.

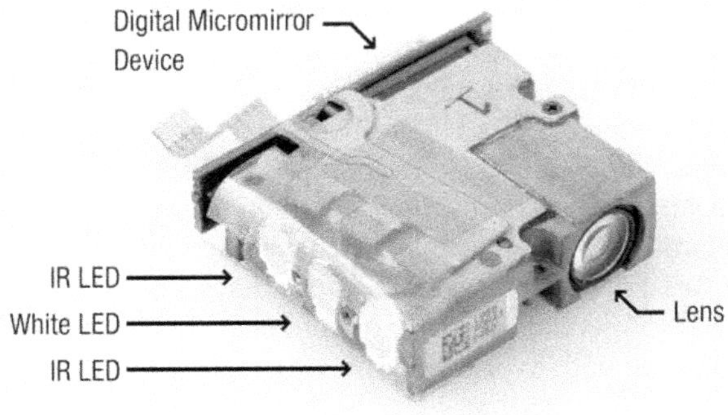

Figure 5: A DLP pico projector engine was modified to project both IR and visible light.

Because tracking visible projected images restricts the type of content that can be projected, we track invisible fiducial markers projected from the handheld projection device (Figure 3 and 4). To achieve this we modify the light sources of a handheld projector to add an IR projection channel. This allows independent visible and invisible content to be combined in a single projected light stream. An on-board IR sensitive camera constantly identifies and tracks the position and orientation of all fiducial markers projected. This data is then used to drive interactive applications. No tracking data is visible to the user, creating a fluid interaction experience.

Lightweight Communication

We enable instant and lightweight communication between devices. Other communication protocols, such as Wi-Fi or Bluetooth, typically require numerous steps to establish an explicit network connection. We use optical communication by projecting symbolic fiducial markers in the invisible IR spectrum. This can be used to communicate events such as button presses, or changes in the state of the application. Optical communication can also be used to initiate other forms of network communication as required.

SIDEBYSIDE HARDWARE PLATFORM

The *SideBySide* hardware platform consists of two core components: a hybrid IR/visible light projector and an on-board sensor assembly. We developed two prototype devices that are currently tethered to the same computer. This greatly simplified the development and evaluation of *SideBySide*. It is important to stress, however, that there is no communication and no data shared between devices – all interaction is based on locally sensed data. Our techniques and applications can therefore be implemented as a standalone handheld device in the future.

Hybrid IR/Visible Light Projector

We modified an off-the-shelf Optoma PK102 handheld projector that uses the Texas Instruments DLP pico chipset (dlp.com/pico), a commonly used light engine found in many commercial handheld projectors. Its optical assembly consists of three high power LED light sources emitting red, green and blue light. We replaced the red and green LEDs with equivalent IR LEDs (Osram SFH4232), allowing us to project an IR image without modifying the projector optics (Figure 5). Two IR LEDs create a sufficiently bright image to be used for marker tracking with the on-board IR camera.

The remaining green LED was replaced with an equivalent white LED (Osram LUWW5AM) to produce a brighter visible projected image. Due to the properties of the projector's optical assembly, undisclosed by the manufacturer, the projected visible image changes to a light green color. To provide the white LED with sufficient voltage (3.2V), we connect it to the blue LED power source that has the highest source voltage (~2.92V). The red and green power sources (~1.6V & ~2.5V respectively) are used with the IR LEDs that have lower voltage requirements (1.5V).

Although our prototype restricts the working color palette to monotone, our aim was not to engineer an entirely new projection device but to evaluate the feasibility of projected IR markers for tracking and registration. Designing a full RGBIR (Red, Green, Blue, Infrared) pico-projector can be achieved by numerous manufacturers, and is therefore beyond the scope of our current work.

On-board Sensor Assembly

We equipped our handheld projector with a PointGrey Flea3 (www.ptgrey.com) IR-sensitive black and white camera mounted above the projector (Figure 6). We use an IR pass filter to cut visible light from the camera image and avoid interference with fiducial marker tracking in the IR spectrum. The camera is fitted with a fixed focal length 3mm wide-angle lens that is mounted directly above the projector lens for optimal optical alignment.

We enable gestural interaction using an IMU with a three-axis accelerometer, gyroscope, and magnetometer. It enables us to measure absolute orientation of the device, as well as relative acceleration and angular velocity. An ultrasonic ranging sensor is used to determine the distance to the projection surface. Because the projected image is much brighter when the device is closer to the projection surface, the ranging sensor allows us to dynamically adjust the image threshold level for more robust marker recognition.

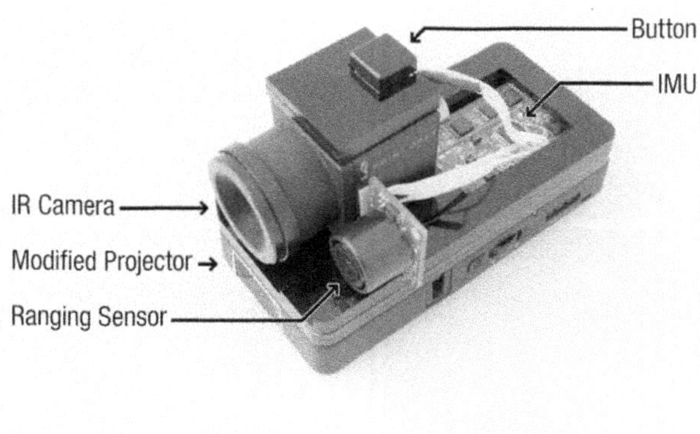

Figure 6: The *SideBySide* prototype with IR/visible light projector and an on-board sensor assembly.

The size of our prototype allows a user to hold and manipulate the device with a single hand. Because the system does not require any additional instrumentation of the environment, the device can be self-contained and reduced in size significantly. Many of the individual components used in our prototype can be found in current generation mobile devices. A compact and relatively inexpensive commercial implementation of our platform is very much possible.

SIDEBYSIDE SOFTWARE PLATFORM

The *SideBySide* software platform provides functionality to combine visible and IR imagery, track and register projected images using fiducial markers, resolve overlapping fiducial markers, and optically communicate arbitrary information between devices. In this section we discuss implementation details of the software platform.

Combining Visible and Infrared Imagery

To project an invisible image in the near-IR spectrum we load a monotone image into the red and green channels of an OpenGL frame buffer. The visible image is loaded from a separate monotone image into the blue channel (Figure 3) using OpenGL's additive blending mode. This combines the channels in real time using the graphics processing unit. Ghosting between channels, i.e. leaking from the IR channel into the visible channel (or vice versa), can be resolved by setting the system display color profile to 'generic RGB'. This allows the projection of clean, separate images in the visible and IR spectrums. Our approach can scale up to work with a full RGBIR image, where the IR channel is handled in a similar way to how alpha channels are used to specify transparency.

Tracking and Registration of Projected Images

To enable multi-user interaction with handheld projectors, each device must know the spatial relationship between its projected image and others nearby. To determine these spatial relationships we have developed tracking and registration techniques using invisible projected fiducial markers.

Each device projects a unique, static, 'reference' marker in the center of its projection frame. The on-board camera has a larger field of view than the projection frame, so it can observe markers from multiple devices (Figure 3). Each device firstly observes its own reference marker, then observes markers projected by other devices, next it determines the location and orientation of each marker in relation to its own marker, and finally estimates the size and orientation of the projection frames.

Our current implementation uses the *ARToolkitPlus* library [22] for marker tracking. A one-time calculation of the intrinsic camera parameters and homography matrix is performed to correct for lens distortion (Figure 7a). Once we have registered the markers in camera coordinates (Figure 7b), we remap them to the projector coordinate system. Remapping is based on the location of the projected marker in the scene and the scale ratio between the original pixel size of the projected marker and the size of the same marker observed by the camera. This process provides us with spatial information in the coordinate system used to design interactions and display graphics (Figure 7c).

Overlapping Markers

In multi-user interaction scenarios with handheld projectors, two projection frames often overlap. This can be accidental or an essential element of the interaction. For example, Cao et.al. used overlapping images for file transfer and magic-lens style navigation of large images [2]. Robust tracking of overlapping projected markers is therefore a key requirement for the *SideBySide* system.

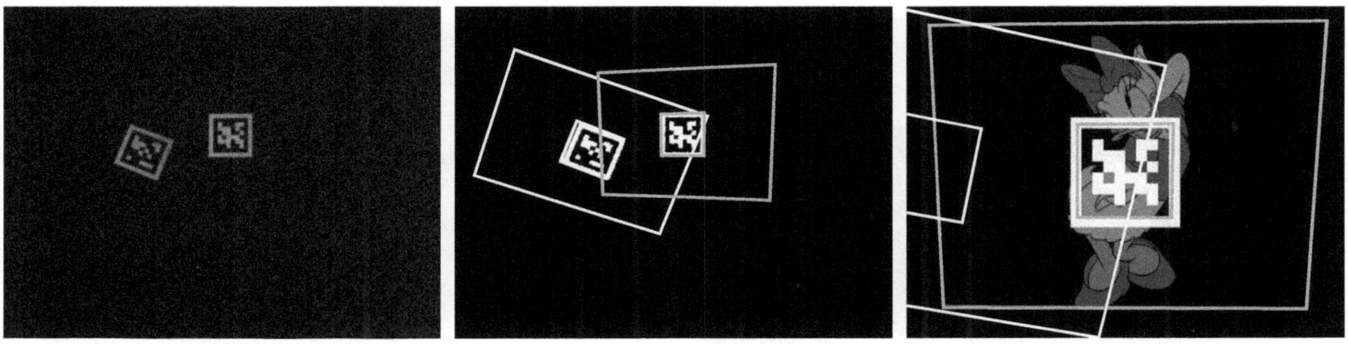

a) IR Camera Image b) Marker Identification c) Map to Projection Space

Figure 7: Invisible projected markers are perceived by an IR camera (a), located and identified (b) and then mapped from the camera coordinate space to the projection coordinate space (c).

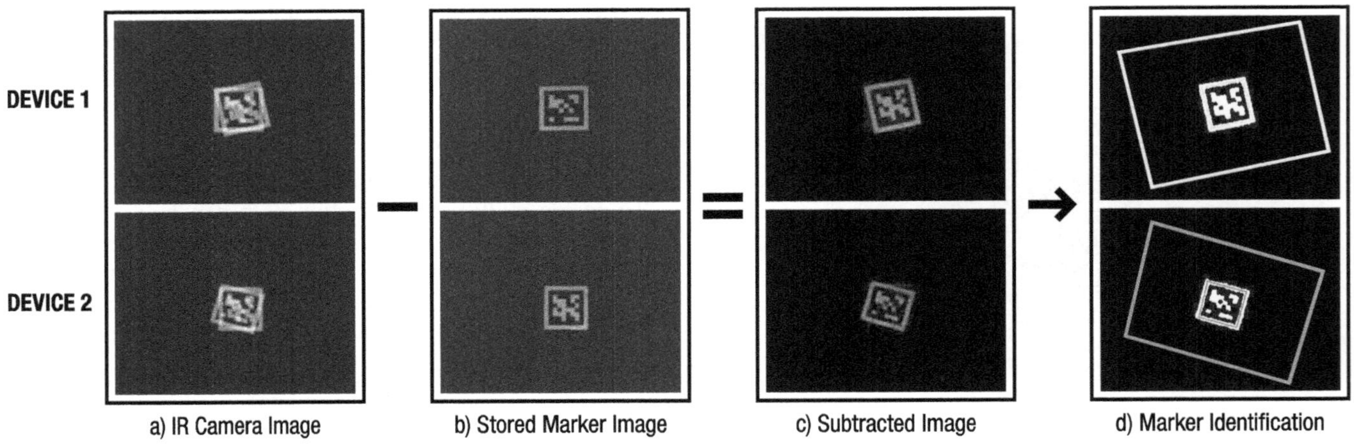

Figure 8: Recovery and tracking of overlapping projected markers.

Unlike printed markers that are typically opaque, projected markers can overlap and still leave adequate information to identify each marker individually. The overlapping region increases in brightness due to the additive nature of projected light (Figure 8a). A reference marker projected in the middle of the projector frame is known, unique and relatively static (Figure 8b). By subtracting it from the scene, we can recover the markers projected on top of it by other devices (Figure 8c). The recovered markers can then be identified and tracked (Figure 8d).

A naïve approach to marker subtraction would be to store a static binary representation of the reference marker in memory. However, environmental conditions such as lighting and properties of the projection surface constantly change as users move throughout the environment. Our marker recovery procedure continuously adapts to the changing environmental conditions by refreshing the stored image of the reference marker when there is no overlap, resulting in more robust performance.

Due to the close optical alignment of the camera and projector axes, projected images observed by the camera are relatively invariant to positional changes of the camera in relation to the projection surface. Even when the user points the device towards the projection surface at an acute angle, the projected markers appear relatively static and rectangular to the camera (Figure 9). Our adaptive marker subtraction technique is robust in situations when the angle of projection is constantly changing.

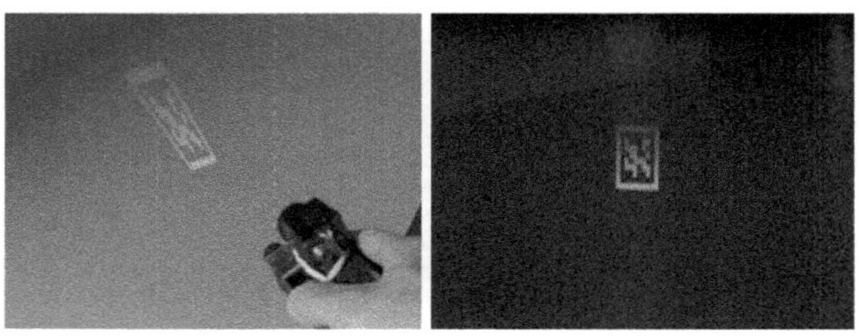

Figure 9: Projected markers that look distorted to the user (left) will appear relatively square when viewed from the device camera (right).

Optical Communication

To communicate events such as button presses, or changes in the state of the application we use optical communication by projecting invisible *event markers*. Event markers are standard fiducial markers used exclusively for symbolic data communication rather than location tracking (Figure 10). To project dynamic event markers, the sender device firstly identifies an empty region in the projection frame. It then projects a marker into this region for a given duration, in our implementation 1000ms. The event marker is projected towards the viewing area of the other device's camera, minimizing the possibility that it will fall outside the camera field of view. The camera on the receiving device observes the marker, recovers its ID, and executes the appropriate application-specific response. A total of 4096 marker IDs can be used with the *ARToolKitPlus* library to communicate between devices.

To measure the time taken for an event marker to be sent from one device and received by another device we performed a simple latency test. We recorded the transmission time of 100 event markers while both projectors were in a static position. All markers were successfully transmitted with a mean latency of 121.45 ms and standard deviation of 8.49 ms. This latency is roughly half the typical minimum human response time of 240 ms [4] and suitable for general-purpose interaction.

Communication bandwidth between handheld projection devices can easily be increased with the use of more so-

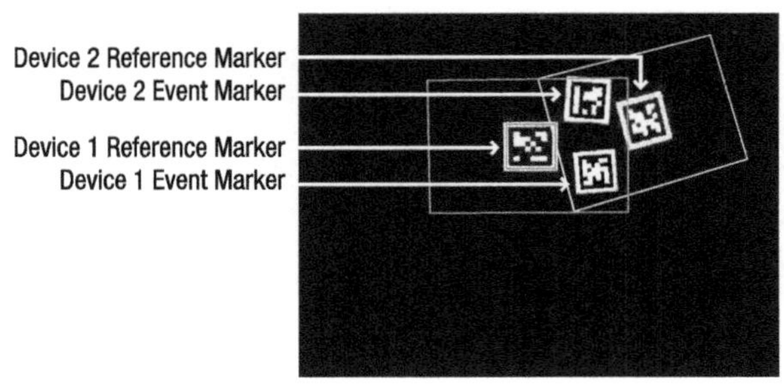

Figure 10: *Event markers* communicate event and state change information between devices.

phisticated spatial encoding techniques, such as QR codes, or temporal encoding techniques, such as modulated IR light. These techniques allow larger amounts of information to be transmitted between handheld projection devices such as URLs, geo locations, address data, status updates, calendar events, and email addresses. Optical communication can also be used to facilitate a 'heavyweight' network connection, such as WiFi or Bluetooth, for even larger files or secure communication between devices.

LIMITATIONS AND TRADEOFFS

Our current prototype has several limitations and tradeoffs.

Accuracy

We conducted an experiment to determine how precisely we could align two shapes projected from different projectors using our tracking system (Figure 11). We measured the distance from each corner of a square shape (Device 1) to each tip of an identically sized 'x' shape (Device 2). We took measurements in ten different locations distributed randomly across the projection area, for a total of 40 measurements. The mean misalignment between the two shapes was 5.28mm, with a standard deviation of 3.34mm. Although this level of accuracy is not ideal for perfect alignment of images, we found it to work well for general-purpose interaction where alignment is not the most critical requirement. Indeed, even professional level motion capture systems struggle to perform with a perfect level of precision [2]. Optimization of the underlying *ARToolKitPlus* tracking library can further improve the accuracy of the *SideBySide* system.

Projection Brightness

Images projected from handheld projectors have limited brightness and it is important for the projection device to remain in close proximity to the projection surface. In our current implementation, increasing the distance beyond 100 cm causes both the visual and IR projected images to dim. This makes it difficult for users to view projected content and decreases the reliability of marker tracking. Handheld projectors are typically used at a range of 60-70cm from the projection surface, where projected imagery is clear and easily seen [26]. Our current implementation functions reliably within this range.

Natural Light

A well-known problem for interactive systems using IR cameras and computer vision techniques is sunlight and other sources of IR light in the environment. This restricts usage of our system to settings without an abundance of natural light, such as indoor spaces with controlled lighting or outside spaces at night.

Camera Setup

A number of general camera decisions need to be made based on the application scenario. Motion blur can be an issue when the device is used for quick gestural interaction. Reducing the camera exposure time can help minimize motion blur; however, this comes at the cost of a dimmer image, decreasing tracking performance. The choice is

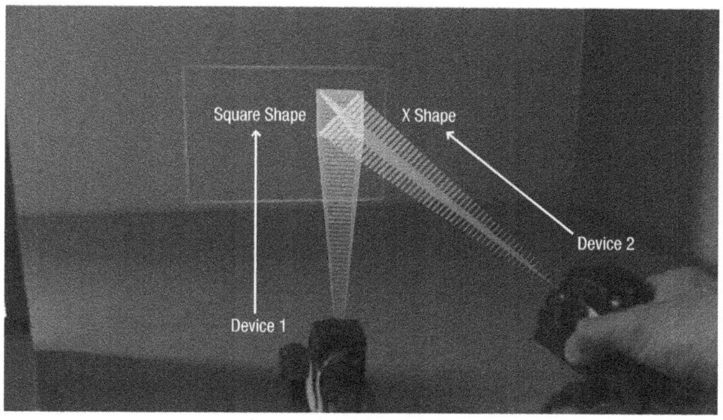

Figure 11: Testing tracking accuracy by aligning two identically sized shapes from different projectors.

therefore application dependent. When quick gestural movements are required, shorter exposure times should be used. When quick gestures are not required, longer exposure times will allow for better tracking performance.

Camera lens selection introduces another trade off. Wide-angle lenses capture a larger area well beyond the bounds of the projected image. This is useful to detect markers even when they are located at relatively large distances apart. However wide-angle lenses cause each marker to occupy fewer pixels of the camera image and result in coarser tracking and reduced accuracy.

Multi-user Interaction

Relative tracking limits the type of interactions that can currently be implemented with the *SideBySide* system. Camera-based systems for absolute localization, however, are a well researched area [11,19] and could easily be combined with our relative tracking approach.

Tracking overlapping markers is currently limited to either two overlapping markers at one time or to multiple markers overlapping different areas of the reference marker. It will fail when two markers overlap on top of the reference marker. This limitation can be overcome by using temporal sequencing of projected markers, so that each device projects a marker in sequence one after the other. Temporal sequencing can be also used to increase the number of projected event markers used at one time. With our current implementation, as the number of event markers increases it becomes increasingly difficult to locate free space for them to be projected. By projecting them one after the other this issue can also be resolved. We elected to leave the investigation of these techniques for future work.

Performance

Our current implementation runs two separate handheld devices on a single Apple MacBook Pro (2.89 GHz Intel Core 2 Duo) at a frame rate of ~45fps. Camera imagery is processed at 640x480 pixels and graphics are outputted at 800x600 pixels before being downscaled to the 480x320 resolution supported by the DLP projection engine. The underlying *ARToolKitPlus* tracking library is designed for use with mobile devices and [22] lists numerous optimizations that are applicable to our system. We believe an embedded version of *SideBySide* will run sufficiently on a current generation mobile device and within 2-4 years will match the performance of our current implementation.

APPLICATIONS

The *SideBySide* system supports a range of co-located multi-user interaction scenarios. By tracking the spatial relationship between multiple projected images, the system is ideally suited to interaction techniques utilizing the distance and angle between projections. Angle and distance can be used for continuous control, e.g. to zoom in/out, or as a binary control to trigger events, e.g. when the two projections overlap. Properties such as the alignment of the projections, the highest/lowest projection, or the relative size of the projections can be used to support further interaction techniques. With these basic building blocks *SideBySide* can support a diverse range of applications. We have developed example applications that focus on three areas: Mobile Content Exchange, Games, and Education.

Mobile Content Exchange

Handheld projectors can be used to support content exchange between devices in ad-hoc interaction scenarios.

Contact Exchange

The *Contact Exchange* application shows how common procedures such as exchanging contact information can be performed with the *SideBySide* system. One user scrolls through their list of contacts by tilting the device up and down. When she finds the contact she wants to exchange she presses a button and drags the contact on to the recipients projected address book (Figure 12, top). At that stage an invisible QR Code with embedded contact information is projected, and the recipient's device scans the code to complete the transfer. This technique can also be adapted for use with multiple devices by projecting the contact information code into open space and having multiple recipients scan the code at the same time.

File Transfer

The *File Transfer* application illustrates how users can transfer files from one device to another. The sender begins by scrolling through the files on her device with simple flick gestures. When she locates the file she wishes to transfer she drags it on to the receivers projected folder (Figure 12, bottom). As with the *Contact Exchange* example, a QR Code is then projected that contains a location where the file can be retrieved. Depending on the implementation this may be a URL or a Bluetooth address.

The *Contact Exchange* and *File Transfer* applications are two specific instances of content exchange. They greatly simplify the often-cumbersome task of locating a specific device to connect to, by providing a direct 'project-and-drop' style interaction. Any digital content, such as photos, videos, music, URLs, applications, and messages, can be transferred using variations of these techniques.

Education

Handheld projectors offer a novel, lightweight platform for learning applications.

Question & Answer

The *Question & Answer* application is designed to teach basic vocabulary to young children as either a first or second language (Figure 13, top). The teacher begins by projecting a question and several written answers from her device. At the same time the student's device depicts a pictorial version of the answer. The student answers the question by pointing to the correct written answer and pressing the button. This activity works both in a one-to-one context

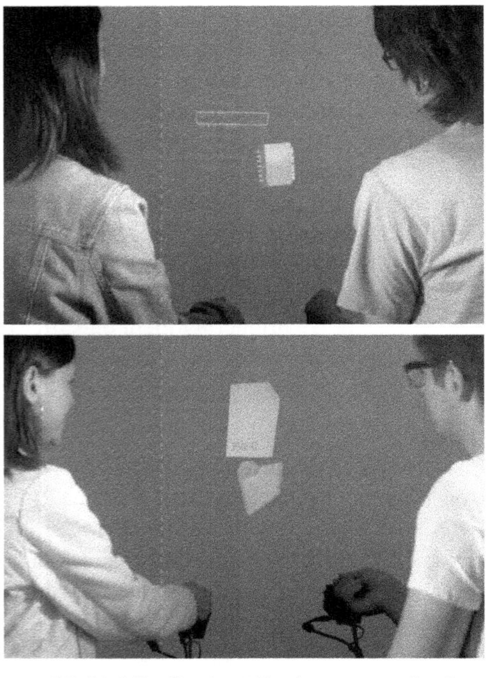

Figure 12: Mobile Content Exchange applications: *Contact Exchange* (top) and *File Transfer* (bottom).

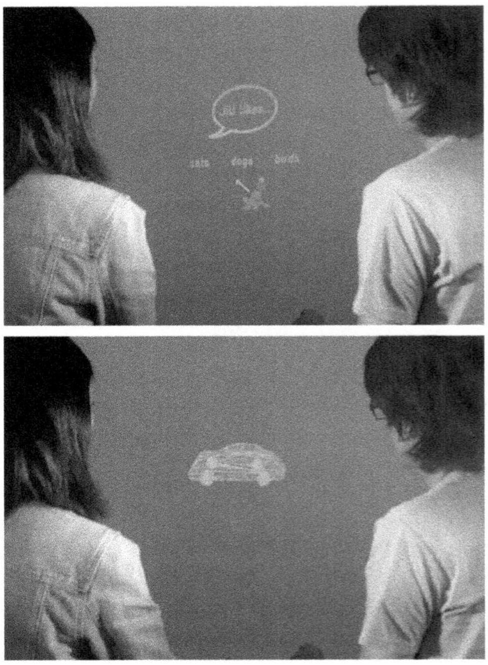

Figure 13: Education applications: *Question & Answer* (top), *3D Viewer* (bottom).

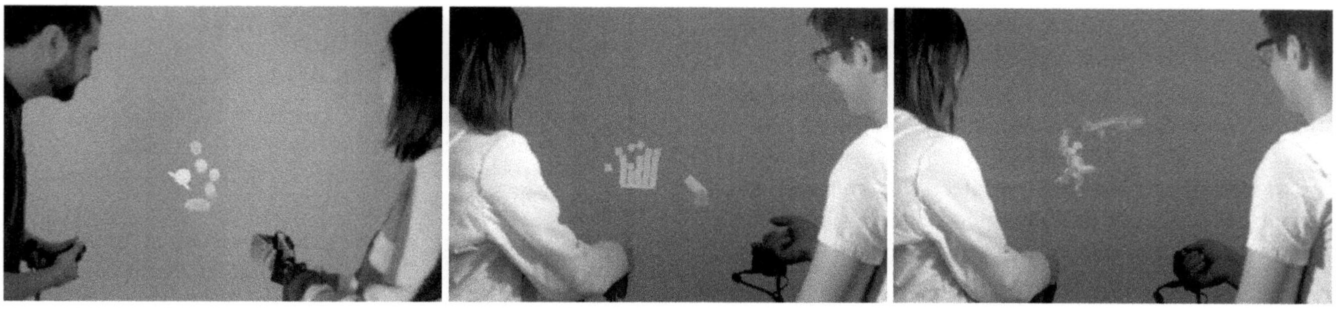

Figure 14: Game applications: *Falling* (left), *Cannon* (middle), *Gorilla* (right).

as well as with small groups of children taking turns to answer the questions. This allows for a more participatory style of interaction when compared to standard computers, but is more intimate than using a large overhead projector.

3D Viewer

The *3D Viewer* application lets two people control and view a 3D model together (Figure 13, bottom). One user projects an image of the 3D model and the other user projects a tool that controls the view. For example, the *orbit* tool maps the x,y difference between the two projection frames to the 3D rotation of the model. The *zoom* tool maps the distance between the two projection frames to the amount of zoom applied to the 3D model. These tools allow both users to actively control the vantage point or zoom level of the model. We envision the *3D Viewer* as a useful way to demonstrate 3D content in situations where a display or projector is not available. Models could range from mechanical objects, to architectural CAD renderings, to 3D molecular structures.

Games

Devices with embedded projectors offer an exciting new modality to play ad-hoc co-located games.

Boxing

The *Boxing* game is a playful rendition of a boxing match. Each player controls a boxer character by moving the projector (Figure 1). A single button on the projector is used to throw punches, but these land only if the player's character is within striking distance of the opponent. The game is played without a boxing ring, meaning the players are free to roam around and make full use of any available space. To communicate a punch being thrown we project event markers for the other device to read. If the distance between the two characters is within striking range, the other device responds to the punch. We found that despite the quick device movement during the game, the tracking system performs well.

Falling

In the *Falling* game two players work together to safely guide falling chicks into their nest. One player controls the nest location and direction of the falling chicks, and the other player controls the 'mama bird' to push the chicks into the nest (Figure 14, left). When one chick falls into the nest, the location of the nest shifts, and both players must re-adjust their positions to guide the next chick into the new nest location. We use a simple physics simulation to animate the falling chicks and IMU sensor data to make sure they are always falling downwards when the projector is rotated. We create an invisible physics object mapped to the location and orientation of the mama bird, so the chicks projected from one device appear to collide and interact with the mama bird projected from the other device.

Cannon

In the *Cannon* game two players work together to knock a stack of bricks off a platform by firing a projected cannon ball from one screen to another (Figure 14, middle). One user controls the location of the bricks by moving their projector, and the other user controls the location of the cannon in a similar manner. Pressing a button on the device fires the cannon ball from one projection frame to the next. Based on the relative location of the two projection frames the ball may miss the bricks or collide to knock them off the platform. To determine the location of the ball we project an event marker when the ball is fired. The device receiving the ball reads this marker and creates another ball with the same location and trajectory in its own projection space. When the ball is about to switch between projection frames, it is removed from one frame and made visible in the other. This gives the impression, due to persistence of vision, that a single ball has traveled across the two frames.

Gorilla

In the *Gorilla* game one player controls a gorilla character and the other controls a rescue plane (Figure 14, right). The rescue plane must try to capture the gorilla by moving in close and launching its net. The gorilla can resist being captured by punching at the rescue plane to destroy it. The button on each device triggers either the gorilla attacks or the rescue plane net. When the net is launched at the right angle and distance, the gorilla is captured and transfers from one projection screen to the other – temporarily hanging from the bottom of the rescue plane in the net.

CONCLUSIONS AND FUTURE WORK

We have presented *SideBySide*, a novel hardware and software platform for ad-hoc multi-user interaction with handheld projectors. Through use of a device-mounted camera and a hybrid visible/IR light handheld projector we have shown the viability of tracking projected content with invisible fiducial markers. Unlike previous systems that dramatically limit mobility by relying on infrastructure embedded in the environment, our system is completely self-contained and can be deployed as a handheld device.

Through the development of a range of example applications we have shown the wide and varied interaction scenarios where *SideBySide* can be put to real world use. Future work on the *SideBySide* project will continue to explore the possibilities of multi-user interaction by developing new applications and conducting formal user studies.

Enabling separate handheld projection devices to interact together is an important step towards truly seamless interaction across the greater ubiquitous computing landscape. We envision a day when digital content can traverse the boundaries of individual screens for fluid interaction between devices, people, and the physical environment.

ACKNOWLEDGMENTS

We thank Christopher Ioffreda, Yu Willis, Cheng Xu and Jo Ana Parker for assistance with photography, Sharon Hoosein for illustration assistance, and Mark D Gross for reviewing an early draft of this paper.

REFERENCES

1. Beardsley, P., van Baar, J., Raskar, R. and Forlines, C. Interaction Using a Handheld Projector. *IEEE Computer Graphics and Applications 25*, 1 (2005), 39-43.
2. Cao, X., Forlines, C. and Balakrishnan, R., Multi-user Interaction Using Handheld Projectors. In Proc. *UIST '07*, ACM (2007), 43-52
3. Cao, X., Massimi, M. and Balakrishnan, R., Flashlight Jigsaw: An Exploratory Study of an Ad-hoc Multi-player Game on Public Displays. In Proc. *CSCW '08*, ACM (2008), 77-86.
4. Card, S.K., Moran, T.P. and Newell, A. The Model Human Processor: An Engineering Model of Human Performance: Vol. 2 Cognitive Processes and Performance. in Boff, K.R., Kaufman, L. and Thomas, J.P. eds. *Handbook of Perception and Human Performance*, 1986, 1-35.
5. Chan, L.-W., Wu, H.-T., Kao, H.-S., Ko, J.-C., Lin, H.-R., Chen, M.Y., Hsu, J. and Hung, Y.-P., Enabling Beyond-surface Interactions for Interactive Surface with an Invisible Projection. *UIST '10*, ACM (2010), 263-272.
6. Grundhöfer, A., Seeger, M., Hantsch, F. and Bimber, O., Dynamic Adaptation of Projected Imperceptible Codes. In Proc. *ISMAR '07*, IEEE (2007), 1-10.
7. Hosoi, K., Dao, V.N., Mori, A. and Sugimoto, M., CoGAME: Manipulation Using a Handheld Projector. In Proc. *SIGGRAPH '07 Emerging Technologies*, ACM (2007), 2.
8. Kane, S.K., Avrahami, D., Wobbrock, J.O., Harrison, B., Rea, A.D., Philipose, M. and LaMarca, A., Bonfire: A Nomadic System for Hybrid Laptop-Tabletop Interaction. In Proc. *UIST '09*, ACM (2009), 129-138.
9. Köhler, M., Patel, S.N., Summet, J.W., Stuntebeck, E.P. and Abowd, G.D., TrackSense: infrastructure free precise indoor positioning using projected patterns. In Proc. *Pervasive '07*, Springer-Verlag (2007), 334-350.
10. Lee, J., Hudson, S. and Dietz, P., Hybrid Infrared and Visible Light Projection for Location Tracking. In Proc. *UIST '07*, ACM (2007), 57-60.
11. Nakazato, Y., Kanbara, M. and Yokoya, N., Localization System for Large Indoor Environments using Invisible Markers. In Proc. *VRST '08*, ACM (2008), 295-296.
12. Ozuysal, M., Calonder, M., Lepetit, V. and Fua, P. Fast Keypoint Recognition Using Random Ferns. *IEEE Transactions on Pattern Analysis and Machine Intelligence 32*, 3 (2010), 448-461.
13. Park, H. and Park, J.-I., Invisible Marker Based Augmented Reality System. In Proc. *VCIP '05*, SPIE (2005), 501-508.
14. Pinhanez, C.S., The Everywhere Displays Projector: A Device to Create Ubiquitous Graphical Interfaces. In Proc. *UbiComp '01*, Springer-Verlag (2001), 315-331.
15. Rekimoto, J., Pick-and-Drop: A Direct Manipulation Technique for Multiple Computer Environments. In Proc. *UIST '97*, ACM (1997), 31-39.
16. Rekimoto, J. and Saitoh, M., Augmented Surfaces: A Spatially Continuous Work Space for Hybrid Computing Environments. In Proc. *CHI '99*, ACM (1999), 378-385.
17. Rukzio, E., Holleis, P. and Gellersen, H. Personal Projectors for Pervasive Computing. *Pervasive Computing* (2011).
18. Rukzio, E., Schöning, J., Rohs, M., Häkkila, J. and Dachselt, R. Ubiprojection 2010: Workshop on Personal Projection. 2010, http://eis.comp.lancs.ac.uk/workshops/ubiproject2010/.
19. Saito, S., Hiyama, A., Tanikawa, T. and Hirose, M., Indoor Marker-based Localization Using Coded Seamless Pattern for Interior Decoration. In Proc. *VR '07*, IEEE (2007), 67-74.
20. Shirai, Y., Matsushita, M. and Ohguro, T., HIEI Projector: Augmenting a Real Environment with Invisible Information. In Proc. *WISS '03* (2003), 115—122.
21. Sugimoto, M., Miyahara, K., Inoue, H. and Tsunesada, Y., Hotaru: Intuitive Manipulation Techniques for Projected Displays of Mobile Devices. In Proc. *INTERACT '05*, Springer (2005), 57-68.
22. Wagner, D. and Schmalstieg, D., ARToolKitPlus for Pose Tracking on Mobile Devices. In Proc. *CVWW '07* (2007), 139-146.
23. Weng, D., Huang, Y., Liu, Y. and Wang, Y., Study on an Indoor Tracking System with Infrared Projected Markers for Large-Area Applications. In Proc. *VRCAI '09* ACM (2009), 239-245.
24. Wienss, C., Nikitin, I., Goebbels, G., Troche, K., Göbel, M., Nikitina, L. and Müller, S., Sceptre: an infrared laser tracking system for virtual environments. In Proc. *VRST '06*, ACM (2006), 45-50.
25. Willis, K.D.D. A Pre-History of Handheld Projector based Interaction. *Journal of Personal and Ubiquitous Computing*, Theme issue on Personal Projection (2011).
26. Willis, K.D.D., Poupyrev, I. and Shiratori, T., MotionBeam: A Metaphor for Character Interaction with Handheld Projectors. In Proc. *CHI '11*, ACM (2011), 1031-1040.
27. Wilson, A.D., PlayAnywhere: A Compact Interactive Tabletop Projection-Vision System. In Proc. *UIST '05*, ACM (2005), 83-92.

OmniTouch: Wearable Multitouch Interaction Everywhere

Chris Harrison[1,2] *Hrvoje Benko*[1] *Andrew D. Wilson*[1]

[1]Microsoft Research
One Microsoft Way
Redmond, WA 98052
{benko,awilson}@microsoft.com

[2]Human-Computer Interaction Institute
Carnegie Mellon University
5000 Forbes Avenue, Pittsburgh PA 15213
chris.harrison@cs.cmu.edu

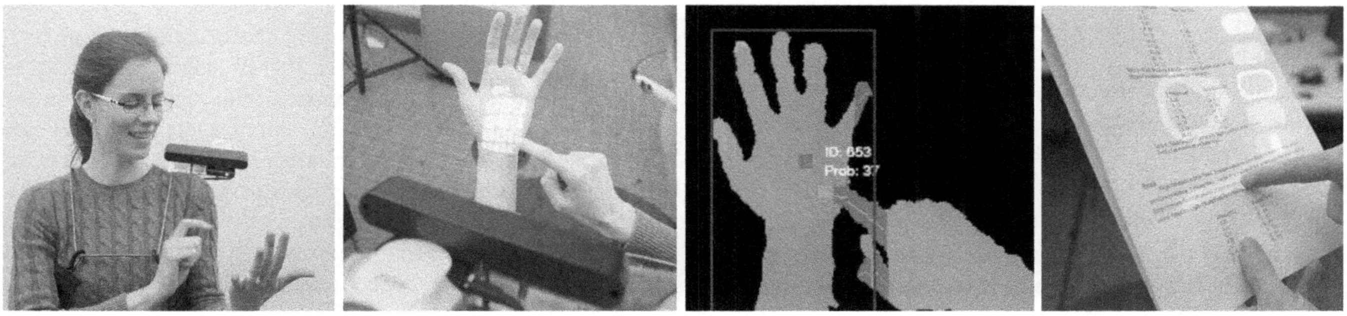

Figure 1. *OmniTouch* is a wearable depth-sensing and projection system that allows everyday surfaces - including a wearer's own body - to be appropriated for graphical multitouch interaction.

ABSTRACT

OmniTouch is a wearable depth-sensing and projection system that enables interactive multitouch applications on everyday surfaces. Beyond the shoulder-worn system, there is no instrumentation of the user or environment. Foremost, the system allows the wearer to use their hands, arms and legs as graphical, interactive surfaces. Users can also transiently appropriate surfaces from the environment to expand the interactive area (e.g., books, walls, tables). On such surfaces - without any calibration - *OmniTouch* provides capabilities similar to that of a mouse or touchscreen: X and Y location in 2D interfaces and whether fingers are "clicked" or hovering, enabling a wide variety of interactions. Reliable operation on the hands, for example, requires buttons to be 2.3cm in diameter. Thus, it is now conceivable that anything one can do on today's mobile devices, they could do in the palm of their hand.

ACM Classification: H.5.2 [Information interfaces and presentation]: User Interfaces - Graphical user interfaces; Input devices and strategies.

General terms: Human Factors

Keywords: On-demand interfaces, finger tracking, on-body computing, appropriated surfaces, object classification.

INTRODUCTION

Today's mobile computers provide omnipresent access to information, creation and communication facilities. It is undeniable that they have forever changed the way we work, play and interact. However, mobile interaction is far from solved. Diminutive screens and buttons mar the user experience, and otherwise prevent us from realizing their full potential.

In this paper we explore and prototype a powerful alternative approach to mobile interaction that uses a body-worn projection/sensing system to capitalize on the tremendous surface area the real world provides. For example, the surface area of one hand alone exceeds that of typical smart phone. Tables are often an order of magnitude larger than a tablet computer. If we could appropriate these ad hoc surfaces in an on-demand way, we could retain all of the benefits of mobility while simultaneously expanding the interactive capability. However, turning everyday surfaces into interactive platforms requires sophisticated hardware and sensing. Further, to be truly mobile, systems must either fit in the pocket or be wearable.

In this paper, we present *OmniTouch*, a novel wearable system that enables graphical, interactive, multitouch input on arbitrary, everyday surfaces. Our shoulder-worn implementation allows users to manipulate interfaces projected onto the environment (e.g., walls, tables), held objects (e.g., notepads, books), and their own bodies (e.g., hands, lap). A key contribution is our depth-driven template matching and clustering approach to multitouch finger tracking. This enables on-the-go interactive capabilities, with no calibration, training or instrumentation of the environment or the user, creating an always-available interface [8,24,28].

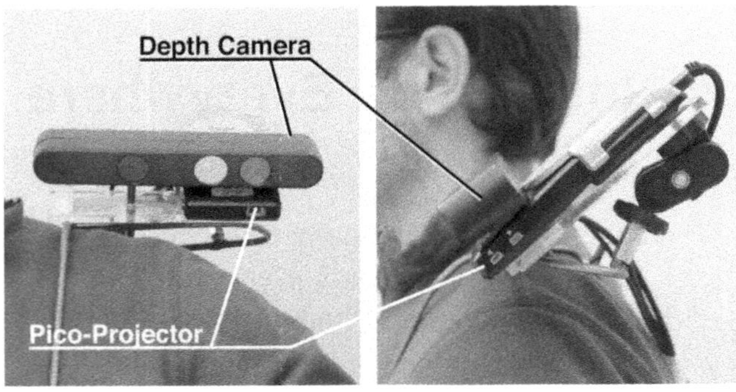

Figure 2. Our prototype shoulder-worn *OmniTouch* System.

RELATED WORK

OmniTouch draws from a variety of fields, including touch interaction techniques, surface computing, free-space gesturing, computer vision, wearables, and ubiquitous computing. Here we focus on highly related, influential work that intersects these fields.

Augmenting the environment with interactive projection interfaces has been a research vision for decades. A variety of approaches are possible, including installing projectors in the environment [20,32], using handheld projectors [3,22], and having users wear mounted projectors [11,17]. Providing touch-based interactivity on arbitrary projected objects is challenging, and generally requires a fixed non-tracking projection [8,17], careful calibration of objects in the environment [20,32,34], or objects to be instrumented with sensing elements [10,14,22]. A small number of such systems have attempted to be truly ad hoc, without requiring permanent instrumentation of the surfaces they operate on [12,17,29,33,34].

The emergence of pico-projectors has enabled a new class of worn, on-body projected interactive systems. SixthSense [18] and Interactive Dirt [17] both featured a worn camera/projector combination. Finger tracking was achieved by wearing fingertip markers (e.g., color or IR reflective). In contrast to our system, true touch interactions were not possible since the two systems could not differentiate between clicked and hovering fingers. This was partially due to the systems' inability to track surfaces in the environment, which also made it impossible to have the projected interface change and follow the surface as it moved. Also of note is Skinput [8], which uses bio-acoustics to detect finger tap events on the skin. Skinput's main limitations were its lack of support for any surface other than the user's body, its inability to detect touch drag movements, and the lack of support for multitouch. Although the system included a pico-projector, no surface tracking was performed, requiring users to position their arms at a predefined position.

Detecting fingers, hands, touches, and gestures has been an active research topic in computer vision [1,6,20,26]. Making computer vision-based tracking work in a wearable, ad-hoc context is challenging due to lack of control of the environment and the general inability to instrument users (e.g., markers [17,18], gloves [27]).

Closely related to our technical approach are systems using the depth-camera tracking without augmenting the user or environment. LightSpace [32] uses an array of depth cameras to track users and arm-level manipulations in an augmented room. At a smaller scale, a single camera can provide conventional touch events by using a per-pixel depth threshold determined from a histogram of the static scene [34]. Both approaches work on a variety of surfaces, but require careful calibration before they can operate.

HARDWARE

Our proof-of-concept *OmniTouch* system, seen in Figures 1 and 2, consists of three principal components. First is a custom, short-range PrimeSense [21] depth camera, which provides a 320x240 depth map at 30 FPS. Objects as close as 20cm can be imaged by this sensor, with relative error in the depth (Z) axis of approximately 5mm. Depth accuracy decreases and noise increases at larger distances. However, for our application, which chiefly considers interaction within a 1m "bubble" in front of the user, noise and accuracy loss was minimal. We initially constructed a prototype using a Microsoft Kinect with good results. However, a minimum sensing distance of ~50cm necessitated awkward placement high above the head to capture the hands.

The second key component is a Microvision ShowWX+ laser pico-projector [16]. This projector has the important property of wide angle, focus-free projection of graphical elements regardless of depth (i.e., distance from projector). Finally, the depth camera and projector are tethered to a desktop computer for prototyping purposes.

Both the depth camera and projector are rigidly mounted to a form-fitting metal frame, which is worn on the shoulders, and secured with a chest strap. We chose the shoulder as it provides a good vantage point (both for sensing and projection) of the arms and held objects, as well as proximate fixed surfaces, such as walls and tables. However, our approach is amenable to other locations (e.g., the upper arm [8] and chest [18]). Additionally, the shoulders tend to be very stable, allowing for projected interfaces with minimal sway and jitter (see Video Figure).

The first person body-stabilized perspective is desirable for sensing and processing, as many simplifying assumptions can be made about the location and orientation of fingers and hands. For example, it is physically impossible for the user's arms to enter the image from the top. The system's field of view also automatically translates with the wearer. Further, camera and projection occlusion issues are minimized, as their fields of view roughly coincide with the wearer's line of sight.

MULTITOUCH FINGER TRACKING

We present a unique approach to ad hoc finger tracking, which enables multitouch input on arbitrary surfaces, both flat and irregular, with no calibration or training. We can resolve the *X, Y and Z position* of fingers, and whether they are *touching* or *hovering* over a surface. Thus, *OmniTouch* produces input events similar to that of mice or touchscreens, enabling a wide variety of applications.

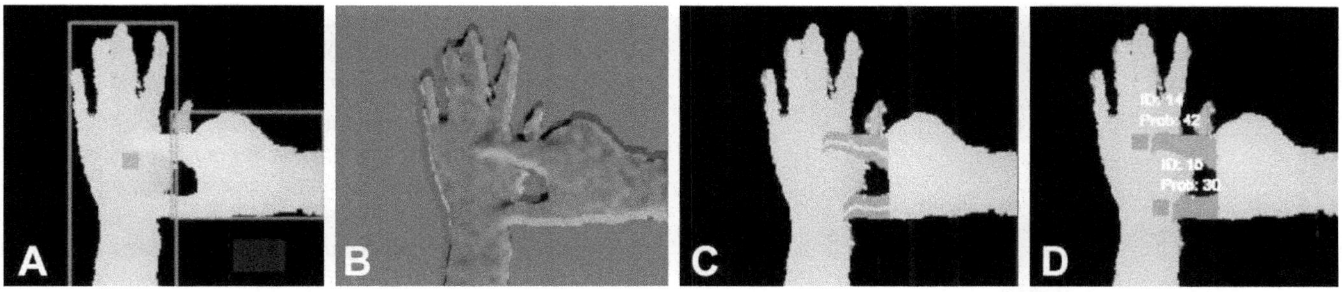

Figure 3. Left to right: depth map, derivative of depth map, finger slices overlaid in blue, path finding and tip estimation.

Finger Segmentation

Identifying finger input is a multistep process. First, we take a depth map of a scene (Figure 3A) and compute the depth derivative in the X- and Y-axes using a sliding, 5x5 pixel window (Figure 3B; X and Y derivative visualized using blue and red channels respectively). We then iterate over this derivative image, looking for vertical slices of cylinder-like objects. This is similar to template matching, but with some dynamic parameters. Put simply, for a slice of pixels to be a candidate, it must show a steep positive derivate, followed by a region of relative smoothness, and finally closed by a steep negative derivative (Figure 4). This ordering is critical; otherwise, concave features (e.g., gaps between fingers) would also be recognized. Also significant is that the depth camera we use represents sensing errors, out-of-range surfaces, and occlusion boundaries as holes in the depth image. As such, they appear as concavities in the derivative, which our process ignores.

To primarily isolate fingers, candidate slices must be between 5 and 25mm in height, a range we found to cover typical finger diameters, including the critical fingertip. Pixel distances can be converted into real world distances (mm) because the depth value is also known. The result of this finger-slice identification process is shown in Figure 3C.

Using the derivative of the depth map has several benefits that make it a key component of our sensing approach. Foremost, this approach suppresses absolute depth information, allowing the scene to be treated as a conventional 2D image, which is easier to process with standard computer vision techniques. Additionally, regardless of the surface the finger is operating on, the derivative profile is mostly invariant, greatly simplifying recognition.

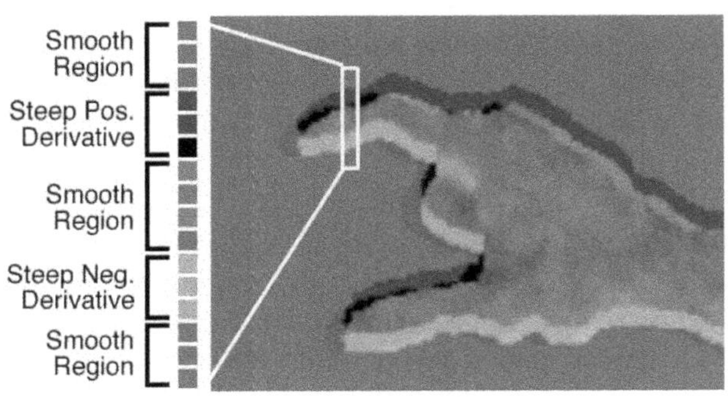

Figure 4. Close up example of a candidate finger slice.

Once all candidate finger slices are identified, we then greedily group proximate slices into contiguous paths. Paths that are shorter or longer than probable fingers are discarded. Even in noisy scenes, this process yields few false positives. The output, seen in Figure 3D, resembles a skeletal model of the fingers. Like other computer vision techniques, fingers that are occluded are not detected. Additionally, and usefully, fingers that are "tucked in" are not tracked. However, our technique is sensitive to approach angle (can neither be too steep nor too shallow) and generally requires fingers be outstretched for reliable recognition.

Many approaches are possible for disambiguating which end of the path is the fingertip. In our proof-of-concept system, we assume a right-handed user, and thus, in almost all cases, the leftmost point in a path is the fingertip. This worked well in practice for our left-shoulder mounted configuration. To eliminate sensing noise and pixel-boundary flicker, fingertip positions are smoothed by a Kalman filter.

Finger Click Detection

The finger segmentation process, described above, yields the spatial location (X, Y and Z) of fingers. A secondary process is used to determine whether these fingers - specifically the tips - are in contact with a surface (i.e., a "click").

We start by computing the midpoint of the finger path, which roughly equates to the location of the minor knuckle. From this point, we flood fill towards the fingertip (i.e., all directions but rightward). This operation is performed on the depth map using a tolerance of 13mm in depth to determine if neighboring pixels can be filled. When the finger is hovering above a surface or in free space, the flood fill expands to encompass the entire finger (Figure 5, left). However, when the finger contacts a surface, the fill operation

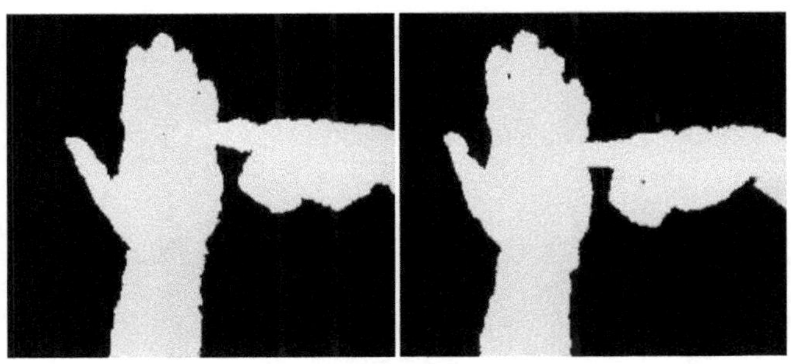

Figure 5. Flood filling result when finger is hovering (left) and "clicked" (right).

Figure 6. In order for interfaces to appear visually aligned and correct when projected onto moving surfaces, the projected image must be dynamically pre-distorted (see inset images).

floods out into the connecting object (Figure 5, right). If a pixel count threshold is passed (e.g., 2000 pixels), the flood fill discontinues and the finger is determined to be clicked. Note, if the surface is very small or lies outside the camera's view, the threshold may not be passed, and the click missed.

This process detects finger clicks robustly, and also maintains a clicked state when dragging a finger across a surface, including irregular ones. In practice, a finger will be seen as "clicked" when its hover distance drops to 1cm or less above a surface; above 2cm is reliably seen as hovering. Hover distances between 1 and 2cm are ambiguous, and largely depend on local noise; we apply hysteresis to reduce flickering between click states. Anecdotally, users did not notice the ambiguity and generally "clicked through" this region on the way to their desired target.

ON-DEMAND PROJECTED INTERFACES

With finger tracking alone, it is possible to support interfaces lacking graphical feedback, or "invisible interfaces" [7]. For example, it would be possible to sketch simple figures or perform graffiti-like text entry on a notepad.

Infusing interactive graphical feedback expands the application space considerably. However, the inherent dynamic nature of objects in the real world makes this complex. Not only must interfaces track which objects they are rendered on, but they must be projected in such a way as to account for their host surface's position and orientation in 3D space (Figure 6). Without these considerations, interfaces would be rendered with inappropriate position, orientation and size, and be subject to perspective visual distortions.

Surface Segmentation and Tracking

In addition to finger tracking, the depth video stream is also used to track surfaces suitable for projection in front of the user. First, distinct surfaces are segmented by performing a 3D connected components operation on the depth map (Figure 7, right). Surfaces smaller than hand size are discarded.

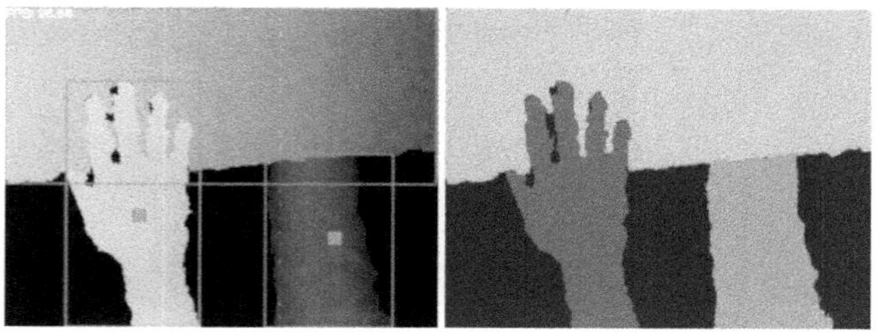

Figure 7. 3D connected components and their lock points.

For each surface, we compute the orientation about the Z-axis (orthogonal to the camera) by taking the covariance of the component's pixels in space, and computing the first and second moments. Orientation about the X- and Y-axes is estimated using the distribution of surface normals, which tend to be Gaussian over the primary orientations.

We also generate a central X/Y/Z "lock point", to which an interface can be attached (Figure 7). This point must be stable regardless of translation and rotation in 3D space. One approach is to take the centroid of an object's pixels. However, because part of the surface may be occluded when the user is interacting with their fingers, this is not reliable. Instead, we move inwards 10cm along the surface's major axis from its upper extent, centered on the midpoint of the minor axis (Figure 8, red). Although more sophisticated techniques are possible, this solution worked well. Finally, a Kalman filter is used to smooth all six degrees of freedom.

Projector/Camera Calibration

To enable authoring and interaction with projected interfaces, it is necessary to calibrate the projector and camera in a unified 3D space. Since our depth camera reports real-world depth values (mm), we chose that as our target coordinate system and calibrate the projector using camera values.

The process requires the intrinsic parameters of the projector, such as the field of view and the center of projection. To find the extrinsic projector parameters we require four non-coplanar calibration points. These four points must be identified by the depth camera and located in the projector image. Once the correspondence of the 2D points in the projected image and their actual 3D location in space (depth camera value) is established, we use the POSIT algorithm [5,32] to find the position and orientation of the projector. Note that this calibration only needs to be performed once, since the spatial relationship between the projector and the camera is fixed (i.e., both are mounted to a rigid frame).

Summoning & Defining Interactive Areas

Determining where to place an interface and how large it should be is non-trivial. For example, consider the hand: Do we center the interface in the middle of the palm, or the centroid of the surface? Or the midpoint between the wrist and finger tips? Or the absolute center of the bounds of the hand? Figure 8 depicts these four (of many possible) options. Sizing the interface has similar challenges: do we fit an interface to just the palm (which is attractive due to its relative flatness), the hand minus the thumb, or the full extent of the hand?

Previous approaches to on-body interfaces [8,17] projected a fixed-sized interface at a fixed image location. In order to use such an interface, a user must raise a physical object into this region at a specified distance, or walk up to a wall. This places the interface localization burden entirely on the user and is ill-suited for many on-the-go mobile scenarios.

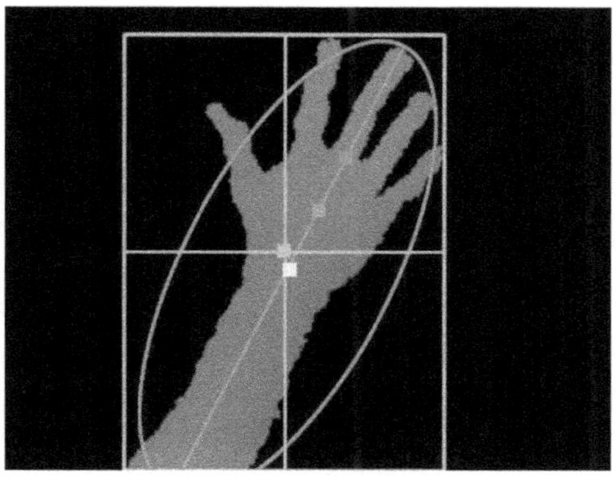

Figure 8. Possible lock points on the hand: Green: absolute center of surface bounds. Yellow: centroid of surface's pixels. Red: 10cm offset along major axis from upper extent. Blue: midpoint between wrist and middle finger tip.

In contrast, *OmniTouch* implements three distinct approaches to define, present, and track interactive areas:

One Size Fits All

OmniTouch can use a surface's lock point and orientation to provide an interface that tracks with a surface. However, because the bounds of the object in 3D space are unknown, the interface can only be as big as the smallest conceivable surface (generally the hand). Thus, even when a projecting on a large table, the interface will still be hand-sized. Additionally, every surface must use a generic lock point, which can lead to sub-optimal centering on asymmetric and organic surfaces, like the hands. These drawbacks motivated us to explore more sophisticated options.

Classification-Driven Placement

Classification-driven placement consists of two stages. First, the system differentiates between a small set of surfaces by performing surface classification. Second, the system automatically sizes, positions and tracks an interface given the available projection area and heuristics describing the appropriate location for that surface.

We perform surface classification among a set of five common surfaces (hand, arm, pad, wall, and table) by considering a variety of features derived from each surface's depth image. For example, to distinguish between planar and organic surfaces, we calculate the standard deviation of the surface normals. Planar objects inherently have a majority of their normals pointing in a common direction, yielding a low standard deviation. On the other hand, organic surfaces tend to be more "rounded" (often symmetrically so), leading to diverse distributions and higher standard deviations. Size is very also descriptive; depth data allows for reasonable approximation of real world size - a notepad is easily distinguished from a table. Additionally, aggregate surface orientation immediately disambiguates tables from walls. These simple features worked well in our prototype implementation given the small set of surfaces to distinguish, but a more general solution would require more sophisticated features (e.g., see [13] for depth-driven object recognition).

Figure 9. To sidestep complexities in automatically positioning and sizing interfaces, users can simply "click-and-drag" interfaces wherever desired.

Each class of surface defines a unique graphics placement heuristic (an offset vector from the surface's lock point) and default size. For example, a hand has a hand-sized interface while a wall has a wall-sized interface. Lastly, once the surface is identified and the interface is placed, we track the surface change frame-to-frame and accordingly adjust the interface to reflect this change. This mimics the expectation of the user, that once the interface is established, it should remain "glued" to the surface it is projected on. Optionally, given the real-world depth data, the interface can be further refined and fitted to the available area on the surface, by performing depth-constrained flood filling from the surface's placement point.

Unfortunately, this classification-driven approach suffers from scalability issues, since it is simply not possible to build a classifier for every conceivable surface. However, for common surfaces that have unique placement considerations, this approach is attractive and viable.

User-Specified Placement

An entirely different approach is to let the user define the interactive area. This sidesteps much of the complexity described above, as users have a good innate sense of where interfaces should be centered and how big they should be. This exposes a high level of customization to users. However, this flexibility comes at the expense of requiring additional user interaction before an interface can be utilized.

In our prototype system, we provide two mechanisms for user specified placement, although many options are possi-

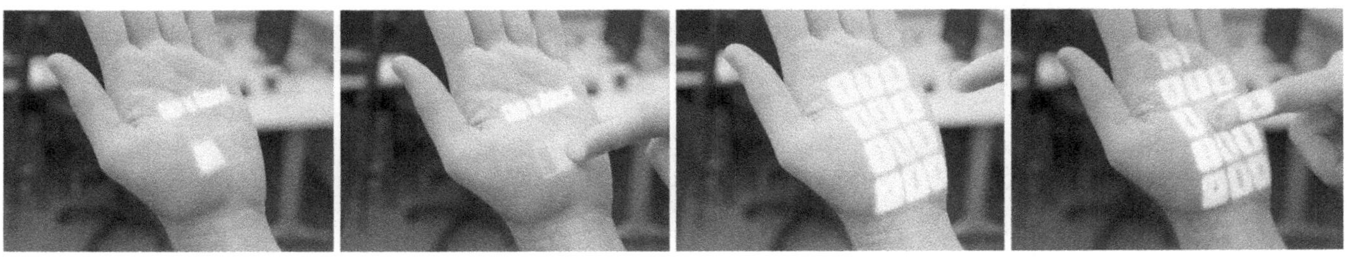

Figure 10. We created a simple phone keypad application; in this sequence, time progresses left to right.

ble. The simplest is for a user to "click" on a surface, causing a generically sized interface to be centered at that location. Alternatively a user can click and drag to position and size in one continuous action (Figure 9). As with the classification-driven approach, once the interface is established, we update its location and orientation frame-by-frame.

Compositing Interfaces in 3D Space

In our proof-of-concept implementation, we model interfaces as planar 2D surfaces, which are positioned and oriented in 3D space. Their 3D placement is computed in relation to the aforementioned lock points and surface orientations so that they are correctly updated as surfaces move. Displaying such interfaces on top of any available surface is straightforward since our projector is precisely calibrated to the depth camera coordinate system. We simply create a 3D scene containing all active surfaces and then render this scene from the perspective of the projector using the projector/camera calibration discussed earlier (Figure 6).While we currently render only planar interfaces, our approach easily lends itself to experimenting with 3D interfaces that take into account the true geometry of the projected surface.

By defining our interfaces in the 3D world space (i.e., using millimeters), they are projected with correct scale and distortion regardless of where the surface is with respect to the camera (as long as it is visible). Our aim is that the interactive surfaces appear to the user "glued" to the physical surface. 3D rendering also automatically takes into account the Z-ordering of our interfaces.

Simultaneously, we use the 3D scene to ray cast fingertip positions onto our planar interfaces. Finger inputs are reported as X/Y coordinates in their local 2D space, which simplifies interface development and enables detection and tracking of finger hover. Although it is possible to use Z distance for click detection, we found our flood-fill heuristic approach to be most accurate.

EXAMPLE APPLICATIONS

With *OmniTouch* providing capabilities similar to that of mice and touchscreens, the application space is expansive. Over the course of development, we created many small, interactive applications that ran on top of our *OmniTouch* engine (Figures 1, 10 and 11). These served both as proof of concept and also as a gauge of input accuracy and real world applicability. We briefly describe a few exemplary applications; please also refer to the Video Figure.

Conventional Interaction

With the ability to click, buttoned interfaces are immediately possible; dragging enables interfaces to be scrolled. As a simple demonstration, we built a phone keypad application (Figure 10). To prevent accidental dialing, a "slide to unlock" feature is included. We also experimented with hierarchical menu navigation, visualized as a scrollable list with clickable items (Figure 11C). This class of interface is prevalent in contemporary mobile devices. Additionally, we built a full keyboard, potentially allowing for text entry on the go (Figure 11A). Lastly, a "post-it" application allows users to write quick notes on their palm (Figure 11E).

To showcase our system's multitouch capabilities, we developed a simple annotation application, where each finger generates a stroke; a small palette of highlight colors is provided (Figure 1). We also implemented the ubiquitous map panning and zooming demo, which is controlled by finger drags and pinching respectively (Figure 11D).

Multi Surface Interaction

As *OmniTouch* can track multiple objects within its field of view, it is possible to support interaction on multiple surfaces and levels. As a proof of concept, we created a painting application for walls. We use the left hand as the color pallet, which can be raised and lowered as needed (Figure 11G). Similarly, when working at a table, the hand may serve as an application switcher (Figure 11F).

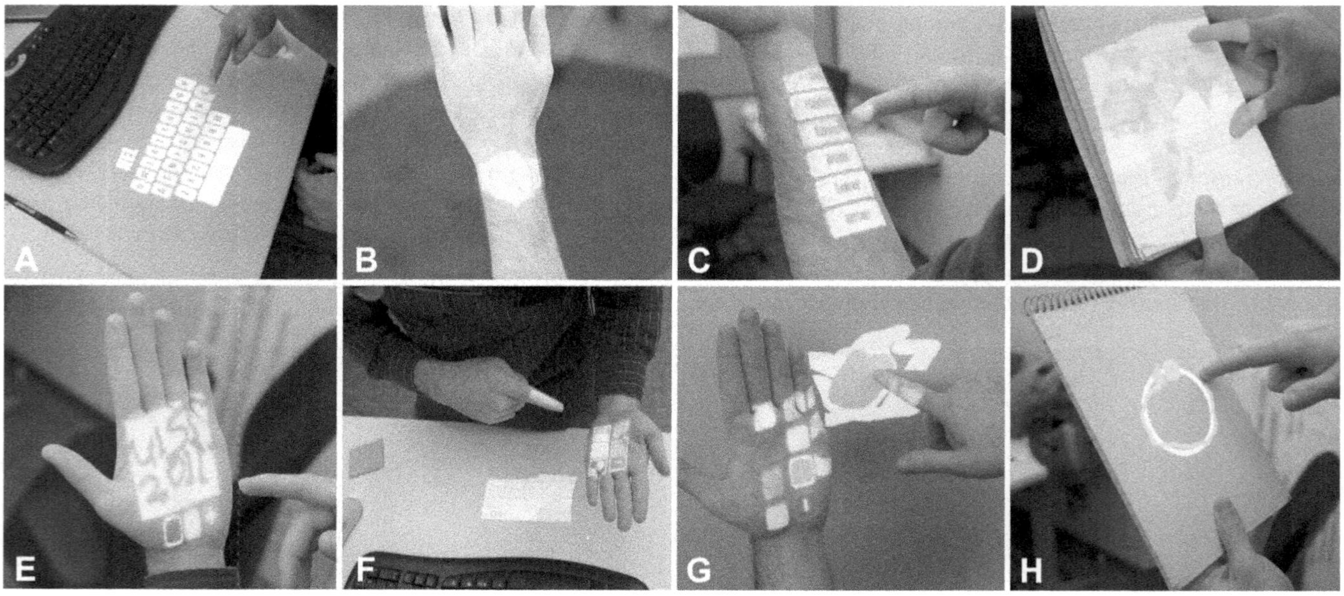

Figure 11. Some of the applications we developed that run on top of *OmniTouch*. See text for descriptions.

Making Use of Rich Metadata

Our surface tracking procedure generates a variety of metadata, such as whether a surface is public or private, organic or flat, big or small, and vertically or horizontally oriented – all of which are exposed to applications wishing to be more context sensitive. For example, the orientation of a hand or handheld surface could be used to determine if the content is visible to only the user or to others (Figure 12) [14]. Additionally, because the geometry between the shoulders and head is fixed, view-dependent VR [31] is possible. Finally, the position of surfaces within the field of view could be used to enable peephole displays [35].

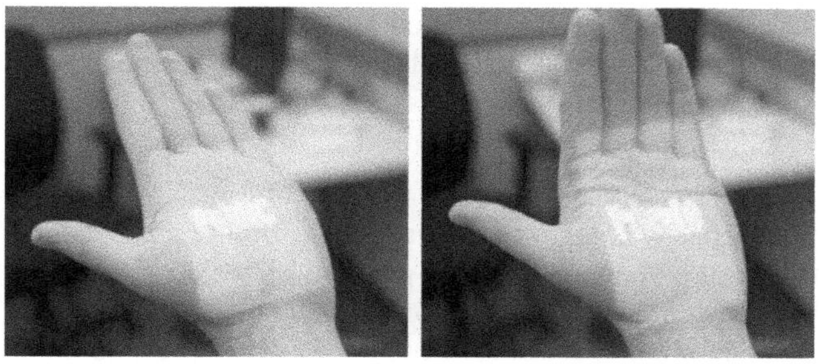

Figure 12. *OmniTouch* can infer if a surface is public or private from orientation features.

USER STUDY

To evaluate and demonstrate the feasibility of our approach, we conducted a user study that sought to quantify the key performance characteristics of our system. At a high level, can *OmniTouch* correctly register touch events and how accurately can they be localized? At a meta-level, how large would interface elements have to be to enable reliable operation of an ad hoc interface rendered on the hand? To place our system's performance in context, we compare our method to the gold standard - capacitive touch screens - drawing performance results from the literature [9,15,25].

Participants

We recruited 12 participants from our local metropolitan area (6 female), ranging in age from 23 to 49, with a mean of 34. All participants were right handed and were required to have some experience with touch screen devices. The study took approximately one hour and included a gratuity.

Test Surfaces

Our goal with *OmniTouch* was to support interaction on three classes of surface: 1) on-body, 2) objects held in the hands, and 3) fixed surfaces in the environment. For our user study, we included one example from each class: the *hand*, a note *pad* held in the hand, and a *wall*. Additionally, we included the forearm (*arm*), as on-body interaction was a particular focus of our work and also challenging from a sensing perspective. Moreover, the *arm* served as a nice contrast to the *hand*, which, although highly irregular, is still fairly planar. Finally, these four surfaces, seen in Figure 13, represent ad hoc surfaces our system would likely use.

Procedure

We first fit participants with our shoulder-mounted system. Once the frame was secured and comfortable, participants were allowed to play with the phone keypad example application. This let them find comfortable positions to hold their arms, both for being rendered on and for pointing, and also to practice using the system. During this period, the experimenters provided feedback to help them become more accurate. This training period lasted a maximum of 10 minutes, though most participants felt confident using the system after just a few minutes of use.

Our primary user study interface consisted of 9 crosshair targets, laid out in a 3x3 pattern (Figure 13). Columns and rows were spaced 3cm apart; the crosshairs were 2x2cm in size (9x9cm total size). In each trial, one crosshair was rendered in red. Users "clicked" this crosshair as accurately as they could. If a click was detected, the system would beep and a green circle was placed around the target crosshair (see Figure 13, wall). The experimenter advanced the inter-

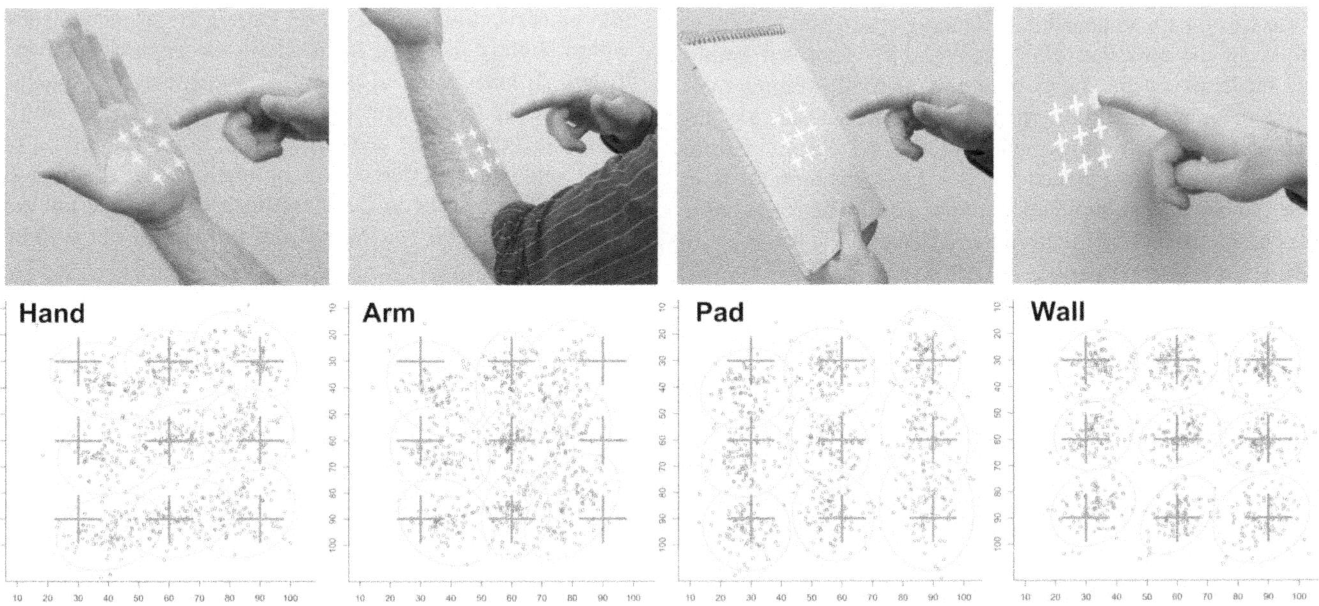

Figure 13. The four surfaces we tested and user click distributions. 95% confidence ellipses shown in green. Axis units in mm.

face to the next trial after each click attempt, regardless of whether or not it was detected. Each of the 9 crosshair locations was repeated 4 times, for a total of 36 click trials; presentation order was randomized.

This interface and procedure was used for each of the four test surfaces: *hand*, *arm*, *pad* and *wall*. Before each surface, users were allowed to briefly practice before data collection began. For the *wall* condition, participants were asked to stand approximately 30cm from the wall. For the other three surfaces, users found a comfortable position. The ordering of the surfaces was randomized to compensate for any order effects. We ran two rounds of data collection to investigate if there were any effects from learning, fatigue, or slight variations in posture. This produced 288 trials (2 rounds x 4 surfaces x 36 click trials) per participant.

To quantify how our system performed at different distances, we included two additional rounds of data collection. Participants were asked to hold their *hands* at arm length (*far*), at an "average and comfortable" distance (*average*), and as close to the system as possible, while still being able to click with their right hand (*close*). We also tested these three distances with the *pad* surface; the ordering of the *pad* and *hand* distance trials was alternated between participants. This procedure produced 216 trials (2 surfaces x 3 distances x 36 click trials) per participant.

The tests described above were primarily designed to isolate click segmentation and spatial accuracy. A key feature of *OmniTouch* is its ability to track fingers while dragging. To better understand the spatial performance of finger drags, we created a drawing experiment interface (Figure 11H). In this application, users were presented one of six possible shapes: up line, down line, left line, right line, clockwise circle, counterclockwise circle. Each shape was repeated 4 times, for a total of 24 drawing trials per participant.

Direction of the stroke was indicated using a green arrow and a red "stop". Participants were asked to draw as closely to the white path as possible, balancing speed and accuracy. Unlike in the crosshair experiments, users received graphical feedback in the form of a red path illustrating their stroke. This allowed participants to compensate for any inaccuracies in their movement and the system's fingertip estimation. We chose to conduct this experiment on the *pad*, as a flat surface minimized external confounds (e.g., user inaccuracy caused by the irregular surface of the hands).

RESULTS & DISCUSSION

Our 12 participants produced 3456 click trials on our four surfaces, a further 2592 in our distance experiment, and 288 drawn shapes. No effect was found between the two rounds of crosshair trials (e.g., from fatigue or learning). Additionally, there were no significant performance differences between participants. Thus, data was combined for each surface. Data from the distance and the dragging trials was kept separate for independent analysis. Ultimately, these results should be considered a performance baseline, as significant improvements in depth camera resolution and sensitivity are forthcoming.

Finger Click Detection

We combined data from all of our crosshair-clicking experiments (two rounds of four surfaces and two rounds of three distances) – a total of 6048 click trials. Of these, 96.5% correctly received exactly one finger click event. Regarding errors, 50 trials (0.8%) had no click event (i.e., the system missed the participant's finger click), 154 trials (2.5%) had two click events (i.e., the system incorrectly thought the user clicked twice, or believed a secondary finger to have clicked), and 8 trials (0.1%) had three click events.

For the user study, we configured *OmniTouch* to record all input events, without any high-level mechanism for click rejection, as typically found in interactive systems. Of the 162 trials receiving double and triple clicks, 94.8% percent occurred within 500ms of the first click event. Thus, with a simple timeout, single finger click segmentation accuracy would be 98.9%.

Of the 50 trials (0.8%) with missed clicks, 33 were contributed by the three left-most crosshairs in the *arm* condition (see Figure 13, arm). As noted in [23], participants tend to hook their fingers when targeting items on reverse slopes, which is the case for the right hand targeting the left most side of the left forearm. One possible explanation for this increased error is that hooking occludes the contact point and also shortens the finger's profile from the camera's perspective, which can cause tracking loss. Otherwise, the distribution of missed-click and multi-click errors was evenly spread over all crosshair positions and surface conditions.

Finally, we compared click segmentation performance at the three distances tested in the user study (*hand*/*pad* surfaces at *close*/*average*/*far* distances). However, no significant effects were found.

Finger Click Spatial Accuracy

Importantly, our results represent the cumulative error of the system and the user. There are three primary sources of error: 1) misalignment and non-linearities in the projector/camera calibration (e.g., a button is projected somewhere slightly different from where the camera believes it to be), 2) inaccuracy in the fingertip estimation, especially when the tip fuses with the surface during clicks, and 3) user inaccuracy when clicking targets, (e.g., due to "fat fingers" and varying perception of one's finger input point [9]). Although some of these factors are outside of our control, they model the *real-world performance* of our system.

There are two important and independent measures for analyzing targeting performance: offset and spread [4,9,25].

Finger Click Spatial Offset

Analysis revealed there was a small systematic offset between where *OmniTouch* believed the user clicked and where the user believed they clicked. Specifically, we found an average offset of 11.7mm to the left of targets across all conditions and participants, in agreement with previous findings in the touchscreen literature [15,25]. Y-offset for the *hand*, *arm* and *pad* surfaces was similarly an average of 1.1mm above the true target. Finger touches on the *wall*, however, were offset downwards an average 10.0mm, pos-

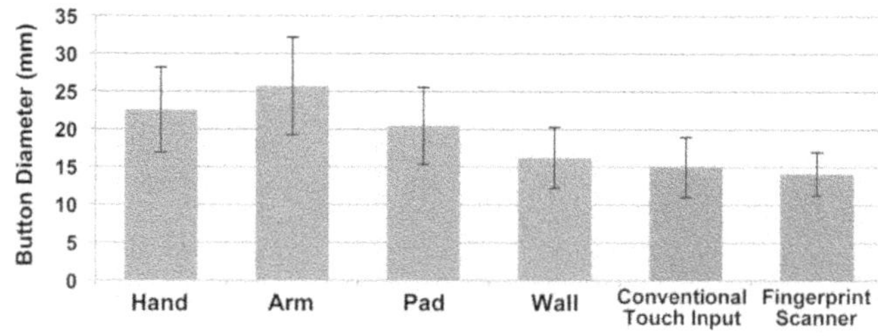

Figure 14. Button diameter necessary to encompass 95% of touches. Error bars denote standard deviation across all trials. Results in orange from [9].

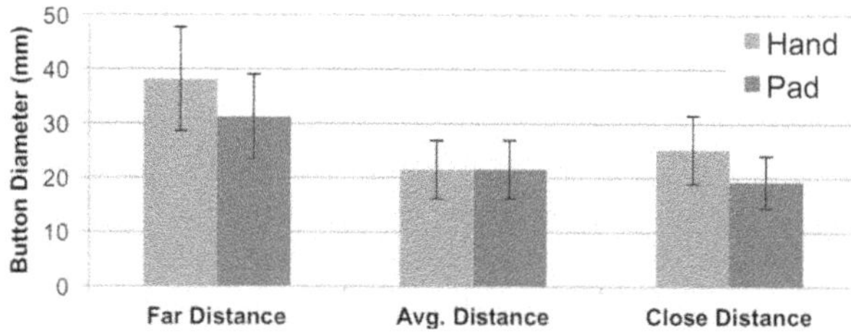

Figure 15. Button diameter needed to encompass 95% of touches. Error bars show standard deviation across trials.

sibly due to its extreme angle (at roughly chest height, and oriented vertically). Finally, distance appears to have no significant effect on offset.

Because offsets are systematic across-users and across-surfaces, we simply apply a post-hoc X/Y offset to our subsequent data analysis. These offset values could be trivially added to our system's real-time finger point estimations. The only case we handle specially is the *wall*, which is recognized by *OmniTouch* using size and orientation information. With the wall, points are shifted upward 10.0mm. For maximum generality, we did not compute or apply any per-user offset, though this has been shown to significantly increase accuracy [9,30].

Finger Click Spatial Precision

The spatial precision of *OmniTouch* is visualized in Figure 13, which depicts 95% confidence ellipses for the nine crosshair targets on our four test surfaces. For analysis, we removed 93 outliers (1.5% of our click trials) in order to plot our results side-by-side with those in [9] (Figure 15). Outliers were defined as points lying greater than three standard deviations away from the mean difference between points and the target. Similar to [9], outliers were a mix of user error, user inaccuracy, and tracking errors.

Figure 14 displays the minimum button diameter necessary to correctly capture 95% of touches for each surface. We also include two points of comparison from [9] - an estimation of conventional touch input (derived from a capacitive touchpad) and results from crosshair trials using a high-resolution optical fingerprint scanner. Exceeding our expectations, *OmniTouch* on a *wall* appears to be nearly as accurate as conventional touchscreens (16.2mm vs. 15.0mm). The *hand* requires buttons to be 22.5mm in diameter, offering the highest un-instrumented, on-body button density to date [8,24,32]. The *pad* performs similarly to the *hand.*

The arm is our least accurate surface, requiring targets approximately 70% larger than a conventional touch screen to achieve the same 95% touch accuracy (25.7mm vs. 15.0mm). This degradation in error comes chiefly from buttons located on the sides of the arms, where curvature is high (see Figure 13). Given that the arm is well suited to narrow, tall interfaces (Figure 11C), we also computed the accuracy using only the center column of crosshair targets, which proved to be quite accurate (20.5mm, SD=5.1mm).

Effects of Distance on Spatial Precision

We previously reported that distance had no significant effect on click segmentation accuracy or on spatial offset. However, there does appear to be a significant loss of precision when interacting at *far* distances. Using a Bonferroni-corrected all-pairs *t*-test, we found no significant difference in performance between the *hand* and *pad* at our three test distances. We then combined *hand* and *pad* distance trials into aggregated *far*, *average* and *close* data sets. Overall, the *far* condition is significantly worse performing than both *average* and *close* distances (both $p<.001$) – requiring buttons to be roughly 60% larger to operate at around arm's length. There is no significant difference between *average* and *close* distances. Figure 15 illustrates these results as button diameters necessary to encompass 95% of touches.

Finger Drag Spatial Accuracy

In our dragging (drawing) experiment (Figure 11H), we included vertical and horizontal lines, as well as circles, in order to assess X, Y and X+Y dragging performance. For both lines and circles, we use the absolute Euclidian distance from the closest point on the desired path as our error distance metric. We did not apply our global X/Y offset to stroke points as live graphical feedback was provided. Such feedback allowed participants to compensate for any system inaccuracies as they performed the task.

On average, participants deviated from the desired path by just 6.3mm (mean SD=3.9mm). There is no significant performance difference between shapes, 1D or 2D trials, or in X- or Y-axes.

FUTURE WORK

Several immediate avenues of future work exist. Foremost, we focused on interfaces that were 2D and primarily rectilinear. Our bodies, however, are neither. If we are to have interfaces on organic surfaces [10], it will be valuable to rethink classic interface paradigms, and consider how our unique form can contribute to a computing experience.

There are also many opportunities to enhance the approaches in this work. For example, it is possible to create 3D meshes of objects, allowing for distortion free projection onto non-planar surfaces (i.e., projective texturing). Additionally, postures and gestures of the arms and hands could be used for input. For example, a "telephone" gesture with hands could summon a keypad on the arm, while a "back of hand" pose could render a watch on the wrist (Figure 11B).

Finally, there are many fascinating qualitative questions surrounding on-body interaction. For example, how comfortable are people using their own bodies as interactive platforms? What are the social implications if other people want to use these interfaces? Is it acceptable to control an interface on someone else's body? Such interactive capabilities may open new questions in proxemics research.

CONCLUSION

In this paper, we described and evaluated our proof-of-concept implementation of *OmniTouch*. Results suggest interactions traditionally reserved for dedicated touch surfaces can now move into the environment, in an ad hoc fashion. Although our current prototype is fairly large, there are no significant barriers to miniaturization. It is entirely possible that a future incarnation of *OmniTouch* could be the size of a box of matches, worn as pendent or watch. Thus, the benefit of extreme portability can be combined with the ease and accuracy of interaction on large, physical surfaces.

The chief goal of the present work is to demonstrate that touch input can be achieved on everyday surfaces, including the human body. This brings to reality many intriguing interactions proposed in earlier work. In this paper, we only graze the surface of interactions enabled by making touch input available everywhere. We answer the fundamental question of whether or not it is possible, but in many ways, the hardest work lies ahead.

ACKNOWLEDGMENTS

We thank PrimeSense and Ohad Shvueli for the short range depth camera used in this research.

REFERENCES

1. Argyros, A.A., and Lourakis, M.I.A. Vision-based interpretation of hand gestures for remote control of a computer mouse. In *Proc. ECCV '06 Workshop on Computer Vision in HCI.* LNCS 3979. 40–51.
2. Benko, H. Saponas, T.S., Morris, D., and Tan, D. Enhancing input on and above the interactive surface with muscle sensing. In *Proc. ITS '09.* 93–100.
3. Cao, X., and Balakrishnan, R. Interacting with dynamically defined information spaces using a handheld projector and a pen. In *Proc. UIST '06.* 225–234.
4. Chapanis, A. Theory and methods for analyzing errors in man-machine systems. Annals of the New York Academy of Science 51, *Human Engineering* (1951), 1179–1203.
5. DeMenthon D. and Davis, L.S. Model-based object pose in 25 lines of code. *International Journal of Computer Vision*, 15, (1995). 123–141.
6. Erol, A., Bebis, G., Nicolescu, M., Boyle, R.D., and Twombly, X. Vision-based hand pose estimation: A review. *Computer Vision and Image Understanding*. 108, (2007), 52–73.
7. Gustafson, S., Bierwirth, D., and Baudisch, P. Imaginary interfaces: spatial interaction with empty hands and without visual feedback. In *Proc. UIST '10.* 3–12.
8. Harrison, C., Tan, D., and Morris, D. Skinput: appropriating the body as an input surface. In *Proc. CHI '10.* 453–462.
9. Holz, C. and Baudisch, P. The generalized perceived input point model and how to double touch accuracy by extracting fingerprints. In *Proc. CHI '10*, 581–590.
10. Holman, D. and Vertegaal, R. Organic user interfaces: designing computers in any way, shape, or form. *Comm. of the ACM,* 51, 6 (2008). 48–55.
11. Hua, H., Brown, L., and Gao, C. Scape: Supporting stereoscopic collaboration in augmented and projective environments. *IEEE Comput. Graph. Appl.* 24, 1 (2004), 66–75.
12. Kane, S., Avrahami, D., Wobbrock, J., Harrison, B., Rea, A., Philipose, M. and LaMarca, A. Bonfire: A nomadic system for hybrid laptop-tabletop interaction. In *Proc. UIST '09.* 129–138.
13. Lai, K., Bo, L., Ren, X., and Fox, D. Sparse Distance Learning for Object Recognition Combining RGB and Depth Information. In *Proc. ICRA '11.*
14. Lee, J.C., Hudson, S.E. and Tse, E. Foldable interactive displays. In *Proc. UIST '08.* 287–290.
15. Lewis, R.J. Literature review of touch-screen research from 1980 to 1992. *IBM Technical Report,* 54.694. Aug 20, 1993.
16. MicroVision, Inc. http://www.microvision.com
17. McFarlane, D., and Wilder, S. Interactive dirt: Increasing mobile work performance with a wearable projector-camera system. In *Proc. UbiComp '09*, 205-214.
18. Mistry, P., Maes, P., and Chang, L. WUW - wear Ur world: a wearable gestural interface. In *CHI '09 Ext. Abst.* 4111–4116.
19. Park, Y. Han, S., Park, J. and Cho, Y. Touch key design for target selection on a mobile phone. *Proc. MobileHCI '08.* 423–426.
20. Pinhanez, C. S. The Everywhere Displays projector: A device to create ubiquitous graphical interfaces. In *Proc. UBICOMP '01.* 315–331.
21. PrimeSense Ltd. http://www.primesense.com.
22. Raskar, R., Beardsley, P., van Baar, J., Wang, Y., Dietz, P., Lee, J., Leigh, D., and Willwacher, T. RFIG lamps: interacting with a self-describing world via photosensing wireless tags and projectors. In *Proc. SIGGRAPH '04.* 406–415.
23. Roudaut, A, Pohl, H. and Baudisch, P. Touch input on curved surfaces. In *Proc. CHI '11.* 1011-1020.
24. Saponas, T.S., Tan, D.S., Morris, D., Balakrishnan, R., Turner, J., and Landay, J. A. Enabling always-available input with muscle-computer interfaces. In *Proc. UIST '09.* 167–176.
25. Sears, A. Improving touchscreen keyboards: Design issues and a comparison with other devices. *IEEE Computer*, 3 (1991), 253–269.
26. Starner, T., Auxier, J., Ashbrook, D., and Gandy, M. The Gesture Pendant: A self-illuminating, wearable, infrared computer vision system for home automation control and medical monitoring. In *Proc. ISWC* '00, 87–94.
27. Sturman, D.J. and Zeltzer, D. A Survey of glove-based input. *IEEE Comp Graph and Appl*, 14, 1 (1994). 30–39.
28. Tan, D., Morris, D., and Saponas, T.S. Interfaces on the go. *ACM XRDS,* 16, 4 (2010), 30–34.
29. Tomasi, C., Rafii, A. and Torunoglu, I. Full-size projection keyboard for handheld devices. *Comm. of the ACM,* 46, 7 (2003), 70–75.
30. Wang, F. and Ren, X. Empirical evaluation for finger input properties in multi-touch interaction. In *Proc. CHI '09.* 1063–1072.
31. Ware, C., Arthur, K. and Booth, K.S. Fish tank virtual reality. In *Proc. CHI '93.* 37–42.
32. Wilson, A. and Benko, H. Combining multiple depth cameras and projectors for interactions on, above and between surfaces. In *Proc. UIST '10.* 273–282.
33. Wilson, A.D. PlayAnywhere: a compact interactive tabletop projection-vision system. In *Proc. UIST '05.* 83–92.
34. Wilson, A.D. Using a depth camera as a touch sensor. In *Proc. ITS '10.* 69–72.
35. Yee, K. Peephole displays: pen interaction on spatially aware handheld computers. In *Proc. CHI '03.* 1–8.

Visual Separation in Mobile Multi-Display Environments

Jessica R. Cauchard[1], Markus Löchtefeld[2], Pourang Irani[3], Johannes Schoening[2], Antonio Krüger[2], Mike Fraser[1], Sriram Subramanian[1]

[1]University of Bristol
Bristol Interaction & Graphics
Dept. of Computer Science
Woodland Rd, Bristol
BS8 1UB, UK
{cauchard, fraser, sriram}@cs.bris.ac.uk

[2]German Research Center for Artificial Intelligence (DFKI)
Stuhlsatzenhausweg 3 66123
Saarbrücken, Germany
{markus.loechtefeld, johannes.schoening, krueger}@dfki.de

[3]University of Manitoba
Computer Science Department,
Human-Computer Interaction lab
Winnipeg, Manitoba,
Canada.
irani@cs.umanitoba.ca

ABSTRACT
Projector phones, handheld game consoles and many other mobile devices increasingly include more than one display, and therefore present a new breed of mobile Multi-Display Environments (MDEs) to users. Existing studies illustrate the effects of visual separation between displays in MDEs and suggest interaction techniques that mitigate these effects. Currently, mobile devices with heterogeneous displays such as projector phones are often designed without reference to visual separation issues; therefore it is critical to establish whether concerns and opportunities raised in the existing MDE literature apply to the emerging category of Mobile MDEs (MMDEs). This paper investigates the effects of visual separation in the context of MMDEs and contrasts these with fixed MDE results, and explores design factors for Mobile MDEs. Our study uses a novel eye-tracking methodology for measuring switches in visual context between displays and identifies that MMDEs offer increased design flexibility over traditional MDEs in terms of visual separation. We discuss these results and identify several design implications.

ACM Classification: H5.2 [Information interfaces and presentation]: User Interfaces. - Graphical user interfaces.

General terms: Design, Experimentation, Human Factors.

Keywords: Mobile Multi-Display Environment, Mobile Projection, Visual Separation, Handheld Devices, Eye Tracking, Visual Search.

INTRODUCTION
Clamshell phones, handheld dual-display game consoles, projector-enhanced tablet PCs and cameras are steadily increasing the number and forms of multi-display mobile devices. In the case of projector phones, it is expected that the market will grow to 20 million units by 2015 [12]. Unlike traditional handsets, these devices offer a large projected display, in addition to the existing display, that can be viewed by more than one person at a time.

Such mobile multi-display environments operate by providing visual information on different screens. Figure 1 illustrates two examples of projecting on the floor or the wall to create a large screen real-estate. Often the larger display allows sharing public information, while private information can be kept on the device's screen for the owner's eyes only, or to principally support input feedback. Additionally, two physical displays on one mobile device can afford more display real estate than a single-display mobile-device. While MMDEs can be used in both, single-user contexts (using multiple displays to partition tasks) and multi-user contexts (e.g. for privacy setting), the design space of MMDEs needs refinement for single-user contexts before considering aspects of multi-user environments.

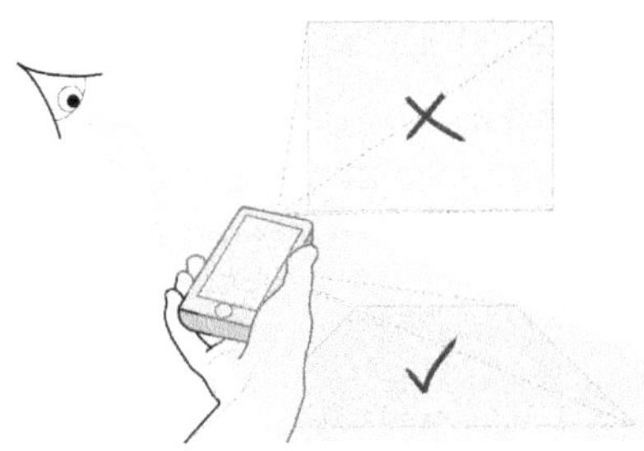

Figure 1 – Design implications: In Mobile Multi-Display environments, displays should ideally be in the same field of view.

The existing MDE literature shows how such device ecologies are affected by the unavoidable visual separation effects caused by multiple displays [28, 29]. Simply defined, visual separation is the division of information across space in MDEs. Non-continuous presentation of information can be inefficient to interact with, if it is not handled properly [5, 18]. Research in fixed multi-display environments has shown that visual separation of content can affect performance [13, 22]. Tan and Czerwinski [29] found a significant detrimental effect when dividing information across multiple displays at different depths for the same separation angle. Likewise, Su and Bailey [28] found that when positioning large displays through workspaces, the relative depth between displays can affect users' performance.

On one hand, direct control over the projection space and the closeness of the display on a mobile device could mitigate the effects of visual separation on mobile MDEs. However, on the other hand, mobile devices can create conditions whereby their mobility accentuates static MDE problems. For example, mobile projector phones have an inherent depth differential between the phone's screen and the projection. Prior work in MDEs would suggest negative visual separation effects due to this depth gap. With a lack of understanding of how visual separation affects usability and performance, it is hard to identify appropriate designs and suitable interaction techniques or adapt these devices to specific applications.

Borrowing on principles derived from research in MDEs, we map out factors that could negatively impact visual separation in MMDEs. This motivated our user study which includes an innovative eye-tracking methodology to measure visual separation effects. Our principal contributions are that: 1. Visual separation does not impair the viability of MMDEs; 2. Displays should ideally be in the same field of view (Figure 1); 3. Factors such as: handling, portability and unsteadiness do not exacerbate visual separation. 4. We present some implications of our study on MMDE design.

TYPES OF MOBILE MULTI-DISPLAY ENVIRONMENTS

In this section we explore existing work in MMDEs. MMDEs are either partially mobile (i.e. a mobile component imported in a traditional MDE) or fully mobile (i.e. a mobile device that supports more than one display).

Partially mobile MDEs include environments where a mobile device is imported inside a traditional MDE, for example Greenberg et al. [14] present an environment in which a PDA is used in conjunction with shared public displays. Since the mobile component can be flexibly reoriented relative to the existing MDE, the visual separation effects of this component in the overall environment may be mitigated by the ability to easily reorient the device. This could minimise visual separation between displays and thus current research in fixed MDEs is likely to hold in the partially mobile MDE case.

There are many existing examples of fully mobile MDEs in the literature, which can be divided into two categories, *multi-device-single-display* and *single-device-multi-display*.

Mobile *multi-device-single-display* environments are created when individual single-display mobile devices are brought together to create a new MDE. For example Lyons et al. [21] present techniques using a network to link multiple single displays in order to share co-located display spaces. Cao et al. [6] present a multi-user interaction technique that allows individual handheld projectors to interact simultaneously. Finally, Siftables [24] provide a set of tangible interactive objects, each equipped with a single display that can be combined in order to manipulate data and information. They support tangible interaction effects, such as removing a physical item from a pile to delete associated virtual data. In all the described cases, each individual display can easily be moved and re-oriented depending on the desired situation. The users can then intuitively reduce visual separation effects.

Mobile *single-device-multi-display* environments provide more than one display on a single mobile device. This type of environment has gained a lot of popularity with the growth of embedded pico-projectors in existing devices such as phones, cameras, camcorders and even tablet PCs. Traditionally these displays have been fixed relative to one another, such as with a mobile projector phone where the projection lens is normally fixed at an orthogonal angle to the mobile phone's screen. Some devices, such as the Nintendo DS™ present reconfigurable hardware capabilities in between the two screens. Unfortunately, these capabilities are not currently exploited by software applications. Nonetheless, increasing numbers of *single-device-multi-display* environments exploit a reconfigurable multi-display layout, as the Codex [17] where two screens are hinged and can be rearranged into different positions. Despite the possibility of re-orienting these devices, many *single-device-multi-display* environments do not allow the user to rearrange displays in order to simultaneously visualise information. This bears the question of whether we can immediately transfer guidelines from research on fixed multi-display contexts to mobile *single-device-multi-display* environments.

FACTORS INTENSIFYING THE IMPACT OF VISUAL SEPARATION

Having reviewed existing MMDEs, in this section we review existing work on visual separation in MDEs and the visual separation challenges for *single-device-multi-display* mobile environments. Factors amplifying the effects of visual separation have been studied for a range of multi-display configurations including when displays are of different sizes, when placed at different distances from the user, if oriented at different relative angles and when separated by surrounding bezels or frames.

Size and Depth

Mandryk et al. [22] show that users are faster at interacting between two identical and continuous monitors compared to using a secondary monitor of smaller size placed with a small gap to the primary screen. Pointer warping techniques such as Mouse Ether [2] and frame memory pointer [4] propose cursor movement techniques that can help reduce the effects of visual separation across displays of different sizes in heterogeneous MDEs.

Early literature in ergonomics [1] advises that documents and screen be kept at the same distance from the user for data-entry tasks that require rapid shifts between both elements, to reduce costs in switching views. Recently, Tan and Czerwinski [29] show a detrimental effect due to visual separation when a screen and a projector are placed at different depths within the same visual field. These negative effects can be reduced with techniques such as the Perspective Cursor [25], that remaps the ordinary mouse cursor in a complex heterogeneous MDE depending on the perspective of each user regardless of their position.

In most *single-device-multi-display* mobile environments, the screens used are set to have similar characteristics and dimensions, and are often at the same distance from the user (i.e. where the device is held). However, in projector-enhanced mobile devices, screens and projections vary in size and distance depending on the proximity to the projection surface. This is the case for mobile projector phones, projector-cameras or camcorders and e-book readers equipped with projectors. This category of devices contains a small personal screen and a larger projection area. Although absolute size and distance can be configured by manipulating the device, relative size and distance between displays are typically fixed and may cause visual separation effects due to angular or focal displacement.

Angular separation / Field of view (FOV)

Tan and Czerwinski [29] show greater visual separation effects of depth when the data is separated by a 55° angle (i.e. outside the useful FOV) compared to a 27° angle (i.e. inside the useful FOV). Su and Bailey [28] studied visual separation for multiple large displays and found negative effects when the secondary screen is situated on the same horizontal plane as the primary screen but at an angle of 70° relative to the user, at the periphery of their field of view. Their study also showed a negative effect when the second screen was completely behind the user (i.e. in a completely separate FOV); however, they found no effect when the secondary screen was oriented at an angle from the first screen and were both at the same distance from the user. Following their experiment, they presented a set of guidelines on how to position two large displays relative to each other: the displays should stay on the same horizontal plane, at no more than a 45° subtended visual angle and should not be placed behind a user; in other words both displays should stay within the user's FOV.

Some *single-device-multi-display* environments are designed with the displays in different fields of view. For example, some clamshell phones are equipped with both an internal and an external display, such as the Samsung Alias™ 2. With this configuration, the screens are on different sides of the phone (i.e. in a different FOV) and cannot be used simultaneously. Codex [17] is a dual-screen device that works with a hinge between the screens and offers different functionalities for different rotational 'postures' of the screens, that can be in same or different FOV depending on context. Z-Agon [23] is another example of *single-device-multi-display* with 6 screens fitted in a cubic arrangement. Held in the palm, it can be moved to explore content on the 2 or 3 faces in front of the user while other faces remain hidden at the back of the cube.

Bezels

In MDEs, Tan and Czerwinski [29] found no effects of visual separation due to bezels and physical distance between screens alone. Yang et al. [30] found minimal visual separation effects between Lens-Mouse (a mouse with screen on top) and the monitor. Task performance in Yang et al.'s study [30] degraded in their dual-monitor condition attributed to distance and not bezels. Contrarily, Bi et al. [5] found that splitting symbols across two displays with a bezel in the middle was detrimental in a search task. Bi et al. [5] also found that interacting with data was faster with no bezel compared to a tiled screen. Forlines et al. [13] show that for an individual user; having information split across multiple vertical screens is detrimental in terms of reaction time to accomplish a visual search task compared to a single vertical screen. Stitching [18] is an interaction technique designed to reduce visual separation effects by using a pen interface to draw interaction lines across multiple displays.

Chen et al. [9] present a dual-display e-book reader and shows advantages of using multiple screens for reading. For example, information can be separated on both screens through the bezel for multi-document reading. Moreover, the device supports interaction techniques that draw on real books, such as moving one screen towards the other to 'turn pages'. In addition, the screens can be detached and reassembled for different modes of use. Devices with dual screens separated by a bezel already exist, such as phones, laptops or even game consoles as the dual-screen Nintendo DSi™ or dual-touch-screen Toshiba Libretto® laptop.

MMDEs vs. MDEs

In all the above designs, MMDEs have very different characteristics to traditional MDEs. We have identified inherent size and depth gaps which create potential angular and focal separation in the case of projector-enhanced mobile devices or individual displays placed in separate fields of view such as clamshell phones. Previous research in MDEs shows that multiple screens need to be placed within the same useful FOV of the user to avoid negative effects of visual separation [28] and also that specific interaction techniques need to be applied if the size of the displays differs. Yet, MMDE designs do not necessarily follow these guidelines because the studies presume a fixed position and orientation and no or limited control over changing display placement during the task. It is therefore essential to determine whether visual separation effects previously demonstrated in fixed MDEs translate to MMDEs. In the remainder of this paper, we explore the design space for MMDEs and we determine if the negative effects of visual separation in MMDEs can be reduced by aligning displays within the same field of view.

DESIGN FACTORS FOR MOBILE MDES

There is a fixed number of ways to position displays together in a *single-device-multi-display* mobile environment. When such devices possess more than two displays, these design considerations apply to each pair of displays individually. The displays can either be separated by: distance vertically (Figure 2a,b,c) or horizontally (Figure 2d,e,f), an angle (Figure 2g,h,i), or any combination of those conditions. The displays can be separated by any distance *d* that will vary depending on the devices' design: from a few centimeters wide such as the size of a bezel or a hinge (Figure 2 left column) up to a few meters wide in the case of a projector enhanced device (Figure 2 middle and right columns). When the displays are separated by an angle α (Figure 2g,h,i), α can be of any value (0-360°) along any axis in the cartesian space.

When the displays are close to each other or at a small angle from each other, they are in the same field of view. However when *d* or α have high values, the displays are in different fields of view. In fixed MDEs, displays tend to be in the same field of view, which is not the case in current mobile MDEs. In our user study, we will determine whether placing the displays in different fields of view increase visual separation effects.

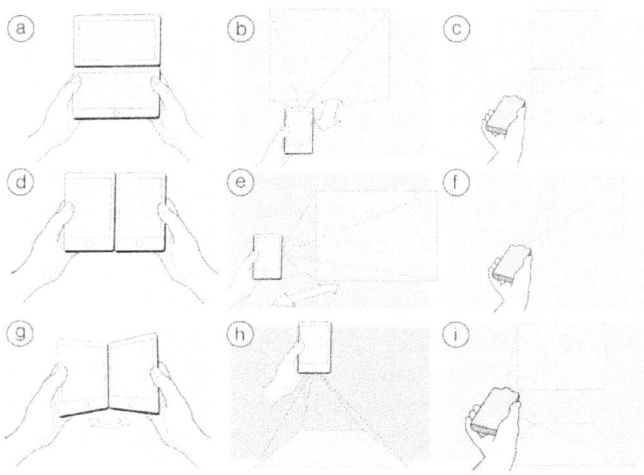

Figure 2 - Possible layouts for two displays on a mobile device for different types of displays: screen-screen (a,d,g); screen-projector (b,e,h) and projector-projector (c,f,i). Displays can be separated horizontally, (a,b,c), vertically (d,e,f), by an angle across any plane (g,h,i) or any combination of the above positions. In the screen-projector cases (b,e,h), the displays are further separated by depth due to the inherent properties of each display

Depending on the design of the device, the displays are either relatively *fixed*: always at the same distance and angle from each other or *reconfigurable*: the distance and angle between the displays is context-dependent such as in Codex [17]. Reconfigurable devices are especially interesting since they can adapt to different contexts by rearranging the displays with respect to one another. Experimentally, reconfigurable displays can be simplified to devices that offer a set of fixed configurations, visual separation effects can then be studied for fixed configurations only.

In Figure 2, we present possible layouts of two displays: two screens (left column), a screen and a projector (middle column) and two projectors (right column).

In the *two screens* case, the screens are unlikely to be more than a few centimetres apart in order for the device to be handheld; the design is therefore similar to traditional screens in MDEs separated by a bezel. The visual separation effects are then likely to be similar to the effects of bezels in MDEs. However, bezels do not affect visual separation as long as information is not cut across the bezel [5] and appropriate interaction techniques are implemented [18]. We have therefore chosen not to explore visual separation effects for this configuration.

In the case of *a screen and a projector*, the displays have by default heterogeneous characteristics, such as different sizes and resolutions and are moreover separated by depth. The literature on MDEs shows that depth can be an important factor when managing visual separation effects. Moreover, the position of the projector lens on the device itself will determine if both displays will be in the same field of view or not. We believe that visual separation effects will be at their strongest in this type of environment, hence our decision to run the user study with a projector enhanced mobile device.

The *two projectors* case is similar in characteristics to traditional large displays MDEs, such as two projection spaces that will display either on the same, on an orthogonal or on opposite planes, characteristics that have already been explored in the MDE literature. Yet, dual-projectors mobile devices present some interesting features such as the ability to display at different depths depending on the surrounding environment, as when displaying on an uneven wall. Nonetheless, in most multi-projector cases, the projections will either be separated in distance (depth), in plane or in size of projection. We believe that those issues are similar to the ones encountered by "a screen and a projector" case and that any experimental results obtained for the former configuration will apply to this category too.

STUDY

The purpose of this study is to identify the effects of visual separation on *single-device-multi-display* mobile environment when the multiple displays are in the same field of view and when they are not, as well as when the device is fixed or mobile. We run the study using a projector-enhanced mobile device since the embedded displays are by design of different sizes and displaying at different depths. We study the "a screen and a projector" case over the "two-projector" case since this configuration is more prominent in current devices. We expect that the lack of physical connection between displays will generate greater effects of visual separation.

Our experimental setup includes the following aspects of mobility: handling (participant can handle the device as they feel comfortable), portability (implies that the size and distance of the projection will vary), unsteadiness (jitter is not compensated as in a real-life scenario) but not actually moving between rooms in order to allow comparison between results in the *fixed* and the *mobile* settings.

Task

The task chosen for this experiment is a visual search task. Visual search is a typical task for analysing visual separation [13]. Tan et al. [29] use different types of task including text comparison as it is "representative of tasks in which the user must cross reference and compare content displayed in multiple locations" (p.4). Chen and Chien [8] use a similar task when looking at effects on visual performance on small screens. In our experiment, we chose an image comparison over a text comparison task, since the laser projector's resolution could affect reading accuracy.

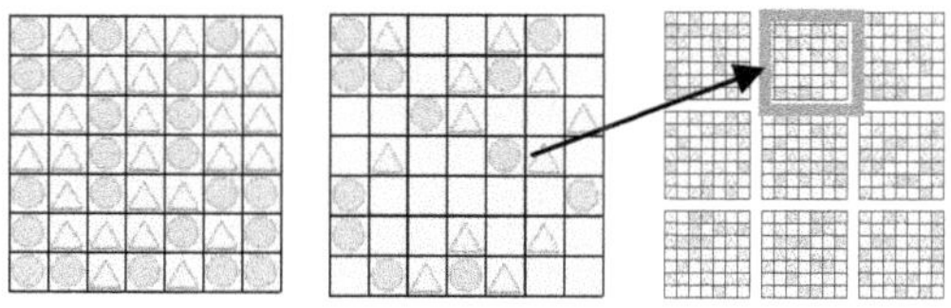

Figure 3 – a. Left: Example of pattern displayed on the screen – b. Centre: Matching sparse version – c. Right: 3x3 grid displayed on the projection.

The task chosen consisted of matching a pattern on the screen (Figure 3a) with a sparse version of the same pattern (Figure 3b) positioned inside a projected 3x3 grid of competing matches (Figure 3c). This makes use of the different display sizes, showing the initial pattern only and a keypad on the small display and the 9-pattern grid on the larger projected display. The sparse versions are randomly created by deleting half of the items from the initial pattern and replacing them with blank cases. The competing patterns in the grid are other sparse versions of the initial pattern for which 5 items are permuted in order to look similar but not match the initial pattern.

In a pilot study with 4 participants we presented the participants with two types of patterns: a matrix filled with letters 'P' and 'B' and a matrix filled with coloured shapes: circles and triangles. The letter-based task was very long to perform and extremely tiring for the user while results obtained were similar to the shape-based task. We then decided to run the study with the shape-based task only.

The participant would select a matching pattern on the projection by pressing the corresponding number on the numeric keypad on the screen below the initial pattern. Depending on the answer, the participant could receive positive audio-feedback and continue to the next trial or receive negative audio-feedback and would have to repeat the same trial until the correct matching pattern was found.

Experimental design

For the study we used a Google Nexus One with touch screen combined to a Microvision ShowWX laser pico-projector (Figure 4). The study makes use of a portable eye tracker since these systems have already been used to measure visual search tasks [19]. The experimental room was darkened to optimize the projector viewing conditions.

Figure 4 – Phone and projector used for the user study fitted with the Floor setting mirror.

The independent variables were:

- Position of the projection relative to the phone's screen: in the same field of view (Floor), in different fields of view separated by one angular plane (Front) or by two angular planes (Side)
- Mobility: whether the device is fixed on a tripod or handheld by the user: mobile setting.

Position

The projection spaces relative to the screen are described on Figure 5: The Front projection corresponds to the alignment of the phone and the projector. A mirror is placed at the top of the projector lens and oriented at 60° downwards for the Floor condition, as shown in Figure 4, and 40° sideways for the Side condition. In order to reduce the keystone effect introduced by the mirror, we projected at a resolution smaller than the projector's maximum one.

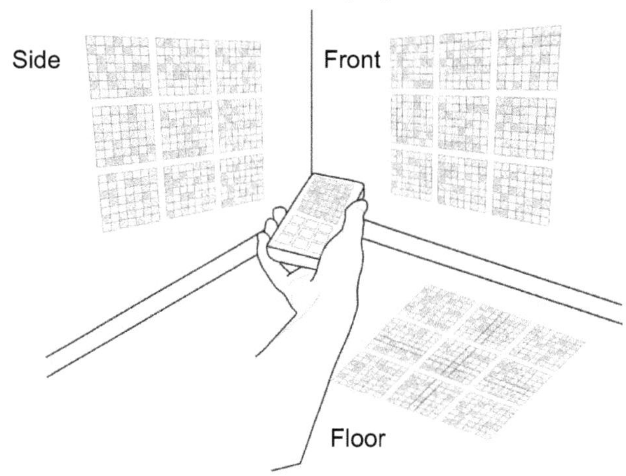

Figure 5 - Example of task pattern and grid of sparse patterns in the three positions in fixed setting: Front, Floor and Side. For each trial, the grid is only displayed in one setting only.

Mobility

In terms of mobility, the device was either set at a fixed position on a tripod (fixed setting) or held by the user (mobile setting).

In the fixed setting, the assembly phone-projector is placed on top of a tripod and the participant had to stand on footsteps marked by the tripod. The position of each projection space (on the floor, front and side walls) was predefined in order to set a constant position and aspect ratio of the projection for all participants. We ensured that all three projection spaces were the same distance from the device (110cm) and would therefore always have the same size (middle of the projected grid fixed at 60cm wide).

In the mobile setting, the user is holding the device and can use any projection surface at any distance or size that they are comfortable with. The user was free to move around the room with the device. The distance to the wall and the size of the projection would then vary depending on user's movements. We did not impose any restriction on how the user would hold the device. Nonetheless, we observed that most users held the device in the non-dominant hand and touched the screen with the dominant hand, while other users held the device in both hands and used their thumbs to touch the screen. None held the device with their dominant hand.

Eye tracking procedure

The context switches were measured using a mobile eye tracker: Tobii® Glasses that recorded eye movements at 30 Hz. This eye tracker is non-intrusive as it is low weight (75 grams glasses) and fully mobile so participants could roam freely. Some InfraRed (IR) markers were positioned around the various display spaces (in the fixed setting) to allow automatic data mapping and help repositioning the projected image at the same place for each participant. The eye tracker records both a video of the scene and where the user is looking in the scene.

Hypothesis

Based on the literature review and our preliminary exploration of the issues, we expected display configurations (relative positions of displays within same or in different fields-of-view), and whether the device is being held (mobility), to significantly affect performance and produce visual separation effects.

We presumed visual separation effects to be less important when the screen and the projection are in the same field of view (floor setting) than when the projection is in a different field of view than the screen (front and side settings). We also expected for participants to compensate visual separation effects when holding the device since they could themselves reconfigure the display areas adaptively.

Procedure

Twelve volunteers (5 men) aged between 24 and 35 years old (μ=28.6) were recruited from within one of our universities. All our participants were familiar with touch-screen technology and all had normal colour vision. We used a within-subjects design where position and mobility were counterbalanced across participants.

We explained the task to each participant individually. To start a trial the user pressed the "Start" button whenever they felt ready. There were 8 trials for each experimental condition. Participants were also told that they should say aloud if they pressed the wrong button in order to identify false negatives. After the experiment, users filled out a NASA TLX satisfaction survey.

In summary the experimental design was: 12 participants x 2 mobility factors x 3 positions x 8 trials = 576 data points.

Measures

- *Number of context switches* between the screen and the projected display. Previous studies on visual separation do not measure the number of context switches. However the problems induced by context switches are quantified in mobile projector-phone studies [16] as well as in some MDE studies [3, 11]. This is measured by the portable eye tracker. The number of context switches is computed by the eye tracking software in the fixed setting using the IR markers and is then manually verified through analysis of the eye tracker video. In the mobile setting, the switches are manually counted at the video analysis stage (Figure 6) since the position of the projection space is not constrained in this setting.

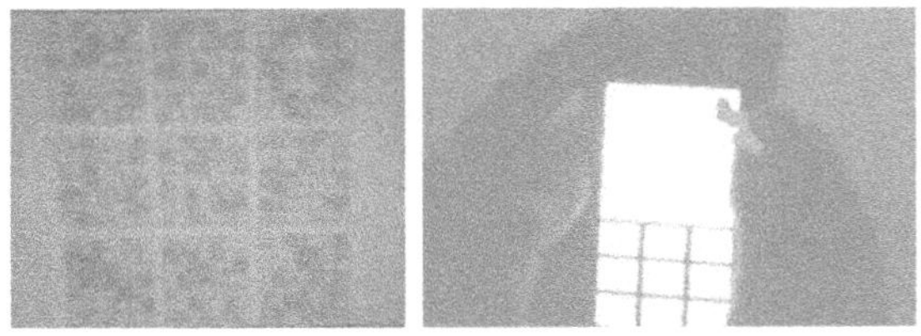

Figure 6 – Snapshots from the eye tracker video
Left: User is looking at the projection.
Right: User is looking at the phone

- *Completion time* and *number of errors* in performing each trial, including number of false positives. These are typical measures in visual separation studies [13, 28, 29] and allow comparing participants' efficiency for different experimental settings. The completion time is timed between the start of the task to its successful completion.
- *Position preferred* - NASA TLX: This test assesses subjective information on a 7-point Likert scale for mental, physical and temporal demand; performance; effort and frustration. We have combined this traditional subjective workload questionnaire with some personalised questions aimed at gathering user preference data.

Results

We used a repeated measures ANOVA test for the number of context switches, completion time and number of errors. We used the univariate ANOVA test for the NASA-TLX results analyses with subject as a random factor.

- *Number of context switches:* We found a main effect for position ($F_{(2,94)}$=62.817, $p<0.001$), pairwise post-hoc comparison showed significant differences between the positions: Front and Floor ($p<0.001$), and Side and Floor ($p<0.001$) and no significant differences between Mobile and Static conditions ($F_{(1,95)}$=1.034, $p>0.05$). The mean for Front and Side were respectively 20.49 and 19.62 context switches, compare to 31.41 for the Floor conditions as shown on Figure 7 (left).
- *Task completion time and number of errors*: Our findings showed no significant difference in trial completion time for position ($F_{(2,94)}$=0.390, $p>0.05$) and mobility

($F_{(1,95)}$=0.057, $p>0.05$), as well as no significant difference in error-rates for the different positions ($F_{(2,94)}$=1.049, $p>0.05$) and mobility ($F_{(1,95)}$=1.143, $p>0.05$). The average error rate across all conditions was 8.9%. Figure 7 right shows the average trial completion times across all conditions.

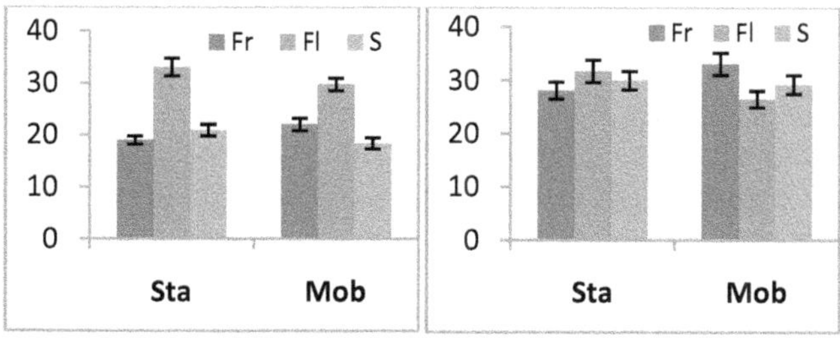

Figure 7 – Average of context switches (left) and average task completion time (right) for each conditions: Fr: Front, Fl: Floor, S: Side.

- *NASA TLX*: We only found a significant difference in temporal demand ("How hurried or rushed was the pace of the task?") for position ($F_{(2,22)}$=4.086, p=0.031). Floor is perceived as faster than Front and both are perceived as faster than Side (means for temporal demand for Floor is 3.67, Front is 3.83 and Side is 4.33 on a 7-point Likert scale). For all other variables no significant effect was found.
- *Position preferred*. In the fixed setting, 75% of participants chose the Front position with the remaining participants preferring the Floor. In the mobile setting, half of the participants preferred the Floor, 42% the Front and 8% the Side. When asked what their favourite position was overall, 75% favoured a mobile position compared to a fixed one (Figure 8).

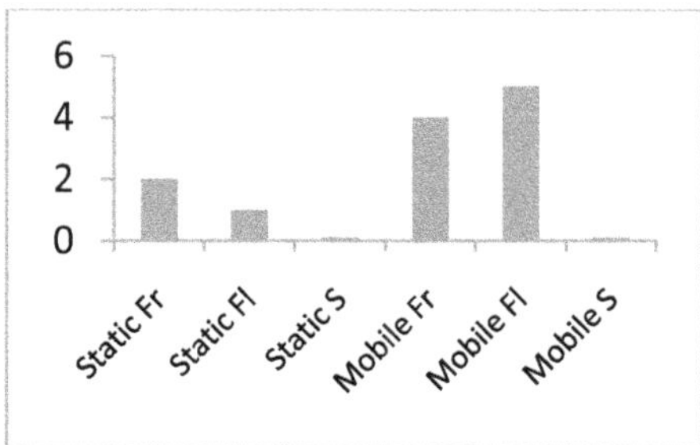

Figure 8 – Overall preferred position for each participant (Fr: Front, Fl: Floor, S: Side)

Discussion

In this section, we discuss the above results on four related themes: A. Viability of mobile MDEs, B. Dual-display configurations, C. Substantiation of mobile uses and D. Design implications

A. Visual separation does not impair the viability of MMDEs

The results of the study show that visual separation effects did not prevent users from carrying out the task, which is reflected through the low error rate of only 8.9% over all tasks and conditions. This result is valid for both the static and the mobile conditions.

During the experiment, participants had no problems using a mobile dual-display device even with very heterogeneous displays in terms of size, resolution and depth of the displays. In a case where tasks are divided across displays, *single-device-multi-display* environments can outperform today's single display devices. Moreover, the tasks can make use of the different displays' characteristics, such as our experiment uses the phone's screen to display a single pattern and a keypad and the large projection space to display a large grid of 9 patterns.

We conclude that mobile multi-display environments with heterogeneous displays are a viable solution.

B. Displays should ideally be in the same field of view.

The eye tracker recorded significantly more eye context switches in the floor condition: over 30% more than in the other positions; whereas we found no significance in completion time and error rate across the three positions in both fixed and mobile settings. This important result would have been overlooked should we have used traditional task performance measures only.

Our task was complex enough that participants could not simply memorise the whole pattern and find the matching pattern on the projection. The results show that the number of eye context switches does not affect task performance and that there is a higher number of context switches when both displays are in the same field of view. This suggests context switches are a lot cheaper to perform when both displays are in the same field of view (Floor setting) as they only require a simple eye movement and little or no head and neck movements, unlike the Side and Front conditions where participants reported discomfort. One participant said about the Side setting: "It was very uncomfortable to constantly turn my head during the experiment". We also believe that the higher number of context switches in the Floor condition is due to the fact that context switches can be considered as epistemic [20], using the active memory to store the position of the geometric shapes in the pattern. Instead of having to remember the positions in the pattern, users could externalise their thought processes by switching context more often. This could also explain why this setting appeared as being faster paced to the participants.

We recommend that as a default displays in MMDEs should have the displays aligned in the same field of view.

C. Mobility factors do not exacerbate visual separation.

Since we found no significant difference between mobile and static setting in terms of error rate, task completion time or context switches, we believe that the following mobility factors: handling, portability, projection size and unsteadiness, have no particular effect on visual separation.

Participants' wrist and hand movements in the mobile setting did not help compensate the effects of visual separation. A possible reason could be that they were already compensating for the jitter of the projection resulting from the participants holding the device in their hands. Since none of the participants mentioned jitter as a problem during the experiment and in the post-study questionnaire, we conclude that they instinctively compensated for any mobility-induced jitter effects. Our experiment showed no more visual separation effects between mobile and static settings, even though the projection space and display size were varying; and since participants showed a strong preference for the mobile setting, the investigation of mobile scenarios is justified.

Factors such as: handling, portability and unsteadiness do not exacerbate visual separation. Although we did not explicitly test fully mobile conditions, we anticipate that those results are transferable to those environments.

D. Design implications

In the following sections, we present some design implications for future MDEs that emerge from our discussion in terms of type of displays, display physical arrangements, flexibility of design and mobility.

Type of displays for MMDEs

Our experiment demonstrates that mobile MDEs are viable, which includes heterogeneous dual-display solutions. Although dual-display solutions for mobile devices are technically possible, they are currently under-exploited by manufacturers. Our study demonstrates that these solutions should be envisaged more often since visual separation effects do not present issues for carrying out activities where tasks are distributed across displays, such as in our experiment. This is also valid for activities wherein the user chooses which display to use depending on application and context needs. Those scenarios of use are consistent with most common uses of MDEs as described by Grudin [15].

Additionally, most existing dual-display mobile devices are designed with multiple displays of similar types, whereas heterogeneous displays offer more potential, such as the ability to choose where to display depending on the context without generating negative visual separation effects. While current usage of heterogeneous dual-display mobile devices is often limited to one display at a time, we encourage designers to consider exploiting both displays simultaneously. This would also allow more flexibility in the choice of interaction technique; such as in Chen's e-book reader [9]

Physical arrangements of displays

Our experiment shows that having both displays in the same field of view is paramount for applications that make use of both displays. There is evidence that users can reduce the amount of information they have to *remember* and can instead use active memory to *recall* information by switching gaze between displays more frequently. This is particularly important for applications that suffer from heavily cluttered displays, such as map applications. This pattern of increased context switches to alleviate cognitive load is equally important when one display is also used to facilitate input to the other display. For example, a projector phone's touch screen can be used to manipulate content in the projected space. In this situation, the displays must be arranged within the same field of view. When both displays are in the same field of view, one display can be partially occluding the second display. This case is especially likely to occur in MMDEs where there is a depth gap between the displays as in mobile projector phones.

Besides, arranging displays in the same field of view is not trivial in a mobile environment where external factors influence how the user holds the device and on which surfaces content can be displayed. These external factors range from luminosity and glare to the available projection spaces, number of users viewing the content and the type of information being displayed. The usage of a steerable projection could overcome these environmental issues, as proposed by Pinhanez [27] for static and by Cauchard et al. [7] for mobile projection. Moreover, a steerable projection can reduce visual separation effects in MDEs by automatically reconfiguring the alignment of the displays according to the context the device is used in.

Flexibility of design

Prior research conducted in MDE suggests that displays arranged on different planes or separated by more than 45° angle result in lower task performance and provide negative visual separation effects [28]. However, in our study, we find no significant task performance differences, whether in time completion or error rate, across the different settings. These results show that guidelines for MDEs are not directly applicable to MMDEs. One explanation could be that MMDEs use a comparably small display, close to the user compared to traditional MDEs. This shows that although it is preferable for the user to have both displays in the same field of view, there is more flexibility in the alignment of displays in MMDEs than in MDEs.

This is especially the case for applications that do not require epistemic actions from the user, and for which the need for rapid context switching is not crucial. For those applications, manufacturers have more freedom to position the projection unit wherever it best suits the device ecology. This could result in smaller devices since the projection unit could be placed where it fits best without generating visual separation effects on performance. In this case, a wide range of interaction techniques can be supported for which displays do not need to be aligned, such as foot interaction on the floor [7] or even shadows on the projection [10] for any other projection setting.

Floor Projection

Our experimental results also illustrates that projecting on the floor is a promising option. When a projector-phone is held horizontally, the user can have both displays in the same field of view by projecting on the floor. This is especially useful for street navigation applications where users can follow directional arrows on the floor instead of reading a map on a small screen. Moreover, unlike a wall, the floor is a surface that is constantly available for projection.

However, projecting on the floor is not straightforward and involves careful technical considerations. As is the case for any projection surface, the floor can be uneven, as for example on a cobbled street. There is also the issue of the user paying attention to the projected display only, while being inattentive to their surroundings. This can be very dangerous, so it is important to design a system that will retain users' awareness to hazards.

The choice of interaction technique will partially depend on the position of the floor projection with respect to the user. Projecting close to the user allows foot interaction or even a full body interaction; projecting further away from the users' body will require indirect input such as through buttons or sensors on the projecting mobile device. The position of the projection can also be adapted to the user's pace. For example, if the person is walking, the projection could be further away from their body [26] and move closer when the user stops walking to allow for direct interaction.

Mobility

In our study we find no more visual separation effects when the device is held than when the device is fixed on a tripod. Most current *single-device-multi-display* environments are built for scenarios of use in which the device is placed on a surface. Our study shows that various factors of mobility are worth investigating, such as when the user is walking while holding the device; or stopping by to obtain contextual information about the area they are walking by; or when using a QR-code on a poster for example. Many contextual applications could benefit from true mobility and new interaction paradigms could be envisaged, such as the use of haptic while on the move.

FUTURE WORK

The focus of the present work has been to explore visual separation issues for a single user working in a mobile multi-display environment. However there are equally interesting future scenarios which involve multi-user collaboration in mobile multi-display environments. Supporting collaboration in a MMDE requires positioning displays in order to improve coordination and awareness while potentially increasing visual separation. One direction of future research is to explore how visual separation issues affect collaboration and coordination between multiple users.

CONCLUSION

In this paper we presented design factors for an emerging category of devices: Mobile Multi-Display Environments (MMDEs). We then investigated visual separation effects for MMDEs compared to the current literature of visual separation in fixed MDEs. Through an innovative eye tracking methodology, we compared different angular separations of a projection and a screen: two displays of different sizes and at different distances from the user. We determined that although task performance was not affected by the displays being in the same or in different fields of view, the number of eye context switches was over 30% higher in the condition where both displays were in the same field of view. We also tested various factors of mobility in our experiment and concluded that they did not affect visual separation. We finally present design implications in terms of types of displays used in MMDEs, physical arrangements of the displays, flexibility of design of MMDEs and mobility.

Additionally, we establish that through the use of an eye tracker, we were able to highlight interesting differences between different physical arrangements of displays; that may not have been revealed with trial completion time and accuracy alone. This further suggests that eye tracking is an interesting way to investigate visual separation issues.

ACKNOWLEDGEMENTS

Partial funding for this work was provided by EPSRC (grant number EP/G058334/1) and MobileVCE (www.mobilevce.com) as part of the User Interactions for Breakthrough Services research program.

We would like to thank Dr Peter Bennett in the Bristol Interaction and Graphics lab for the illustrations.

REFERENCES

[1] Ankrum, D. R. Visual Ergonomics in the Office — Guidelines. Technical Report, 1999.

[2] Baudisch, P., Cutrell, E., Hinckley, K. and Gruen, R. Mouse ether: accelerating the acquisition of targets across multi-monitor displays. In *CHI '04 EA*, ACM, 2004, pp. 1379-1382.

[3] Benko, H. and Feiner, S. Multi-monitor mouse. In *CHI '05 EA*, ACM, 2005, pp. 1208-1211.

[4] Benko, H. and Feiner, S. Pointer warping in heterogeneous multi-monitor environments. In *Proceedings of Graphics Interface 2007*, ACM, 2007, pp. 111-117.

[5] Bi, X., Bae, S.-H. and Balakrishnan, R. Effects of interior bezels of tiled-monitor large displays on visual search, tunnel steering, and target selection. In *CHI 2010*, ACM, 2010, pp. 65-74.

[6] Cao, X., Forlines, C. and Balakrishnan, R. Multi-user interaction using handheld projectors. In *UIST 2007*, ACM, 2007, pp. 43-52.

[7] Cauchard, J. R., Fraser, M. and Subramanian, S. Offsetting Displays on Mobile Projector Phones. In *Ubiprojection Workshop on Personal Projection at Pervasive 2010*, pp. 3.

[8] Chen, C.-H. and Chien, Y.-H. Effects of RSVP display design on visual performance in accomplishing dual tasks with small screens. *International Journal of Design*, 1, 2007, pp. 27-35.

[9] Chen, N., Guimbretiere, F., Dixon, M., Lewis, C. and Agrawala, M. Navigation techniques for dual-display e-book readers. In *CHI'08*, ACM, pp. 1779-1788.

[10] Cowan, L. and Li, K. ShadowPuppets: Supporting Collocated Interaction with Mobile Projector Phones Using Hand Shadows. In *CHI 2011*, ACM

[11] Dickie, C., Hart, J., Vertegaal, R. and Eiser, A. LookPoint: an evaluation of eye input for hands-free switching of input devices between multiple computers. In *OZCHI '06*, ACM, 2006, pp. 119-126.

[12] Dickson, F. Pico Projectors: One Reason Bigger Isn't Better. Technical Report IN1004722WH, In-Stat, 2010.

[13] Forlines, C., Shen, C., Wigdor, D. and Balakrishnan, R. Exploring the effects of group size and display configuration on visual search. In *CSCW '06*, ACM, 2006, pp. 11-20.

[14] Greenberg, S., Boyle, M. and Laberge, J. PDAs and shared public displays: Making personal information public, and public information personal. *Personal and Ubiquitous Computing*, 3, 1999, pp. 54-64.

[15] Grudin, J. Partitioning digital worlds: focal and peripheral awareness in multiple monitor use. In *CHI 2001*, ACM, 2001, pp. 458-465.

[16] Hang, A., Rukzio, E. and Greaves, A. Projector phone: a study of using mobile phones with integrated projector for interaction with maps. In *MobileHCI 2008*, ACM, 2008, pp. 207-216.

[17] Hinckley, K., Dixon, M., Sarin, R., Guimbretiere, F. and Balakrishnan, R. Codex: a dual screen tablet computer. In *CHI'09*, ACM, 2009, pp. 1933-1942.

[18] Hinckley, K., Ramos, G., Guimbretiere, F., Baudisch, P. and Smith, M. Stitching: pen gestures that span multiple displays. In *AVI 2004*, ACM, pp. 23-31.

[19] Kern, D., Marshall, P. and Schmidt, A. Gazemarks: gaze-based visual placeholders to ease attention switching. In *CHI 2010*, ACM, 2010, pp. 2093-2102.

[20] Kirsh, D. and Maglio, P. On Distinguishing Epistemic from Pragmatic Action. *Cognitive Science*, 18, 1994, pp. 513-549.

[21] Lyons, K., Pering, T., Rosario, B., Sud, S. and Want, R. Multi-display Composition: Supporting Display Sharing for Collocated Mobile Devices. In *Proceedings of the 12th IFIP TC 13 International Conference on Human-Computer Interaction: Part I*, Springer-Verlag, 2009, pp. 758-771.

[22] Mandryk, R. L., Rodgers, M. E. and Inkpen, K. M. Sticky widgets: pseudo-haptic widget enhancements for multi-monitor displays. In *CHI '05 EA*, ACM, 2005, pp. 1621-1624.

[23] Matsumoto, T., Horiguchi, D., Nakashima, S. and Okude, N. Z-agon: mobile multi-display browser cube. In *CHI '06 EA*, ACM, 2006, pp. 351-356.

[24] Merrill, D., Kalanithi, J. and Maes, P. Siftables: towards sensor network user interfaces. In *TEI'07* ACM, 2007, pp. 75-78.

[25] Nacenta, M. A., Sallam, S., Champoux, B., Subramanian, S. and Gutwin, C. Perspective cursor: perspective-based interaction for multi-display environments. In *CHI'06*, ACM, 2006, pp. 289-298.

[26] Ota, S., Takegawa, Y., Terada, T. and Tsukamoto, M. A Method for Wearable Projector Selection that Considers the Viewability of Projected Images. *Comput. Entertain.* 8, 2010, pp. 1-16.

[27] Pinhanez, C., Kjeldsen, R., Levas, A., Pingali, G., Podlaseck, M. and Sukaviriya, N. Applications of steerable projector-camera systems. In *IEEE International Workshop on Projector-Camera Systems at ICCV 2003*, IEEE Computer Society Press.

[28] Su, R. and Bailey, B. P. Put Them Where? Towards Guidelines for Positioning Large Displays. In *Proc. of Graphics Interface '05*, 2005, pp. 337-349.

[29] Tan, D. S. and Czerwinski, M. Effects of Visual Separation and Physical Discontinuities when Distributing Information across Multiple Displays. In *Interact 2003*, pp. 252-255.

[30] Yang, X.-D., Mak, E., McCallum, D., Irani, P., Cao, X. and Izadi, S. LensMouse: augmenting the mouse with an interactive touch display. In *CHI 2010*, ACM, 2010, pp. 2431-2440.

The 1Line Keyboard: A QWERTY Layout in a Single Line

Frank Chun Yat Li, Richard T. Guy, Koji Yatani, and Khai N. Truong
Department of Computer Science
University of Toronto
Toronto, ON M5S 3G4, Canada
{frankli, guy, koji, khai}@dgp.toronto.edu

Figure 1: The 1Line Keyboard. It consists of only eight character keys, flick gestures, and a novel approach for integrating the spacebar into the bezel. It is 140px tall (26.9mm) and 39.8% of the size of the native landscape iPad keyboard.

ABSTRACT

Current soft QWERTY keyboards often consume a large portion of the screen space on portable touchscreens. This space consumption can diminish the overall user experience on these devices. In this paper, we present the 1Line keyboard, a soft QWERTY keyboard that is 140 pixels tall (in landscape mode) and 40% of the height of the native iPad QWERTY keyboard. Our keyboard condenses the three rows of keys in the normal QWERTY layout into a single line with eight keys. The sizing of the eight keys is based on users' mental layout of a QWERTY keyboard on an iPad. The system disambiguates the word the user types based on the sequence of keys pressed. The user can use flick gestures to perform backspace and enter, and tap on the bezel below the keyboard to input a space. Through an evaluation, we show that participants are able to quickly learn how to use the 1Line keyboard and type at a rate of over 30 WPM after just five 20-minute typing sessions. Using a keystroke level model, we predict the peak expert text entry rate with the 1Line keyboard to be 66-68 WPM.

ACM Classification: H5.2 [Information interfaces and presentation]: User Interfaces – Input devices and strategies

General terms: Design, Experimentation, Human Factors

Keywords: Text entry, soft keyboard, reduced keyboard, word disambiguation, keystroke level model

INTRODUCTION

Touchscreens allow the input and output space to be completely overlapped. This removes the need for physical input keys. Unfortunately, to support typing on touchscreens without additional hardware, many touchscreen devices, such as the iPad, implement a soft QWERTY keyboard that consumes a significant amount of screen space.

We conducted a small survey with 50 iPad owners (26 male, 24 female) to understand their user experience. Although survey respondents reported very frequent usage of their iPads and liked their overall experience, they also indicated a desire to minimize the space occupied by the soft QWERTY keyboard. Respondents rated the display size of the iPad with a median of 5 (1: very unsatisfied, 5: very satisfied); however, the rating significantly dropped to a median of 4 for the display size with the keyboard visible (Friedman, $\chi^2_{(1)}=21.2$, $p<.001$). Comments from the survey highlighted a common reason for this drop.

"The keyboard size is great to type on, but the remaining screen real estate is too small to work on properly. You have to scroll up and down all the time."

Feedback from survey respondents inspired us to design a keyboard that consumes less space than the current solutions. Motivated by evidence that users rarely want to spend the time needed to learn a new keyboard layout [1, 17], we decided to leverage the QWERTY keyboard layout instead of using different layouts and input modalities. In doing so, we hope that users can adapt their familiarity and existing experiences with physical keyboards for desktops, laptops or other computer devices to our keyboard. The design we developed, called the 1Line keyboard, condenses the three rows of character keys in the QWERTY layout into a single line with eight keys (Figure 1). In this manner,

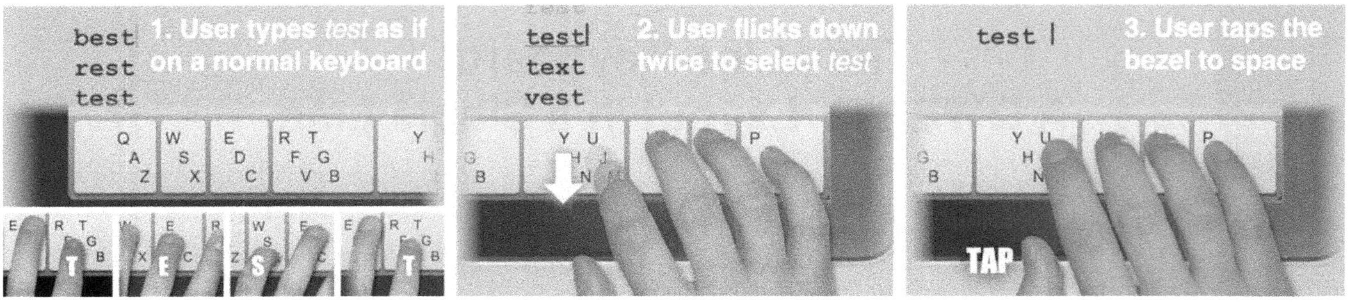

Figure 2: A storyboard illustrating a user typing *test*. As the user types, a word disambiguation algorithm tries to identify words she wishes to type. If the word she wants is not first in the disambiguation list, she flicks down to select it.

our keyboard is about 40% of the height of the native iPad keyboard (in landscape mode). The sizing of the eight keys is based on users' mental layout of a QWERTY keyboard on an iPad. The system disambiguates the word the user types based on the sequence of the keys pressed and using word frequencies calculated from an English corpus. If her desired word is not the first disambiguated word, she can flick through a list of possible words to select the intended text. This concept is similar to other works that condense multiple letters into one key [4, 5, 6] and list disambiguated words [6, 11, 21]. Our keyboard goes one step further by supporting flick gestures for backspaces and enters, and taps on the bezel below the keyboard for space (Figure 2).

In this paper, we describe our implementation and our user studies and analysis of the 1Line keyboard. Our participants were able to achieve 30.7 WPM (SD: 10.8) on the 1Line keyboard after five 20-minute typing sessions. While this rate is 57% of the participants' rate using the native iPad QWERTY keyboard (iPad: 53.9 WPM (SD: 19.8)), our 1Line keyboard saves 60% of the space occupied by the iPad keyboard. Our study also included the task of creating presentation slides and revealed that participants needed to perform significantly more scrolling with the iPad keyboard than the 1Line keyboard. Finally, we discuss a keystroke level model of our keyboard design which predicts the peak expert text entry rate to be 66.8-68.6 WPM.

RELATED WORK

The 1Line keyboard builds on prior work in keyboards with reduced layouts and gestures to replace buttons or keys.

Keyboards with Reduced Layouts

The limited space available in portable devices motivated researchers to reduce the number of buttons required to support a full alphabetic keyboard [4, 5, 6]. These systems must employ word disambiguation techniques to address the fact that a reduced key set requires that each key represent more than one character. Letterwise [14] and the commercially available T9 [21] represent attempts to support text entry on the 12 keys of a numeric keypad on a mobile device. The primary difference between these systems is the word disambiguation strategy: Letterwise orders the possible meanings of a key sequence by prefix probability while T9 orders possible meanings using whole word probabilities. In T9's disambiguation algorithm, 93.5% of the corpus of the top 9025 most frequent English words can be typed uniquely [19], whereas in our algorithm, 94.3% of the top 10,000 words can be typed uniquely.

Brailletouch is a 6-key chording keyboard for text entry [4] but requires knowledge of braille. Green *et al.* introduced the "stick keyboard" which consists of the home keys on the QWERTY keyboard along with a second row of modifier keys [6]. While their design is similar to ours, we reduce the keyset even more by introducing bezel taps and swipe gestures. Furthermore, our layout is based on users' mental layout of a QWERTY keyboard on an iPad.

Gesture Support to Replace Buttons or Keys

Researchers have previously explored gestures both on and off the screen to replace touch button inputs. The Non-Keyboard is a concept that maps a QWERTY layout into a glove [5]. The Non-Keyboard disambiguates words using three levels: lexical (tri-grams), syntactic (part of speech) and frequency rankings (corpus). However, due to the limited computing power available at the time of the research, the authors evaluated the system in a Wizard of Oz study. The authors were not able to show the performance and learning effects of their concept in a multi-session study. With the 1Line keyboard, we choose to use gestures to augment the input keypad rather than completely eliminate the touch keypad.

Flick and swipe gestures have been used to replace touchscreen buttons [2, 10, 12, 13, 18]. These projects uncover the fact that swipe gestures need not rely on a starting spot on the screen, which lets us reuse screen real-estate for both taps and swipes. Another approach to replace on-screen buttons is to interact with devices by tapping off the screen. Tap detection using accelerometers has been investigated before with Whack gestures [8] and Bonfire [9]. We use tap detection to replace the spacebar. Our 1Line keyboard utilizes commodity hardware (touchscreen and accelerometer) to provide a reduced-size keyboard that leverages prior experiences with the QWERTY layout.

DESIGN AND IMPLEMENTATION

The basic concept of the 1Line keyboard is to combine each column of the keys in the QWERTY keyboard into one key in order to save space while maintaining the familiar QWERTY layout. Because each key is now associated with multiple letters, this design needs to perform word disambiguation. We also introduce flick gestures to replace backspace and enter keys, and a tapping gesture on the bezel below the keyboard to replace the space bar. Figure 2 shows a walkthrough of typing the word *test*. We explain the implementations of these components in this section.

Key Layout and Size

To inform the design of the 1Line keyboard, we conducted a small study with nine participants (6 males, 3 females) in order to understand the spatial distribution of typing on the QWERTY layout. Findlater *et al.*'s work on touch typing patterns suggests that the user's fingers do not necessary line up in a straight line when typing on the Microsoft Surface [3]. Furthermore, different fingers had different spreads in target selection. We thus decided to empirically identify the optimal key size and layout.

Setup and Methods. Similar to the *Asterisk feedback, no keyboard* condition in Findlater *et al.*'s study [3], we asked the participants to type test phrases on a blank keyboard (Figure 3). Two coloured bars were marked on the blank keyboard for participants to home their index fingers, similar to the bars on the *F* and *J* keys on most QWERTY keyboards. The gray bounding box in Figure 3 is of the exact size of the three rows of keys in the native iPad keyboard. To prevent participants' hands from drifting over the course of the study, the space bar was condensed into two small yellow buttons, one for each thumb. Participants had to touch one of these small buttons with the thumb in order to enter a space. Also, to facilitate our analysis of the gathered data, we disabled multi-touch on the device, and participants were instructed to type as accurately as possible.

Participants were required to type 50 phrases. Thirty of the phrases were randomly picked from the MacKenzie & Soukoreff set [16]. In order to mitigate the imbalance on the number of occurrences of letters like *j*, *y*, and *z*, we created 20 special phrases. These 20 phrases were created using the following steps. First, we looked for the most frequent words that use infrequent letters in the Corpus of Contemporary American English[1] (COCA). Then we manually identified meaningful phrases containing these words. For example, one of the phrases *"the grey zone of justice"* contains three infrequent letters: *j*, *y*, and *z*. The final set of 50 phrases had at least 13 appearances of each letter and had a correlation with English of 0.9205 (calculated using AnalysePhrases [16]; first 50 phrases from the MacKenzie & Soukoreff set had a correlation of 0.939).

Participants were given five practice phrases at the beginning of the session. To ensure a consistent starting hand position, users had to press both the space buttons with their thumbs to activate a test phrase. As feedback, we showed an asterisk for a non-space character and an underscore for a space character (see Figure 3). We collected the contact points for every alphabetic character that was not backspaced along with

[1] The version we used contained 500k of the most frequent words used in the American English. Each word is given a frequency as indications of how popular the word is in American English.

Figure 3: Interface used to record the participants' mental layout of a QWERTY keyboard on an iPad.

the label of the corresponding letter in the test phrase. This study took around 25 minutes to complete.

Results. Contact points for each character beyond 3SD of the respective participant mean were removed as outliers. The remaining points for each character were averaged across all participants and are presented in Figure 4. The error bars in the Figure 4 represent 2SD. Instead of the distinct hand curvatures seen in the results from Findlater *et al.*'s study [3] (keys using the middle and ring fingers were higher than keys using the index and pinky finger), our results show that the middle row of the keyboard is relatively flat. We believe that this is due to the constrained size of the interaction space. In Findlater *et al.*'s study, participants typed on a Microsoft Surface and were not constrained for space. However, in our study, because the input space on the iPad is confined, the participants had to angle their hands slightly inward and curl their fingers closer than normally needed for a full sized keyboard.

Design of the keys. Our objective for this study was to find a comfortable size and position for each of the eight keys in the 1Line keyboard. We looked closely at the results of the keys located in the home row. To instruct the height of the keys, we took the distance between the highest and lowest error bars of the home row (*L* and *D* ~120 pixels). To divide the horizontal space into different buttons, we used the midpoint between the ends of adjacent errors bars for the points of *A*, *S*, *D*, and *F* (see Figure 4). These divisions gave a layout for the four left hand keys. We then mirrored the layout to the right half. This symmetry keeps the layout consistent and clean. We based our calculations on the left handed letters (*i.e.*, *A*, *S*, *D*, and *F*) instead of the right because the most frequently used letters in the alphabet are located on the left side of the QWERTY keyboard.

Word Disambiguation

Because each of the eight keys is associated with multiple letters (*e.g.*, the leftmost key can type the letters *q*, *a*, or *z*), word disambiguation is necessary for successful typing. We implemented our algorithm for word disambiguation based on the COCA. We first removed all entries in the COCA containing non-alphabetic characters. We then built a hash table of all remaining words using the finger sequence as the key and the word as the value. For example, the word *test* is assigned to a finger sequence of *left-index*, *left-*

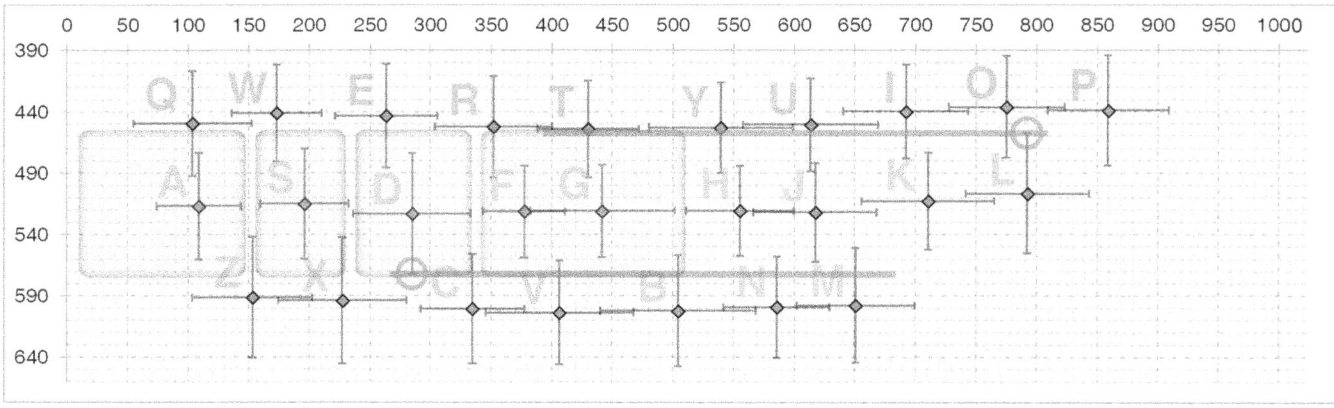

Figure 4: Participants' mental layout of a QWERTY keyboard on an iPad. The units are in pixels. The error bars show 2 SD of the means. The four boxes show how we designed the layout of the buttons in the 1Line keyboard. The height of the buttons was chosen to reflect the highest and lowest error bars of the home row (circled in red). To maintain symmetry we designed the left-handed buttons and mirrored them to the right (only left-handed buttons are shown here).

middle, *left-ring, and left-index*. We sorted all the words that have the same finger sequence by their frequency in the COCA. Thus, our word disambiguation algorithm suggests the most frequently-used word first depending on the sequence of the key pressed.

Coverage. Figure 5 shows the coverage of the alphabetic only words in COCA using our algorithm. To calculate coverage, we found the percentage of words that appear as the most likely word for its key sequence and the percentage of words that appear in the top two and three most likely words for its key sequence. These results show that in the top 10,000 words, 94.28% can be typed without the need for disambiguation and 99.23% appear in the top three most likely words for any key sequence.

Flick Gestures

We implemented some common operations in text entry as flick gestures. The entire keyboard space is a gesture area. We currently support the following gestures:

- *One-finger left flick*: Backspace (hold to repeat)
- *One-finger right flick*: Enter
- *One-finger down flick*: Navigates to the next word in the word disambiguation list (hold to repeat)
- *One-finger up flick*: Navigates to the previous word in the word disambiguation list (hold to repeat)
- *Two-finger left flick*: Deletes the whole word

Bezel Tap Detection

Like most mobile devices on the market today, the iPad is packaged with a MEMS accelerometer. For the 1Line keyboard, we took advantage of this existing hardware to detect tapping gestures on the bezel. We sampled the accelerometer at 100 Hz and computed the 2nd order finite difference ($fd_{[n]}$) using the values in the Z-axis (the axis perpendicular to the device screen). Each accelerometer measurement provides the system time ($t_{[n]}$) and the acceleration along the z axis ($z_{[n]}$). The formula for $fd_{[n]}$ is:

$$fd_{[n]} = \frac{z_{[n-2]} - 2z_{[n-1]} + z_n}{(t_{[n-1]} - t_{[n-2]})(t_{[n]} - t_{[n-1]})} \quad (1)$$

Figure 6 shows the $fd_{[n]}$ over the course of two taps. We set a window of ten previous values (equivalent to 100ms) to watch for a significant positive and negative deviation from zero in the finite difference. Empirical evidence suggests 800 m/s^4 as an acceptable threshold. The system also monitors all touch events on the screen. When an acceleration spike occurs and a touch-down event does not happen con-

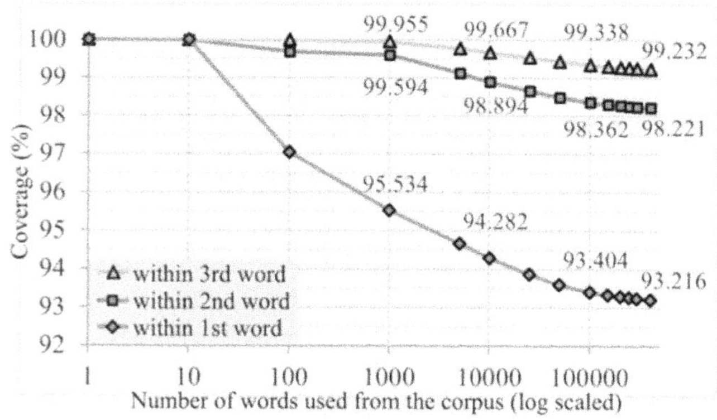

Figure 5: Coverage of our word disambiguation algorithm. Each line shows the coverage of words that are returned within the first, second, or third word of the word disambiguation list. There were a total of 406912 alphabetic only words in the corpus.

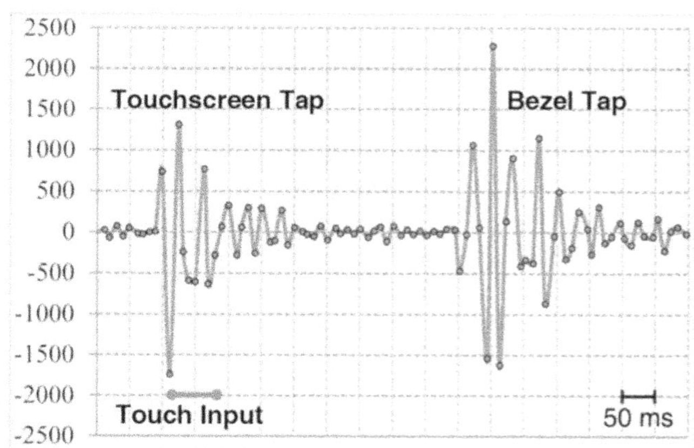

Figure 6: This graph of $fd_{[n]}$ shows a tap on the touchscreen followed by a tap on the bezel. The touch input is labelled in red.

currently, the system considers the spike as a tap on the bezel. When the difference becomes greater than 10,000 m/s^4, the system ignores the acceleration data. This can happen when, for instance, the user moves the device. The system ignores acceleration data while the user is touching the screen and again for the first five samples after detecting any tap to avoid false detection of multiple taps. Our algorithm is computationally inexpensive and can keep up with the fast typing speed of expert users.

USER EVALUATION

In this study, we wanted to validate the usability of the 1Line keyboard and to compare it to a soft QWERTY keyboard. We conducted our study using the Apple iPad because it is currently the most popular tablet on the market. Because of the similarity to the QWERTY layout, we expected the learning curve to level fairly quickly. Our pilot studies confirm that although typing speed still continues to improve after 15 sessions of typing, it diminishes significantly after the first 5 sessions. Thus, we decided to format the study into 5+2 sessions. In the following section, we will refer to these 5+2 sessions as the five *typing sessions*, an *application session* and the *spacebar session.*

The *typing sessions* were used to gain an understanding of the initial usability of the 1Line keyboard and its learning curve. The *application session* was designed to collect both qualitative and quantitative data of the participants' experience with using the 1Line keyboard to make presentation slides. In our exploratory survey, creating presentation slides was the least preferred activity on the iPad by the responders. The inclusion of this session in the experimental design allows us to understand how the 1Line keyboard could benefit users in a realistic scenario in which the limited visual working space can cause interaction breakdowns that affect the ease in which the user completes a task. The *spacebar session* was designed to evaluate our bezel tap detection.

Participants

Ten participants (referred to as *P0-P9;* 8 males; 8 right handed) from age 20 to 35 (mean: 23.7, SD: 4.4) were recruited for our study. All but one participant had at least one touchscreen device (mobile phones and/or music players) and regularly engaged in text entry on these devices. However, none had significant prior experience typing on the native iPad keyboard. All participants showed expert typing speed on a physical QWERTY keyboard using TextTest [22]; the average typing speed was 82.6 WPM (SD: 23.0) with about 4% error rate. They were compensated $120 for their participation in this study.

Instruments and Setup

We used a 9.7" 16GB iPad. The iPad was placed on a desk in front of the participants, who could choose to prop the iPad up to any angle they felt comfortable. They could also freely adjust the height of their chairs.

The Typing Sessions. The *typing sessions* used a custom iPad application. The application presented short test phrases above either the 1Line keyboard or the iPad keyboard. Aside from the keyboards, the participants were not able to interact with any other part of the screen. We presented the iPad keyboard in the default factory state with the auto-correction enabled. The phrases used in the typing tasks are from the set of 500 test phrases developed by MacKenzie & Soukoreff [16]. We randomized the order of these phrases and added them to a list. We continued this until we had 5000 phrases in two lists, one for each keyboard. We then grouped every ten phrases into a block, making 500 blocks for each list. These two sets of blocks were pre-loaded into the iPad application. The application kept track of the progress for each participant. When a participant started a new session, the system always presented the first phrase in the next block even if she did not complete all the phrases in the previous block during the previous session.

The Application Session. In the *application session*, the participants were asked to complete presentation slides on our simplified presentation application. Figure 7 shows a screenshot of our presentation application. The design of this application was based on Keynote, which is an existing presentation application on the iPad. Aside from interacting with the keyboard, participants could pan the slide up and down to view the portion of the slide occluded by the keyboard as well as minimize the keyboard entirely by tapping on the slide. Tapping the title bar reactivated the keyboard.

The Spacebar Session. The app used in the *spacebar session* was very similar to the one used in the *typing sessions.* However, we disabled the bezel tap detection and the single row of keys was shifted up to accommodate a touchscreen spacebar. The spacebar had the exact same height as the bezel (117 pixels tall, ~22mm) and extend from the *left-middle* finger key to *right-middle* finger key.

Study Design and Procedure

The Typing Sessions. In each of the *typing sessions*, participants used both the 1Line and the iPad keyboard to type the test phrases. In each session, participants completed 20 minutes of typing with each keyboard. Each time partici-

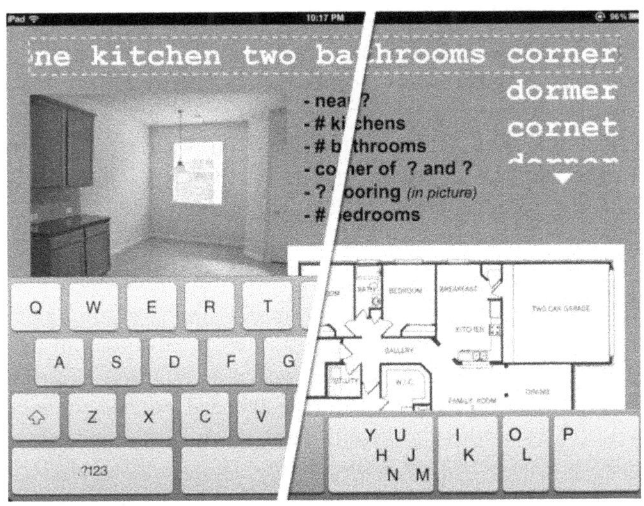

Figure 7: The Keynote imitation app used in the *application session* with the native iPad keyboard (left) and 1Line keyboard (right).

pants finished a 20-minute typing condition, they were asked to complete a NASA TLX workload assessment [7]. The presentation order of the two keyboards was counter-balanced across participants in the first sessions and alternated in each session thereafter. Each session took around 45 minutes to complete. Any two of the sessions were scheduled at least 2 and at most 72 hours apart so that participants could carry over their experience on the 1Line keyboard throughout the study.

The Application Session. Participants in this session had to add the title to a series of slides for a real-estate presentation. Each slide contained three images: a map, a floor plan, and a picture showing interior images from a house. Bullet points above the floor plan described what characteristics of the house to put in the title. Each of these points required the participants to look at the one of the three images. Participants had to follow the order given in the bullet points. For example, for the slide shown in Figure 7, they would have to type *"near school one kitchen two bathrooms corner of county and meadow tile flooring three bedrooms"*. There were seven slides in total: one for practice and three for each keyboard. The presentation order of the keyboards was counter-balanced across participants. Participants were given as much time as they needed to complete the tasks and were allowed to stop and ask questions at any time. A short interview was conducted right after to probe their experiences with the two keyboards in this application. They were encouraged to make comments in the context of the presentation titling tasks.

The Spacebar Session. Participants carried out another 20-minute typing exercise using a slightly modified 1Line keyboard. In this session, we included a spacebar in the touchscreen and disabled the bezel tap detection. We administered this extra typing session to check whether our bezel tap detection could have degraded the typing speed. After the typing, we administered a workload assessment and conducted a final exit interview. The *application session* and this *spacebar session* were scheduled together and took 45 minutes to complete in total.

Results: Typing Sessions

For our analysis, we modified the StreamAnalyzer from Wobbrock and Myers [23] to account for word-level operations like word deletion and word corrections. Also the native keyboard's auto-correct function can potentially lower the keystroke per character (KSPC) below 1.0. We accounted for these cases in our analysis.

Overall Performance. We removed any data point over 3SD from the average typing rate and over 4SD from the average error rate for each participant in each session as an outlier (0.95% of the data points removed). Running a repeated-measures ANOVA for each keyboard against the sessions, we found a significant main effect of the number of the sessions on typing speed (1Line: $F_{(4,36)}$=30.82, p<.001, iPad: $F_{(1.937,17.434)}$=4.54, p=.027 with Greenhouse-Geisser correction ε =.48). However, the post-hoc pairwise comparisons show no significant differences between sessions 3 to 5 for each of the techniques (1Line: p>.64 iPad: p>.99 for all pairs). Because both the QWERTY keyboard and the 1Line keyboard use the QWERTY layout, we expected a shallow learning curve. Moreover, we found no significant main effect of session on the differences in speed between the two techniques ($F_{(4,36)}$=7.35, p=.80). In other words, participants displayed a similar learning curve as the iPad keyboard, which affirmed that they were able to transfer their existing experiences from using QWERTY keyboards in desktops, laptops and other devices.

With paired t-tests, the 1Line keyboard performed significantly slower ($t_{(9)}$=7.74, p<.001) than the iPad keyboard in each of the 5 sessions (see Figure 8 left). At the 5th session, participants averaged 30.7 WPM (SD: 10.8) on the 1Line keyboard and 53.9 WPM (SD: 19.8) on the iPad keyboard. They were able to reach 57% of the performance on the iPad keyboard using a keyboard that is 60% smaller.

The NASA TLX workload assessments were analyzed with paired t-tests (the normality of mental and total workloads in each session passed the Shapiro-Wilk tests). We found no significant differences between the 1Line and iPad keyboards in any of the 5 sessions at the 95% confidence level. Looking at individual components of the assessments, we only found a trend in mental demand (see Figure 8 right). The differences in mental demand between the two keyboards in the first four sessions was significant (p<.036 for all sessions). But at the 5th session, the differences were not significant ($t_{(9)}$=2.09, p=.066). While our participants had more mental demand when typing on the 1Line keyboard compared to the iPad keyboard, the cognitive effort became comparable after the 5th session.

Error Rates. The final error rate [22] is computed using the minimum string distance (MSD) [20]. Participants had a final error rate of 1.7% (SD: 2.4) with the 1Line keyboard and 1.2% (SD: 2.0) with the iPad keyboard. A Wilcoxon signed ranks test showed no significant difference on the final error rate between the 1Line keyboard and the native iPad keyboard (Z=-0.87, p=.386). On average, the KSPC for the 1Line keyboard was 1.31 (SD: 0.35) and the iPad key-

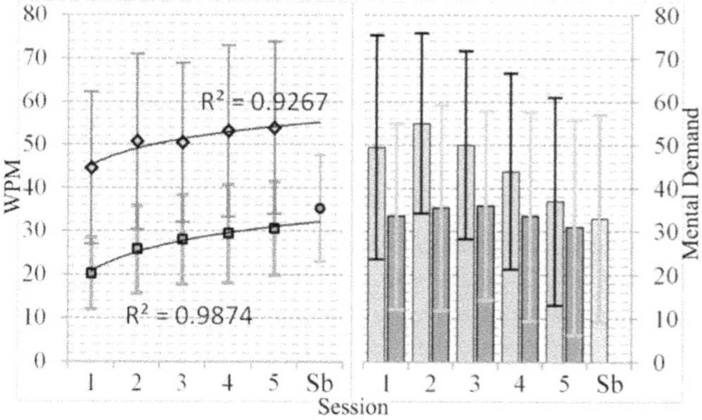

Figure 8: Left shows the overall text entry rate for both keyboards (iPad: top, 1Line: bottom) for each session. Right shows the mental demand for both keyboards (iPad: dark, 1Line: light) in each session.

board was 1.26 (SD: 0.36). Pairwise t-tests show significant differences in KSPC between the two keyboards in each of sessions 3 to 5 (p<.05 for all pairs). This is not surprising once we look at the corrected error rate. On average, participants had a corrected error rate of 10.8% (SD: 10.8%) with the 1Line keyboard and 9.0% (SD: 10.6%) with the iPad keyboard. A Wilcoxon test showed a significant difference in the corrected error rate [20] between the two keyboards (Z=-2.40, p=.017). There were fewer manual corrections with the iPad keyboard and, hence, a lower KSPC. This is because the factory auto-correct function was enabled for the native iPad keyboard condition. On average the iPad automatically corrected 7.5% (SD: 10.1%) of the input stream. This auto-correction rate translates to one correction every 13.3 characters or roughly once every 3 words.

Results: Application Session

Because participants could type faster on the iPad keyboard, we found a significant difference in completion time between the keyboards ($t_{(9)}$=-5.45, p<.001). Participants used on average 105.6s (SD: 26.0) with the 1Line keyboard and 77.8s (SD: 20.2) with the iPad keyboard to title each slide. The 35.7% slowdown with using the 1Line keyboard in this task almost directly reflects the 43% slowdown observed in the *typing sessions*.

However, our main objective of this task was to measure how likely the user would need to perform interactions on the visual working space (*e.g.*, scrolling) to gain information to complete the task. The average distance scrolled while completing the tasks for each slide was 1325 pixels (SD: 846) using the 1Line keyboard and 2828 pixels (SD: 1819) using the iPad keyboard. The distances scrolled between the two techniques are significantly different ($t_{(9)}$=3.84, p=.004). This result indicates that a larger visual working space offered by the 1Line keyboard allowed participants to focus on completing the task rather than navigating the working space.

Results: Spacebar Session

In this last session, we added a soft spacebar. On average, participants achieved 35.3 WPM (SD: 12.3). The data from the first five sessions fits a logarithmic growth (R^2=0.9874, Figure 8 left). Using the fit, the text entry speed can be extrapolated to 32.2 WPM for the next session. Thus, our bezel spacebar only degraded performance by about 8.8% and saves the space used by the soft spacebar (117 pixels tall or ~22mm in our implementation).

Discussion on Performance Differences

At the fifth session, our participants performed 43% slower on the 1Line keyboard than the iPad keyboard. Aside from the fundamental trade-off between keyboard size and performance (1Line keyboard is 60% smaller than the iPad keyboard), we examined the results and found three main sources for the performance drop.

First, the inaccuracies of the bezel spacebar detection algorithm caused some false positives and false negatives. The results of the *spacebar session* showed that the inaccuracies attributed to 8.8% of the performance degrade. Furthermore, we estimated the frequency of false positives by counting space characters that were backspaced. On average 5.2 (SD: 1.1) space characters were backspaced per block (10 lines). Thus, a false positive is estimated to have occurred roughly once every 2 lines. The bezel spacebar also had false negatives; however, we were not able to quantify the amount of false negative with the data we collected.

Second, with disambiguation, it was difficult to catch a typo in the beginning of a word (*e.g.*, a mistype of finger, *fonger*, disambiguates to *bomber*). Five participants said they often needed to delete the entire word to start over. On average, participants used the word backspace function 2.7 (SD: 1.0) times per block. The phrase set we used contained an average of 64 words per block. Participants thus threw out about 4.2% of all words they typed.

Lastly, the current implementation does not remember the word the user selected in the disambiguation list. If a wrong word is selected by accident, the user would need to backspace and start from the very top of the list again. Four participants raised this concern during the interview. Further analyses showed that participants used an average of 3.5% (SD: 6.0) of their typing time interacting with the list.

Qualitative Results of User Preference

All participants but one thought they were faster with the iPad keyboard. But in the context of making presentation slides, five explicitly said they needed to scroll less with the 1Line keyboard.

"I spent a lot of time going back and forth on the slides for the iPad keyboard, like going up and down, because the keyboard takes up half the screen." (P1)

After the slides, participants even began to envision other scenarios where the 1Line keyboard would be useful.

"When we compare it with the other keyboard, well I can say that it just holds a big portion of the screen. That's maybe a bit disturbing if you are typing a long piece of document, instead of just single sentences." (P4)

While the entire size of the 1Line keyboard is 40% of the size of the iPad keyboard, the individual keys are actually much larger. Our participants found the larger keys more comfortable to touch.

"The [1Line keyboard], it's really convenient, because I can just place my hands like this. And basically, I don't have to move them a lot. I just move my fingers. I find this more comfortable than the regular one. I sometimes have to get my hand out of the way to see some of the keys on the normal one." (P7)

Another advantage we found with the keys of the 1Line keyboard is that it facilitates typing with long nails.

"And like when I curl my fingers for the lower keys, my nail hit and then I don't touch the [iPad] keyboard or the screen and then I don't touch anything, which doesn't happen with the [1Line] one." (P1)

The 1Line keyboard reduces the screen space needed while maintaining the QWERTY layout. This liberates the effort needed for users to learn a completely new layout.

"I was still typing sort of like a smaller version of regular typing. So if it's a top row key, my fingers will actually open up a little..." (P1)

The disambiguation list was the least preferred aspect of the 1Line keyboard.

"I find it difficult in doing sort of longer words. I find it difficult trying to keep my position inline where I was in the word. [...] So I found myself sort of having to spell the word letter by letter in my head as I was typing. So it required a bit more mental effort." (P0)

Because the system does not support word prediction, the target word might not appear in the disambiguation list until the final character has been typed. This might have caused extra mental effort in our participants. Our participants also expressed difficulty in cases where the same key needs to be pressed multiple times (*e.g.*, the word "indeed" requires users use the left middle finger four times).

"On the single row one, when I am typing sometimes, when I have to press one of the keys too many times, I usually make mistakes there." (P7)

Another major difference between the 1Line and the iPad keyboard was the flick gestures for backspace and enter. Participants adapted to these gestures without troubles. Four participants mentioned swipe gestures when asked what they liked in the 1Line keyboard.

"The swiping, I thought that was really cool. It really makes it easier. It's more like a reflex rather than I have to go and find another key. Because when you are tapping you just want to worry about the letters, nothing else. You don't want to use another key for enter or backspace." (P8)

PREDICTING PEAK EXPERT PERFORMANCE

The peak expert performance is another metric to understand a new text entry method. Instead of extending our user study, we predict the expert performance of the 1Line keyboard using a keystroke level model (KLM). A KLM is built from the times of individual keystrokes. But because there are no existing time measurements for multi-finger touchscreen keystrokes, we ran an additional study with the same participants as our user study to collect keystroke and flick gesture timing data for building the KLM. This study took place right after the last session of the user evaluation.

We did not build a similar KLM for the iPad keyboard because we would need to measure (26 letters + 2 thumbs)^2 = 784 transitions. Such a study would be too fatiguing for our participants. Because our main contribution is not proposing models of different keyboards, we decided not to pursue a model for the iPad keyboard in this work.

Keystroke Level Model

Consider typing the word *wpm*. The first letter *w* is typed with the *left-ring* finger. After typing *w*, the user will hit the letter *p* with the *right-pinky* finger. This sequence of typing two letters then consists of three elements: pressing the *left-ring* key, transitioning from the *left-ring* key to the *right-pinky* key, and pressing the *right-pinky* key. Thus, the time to type *wp* can be modeled as the sum of these two key press times and one transition time. Even after the user types the whole word, she may need to select a word from the disambiguated list. For this, she would perform downward flick gesture(s) to reach the desired word. In the example of *wpm*, it appears third in the list. Thus, the user has to perform a flick gesture twice. Our KLM takes the flick gesture and transition times into account.

In typical typing situations, every word is followed by a space. Our KLM assumes that every word ends with a space and starts from a space. A space character can be entered by either the *right-* or *left-thumb*. Depending on the last keystroke of the word, the time for entering a space character with the *right-thumb* or the *left-thumb* will be different. In the example of *wpm(flick)(flick)*, the last interaction before entering a space is a flick gesture. The transition time from a flick gesture to the *right-thumb* can be different from one to the *left-thumb*. The key press time can also be different between the two thumbs. Similarly, because we assume every word starts from a space, our KLM needs to add the transition time from a space to the first keystroke of the word. We generated two models; the *ideal thumb policy* KLM and the *non-ideal thumb policy* KLM. The *ideal thumb policy* KLM uses the fastest times to account for the space characters. On the other hand, the *non-ideal thumb policy* KLM uses the slowest times.

Experimental Setup and Methods

We developed an iPad application to measure the timing of keystrokes on the 1Line keyboard. The bottom portion of the screen showed the 1Line keyboard with unlabelled keys. We added two spacebars below the buttons for each of the thumbs and disabled the tap detection algorithm. The top portion displayed a disabled copy of the bottom portion and was used to present the tasks to the participants.

Each task consisted of three consecutive interaction steps. An interaction step can be either tapping a key or performing a flick gesture. For example, one of the tasks consisted of tapping the *right-middle* finger button, flicking down, and then tapping the *left-thumb* button. These interaction steps were illustrated at the top of the screen. Because multi-touch was enabled, participants could begin the next interaction step (*i.e.*, putting a finger down on the screen) without completing the previous interaction step (*i.e.*, lifting a finger up on the screen) as long as they finished the previous interaction step before finishing the next interaction. Each task had to be completed correctly; otherwise, participants were asked to complete the same task again. Participants were instructed to only use the corresponding finger for each key (but they were allowed to perform flick gestures with any finger) and to complete each task as fast as they could. We collected the key press times for all keys, the transition times for all possible pairing of keys and flick gestures, and the times for flick gestures. Unreachable transitions were not collected (*e.g.*, transition for a space to a space). This experimental design allowed us to measure the time for different interaction components without a mental

	l-pinky	*l-ring*	*l-middle*	*l-index*	*l-thumb*	*r-thumb*	*r-index*	*r-middle*	*r-ring*	*r-pinky*	*flick UP*	*flick DN*
l-p	**86**±30	**71**±87	**72**±115	**56**±97	**81**±151	**57**±93	**69**±146	**74**±94	**61**±87	**52**±92	-	-
l-r	**64**±83	**87**±43	**64**±84	**62**±102	**91**±141	**75**±127	**89**±126	**95**±134	**69**±117	**66**±100	-	-
l-m	**83**±123	**72**±130	**92**±33	**52**±69	**87**±121	**83**±126	**112**±164	**88**±139	**104**±137	**72**±96	-	-
l-i	**83**±109	**79**±96	**52**±77	**99**±52	**94**±111	**85**±112	**63**±80	**95**±150	**106**±161	**67**±87	-	-
l-t	**59**±85	**80**±88	**70**±93	**74**±90	-	-	**67**±90	**84**±158	**78**±140	**74**±99	**232**±105	**224**±124
r-t	**61**±113	**83**±120	**93**±137	**70**±102	-	-	**50**±82	**67**±98	**80**±130	**86**±101	**248**±106	**229**±107
r-i	**76**±122	**96**±138	**85**±115	**62**±98	**67**±96	**73**±117	**91**±33	**53**±74	**62**±88	**70**±113	-	-
r-m	**76**±146	**77**±90	**85**±133	**89**±108	**69**±102	**81**±114	**69**±91	**94**±53	**58**±93	**95**±107	-	-
r-r	**78**±122	**61**±91	**78**±130	**92**±135	**59**±93	**83**±121	**88**±155	**66**±88	**91**±39	**81**±138	-	-
r-p	**56**±102	**71**±132	**75**±114	**79**±113	**61**±88	**76**±121	**77**±162	**86**±160	**93**±131	**92**±50	-	-
UP	**271**±284	**230**±161	**235**±185	**200**±116	-	-	**213**±131	**336**±334	**315**±313	**295**±241	**158**±82	-
DN	**255**±196	**237**±163	**243**±222	**200**±115	-	-	**248**±237	**276**±212	**270**±191	**254**±154	-	**143**±103
KP	**108**±37	**102**±33	**91**±30	**83**±26	**101**±28	**92**±30	**85**±27	**92**±28	**94**±31	**99**±33	**108**±42	**111**±46

Table 1: The units are in ms (mean: bolded, SD: unbolded). The bottom row shows the average times of different keystrokes. The top rows show the transitions times from a keystroke to another; columns are the starting keystroke. For example the transition time from *left-ring* to *left-pinky* is 71±87 ms, but the time from *left-pinky* to *left-ring* is 64±83 ms.

overhead. We therefore believe that this performance could be used to predict the peak performance of an expert user.

Results

Outliers beyond 4SD of the means in each category were removed per participant (1.0% removed). Table 1 shows the resulting means. To come up with the predicted WPM, we followed a method used by MacKenzie & Soukoreff [15]. We first calculated the time to type each word in COCA. Summing up all words, our model used 3.89×10^8 (*non-ideal thumb policy* KLM) to 4.00×10^8 (*ideal thumb policy* KLM) seconds to type the entire corpus (weighted by frequency). There are 2.23×10^9 characters in the corpus (weighted by frequency). The average time required to type a character in the corpus (t_{CHAR}) is then 0.17 to 0.18 *seconds per character.* Finally, words per minute (WPM) is calculated by $1/t_{CHAR} \times 60$ *seconds per minute* / *5 characters per word.* The resulting predicted peak expert performance of the 1Line keyboard is 66.8 (*non-ideal thumb policy* KLM) to 68.6 (*ideal thumb policy* KLM) WPM.

This prediction does not include using the bezel spacebar. While there is a degradation of performance when using the bezel spacebar, our user evaluation showed that the lost in performance was 8.8%. Thus, the estimated peak expert performance with the bezel spacebar would be around 61-63 WPM. Referencing back to the results of the *typing sessions*, the fastest line completed by our fastest participant using the 1Line keyboard was done with 73.8 WPM, the fastest block (10 lines) was done with 48.0 WPM, and the fastest 20-minute session (12 blocks) was done with 40.6 WPM. Our KLM is in line with actual user data.

AREAS OF IMPROVEMENTS

The current prototype on the iPad was the first step in realizing the concept of the 1Line keyboard. In this section, we discuss a few areas of improvements.

Adaptive Word Disambiguation

Our current disambiguation approach simply uses the frequency of occurrence of each word appeared in an English corpus (COCA in this work). Adaptively changing the behaviour of the word disambiguation could improve the typing speed. For example, if the user types a lower frequency word (according to COCA) repeatedly, 1Line could give that word higher priority in the disambiguation. There also needs to be ways for the user to enter her own words (those not found in COCA) into the algorithm.

Integration of Auto-correction

The current 1Line keyboard prototype does not have auto-correction. One problem participants expressed about our keyboard was that when they needed to press the same key a few times in order to type correctly, their typing resulted in an error. Thus, among different auto-correction features, omission correction could greatly contribute to improvements on the user experience on the 1Line keyboard.

Richer Gesture Set

The current prototype only supports five flick gestures. But the underlying hardware supports other types of gestures, and they could be used to enrich our keyboard. In future implementations, the user could toggle the caps-lock by flicking up or down with two fingers. The user also could switch to a numeric or symbolic layout with 3-finger flicks upward or downward. Future work will investigate an efficient layout for numbers and symbols.

More Robust Tap Detection

The tap detection algorithm we employ rests on the hypothesis that a user's finger press moves the device. As deployed, with the device resting on its bevelled back casing, any movement that is not perfectly centered on the device causes the device to pivot and register a tap. Future work will investigate whether other configurations, including devices whose case is not bevelled, are good candidates for an accelerometer based tap detection approach. We also found that elevating the device on a soft surface, such as a rubberized case, will lower false positives.

Taps that are not along the central plane of the device register a change in the acceleration along the X and, to a lesser extent, the Y-axis. Our preliminary work suggests that movement in the X-axis can be used to distinguish *left*, *right* and *center* bezel taps, which enables a richer keyboard experience without the expense of extra screen real estate or smaller keys. For example, users could tap the center of the device to enter a space, but tap its left side to toggle caps-lock and the right side to toggle num-lock.

CONCLUSIONS AND FUTURE WORK

The objective of this work is to reduce the size of touchscreen tablet keyboards. The result of our work is the 1Line keyboard. It is 140 pixels tall and 39.8% the height of the native keyboard found on an iPad in the landscape mode. The 1Line keyboard has only 8 keys, one for each finger. The key sizes are designed based on participants' mental layout of a QWERTY keyboard on an iPad. All character operation keys are replaced by multitouch flick gestures. The spacebar is integrated into the bezel of the device with the support of a novel tap detection algorithm. Our user study indicates that the 1Line keyboard can reduce interaction breakdowns in tasks involving both visual exploration and text entry in portable tablet devices.

We plan to extend this 1Line keyboard to other types of devices using touchscreens. For example, an adaptation of the 1Line keyboard to a handheld touchscreen device could be beneficial because the real estate of the screen in these devices is even more limited than a tablet device. We also believe that the 1Line keyboard could offer some benefits even in a tabletop surface. In this type of device, visual space would not be an issue. However, as our investigation indicates, our system would allow the user to type accurately as long as it detects which finger is used for typing each letter instead of which key is pressed. Thus, the 1Line keyboard on a tabletop surface could liberate the user from concerns about hitting the wrong keys or homing the hand to a generic keyboard layout given by the system.

REFERENCES

1. Bi, X., Smith, B. A., and Zhai, S. 2010. Quasi-qwerty soft keyboard optimization. In *Proc. of CHI '10*. ACM, NY, USA, 283-286.
2. Bonner, M.N., Brudvik, J.T., Abowd, G.D. and Edwards, W.K. 2010. No-Look Notes: Accessible Eyes-Free Multi-touch Text Entry. In *Proc of Pervasive 2010*. Springer-Verlag, Berlin, Germany, 409-426.
3. Findlater, L., Wobbrock, J., Wigdor, D. 2011. Typing on flat glass: Examining ten-finger expert typing patterns on touch surfaces. In *Proc. of CHI '11*. ACM, NY, USA, 2453-2462.
4. Frey, B., Southern, C., and Romero, M. 2011. BrailleTouch: Mobile Texting for the Visually Impaired. In *Proc. HCII'11*. To appear.
5. Goldstein, M., Book, R., Alsiö, G., and Tessa, S. 1999. Non-keyboard QWERTY touch typing: a portable input interface for the mobile user. In *Proc. of CHI '99*. ACM, NY, USA, 32-39.
6. Green, H., Kruger, J., Faldu, C., and St. Amant, R. 2004. A Reduced QWERTY Keyboard for Mobile Text Entry. In *Proc. of CHI '04*. ACM, NY, USA, 1429-1432.
7. Hart, S. and Staveland, L. 1988. Development of NASA-TLX (Task Load Index): Results of empirical and theoretical research. In *Human Mental Workload, P. A. Hancock and N. Meshkati, Eds.*, North-Holland: Elsevier Science, 139-183.
8. Hudson, S.E., Harrison, C., Harrison, B.L., and LaMarca, A. 2010. Whack gestures: inexact and inattentive interaction with mobile devices. In *Proc. of TEI '10*. ACM, NY, USA, 109-112.
9. Kane, S.K., Avrahami, D., Wobbrock, J.O., Harrison, B., Rea, A.D., Philipose, M., and LaMarca, A. 2009. Bonfire: a nomadic system for hybrid laptop-tabletop interaction. In *Proc. of UIST '09*. ACM, NY, USA, 129-138.
10. Kane, S.K., Bigham, J.P., and Wobbrock, J.O. 2008. Slide rule: making mobile touch screens accessible to blind people using multi-touch interaction techniques. In *Proc. of Assets '08*. ACM, NY, USA, 73-80.
11. Kane, S.K., Wobbrock J.O., Harniss, M., and Johnson, K.L. 2008. TrueKeys: identifying and correcting typing errors for people with motor impairments. In *Proc. of IUI'08*. ACM, NY, USA, 349-352.
12. Karlson, A.K., Bederson, B.B., and SanGiovanni, J. 2005. AppLens and launchTile: two designs for one-handed thumb use on small devices. In *Proc. of CHI '05*. ACM, NY, USA, 201-210.
13. Kristensson, P. and Zhai, S. 2005. Relaxing stylus typing precision by geometric pattern matching. In *Proc. of IUI'05*. ACM, NY, USA, 151-158.
14. MacKenzie, I.S., Kober, H., Smith, D., Jones, T., Skepner, E. 2001. LetterWise: Prefix-based Disambiguation for Mobile Text Input. In *Proc. of UIST '01*. ACM, NY, USA, 111-120.
15. MacKenzie, I.S. and Soukoreff, R.W. 2002. A model of two-thumb text entry. In *Proc. of GI'02*. 117-124.
16. MacKenzie, I.S. and Soukoreff, R.W. 2003. Phrase sets for evaluating text entry techniques. In *Extended Abstracts of CHI '03*. ACM, NY, USA, 754-755.
17. MacKenzie, I.S., Zhang, S.X., and Soukoreff, R.W. Text entry using soft keyboards, *Behaviour & Information Technology, 18* (1999), 235-244.
18. Pirhonen, A., Brewster, S., and Holguin, C. 2002. Gestural and audio metaphors as a means of control for mobile devices. In *Proc. of CHI '02*. ACM, NY, USA, 291-298.
19. Silfverberg, M., MacKenzie, I. S., & Korhonen, P. 2000. Predicting text entry speed on mobile phones. In *Proc. of CHI'00*. ACM, NY, USA, 9-16.
20. Soukoreff, R.W. and MacKenzie, I.S. 2003. Metrics for text entry research: an evaluation of MSD and KSPC, and a new unified error metric. In *Proc. of CHI '03*. ACM, NY, USA, 113-120.
21. T9. http://www.t9.com/
22. Tinwala, H. and MacKenzie, I.S. 2010. Eyes-free text entry with error correction on touchscreen mobile devices. In *Proc. of NordiCHI '10*. ACM, NY, USA, 511-520.
23. Wobbrock, J.O. and Myers, B.A. 2006. Analyzing the input stream for character- level errors in unconstrained text entry evaluations. *ACM Trans. Comput.-Hum. Interact.* 13, 4 (December 2006), 458-489.

1 Thumb, 4 Buttons, 20 Words Per Minute: Design and Evaluation of H4-Writer

I. Scott MacKenzie[1], *R. William Soukoreff*[2], *Joanna Helga*[1]

[1]Dept. of Computer Science and Engineering
York University
4700 Keele Street
Toronto, Ontario, M3J 1P3 Canada
+1 416 736-2100
{ mack, joanna }@cse.yorku.ca

[2]Dept. of Computer Science
University of Toronto
10 King's College Road
Toronto, Ontario, M5S 3G4 Canada
+1 416 978-3619
will@dgp.toronto.edu

ABSTRACT

We present what we believe is the most efficient and quickest four-key text entry method available. *H4-Writer* uses Huffman coding to assign minimized key sequences to letters, with full access to error correction, punctuation, digits, modes, etc. The key sequences are learned quickly, and support eyes-free entry. With *KSPC* = 2.321, the effort to enter text is comparable to multitap on a mobile phone keypad; yet multitap requires nine keys. In a longitudinal study with six participants, an average text entry speed of 20.4 wpm was observed in the 10th session. Error rates were under 1%. To improve external validity, an extended session was included that required input of punctuation and other symbols. Entry speed dropped only by about 3 wpm, suggesting participants quickly leveraged their acquired skill with *H4-Writer* to access advanced features.

ACM Classification: H.5.2 [Information Interfaces and Presentation]: User Interfaces – input devices and strategies (e.g., mouse, touchscreen)

General Terms: Performance, Design, Experimentation, Human Factors

Keywords: Text entry, Huffman coding, mobile text entry, small devices

INTRODUCTION

New methods of text entry appear with great frequency these days. This is due in large part to a heightened interest in small hand-held devices. While texting on mobile phones is the most obvious example, small or reduced form-factor devices are of interest in other domains, such as ubiquitous computing, wearable computing, gaming, and accessible computing. These environments often require an input mechanism that is physically constrained and that requires only a few keys or a small set of input primitives.

Text entry methods generally fall within one of two categories: methods using discrete actions on a keyed device (virtual or physical) and methods using continuous actions on a digitizing surface. The focus in this paper is the former: text entry using keys or buttons.

In the following sections, we present a new method for designing optimized small keyboards. The result is a family of reduced-key keyboards. We present and analyse the design space for keyboards with 2 to 27 keys. A 4-key design is chosen for detailed analysis and empirical evaluation.

Symbols, Codes, and Keys

Most previous research in designing optimized keyboards takes the approach of assigning letters to keys, typically by exploiting the statistical properties of a language [e.g., 1, 3-5, 7, 16, 19, 22]. We take the opposite approach: assigning keys to letters.

The keys-to-letters idea is somewhat like assigning codes to symbols, as, for example, assigning binary codes to letters in the UTF-8 character encoding system. Figure 1a shows the code corresponding to "a". Since the encoding is binary, the code consists of 0s and 1s only. We could, however, interpret the 0s and 1s as key presses on a 2-key keyboard, in which case entering "a" would require 8 key presses, as depicted in Figure 1b.

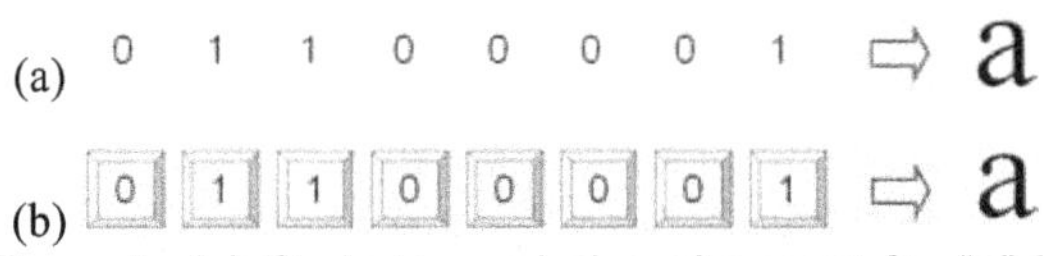

Figure 1. (a) Code-to-symbol assignment for "a" in UTF-8. (b) Equivalent key sequence.

Clearly, this exercise has little practical value, since input requires numerous key presses for each letter of input. However, it is noteworthy that only two keys are required. A simple question is this: Is there a more efficient coding system to reduce the number of key presses? The answer is equally simple: yes.

Huffman Codes

In 1952, Huffman described an algorithm to generate a "minimum-redundancy code" such that "the average number of digits per message is minimized" [6, p. 1098]. The algorithm builds a code tree from a set of symbols and their relative probabilities or frequencies in a language. Frequent symbols get shorter codes; in-frequent symbols get longer codes. As an example, the codes generated by Huffman's algorithm for the letters of the English alphabet, with the addition of a SPACE character, are given in Figure 2. The symbol frequencies are from a version of the British National Corpus[1] containing 67 million words [20].

Symbol	Frequency	Huffman Code
[space]	67962112	111
e	37907119	010
t	28691274	1101
a	24373121	1011
o	23215532	1001
i	21820970	1000
n	21402466	0111
s	19059775	0011
h	18058207	0010
r	17897352	0001
l	11730498	10101
d	10805580	01101
c	8982417	00001
u	8022379	00000
f	7486889	110011
m	7391366	110010
w	6505294	110001
y	5910495	101001
p	5719422	101000
g	5143059	011001
b	4762938	011000
v	2835696	1100000
k	1720909	11000011
x	562732	110000100
j	474021	1100001011
q	297237	11000010101
z	93172	11000010100

Figure 2. Huffman codes built from the frequencies and letter symbols (including SPACE) in English.

The lengths of the codes vary from 3 to 11 bits (or "digits", in Huffman's terms). The mean code length, weighted by frequency, is 4.117 bits. The code length is equivalent to keystrokes per character (*KSPC*) if the digits are viewed as keystrokes, as per the example in Figure 1b. *KSPC* is a common metric for text entry research [9]. It is the average number of keystrokes required to produce each character of text in a given language using a given input method. While *KSPC* = 4.117 is still quite high, it is only about half the *KSPC* of the UTF-8 example above, and only two keys are required.

The codes in a Huffman tree are called *prefix codes*, since they are at leaf nodes in the tree. This means, for example, if the code 010 represents a symbol, no other symbol has a code beginning with 010 (see "e" in Figure 2). The importance for text entry is that delimiting actions are not necessary to uniquely identify the meaning of a sequence of input actions.

[1] ftp://ftp.itri.bton.ac.uk/

Design Space

Huffman's algorithm is most-commonly used for binary, or base-2, codes for electronic communications systems. Although rarely done, the algorithm can also generate codes using other bases.

To explore the design space of optimized small keyboards using Huffman code-to-symbol assignments, Figure 3 shows the mean code length, or *KSPC*, for Huffman code trees built for bases 2 through 27 supporting the 27 symbols in Figure 2. (Other points in the design space are plotted for comparison, as discussed later.) As expected, there is a relationship between the base of the codes and the mean code length. The lower the base, the longer the mean code length; the higher the base, the shorter the mean code length. This is relevant for text entry. A lower base means more keystrokes but fewer keys. A higher base means fewer keystrokes but more keys.

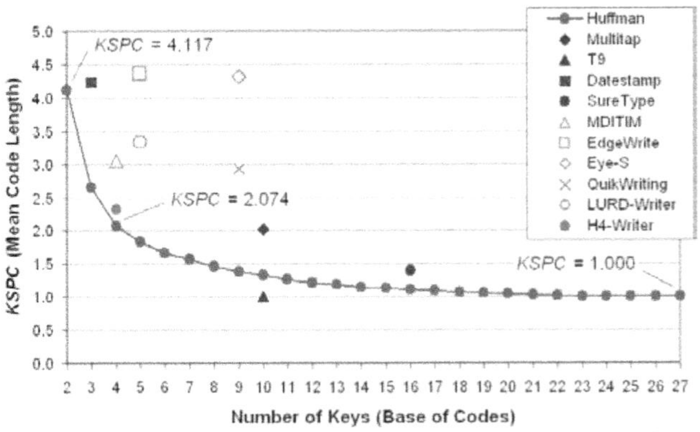

Figure 3. *KSPC* (mean code length) vs. number of keys (base of codes) for Huffman codes using the 27 symbols in Figure 2.

The right-most point in Figure 3 represents the Huffman code tree for base-27. The result is a conventional keyboard, with *KSPC* = 1. There are 27 keys but only one keystroke is required to produce each character. At the other extreme, we see the base-2 example discussed earlier, with *KSPC* = 4.117. These two points encompass the design space of interest in this paper.

The base-4 Huffman value has *KSPC* = 2.074 (see figure). This is close to *KSPC* = 2.032, the value for multi-tap on a mobile phone keyboard [9] (see ◆ in figure). This is interesting since multi-tap requires 10 keys: 9 keys for a-z and SPACE and a 10th key to delimit successive letters on the same key (e.g., "cab" = "222n2n22" where "n" is a designated "next" key).[2] So, the prospect of a 4-key keyboard producing English text in just over two keystrokes per character is provocative.

It is possible to have points below the line in Figure 3, but they require predictive techniques of some form. An

[2] A timeout may also serve as a delimiter. In a sense, the timeout is like a 10th key, since it produces a discrete event not available with the 9 keys used for text input.

example is T9 on a mobile phone, which has a very low *KSPC* = 1.007 [9] (see ▲ in figure). T9 requires a dictionary as well as a 10th key ("next") to cycle through alternate words when there are multiple matches for a key sequence. However, visual attention is imposed on the user who must view the display to determine if the correct word appears at the end of each key sequence [20]. In general, predictive techniques do not support eyes-free input.

Both multi-tap and T9 require additional keys and interaction methods to correct errors or to enter punctuation symbols, uppercase letters, digits, etc. As demonstrated later in this paper, a keyboard designed using Huffman codes can provide these same features without additional keys.

Besides the multi-tap and T9 points, there are additional points that could be added to Figure 3 for the many phone-like and other keypads and text entry methods proposed in the literature (see [11, 13] for reviews). A few points have been selected for discussion here.

Text entry is possible using three keys (base-3) using the "date stamp" method [10]. Letters appear on a virtual keyboard. Left and right cursor keys navigate the virtual keyboard and ENTER selects letters (see Figure 4a). *KSPC* = 4.230 using a fluctuating optimized letter arrangement (■ in Figure 3).

(a)

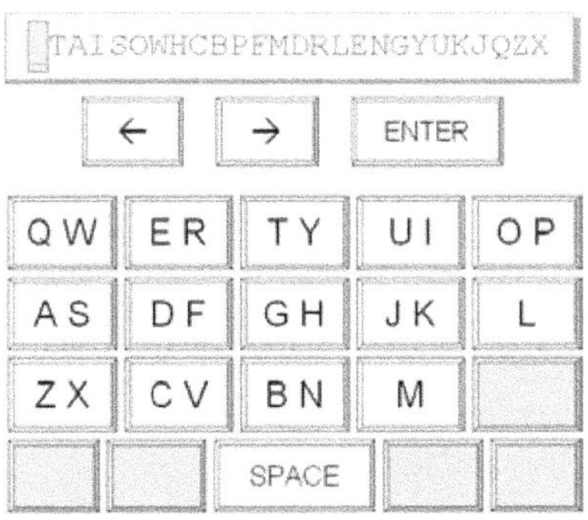

(b)

Figure 4. Example text entry methods. (a) 3-key date stamp method [10]. (b) SureType letter arrangement on RIM's *Blackberry 7100.*

The Qwerty-like keyboard on RIM's *Blackberry 7100* – called SureType – uses a five-column arrangement with two letters per key (see Figure 4b). This form factor allows for bigger keys but introduces ambiguity. In all, 16 keys are required: 14 letter keys, 1 SPACE key, and 1 "next" key (not shown). Using T9-like input, *KSPC* is close to 1. Using multi-tap, *KSPC* = 1.404 (● in Figure 3).

There are two points in Figure 3 for the base-9 condition. Although described as gesture systems by the authors, comparisons are relevant here since the gestures involve navigating between discrete regions on a display. *Eye-S* is shown in Figure 5a [18]. Used with an eye tracker, text entry involves fixating on targets in a sequence defined for each letter. The sequence for "c" (248) is shown in the figure.

(a)

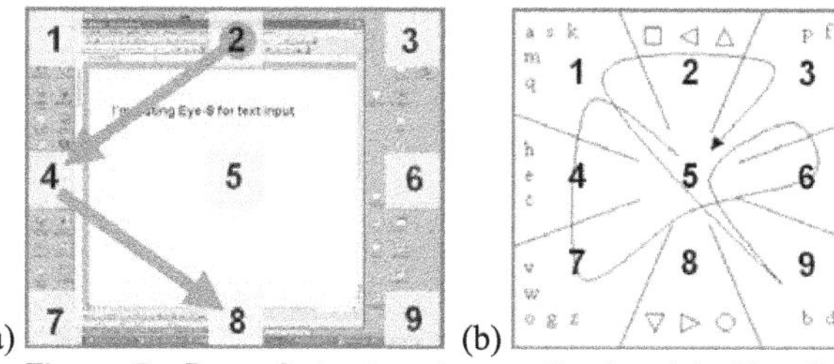

(b)

Figure 5. Base-9 text entry methods. (a) *Eye-S* [18]. (b) *Quikwriting* [17].

Quikwriting is a stylus input method [17]. As with *Eye-S*, it involves navigating around discrete regions on a display. Two gestures are necessary to enter a letter; the first selects a group of letters, and the second selects a letter within the group, with the center (region 5 in the figure) delimiting the letter gestures. Moving the stylus from the center into a perimeter region selects the respective group of letters. A letter within the group is selected by moving the stylus either back to the center region (selecting the middle letter of a group) or first through 1 or 2 perimeter regions (denoting the other letters in the group, respectively). The sequence for "quik" (517 563 59 513) is shown in the figure.

Eye-S and *Quikwriting* have specific target sequences for each letter, including SPACE, thus *KSPC* is easily calculated. The results are *KSPC* = 4.318 for Eye-S and *KSPC* = 2.929 for *Quikwriting* (◇ and × in Figure 3, respectively). These values are substantially higher than *KSPC* = 1.391, the base-9 statistic using Huffman codes. Of course, any comparison must acknowledge the different design goals.

Eye-S was designed to create patterns that mimic Roman letters. For example, the target sequence in Figure 5a is similar in shape to "c". The result, although sub-optimal in terms of *KSPC*, is easier for users to learn.

A design goal for *Quikwriting* was to devise a stylus input method that avoided the thorny problem of handwriting recognition. Clearly, this goal was met. With *Quikwriting*, recognition is a simple matter of detecting stylus transitions through discrete zones (viz. targets). There is a one-to-one correspondence between target sequences and letters in the alphabet. Recognizing handwritten strokes, on the other hand, requires computing a set of shape features for a user-entered stroke and comparing the features to entries in a lookup table to find the best match – a much harder problem.

The Huffman design objective is simple: minimize the mean code length or *KSPC*. While this is a notable pursuit, there are many outstanding issues, such as implementation, ease of learning, and human performance. We will examine these issues shortly. But, first, we focus on the base-4 and base-5 conditions in Figure 3.

BASE 4 AND BASE 5

The codes and *KSPC* values for several text entry methods are shown in Figure 6. These methods were chosen since they all involve (about) four primitive input actions. Thus, they are reasonable points of comparison for the base-4 condition in Figure 3. The second column, labeled H4, gives the Huffman codes for the base-4 condition discussed above. *KSPC* = 2.074 (see Figure 3).

Symbol	H4	MDITIM	LURD-Writer[1]	Edge-Write[1]	H4-Writer
[space]	0	NE	L*	21*	DD
e	32	WES	LL*	2134*	UU
t	31	SNE	UU*	124*	RR
a	23	NSW	RR*	324*	RD
o	22	WSEN	LUUR*	21342*	RL
i	21	WNS	LU*	13*	UD
n	13	NSN	RD*	3142*	UR
s	12	ESE	UR*	2143*	DU
h	11	WSWS	URR*	1324*	UL
r	10	WSN	LUR*	213*	DRR
l	333	SNS	DLL*	134*	DLL
d	332	SWE	LUU*	2434*	DRU
c	331	ESW	LURR*	234*	DLD
u	330	SEN	UUR*	1342*	DLR
f	303	ESNE	DDL*	213*	DLU
m	302	WSWN	LLU*	31424*	DRD
w	301	WNWN	RDD*	13242*	RUD
y	203	SWSE	DLLU*	1424*	RUR
p	202	WNEN	URRD*	3123*	RUU
g	201	ESNS	URD*	21343*	RUL
b	200	SEW	RDL*	1343*	DRLD
v	3003	WNWS	DLU*	134*	DRLR
k	3002	WSWE	RRD*	13234*	DRLU
x	3000	SWSN	URDD*	1423*	DRLLD
j	30012	SESW	RDLL*	243*	DRLLR
q	30011	WSES	RDLU*	213424*	DRLLU
z	30010	SWSW	RDDL*	1234*	DRLLL
KSPC =	2.074	3.047	3.339	4.356	2.321

[1] The asterisk (*) is a delimiting action

Figure 6. Code-to-symbol assignments and *KSPC* for several base-4 or base-5 text input methods. (Figure 7 explains the labels).

Figure 7 shows the mapping between the labels used in Figure 6 and the buttons, stoke directions, or corners, used in the original research.

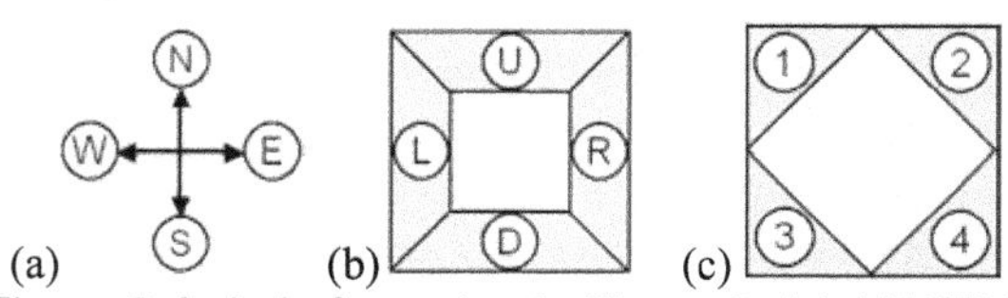

Figure 7. Labels for codes in Figure 6. (a) *MDITIM*. (b) *LURD-Writer* and *H4-Writer*. (c) *EdgeWrite*.

Minimal Device Independent Text Input Method

One example of base-4 prefix codes is Isokoski and Raisamo's Minimal Device Independent Text Input Method (*MDITIM*) [8]. Their system was designed both for keyed input and gesture input. Only four keys or zones were used, one for each compass direction (N, S, E, W). Rather than use an optimized code set, however, they selected codes based on a few design heuristics, primarily to support gesture input. For example, where possible, they choose sequences that were spatially similar to the intended letter, as shown in Figure 8a for the letter "b". Figure 8b shows the equivalent key sequence.

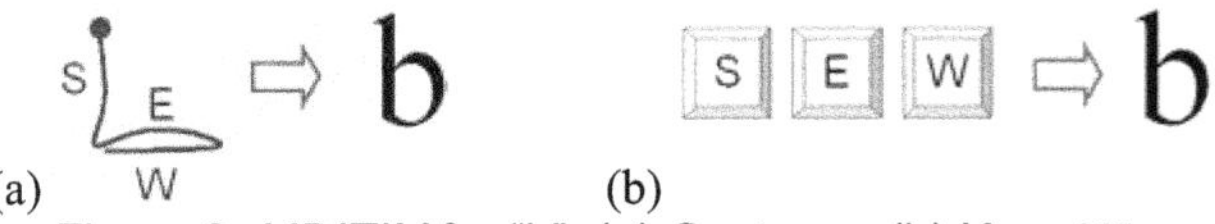

Figure 8. *MDITIM* for "b". (a) Gestures. (b) Keys [8].

As well, Isokoaki and Raisamo avoided codes with the same gesture used consecutively, such as WW, since it is hard to distinguish consecutive strokes in the same direction (without a delimiting action, such as pen up). This heuristic, while reasonable for gesture input, has the opposite effect for keyed input. Consecutive presses on the same key are fast, so repeating "digits" in the code have a positive effect for keyed input.

MDITIM includes additional codes for numerals and punctuation symbols (not shown). The *MDITIM* key-to-symbol assignments are shown in the third column in Figure 6. In the end, *MDITIM* yields *KSPC* = 3.047 (△ in Figure 3). This is 47% higher than *KSPC* = 2.074 for the base-4 Huffman code-to-symbol assignments in the second column of Figure 6.

LURD-Writer

With Felzer and Nordmann's *LURD-Writer* [2], the user moves the mouse cursor left, up, right, or down to hit the edges of an input square. Although the mouse movements are like gestures, the edges are like soft keys, which are selected when contacted by the mouse cursor. The initial state of the input square is shown in Figure 9a. Each hit selects a group of characters, which are then rearranged along the edges. As edges are hit, characters are pre-selected and displayed in the lower left and right corners of the input square. The user may select a character with a left or right mouse button click, or hit another edge to further narrow in on the desired character. The input of "e" involves three actions: LEFT, LEFT, CLICK, as illustrated in Figure 9.

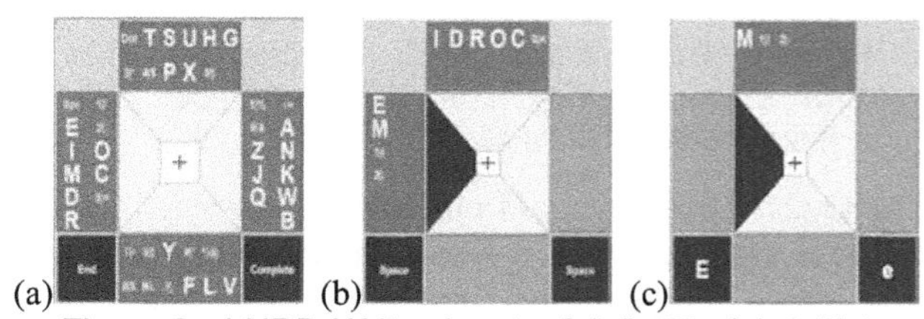

Figure 9. *LURD-Writer* input of "e" [2]. (a) Initial state. (b) After selecting left edge. (c) After selecting left edge again. Final selection of "e" occurs with a right mouse button click (left button for uppercase).

The LURD codes for a-z and SPACE are given in Figure 6, fourth column. The choice of codes was based on design heuristics supporting a hands-free mouse emulator for users with physical disabilities. Input used a headband and sensor that generated pulses in response to intentional muscle contractions in the user's brow. Single or double contractions evoked state changes in the "mouse". One heuristic imposed was to only use clockwise changes in the movement direction. As seen in Figure 6, clockwise patterns, such as LU or LUR, are used, whereas counter-clockwise patterns, such as UL or RUL, are not.

For each code, a final asterisk (*) is added to represent the mouse button click for selection. Since *LURD-Writer* does not use prefix codes, a delimiter is needed to distinguish, for example, L (SPACE) from LL (e). The button click effectively adds 1 to the code length for each symbol, since the button click is akin to a 5th key. For this reason, we consider *LURD-Writer* a base-5 text entry method.

LURD-Writer includes codes for the entry of digits and punctuation symbols and also includes a word completion mode (not shown). For the core 27 symbols (a-z, SPACE), *KSPC* = 3.339 (○ in Figure 3) making *LURD-Writer* slightly less efficient than *MDITIM*.

EdgeWrite

Another text input method of interest is Wobbrock et al.'s *EdgeWrite* [24]. *EdgeWrite* is a gestural input method that uses patterns of movement between the four corners of an input square. A goal was to design each gesture to mimic the letter it represents, as this criterion is known to quicken users' learning of the gestures [14]. The gestures for the letters a-e are shown in Figure 10.

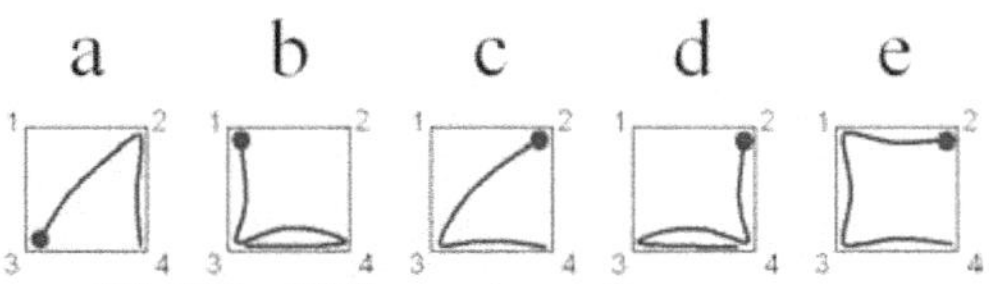

Figure 10. *EdgeWrite* gestures for a-e.

EdgeWrite has been implemented with a variety of devices and methods. One method involves "typing on four keys" [25]. In this case, each gesture is a series of key presses. Using the authors' labels for the corners (see Figure 10), inputting the "e" involves pressing in sequence the keys 2, 1, 3, and 4. The *EdgeWrite* codes for a-z and SPACE are given in Figure 6, fifth column.

As with *LURD-Writer*, the *EdgeWrite* codes are not prefix codes, so a delimiting action is needed to distinguish, for example, 21 (SPACE) from 2134 (e). The authors used an "adaptive timeout" as a delimiter. The duration of the timeout was between 1.2× and 2.0× the duration of key presses; thus, the timeout amounts to a discrete action taking at least as long as one key press. Again, this is akin to a 5th key and is represented in Figure 6 as an asterisk after each code. As with *LURD-Writer*, the need for a distinct delimiting action makes *EdgeWrite* a base-5 text entry method.

The four-key input mode for *EdgeWrite* has *KSPC* = 4.356 (□ in Figure 3). Although this is high, it is important to remember that *EdgeWrite* is primarily a gesture input method. Optimizing the codes for keyed entry was not a design criterion.[3]

Our proposed base-4 text entry method using Huffman coding is *H4-Writer*, shown in the right-most column in Figure 6. Before describing *H4-Writer*, the performance evaluations of *MDITIM*, *LURD-Writer*, and *EdgeWrite* are summarized.

Performance Comparison

Isokoski and Raisamo conducted a longitudinal study of *MDITIM* with five participants [8]. Entry speeds were about 2-3 wpm for the 1st session, representing about 30 minutes of practice. Speeds increased to about 7-8 wpm in the 10th session.

Torsten and Nordmann reported entry speeds for *LURD-Writer* of 1-3 wpm [2]. Testing involved a single physically-disabled participant. Input used pulses generated by a sensor connected to the user's forehead. The pulses controlled a state machine to generate L, U, R, and D commands. No doubt, higher entry speeds are possible using a manually operated mouse or keyboard.

Wobbrock et al. evaluated their 4-key implementation of *EdgeWrite* in a longitudinal study with five participants. Input used keys on the numeric keypad of a standard keyboard. Participants pressed keys using multiple fingers on their dominant hand. Entry speeds were about 6.5 wpm in the 1st session, increasing to 16.9 wpm in the 10th session.

Taking Stock

The H4 column in Figure 6, at *KSPC* = 2.074, gives what we believe are the most efficient code-to-symbol assignments for 4-key English text entry. There are several caveats, however. One is the tag "non-predictive". This is important because predictive text entry methods (e.g., T9) do no support eyes-free input: The user must attend to the on-going predictive process. The H4 assignments in Figure 3 are non-predictive, and therefore support eyes-free input. Of course, the code-to-symbol assignments must be learned, and this takes time.

Another issue is the limited reach of a model that reduces English to 27 symbols. English, or any other language, is much more than 26 letters and SPACE. Many other symbols are important for text entry, such as accented symbols, punctuation symbols, numerals, and so on. Furthermore, editing commands (e.g., BACKSPACE, DELETE) and mode shifts (e.g., SHIFT, CAPSLOCK) are required to support comprehensive text entry. However, it is difficult to include these in the model, since frequency data for symbols and commands are either

[3] Later refinements in the *EdgeWrite* gesture set by Wobbrock and Myers yield *KSPC* rates of 4.483 [23] and 4.258 wpm (see http://depts.washington.edu/ewrite/downloads/EwChart.pdf).

unavailable or domain specific. So, while the modeling process above is robust, it is limited. Clearly, converting the H4 code-to-symbol assignments in Figure 6 into a comprehensive text entry method requires further design. For this, we introduce *H4-Writer*.

Design of H4-Writer

The right-most column in Figure 6 shows the code-to-symbol assignments for *H4-Writer*. The same algorithm was used as for the H4 codes in the second column; however, a trick was used. Note the absence of any code beginning with "L" for *H4-Writer*. Thus, the top-level node in the tree has three branches (URD), instead of four. This was achieved by tricking the algorithm: A fake symbol with an arbitrarily high frequency was inserted in the symbol-frequency list. With this mutation, the algorithm assigned an entire top-level branch to the fake symbol. Of course, this reduces the efficiency of the codes for the core symbols (a-z, SPACE). The loss in efficiency appears as an increase in *KSPC*. As seen in Figure 6, *KSPC* = 2.321 for *H4-Writer*. Remarkably, this is only 12% higher than *KSPC* = 2.074 for the base-4 Huffman codes. This occurs simply because the top nine symbols for *H4-Writer* require only two codes (viz. keystrokes) yet encompass 72% of English (see frequencies in Figure 2). By comparison to H4, the *KSPC*s for the other methods in Figure 6 are higher by 47% (*MDITIM*), 61% (*LURD-Writer*), and 110% (*EdgeWrite*).

The L-branch for *H4-Writer* was hand-coded, with the goal of designing a comprehensive and consistent 4-key text entry method. A hand approach was used due to the absence of reliable frequency data for special symbols and commands, as noted above. Examples from the L-branch for *H4-Writer* are given in Figure 11. BKSP, ENTER, and SHIFT are assigned short two-key sequences, since it is known that these keys are among the most frequent of all keys used in desktop applications [21]. CAPS_LOCK, period, and comma are assigned three-key sequences.

Symbol	H4-Writer L Branch	Symbol	H4-Writer L Branch
[Bksp]	LL	-	LDDLD
[Enter]	LU	%	LDDUL
[Shift]	LR	$	LDDUU
[CapsLock]	LDL	[SymLock]	LDDUR
.	LDU	0	LDDDUL
,	LDR	1	LDDDUU
?	LDDLL	2	LDDDUR
:	LDDLU	3	LDDDUD
'	LDDLR	etc.	

Figure 11. Coding for *H4-Writer* commands and special symbols.

At *KSPC* = 2.321, *H4-Writer* is positioned very close to Huffman's "minimum redundancy line" in Figure 3 (see ● in figure). Although this is promising, it remains to be seen how well *H4-Writer* will perform for text entry. We are interested in the usual metrics for speed and accuracy, but also in the learning process and in the entry of uppercase letters, numerals, and punctuation symbols.

METHOD

The evaluation of *H4-Writer* proceeded in two parts. The first part was a longitudinal study with ten sessions. Users entered phrases of text selected at random from a set. The phrases included only lowercase letters and the SPACE character. Such a procedure is high in internal validity, but low in external validity, necessitating the second part of the study. The second part involved an additional session using a phrase set that included uppercase letters, digits, and punctuation symbols. This final session provided an opportunity to test *H4-Writer*'s viability as a general-purpose text entry method.

Participants

As is customary with longitudinal evaluations [e.g., 8, 15, 25], fewer participants were used but testing involved many sessions. Six participants were recruited from two local university communities. There were 4 males and 2 females with a mean age of 27 (*SD* = 11.0). All were experienced users of desktop computers, reporting 10-16 hours of daily usage. None had prior experience with *H4-Writer* or the other methods in Figure 6.

Apparatus

The apparatus included hardware and software. The software was written in Java and ran on a notebook PC running Microsoft *Windows XP*. Figure 12 shows a screen snap of the software midway through the input of a phrase of text. Four virtual keys (in red boxes) show the symbols accessible along each branch of the Huffman code tree. The contents of the virtual keys are updated with each key press, reflected the decent through the Huffman tree. The key renderings are important for novices, who visually follow the progression of symbols on the virtual keys during input. However, as learning

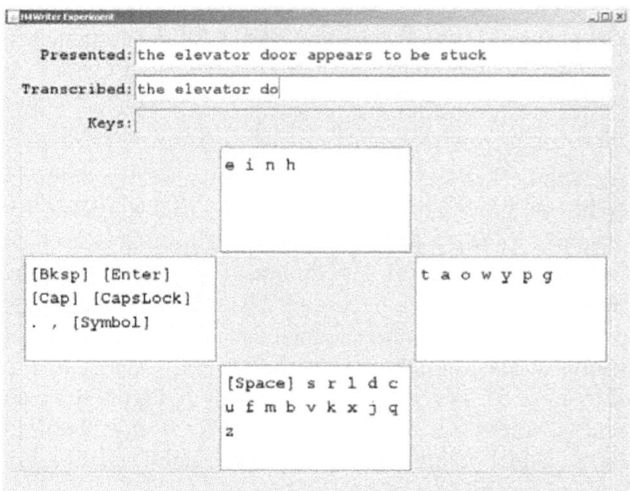

Figure 12. Screen snap of the *H4-Writer* software.

progresses, the need to view the virtual keys diminishes. For example, "the" requires RR (t), UL (h), UU (e), DD (SPACE), as given in Figure 6. These patterns are quickly learned. Words involving less common letters take more time to learn. An important motivation for the experiment was to empirically measure the learning progression.

Mistakes, if noticed, were corrected by entering BKSP (LL) followed by the button presses for the correct character. At the end of the trial, the ENTER (LU) had to be typed. Following each trial, to help motivate participants, a pop-up window appeared showing the presented and transcribed text phrases, as well as the entry speed and error rate.

User input to *H4-Writer* requires four physical keys or buttons. For this, we used an Xtreme Gaming *Sector 7* game controller, as seen in Figure 13.

Figure 13. Xtreme Gaming *Sector 7* game controller. Physical input uses the four thumb-operated buttons on the right-hand side.

The game controller was held in the usual manner with both hands. Text was entered by the right thumb using the four buttons on the right side of the controller. The button assignments were as expected (e.g., 4 = L; see Figure 13).

The game controller interfaced to the host via a USB connection. Software from Xpadder (www.xpadder.com) provided the necessary mapping of game controller button presses to system key events, as required for the *H4-Writer* experiment software.

Procedure

Each participant was briefed on the goals of the experiment and on the operation of *H4-Writer*. The system was demonstrated by the experimenter, after which the participant entered a few warm-up phrases.

Sessions were scheduled with no more than two sessions on one day and no more that two intervening days between sessions. Each session was divided into 12 blocks with 5 phrases/block. The first two blocks were deemed warm-up and discarded. Rest breaks were allowed between phrases and blocks at the discretion of the participant. Sessions at the beginning of the experiment lasted about 50 minutes. Toward the end, sessions lasted about 35 minutes.

Overall there were 11 sessions of text entry. These were divided into two parts, described as follows.

Part I – Basic Test of H4-Writer

Sessions 1-10 used phrases drawn at random from a set of 500 phrases [12]. The phrases included only lowercase letters, with no punctuation. Part I constituted a longitudinal study and was intended as a basic test of *H4-Writer*, focusing on learning, and on input of the core 26 letters, as well as SPACE, BACKSPACE, and ENTER.

Part II – Extended Session

A single extended session was performed after completion of Part I to test the viability of *H4-Writer* as a comprehensive text entry method. The 11th session used a different phrase set containing 100 phrases. The phrases included a mixture of uppercase and lowercase letters, as well as special symbols. A few examples follow:

```
Can I skate with my sister today?
Beware the ides of March!
Don't say anything.
Play it again, Sam.
Yes - you are very smart!
```

The goal for Part II was to improve external validity by using *H4-Writer* in a context typical of expected usage. Input involved accessing the L-branch of the *H4-Writer* code tree to input special symbols (see Figure 11).

For both parts, participants were instructed to proceed as quickly and accurately as possible and to correct any errors they noticed as input proceeded. Error-free transcribed text was desired, but not essential.

Design

As the experiment was longitudinal and was intended as an initial test of *H4-Writer*, there was no alternative input method as a point of comparison. Session, however, served as an independent variable, primarily to gauge the progress of learning of the participants. The dependent variables were entry speed (words per minute), error rate (%), and keystrokes per character (*KSPC*).

Overall, the analyses were based on 6 participants × 11 sessions × 10 blocks/session × 5 phrases/block = 3,300 phrases of input.

RESULTS AND DISCUSSION

Part I – Basic Test of H4-Writer

Text entry speed in Part I started with a mean of 7.7 wpm in Session 1 and finished at 20.4 wpm in Session 10 – an increase of 165%. The improvement with practice is evident in Figure 14, which shows the progress overall and for each participant.

We consider the session-ten entry speed in Figure 14 the most important overall result of this experiment. Not only is 20.4 wpm a respectable text entry speed, it was achieved using one thumb on four buttons (see title of this paper).

Figure 14 also shows the power law of learning over the ten sessions:

$$\text{Entry Speed} = 10.0\, n^{0.33} \text{ wpm}$$

where n is a unit of about 40 minutes of practice. The model explains 96.3% of the variation in observations, according to R^2.

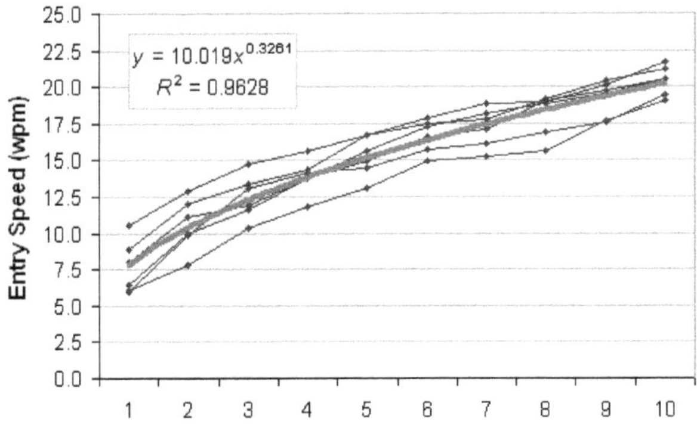

Figure 14. Entry speed (wpm) by Session, overall and for each participant.

The closest point of comparison to our result is in Wobbrock et al.'s test of *EdgeWrite* using four-keys on a numeric keypad [25]. Using 5 participants, they reported a mean of 16.9 wpm on session 10. However, entry involved the use of four fingers. For our experiment, by contrast, text entry involved one thumb only. Nevertheless, *H4-Writer* is about 20% faster. This is expected given the differences in the computed *KSPC* between *EdgeWrite* and *H4-Writer* noted earlier (see Figure 6). Simply put, in terms of key-stroking requirements, *H4-Writer* is more efficient than *EdgeWrite*. So, a higher entry speed is fully expected. Of course, it takes an experiment with users, such as reported here, to put an empirical perspective on this.

Entry speed alone does not provide a complete story. It is important also to consider accuracy or error rates. Over the 10 sessions, the mean error rate was very low: 0.69%. This figure is based on the mean of the minimum string distances (MSD), computed as character-wise comparisons between the presented and transcribed text phrases. Figure 15 shows the error rate result overall and by participant.

The result for participant P3 is highlighted in Figure 15. This participant seemed to have a preoccupation with speed and this surfaced as a swelling in error rates, with a Session-5 high of 5.2%. This was pointed out to the participant, along with a suggestion to relax and focus a bit more on accuracy. The effect was immediate. P3's error rates were in line with the other participants for Sessions 6-10. Although it might be reasonable to label P3 an outlier and exclude the data, the effect overall seemed minor, so the data stand.

Although the error rate results in Figure 15 look slightly more erratic than the entry speed results in Figure 14, this is typical. Errors are discrete events and tend to occur in clusters. In fact, of the 3,000 total phrases represented in Figure 15, 2,588 (86.3%) were error free; i.e., error rate = 0%. Errors when they did occur tended to produce single-phrase chunks.

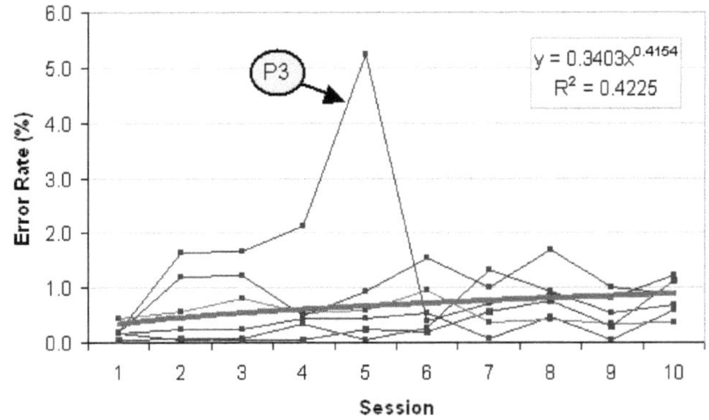

Figure 15. Error rate (%) by session, overall and for each participant. See text for discussion.

Keystrokes per character (*KSPC*) is not only a useful statistic to compare text entry methods a priori (see Figure 6), it is a useful dependent measure. If a participant enters text perfectly, then the observed *KSPC* equals the predicted (i.e., calculated) *KSPC*. However, if errors occur, the situation is different. Errors that remain are reflected in the MSD statistics, as just examined. Errors that are corrected require extra keystrokes and this yields an increase in *KSPC* above the predicted *KSPC*. The result for *KSPC* is given in Figure 16.

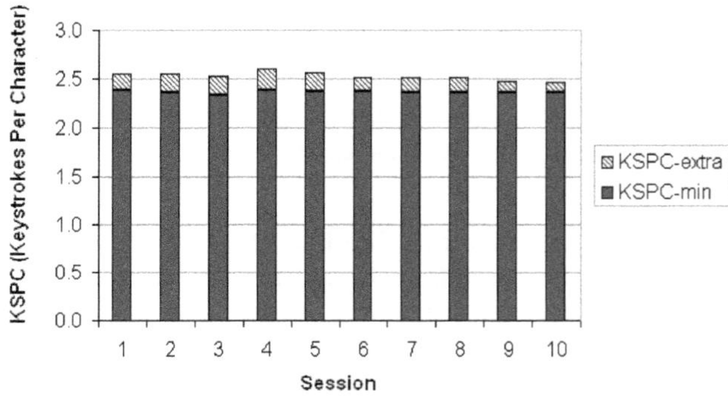

Figure 16. *KSPC* (keystrokes per character) by session.

The observed *KSPC* is divided into two parts: *KSPC-min* and *KSPC-extra*. *KSPC-min* is the predicted *KSPC* based on the actual phrases entered. The heights of the solid bars for *KSPC-min* are close to the value of *KSPC* = 2.321 given earlier (see *KSPC* value for *H4-Writer* in Figure 6). Slight deviations occur because the values are computed from the actual phrases entered, rather than for English in general.

Of more interest here is *KSPC-extra*, which quantifies the additional keystrokes to correct errors. These keystrokes are combinations of BKSP (LL) and the keystrokes for the correct characters. The added height to the bars in Figure 16 is small. The mean of the *KSPC-extra* values is 0.134, suggesting an overhead of approximately 1 keystroke every 7.4 keystrokes to correct errors. Our conclusion is simply that participants' behaviour overall was neither reckless nor untoward. Participants made a small number of errors and they tended to correct most of those that did occur.

Although we consider *KSPC* to provide a suitable perspective of error correction performance (because our design was directed at reducing *KSPC*), we also calculated the corrected error rate, which averaged 3.7%.

The on-screen keyboard was visible throughout the experiment. This was essential while learning *H4-Writer*; however, visual access of the on-screen keyboard diminished as expertise developed and entry speeds increased. Once entry speeds exceeded about 15 wpm, *H4-Writer* became fully eyes-free as the keying rate (3-4 keystrokes per second) was too high for any visual search to occur.

Part II – Extended Session

By the time participants reached the 10th session, they were well versed in the operation of *H4-Writer*, having reached an average entry speed just over 20 wpm. The 11th session was designed to test their ability to leverage existing skill and delve into the L-branch of the *H4-Writer* code tree to input special symbols.

Session 11 proceeded just like Sessions 1-10, except a different phrase set was used. Punctuation and other special symbols were required (examples given earlier). Clearly, performance would suffer, but how much so? The result for entry speed is shown in Figure 17.

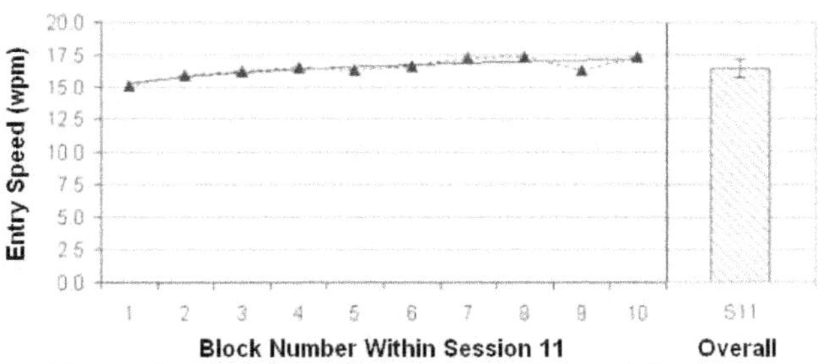

Figure 17. Session 11 entry speed (wpm) by block and overall.

The overall entry speed for Session 11 was 16.5 wpm, varying from 15.1 wpm in the 1st block to 17.4 wpm in the 10th block. Bear in mind that there were two warm-up blocks for which the data were discarded. (This was true for all sessions, as noted earlier.) Therefore, the initial performance while entering special characters was slightly worse than revealed in Figure 17. However, given that the total time for Session 11 was about 35 minutes, participants clearly adjusted quickly to the added demand of entering special symbols. By the end of Session 11, entry speeds were within 3 wpm of the speeds in Session 10 with the lowercase-only phrase set.

Error rates and *KSPC* results were also encouraging for Session 11. The error rate overall was <1% and *KSPC-extra* was similar to that observed in Sessions 1-10.

Participants liked *H4-Writer*, but found the experiment long and demanding. An alternative methodology for the longitudinal study might have worked better. For example, participants could have used *H4-Writer* daily in an unstructured manner, with formal testing occurring at designated intervals, such as one test per week over a few months of use.

CONCLUSIONS

We have presented the design and evaluation of *H4-Writer*, a text entry method that uses one thumb and four buttons. Given the small form factor, the observed entry speed of just over 20 words per minute after 10 sessions of practice (≈40 minutes each) is encouraging.

H4-Writer is one example in a family of keyed input methods using Huffman coding to minimize *KSPC* for non-predictive text entry. A variety of other implementations are being considered, for example, using stylus input, a joystick, a touchpad, head tracking, and eye tracking.

As demonstrated in our design analysis, the use of a Huffman code tree allows extra symbols and extra commands to be added without the need for additional buttons. And so, the method has potential for use in any situation where only a small number of input primitives are available yet comprehensive text entry is required.

ACKNOWLEDGEMENT

Thanks are offered to Torsten Felzer for providing the enhanced phrase set for the 11th session.

REFERENCES

1. Dunlop, M. D., Watch-top text-entry: Can phone-style predictive text entry work with only 5 buttons? *Proceedings of MobileHCI 2004*, (Heidelberg, Germany: Springer-Verlag, 2004), 342-346.
2. Felzer, T. and Nordmann, R., Alternative text entry using different input methods, *Proceedings of the ACM SIGACCESS Conference on Computers and Accessibility - ASSETS 2006*, (New York: ACM, 2006), 10-17.
3. Gong, J. and Tarasewich, P., Alphabetically constrained keypad designs for text entry on mobile phones, *Proceedings of the ACM SIGCHI Conference on Human Factors in Computing Systems - CHI 2005*, (New York: ACM, 2005), 211-220.
4. Green, N., Kruger, J., Faldu, C., and Amant, R. S., A reduced QWERTY keyboard for mobile text entry, *Extended Abstracts of the ACM SIGCHI Conference on Human Factors in Computing Systems - CHI 2004*, (New York: ACM, 2004), 1429-1432.
5. Harbusch, K. and Kühn, M., Towards an adaptive communication aid with text input from ambiguous keyboards, *Proceedings of the European Association for Computational Linguistics - EACL 2003*, (Cambridge, MA: MIT Press, 2003), 207-210.
6. Huffman, D. A., A method for the construction of minimum redundancy codes, *Proceedings of the IRE*, *40*, 1952, 1098-1101.

7. Hwang, S. and Lee, G., Qwerty-like 3x4 keypad layouts for mobile phone, *Extended Abstracts of the ACM SIGCHI Conference on Human Factors in Computing Systems - CHI 2005*, (New York: ACM, 2005), 1479-1482.

8. Isokoski, P. and Raisamo, R., Device independent text input: A rationale and an example, *Proceedings of the Working Conference on Advanced Visual Interfaces - AVI 2000*, (New York: ACM, 2000), 76-83.

9. MacKenzie, I. S., KSPC (keystrokes per character) as a characteristic of text entry techniques, *Proceedings of the Fourth International Symposium on Human-Computer Interaction with Mobile Devices - MobileHCI 2002*, (Berlin: Springer, 2002), 195-210.

10. MacKenzie, I. S., Mobile text entry using three keys, *Proceedings of the Second Nordic Conference on Human-Computer Interaction - NordiCHI 2002*, (New York: ACM, 2002), 27-34.

11. MacKenzie, I. S. and Soukoreff, R. W., Text entry for mobile computing: Models and methods, theory and practice, *Human-Computer Interaction*, *17*, 2002, 147-198.

12. MacKenzie, I. S. and Soukoreff, R. W., Phrase sets for evaluating text entry techniques, *Extended Abstracts of the ACM SIGCHI Conference on Human Factors in Computing Systems - CHI 2003*, (New York: ACM, 2003), 754-755.

13. MacKenzie, I. S. and Tanaka-Ishii, K., Text entry with a small number of buttons, in *Text entry systems: Mobility, accessibility, universality*, (I. S. MacKenzie, and Tanaka-Ishii, K., Eds.). San Francisco, Morgan Kaufmann, 2007, 105-121.

14. MacKenzie, I. S. and Zhang, S. X., The immediate usability of Graffiti, *Proceedings of Graphics Interface '97*, (Toronto: Canadian Information Processing Society, 1997), 120-137.

15. MacKenzie, I. S., Zhang, S. X., and Soukoreff, R. W., Text entry using soft keyboards, *Behaviour & Information Technology*, *18*, 1999, 235-244.

16. Pavlovych, A. and Stuerzlinger, W., Less-Tap: A fast and easy-to-learn text input technique for phones, *Proceedings of Graphics Interface 2003*, (Toronto: Canadian Information Processing Society, 2003), 97-104.

17. Perlin, K., Quikwriting: Continuous stylus-based text entry, *Proceedings of the ACM Symposium on User Interface Software and Technology - UIST '98*, (New York: ACM, 1998), 215-216.

18. Porta, M. and Turina, M., Eye-S: A full-screen input modality for pure eye-based communication, *Proceedings of the ACM Symposium on Eye Tracking Research and Applications - ETRA 2008*, (New York: ACM, 2008), 27-34.

19. Ryu, H. and Cruz, K., LetterEase: Improving text entry on a handheld device via letter reassignment, *Proceedings of the 19th Conference of the Computer-Human Interaction Special Interaction Group (CHISIG) of Australia - OZCHI 2005*, (New York: ACM, 2005), 1-10.

20. Silfverberg, M., MacKenzie, I. S., and Korhonen, P., Predicting text entry speed on mobile phones, *Proceedings of the ACM SIGCHI Conference on Human Factors in Computing Systems - CHI 2000*, (New York: ACM, 2000), 9-16.

21. Soukoreff, R. W. and MacKenzie, I. S., Input-based language modeling in the design of high performance input systems, *Proceedings of Graphics Interface 2003*, (Toronto: CIPS, 2003), 89-96.

22. Tanaka-Ishii, K., Inutsuka, Y., and Takeichi, M., Entering text with a four-button device, *Proceedings of the 19th International Conference on Computational Linguistics - Vol. 1*, (Morristown, NJ: Association for Computational Linguistics, 2002), 1-7.

23. Wobbrock, J. O. and Myers, B. A., Trackball text entry for people with motor impairments, *Proceedings of the ACM SIGCHI Conference on Human Factors in Computing Systems - CHI 2006*, (New York: ACM, 2006), 479-488.

24. Wobbrock, J. O., Myers, B. A., and Kembel, J. A., EdgeWrite: A stylus-based text entry method designed for high accuracy and stability of motion, *Proceedings of the ACM Symposium on User Interface Software and Technology - UIST 2003*, (New York: ACM, 2003), 61-70.

25. Wobbrock, J. O., Myers, B. A., and Rothrock, B., Few-key text entry revisited: Mnemonic gestures on four keys, *Extended Abstracts of the ACM SIGCHI Conference on Human Factors in Computing Systems - CHI 2006*, (New York: ACM, 2006), 489-492.

PUB - Point Upon Body: Exploring Eyes-Free Interaction and Methods on an Arm

Shu-Yang Lin[*] *Chao-Huai Su*[*] *Kai-Yin Cheng*[*] *Rong-Hao Liang*[†] *Tzu-Hao Kuo*[*] *Bing-Yu Chen*[‡]
[*†‡]National Taiwan University [†]Academia Sinica
[*†]{young,domossu,keynes,howieliang,kakukogou}@cmlab.csie.ntu.edu.tw [‡]robin@ntu.edu.tw

ABSTRACT
This paper presents a novel interaction system, *PUB* (Point Upon Body), to explore eyes-free interaction in a personal space by allowing users tapping on their own arms to be provided with haptic feedback from their skin. Two user studies determine how users can interact precisely with their forearms and how users behave when operating in their arm space. According to those results, normal users can divide their arm space at most into 6 points between their wrists and elbows with iterative practice. Experimental results also indicate that the divided pattern of each user is unique from that of other ones. Based on the design principles from the observations, an interaction system, *PUB*, is designed to demonstrate how interaction design benefits from those findings. Two scenarios, remote display control and mobile device control, are demonstrated through the *UltraSonic* device attached on the users' wrists to detect their tapped positions.

ACM Classification: H5.2 [Information interfaces and presentation]: User Interfaces. - Graphical user interfaces.

General terms: Design, Human Factors, Experimentation.

Keywords: Kinetic User Interface, eyes-free interaction, natural haptic feedback.

INTRODUCTION

Several approaches have been developed to utilize a user's forearm's skin [7] or muscle [21] to explore the interaction through the eyes-free manner. Despite the availability of such approaches, the human factors that influence how users interact with their forearms remain unknown. Therefore, we conducted a series of user studies to explore the design space for the interaction with the forearm.

The results of the user studies confirm the following principles for designing an eyes-free manner on an arm. The haptic feedback from a user's skin allows her/him to increase the accuracy of the tapped positions. The elbow joint is deemed as the central point of the full arm from the shoulder joint to the wrist joint. The discriminated points for normal users can reach to at most 6 points between the elbow joint to the wrist joint. Some users can even discriminate 8 points. However, distributions of the tapped positions differ from user to user. Therefore, a calibration procedure is required if more than 5 accessed points are available. Experimental results indicate that the central area between the elbow joint and the wrist joint has a larger variation than the two joint points. The tapped behavior also varies from user to user. While tapping on the desired position, before confirming, they attempt to locally shift their fingers to fine-tune the imagined results. Hence, the waiting time for final confirmation is required.

Figure 1: A user operated the *UltraSonic* device to interact with a hierarchical GUI system on a remote display through the designed prototype system, *PUB*.

We then developed a novel prototype system, *PUB* (Point Upon Body), to demonstrate the applicability of the derived principles. Two scenarios based on the prototyped *UltraSonic* device are provided. One is for controlling a music player on a mobile device (Figure 9), and the other is for selecting a hierarchical graphical user interface (GUI) system on a remote display (Figure 1). Through those demo scenarios, designers and researchers can know more about how to utilize people's arms as a kinetic input device.

The rest of this paper is organized as follows. Two user studies were conducted to explore the human factors about the eyes-free interaction on a user's arm. The EXPLORING DESIGN SPACE section describes the user studies' procedures, results and subsequently derived design principles. Based on those principles, the PUB DESIGN section introduces the design of the prototype system, *PUB*, to demonstrate the possible scenarios. Next, the DISCUSSION section discusses the limitations and possible generalizations. Conclusions are finally drawn in the CONCLUSION section, along with recommendations for future research.

RELATED WORK

Neuropsychological studies suggest that the human brain constructs three representations of space: extrapersonal space, peripersonal space and personal space [20, 14, 19]. Extrapersonal space is constructed in the human brain to be the space distant from the body. Peripersonal space encompasses the space surrounding human bodies and can be reached easily with the limbs. Personal space (a.k.a. pericutaneous space), refers to the surface immediately above the skin of the human body and the space that human bodies occupy. Related literature is summarized as follows.

Extrapersonal Space

Contents or objects beyond user reach can be controlled by using a hand gesture or the user's shadow. Pointing is the most used and intuitive gesture. Bolt [5] studied the pointing gesture by combining voice commands to interact with a distant large screen. The pointing gesture can be recognized through stereo images [9], glove [4], motion capture [27] and laser pointer [10].

Even the orientation of a user's head can help to recognize the pointing gesture [17]. Various ways of performing ray-casting gestures were also thoroughly studied [27, 11]. Through a user's shadow, remote contents can also be interacted with [12, 23]. Moreover, functions can be further anchored on the shadow to achieve body-centric interaction with the remote display [24]. Nevertheless, users must normally pay attention to the remote display because those interaction methods are designed for remote content interaction.

Peripersonal Space

The interactive techniques designed for peripersonal space are normally intended for interacting with reachable contents. Mistry *et al.* [16] demonstrated that by integrating with a camera and a pico-projector, a user can use the predefined gestures to interact with the projected nearby gesture. Li *et al.* [13] utilized human's proprioception kinesthetic memory to trigger shortcuts on a mobile device in an eyes-free manner. Mine *et al.* [15] also exploited proprioception to interact with virtual objects. Gustafson *et al.* [6] further explored the imaginary space in front of users to allow them to interact with "nearby imaginary" results. However, the lack of haptic feedback may lower the accuracy of pointing or selecting [27]; in addition, users may become fatigued by hanging their hands in the air.

Personal Space

In this category, the input is simply on a user's body. Marisil [2] is designed by projecting the phone's keypad on a user's fingers. Brainy hand [25] adopted a similar concept by projecting images and words on a user's arm; a user can then select the desired function by directly tapping on the projected region. By equipping the user with wearable devices, user interaction can be detected by rotating a user's wrist or by pressing on the clothes next to the skin [18]. Saponas *et al.* [21] and Harrison *et al.* [7] further explored the technologies capable of detecting a user's tapped position on the forearm's skin by analyzing the forearm's electromyography (EMG) data or transmitted acoustic data through a custom made bio-acoustic sensing array.

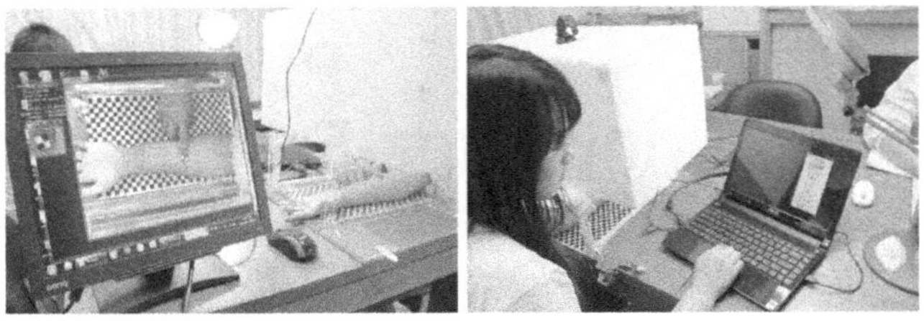

(a) (b)

Figure 2: (a) Vision-based procedure used to measure automatically where a participant taps. (b) User study environment. The acrylic case is used to shelter a participant's visual attention on the forearm. The display shows the tasks to be executed.

Using a human body as the input interface can provide haptic feedback. Meanwhile, tapping on the body gives users the feeling of being touched. In doing so, an eyes-free manner interaction utilizing the user's kinesthetic sense can be achieved [8, 3, 26, 22]. Although studies have demonstrated that the forearm can be a usable interaction area, the human factors about how users can take the benefits from a user's spatial knowledge of the personal space remains unknown. Therefore, motivated by those enabled technologies, this work explores the design space on a human arm.

EXPLORING DESIGN SPACE

To know how users can interact with their arms, we conducted two user studies to explore the design space. Before those, we conducted a prior user study to examine how participants perceive their full arms first. By confirming that the elbow joint was deemed as the middle point of the arm, the first user study investigated how participants can divide their forearms. Thereafter, the second user study verified the importance of haptic feedback and the feeling of being touched from the skin.

Participants and Experiment Conditions

12 paid participants (5 females) were recruited, ranging from 21 to 30 years old (mean age=23.67, s=2.90). All participants are right-handed, and the measured personal space was focused on the left forearm. Each participant was tested in an isolated room, in which only the tester and the participant were located.

Figure 2(b) illustrates the test environment. Each participant was instructed to sit in front of the table and place her/his left forearm in an acrylic case, which was used to shelter the participant's visual attention from the forearm. The screen shows the task to be executed. A camera was set above the participant's forearm to measure where a user tapped automatically through the developed vision-based procedure (Figure 2(a)). A user's index finger was used to perform the tap tasks, and a marker was stuck on the nail of the index finger for tracking. Experimental results indicate that the tracking error of the developed vision-based procedure is 3 *mm*.

User Study 1: Explore the Division on the Forearm

The first user study explores how a participant perceives the forearm is divided and how precisely the forearm can be di-

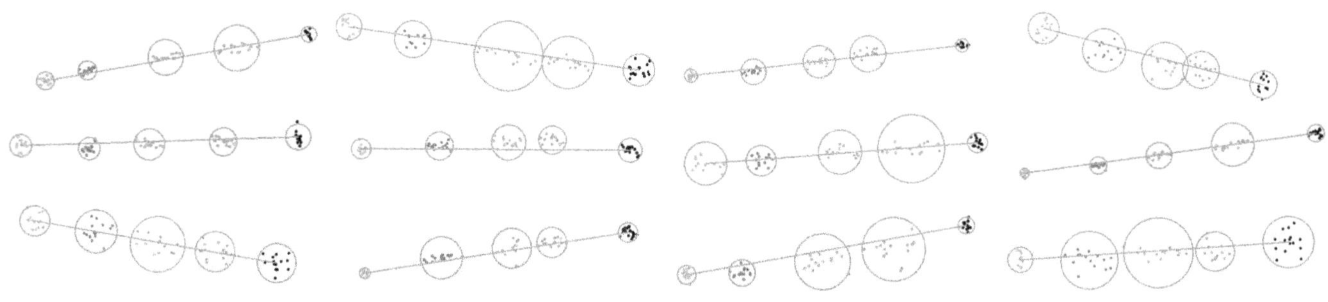

Figure 3: Point distribution of each participant, who performed 5 points division task in the first user study. The covered area inside the circle refers to the points within two standard deviations.

vided by the participant through an eyes-free manner. The two end points are the elbow joint and wrist joint. Before the formal user study, a pilot study was conducted by recruiting 4 participants to perform the test. Experimental results indicate that the participants can easily discriminate 4 points. One participant can successfully divide the forearm into 8 points. Therefore, the test divided levels range from 5 to 9 points are set in this user study. Although the learning effect may exist, only the limit in which a participant can achieve – even through the iterative practices – is tested.

Tasks and Procedures. For each level, participants were shown a picture displaying how many points were divided on their forearms in the task. Each point on the forearm was registered with a serial number. Notably, the wrist joint represents the number 1 and the elbow point refers to the final number. A random number was displayed on the screen to indicate to the participants which point they should tap on. Then, the participants had to move their index fingers to press the space key to proceed to the next task. Therefore, the index finger is forced to leave the left forearm while pressing the space key, and the processed time was also recorded. Each point should be tested for 15 times in each level. Therefore, there are a total of 525 tapping tasks (75+90+105+120+135) for all levels in this user study.

Hypotheses. Some expectations are made for the calculated accuracy rate. The accuracy rate refers to the portion of the non-overlapping tapped points in one category in each level. The non-overlapping points imply that the positions of the tapped points does not cause any ambiguity. We thus hypothesize the following:

H1: Wrist joint and elbow joint have the highest accuracies.

H2: The level with odd number points has a higher accuracy on average than with even number ones.

H3: The accuracy rate on average decreases with an increasing number of points placed on the forearm.

H4: The time spent to determine the imagined position will be increased when the number of points placed on the forearm increases.

Data Processing. Before the tests were examined, the measured and recorded data was first normalized based on the forearm length of the participants. 356 outliers (5.3% of the total points) were then removed from the data recorded. A measured position that is not within the two standard deviations from the categorized points is treated as an outlier.

Result. Figure 3 shows the point distribution of each participant for the level with 5 points. The ellipses were drawn by calculating two standard deviations from the center of the tapped locations. Figure 6 shows the projected data on the line in the level with 7 points. According to this figure, each participant has an individual divisions pattern. Closely examining the raw data in each level reveals that while the divided points is under 5 (including), a uniform design for the divided region for general users is possible. However, while the divided points exceed 6, a personalized setting must be calibrated. Reviewing the statistics indicates that normal participants can successfully divide their forearms into 6 points. However, only 2 participants can divide the forearm into 7 points, while 1 participant can achieve the 8 points. None of the participants can successfully divide the forearm into 9 points, even through the iterative practice. Therefore, our results confirm that the 6 points are the limit for normal users; in addition, for extreme users, 8 points are the upper limit. For the each hypothesis, we examined it by using the F-test.

For H1, a series of F-tests was performed, indicating that all end points and the other points significantly differ in accuracy except for the elbow points in the level with 7 points (Figure 4). Closely examining the data reveals that the first user's accuracy rate of the 7-th point is extremely low. By replacing the data with the average from the other participants' ensures that the end points yield the highest accuracies.

For H2, odd and even number of points ($F_{0.05,1,22} = 0.81, p = 0.36$) do not significantly differ in accuracy rate. This appears to be due to the fact that the middle points in the level with odd numbers do NOT provide a higher accuracy rate than originally expected. We assume that the middle point in the level with odd points can play as a critical reference point such as the two end joints performed. Hence, the data from the level with odd points are examined further. A series of F-tests reveals extremely low accuracy rates on middle points in the levels with odd points. The result confirms the hypothesis in which odd and even points do not significantly differ accuracy. This may be due to the fact that the center area on the forearm has fewer nerves than the two ended points.

For H3, both 6 and 7 points ($t_{15} = 3.15, p = 0.003$) and 7 and 8 points significantly differed from each other ($t_{14} = 2.41, p = 0.015$). Meanwhile, no other pair of points significantly differed from each other. We can thus infer that

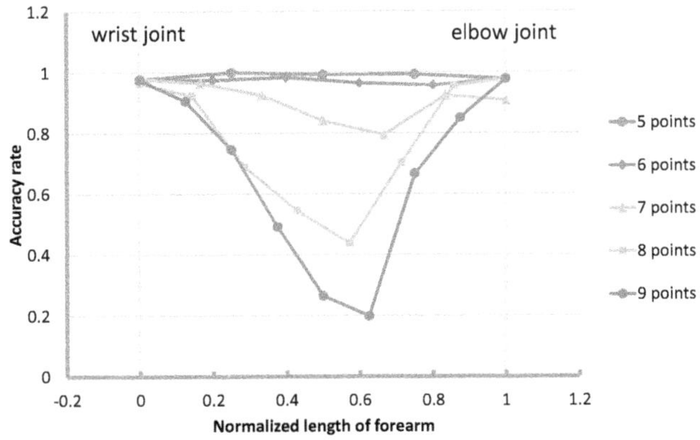

Figure 4: Broken-line graph that presents the accuracy rates for each point in each stage.

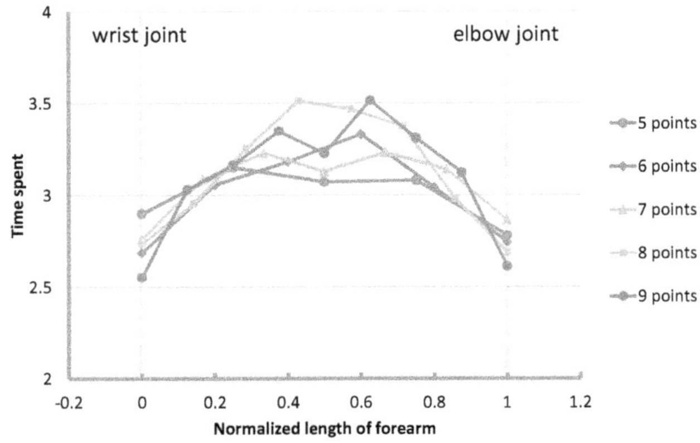

Figure 5: Broken-line graph that presents the time spent for each point in each stage.

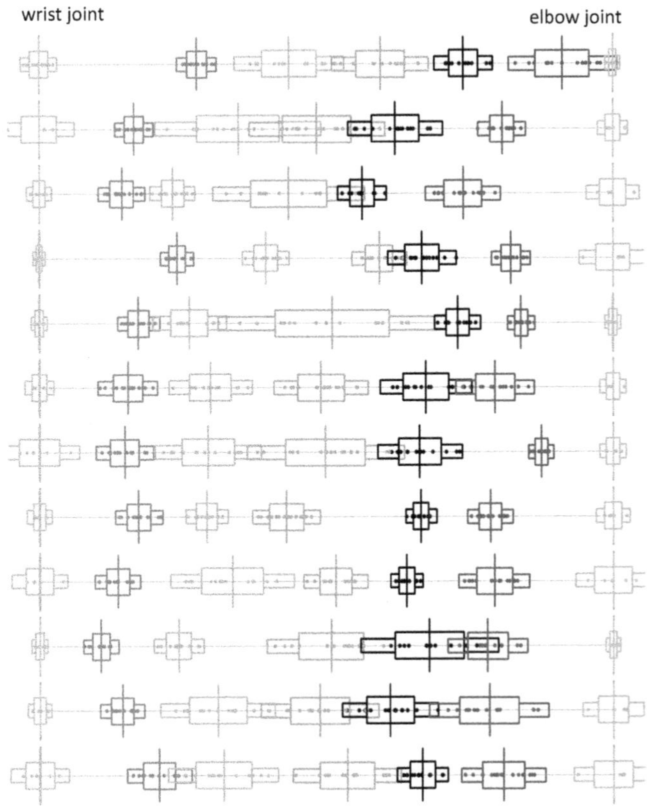

Figure 6: The projected point distribution of the 12 participants for the level with 7 points in the first user study. A thicker box represents the cover area of a standard deviation, while the flatter one represents the cover area of two standard deviations.

the accuracy rate of the level of 6 points is higher than that of 7 points; in addition, the accuracy rate of the level of 7 points is higher than that of 8 points. Although not all results can pass the examination, the above results still exhibit this trend. Naturally, participants normally become confused with an increasing number of divided points.

For H4, all levels did not differ in time spent. Combining the results from H3 suggests that while increasing the divided points, although the response time does not increase, the variations of the tapped positions increase. This phenomenon may suggest that participants always have confidence when tapping the desired positions in each level. They may assume that the tapped position is right, while it may be actually wrong while the number of divisions increases. Closely examining the data reveals that while the points approach the two ended points, the time spent decreases (Figure 5). These findings also suggested that the two endpoints provide strong spatial hints to strengthen the participants' confidence.

User Study 2: Importance of the Feedback from Skin

The first user study indicates that 7 points can still be manipulated for some participants with an excellent sense of body. We believe that the body sense is provided by two main aspects, i.e., the haptic feedback provided by the forearm (i.e., exteroception) and perception of reference provided by two end joints (i.e., proprioception).

Tasks and Procedures. This user study instructed participants to perform the tapping task with 5, 6, and 7 divided points. The procedures resemble those in the first user study. However, the participants were not allowed to touch their skin, but could tap on the desktop besides their left forearms. The left forearm is simply placed besides as a reference, to allow users to feel where the two end points are. Each point was randomly indicated for 15 times. This user study contains a total of 270 tapping tasks (75+90+105).

Hypothesis. The hypothesis is set as below:

H1: The accuracy rate with haptic feedback is higher than that without it.

Result. The F-test was performed, with those results indicating significant difference in each level without the aid of haptic feedback. The results further demonstrate that the participants' ability to manipulate their forearms as an input device declines in accuracy by 23.26%. This finding confirms that the feeling of being touched on the skin can provide spatial intelligence to allow participants to discriminate where the forearm is touched without paying any eye-attention.

Tapping Behaviors

During the user studies, in addition to recording the tapped data, our results also indicated how participants behaved. It

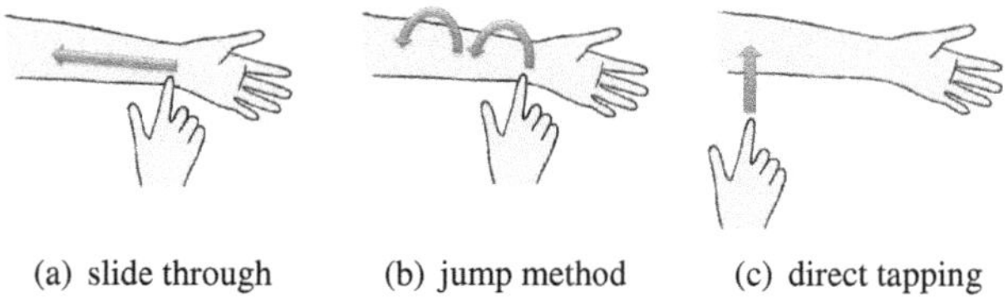

Figure 7: Three different tapping methods

shows that the tapped behaviors can be categorized into three types (Figure 7). In the first type, participants slid the index finger on the skin of the forearm until they felt as if they had reached the indicated point (Figure 7(a)). Participants belonging to the second type reached the indicated point by first tapping on the confident point, normally the wrist joint or elbow joint. Next, the participants simply used the jump gesture to measure the distance of the desired position (Figure 7(b)). The third type of participants just tapped the target point directly without any strategy (Figure 7(c)). The different types generated different accuracy rates. Figure 8 indicates that direct tapping method generates the lowest accuracy rate; in addition, the sliding through method generates the highest overall accuracy rates. This finding may confirm that the feeling of being touched on the skin provides spatial intelligence to the participants. While the index fingers of the participants take more time to contact with the skin, the accuracy rate becomes higher. While observing participants' behaviors reveals that each participant locally shifts the index finger to adjust the position around the desired location. Above results provide implications for interaction design.

Design Implications

Based on the experimental results and observations of these user studies, the following design implications are derived:

1. *Mentally perceived positions normally differ from the actual measurements.* Middle points of the arm are treated as the elbow joint, but not the actual middle point in measurements. The divided region is disproportionate. The two ended points typically have the smallest area, and the points in the middle of the forearm require a larger area than other points.

2. *Users have their own unique tapping patterns.* A personalized interface might be preferable over attempting to construct a general user interface for the forearm. However, a general design is possible if the divided points are below 5.

3. *The tapped position should not be confirmed immediately.* According to the observations, the participants often locally shift their fingers to adjust the final positions. Therefore, waiting for a certain time is preferred over responding to the gesture immediately.

4. *Individuals have their limitations.* Most users are limited to 6, but an extreme user can achieve 8 divided points.

5. *Hierarchical UI can benefit from the discrete points.* Because the normal participants can sense the discrete points at most 6, the adapted user interface may take the advantage of the characteristics of direct and discrete tapping.

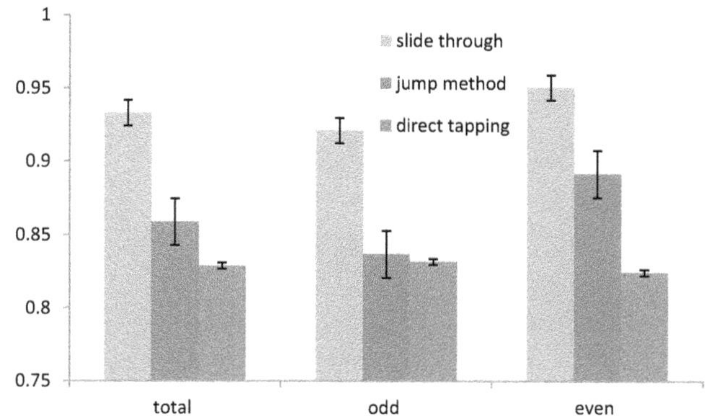

Figure 8: Accuracy rates of the three tapping methods

PUB DESIGN

According to our user study results, interfaces in the personal space (or so-called KUI) can be manipulated in an eyes-free manner and provide users with important natural haptic feedback. Moreover, a body is always portable and reachable to be utilized as an input device. A user's forearm is a desirable input space owing to that it is a rather easily reachable part of a body. Based on an examination of how human factors influence how a user interacts with her/his forearm, the concluded design implications may help designers to devise appropriate interactive manners and help researchers to enable the technologies that can fit human's mental models. This section demonstrates how technologies and interactions can be developed to utilize the derived implications.

UltraSonic Device

Since *PUB* is designed to demonstrate the advantages of the concluded design implications, the chosen detection solution should be sufficiently accurate, mobile and should not physically cover the forearm's skin. According to the results of the user studies, users can discriminate a maximum of 8 points. Hence, a sensor capable of successfully discriminating the different 7 ranges, excluding the point that the device situated at, can be a candidate detection solution.

Ultrasonic Sensor. Motivated by the prototype of Ahmad and Musilek [1], which mounts a camera on the wrist to detect the movement of the fingers, we can infer that an ultrasonic sensor is a viable candidate. The small ultrasonic sensor can be attached on a watch or a wrist band to make it portable. Moreover, the detection method still allows a user to directly tap on the skin. Closely examining the Devantech SRF10 ultrasonic rangefinder reveals that the sensed values can be provided from 6 *cm.* to 6 *m.*, which is longer than the forearm of a normal user. It can discriminate 7 points on the forearm of a user. The Arduino platform with an ATmega328 microprocessor is connected with the ultrasonic sensor to form our hardware prototype, *UltraSonic*.

Algorithm. Since every user has different tapping intervals, our system requires users to tap each location 10 times first for calibration. Then we calculate the optimal intervals that separate each location. Due to the limitations of the ultrasonic sensor, users also need to be fully trained. Here are some characteristics of the used *UltraSonic* device: When a user performs gestures, the sensed data sequence during the

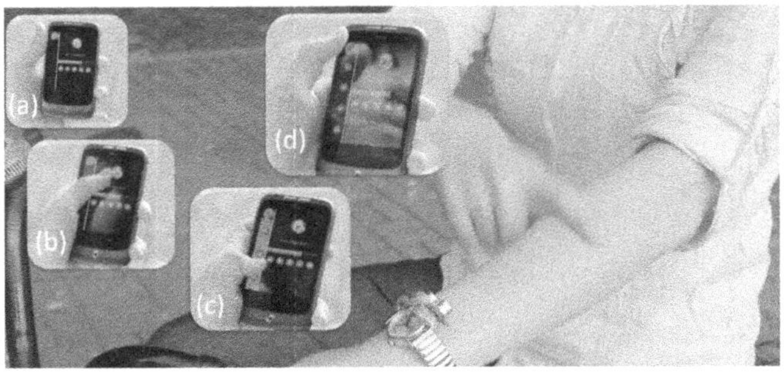

Figure 9: A user utilized *PUB* to bind the music controls on the forearm through her mobile device, allowing her to control the music player in an eyes-free manner through the *UltraSonic* device attached on her watch.

first second tend to be very unstable and very noisy. However, the sensed data will be stable and reliable after that, though some noise still exists. The reason is that the sensed range is quite long and everything inside the virtual emitting frontal cone may cause error in the data.

The algorithm is designed as follows:

1. If the sensed value exceeds the upper bound (typically 22 *cm.*, the average forearm length), discard it.
2. Start to record when 3 consecutive sample values are below the upper bound.
3. Discard the data sequence within the first second.
4. Collect sensed values between 1 and 1.5 *sec.*
5. Remove the outliers of the data.
6. Analyze the average and gradient of the sensed values for determining which gesture it is.

Through the consecutively sensed values, *PUB* can recognize a user's gestures, tapping or sliding. Since users may locally shift their fingers before confirmation, the system is designed to listen for 500 *ms.* while the fingers are tapped on the skin.

Performance. We tested the performance by attaching the device on a user's wrist, and asked him to use his index finger to tap the designated location except the wrist point. The accuracies are 84%, 66.6% and 65.7% for 5, 6 and 7 points, respectively, excluding the wrist point. If we attach the sensor facing to the inner side of the forearm, we found that the movement of the upper arm will easily disturb the system, especially when users are in the outdoor. Therefore, we suggest that attaching the sensor facing to the outside of the forearm to alleviate the problem.

Mobile Eyes-Free Interaction

While mobile, a user can perform multiple tasks simultaneously, such as riding a bicycle and listening to music. Therefore, a user's eye attention may focus on the primary task and use the peripheral senses to perform the secondary tasks. The exteroception and haptic feedback from a user's skin may be an excellent candidate for the peripheral senses. Moreover, in this paper, *PUB* is implemented on a smart phone, HTC Wildfire, to demonstrate how the concluded implications can help users in a mobile scenario.

Figure 9 shows that a user utilized *PUB* to bind the music controls on her forearm by dragging the desired icons into the left column. If there are more than five bound controls, then further calibration procedures are required to fit the user's tap pattern. While finishing binding, the user can trigger play/pause, stop and switch to a previous/next song by tapping on the forearm without taking out the music player from the pocket. The user can also perform a sliding gesture forward or backward on her forearm to increase or decrease the volume. In this manner, a multi-tasking and eyes-free interaction is achieved.

Remote Display Interaction

Since users can accurately discriminate discrete points upon forearms, this work develops a hierarchical GUI system by rearranging the layout of the icons as a discrete and organized structure to take the advantages of the explored human factors. Rather than raising a hand in the air to control the remote display, a user can tap on the forearm to click on the desired icon or slide to scroll the list (Figure 1). In doing so, a user may feel less fatigued. Meanwhile, over long-term use, the accuracy may increase due to the provided haptic feedback on the skin.

CONCLUSION

In this paper, we presented a novel interaction system, *PUB* (point upon body), to explore the human factors with respect to how users can interact with their forearms. Based on the user studies, we recommend the design implications and suggest that the enabled technologies should consider the mental models of users. The prototype system, *PUB*, demonstrates how to use the derived implications in order to enable feasible technologies and interactions. Although this paper explores only the design space on a forearm, the proposed methods can be generalized to explore other parts of the human body. Restated, this paper presents a highly effective method to understand human factors in a personal space. Importantly, the derived implications significantly contribute to efforts of designers and researchers to create more intuitive interactions and user friendly technologies.

FUTURE WORK

Although this work has derived the implications of the design guidelines and demonstrated appropriate scenarios, a user study may be necessary to evaluate the design guidelines and the claimed benefits. Furthermore, the social issue should also be considered. The ability of users to interact with their forearms does not necessarily imply that they must interact with them. We recommend that future researches examine the acceptable gestures on an arm. Moreover, we only investigate the tapping behaviors longways, and the lateral division across the arm can be accessed in the future.

The proposed interaction scenarios and design implications can also be generalized. For instance, applying *PUB* to document viewing software allows users to slide on their arms to go through pages when reading documents. By binding *PUB* to hand-held devices (e.g., smart phone), functions on screen of the device can be placed on a user's arm, which functions like the extended input pad of a small screen device.

ACKNOWLEDGEMENTS

This paper is partially supported by the National Science Council of Taiwan under NSC100-2622-E-002-016-CC2, the Excellent Research Projects of the National Taiwan University under NTU99R80303, and MediaTek Inc. We also thank Li-Wei Chan, Mike Y. Chen, and Rung-Huei Liang for their precious comments, and Paulo Silva for proofreading.

REFERENCES

1. AHMAD, F., AND MUSILEK, P. A keystroke and pointer control input interface for wearable computers. In *Proc. IEEE PerCom '06*, pp. 2–11.
2. ANTONIAC, P., AND PULLI, P. Marisil - mobile user interface framework for virtual enterprise. In *Proc. ICE '01*, pp. 171–180.
3. BALAKRISHNAN, R., AND HINCKLEY, K. The role of kinesthetic reference frames in two-handed input performance. In *Proc. ACM UIST '99*, pp. 171–178.
4. BAUDEL, T., AND BEAUDOUIN-LAFON, M. Charade: remote control of objects using free-hand gestures. *CACM 36*, 7 (1993), 28–35.
5. BOLT, R. A. Put-that-there: Voice and gesture at the graphics interface. In *Proc. ACM SIGGRAPH '80*, pp. 262–270.
6. GUSTAFSON, S., BIERWIRTH, D., AND BAUDISCH, P. Imaginary interfaces: spatial interaction with empty hands and without visual feedback. In *Proc. ACM UIST '10*, pp. 3–12.
7. HARRISON, C., TAN, D., AND MORRIS, D. Skinput: appropriating the body as an input surface. In *Proc. ACM CHI '10*, pp. 453–462.
8. HINCKLEY, K., PAUSCH, R., AND PROFFITT, D. Attention and visual feedback: the bimanual frame of reference. In *Proc. I3D '97*, pp. 121–126.
9. HUNG, Y.-P., YANG, Y.-S., CHEN, Y.-S., HSIEH, I.-B., AND FUH, C.-S. Free-hand pointer by use of an active stereo vision system. In *Proc. IEEE ICPR '98*, vol. 2, pp. 1244–1246.
10. ISHII, K., ZHAO, S., INAMI, M., IGARASHI, T., AND IMAI, M. Designing laser gesture interface for robot control. In *Proc. Interact '09*, pp. 479–492.
11. JOTA, R., NACENTA, M. A., JORGE, J. A., CARPENDALE, S., AND GREENBERG, S. A comparison of ray pointing techniques for very large displays. In *Proc. GI '10*, pp. 269–276.
12. KRUEGER, M. W., GIONFRIDDO, T., AND HINRICHSEN, K. VIDEOPLACE: an artificial reality. In *Proc. ACM CHI '85*, pp. 35–40.
13. LI, F. C. Y., DEARMAN, D., AND TRUONG, K. N. Virtual shelves: interactions with orientation aware devices. In *Proc. ACM UIST '09*, pp. 125–128.
14. LONGO, M. R., AND LOURENCO, S. F. On the nature of near space: Effects of tool use and the transition to far space. *Neuropsychologia 44*, 6 (2006), 977–981.
15. MINE, M. R., BROOKS, JR., F. P., AND SEQUIN, C. H. Moving objects in space: exploiting proprioception in virtual-environment interaction. In *Proc. ACM SIGGRAPH '97*, pp. 19–26.
16. MISTRY, P., MAES, P., AND CHANG, L. WUW - wear Ur world: a wearable gestural interface. In *Ext. Abs. ACM CHI '09*, pp. 4111–4116.
17. NICKEL, K., AND STIEFELHAGEN, R. Pointing gesture recognition based on 3D-tracking of face, hands and head orientation. In *Proc. ICMI '03*, pp. 140–146.
18. REKIMOTO, J. GestureWrist and gesturePad: Unobtrusive wearable interaction devices. In *Proc. ISWC '01*, pp. 21–27.
19. RIZZOLATTI, G., SCANDOLARA, C., MATELLI, M., AND GENTILUCCI, M. Afferent properties of periarcuate neurons in macaque monkeys. *Behav. Brain Res. 2*, 2 (1981), 147–163.
20. SAKATA, H., AND KUSUNOKI, M. Organization of space perception: neural representation of three-dimensional space in the posterior parietal cortex. *Curr. Opin. Neurobiol. 2*, 2 (1992), 170–174.
21. SAPONAS, T. S., TAN, D. S., MORRIS, D., BALAKRISHNAN, R., TURNER, J., AND LANDAY, J. A. Enabling always-available input with muscle-computer interfaces. In *Proc. ACM UIST '09*, pp. 167–176.
22. SELLEN, A., KURTENBACH, G., AND BUXTON, W. The role of visual and kinesthetic feedback in the prevention of mode errors. In *Proc. Interact '90*, pp. 667–673.
23. SHOEMAKER, G., TANG, A., AND BOOTH, K. S. Shadow reaching: a new perspective on interaction for large displays. In *Proc. ACM UIST '07*, pp. 53–56.
24. SHOEMAKER, G., TSUKITANI, T., KITAMURA, Y., AND BOOTH, K. S. Body-centric interaction techniques for very large wall displays. In *Proc. NordiCHI '10*, pp. 463–472.
25. TAMAKI, E., MIYAKI, T., AND REKIMOTO, J. Brainy hand: an ear-worn hand gesture interaction device. In *Ext. Abs. ACM CHI '09*, pp. 4255–4260.
26. TAN, D. S., PAUSCH, R., STEFANUCCI, J. K., AND PROFFITT, D. R. Kinesthetic cues aid spatial memory. In *Ext. Abs. ACM CHI '02*, pp. 806–807.
27. VOGEL, D., AND BALAKRISHNAN, R. Distant freehand pointing and clicking on very large, high resolution displays. In *Proc. ACM UIST '05*, pp. 33–42.

SpeckleSense: Fast, Precise, Low-cost and Compact Motion Sensing using Laser Speckle

Jan Zizka [1,2] Alex Olwal [1] Ramesh Raskar [1]

[1] MIT Media Lab
77 Mass. Ave., E14
Cambridge, MA, USA

[2] Comenius University DAI
Mlynska dolina
Bratislava, Slovakia

{zizka, olwal, raskar}@media.mit.edu, http://specklesense.media.mit.edu/

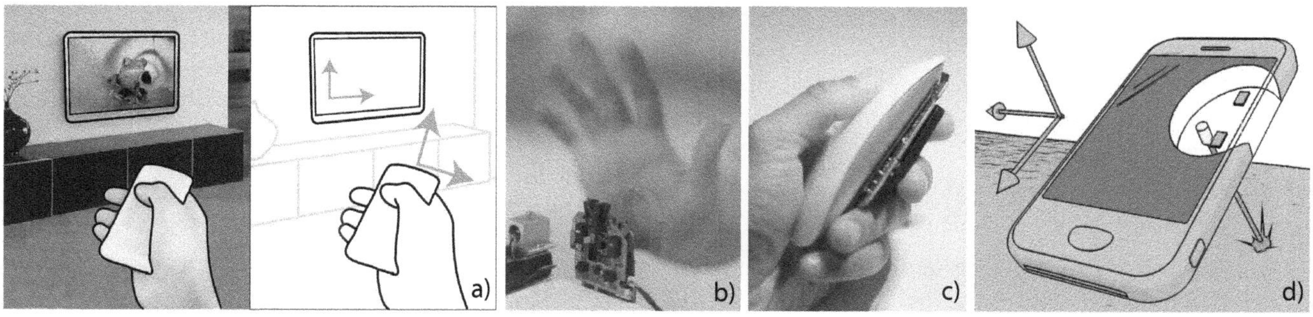

Figure 1: SpeckleSense uses laser speckle sensing to enable effective motion-based interaction that is applicable to many scenarios, such as a) motion-sensing remote controls, b) interaction with public displays, c) 3D input devices, and d) as the next-generation sensors for mobile devices.

ABSTRACT

Motion sensing is of fundamental importance for user interfaces and input devices. In applications, where optical sensing is preferred, traditional camera-based approaches can be prohibitive due to limited resolution, low frame rates and the required computational power for image processing.

We introduce a novel set of motion-sensing configurations based on laser speckle sensing that are particularly suitable for human-computer interaction. The underlying principles allow these configurations to be fast, precise, extremely compact and low cost.

We provide an overview and design guidelines for laser speckle sensing for user interaction and introduce four general speckle projector/sensor configurations. We describe a set of prototypes and applications that demonstrate the versatility of our laser speckle sensing techniques.

ACM Classification: H5.2 [Information interfaces and presentation]: User Interfaces. - Graphical user interfaces.

General terms: Design, Human Factors, Experimentation.

Keywords: Input devices, tracking, mouse, laser speckle

INTRODUCTION

Motion-based interaction has recently received widespread popularity thanks to low-cost camera-based technologies and an abundance of inertial sensors in consumer electronics. Today, all major video console platforms have the ability to sense human motion images using special-purpose cameras. Hundreds of millions of cell phone cameras have made image sensors extremely affordable, but their use for real-time motion tracking is limited by low pixel throughput (the product of resolution and frame rate). While special-purpose cameras can achieve higher frame rates, resolution is limited by image processing demands, which in turn affects the possible accuracy.

Many projects have explored creative usage of image sensors that avoid the implicit limitations when a camera is used to form an image of a scene in the classical sense. This has, for example, enabled compact imaging systems that can read extremely small patterns, such as Bokode [23].

Laser speckles are micro-patterns that are formed from the interference of scattered coherent light. Laser speckle tracking techniques have traditionally been used for applications like measurements and particle tracking in mechanical engineering and biology [12]. This paper explores the application of laser speckle to user interfaces and motion tracking, as their unique characteristics make them an interesting alternative or complement to classical camera- or sensor-based tracking techniques.

CONTRIBUTIONS

We exploit the high frequency interference patterns caused by lasers and sense direct or reflected light using a high framerate lensless 2D image sensor. Fast optical flow computation helps us track laser or sensor motion to enable new

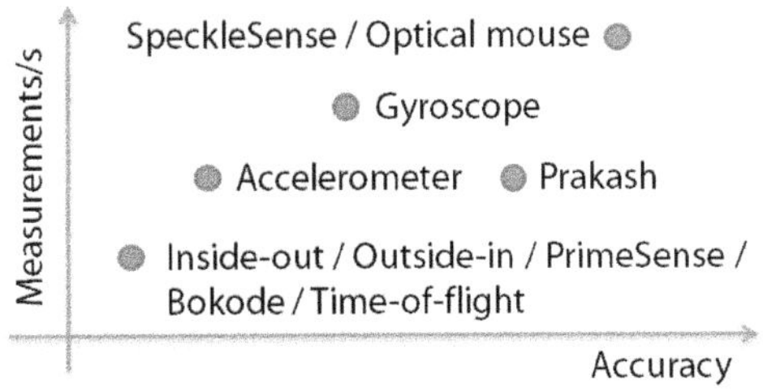

Figure 2: SpeckleSense's relative motion tracking combines high accuracy with fast update rates.

input devices and interaction techniques. Our contributions are:

- A novel laser speckle sensing technique that is particularly suitable for motion-based input. It is fast, precise, can be extremely compact, is low cost, and requires little computational power.
- An overview and design guidelines for using laser speckle sensing in human-computer interaction.
- Four general speckle projector/sensor tracking configurations for motion-based input.
- Two practical implementations of laser speckle tracking for human-computer interaction. The first type is based on a high-speed, low-resolution digital camera. The second type is based on readily available consumer electronics and optics, where we exploit the capabilities of optical sensors from computer mice.
- A set of prototypes and applications that demonstrate how laser speckle sensing can be used both standalone as well as in combination with other devices.

RELATED WORK

Surface interaction

Motion sensing is relevant to all classical pointing devices; mice, (multi-)touch displays, touchpads, pointing sticks, styli, joysticks, and others. The optical mouse is probably one of the most popular input devices. It uses a small camera that images and tracks the naturally occurring texture of the surface to establish its 2D motion on the surface.

Considerable effort has been invested in supporting additional degrees-of-freedom (DOF), beyond just two, for computer mice. MacKenzie et al. use two balls to add one DOF [22], whereas VideoMouse [18] uses a special mouse pad, camera and computer vision. The Rockin' Mouse [5] is augmented by inertial sensors and Baudish et al. create a mid-air mouse using a flexible "skin" [7]. Villar et al.'s five prototypes [38] and Apple's Magic mouse [2] replace the mouse wheel with a multitouch surface that enables sensing of 2D multi-finger gestures. Integral 3D mice [1, 4] are intended for effective spatial manipulation.

Table 1: SpeckleSense tracks motion velocity using a projector-based approach.

	Camera	Inertia	Projector / Structured light
Acceleration		Accelerometer	
Velocity	Optical mouse	Gyroscope	**SpeckleSense**
Position	Inside-out (Wii)		Bokode
	Outside-in		Prakash
	Time-of-Flight		PrimeSense

Mid-air interaction

As discussed in a survey by Welch and Foxlin [40], several options for optical and non-optical motion tracking are available. Sony PS Move[1] and Xwand [41] demonstrate the advantages in combining optical and inertial tracking. Similarly, Nintendo Wii[2] tracks fixed markers with a moving camera and inertial sensors. Commercially available mid-air mice [21] and [13] use inertial sensors only. The PrimeSense [29] sensor used in Microsoft Kinect[3] recovers depth images with structured IR light to enable markerless and deviceless user interaction.

Motion-based interaction

Several projects investigate the use of sensing to create spatially aware displays [11, 25, 26, 34, 36, 43, 32] for new forms of human-computer interaction with handheld displays. Motion-based input for small displays has also been explored as a promising direction to expand the possible interaction [8, 14, 15, 17, 39, 24, 35, 42] for portable devices.

The SpeckleSense principle is related to other projector-based tracking techniques, where the environment is spatially divided and coded using special lightning (See Figure 2 and Table 1) . The Office of the Future [31], Bokode [23] and Prakash [30] projects use incoherent structured light, while PrimeSense [29] uses special diffraction gratings to form a desired pattern.

Speckle phenomena and HCI

After its theoretical development in the 1970's and 1980's, speckle-based techniques have begun to find their way from controlled laboratory conditions to practical applications and user interaction. Popov et al. [28] describe the design and simulation of optical computer mice, where five photodiodes track the speckle pattern, and Schroeder et al. present a similar solution [37]. DePue et al. [10] estimate the device's distance to the surface using two detectors and two lasers with different wavelengths, and Bathiche et al. [6] describe a technique to suspend tracking when the device is lifted. Liao at al. investigate designs with lenses and limiting apertures [20] and these principles are also used to track a mechanical finger-controlled pad [19]. Reilly and Hanson [33] use CCD linear arrays and collection optics to capture speckle pattern that is reflected off the skin. The Philips Laser Doppler [27] is different from speckle sensing, as it uses interferometry techniques to measure the Doppler shift in the frequency of laser light, which is proportional to velocity.

[1] http://us.playstation.com/ps3/playstation-move/
[2] http://www.nintendo.com/wii
[3] http://www.xbox.com/kinect

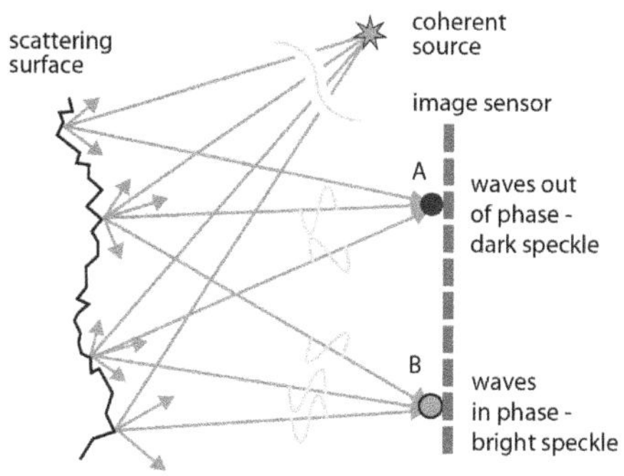

Figure 3: The laser speckle phenomena. Light from a coherent light source scatter on a surface's microstructure and the resulting reflected waves reach an image sensor in different phases, due to differences in their travel paths. The interference from each wave contributes to the intensity at each pixel.

LASER SPECKLE: EXPLOITING COHERENT LIGHT FOR FAST, PRECISE TRACKING

When a diffuse object is illuminated with coherent light, the resulting interference forms a speckle pattern, as illustrated in Figure 3. In the ideal case, each point of the surface scatters the incoming light waves in all directions. Each pixel in an image sensor placed in the field would thus receive contributions from multiple reflected waves. More importantly, the measured intensity in each pixel is a result of the interference from each wave, as they all have traveled different path lengths from the surface to the sensor. These waves have different, theoretically random, phases. Most surfaces (except e.g., glass) are sufficiently rough to produce statistically independent phases of waves. The resulting images contain grainy, high-contrast structures that are referred to as "speckle" (See Figures 4–7).

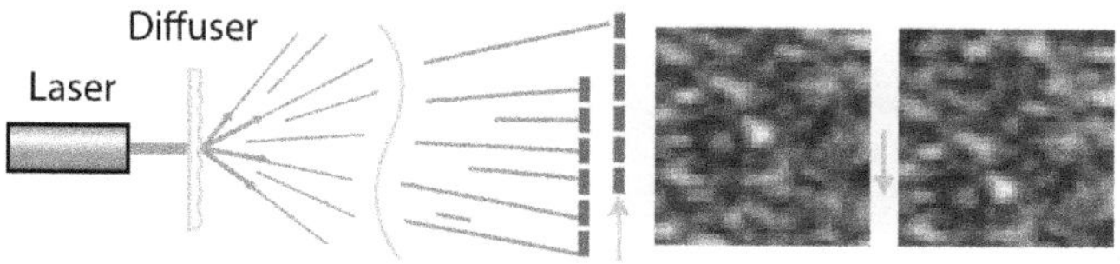

Figure 4: The speckle pattern motion can be tracked with image processing algorithms as the speckle sensor or projector move.

Speckle Projector: Generating speckle patterns with laser + diffuser

Speckle patterns can also be generated by integrating a laser diode with an optical diffuser, to create a *Speckle Projector*, as illustrated in Figure 4.

The light from such a speckle projector has similar characteristics to a point light source, if the diameter of the diffuser's illuminated area is significantly smaller than its distance to the image sensor (i.e., at least one order of magnitude smaller). This makes it possible to project a dense (but unknown) pattern into space, which can be sensed using a lensless image sensor.

The diffuser controls the projection angle, which also affects energy distribution and intensity.

Speckle tracking

While we have no control of the projected speckle pattern, we can use image processing and computer vision techniques to analyze its properties.

Relative motion tracking

A small translation v of the image sensor will translate the captured image by $-v$. Similarly, a translation v of the speckle projector in a plane parallel to the sensor would shift the image by v, as shown in Figure 6. On the other

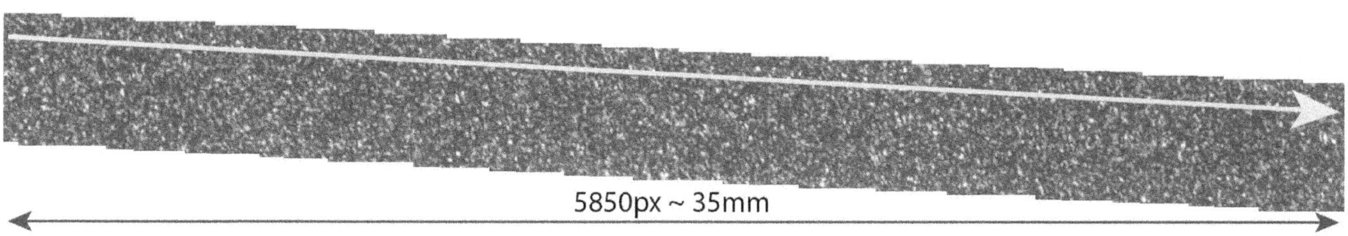

Figure 5: Frame-to-frame tracking of 22 speckle patterns, displayed in a stitched panorama image.

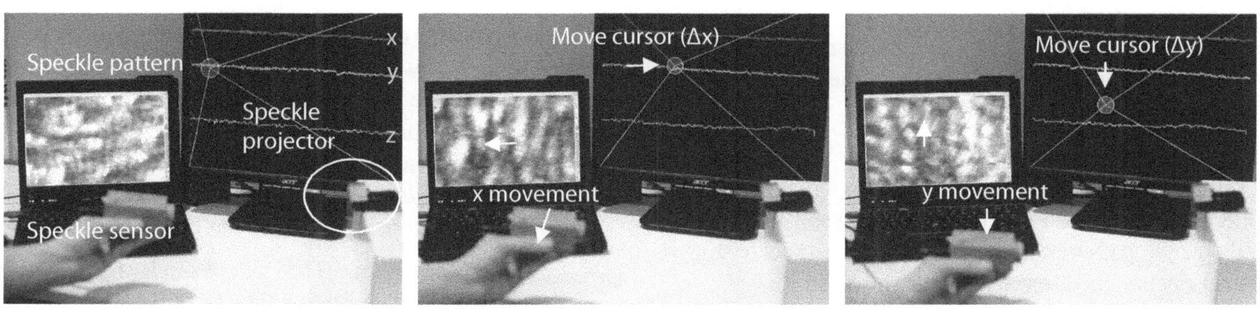

Figure 6: The speckle sensor is sensitive to small translations relative to the projected speckle pattern. A high frame-rate camera that is matched with the laser speckle characteristics can be used to track fine frame-to-frame movement. Here, the movement controls a cursor in our software.

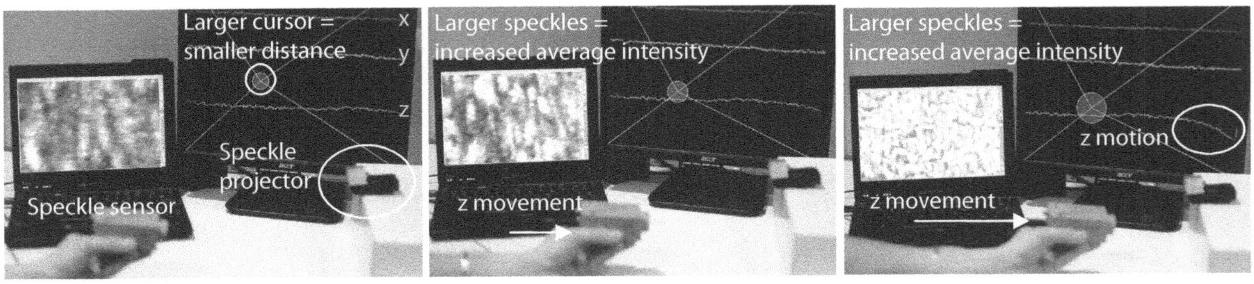

Figure 7: As the speckle sensor is moved closer to the speckle projector, speckles become larger in the image. While the speckle pattern is unknown, the statistically consistent distribution allows us to estimate distance with average intensity. Here, the distance controls the circle's radius in our software.

hand, a small change in the speckle projector's orientation will move the speckle image by θd, where θ is the angle, and d is the distance to the image sensor.

Distance approximation through speckle structure

As with any beam, the projected laser speckle will increase with size as the speckle projector gets closer to the sensor. The specific speckle pattern is, however, neither controlled nor known, as both the distribution of speckles and their sizes vary. The average sizes and distribution is, however, consistent, which allows us to approximate distance by analyzing the average image intensity. The size of speckle varies in space according to the following equation [9]:

$$s \sim \lambda \times d / a \qquad (1)$$

where d is distance to the illuminated surface of diameter a and λ is the laser's wavelength. We can thus estimate the absolute distance between the speckle projector and sensor if λ, a and pixel size is known. See Figure 7.

Design criteria for the speckle sensor apparatus

To track speckles we must ensure that they are larger than the sensor's pixel size, to avoid the averaging that would happen if several speckles (bright and dark) would be captured in the same pixel, as the needed contrast would be lost. On the other hand, the speckles must be smaller than the sensor, over the whole tracking range.

The image motion computations depend on how fast the camera can acquire subsequent images for frame-to-frame comparisons. The maximum speed (mm/s) at which a system can correctly track is given by the following equation:

$$Speed_{max} = PixelSize \times Overlap_{max} \times FPS_{max} \qquad (2)$$

where $PixelSize$ is in mm, $Overlap_{max}$ is maximal frame-to-frame translation in pixels and FPS_{max} is the camera's highest frame rate.

Creating speckles on external surfaces

A collimated laser beam can be used to create a virtual speckle projector on an external surface, such that the reflected speckle pattern can be tracked with a speckle sensor that is rigidly attached to the laser, as shown in Figure 8.

As the laser beam hits the surface, reflected waves reach the sensor's pixels, and their interferences generate the measured per-pixel intensities. Let us assume that this device is translated by p, the sensor's pixel size. Then, the projected laser beams P_1 (before movement) and P_2 (after movement), will have an overlapping area Q. In-between frames Q will generate a static speckle pattern, which can be tracked with motion estimation algorithms. The speckle pattern variation due to the difference between P_1 and P_2 will have a negligible influence on the tracking as long as Q is significantly larger than p. Thus, for detection of one-pixel speckle motion, the sensor frame rate must be sufficiently high.

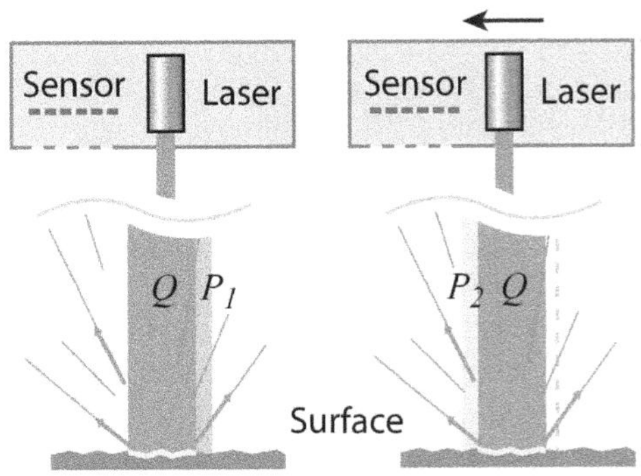

Figure 8: A device with an embedded speckle sensor and laser can detect its relative motion along a surface if the sensed inter-frame motion (P_1-P_2) is significantly smaller than the laser beam's width. The speckles generated by the area Q will thus dominate the speckle pattern with frame-to-frame trackable patches.

SPECKLE TRACKING CONFIGURATIONS

Our speckle tracking relies on active illumination (speckle projector) combined with an optical sensor (speckle sensor), but differs from traditional camera-based motion tracking systems, due to the flexible configurations possible with simple hardware. Before we describe a number of prototypes where we use multiple speckle projectors and sensors as building blocks for novel input devices, we will explore four general tracking configurations using a single speckle projector/sensor pair. Speckle tracking provides the following characteristics in all of our configurations:

- *High sampling rate.* The optical sensor has a very high sampling rate (approximately 10,000 Hz) compared to traditional digital cameras (30–100 Hz).
- *High sensitivity.* The dense speckle pattern allows tracking down to 50 μm.

- *Extremely small.* The active components of the speckle projector and sensor are only a few millimeters in diameter, making them suitable for integration in embedded systems, like mobile devices. Displays that are too small to fit touch-screens or other input controls may especially benefit from the ability of using the space in front and around them for user interaction [8, 15].
- *Flexible choices for projection angles — ultra-wide or narrow.* In our experiments we use optical diffusers that project the speckles ultra-wide and uniformly over 80–120 degrees. Narrower diffusers can be chosen if it is desirable to limit the field-of-view or to increase the range (as the energy will be less diffused).
- *Flexible choices for sensor field-of-view — ultra-wide or narrow.* Light falls directly on the surface of the lensless image sensor and from all directions (180°). Narrower field-of-view can be achieved with small apertures or masks.
- *Compatible with legacy applications.* Laser speckle can be sensed using modified optical mouse sensors, for direct compatibility with mouse-controlled applications (avoiding drivers or intermediate software).

Handheld Speckle Projector (A)

Digital Pointing Device, Purely Optical Communication

A fixed optical sensor can be used for precise motion tracking of a handheld speckle projector to create a digital pointer for relative 2D input. This configuration does not require any other communication between the handheld input device and the system, besides the motion data that is optically transmitted with the projected speckle pattern. Several characteristics distinguishes it from the on-board sensors (e.g., accelerometers or gyroscopes) that are typically used in current digital pointing devices.

- *Relative tracking solely through optical tracking.* Lack of radio and active electronics greatly simplifies hardware design, making the design low-cost and power efficient.
- *Fast transmission.* Motion data is transmitted at the speed of light, which eliminates the limitations and lag associated with radio-based communication.
- *Directional.* The optical communication allows a single speckle projector to be used for control of multiple devices without the need for radio-based pairing or connections. The speckle projector could thus be used for casual control of multiple simple devices around one's home, e.g., communicating directly with a light bulb with an embedded speckle sensor.

We could also augment the optical communication with additional data, to enable actuation and mode switching, while preserving the minimalistic design. For this purpose, one could simply use the light modulation techniques that are found in standard IR remote controls and encode commands by pulsing the laser at high frequencies. We, for example, envision a low-cost approach for adding continuous motion to traditional remote controls. A user could thus turn on a TV using standard remote control buttons, and use relative motion with its embedded speckle projector to increase/decrease volume.

Similarly, unique device IDs could be optically encoded to enable device-specific functionality, e.g., when switching between input devices. A limitation of the minimalistic design is that *simultaneous* multi-device input is a bit more complex. One approach for a small set of speckle projectors at different wavelengths could be to separate the input using matching infrared filters for a corresponding set of speckle sensors. With different infrared filters, this approach scales well under the assumption that speckle projectors and sensors are available at low cost and with negligible additional computational requirements.

Handheld Speckle Sensor (B)

Speckle Sensor in Handheld Device → Long-range, Mid-air Tracking

An input device with a speckle sensor can be used to track its relative movement in a projected speckle pattern. In this configuration, we fix a speckle projector in the environment, directed towards the user, who interacts by moving an input device with an embedded speckle sensor. A portable device (e.g., a mobile phone) can use the motion data independently, whereas an input device that controls a remote system would rely on radio, cable or optical communication to report the sensor data. While this introduces more complexity, it adds the inherent support for unique identification of multiple devices and the use of additional physical controls (e.g., buttons, scroll wheels, and touch pads).

- *Rotation-invariant translation.* The motion estimation is only sensitive to global translations since the sensor tracks the speckle pattern's vector field. Rotation of the sensor will results in a skewed image with negligible motion, as parts of the pattern will either move in opposite directions, or not move at all. This enables precise translational movements while avoiding influences from unintentional rotational motion.

Self-tracked Device (C)

Embedded Laser + Speckle Sensor → Device Tracked On & Above Surface

The speckle phenomena can also be exploited in a standalone configuration where both sensor and light source are embedded in the input device, similar to the configuration of a traditional optical mouse. In our configuration, however, the speckle sensor tracks the resulting speckle pattern produced by an embedded laser's coherent light when it reflects off the surface. Such a mouse works both on and above the surface, depending on the effect of the laser and the aperture of the optical sensor.

- *Standalone configuration.* Only needs surface for operation and works both on and above the surface.

Speckle Tracking of Hands (D)

Laser + Sensor in Environment → Tracking Hand Motion

For gestural interaction, we can exploit the body as a speckle generating surface when illuminated with a laser. In this configuration, the laser and speckle sensor are integrated in the device to support hand interaction in front of it. It allows unencumbered interaction without special-purpose input devices and is suitable for integration in small form factors or in public displays where it may not be desirable or feasible to use physical controls.

HYBRID TRACKING CONFIGURATIONS

The four general configurations consisting of a single speckle projector/sensor, described above, could be extended for additional functionality using multiple lasers/diffusers and optical sensors. Here, we describe a few interesting examples that we have started to explore.

Tracking Both on Surface and for Mid-air Gestures (E)

On-surface + Longe-range, Mid-air Input

The handheld speckle sensor in the long-range configuration (B) can be reused to also support traditional on-surface input, by mounting the sensor at a 45° angle and adding a downward-pointing low-effect laser (See Figure 9). When moved on the surface, the embedded laser will hit the surface and create a speckle pattern that will be seen by the speckle sensor. When the device is lifted from the surface, the low effect of the embedded laser will not create a sufficiently bright pattern, and instead, a speckle projector in the environment (e.g., integrated with a large display) will provide lateral motion tracking.

It may be desirable to avoid simultaneous sensing of speckle from the embedded laser and the source in the environment. This could be addressed with a proximity sensor at the bottom of the input device to control the projections, or by arranging the laser and speckle sensor such that lift-off would limit the visibility of the embedded laser light [6].

Two Sensors for Relative Tracking in 3D Space (F)

Standalone Relative 3D Tracking

By adding a second optical sensor to the Speckle-sensing mouse configuration at an angle (e.g., 45°), we can also recover relative motion above the surface.

When the device moves perpendicular to the surface, the sensor aligned with the laser is only observing speckle scaling, whereas the second off-axis sensor senses vertical motion, which corresponding to change in depth. See Figure 10a. The use of two sensors also works in other configuration, e.g., hand tracking, as shown in Figure 10b.

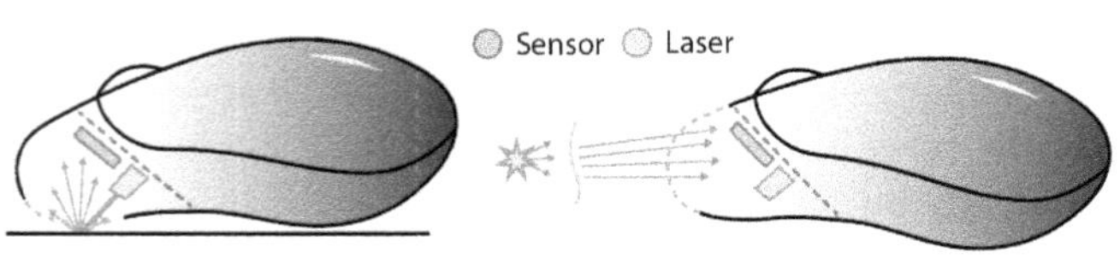

Figure 9: *Hybrid tracking configuration E* uses a speckle sensor at 45° to allow tracking both on the surface and in mid-air. An embedded laser creates speckle that can be sensed when the mouse is on the surface, while a speckle projector installed in the environment allows tracking in mid-air.

a) b)

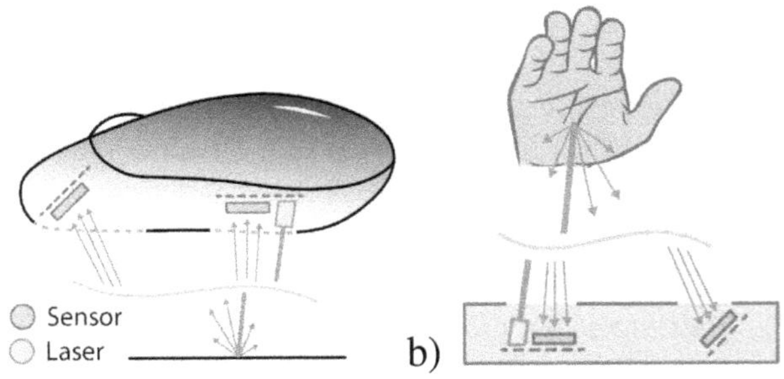

Figure 10: *Hybrid tracking configuration F* uses two speckle sensors to estimate relative motion orthogonal to a surface. a) Distance estimation with two embedded sensors in a mouse. b) The user's hand is used as a speckle generating surface when illuminated with colliminated light, allowing its 3D motion to be tracked with two fixed speckle sensors.

IMPLEMENTATION

Our initial experiments, shown in Figures 6 and 7 were conducted using a PixeLINK PLA741 firewire camera (http://www.pixelink.com), set to an image resolution of 160×120 pixels at 300 fps. The configuration makes it possible to demonstrate and experiment with speckle tracking, even if it the amount of motion velocity that can be tracked is limited by hardware.

The limited frame rate (30–100 fps) of typical digital cameras prohibits speckle motion tracking due to small sensor sizes. While it is impractical to dramatically increase the sensor size, we can use a fast camera (compared to motion velocity) to estimate the relative 2D motion of either the sensor or speckle projector.

Optical sensors in modern mice have small, but fast sensors with dedicated optical flow calculations in hardware. The gaming grade sensor Avago ADNS-9500 [3] captures images at 10,000 fps, and computes and reports the frame-to-frame motion vector at 1,000 Hz. In several of our prototypes, we repurpose the components from wireless (Logitech M505) or wired (Logitech G500) optical mice, and use the optical sensors with lenses removed as speckle sensors..

a) b)

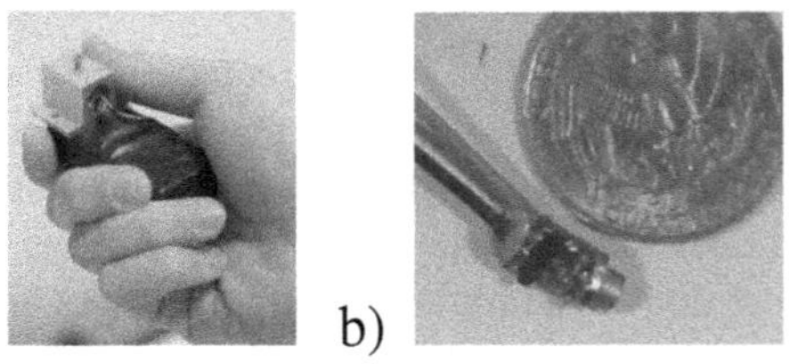

Figure 11. a) Our handheld Speckle Projector consists of a 50 mW laser (780 nm), diffuser (80°) and battery. With our speckle sensors it has a 3 m range. b) The laser diode is only a few millimeters wide and could be integrated into various hardware configurations.

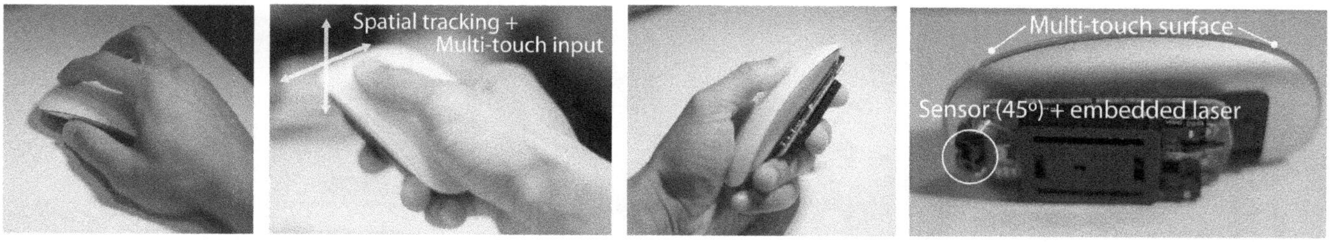

Figure 12: The TouchController works both as a regular mouse and in mid-air, tracked through a speckle projector in the environment. Its multi-touch surface enables a combination of spatial gestures and multi-touch interaction.

To optimize our results according to Equation 1 and 2, we use two types of lasers in our prototypes. For short-range interactions we use a 5 mW, 650 nm laser without diffuser. For long-range interactions (3 m tracking range), we use a 50 mW, 780 nm laser combined with a diffuser from Luminit (http://www.luminitco.com/) that provides a uniform 80° distribution (See Figure 11).

PROTOTYPES AND APPLICATIONS

Using our toolbox of tracking configurations we developed a set of prototypes and applications to explore the possibilities of laser speckle sensing, combining it with different physical controls and form factors.

TouchController: Remote Translation + Multi-touch

Numerous input devices exist where accelerometers and/or gyroscopes map device orientation to mouse translation on large displays, for example, during presentations.

Our TouchController, shown in Figure 12, instead allows the use of small, rotation-invariant translations. It uses a sensor from an optical mouse with the lens removed, and pointed at 45°. This allows both ordinary surface tracking of the speckle pattern created by the embedded laser, and tracking when lifted up and pointed in the direction of a speckle projector (See Hybrid Configuration E, above).

We augmented the device with a multi-touch surface (from an Apple Magic Mouse), such that mid-air motion could be combined with multi-touch gestures on its surface.

To explore interactions with the prototype, we implemented a 3D viewer using Java and the Processing environment (http://www.processing.org) and used Python on Mac OS X and its native multi-touch libraries to track finger position, orientation and contact size on the multi-touch surface. The speckle tracking was implemented with C# on Windows XP using the Raw Input libraries. Both tracking applications stream their data to the 3D viewer over UDP and control rotation, scale and translation of a 3D model:

- *Single-finger drag:* Rotates the model.
- *Pinch-zoom:* Scales the model.
- *Moving the device in air while touching surface:* Designed to simulate "grabbing" the model and translating it in the screen plane.

Mobile Viewport: Spatially Tracked Multi-touch Display

Inspired by previous work [11, 16, 25, 26, 34, 36, 43] on spatially aware handheld displays, we combined our 3D tracking (Configuration F, above) with a mobile phone. See Figure 13.

Relative tracking in the space above a surface is performed using two optical sensors, a small laser (5 mW) and a mirror for compactness, which were integrated with the bottom part of an Android OS phone (Motorola Droid X).

We implemented two applications. In a medical imaging viewer, we allow exploration of the slices in a CT stack by moving the device in 3D space. In an image viewer application, distance from the surface instead controls zoom level. The software was implemented in Java for the Android platform. Currently, it receives tracking events over UDP from a PC that interfaces with the wireless mouse sensors and calculates relative 3D motion. In an integrated solution, we expect the speckle tracking components to be embedded directly on the device, similarly to currently popular onboard sensors (accelerometers, gyroscopes, camera, etc.).

The graphics can be manipulated both with multi-touch gestures and spatial motion:

- *Move the device orthogonally to the surface:* Pan in current slice or image.

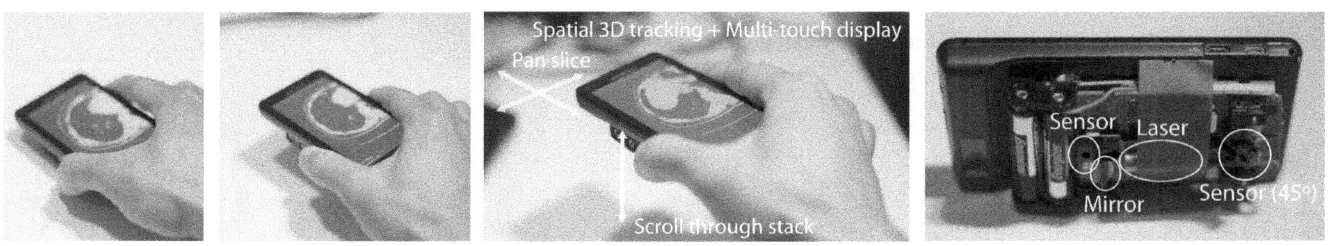

Figure 13: The Mobile Viewport adds relative 3D tracking to a mobile phone. Interaction is supported both by moving the device in 3D space and through multi-touch interaction on the display. A user can pan around in a medical image viewer and scroll through a CT stack by moving the device in 3D, or pan around in the view of a web page and control zoom level with distance

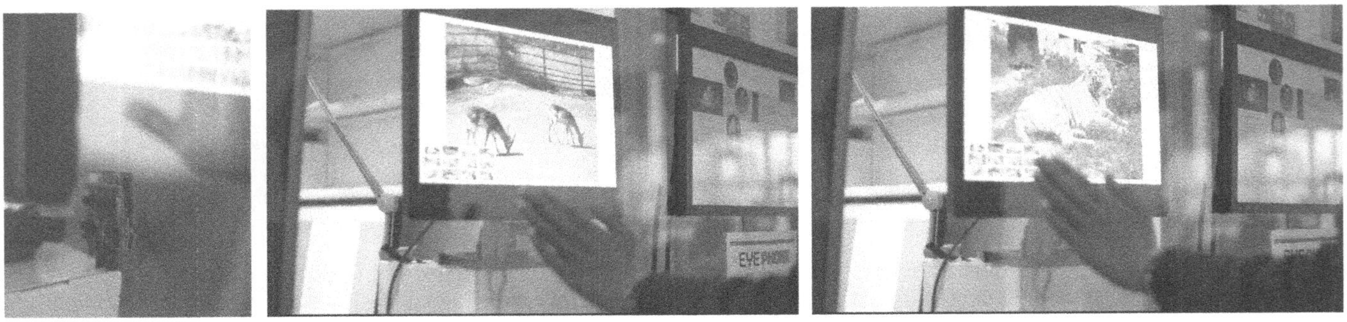

Figure 14. Low-cost motion tracking for public displays using an embedded Speckle projector and sensor (configuration D). The user's 2D hand movement selects the fullscreen image from a matrix of thumbnails in the lower left corner.

- *Move the device closer/further from surface:* Go up/down in medical image stack, or zoom in image viewer.
- *Pinch-zoom:* Zoom in the medical slice, and alternative method to zoom in image viewer.
- *Two-finger drag:* Alternative way to pan current slice.
- *Single-finger drag:* Add annotations (draw).

Motion input for public displays

To enable natural interaction in public displays without requiring physical input devices or touch-sensitive surfaces, we integrated a speckle sensor (optical mouse sensor) and laser (Configuration D) behind a glass window.

When hit by the laser, the user's hand creates speckles that are reflected to the speckle sensor. This allows non-contact interaction with the display, which may be desirable, both for sanitary reasons and to protect the input technology from users and environment.

We developed an image browser application in C# that interfaces with the speckle sensor, allowing it to be controlled with the hand, as shown in Figure 14. The user's 2D hand movement controls the selection in a matrix of thumbnails in the lower left corner. The currently selected photo is shown in full-screen, and to keep the current selection, the user pulls back the hand. Currently, we do not provide actuation in this configuration, but it would be possible to combine the sensing with swiping gestures, for example.

PERFORMANCE AND LIMITATIONS

Accuracy. The mouse sensor and our algorithm integrate huge amount of small shifts each second (10 kHz). This results in an accumulative error which increases over time. We used a linear actuator controlled by a stepper motor as a ground truth reference in an experiment to recover the accumulative error. The trajectory was 35 cm, movement took 1 s and we ran 10 experiments. The average deviation was 0.0217% (0.076 mm).

Effective range. The effective range for the mid-air configurations (A, B) was ~3 m (diffused 50 mw laser). In reflective mode, effective range depends on the reflectivity of the surface. With our 5 mw laser, we are able to precisely track 20 cm above a reference sheet of white paper. When the reflectivity of the surface is k times lower than our reference, the effective range is $sqrt(k)$ times smaller, as the incoming energy decreases with the square of the distance. As a comparison, we tracked ~6 cm above black plastic.

Ambient light. The combination of a lensless image sensor and coherent light ensures robustness to ambient light. Since incoherent light (e.g., light bulbs and LEDs) will not be focused in a lensless configuration, it will be blurred, as each light source produces an equal contribution to each image sensor element, and the sum of all such sources produces an average intensity signal. The laser speckle is added to this average intensity and creates a lower contrast image, but even with a high average intensity component in our experiments, we would typically have sufficient information to compute frame-to-frame motion.

PRELIMINARY USER FEEDBACK

For initial informal qualitative feedback on our prototypes, we invited five colleagues (25–35 years, all male) from our department to test our hardware prototypes and applications. All participants had used motion controllers and regularly used mobile phones with multi-touch displays.

For each interface we demonstrated how to use the input device to control an application and then allowed them to get familiar with it for a few minutes.

For each of the prototypes, we asked them to perform a set

Figure 15: A participant in our informal feedback sessions zooms into a web page with the Mobile Viewport interface by varying the device's distance to the surface.

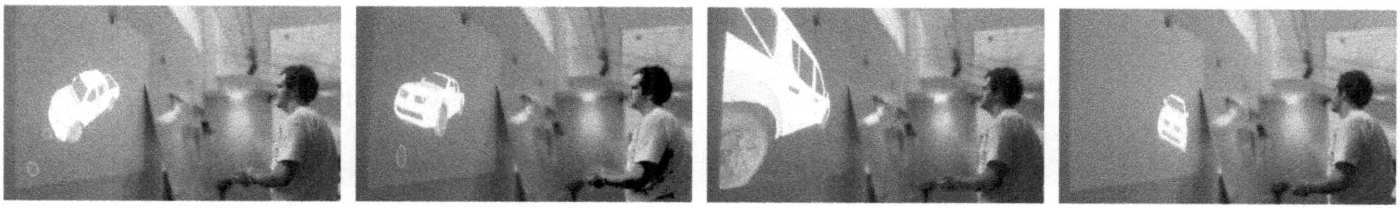

Figure 16: A participant exploring the TouchController for translation, rotation and scale of a model in our 3D viewer.

of tasks based on navigating, positioning, orienting or selecting objects, depending on the application. We asked the participants to think aloud and encouraged them to provide both positive and negative comments.

Participants liked the concept but found the public display prototype the hardest to use. The lack of actuation made it difficult to get in/out of tracking mode or reposition the hand. It also required a bit of practice for browsing the images, as the interaction area is quite small. All participants were able to control the imagery in the end, but had difficulties moving out of the tracking range without activating another image. One participant said that the continuous "Midas touch"-like tracking would not be a problem if the hand could be held still in a comfortable location. He also suggested the use of multiple sensors to expand the tracking area. Another participant initially tried swiping gestures, which we had not adapted the user interface for. For the next steps with this prototype, we plan to use multiple speckle sensors to both expand the tracking area and provide depth sensing, which could allow better visual feedback for entering/exiting the tracking area, and support actuation through proximity. A fast speckle-sensing image sensor where we have access to the image buffer (as in the experiments shown in Figures 6 and 7) would also allow us to recover absolute depth in a calibrated installation.

Participants appreciated the Mobile Viewport (See Figure 15), where they panned around and zoomed in a 1920×1200 screenshot of a news website on the 480×854 pixel mobile display. All participants were able to pan and zoom into different areas when asked. Several participants especially liked the single-handed zoom when moving the mobile phone closer or further from the surface. Based on the feedback we plan to also add smoothing to the tracking as it became clear how critical this was in tracking mode, as small pixel shifts disturbed the reading experience. We plan to create a more compact version of the sensors, as the current version affected the possibilities for grip.

The TouchController for controlling a 3D model on a projected wall was the most appreciated prototype (shown in Figure 16). One participant had initial difficulties in moving the model as he was swiping very fast and with a rotational motion, which resulting in the handheld device pointing away from the speckle projector. After additional instruction, he was able to successfully control the model. The combination of multi-touch input and spatial manipulation worked well for the participants, and two of them suggested that we also added depth control.

CONCLUSIONS AND FUTURE WORK

In this paper we introduced laser speckle sensing as a powerful and effective technique for motion sensing in human-computer interaction. It overcomes many of the limitations of traditional camera based systems and allows fast and precise tracking with a compact, low-cost technology that can perform the computations in embedded hardware.

We have also presented a set of prototypes and applications that demonstrate the potential of laser speckle sensing for different human-computer interaction scenarios. In future work, we plan to refine our prototypes and evaluate them in comparison with established technology and devices based on accelerometers, gyroscopes and other approaches to motion sensing. We also plan to further develop our speckle analysis methods, by switching to developer hardware, where we can access raw image data from fast (10,000 fps) image sensors.

A formal user study that evaluates the performance of our input devices and techniques will also provide additional insight into the benefit of our sensing technology's high precision to user interaction in a variety of applications.

ACKNOWLEDGMENTS

Jan Zizka was supported by Comenius University and ME-Inspection, Alex Olwal was supported by a Swedish Research Council Fellowship and a Blanceflor Foundation Scholarship, and Ramesh Raskar was supported by an Alfred P. Sloan Research Fellowship. We thank Samsung Electronics for support, the members of the MIT Media Lab Camera Culture group, the participants in our preliminary evaluation, and our reviewers for their insightful feedback.

REFERENCES

1. 3Dconnexion. Space 3d mice. http://www.3dconnexion.com/. July 2011.
2. Apple Magic Mouse. http://www.apple.com/magicmouse/. July 2011.
3. Avago Technologies. Adns-9500 sensor. http://www.avagotech.com/docs/AV02-1726EN. July 2011.
4. Axsotic. 3d-spheric-mouse. http://www.axsotic.com/. July 2011.
5. Balakrishnan, R., Baudel, T., Kurtenbach, G., and Fitzmaurice, G.. The Rockin' Mouse: Integral 3D Manipulation on a Plane. *Proc. CHI '97* (1997), 311–318.
6. Bathiche, S. N., and Starkweather, G. K., Data input device for tracking and detecting lift-off from a tracking surface by a reflected laser speckle pattern, U.S. Patent 7,161,582., 2007
7. Baudisch, P., Sinclair, M., and Wilson, A., Soap: a pointing device that works in mid-air. *Proc. UIST '06* (2006), 43–46.

8. Butler, A., Izadi, S., and Hodges, S. SideSight: multi-"touch" interaction around small devices. *Proc. UIST '08* (2008), 201-204.
9. Dainty, J. C. Laser Speckle and Related Phenomena. Springer-Verlag, Berlin (1984).
10. DePue, M. T., Schroeder, D. W., and Xie, T., Optical device that measures distance between the device and a surface, U.S. Patent 7,427,981, 2008.
11. Fitzmaurice, G. W. Situated information spaces and spatially aware palmtop computers. *Commun. ACM 36, 7* (Jul. 1993), 39–49.
12. Goodman, J. W.. Speckle phenomena in Optics: Theory and Applications. Roberts and Company, Englewood, 2007.
13. Gyration. Air mouse. http://www.gyration.com/. July 2011.
14. Hachet, M., Pouderoux, J., and Guitton, P. A camera-based interface for interaction with mobile handheld computers. *Proc. I3D '05* (2005), 65–72.
15. Harrison, C. and Hudson, S. E., Abracadabra: wireless, high-precision, and unpowered finger input for very small mobile devices, *Proc. UIST '09* (2009), 121–124.
16. Harrison, C. and Hudson, S. E., Minput: enabling interaction on small mobile devices with high-precision, low-cost, multipoint optical tracking, *Proc. CHI '10* (2010), 1661–1664.
17. Hinckley, K., Pierce, J., Sinclair, M., and Horvitz, E. Sensing techniques for mobile interaction. *Proc. UIST '00* (2000), 91–100.
18. Hinckley, K., Sinclair, M., Hanson, E., Szeliski, R., and Conway, M. The Videomouse: A Camera-based Multi-degree-of-freedom Input Device. *Proc. UIST '99* (1999), 103–112.
19. Liao, C.-M., Huang, P. S., Chiu, C.-C., Hwang, Y.-Y., Ma, S.-I. Real-time finger-controlled navigation system using laser speckle patterns, Optical Engineering, Volume 49, Issue 5 (2010).
20. Liao, C.-M., Huang, P. S., Hwang, Y.-Y., Chen, M., Chiu, C.-C. Robust technique of analyzing and locating laser speckle patterns for optical computer mice, Optics and Lasers in Engineering, 47, 7-8 (2009), 875–883.
21. Logitech. Mx air mouse. http://www.logitech.com/en-us/mice-pointers/mice/devices/3443/. July 2011.
22. MacKenzie, S., Soukoreff, R., and Pal, C. A Two-ball Mouse Affords Three Degrees of Freedom. *CHI EA '97* (1997) 303–304.
23. Mohan, A., Woo, G., Hiura, S., Smithwick, Q., Raskar, R. Bokode: imperceptible visual tags for camera based interaction from a distance. *Proc. SIGGRAPH '09* (2009).
24. Ni, T. and Baudisch, P., Disappearing mobile devices. *Proc. UIST '09* (2009), 101–110.
25. Olwal, A. LightSense: Enabling spatially aware handheld interaction devices. *Proc. ISMAR '06* (2006). 119–122.
26. Olwal, A., and Feiner, S. Spatially Aware Handhelds for High-Precision Tangible Interaction with Large Displays. *Proc. TEI '09* (2009), 181–188.
27. Philips. Laser Doppler technology. http://lasersensors.philips.com/. July 2011.
28. Popov, P., Pulov, S., and Pulov, V. A laser speckle pattern technique for designing an optical computer mouse, Optics and Lasers in Engineering, 42, 1 (2004), 21–26.
29. PrimeSense. http://www.primesense.com/. July 2011.
30. Raskar, R., Nii, H., deDecker, B., Hashimoto, Y., Summet, J., Moore, D., Zhao, Y., Westhues, J., Dietz, P., Barnwell, J., Nayar, S., Inami, M., Bekaert, P., Noland, M., Branzoi, V., and Bruns, E. 2007. Prakash: lighting aware motion capture using photosensing markers and multiplexed illuminators. *Proc. SIGGRAPH '07* (2007), Article 36.
31. Raskar, R., Welch, G., Cutts, M., Lake, A., Stesin, L., and Fuchs, H. The office of the future: a unified approach to image-based modeling and spatially immersive displays. *Proc. SIGGRAPH '98* (1998). 179-188.
32. Reilly, D., Rodgers, M., Argue, R., Nunes, M., and Inkpen, K. Marked-up maps: Combining paper maps and electronic information resources. Personal and Ubiquitous Computing, 10, 4 (2006), 215–226.
33. Reilly, R. and Hanson, A. Gesture recognition for augmentative human computer interaction, Engineering in Medicine and Biology Society, 2 (1995), 1275–1276.
34. Rekimoto, J. and Nagao, K. The world through the computer: Computer augmented interaction with real world environments. *Proc. UIST '95* (1995), 29–36.
35. Rekimoto, J. Tilting operations for small screen interfaces. *Proc. UIST '96* (1996), 167–168.
36. Sanneblad, J. and Holmquist, L. E., Ubiquitous graphics: combining hand-held and wall-size displays to interact with large images. *Proc. AVI '06* (2006), 373–377.
37. Schroeder, D. W., DePue, M. T., Kakarala, R., Xie, T., VanWiggeren, G. D. Tracking motion using an interference pattern, U.S. Patent 7,737,947, 2010.
38. Villar, N., Izadi, S., Rosenfeld, D., Benko, H., Helmes, J., Westhues, J., Hodges, S., Ofek, E., Butler, A., Cao, X., and Chen, B. Mouse 2.0: Multi-touch Meets the Mouse. *Proc. UIST '09* (2009), 33-42.
39. Wang, J. and Canny, J. TinyMotion: camera phone based interaction methods. *CHI '06 EA*, 339-344, 2006.
40. Welch, G. and Foxlin, E. Motion Tracking: No Silver Bullet, but a Respectable Arsenal. *Computer Graphics and Applications*, 22, 6 (2002), 24-38.
41. Wilson, A. and Shafer, S., Xwand: UI for intelligent spaces, in *Proc CHI '03* (2003), 545–552
42. Yang, X.-D., Mak, E., McCallum, D., Irani, P., Cao, X., and Izadi, S. Lensmouse: augmenting the mouse with an interactive touch display, *Proc. CHI '10* (2010), 2431–2440.
43. Yee, K. Peephole displays: Pen interaction on spatially aware hand-held computers. *Proc. CHI '03* (2003), 1–8.

Area-Based Photo-Plethysmographic Sensing Method for the Surfaces of Handheld Devices

Hiroshi Chigira, Atsuhiko Maeda, Minoru Kobayashi
NTT Cyber Solutions Laboratories, NTT Corporation
Yokosuka-Shi, Kanagawa, Japan
{lastname.firstname}@lab.ntt.co.jp

ABSTRACT
Capturing the user's vital signs is an urgent goal in the HCI community. Photo-plethysmography (PPG) is one approach; it can collect data from the finger tips that indicate the user's autonomic nervous system (ANS) and offers new potentials such as mental stress measurement and drowsy state detection. Our goal is to set PPG sensors on the surfaces of ordinary devices such as mice, smartphones, and steering wheels. This will offer smart monitoring without the burden of additional wearable sensors. Unfortunately, current PPG sensors are very narrow, and even if the sensor is attached to the surface of a device, the user is forced to align and hold the finger to the sensor point, which degrades device usability. To solve this problem, we propose an area-based sensing method that relaxes the alignment requirement. The proposed method uses two thin acrylic plates, a diffuser plate and a detection plate, as an IR waveguide. The proposed method can yield very thin sensing surfaces and gentle curvatures are possible. An experiment compares the proposed method to the conventional point-sensor in terms of LF/HF discrimination performance with the participant in the resting state, and the proposed method is shown to offer comparable sensing performance with superior usability.

ACM Classification: H5.2 [Information interfaces and presentation]: User Interfaces. - Input devices and strategies.

General terms: Human Factors

Keywords: vital sensing, photo-plethysmography, heart rate variability, autonomic nervous system, LF/HF, mental stress, drowsiness, light guide, wave guide

INTRODUCTION

The user's vital signs are a rich information source for the HCI community, not just for clinical use. Sensing techniques, analysis methods, and applications are being widely developed, and they have expanded the possibilities of emerging human-computer interaction techniques, as well as providing good insights for evaluating and designing interfaces.

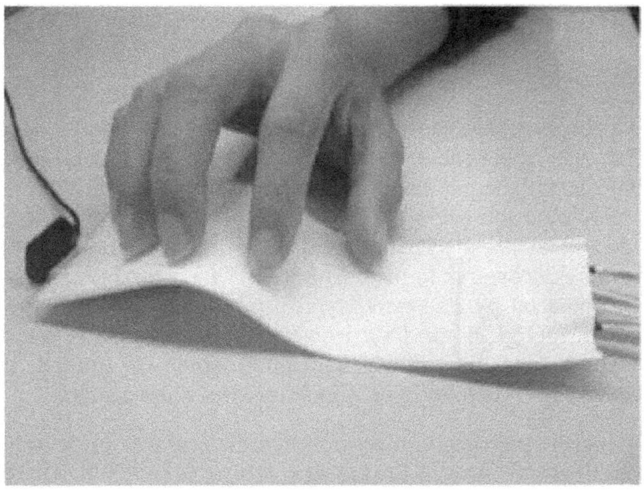

Figure 1: Area-based photo-plethysmographic sensing method can catch the user's photo-plethysmography (PPG) waveform regardless of where the user's finger is on the sensing surface. This surface can be realized as thin, flat or curved plates.

Picard discussed the importance of sensing the user's vital signs for better human-computer interfaces [27]. Electrocardiography (ECG), galvanic skin response (GSR), body temperature, electroencephalogram (EEG), functional near infrared spectroscopy (fNIRs), and many other methods are used alone or together to gather data. They are being utilized to enhance the quality of distant communication [10], and to measure the user's mental stress, user experience, and mental workload in various tasks and situations [5, 18, 3, 12, 13, 25, 1, 16].

Photo-plethysmography (PPG) targets one vital sign, the change in blood volume in peripheral body parts such as finger tips or earlobes. PPG is affected by the cardiovascular state, i.e. the activity of the autonomous nervous system (ANS) [11], and it has the potential to detect valuable user information such as the mental stress [19, 15] and drowsiness [9]. PPG can be observed with an IR-LED and a photo detector (photo diode or photo transistor), and so can be integrated into a simple, low cost, small package. These attributes are very attractive for designing vital sensing systems that suit our daily life.

Most current PPG systems employ wearable sensors. This approach has the advantage of continuous, precise monitor-

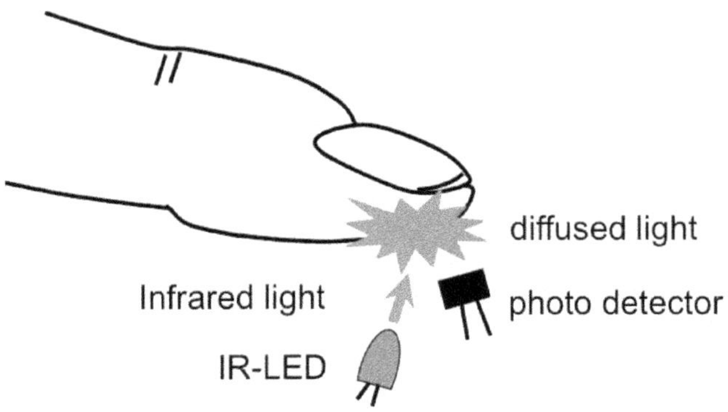

Figure 2: Photo-Plethysmography: method to acquire plethysmographic data of finger tips by R-LED and photo detector.

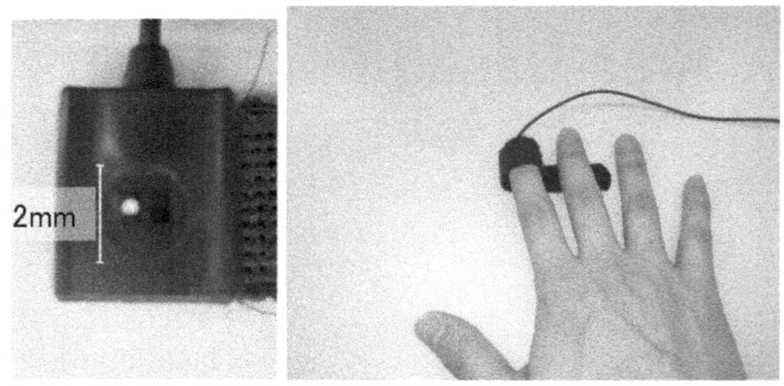

Figure 3: Point PPG sensor (B PAC TSD200).The sensor size, including R-LED and photo detector, is about 2 mm.

ing because the sensors are attached firmly to the user's body. However, this benefit comes at a high cost: the typical user objects to the equipment resulting in a loss of usability. Several remote approaches [29, 6, 34, 17, 8] have been proposed, and especially, the vision-based PPG approach [14, 30, 20] is more acceptable to the user because the wearable sensors are replaced by a camera (typically mounted on the monitor of laptop PC or TV). However, this approach is weak against occlusion and sensing opportunities are limited; it works only when the user is looking toward the camera.

Using the physical contact between the surfaces of devices and the user's hand is the key to solving this problem. There have been early studies on this approach. The sentic mouse by Kirsch and Picard [4] is an ordinary mouse that can sense GSR. Ark et al. proposed the emotion mouse to sense GSR and body temperature [31]. Nakazono et al. described a mouse that could sense PPG [33]. A natural extension is to increase the sensing frequency by turning all surfaces of everyday objects such as mice, smartphones, and steering wheels into sensors. This approach is attractive, but hard to implement. The biggest challenge is how to design practical surfaces that can accurately gather PPG data. The conventional PPG sensor is very small, and even if it is integrated into the devices, the user has to align his/her hand or finger tip to the sensor point. This degrades usability.

In this paper, as a first step to realize PPG sensing from device surfaces, we propose an area-based PPG sensor (Figure 1). The proposed method combines a conventional point-type PPG sensor with two different types of acrylic plates that form a very thin light guide. The proposed method yields wide sensing areas that can be given gentle curvatures and so are readily integrated into existing devices without loss of their original shape or usability. We implement two prototypes, a flat surface and a curved surface, and evaluate their performance against that of a conventional point PPG sensor by LF/HF value, a measure of ANS activity.

RELATED WORK

Photo-Plethysmography

Photo-plethysmography (PPG) is an electro-optic method for measuring the cardiovascular waveform at peripheral parts of the body such as finger tips or earlobes. This waveform, initially generated by heartbeat, propagates throughout the whole body via the arteries, as a change in blood volume. PPG waveform data is gathered by illuminating the body part with near infrared light from an IR-LED and capturing the reflected light by a photo detector such as photo diode or photo transistor (see Figure 2). At the wavelengths used, 700-1000 nm, human tissue has relatively good transparency while hemoglobin has strong absorbance [7]. The amount of light captured by the photo detector is determined, to some extent, by the amount of hemoglobin, so PPG waveform can be detected as an electrical signal. This sensing method eliminates the electrodes used in ECG or GSR that are likely to irritate the skin.

PPG waveform is affected by the activity of ANS [11], thus it holds a lot of information about the user. One of the envisioned applications is stress measurement based on heart rate variability (HRV) [5], which means the variance in the time intervals of adjacent PPG peaks. Frequency analyses of HRV such as LF/HF have been used to detect mental stress during particular tasks or work [19, 15]. A drowsy state detection method utilizing the peak intervals and the amplitude of PPG waveform has also been attempted [9]. These findings elucidate potential applications such as a stress monitoring system that makes the work environment healthy and a safe driving system that prevents accidents while driving.

Current Sensing Technique

We briefly summarize the current vital sensing methods, especially those related to PPG sensing. There are three main types: *Wearable Sensor, Contact-Free Approach,* and *Approach of Touching Ordinary Devices.*

Wearable Sensor PPG is, together with other vital signs, generally captured by wearable sensors. Renevey et al. proposed a wrist type PPG sensor [24]. iCalm of Flecher et al. is a wrist-band sensor that also captures GSR, body temperature, and motor activity [26]. A forehead sensor was proposed by Mendelson et al. [32]. Finger ring type wearable sensor was proposed by Rhee et al. [28]. Poh et al. proposed an earlobe type PPG sensor [22]. These wearable sensors have several advantages chiefly good accuracy and continuous monitoring. Both are achieved because they are attached firmly to the user's body. Because of this feature, wearable sensors are especially good for clinical use, professionals such as firefighters who need vital monitoring in dangerous places, and athletes who want to know their physical condition during training. However, wearable sensors have one serious disadvantage, they are obtrusive. Even though sensor size continues to shrink, force is still needed to attach them, and they are likely to interrupt the user's original state. Poh et al.'s heartphone [21] is efficient approach in this regard. Since this earphone type PPG sensor can be used as ordinary earphones, it fits into daily life. However, usage is forbidden while driving and is disruptive when working and talking to other people.

Contact-Free Approach Contact-free sensors, which have been attempted by several studies, are good because they offer reasonable usability. Laser Doppler [29], microwave radar [6, 8], thermal imaging [17] have been used, however, these techniques are expensive and demand extra hardware. Vision-based techniques, using a camera to detect the change in color of blood flows, have been proposed in recent years [14, 30, 20]. They offer the ability of acquiring PPG waveforms of multiple users simultaneously. In addition, many recent devices like laptop PCs, TVs, and smartphones are equipped with a front-side camera. Unfortunately, this approach is weak against occlusion, and the user must remain in the viewing angle of the camera.

Approach of Touching Ordinary Devices There are several studies on sensors that create tactile interfaces on ordinary devices. Kirsch proposed the sentic mouse [4]. The body of the mouse mounts a GSR sensor enabling data capture during mouse use. The emotion mouse of Ark et al. is another mouse-based sensing technique [31]; GSR and body temperature data are collected from the surface of the mouse. Attempts have also been made at PPG. Nakazono et al. proposed a mouse-based PPG sensing method [33], and Park et al. proposed a steering wheel with PPG sensor [9].

Our Goal

Our approach is inspired by the third approach, touching ordinary devices. This approach is of course less continuous and less accurate than wearable sensors, but it is far less obtrusive. Sensing PPG from the surface of a device is, however, challenging. The main reason is the small size of current PPG sensors. In clinical use, patients accept that the small sensor must be carefully positioned and then fixed in position (Figure 3). In daily life, however, it is unrealistic to force the user to carefully align a fingertip to just one part of an ordinary device and to keep it there. It will disrupt the user's willingness to use the device. Figure 4 compares the sizes of typical components of point sensors and mice, one of the targets for PPG sensor application. There is another challenge. The original appearance of the device should not be compromised.

DESIGN PRINCIPLES

To reach our goal, we considered the surface type PPG sensor and identified the two key requirements that the sensor should satisfy.

1. Alignment-free: the loss of usability must be minimized, and there must be no need for the user to continuously cover one sensor point with a fingertip.
2. Aesthetically pleasing: easily integrated into the devices while keeping their original shape, appearance, and functionality.

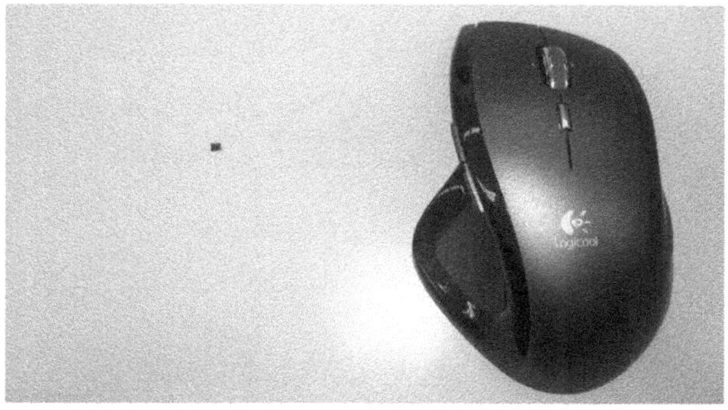

Figure 4: Typical R-LED and photo detectors are relatively small compared to handheld devices or controllers.

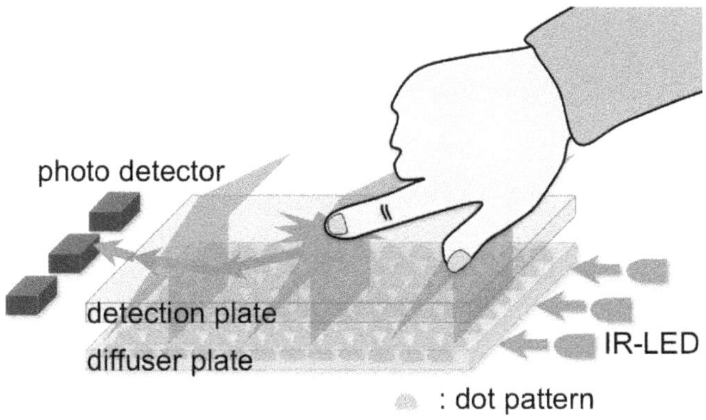

Figure 5: The proposed method is a sensing surface constructed by a diffuser plate (brown), detection plate (blue), R-LED, and photo detector.

In addition, the proposed interface should be robust enough to support the environments in which the devices are used. For example, PPG is an electro-optic method and so should be robust against ambient light.

Area Sensing Surface

The proposed sensor has a wide sensing area and satisfies the two above requirements. Figure 5 shows an overall view of its arrangement. The key advance is the light guide. The IR-LED and photo detector are carried over from the conventional point PPG sensor. The detection plate overlays the diffuser plate with a thin air (or void) layer between them. The top of the detection plate is the surface that the user touches. These light guide plates act as a waveguide that links the IR-LED, the photo detector, and the user's fingertip. Both plates are acrylic with high refractive index (1.49).

We explain the proposed method in more detail with reference to Figure 6. The bottom surface of the diffuser plate has many dot patterns. The lights from the entrance experience several total internal reflections (TIRs) and pass to the detection plate via these dot patterns. This technique is well-known in edge-lit type LCD backlight schemes.

The detection plate is a simple acrylic plate that is highly

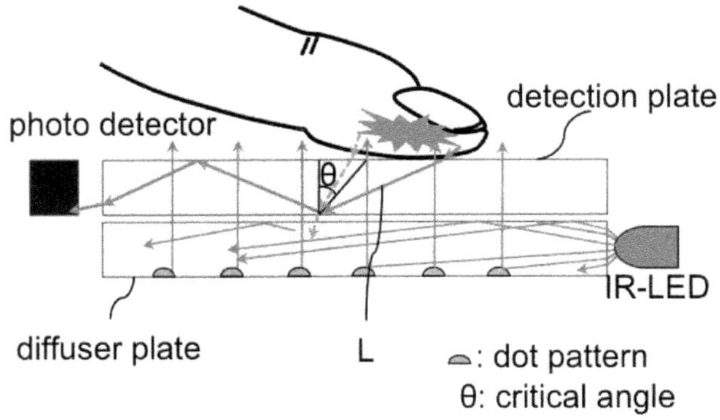

Figure 6: Cross section of the proposed sensor. Scattered lights whose incident angle is greater than θ experience repeated TIRs until they reach the photo detector (Like L).

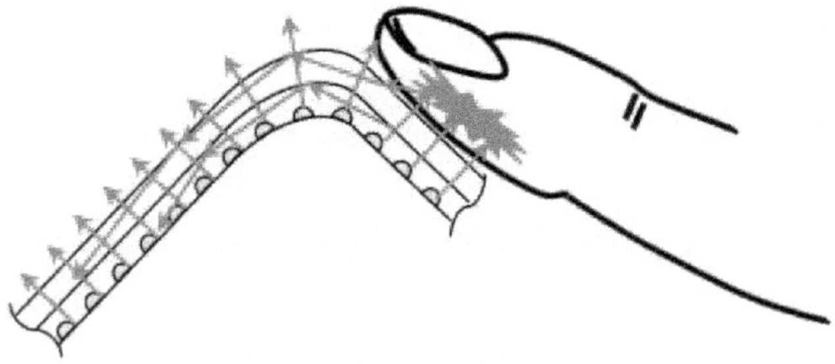

Figure 7: Proposed method supports thin, curved surfaces provided the TIR requirement is satisfied.

transparent to IR-light. Because of this feature, about 90% of the light from the diffuser plate can pass through this detection plate. Light that reaches the fingertip enters the skin and is reflected to reenter the detection plate. The back-scattered light whose incident angle is greater than θ reaches the photo detector through the detection plate after experiencing several TIRs like L in Figure 6. θ is the critical angle for the acrylic-air boundary, calculated to be about 42.2 degrees by Snell's law, taking the refractive index of air as 1.

Advantages

The proposed method has the following advantages.

Alignment-free: Proposed method can catch the user's PPG waveform regardless of where the user's finger is on the sensing surface. This offers high usability since the user does not have to be conscious of finger-sensor alignment.

Applicable as thin, curved surfaces: Proposed method can be realized as thin flat or curved plates (figure 7). This greatly widens the range of device surfaces that can act as PPG sensors without loss of original design or appearance.

Prototype

We implemented two prototypes based on the proposed method: a flat surface and a curved surface (Figure 8). The flat surface sensor consists of diffuser plate, detection plate, IR-LED, and photo detector. The surface is 100 mm by 35 mm. As the diffuser plate, we selected the light guide plate

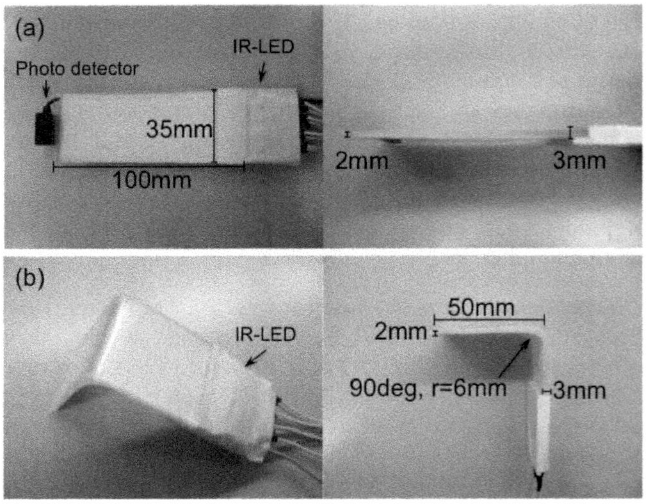

Figure 8: Two prototypes: (a) shows the flat surface. The diffuser plate and detection plate are transparent, but the surface looks white because of the reflection sheet. (b) shows the uni-axial curved surface, components are basically the same. The radius of curvature is 6 mm.

used as the back light panel in a SHARP 8.9-inch back-lit type LCD (LQ089B1LS01) shown in Figure 9 (a). This light guide plate is tapered. The thickest part (light entrance) is 2 mm and the thinnest part is 1 mm. We also used the reflection sheet of the SHARP LCD (Figure 9 (b)). This sheet increases the emitting efficiency of the diffuser plate. At the light entrance of the diffuser plate, we arranged a set of 4 IR-LEDs (OptoSupply OSI5FU5111C-40, peak wavelength is 940 nm) and drove them at 100 mA (Figure 9 (c)). The detection plate is a 0.8 mm thick acrylic plate. Its exit surface was polished in order to reduce light loss. As the photo detector, we used a point PPG sensor (BIOPAC TSD200 sensor head often used in research, its peak wavelength is 870 nm). We used this sensor to acquire PPG waveform data that was then passed through a data acquisition system (BIOPAC MP150 sensor system with sampling frequency of 1 kHz) for storage in a PC (Windows 7). This system also included a low pass filter (10 Hz cutoff) and a notch filter to cancel AC noise during acquisition.

These two prototypes are 2.8 mm thick at most, but this dimension can, in theory, be reduced.

EVALUATION

We conducted several experiments on both prototypes to elucidate their performance. We used a point PPG sensor (BIOPAC TSD 200, Figure 3) as the reference, and evaluated the performance of PPG acquisition in enough detail to precisely calculate LF/HF, one of the widely used indices of autonomic nervous system (ANS) activity. Precise ANS activity measurement enables the creation of various applications that utilize the user's mental state. In addition to LF/HF, we also analyzed the correctness of peaks as identified by the prototypes. For the sake of this analysis, we first define two errors associated with peak detection: missing peak (MP) and false peak (FP) (Figure 10). MP means that a peak on the waveform output by the point sensor has no correspond-

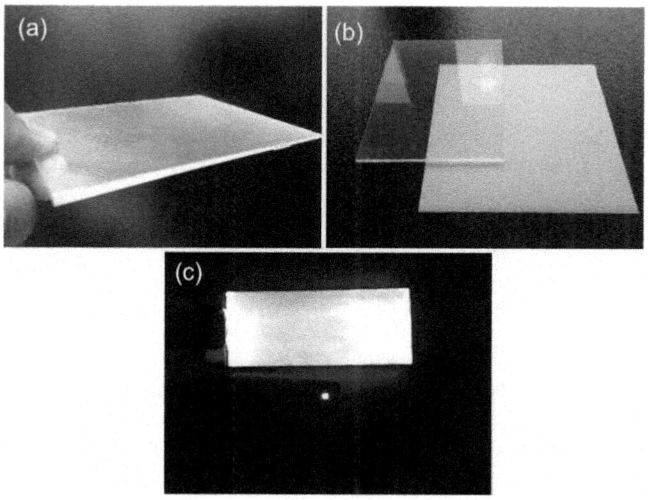

Figure 9: (a): Light guide panel from SHARP 8.9-inch LCD. It has tapered shape. (b): Reflection sheet (white) and Light guide panel (semi-transparent). (c): IR-light emission over entire surface. The small dot light is the IR-light emitted by the point PPG sensor (BIOPAC TSD200). We captured this using an IR-camera.

ing peak in the waveform output by our prototypes, and FP means that a peak in the waveform of our prototypes has no corresponding peak in the waveform of the point sensor. In order to detect MP and FP, we defined window w as the region of corresponding peak. If there was no corresponding peak in the $\pm w$ area around a peak in point sensor data (surface sensor data), then we set that peak as MP (FP). We used LF/HF, MP, FP to confirm if our prototypes satisfied the following factors.

- Realization of two requirements
  - Alignment free: we evaluated this by changing the distance from photo detector to the point of finger touch.
  - Acquisition on curved surfaces: we confirmed this using the curved surface prototype.
- Robustness
  - Type of touch: we evaluated the impact of three types of touch on system performance.
  - Ambient light: we evaluated the impact of several ambient light conditions, including TV and sunlight, on system performance.
  - Age: we confirmed that the prototypes were well utilized by young people and mature people.

Variables

Independent variables in our evaluation are shown below.

- *Distance*: 10, 30, 50, 70 mm

Index finger tip touching the surface (Figure 11).

- *Shape of surface*: flat, curved

Index finger tip touching the surface at the distance of 70 mm for flat surface, the same as the 70 mm in the experiment on *Distance* (Figure 12).

- *Type of touch*: one tip, three tips, entire fingers (Figure 13)

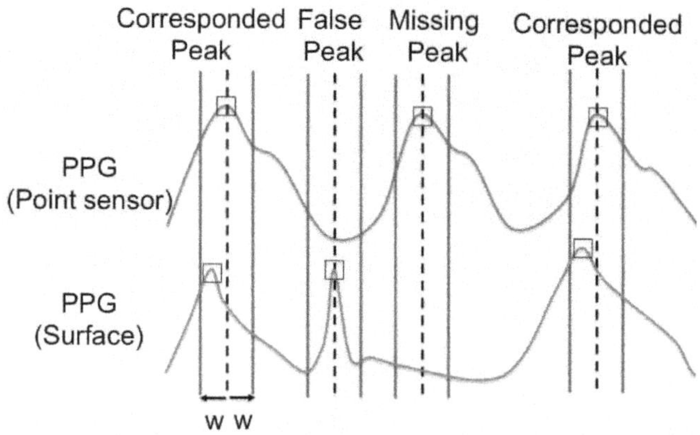

Figure 10: MP and FP were counted using window w. Square plot means detected peak. If there was no corresponding peak in the $\pm w$ area from a peak in point sensor data (surface), then the peak was set as MP (FP).

Figure 11: Examples of distance: 10 mm (left) and 70 mm (right)

- *Ambient light*: halogen light (100 lux), fluorescent light (1400 lux), TV (1405-1410 lux), sunlight (over 8400 lux).
- *Age group*: young, mature

Unless otherwise noted, all experiments used the flat prototype under fluorescent light. In the *Ambient light* and *Age group* experiments, all participants used three tips for touching.

As the video image on the TV in the ambient light experiment, we used a black-white pattern transition with a cycle time of 1 second. Luxmeter values were 1405 lux for the black image, and 1410 lux for the white image. We also observed the IR-light emitted by the TV using an IR-camera. The TV (a 42-inch cold-cathode tube type set) was placed 1 m from the prototype.

Participants

Eleven participants joined our experiments (young participants, five males and two females, 25-27 years old, mature participants, one male, three females, 62-74 years old). One young participant (male, 26 years old) participated in the experiments of *Distance, Shape, Type of touch, Ambient light,* and all eleven participants participated in the *Age group experiment*. Informed consent was obtained from all participants prior to the start of the experiments.

Procedure

Participants were asked to sit on a chair calmly and not to move their body, arm, or fingers during the experiment. Our prototypes were placed on the table and the participants put

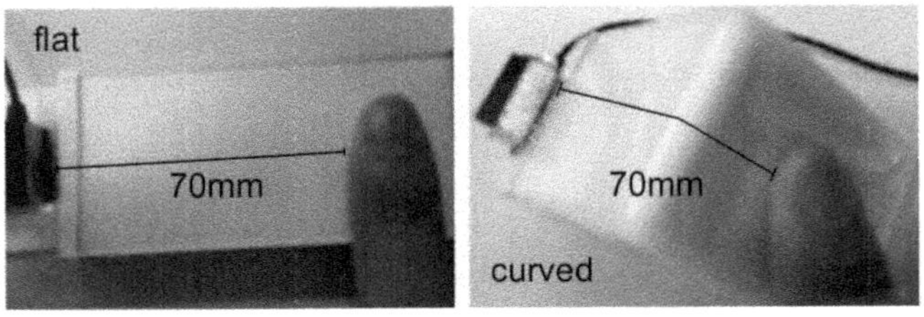

Figure 12: Shape of surface: flat (left) and curved (right).

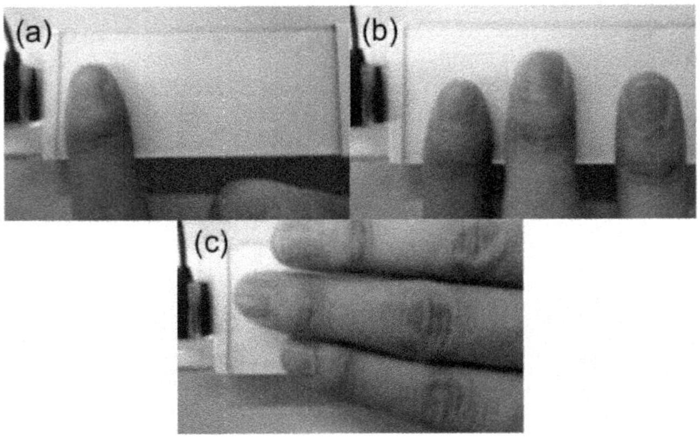

Figure 13: Type of touch. (a): one tip. (b): three tips. (c): entire fingers.

their right hand on it softly, with no undue pressure. A point PPG sensor was attached to the index fingertip of their left hand. After staying calm for 1 minute, PPG data was acquired in three periods, each 180 seconds long, with inter-period interval of 30 seconds.

Data Analysis

All the PPG waveform datasets (point sensor and prototypes) were loaded into the PC, then peak detection and calculation of MP, FP, LF/HF were performed by modules written in C# and Visual Studio .NET [23].

Peak Detection Our peak detection algorithm detected peaks using a simple numerical derivation of waveform and peaks separated by less than 0.5 seconds were eliminated as artifacts. This is because our experiments were performed in the rest state, so short adjacent peak intervals (0.5 seconds represent an average pulse rate of 120 beats per minutes) are most unlikely.

MP and FP As w, window size used to detect MP and FP, we chose 0.45 seconds. This setting helped to absorb the time lag between the point sensor and the prototype (the position of peaks can not be exactly the same) and to count the number of corresponding peaks correctly (wider window sizes such as 1 second can fail to detect missing peaks and false peaks correctly). After counting all MPs and FPs, we calculated the rate of MP (MPR) and the rate of FP (FPR) as below.

$$MPR = \frac{N_{missing}}{N_{point}} \quad (1)$$

$$FPR = \frac{N_{false}}{N_{prototype}} \quad (2)$$

$N_{missing}, N_{false}, N_{point}, N_{prototype}$ is the number of missing peak, false peak, peaks of point sensor, and peaks of prototype, respectively.

LF/HF LF/HF is a frequency-based index that assesses the ANS activity via the heart rate variability (HRV) [5] expressed as the adjacent peak to peak interval (PPI) of PPG waveform [19, 15]. Extracted PPIs were handled as time series data, plotted and interpolated by spline interpolation. Frequency analysis was then conducted by the max entropy method (MEM) to extract the spectrum of the PPI plot. In this spectrum, the power of the low-frequency range (LF: 0.04-0.15 Hz) is influenced by both the sympathetic and parasympathetic nerve, while that of the high-frequency range (HF: 0.15-0.4 Hz) is influenced by only the parasympathetic nerve. LF/HF is the ratio of these powers.

Several studies have shown that the LF/HF value under a task or work is around 3 while it is around 1 in the relaxed state[19, 15]. These findings imply that the LF/HF differences between our prototypes and the point sensor should be at least below 1, thus we set this value as a performance requirement in our study.

RESULTS

One of the results of our experiment is shown in Figure 14; PPG waveform, PPI plot, and power spectrum of PPI plot of point sensor and flat sensor. In the graph of PPG waveform, yellow square plots mean the detected peaks. In this result, there was no MP or FP.

All LF/HF differences between our prototypes and the point sensor seen in the five experiments are shown in Figure 15. In the five experiments, the largest value of reference LF/HF value (from the point sensor) was observed as 2.42, and other reference LF/HF values were below 2. The largest difference in LF/HF (1.86), was observed from a participant of the young group in the *Age group* experiment. Sunlight in the *Ambient light* was second largest difference (1.18); other LF/HF differences were below 1, and so satisfied our performance requirement. One-way ANOVA tests showed no significant difference in all five experiments (F value of each experiments were 0.22, 1.47, 1.23, 3.08, 1.92 respectively, all $p > 0.09$). The results of MPR and FPR in all five experiments are shown in Figure 16. All MPR and FPR values were below 0.03.

DISCUSSION

We discuss, with respect to each independent variable *Distance, Shape, Type of touch, Ambient light,* and *Age group*, the results of the dependent variables: LF/HF difference, MPR, and FPR. We then briefly examine the main factors influencing the performance of our prototypes and what can be done to improve PPG acquisition.

Distance All LF/HF differences were below 0.5, and there was no significant difference (Figure 15 (a)). Both MPR and FPR were very low, but there was a slight increase at 50 mm and 70 mm (Figure 16 (a)). For further analysis, we carefully examined the PPG waveform acquired from the proto-

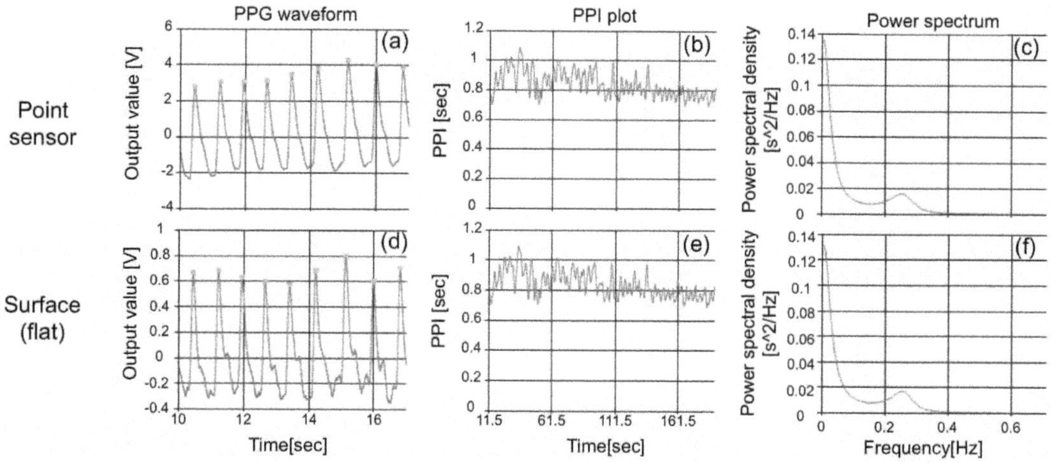

Figure 14: The result acquired from young participant. (a)-(c) are the results of point sensor, PPG waveform, PPI plot, and power spectrum of PPI plot, respectively. (d)-(f) are the results of flat sensor. Yellow squares in PPG waveforms represent the detected peaks.

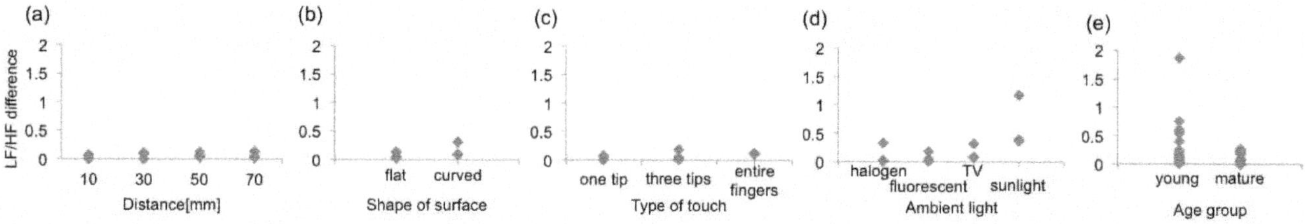

Figure 15: Differences of LF/HF in five experiments. The largest difference (1.89), was observed from a young participant in the age experiment. Using sunlight in the Ambient light experiment yielded the second largest value(1.18). All other differences were below 1.

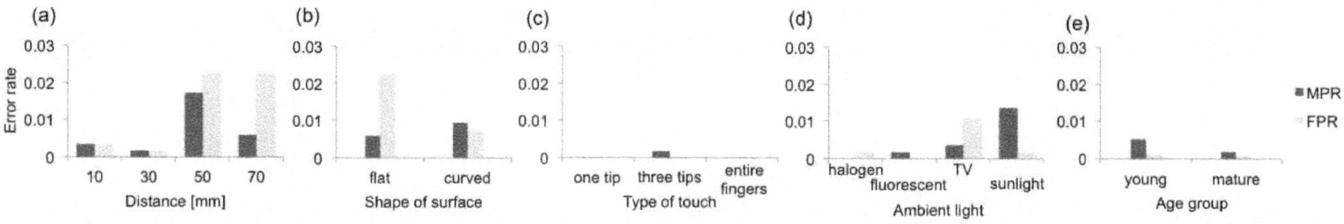

Figure 16: MPR and FPR from all experiments. All rates were below 0.03.

type. Figure 17 shows the PPG waveforms acquired at the distances of 10 mm and 70 mm; a difference in gain can be seen. This implies that we should restrict sensor size. However, assuming a realistic size of ordinary devices such as mice, the proposed method is feasible.

Shape of surface The curved surface showed a comparably small LF/HF difference, which satisfied our performance requirement (Figure 15 (b)).Thus our curved shape prototype is practical. The surface curvatures seen in most handheld devices is gentler than that of our curved prototype, so the proposed method is suitable for most devices.

Type of touch The three types of touch yielded very small LF/HF differences that were far below 1 (Figure 15 (c)). They also exhibited very low MPR and FPR (Figure 16 (c)), thus our prototype turned out to be very stable with regard to the type of touch, one tip, several tips, or entire fingers. This also implies a good advantage: touching by multiple points or large skin areas returns more light to the photo detector, and this helps to ensure accurate waveform data. This can increase the stability of PPG waveform acquisition.

Ambient light In the results of ambient light (Figure 15 (d)), halogen light and fluorescent light yielded low LF/HF differences, MPR, and FPR. The LF/HF difference under TV was not significantly different from halogen light and fluorescent light, but FPR was slightly increased (Figure 16 (d)). By examining the effect of TV noise in detail (see Figure 18 (a), (d)), we found that artifacts, and thus false peaks, may be created by changes in the TV images. Under sunlight, the LF/HF difference was relatively high, and MPR was somewhat high (Figures 15 (d), 16 (d)). This seems to due to the relatively strong IR component of sunlight saturating the photo detector, which can be expected to decrease waveform

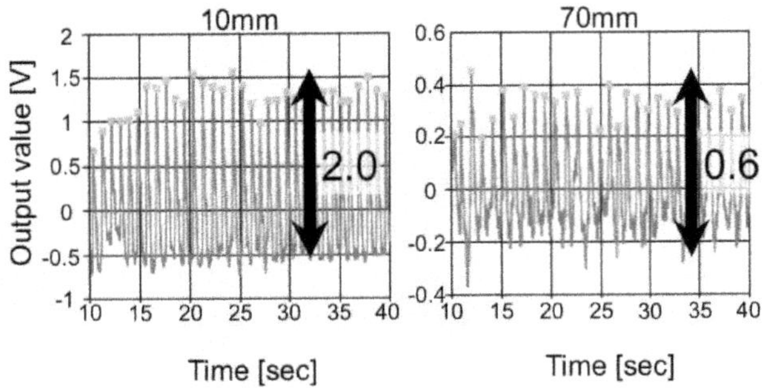

Figure 17: Result at 10 mm (left) and 70 mm (right) from Distance experiment. A gain decrease was observed.

gain and stability (Figure 18 (b) and (e)). This is also due to the experimental setting; the prototypes were placed face up on a table. This result implies that we should choose areas relatively protected from ambient light to improve acquisition performance. For a smartphone, for example, the sensor face could be mounted on the side of the phone. These locations are not directly exposed to sunlight or TV images.

Age group In the *Age group* experiment (Figure 15 (e)), there were no significant differences in terms of LF/HF, and MPR and FPR were small (Figure 16 (e)). However, the results of one participant in the young group exhibited large differences in LF/HF that did not satisfy our requirement. We examined the waveform of that participant, and found a disturbance in his waveform as captured by the prototype (Figure 18(c), (f)). This disturbance implies that unconscious finger movements can yield motion artifacts.

As described above, most differences in LF/HF satisfied our performance requirement, and both MPR and FPR were rather small. Our prototypes supported larger distances from the photo detector, and curved sensor surfaces. This means that our prototypes satisfy our design requirements. They were also valid with several types of touch, and different ambient lighting conditions. In addition, our prototypes are suitable for both young and mature age groups. This stability against age is seen as an important advantage.

The negative effects such as finger motion artifacts, light artifacts created by TV programs, saturation by sunlight, and gain reduction by distance, indicate the need to further improve the proposed method. One important issue is the need for an alternative approach to obtaining the activity of ANS, because peak detection is inherently weak against disturbances and artifacts. The approach of directly calculating the PPIs, such as that of Barros and Ohnishi [2], appears promising.

This study is merely the first step. To provide a better reference, we should compare the prototypes to a clinical ECG system. Also, the experiments were performed while the participants were in the rest state. Data collection during movement and active mental states must be examined. Another issue is the rather high energy consumption of the prototypes, 100mA. Greater efficiencies are needed to support their use in handheld devices. Despite these limitations, our experiments are useful in terms of providing an initial evaluation.

CONCLUSION

The importance of sensing vital signs continues to increase in the HCI community, and many techniques or methods have been proposed. Our approach is a vital sign sensor that offers excellent usability in daily life. In this paper, we focused on allowing ordinary devices to realize PPG via physical contact. This approach will enable us to measure the worker's mental stress through mouse usage and detect the driver's drowsiness through the steering wheel, which suggests excellent usability. As the first step in realizing this goal, we presented an area-based sensing surface created around two light guide plates. This surface can be thin and curved, and so is a considerable advancement over the original point PPG sensors; it can be added to ordinary handheld devices with no drop in usability. A pilot study with eleven participants was performed, and the results showed that the proposed method matches the performance of a traditional point PPG sensor. Future work will tackle the improvement of robustness against motion and light artifacts and reducing the power consumption. We will also implement our method into handheld devices such as mice and steering wheels, and evaluate its feasibility when performing various tasks with the devices. This study will contribute to the design and evaluation of future interfaces and human-computer interaction.

REFERENCES

1. Brogni A., Vinayagamoorthy V., Steed A., and Slater M. Variations in physiological responses of participants during different stages of an immersive virtual environment experiment. In *Proc. VRST 2006*, pages 376–382. ACM Press, 2006.

2. Barros A. K. and Ohnishi N. Heart instantaneous frequency (hif): an alternative approach to extract heart rate variability. *Biomedical Engineering, IEEE Trans.*, 48:850–855, 2001.

3. Chen D. and Vertegaal R. Using mental load for managing interruptions in physiologically attentive user interfaces. In *Proc. CHI 2004*, pages 1513–1516. ACM Press, 2004.

4. Kirsch D. The sentic mouse: Developing a tool for measuring emotional valence. Technical report, MIT Media Laboratory Perceptual Computing Section, 1997.

5. Rowe D. W., Sibert J., and Irwin D. Heart rate variability: indicator of user state as an aid to human-computer interaction. In *Proc. CHI 1998*, pages 480–487. ACM Press, 1998.

6. Greneker E. F. Radar sensing of heartbeat and respiration at a distance with applications of the technology. In *Radar 97*, number 449, pages 150–154, 1997.

7. JOBSIS F. F. Noninvasive infrared monitoring of cerebral, and myocardial oxygen sufficiency and

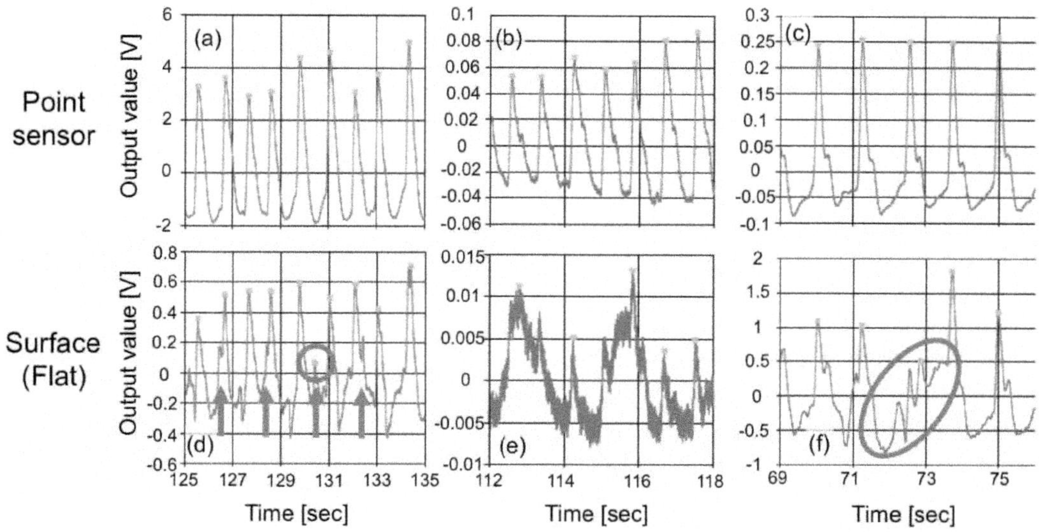

Figure 18: (a), (d) are the results of TV, and (b), (e) are the results of sunlight , in Ambient light experiment. (c), (f) are the results of one young participant in the Age group experiment.

circulatory parameters. *Science*, 198:1264–1267, 1977.

8. Lu G., Yang F., Tian Y., Jing X., and Wang J. Contact-free measurement of heart rate variability via a microwave sensor. *Sensors*, 9(12):9572–9581, 2009.

9. Park H., Oh S., and Hahn M. Drowsy driving detection based on human pulse wave by photoplethysmography signal processing. In *Proc. IUCS 2009*, pages 89–92. IEEE, 2009.

10. Wang H., Prendinger H., and Igarashi T. Communicating emotions in online chat using physiological sensors and animated text. In *Proc. CHI 2004*, pages 1171–1174. ACM Press, 2004.

11. Allen J. Photoplethysmography and its application in clinical physiological measurement. *Physiological Measurement*, 28(3), 2007.

12. Healey J. A. and Picard R. W. Detecting stress during real-world driving tasks using physiological sensors. *Intelligent Transportation Systems, IEEE Trans.*, 6:156–166, 2005.

13. Lee J. C. and Tan D. S. Using a low-cost electroencephalograph for task classification in hci research. In *Proc. UIST 2006*, pages 81–90. ACM Press, 2006.

14. Humphreys K., Ward T., and Markham C. A cmos camera-based pulse oximetry imaging system. In *Proc. EMBS 2005*, pages 3494 –3497. IEEE, 2005.

15. Mizuno K, Tanaka M, Yamaguti K, Kajimoto O, Kuratsune H, and Watanabe Y. Mental fatigue caused by prolonged cognitive load associated with sympathetic hyperactivity. *Behavioral and Brain Functions*, 17(7), 2011.

16. Hirshfield L. M., Solovey E. T., Girouard A., Kebinger J., Jacob R. J. K., Sassaroli A., and Fantini S. Brain measurement for usability testing and adaptive interfaces: an example of uncovering syntactic workload with functional near infrared spectroscopy. In *Proc. CHI 2009*, pages 2185–2194. ACM Press, 2009.

17. Garbey M., Sun N., Merla A., and Pavlidis I. Contact-free measurement of cardiac pulse based on the analysis of thermal imagery. *Biomedical Engineering, IEEE Trans.*, 54(8):1418 –1426, 2007.

18. Meehan M., Insko B., Whitton M., and Brooks F. P. J. Physiological measures of presence in stressful virtual environments. *ACM Trans. Graph.*, 21:645–652, 2002.

19. Takada M., Ebara T., and Kamijima M. Heart rate variability assessment in japanese workers recovered from depressive disorders resulting from job stress: measurements in the workplace. *International Archives of Occupational and Environmental Health*, 83:521–529, 2010.

20. Poh M-Z., McDuff D. J., and Picard R. W. Advancements in noncontact, multiparameter physiological measurements using a webcam. *Biomedical Engineering, IEEE Trans.*, 58(1):7–11, 2011.

21. Poh M-Z., Kim K., Goessling A., Swenson N., and Picard R. W. Cardiovascular monitoring using earphones and a mobile device. *IEEE pervasive computing*, 24:54–67, 2011.

22. Poh M-Z., Swenson N. C., and Picard R. W. Motion-tolerant magnetic earring sensor and wireless earpiece for wearable photoplethysmography. *Information Technology in Biomedicine, IEEE Trans.*, 14(3):786 –794, 2010.

23. Microsoft. Visual studio .net. http://www.microsoft.com/visualstudio/.

24. Renevey P., Vetter R., Krauss J., Celka P., and Depeursinge Y. Wrist-located pulse detection using ir signals, activity and nonlinear artifact cancellation. In *Proc. EMBS 2001*, volume 3, pages 3030 – 3033. IEEE, 2001.

25. Mandrik R. L., Inkpen K. M., and Clvert T. W. Using psychophysiological techniques to measure user experience with entertainment technologies. *Behaviour and Information Technology*, 25:141–158, 2006.

26. Fletcher R. R., Dobson K., Goodwin M. S., Eydgahi H., Smith O. W., Fernholz D., Kuboyama Y., Hedman E. B., Poh M-Z., and Picard R. W. icalm: Wearable sensor and network architecture for wirelessly communicating and logging autonomic activity. *Information Technology in Biomedicine, IEEE Trans.*, 14(2):215 –223, 2010.

27. Picard R. W. and Healey J. Affective wearables. *Personal and Ubiquitous Computing*, 1:231–240, 1997.

28. Rhee S., Yang B-H., and Asada H. H. Artifact-resistant, power-efficient design of finger-ring plethysmographic sensors. i. design and analysis. In *Proc. EMBS 2000*, pages 2792–2795. IEEE, 2000.

29. Ulyanov S. S. and Tuchin V. V. Pulse-wave monitoring by means of focused laser beams scattered by skin surface and membranes. In *SPIE*, number 1884, pages 160–167.

30. Verkruysse W., Svaasand L. O., and Nelson J. S. Remote plethysmographic imaging using ambient light. *Opt. Express*, 16(26):21434–21445, 2008.

31. Ark W. S., Dryer D. C., and Lu D. J. The emotion mouse. In *Proc. HCII 1999*, pages 818–823, 1999.

32. Mendelson Y., Duckworth R. J., and Comtois G. A wearable reflectance pulse oximeter for remote physiological monitoring. In *Proc. EMBS 2006*, pages 912–915. IEEE, 2006.

33. Nakazono Y., Ozeki H., and Mizusawa J. Non-invasive measurement of cardiovascular stress responses by a photoplethysmography-built-in pc mouse. *Journal of the Society of Biomechanisms*, 1(33):80–84, 2009.

34. Qiu Y., Hu S., Cheang P. Y. S., Crabtree V. P., Smith P. R., Cai Y., and Zhu Y. Poincare plot analysis for pulse interval extracted from non-contact photoplethysmography. In *Proc. EMBS 2005*, pages 1964–1967. IEEE, 2005.

Detecting Shape Deformation of Soft Objects Using Directional Photoreflectivity Measurement

Yuta Sugiura[1&2], *Gota Kakehi*[1], *Anusha Withana*[1&2], *Calista Lee*[1], *Daisuke Sakamoto*[2&3], *Maki Sugimoto*[1&2], *Masahiko Inami*[1&2] *and Takeo Igarashi*[2&3]

[1]Graduate School of Media Design, Keio University (KMD), 4-1-1 Hiyoshi, Kohoku, Yokohama, 223-8526 Japan

[2]JST, ERATO, IGARASHI Design Interface Project, 1-28-1-7F, Koishikawa, Bunkyo, Tokyo, 112-0002 Japan

[3]Dept of Computer Science, The University of Tokyo, 7-3-1 Hongo, Bunkyo, Tokyo, 113-0033 Japan

{y-sugiura | g.kakehi | anusha | calista | inami}@kmd.keio.ac.jp, {sakamoto | sugimoto}@designinterface.jp, takeo@acm.org

ABSTRACT

We present the FuwaFuwa sensor module, a round, hand-size, wireless device for measuring the shape deformations of soft objects such as cushions and plush toys. It can be embedded in typical soft objects in the household without complex installation procedures and without spoiling the softness of the object because it requires no physical connection. Six LEDs in the module emit IR light in six orthogonal directions, and six corresponding photosensors measure the reflected light energy. One can easily convert almost any soft object into a touch-input device that can detect both touch position and surface displacement by embedding multiple FuwaFuwa sensor modules in the object. A variety of example applications illustrate the utility of the FuwaFuwa sensor module. An evaluation of the proposed deformation measurement technique confirms its effectiveness.

ACM Classification: H5.m. Information interfaces and presentation (e.g., HCI): Miscellaneous.

General terms: Design, Measurement

Keywords: Soft User Interface, Density Measurement, Photoreflectivity, Tangible User Interface, Multiple Sensors

INTRODUCTION

While traditional input devices such as buttons and handles are made of hard materials, ones made of soft materials are now being introduced for use in interactive systems to provide an emotionally richer user experience [8, 10]. Soft input devices are especially suitable for children because they are safer than hard ones. However, the sensing techniques used for soft input devices typically require the attachment of electromechanical sensors to soft surfaces to physically measure the deformation. This approach unfortunately spoils the softness of the original material.

In this paper, we present a FuwaFuwa sensor module for detecting shape changes in soft objects. The FuwaFuwa module contains six photoreflectors (each comprising a photosensor and IR light emitter), pointing in six orthogonal directions. The measured photoreflectivities are used to determine the density of the padding material in the object (e.g., cotton and wool).

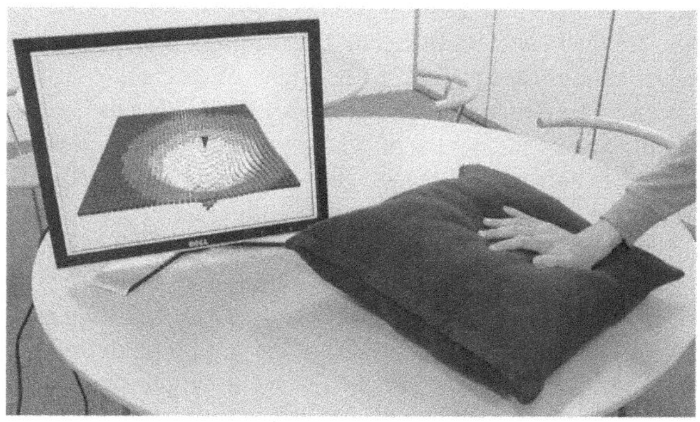

Figure 1: Detecting shape deformation of soft object using directional photoreflectivity measurement

Our experimental results showed that the photoreflectivity of such materials is a reliable measure for use in determining the density. The user's interactions with a soft object change the shape of the object, resulting in a change in the density of the padding material. The sensors in the FuwaFuwa module detect the degree of this change. As shown in Figure 1, the position of a displacement can be determined by placing several FuwaFuwa modules in the object.

Since it is battery-powered and equipped with wireless communication, the FuwaFuwa sensor module can easily be placed in typical soft objects (e.g. cushions, sofas, pillows, beds) without affecting their softness. This is the main advantage that the FuwaFuwa sensor module has over typical sensors.

The work described in this paper has resulted in four significant contributions to shape deformation detection for soft objects:

- A method using directional photoreflectivity measurement for detecting pressure changes in soft objects.
- A hand-sized, battery-operated sensor module equipped with wireless communication that can easily be embedded in a soft object without affecting its softness.
- A multi-sensor network system that can detect the barycenter of large soft objects and measure the amount of pressure exerted by the user as input.
- Several example application scenarios for the sensor system.

RELATED WORK

Many researchers have explored different types of sensing techniques and applications for soft objects as interfaces in today's world.

Plush Toy Interfaces

The transition from infancy to childhood to adolescence is characterized by certain behaviors, such as remaining attached to a plush toy [26]. Even adults often display an instinctive desire to touch a plush toy. This has led to the recent introduction of interactive plush toys to provide an emotionally richer user experience [8, 10]. Yonezawa et al. made an interactive plush toy by equipping it with seven types of sensors (bend sensor, microphone, etc.) [28]. They have also created an application to be used with this toy that composes music on the basis of the intensity and frequency of interaction. While their approach preserves the soft properties of the plush toy, installing the sensors is not a simple operation, making its use problematic for typical soft household objects.

Foam Interfaces

Murakami et al. had developed a device that enabled one to intuitively manipulate 3D CG models [12]. A block of non-conductive urethane foam was cut into a cube, and 90 pieces of conductive urethane foam were attached to it. The resistance of the foam pieces changed in accordance with the deformation of the cube, and the relationship between the resistance and length of the foam pieces was calculated beforehand. In accordance with the lengths recorded for 90 points, the user is able to manipulate the 3D object by deforming the cube.

Smith et al. developed "Digital Foam" (DF) an input device with which one is able to manipulate a 3D object in a manner similar to the way one manipulates clay [20]. It consists of a number of units created using a combination of conductive cloth and conductive urethane foam. The resistance of each unit changes in accordance with changes in the pressure applied to it. The main difference between DF and FuwaFuwa is that the goal of DF is to create a soft sensor to detect pressure, whereas the FuwaFuwa is a sensor designed to convert existing soft objects into sensing platforms.

Fur-like and Fabric Interfaces

Various other types of interfaces have been proposed, such as a fur-like interface [2, 4, 13]. Baudisch et al. developed Soap, an input device enclosed in elastic fabric that is based on an optical sensor used for cursor control [1]. The device can be used in various applications, such as for pointing and game control. Although its structure is simple, it cannot measure pressure because the device is made specifically for x-y movement.

Elastic Material Interfaces

Elastic material is a commonly used material in human computer interaction [5, 19, 24, 25]. There have been several attempts at detecting shape deformation using cameras. Sato et al. designed a tabletop system comprising an LCD and an overhead camera for use in detecting the orientation and power of the force [17]. This approach can work well in a limited environment such as a tabletop. However, problems such as camera occlusion occur when it is used in a daily life environment, which is ever-changing.

In the field of robotics, elastic material has been used for developing a robot surface similar to human skin. There have also been several sensors proposed for sensing the touch interaction on the robot's skin [7, 11]. Kadowaki et al. have developed a method that uses a sensor attached to a soft body to sense and differentiate between interactions (such as push, pinch, and rub) with the object [9]. The soft object used was a piece of urethane foam, with five phototransistors attached at the top and three infrared light-emitting diodes (IR LEDs) attached at the bottom. The electric currents flowing through the phototransistors change in accordance with deformation in the soft body, and these changes are measured and used to determine the amount of deformation. Although this method is sensitive enough to detect very slight changes in deformation, the thickness of the soft body must remain fixed, which makes the method rather inflexible.

Air Pressure Interfaces

Air itself can create a soft tactile impression. Hiramatsu et al. developed a soft ball-shaped device that reacts to being squeezed, thrown, and shaken [6]. The device has airbag-filled cushions located in a radial fashion at 19 points, and a pneumatic sensor detects the pressure applied. Sponges in the device fill the voids. However, the sensor must be attached to the surface of the device, thus making this approach difficult to apply to many soft objects. Yasumoto et al. proposed a balance-ball-shaped interface as a game controller [27]. Eight pressure sensors attached to the surface of a soft object enable its center of gravity to be measured. As a form of media art, Ueki designed "Tabby," a light that appears to breathe due to the use of an air compressor [22]. A pyroelectric IR sensor inside the lampshade detects the user's touch, but differences in touch pressure are not detected.

Our Interface

Our FuwaFuwa sensor module has three properties in particular that distinguish it from the sensors described above.

- It is small and wireless, so it can be inserted into simple small objects.
- It can continuously measure pressure.

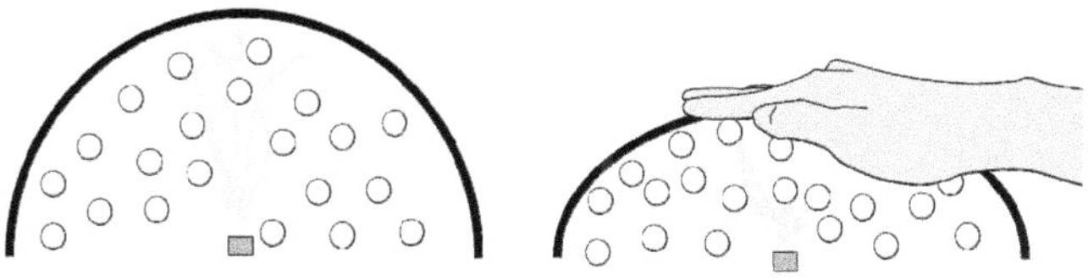

Figure 2: Directionality of reflected light is lower at low density (left) than at high density (right)

- A configuration of such modules can determine the position of touch on a surface.

DIRECTIONAL PHOTOREFLECTIVITY BASED MATERIAL DENSITY MEASUREMENT

Principle

Soft objects such as stuffed toys and pillows usually consist of light materials such as wool, feathers, and cotton as stuffing. The random arrangement and grainy structure of such materials cause incident light to be scattered, resulting in a diffused energy pattern. When these materials are tightly packed (i.e., when the density is increased), they create a considerable amount of directed and specular reflected light. This phenomenon is illustrated in Figure 2.

The IR LED in each photoreflector in the FuwaFuwa sensor module directs a beam towards the stuffing material, and the corresponding photosensor measures the reflected light energy. This measurement indicates the density of the soft material and can be used to detect user interactions with the object.

Relationship between Photoreflectivity and Density

We conducted an experiment to investigate the relationship between the change in density and the photoreflective properties of soft material. A KODENSHI SG-105 photoreflector (comprising an IR LED and a photosensor) was positioned at the bottom of a clear acrylic box (10.4 x 10.4 x 14.6 cm) with a cover that could be set at different heights (Figure 3). The box was filled with soft material, the cover height was varied from 12 to 5.2 cm in intervals of 2 mm, and the light energy reflected on the sensor was measured at each height. The experiment was repeated for three soft materials with different densities: a polyester cotton called "thubuthubu-shugei-wata" [21], small feathers, and natural cotton (Figure 4).

Experiment Procedure

1. Place 10.0 g of soft material in the box.
2. Set the cover to be 12 cm from the bottom.
3. Record the photosensor output at 1 Hz for 10 s, collecting a total of ten records.
4. Lower the cover by 2 mm.
5. Repeat steps 3 and 4 until the cover is under the 3.4 cm from the bottom.
6. Raise the cover by 2 mm.
7. Record the photosensor output at 1 Hz for 10 s, collecting a total of ten records.

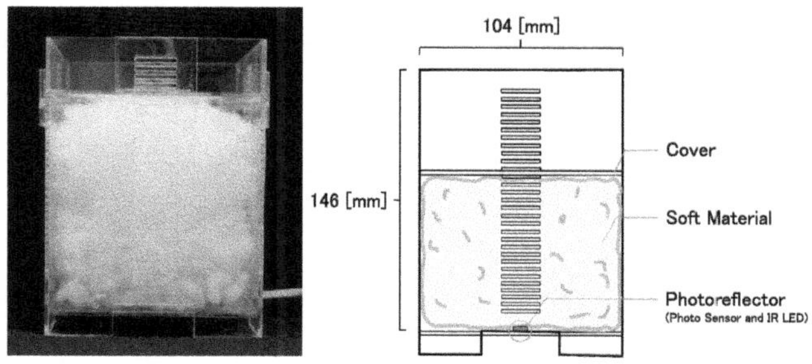

Figure 3: Experimental sensor apparatus

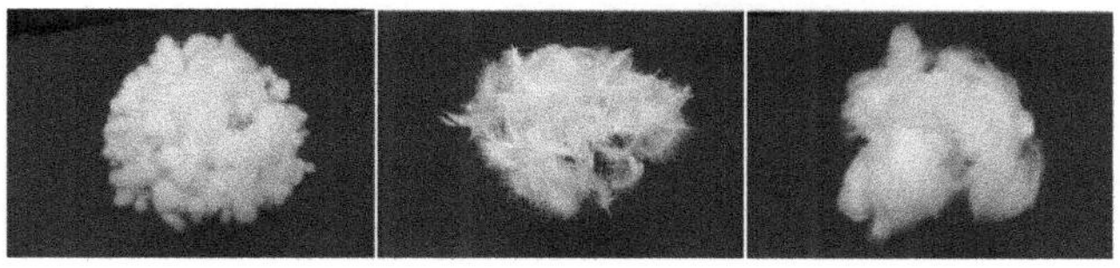

Figure 4: Soft materials: polyester cotton (left), small feathers (center), and natural cotton (right)

8. Repeat steps 6 and 7 until the cover is again at a height of 12 cm from the bottom.

Experiment Conditions

Since the density of a cushion is typically about 0.01 [g/cm^3], we used a density range of 0.0078 to 0.0257 [g/cm^3] for our experiment. The material was weighed using a Tanita KP-103 electronic scale (maximum weight: 120 g, accuracy: 0.1 g), and the photosensor measurements were recorded using an Atmel ATmega328 microcontroller. To check for the effect of hysteresis, we made identical measurements after both lowering and raising the cover. A phototransistor was included in the voltage-divider circuit so that the measured output voltage was inversely proportional to the light reflected on the sensor.

Results

Figure 5 shows a plot of the average measured voltage against the material density for the polyester cotton. The voltage increased with the pressure created by pushing, and it decreased as the pressure was reduced by pulling. But we can observe certain level of hysteresis. Finally, the voltage is saturated at the 0.0257 [g/cm^3]. There was a negligible change in the average measured voltage in the 0.0077 to 0.0092 [g/cm^3] density range. Therefore, we use polyester cotton density higher than 0.0092 [g/cm^3].

In the case of the small feathers (Figure 6) and the natural cotton, the voltage is mostly saturated in the measured range, so it is difficult to measure the density of these materials in a cushion using our method. We found that it is possible to measure the density of these materials when the density is low as in feather quilt blanket or down jacket (see Figure 7 and 8). However, we did not use them in our prototype because the weight of the current sensor module is too heavy for such low-density objects. The sensor module might slide according to gravity and cannot stably detect the density.

Other Materials

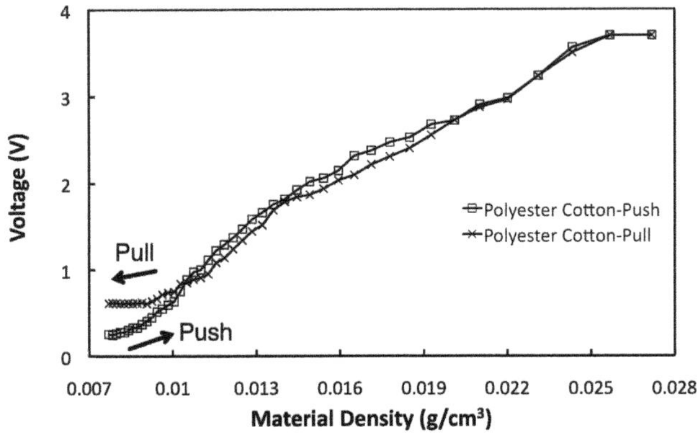

Figure 5: Average measured voltage against material density polyester cotton

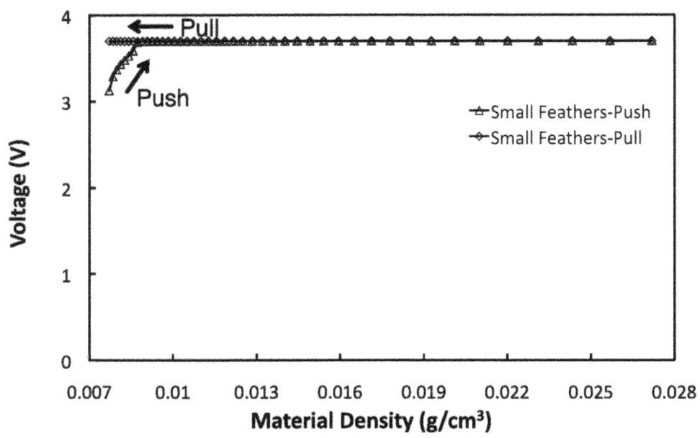

Figure 6: Average measured voltage against material density small feathers

We checked the feasibility of using urethane sponge and polystyrene foam cut at about ϕ 2 mm as the stuffing material, and found that it was difficult to measure the pressure with such materials because the voltage saturated when they were used.

IMPLEMENTATION

System Overview

The hardware configuration used for the prototype implementation is shown in Figure 9. The FuwaFuwa sensor module (or modules) to be installed in various types of soft objects connects wirelessly to a server (MacBook Pro). The server sends data to one or more clients through a TCP/IP network. The clients process the data and display the results.

FuwaFuwa Sensor Module

Figure 10 shows a photograph of the FuwaFuwa sensor module, and Figure 11 shows the main components. Its six orthogonally arranged photoreflectors enable the energy of the light reflected from each direction to be independently measured. The module requires no physical connection since it is equipped with a wireless communication module (XBee Series1) and a Li-Po battery (3.7 V, 350 mA). Its diameter is 64 mm. The cover is made of acrylonitrile butadiene styrene

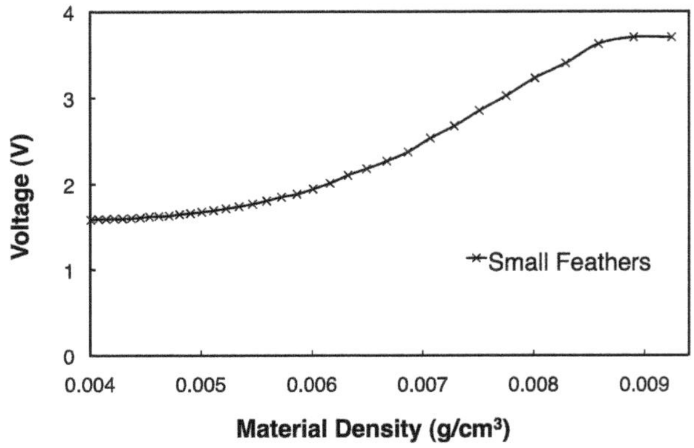

Figure 7: Average measured voltage against low-level density of small feathers

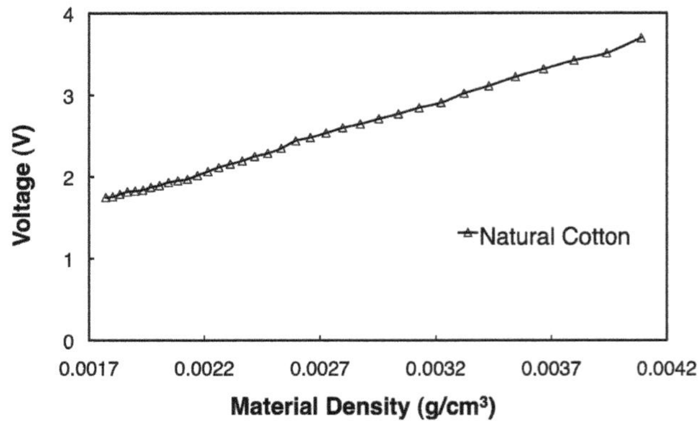

Figure 8: Average measured voltage against low-level density of natural cotton

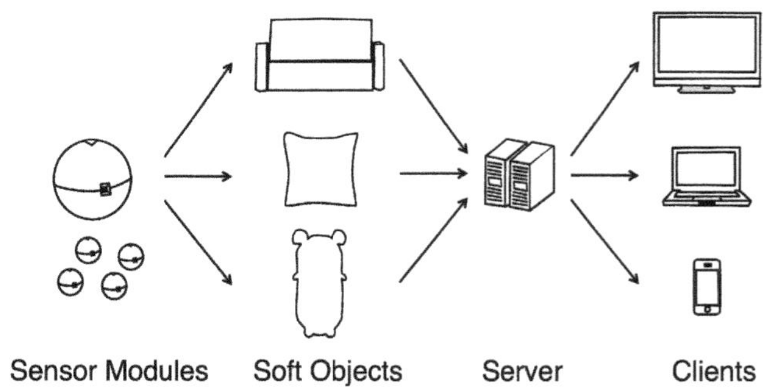

Figure 9: System overview

(ABS) plastic using a 3D printing machine. It can be easily placed in any soft object to create a soft interface.

Data Processing

An Arduino Pro mini microcontroller (based on ATmega328) is embedded in each FuwaFuwa sensor module for processing the data. It has a 10-bit A/D converter so that each photoreflector outputs from the value of 0 to 1023, and is connected to the ZigBee module. Since an ID number can be assigned to each ZigBee module, multiple sensor modules can be used at the same time.

Figure 10: Photograph of FuwaFuwa sensor module (3 of the 6 photoreflectors are visible)

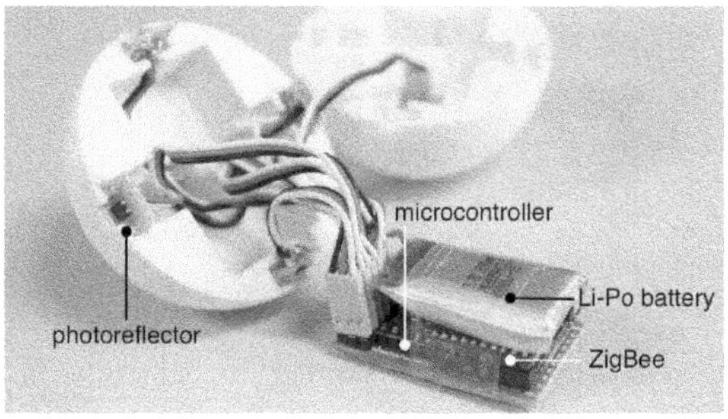

Figure 11: Main components of FuwaFuwa sensor module

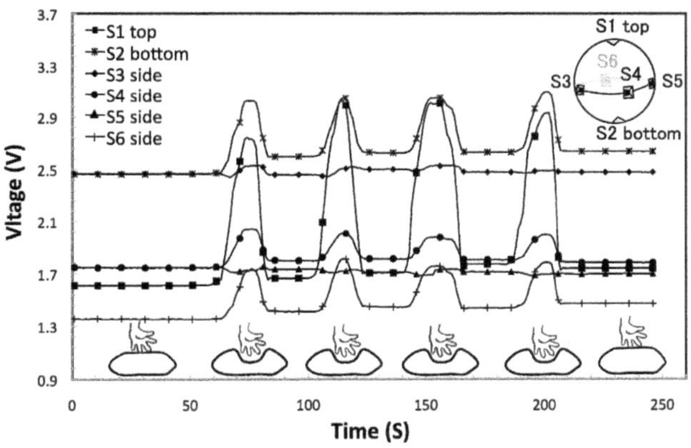

Figure 12: Each sensor values in the module

2 Bytes	1 Byte	1 Byte	2 × N Bytes
START	Module ID	No. of Photore-flector in the module	Photoreflector Value

Table 1: User datagram protocol for server-client connection

Figure 12 shows the individual sensor readings when Fuwa-Fuwa is embedded in a spherical soft object and the object is pushed along the axis of sensor 1 and 2 (S1 and S2) towards S1. According to the graph, S1 has the highest voltage variations and S2 has the second highest variations due to the directionality of the density variation inside the object.

Proxy Server

A proxy server connects the FuwaFuwa sensor module with the client software using serial communication at 57,600 bps.

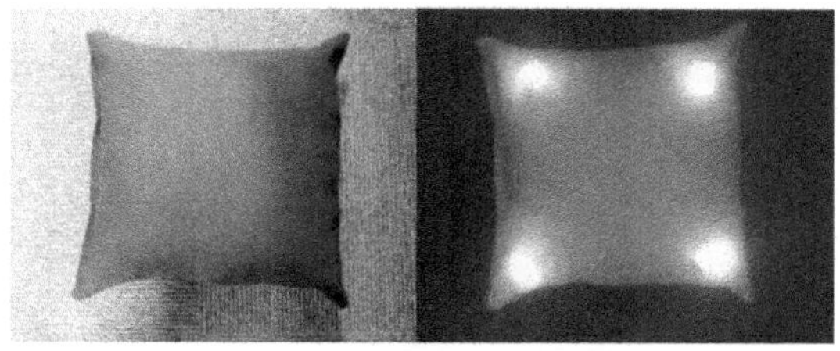

Figure 13: Detecting locations of FuwaFuwa sensor modules: image with normal camera (left) and IR camera (right)

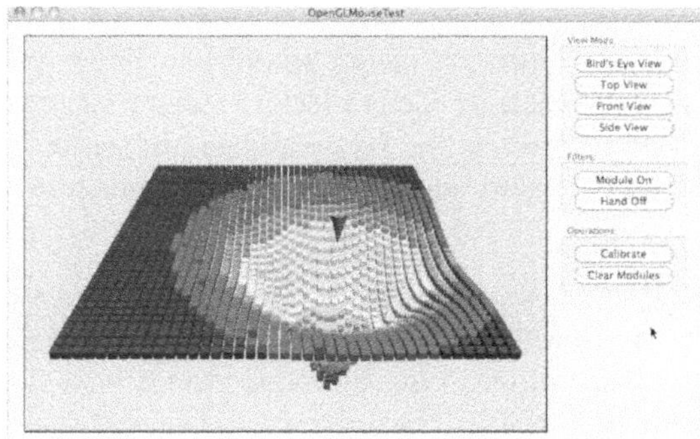

Figure 14: Visualized sensor data

The server processes the received data and sends it to one or more clients using the user datagram protocol (Table 1).

Multiple FuwaFuwa Sensor Modules

By installing multiple FuwaFuwa sensor modules in a larger soft object, collected sensor measurements can be used to indentify the point of touch on the surface. This means that any soft object can be converted used as a touch-sensitive surface. Moreover, it enables the strength of the touch to be measured, which is difficult with a hard touch surface. Next we explain the method for calibrating the module locations, the method for calculating the touch point, and the software used for visualizing the sensor data.

Module Location Calibration

When multiple sensor modules are placed in an object, their locations must be calibrated before they can be used. The LED in each module emits IR light in a particular direction. An IR camera can detect these high-intensity light beams even through the object's stuffing and covering, as shown in Figure 13. When a sensor-embedded object is placed within the camera's field of view, the user can specify the location of the embedded sensors by clicking on them in the software.

Barycenter Calculation

The touch point is detected by calculating the barycenter of the sensor modules using the calibrated sensor locations and the photorefractive values. The coordinates on the soft object are the same as the coordinates that are calibrated using the IR camera. This means that the user's input will become the barycenter of the calibrated coordinate by the module location calibration process. The system detects 1) two-dimensional point and 2) pressure level of user's pressing gesture. The formula is:

$$M = \sum_{i=1}^{n} p_i \quad (1)$$

$$x = (\sum_{i=1}^{n} p_i x_i) / M \quad (2)$$

$$y = (\sum_{i=1}^{n} p_i y_i) / M \quad (3)$$

where n is the number of sensor modules. p_i is the pressure that is the total value of photoreflector values at sensor module i. x_i and y_i represent the x-y coordinates of sensor i. M is total value of pressure, and will be used as the pressure level.

Data Visualization

We designed software for visualizing the sensor data based on the pressure widgets developed by Ramos et al. [15]. The color and shape of the displayed image change with changes in pressure (Figure 14). The image can be viewed from various viewpoints such as the top, side and front.

EXAMPLE APPLICATIONS

To help illustrate the utility of the FuwaFuwa sensor module, we present several example domains where the technology could be deployed.

Music Instrument

We converted a cushion into a music composer using FuwaFuwa (Figure 15). Two sensors were embedded in the either side of the cushion and it can detect the touch position and applied pressure. Keys are shown in different colors (projected) and the pitch of each key can be changed using the amount of pressure applied. Multiple cushions can be combined to make a multi-user music composer application.

Soft Interactive Robot

Many researchers have been exploring the usage of soft robots because softness would help to reduce the psychological distance between robots and humans [16, 23]. With this in mind, we developed a soft pet robot named "sofmo" using one FuwaFuwa sensor module. The robot detects user actions and reacts accordingly. The robot changes its voice in accordance with changes in touch pressure (Figure 16) and moves its eyes (actuated by servo motors) towards the touch position (Figure 17). It can thus support physical interactions such as hitting, throwing, and hugging, and can be used as a safe robotic toy for children or to provide therapy for elderly people. Additionally, robots located remotely can be synchronized to provide a new form of communication media [18].

Gaming Peripherals

We installed a FuwaFuwa sensor module in a small spherical cushion to create a game controller for a simple game (Figure 18). The user controls the game character by manipulating the surface of the cushion. Different actions such as squeeze, hit, push, and rub are used to trigger different actions.

Figure 15: Music instrument

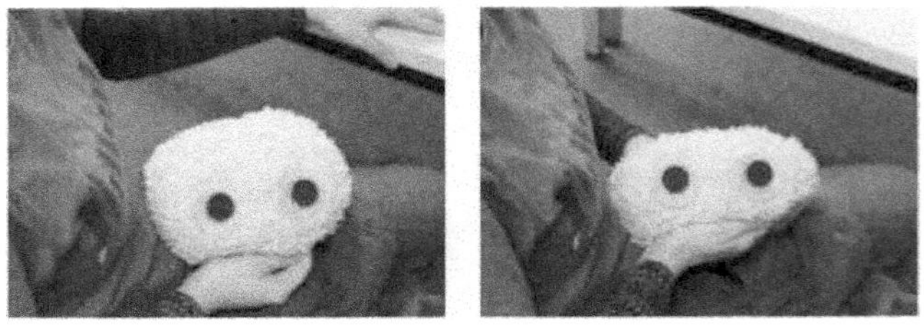

Figure 16: Voice changes with change in touch pressure

Figure 17: Eyes move toward touch position

We also developed an entertainment application—a balancing game. An ice floe carrying some penguins tips when the user shifts his/her center of gravity on the beanbag chair, which used as the game controller (Figure 19). The size of the beanbag chair is 1 m in diameter, and four sensor modules in the chair are used to measure the axis of the center of gravity of the user. The FuwaFuwa sensor module can also be applied to health-related games incorporating body movements [14, 27].

Domestic Media Controller

Soft objects are commonly found in home environments. We created a media controller application for a living room by converting a cushion into a remote controller for a digital home theatre system. Three FuwaFuwa sensor modules are installed in the cushion, and a media control menu is projected onto the cushion (Figure 20). The user pushes the cushion in the appropriate places to select the desired functions.

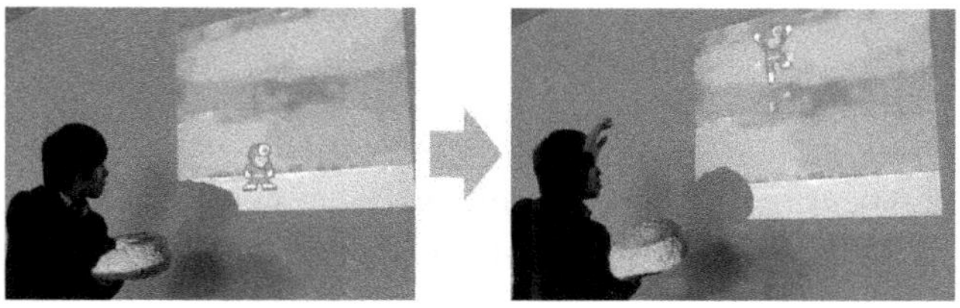

Figure 18: Game controller

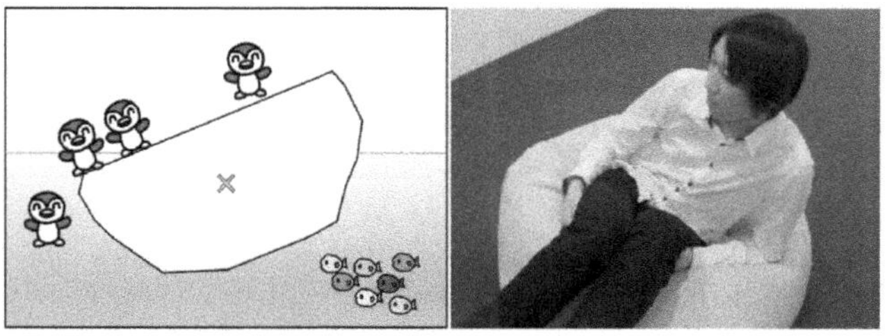

Figure 19: Balancing game display (left); beanbag chair as game controller (right)

Figure 20: Media controller

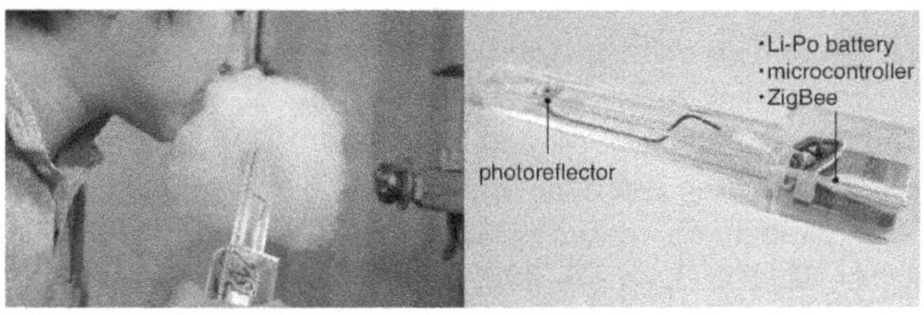

Figure 21: Stick for holding candy floss

Entertainment Candy Floss

Candy floss (or cotton candy) has properties very similar to those of cotton. We attached a photoreflector to a stick holding candy floss (Figure 21). The stick (made from acrylic) was embedded with a microcontroller, wireless module, and a small battery. The stick detects when the user eats the floss and responds by playing a sound.

These are but a few examples of possible usages, showing how the FuwaFuwa sensor module can be used to enhance our daily life in a pleasurable manner.

Human Activity Sensors

Because the FuwaFuwa sensor module is small, it can be installed in such household objects as sofas, pillows, and beds. Moreover, it can detect a person's behavior and condition [3]. For example, a module installed in a pillow was used to detect a user's behavior. When the user falls asleep, the surrounding lights are automatically dimmed.

DISCUSSION

Advantages

The FuwaFuwa sensor module has three important advantages over existing technologies for soft interfaces. Firstly, it does not spoil the softness of the object into which it is embedded, mainly because it requires no physical connection and is relatively small. Secondly, it can detect a wide range of variations in deformation. As shown in the experimental results, it can detect gradual changes in polyester cotton density and thus different deformation levels. Finally, it can be easily installed in almost any soft object because no physical connections are required. We believe that these features of the FuwaFuwa sensor module enable it to be used to create powerful and economical ambient sensor environments for household applications.

Accuracy

Overall, the system recognized the user input (points and pressure levels) on the soft object's surface accurately. In the media controller application, which provides four selections on the object's surface, the system recognized every user selection with four sensor modules. In the game controller application, the user could select various types of shotguns by adjusting the pushing time. However, there were cases of incorrect operations. In one case, for example, lengthy use shifted the orientation of the modules in the object, which distorted their calibration. In another case, the cotton stuffing clogged up a photoreactor opening.

Limitation and Future Work

Our FuwaFuwa sensor module is a "proof-of-concept" implementation, so that it has some hardware limitations. The Li-Po battery can supply power for only up to 3 hours, after which the user has to remove and charge the battery. Because the sensor module is installed within a soft object, removing it to charge the battery is inconvenient, especially when it is located deep in the object such as a beanbag chair. Also, its diameter is 64 mm, meaning that it cannot be installed it in very small and/or thin objects such as small plush toys, comforters, rugs, and clothing. There is thus a trade-off between available usage time and module size (current battery, 350mAh Li-Po battery 36mm vs. smaller 110mAh 28mm). The current implementation of FuwaFuwa uses a general-purpose microcontroller (arduino) and a commercial ZigBee module. In a more customized implementation however, we can select components with smaller footprint and integrate them into a more power-efficient system with smaller form factor. For larger objects such as beanbag chairs that are not normally moved, an external power supply might be more appropriate. Furthermore, we plan to use power-saving mechanisms such as activity detection using an accelerometer or a single IR sensor, power hopping, and so on. Currently, the sensor's cover is made of hard plastic. In the future, we plan to use soft materials such as polyurethane rubber.

An IR camera is used to calibrate the module locations. However, fabrics that are tightly woven or are heavy (such as velour and leather) block IR light. Moreover, if the modules are installed deep in the soft material, it is hard for the IR camera to recognize the IR light. Additionally, having to hold the camera over the object to capture the image is inconvenient, intrusive, and troublesome for the user. A better calibration method would be to have the modules detect their location automatically simply by having the user touch the object a few times.

CONCLUSION

We have developed a sensor module that enables a user to interact directly with soft objects. Our FuwaFuwa sensor module can be embedded in typical soft objects in the household without complex installation procedures and without spoiling the softness of the object because it requires no physical connection. Using a directional, photoreflectivity-based shape deformation measurement technique, it can detect a wide range of deformations. A variety of example applications illustrate the utility of the FuwaFuwa sensor module. An evaluation of the proposed deformation measurement technique confirmed its effectiveness.

REFERENCES

1. Baudisch, P., Sinclair, M. and Wilson, A. Soap: a pointing device that works in mid-air. In *Proc. UIST '06*, ACM (2006), pp. 43–46.
2. Chang, J., MacLean, K. and Yohanan, S. Gesture Recognition in the Haptic Creature. In *Proc. EuroHaptics '10*, pp. 385–391.
3. Choe, E. K., Kientz, J. A., Halko, S., Fonville, A., Sakaguchi, D. and Watson, N. F. Opportunities for computing to support healthy sleep behavior. In *Ext. Abst. CHI '10*, ACM (2010), pp. 3661–3666.
4. Furukawa, M., Uema, Y., Sugimoto, M. and Inami, M. Fur interface with bristling effect induced by vibration. In *Proc. AH '10*, ACM (2010), Article 17, 6 pages.
5. Harrison, C. and Hudson, S. E. Providing Dynamically Changeable Physical Buttons on a Visual Display. In *Proc. CHI '09*, ACM (2009), pp. 299–308.
6. Hiramatsu, R. Puyo-con. In *ACM SIGGRAPH ASIA 2009 Art Gallery & Emerging Technologies*, ACM (2009), pp. 81–81.
7. Inaba, M., Hoshino, Y., Nagasaka, K., Kagami, S. and Inoue, H. A full-body tactile sensor suit using electrically conductive fabric and strings. In *Proc. IROS '96*, IEEE (1996), pp. 450–457.
8. Johnson, M. P., Wilson, A., Blumberg, B., Kline, C. and Bobick, A. Sympathetic interfaces: using a plush toy to direct synthetic characters. In *Proc. CHI '99*, ACM (1999), pp. 152–158.
9. Kadowaki, A., Yoshikai, T., Hayashi, M., Inaba, M. Development of Soft Sensor Exterior Embedded with Multi-axis Deformable Tactile Sensor System. In *Proc. Ro-Man '09*, IEEE (2009), pp.1093–1098.
10. Marti, S. and Schmandt, C. Physical embodiments for mobile communication agents. In *Proc. UIST '05*, ACM (2005), pp. 231–240.
11. Miyashita, T., Tajika, T., Ishiguro, H., Kogure, K. and Hagita, N. Haptic communication between humans and robots. In *Proc. ISRR '05*, 2005.
12. Murakami, T. and Nakajima, N. Direct and intuitive input device for 3-D shape deformation. In *Proc. CHI '94*, ACM (1994), pp. 233–236.
13. Nakajima, K., Itoh, Y., Yoshida, A., Takashima, K., Kitamura, Y. and Kishino, F. FuSA2 touch display. In *ACM SIGGRAPH 2010 Emerging Technologies*, ACM (2010), Article 11, 1 pages.
14. Nintendo, Wii Fit, http://www.nintendo.co.jp/wii/rfnj/
15. Ramos, G., Boulos, M. and Balakrishnan, R. Pressure widgets. In *Proc. CHI '04*, ACM (2004), pp. 487–494.
16. Samani, H. A., et al. A Design Process for Lovotics. Human - Robot Personal Relationships. In *Proc. HRPR '10*, Springer LNICST series, Volume 59, pp. 118–125.
17. Sato, T., Mamiya, H., Koike, H. and Fukuchi, K. Photoelastictouch: transparent rubbery tangible interface using an lcd and photoelasticity. In *Proc. UIST '09*, ACM (2009), pp. 43–50.
18. Sekiguchi, D., Inami, M. and Tachi, S. RobotPHONE: RUI for Interpersonal Communication. In *Ext. Abst. CHI '01*, ACM (2001), pp. 277–278.
19. Slyper, R., Poupyrev, I. and Hodgins, J. Sensing through structure: designing soft silicone sensors. In *Proc. TEI '11*, ACM (2011), pp. 213–220.
20. Smith, R. T., Thomas, B. H. and Piekarski, W. Digital foam interaction techniques for 3D modeling. In *Proc. VRST '08*, ACM (2008), pp. 61–68.
21. Thubuthubu-shugei-wata, Arai Corporation, http://www.sofiapack.com/hobby.html
22. Ueki, A., Kamata, M. and Inakage, M. Tabby: designing of coexisting entertainment content in everyday life by expanding the design of furniture. In *Proc. ACE '07*, ACM (2007), pp. 72–78.
23. Wada, K. and Shibata, T. Social effects of robot therapy in a care house - change of social network of the residents for two months. In *Proc. ICRA '07*, IEEE (2007), pp. 1250–1255.
24. Weinberg, G. Orth, M. and Russo, P. The embroidered musical ball: a squeezable instrument for expressive performance. In *Ext. Abst. CHI '00*, ACM (2000), pp. 283–284.
25. Weiss, M., Wagner, J., Jansen, Y., Jennings, R., Khoshabeh, R., Hollan, J. D. and Borchers, J. 2009. SLAP widgets: bridging the gap between virtual and physical controls on tabletops. In *Proc. CHI '09*, ACM (2009), pp. 481–490.
26. Winnicott, D. (1953). Transitional objects and transitional phenomena, *Int. J. Psychoanal*, 34, pp. 89–97.
27. Yasumoto, M. Balance ball interface. In *ACM SIGGRAPH ASIA 2008 Art Gallery & Emerging Technologies*, ACM (2008), pp. 41–41.
28. Yonezawa, T., Clarkson, B., Yasumura, M. and Mase, K. Context-aware sensor-doll as a music expression device. In *Ext. Abst. CHI '01*, ACM (2001), pp. 307–308.

Modular and Deformable Touch-Sensitive Surfaces Based on Time Domain Reflectometry

Raphael Wimmer
University of Munich
Amalienstr. 17, 80333 Munich, Germany
raphael.wimmer@ifi.lmu.de

Patrick Baudisch
Hasso Plattner Institute
Potsdam, Germany
patrick.baudisch@hpi.uni-potsdam.de

ABSTRACT
Time domain reflectometry, a technique originally used in diagnosing cable faults, can also locate where a cable is being *touched*. In this paper, we explore how to extend time domain reflectometry in order to touch-enable thin, modular, and deformable surfaces and devices. We demonstrate how to use this approach to make smart clothing and to rapid prototype touch sensitive objects of arbitrary shape. To accomplish this, we extend time domain reflectometry in three ways: (1) *Thin:* We demonstrate how to run time domain reflectometry on a single wire. This allows us to touch-enable thin metal objects, such as guitar strings. (2) *Modularity:* We present a two-pin connector system that allows users to daisy chain touch-sensitive segments. We illustrate these enhancements with 13 prototypes and a series of performance measurements. (3) *Deformability*: We create deformable touch devices by mounting stretchable wire patterns onto elastic tape and meshes. We present selected performance measurements.

ACM Classification: H5.2 [Information interfaces and presentation]: User Interfaces: Input Devices and Strategies, Interaction Styles.

Keywords: touch sensing, time domain reflectometry, TDR, wearable, deformable, input, capacitive sensing.

General terms: Design, Human factors.

INTRODUCTION
Traditional touch sensing technologies, such as capacitive [4] or resistive sensing [16], require at least *O(n)* cable connections to drive an *n* x *n* sensing grid [1]. Large numbers of cables, however, result in thick and inflexible connections. This becomes an issue when touch-enabling deformable objects, such as smart clothing [20], where deformability, modularity, and form factor are essential.

In this paper, we propose adapting touch sensing based on *time domain reflectometry* (*TDR* [22]) to overcome these limitations. In TDR, a controller injects an electric pulse into a cable. As the impulse travels down the wire, any defect along the cable causes a partial echo, a pulse of reduced amplitude that travels back to the controller.

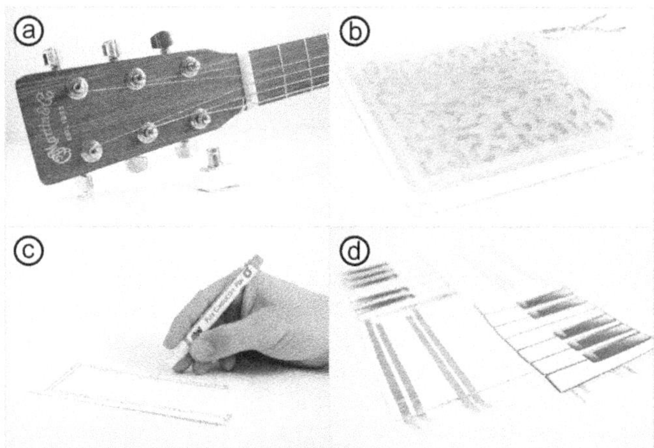

Figure 1: We use time domain reflectometry to touch-enable new devices and form factors including (a) *very thin* objects, such as guitar strings. (b) We use fractal wire layouts to create touch sensors that are *flexible* and *stretchable*. (c) Using conductive ink, we allow users to *sketch* touch-sensitive interfaces. (d) By daisy chaining wires, we create *modular* touch-sensors, such as this paper piano.

This echo allows computing the location of the defect: we obtain the distance to the defect by dividing the time delay between injection and echo by twice the speed of electricity in cables (50-70% of the speed of light, depending on cable type).

While TDR was originally used to diagnose defects in electric cables, engineers discovered as early as 1964 that TDR also responds to a cable being *touched* [22]. A recent US patent [6] proposes using the effect to touch-enable keypads by routing a cable in a serpentine layout behind the buttons. In a recent poster submission [15] Huang et al. propose using the same design on a printed circuit board to touch-enable a letter-size touchpad.

We argue that the possibility of sensing touches along a single pair of wires makes TDR a promising candidate for ultra mobile/wearable devices and smart clothing. To enable this, we present three extensions to TDR, which together allow for a range of new device designs, including the ones shown in Figure 1.

(1) *Thin:* We demonstrate how to use time domain reflectometry on a single wire. This allows us to touch-enable thin metal objects, such as guitar strings. (2) *Modularity:* We present a two-pin connector system that allows users to daisy chain devices. (3) *Deformability*: We create deformable touch devices by mounting fractal wire patterns onto

elastic tape and meshes. Then we demonstrate how to use TDR to allow users to rapidly prototype touch sensitive objects.

We also present selected performance measurements. Using a reflectometer built in 1975 (*Tektronix 1502*), we obtain a precision of one millimeter and a latency of 100ms. Using parallel traces of copper foil, we obtain a signal-to-noise ratio of up to 27 dB, which is similar to common capacitive touchscreen controllers. Applying an adaptive moving average filter we obtain a signal-to-noise-ratio of 37 dB without affecting responsiveness (the filter does introduce lag when recognizing dragging though; we thus recommend the filter for touch recognition only).

While today's high-resolution reflectometers are bulky and expensive, we anticipate that the required functionality may soon be achieved using affordable off-the-shelf time-to-digital converter ICs.

RELATED WORK

The work presented in this paper is related to touch sensing, smart clothing, and time domain reflectometry.

Touch Sensing on Curved or Flexible Surfaces

Today, the two predominant touch-sensing technologies are capacitive [4] and resistive [16] technologies. Unlike resistive touch sensors, capacitive sensors activate even on light touch. According to Dijkstra et al. [8], for example, operating surfaces based on the resistive *Touchco* requires a significant amount of force. Grasping capacitive *Displax* film renders a large part of the surface insensitive to touch [8].

Most touch-sensitive surfaces in use today are planar. However, interaction on non-planar surfaces has gained interest among researchers [25]. Flexible touch-sensitive films, such as *Displax* and *Touchco*, can be bent along a single axis only. Custom designs based on capacitive sensors allow touch-enabling arbitrary shapes, but their shape cannot be modified later [34]. Also, connecting individual sensors to the controller results in a large number of connecting wires [32].

Also optical touch sensing methods (e.g. [21, 37]) require a number of optical fibers proportional to the desired resolution. Range finders (e.g., *SideSight* [5]) allow sensing touch using a compact form factor, but strongly convex shapes are subject to occlusion. Sensing based on microphone arrays (e.g., *Skinput* [12]), allows users to tap, but offer only limited support for dragging.

Wearables and Smart Clothes

In wearable computing, touch-enabled fabrics allow users to interact anywhere. To allow for optimal integration, touch sensors should to be as compliant as the fabric. So far, there are two layout approaches for touch-enabling fabric: (a) a matrix of orthogonally overlapping conductive strips separated by a non-conductive insulator [14], or (b) arrays of distinct sensors [23]. *Pinstripe* by Karrer et al. [17] detects pinching and rolling of cloth between the fingers by scanning for connections between parallel conductive threads sewn into the fabric. Wagner et al. [35] propose an 'electronic skin' where small rigid subcircuit islands are connected by stretchable thin-film conductors and embedded in a silicone sheet.

Cord input [28] allows using a cord as an input device. However, the membrane potentiometers used in this prototype offer only single-touch tracking and are both expensive and susceptible to bending and force.

Time Domain Reflectometry

As discussed earlier, TDR works by sending an electric pulse along a wire. In reality, TDR uses two wires: One wire is connected to the pulse generator and measurement circuit; the other wire is connected to ground, thereby coupling the sensing wire to ground with a constant capacitance. At discontinuities, where the *characteristic impedance* changes along the cable, a part of the pulse is reflected back to the measuring device.

Such changes in characteristic impedance are caused by changes in the resistance, the inductance, or the capacitance of the wire pair. While initially developed to test cables, this has allowed TDR to also be used to measure soil humidity and detect soil movement [19], to locate microscopic defects in integrated circuits [11], and to recognize strains and fractures in buildings and bridges [31].

Engineers distinguish three termination types of TDR [33]. At the end of the cable, the pulse is reflected at *open ends*; the pulse may disappear when wires are terminated with *matching impedance*; or an inverted pulse is reflected when ends are *short circuited*. As the reflectometer has high impedance inputs, a pulse in a cable with open ends may travel back and forth several times, causing erroneous detection of faults.

In this paper, we use a time domain reflectometer that injects a short electric pulse into the cable. Some reflectometers use a step function instead. While the resulting signal looks differently, it contains the same information.

UNDERLYING PHYSICS & DESIGN IMPLICATIONS

In the remainder of this paper we present several circuit designs for TDR touch sensors. The functioning of these designs relies on optimizing a range of parameters, such as wire thicknesses, minimum distances, and dimensions of insulation layers. Since the aforementioned related work [6, 15] lacks a description of the underlying physics, we provide one here. Throughout the paper, this discussion helps us explain which designs work best and why.

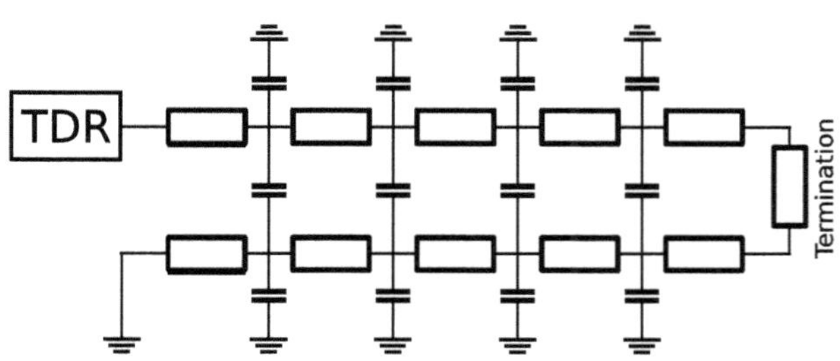

Figure 2: Lumped circuit model of wire pair connected to a time domain reflectometer. Each wire is capacitively coupled to the environment and to the other wire.

Underlying Physics

Figure 2 shows a lumped circuit model of the wire pair. Each wire can be modeled as a series of resistors with very low resistance. In addition, each wire segment forms a capacitor with the parallel wire segment. If the wire diameter, the distance between wires, and the properties of the dielectric between the wires are constant along the cable, the capacitance values between the segments are equal.

TDR touch sensing relies on detecting capacitance changes caused by conductive objects near the wire pair. The user's finger capacitively couples to each wire and thus creates a capacitive shunt between the wire pair. This increases the capacitance at the touch location, causing a partial (inverted) reflection of the TDR pulse (Figure 3). The larger the capacitance change, the greater the amplitude of the reflection. This effect is somewhat similar to *transmit mode* electric field sensing [30], used e.g. by *DiamondTouch* [7]. This allows for simultaneous multi-touch sensing, because only a part of the pulse energy gets reflected back at each touch location.

While it is also possible to measure cables with junctions using TDR, common approaches require simultaneous measurements from multiple ends to distinguish between reflections from different branches [9]. In this paper, we limit our discussion to the case of a single continuous wire pair without junctions.

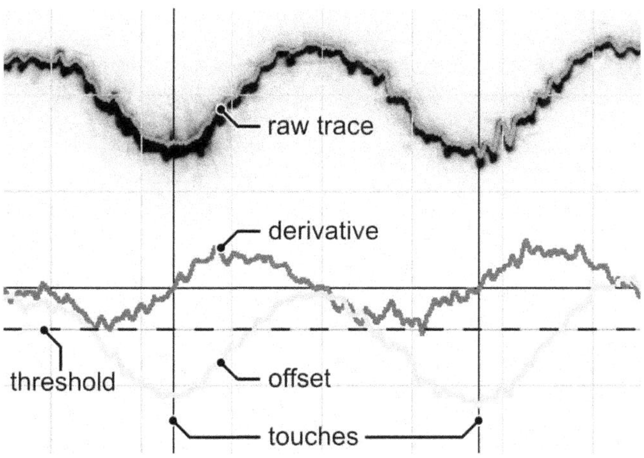

Figure 3: Our approach allows detecting multiple touches on a cable: In this TDR trace two touches were detected by locating negative peaks in the raw trace that also form a local minimum, i.e., derivative is zero.

Implications for Device Design

The principles discussed above have implications for device designers. By increasing the relative change in capacitance effected by a touch, we can enhance touch sensitivity. This is the case …

(1) with increasing distance between both wires, which also decreases the capacitance between wires,

(2) with decreasing distance between wires and the touching finger, and

(3) with increasing size of the contact area between finger and wire.

This means, for example, that parallel strips of copper foil (Figure 4b) are more sensitive to touch than round wires (Figure 4a). We can also increase touch sensitivity by using wires spaced out more widely—up to a maximum of a human finger width, after which point users cannot make contact with both wires at the same time anymore. However, there is a tradeoff between cable width and flexibility, which needs to be evaluated depending on the application.

Coaxial cable (Figure 4c) is barely touch-sensitive, because the finger causes barely any capacitive coupling between inner wire and shield. Deforming a coaxial cable locally, however, changes its impedance, generating a weak, wide echo.

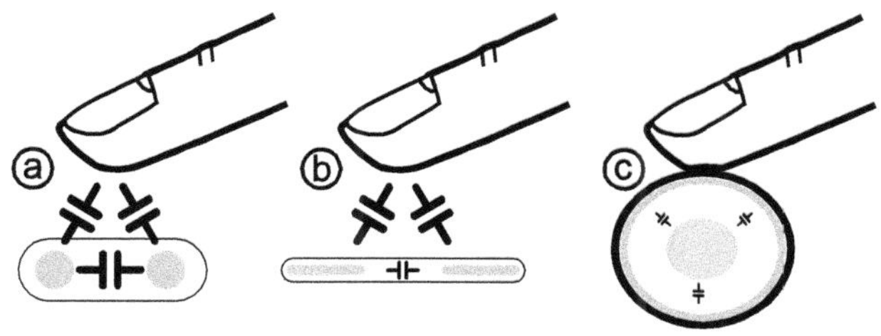

Figure 4: Capacitances between finger and cable: (a) two-wire cable, (b) wide copper traces or foil, and (c) coaxial cable.

Another adverse effect is crosstalk between a wire pair that runs parallel to or crosses another wire pair. A common countermeasure is to employ *coplanar waveguides*, where the active wire is shielded by *two* parallel grounded wires instead of one [15]. Also appropriate spacing of parallel cables mitigates crosstalk. We suggest a spacing of at least twice the distance between the wire pair.

Based on this understanding, we can now discuss our prototypical implementation.

OUR IMPLEMENTATION 1975

The need to process electrical signals in the pico-second range makes reflectometers still comparably expensive to date. However, reflectometers with millimeter resolution have been in use for decades. We conducted the research presented in this paper using a used Tektronix 1502 Reflectometer built around 1975 (Figure 5), which we bought online for €300. The reflectometer was calibrated in 2010.

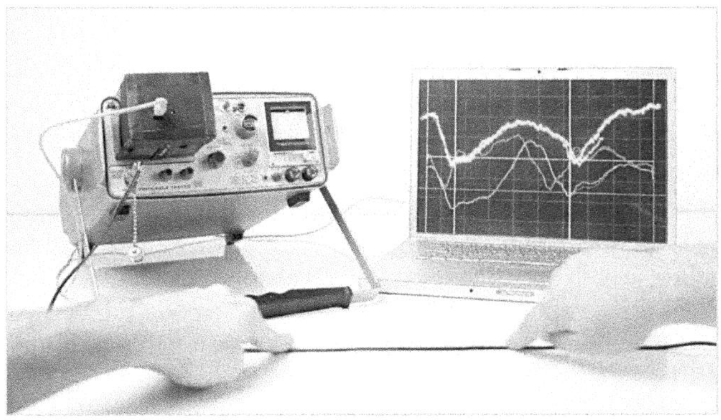

Figure 5: Our experimental setup is based on a *Tektronix 1502* reflectometer built in 1975.

The device offers no digital output and instead graphs the signal on its CRT screen. We bypass the lack of a digital output by capturing the CRT screen using a Point Grey FireFly FireWire camera (640x480px, 20fps). We then reconstruct the graph from the camera image using OpenCV and NumPy by locating the brightest pixel in each column. We extract the delta between current and untouched state by applying background subtraction. Finally, we smooth the signal using a weak low-pass filter over each trace and apply an adaptive moving average filter.

Adaptive moving average (AMA) filters are moving average filters that adjust sample weights dynamically [38]. Our implementation weights samples whose value changes a lot between frames stronger than others. Consequently, the filter smoothes low-amplitude noise strongly, while preserving rapid changes, as they occur during touch events or when users are dragging. The main benefit of AMA filters is therefore that they offer low latency for fast movements while keeping noise low for slow movement.

The screen shown in Figure 3 illustrates how our prototype senses touch. The system reports touches at negative peaks, i.e. wherever the signal (green line) drops below a certain threshold (gray horizontal line) and the first derivative is zero (blue line). In the shown example there are two such points and the system indicates their locations on the cable using vertical lines.

As the Tektronix CRT screen shows only a limited time window, we can see only a limited distance range of the cable. Zooming all the way in, we can capture a 21cm cable segment with a theoretical maximum resolution of 0.3mm. On the other end of the zooming range, we can capture a 400m segment with a maximum resolution of 60cm. Modern digital reflectometers, such as the *Mohr CT100* series, suffer neither of these limitations.

Using this experimental setup we have touch-enabled ultra-thin objects, modular devices, and stretchable 2D surfaces.

ULTRA-THIN TOUCH SENSORS

In this section, we demonstrate how to touch-enable cables and wires and in particular how to do so using a single wire.

Overloading Touch onto Everyday Objects

Touch-enabling objects that already contain a wire pair requires only little effort; we simply overload touch sensing onto the existing wires pair.

In one instance, we have retrofitted a pair of off-the-shelf headphones with TDR-based touch sensing. This design allows users to pause, play, and skip tracks by squeezing the respective locations on the headphone cable; users adjust volume by sliding fingers or the entire hand along the cable.

We implemented this by connecting the left and right channels of the headphone to the reflectometer. The ground wires, which are connected to the headphone plug, were not used for sensing. We found the capacitive coupling caused by the common ground wires to decrease touch sensitivity only slightly.

We obtained best results with headphones that use standard "ribbon" cables, i.e., two unshielded wires located next to each other. Coaxial cables worked as well, but as discussed earlier were much less sensitive, because touches had less of an effect on local capacitance. The two wires of the cable we used were 2.5mm apart, which worked well.

Another limitation of our outdated reflectometer is that it is not capable of testing live wires (its pulse generator might can get damaged even by small currents). To protect the device, we therefore did not connect the headphone to an actual audio source in this demo. More modern reflectometers do not suffer from this limitation.

Application to Metal Objects—Extension to Single Wire

As mentioned above, TDR generally uses two parallel wires. This works fine for most applications, such as the headphones. However, when we want to touch-enable individual wires, such as a guitar string, the two-wire approach reaches its limit.

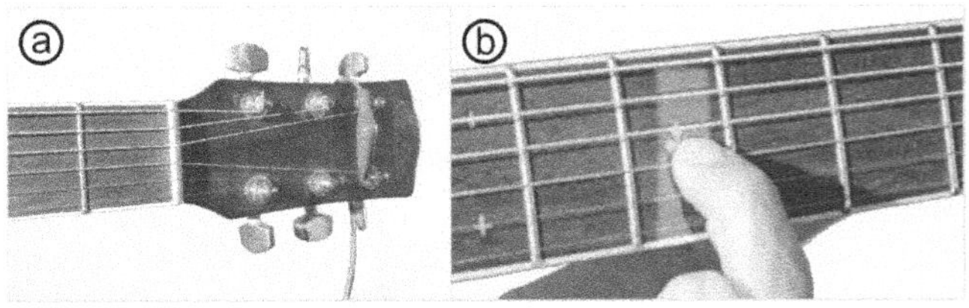

Figure 6: (a) We have touch-enabled a guitar string of an otherwise unmodified acoustic guitar. (b) In the shown demo application, the touch location is highlighted in real-time using a projected white bar.

To address this, we have developed a TDR version that locates touch along a single wire. We demonstrate this by touch-enabling a guitar string (Figure 6). Applied to all strings, this approach could be used to capture the user's grip patterns while playing a guitar without applying any modifications to the instrument itself.

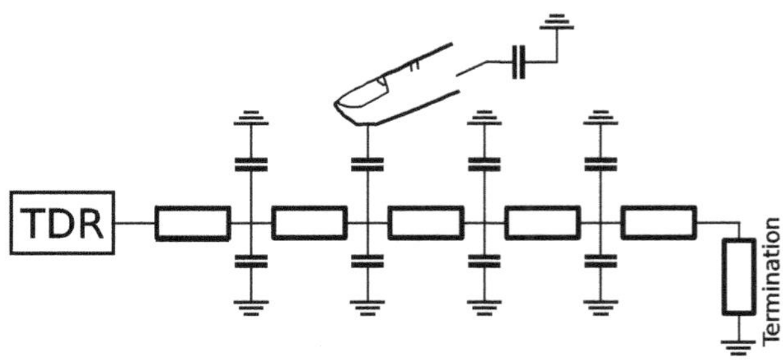

Figure 7: A lumped circuit model of a single wire touch-enabled using TDR. Touching the wire increases its capacitive coupling to the environment at the touch location.

The lumped circuit model in Figure 7 illustrates the underlying physical effect we exploit. A single wire is capacitively coupled to ground via the environment. This coupling is very weak, however. A finger touching the wire will increase the capacitive coupling, increasing the characteristic impedance at the touch location. This works for both bare and insulated wires. Grounding the wire's end prevents spurious touches and the touching object needs to be grounded or offer good capacitive coupling to the environment. Overall, this makes the properties of single-wire TDR similar to those of traditional *loading mode electric field sensing* [30].

Single-wire TDR is subject to two limitations. As most of the pulse gets absorbed by the touching finger, only the touch location closest to the reflectometer can be determined reliably. We therefore modified our algorithm so as to detect only the first touch (Figure 8). Finally, the single-wire approach only works as long as there are no large conductive objects close by, which prevents certain applications, such as touch-enabling the frames of glasses.

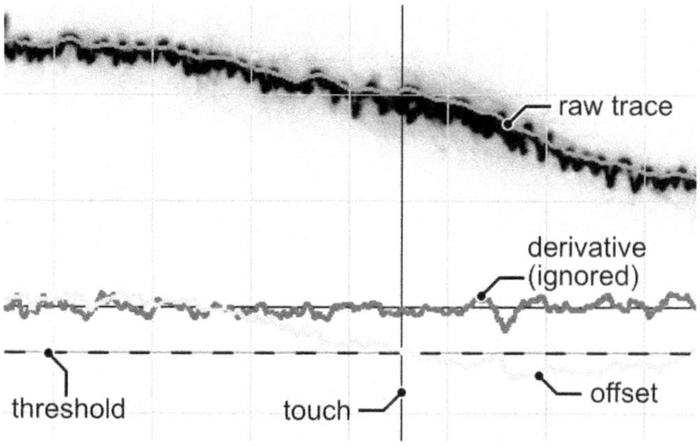

Figure 8: With single-wire sensing, our system detects touch at the location where the characteristic impedance drops below a threshold. Since the signal continues to drop after the touch location, we do not consider the first derivative in single-wire sensing.

MODULAR TOUCH SENSORS

The above examples are exceptions in that they readily offer a set of wires to appropriate. In the more typical case, we touch-enable objects and clothing by applying a touch sensitive strip or sheet.

Tear-Off, Adhesive Touch Strip for Prototyping

To allow users to touch-enable arbitrary objects quickly, e.g., when prototyping touch sensitive devices, we created the *touch tape* shown in Figure 9. It consists of masking tape with two embedded strips of copper foil. The adhesive coating allows users to apply the tape to any flat or curved surface. The tape roller helps users obtain the desired amount.

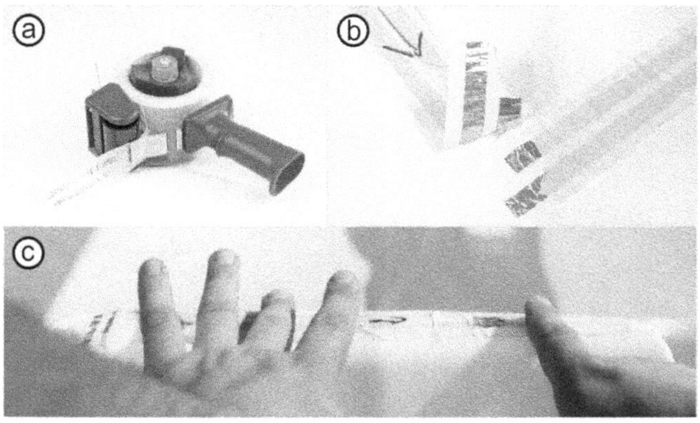

Figure 9: (a) *Touch tape* is masking tape with embedded copper traces. (b) Users can join multiple strips by connecting the trace pairs. (c) We used this setup to control a first person shooter and a racing game in an impromptu gaming session. Note the bimanual use.

Application designers link touch locations to actions by entering a calibration mode, tapping an area on the tape, and then picking the action to be executed on the computer. To give users a sense of where to touch, the application designer may also mark locations or draw widgets such as buttons or sliders onto the tape.

Using thin strips of copper foil with a distance of about 1cm, we minimize capacitance between strips and maximize capacitive coupling to the finger, resulting in a better signal-to-noise ratio. Therefore, the shown parallel strip design is so sensitive that it allows sensing a hovering finger up to about 1cm above the strip. This allows detecting and locating gestures before the finger actually touches the tape (similar to e.g., *PreSense* [24]).

Daisy-Chaining TDR Touch Sensors

Touch tape allows users to (re)assemble multiple pieces of tape into a larger piece by pressing one wire pair onto the other (Figure 9b). This allows creating larger touch-sensitive surfaces or changing their configuration.

As a first proof-of-concept prototype, we applied parallel strips of copper foil to paper piano tiles (Figure 1b). The prototype allows users to add additional octaves by attaching additional 12-key tiles to the end of their keyboard.

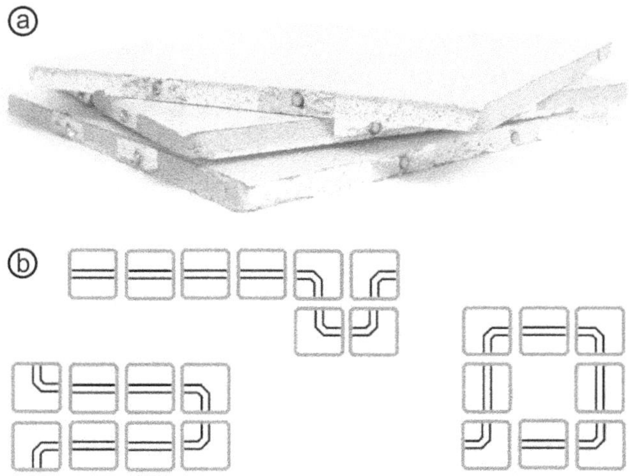

Figure 10: (a) Each floor tile bears electric contacts and magnetic connectors on each of its four sides. The magnets help users connect tiles quickly. (b) Three example layouts created using the same eight floor tiles. Only the first tile needs to be connected to the reflectometer.

We have obtained best sensing results using a short circuit termination. Alternatively, we have achieved less accurate but acceptable tracking using "open ends" (i.e., no termination) which saves users the effort of attaching the terminator.

Floor Tiles

Figure 10 shows a set of eight floor tiles measuring 30cm x 30cm each. Each tile contains a pair of straight or curved metal strips. This design allows users to assemble differently shaped touch-sensitive surfaces. Magnetic connectors hold the tiles together and act as conductive bridges between tiles.

Cable Identifiers Allow Auto-Configuring Device Sets

To allow the system to recognize how a set of modular segments is currently reconfigured, we provide each segment with a unique arrangement of "markers". Markers are simple pieces of copper foil wrapped around the cable segments at object-specific intervals. In the signal trace, markers show up as dents. This allows the system to identify cable segments attached to the reflectometer and, if we avoid symmetries, to determine which side of the segment is connected.

A cable segment's marker pattern remains largely visible when segments are daisy chained. We have exploited this in order to distinguish different 'devices' plugged into a headphone jack (Figure 11). In the shown example, markers were placed at multiples of 14 cm along the wire.

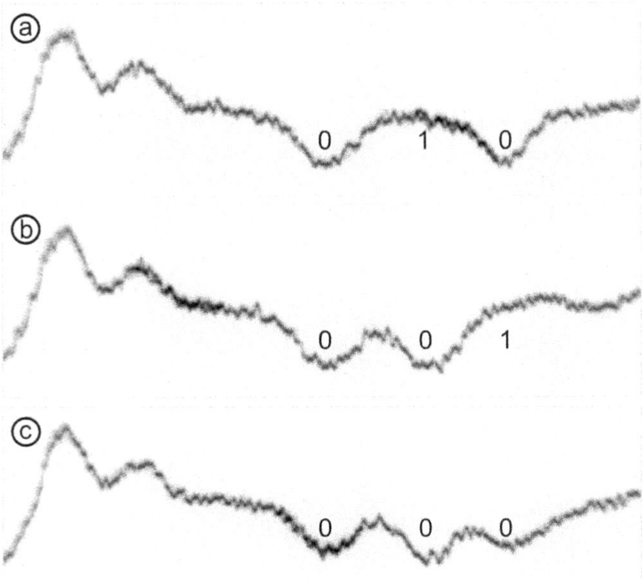

Figure 11: We identify cables by unique patterns of discontinuities. These raw traces belong to three different modules, each of which was marked with a different 3-bit sequence. Binary values are encoded by wrapping short strips of copper foil around the wire pair.

TOUCH-ENABLING DEFORMABLE 2D SURFACES

Touch-enabling surfaces using TDR requires covering the area with the wire pair in a space-filling pattern. Replacing the serpentine pattern proposed by Huang [15] (Figure 12a) we use a Hilbert Curve layout [13] in most of our prototypes (Figure 12b). In our prototypes, we use Hilbert Curves with mitered corners instead of rounded or straight corners. This avoids signal reflection at corners and keeps the diameter—and thus the impedance—of the trace approximately constant.

Hilbert curves offer several benefits:

(1) They offer consistent touch resolution in x and y directions, whereas serpentines offer high resolution along the main direction of the wire, but not perpendicular to it. (2) Hilbert curves ensure that successive wire segments are also close together on the surface. This limits the x/y error resulting from sensing inaccuracies along the wire. (3) Hilbert Curves allow for better differentiation between adjacent touches, as the probability of two adjacent touches falling onto the same wire segment is lower than with the serpentine layout. (4) Hilbert Curves support modularity. Since they are self-similar, users can (repeatedly) cut a Hilbert Curve in half, always resulting in a functional touch-sensitive surface. Similarly, tiles made from Hilbert Curves can be combined to form larger touch-sensitive surfaces. (5) Hilbert Curves result in stretchable layouts, as we discuss in the following section.

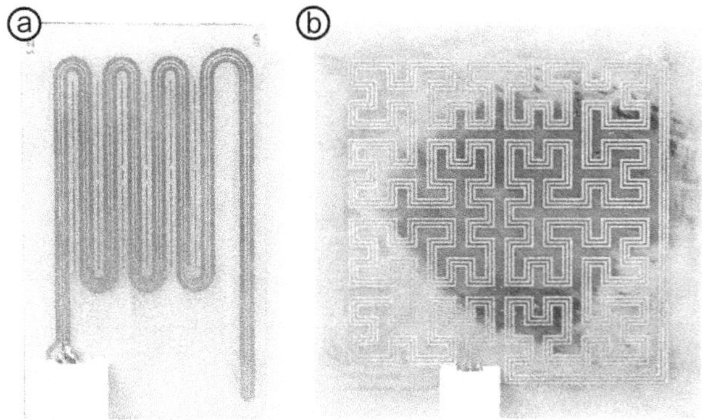

Figure 12: We touch-enable surfaces not (a) using serpentines but (b) using Hilbert curves. In both prototypes, traces are spaced 5mm apart, so that a finger touches at least two different locations along the trace.

Stretchable Strips

A serpentine layout also works fine, as long as the touch-enabled object is stretched along only a single dimension. Figure 13 shows a prototype of a stretchable wristband that we have used to temporarily touch-enable arbitrary objects of different sizes. It is made of conductive thread embedded into a stretchable mesh material.

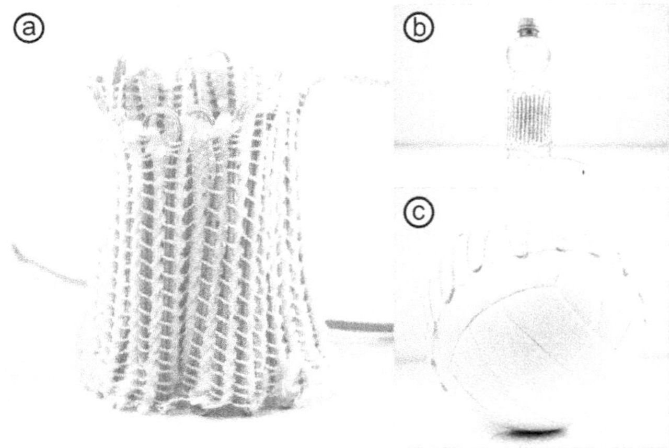

Figure 13: Embedding a cable laid out in a zigzag pattern into a strip of stretchable mesh allows mounting the strip to objects of different sizes.

Note how spatial resolution decreases when the mesh is being stretched, and increases when it is released.

Figure 14 shows a similar prototype, only this time we used conductive thread embedded into strips of a soft silicone support material. When the strip is stretched, the thread is pulled to its full length; upon relaxation, the thread crinkles.

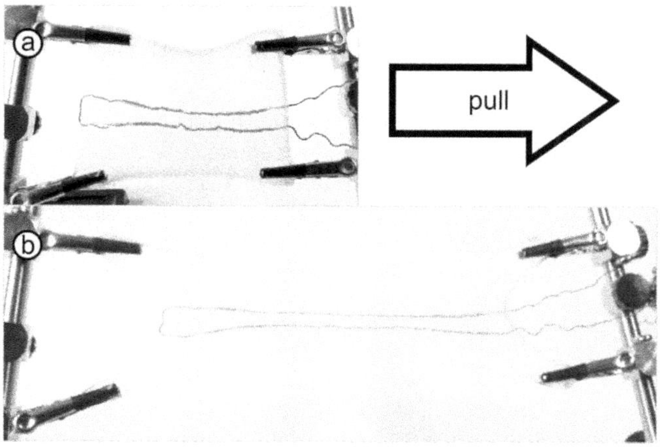

Figure 14: Conductive thread embedded into a silicone strip: (a) relaxed, (b) stretched

Figure 15 shows a touchpad based on the Hilbert Curve; unlike the serpentine designs, it is stretchable in both x and y.

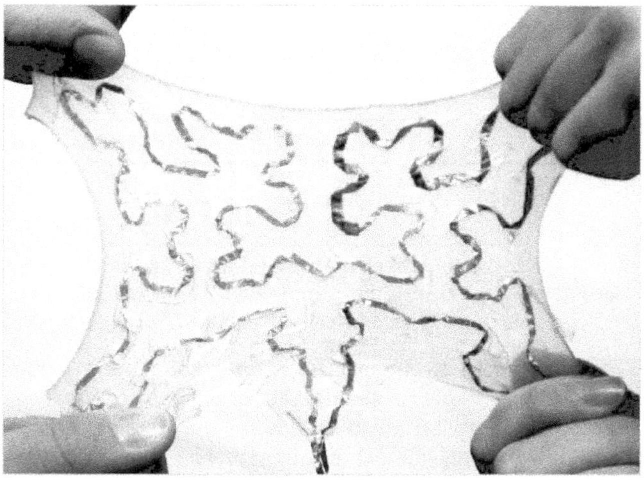

Figure 15: Wire layouts based on the Hilbert Curve are stretchable in x and y direction.

In addition to sensing touch, the design shown in Figure 15 also detects pressure. We achieved this by embedding *two* Hilbert Curves made from copper foil into the silicone, using a technique proposed by Slyper et al. [29]. The two copper foil layers are separated by a thin silicone layer. When a finger applies force to the pad, the two copper layers are pressed together, locally increasing their capacitive coupling. This shows up in the TDR trace. Again, the Hilbert Curve is a beneficial layout, as deformations stay locally confined.

Sketching Touch Sensors

To provide even more flexibility when rapid prototyping interfaces using TDR, we have created interfaces using conductive ink (*Circuitworks CW2200MTP pen*). As illustrated by Figure 16a, this approach allows users to touch-enable an arbitrary surface by drawing parallel conductive traces on a sheet of paper and connecting these to the reflectometer. This allows sketching arbitrary touch-sensitive shapes, allowing designers to create exactly the shapes required by the application (Figure 16b). As we only track impedance changes over time, minor fluctuations in line width and spacing have no effect on sensitivity. Actions can be mapped to touch locations using the same approach as described for the masking tape.

The resulting widgets continue to work when users touch the backside of the paper. We exploit this in order to achieve better affordance: we let users flip the paper around and draw or print GUI widgets that explain the desired interaction onto the sheet. The result is an interactive paper prototype.

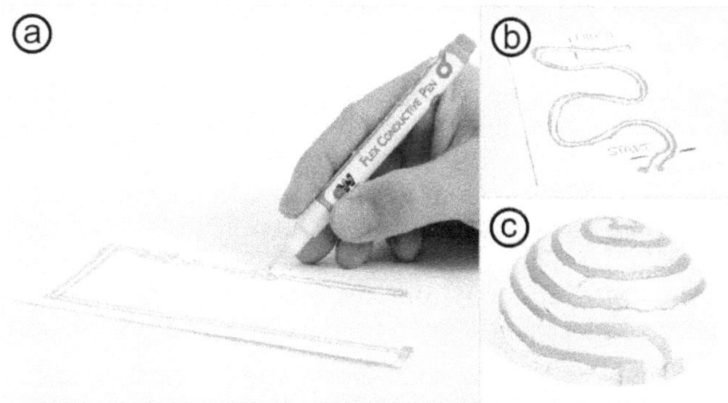

Figure 16: (a) Sketching a TDR touch interface using conductive ink. (b) This allows creating ad-hoc UIs like this path-following game. (c) Using conductive spray paint and hand-cut stencils, arbitrarily shaped objects can be touch-enabled.

Conductive paint is also well suited for making non-planar surfaces touch-sensitive, such as the one shown in Figure 16c. This version was created using a stencil, offering additional precision: (a) Draw rough traces onto the surface using a sharpie pen, (b) apply a thin silicone layer, (c) cut parallel lines into the silicon, following the drawn trace. (d) remove the silicone from the traces, (e) spray-paint the surface with conductive paint (*CRC Industries EMV35*), and finally (e) pull off the remaining silicone.

Using appropriate printing techniques [36], touch-sensitive paper based on TDR might also be mass-produced, e.g. using transparent indium tin oxide (ITO) for the traces.

MEASUREMENTS: SENSITIVITY, PRECISION, LATENCY

To obtain a better understanding of the accuracy and limitations of our approach, we conducted a series of measurements using the following five cable types.

A: flexprint ribbon cable, 0.8mm wide, 0.5mm gap, 0.5m

B: copper foil traces, 8mm wide, 10mm gap, 0.5m long

C: copper foil traces, 20mm wide, 20mm gap, 0.5m long

D: ribbon cable, ∅0.4mm, 0.9 mm gap, length 2.5m long

E: loudspeaker cable, ∅1.5mm, 1.2mm gap, 11m long

We report amplitude changes in a TDR trace in units of mρ (millirho). Here, $\rho = V_{reflected} / V_{pulse}$, i.e. the relation between the amplitudes of reflected pulse and injected pulse. As our reflectometer emits 300 mV pulses, 1 mρ ≙ 0.3 mV.

Figure 17: Cable types tested in our evaluation of sensor characteristics. A-C consist of flat copper foil traces, D and E use stranded wires.

Setup

Cables A to D were connected to the reflectometer using a 95cm cable with alligator clips. Cable E already had a BNC connector. Cables were laid out in a straight line, as shown in Figure 17.

For consistency, we simulated touches using metal weights placed across the cable's wires or traces: For cables A to C we simulated the touch of an index finger at 1 Newton using a 10g 28mm x 14mm x 8mm ferrite block. For cables D and E, we simulated a finger slightly enclosing the cable using a 10g 22mm x 26mm x 3mm steel plate. Weights were placed 250mm from the start of the cable/traces, which was located 1200mm from the reflectometer's input.

In order to reflect the noise levels *along* a cable segment, we calculated the root-mean-square (RMS, similar to standard deviation) changes in mρ for a single trace of 400px width. We then took the maximum noise level of 200 frames. For a discussion of signal to noise ratios, see Atmel's Touch Sensor Design Guide [1]. To give a better overview of the expected performance, we computed all results without filtering (respective first row) and using a 32 sample adaptive moving average filter (respective second rows).

For each cable we also recorded 800 samples of the touch location and determined the jitter. We also determined the minimum distance of adjacent touches by placing *two* weights on the cable, and decreased their distance until our algorithm started to merge the two peaks into one.

For determining the latency of our setup, we simultaneously captured the cable and our visualization on video with 25 frames per second. Touch latency was determined as the time between the finger first touching the cable and our software detecting a touch. Dragging latency is the time between the finger stopping at a defined point and our software reporting a touch at that point. The speed of slow touches (1Hz), fast touches (2Hz), slow dragging (12.5cm/s), and fast dragging (50cm/s) was defined by audible clicks at intervals of 1s and 0.5s. We measured 20 instances of each touch and dragging movement, ignoring a total of 4 instances where no touch was detected.

Results

Table 1 shows our results for the five different cable types. Overall, we got a very good signal-to-noise, especially for cable types B and C, which also provided very good precision. Touches were between 1-5mm (RMS) off.

Due to their plastics coating, cables D and E are significantly less sensitive. The minimum distance between touches consequently depends greatly on the cable type and is limited by the ~140ps risetime of the Tektronix 1502. Newer reflectometers like the Mohr CT100HF generate pulses with half the risetime. Note that the values in the table may be understood as lower bounds; touches with a force of more than 1 Newton or users holding the cable between two fingers result in much larger signal changes and thus better recognition.

In addition, we measured the impact of position (= distance from reflectometer) onto touch recognition with cable E in 50cm steps. We found amplitude to decrease in a linear fashion. At a distance of about 6m, the peak started to blend with the background noise. When grasping the cable with the whole hand, we were able to recognize touch at distances of up to 20m.

Cable	Resistivity Signal change on touch (mρ)	Noise RMS (mρ)	Signal to noise (dB)	Error offset RMS (mm)	Min. touch spacing (mm)
A	30	5	15		
		2	23	5	150
B	220	9	27		
		3	37	1	25
C	150	7	26		
		3	34	1	25
D	40	7	15		
		3	22	1	40
E	30	7	12		
		3	20	4	20

Table 1: Sensitivity and spatial resolution of five cable types. Second rows are results after applying a 32-sample adaptive moving average filter. $\rho = V_{reflected} / V_{pulse}$,

The base latency of our specific setup is about 120ms. This is the result of the 20fps update rate of the camera (on average 25ms delay) and about 100ms for transferring, buffering and processing the camera image. The delay is the result of our low-cost implementation; the reflectometer itself reacts instantly to changes.

For cables B and C, signal-to-noise-ratio without filtering is comparable to that of standard capacitive touchscreen controllers (25:1, [3]). For touches, latency is roughly comparable to standard touchscreen setups (80ms, [1]) and seems adequate for many applications [1]. We can stabilize the recognized touch location using the aforementioned filter without adding any latency.

For dragging, in contrast, only light or no filtering should be used. In earlier versions, we experimented with a 32-sample filtering window, i.e. a filter looking back 1.5 seconds. For slow dragging this added about 700ms of latency and about 300ms for fast dragging. Both were quite noticeable, which is why we do not recommend using the filter for dragging.

BENEFITS AND LIMITATIONS

The sensing approach presented in this paper offers four benefits:

1. Touch-enable non-planar and deformable objects. Since cables are compliant and robust, our approach allows us to create stretchable and deformable touch sensitive objects and bringing touch input to novel form factors.

2. In particular, the proposed approach allows *touch-enabling single-wire devices,* such as guitar strings, by switching to single-cable sensing.

3. *Easy to prototype and rearrange.* TDR allows chaining modular sensors without the need for additional controllers. Extensions require only additional cable; touch-sensitive fabric can be mass-produced inexpensively.

4. *Suitable for large installations.* While the prototypes shown in this paper were limited by our outdated reflectometer hardware, devices with higher power and digital interfaces allow applying the concept to installations of much larger scale. In particular, the concept allows tracking a large number of contact points using a single cable. While sensitivity decreases over distance, generating pulses with greater power and shorter risetime can counter this effect.

Limitations

1. Traditional TDR sensing is *susceptible to radio interference.* Mobile phones and other wireless devices (GSM, CDMA, 3G/UMTS, Wifi/Bluetooth) transmit in the GHz range, which can add noise to the TDR signal, reducing sensitivity. Future devices might evade interference by listening to traffic and actively waiting for pauses between packets for sensing. Additionally, TDR variants like spread-spectrum TDR are more robust against noise [10].

2. Time domain reflectometers with high spatial resolution are still *bulky and expensive.* Prices and size can be expected to drop with wider distribution, however. Another alternative might be to make the required hardware from off-the-shelf time-to-digital converter ICs, such as the *acam TDC-GP21*, which already offers a resolution of <50ps, which could enable TDR resolutions of <1cm.

CONCLUSIONS AND FUTURE WORK

In this paper we have demonstrated how to apply time domain reflectometry in order to create thin, modular, and flexible touch strips and surfaces for use in wearable computing and to allow rapid prototyping touch sensitive surfaces. Unlike existing solutions, all sensing takes place over a single pair of wires (or even a single wire), enabling a multitude of new shapes for touch-sensitive surfaces.

As future work, we plan to investigate touch sensing using *optical* TDR. We are also working on a low-cost TDR sensing circuit that can be used for applications where limited resolution is acceptable.

ACKNOWLEDGMENTS

We thank Kay Herschelmann, Doris Hausen and Sebastian Löhmann for their help with filming and/or photographing, and Dominikus Baur, Doris Hausen and Christian Holz for their comments on earlier versions of this paper.

NOTES & SUPPORTING DOCUMENTATION

Source code and further documentation can be found online at http://tdr.wikia.com

REFERENCES

1. Anderson, G., Doherty, R., and Ganapathy, S. User Perception of Touch Screen Latency. In *Marcus, A. Design, User Experience, and Usability. Theory, Methods, Tools and Practice (LNCS 6769)*, Springer, 2011, pp. 195-202.
2. Atmel, Touch Sensors Design Guide, Atmel Corporation, 10620D-AT42-04/09, 2009, p. 9.
3. Barrett, G. and Omote, R. Projected-Capacitive Touch Technology, *Information Display Magazine*, 26(3). 2010, pp. 16-21.
4. Beck, F. and Stumpe, B. Two Devices for Operator Interaction in the Central Control of the New CERN Accelerator, *CERN 73-6*, 1973
5. Butler, A., Izadi, S., and Hodges, S. SideSight: multi-"touch" interaction around small devices. In *Proc. UIST '08,* pp. 201-204.
6. Collins, Ryan V. Methods and apparatus for receiving user input via time domain reflectometry. *US-Patent 2004/0239616 A1,* 2004.
7. Dietz, P. and Leigh, D. DiamondTouch: a multi-user touch technology, In *Proc UIST '01*, pp. 219-226
8. Dijkstra, J., Perez, C., and Vertegaal, R. Evaluating Effects of Structural Holds on Pointing and Dragging Performance with Flexible Displays. In *Proc CHI '11,* pp. 1293-1302.
9. Doorn, E., Tolani, D. Radical Extension of Time Domain Reflectometry for Detection and Location of Flows in Aircraft Wiring Systems, *9th Joint FAA/DoD/NASA Conference on Aging Aircraft*, 2006.
10. Furse, C., Chung, Y.C., Lo, C., and Pendayala, P. A Critical Comparison of Reflectometry Methods for Location of Wiring Faults, *Journal of Smart Structures and Systems*, 2(1), 2006, pp. 25-46
11. Han, D.H., Xu, B.S., Choi, M.J., He, J., Gardiner, S., and Lee, C. Realization of Ultra-Wideband, High-Resolution TDR for Chip-Carrier Packages. In *Proc ASME InterPACK '05*, pp. 1499-1503
12. Harrison, C., Tan, D., and Morris, D. Skinput: appropriating the body as an input surface. In *Proc CHI '10*, pp. 453-462.
13. Hilbert, D. Ueber die stetige Abbildung einer Linie auf ein Flächenstück, Mathematische Annalen, 38, 1891, pp. 459-460.
14. Holleis, P., Schmidt, A., Paasovaara, S., Puikkonen, A., and Häkkila, J. Evaluating capacitive touch input on clothes. *In Proc MobileHCI '08*, pp. 81–90.
15. Huang, C.F. Precise Location of Touch Panel by Employing the Time-Domain Reflectometry. *SID Symposium Digest of Technical Papers,* 40(1), 2009, pp. 1291-1293.
16. Hurst, S. and Parks, J. Electrical Sensor Of Plane Coordinates. *US Patent 3,662,105,* 1972.
17. Karrer, T., Wittenhagen, M., Lichtschlag, L., Heller, F., and Borchers, J. Pinstripe: Eyes-free Continuous Input on Interactive Clothing. *In Proc CHI '11.* pp. 1313-1322.
18. Linz, T., Vieroth, R., Dils, C., Koch, M., Braun, T., Becker, K. F., Kallmayer, C., and Hong. S. Embroidered Interconnections and Encapsulation for Electronics in Textiles for Wearable Electronics Applications. *Advances in Science and Technology*, 60, 2008, pp. 85-94.
19. Malicki, M. A., Plagge, R., Renger, M., and Walczak, R. T. Application of time-domain reflectometry (TDR) soil moisture miniprobe for the determination of unsaturated soil water characteristics from undisturbed soil cores, *Irrigation Science*, 13(2), 1992, pp. 65-72.
20. Mann, S. "Smart clothing": wearable multimedia computing and "personal imaging" to restore the balance between people and their intelligent environments. In *Proc. Multimedia '96*, pp. 163-174.

21. Missinne, J., Van Steenberge, G. , Van Hoe, B. Van Coillie, K., Van Gijseghem, T., Dubruel, P., Vanfleteren, J., and Van Daele, P. An array waveguide sensor for artificial optical skins. *In Proc SPIE 7221*, 722105, 2009.
22. Oliver, B. M. Time Domain Reflectometry, *HP Journal* 15(6), 1964.
23. Perner-Wilson, H., Buechley, L., and Satomi, M. Handcrafting textile interfaces from a kit-of-no-parts. *In Proc TEI '11*, pp. 61-68.
24. Poupyrev, I., Yeo, Z., Griffin, J., and Hudson, S. Sensing Human Activities with Resonant Tuning. In *CHI'10 Extended Abstracts*, pp. 4135-4140.
25. Rekimoto, J., Ishizawa, T., Schwesig, C., and Oba, H. PreSense: interaction techniques for finger sensing input devices. In *Proc UIST '03*, pp. 203-212.
26. Roudaut, A., Pohl, H., and Baudisch, P. Touch on Curved Surfaces. In *Proc CHI '11*, pp. 1011-1020
27. Schwarz, J., Harrison, C., Hudson, S., and Mankoff, J. Cord input: an intuitive, high-accuracy, multi-degree-of-freedom input method for mobile devices. In *Proc. CHI '10,* pp. 1657-1660.
28. Schwarz, J., Harrison, C., Mankoff, J., and Hudson, S. E. Cord Input: An Intuitive, High-Accuracy, Multi-Degree-of-Freedom Input Method for Mobile Devices. *In Proc CHI'10*, pp. 1657-1660.
29. Slyper, R., Poupyrev, I., and Hodgins, J. Sensing through structure: designing soft silicone sensors. *In Proc TEI '11*, pp. 213-220.
30. Smith, J., White, T., Dodge, C., Paradiso, J., Gershenfeld, N., and Allport, D. Electric field sensing for graphical interfaces. *Computer Graphics and Applications, 18*(3), IEEE, 1998, pp. 54–60.
31. Sun, S. Pommerenke, D., Drewniak, J., Chen, G., Xue, L., Brower, M., and Koledintseva, M. A novel TDR-based coaxial cable sensor for crack/strain sensing in reinforced concrete structures. *IEEE Transactions on Instrumentation and Measurement*, 58(8), 2009, pp. 2714-2725
32. Taylor, B. T. and Bove, V. M. Graspables: grasp-recognition as a user interface. In *Proc CHI '09*. pp. 917-926..
33. Tektronix. TDR Impedance Measurements: A Foundation for Signal Integrity. *Application Note*, 2008.
34. Villar, N., Izadi, S., Rosenfeld, D., Benko, H., Helmes, J., Westhues, J., Hodges, S., Butler, A., Ofek, E., Cao, X., and Chen, B. Mouse 2.0: Multi-touch Meets the Mouse. *In Proc. UIST '09*, pp. 33-42.
35. Wagner, S., Lacour, S., Jonesa, J., Hsu, P., Sturm, J., Li, T., and Suo, Z. Electronic skin: architecture and components, *Physica*, E 25, 2004, pp. 326–334.
36. Weigelt, C., Hübler, A. Printed Near Field Communication System. *Lecture Notes in Informatics*, Nr. 133, 2008, pp. 301-306.
37. Wimmer, R. FlyEye: grasp-sensitive surfaces using optical fiber. *In Proc TEI '10*. pp. 245-248.
38. Wimmer, R. Capacitive Sensors for Whole Body Interaction In: *David England (Ed.): Whole Body Interaction*. Springer, Berlin, Germany, 2011, pp. 121-133.

deForm: An Interactive Malleable Surface For Capturing 2.5D Arbitrary Objects, Tools and Touch

Sean Follmer[1], *Micah K. Johnson*[2], *Edward H. Adelson*[2], *Hiroshi Ishii*[1]

[1] MIT Media Lab
Cambridge, MA
{sfollmer, ishii}@media.mit.edu

[2] MIT CSAIL
Cambridge, MA
{kimo, adelson}@csail.mit.edu

ABSTRACT

We introduce a novel input device, deForm, that supports 2.5D touch gestures, tangible tools, and arbitrary objects through real-time structured light scanning of a malleable surface of interaction. deForm captures high-resolution surface deformations and 2D grey-scale textures of a gel surface through a three-phase structured light 3D scanner. This technique can be combined with IR projection to allow for invisible capture, providing the opportunity for co-located visual feedback on the deformable surface. We describe methods for tracking fingers, whole hand gestures, and arbitrary tangible tools. We outline a method for physically encoding fiducial marker information in the height map of tangible tools. In addition, we describe a novel method for distinguishing between human touch and tangible tools, through capacitive sensing on top of the input surface. Finally we motivate our device through a number of sample applications.

ACM Classification: H5.2 [Information interfaces and presentation]: User Interfaces. - Graphical user interfaces.

General terms: Design, Human Factors.

Keywords: 2.5D input device, Malleable Surface, Deformable Interfaces, Sculpting Interfaces.

INTRODUCTION

When interacting with highly malleable and deformable physical surfaces and forms in the real world, such as clay, there are diverse possibilities for input. Sculptors use their entire hands to shape and deform, not just their fingertips, providing nuanced control. Sculptors also use a variety of tools with complex shapes to displace clay or to add texture. These tools afford higher precision and more variety than hands alone. But in addition to sculpting tools, any arbitrary object can be used to deform clay.

When sculptors deform clay, they also feel the feedback of the clay pressing back. This enables sculptors to accurately gauge how much material they are removing or the manner in which they are shaping the medium. By combining these various inputs, sculptors transform blocks of clay into expressive and meaningful forms.

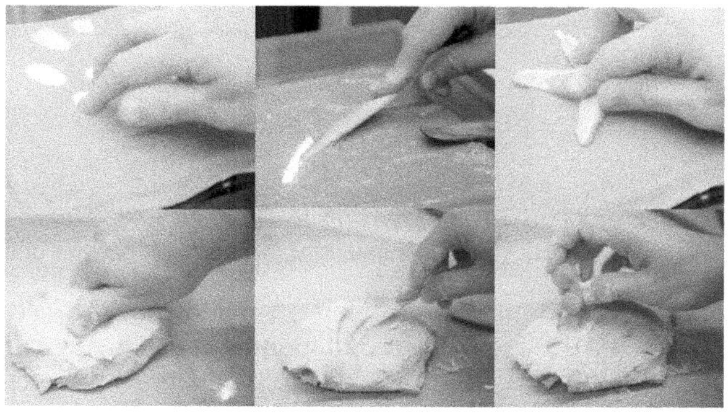

Figure 1. Above: Using hands, tools and arbitrary objects to input with deForm. Below: Using hands, tools and arbitrary objects to deform clay.

What if we could combine the expressivity of clay with the benefits of digital interaction to allow for input from hands, tools and arbitrary objects with co-located visual feedback? Users could use their fingers and hands to pinch and depress the form. They could use a physical sculpting tool to add fine detail, find a physical object to imprint a complex texture into the form. Users could also feel the deformations while producing them, because of the immediate feedback from an elastic input surface.

To capture complex interactions of hands, tools and arbitrary objects, we propose using high resolution real-time 3D scanning. Dense real-time 2.5D/3D input has only recently become available and affordable, bringing the flexibility to use arbitrary objects as input. Some camera-based solutions often focus on mid-air interaction, and lack the physical feedback of real-world malleable surfaces. Other researchers have shown that passive haptic feedback can enhance precise, expressive input [16,27,33].

Our solution combines a passive deformable surface with real-time 2.5D capture to support a wide variety of input. Instead of directly tracking tools, objects, or hands, our system indirectly senses them through deformations of a highly pliable surface. This approach provides passive haptic feedback, and makes clear to the user where the surface of interaction begins and when objects are being scanned. Any object can be used as input, and its shape and 2D gray

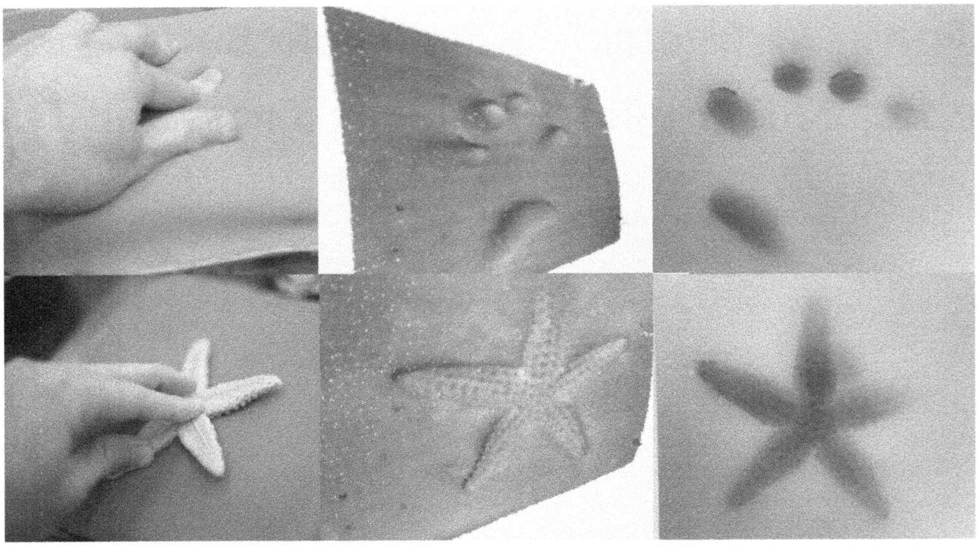

Figure 2. Left to Right, Above, Hand deforming gel surface, 3D view and depth map. Below, starfish toy, 3D reconstruction and depth map.

scale texture, or albedo, are captured as it deforms the surface of the device. A high-resolution 2.5D capture system allows for increased complexity, overcoming the limitations of low-resolution generic deformations in order to achieve the desired clay-like sculpting.

We introduce deForm, a real-time 2.5D surface interface that uses infrared (IR) structured light scanning and projected visual feedback. We also detail our solution for tracking arbitrary and tagged tangible tools, touch and hand gestures. We then describe our method for discerning human touch from contact with tangible tools. A number of sample applications highlight the flexibility of input provided by our system; emulating a six-degree of freedom mouse, a sculpting application that uses real sculpting tools, and an application for remixing objects. A discussion of limitations and future work follows.

RELATED WORK

In this section we summarize 3D input and its limitations. We then describe how related work has sought to bring 3D input to 2D surface input.

3D Input

Advances in Stereo Vision and structured light scanning have made 2.5D real-time video capture a possibility. Most recently the Microsoft Kinect, made by Primesense, uses structured lighting to capture real-time, 30hz, 2.5D geometry at a 640x480 resolution, but is tuned for room scale interactions with a wide angle lens [1]. Custom structured lighting systems have been shown to capture realistic geometry at very high frame rates, by projecting fixed or time sequenced patterns onto objects [40].

One disadvantage of using 3D capture of points or video for input is that it does not provide physical feedback. In addition, these systems provide no physical mechanism to highlight to the user which information is being captured; there is only, in some cases, on-screen feedback. The work of haptic interfaces such as The Phantom, have explored adding mechanical actuators to 3D input to provide tactile feedback [19]. But these systems only allow for single point interactions and contain many moving parts.

One successful approach has been to combine materials that can provide unactuated, passive haptic feedback with 3D sensing. Illuminating Clay used a laser scanner to scan the front of a clay surface at 1 Hz and projected feedback directly onto the clay [23]. However, the user's hands interfered with scanning, as a result of the camera's location above the surface. Passive foam blocks tracked with a vicon system and tracked fingers and tools have been used to enable 3D sculpting [26]. However, this system required augmenting hands and tools with markers, and only provided a simulation of deformations, as opposed to capturing true deformations in the surface. We hope to expand on this work by adding real-time 2.5D scanning to a passive malleable surface to capture real deformations with any object.

Extending Surface Input to 2.5D

There has been a wealth of research on 2D surface interaction [5]. Recently many researchers have explored adding more dimensionality to surface input through both *above the surface* interactions and *into the surface* interactions.

Visual Touchpad used stereovision to enable *above the surface* 2.5D interaction [18]. More recent work has harnessed depth-sensing cameras to facilitate *above the surface* interaction [6,10]. Although these systems allow for much larger areas of interaction, they lose some of the advantages of tabletop surface systems, such as passive haptic feedback, and co-located input and output.

More closely related to our work, into the surface 2.5D interaction allows users to press hands and objects against or into the surface to capture more dimensionality, see table 1 for a comparison of the most relevant systems. Some of these systems measure pressure through force sensitive

	Deformable Material	Sensing Method	Resolution	Input Tracking
deForm	Thermo-plastic Elastomer	IR 3-Phase Structured Light Scanning	640 x 480 @20hz	3D + 2D surface
GelSight [12]	Thermo-plastic Elastomer	RGB Photometric Stereo	640 x 480 @30hz	3D
GelForce [34]	Silicone	Camera tracked embedded dots	24 x 24 3D vectors @30hz	6DoF
Photoelastic Touch [25]	Polyethylene or Silicone	Photoelastic effect with polarized Camera	Low @ 200hz	2D + Pressure
Haptic Lens [28]	Liquid Bladder with pigment	Reflected Pixel Intensity	Unknown	3D
Hook et al. [8]	Ferrofluid Bladder	Ferromagnetic Sensors	8 x 8@55hz	2D + Pressure
Matrix [22]	Mechanical Rods on springs	Matrix of Linear Encoders	12 x 12@30hz	3D
Unmousepad [24]	None	IFSR	87dpi (interpolated) @60hz 40 x 30raw	2D + Pressure

Table 1. A comparison of some existing malleable input devices. DeForm also supports tools, touch, collocated projection and 2D texture capture. Gelforce and Photoelastic Touch also have visual feedback.

resistors [24], or mechanical deformations [22]. Other systems employ magnetic sensors and deformable magnetic material [8,11,31].

Another approach is to allow the surface to be deformable and to measure its deformation with a camera. Our system takes this approach, and as such we closely review other systems in this domain. One approach uses a deformable projection screen made of lycra fabric or latex rubber, which stretches when force is applied to it, either tracked by reflected pixel intensity [3] or by tracking dots on the surface[35].

A number of these 2.5D surfaces have used a deformable liquid bag or gel as their basis. These systems can more clearly resolve concave shapes. This occurs because the gel or liquid applies a stronger force back on the surface to fill in concavities.

One category of gel/liquid based 2.5D systems provide pressure-sensitive input through pixel intensity from a camera mounted below the surface. Pigment dispersed in a liquid contained in a bag reflects more light the deeper an object is pressed [28,30]. The liquid-based approach does not provide for high-resolution 3D scans, cannot allow 2D texture information to be captured, and has physical stability issues due to fluid movement [7].

Gel-based input systems provide a stable deformable surface to interact with. Photoelastic Touch, utilizes polarizers to measure the photoelastic effect of deformations into gel surfaces [25]. This provides a fairly low resolution spatial pressure map, limited to finger scale detail. Furthermore, spatial resolution decreases dramatically with increased input force. Smith et al. showed that a deformable gel on top of an FTIR multitouch system can provide pressure information [29].

A more sophisticated marker-based system, Gelforce uses two grids of visible markers vertically offset in the gel and a single camera to derive true 3D force vectors applied to the gel [34]. This system has many benefits, but its resolution is limited by the size of the dots. These optical dots also obscure the surface and preclude 2D texture reconstruction.

GelSight uses a gel with a painted surface and a photometric stereo system to capture 2.5D surface normals [12]. This system is limited to only accurately reconstructing shallow surfaces because photometric stereo does not capture precise depth disparities [20]. In addition Gelsight is highly dependent on surface color, requiring a thick layer of paint. Furthermore it cannot capture independent 2D texture of an object. Our system uses structured lighting to triangulate surface geometry and is less sensitive to depth discontinuities.

Our system provides many benefits beyond existing work in *into the surface* 2.5D input. It allows for high-resolution dense surface reconstruction, 2D texture capture in the IR spectrum, to allow for simultaneous 2D visible light feedback at interactive rates. This paper also introduces depth-based fiducials, and a method for discerning touch from passive tools.

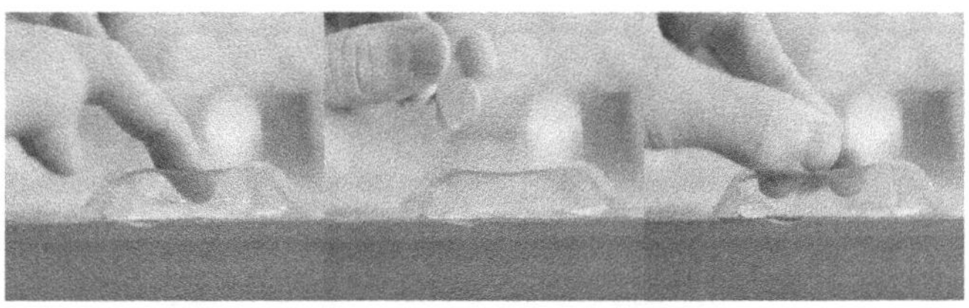

Figure 3. The thermoplastic Elastomer deforms when force is applied but returns to normal state quickly, as seen in the middle image.

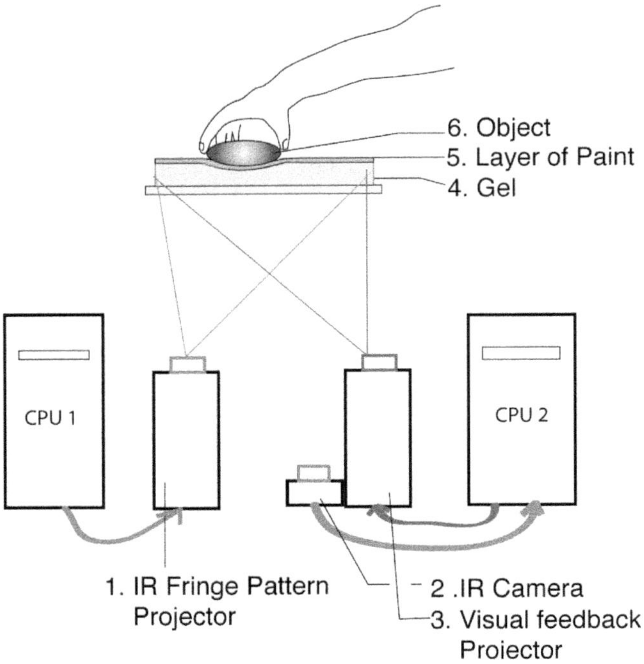

Figure 4. deForm system Diagram. CPU 1 generates IR fringe patterns, which are projected through the glass and onto the gel surface. An IR camera attached to CPU2 captures deformations in the gel, and CPU2 reconstructs 2.5D geometry. CPU2 provides visible light projection on the gel surface to the user.

SYSTEM DESCRIPTION

Our system for 2.5D input consists of two parts: a passive, deformable gel surface coated with a thin layer of paint, and a camera projector system for real-time 3D scanning of the paint surface from below.

We use a 1 inch thick gel surface, which is cut into a square measuring 8 by 8 inches. The gel is deformable, but very elastic, and returns to its normal state after the object is removed. The gel is optically transparent and the surface is painted with a gray paint to capture only the geometry of the surface of the gel as opposed to objects above the gel. The painted surface can also be used as a projection screen. The gel sits on a piece of clear glass through which the pattern is projected onto the gel, see figure 4.

deForm uses a structured light system to capture deformations in the surface of the gel in 3D. Our system implements the Three-Phase structured light scanning techniques described by Zhang [40]. Three sinusoidal fringe patterns are projected on to the gel surface in sequence and captured by a high-speed point grey camera. The patterns are time sequenced, which means our system requires three projected and captured frames for one 2.5D reconstruction.

With this system we are able to achieve a high-resolution, 640 by 480, depth map at interactive rates of 20 Hz. Figure 5 shows a single reconstruction captured in three frames at 60fps.

Three-phase structured light scanning can also reconstruct a greyscale texture image of the surface of the gel from the three phase images without requiring an additional camera or a reduction in frame rate [40]. The thin paint used lets through much of the surface color and texture, allowing us to simultaneously map the surface image of the object to its 3D scan.

Instead of projecting patterns in the visible light spectrum, the IR light spectrum is used to "invisibly" capture geometry. This allows for simultaneous 2.5D input in IR and projection of visible light interfaces on the gel surface for the user to interact with.

We initially attempted to use a Microsoft Kinect camera [1] for our 3D input, but found that it was not appropriate because it was designed for room scale interactions. The 70 degree field of view, combined with an active sensing area

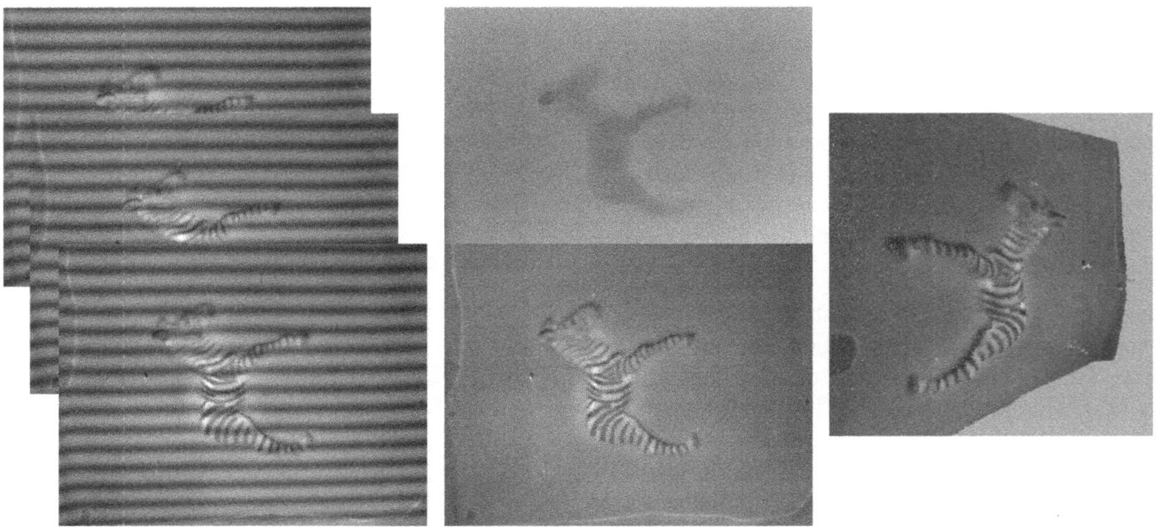

Figure 5. 2.5D structured light reconstruction. Left: 3 different 120deg. phase-shifted sinusoidal fringe patterns projected in IR on gel surface, sequentially captured. Middle Top: 2.5D depth map of Zebra toy. Middle Bottom: greyscale 2D texture reconstructed from fringe patterns. Right: 3D view with 2D texture applied.

starting 30in from the device, results in a minimum sensing area of roughly 42X31 inches. At its 640 by 480 resolution the maximum spatial resolution is roughly 15PPI, far lower than our system's 80PPI. The Kinect also has a very limited z-depth resolution, at close to 0.5cm accuracy.

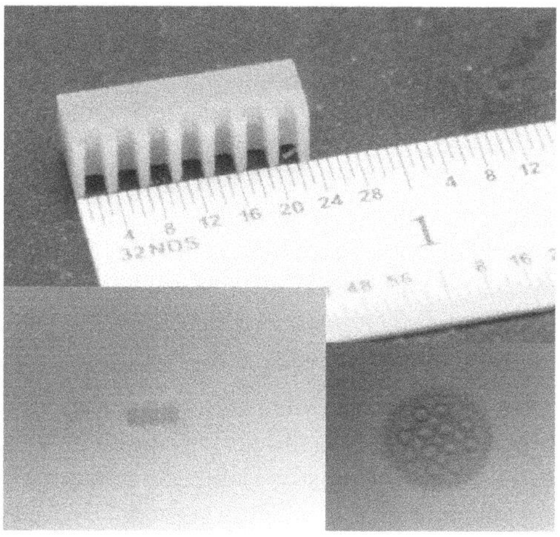

Figure 6. Above: A target used to measure accuracy with 0.8mm pins with 1.6mm spacing. Below: Left: target clearly resolved. Right: Lego gear clearly resolved

Accuracy

Our system is currently able to capture surface geometry with features as small as 0.8mm with spacing between features as small as 1.6mm. We evaluated out system using a number of lasercut depth targets, see figure 6. We are able to capture the overall geometry of a Lego gear, a fairly complex 2.5D object. There is some reduced accuracy due to the gel surface, but this is minimal. Deep concavities are not accurately reconstructed.

Tracking

Using a background subtraction algorithm on the reconstructed depth map, our system is able to easily detect objects, fingers and tangible tools pressed into the surface. After segmentation and labeling, we are able to track these objects and classify their average and maximum depth if necessary.

We can also estimate the relative rotation and orientation of the object, providing 6 Degree of Freedom input. We estimate the pitch and roll, by averaging the normal vectors over the object. The rotation or yaw can be estimated by finding the major axes, but this approach only works with non-rotationally symmetric objects.

The system can also estimate the force applied by the object, based on both its depth in the gel and the surface area of the object in contact with the gel. The gel has a uniform durometer and so requires a relatively uniform force to deform it. By integrating the area bounded by the object in the depth map, we can estimate the relative force in the Z direction. This could be useful for determining the pressure applied to a stylus as opposed to a flat hand.

TANGIBLE TOOLS

Our system can support input from both arbitrary objects and tagged objects such as tangible phicons (physical icons) [9]. Deformations from arbitrary objects can be mapped directly to input, while using special tagged tangible controllers to pre-form specific operations.

Arbitrary objects/tools

deForm can capture, in 2.5D, arbitrary objects pressed into the gel surface. We can use these 2.5D geometries to deform virtual meshes or to control 3D scenes. A wide variety of objects can be used to deform the surface, allowing for a diverse set of input means, beyond a single stylus. Multiple shapes can be captured at the same time.

For example, traditional wooden sculpting tools could be used to deform digital models. Many projects have sought to use traditional paintbrushes with digital interfaces [21,32], to capture particular properties and styles.

Since deForm can capture both 2.5D geometry and 2D grayscale texture information, the system can function as a fast 3D scanner. Optical multitouch systems have used scans of 2D graphics, such as real photographs and documents [38], to create an easy, direct way to input information. Our system adds another dimension to that intuitive approach. For example, a child could copy her toy by pressing it into the gel. The toy could then be modified in the digital world or uploaded to represent a digital avatar in a game. We discuss the concept of "remixing" toys in the application section below.

Tangible Controls

In some applications, developers may require specific tangible tools to perform predefined operations. Many systems for tangible interaction choose optical markers to track tangible tools quickly and easily [13].

Our system is able to use 2D optical markers by detecting objects' 2D greyscale textures. We have used Reactivision markers with our system and tracked them when pressed

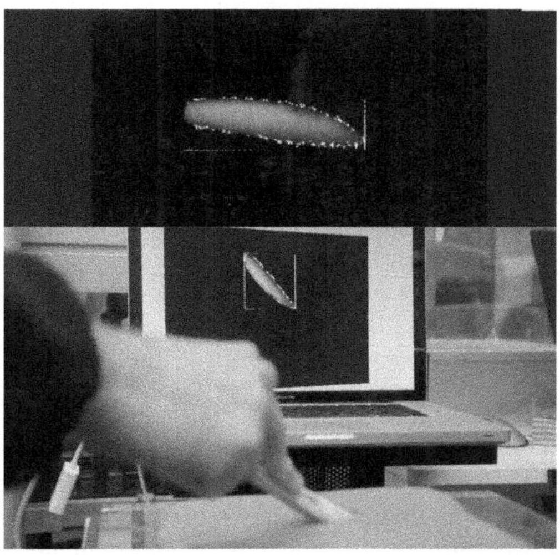

Figure 7. Tangible tools can be tracked as well from the depth map. Here a sculpting tool is background subtracted and labeled.

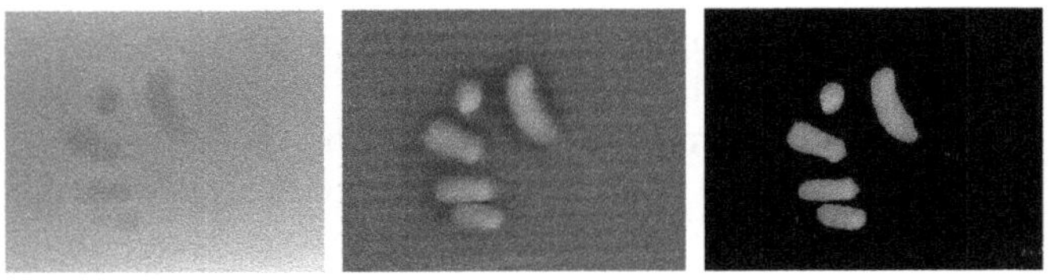

Figure 8. Left to right: Raw depth map of fingers pressed into gel, Background subtraction, Thresholded 2.5D image

Figure 9. Depth encoded markers, designed for deForm. Left: two laser cut reactivision markers modified to encode pattern in height. Middle: depthmap of depressed marker. Right: tracked and labeled marker.

into the gel surface and on the surface. In addition, our system can estimate the pitch and roll of the markers through the techniques described above.

deForm also encodes marker information in physical depth rather than visible light, which can be tracked in a depth map. This approach allows for other information to be encoded beyond a 2D pattern. In addition, the physical shape of a marker is easily changed, allowing for dynamic tags. This technique could also be applied to other depth-based input devices that do not capture 2D texture.

We encoded Reactivison information into depth markers by laser etching acrylic plastic, mapping black and white to height values. Using depth-encoded Reactivision markers, we are able to easily track these tags using just the depth map image, see figure 9. As a result of to the gel surface some error remains due to poor reconstruction of small, interior details . A modified Reactivision tag, with larger holes and fewer interior graphics, shown in figure 9, allows for a recognition accuracy of 95% when directly pressed into the material. The adjustment limits the address space but greatly improves tracking performance.

Mechanical components, such as buttons and sliders, could be added to these tangible controllers, as implemented for Slap Widgets [36]. We could encode different information into the depth of a single mechanical pin. For example, instead of a single on/off button we can have pressure sensitive buttons. Alternatively, rotation could be encoded in a pin by using a cam type system.

TOUCH INTERACTIONS

Our system supports traditional multitouch input, but due to its depth, it can capture more complex hand interaction.

Into the Surface Touch interactions

Iconic Gestures

Using the 2.5D depth map deForm is able to support a number of different pressure-sensitive touch gestures, such as pinching and rotating, by tracking finger positions in 3D. We can extract finger locations from the threshold depth map through thresholding and blob detection.

Beyond simply detecting gestures by finger tracking, we are able to detect certain gestures from the displacement of the gel. When an object or finger is pressed into the gel, the gel deforms around the object, increasing in height surrounding the perimeter of the object. When pinching, the gel is displaced between the fingers greatly. This provides an easy way to detect pinching, by looking for areas in the depth map that have increased in height. This is just one example that highlights the differences between our system which captures the geometry of deformation, and a system which merely senses pressure.

The friction that occurs when users articulate their fingers while pressed deeply into the gel, necessitates a vocabulary of gestures based on mostly isometric relative change, rather than absolute positions. This approach would also benefit from the passive haptic feedback that the gel provides.

Beyond iconic gestures

Because our system can detect more complex hand poses than simple touch points, there is a large opportunity to support touch interactions beyond iconic gestures. We can use the 2.5D geometry of the hands to directly manipulate a mesh, much as one would manipulate clay. This type of interaction is explored in later discussion.

Touch Interactions on top the surface

We can use the reconstructed 2D texture image of the gel surface to do basic diffuse IR multitouch sensing. In the texture image we can clearly see finger-tips finely resolved even before they greatly deform the surface, as shown in figure 10. We can use simple background subtraction and thresholding to find the finger or hand points in contact with the surface. This 2D image can then be compared to the background subtracted depth image to find touch points that are not pressing into the surface. This allows for touch interactions both on the surface and into the surface. For example, touch on the surface could be used as a hover mode, and pressing into the screen could select. Alternatively, touch gestures on the surface could change global application parameters, but touch gestures into the surface could change local parameters.

DISCERNING TOUCH FROM TOOLS

Many optical systems that support multitouch interaction discern touch points from other objects by looking for the size of the blobs [5]. This method is fairly robust, but is not foolproof. Un-tagged tangible tools, such as a sculpting tool, may appear similar to a finger. To resolve this ambiguity, we propose the use of capacitive sensing in addition to optical sensing. Capacitive sensing relies on the change in capacitance between an electrode and the environment. Unlike human hands, non-conductive objects do not change the capacitance greatly. This allows deForm to distinguish between touch and tools.

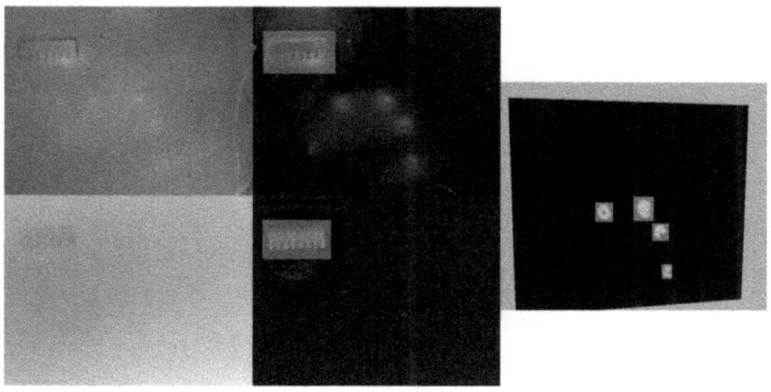

Figure 10. Using the reconstructed 2D grey scale texture to provide on-the-surface multitouch. Above: Images are 2D greyscale and background subtracted greyscale image. Below: Depth information. Right: Depth information is subtracted from the greyscale image to find touches only on the surface, which are highlighted in red.

Because our system relies on a very deformable and flexible surface, embedding traditional capacitive sensors on the surface is not ideal. Rather, we use conductive paint on the surface. A thin layer of silver-based conductive paint is applied to surface of the gel. With this set-up the system distinguishes between the presence of a hand and a non-conductive tool.

TECHNICAL IMPLEMENTATION

The gel structure is a soft, shor 00 durometer, thermo plastic elastomer called Ultraflex sold by Douglas and Sturges, which is heated and cast. We have explored different durometer gels and found a narrow range acceptable; if the gel is too stiff, it will be more difficult to use, too loose and the gel surface will deform too easily and not retain its shape. Once painted, talc powder or cornstarch is applied to lessen the gel's stickiness.

In order to capture each projected fringe pattern frame we synchronized the camera with the vsync line of the VGA input of a projector. We used a DLP projector because the mirror arrays can update within the frame interval, unlike many LCD projectors. Using a DLP projector, we were able to achieve rates of reconstruction at 20 Hz, by projecting and capturing at 60 Hz. This technique should scale to much higher frame rates, as described in [40].

We calibrated the projector and cameras to correct for lens distortion using standard techniques [14]. To correct for gamma differences between projector and camera and phase errors, we implemented Zhang's calibration for phase error correction, which uses a look up table to match the recorded phase with the ideal phase [39].

To project IR patterns, we modified our DLP by removing the IR cut filter in front of the bulb and replacing it with a cold mirror that reflects visible light and allows IR to pass [4]. We attached a IR pass filter to our Point Grey grayscale camera so as to capture only IR light.

We mounted the two projectors, IR and visible light, on the inside of a box shown in fig. 11. We mounted the camera

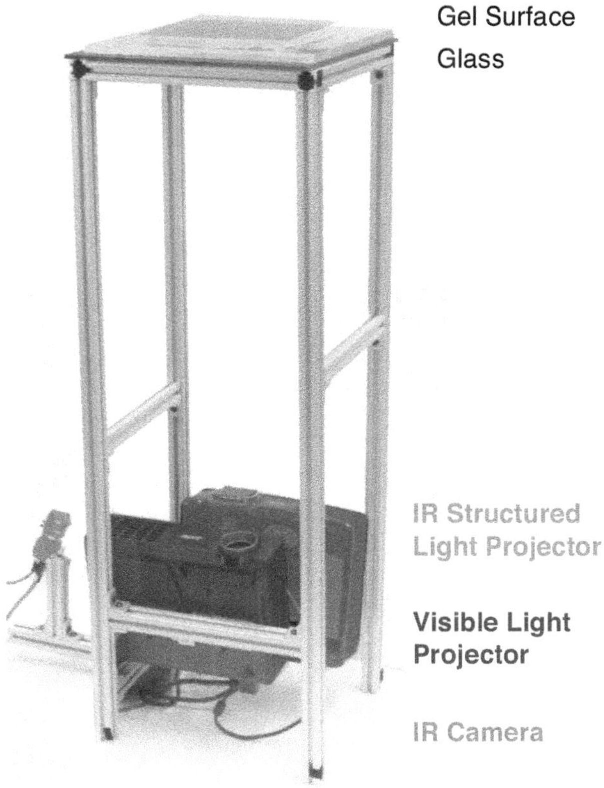

Figure 11. An image of the deForm setup. IR and Visible Light projectors mounted in 80/20 box project upwards through glass to gel surface. An IR camera off to the side captures deformations in the gel.

off to the side to observe deformations in the pattern projected on the gel surface. We placed the painted gel surface on top of the box on a piece of glass.

One computer generates the patterns and another captures the geometry and displays interface elements. We created the software using C++, using Open Frameworks and openCV. We built our system on top of the open frameworks structured lighting library, ofxStructuredLighting [2].

DEMONSTRATION APPLICATIONS

We developed a number of sample applications to explore the possibilities of 2.5D input from hands, tools and arbitrary objects.

6 Degree of Freedom Mouse

Using our depth based fiducial markers we were able to emulate a 6 DOF mouse. This type of interaction is mostly isometric and relies on relative input. In this sample application a 3D scene can be navigated by moving the tangible marker relative to its starting point in the gel. Pitch, roll and yaw are mapped to the rotation of the marker, and the camera can be dollied by moving the controller forward, back, right, left, up or down. This demonstrates the possibilities for using deForm to prototype new and varied 3D input devices quickly.

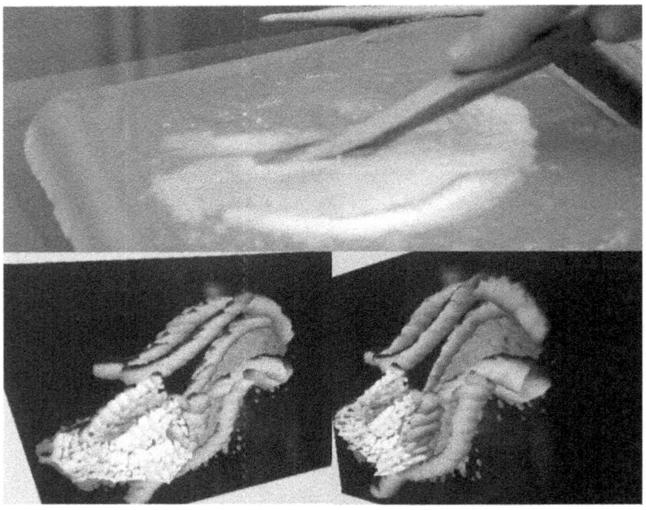

Figure 12. An example sculpting application. Above, users can deform 3D shapes with real sculpting tools and projected feedback. Below, two views of a sea dragon sculpted with the system.

Sculpting Application

We also created a sculpting application that allows for use of real wooden sculpting tools and hands to deform digital clay. This application highlights the flexibility of the deForm system to allow any object to deform a virtual clay model. The user views a model projected on the surface of the gel and can directly edit it through deformations. A secondary display provides an additional 3D view.

To use the raw depth map as input, we background subtract and threshold the depth image. We then break up the interaction into sections where an object or multiple objects are deforming the surface. During the time that any object is deforming the surface, we currently find the maximum depth per pixel over that time. Once the object is removed, we add that maximum depth per pixel to the model and preview this to the user as they are deforming it.

Tangible tagged tools can be used to add reflective symmetry, or undo actions. Hand gestures on the surface can be used to scale and rotate the scene. Currently the system is limited to only deforming a height map, but the system could be extended to manipulating and deforming a full 3D object, by rotating the model virtually.

Remixing Toys

A third application highlights the ease of 3D scanning with the deForm system. Current systems for 3D modeling are very complicated and not readily accessible to children. We present an interface for children to create their own toys. Instead of designing toys from scratch, children can copy different parts from existing toys and combine them to create a new toy.

In this application 2.5D geometry and 2D textures are captured to allow children to scan their toys easily. Once copied, children can erase, modify and add new geometry to make a new "remixed" toy which can be 3D printed.

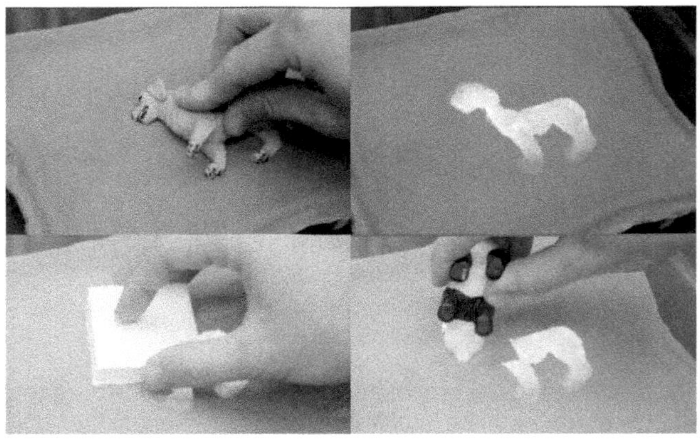

Figure 13. Children can create new toys by scanning and modifying with direct interaction. Left to Right: Pressing in a dog toy to scan it; projected feedback of the dog shape; eraser tool tracked with marker; copying a new panda head for a toy.

Children can scan an object by pressing it into the surface. It then appears directly on the surface. Then they can use a tagged eraser tool to erase geometry, and stamp down other shapes. By making 3D scanning much easier, faster and more direct, copying can become a means for creation.

DISCUSSION AND FUTURE WORK

System limitations

The resolution of our reconstruction is dependent on both the camera and projector, which makes this system limited or unsuitable for reconstructing large surfaces. The trade-off between size of the reconstructed area and the PPI is quite clear, so a table size system would have a less appeal. However, the system could be combined with a digital SLR to capture single higher resolution scans, especially when combined with projector defocusing, which removes the constraint of projector resolution [17].

Currently we are using a time-multiplexed approach to capture the three required patterns to reconstruct the geometry. As a result of the time delay between each frame, large amounts of motion causes errors in reconstruction. This makes the current system ill-suited for applications such as gaming. However, smaller errors are corrected by replacing erroneous data points with information from the previous frame. Increasing frame rates could improve this problem. In addition, other phase-based structured lighting techniques have been developed to solve this problem. The 2 plus 1 phase approach is less sensitive to motion [40]. Another approach is to separate the patterns by color (often Red, Green and Blue channels) as opposed to time.

The current system requires a large total height due to the use of a camera and projector system, which can rarely be as thin as other approaches such as capacitive or FSR based input devices. It may be possible to reduce the height required by using wider field of view cameras and short throw projectors, or by introducing some sort of wave guide, such as [15].

Currently the system requires paint on the surface of the gel both to aid in reconstruction and as a projection surface. Heavy use degrades the paint over time, causing problems such as light leaks and lower quality reconstruction. Improving the robustness of the paint would lead to a more durable solution, and might also limit friction. Sliding and dragging are more difficult due to the friction caused by the gel and paint. Currently, we apply a lubricant, but this is an insufficient solution outside of the lab setting.

Future work

We believe that deForm points towards more flexibility and fluidity of input. Camera based systems open broad possibilities for novel input modalities. By combing high resolution capture with a deformable, elastic surface we can begin to estimate interactions similar to sculpting clay. So much expressivity in hands that is lost when only using touch points. Previous work combined touch and 2.5D capture with physics based simulations [37], and we think deForm could be a great platform for further exploration.

We would also like to explore more interaction techniques for bimanual input, using a tool in one hand and touch input in another. By extending our capacitive sensing to a matrix-based approach we could locate the positions of hands and tools simultaneously to create interesting interactions.

We would also like to explore the use of arbitrary gel shapes as tangible controllers rather than a surface input device. The gel can be cast in any shape, such as the shape of a computer mouse. Physical affordances or buttons could be included in the form. These tools could be used on top of a traditional surface rear projection table, by using a technique similar to the Second Light system to project through the surface and onto the gel. This could be a good tool for prototyping 2.5D tangible input devices.

Finally we would like to explore how real users could interact with deForm. During an informal open house 50 participants including 4 children used the remixing toys example application. Initial feedback was encouraging; children particularly took to the direct manipulation provided by the system. We would like to run further evaluations of that interface and how users respond to the 2.5D input and passive haptic feedback provided by deForm.

CONCLUSION

We have demonstrated a high-resolution 2.5D surface input device that can support a wide variety of input types including arbitrary objects, tangible phicon tools and touch. It can provide passive haptic feedback through a gel surface, while capturing 2.5D deformations in its surface and its 2D greyscale texture. We have shown this can be combined with invisible projection to create a 2.5D interactive deformable surface interface, and have highlighted the tool's strengths in 3D manipulation and digital sculpting through a number of sample applications.

ACKNOWLEDGMENTS

The authors would like to thank Matt Hirsch for his help troubleshooting computer vision problems and being generous with his time, and Hannah Perner-Wilson for her help with conductive paint. We would also like to thank Daniel Leithinger and the rest of the Tangible Media Group for their help and valuable input.

REFERENCES

1. Xbox.com | Kinect. 2010. http://www.xbox.com/en-US/kinect.
2. ofxStructured Light. http://code.google.com/p/structured-light/.
3. Cassinelli, A. and Ishikawa, M. Khronos projector. *ACM SIGGRAPH 2005 Emerging Technologies*, ACM Press (2005), 10.
4. Chan, L.W., Wu, H.T., Kao, H.S., Lin, H.R., Chen, M.Y,Hsu, Jane, Hung, Y.P. Enabling beyond-surface interactions for interactive surface with an invisible projection. *Proc. UIST 2010*, ACM Press (2010), 263–272.
5. Han, J.Y. Low-cost multi-touch sensing through frustrated total internal reflection. *Proc. UIST 2005*, ACM Press (2005), 115.
6. Hilliges, O., Izadi, S., Wilson, A.D., Hodges, S., Garcia-Mendoza, A., and Butz, A. Interactions in the Air : Adding Further Depth to Interactive Tabletops. *Proc. UIST 2009*, ACM Press (2009), 139–148.
7. Hilliges, O., Kim, D., and Izadi, S. Creating malleable interactive surfaces using liquid displacement sensing. *Proc. Tabletop 2008*, IEEE Press (2008), 157-160.
8. Hook, J., Taylor, S., Butler, A., Villar, N., and Izadi, S. A reconfigurable ferromagnetic input device. *Proc. UIST 2009*, ACM Press (2009), 51.
9. Ishii, H. and Ullmer, B. Tangible bits. *Proc. CHI 1997*, ACM Press (1997), 234-241.
10. Izadi, S., Hodges, S., Taylor, S., et al. Going beyond the display. *Proc. UIST 2008*, ACM Press (2008), 269.
11. Jansen, Y., Karrer, T., and Borchers, J. MudPad: tactile feedback and haptic texture overlay for touch surfaces. *Proc. ITS 2010*, ACM Press (2010), 11–14.
12. Johnson, M.K. and Adelson, E.H. Retrographic sensing for the measurement of surface texture and shape. *Proc. IEEE CVPR 2009*, IEEE Press (2009), 1070-1077.
13. Kaltenbrunner, M. and Bencina, R. reacTIVision. *Proc. TEI 2007*, ACM Press (2007), 69.
14. Lanman, D. and Taubin, G. Build your own 3D scanner. *ACM SIGGRAPH 2009 Courses*, ACM Press (2009), 1-94.
15. Large, M.J., Large, T., and Travis, A.R.L. Parallel Optics in Waveguide Displays: A Flat Panel Autostereoscopic Display. *Journal of Display Technology 6*, 10 (2010), 431-437.

16. Lecuyer, A., Coquillart, S., Kheddar, A., Richard, P., and Coiffet, P. Pseudo-haptic feedback: can isometric input devices simulate force feedback? *Proc. IEEE Virtual Reality 2000*, IEEE Comput. Soc, 83-90.

17. Lei, S. and Zhang, S. Flexible 3-D shape measurement using projector defocusing. *Optics Letters 34*, 20 (2009), 3080.

18. Malik, S. and Laszlo, J. Visual touchpad. *Proc. ICMI 2004*, ACM Press (2004), 289.

19. Massie, T.H. and Salisbury, J.K. The PHANTOM Haptic Interface: A Device for Probing Virtual Objects. *Proceedings of the ASME Winter Annual Meeting Symposium on Haptic Interfaces for Virtual Environment and Teleoperator Systems*, (1994), 295–300.

20. Nehab, D., Rusinkiewicz, S., Davis, J., and Ramamoorthi, R. Efficiently combining positions and normals for precise 3D geometry. *ACM Transactions on Graphics 24*, 3 (2005), 536.

21. Otsuki, M., Sugihara, K., Kimura, A., Shibata, F., and Tamura, H. MAI painting brush: an interactive device that realizes the feeling of real painting. *Proc. UIST 2010*, ACM Press (2010), 97–100.

22. Overholt, D. The MATRIX: a novel controller for musical expression. *Proc. NIME 2001*, AMC (2001), 1–4.

23. Piper, B., Ratti, C., and Ishii, H. Illuminating clay. *Proc. CHI 2002*, ACM Press (2002), 355.

24. Rosenberg, I. and Perlin, K. The UnMousePad. *Proc. SIGGRAPH 2009*, ACM Press (2009), 1.

25. Sato, T., Mamiya, H., Tokui, T., Koike, H., and Fukuchi, K. PhotoelasticTouch: transparent rubbery interface using a LCD and photoelasticity. *ACM SIGGRAPH 2009 Emerging Technologies*, ACM (2009), 1–1.

26. Sheng, J., Balakrishnan, R., and Singh, K. An interface for virtual 3D sculpting via physical proxy. *Computer graphics and interactive techniques in Australasia and South East Asia*, (2006), 213.

27. Sile O'Modhrain. Playing by Feel: Incorporating Haptic Feedback into Computer-Based musical Instruments. 2000. https://ccrma.stanford.edu/~sile/thesis.html.

28. Sinclair, M. The haptic lens. *Ext. Abstracts ACM SIGGRAPH '97*, ACM Press (1997), 179.

29. Smith, J.D., Graham, T.C.N., Holman, D., and Borchers, J. Low-Cost Malleable Surfaces with Multi-Touch Pressure Sensitivity. *TABLETOP 2007*, IEEE (2007), 205-208.

30. Tom White. Introducing Liquid Haptics in High Bandwidth Human Computer Interfaces. 1998. http://dspace.mit.edu/handle/1721.1/62938.

31. Valino Koh, J.T.K., Karunanayaka, K., Sepulveda, J., Tharakan, M.J., Krishnan, M., and Cheok, A.D. Liquid interface. *Proc. ACE 2010*, ACM Press (2010), 45.

32. Vandoren, P., Van Laerhoven, T., Claesen, L., Taelman, J., Raymaekers, C., and Van Reeth, F. IntuPaint: Bridging the gap between physical and digital painting. *TABLETOP 2008*, IEEE (2008), 65-72.

33. Viciana-Abad, R., Lecuona, A.R., and Poyade, M. The Influence of Passive Haptic Feedback and Difference Interaction Metaphors on Presence and Task Performance. *Presence: Teleoperators and Virtual Environments 19*, 3 (2010), 197-212.

34. Vlack, K., Mizota, T., Kawakami, N., Kamiyama, K., Kajimoto, H., and Tachi, S. Gelforce: a vision-based traction field computer interface. *Ext. Abstracts CHI 2005*, ACM Press (2005), 1154–1155.

35. Vogt, F., Chen, T., Hoskinson, R., and Fels, S. A malleable surface touch interface. *ACM SIGGRAPH 2004 Sketches*, ACM Press (2004), 36.

36. Weiss, M., Wagner, J., Jansen, Y., et al. SLAP widgets. *Proc. CHI 2009*, ACM Press (2009), 481.

37. Wilson, A.D., Izadi, S., Hilliges, O., Garcia-Mendoza, A., and Kirk, D. Bringing physics to the surface. *Proc. UIST 2008*, ACM Press (2008), 67.

38. Wilson, A.D. TouchLight. *Proc. ICMI 2004*, ACM Press (2004), 69.

39. Zhang, S. and Yau, S.-T. Generic nonsinusoidal phase error correction for three-dimensional shape measurement using a digital video projector. *Applied Optics 46*, 1 (2007), 36.

40. Zhang, S. Recent progresses on real-time 3D shape measurement using digital fringe projection techniques. *Optics and Lasers in Engineering 48*, 2 (2010), 149-158.

A New Angle on Cheap LCDs: Making Positive Use of Optical Distortion

Chris Harrison *Scott E. Hudson*
Human-Computer Interaction Institute and Heinz College Center for the Future of Work
Carnegie Mellon University, 5000 Forbes Avenue, Pittsburgh, PA 15213
{chris.harrison,scott.hudson}@cs.cmu.edu

ABSTRACT
Most LCD screens exhibit color distortions when viewed at oblique angles. Engineers have invested significant time and resources to alleviate this effect. However, the massive manufacturing base, as well as millions of in-the-wild monitors, means this effect will be common for many years to come. We take an opposite stance, embracing these optical peculiarities, and consider how they can be used in productive ways. This paper discusses how a special palette of colors can yield visual elements that are invisible when viewed straight-on, but visible at oblique angles. In essence, this allows conventional, unmodified LCD screens to output two images simultaneously – a feature normally only available in far more complex setups. We enumerate several applications that could take advantage of this ability.

ACM Classification: H.5.2 [Information interfaces and presentation]: User Interfaces - Graphical user interfaces, screen design. B.4.2 [Input/Output and Data Communications]: Input/Output Devices - Image Display.

General Terms: Human Factors.

Keywords: Displays, dual output, multiuser, privacy.

INTRODUCTION
When viewing LCD monitors from an oblique angle, it is not uncommon to witness a dramatic color shift. Occasionally, this can appear as a total color inversion. Although hues can shift, there are also complex interactions that affect saturation and luminance, causing, for example, light shades to become dark [2,7]. This is primarily caused by a polarization asymmetry, where light rays passing through the pixel matrix at oblique angles are influenced by the relative orientation of the liquid crystal (see Figure 1 and [7], chapter 6).

Engineers and designers have sought to reduce these effects for more than two decades. This effort has been further driven by the popularity of LCD televisions, which have viewers located at wider angles than seen in typical computing setups. This has led to the emergence of more advanced LCD technologies, such as In-Plane Switching (IPS) and Vertical Alignment (VA) screens, which have superior field of view [2]. However, this benefit comes with a higher price tag, slower refresh rate, and increased power consumption.

Most of the LCD screens manufactured today are of the Twisted Nematic (TN) variety. Although more susceptible to color distortion, the technology has superior response times and is inexpensive. For most uses, the color distortion (and in general, poorer color reproduction) is acceptable to consumers. The installed manufacturing capacity is enormous, and is unlikely to evolve at a dramatic rate due to the huge costs in shifting production to a new technology.

CONCEPT
Rather than fight against the optical effects found in TN LCD screens, we embrace them. In particular, we take advantage of the fact that very light colors are almost indiscernible from white when viewed straight-on, but dramatically darken at oblique angles. This effect allows the LCD panel to output two images at once: one that is visible from conventional viewing angles (i.e., <30° from perpendicular) and another from oblique angles (>30° off perpendicular).

This ability has a similar flavor to that of much more advanced and expensive multi-output display technologies. These include lenticular and parallax barrier displays [9,11], shutter glasses [1,12], polarized glasses [10], switchable diffusers [5], retro-reflective surfaces [4], and highly engineered optical films [8,13]. An alternate approach is to use movable, spatially aware displays [3] to present different information depending on how the screen is positioned (e.g., a shared screen that can be tilted towards one user or another, and present different information accordingly [6]).

Without such special hardware to tightly control aspects, such as viewing angle and color reproduction, advanced techniques (e.g. stereoscopy) are not possible. However, with careful design, we believe there are numerous applications where the distortion can be put to productive use. These new abilities are essentially free, require no modification to LCD screens, and could be provided with little more than a software update.

AXIS OF USE
LCD screens tend to be viewed at more diverse angles along the horizontal axis; it is far less common to view screens from steep downward or upward angle. This is primarily because we sit or stand at fairly uniform heights, but our position in the room can change. When there are multiple viewers, as might be seen in a conference or living room, they also tend to be spread out along the horizontal axis. In response, LCD manufacturers have attempted to minimize color distortion primarily in the horizontal axis. High quality TN screens show almost no color variance from side to

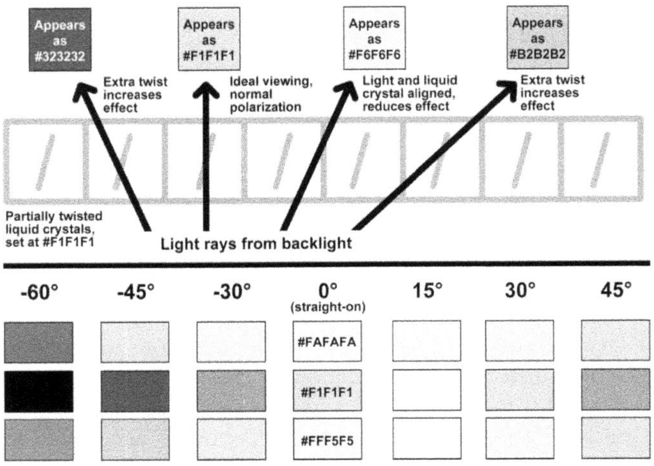

Figure 1. Colors are distorted when viewed off-axis.

side. However, even high quality screens show dramatic color effects in the vertical axis.

APPROACH

We employ a simple color palette to achieve our dual-output effect (partial set shown in Figure 1). This relies on three key phenomena: 1) white pixels remain white, even at oblique angles (though occasional inverting); 2) black pixels remain black, even at oblique angles; and 3) greys between pure white and pure black will darken at oblique angles (colors will also darken, and invert in one direction).

The effect seen in Figure 2 is achieved by rendering a very faint red box underneath pure white text. Both of these elements are imperceptible to the primary user. When viewed from the side, the red box darkens, allowing the pure white text (which remains white) to become readable. The same effect also causes the dark purple "print" and "return" buttons to darken to black. In Figure 3, light gray text is rendered underneath black text. When viewed from an angle, the black text remains black. However, the gray masking text becomes darker, fusing with the black text.

EXAMPLE APPLICATIONS

To help motivate our idea and illustrate the optical effect we employ, we devised a series of example applications. These were a built on a variety of monitors and brands, including Sony, Philips, and Samsung. As noted previously, TN LCD

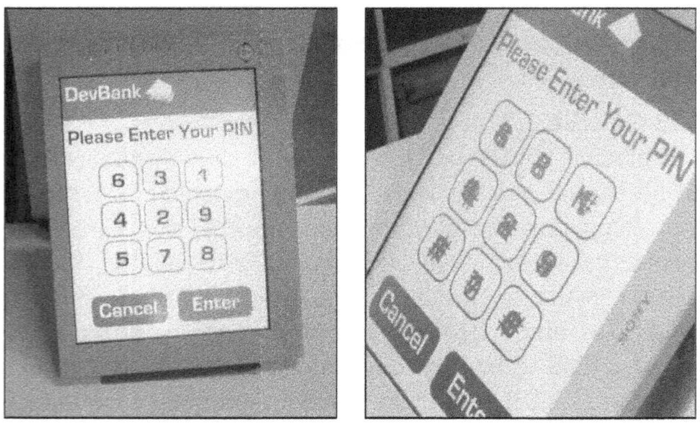

Figure 3. ATM PIN entry keypad with randomized digit locations. From side angles, the keypad buttons are masked, preventing onlookers from deducing the PIN.

Figure 2. Warning messages could be displayed to people snooping behind and to the side of the ATM.

screen tend to have severe color distortion in one axis. Most of our examples assume secondary viewers in the horizontal plane, and thus, we place monitors in a portrait configuration (90° from typical use) to maximize the optical effect.

Note: Figures in this paper have not been graphically post-edited in any manner (e.g., contrast, white balance). The embedded photos are directly from the camera for maximum fidelity. The effect is more prominent in real life as human eyes have a superior dynamic range to that of a camera. All images were taken indoors with standard lighting to simulate realistic use. Please also view the Video Figure.

Privacy

One simple use of this phenomenon is for visual warnings for snooping onlookers. For example, while using an ATM, people floating behind and to the side of the user might see "please move back behind the yellow line" or "you are being filmed" on the screen in bold letters (Figure 1). The primary user, however, cannot see this text and goes about his or her banking business undisturbed.

It is also possible to mask sensitive information by employing a watermark. To the primary user, this is essentially invisible (very light grey text rendered behind black text). However, onlookers see the watermark rendered with a dark appearance. This visually fuses with the original text, making it difficult to read. Returning to our ATM example, this could be used to mask information such as account balance and credit card transactions.

This technique of masking elements could also be used for secure password entry. A simple approach could employ a

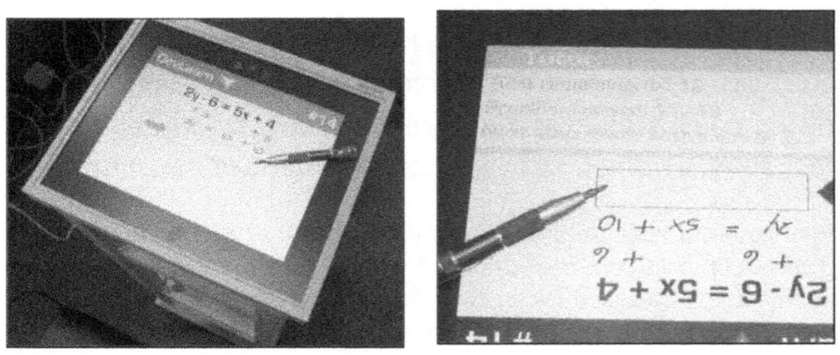

Figure 4. Left: a tutoring system displays a series of algebra problems to students. Right: the tutor, sitting opposite, can see additional information, such as time remaining.

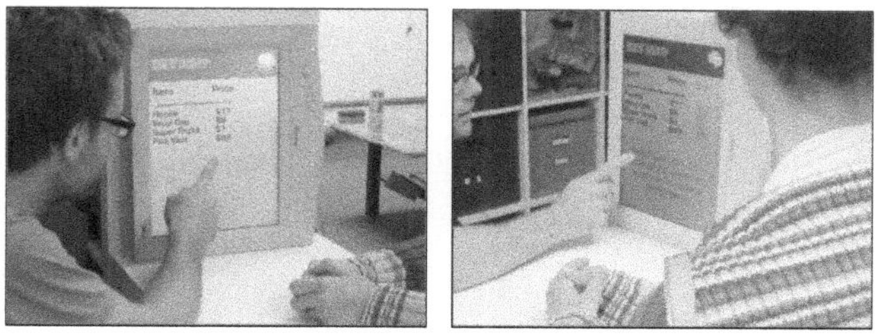

Figure 5. In a point of sale setup, customers could be shown inventory and prices, while the salesperson views additional, private information, such as cost or potential discounts.

touch screen number keypad with randomized digit locations (Figure 3). An off-angle onlooker could view the sequence of button presses, but would be unable to deduce the PIN without knowing the digit-to-button mapping (which is random and masked visually).

Multi-User

There are many situations where presenting differing information to two distinct parties is valuable [6,13]. For example, consider a tutor working closely with a student. A common computer and screen could be used to facilitate close interaction. However, it may be beneficial for the tutor to see the answer, problem difficulty, number of correct answers thus far, the next question, remaining time in the session, and so on. A LCD panel could be set up to provide this information to the tutor only, as depicted in Figure 4.

A similar setup could be deployed in point of sale applications, where, for example, prices could be shown to the customer, while costs are shown to the employee, who can then negotiate a final price. Stores, banks and similar facilities sometimes use privacy preserving grills to hide this information. Not only does this cost more in materials and retrofitting, but also comes at a total loss of information presentation ability to the consumer (Figure 5). A well-positioned LCD could achieve this effect for free.

A final example is that of the viewer peeking over a display from behind and above. This might happen if a teacher was walking around a classroom and checking on student progress by peeking over their laptop screens. This oblique angle opens the possibility to display information like that in the tutoring example. Alternatively, a parent could peek over their child's laptop to see what they have been working on and for how long.

Secondary Information Display

Screens with two viewing angles could also be used for primary and secondary information display to a single user. For example, when sitting in front of a screen, a user could see their email client as usual. However, when seated on a couch with an oblique and far view to the computer monitor, the screen could display "4 Unread Emails" in a large font (Figure 6). In this way, the monitor can serve an additional role as a naïve, context-sensitive ambient display, with no sensing, tracking or knowledge necessary.

There could also be opportunities to engage users on oblique approach trajectories, common with wall-mounted

Figure 6. Typical email interface is visible when looking head on; when seated at or approaching from an oblique angle, the display could operate as an ambient display.

displays in hallways. Lastly, use in handheld displays, like those in mobile phones, could be fruitful. Tilting the device could reveal secondary information [6] or a control panel.

CONCLUSION

We have presented our novel use of the color distortion inherent in most LCD displays, especially prominent in the common Twisted Nematic variety. We discussed how our approach can be employed and articulate numerous example applications to help motivate our ideas. A meta-contribution of this work is to encourage researchers to reconsider what might at first glance be seen as a negative aspect or limitation of a technology, and instead, find ways to appropriate and make use of it.

REFERENCES

1. Agrawala, M., Beers, A.C., McDowall, I., Fröhlich, B., Bolas, M., and Hanrahan, P. The two-user Responsive Workbench: support for collaboration through individual views of a shared space. In *Proc. SIGGRAPH '97*. 327-332.
2. Baker, S. Panel Technologies - TN Film, MVA, PVA and IPS Explained. http://tftcentral.co.uk/articles/panel_technologies.htm. 7/25/11
3. Fitzmaurice, G.W. Situated Information Spaces and Spatially Aware Palmtop Computers. *Comm. of the ACM*, 36(7), '93. 38-49.
4. Hua H., Brown L.D., Gao C., Ahuja N. A new collaborative infrastructure: SCAPE. In *Proc. IEEE VR '03*. 171–179.
5. Izadi, S., Hodges, S., Taylor, S., Rosenfeld, D., Villar, N., Butler, A., and Westhues, J. Going beyond the display: a surface technology with an electronically switchable diffuser. *Proc. UIST '08*, 269–278.
6. Lee, J., and Hudson, S. Foldable Interactive Displays. In *Proc. UIST '08*. 287-290.
7. Lueder, E. (2010). *Liquid Crystal Displays: Addressing Schemes and Electro-Optical Effects* (2nd Ed). Wiley.
8. Matsushita, M., Iida, M., Ohguro, T., Shirai, Y., Kakehi, Y., and Naemura, T. Lumisight table: a face-to-face collaboration support system that optimizes direction of projected information to each stakeholder. In *Proc. CSCW '04*. 274-283.
9. Perlin, K., Paxia, S., and Kollin, J. An Autostereoscopic Display. In *Proc. SIGGRAPH '00*. 319-326.
10. Sakurai, S., Kitamura, Y., Subramanian, S., and Kishino, F. A visibility control system for collaborative digital table. *Personal Ubiquitous Computing*. 13, 8 (Nov. 2009), 619-632.
11. Schwerdtner, A. and Heidrich, H. Dresden 3D display (D4D). *Stereoscopic Display and V.R. Systems V*. SPIE Vol. 3295, 1998. 203-210.
12. Shoemaker, G.B. and Inkpen, K.M. Single display privacyware: augmenting public displays with private information. In *Proc. CHI '01*. 522-529.
13. Smith, R.T. and Piekarski, W. Public and private workspaces on tabletop displays. In *Proc. AUIC '08*. 51-54.

Direct and Gestural Interaction with Relief: A 2.5D Shape Display

Daniel Leithinger, David Lakatos, Anthony DeVincenzi, Matthew Blackshaw, Hiroshi Ishii
MIT Media Lab
75 Amherst Street, Cambridge, MA 02139, USA
{daniell, dlakatos, tonyd, mab, ishii}@media.mit.edu

ABSTRACT

Actuated shape output provides novel opportunities for experiencing, creating and manipulating 3D content in the physical world. While various shape displays have been proposed, a common approach utilizes an array of linear actuators to form 2.5D surfaces. Through identifying a set of common interactions for viewing and manipulating content on shape displays, we argue why input modalities beyond direct touch are required. The combination of freehand gestures and direct touch provides additional degrees of freedom and resolves input ambiguities, while keeping the locus of interaction on the shape output. To demonstrate the proposed combination of input modalities and explore applications for 2.5D shape displays, two example scenarios are implemented on a prototype system.

ACM Classification: H5.2 [Information interfaces and presentation]: User Interfaces: Input devices and strategies; Haptic I/O; I.3.6 [Methodology and techniques]: Interaction techniques.

General terms: Design, Human Factors

Keywords: Gestural Input, Tangible Input, Direct Manipulation, Actuated Surface, Shape Display

INTRODUCTION

Shape displays generate dynamic physical forms controlled by a computer. While today's shape displays are unable to render arbitrary objects in space, current implementations succeed in generating approximations of an object's shape. As computer interfaces, they inherit the benefits of Tangible User Interfaces (TUI) [11], allowing multiple users to simultaneously view, feel and manipulate a physical shape instead of an abstract graphical representation. This enables novel, currently unexplored uses in areas such as computer-aided design (CAD). Review of related work, reveals that most shape output mechanisms are comprised of a 2D array of linear actuators. This arrangement forms a 2.5D approximation of an object's shape, similar to a relief sculpture (Fig. 2). The term 2.5D in this context follows a common

Figure 1: We propose to extend direct touch interaction with 2.5D shape displays by a set of freehand gestures

definition used for digital elevation models [26]. Current 2.5D shape displays allow user input by touching and pressing into the interface surface. We argue that additional input modalities enable 2.5D shape displays to perform a wider range of applications: by extending touching and pressing with freehand gestural input, we keep the locus of interaction on the shape output. We define a set of gestures for selecting, translating, and rotating the shape of an object. Through our implementation we demonstrate the use of these gestures in two applications. The first application explores the rendering of arbitrary 3D models augmented with graphics. In the second application, we investigate the mixed input capabilities of direct touch and freehand ges-

Figure 2: Relief sculpture (image courtesy of Chez Căsver)

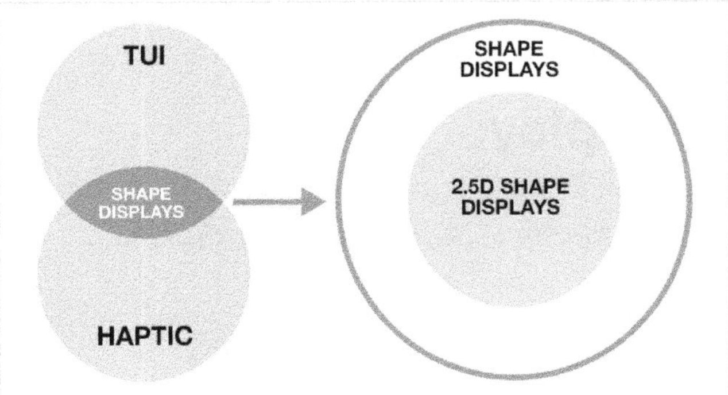

Figure 3: Overview of shape displays

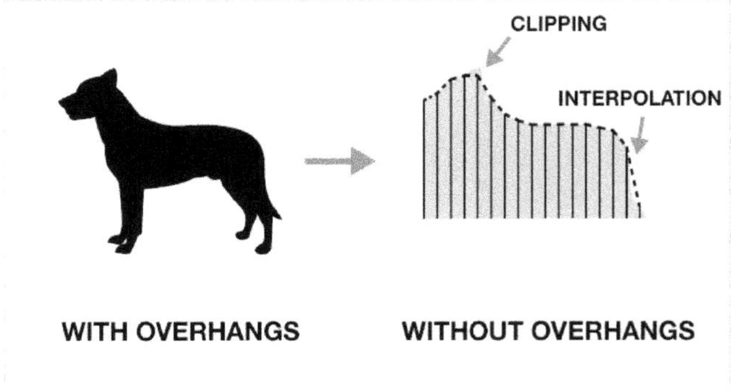

Figure 4: 2.5D shape displays are not able to render overhangs

tures for CAD.

RELATED WORK

Shape Displays: Actuated Tangible Interfaces

Shape displays are haptic interfaces with the ability to create and deform physical shapes in real time. The idea of computationally controlled matter to create an immersive visual and haptic sensation was first described by Sutherland in 1965 as the ultimate display [24]. Most shape displays are not only output devices, but also allow user input. The approach of interacting with computers through physical embodiments of information is similar to the concept of Tangible User Interfaces (TUI) introduced by Ishii et al. [10]. Poupyrev et al. identify shape displays as an emerging field in the context of TUI [21].

Future shape displays might be able to generate arbitrary shapes through self-arranging independent modules [6]. However, current approaches consist of fixed arrangements of actuators forming a surface. These actuators can be embedded into the surface, such as the Nitinol actuators of Surflex [3] or the hinge elements of the Formable Crust project [22]. Other arrangements include volumetric actuators attached to a column, as proposed by Volflex [13]. However, the majority of shape displays utilize a 2D array of linear actuators, which form 2.5D shapes similar to relief sculptures.

2.5D Shape Displays

While 2.5D shape displays vary in size, type of actuation, and speed of shape output they all follow the same principle of shape generation. An array of actuated pins forms a surface, similar to pin screen toys [25]. This layout of actuators allows simple mechanical design, since the actuators can be hidden under the surface, compared to the complexity of embedding them into the surface.

Limitations

2.5D shape displays are limited in the types of shapes they can generate. Most fundamentally they do not allow overhangs (Fig. 4). Another limitation is the resolution of the actuated points. Due to the size and complexity of the actuators, they cannot be packed densely enough to create a resolution capable of outputting a perceived continuous shape [23, 16]. Perceived resolution can be increased by stretching a malleable surface over the pin array producing the illusion of continuous shape.

Actuators have a limited linear range. If the shape formed by the interface exceeds this range, it will be clipped. The generated shape may be augmented with visuals: either through LED's embedded in the pins or top-down projection on the surface.

History

The "surface display", created by Hirota and Hirose in 1993 [10] consists of a 4 x 4 linear actuator array. The actuators form a physical surface from the depth buffer of arbitrary 3D geometry.

Iwata et al. developed FEELEX in 1995 to overcome shortcomings they identified in their previously constructed haptic interfaces tethered to the human body [12]. FEELEX consists of a malleable surface deformed by an array of 6 x 6 linear actuators. A top-down projector is used to create visual feedback on the surface. Through embedded pressure sensors the system reacts to the user's push. An example application renders a moving creature reacting to touch

Name	Actuation method	Number of actuators	Display size	Actuator travel
FEELEX	Motor driven screws	6 x 6	240 x 240 mm	8 cm
FEELEX 2	Piston-crank mechanism	23	50 x 50 mm	1.8 cm
Lumen	Nitinol actuators	13 x 13	84 x 84 mm	6 mm
Digital Clay	Hydraulic	5 x 5	25 x 25 mm	48 mm
Surface display	Slider-crank mechanism	4 x 4	120 x 120 mm	5 cm
Xeno-Vision Mark III	Electric	7000	91 x 122 cm	15 cm
Relief	Belt actuation	12 x 12	45 x 45 cm	13 cm

Table 1: Comparison of 2.5D shape displays

input of a single user. A second version, FEELEX 2 decreases the spacing between the actuators for use as a medical palpation simulation device. While FEELEX displays are able to sense user input through touch, they do not allow additional input techniques.

Digital Clay is a research initiative at Georgia Tech investigating various shape rendering devices and their application as human computer interfaces. One of the proposed mechanisms is a 2.5D shape display [22], with applications proposed for 3D modeling by sculpting with fingers. A functional prototype with a 5 x 5 array of hydraulically driven actuators was developed. Potential user interactions for the system were investigated with PHANTOM haptic devices [5]. The proposed interactions are not evaluated on an actual 2.5D shape display, as they would require resolution and sensing capabilities that have not yet been achieved.

Lumen by Poupyrev et al. [20] is a shape rendering apparatus driven by a 13 x 13 nitinol actuator array, similar to the apparatus of Pop-Up [15]. Graphic overlay is integrated into the device by lighting each actuated pin with a monochrome LED. Applications for Lumen include animated shapes, reconfigurable tangible user interface elements, and connected shapes for remote presence. The input mode is similar to that of a touch screen with tactile feedback, thus it does not explore additional interactions, beyond direct touch.

The XenoVision Mark III Dynamic Sand Table trades output speed for a simplified actuation mechanism, which enables a high resolution through 7000 actuators [19, 4]. As rendering a complete shape on the current system takes more than 30 seconds, users cannot interact with the physical shape in real-time.

Gemotion Screen by Niiyama and Kawaguchi [17] utilizes pneumatically actuated flexible fabric screens with front projected graphics to display organic art.

Photonastic Surface by Oguchi et al. proposes a novel mechanism to address individual actuators of 2.5D shape displays using projected light [18].

Relief, developed by Leithinger and Ishii [14] proposes an actuator apparatus based on commercial hardware and open-source components for low cost and scalability.

Actuator arrangements similar to 2.5D shape displays exist on different scales, from fingertip sized tactile displays [1] to wall-sized displays [7]. However, the focus of this paper is on shape displays at the scale of the users hands.

Freehand Gestures

To date, 2.5D shape displays have only utilized touch as an input modality. Based on our investigation of the limitations of direct touch, we propose to extend this modality with freehand gestures. Our proposed gestures have been inspired by previous research using pinching to interact with 3D data.

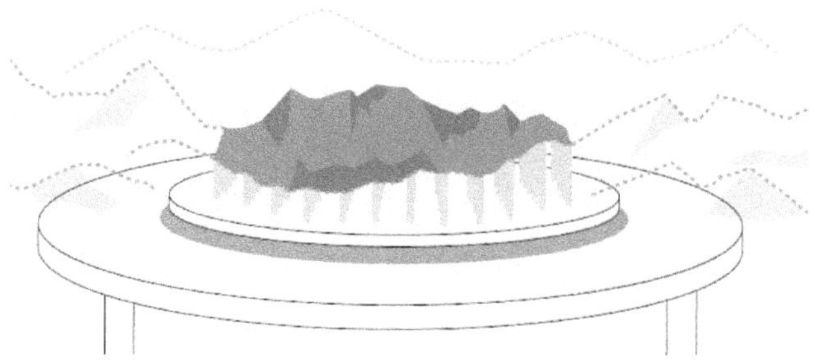

Figure 5: 2.5D shape displays output a subset of total geometry

Wilson proposes a robust computer-vision algorithm for detect freehand pinching gestures [27] to zoom, translate and rotate digital content. This method has been applied for large screen interaction, such as dome-shaped displays [2] and to complement touch on interactive tabletops [9]. The metaphor of pinching a virtual string connected to a 3D object has also been applied by Grossman et al. to interact with volumetric displays [8] and by Zigelbaum et al. to interact with large screens [28].

INTERACTIONS

Due to the limited resolution of current 2.5D shape displays, they can only generate an approximation of the actual model. Therefore, only a subset of the total model geometry might be shown at a time (Fig. 5). Thus global operations such as zoom, translation and rotation are essential, in order to view details of the model.

3D modeling software (e.g. AutoCAD), allows modification of model geometry through transformation of individual vertices. These operations require the selection of a subset of pins on the display.

To summarize, the following interactions need to be supported:

- Transformation of scene view
- Selection of model vertices
- Transformation of selected vertices

In order to implement these interactions, first we demonstrate the limitations of direct touch, followed by a discussion of other input modalities.

Limitations of Touch and Deformation

Touch input on 2.5D shape displays has been previously limited to buttons [21] or button like behavior [12]. Touching the surface acts like a mouse click in traditional graphical user interfaces (GUI). Interpretation of touch input varies greatly between applications. Proposed interactions have also explored behaviors similar to a touch screen: users can swipe their hand, leaving a shape trace on the interface [21].

Because touch can perform many different functions, its implied use becomes ambiguous. Problems arise when we examine the requirements of a simple 3D modeling application. We define the most basic set of user interactions as the transformation and deformation of an object. Deformation

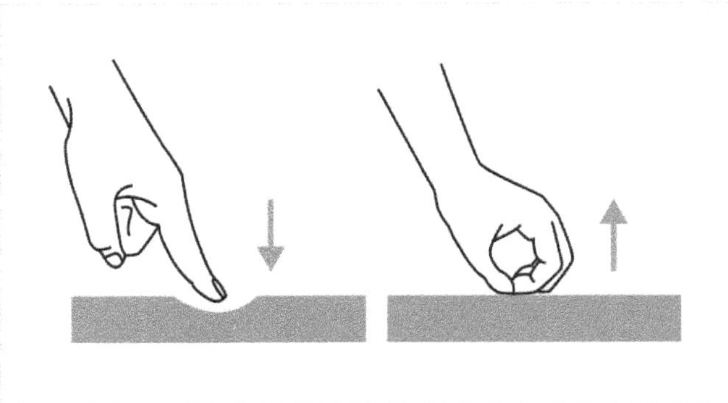

Figure 6: Ambiguities of direct manipulation: pushing and pulling pins

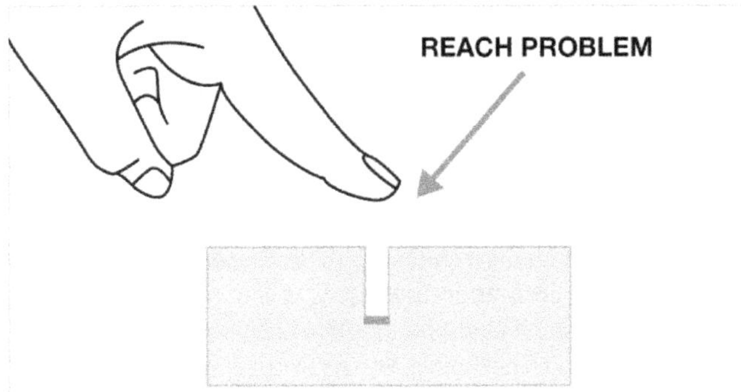

Figure 7: Reach problem – the shape of the interface surface may hinder direct touch

of object geometry can be achieved by mapping surface changes to the object mesh. This creates a clay-like behavior, allowing the user to push and pull on the surface. While this interaction performs well when pushing, it is practically difficult to pull the surface to a desired height (Fig. 6).

Once object transformations are added to program functionality, input through touch becomes ambiguous. When a user presses onto an object, it is no longer clear whether the object should be moved or deformed. With each additional feature both the complexity of interaction and input ambiguity are increased. In order to keep low input ambiguity, while retaining the locus of interaction at the surface, we propose that a 2.5D shape display requires an additional mode of input.

An interesting design challenge of direct touch interaction is the "reach problem". The resolution of the 2.5D shape display may hinder users to reach for certain areas due to surface topology (Fig. 7).

External Controller as Additional Input

We experimented with interaction modalities beyond direct touch by connecting a standard trackball mouse for global surface navigation. A series of interactions map to the features of the trackball. Rolling the ball in any direction pans the surface accordingly. Similarly, pressing either mouse button activates standard zoom in and out commands across the entire surface. In order to compare the use of an external controller against direct touch, the input features of pan and zoom were implemented directly onto the 2.5D shape display itself. The edge pins of the interface activate panning. Pushing the pins the user can pan the scene according to location of the push along the edge. Zooming in is achieved by pushing on center pins, while zooming out by pushing on opposing edge pins.

Upon comparing the two implementations we argue that while an external controller reduces interaction ambiguity, it also it removes the locus of interaction from the table, thus interrupting the user from performing actions efficiently.

Gestures as Additional Input

Learning from our previous tests, we identify gestural input as the best additional interaction modality with a 2.5D shape display. Gestures can be utilized to perform functional commands over the entire surface without altering the locus of interaction. By expressing gestures directly above the surface, a user can seamlessly switch between selection, manipulation, and translation of objects on a 2.5D shape display. When coupled with direct touch, a user is able to maximize functionality without creating input ambiguity.

A grammar of gestures has been implemented to explore basic functions used to interact with a 2.5D shape display. We have found that the most fundamental set of gestures includes: selection of an area, translation of the selection, rotation of the selection, and scaling of the selection. Further description of these techniques follows:

Selection

In order to select a subset of the surface the user forms two parallel vertical planes with their hands (Fig. 9) - a gesture commonly used to indicate the dimension of an object (e.g. "I caught a fish this big!"). The system indicates a selected area with a projected square selection rectangle. A two-finger pinch on either hand locks the selection dimensions, enabling manipulation through a number of gestures.

Translation

By adjusting hand position along the X, Y, or Z-axis, the user can simultaneously manipulate the height and position of the selection (Fig. 10). After reaching the desired height and position the user can release the pinch gesture, saving surface state, and resetting the interaction state back to selection mode.

Rotation

By rotating the locked hands about the X, Y or Z-axis, the selection rotates accordingly (Fig. 11).

Scaling

By changing the distance between the locked hands, the selection scales proportionally (Fig. 12). This gesture is an evolution of the ubiquitously popular pinch-zoom in natural user interfaces.

Figure 8: Viewing terrain on a 2.5D shape display

Figure 9: Gesture for selection

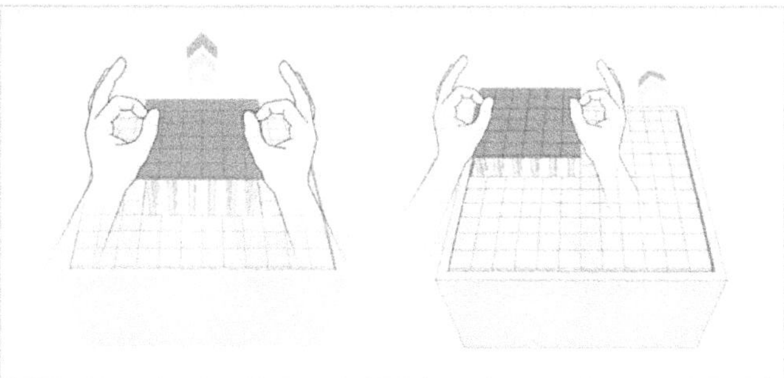

Figure 10: Gesture for translation

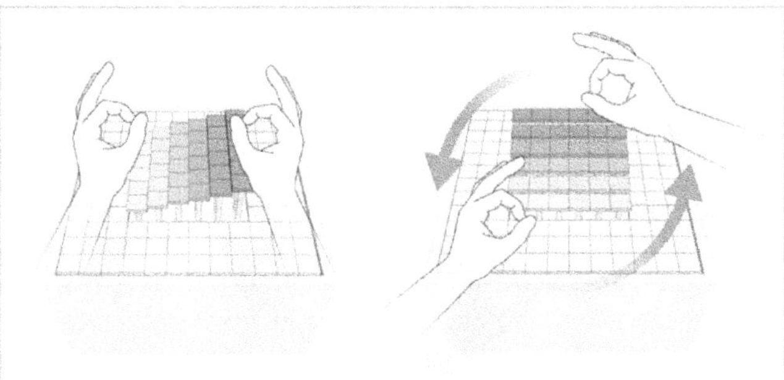

Figure 11: Gesture for rotation

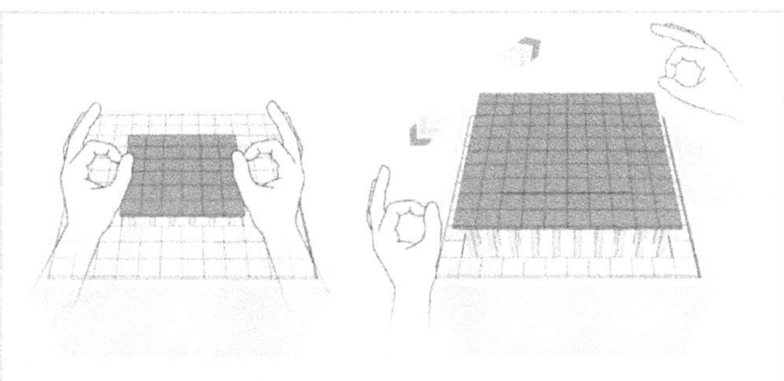

Figure 12: Gesture for scale

APPLICATIONS

Through two applications we show how gestural input and direct manipulation can be used to navigate and to manipulate a 2.5D shape display.

Viewing 3D models

As discussed in related work, 2.5D shape displays are unable to create arbitrary shapes. However, shapes without overhangs, such as terrain data, can be formed with reasonable accuracy as previously proposed [4]. To explore the advantages of interactive shape output, we developed a geospatial application, equivalent to a tangible version of Google Maps (Fig. 8). Users can translate, scale and rotate terrain in 2 dimensions through use of the previously described freehand gestures. In addition to terrain data, our application is able to load geometry from a 3DS file and output an approximation of the physical shape on the surface. Similar to the terrain scenario, the object can be translated, rotated and scaled, however these transformations can be applied in all dimensions.

Recompose

Recompose explores the potential as an input device through a system that allows expression of volumetric structures. While designing the system we adhered to the following criteria:

Re-purpose methods from traditional digital design

Methods such as translate, rotate and scale are computational manipulations of data that aid the efficiency of digital design. Previously, as physical matter could not be informed by digital data (it is impossible to scale a mass of clay), such methods could not be applied when designing with physical materials. However, as the surface of the 2.5D shape display is computationally informed, such methods can be utilized freeing the user of constraints imposed by physical matter and speeding up the process of design.

Direct Manipulation

Haptic sensation remains our primary feedback mechanism in traditional surface manipulation (e.g. clay sculpting). We designed a system where direct haptic manipulation is a core component of the interaction. By allowing direct manipulation of pin height, users are afforded such haptic feedback.

Modality

The modality change between direct manipulation and gestural input must be complementary and seamless. In order for direct manipulation and digital design methods to coexist, we need a clear dividing line between each functional mode; a design that allows users to seamlessly change between them.

Metaphors

Functional gestures should be rooted in metaphor to aid intuition. By having strong metaphors to existing interaction paradigms, gestural interaction with the system can be made more intuitive.

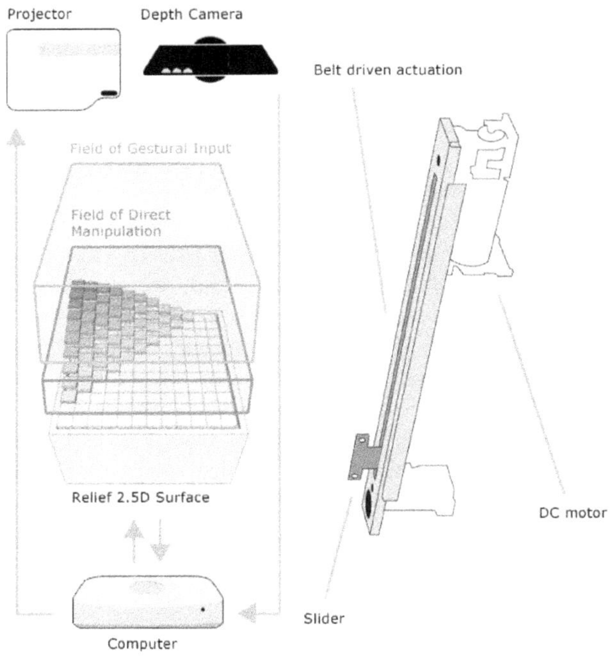

Figure 13: a) System overview b) Actuator element

SYSTEM DESIGN

Hardware

We utilize a 2.5D shape display similar to the system proposed by Leithinger and Ishii [14]. The table consists of an array of 120 individually addressable pins, whose height can be actuated and read back simultaneously, thus allowing the user to utilize them as both input and output. We have furthered the design by placing a depth camera above the tabletop surface. Through gaining access to the depth information we are able to detect basic gestures from the user (Fig. 13a).

The pins are actuated with ALPS motorized slide potentiometers, widely used in audio mixing boards (Fig. 13b). Each pin has a reach of 13 cm vertically with a resolution of 7 bits, thus the pins can be controlled in 1 mm increments. While trying to achieve minimal spacing between actuators we were limited by the dimensions of the slide potentiometers. Currently, the actuators are arranged in a square grid with 5 cm spacing.

Arduino Duemilanove boards with attached Ladyada motor driver shields control the actuators. Instead of daisy-chaining the modules as previously proposed, our system utilizes I2C bus configurations for faster, more reliable communication. Our software application communicates over a serial connection with three Arduino master modules, which control up to 12 slave modules over an I2C bus. Using this method, the apparatus achieves a speed of 15 fps for communication between an application and the target positions on the microcontrollers. Though considerably slower than commercial haptic devices like the Phantom, this speed proves sufficient for the interface.

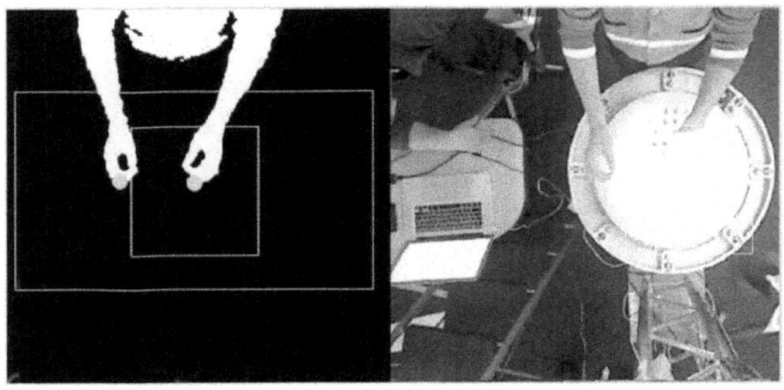

Figure 14: Image seen by the depth camera processed to extract gestures and same view with RGB camera

In order to provide the user visual feedback a projector is mounted 150 cm above the table. A projected graphical user interface guides the user through the interaction and colors the individual pin platforms corresponding to their actuated height.

Depth reading is achieved through a Microsoft Kinect depth camera. The camera is located inline with the projector centered to the table in order to minimize the parallax error arising from asymmetrical placement. The camera is mounted at a distance of 135 cm from the tabletop surface as a compromise between maximum covered area and sufficient precision to accurately detect the pinch gesture.

Both the depth camera and the actuated surface control system are connected to a Unix based operating system, where the custom host software written by the authors processes the required computation.

Software

Software on the control machine is written in OpenFrameworks. Rendering on the actuated surface is achieved by processing the depth buffer of the 3D mesh and sending the depth values to the hardware actuators. Direct touch input is detected by computing the difference of the last actuated and currently reported height.

Computer Vision

Freehand gesture input is sensed with a depth camera. The software uses a community contributed set of libraries to access the camera. After acquiring the depth image of the camera, the users contour is computed from the depth values (Fig. 14). For gesture recognition a state-machine is implemented that stores the current gesture state and reacts to changes in hand posture accordingly. After extracting curvature of the blobs corresponding to the hands of the user, our algorithm finds fingers and determines the current height of the hands.

DISCUSSION

Direct manipulation of an actuated surface allows us to precisely affect the material world, where the user is guided throughout the interaction by natural haptic feedback. However, direct manipulation is incapable of affecting large areas of a surface or small sections unreachable due to the reach problem. We demonstrate how free hand gesture input can solve this problem without requiring the user to shift their focus to an external controller. We designed the system so users can fluidly change between gestural and direct manipulation.

After implementing two applications to demonstrate the interactions presented in this paper, they were tried by over 300 different visitors during various demonstrations in our research laboratory and at Siggraph Emerging Techologies 2011. While we have not conducted formal experiments, we where able to gather interesting feedback and observations:

In the application to view 3D models, many users commented on how they found it easier to understand the shape of the model when shown on the interface compared to a 2D display. While we expected this feedback, it was remarkable how the low resolution of the output apparatus was sufficient to present a perceptual advantage. Projected graphics were key to aiding users in identifying the 3D models. Without projection, the rendered shapes were too low in resolution for the user to perceive the underlying 3D model.

In the Recompose application users found direct manipulation to be intuitive. While users understood selection feedback, it was not apparent that a pinching gesture would be required to transform a shape. Once demonstrated, all users were able to replicate this functionality and many could relate to the interaction metaphor of pinching strings. However, the tracking of small hands was sometimes inconsistent due to the camera resolution.

These observations of visitors using both touch and freehand gestures are encouraging indicators that the proposed interactions are intuitive and efficient for interacting with 2.5D shape displays. The proposed freehand gestures have been utilized previously for spatially transforming data, but our applications demonstrate that they work well in the context of 2.5D shape displays.

CONCLUSION AND FUTURE WORK

In this paper we have identified 2.5D shape interfaces as a distinct subcategory of shape displays. We found properties common to all 2.5D shape displays and listed their advantages and limitations.

We have presented interaction techniques for 2.5D shape displays, which extend manipulation through touch with freehand gestures. After identifying a set of common interactions for viewing and manipulating content on shape displays, we proposed freehand gestures to implement them.

We intend to further the system by implementing a number of additional interaction features beyond the previously explored select, translate, and transform functions. We would like to explore the following set of features:

Copy and Paste

Additional gestures would allow users to quickly duplicate shapes. The duplicated shapes could be both digital models and physical objects captured by the depth-sensing camera.

Timeline Controls

A timeline of all surface manipulation captured during a session allowing for time reversal, state saving, and undo type functions. We believe that implementing a set of gestures to explore the dimension of time grants the user additional power currently impossible by the constraints of the physical world.

Advanced Drafting Techniques

We plan to implement techniques commonly found in drafting and 3D modeling tools, such as spline lofting and Boolean operations.

System design

We intend to pursue both higher fidelity gesture recognition coupled with higher resolution actuated surfaces to allow for a greater range of expression and interpretation.

ACKNOWLEDGEMENTS

We would like to thank our colleagues at the MIT Media Lab, especially Adam Kumpf and Sean Follmer for ideas and insights.

REFERENCES

1. Benali Khoudja, M., Hafez, M., Alexandre, J.M., Kheddar, A. Tactile Interfaces: A State of the Art Survey. In *Proceedings of the International Symposium on Robotics (2004)*, 721-726
2. Benko, H., and Wilson, A. 2010. Multi-point interactions with immersive omnidirectional visualizations in a dome. In *ACM International Conference on Interactive Tabletops and Surfaces* (ITS '10). ACM, New York, NY, USA, 19-28.
3. Coelho, M., Ishii, H., and Maes, P. 2008. Surflex: a programmable surface for the design of tangible interfaces. In *CHI '08 extended abstracts on Human factors in computing systems* (CHI EA '08). ACM, New York, NY, USA, 3429-3434.
4. Francica, J., 2004. Interview with Xenotran Founder, Dr. Derrick Page. In *Directions Magazine*. November 21st 2004, http://www.directionsmag.com/articles/interview-with-xenotran-founder-drderrick-page/123593
5. Gargus, J., Kim, B., Rossignac, R., and Shaw, D. 2002. Finger Sculpting with Digital Clay. GVU Technical Report, GIT-GVU-02-22
6. Goldstein, S., Campbell, J., and Mowry, T. Programmable Matter. In *IEEE Computer*, 38(6): 99–101, June, 2005.
7. Goulthorpe, M., Burry, M., and Dunlop, G. Aegis Hyposurface: The Bordering of University and Practice. In *Proc. of ACADIA*, 2001, Association for Computer--Aided Design in Architecture, pp. 344--349.
8. Grossman, T., Wigdor, D., and Balakrishnan, R. 2004. Multi-finger gestural interaction with 3d volumetric displays. In *Proceedings of the 17th annual ACM symposium on User interface software and technology* (UIST '04). ACM, New York, NY, USA, 61-70.

9. Hilliges, O., Izadi, S., Wilson, A., Hodges, S., Garcia-Mendoza, A., and Butz, A. 2009. Interactions in the air: adding further depth to interactive tabletops. In *Proceedings of the 22nd annual ACM symposium on User interface software and technology* (UIST '09). ACM, New York, NY, USA, 139-148.
10. Hirota, K., Hirose, M. Simulation and presentation of curved surface in virtual reality environment through surface display. In *Proceedings of the Virtual Reality Annual International Symposium* (VRAIS '95). IEEE Computer Society, Washington, DC, USA, 211-216
11. Ishii, H. and Ullmer, B. 1997. Tangible bits: towards seamless interfaces between people, bits and atoms. In *Proceedings of the SIGCHI conference on Human factors in computing systems* (CHI '97). ACM, New York, NY, USA, 234-241.
12. Iwata, H., Yano, H., Nakaizumi, F., and Kawamura, R. 2001. Project FEELEX: adding haptic surface to graphics. In Proceedings of the 28th Annual Conference on Computer Graphics and interactive Techniques SIGGRAPH '01. ACM, New York, NY, 469-476.
13. Iwata, H., Yano, H., and Ono, N. 2005. Volflex. In *ACM SIGGRAPH 2005 Emerging technologies* (SIGGRAPH '05), Donna Cox (Ed.). ACM, New York, NY, USA, 2005, Article 31
14. Leithinger, D., and Ishii, H. 2010. Relief: a scalable actuated shape display. In *Proceedings of the fourth international conference on Tangible, embedded, and embodied interaction* (TEI '10). ACM, New York, NY, USA, 221-222.
15. Nakatani, M., Kajimoto, H., Sekiguchi, D., Kawakami, N., and Tachi, S. 3D form display with shape memory alloy. In Proc. 13th International Conference on Artificial Reality and Telexistence, Tokyo, Japan, 2003, pp. 179-184
16. Nakatani, M., Kajimoto, H., Kawakami, N., and Tachi, S. 2005. Tactile sensation with high-density pin-matrix. In *Proceedings of the 2nd symposium on Applied perception in graphics and visualization* (APGV '05). ACM, New York, NY, USA, 169-169.
17. Niiyama, R. and Kawaguchi, Y. Gemotion Screen: A Generative, Emotional, Interactive 3D Display. In *Proceeding of the ASIAGRAPH 2008* in Shanghai, pp.115–120, Shanghai, China, July 2008
18. Oguchi, R., Kakehi, Y., Takahashi, K., and Naemura, T. 2008. Photonastic surface: pin matrix type display controlled with light. In *Proceedings of the 2008 International Conference on Advances in Computer Entertainment Technology* (ACE '08). ACM, New York, NY, USA, 396-396.
19. Page, D. J. (2005). Reconfigurable Surface. US Patent No. 6903871 B2.
20. Poupyrev, I., Nashida, T., Maruyama, S., Rekimoto, J., and Yamaji, Y. 2004. Lumen: interactive visual and shape display for calm computing. In *ACM SIGGRAPH 2004 Emerging Technologies* (Los Angeles, California, August 08 - 12, 2004). H. Elliott-Famularo, Ed. SIGGRAPH '04. ACM, New York, NY, 17.
21. Poupyrev, I., Nashida, T., Okabe, M. Actuation and Tangible User Interfaces: the Vaucanson Duck, Robots, and Shape Displays. Proceedings of TEI'07. 2007: ACM: pp. 205-212.
22. Rossignac, J., Allen, M., Book, W., Glezer, A., Ebert-Uphoff, I., Shaw, C., Rosen, D., Askins, S., Bai, J., Bosscher, P., Gargus, J., Kim, B.-M., Llamas, I., Nguyen, A., Yuan, G., Zhu, H. 2003. Finger Sculpting with Digital Clay: 3D Shape Input and Output through a Computer-Controlled Real Surface. smi, International Conference on Shape Modeling and Applications 2003, pp. 296
23. Shimojo, M.; Shinohara, M.; Fukui, Y. Human shape recognition performance for 3D tactile display. In *IEEE International Conference on Systems, Man, and Cybernetics, 1997*, vol.4, no., pp.3192-3197 vol.4, 12-15 Oct 1997
24. Sutherland, I. The Ultimate Display. In *International Federation of Information Processing*, Vol. 2, 1965, pp. 506-508.
25. Ward, F. (1985). Pin Screen. US Patent No. 4536980.
26. Weibel, R. & Heller, M. 1991. Digital Terrain Modeling. In: *Maguire, D.J., Goodchild, M.F. and Rhind, D.W. (eds.). Geographical Information Systems: Principles and Applications.* London: Longman, 269-297.
27. Wilson, A. 2006. Robust computer vision-based detection of pinching for one and two-handed gesture input. In *Proceedings of the 19th annual ACM symposium on User interface software and technology* (UIST '06). ACM, New York, NY, USA, 255-258.
28. Zigelbaum, J., Browning, A., Leithinger, D., Bau, O., and Ishii, H. 2010. g-stalt: a chirocentric, spatiotemporal, and telekinetic gestural interface. In *Proceedings of the fourth international conference on Tangible, embedded, and embodied interaction* (TEI '10). ACM, New York, NY, USA, 261-264.

6D Hands: Markerless Hand Tracking for Computer Aided Design

Robert Y. Wang[1,] , *Sylvain Paris* , *Jovan Popović* [,4]

[1]3Gear Systems
Foster City, CA
rywang@threegear.com

Adobe Systems, Inc.
Cambridge, MA
{sparis,jovan}@adobe.com

MIT CSAIL
Cambridge, MA

[4]Univ. of Washington
Seattle, WA

ABSTRACT

Computer Aided Design (CAD) typically involves tasks such as adjusting the camera perspective and assembling pieces in free space that require specifying 6 degrees of freedom (DOF). The standard approach is to factor these DOFs into 2D subspaces that are mapped to the x and y axes of a mouse. This metaphor is inherently modal because one needs to switch between subspaces, and disconnects the input space from the modeling space. In this paper, we propose a bimanual hand tracking system that provides physically-motivated 6-DOF control for 3D assembly. First, we discuss a set of principles that guide the design of our precise, easy-to-use, and comfortable-to-use system. Based on these guidelines, we describe a 3D input metaphor that supports constraint specification classically used in CAD software, is based on only a few simple gestures, lets users rest their elbows on their desk, and works alongside the keyboard and mouse. Our approach uses two consumer-grade webcams to observe the user's hands. We solve the pose estimation problem with efficient queries of a precomputed database that relates hand silhouettes to their 3D configuration. We demonstrate efficient 3D mechanical assembly of several CAD models using our hand-tracking system.

ACM Classification: H5.2 [Information Interfaces and Presentation]: User Interfaces–*Input devices and strategies*

General terms: Design, Human Factors, Algorithms

Keywords: computer aided design, hand-tracking, 3D object manipulation

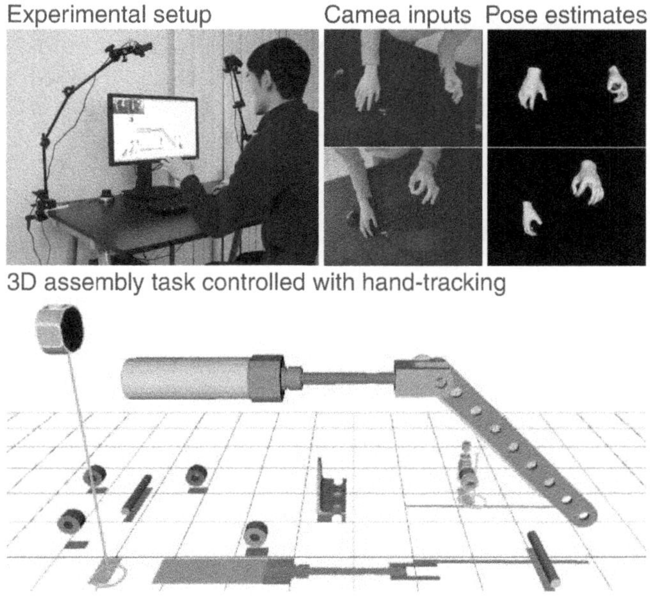

Figure 1: We propose a markerless hand-tracking system using two webcams for 3D assembly in the context of Computer Aided Design.

INTRODUCTION

Computer Aided Design (CAD) is an essential component of modern mechanical engineering, architectural design and visual effects design. 3D CAD software enables a user to digitally specify shapes, positions and orientations of objects in a virtual 3D scene. Formally, most of these tasks require users to specify 3 or more variables, for instance, the xyz components of a translation or the three angles of a rotation. However, a 2D mouse is still the predominate method by which users interact with CAD software. It is typically controlled unimanually by the dominant (right) hand and used for both adjusting the camera perspective and moving objects in a 3D scene. In this paper, we propose a new input method that is complimentary to the mouse and better matches the dimensionality of 3D assembly tasks.

We facilitate more efficient interactions for CAD by enabling the user to manipulate the camera perspective and objects in the scene with both hands in 3D. We can track 6 degrees of freedom for each hand and a pinching gesture for selection. To avoid wrist-strain, we primarily use the three translational degrees of freedom of each hand tracked at the tip of the thumb. We propose comfortable, memorable and efficient gestures that map unimanual translation to 3D translation in the virtual world and bimanual translation to 3D rotation.

A complete CAD software system typically includes functionality for modeling 3D parts, assembling the parts into a whole, and, in the case of engineering CAD, laying out views of the assembly on a paper blueprint. In this work, we focus on the assembly component of CAD, which primarily involves the 3D positioning of parts, a task well suited for direct hand manipulation.

A major feature of our system is that it tracks the hands without gloves or markers, leaving them unencumbered to use the keyboard and mouse. This enables users to transition seamlessly to existing functionality in the CAD software such as navigating a menu with the mouse and typing coordinates on the keyboard. By facilitating these mixed-mode operations, our system serves as a practical complement to the mouse and keyboard for 3D assembly interactions.

RELATED WORK

Many methods have been proposed for markerless or gloveless hand tracking, but they are either too slow for interactive applications, e.g. [24, 7], or the range of poses that they can detect do not permit the precise selection required in CAD applications, e.g. [14, 13, 20]. In comparison, our system achieves bimanual 6-DOF pose estimation at interactive rates and reliably detects poses suited for discrete selection such as pinching and pointing.

Glove tracking has been proposed to ease and speed up the problem of hand tracking, e.g. [27, 25]. However, gloves are a significant drawback if one wants to also use the keyboard and mouse. Users may be reluctant to put on a glove when switching from a 2D task such as menu navigation to a 3D task such as object assembly. Wearing a glove may also become uncomfortable during long work sessions.

Dedicated 6-DOF rate-control devices such as the 3DConnexion SpaceNavigator are used for smooth camera control, but are generally not suited for or used for object selection or manipulation in CAD. We propose a set of hand gestures that works well for both camera adjustment and object manipulation.

Recently Microsoft introduced and deployed the Kinect motion capture system. While successful results have been shown for whole body tracking [21], it is unclear if the Kinect system can be used to track hands. In particular, occlusions of the fingers are difficult to resolve using a single viewpoint.

Pinching has been shown to be an effective gesture for "clicking" in 3D space. Hilliges and colleagues use a single depth camera to detect pinches above a table top [9]. Benko and Wilson [4] track pinches using an infrared camera above a projector. Wilson uses a webcam to detect pinches above the keyboard [26]. However, all three approaches rely on a single-view pinch detection technique that suffers from occlusions, restricting the hand orientations that can be tracked. A unique feature of our approach is the use of two wide-baseline viewpoints. Our two-view approach resolves occlusions from one view using information from the other, enabling robust gesture (e.g. pinch) detection. Our contribution is independent of the particular type of camera used (depth or RGB).

Recent work on 3D assembly by Kin and colleagues [11] addressed the construction of organic sets on a multi-touch surface. In organic set dressing, the artistic look and feel of a scene is more important than precise placement of parts. In comparison, we focus primarily on 3D assembly for mechanical engineering where exact relationships between parts is crucial.

A large body of HCI research has used various forms of 3D input for virtual reality applications [1, 10, 3] but studies have shown that 3D input usability is often inferior to the mouse [5, 23]. Based on this observation, we designed our system to limit the duration of 3D input sessions and to be complementary to existing input devices so that users can fall back to standard mouse+keyboard interaction at any time. We envision that our hand tracking will be used only for 3D assembly tasks where it offers a natural and intuitive three-dimensional interaction, while other tasks such as menu navigation will continue to be done with the mouse.

TRADITIONAL 3D ASSEMBLY WORKFLOW

3D assembly refers to positioning a set of 3D parts to create a larger whole. It is used to construct a set from a collection of props or to assemble mechanical pieces into a machine. It is performed in two main ways.

Coarse 3D placement is used primarily in the context of computer animation or special effects, where the location of an object is only important so much as it generates a convincing image or effect. For such placement, users mostly rely on the translation manipulator to specify position in 3D space with a 2D mouse. A translation manipulator multiplexes 3D translation onto three 1D components projected as axes on the screen (Figure 2). The user selects an arrow and drags along each axis, one at a time, to move an object to its desired location. CAD software also lets users drag objects freely in the image plane. These manipulators are good at specifying axis-aligned and in-plane translations, but require more effort for other directions. Equivalent metaphors with similar pros and cons exist for rotations.

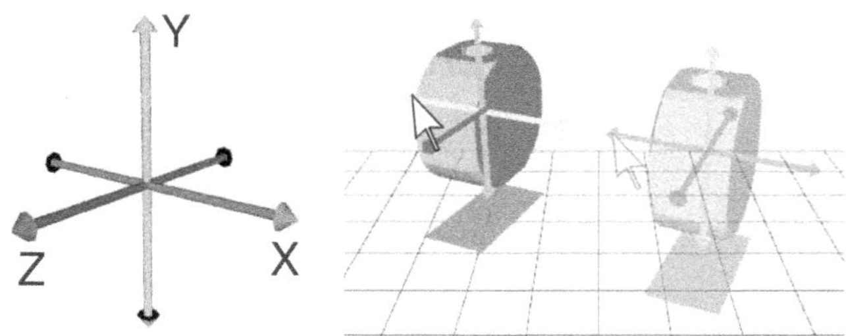

Figure 2: A traditional translation manipulator multiplexes 3D translation onto three 1-D translation modes. The user enters the x translation mode by dragging along the projected x-axis.

These manipulators provide a continuous and thus imprecise translation control. For precise placement of mechanical parts, a process of specifying constraints between faces and boundaries (or "mates") is used to define the position of a part exactly. Such positioning is crucial in manufacturing, and mating is the primary mode for 3D assembly in all mechanical engineering CAD software (e.g. SolidWorks, Autodesk Inventor, CATIA). A mate is specified with the mouse by selecting two of the features to align, and defining the relationship between them (Figure 3). For instance, if two circular boundaries are required to lie along the same axis, a user would click each boundary successively and select the concentric mate option. Specifying mates requires significant adjustments to the camera perspective because mates often involve occluded features. For instance, when specifying that two faces should be coincident, one of the faces is often facing away from the user, and thus not directly selectable.

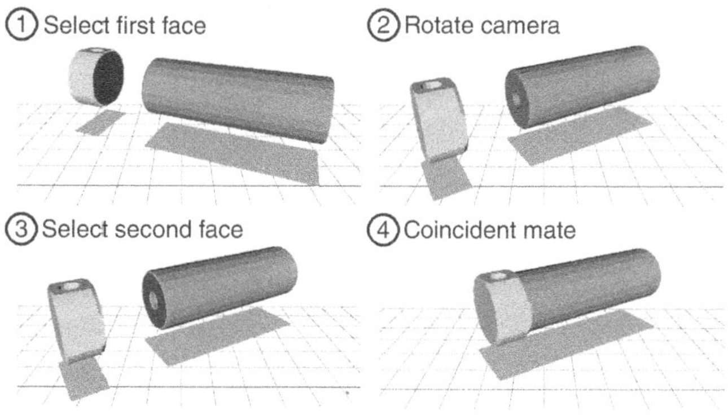

Figure 3: To specify a constraint or "mate" using a traditional 2D mouse, the user clicks on one face, rotates the camera, clicks on the other face, and indicates that they should be coincident.

In addition to manipulating objects, users also adjust the camera perspective to visualize the assembly from different view points or to select occluded features. This is classically done with the mouse using an arcball rotation control. This tool maps x and y mouse translations to the rotations around the y and x screen axes respectively. z-axis rotation, when available, is modal and involves either a different mouse button or a modifier key.

We observed several mechanical engineers using the Solidworks 2009 CAD software. Other functions often used in 3D assembly include importing parts from the file system into the scene, hiding or isolating parts in complex assemblies, and performing specialized shape modifications to a part (e.g. adding threads to a screw). These actions are accessed through mouse-driven menus, and would be more difficult to map to hand tracking.

We contribute a system that uses hand gestures for the positioning of parts for 3D assembly while other tasks such as entry of numerical values, annotations, or menu navigation are still performed with the keyboard and the mouse. Our gestures allow users to efficiently reposition pieces in 3D by selecting and moving them with their hands. Users can also adjust the camera perspective to access pieces and explore the 3D scene. Furthermore, our system enables modeless specification of exact relationships, making it suitable for the assembly of mechanical parts for engineering.

HAND GESTURES FOR 3D ASSEMBLY

Based on the observations made in the previous section, we first describe the design principles that guided how we built our system. Then, we propose a set of gestures that follow these guidelines.

Design Principles

Before describing the gestures that we implemented in our system, we first discuss the challenges that we faced while we designed our system and the high-level principles that we followed to address them.

A small number of simple hand poses Although a human hand has 27 DOFs, only a few poses are comfortable and can be reproduced without training. Guided by this idea, we built our system mostly on the pinch pose inspired by Andrew Wilson's [26] Thumb and Fore-Finger Interface. We use pinching as an analog of the mouse click to indicate the selection of an object. We also explore pointing for specifying remote locations, and touching the desktop with fingers to turn the desk surface into a multi-touch interface.

Use precise and memorable gestures To create precise and memorable gestures, we use metaphors that correspond closely to physical actions. We directly map 3D physical positions to virtual positions. Once a user understands a virtual scene, reaching for the object leverages his physical intuition to reach for a point in 3D space. We also adopt a physically-based mental model to design hand gestures for rotation. Motivated by work showing that users tend to perform rotation and translation separately [15], we decouple camera rotation and camera translation as two distinct gestures to provide precise and physically-based control for both.

Limited hand motion Unrestricted 3D interactions and large movements are tiring and only useful for short periods of time. We exploit the desktop environment to address the fatigue issue and design our system such that users can rest their elbows or forearms on the desk most of the time. Inspired by the Eden system, [11], we also allow the user to pass objects between the hands (throw-and-catch) to minimize dragging. We also amplify the user's 3D motion so that only small gestures are needed, e.g. we map a 10° hand rotation to 20° in the modeler.

Specification of exact constraints Exact constraints, or *mates*, are crucial in mechanical engineering applications to align pieces or put objects in exact contact. Specifying these mates explicitly involves selecting small features such as boundaries and faces. This is already challenging in 2D with a mouse, and even more difficult with 3D selection. Instead, we "snap" a part into place when it is sufficiently close to satisfying a concentric or a coincident mate. This feature enables our prototype CAD system to facilitate the precise alignment and contact specification required in mechanical engineering.

Concentric and coincident mates account for a large proportion of mates between mechanical parts. For instance, any mechanical assembly held together by screws and nuts use concentric and coincident mates. However, we hope to address more general mates (e.g. distance mates, curved surfaces) in future work. Presently, we fall back to traditional mouse and keyboard input for more complex mates.

Cues for 3D positioning We need to provide visual cues that relate the physical space where the user's hands are with the virtual space where modeling occurs. Since we do not want to assume that a 3D display is available, a simple "3D pointer", e.g. a small 3D arrow, is not enough because of the depth ambiguity inherent in 2D displays that makes it difficult to know if the pointer is at the same depth as another object. We address this challenge with a shadow metaphor that provides unambiguous depth cues in addition to the main 3D view. We render a virtual ground plane on which each piece projects a shadow, and we augment our pointer with a stem and base that shows its projection on the same plane [8], thereby resolving the depth ambiguity. Further, we also highlight the closest object to each hand to show which object can be selected in the current configuration.

Seamless transition between tracking and other modalities 3D assembly in CAD software is performed in conjunction with other activities that require the use of the keyboard and mouse such as structural analysis, reading documentation, or even just checking e-mail. Hand tracking should not interfere with other input modalities and should be an addition to them, not a replacement. We designed our system so that it can track bare hands since gloves and markers would impede the users' ability to type and use a mouse comfortably. We also automatically stop tracking when the hands approach the keyboard or the mouse, which allows the user to seamlessly go back to a classical keyboard-and-mouse interaction at any time.

Gestures

We support several gestures for object and camera manipulation (Figure 4). These are designed according the guidelines previously discussed.

Object translation When the user pinches with one hand, we select the closest object, and translate according to the pinching hand. If the user drags the object sufficiently close to another object, we examine the shapes of both objects and consider snapping the dragged object to generate a mate.

In our prototype CAD system, we focus on two common mates, concentric mates between circular boundaries and coincident mates between two faces. We detect approximate alignment of circular boundaries [16, 12] to snap the object into an exact alignment. Similarly, we snap together parallel faces that are almost touching to generate a coincident mate. Our 3D snapping generalizes snapping with 2D input devices [17] by generating the same mates used in CAD software.

Long-distance object translation Dragging objects is suitable for small translations but becomes tedious for large displacements, for example to go from one side of the workspace to the other. We address this with a throw-and-catch gesture akin to the Eden system [11]. The user pinches with one hand next to an object, which selects it, then pinches with the other hand where the object should go, and finally opens again the first hand, i.e. stops pinching, which transports the object where the second hand is. This gesture may be better seen in the companion video.

Camera translation When the user double-pinches with the two hands, we "attach" the camera to the two hands and translate it according to the average hand motion.

Camera and object rotation The user can control rotation by pinching with both hands, using a new *sheet-of-paper* metaphor. The motion is inspired by the grab-and-twirl gesture developed by Cutler and colleagues [6], and reproduces what users would experience if they were handling a sheet of paper as shown in Figure 5. Compared to grab-and-twirl, we remove the dependence on the hand orientation completely. Because we can track the 3D pinch points more accurately than hand orientation, we can amplify the rotated angles to minimize motion. We detail the formulas to derive the rotation angles from these gestures in the appendix.

When nothing is selected, a two-handed pinch rotates the viewpoint direction. When an object is selected with one of the hands, the rotation affects that object. Because CAD models are almost always axis-aligned, we snap object rotations to 90 degree increments.

Discussion We also experimented with a direct mapping of hand orientation to camera and object rotation. Direct orientation mapping worked well for small rotations, but large rotations led to significant strain on the wrists. This was problematic because camera viewpoint changes and object reorientations in CAD typically involve rotations of 90 degrees or more. In comparison, our two-handed pinching gestures do not require uncomfortable extreme wrist rotations and distributes effort across the larger muscles of the arm. Overall, we found our sheet-of-paper metaphor as easy-to-learn as a direct mapping while being more accurate and less straining on the wrists.

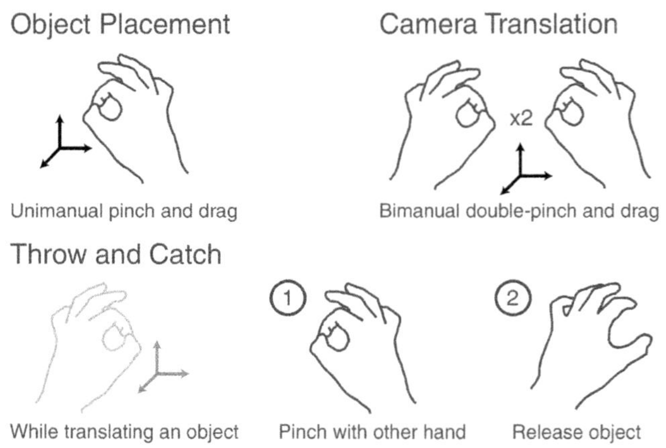

Figure 4: We support a few simple gestures for 3D manipulation and camera adjustment

MARKERLESS HAND-TRACKING

The main technical contribution of this work is a markerless hand tracking system that accurately and robustly recognizes the gestures previously described. As discussed in the previous work section, real-time markerless hand tracking is still an unsolved problem, and our approach leverages a wide-baseline camera setup, our constrained set of gestures, and the calibrated desktop environment to make this problem tractable.

Physical Setup

We designed our setup with several factors in mind. We ensure that both cameras can see the hands over a large 3D

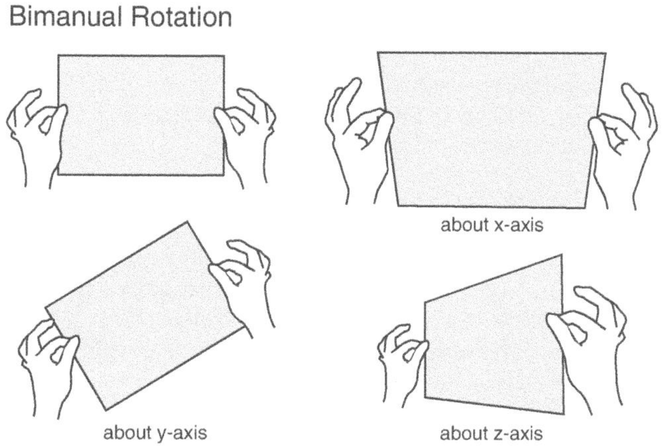

Figure 5: We mimic the physical actions of rotating an imaginary piece of paper with two hands to define our gestures for bimanual rotation. Rotating the sheet about the y or z-axis involves moving the hands in opposite directions along the xz or xy-plane respectively. To rotate the paper about the x-axis, one lifts or lowers the hands while bending the wrists (resulting in a translation along the y-axis about the elbow pivot)

capture volume. Our pose estimation algorithm benefits from two significantly different viewpoints to maximize information and minimize self-occlusion of the hand. The cameras are placed so that one hand does not occlude the other from either view. In particular, this could be a problem when one hand is raised above the other (Figure 6).

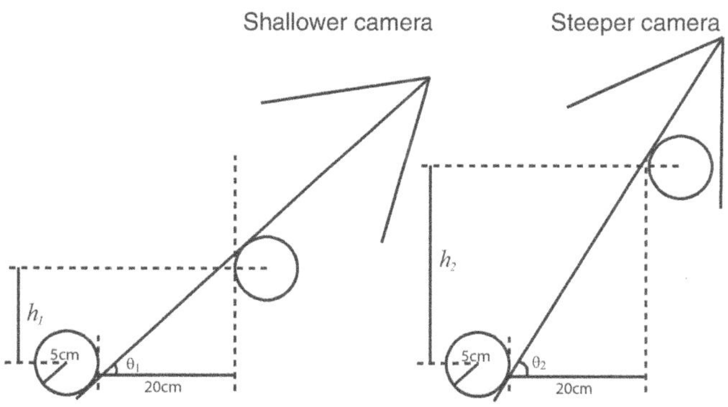

Figure 6: The most common occlusion case is when one hand (approximated as the circle on the right) is raised above another (the left circle). A steeper camera angle $\theta_2 > \theta_1$ allows a larger vertical separation $h_2 > h_1$ between the hands without occlusion.

Given these constraints, we propose a configuration such that a 34cm $\times$ 46cm $\times$ 24cm rectangular operating region is completely visible from both cameras. The cameras are placed so that their principal axes differ by an angle of 45°, which yields significantly different viewpoints. Each camera also forms a steep 67° angle with the ground plane. Given a spacing of 20 cm between the two hands, this allows one hand to be 10 cm above the other without inter-hand occlusion.

Markerless Pose Estimation

Our technique applies a data-driven pose estimation algorithm inspired by the marker-based technique of Wang et

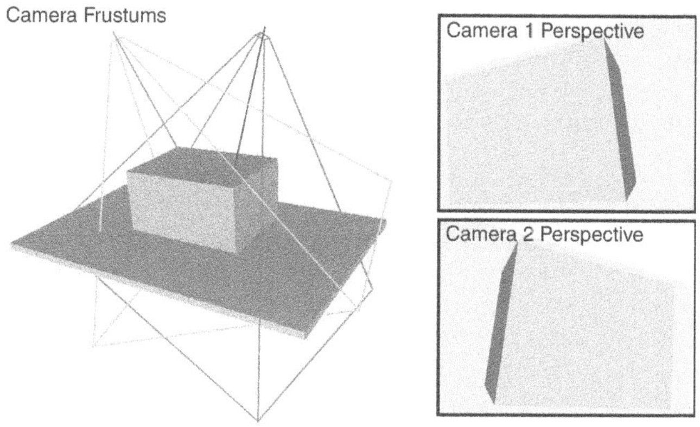

Figure 7: Our cameras are arranged so that both cameras observe the hand in a rectangular operating region (green).

al. [25]. However, using Wang's color glove would greatly impede users' interaction with other input devices such as a mouse or a keyboard, and we opted for a markerless approach, which makes the tracking problem much more challenging. We extend Wang's technique in several ways to address our needs and leverage our specific configuration. First, we sample only the limited set of hand poses relevant to our gestures rather than arbitrary configurations of the hand. We also consider only comfortable hand orientations and positions within our rectangular area. Finally, we modify the pose estimation algorithm to use two cameras rather than one.

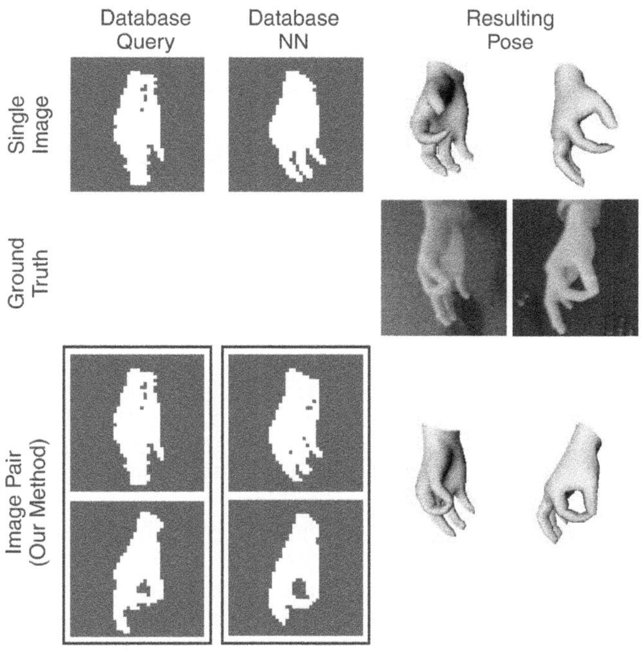

Figure 8: Given only silhouette data, a single camera view does not provide information to resolve ambiguities in orientation and finger configuration. Two cameras from different view points provides much less ambiguous data.

Two Camera Pose Estimation Our system builds upon recent work in data-driven pose estimation that uses a precomputed database to map image features to poses, e.g. [2, 19]. Specifically we adapt a technique designed to track color gloves using a database that maps tiny 40×40 pixel images of the hand to their associated 3D poses [25].

For background subtraction, we build a Gaussian mixture model for the background [22] and segment the two largest connected skin-toned regions (from the left and right hand). We encode the hand regions from each camera as a *pair* of tiny images, and query for the nearest neighbors in a precomputed database mapping hand image pairs to their associated 3D poses. Finally, we solve a 6-DOF inverse kinematics (IK) problem to place the resulting 3D hand pose to match the hand region locations (Figure 9).

A pair of hand images from different viewpoints provides much more information than a single image, but storing a database of image pairs requires twice as much memory for the same density of hand poses. To reduce memory usage, we exploit the redundancy of hand images of the image pair set. Given a set of $N = 2.1 \times 10^6$ relevant hand poses, we render these poses from two camera viewpoints to obtain tiny image pairs $\{(\mathbf{r}_i, \mathbf{r}_i^1)\}_{1...N}$. We then sample K = 30,000 of the most different (i.e. least redundant) images from these image pairs $\{\tilde{\mathbf{r}_k}\}_{1...K}$ using low dispersion sampling. These K images approximate the original set of image pairs, mapping them to a much smaller set of approximations $\{(\tilde{\mathbf{r}}_i, \tilde{\mathbf{r}}_i^1)\}_i$, thus making image-pair-based pose estimation efficient.

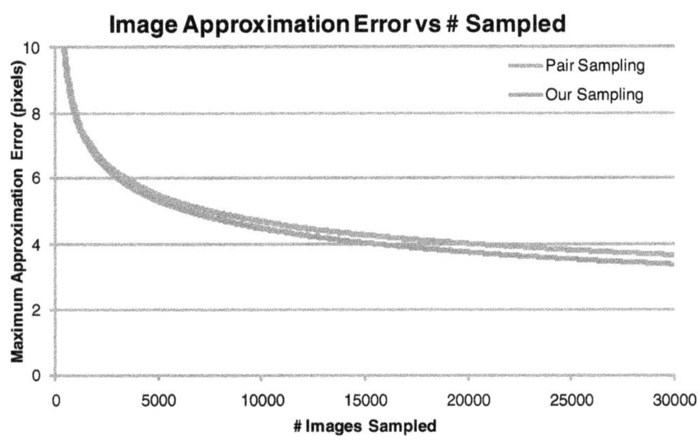

Figure 10: We compared our proposed image sampling approach that exploits redundancy between cameras and decouples sampling with a naive approach that samples pairs of images. Our approach yields a savings of 27% for equal quality at 30,000 samples.

We compared our sampling approach to a naive image-pair sampling approach that does not exploit redundancy of images between cameras (See Figure 10). Both curves converge slowly, but to achieve equal quality with 30,000 samples from the naive approach, our approach only requires 22,000 samples. To achieve equality quality with 30,000 samples taken with our approach, the naive approach would require 50% more samples (45,500).

Gesture and Desktop-Specific Sampling Because our system relies on only a few gestures, we only need to track a small set of hand poses. Hand poses outside of this relevant set are ignored during tracking because they do not correspond to actions in our CAD system. While the work of Wang and colleagues sampled a large variety of hand poses for general purpose tracking, we restrict our sampling to only the set of relevant hand poses for our gestures and for our particular desktop environment.

Our technique concentrates on the finger configurations required by our gestures. We use a relaxed hand pose, a pinching hand pose, and a pointing hand pose as a finger configuration basis $\{\mathbf{q}_i\}$. We then take pairwise blends between each of these poses $\{\mathbf{q}|\mathbf{q} = \alpha\mathbf{q}_i + (1-\alpha)\mathbf{q}_j\}$ for $\alpha \in [0, 1]$ to generate a dense set of finger configuration transitions between basis poses.

Our model assumes that the hand is in a 34cm×46cm×24cm box above the keyboard, and we only sample hand positions in this region. The principal axis of the hand can move in a cone subtending an angle of $\theta = 60°$ and the hand can twist about that axis $\phi = 130°$. While most people can twist their hands more, these ranges are sufficient to cover the set of comfortable poses. With this restrictive sampling, we are able to make markerless hand-tracking feasible.

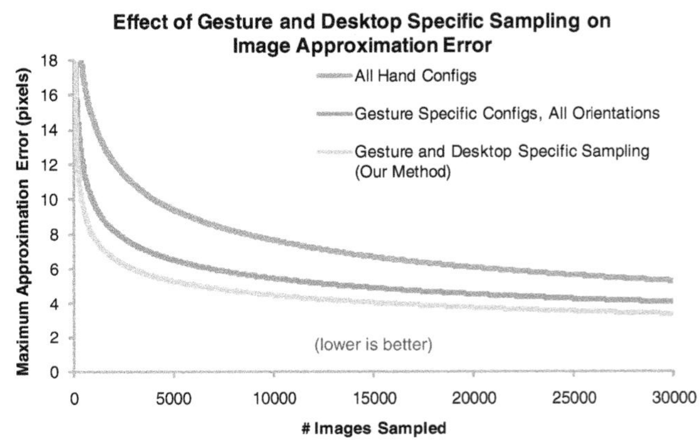

Figure 11: Our gesture-specific and desktop-specific sampling allows us to use as much as 80% fewer samples to achieve equal sampling quality with a gesture and desktop agnostic approach.

In Figure 11, we quantify the benefits of our gesture-specific, desktop-specific sampling, compared to sampling all hand configurations and all orientations, many of which are impossible given the user and camera placement. A gesture-agnostic sampling requires 30,000 samples to achieve equal quality with 5,000 samples taken with our approach. A desktop-agnostic sampling requires 30,000 samples to achieve equal quality with 15,000 samples from our approach.

Pinch / Click Detection A robust pinch detector is the basis of our gestures, and we address it separately from 3D tracking. Our pinch detection is based on detecting separation of the tips of the index finger and thumb in at least one of the two camera images. First, we check for extrema [18] of the silhouette close to the predicted locations of the index finger and thumb from our 3D pose estimate. Thumb-index separation is detected if the geodesic distance between the extrema is longer than the Euclidean distance. If no separation is detected in either view, we register a pinch (Figure 12).

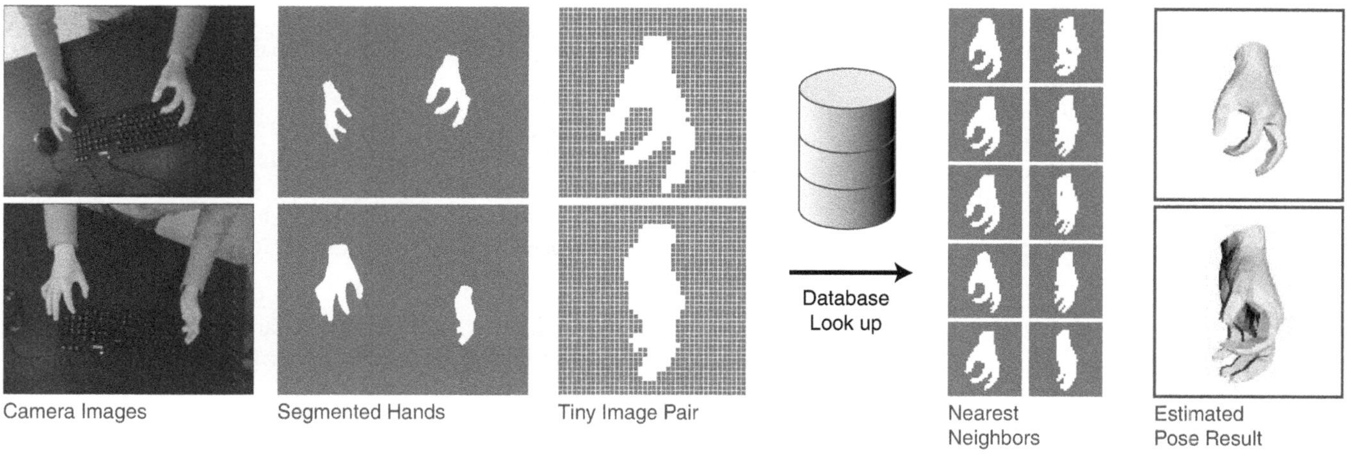

Figure 9: We segment the hands using background subtraction and skin-tone detection. We take the resulting hand regions and encode them as tiny images. We use a pair of tiny images to query the database, blend the nearest neighbors, and solve a 6-DOF IK problem to obtain the 3D hand pose.

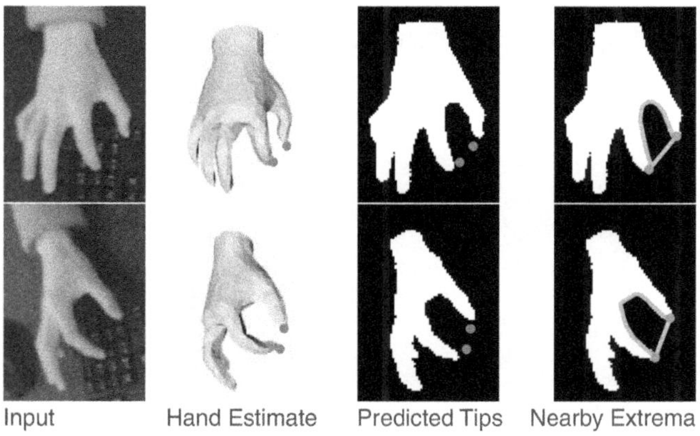

Figure 12: We look for extrema (red points) in the silhouette that match the predicted locations of the thumb and index finger tips (blue points). If the geodesic distance (orange line) between the extrema is larger than the Euclidean distance (green line), we detect a separation.

To evaluate our approach, we recorded 8 sequences from 4 people consisting of pinching gestures performed at various locations in the capture volume. We found that we could track pinching with about 99% accuracy. Further analysis, showed that the occasional missed detections and false pinch detections mostly occur at extreme poses or at extreme positions of our capture volume. As demonstrated in our companion video, our robust detection mechanism enables complex interaction.

Limitations and User Calibration Our computer-vision-based approach is currently limited to environments where the hands can be segmented from the background with skin-tone detection and background subtraction. Presently, we also ask the user to wear a long-sleeved top because we do not model the skin-toned arms. Both of these issues can be resolved with the use of depth cameras, and we hope to explore two-depth-camera setups in future work.

Unlike the technique of Wang and Popović, our database sampling is specific to the camera setup and needs to be regenerated when the cameras are moved. This requires approximately 30 minutes.

For best results, we also manually calibrate three hand poses of the user. Differently shaped hands tend to pinch and point differently. We kinematically adjust the joint angles of our basis poses to reflect the user-specific pinching, pointing and resting gestures. This takes approximately ten minutes of manual calibration, and we hope to incorporate a more accurate and automatic technique in the future [7].

EVALUATION

We tested our system on an Intel Core i7 desktop computer with two PlayStation 3 Eye cameras. Our hand-tracking system runs at interactive rates (20 Hz) on two threads of the processor. Our complete 3D assembly system runs at a slower rate of 17 Hz on the models we tested.

We measured precision (jitter) of the tracked thumb tips to be approximately 3mm. Using known rotation sequences, we also estimated the rotation precision to be between 1 and 3 degrees around the x and y axes, and about 6 degrees around the z axis.

We tested our assembly system on several models used to teach 3D assembly included as part of the SolidWorks CAD software. We show that these models can be efficiently assembled using hand gestures alone. In the hands of an expert user of both our system and a traditional CAD mating interface, we have observed time savings of up to 40%. This comes from significantly fewer modal transitions from selecting parts to adjusting the camera. We also evaluated our bimanual rotation gestures on a rotation-matching task. While not quite as efficient as an expert arcball user, our bimanual gestures provides a comfortable and easy-to-use rotational mapping. In another sequence, we show that our system works well alongside a mouse, keyboard and 3DConnexion SpaceNavigator.

In an early pilot study with three novice users, we found that due to the lack of tactile feedback, visual feedback is crucial for keeping the user in sync with the state of the assembly system. Users would often mis-select objects or confuse being in object translation mode versus camera rotation mode. In response, we gave each assembly action, including camera rotation, camera translation, object selection, and object release, a distinct visual cue. For instance, we draw a bounding box around the scene and a 3D manipulator for camera rotation and translation. We higlight the active object with a golden halo when it has been selected for manipulation.

We also found that shadows were an insufficient depth cue for 3D object selection on a 2D display. Users would often select a different object than the one they had intended. We addressed this by brightening objects near each hand and always outlining the closest object that would be selected if the user were to pinch. These cues inform the user about the relative position of his hands in the scene without having to look down at shadows before selecting an object, reducing the incidence of mis-selections.

Extensions

In addition to 3D CAD assembly, our hand-tracking system can be used to turn the desk plane into a touch-sensitive device. We use our two-camera setup to triangulate the 3D location of the index finger and detect intersection with the calibrated desk plane. We demonstrated this system on a 2D multi-touch photo rotation task. While our touch detection is only accurate within five millimeters, this is sufficient for simple multi-touch applications at the desktop.

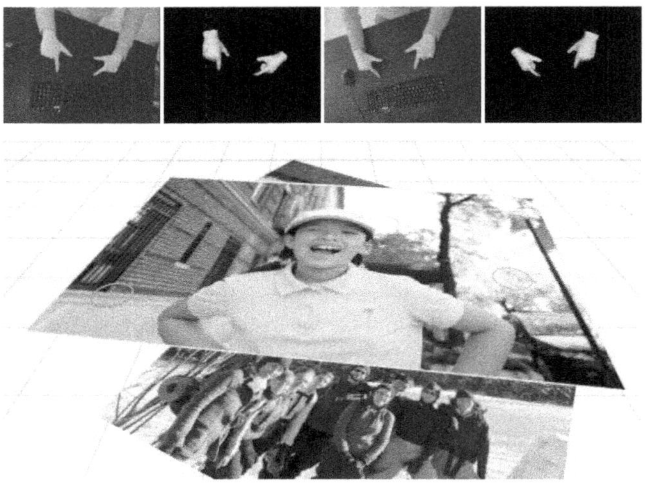

Figure 13: We detect touch with a calibrated desk to enable a virtual multi-touch surface.

CONCLUSION

We have developed a hand-tracking system tailored for a fundamental task in computer aided design, 3D assembly. Our system relies on a small set of gestures that are comfortable to use, precise, and easy to remember. To recognize these gestures, we built a data-driven pose-estimation system that uses a wide-baseline camera setup and an efficiently sampled database to track the hands without markers, alongside the keyboard and mouse. Furthermore, our prototype CAD system generates the exact positioning constraints used in traditional CAD for mechanical engineering. In summary, we have developed a complementary user input device for efficient 3D assembly of mechanical parts.

REFERENCES

1. Maneesh Agrawala, Andrew C. Beers, Bernd Fröhlich, Patrick M. Hanrahan, Ian McDowall, and Mark Bolas. The two-user responsive workbench: Support for collaboration through independent views of a shared space. In *Proceedings of SIGGRAPH 97*, pages 327–332, 1997. 2

2. Vassilis Athitsos and Stan Sclaroff. Estimating 3D hand pose from a cluttered image. In *Computer Vision and Pattern Recognition (CVPR)*, volume 2, pages 432–439, 2003. 6

3. Hrvoje Benko and Andrew Wilson. Depthtouch: Using depth-sensing camera to enable freehand interactions on and above the interactive surface. Technical Report MSR-TR-2009-23, Microsoft, 2009. 2

4. Hrvoje Benko and Andrew D. Wilson. Multi-point interactions with immersive omnidirectional visualizations in a dome. In *Interactive Tabletops and Surfaces (ITS)*, pages 19–28, 2010. 2

5. Francois Bérard, Jessica Ip, Mitchel Benovoy, Dalia El-Shimy, Jeffrey Blum, and Jeremy Cooperstock. Did "Minority Report" Get it Wrong? Superiority of the Mouse over 3D Input Devices in a 3D Placement Task. *Human-Computer Interaction–INTERACT 2009*, pages 400–414, 2009. 2

6. Lawrence D. Cutler, Bernd Fröhlich, and Pat Hanrahan. Two-handed direct manipulation on the responsive workbench. In *Proc. of Interactive 3D Graphics (I3D)*, 1997. 4

7. Martin de La Gorce, Nikos Paragios, and David J. Fleet. Model-Based Hand Tracking with Texture, Shading and Self-occlusions. In *Computer Vision and Pattern Recognition (CVPR)*, pages 1–8, 2008. 2, 7

8. Michael Glueck, Keenan Crane, Sean Anderson, Andres Rutnik, and Azam Khan. Multiscale 3D reference visualization. In *Proc. of Interactive 3D Graphics and Games (I3D)*, pages 225–232, 2009. 4

9. Otmar Hilliges, Shahram Izadi, Andrew D. Wilson, Steve Hodges, Armando Garcia-Mendoza, and Andreas Butz. Interactions in the air: adding further depth to interactive tabletops. In *User Interface Software and Technology (UIST)*, pages 139–148, 2009. 2

10. Daniel F. Keefe, David B. Karelitz, Eileen L. Vote, and David H. Laidlaw. Artistic collaboration in designing vr visualizations. *IEEE Computer Graphics and Applications*, 25(2):18–23, 2005. 2

11. Kenrick Kin, Tom Miller, Björn Bollensdorff, Tony DeRose, Björn Hartmann, and Maneesh Agrawala. Eden: A professional multitouch tool for constructing virtual organic environments. In *Human Factors in Computing Systems (CHI)*, 2011. 2, 3, 4

12. Wilmot Li, Maneesh Agrawala, Brian Curless, and David Salesin. Automated generation of interactive 3D exploded view diagrams. *ACM Trans. on Graphics*, 27(3), 2008. 4

13. S. Malik and J. Laszlo. Visual touchpad: a two-handed gestural input device. In *Int. Conf. on Multimodal interfaces*, pages 13–15, 2004. 2

14. Cristina Manresa, Javier Varona, Ramon Mas, and Francisco J. Perale. Real-time hand tracking and gesture recognition for human-computer interaction. *Electronic Letters on Computer Vision and Image Analysis*, 2000. 2

15. Maurice Masliah and Paul Milgram. Measuring the allocation of control in a 6 degree-of-freedom docking experiment. In *Human Factors in Computing Systems (CHI)*, pages 25–32, 2000. 3

16. Niloy J. Mitra, Yong-Liang Yang, Dong-Ming Yan, Wilmot Li, and Maneesh Agrawala. Illustrating how mechanical assemblies work. *ACM Trans. on Graphics*, 29(3), 2010. 4

17. Ji-Young Oh and Wolfgang Stuerzlinger. Moving objects with 2D input devices in cad systems and desktop virtual environments. *Proc. of Graphics Interface*, pages 195–202, 2005. 4

18. Christian Plagemann, Varun Ganapathi, Daphne Koller, and Sebastian Thrun. Real time identification and localization of body parts from depth images. In *Int. Conf. on Robotics and Automation (ICRA)*, 2010. 6

19. Javier Romero, Hedvig Kjellstrm, and Danica Kragic. Hands in action: real-time 3D reconstruction of hands in interaction with objects. In *Int. Conf. on Robotics and Automation (ICRA)*, pages 458–463, 2010. 6

20. Markus Schlattmann and Reinhard Klein. Efficient bimanual symmetric 3D manipulation for markerless hand-tracking. In *Virtual Reality International Conference (VRIC)*, 2009. 2

21. Jamie Shotton, Andrew Fitzgibbon, Mat Cook, Toby Sharp, Mark Finocchio, Richard Moore, Alex Kipman, and Andrew Blake. Real-Time Human Pose Recognition in Parts from Single Depth Images. In *Computer Vision and Pattern Recognition (CVPR)*, 2011. 2

22. Chris Stauffer and W.E.L. Grimson. Adaptive background mixture models for real-time tracking. In *Computer Vision and Pattern Recognition (CVPR)*, volume 2, pages 246–252, 1999. 6

23. Wolfgang Stuerzlinger and Chadwick Wingrave. The Value of Constraints for 3D User Interfaces. *Dagstuhl Seminar on VR*, 2010. 2

24. Erik B. Sudderth, Michael I. Mandel, T. Freeman, and S. Willsky. Distributed occlusion reasoning for tracking with nonparametric belief propagation. In *Neural Information Processing Systems (NIPS)*, pages 1369–1376, 2004. 2

25. Robert Y. Wang and Jovan Popović. Real-time handtacking with a color glove. *ACM Trans. on Graphics*, 28(3):1–8, 2009. 2, 5, 6

26. Andrew D. Wilson. Robust computer vision-based detection of pinching for one and two-handed gesture input. In *User Interface Software and Technology (UIST)*, pages 255–258, 2006. 2, 3

27. Thomas G. Zimmerman, Jaron Lanier, Chuck Blanchard, Steve Bryson, and Young Harvill. A hand gesture interface device. In *Human Factors in Computing Systems (CHI)*, pages 189–192, 1987. 2

Appendix: Formulas for camera rotation

Given previous click points $(\mathbf{p}_0, \mathbf{p}_1)$ and current click points $(\mathbf{p}'_0, \mathbf{p}'_1)$, the bimanual rotation is specified by $R_1 R_2$. The rotation R_1 corresponds to the elbow rotation about the x-axis of $\arctan((((\mathbf{p}'_0 + \mathbf{p}'_1) - (\mathbf{p}_0 + \mathbf{p}_1))/2)_y, f)$, where f is the forearm length. The rotation R_2 corresponds to rotating the sheet about its center axis. Let the normalized vector between the click points be $\mathbf{n} = (\mathbf{p}_1 - \mathbf{p}_0)/\|\mathbf{p}_1 - \mathbf{p}_0\|$ and $\mathbf{n}' = (\mathbf{p}'_1 - \mathbf{p}'_0)/\|\mathbf{p}'_1 - \mathbf{p}'_0\|$. Then R_2 is a rotation about the sheet's center axis $\mathbf{n} \times \mathbf{n}'$ with an angle of $\arctan(\|\mathbf{n} \times \mathbf{n}'\|, \mathbf{n} \cdot \mathbf{n}')$.

KinectFusion: Real-time 3D Reconstruction and Interaction Using a Moving Depth Camera*

Shahram Izadi[1], *David Kim*[1,3], *Otmar Hilliges*[1], *David Molyneaux*[1,4], *Richard Newcombe*[2], *Pushmeet Kohli*[1], *Jamie Shotton*[1], *Steve Hodges*[1], *Dustin Freeman*[1,5], *Andrew Davison*[2], *Andrew Fitzgibbon*[1]

[1]Microsoft Research Cambridge, UK [2]Imperial College London, UK
[3]Newcastle University, UK [4]Lancaster University, UK [5]University of Toronto, Canada

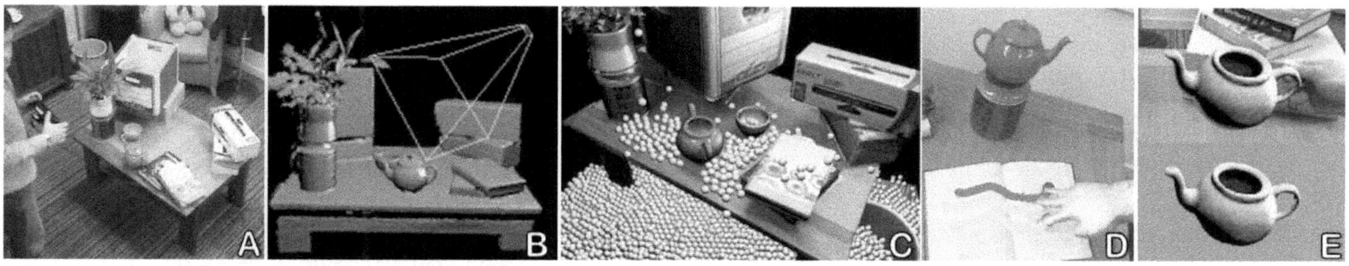

Figure 1: KinectFusion enables real-time detailed 3D reconstructions of indoor scenes using only the depth data from a standard Kinect camera. A) user points Kinect at coffee table scene. B) Phong shaded reconstructed 3D model (the wireframe frustum shows current tracked 3D pose of Kinect). C) 3D model texture mapped using Kinect RGB data with real-time particles simulated on the 3D model as reconstruction occurs. D) Multi-touch interactions performed on any reconstructed surface. E) Real-time segmentation and 3D tracking of a physical object.

ABSTRACT

KinectFusion enables a user holding and moving a standard Kinect camera to rapidly create detailed 3D reconstructions of an indoor scene. Only the depth data from Kinect is used to *track* the 3D pose of the sensor and *reconstruct*, geometrically precise, 3D models of the physical scene in *real-time*. The capabilities of KinectFusion, as well as the novel GPU-based pipeline are described in full. We show uses of the core system for low-cost handheld scanning, and geometry-aware augmented reality and physics-based interactions. Novel extensions to the core GPU pipeline demonstrate object segmentation and user interaction directly in front of the sensor, without degrading camera tracking or reconstruction. These extensions are used to enable real-time multi-touch interactions *anywhere*, allowing any planar or non-planar reconstructed physical surface to be appropriated for touch.

ACM Classification: H5.2 [Information Interfaces and Presentation]: User Interfaces. I4.5 [Image Processing and Computer Vision]: Reconstruction. I3.7 [Computer Graphics]: Three-Dimensional Graphics and Realism.

General terms: Algorithms, Design, Human Factors.

Keywords: 3D, GPU, Surface Reconstruction, Tracking, Depth Cameras, AR, Physics, Geometry-Aware Interactions

* Research conducted at Microsoft Research Cambridge, UK

INTRODUCTION

While depth cameras are not conceptually new, Kinect has made such sensors accessible to all. The quality of the depth sensing, given the low-cost and real-time nature of the device, is compelling, and has made the sensor instantly popular with researchers and enthusiasts alike.

The Kinect camera uses a structured light technique [ ] to generate real-time *depth maps* containing discrete range measurements of the physical scene. This data can be reprojected as a set of discrete 3D points (or *point cloud*). Even though the Kinect depth data is compelling, particularly compared to other commercially available depth cameras, it is still inherently noisy (see Figures 2B and 3 left). Depth measurements often fluctuate and depth maps contain numerous 'holes' where no readings were obtained.

To generate 3D models for use in applications such as gaming, physics, or CAD, higher-level *surface* geometry needs to be inferred from this noisy point-based data. One simple approach makes strong assumptions about the connectivity of neighboring points within the Kinect depth map to generate a *mesh* representation. This, however, leads to noisy and low-quality meshes as shown in Figure 2C. As importantly, this approach creates an incomplete mesh, from only a single, fixed viewpoint. To create a complete (or even watertight) 3D model, different viewpoints of the physical scene must be captured and *fused* into a single representation.

This paper presents a novel interactive reconstruction system called KinectFusion (see Figure 1). The system takes live depth data from a moving Kinect camera and, in real-time, creates a single high-quality, geometrically accurate, 3D model. A user holding a standard Kinect camera can move within any indoor space, and reconstruct a 3D model of the physical scene within seconds. The system contin-

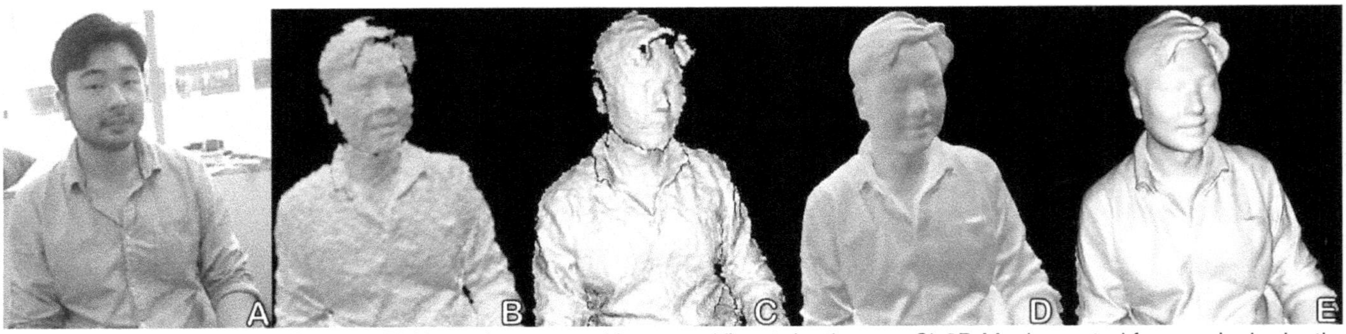

Figure 2: A) RGB image of scene. B) Normals extracted from raw Kinect depth map. C) 3D Mesh created from a single depth map. D and E) 3D model generated from KinectFusion showing surface normals (D) and rendered with Phong shading (E).

uously tracks the 6 degrees-of-freedom (DOF) pose of the camera and fuses new viewpoints of the scene into a global surface-based representation. A novel GPU pipeline allows for accurate camera tracking and surface reconstruction at interactive real-time rates. This paper details the capabilities of our novel system, as well as the implementation of the GPU pipeline in full.

We demonstrate core uses of KinectFusion as a low-cost handheld scanner, and present novel interactive methods for *segmenting* physical objects of interest from the reconstructed scene. We show how a real-time 3D model can be leveraged for *geometry-aware* augmented reality (AR) and physics-based interactions, where virtual worlds more realistically merge and interact with the real.

Placing such systems into an interaction context, where users need to dynamically interact in front of the sensor, reveals a fundamental challenge – no longer can we assume a static scene for camera tracking or reconstruction. We illustrate failure cases caused by a user moving in front of the sensor. We describe new methods to overcome these limitations, allowing camera tracking and reconstruction of a static background scene, while simultaneously segmenting, reconstructing and tracking foreground objects, including the user. We use this approach to demonstrate real-time multi-touch interactions *anywhere*, allowing a user to appropriate any physical surface, be it planar or non-planar, for touch.

RELATED WORK

Reconstructing geometry using active sensors [ ], passive cameras [,], online images [ ], or from unordered 3D points [,] are well-studied areas of research in computer graphics and vision. There is also extensive literature within the AR and robotics community on Simultaneous Localization and Mapping (SLAM), aimed at tracking a user or robot while creating a map of the surrounding physical environment (see [ ]). Given this broad topic, and our desire to build a system for *interaction*, this section is structured around specific design goals that differentiate KinectFusion from prior work. The combination of these features makes our interactive reconstruction system unique.

Interactive rates Our primary goal with KinectFusion is to achieve real-time interactive rates for *both* camera tracking *and* 3D reconstruction. This speed is critical for permitting direct feedback and user interaction. This differentiates us from many existing reconstruction systems that support only offline reconstructions [ ], real-time but non-interactive rates (e.g. the Kinect-based system of [ ] reconstructs at ~2Hz), or support real-time camera tracking but non real-time reconstruction or mapping phases [, ,].

No explicit feature detection Unlike structure from motion (SfM) systems (e.g. [ ]) or RGB plus depth (RGBD) techniques (e.g. [,]), which need to robustly and continuously detect sparse scene features, our approach to camera tracking avoids an explicit detection step, and directly works on the full depth maps acquired from the Kinect sensor. Our system also avoids the reliance on RGB (used in recent Kinect RGBD systems e.g. [ ]) allowing use in indoor spaces with variable lighting conditions.

High-quality reconstruction of geometry A core goal of our work is to capture detailed (or *dense*) 3D models of the real scene. Many SLAM systems (e.g. [ ]) focus on real-time tracking, using *sparse* maps for localization rather than reconstruction. Others have used simple point-based representations (such as surfels [ ] or aligned point-clouds [ ]) for reconstruction. KinectFusion goes beyond these point-based representations by reconstructing *surfaces*, which more accurately approximate real-world geometry.

Dynamic interaction assumed We explore tracking and reconstruction in the context of *user interaction*. Given this requirement, it is critical that the representation we use can deal with dynamically changing scenes, where users directly interact in front of the camera. While there has been work on using mesh-based representations for live reconstruction from passive RGB [, ,] or active Time-of-Flight (ToF) cameras [,], these do not readily deal with changing, dynamic scenes.

Infrastructure-less We aim to allow users to explore and reconstruct arbitrary indoor spaces. This suggests a level of mobility, and contrasts with systems that use fixed or large sensors (e.g. [,]) or are fully embedded in the environment (e.g. [ ]). We also aim to perform camera tracking without the need for prior augmentation of the space, whether this is the use of infrastructure-heavy tracking systems (e.g. [ ]) or fiducial markers (e.g. [ ]).

Room scale One final requirement is to support whole room reconstructions and interaction. This differentiates KinectFusion from prior dense reconstruction systems, which have either focused on smaller desktop scenes [,] or scanning of small physical objects [,].

The remainder of this paper is structured into two parts: The first provides a high-level description of the capabilities of KinectFusion. The second describes the technical aspects of the system, focusing on our novel GPU pipeline.

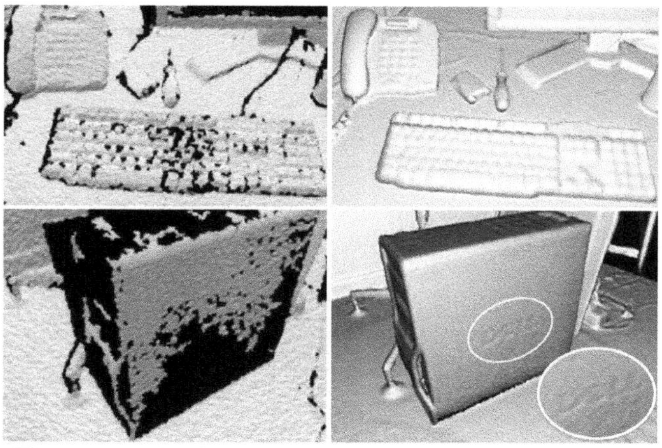

Figure 3: Left: Raw Kinect data (shown as surface normals). Right: Reconstruction shows hole filling and high-quality details such as keys on keyboard, phone number pad, wires, and even a DELL logo on the side of a PC (an engraving less than 1mm deep).

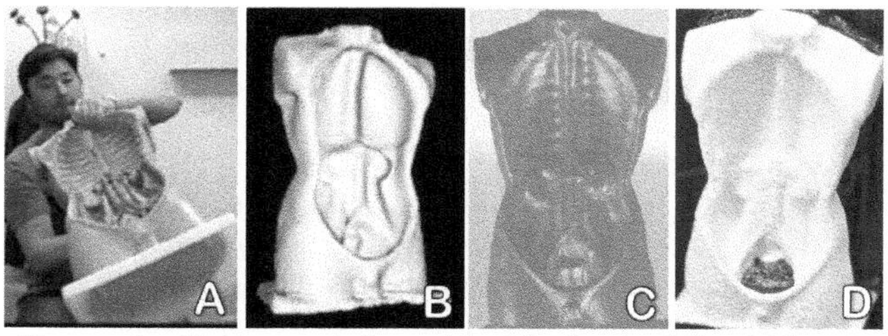

Figure 4: A) User rotating object in front of fixed Kinect. B) 360° 3D reconstruction. C) 3D model imported into SolidWorks. D) 3D printout from reconstruction.

KINECTFUSION

Our system allows a user to pickup a standard Kinect camera and move rapidly within a room to reconstruct a high-quality, geometrically precise 3D model of the scene. To achieve this, our system continually tracks the 6DOF pose of the camera and fuses live depth data from the camera into a single global 3D model in real-time. As the user explores the space, new views of the physical scene are revealed and these are fused into the same model. The reconstruction therefore grows in detail as new depth measurements are added. Holes are filled, and the model becomes more complete and refined over time (see Figure 3).

Even small motions, caused for example by camera shake, result in new viewpoints of the scene and hence refinements to the model. This creates an effect similar to image super-resolution [ ] – adding greater detail than appears visible in the raw signal (see Figure 3). As illustrated in Figures 2 and 3, the reconstructions are high-quality, particularly given the noisy input data and speed of reconstruction. The reconstructed model can also be texture mapped using the Kinect RGB camera (see Figures 1C, 5B and 6A).

Low-cost Handheld Scanning A basic and yet compelling use for KinectFusion is as a low-cost object scanner. Although there is a body of research focusing on object scanning using passive and active cameras [,], the speed, quality, and scale of reconstructions have not been demonstrated previously with such low-cost commodity hardware. The mobile and real-time nature of our system allows users to rapidly capture an object from different viewpoints, and see onscreen feedback immediately. Reconstructed 3D models can be imported into CAD or other 3D modeling applications, or even 3D printed (see Figure 4 C and D).

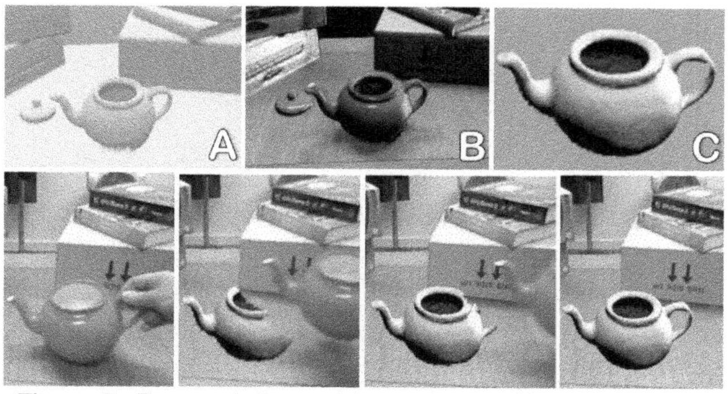

Figure 5: Fast and direct object segmentation. First entire scene is scanned including object of interest – the teapot. 3D reconstruction shows surface normals (A) and texture mapped model (B). Bottom left to right: Teapot physically removed. System monitors real-time changes in reconstruction and colors large changes yellow. C) This achieves accurate segmentation of teapot 3D model from initial scan.

As also shown in Figure 4, our system can also be used in 'reverse' – without any code changes – whereby the system tracks the 6DOF pose of a handheld rigid object that is rotated in front of a fixed Kinect camera (as long as the object occupies the majority of the depth map). While fingers and hands may initially form part of the 3D reconstruction, they are gradually integrated out of the 3D model, because they naturally move as a process of rotating the object.

Object Segmentation through Direct Interaction Users may also wish to scan a specific smaller physical object rather than the entire scene. To support this, KinectFusion allows a user to first reconstruct the entire scene, and then accurately *segment* the desired object by moving it physically. The system continuously monitors the 3D reconstruction and observes changes over time. If an object is physically removed from view or moved within the scene by the user, rapid and large changes in the 3D model are observed. Such changes are detected in real-time, allowing the repositioned object to be cleanly segmented from the background model. This approach allows a user to perform segmentation rapidly and without any explicit GUI input, simply by moving the object directly (see Figure 5).

Geometry-Aware Augmented Reality Beyond scanning, KinectFusion enables more realistic forms of AR, where a 3D virtual world is overlaid onto and interacts with the real-world representation. Figure 6 (top row) shows a virtual metallic sphere composited directly onto the 3D model, as well as the registered live RGB data from Kinect. The virtual sphere can be rendered from the same perspective as the tracked physical camera, enabling it to be spatially registered as the Kinect moves. As shown in Figure 6 (B, C and D), the live 3D model allows composited virtual graphics to be precisely occluded by the real-world, including geometrically complex objects. This quality of occlusion handling is not possible with the raw depth map (Figure 6E), especially around the edges of objects due to significant noise along depth discontinuities. Precise occlusions are critical for truly immersive AR experiences, and have not been achieved in sparsely mapped real-time AR systems (e.g. [ ]).

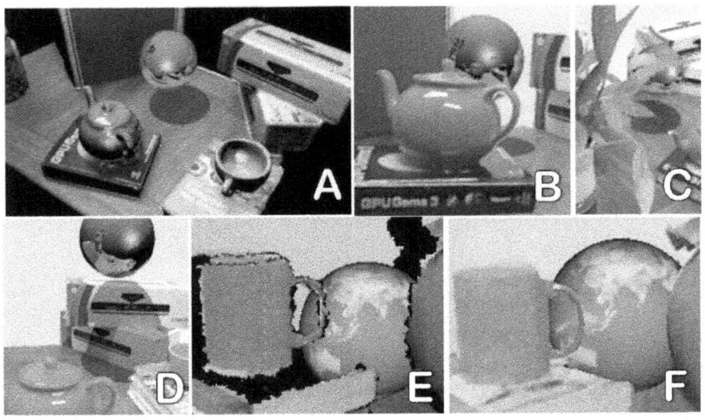

Figure 6: Virtual sphere composited onto texture mapped 3D model (A) and calibrated live Kinect RGB (B, C and D). Real-time 3D model used to handle precise occlusions of the virtual by complex physical geometries (B and C). Comparing occlusion handling using live depth map (E) versus 3D reconstruction (F). Note noise at depth edges, shadows and incomplete data (e.g. book) in live depth map. Virtual sphere casts shadows on physical (D) and reflects parts of the real scene (B and D).

Figure 7: Interactive simulation of physics directly on 3D model even during reconstruction. Thousands of particles interact with reconstructed scene. Reconstruction, camera tracking, and physics simulation all performed in real-time.

Raytraced rendering effects can be calculated in real-time to create realistic shadows, lighting and reflections that consider both virtual and real geometries. For example, Figure 6 (B and D) shows how the virtual can cast shadows onto the real geometry, as well as reflect parts of the real scene onto the virtual. The latter can even be parts of the scene that are occluded from the current perspective of the physical camera.

Taking Physics Beyond the 'Surface' Taking this ability of combining and spatially aligning real and virtual worlds one step further, the virtual can also begin to interact dynamically with the reconstructed scene by simulating aspects of real-world physics. Many types of applications such as gaming and robotics can benefit from such physically precise real-time simulation. Rigid body collisions can be simulated live even as the 3D model is being reconstructed. Figure 7 shows thousands of particles interacting with the 3D model as it is reconstructed, all in real-time. This ability to both reconstruct a scene and simultaneously perform physics computations on the model is *unique*, and opens up a potential for more physically realistic AR applications.

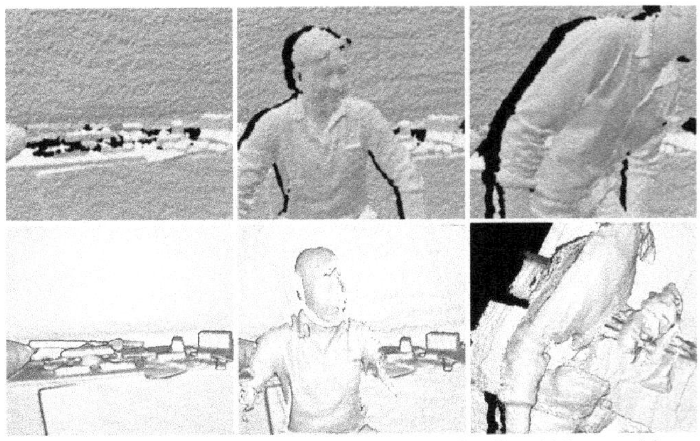

Figure 8: A user moves freely in front of a fixed Kinect. Live raw data (top) and shaded reconstruction (bottom). Left: Scene without user. Middle: User enters scene, but is only partially reconstructed due to motion. Right: Continued scene motions cause tracking failure.

Reaching into the Scene

It is important to note that, like most of the related literature on SLAM and camera-based reconstruction, our core system described so far makes a fundamental assumption – that camera tracking will be performed on a *static* scene. Once we switch focus from *reconstructing* the scene towards *interacting* within it, these assumptions no longer hold true. Physical objects such as the user's hands, will inevitably appear in the scene, move dynamically and impact tracking and reconstruction. Our camera tracking is robust to transient and rapid scene motions (such as the earlier example in Figure 5). However, prolonged interactions with the scene are problematic as illustrated in Figure 8.

While this is clearly a challenging problem within computer vision, our GPU-based pipeline is extended to approximate *camera motion* from *scene motion* for certain user interaction scenarios. When a user is interacting in the scene, the camera tracking 'locks' onto the background and ignores the foreground user for camera pose prediction (shown later in Figure 15). This foreground data can be tracked (in 6DOF) and reconstructed independently of camera tracking and reconstruction of the static background.

This ability to reconstruct and track the user in the scene can enable novel extensions to our physics-based simulation shown earlier. Rigid particles can now collide with the rapidly changing dynamic foreground. Figure 9 demonstrates particles interacting with a dynamically updated reconstruction of a moving user. This enables direct interaction between the user and the physics-enabled virtual objects.

Furthermore, as we have captured geometry of both the background scene and foreground user (e.g. hands or potentially the full body), we can determine *intersections* between the two. These points of intersection indicate when the foreground 'comes into contact with' the background, and forms a robust method to detect when a user is touching any arbitrarily shaped surface – including non-planar geometries. This allows direct multi-touch interactions, such as those

Figure 9: Interactive simulation of particle physics on dynamic scenes. Particles interact with dynamically moving foreground user, whilst physical camera and user move. User can collide with the physics-enabled virtual objects.

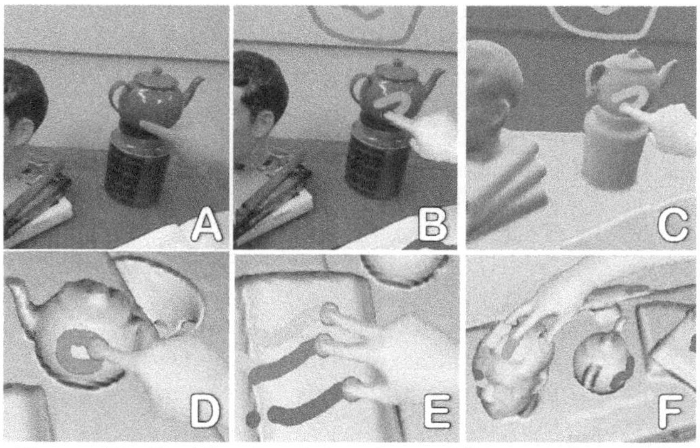

Figure 10: Enabling touch input on arbitrary surfaces with a moving camera. A) Live RGB. B) Composited view with segmented hand and single finger touching curved surface. C) rendered as surface normals. D) Single finger drawing on a curved surface. E) Multi-touch on regular planar book surface. F) Multi-touch on an arbitrarily shaped surface.

demonstrated in the interactive tabletop community, to reach *any* surface in the user's environment (see Figure 10).

GPU IMPLEMENTATION

Our approach for real-time camera tracking and surface reconstruction is based on two well-studied algorithms [, ,], which have been designed from the ground-up for parallel execution on the GPU. A full formulation of our method is provided in [ ], as well as quantitative evaluation of reconstruction performance. The focus of this section is on the implementation of our novel core and extended GPU pipeline, which is critical in enabling interactive rates.

The main system pipeline consists of four main stages (labeled appropriately in Figure 11):

a) Depth Map Conversion The live depth map is converted from image coordinates into 3D points (referred to as vertices) and normals in the coordinate space of the camera.

b) Camera Tracking In the tracking phase, a rigid 6DOF transform is computed to closely align the current oriented points with the previous frame, using a GPU implementation of the Iterative Closest Point (ICP) algorithm [ ]. Relative transforms are incrementally applied to a single transform that defines the global pose of the Kinect.

c) Volumetric Integration Instead of fusing point clouds or creating a mesh, we use a volumetric surface representation based on [ ]. Given the global pose of the camera, oriented points are converted into global coordinates, and a single 3D voxel grid is updated. Each voxel stores a running average of its distance to the assumed position of a physical surface.

d) Raycasting Finally, the volume is raycast to extract views of the implicit surface, for rendering to the user. When using the global pose of the camera, this raycasted view of the

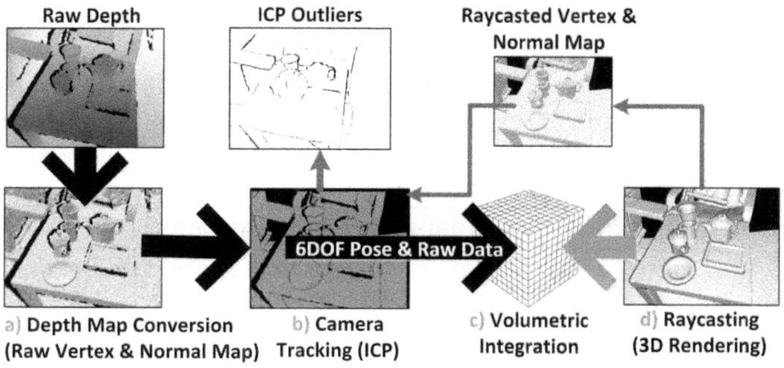

Figure 11: Overview of tracking and reconstruction pipeline from raw depth map to rendered view of 3D scene.

volume also equates to a synthetic depth map, which can be used as a less noisy more globally consistent reference frame for the next iteration of ICP. This allows tracking by aligning the current live depth map with our less noisy raycasted view of the model, as opposed to using only the live depth maps frame-to-frame.

Each of these steps is executed in parallel on the GPU using the CUDA language. We describe each of these steps of the pipeline in the following sections.

Depth Map Conversion

At time i, each CUDA thread operates in parallel on a separate pixel $\mathbf{u} = (x, y)$ in the incoming depth map $\mathbf{D}_i(\mathbf{u})$. Given the intrinsic calibration matrix $\mathbf{K}$ (of the Kinect infrared camera), each GPU thread reprojects a specific depth measurement as a 3D vertex in the camera's coordinate space as follows: $\mathbf{v}_i(\mathbf{u}) = \mathbf{D}_i(\mathbf{u})\,\mathbf{K}^{-1}[\mathbf{u}, 1]$. This results in a single vertex map $\mathbf{V}_i$ computed in parallel.

Corresponding normal vectors for each vertex are computed by each GPU thread using neighboring reprojected points: $\mathbf{n}_i(\mathbf{u}) = (\mathbf{v}_i(x+1, y) - \mathbf{v}_i(x, y)) \times (\mathbf{v}_i(x, y+1) - \mathbf{v}_i(x, y))$ (normalized to unit length $\mathbf{n}_i/||\mathbf{n}_i||$). This results in a single normal map $\mathbf{N}_i$ computed in parallel.

The 6DOF camera pose at time i is a rigid body transform matrix $\mathbf{T}_i = [\mathbf{R}_i|\mathbf{t}_i]$ containing a 3x3 rotation matrix ($\mathbf{R}_i$) and 3D translation vector ($\mathbf{t}_i$). Given this transform, a vertex and normal can be converted into global coordinates: $\mathbf{v}_i^{\mathrm{g}}(\mathbf{u}) = \mathbf{T}_i\mathbf{v}_i(\mathbf{u})$ and $\mathbf{n}_i^{\mathrm{g}}(\mathbf{u}) = \mathbf{R}_i\mathbf{n}_i(\mathbf{u})$ respectively.

Camera Tracking

ICP is a popular and well-studied algorithm for 3D shape alignment (see [ ] for a detailed study). In KinectFusion, ICP is instead leveraged to track the camera pose for each new depth frame, by estimating a single 6DOF transform that closely aligns the current oriented points with those of the previous frame. This gives a relative 6DOF transform $\mathbf{T}^{\mathrm{rel}}$ which can be incrementally applied together to give the single global camera pose $\mathbf{T}_i$.

The important first step of ICP is to find correspondences between the current oriented points at time i with the previous at $i-1$. In our system we use *projective data association* [ ] to find these correspondences. This part of the GPU-based algorithm is shown as pseudocode in Listing 1. Given the previous global camera pose $\mathbf{T}_{i-1}$, each GPU thread transforms a unique point $\mathbf{v}_{i-1}$ into camera coordinate space, and perspective projects it into image coordinates. It then uses this 2D point as a lookup into the current vertex ($\mathbf{V}_i$) and normal maps ($\mathbf{N}_i$), finding corresponding points along the *ray* (i.e. projected onto the same image coordinates). Finally, each GPU thread tests the compatibility of corresponding points to reject *outliers*, by first converting both into global coordinates, and then testing that the Euclidean distance and angle between them are within a threshold.

Listing 1 Projective point-plane data association.

for each image pixel $\mathbf{u} \in$ depth map $\mathbf{D_i}$ **in parallel do**
  if $\mathbf{D}_i(\mathbf{u}) > \mathbf{0}$ **then**
    $\mathbf{v}_{i-1} \leftarrow \mathbf{T}_{i-1}^{-1}\mathbf{v}_{i-1}^{\mathrm{g}}$
    $\mathbf{p} \leftarrow$ perspective project vertex $\mathbf{v}_{i-1}$
    if $\mathbf{p} \in$ vertex map $\mathbf{V}_i$ **then**
      $\mathbf{v} \leftarrow \mathbf{T}_{i-1}\mathbf{V}_i(\mathbf{p})$
      $\mathbf{n} \leftarrow \mathbf{R}_{i-1}\mathbf{N}_i(\mathbf{p})$
      if $||\mathbf{v} - \mathbf{v}_{i-1}^{\mathrm{g}}|| <$ distance threshold **and** $\mathbf{n} \,.\, \mathbf{n}_{i-1}^{\mathrm{g}} <$ normal threshold **then**
        point correspondence found

Given these set of corresponding oriented points, the output of each ICP iteration is a single relative transformation matrix $\mathbf{T}^{\mathrm{rel}}$ that minimizes the point-to-plane error metric [ ], defined as the sum of squared distances between each point in the current frame and the tangent plane at its corresponding point in the previous frame:

$$\arg\min \sum_{\substack{\mathbf{u} \\ \mathbf{D}_i(\mathbf{u})>0}} ||(\mathbf{T}^{\mathrm{rel}}\mathbf{v}_i(\mathbf{u}) - \mathbf{v}_{i-1}^{\mathrm{g}}(\mathbf{u})) \cdot \mathbf{n}_{i-1}^{\mathrm{g}}(\mathbf{u})||^2 \quad (1)$$

We make a linear approximation to solve this system, by assuming only an incremental transformation occurs between frames [,]. The linear system is computed and summed in parallel on the GPU using a tree reduction. The solution to this 6x6 linear system is then solved on the CPU using a Cholesky decomposition.

One of the key novel contributions of our GPU-based camera tracking implementation is that ICP is performed on *all* the measurements provided in each 640×480 Kinect depth map. There is no sparse sampling of points or need to explicitly extract features (although of course ICP does implicitly require depth features to converge). This type of *dense* tracking is only feasible due to our novel GPU implementation, and plays a central role in enabling segmentation and user interaction in KinectFusion, as described later.

Volumetric Representation

By predicting the global pose of the camera using ICP, any depth measurement can be converted from image coordinates into a single consistent global coordinate space. We integrate this data using a *volumetric* representation based on [ ]. A 3D volume of fixed resolution is predefined, which maps to specific dimensions of a 3D physical space. This volume is subdivided uniformly into a 3D grid of voxels. Global 3D vertices are integrated into voxels using a variant of Signed Distance Functions (SDFs) [ ], specifying a relative distance to the actual surface. These values are positive in-front of the surface, negative behind, with the surface interface defined by the *zero-crossing* where the values change sign.

In practice, we only store a truncated region around the actual surface [ ] – referred to in this paper as Truncated Signed Distance Functions (TSDFs). Whilst this approach has been studied in the context of laser range finders, we have found this representation also has many advantages for the Kinect sensor data, particularly when compared to other representations such as meshes. It implicitly encodes uncertainty in the range data, efficiently deals with multiple measurements, fills holes as new measurements are added, accommodates sensor motion, and implicitly stores surface geometry.

Listing 2 Projective TSDF integration leveraging coalesced memory access.

for each voxel g in x,y volume slice **in parallel do**
  while sweeping from front slice to back **do**
    $\mathbf{v}^{\mathrm{g}} \leftarrow$ convert $\mathbf{g}$ from grid to global 3D position
    $\mathbf{v} \leftarrow \mathbf{T}_i^{-1}\mathbf{v}^{\mathrm{g}}$
    $\mathbf{p} \leftarrow$ perspective project vertex $\mathbf{v}$
    if $\mathbf{v}$ in camera view frustum **then**
      $\mathbf{sdf}_i \leftarrow ||\mathbf{t}_i - \mathbf{v}^{\mathrm{g}}|| - \mathbf{D}_i(\mathbf{p})$
      if ($\mathbf{sdf}_i > 0$) **then**
        $\mathbf{tsdf}_i \leftarrow min(1, \mathbf{sdf}_i /$ max truncation$)$
      else
        $\mathbf{tsdf}_i \leftarrow max(-1, \mathbf{sdf}_i /$ min truncation$)$
      $\mathbf{w}_i \leftarrow$min(max weight, $\mathbf{w}_{i-1}$ + 1)
      $\mathbf{tsdf}^{\mathrm{avg}} \leftarrow (\mathbf{tsdf}_{i-1}\mathbf{w}_{i-1} + \mathbf{tsdf}_i\mathbf{w}_i)/\mathbf{w}_i$
      store $\mathbf{w}_i$ and $\mathbf{tsdf}^{\mathrm{avg}}$ at voxel $\mathbf{g}$

Volumetric Integration To achieve real-time rates, we describe a novel GPU implementation of volumetric TSDFs. The full 3D voxel grid is allocated on the GPU as aligned linear memory. Whilst clearly not memory efficient (a 512^3 volume containing 32-bit voxels requires 512MB of memory), our approach is *speed* efficient. Given the memory is aligned, access from parallel threads can be *coalesced* to increase memory throughput. This allows a full sweep of a volume (reading and writing to every voxel) to be performed incredibly quickly on commodity graphics hardware (e.g. a 512^3 sweep, accessing over 130 gigavoxels, takes $\sim 2ms$ on a NVIDIA GTX470).

Our algorithm provides three novel contributions. First, it ensures real-time coalesced access to the voxel grid, whilst integrating depth data *projectively*. Second, it generates TSDF values for voxels within the current camera frustum that do not contain a direct measurement in the current depth map. This allows continuous surface estimates to be discretized into the voxel grid, from the point-based Kinect depth maps. Third, it is *much* simpler to implement than hierarchical techniques (e.g. [ ]), but with the increased available memory on commodity GPUs, can scale to modeling a whole room.

The pseudocode Listing 2 illustrates the main steps of our algorithm. Due to the large number of voxels typically within a volume, it is not feasible to launch a GPU thread per voxel. To ensure coalesced memory access, a GPU thread is assigned to each (x, y) position on the front slice of the volume. In parallel, GPU threads then sweep through the volume, moving along each slice on the Z-axis. Given the resolution of the volume, and the physical dimensions this maps to, each discrete 3D grid location can be converted into a vertex in global coordinates. A metric distance from the camera center (the translation vector of the global camera transform) to this vertex can be calculated. This 3D vertex can also be perspective projected back into image coordinates to lookup the actual depth measurement along the ray. The difference between measured and calculated distances gives a new SDF value for the voxel (line 7). This is normalized to a TSDF (lines 9 and 11) and averaged with the previous stored value using a simple running weighted average (line 13) [ ]. Both the new weight and averaged TSDF are stored at the voxel.

Raycasting for Rendering and Tracking A GPU-based raycaster is implemented to generate views of the implicit surface within the volume for rendering and tracking (see pseudocode Listing 3). In parallel, each GPU thread walks a single ray and renders a single pixel in the output image. Given a starting position and direction of the ray, each GPU thread traverses voxels along the ray, and extracts the position of the implicit surface by observing a zero-crossing (a change in the sign of TSDF values stored along the ray). The final surface intersection point is computed using a simple linear interpolation given the trilinearly sampled points either side of the zero-crossing. Assuming the gradient is orthogonal to the surface interface, the surface normal is computed directly as the derivative of the TSDF at the zero-crossing [ ]. Therefore each GPU thread that finds a ray/surface intersection can calculate a single interpolated vertex and normal, which can used as parameters for lighting calculations on the output pixel, in order to render the surface.

Listing 3 Raycasting to extract the implicit surface, composite virtual 3D graphics, and perform lighting operations.

1: **for** each pixel $\mathbf{u} \in$ output image **in parallel do**
2: $\quad \mathbf{ray}^{\text{start}} \leftarrow$ back project $[\mathbf{u}, 0]$; convert to grid pos
3: $\quad \mathbf{ray}^{\text{next}} \leftarrow$ back project $[\mathbf{u}, 1]$; convert to grid pos
4: $\quad \mathbf{ray}^{\text{dir}} \leftarrow$ normalize $(\mathbf{ray}^{\text{next}} - \mathbf{ray}^{\text{start}})$
5: $\quad \mathbf{ray}^{\text{len}} \leftarrow \mathbf{0}$
6: $\quad \mathbf{g} \leftarrow$ first voxel along $\mathbf{ray}^{\text{dir}}$
7: $\quad \mathbf{m} \leftarrow$ convert global mesh vertex to grid pos
8: $\quad \mathbf{m}^{\text{dist}} \leftarrow ||\mathbf{ray}^{\text{start}} - \mathbf{m}||$
9: $\quad$ **while** voxel $\mathbf{g}$ within volume bounds **do**
10: $\qquad \mathbf{ray}^{\text{len}} \leftarrow \mathbf{ray}^{\text{len}} + \mathbf{1}$
11: $\qquad \mathbf{g}^{\text{prev}} \leftarrow \mathbf{g}$
12: $\qquad \mathbf{g} \leftarrow$ traverse next voxel along $\mathbf{ray}^{\text{dir}}$
13: $\qquad$ **if** zero crossing from $\mathbf{g}$ to $\mathbf{g}^{\text{prev}}$ **then**
14: $\qquad\quad \mathbf{p} \leftarrow$ extract trilinear interpolated grid position
15: $\qquad\quad \mathbf{v} \leftarrow$ convert $\mathbf{p}$ from grid to global 3D position
16: $\qquad\quad \mathbf{n} \leftarrow$ extract surface gradient as $\nabla \mathbf{tsdf}(\mathbf{p})$
17: $\qquad\quad$ shade pixel for oriented point $(\mathbf{v}, \mathbf{n})$ **or**
18: $\qquad\quad$ follow secondary ray (shadows, reflections, etc)
19: $\qquad$ **if** $\mathbf{ray}^{\text{len}} > \mathbf{m}^{\text{dist}}$ **then**
20: $\qquad\quad$ shade pixel using inputed mesh maps **or**
21: $\qquad\quad$ follow secondary ray (shadows, reflections, etc)

Our rendering pipeline shown in Figure 12 also allows conventional polygon-based graphics to be *composited* on the raycasted view, enabling blending of virtual and real scenes with correct occlusion handling (see Figure 6). In the first step (labeled a), a mesh-based scene is rendered with *graphics camera* parameters identical to the physical global camera pose ($\mathbf{T}_i$) and intrinsics ($\mathbf{K}$). Instead of rendering to the framebuffer, the vertex buffer, surface normals and unshaded color data are stored in off-screen vertex, normal and color maps respectively (labeled b), and used as input during raycasting (labeled c). For each GPU thread, a distance from the associated mesh vertex to the camera center is calculated in grid coordinates (Listing 3 lines 7 and 8). This distance acts

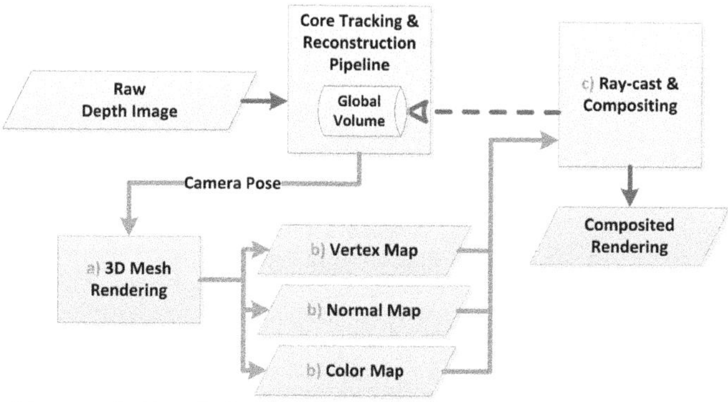

Figure 12: Rendering pipeline combining raycasting of volume with compositing of virtual polygon-based graphics.

as an additional termination condition while stepping along each ray (line 19), allowing accurate occlusion testing between volumetric and mesh surface geometries.

Ambient, diffuse and specular lighting contributions can be calculated *across* reconstructed and virtual geometries (see Figure 6). More advanced shading calculations can be performed by walking along the second (and possibly further) bounce of each ray. Shadows are calculated after the first ray hits a voxel or mesh surface (Listing 3 line 13 and 19), by walking a secondary ray from the surface to light position (using grid coordinates). If a surface is hit before ray termination then the vertex is shadowed. For reflections, once the first ray hits a surface, a new ray direction is calculated, based on the surface normal and initial ray direction.

A novel contribution of our raycaster is the ability to view the implicit surface of the reconstructed 3D model, composite polygon geometry with correct occlusion handling, and provide advanced shading requiring raytraced operations, all in real-time, through a single algorithm. Any 6DOF graphics camera transform can be used to raycast the volume, including arbitrary third-person views allowing user navigation of the 3D model. However, another *key* contribution of our raycaster, is in generating higher-quality data for ICP camera tracking. When the raycast camera transform equates to the physical camera pose, the extracted vertices and normals equate to depth and normal maps (from the same perspective as the physical camera) but with considerably less noise, shadows and holes than the raw Kinect data. As shown in [ ], this allows us to mitigate issues of drift and reduce ICP errors, by tracking directly from the raycasted model as opposed to frame-to-frame ICP tracking.

Simulating Real-World Physics

Taking the merging of real and virtual geometries further, the GPU pipeline is extended to support simulation of physically realistic collisions between virtual objects and the reconstructed scene. A particle simulation is implemented on the GPU, based on [ ] and [ ]. Scene geometry is represented within the simulation by a set of static particles (see Figure 13). These are spheres of identical size, which remain stationary but can collide with other dynamically simulated particles. Whilst an approximation, this technique models every discrete surface voxel within the volume in real-time, achieving compelling results even for very small and arbitrarily shaped objects such as a book's edges or a teapot's handle in Figures 7 (bottom right) and 13.

Figure 13: Simulating physics on the real-time reconstruction. Left: Surface is approximated as series of static particles (updated per integration sweep) which interact with dynamic particles. Every surface voxel is represented by a static particle. Middle: Surface normals of static and dynamic particles. Right: Shaded scene with only dynamic particles composited.

Static particles are created during volume integration. As the volume is swept, TSDF values within an adaptive threshold close to zero (defining the surface interface or *zero level set*) are extracted. For each surface voxel, a static particle is instantiated. Each particle contains a 3D vertex in global (metric) space, a velocity vector (always empty for static particles), and an ID. One key challenge then becomes detecting collisions. We use a spatially subdivided uniform grid to identify neighboring particles [ ]. Each cell in the grid has a unique ID. Each dynamic or static particle is assigned a grid cell ID by converting the particle's global vertex to grid coordinates. Our system then maintains two lists – one containing static particles; the other dynamic. In both, particles are binned into the grid cells by sorting them by their current grid ID (using a GPU-based radix sort). During each simulation step, a GPU thread is launched per dynamic particle. Each thread processes collisions by examining (3^3) neighborhood of cells (first for dynamic-dynamic collisions and then dynamic-static). The Discrete Element Method (DEM) [ ] is used to calculate a velocity vector when two particles collide. The particle's global velocity is incremented based on all neighboring collisions, gravity, and interactions with the bounding volume. Each particle is then repositioned based on the accumulated velocity per simulation step.

Figure 7 shows thousands of particles interacting with the reconstructed scene. A major contribution of our GPU-based pipeline is that it maintains interactive rates despite the overhead of physics simulation, whilst performing real-time camera tracking and reconstruction. By default, only dynamic particles are rendered during raycasting and again can be correctly occluded by the reconstructed geometry (see Figure 7).

INTERACTING IN THE SCENE

The core system described so far makes assumptions that the scene will remain reasonably static. Clearly in an interaction context, users want to move freely in front of the sensor, and interact in the scene. This opens up two main challenges.

First, ICP tracking assumes a single rigid transform occurred per frame due to camera motion. User interaction in front of the sensor will cause scene motion *independent* of camera motion, which breaks this assumption. Because our ICP tracking is dense (i.e. uses all available points) our system is resilient to transient scene motions. For example, in Figure 5, even when the user moves the object, enough *background* points will remain for ICP to converge. However, large or longer-term scene motions will cause tracking failure.

Second, whilst our system supports real-time reconstruction, surface predictions are refined over time using a running

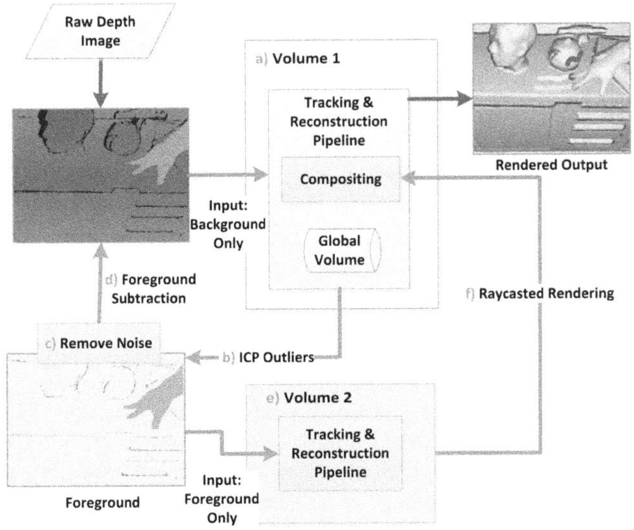

Figure 14: Extended GPU pipeline for real-time foreground and background segmentation, tracking and reconstruction.

weighted average of distance values. By adapting the weighting, higher precedence can be given to new TSDF values, allowing for faster model updates, but the trade-off is additional noise being introduced to the reconstruction. In practice, a weight is chosen to balance quality of reconstruction with regular updates to the reconstruction based on scene changes. However, this does not support a continuously moving scene. Typically a user freely moving in the scene leads to associated depth data being partially integrated into the volume (Figure 8 middle). As camera tracking relies directly on this model, which is now inconsistent with the live data, failures will occur (Figure 8 right).

ICP Outliers for Segmentation To begin to explore dynamic user interaction with the reconstructed scene, a novel extension to the core GPU pipeline is provided (shown in Figure 14). The technique leverages a unique property of dense ICP tracking. When *all* depth measurements are used, *outliers* from projective data association can form a strong initial predication as to parts of the scene moving independent of camera motion – if enough rigid background points are present for ICP still to converge. Our solution robustly *segments* a moving foreground object from the background, allowing tracking failures to be reduced, and enabling users to interact directly in the scene.

This pipeline assumes that at least parts of a rigid scene have been initially reconstructed using the core reconstruction pipeline (labeled a). After this initial scan, a moving object entering the scene contains oriented points with significant disparity to already reconstructed surfaces. These fail ICP projective data association and are copied into an *outlier map* (labeled b). Next, a depth-aware connected component analysis is performed on the outlier map to cluster large connected patches and remove smaller outliers due to sensor noise (labeled c). Large connected patches, where foreground scene motion has been detected, are masked in the input depth map for core 'background' reconstruction (labeled d). This stops associated foreground depth measurements being used for reconstruction or tracking in the core pipeline. Large patches of outliers can be additionally reconstructed using a second volume (labeled e) – potentially running on a

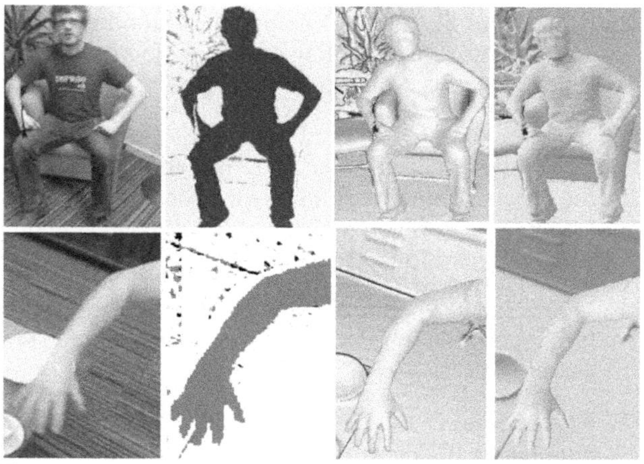

Figure 15: Moving user is segmented and reconstructed, independent of background. Left to right: 1) Live RGB. 2) ICP outliers (for initial segmentation prediction). 3) final composited scene showing foreground shaded differently to background. 4) Composited normal maps.

separate GPU with different reconstruction settings. A final step raycasts the two separate volumes and composites the output (labeled f), using the same method as Figure 12.

Overall our technique yields compelling results in stabilizing tracking and therefore improving reconstruction quality for a static background, even when parts of the scene continually move in front of the camera. Furthermore, it allows a foreground object to be robustly segmented, and potentially reconstructed separately of the background (see Figure 15).

Listing 4 Create touch map – testing if foreground and background vertices overlap.

1: $\mathbf{V}^{g}_{fg} \leftarrow$ raycasted vertex map from foreground volume
2: **for** each pixel $\mathbf{u} \in \mathbf{O}$ (touch map) **in parallel do**
3:    cast single ray for $\mathbf{u}$ (as Listing 3)
4:    **if** zero crossing when walking ray **then**
5:       $\mathbf{v}^{g}_{bg} \leftarrow$ interpolated global zero crossing position
6:       **if** $||\mathbf{v}^{g}_{bg} - \mathbf{V}^{g}_{fg}(\mathbf{u})|| <$ adaptive threshold **then**
7:          $\mathbf{O}(\mathbf{u}) \leftarrow \mathbf{V}^{g}_{fg}(\mathbf{u})$

Detecting Touch on Arbitrary Surfaces The pipeline can be further extended to support multi-touch input by observing intersections between foreground and background. We extend the default raycasting of the background volume to output a touch map, as shown in pseudocode Listing 4. Using the raycasted foreground vertex map as input, each GPU thread again walks a ray through the background volume. If a zero crossing is located, the corresponding foreground vertex (along the same ray) is tested (line 6). If foreground and background are within range, the foreground position is output in the touch map. A depth-aware connected component analysis of the touch map suppresses noise and labels fingertip candidates, which are tracked over time. Examples of enabling multi-touch on both planar and non-planar surfaces are shown in Figures 10 and 16.

Towards Modeling of Dynamic Scenes

The ability of now distinguishing moving foreground robustly from background raises interesting questions regarding how best to reconstruct such moving surfaces. The key challenge becomes how to integrate foreground data into a second volume so that correspondence between surface measurements can be ensured over time. As an initial exploration, we have experimented with independently predicting the pose of the foreground object using another instance of ICP. Again *dense* ICP is performed but only using the *foreground* oriented points (from the live depth map and raycasted second volume). In practice we have found that dense ICP converges even if small parts of the foreground are moving non-rigidly. A compelling example is a user's arm (Figure 15) where ICP converges on the rigid parts even if fingers are moving non-rigidly. This offers a coarse method for predicting the pose of the foreground object, relative to the global camera transform.

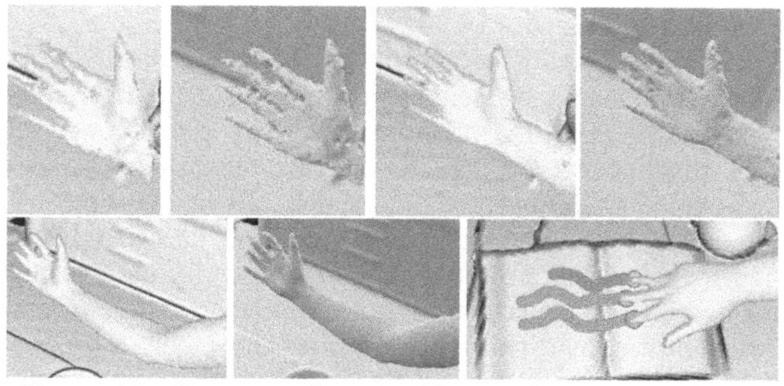

Figure 16: Segmentation, tracking and reconstruction of user's arm with moving Kinect. Top left: Arm is first introduced and reconstruction contains a great deal of noise. Top right: surface is refined based on separate ICP-based pose prediction. Bottom left: the moving surface is rapidly reconstructed to a much higher quality than the raw Kinect signal. Bottom right: The intersection between foreground and background surfaces are used for multi-touch detection.

Using this predicted pose, depth measurements can be aligned and fused into the second volume. A surface prediction of the foreground, which becomes more refined and complete, can be built up over time. Because the foreground surface will likely be moving, we give more weight to new measurements being integrated. One simple extension uses a per-voxel weighting, adapted based on a running average of the derivative of the TSDF (prior to integration). This allows us to adapt the weight of individual surface voxels, giving higher priority to new measurements when the rate of change is high (e.g. fingers or hands), and lower if the TSDF measurements are stable (e.g. the forearm). Figures 16 and 15 shows our initial results based on foreground ICP tracking and per-voxel adaptive weighting. Note there is considerably less noise than the raw Kinect data – the user's arms, hand and fingers are clearly identifiable – and that this foreground reconstruction occurs alongside camera tracking and refinement of the background reconstruction.

For our physics simulation, we can now represent the entire foreground reconstruction as static particles, allowing collisions between the moving user, and the dynamic particles, to be modeled per frame (as shown in Figure 9). This approach of reconstructing a moving foreground, can also be used purely to *track* the pose of rigid objects held in the user's hand – enabling tracking independent of camera motion and without markers or prior knowledge of the object. One example is shown in Figure 1 (far right) where an already reconstructed teapot (from Figure 5) is tracked in 6DOF and re-registered with the real physical object.

CONCLUSIONS

We have presented KinectFusion, a real-time 3D reconstruction and interaction system using a moving standard Kinect. Our contributions are threefold. First, we detailed a novel GPU pipeline that achieves 3D tracking, reconstruction, segmentation, rendering, and interaction, all in real-time using only a commodity camera and graphics hardware. Second, we have demonstrated core novel uses for our system: for low-cost object scanning and advanced AR and physics-based interactions. Third, we described new methods for segmenting, tracking and reconstructing dynamic users and the background scene simultaneously, enabling multi-touch on any indoor scene with arbitrary surface geometries. We believe this is the first time that a reconstruction system has shown this level of user interaction directly in the scene.

Our hope is to scale the system further, reconstructing larger scenes where more memory efficient representations such as octrees might be needed [ ]. Encouraged by our initial results, we also wish to explore more fine-grained methods for tracking and reconstruction of moving deformable surfaces, including the user. Our hope is that KinectFusion will open many new topics for research both in terms of the underlying technology, as well as the interactive possibilities it enables.

REFERENCES

1. P. J. Besl and N. D. McKay. A method for registration of 3-d shapes. *IEEE Trans. Pattern Anal. Mach. Intell.*, 14:239–256, February 1992.
2. X. Cao and R. Balakrishnan. Interacting with dynamically defined information spaces using a handheld projector and a pen. In *UIST*, pages 225–234, 2006.
3. Y. Chen and G. Medioni. Object modeling by registration of multiple range images. *Image and Vision Computing (IVC)*, 10(3):145–155, 1992.
4. Y. Cui et al. 3d shape scanning with a time-of-flight camera. In *Computer Vision and Pattern Recognition (CVPR)*, pages 1173 –1180, June 2010.
5. B. Curless and M. Levoy. A volumetric method for building complex models from range images. *ACM Trans. Graph.*, 1996.
6. S. Farsiu et al. Fast and robust multiframe super resolution. *IEEE Transactions on Image Processing*, 13(10):1327–1344, 2004.
7. J. Frahm et al. Building Rome on a cloudless day. In *Proc. Europ. Conf. on Computer Vision (ECCV)*, 2010.
8. B. Freedman, A. Shpunt, M. Machline, and Y. Arieli. Depth Mapping Using Projected Patterns. Patent Application, 10 2008. WO 2008/120217 A2.
9. S. L. Grand. Broad-phase collision detection with CUDA. In *GPU Gems 3*. Addison-Wesley, 2007.
10. T. Harada. Real-time rigid body simulation on gpus. In *GPU Gems 3*. Addison-Wesley Professional, 2007.
11. R. Hartley and A. Zisserman. *Multiple View Geometry in Computer Vision*. Cambridge University Press, second edition, 2004.
12. P. Henry et al. RGB-D mapping: Using depth cameras for dense 3D modeling of indoor environments. In *Proc. of the Int. Symposium on Experimental Robotics (ISER)*, 2010.
13. B. Huhle et al. Fusion of range and color images for denoising and resolution enhancement with a non-local filter. *Computer Vision and Image Understanding*, 114(12):1336–1345, 2010.
14. M. Kazhdan, M. Bolitho, and H. Hoppe. Poisson surface reconstruction. In *Proc. of the Eurographics Symposium on Geometry Processing*, 2006.
15. G. Klein and D. W. Murray. Parallel tracking and mapping for small AR workspaces. In *ISMAR*, 2007.
16. M. Levoy et al. The digital Michelangelo Project: 3D scanning of large statues. *ACM Trans. Graph.*, 2000.
17. K. Low. Linear least-squares optimization for point-to-plane icp surface registration. Technical report, TR04-004, University of North Carolina, 2004.
18. P. Merrell et al. Real-time visibility-based fusion of depth maps. In *Proc. of the Int. Conf. on Computer Vision (ICCV)*, 2007.
19. R. A. Newcombe and A. J. Davison. Live dense reconstruction with a single moving camera. In *Proc. of the IEEE (CVPR)*, 2010.
20. R. A. Newcombe, S. Lovegrove, and A. J. Davison. Dense tracking and mapping in real-time. In *Proc. of the Int. Conf. on Computer Vision (ICCV)*, 2011.
21. R. A. Newcombe et al. Real-Time Dense Surface Mapping and Tracking with Kinect. In *ISMAR*, 2011.
22. S. Osher and R. Fedkiw. *Level Set Methods and Dynamic Implicit Surfaces*. Springer, 2002.
23. S. Rusinkiewicz, O. Hall-Holt, and M. Levoy. Real-time 3D model acquisition. *ACM Trans. Graph.*, 2002.
24. S. Rusinkiewicz and M. Levoy. Efficient variants of the ICP algorithm. *3D Digital Imaging and Modeling, Int. Conf. on*, 0:145, 2001.
25. S. Thrun. Robotic mapping: A survey. In *Exploring Artificial Intelligence in the New Millenium*. 2002.
26. D. Vlasic et al. Dynamic shape capture using multi-view photometric stereo. *ACM Trans. Graph.*, 28(5), 2009.
27. D. Wagner, T. Langlotz, and D. Schmalstieg. Robust and unobtrusive marker tracking on mobile phones. In *ISMAR*, pages 121–124, 2008.
28. T. Weise, T. Wismer, B. Leibe, and L. V. Gool. In-hand scanning with online loop closure. In *IEEE Int. Workshop on 3-D Digital Imaging and Modeling*, 2009.
29. K. Zhou, M. Gong, X. Huang, and B. Guo. Data-parallel octrees for surface reconstruction. *IEEE Trans. on Visualization and Computer Graphics*, 17, 2011.

Vermeer: Direct Interaction with a 360° Viewable 3D Display

Alex Butler[1], *Otmar Hilliges*[1], *Shahram Izadi*[1], *Steve Hodges*[1], *David Molyneaux*[1,2], *David Kim*[1,3], *Danny Kong*[1]

[1]Microsoft Research
7 J J Thomson Avenue
Cambridge, CB3 0FB, UK

[2]Computing and Communications,
Lancaster University,
Lancaster, LA1 4WA, UK

[3]Computing Sciences
Newcastle University,
Newcastle, NE1 7RU, UK

{dab,otmarh,shahrami,shodges,a-davmo,b-davidk}@microsoft.com, d.l.kong.01@cantab.net

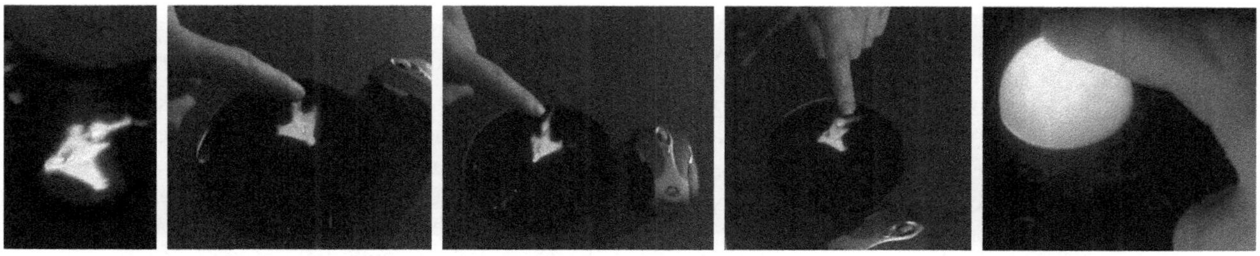

Figure 1: Vermeer allows direct interaction within the volume of a 360° viewable 3D display. Far left: 3D model rendered using our 3D display. Middle sequence: user places finger in the volume to interact directly with 3D model. Note how the perspective of the 3D model changes, depending on the viewer position (without requiring any head tracking or specialized eyewear). Far right: the user interacts with a spherical display using the same optical arrangement.

ABSTRACT

We present Vermeer, a novel interactive 360° viewable 3D display. Like prior systems in this area, Vermeer provides viewpoint-corrected, stereoscopic 3D graphics to simultaneous users, 360° around the display, without the need for eyewear or other user instrumentation. Our goal is to overcome an issue inherent in these prior systems which – typically due to moving parts – restrict interactions to *outside* the display volume. Our system leverages a known optical illusion to demonstrate, for the first time, how users can reach into and directly touch 3D objects *inside* the display volume. Vermeer is intended to be a new enabling technology for interaction, and we therefore describe our hardware implementation in full, focusing on the challenges of combining this optical configuration with an existing approach for creating a 360° viewable 3D display. Initially we demonstrate direct in-volume interaction by sensing user input with a Kinect camera placed above the display. However, by exploiting the properties of the optical configuration, we also demonstrate novel prototypes for fully integrated input sensing alongside simultaneous display. We conclude by discussing limitations, implications for interaction, and ideas for future work.

ACM Classification: H5.2 [Information interfaces and presentation]: User Interfaces. - Graphical user interfaces.

General terms: Design, Human Factors, Algorithms

Keywords: 360° Viewable 3D Display, In-Volume Interaction, Input Sensing, Optical Illusion, Tabletop.

INTRODUCTION

There is a growing body of research into 360° viewable 3D displays [5,8,10,13,19,20,29,32]. Such systems provide viewpoint-corrected, stereoscopic 3D graphics to simultaneous users, 360° around the display, without the need for eyewear or other user instrumentation. These technologies also tend to provide depth cues such as vergence, correct eye-accommodation and horizontal motion parallax – the latter without the need for head tracking – which provide a perception of depth even for those without stereopsis. They have been shown to improve viewer perception of 3D when compared with stereo-only displays [14].

Most implementations of such displays restrict the user from interacting within the display volume. Indeed, users are typically separated from the displayed 3D objects by a glass or acrylic shield (due to moving parts [10,19] or hazardous [20] or fragile optical elements [29]). Current user interface research within this domain has therefore focused on enabling *outside* of the volume interaction [15,16].

We introduce a novel interactive display system called Vermeer, which allows users to reach into and directly touch 3D objects within the display volume. The system builds on the 3D display research of [19] and therefore has similar benefits for viewing 3D graphics. However, Vermeer also supports *direct* interactions *within* the display volume, where users can now place their fingers (or indeed any object) to interact, as shown in Figure 1. This has not been demonstrated previously by other 360° viewable 3D displays because of their physical constraints.

To achieve this, the system exploits a known optical illusion using two parabolic mirrors [11,24]. This optical configuration allows a 360° viewable 3D display to be *reimaged* [1] such that the graphics appear to be floating in a user-accessible region above the unit. We first show how a Kinect camera, placed above the display, can be used to detect fingers inside the display volume, and demonstrate simple proof-of-concept in-volume interactions. Next we leverage the unique properties of the parabolic mirror configuration and demonstrate novel prototypes that support fully integrated input sensing alongside simultaneous display. We conclude by discussing limitations, implications for interaction, and ideas for future work.

RELATED WORK

Detailed surveys of 3D display technologies are provided by [5,6,9,17,19,30]. Our aim is to enable direct interaction with a particular class of 3D display. Such technologies are referred to as volumetric [5,10,13,29], multiview [8,12,22] or 360° light field displays [12,19,32] within the literature. Whilst there are clearly distinctions between these types of displays, for our purposes we characterize these displays as exhibiting the following properties:

- *A 360° horizontal field-of-view and omnidirectional viewing,* where users receive differing views of the 3D scene depending on their position around the display.
- *Horizontal parallax without head tracking.*
- *Simultaneous support for multiple viewers.*
- *Stereoscopic imagery* without the need for eyewear or other user instrumentation.
- *Non-planar characteristics* where the display is bound to an entire 3D volume rather than a single plane.

Such systems clearly contrast with *stereo* only displays which require specialized glasses and support a single stereoscopic depth cue. They also contrast with *autostereo* only displays (e.g. based on lenticular arrays or parallax barriers [9,17]), which remove the need for glasses, but again only deliver stereoscopic-cues and typically support limited viewing positions.

Many different techniques have been proposed to enable such 360° viewable 3D displays (see [5,13,19] for a detailed overview). These include swept volume approaches which use moving parts, such as rotating display elements to render slices of volumetric data at high speed, and form full 3D imagery through persistence of vision [6,13]. An extension to these approaches are systems that rotate a high speed LCD [22], LED [12,32] or projected display [19], and restrict viewing angles to create perspective-corrected renderings of a 3D scene in different directions. Solid state displays that render slices of 3D data onto a stack of dynamically switching diffuser planes [29] have been proposed as well as more unconventional approaches that use multiple lasers to stimulate points or regions within photonically excitable mediums [20].

Whilst these systems offer steps towards realistic 3D display, they do not naturally allow a user to interact directly within the display volume, either because of rapidly moving mechanical elements, physical encasing of optical components, or hazardous or fragile materials. Typically a transparent glass or acrylic dome or other barrier separates the physical display volume from the user.

Despite these limitations, previous work has reported different approaches to interact with virtual 3D content rendered by such displays from *outside* of the volume. In [16] the 6DOF pose of fingers are tracked using a Vicon motion capture system to support interactions outside and on the dome of an Actuality volumetric display [10]. [15] presents an evaluation of targeting tasks using a Vicon tracked stylus to point into the volumetric display from the outside.

Our goal is to remove this limitation on 360° viewable 3D displays, and allow direct interaction within the volume.

Aside from spatial 3D displays, there is also considerable literature on head-worn optical or video see-through 3D display systems (see [3] for a detailed overview). Whilst enabling greater user mobility and novel AR and VR scenarios, many head-worn displays have a number of drawbacks including small field-of-view, continually forcing the user to refocus between virtual graphics close to the eye and real-world objects far away (an issue for optical see though displays), inherent latency, and inaccuracies in tracking, which can result in sickness and fatigue during use [7,18]. Perhaps the biggest drawback of head-worn solutions is ergonomics; many available devices are still heavy and require tethered hardware to be worn.

Another approach is to present stereoscopic imagery to a limited number of users is to leverage a horizontal projection screen and tracked shutter glasses, as in [2]. In addition to head-worn glasses, the system also tracks styli for input. While less intrusive this approach still suffers from missing depth cues and possible distortions in depth perception [18]. Also it is non-trivial to scale such systems to many users due to frame rate limitations of projection and glasses hardware [2].

In contrast to these previous approaches, we wish to support even more lightweight 'walk up and use' tabletop scenarios, without any user instrumentation, eyewear or otherwise, or the use of tracked input devices.

Another means of co-locating 3D graphics and input without glasses is to use an optical combiner such as a beam-splitter [4,25,26,31]. In these arrangements 3D graphics produced on a CRT or LCD screen are reflected as a virtual image displayed to the user through a beam splitter. This co-locates the virtual reflected scene with the user's interaction space. Input is typically provided using a stylus [25,31] or force-feedback device [26].

While these setups provide many depth cues including full motion parallax when employing head-tracking they are inherently single user and cannot easily provide omnidirectional views of the scene. The virtual showcase [4] circumvents some of these limitations by utilizing several or a single curved beam-splitter. This provides a more omni-directional viewing experience but fully encases the display preventing users from reaching into the volume.

VERMEER PROTOTYPE

In order to enable direct, unencumbered interaction with a 360° viewable 3D display we exploit a known optical illusion used in the commercially available Opti-Gone Mirage product [24]. When two equally-sized parabolic mirrors are placed in a 'clamshell' setup (facing each other with the center of each mirror coinciding with the focal point of the other) any object that can be placed in the central region of the lower mirror is *reimaged* so that an image of that object can be observed 'floating' just above the upper mirror, as if it were real. This well-known phenomenon (described fully in [1,11]), forms the basis of our display.

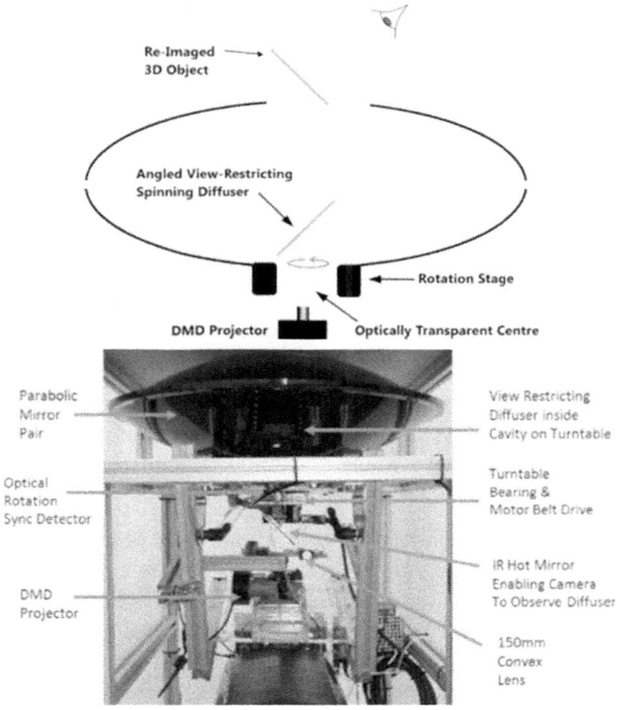

Figure 2: The Vermeer Display. Top: shows basic principle of operation. A 360° viewable 3D display based on spinning optics is placed at the bottom of a pair of parabolic mirrors. The display is reimaged above the mirrors, where it can be observed by multiple users who can then place their fingers inside the view volume. Bottom: hardware configuration showing main components.

The basic architecture of Vermeer is a 360° viewable 3D display sited between these two parabolic mirrors as depicted in Figure 2. Users can view content 360° around the reimaged display and can also touch anywhere within the perceived display volume to interact with the 3D content directly. Users must view the image from around 45° relative to the center axis above the top aperture in order to see into the mirror cavity.

Building this configuration is non-trivial, particularly as it requires us to build and extend the 360° viewable 3D display described in [19] to support both projection and imaging from below. The previous system used top-down projection onto an anisotropic mirror [19]. However, top-down projection is not feasible for our requirements, as fingers interacting within the volume will occlude the projection. In the remainder of this section we describe the salient parts of our hardware and software implementation.

We sourced the Opti-Gone Mirage Model 22 consumer product [24], which provides 56cm diameter parabolic mirrors with a 15cm diameter opening in both mirrors. This setup provides a cylindrical view volume of about 50 mm diameter and 55 mm height for the 3D display to appear. Inside this volume, a projection screen (35 mm wide and 70 mm high) is mounted at a 45° angle upon a rotating stage, with circular cut-out at its center. This is driven by belt using an Animatics SM2316D SmartMotor. This allows us to control the orientation of the projection screen without obstructing the optical path from the projector mounted underneath the diffuser.

A high speed DMD projector is utilized to display multiple renderings of the 3D scene at very high frame rates – the projection is synchronized with the SmartMotor to ensure that the correct view is displayed at the correct time (or rather when the diffuser is positioned in the corresponding orientation). The projector is mounted so that additional, optical elements can be positioned in the optical path. For example, lenses to focus the projection for a shorter throw distance. Additionally a hot mirror enables an infrared (IR) camera to sense user input (as described later).

View Restrictive Diffuser

A narrow view angle is required to present sufficiently different views to multiple users around the display and to ensure inter-ocular separation of images for stereopsis. Previous work [19] used a reflective mirror with anisotropic characteristics (to provide a narrow viewing angle in the horizontal direction) coupled with projection from above. Our current implementation uses a back-projection diffuser with a stack of off-the-shelf privacy films [27] on top (we use 7 in our current implementation). The stacked arrangement simulates deeper micro-louvres and generates the narrow viewing angle required.

This solution greatly minimizes the visibility of vertical dead banding, as apparent in other parallax barrier techniques such as macro scale venetian blinds. Our stacked arrangement can lead to small Moiré artifacts in the image although these are not as apparent when the diffuser is spinning. We have also recently sourced a custom single substrate *view control film* (from Shin-Etsu) with a narrower field-of-view and no visible Moiré. However, the stacked arrangement is a more readily available solution.

High-speed Projection and Rendering Pipeline

To display multiple viewpoints per full rotation of the spinning diffuser, we use a Texas Instruments DMD Discovery 0.7" XGA D4100 high speed projector. We target a horizontal view angle of ~1.875° such that a full 360° rotation is made up of 192 independent viewpoints. We use a DLi D4100 DVI interface daughterboard in combination with a custom FPGA to split each outgoing 24-bit DVI frame into 24 binary DMD images on the projector. Each single 24-bit RGB DVI frame transmitted from the PC to the projector therefore can contain 24 binary images each containing 24 different projections of the 3D scene. Our DVI connection runs at 120Hz, totaling 2880 binary projector frames per second, achieving a total refresh rate of 15Hz for the entire display.

Our focus is on the novel use of the mirrors for input so for our display we employ a much simpler 3D perspective rendering than that proposed by [19]. A virtual camera circles the scene looking down at a 45° angle to compensate for the diffuser mounted at the same angle. The virtual camera also rotates about its own up vector to correct for the rotation of the diffuser stage. A custom rendering technique writes 24 consecutive views into an off-screen render target. A final post-processing pass combines these views into a single 24-bit RGB image.

Synchronization

Synchronization between the mechanically rotating element and the projected image stream is critical to ensure that the 360° generated viewpoints remain consistent. The FPGA decoding incoming DVI frames was designed to detect a pattern embedded in the first 15 lines of the very first binary image of a 360° cycle. A 2μs pulse is generated at each start of a full rotation. A simple LED and photodiode optical detector generates a second pulse whenever the angled diffuser passes a reference (0°) position. A TI MSP430 embedded microprocessor monitors the difference in time between the incoming pulses. A simple control loop adjusts the speed of rotation of the motor to ensure that the first frame of the series is projected at the diffuser's zero angle position.

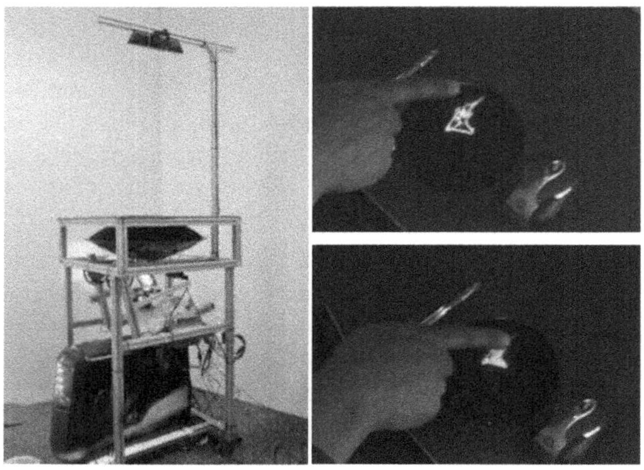

Figure 3 Left: The Vermeer display with Kinect depth sensor mounted above. Right: the user's finger is sensed within the volume using the Kinect sensor and causes the ship to switch from wireframe to dithered rendering.

IN-VOLUME INTERACTION

Figure 1 shows interactive graphics rendered on Vermeer as seen from different viewpoints around the setup. Note how the virtual 3D model shares the same perspective foreshortening with real objects in the scene such as the mouse and a user's finger. Also note how the position of the 3D model stays steady in relation to the fingertip illustrating correct spatial registration. The graphics are reimaged from the bottom of the parabolic mirror pair, allowing users to directly touch the 3D model.

To first explore the possibilities for interaction with dynamic 3D scenes we mounted a Kinect camera directly above the mirror pair (Figure 3, left).

We implemented a fingertip tracking technique using the depth data from the Kinect camera. Using the depth data, it is relatively straightforward to segment the user's hand from the background once it enters the volume, trace the contour of the user's hand and detect fingertips using a peak-and-valley image processing algorithm [23] at 30Hz (Figure 4). Detected fingertip positions are Kalman filtered and tracked over time to be used as spatial input for our demonstrators. Once fingertips are found, we average the depth values of a patch of pixels around the fingertip to infer its 3D position. To avoid depth distortions only pixels lying within the contour are considered.

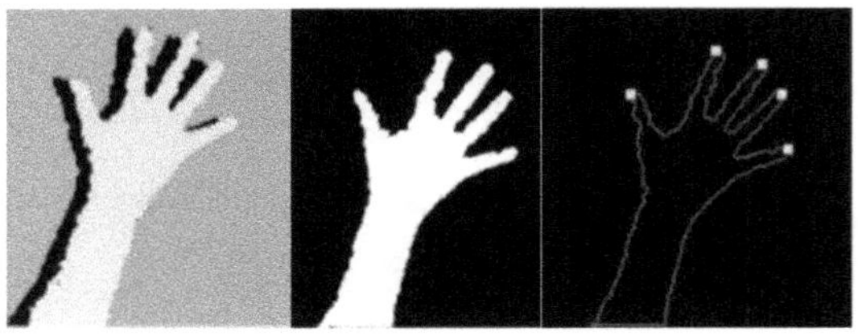

Figure 4 left to right: depth map real-world converted; foreground extracted; contour traced and fingertips detected using peak-and-valley algorithm.

In the most simplistic scenario a user may place a finger within the display volume in order to animate a 3D character or change the rendering used (Figure 3, right). However, it is possible to implement more fine-grained interactions than this simplistic binary touch/no-touch scenario. The actual spatial location of the fingertip can be used to make better use of the 3D nature of our system. When a user touches the center of the 3D character the rendered model will start to walk following a pre-defined animation. In contrast, if the user touches the top of the model the animated character waves his arm and lowers it back once the finger retracts from the volume.

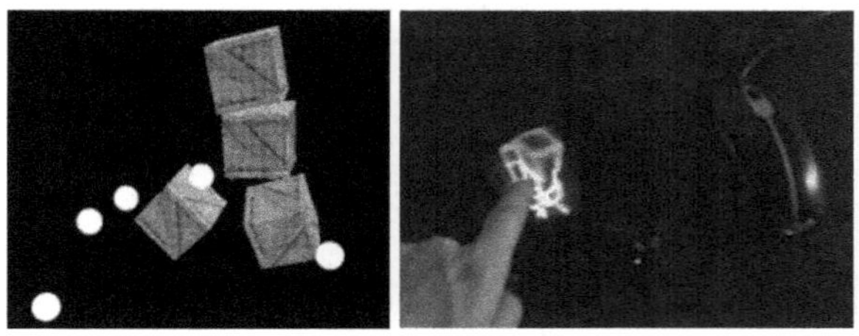

Figure 5 Left: On screen physics-enabled scene with dithered gray-scale rendering; white spheres serve as proxy for fingers and interact with virtual objects. Right: Scene as viewed by the user.

A final example demonstrates more fine-grained interactive capabilities of our system. Rather than interacting with pre-defined animations it is possible to use a physics simulation (in our case NVIDIA PhysX) to control the position of virtual objects via real-world concepts such as forces, collisions and friction. In this instance we use the 3D fingertip position data and model the users' fingers as spherical proxy objects within the simulation. This allows users to knock over stacks of virtual spheres or boxes by directly intersecting their fingers with the virtual objects inside the volume (see Figure 5).

INTEGRATED SENSING

So far we have demonstrated how the reimaged graphics of a 360° viewable 3D display can be directly interacted with using fingertips sensed using a Kinect camera. This arrangement, while enabling some interesting interaction possibilities, increases the complexity of the setup, and suffers from many of the issues of top-down camera systems, in particular additional bulk and occlusions. In this section, we demonstrate two novel prototypes that further leverage the optical properties of the mirrors to sense user input from *within* the display arrangement – making it more appealing as a self-contained tabletop form-factor.

Infrared Reimaging

One optical property of the parabolic mirrors, particularly interesting for finger sensing, is the ability to reimage light in the near-IR range. This can be confirmed by placing an IR diffusing object inside the mirror-pair and illuminating the object using IR LEDs. The example in Figure 6 left shows a dome (hemispherical object) being illuminated and reimaged in this way. Here a handheld IR camera observes a reimaged 3D IR object floating above the mirror.

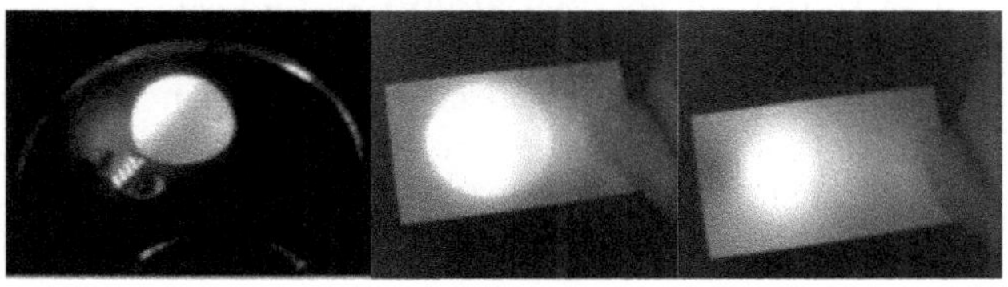

Figure 6 Left: A reimaged IR illuminated dome, as seen from a handheld IR camera above the mirrors. Middle and right: A diffuser sheet is intersected with this IR dome at different heights, and imaged from below.

One interesting aspect is that the floating IR object is *optically real*. We illustrate this in Figure 6 right, by moving a diffuser sheet (tracing paper) above the top mirror aperture, and using an IR camera to image this area from below. The figure clearly shows a circular spot where the diffuser intersects with a cross-section of the reimaged IR dome. The IR light is scattered downwards and imaged by the camera. Moreover, the size of the spot changes as the diffuser is moved up and down, intersecting with different slices of the reimaged 3D IR dome. This optical property can be leveraged for in-volume touch sensing. An arbitrary 3D surface, reimaged using IR, can float in the display area. Fingertips intersecting with this reimaged IR object will be clearly illuminated and detected with an IR camera.

Figure 7 (top left) shows our first novel prototype exploiting this optical property. Figure 7 (top right) shows the setup more clearly. A dome object is placed at the base of the mirror cavity. A video projector is used to render visible graphical output onto the dome. Graphics are predistorted to compensate for the non-planar projection screen. To sense user input, an IR camera (located at the base of the mirror pairs) images through the aperture in the top mirror half.

From above, in visible light, the user can see the reimaged dome object and projected graphics. However the IR camera below is directly imaging this same space (without observing the reimaged visible object). When the user's fingers are placed inside the display volume, they intersect the reimaged IR dome, and IR light will be scattered downwards, where the camera can image a bright reflection of the fingertip, as illustrated in Figure 7.

A user interacting with the system is thus presented with interactive full-color graphics floating above the mirror. When touching (or rather intersecting) the surface of the reimaged projection surface we can detect and track the resulting bright IR blobs in the camera image for user input. In our proof-of-concept implementation a map of the earth is projected, as shown in Figure 7, bottom.

A finger moving along the surface of the reimaged hemisphere spins the globe about an imagined axis perpendicular to the motion trajectory. It is worthwhile noting that only the section of the finger actually intersecting the reimaged sphere is IR illuminated so that fingers hovering above the sphere's surface can be distinguished from ones touching. This prototype demonstrates how we can sense intersections between physical objects above the mirror and IR illuminated objects inside. These objects do not need to be planar as demonstrated here.

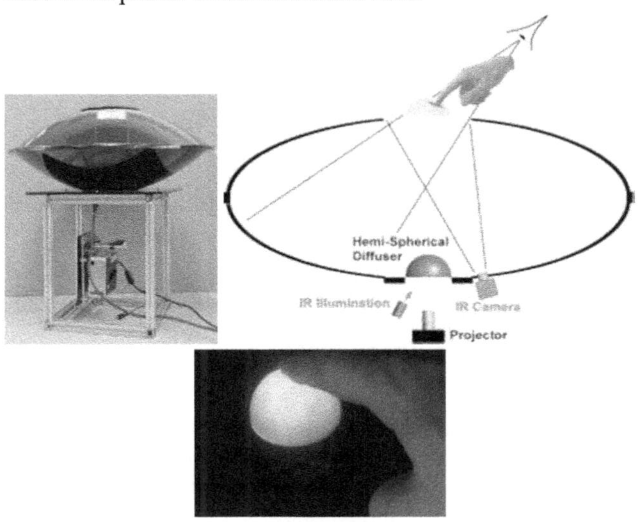

Figure 7: Top left: Prototype of integrated fingertip sensing. Top right: Schematic overview. A rear-projected hemispherical diffuse surface is also illuminated from below with IR. Bottom: A user spins the rendered map of the earth by dragging a finger across the surface of the reimaged globe.

Fully Integrated Touch Sensing and 3D Display

The previous prototype shows how the optical properties of the parabolic mirror pair extend to IR based fingertip sensing. A more well-known but rarely exploited property of the mirror arrangement is that the floating reimaged object can in fact be re-illuminated (e.g. using a small torch or laser) under certain circumstances [1, 28]. If a laser is shone onto the floating reimaged object, but aimed to ensure that the light actually passes down into the aperture of the upper mirror, the bright laser spot will appear on the reimaged object as if it were real (this is described in [28], page 28).

This demonstrates the basic reversibility of the optical setup, and highlights that light emitted by, or diffusely scattered off, any object above the top cavity can be reimaged downwards into the bottom cavity. We use both these properties of the optical arrangement to support fully integrated sensing in our 360° viewable 3D display.

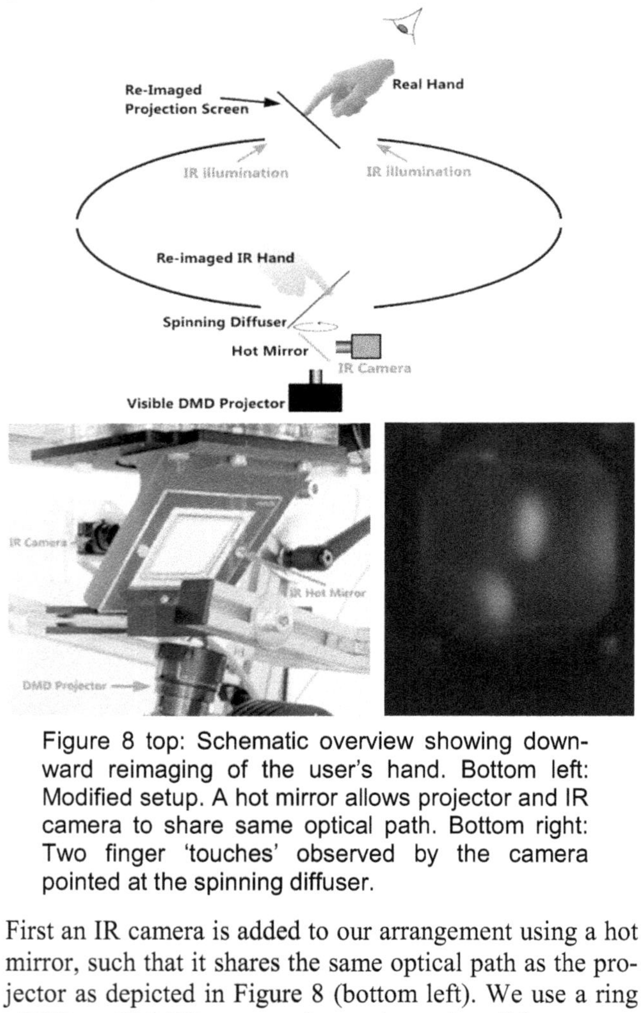

Figure 8 top: Schematic overview showing downward reimaging of the user's hand. Bottom left: Modified setup. A hot mirror allows projector and IR camera to share same optical path. Bottom right: Two finger 'touches' observed by the camera pointed at the spinning diffuser.

First an IR camera is added to our arrangement using a hot mirror, such that it shares the same optical path as the projector as depicted in Figure 8 (bottom left). We use a ring of 850nm IR LEDs mounted onto the cavity of the top parabolic mirror to flood the area above the mirror pair with diffuse IR light. When a user's finger moves into this area it will scatter some of this light into the mirror.

The illuminated part of the finger will be reimaged downwards into the mirror cavity. Much in the same way that the diffuser intersected with the IR dome in our previous system, the spinning diffuser can intersect with the optically real image of the finger at the bottom of the parabolic mirrors. This is then visible to the IR camera underneath. Fingertips are readily detected by an IR camera pointing at the diffuser. The full setup is summarized in Figure 8.

At first the fact that the diffuser is spinning at high speeds seems to pose a major problem, but in practice using a regular 30fps camera we have observed minimal motion blur and fingertips are clearly discernible as shown in Figure 8 (bottom right).

DISCUSSION

Our Vermeer prototype generates 360° views of a 3D object which can be observed by multiple people around a tabletop surface without the need for glasses. Depending on the chosen 3D volumetric display at the heart of the parabolic mirror pair such a display can provide several depth cues: vergence, accommodation, horizontal motion parallax and stereopsis. We developed this specific 3D display based on the design proposed by Jones et al. [19]. Although many of the display's features have been demonstrated in the context of light-field and volumetric displays in the past, our system, to our knowledge for the first time, demonstrates the additional feature of direct-touch interaction within the display volume. We built a fully-functional 3D display and illustrated the design changes necessary to allow for a new rear-projected optical configuration. This configuration utilizes a commercially available optical illusion to support reimaging of the displayed content.

We have demonstrated how a depth-sensing technology such as Kinect can be used to provide 'in-display' touch input. However, perhaps more interestingly, we have demonstrated how the optical configuration can itself be leveraged, to support novel means for integrated in-volume touch sensing, whilst simultaneously displaying content. This reduces the complexity and size of the setup.

Our prototypes demonstrate proof-of-concept manipulations of 3D virtual models within the display volume. However, we have to contrast this against the relatively small dimensions of the viewable volume. This small size limits the number of fingers interacting simultaneously in the volume. It is however interesting to note that the Kinect sensing mechanism is capable of sensing a much larger volume than the viewable area. This enables us to combine indirect interaction techniques that have previously been proposed in the literature [15,16] with direct in-volume interactions. For example, a bi-manual technique could be implemented where one hand is used to select objects in the volume (by touching them) and the other hand is used to manipulate parameters from further away.

Another interesting opportunity that arises from the combination of input with our display setup has to do with the optical properties of the illusion. When a finger enters the image formed above the mirror it does not occlude the object as expected which leads to severe distortions in depth perception. Since we have full programmatic control of the displayed graphics and information about the users' fingers location, and spatial configuration, it is conceivable to mitigate this issue by providing interesting feedback to the user. One simple solution would be to move graphical elements out of the way so that they can never intersect with a physical object within the viewable volume, or perhaps add interesting effects causing 3D models to morph as fingers enter the display volume.

Finally the combination of a multi-view omnidirectional display and direct input could be used in a number of multi-user scenarios. For example, the system can show different views to users located at opposing sides of the setup (e.g., different decks of cards), allowing them to view personalized content privately.

As well as these implications for interaction, there are of course a number of limitations of Vermeer currently, which may be interesting to overcome in the future:

- *Display size* is small compared to the size of the parabolic mirrors currently.
- *Viewpoint constraints* exist even though the display is essentially walk-up-and-use; in particular view truncation is apparent when the viewpoint is too high or too low and the auto-stereo nature of the display works best at a certain distance from the display.
- *Distortion* of the displayed image occurs as only one point on the rotating projection surface is at mirror's focal point; the rest of the surface will not be reimaged without distortion. In addition, the mirrors we used in our prototype are not manufactured perfectly and cause additional (albeit minor) distortion.
- *Rendering fidelity* is essentially limited by the end-to-end speed of the rendering pipeline. With a higher DVI frame rate and correspondingly faster projector interface it would be possible to render at a higher frame-rate. A higher resolution and/or color projection system would also improve the displayed image.

FUTURE WORK

Perhaps the most obvious future work is in making the Vermeer display bigger and enabling higher fidelity. Clearly, in order to scale such an interactive display system to accommodate larger 3D scenes a larger parabolic mirror pair would be required. However in such a case the user may become too far away from the central hole to reach and interact with the 3D display. To mitigate this we have experimented with truncating the optics, i.e. using partial parabolic mirror sectors. We have cut a mirror pair in half diametrically and verified this provides a 180° viewing angle with the user situated within the truncated half - close enough to glance into the bottom mirror and touch the display volume. This is a compromise which may be acceptable to some users for the benefit of obtaining much larger 3D content displays whilst being close to the displayed objects to manipulate and interact with them.

Another area of future work which we have begun to experiment with is the possibility of extending the integrated sensing approach to image the environment around the display. We have observed an interesting effect that occurs when we place a webcam into the parabolic mirror arrangement. As depicted in Figure 9, this generates a reimaged virtual camera at the top of the mirror pair. When we view the live video from the webcam, we have observed that the image generated corresponds not to the real camera's location, but to the reimaged device (ignoring geometric distortions due to the mirror). Any object such as a playing card held in the field of view of the reimaged webcam is captured – as if the camera were physically at that reimaged location (Figure 9).

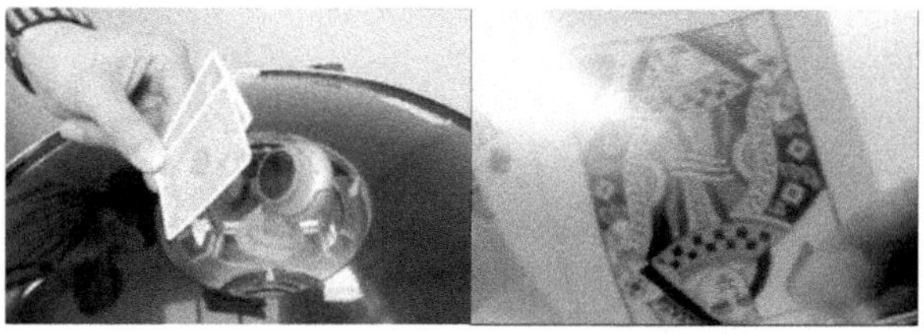

Figure 9 Left: a webcam placed at the bottom of the lower mirror will be reimaged and therefore viewable above the upper mirror. Right: any objects in the field of view of the floating webcam will actually be imaged by the sensor.

In our moving diffuser 3D display, we could imagine an arrangement where a high speed camera and mirror are used to image the scene from the revolving stage within the volume. This could allow us to capture the real lighting conditions and appropriately relight the virtual scene or sense the upper body of users interacting with the display, tracking their heads to correct for vertical perspective.

One final area of future work is to consider how a high speed camera could be used for our prototype in Figure 8 for more accurate 3D touch sensing. Here if such a camera is synchronized with the revolving diffuser, it should be possible to capture true 3D intersections between illuminated fingertips and each different diffuser orientation. This provides us with the possibility to sense more than just the presence or 2D location of fingertips in the volume, but instead accurately determine intersections between touch-points and the virtual 3D model. Other styles of volumetric display, in particular [29], with uniform layered switching diffuser planes may have advantages over a rotating angled diffuser in such a scenario.

CONCLUSIONS

We have shown that it is possible to use a pair of parabolic mirrors to reimage a 360° viewable 3D display enabling the use of direct in-volume interaction, which has not previously been possible with such displays. We have refined the design used in previously reported 3D displays to support our approach, and have presented our prototype system, Vermeer, in some detail. We have augmented the Vermeer display initially with a Kinect depth sensor to illustrate interaction with the displayed image.

In addition, we have demonstrated novel prototypes that replace the external Kinect sensor with integrated sensing configurations where cameras inside or adjacent to the parabolic mirror system can detect fingertip interactions within the floating display volume.

Our aim has been to introduce a new platform for interaction, enabling others to explore new interactive possibilities with such emerging 3D displays.

REFERENCES

1. Adhya, S. and Noé, J. A Complete Ray-trace Analysis of the 'Mirage' Toy. *In SPIE Education and Training in Optics and Photonics Conference (ETOP)*. 2007.
2. Agrawala, M., Beers, A., McDowall, I., Froehhlich, B., Bolas, M., Hanrahan, P. The two-user Responsive Workbench: support for collaboration through individual views of a shared space. *In ACM SIGGRAPH '97.*
3. Bimber, O. and Raskar, R. 2005. Spatial Augmented Reality: Merging Real and Virtual Worlds. *A. K. Peters*, Natick, MA, USA.
4. Bimber, O. Fröhlich, B., Schmalstieg, D. Encarnacao, L.M. The virtual showcase: a projection-based multi-user augmented reality display. *In ACM SIGGRAPH'02*
5. Blundell, B. and Schwarz, A.J. *Volumetric Three-Dimensional Display Systems*, Wiley-IEEE Press, 2000
6. Blundell, B. and Schwarz, A.J. *Creative 3-D Display and Interaction Interfaces: A Trans-Disciplinary Approach*, Wily-Interscience, 2005.
7. Cobb, S., Nichols, S., Ramsey, A., Wilson, J. Virtual Reality-Induced Symptoms and Effects (VRISE). *Presence: Teleoper. Virtual Environ. 8*, 2 (April 1999)
8. Cossairt, O.S., Napoli, J., Hill, S.L., Dorval, R.K., Favalora, E. Occlusion-capable multiview three-dimensional display. *In Applied Optics (46)*. (2007).
9. Dodgson, N. A. 2005. Autostereoscopic 3D displays. *Computer 38, 8, 31–36.*
10. Dorval, R.K., Thomas, M., Bareau, J. Volumetric three-dimensional display system. *US Patent #6,554,430* (issued 29 Apr 2003).
11. Elings, V.B., Landry, C.J. Optical Display Device. *US Patent #3647284*. Issued March 7, 1972.
12. Endo, T., Sato, M., Kajiki, Y., Honda, T. Cylindrical 3D Video Display Observable from All Directions. *In Proc Pacific Conference on Computer Graphics and Applications (PG '00).*
13. Favalora, G. E. 2005. Volumetric 3D displays and application infrastructure. In *Computer 38, 8, 37–44.*
14. Grossman, T. and Balakrishnan, R., An Evaluation of Depth Perception on Volumetric Displays, In *AVI 2006*
15. Grossman, T. and Balakrishnan, R., The Design and Evaluation of Selection Techniques for 3D Volumetric Displays, In *Proceedings of UIST 2006.*
16. Grossman, T., Wigdor, D. and Balakrishnan, R., Multi-Finger Gestural Interaction with 3D Volumetric Displays, In *Proceedings of UIST 2004.*
17. Halle, M., Autostereoscopic displays and computer graphics. In Proceedings of *ACM SIGGRAPH* '97
18. Hoffman, D., Girshick, A., Akeley, K. and Banks, S. 2008. Vergence–accommodation conflicts hinder visual performance and cause visual fatigue. *In Journal of Vision* 2008 8(3): 33
19. Jones, A., Bolas, M., McDowall, I., Yamada, H., & Debevec, P. Rendering for an Interactive 360 Degree Light Field Display, In *Proceedings of ACM SIGGRAPH 2007.*
20. Kimura, H., Uchiyama, T., and Yoshikawa, H. 2006. Laser produced 3D display in the air. In *Proceedings of ACM SIGGRAPH 2006 Emerging Technologies.*
21. Kiyokawa, K. , Kurata, K., Ohno, H. An Optical See-Through Display for Mutual Occlusion of Real and Virtual Environments. *In Proc ACM ISAR 2000.*
22. Maeda, H., Hirose, K., Yamashita, J., Hirota, K., and Hirose, M. 2003. All-around display for video avatar in real world. In *Proceedings of ISMAR 2003.*
23. Malik, S., McDonald, C. and Roth, G. "Hand Tracking for Interactive Pattern-based Augmented Reality". In *Proceedings of ISMAR 2002.*
24. Opti-Gone, http://www.optigone.com/m22.htm (verified July 2011).
25. Poston, T., Serra, L. Dextrous virtual work. *Commun. ACM 39, 5 (May 1996)*, 37-45.
26. Scharver, C., Evenhouse, R., Johnson, A., Leigh, J. Designing Cranial Implants in a Haptic Augmented Reality Environment. *Comm. of the ACM, Volume 47, Issue 8*, August 2004
27. Shin-Etsu View Control Film, http://www.shinetsu.info/index.php/products/view-control-film/view-control-film
28. Suffern, K., Ray tracing from the Ground-up. AK Peters, pp. 22, 2007.
29. Sullivan, A. A Solid-State Multi-Planar Volumetric Display, SID Symposium Digest Tech Papers 34, 1531-1533 (2003).
30. Travis, A. R. L. The display of three-dimensional video images. *Proceedings of the IEEE 85, 11 (Nov).*
31. von Wiegand, T., Schloerb, D., Sachtler, W.L. Virtual Workbench: Near-Field Virtual Environment System with Applications. *Presence: Virt. Environ. 8, 5 (October 1999).*
32. Yendo, T., Kawakami, N., and Tachi, S. 2005. Seelinder: the cylindrical lightfield display. In *Proceedings of SIGGRAPH 2005 Emerging Technologies.*

IrCube Tracker: An Optical 6-DOF Tracker based on LED Directivity

Seongkook Heo, Jaehyun Han, Sangwon Choi, Seunghwan Lee, and Geehyuk Lee
Human-Computer Interaction Lab, KAIST
Daejeon, South Korea
{leodic, jay.jaehyun, sangwonchoi7, rigelsh, geehyuk}@gmail.com

Hyong-Euk Lee, SangHyun Kim, Won-Chul Bang, DoKyoon Kim, and ChangYeong Kim
Samsung Advanced Institute of Technology
Giheung, South Korea
{hyongeuk.lee, sanghyun80.kim, wc.bang, jamesdk.kim, cykim}@samsung.com

ABSTRACT
Six-degrees-of-freedom (6-DOF) trackers, which were mainly for professional computer applications, are now in demand by everyday consumer applications. With the requirements of consumer electronics in mind, we designed an optical 6-DOF tracker where a few photo-sensors can track the position and orientation of an LED cluster. The operating principle of the tracker is basically source localization by solving an inverse problem. We implemented a prototype system for a TV viewing environment, verified the feasibility of the operating principle, and evaluated the basic performance of the prototype system in terms of accuracy and speed. We also examined its application possibility to different environments, such as a tabletop computer, a tablet computer, and a mobile spatial interaction environment.

ACM Classification: H5.2 [Information interfaces and presentation]: User Interfaces. - Input devices and strategies.

General terms: Design, Human Factors

Keywords: IrCube, optical 6-DOF tracker, LED directivity, source localization

INTRODUCTION
Six-degrees-of-freedom (DOF) trackers, which were mainly used for professional computer applications, are now in demand by everyday consumer applications, such as tracking player motions in an exertion computer game, tracking eyeglasses for stereoscopic displays, tracking a mobile phone in mobile spatial interaction (MSI) applications. Recently, 6-DOF tracker technologies developed for professional computer applications are being adapted for everyday consumer applications. Some examples are Sixense TrueMotion magnetic tracker [4], InterSense PCTracker ultrasound tracker [10], and PlayStation Move optical tracker [3]. However, these solutions do not seem to satisfy the requirements of frugal consumer electronics yet. They are still too expensive to be adopted by consumer electronics. They are often too big to fit in a small device such as a tablet computer or a smartphone. They also have other limitations specific to the type of technology. Ultrasound trackers are not usually good at tracking a fast-moving object [6], and have limitation for miniaturization. Magnetic trackers are in a better position for miniaturization, but have the drawback of being sensitive to nearby ferromagnetic materials or external magnetic fields. Optical trackers using a camera and markers are now popular for TV game consoles. One of their drawbacks is that their tracking volume is limited by the field of view and the depth of field of a camera.

We conducted a survey to find appropriate tracker technologies for consumer products such as a smart TV, a tabletop computer, and a tablet computer. Many of them satisfied the performance needs of consumer electronics, but our concern was their cost and size. None of them seemed to satisfy the tight cost and size requirements of consumer electronics. This was the motivation for the design of the IrCube tracker, a new 6-DOF tracker that we introduce in this paper. From the beginning of the design, we precluded the use of any expensive or bulky components. The result was an optical 6-DOF tracker that tracks the position and orientation of an LED cluster, with a few optical sensors. The operating principle of the tracker is basically source localization by solving an inverse problem. While both the optical sensors and the LED cluster appear bulky in the current prototype system, their miniaturization is already in progress. Its advantages in cost and size will make it a valuable alternative in consumer electronics applications where other tracker technologies may fail to fit in.

In the rest of the paper, we describe the operating principle of the IrCube tracker, the implementation details of a prototype, and the evaluation results of the prototype. We also describe extended experiments where we investigated the applicability of the IrCube tracker to diverse application environments.

OPERATING PRINCIPLE
The estimation of the position and orientation of a source from the measurements of its field strengths is a common problem in science and engineering, known as an inverse problem for source localization. Typical examples are localization of an effective electric dipole from electroencephalogram (EEG) measurements [7] and localization of a mag-

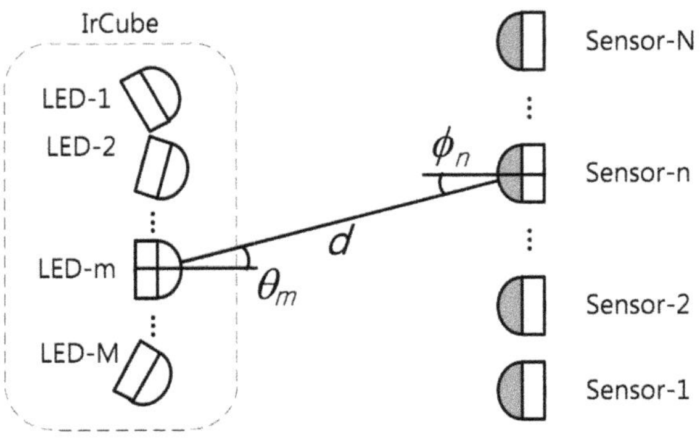

Figure 1: The forward model from an LED to a photo-sensor.

netic dipole from magnetic field measurements [9]. The use of the directivity of an LED is also often found in literature. For example, Roufas, et al. [16] implemented an automatic docking system that uses the directivity of infrared LEDs. Evans, et al. [5] implemented a head-operated joystick that uses the directivity of infrared LEDs. The operating principle of the IrCube tracker is the combination of these two themes: a source localization problem where a source is a cluster of LEDs and the field of the source is governed by LED directivity.

In order to formulate an inverse problem, we need to have a forward model first that predicts light intensities at the sensors given the position and orientation of an LED cluster. Given a forward model, we can define an optimization problem that is to minimize the difference between intensity measurements by the sensors and intensity predictions by the forward model. A solution to the optimization problem will give the most likely position and orientation estimation of the LED cluster. We call the LED cluster an IrCube since its structure is derived from a cube as shown in Figure 3.

Forward model

Figure 1 explains the relationship between the LEDs and the photo-sensors in the IrCube system. The light power F received by the n-th photo-sensor when the m-th LED is on is determined by the two angles, θ_m and ϕ_n, and the distance d:

$$F = F_0 \times \frac{1}{d^2} \times D_{LED}(\theta_m) \times D_{diode}(\phi_n) \qquad (1)$$

where F_0 is a constant, and $D_{LED}(\cdot)$ and $D_{diode}(\cdot)$ are the directivity functions of the LEDs and the photo-sensors, respectively. It is assumed here that all LEDs and all photo-sensors are identical and their directivity functions have an axial symmetry. In the case of Lambertian directivity, the directivity function is in the following form: $D_{LED}(\theta_m) = \cos\theta_m$ and $D_{diode}(\phi_n) = \cos\phi_n$. In practice, however, no device directivity follows an ideal mathematical curve, and the directivity functions should be determined empirically.

Inverse problem

An IrCube consists of M infrared LEDs with different orientations. While these LEDs are turned on and off sequentially one at a time, their intensities are measured by the N photo-sensors, resulting in $M \times N$ measurements. These measurements, by the way, can be predicted fairly precisely using the forward model given by Eq. (1). Let E be the error function between the measurements and the predictions:

$$E(\vec{x}, \vec{q}) = \sum_{m=1}^{M} \sum_{n=1}^{N} \left(O_{mn} - F(\vec{x}_m - \vec{X}_n, \vec{q}_m)\right)^2 \qquad (2)$$

where O_{mn} and $F(\vec{x}_m - \vec{X}_n, \vec{q}_m)$ are the measurements and the forward-model predictions of the output of the n-th sensor when the m-th LED is on, $\vec{x}_m$ and $\vec{q}_m$ are the position and orientation of the m-th LED, and $\vec{X}_n$ is the position of the n-th sensor. Since all LEDs have fixed positions and orientations in the IrCube, x_m and q_m are determined by the position $\vec{x}$ and the orientation $\vec{q}$ of the IrCube. Also, the positions and orientations of all sensors are fixed and known. Therefore, the error function is dependent only on $\vec{x}$ and $\vec{q}$, and its minimization with respect to these variables determines the position and orientation of the IrCube.

EARLY INVESTIGATION

Before we start to design a prototype realizing the IrCube tracker, we examined a few technical requirements and design parameters by experiment or by computer simulation. We summarize below some of the important considerations that we made for the design of a prototype.

LED directivity

One of the important design parameters was the directivity of the LEDs. We assumed that all LEDs have an axial symmetry in their directivity although they do not have an axial symmetry in their die structure. We could convince ourselves that this is a reasonable assumption through many actual measurements of LED directivity. We also assumed that all LEDs in an IrCube have the same directivity. We expected that LEDs with high directivity would make the resulting design more direction-sensitive but would require more LEDs since their radiation field is narrow. While high angular resolution was an important goal, it was more important to limit the number of required LEDs since the cost of an IrCube and the computing time would increase with this number. Therefore, we decided to fix the number of LEDs first and find the best directivity by computer simulation. We considered a cluster of 5 LEDs where one is facing forward and the other four are tilted by 45° to the four perpendicular directions, and estimated the positional and angular errors of the tracker system for different directivity conditions. It was not easy to derive a single best directivity value from these experiments since it depended on many environmental parameters such as the amount of ambient optical noise. One of our observations was that the tracker error did not depend sensitively on LED directivity when the directivity is near Lambertian (half angle = 60°), and it started to increase significantly when the directivity is doubled (half angle = 30°). In some cases, simulation

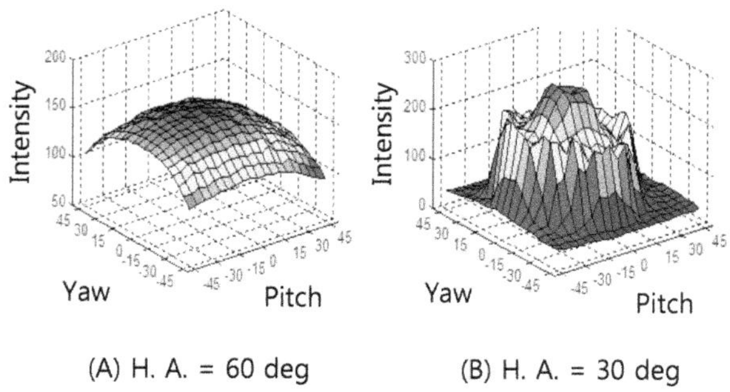

Figure 2: The directivity measurements of two off-the-shelf LEDs (H.A. = half angle).

results appeared to favor some intermediate directivity levels but the difference was not significant. We were in fact glad that Lambertian directivity turned out to be as good as other possibilities since Lambertian directivity meant no need to have a lens structure in an LED, which is a potential source of tracker errors. Figure 2 shows the directivity measurements of two LEDs. The measured data were significantly different from the ideal curves given in the data sheets. Our final decision was to go with LEDs without a lens structure, i.e., with Lambertian directivity.

Sensor & LED constellations

Other important design parameters were the number and the spatial arrangement of the sensors and the LEDs. In fact, these parameters are interrelated, and determination of these parameters at the same time would be a difficult optimization problem. Therefore, we fixed sensor parameters and tried to optimize LED parameters. Later, we came back to verify whether the sensor parameters were not too bad choices.

We assumed that four sensors are at the four corners of a rectangle, which may be a TV or a tabletop computer in a real situation. We decided to use four sensors since the IrCube tracker is basically a triangularization-based method that requires measurements at least at three different places. With four sensors, the tracker will be able to tolerate the occlusion of one sensor. Next, we considered five different LED constellations in an IrCube as shown in Figure 3. We estimated position errors, orientation errors, and computation times for each of these constellations by computer simulations. The graph in Figure 3 shows the simulation results. We chose the 18-LED constellation as the best trade-off between computation time and tracker errors.

After fixing the LED constellations, we tested variations to the sensor constellation by adding more sensors between the current sensors or by tilting the sensors inwards or outwards. Adding more sensors resulted in a slight improvement in tracking errors but required more computation time. Tilting sensors did not result in any positive change in the tracking errors and computation time unless the IrCube is very close to the sensor plane. Our conclusion was that the initial sensor placement was a reasonable, though not optimal, choice.

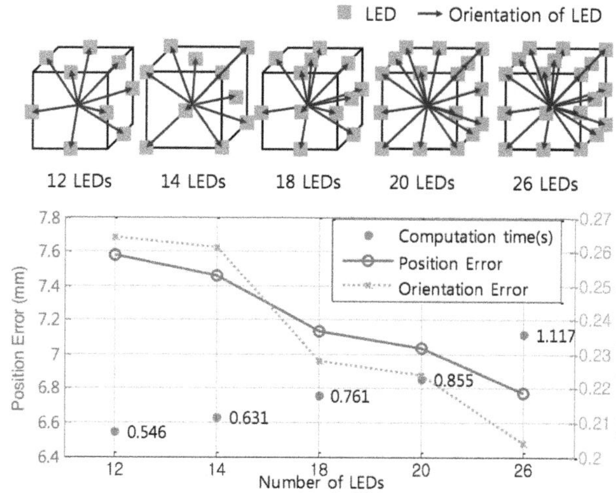

Figure 3: Comparison of five LED constellations.

Optical sensors

The operating principle assumes the availability of a low-noise, linear optical sensor that is sensitive and fast enough to handle modulated light from an LED at a distance. At first, we searched diligently for an off-the-shelf optical sensor that would meet our need, but were not successful. There were some optical sensors that output an analog voltage proportional to light intensity, but they were not fast enough to handle modulated light. Other optical sensors, for example sensors designed for optical communication, were fast enough, but were too insensitive or too noisy to measure the intensity of an LED in a few meters. Other sensors designed for free-space optical communication, such as IrDA, were both fast and sensitive, but did not output an analog voltage. After convincing ourselves that no off-the-shelf sensor meets our need, we decided to design an optical sensor with discrete components meeting our requirements.

From computer simulations, we could set requirements for the optical sensors for the IrCube tracker. Two main requirements were 1) an SNR of 45dB when an LED is in 3 meters from the sensors under a fluorescent lighting condition, and 2) a linearity of 1% over the full output range. In order to filter out optical noise from a fluorescent lamp, it was necessary to use modulated light. Since the optical noise spectrum of a fluorescent lamp extends well beyond 500kHz[1], we set the modulation frequency to 1MHz. This imposed another requirement of high-speedness to the optical sensor. We started with a front-end circuit for an optical sensor given in Hobbs[8] and arrived at an optical sensor design described in the next section satisfying these requirements.

Optimization algorithm

The operating principle assumes the existence of a good optimization algorithm that can solve the optimization problem defined by Eq. (2) in real time. In the computer simulations that we ran in the investigation phase, we used a simplex method[13] since it is one of the most general methods for a continuous error function. After we were convinced of the feasibility of the inverse problem, we tried more efficient algorithms for the implementation of a pro-

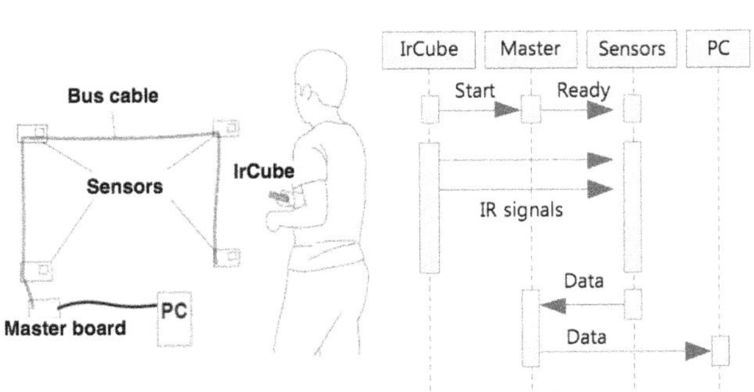

Figure 4: The IrCube tracker prototype: (a) the system configuration and (b) the interaction sequence for data acquisition.

totype. We conducted numerical experiments to compare a simplex method, a quasi-Newton method[17], and a trust-region-reflective method[2] assuming various conditions, for instance, with different amount of simulated noise. The computation time of the trust-region reflective method was about 1/3 that of the quasi-Newton method, and was about 1/5 that of the simplex method. The trust-region reflective method was also the best in terms of the position and orientation accuracy among the three algorithms. Based on these experiment results, we decided to use the trust-region reflective method in the prototype. The computation time of this method could be further reduced to 1/3 when a good initial guess was given, which is in fact possible since a tracking target is in a continuous motion.

IRCUBE TRACKER PROTOTYPE

System overview

We implemented a prototype system as shown in Figure 4 consisting of four sensors, a master board, and an IrCube. The four sensors are placed at the four corners of a 102cm x 63cm rectangular frame. All sensors are connected to the master board by a ribbon cable that carries an I2C data bus and power lines. The sequence diagram in Figure 4b shows the interaction among the IrCube, the master board, the sensors and the PC. A data acquisition cycle is initiated by a start signal from the IrCube. A start signal is a 500μs burst of light modulated at 455kHz, and is received by the master board via a remote control sensor (TSOP7000, Vishay). On a start signal, the master board relays it to the four sensors. The four sensors then measure in parallel the intensities of the IrCube LEDs synchronized to their blinkings, and send the measurements to the master board. After a complete round of the LED blinkings, which takes about 7 ms, the master board transfers collected data to the PC. The PC then estimates the position and orientation of the IrCube by solving an inverse problem.

The IrCube

Figure 5 shows the first and the second prototype of the IrCube. We followed the 18-LED constellation shown in Figure 3 in both prototypes, but the actual number of LEDs in both prototypes was 13 since we omitted 5 LEDs on the rear side of the IrCube. Note in Figure 5 that 4 LEDs wired in parallel were used instead of a single LED in the first prototype.

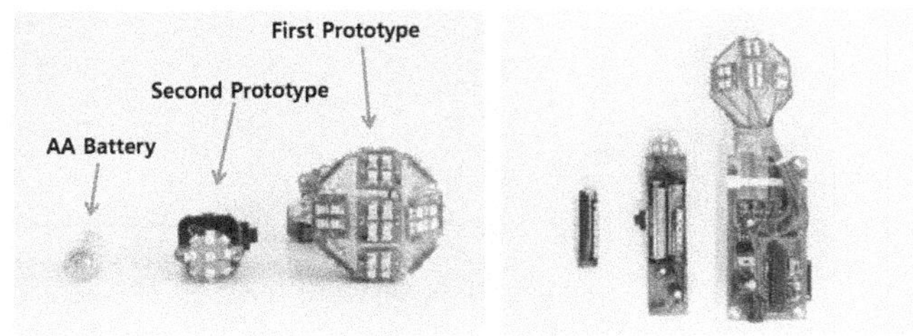

Figure 5: The IrCube prototypes: (a) the first and (b) the second prototype (An AA-size battery is shown together for size comparison).

The same LEDs (SFH4243, OSRAM) with the Lambertian directivity were used in both prototypes. The second prototype has a button for a selection operation, and button events are sent to the master encoded in the start signal.

Optical sensors

The optical sensor is a linear, programmable gain, optical sensor tuned to the modulation frequency of 1MHz. The front-end amplifier shown in Figure 6c consists of a photodiode (in fact, two photo-diodes wired in parallel for a larger receiving area) supported by a bootstrapped bootstrap followed by a capacitive feedback trans-impedance amplifier. The bootstrapped bootstrap was for minimizing the effect of the photo-diode capacitance and achieving the operating frequency of 1MHz. The capacitive feedback trans-impedance amplifier was for the goal of low-noise, high sensitivity optical sensing. We could verify that the design satisfies the bandwidth and linearity requirements through a series of SPICE simulations. We could verify the SNR requirement by actually observing the output of the receiver under diverse ambient lighting conditions after we implemented the whole system.

The programmable gain amplifier (PGA) is required to handle dynamic, wide-range light inputs. The gain of the PGA needs to be adjusted occasionally when the tracking distance changes, and therefore, it is not controlled by an internal feedback loop in the circuit but is controlled externally by an algorithm running on the PC. The gain of the PGA can be adjusted from 1 to 128 in binary steps. The next stage is a band-pass filter with a center frequency of 1MHz and a bandwidth of $\pm$8kHz. While the filter is shown by a single ceramic filter symbol in Figure 6a, it was realized using a superheterodyne circuit with a 1.455MHz local oscillator and a 455kHz ceramic filter as no 1MHz ceramic filter is available off-the-shelf. The last stage of the sensor is an envelope detector that demodulates the modulated signal and outputs an analog signal proportional to the received light power. Figure 6b shows the picture of the implemented sensor module. In order to block scattered light from surrounding components, we had to attach a black circular wall covered with anti-reflection paint around the photo-diodes.

Signal processing

Figure 7 shows the signal processing steps that the tracker program on the PC performs to compute a tracker output

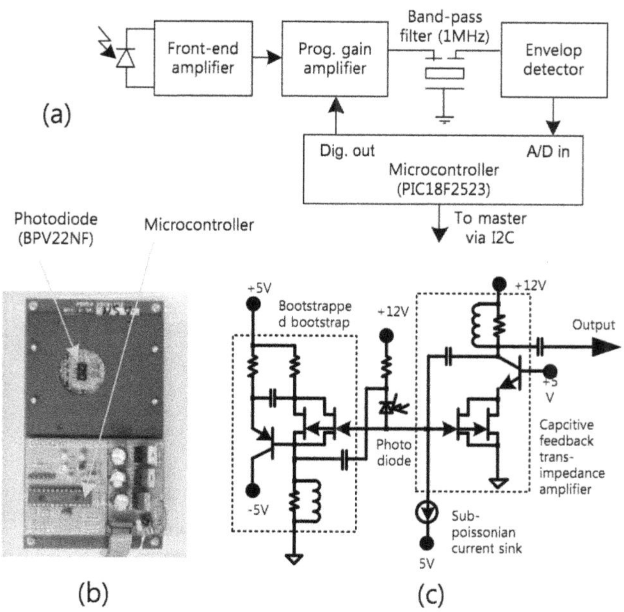

Figure 6: The sensor prototype: (a) the functional block diagram,(b) the implemented sensor board, and (c) the skeletal circuit diagram of the front-end.

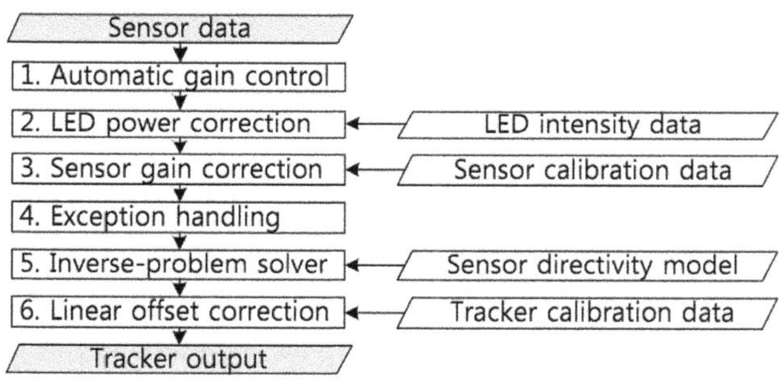

Figure 7: Signal processing steps from data acquisition to the tracker output.

from an acquired sensor data. Each step is explained in details in the following.

Automatic gain control: The program checks whether the sensor outputs are in a proper range and adjust sensor gains otherwise. The gains of all sensors are changed together. The gains are halved when saturation occurs in the sensor outputs, and are doubled when the maximum of the sensor outputs goes below one third the full scale.

LED power correction: The LEDs in the IrCube have individual differences in their intensities. The differences are not negligible (up to 6%), and therefore it was necessary to compensate the differences by scaling sensor outputs. The program scales sensor outputs using LED calibration data that we prepared by actually measuring the intensities of individual LEDs in the IrCube.

Sensor gain correction: The sensors have small individual differences in their gains. Also, their gains in each of the PGA levels are not precise. Therefore, we had to create a mapping function to correct gain errors for each of the sensors and for each of the PGA levels. We measured sensor outputs varying the distance between a sensor and the IrCube, and used these data to find linear mapping functions between light intensities and sensor outputs. Linear mapping functions could fit the measured data well due to the good linear characteristics of the sensors.

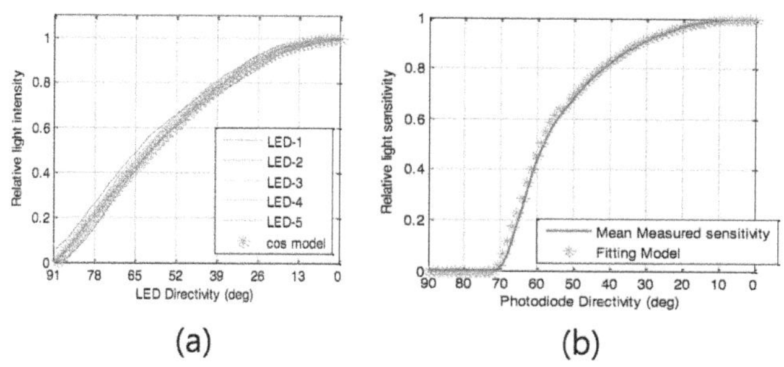

Figure 8: Measured directivity curves of (a) the LED (SFH4243) and (b) the sensors.

Exception handling: Exceptional conditions that we tried to handle were an LED failure and a sensor occlusion. The current prototype has 4 sensors and 13 LEDs, thereby giving a total of 52 sensor measurements in each frame. Among 52 samples, the program selects top 30 samples and excludes 22 weak samples. Bad samples due to a dead LED or an occluded sensor may be automatically filtered out in this process. However, to make sure that all samples for an occluded sensor are excluded the program check the excluded samples again, infer an occluded sensor, and exclude all samples for the occluded sensor. We verified by simulation and by experiment that 30 samples are sufficient to determine the 6-DOF of the IrCube.

Inverse problem solver: The program solves the inverse problem defined by the error function (2) using a trust-region-reflective method. The summation in the error function (2) was of course modified to include only top 30 samples as mentioned above. When the solution of the previous time frame is available, the program uses it as an initial guess for the optimization algorithm. Otherwise, the program tries a few random initial guesses, and chooses the best result as the solution of the inverse problem. The accuracy of the tracker depended a lot on the directivity models of the LEDs and the sensors. We measured the actual directivity curves of the LEDs and the sensors. As shown in Figure 8, the directivity of the LEDs was very close to the ideal Lambertian model. On the other hand, the directivity of the sensors showed a considerable deviation from the Lambertian model. We approximated the directivity curve of the sensors using a cosine function in the first interval (0°–26°), two polynomial functions in the second (26°–52°) and third intervals (52°–71.5°), and a constant in the last interval (71.5°–90°). The rapid decrease of sensitivity over 70° was due to the dark wall around the photo-diodes that was added to block reflections from nearby components.

Linear offset correction: The inverse problem solver outputs the 6-DOF data of the IrCube. As these data are not

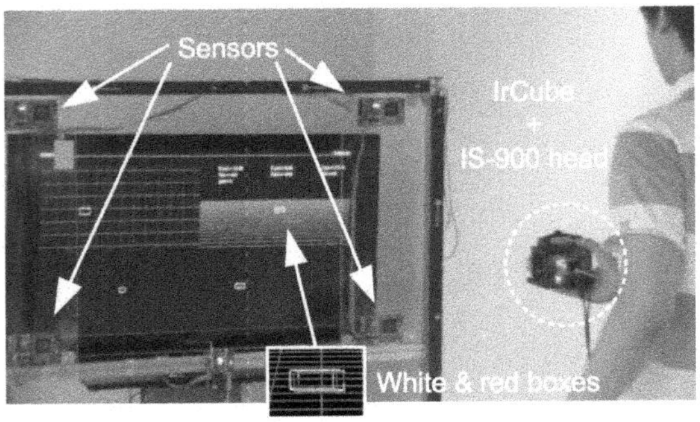

Figure 9: The experimental setup for the measurement of tracker errors.

		Static cond.		Dynamic cond.	
		Mean	S. D.	Mean	S. D.
Position error (cm)	x	2.35	1.67	2.82	1.86
	y	2.02	1.71	3.41	3.12
	z	2.75	1.31	1.81	1.53
Orientation error (deg)	yaw	1.73	1.54	2.90	1.95
	pitch	1.27	1.08	1.68	1.31
	roll	1.38	1.34	1.94	1.66

Table 1: The position and the orientation errors of the prototype.

noise-free, we expected that they would be distributed around a true value. However, measurements showed that their center is shifted slightly from the true value and the amount of shift is different for different positions and orientations. The shifts seemed to be mainly due to ambient light reflection. We could model the shifts by a linear transformation. This linear transformation is the last step that the tracker program performs. No further signal processing steps, such as a smoothing filter and a stabilization filter, follow.

The accuracy of the tracker was improved as we add the LED power correction step, the sensor gain correction step, and the linear offset correction step. It is not easy to rate their relative importance since different step affected different components of the tracker output. For instance, the LED power correction reduced the position error most while the sensor gain correction affected the angular accuracy most. The three steps together contributed to reduce the positional errors to one half the original level and the angular errors to one third the original level.

EVALUATION

Figure 9 is a snapshot of the experimental setup for the measurement of tracker errors. We used InterSense IS-900 [10], a 6-DOF inertial/acoustic tracker, to provide reference data. The experimenter is holding a structure that houses both the IrCube and the IS-900 head. The structure enforces a rigid spatial relationship between the IrCube and the IS-900 head so that the position and orientation of the IrCube could be calculated from IS-900 data. The white box in the display shows the position and orientation of the IrCube by the IrCube tracker while the red box overlapping the white box shows the position and orientation of the IrCube by the IS-900 tracker.

We measured tracker errors both in a static condition and a dynamic condition. In the static condition, we measured 20 static positions and postures of the IrCube in the volume of 2m(X) x 1m(Y) x 2m(Z) whose center is 2 m away from the sensor plane. At every position, we made 100 measurements, and calculated differences between these measurements and the reference data by the IS-900 tracker. In the dynamic condition, we collected three IrCube trajectories from three different participants. They were allowed to move freely for 2–3 minutes in the volume of 2m(X) x 1m(Y) x 2.5m(Z) whose center is 2m away from the sensor plane. Table 1 shows the root mean square (RMS) values of the position and orientation errors in the static and the dynamic conditions. The RMS errors were about 2–3 cm in position and less than 2° in orientation in the static condition. The RMS errors in the dynamic condition were slightly larger than that of the static condition.

We were satisfied with these results since our goal was to design a cost-effective tracker for consumer electronics. For other applications, however, these results may not be sufficient. A position error of 3cm may be acceptable for a game controller, but may be too large for a tablet application. An obvious way to improve the accuracy of the current prototype is to increase the output of the LEDs since the operating principle of our system is based on intensity measurements; its accuracy will improve when the SNR of the intensity measurements improves. Another way to improve the accuracy of our system is to reduce the distance between LEDs and sensors and thereby increasing the light intensity at the sensors. In other words, tracker error will become smaller for a tabletop computer environment and will become even smaller for a tablet computer environment. This is in fact a nice feature since accuracy tolerance is often proportional to the tracking volume. By the way, the numbers in Table 1 represent tracker errors in the raw outputs without any stabilizing filtering. Most trackers use a stabilizing filter, such as a low-pass filter and a Kalman filter, to reduce noise in the outputs. We expect that the IrCube tracker will also benefit from such a post-processing step in the next prototype.

We also tested the behavior of the IrCube system in exceptional cases, e.g., when one of the four sensors was occluded by an obstacle. While the IrCube was held fixed, we covered one of the sensors with a hand, and observed changes in the tracker output. Figure 10 shows changes in the X-position data in this case. The tracker output changes slowly as the hand approaches the sensor, jumps to a wrong value as the hand approaches the sensor further, but recovers tracking eventually at some point. At this point, the tracker must have abandoned values from the occluded sensor and start to track the IrCube using only the data from the remaining three sensors. However, the X position after the occlusion was shifted by approximately 2cm. We repeated similar trials and convinced ourselves that our tracker can continue to track the IrCube reasonably well even one of the sensors is occluded.

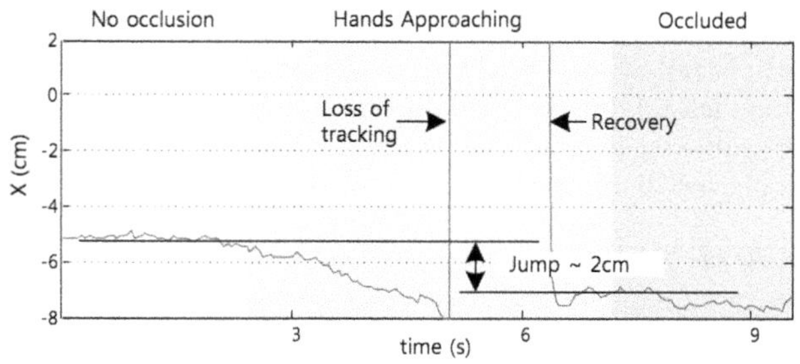

Figure 10: The tracker output when one of the sensors was approached and occluded by the hand.

As well as the tracker accuracy, we were concerned about the computation time of the tracker since the tracker should solve an optimization problem every time frame. The computation time for solving an optimization problem depends on many factors such as a chosen optimization algorithm and the quality of an initial guess. Therefore, it was not easy to predict actual computation time before we could actually run the system. We measured the computation time of our tracker in the dynamic cases while we measured the tracker errors. The mean computation time for each frame was about 21.6 ms (Core2Duo 2.4GHz CPU, 2GB of RAM). This computation time means that we will be able to achieve a frame rate of 50Hz if we pipeline measurements, data transfer and computation properly.

APPLICABLE ENVIRONMENTS

The IrCube system was designed to be a cheap and compact 6-DOF tracker for diverse consumer electronics applications. The first target application was a TV remote controller, and therefore the prototyping and evaluation so far were done in a TV viewing environment. In order to study the applicability of the IrCube tracker to other applications, we set up different application environments, such as a tabletop computer, a tablet computer, and a mobile spatial interaction environment, and test-drove the IrCube tracker adapted to the respective environments. Our goal in these experiments was to discover any potential problems or limitations of the IrCube tracker in the new environments. A discussion of a TV viewing environment is also included in this section for completeness.

TV environment

The IrCube tracker can be easily applied to a TV environment or other vertical display environments by attaching the sensors at the corners of the display as shown in the Figure 11a. This was in fact the environment that we used so far for the prototyping and evaluation of the IrCube tracker; we have already shown the basic applicability of the IrCube tracker to this type of environment.

The most important issue in this environment seems to be the reflection of the IrCube light by the floor. Reflection by all walls can affect the tracker but reflection by the floor affect the tracker most since it is usually the wall nearest to the IrCube and the sensors. We experimented with different floor materials and could see that diffusively reflecting materials affect the tracker more than specularly reflecting materials.

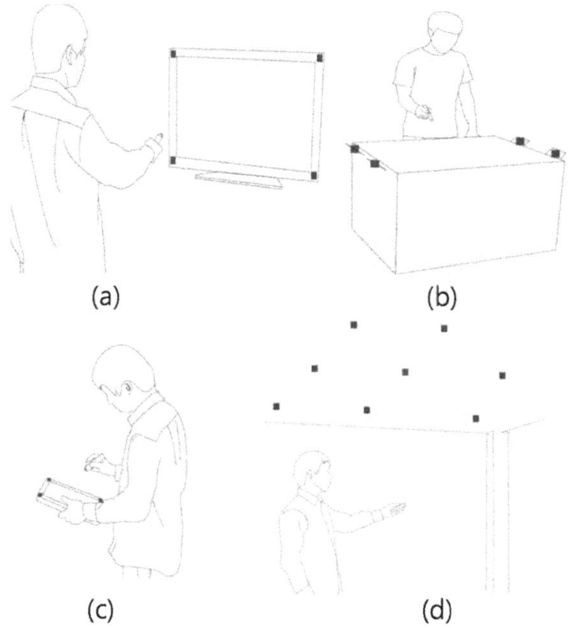

Figure 11: The IrCube tracker applied to different environments: (a) a TV environment, (b) a tabletop computer, (c) a tablet computer, and (d) mobile spatial interaction. Black square dots represent the optical sensors.

Of course, bright materials affect the tracker more than dark materials. A bright and large surface could induce a large tracker error, as large as 10cm, in the direction to the TV.

The field-of-view limitation of the sensors will be a common issue in all application environments, but did not seem to be a serious problem in this case since people usually watch TV at some distance. The field-of-view of the sensors was about 140°, and blind spots could be found only near the TV screen. The line-of-sight problem will be also a common issue in all application environments, but did not seem to be a serious problem in this case since people usually have a good line-of-sight when they watch TV. Some objects in the view may block one of the sensors, but the tracker could handle this well as we showed earlier.

Tabletop computer

The main difference of this environment compared with the TV environment is that the display is now horizontal and most interaction occurs near the display. The field-of-view limitation of the sensors, which resulted in blind spots near the TV in the previous case, was now a major problem that we had to solve first. Our solution was to tilt the sensors toward the screen center by 45° as shown in Figure 11b. This simple solution could be possible since the field-of-view of the sensor was as wide as about 140°.

The most important issue in this case seems to be the reflection of LED light by the display surface. In order to reduce the effect of the surface reflection, we placed the sensors at the same height as the display surface. In this configuration, the sensors could receive reflected light from the IrCube only when it was very near the surface since the reflection by the display surface was mostly specular. We could verify by experiment that the IrCube could be tracked fairly well unless it was very close to the surface, e.g., within 5cm from the surface.

Since our tabletop computer uses an infrared illumination and infrared camera combination to detect fingers, the IrCube was sometimes mis-detected as a finger blob on the tabletop. To avoid this problem, we may use infrared light sources of different wavelengths for the infrared illumination and the IrCube (e.g., 850nm for the illumination and 950nm for the IrCube) and add a narrow band, infrared-passing filter to the touch detection camera. On the other hand, infrared light from the tabletop computer did not affect the IrCube tracker because the IrCube sensors respond only to 1MHz-modulated light.

Since a tabletop computer is a collaborative device, there is a large possibility of the sensors being occluded by other users' hands. This occlusion problem may be only handled by adding more sensors to the edges of the tabletop computer.

Tablet computer

We expect that the IrCube tracker will be a particularly useful option for small computers such as a smartphone and a tablet computer when the IrCube sensors become available as a compact IC. What we will need to do to enable 6-DOF tracking over the device will be to add a few IrCube sensors on the frame of the device. In order to test the feasibility of this case, we installed the sensors near the four corners of a UMPC as shown in Figure 11c. The sensors are tilted to the screen center as in the case of a tabletop computer. The only difference of this case compared with the tabletop computer case was that the screen is small. An obvious problem was that the IrCube sensors were not small enough to be placed at the exact corners of the UMPC, but this will be solved when the sensors become available as a compact IC. The tracker worked well as in the case of a tabletop computer. We did not observe any additional issue specific to this environment.

Mobile spatial interaction

The IrCube sensors may be deployed on the ceiling as shown in Figure 11d for an indoor spatial location purpose. In order to cover a large area, it will be necessary to install a matrix of sensors, but the matrix will not need to be dense. It was expected that the situation would be similar to that of a TV environment except that all sensors are now on a horizontal plane. From the previous experience with the IrCube system in a TV environment, we expected that placement of a sensor every 1 or 2 m would be sufficient.

We installed four sensors on the ceiling which is 270cm high. The four sensors formed a 120cm x 60cm rectangle on the ceiling. For ease of illustration, let the long(short) side of the rectangle be the X(Y)-axis, and let the vertical direction be the Z-axis. The tracker could track the IrCube well as in the case of a TV environment. Even when the IrCube was away from the center of the sensor rectangle as much as by (110cm, 100cm, 50cm) in (X, Y, Z) directions, the position error remained within 3cm in all axes.

One of the unexpected problems that we discovered in the experiment was that there were more obstacles than we expected in an indoor environment. They caused occlusions and light reflections. We expect that occlusion problems may be handled relatively easily by adding more sensors. Reflection problems seemed to be more fundamental, but its effect was not too disruptive.

RELATED WORK

There are many previous works where optical sensors and/or LEDs are used for implementing an optical tracker. In this section, we list up a few representative such examples and explain how our tracker system differs from them.

The HiBall Tracker[19] is a classic example of an optical tracker using LED beacons and optical sensors. A sensor called HiBall measures the relative directions of multiple LED beacons using multiple LEPD sensors and determines the position and the attitude of HiBall. This system is outward looking while IrCube is inward looking, and its operating principle does not rely on the intensity field model of an LED. The HiBall was based on LEPD sensors instead of photo-diodes. While an LEPD sensor is simpler than a camera, it is not as simple as a photo-sensor. Also, the HiBall had 6 LEPDs and each LEPD needs 4 trans-impedance amplifiers, meaning that a HiBall required 24 trans-impedance amplifiers for a pre-amplifying stage alone, and could not be made small and light. According to its operating principle, they needed a dense array of LEDs on the ceiling (about 3000 LEDs to cover a 5.5m x 8.5m area), while our system will require a relatively sparser sensor array.

Prakash system[15] is an optical tracker whose operating principle is most similar to IrCube. This system is outward looking while IrCube is inward looking. In the Prakash system, the orientation of a marker (optical sensor) was determined by the directivity of the sensor as in our system, but the location of a marker was determined by spatial labeling by a set of LED beamers. The LED beamers were basically optical pattern projectors and therefore are much larger and more complex than single LEDs. In contrast, IrCube uses Lambertian LEDs and photo-sensors without requiring any optical components or structures.

In Tokiwa, et al.[18], they showed empirically that the horizontal orientation of a photo-sensor in a light field formed by two mutually orthogonal planar light sources (LED arrays) could be determined by the phase of the received signal that the photo-sensor receives. They used LEDs and photo-sensors as we did but their operating principle and results were different from that of IrCube. First of all, their system is not a 6-DOF tracker. In addition, it requires planar light sources in the environment and its marker is a sensor rather than a light source (outward looking instead of inward looking).

PhaseSpace system[14] is a camera-based motion capture system consisting of a camera and multiple active LED markers. The advantage of LED markers over reflective markers is that detection of occlusion is easier with them because they can be distinguished among each other unlike reflective markers. The role of LEDs in this case is clearly different from the role of LEDs in IrCube.

Bokode[12] is an imperceptible (small) visual tag that can send out a pattern to a camera that is focused at infinity. Since the pattern that a camera receives from a Bokode is dependent on the viewing angle, a camera can determine the orientation of a Bokode. However, the principle of orientation detection in this case is not based on the directivity of a light source or of a sensor and is different from that of IrCube.

The use of LED directivity, source localization concept, and an optimization algorithm in the IrCube tracker are not novel. Especially, there are many previous works where LEDs and photo-sensors were utilized for implementing a tracker as some examples are shown above. However, we believe that our system is the first example where a 6-DOF tracker based on LED intensity field model alone was realized and tested.

DISCUSSION

A reflection problem is one of the fundamental limitations of intensity-based trackers, and the IrCube tracker is not an exception. We are aware of this problem as we mentioned before and are seeking a solution. Meanwhile, we would like to point out that the effect of reflection is not as disruptive as to make the system unstable. In the experiment to evaluate the prototype system, we lined the surrounding walls with non-reflective material to avoid a reflection problem. The sensor outputs decreased by about 3% in magnitude after the lining. These output changes resulted in more a positional error than an angular error, and the positional error was largest in the Z-axis (about 5cm). The errors were smooth and continuous; we spent a lot of time testing the prototype before the non-reflective lining, but were not very aware of or concerned about a reflection problem. Of course, this experience may not be generalized to different environments.

We do not expect to find a general cure to the reflection problem. Instead, we hope to find work-arounds for specific cases. In the case of a TV environment, reflection by the floor is most serious. The reflection problem in this case may be eased by adding a shade structure below a sensor to block reflected light off the floor. The shade structure will limit the tracking volume of the tracker, but this may be tolerable unless controlling a TV from near the floor is required. Another case where the reflection problem was severe was seen in the tabletop computer case. The tracker could not track the IrCube when it was very near the tabletop surface due to reflection by the surface. This problem may be eased by making the sensors polarization-selective because light reflected at a glazing angle is known to be highly polarized.

Another limitation of the IrCube tracker is the power consumption of the LEDs. The second IrCube prototype shown in Figure 5 can run continuously for about 5 hours when powered by a 3.7V / 400mAh battery. Five hours of continuous operation may be too short for some applications but may not for others, e.g. a TV remote, as the IrCube can be in a sleep mode most of the time. Also, the LED intensity may be controlled adaptively. In the current prototype, the LEDs are driven at their maximum capacity for the worst-case condition. The LED power may be controlled adaptively based on the required accuracy of an application. A more fundamental solution may be by exchanging the LEDs and the photo sensors. The same operating principle will be still valid in this reversed case due to an optical symmetry between an LED and a photo-diode. More powerful LEDs in the environment may also help the tracker extend its operating range. The reversed case is not currently possible since the current sensors are too big to form a handy cluster, but will be an attractive option when the sensors are fabricated as a small IC.

Another important technical issue was ambient light noise. We conducted many experiments to examine the effect of different light sources such as a halogen lamp and a fluorescent lamp. While a halogen lamp emits a lot of infrared light, it did not influence the tracker much because the tracker sensor has a band-pass filter. However, the band-pass filter is located after the front-end amplifier, and therefore a direct and close illumination of a halogen lamp on the sensor could make it saturated and blind. A fluorescent lamp was different because its light is modulated by the AC line frequency or an internal oscillator frequency, and can leak through the band-pass filter. In the first design of the tracker sensor, which was originally for a simple pointing device [11], the center frequency of the band-pass filter was 11kHz. It was later raised to 208kHz, to 455kHz, and finally to 1MHz. We could see a significant improvement every time we raised the band frequency and expect a better result with a higher band frequency. The choice of 1MHz is a trade-off between two goals of optical noise suppression and low-noise front-end circuit design. The effect of a fluorescent lamp on the current prototype is a slight increase of jitter noise in the tracker output.

As an intensity-based tracker, the IrCube tracker has limitations in its tracking volume. First, the tracking volume is limited to the front side of the sensors because the sensors are directional. Second, its tracking accuracy will drop as the IrCube is moved away from the sensors since light intensity at the sensors is governed by an inverse square law. Third, the sensors should be distributed spatially for triangulization, which implies that the tracking volume will be only proportional to the separation between the sensors. This last one is in contrast to a camera-based system since a camera-based system can track a marker with a single camera. On the other hand, the IrCube tracker may cover a tracking volume that may not be covered by a camera since the IrCube sensors have wider field of view (FOV) and larger depth of field (DOF). The FOV of the IrCube sensor can approach 180° in principle since the sensor has the Lambertian directivity. The DOF of the IrCube sensor is limited not by a lens design but by the dynamic range of the sensor. The current sensor works well over the entire gain range from 1 to 128, which means that the sensor can track a light source at a distance ranging from 1 to $\sqrt{128}$ (a relative scale) without saturation.

We emphasized that both the sensors and the IrCube can be made small, but did not have a chance to discuss this possibility quantitatively. The current IrCube is a cluster of 13 LEDs in the form of a ball with a diameter of about 20mm. This was the size that we could achieve using SMD-type LEDs on a lab workbench. Considering that the size of an LED die is usually as small as 0.5mm x 0.5mm, we expect that the LED cluster can be shrunk to a ball of a few millimeters in diameter. Also, we do not see any technical hurdle to the miniaturization of the sensors. The current sensor is in the form of a large PCB containing a photo-diode, a front-end amplifier, a programmable gain amplifier, a band-pass filter, an envelope detector, and a micro-controller. We estimate that the analog part of the circuit can be implemented on a die area of 2mm x 2mm, and everything will not require a die area larger than 5mm x 5mm. The resulting sensor will be in the form of a small IC similar to an optical sensor for a remote receiver. The sensor as a chip will suffer less from white noise while its linearity may degrade a little bit.

With a tiny LED cluster and a handy sensor chip, we could have shown better application scenarios. For instance, the tabletop computer and the tablet computer application scenarios that we demonstrated could have been more persuading with an LED cluster embedded in at the tip of a stylus and with the sensors embedded in the frames. As another application, we may add a tiny LED cluster to a smartphone without spoiling its appearance, and then turn the smartphone into a 6-DOF controller for a TV. As yet another application, we may add multiple IrCubes to multiple points on the hand including fingertips and capture hand movements. This of course requires the simultaneous use of multiple IrCubes, which may become possible with a time sharing scheme. We expect that the IrCube tracker will be able to reach wider applications when the sensors become available as a compact IC.

CONCLUSION

We designed an IrCube prototype and showed that the IrCube design so far is approaching the initial goal of a cost-effective tracker system for consumer electronics. Its performance in terms of accuracy and frame rate was shown to be good enough for many consumer electronics applications. Also, it was shown to be applicable to diverse application environments, such as a tabletop computer, a tablet computer, and a mobile spatial interaction environment.

All 6-DOF technologies can become cheaper as market demands increase, but we expect that IrCube will be in a better position in the race due to its structural simplicity. We know how much small and cheap sensors contributed to the advance of user interface design. We also expect that small and cheap 6-DOF solutions will contribute to make 6-DOF tracking more available and affordable option for user interface design.

REFERENCES

1. Boucouvalas, A. C. Indoor ambient light noise and its effect on wireless optical links. *IEE Proc.-Optoelectron. 143*, 6 (1996), 334–338.
2. Coleman, T. F., and Li, Y. An interior trust region approach for nonlinear minimization subject to bounds. *SIAM Journal on Optimization 6*, 2 (1996), 418–445.
3. Engadget. PlayStation Move first hands-on. `http://www.engadget.com`.
4. Engadget. Razer and Sixense hook up for motion sensing PC gaming peripheral. `http://www.engadget.com`.
5. Evans, M. J., Drew, R., and Blenkhorn, P. Controlling mouse pointer position using an infrared head-operated joystick. *IEEE Transactions on Rehabilitation Engineering 8*, 1 (2000), 107–117.
6. Gilson, S. J., Fitzgibbon, A. W., and Glennerster, A. Quantitative analysis of accuracy of an inertial/acoustic 6-DOF tracking system in motion. *Journal of Neuroscience Methods 154*, 1–2 (2006), 175–82.
7. Henderson, C. J., Butler, S. R., and Glass, A. The localization of equivalent dipoles of EEG sources by the application of electrical field theory. *Electroencephalography and Clinical Neurophysiology 39* (1975), 117–130.
8. Hobbs, P. C. D. Photodiode front ends: The REAL story. *Optics and Photonics News*, April (2001), 42–45.
9. Hu, C., Meng, M. Q., and Mandal, M. Efficient magnetic localization and orientation technique for capsule endoscopy. *IEEE/RSJ International Conference on Intelligent Robots and Systems (IROS)* (2005), 628–633.
10. InterSense Inc. Precision Motion Tracking Solutions - IS-900 System. `http://www.inters.com/pages/20/14/`.
11. Lee, G., Lee, S., et al. A TV pointing device using LED directivity. *IEEE International Conference on Consumer Electronics (ICCE)* (2011), 619–620.
12. Mohan, A., Woo, G., et al. Bokode: Imperceptible visual tags for camera based interaction from a distance. *ACM Transactions on Graphics 28*, 3 (2009).
13. Nelder, J. A., and Mead, R. A simplex method for function minimization. *The Computer Journal 7*, 4 (1965), 308–313.
14. PhaseSpace Inc. PhaseSpace Motion Capture. `http://www.phasespace.com/`.
15. Raskar, R., et al. Prakash: Lighting aware motion capture using photosensing markers and multiplexed illuminators. *ACM Transactions on Graphics 26*, 3 (2007).
16. Roufas, K., Zhang, Y., et al. Six degree of freedom sensing for docking using IR LED emitters and receivers. *Lecture Notes in Control and Information Sciences 271* (2001), 91–100.
17. Shanno, D. F. Conditioning of quasi-Newton methods for function minimization. *Mathematics of Computation 24*, 111 (1970), 647–656.
18. Tokiwa, T., Yoshidzumi, M., et al. Motion capture system using an optical resolver. *Lecture Notes in Computer Science 5612* (2009), 536–543.
19. Welch, G., Bishop, G., et al. The HiBall Tracker: high-performance wide-area tracking for virtual and augmented environments. *ACM Symposium on Virtual Reality Software and Technology (VRST 1999)* (1999), 1–10.

Toucheo: Multitouch and Stereo Combined in a Seamless Workspace

Martin Hachet *Benoit Bossavit* *Aurélie Cohé*
Inria Bordeaux
LaBRI, 351 Cours de la Liberation, 33405 Talence, France
FirstName.LastName@inria.fr

Jean-Baptiste de la Rivière
Immersion SAS
12 rue Feaugas, 33100 Bordeaux, France
jb.delariviere@immersion.fr

ABSTRACT
We propose a new system that efficiently combines direct multitouch interaction with co-located 3D stereoscopic visualization. In our approach, users benefit from well-known 2D metaphors and widgets displayed on a monoscopic touchscreen, while visualizing occlusion-free 3D objects floating above the surface at an optically correct distance. Technically, a horizontal semi-transparent mirror is used to reflect 3D images produced by a stereoscopic screen, while the user's hand as well as a multitouch screen located below this mirror remain visible. By registering the 3D virtual space and the physical space, we produce a rich and unified workspace where users benefit simultaneously from the advantages of both direct and indirect interaction, and from 2D and 3D visualizations. A pilot usability study shows that this combination of technology provides a good user experience.

ACM Classification: H5.1 [Information interfaces and presentation]: Multimedia Information Systems. - Artificial, augmented, and virtual realities. H5.2 [Information interfaces and presentation]: User Interfaces. - Input devices and strategies.

General terms: Design, Human Factors

Keywords: Multitouch, stereoscopic display, 3D user interfaces

INTRODUCTION
Recent years have witnessed a keen interest for new input and output technologies. In particular, a widespread boom has occurred surrounding multitouch interaction on the one hand, and stereoscopic visualization on the other hand, noticeably with the extremely rapid market penetration of these technologies for the general public mass market. Direct multitouch interaction has shown many benefits for interaction with digital content. With good mappings, the intuitiveness of multitouch interfaces favors fast and easy interaction. At the same time, stereoscopic visualization, that has been dedicated to specific audiences and applications for a long time, is now becoming a standard display, and it tends to be well accepted by large audiences. In this work, we lean on these current trends and we merge the benefits of both multitouch interaction and stereoscopic visualization into a new original unified workspace. Our system combines efficient direct multitouch interaction with co-located 3D stereoscopic visualization. Hence, users benefit from an immersive visualization of data while being able to interact with both 2D and 3D elements thanks to well-known, or new, touch-based 2D metaphors and widgets, within a seamless workspace. Figure 1 illustrates this workspace, where a user manipulates a 3D stereoscopic object from 2D gestures on a touchscreen.

UIST'11, October 16-19, 2011, Santa Barbara, CA, USA.

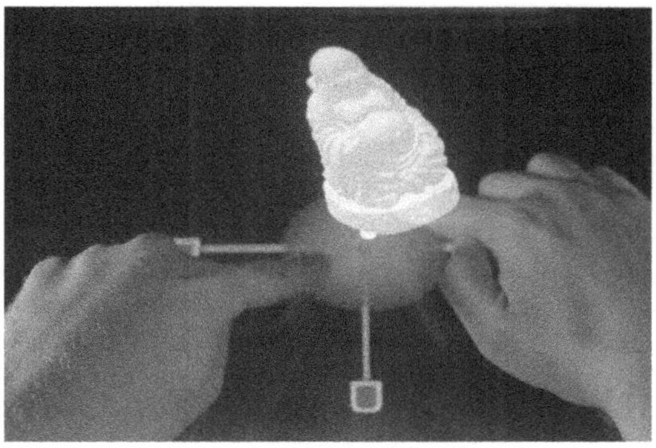

Figure 1: 3D stereoscopic objects and 2D monoscopic content are combined in a unified multitouch workspace.

In this paper, we first review the related work and technologies, and discuss their advantages and drawbacks. Afterwards, we describe both the hardware and software components of our setup. We then focus on interaction techniques and we present the dedicated transformation widget we have designed. A user study allows us to highlight the strengths and weaknesses of our setup. Finally, we describe an applicative scenario before concluding.

RELATED WORK
Interacting with 3D content on touchscreens is an inspiring challenge that has recently motivated interesting research work. Hancock et al. [12] proposed a technique where users manipulate 3D objects with one, two, or three fingers in shallow depth. Reisman et al. [18] extended the well known Rotate-Scale-Translate (RST) multi-touch technique to 3D. Martinet et al. have compared and improved these techniques [16]. In their approaches, Cohé et al. [8] and Kin et al. [14] adapted standard desktop interfaces to the multitouch paradigm. Hilliges et al. added *above-the-surface* interac-

tion paradigms [13]. Even if these techniques enhance interaction with 3D scenes, they generally face the problem of 3D content being visualized on 2D flat screens.

Stereoscopic visualization associated with head tracking favors good perception of 3D content. This technology has been extensively used in VR, and it is now becoming widely available. One of the problems with such a display is the difficulty for the user to interact with, let alone to touch. Dedicated input devices and interaction techniques have been designed (see VR and 3DUI literature, e.g. [5]), but they are generally not integrated within widely distributed applications. Mirror-based display systems, such as the one presented by Schmandt [19], enable co-location between the interaction space and the visually perceived 3D scene. This allows exploiting proprioception and hand-eye coordination [1]. These systems are generally used with haptic devices, e.g. [15]. Such configurations allow one to directly address 3D points within the registered virtual and physical spaces, as well as to feel virtual shapes. With a semi-transparent mirror, the user can see both the real and the virtual environment at the same time. This has been exploited in AR scenarios, e.g. [4][17]. However, the applicative scenarios for such configurations are generally restricted to specific use, and the level of interaction is quite poor. As far as we know, mirror-based stereoscopic systems have never been exploited in conjunction with an additional touchscreen.

Recently, Benko et al. have proposed to combine touchscreens with stereoscopic visualization [3]. Their system is based on a DiamondTouch table used in conjunction with SeeThrough AR head-worn displays, and 3D tracked gloves. This system manages both 2D images projected on the table, and 3D visualization through the head-worn displays. Our approach shares some similar concepts with their work, and it is complementary. Whereas they have conceived their system to favor collaborative work, we have concentrate on a setup that maximizes the consistency and the seamless integration of 2D and 3D stereoscopic displays. Head-worn displays as used in [3] have substantial advantages, but they also suffer from many weaknesses, including a limited field-of-view and resolution, problems of lag and calibration, and so on. Our proposal oversteps these limitations by leaning on a new original optical configuration. Users wear light glasses, and they can interactively observe high-resolution monoscopic and stereoscopic content with a good visual comfort. We have also introduced new 9 DOF interaction widgets that take benefit of such a rich visualization space.

De la Riviere et al. have demonstrated a stereoscopic multitouch system [9]. In their approach, two head-tracked users directly interact on a large stereoscopic multitouch table. This setup revealed many promising uses. On the other hand, it suffers from some limitations. In particular, content occlusion is problematic when visualizing stereoscopic images. Selection is also a critical issue when stereoscopic visualization and touch input are jointly used in a unique setup. Valkov et al. [21][20] have focused on this problem, and they give recommendations for 2D touching of 3D stereoscopic objects. In their work, Coffey et al. [6][7] proposed an immersive setup where users interact on a horizontal touchscreen, while visualizing virtual environments displayed from a large vertical display located in front of them. Veit et al. [22] used a similar approach with a two-side workbench. The limitation of such approaches is that users need to change the focus between the interaction plane, and the 3D display. With our setup, users can refocus at two different depths without changing their viewing direction. This allows concentrating at visual content displayed at given depth, while keeping the context provided by the second depth plane.

All those attempts show that the conjunction of multitouch interaction and stereoscopic visualization is very promising. On the other hand, the previous work also shows that merging these technologies may be hard to perform, both in terms of hardware developments and design of efficient interaction techniques. Indeed, their achievements seem to be conflicting: immersive visualization makes the screen disappear and gives the feeling an object is located ahead of or behind the screen, while the touch input enables efficient interaction with any content that is displayed on the screen or the interaction plane. Moreover, the very nature of stereoscopic images conflicts with touch input, as two images are generated to force the eyes convergence and the associated depth perception, which is contradictory with single images displayed at screen depth to enable efficient and precise touch.

SETUP

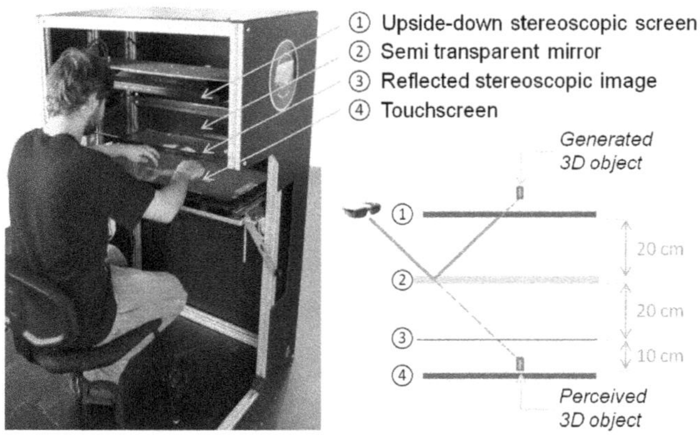

Figure 2: Physical setup

To overcome the limitations of the systems described in the previous section, we propose a new original setup. It relies on a multitouch screen on which users see a visualization and interact with monoscopic content. The stereoscopic visualization is provided by another 3D screen that is hung upside-down at the top of the system, and that is reflected on a semi-transparent mirror located between the user's head and the multitouch screen (see Figure 2). Hence, stereoscopic objects are perceived as if they were displayed above the hands, between the mirror and the touchscreen. The geometry of the system provides a large volume above the touchscreen where stereoscopic objects can be perceived. Head tracking ensures that virtual objects are displayed from a correct point of view, and that the parallax is physically correct for any of the real or virtual object within the workspace. By mapping the virtual stereoscopic volume to the physical space, we can then produce a rich and consistent interactive visualization space.

Regarding the taxonomy of Grossman and Wigdor [11], the input space is *2D Planar*, and both *2D Table* (perceived as *2D*) and *2D Heads Up* (percieved as *3D Volume*) are jointly exploited.

With this setup, users see in the same space the floating 3D objects, their hands, and the data displayed on the touchscreen. Our system inherently provides relevant occlusions clues. Indeed, the stereoscopic objects appear above the user's hands, while the monoscopic content remains below (see Figure 1). Contrary to standard immersive 3D systems that only rely on affecting the eyes convergence to simulate 3D objects depth, our proposal also takes advantage of eye accomodation, and its capability to focus at two different depths. This is illustrated in Figure 3. By changing the lighting conditions inside the system, as well as the brightness of the two screens, we are able to modify the ratio between reflection and transparency and, consequently, we can adjust the visibility of the 2D images, 3D images, and physical objects (e.g. hands).

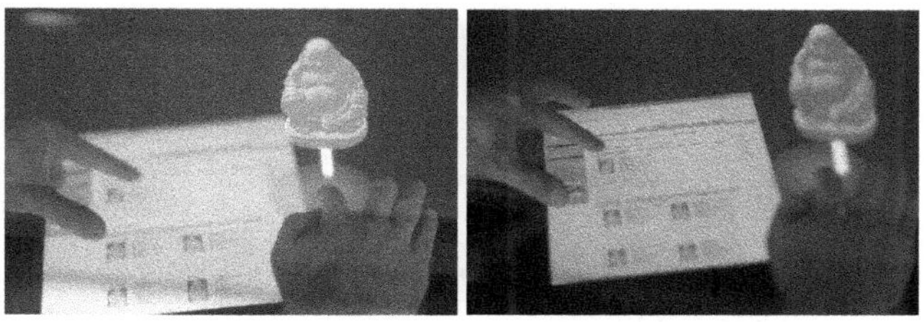

(a) Focus on the 3D object (b) Focus on the touchscreen

Figure 3: The setup based on two physical displays provides natural focus separation.

Our current implementation is based on two 32" 1080p LCD screens, which are capable of stereoscopic visualization with shutter-glasses. We chose identical screens for colorimetric consistency purposes, even if stereo is enabled on the top screen only. A PQLab 32" multitouch sensor that is mounted on the bottom screen is used to detect finger gestures. The semi-transparent mirror reflects 70% of the light. Head-tracking is currently achieved with an electromagnetic sensor, but it will be replaced by an optical tracking solution to avoid wires. Our software plateform is based on Ogre3D and QT. It runs on a unique PC equipped with a Nvidia Quadro Fx 3800 graphic board. The user is sitting when interacting.

INTERACTION TECHNIQUES

The monoscopic touchscreen provides a direct multitouch interaction surface. Consequently, we benefit from the large variety of user interfaces that were previously designed for such systems. In particular, we take advantage of well known multitouch gestures for zooming and panning operations, for item selection, and even for application control. For example, Figure 3 illustrates the use of a web browser that is displayed on the touchscreen, and Figure 4 shows a standard color editor. Such widgets are embedded inside the immersive workspace, and they can be manipulated with standard touch gestures. Users are therefore able to interact in a fast and easy way with the content beneath the fingers, as they would do with a standard touchscreen.

By default, the 3D objects are displayed and move on the monoscopic screen. They are therefore seen as 2D projection of 3D objects just like on any standard screen. A *double tap* gesture on a 3D object makes it appear as a stereoscopic object floating above the surface. A simple z-translation animation gives the impression that the object comes out of the touchscreen. The 3D representation of the object on the touchscreen disappears, and it is replaced by a 3D transformation widget located below the floating object. This widget is used to select the floating object, and to manipulate it. A virtual ray, similar to Glueck et al.'s position pegs [10], enforces the link between the manipulated 3D object and its associated transformation widget, as can be seen in Figure 3. It strengthens the direct relationship between the finger gestures and the object motion, giving an impression of "pseudo-direct" interaction, even if the object is not manipulated directly as in, e.g., [18].

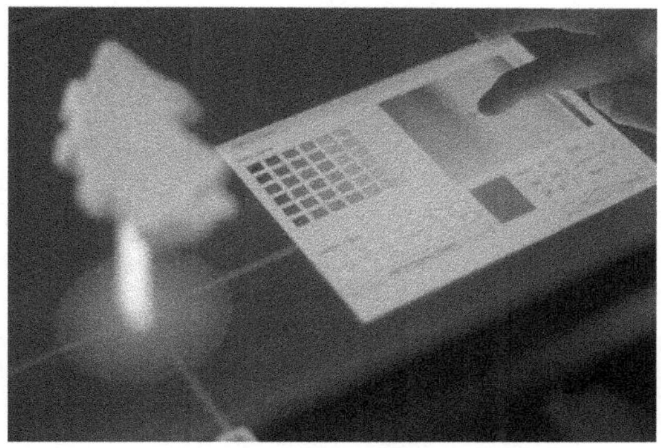

Figure 4: Both standard 2D widgets and 3D widgets are used in the same workspace.

The 3D transformation widget is composed of a central disk and additional virtual controllers (see Figure 5). Dual-touch gestures on the central disk of the widget result in *RST* operations on a plane parallel to the touchscreen (x-y plane). x and y rotations are controlled by way of virtual rods located on the sides of the disk. The fingers crossing the rod would launch an inertial rotation around the rod axis, allowing the control of a single degree of freedom without affecting the others. Similarly, scaling widgets allow the control of the x and y scale factors. For z translations and scaling operations, we use an approach inspired from the balloon metaphor [2]. The user first touches the center of the disk with one finger, and then she or he adjusts the height and the size with a second finger. Hence, users are able to control 9 DOF (plus uniform scaling) of the manipulated 3D object. Figure 5 summarizes these control gestures. Note that all the transformations occur in the camera view frame. The transformation widget can be manipulated with multiple fingers at the same time. Two widgets can also be controlled with two hands for simultaneous manipulation of various objects.

USABILITY TESTING

We conducted an experiment to obtain user feedback about our prototype. Sixteen volunteers (13 males, 3 females, mean age 27) participated in this study. None of them was familiar with stereoscopic visualization nor with large multitouch interaction. The participants were asked to complete a 3D docking task implying 9 Degree-Of-Freedom (3 translations, 3 rotations, 3 scaling), as illustrated in Figure 6. Note that

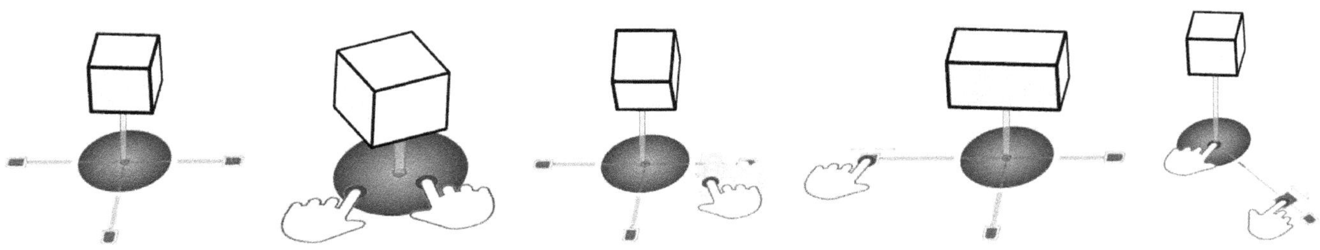

(a) (b) (c) (d) (e)

Figure 5: Gestures and corresponding transformations. (a) The widget is displayed on the touchscreen, below the floating object. A virtual ray links both the object and the widget. (b) One or two fingers on the central disk controls RST movements on the x-y plane. (c) Virtual rods are used for x and y rotations. (d) x and y scaling are controlled with dedicated widgets. (d) When touching the center of the disk, a new control widget appears. It allows controlling z translations and scaling.

we did not focus on precise manipulation in this pilot study, therefore the matching between the target and the manipulated object was quite tolerant. Each participant had to complete the task five times, with various target sizes, orientations and locations. Before starting, the participants were shown the basic usage of the interface. The whole experiment took approximatively between five and ten minutes by participant. After the experiment, the participants were asked to complete a questionnaire based on a five-point Likert scale. We also collected free-form comments.

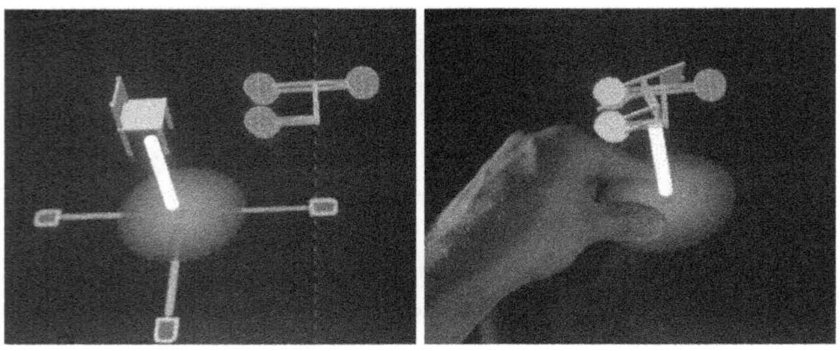

(a) (b)

Figure 6: The 3D docking task. The spheres move from red to green when the alignment is correct within a tolerance area.

In this experiment, we were interested in the general feeling of the participants regarding the system. The participants reported they liked the system with an average score of 4.6, which demonstrates a stimulating and satisfying overall experience. The score for the global intuitiveness is 4. Almost none of the participants reported fatigue or sickness (1.1).

The perception of the depth was rated with an average score of 4.5, and the perception of the 3D objects obtained a 4.6. We did not use shadows nor specific shading to enhance depth perception. Even with our current basic experimental environment, participants did not encounter problems with the perception of the 3D environment. The need to move the head for observing the 3D scene has been rated as low (1.8). The participants tended to keep a fixed head-position. This may indicate that head-tracking is not mandatory once the initial head position has been detected. Note that we need to know the initial head position to correctly map the stereoscopic objects with the monoscopic ones. The low use of head movements may be explained by the inexperience of the participants. Also, the completion of the task did not require extensive head motion. The related mean scores are illustrated in Figure 7.

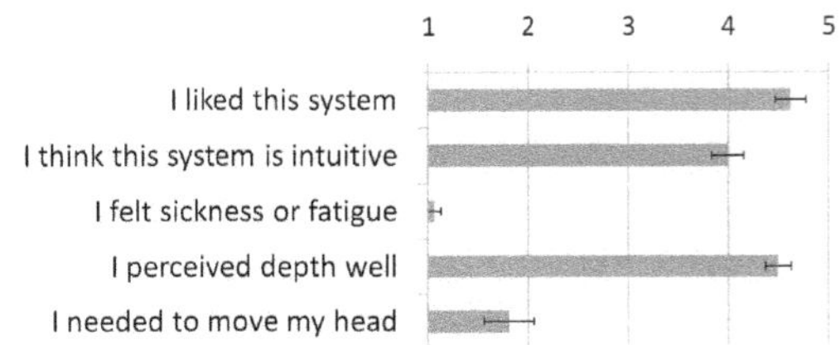

Figure 7: General feeling. Mean scores (1-fully disagree, 5-fully agree) and standard errors (1 SE above and below the mean).

We were also interested in interactions between the visualization of floating objects, the hands, and the widget displayed on the touch screen. The participants answered they were able to visualize well their hand with a score of 4.6. When asking if the hands were too much (resp. too little) visible, the score was 1.6 (resp. 1.5). The hands have not appeared to disturb the visualization of the 3D objects (1.4), nor the 2D objects (2). These results tend to show that the simultaneous visualization of real and virtual elements at different depths do not perturb users (see Figure 8). The simultaneous visualization of their hands and virtual environments may even help users complete the task. This should be studied in more depth in future experiments.

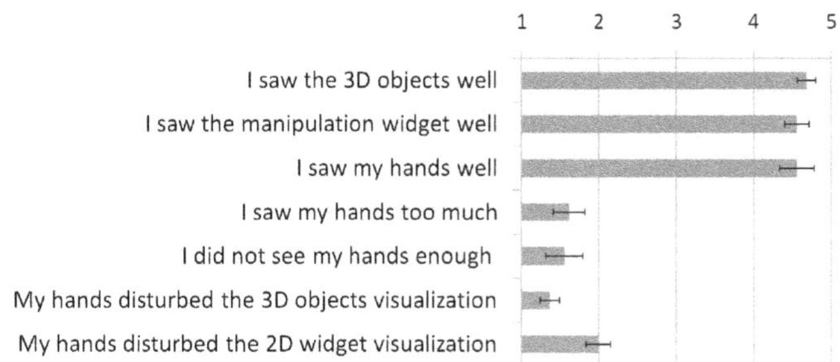

Figure 8: Interactions between the visual elements.

Concerning the widget and the manipulation metaphors (Figure 9), the participants reported they were mainly able to perform what they wanted to (4.2). The RST interface has been rated as easy to use with a score of 4.3. The score for the rotation (resp. scaling) widgets was 4 (resp. 3.9). The z widgets obtained a lower score (3.5). We think that one of the reasons is that the finger movements were sometimes stopped by the borders of the touchscreen. To solve this limitation, we afterwards replaced the initial z movements by circular movements. After having caught a dedicated handle, the user can now turn it around the center of the widget, as she or he would do with a crank handle, to modify the z parameter. Another problem was linked to the selection of the widget due to the parallax between the displayed 2D images and the sensitive surface where the touch inputs were detected. Because we know the position of the user's head, we could solve this problem by warping the input so it could fit exactly with the perceived display space. Note that the participants have practiced no more than 10 minutes with the widget before assessing it. From our experience, the use of the widget become very efficient after a short period of practice. This needs to be better evaluated in future longer experiments.

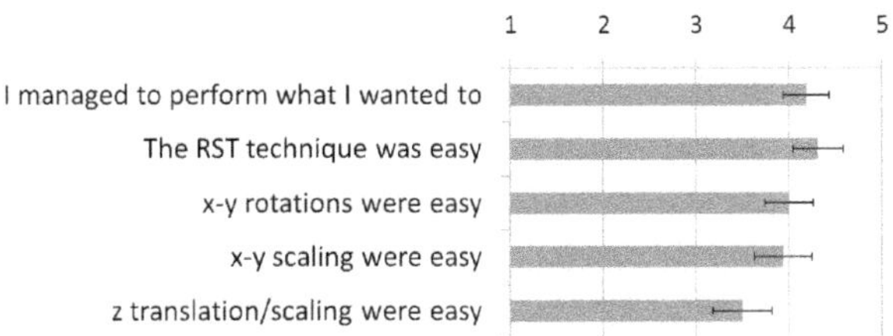

Figure 9: Manipulation widget.

3D docking tasks are generally hard to perform. One of the reason is the difficulty to perceive well the 3D structure of the objects and their relative positioning. Another one is linked to the control of 9 DOF. Our proposal address both of these difficulties. The participants had few problems with perceptual issues thanks to the immersive aspect of our system. They manage to complete the task quite easily thanks to the 2D widget and the associated touch gestures.

LIMITATIONS

In the free-form comments section of the experiment, some participants said that the overall environment was too dark. Indeed, the light coming from the stereoscopic screen is attenuated by the reflection on the semi-transparent mirror, as well as by the shutter glasses needed to produce stereo. In the future versions of our prototype, we will seek for screens that maintain a comfortable overall brightness. We also need to study in more depth colorimetric issues to ensure a perfect consistency taking into account the perturbation induced by the reflection. None of the subjects complained about the possible overlapping between the stereoscopic and the monoscopic content, maybe because the test application we proposed was quite simple. We nevertheless think that such conflicts may be problematic. Because we know the position of the viewer and the position of the 3D objects, we can compute the part of the 2D content that is supposed to be visible (resp. invisible). Hence, we can avoid conflicts, and provide very plausible environments.

Some participants also reported that they found the system bulky, and that they had difficulties to reach the rear part of the touchscreen because of the mirror. We will take these comments into consideration and we will work on ergonomics issues for the design of our future prototype. In particular, we will explore different touchscreen and mirror orientations. We will also work on different form-factors that would avoid the system to be perceived as bulky.

Finally, one of the limitations of our setup is the size of the stereoscopic volume. Compared to large VR screen installations [7] and HMD-based configurations [3], this volume is reduced with our setup. Note however that this volume is bigger than if the stereoscopic display was coming directly from a touchscreen having the same dimensions.

APPLICATION SCENARIO

To illustrate the benefit of our system, we have developed a demo application for a cultural heritage scenario where archaeologists have to reassemble broken objects by manipulating numerous virtual fragments. To complete this task, archaeologists first need to easily access libraries of objects. Then, they may want to sort, arrange, or annotate them. To do this, direct-touch interaction on a multitouch screen is particularly well suited. Similar tasks in fully immersive VR environments may be harder to complete. On the other hand, archaeologists need to precisely perceive all the shape irregularities or the texture variations of the 3D fragments to understand how they can fit together. This can be favored thanks to the immersive aspect of our system. Both stereoscopic visualization and head-tracking provide powerful visualization. The 3D transformation widget we have designed allows the full manipulation of any 3D object. By using two hands, archaeologists can manipulate two objects at the same time to estimate how well they match together (see Figure 10). This would be difficult to complete with a standard multitouch configuration as depth perception may be a true problem. While manipulating stereoscopic objects, archaeologists can still access various standard controls such as color editors, 2D documents, and so on. We believe that numerous other scenarios where the conjunction of both efficient interaction and good visual immersion would benefit from our setup, e.g. in architecture and medicine scenarios.

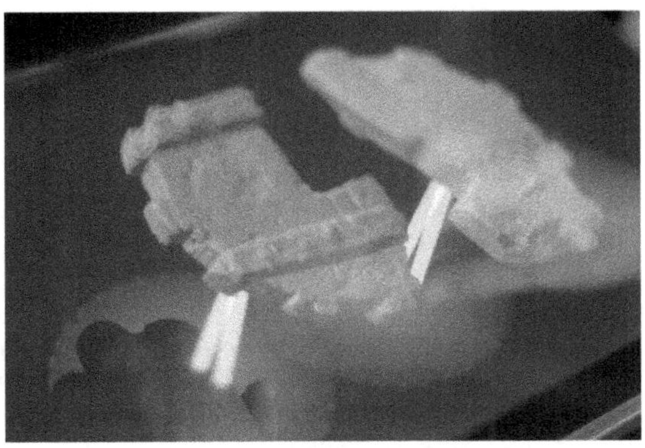

Figure 10: Two virtual fragments being manipulated with both hands for a reassembly task. *This figure is rendered in stereo with the views for both eyes visible.*

CONCLUSION AND FUTURE WORK

We have proposed a new system that combines both multitouch input and immersive visualization into a single unified workspace. This system relies on the strengths of each technology. It favors at the same time fast and easy interaction, 3D manipulation and camera controls, 2D system control, bimanual interaction, and immersive visualization. The original design of our setup takes advantage of eye accomodation and its capability to focus at different depths. Our first usability testing was very positive. The participants enjoyed their experience with the system. This study has shown that the blending of stereoscopic display, monoscopic display, and real elements in the same workspace does not cause perceptual conflicts. It has also shown that our setup allows novice users to complete a 9-DOF docking task without many difficulties. User comments have highlighted some limitations of the system. Our future work will consist in improving the design of our prototype by leaning on ergonomics studies. In addition, we want to continue improving and inventing new interaction techniques to push forward the strengths of our system. We also plan to add a depth-camera to mix touch-based and 3D spatial interaction inside the same workspace.

Despite some current areas of improvement, we are convinced that, thanks to its unique blend of complementary displays and simple multitouch interaction schemes, our proposal could bridge the gap between powerful immersive virtual environments and efficient 2D desktop paradigms within a unified workspace.

Acknowledgements
This work was supported by the ANR project ANR-09-CORD-013 InSTInCT - http://anr-instinct.cap-sciences.net. 3D models: courtesy of VCG-ISTI (Buddha) and Archeovision (virtual fragments).

REFERENCES

1. Roland Arsenault and Colin Ware. The importance of stereo and eye-coupled perspective for eye-hand coordination in fish tank vr. *Presence: Teleoper. Virtual Environ.*, 13:549–559, October 2004.
2. Hrvoje Benko and Steven Feiner. Balloon selection: A multi-finger technique for accurate low-fatigue 3d selections. In *Proc. IEEE Symposium on 3D User Interfaces (3DUI)*, 2007.
3. Hrvoje Benko, Edward W. Ishak, and Steven Feiner. Cross-dimensional gestural interaction techniques for hybrid immersive environments. In *Proceedings of the IEEE Virtual Reality. Conference*, pages 209–216, 2005.
4. Oliver Bimber. Interactive rendering for projection-based augmented reality displays, 2002.
5. Doug A. Bowman, Ernst Kruijff, Joseph J. LaViola, and Ivan Poupyrev. *3D User Interfaces: Theory and Practice*. Addison Wesley Longman Publishing Co., Inc., Redwood City, CA, USA, 2004.
6. Dane Coffey, Fedor Korsakov, and Daniel Keefe. Low cost vr meets low cost multi-touch. In *Advances in Visual Computing*, volume 6454 of *Lecture Notes in Computer Science*, pages 351–360. Springer Berlin / Heidelberg, 2010.
7. Dane Coffey, Nicholas Malbraaten, Trung Le, Iman Borazjani, Fotis Sotiropoulos, and Daniel F. Keefe. Slice wim: a multi-surface, multi-touch interface for overview+detail exploration of volume datasets in virtual reality. In *Symposium on Interactive 3D Graphics and Games*, I3D '11, pages 191–198, 2011.
8. Aurélie Cohé, Fabrice Dècle, and Martin Hachet. tbox: A 3d transformation widget designed for touch-screens. In *ACM Proceedings of CHI 2011 Conference on Human Factors in Computing Systems*. ACM, 2011.
9. J.B. de la Rivière, C. Kervégant, E. Orvain, N. Dittlo, and M. Courtois. 3d multitouch : when tactile tables meet immersive visualization technologies. In *Siggraph 2010 Emerging Technologies, Siggraph 2010 Talk*, 2010.
10. Michael Glueck, Keenan Crane, Sean Anderson, Andres Rutnik, and Azam Khan. Multiscale 3d reference visualization. In *Proceedings of the 2009 symposium on Interactive 3D graphics and games*, I3D '09, pages 225–232, 2009.
11. Tovi Grossman and Daniel Wigdor. Going deeper: a taxonomy of 3d on the tabletop. In *Tabletop'07*, pages 137–144, 2007.
12. Mark Hancock, Thomas ten Cate, and Sheelagh Carpendale. Sticky tools: Full 6DOF force-based interaction for multi-touch tables. In *Proc. ITS*, pages 145–152, 2009.
13. Otmar Hilliges, Shahram Izadi, Andrew D. Wilson, Steve Hodges, Armando Garcia-Mendoza, and Andreas Butz. Interactions in the air: adding further depth to interactive tabletops. In *Proceedings of the 22nd annual ACM symposium on User interface software and technology*, UIST '09, pages 139–148. ACM, 2009.
14. Kenrick Kin, Bollensdorff Bjorn Miller, Tom and, Tony DeRose, and Bjorn Hartmann. Eden: A professional multi-touch tool for constructing virtual organic environments. In *ACM Proceedings of CHI 2011 Conference on Human Factors in Computing Systems*. ACM, 2011.
15. Rick Komerska and Colin Ware. Haptic task constraints fo 3d interaction. In *Proceedings of the 11th Symposium on Haptic Interfaces for Virtual Environment and Teleoperator Systems (HAPTICS'03)*, pages 270–, Washington, DC, USA, 2003. IEEE Computer Society.
16. Anthony Martinet, Géry Casiez, and Laurent Grisoni. The effect of dof separation in 3d manipulation tasks with multi-touch displays. In *Proceedings of the 17th ACM Symposium on Virtual Reality Software and Technology*, VRST '10, pages 111–118, 2010.
17. Jurriaan D. Mulder and Breght R. Boschker. A modular system for collaborative desktop vr/ar with a shared workspace. In *Proceedings of the IEEE Virtual Reality 2004*, pages 75–, Washington, DC, USA, 2004. IEEE Computer Society.
18. Jason L. Reisman, Philip L. Davidson, and Jefferson Y. Han. A screen-space formulation for 2d and 3d direct manipulation. In *UIST '09: Proceedings of the 22nd annual ACM symposium on User interface software and technology*, pages 69–78. ACM, 2009.
19. Christopher Schmandt. Spatial input/display correspondence in a stereoscopic computer graphic work station. *SIGGRAPH Comput. Graph.*, 17:253–261, July 1983.
20. Dimitar Valkov, Frank Steinicke, Gerd Bruder, and Klaus H. Hinrichs. 2d touching of 3d stereoscopic objects. In *ACM Proceedings of CHI 2011 Conference on Human Factors in Computing Systems*. ACM, 2011.
21. Dimitar Valkov, Frank Steinicke, Gerd Bruder, Klaus H. Hinrichs, Johannes Schöning, Florian Daiber, and Antonio Krüger. Touching floating objects in projection-based virtual reality environments. In *Proceedings of Joint Virtual Reality Conference (JVRC 2010)*, pages 17–24. Eurographics, 2010.
22. Manuel Veit, Antonio Capobianco, and Dominique Bechmann. Experimental analysis of the impact of touch screen interaction techniques for 3d positioning tasks. In *IEEE Virtual Reality*, IEEE Conference on Virtual Reality 2011, pages 1–8. IEEE, Springer, 2011.

Harpoon Selection: Efficient Selections for Ungrouped Content on Large Pen-based Surfaces

Jakob Leitner, Michael Haller
Media Interaction Lab, University of Applied Sciences Upper Austria
Hagenberg, Austria
mi-lab@fh-hagenberg.at

ABSTRACT
In this paper, we present the *Harpoon* selection tool, a novel selection technique specifically designed for interactive whiteboards. The tool combines area cursors and crossing to perform complex selections amongst a large number of unsorted, ungrouped items. It is optimized for large-scale pen-based surfaces and works well in both dense and sparse surroundings. We describe a list of key features relevant to the design of the tool and provide a detailed description of both the mechanics as well as the feedback of the tool. The results of a user study are described and analyzed to confirm our design. The study shows that the Harpoon tool performs significantly faster than *Tapping* and *Lassoing*.

ACM Classification: H5.2 [Information interfaces and presentation]: User Interfaces. - Graphical user interfaces.

General terms: Design, Human Factors.

Keywords: Selection Tool, Lasso, Crossing, Pen Input

INTRODUCTION
The interaction design for pen-based interactive whiteboards is challenging due to various reasons. In this paper, we specifically look at challenges concerning interaction techniques for selecting a large number of ungrouped items (e.g., separate ink strokes in handwritten notes or sketches). Interactive whiteboards often lack interaction possibilities (e.g., no hover state, low tracking resolution, lack of modifier keys), which might be required to use selection techniques to their full extend. Tracking data might be less reliable, causing unintended results like premature cancelation of existing selections. Selection techniques optimized for desktop environments do not provide means to easily compensate for such errors. Additional challenges arise due to the size of such surfaces. Frequent mode changes might require users to take round trips to access menus which can be time consuming. Existing selections might be hard to see and modify on large screens. Also selection techniques (e.g., Tapping, traditional Rubber-Band selections) often rely on keyboard-shortcuts for quickly accessing certain functionality (e.g., for adding or removing items). These options are inaccessible on whiteboards as they often do not have supplementary buttons. Even techniques like *Lassoing* that are designed for pen input [9, 13, 15, 16] may rely on supplementary buttons and may also require difficult steering tasks that are highly constrained and error prone [1, 14].

Figure 1: The Harpoon selection tool in action on an interactive whiteboard.

We analyzed these challenges and present several key features that should be considered in the design process of new selection tools. We also present the *Harpoon* selection tool that addresses the aforementioned challenges. We validate our design through a user study and present further improvements based on the results.

Summarizing, the main contributions of this paper are:

- A list of key features that should be considered when designing a selection tool for interactive whiteboards.
- A detailed description of our selection technique and visualization that is based on the aforementioned key features.
- A novel way to implicitly change selection mode, which facilitates fluid modifications of existing selections.
- Description and discussion of study results that confirm our design.

RELATED WORK
The interaction techniques on pen-based surfaces differ greatly from traditional desktop environments. Ren et al. [19] state that *"...current target selection strategies for pen-based systems are mostly only imitations of selection techniques for mouse and touch-screen devices."* In their paper, the authors present detailed design recommendations

for selection strategies for pen-based systems, stating that crossing outperforms other tested selection methods in speed, error-rate, and user-preference. More recently, Apitz et al. [3] formulate design recommendations for user interfaces based on the crossing paradigm. They also provide an extensive list of related work, which we recommend for further reading. In contrast, our work focuses on selection tasks of large groups of randomly arranged items that can have different sizes.

Crossing has been explored for selection of single [1, 19] as well as multiple objects [22]. However, it can be difficult to cross every single stroke in a sketch or a handwritten word. This is especially the case for small targets (e.g., dots, commas, or quotation marks). Area cursors [12] help selecting single targets. DynaSpot [6] extends the idea of area cursors by dynamically resizing the area cursor based on the movement speed but it is also designed for only selecting single targets. Land et al. [14] analyze input and dynamically change selection properties for lasso selections. Some problems with lasso selections like overlapping items however are not addressed with this approach.

We take the idea of dynamic area cursors and crossing and extend it to facilitate efficient selections of very large numbers of items in various conditions. Based on our experience with pen-based interactive surfaces [10] as well as related work, we identified the several key factors that have been considered when designing the Harpoon tool. In the following paragraphs, we present these key factors together with related publications and present implications for the *Harpoon* tool.

Button and hover free: Most interactive whiteboard systems (e.g., Smartboard) do not offer barrel buttons or hover states on pens. If available, buttons located at the pen still might require from users to shift their grip, interrupting the users' input flow [11]. They can also be hit accidently, which may result in unexpected behavior. *Harpooning* does not rely on hardware-dependent tracking data like button-presses, hover information or pressure values.

Support discontinued drag operations: It can be difficult to perform long drag operations with a pen [18]. Bezels in multiscreen-setups prohibit a smooth and continuous dragging across the entire workspace. To support pen usage on large, multi-screen surfaces and to minimize unintended premature selection cancelation, *Harpoon* selections can be comprised of several short drag operations.

Compatibility with established techniques: To alleviate operation for novice users, common interactions should be supported. The *Harpoon* selection tool integrates established selection techniques like tapping [15, 21] and *Lasso* selections [5, 13] to exploit each technique's benefit while compensating for possible weaknesses.

Localized: If required, user interface elements should be placed close to the users' current input position to minimize long, interruptive round trips [7, 10]. The positioning should be dynamic yet predictable to enable fluid interaction. In our application an explicit mode-change is required to switch between different tools. For example, users explicitly need to switch between *Inking* and *Selecting*. We offer two different ways to perform this mode change. Each user can open a localized, digital menu at any location on the drawing canvas. Alternatively a physical tool palette can be used. This initial mode change, while crucial for a pleasurable experience, will not be further discussed in this paper as the focus of this paper is the selection process itself. Further information on our digital menu as well as the physical tool palette can be found in [10]. An overview of tool-switching techniques is given in [8]. Implicit mode changes can be used to avoid explicit mode changes altogether and effectively removing UI placement problems and visual clutter [20]. Once engaged, *Harpooning* does not require any more explicit mode changes during operation.

Support modifications of selections: To minimize interruptions, users should be able to quickly specify whether items should be added or removed from the current selection without explicitly pressing a button or changing mode [16]. *Harpooning* uses implicit mode changes to allow users to quickly modify existing selections.

Large numbers of ungrouped items: Automatic parsing to select high-level structures in ink-based documents [4, 17] is used in several systems [8] to enable a quick selection of pre-defined groups. However, as robust automatic parsing cannot be assumed in all applications and for all domains, the *Harpoon* selection tool supports fast selection of large numbers of ungrouped items.

Support selection in dense surroundings: Lassoing within a dense surround of notes is tedious, because steering [1] along a winding path is slow and error prone for *Lassos* with accuracy constraints [14]. The *Harpoon* selection tool is designed to improve selection speed and accuracy for item-clusters as well as overlapping items.

HARPOON SELECTION

The *Harpoon* selection tool is designed to combine and extend several selection methods for an easy and fast selection of single targets as well as collection of ungrouped items. It is based on the "Slide Touch" strategy as proposed by Ren et al. [19]. Targets are selected when the pen-tip touches the target for the first time after landing on the screen surface. In contrast to the strategy described in [19], a selection area (which we term *spot* from now on, cf. [6]) instead of a single point is used for hit-testing.

Basic Selection

A new selection is started by dragging the pen anywhere on the surface. A yellow dotted line shows the path covered by the stylus tip (see Figure 2). The current spot size is indicated with a circle in the same color. The target is selected as soon as the spot touches it. A small "+"-sign appears indicating that all hit items are added to the current selection. The spot, the dotted selection path as well as the "+"-sign change to the same color (*green*) to provide additional feedback. All selected objects are outlined with a border and they turn semitransparent. A convex hull enclosing all selected objects appears. Continuing the movement in a straight line selects the whole phrase. Note that all strokes (even the small once like the dot on the "i") are added to the selected group. Once the pen is lifted from the surface, the spot, the selection path, and the cursor fade out. Finally, the color of the convex hull changes back to default (see Figure 2).

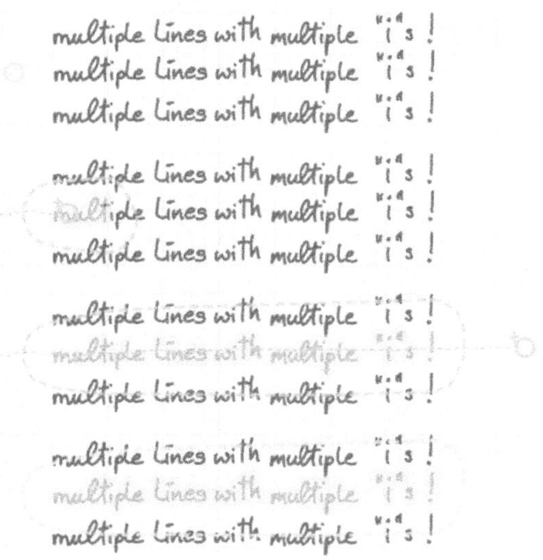

Figure 2: Performing a new selection with the Harpoon tool.

Speed-dependent spot size

It is impossible to predefine a spot size that works well for all purposes. On the one hand, a small diameter is well suited for precise selection operations, giving users fine-grain control over which individual objects to select. However, a small diameter makes selection of larger groups of objects cumbersome since all targets have to be crossed separately. Figure 3 (*top*) for example, shows that small objects (e.g., quotation marks or the dots on the "i") are easily missed. On the other hand, choosing a large diameter prohibits fine-grain operations and might result in the selection of unwanted objects as depicted in Figure 3 (*bottom*).

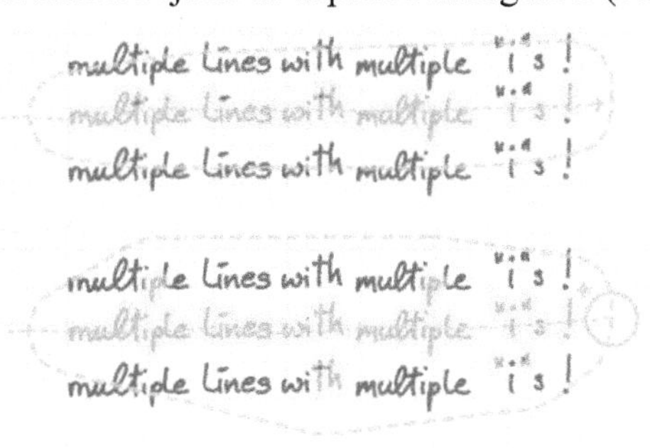

Figure 3: If the spot is too small, small strokes in the phrase might not be selected (*top*). If the cursor size is too large, close by strokes might get selected unintentionally (*bottom*).

Offering multiple different diameters in a menu would allow users to choose an appropriate diameter. However, this mode switch requires additional time and interrupts interaction flow. Also different diameters might be beneficial during a single drag operation.

Hence our *Harpoon* selection tool *dynamically resizes* the spot size based on the current movement speed. We assume that coarse selection operations result in higher input speed. In this case, we chose a large spot size. Precise selection operations require precise pen steering, resulting in slow pen movement. In this case, we choose a small spot diameter. We constantly update the spot size during movement. This results in a fluent transition between coarse and fine-grain actions without the introduction of artificial delays.

We tested several speed to spot-size transfer-functions and noticed that selecting targets in dense environments often requires the users to maintain a constant spot size. Erratic size changes lead to the selection of unwanted targets and should hence be avoided. We also noticed that it is impossible to predefine an input speed at which the system should be most sensitive as selection target sizes vary. The same amount of control is required over a large range of input speeds. Finally, to prevent selection of targets outside the user's attention area, the spot size has to be limited. To avoid erratic size-changes, which can result from noisy input values, we smooth the values using a running average. While this introduces a certain amount of delay, it greatly reduces the number of unwanted selection operations. We chose a linear function instead of an exponential one [6], as this results in the same degree of control for the whole range of movement velocities. Initial empirical tests showed that this worked well, but further experiments might be needed to validate this decision. A maximal threshold for the average speed is used. Values above the threshold are simply clamped. This upper threshold largely depends on the dimensions of the physical setup as well as the display resolution and can be configured in our system.

Figure 4 shows both raw input values as well as smoothed output values. In contrast to [6], we also allow the spot to shrink while moving.

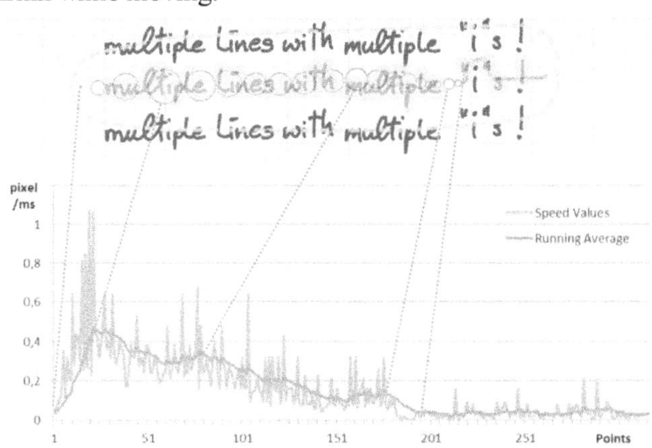

Figure 4: The orange circles represent the spot size during the selection operation (top). The graph (bottom) shows the raw input values (blue), and the resulting smoothed values (orange) used to calculate the spot size.

Selection modifications

Starting a new selection in the *Harpoon* tool leaves already existing selections unchanged, even if no items are selected in the new selection operation. For most other selection techniques (e.g., *Lasso*) starting a new selection automatically resets the last selection. For the *Harpoon* tool, a selection can only be reset when a single tap on the drawing canvas is performed. This minimizes the risk of accidently cancelling the current selection.

Adding items to an existing selection is usually achieved by switching to a dedicated mode (e.g., by pressing the "shift"-key on a keyboard). Removing objects from a current selection is achieved in a similar way. With the *Harpoon* tool, existing selections can be modified without an explicit switch to a different mode.

Single tap

A single tap on any object (e.g., ink) toggles its selection status. Figure 5 shows the result after two separate *single-taps*. Tapping the previously unselected *"h"* in the line above adds it to the current selection, clicking the *"m"* of the current selection removes it.

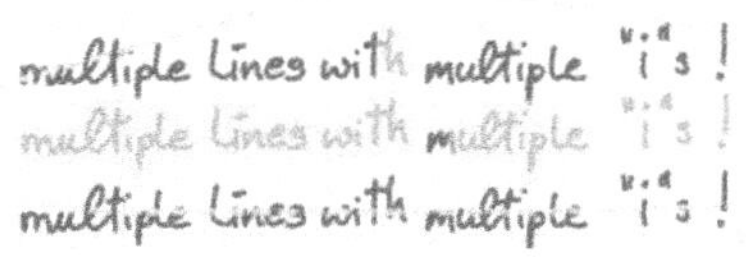

Figure 5: Adding and removing objects can be achieved with a single tap.

If a user clicks on overlapping targets, only the topmost object is selected or deselected. This allows users to achieve very precise modifications and quickly add or remove only a single item to/from the current group.

Dragging

Tapping is well suited for single targets [15]. However, it is cumbersome for large groups. Hence, a dragging operation can also be used to modify the current selection. We explored different methods how to add and remove items. Initially both operations could be performed in a single drag operation. Each items status was simply toggled upon hit. Already selected items were deselected and vice versa. However, early user tests quickly showed that this required a very precise steering during the whole operation and often resulted in unwanted *select* or *deselect* operations. For the *Harpoon* tool, the type of selection operation is determined upon touching the first item. We call the implicit mode-change *"first hit"*.

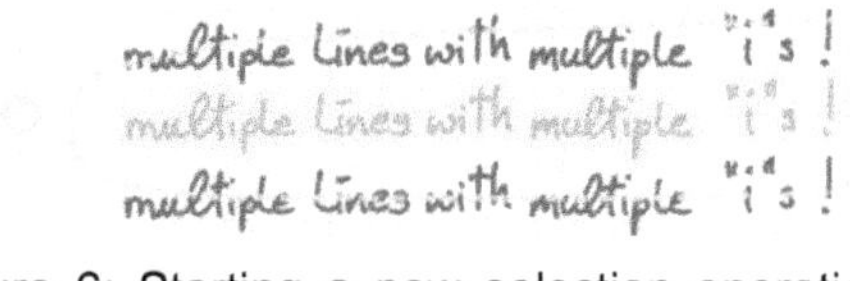

Figure 6: Starting a new selection operation does not reset the previous selection.

Figure 6 shows an existing selection as well as the start of a new selection. At this point the type of operation is not yet determined, the selection path, the spot and the convex hull are rendered in the default color (*yellow*). If at this point the pen would be lifted, the current selection will remain unchanged. The mode-change happens as soon as an item is hit (cf. Figure 7). If the *first hit* item was already part of the selection, the *Harpoon* selection tool enters the *deselect*-mode. A small "-"-icon appears above the cursor and the tools visuals change their color to provide additional feedback, cf. Figure 7 (*top*).

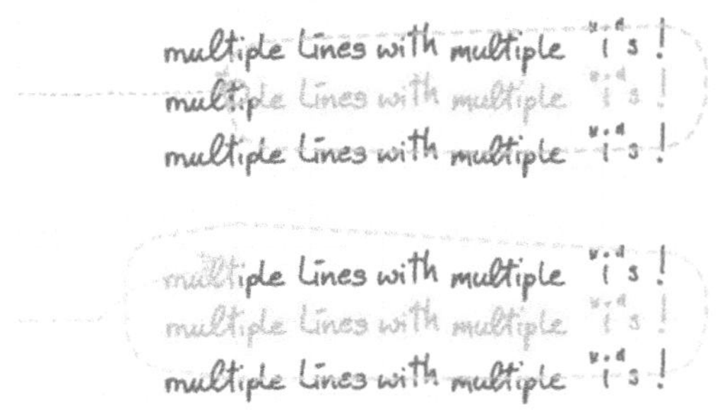

Figure 7: Larger modifications can be achieved through dragging. The first hit object determines selection mode.

Any hit item that was already part of the selection is now removed from it. Objects that are not part of the current selection remain unaffected and cannot be added accidently. If instead the first hit item is not part of the current selection, *select*-mode is activated, see Figure 7 (*bottom*). In this mode, all elements that are already selected remain unaffected and cannot accidently be removed.

After lifting the pen, the *Harpoon* tool automatically switches back to default mode. For each new operation the mode is again decided upon "first hit". This way, it is possible to quickly achieve complex selections by chaining together several separate *select* and *deselect* operations.

Overlapping selection targets

Lasso selections often require a certain percentage of the target (e.g. 50%) to be contained within the *Lasso*-region. This can result in problems when users are trying to select overlapping targets. In contrast to *Lasso* selections it is easy to select several overlapping selection targets with the *Harpoon* selection tool. Any target has to be hit only once with the selection spot. This results in a less constrained and a less complex selection path. In Figure 8 only a single vertical stroke is required to select all three overlapping targets. If errors are made, the previously described options to quickly modify existing selections further improve selection of overlapping strokes.

Figure 8: Multiple overlapping strokes (red) can be selected efficiently without selecting any underlying strokes (blue).

EXPERIMENT

To validate our design we conducted a user study comparing our design to other selection techniques. The techniques are described below. Visual feedback on which items were selected was the same for all described techniques.

Selection Techniques

Four different techniques were tested to compare the performance of our proposed selection technique: *Tapping*, *Lassoing*, *Crossing*, and *Harpooning*.

Tapping

Targets are selected by tapping on individual targets. Selected targets can be deselected with a second click. Clicking on the canvas resets the current selection.

Lassoing

For the *Lasso* tool, targets had to be contained 50% within the *Lasso* region to be selected. To allow users to correct selection errors, new *Lasso*-selections did not reset the current selection, but modify the existing selection by toggling the selection state of each object in the new *Lasso* selection. Items that were not part of the existing selection were added to the selection and vice versa. As with all other techniques a single click on the canvas could be used to reset the current selection.

Crossing

Targets are selected by crossing them with the tip of the pen. Several targets can be selected in a single dragging operation. In contrast to the harpoon selection technique for this technique hit testing was only performed for a single point instead of a larger cursor area. Selections could be modified the same way as described for the *Harpoon* tool. Again a single click on the canvas reset the current selection.

Harpooning

The *Harpoon* tool in the experiment worked as described in the previous section. Targets are selected by touching (crossing) them with the spot during a dragging operation. Cursor size was defined by movement-speed and ranged from 1 pixel to 50 pixels in diameter.

HYPOTHESIS

Before conducting the experiment the following experimental hypotheses were developed:

- *Tapping* will be the slowest technique overall.
- *Harpooning* will be the fastest technique overall.
- *Harpooning* will be best for objects within dense surroundings.
- *Lassoing* will be best for objects within sparse surroundings.
- *Crossing* will be best for single objects.

The corresponding null hypotheses to be tested were that none of the differences predicted in the experimental hypotheses would in fact exist.

EXPERIMENT METHOD

Participants

12 participants (2 females) were recruited from the local university as well as from a local company. Participants' age ranged from 20 to 31 years. All had experience with image editing software; 7 had used interactive whiteboards before. All participants (one left-handed) controlled the stylus with their dominant hand.

Apparatus

The experiment was conducted in a quiet room equipped with an 80" Polyvision Eno 2610 interactive whiteboard. A Toshiba ex20 short throw projector with a resolution of 1024×768 was used for projection. The board was calibrated at the beginning of user testing.

Task

Our experiment task is based on the experiment of Grossman et al. [8]. Our task environment consists of a red start-button, a 6×6 grid of targets, as well as a green finish button. Similar to [8], only the 16 internal targets are candidates for the selection. The border targets are present to ensure the same distance constraints for all 16 internal targets. At the beginning of each trial, all targets are inactive (*black*). The finish button is deactivated and the start button is activated. Each trial begins by pressing the red start button, which turns a set of targets red. Participants now have to select all red targets as quickly as possible using the currently active selection technique.

Figure 9: The experimental environment after successfully selecting all targets.

A semitransparent yellow overlay is used to highlight all selected targets. Once all active targets have been selected successfully, the finish button turns green. This happens only after the selection operation is finished and the pen is lifted from the board. If the wrong targets had been selected, the finish button remains inactive. Participants have to correct their selection before being able to press the finish button. Sets of targets varied in terms of *complexity, difficulty,* and *distance.* Three different levels of complexity, two difficulty levels, and two distances were tested.

Figure 10 shows the different target sets for a distance of 27-pixel. The distance is measured between the centers of the crosses. The complexity levels were *Single*, *Line,* and *Corner*. In the first difficulty setting, crosses were used as targets. Both target's width and height were 25 pixels, which results in a target-size of 40mm on the whiteboard. In the second difficulty setting, four circles with five pixels (8mm) diameter each where placed around the center of the cross. All circles had to be selected. The second difficulty setting was added to simulate selection of ungrouped items like unparsed, handwritten text, which often consists of multiple separate strokes. Participants were told to complete each trial as fast as possible. Trial times were measured between pressing the start and the end button.

Figure 10: In the experiment, we implemented three different complexity levels. All red-colored items had to be selected. In the scenarios at the bottom, participants also had to select the four dots.

All trials could only be completed if all active targets were selected. Consequently trial times included the time necessary to correct errors. This approach to collect quantitative data was taken as the design of the *Harpoon* tool offers many different strategies (sequences of select and deselect operations) to get a correct selection. As a result it is impossible to quantitatively count errors. Instead, we used the qualitative measurements as an indicator for how often the different techniques produced unwanted or unexpected selection results that required the participant to modify the selection.

Experimental Design

A repeated measures within-subject design was used. Technique (*Tapping, Lassoing, Crossing, Harpooning*), Complexity (*Single, Line, Corner),* Difficulty (*cross without dots, cross with dots*), and Distance (*27px, 50px)* were used as independent variables. Presentation order for the techniques was counterbalanced using a 4×4 Latin Square. Before starting the actual trials for each technique the technique was explained to the participants. They were then allowed to familiarize themselves with each technique for an unlimited training period. For each technique, a total of 36 trials had to be completed. Summarizing, each participant completed a total of 144 trials (4 techniques × 2 distances × 3 complexities × 2 difficulties × 3 trials).

In addition, qualitative feedback was collected after each technique using a questionnaire. Participants had to rate each technique in regards to *ease of learning, speed, error rate, error correction* and *overall usability* on a 7-point Likert scale. After completing the whole test, participants were also asked to choose the best and worst techniques for each category. The whole test including training sessions and questionnaires lasted for approximately 30 minutes per person.

QUANTITATIVE RESULTS

Due to our task design, all trials could be used for evaluation. For all tests an alpha level of 0.05 was used. The Greenhouse-Geisser correction was used if the assumption of sphericity was violated. A repeated measures analysis of variance showed main effects for *Technique* ($F_{3,44}$ = 35.046, $p < .0001$), *Distance* ($F_{1,22}$ = 22.355, $p < .001$), *Difficulty* ($F_{1,22}$ = 548.549, $p < .0001$), *Complexity* ($F_{2,33}$ = 384.323, $p < .0001$), and *Trials* ($F_{2,33}$ = 22.132, $p < .0001$)

Hypothesis

Post-hoc analyses on the main effects were conducted in order to confirm/reject the formulated hypotheses. These consisted of paired-samples *t*-tests with family wise error rate controlled across the test using Holm's sequential Bonferroni approach. For all bar charts, the error bars indicate the range of two standard errors of the mean (above and below the mean).

Hypothesis 1: Tapping will be the slowest technique overall

Post-hoc analysis showed that Tapping was significantly slower than all other techniques ($p < .0001$). Hence the first Hypothesis can be confirmed. Tapping was also voted the slowest technique by all 12 participants. Figure 11 shows the overall mean selection times by technique. Overall selection times for all techniques were 5.40s (*SD* = 0.81) for *Tapping*, 4.10s (*SD* = 0.71) for *Lassoing*, 3.80s (*SD* = 0.63) for *Crossing* and 3.48s (*SD* = 0.44) for *Harpooning*. On average targets took 1.6s longer to select all targets using *Tapping*.

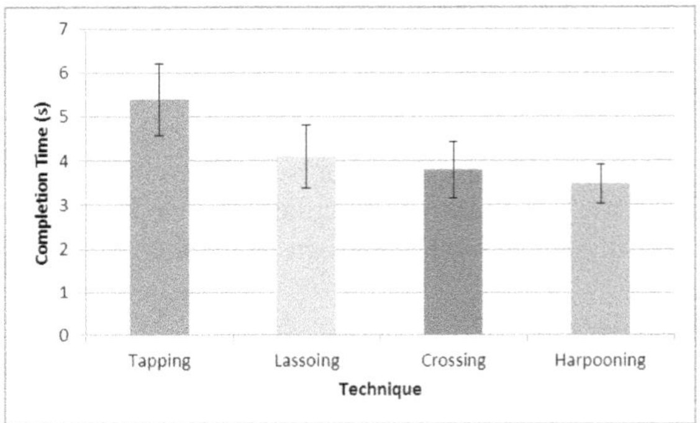

Figure 11: Overall completion times by technique.

Hypothesis 2: Harpooning will be the fastest technique overall

Overall *Harpooning* was significantly faster than *Tapping* and *Lassoing* ($p < .01$). *Harpooning* in our experiment also was on average 0.32s faster than *Crossing*, however pairwise comparison showed no statistical significance (p = .121). Hence the hypothesis has to be rejected.

Hypothesis 3: Harpooning will be best for objects within dense surroundings

Harpooning did not perform best for selections within dense surroundings, the hypothesis has to be rejected. Average completion times were 5.04s (*SD* = 0.72) for *Tapping*, 5.01s (*SD* = 1.02) for *Lassoing*, 3.89s (*SD* = 0.55) for *Crossing,* and 4.06s (*SD* = 0.65) for *Harpooning*.

Crossing performed significantly better than *Tapping* and *Lassoing* ($p < .01$), *Harpooning* performed significantly better than *Tapping* ($p < .01$). There was no significant difference in performance between *Crossing* and *Harpooning*. Figure 12 shows completion times for different distances.

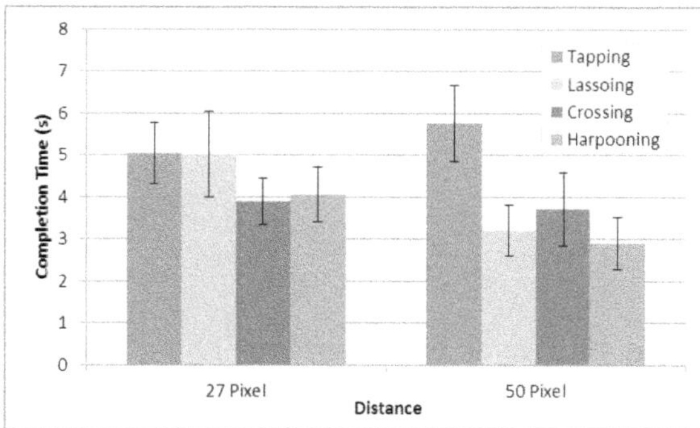

Figure 12: Completion times by technique and distance.

Hypothesis 4: Lassoing will be best for objects within sparse surroundings

Lassoing resulted only in the second fastest completion time. Hence the hypothesis has to be rejected. Instead *Harpooning* was significantly faster than all other techniques ($p < .01$) for the 50 pixel distance trials. Completion times were 5.76s ($SD = 0.91$) for *Tapping*, 3.20s ($SD = 0.61$) for *Lassoing*, 3.70s ($SD = 0.86$) for *Crossing,* and 2.90s ($SD = 0.62$) for *Harpooning*.

Hypothesis 5: Crossing will be best for single objects

Crossing was fastest for single objects however this did not reach significance. Completion times for single objects were 1.86s ($SD = 0.27$) for *Tapping*, 2.55s ($SD = 0.47$) for *Lassoing*, 1.80s ($SD = 0.37$) for *Crossing,* and 1.81s ($SD = 0.22$) for *Harpooning*, cf., Figure 13.

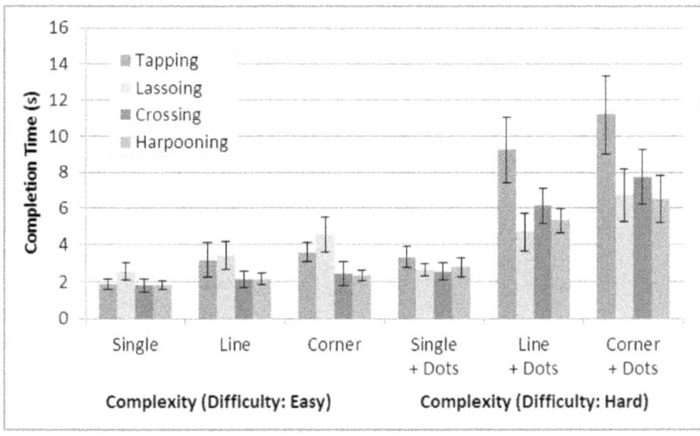

Figure 13: Completion times for both difficulty settings by technique and complexity

Lassoing was significantly slower than all other techniques ($p < .001$) for selecting single objects. No other significant differences were found. Figure 13 shows completion times by technique and complexity separated by difficulty setting.

Discussion

Looking at the quantitative data, the *Harpoon* selection tool shows very promising results with a significant overall speed improvement over the more traditional methods of *Tapping* and *Lassoing*. Instead of excelling at one specific category, *Harpooning* has proven to result in consistently fast completion times for very diverse selection tasks. Even in cases where other techniques might have performed better, the *Harpoon* tool never was significantly slower. This characteristic is especially beneficial for environments, where tool changes are time-consuming (such as interactive whiteboards).

Performance gains might be even larger in real life situations, as the following two examples will show. In a first pilot test using the same minimal distance of 25 pixels as in [8] (compared to 27 pixels used in the actual experiment), trials took very long to complete for *Lassoing*. Participants got really frustrated, even claiming to quit the test if it would stay this difficult. No such problems were noticed with the other techniques. While keeping the 25-pixel scenario might have resulted in much greater completion time differences we did not want to risk annoying participants and as a result distorting trial results. For the same reason, trials using overlapping targets where omitted. Consequently, in the final study design a two-pixel gap remained between the targets in the 27-pixel distance trials. However, in everyday use overlapping items are very well possible, which would suggest an even greater benefit for alternative tools like the *Harpoon* tool over the lasso tool. We are especially pleased that *Harpooning* even offers a significant speed improvement over *Lassoing* in the 50-pixel scenarios. These results are achieved even with qualitative results indicating that the *Harpoon* tool is the most difficult to learn. We believe that as participants become more familiar with the speed-dependent spot size, selection times in sparse environments can be reduced even further.

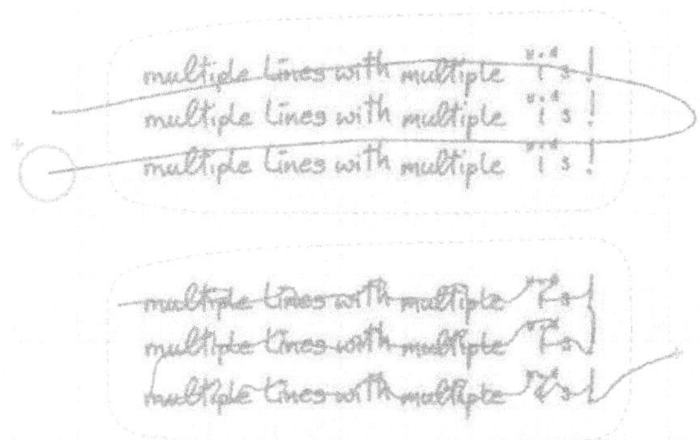

Figure 14: *Harpooning* (*top*) takes considerable less time and effort than *Crossing* (*bottom*). For better visibility the selection path is displayed in red.

Surprisingly, the overall completion time results show only a small difference between *Harpooning* and *Crossing*. We strongly believe that this difference will get larger in real world use-cases especially for sparse ink strokes. Figure 12 shows that already in the 50-pixel scenarios *Harpooning* offers a significant performance improvement over *Crossing*. With larger numbers of (potentially smaller) targets, this gap would get even larger.

The three handwritten phrases "*multiple lines with multiple "i" s!*" as seen in Figure 14 already consist of 3×36 = 108 separate strokes, many of which have only half the size of the dots used in the study. Also the layout of the individual objects is not fixed like in the study, requiring users to constantly plan their selection path and check not to forget any objects. *Crossing* each individual object consequently results in a very complex steering task that requires constant user attention. (cf., Figure 14 *bottom*). In contrast one swift movement with the *Harpoon* tool selects all objects (cf., Figure 14 *top*). Also *Tapping* all 108 separate strokes would result in a much more tedious and time consuming experiment. Then again looking at a different selection scenario, selecting only a single, overlapping stroke could be virtually impossible using the *Lasso*-tool.

Consequently using similar selection targets as depicted in Figure 14 in the study would have biased the study towards *Harpooning* and would also most likely required exclusion of *Lassoing* and *Tapping*. While both *Tapping* and *Lassoing* are well studied techniques they still represent the standard selection tool in many applications to date and hence were included as base-line techniques. However based on the insights of this study a follow up experiment comparing *Crossing* and *Harpooning* using free from ink selection targets might help show the benefits of *Harpooning* even more clearly. Such a comparison as well as follow up studies concerning learning- or fatigue effects, error rates and error correction is seen as future work.

Summarizing we believe that based on the insights gained through the study as well as additional user observations as described earlier, *Harpooning* successfully combines properties that allow users to quickly select ungrouped objects in various different situations. While further testing will show how the tool will perform in real-world scenarios, first indicators already look very promising.

QUALITATIVE RESULTS

After each set of trials participants had to rate each technique concerning *ease of learning, speed, error rate,* and *error correction.* Additionally participants were asked to rate overall usability. Each questions was answered using a Likert scale from 1 to 7 (1 = very good and 7 = not very good). The results for the first four categories are summarized in Figure 15. Overall results are shown in Figure 16.

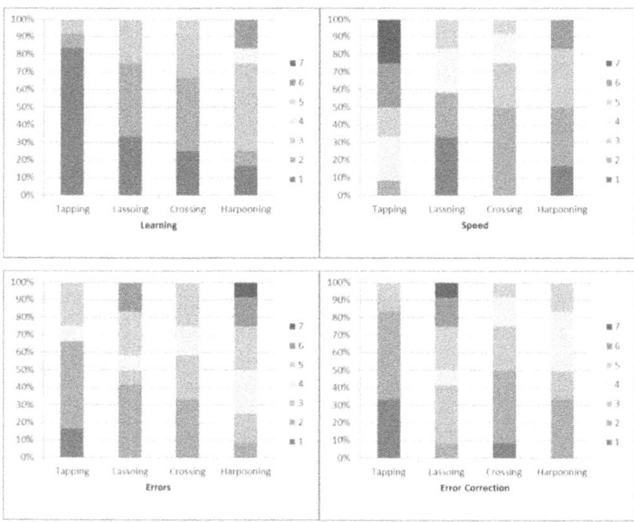

Figure 15: Ratings on *ease of learning, speed, error rate,* and *error correction* based on a 7-point Likert scale (1 = very good).

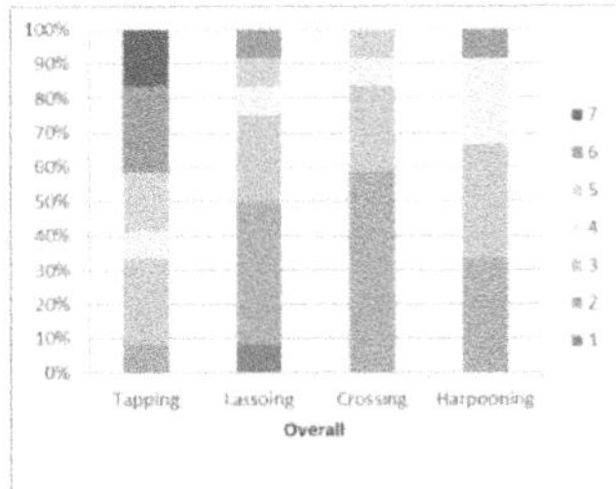

Figure 16: Overall usability ratings of the different techniques (1 = very good).

After completing all trials, participants were also asked to select their favorite and least favorite techniques for each of the aforementioned categories. These results are presented in Figure 17. The qualitative data suggests that *speed* was most influential factor on the participants' *overall* rating. Looking at the raw data shows that for 10 out of 12 participants the fastest technique was also their most favorite overall. For the slowest technique, we get similar results. 8 out of 12 participants selected the same technique as the slowest technique as well as least favorite overall. This can also be seen in Figure 17 (relevant bars are highlighted). At first glance other factors like ease of learning, error rate, or error correction seem to play only a secondary role. The majority of participants said that *Tapping* performed best on ease of learning, error rate, and error correction. Nevertheless, no participant chose *Tapping* as his/her favorite.

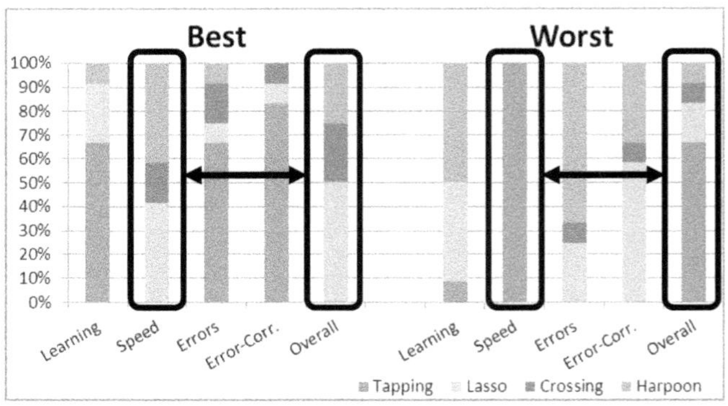

Figure 17: After completing all trials participants were asked to choose the best and worst technique. Overall rating was most influenced by the participants' speed rating.

The quantitative results as well as qualitative speed ratings are in favor of *Harpooning.* Still *Lassoing* was selected as the overall favorite tool by most participants. This is because both error rate and error correction performance indirectly influenced speed ratings and consequently overall ratings. This can be explained with the chosen experimental design: participants could only press the finish button after all targets have been selected correctly: Therefore, both errors and the ability to quickly correct them influenced the overall time. Consequently, techniques resulting in fewer errors required less additional time to complete the trial. Looking again at the raw data, we noticed that participants who rated a technique's error rate poorly also gave poor speed ratings. By reducing the number of errors, not only the measured completion time would be reduced, but most likely also subjective speed assessments and overall usability. The qualitative results show that *Harpooning* resulted in a higher error rate. We have identified several problems that contributed to this high error-rate:

- The current spot-size for the *Harpoon* selection was very hard to see, especially for faster movement. As a result choosing the correct movement speed to achieve an optimal spot size was very difficult.
- It was impossible to notice exactly, which areas have already been visited. Thus, it was hard to quickly spot objects that have been missed.
- Smoothing the input values caused spot size to grow too slowly.

Based on these results, we made several changes to the *Harpoon* selection tool as described in the next session.

IMPROVEMENTS

Several participants commented that the current feedback of the *Harpoon* tool made it very difficult to see which areas have been selected. This made it more difficult to quickly see whether any objects had been missed. As a result, we changed the feedback of the selection path from a dotted line to a semitransparent stroke with its thickness defined by the spot diameter, cf., Figure 19.

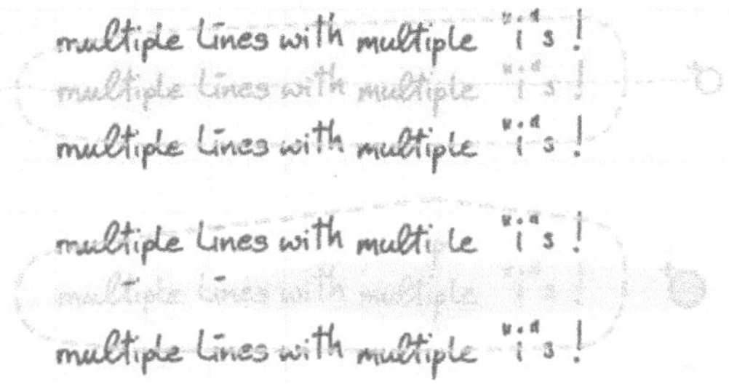

Figure 18: Instead of a dotted line (*top*), a semi-transparent stroke with varying thickness is drawn (*bottom*). This makes it a lot easier to notice which areas have been visited and helps spotting objects that might have been missed.

In addition, the spot is now filled to improve visibility during fast movement. During the selection operation, all selected objects turn even more transparent to highlight missed objects, cf. Figure 18 (*bottom*).

In the *deselect*-mode, selected items turn opaque to stand out more against the background (see Figure 19). We also render a semitransparent white area between the current selection and the background to further improve this contrast.

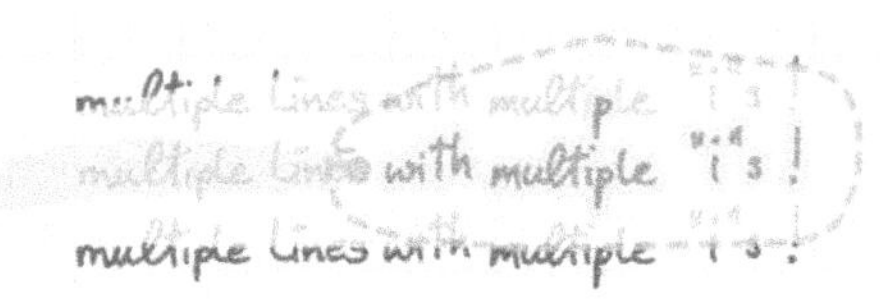

Figure 19: When deselect-mode is engaged, all selected items turn completely opaque to stand out more against the background.

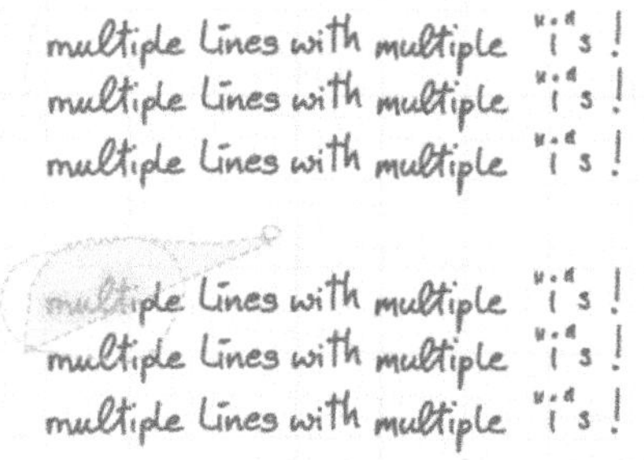

Figure 20: If a user starts circling around objects, the tool automatically switches to the Lasso mode. If a stroke is crossed directly, the Harpoon mode is engaged.

First informal user tests show that these improvements help users finding missed objects more quickly. The changes also help to find overlapped strokes.

In certain cases, participants would lasso objects even in a different selection technique (e.g. *Harpooning*). We automatically detect this and switch mode accordingly. When a new selection is started, the *Harpoon* selection tool also simultaneously performs *Lasso* hit-tests during movement. If users are starting to circle an object without directly crossing it, the harpoon tool automatically switches to *Lasso* mode as soon as the first object is contained (e.g. 50%). However, if the first stroke is hit directly with the spot, *Lasso* hit-testing is disabled and the *Harpoon* tool acts as described before (see Figure 20).

We also noticed that smoothing the input values sometimes caused the spot size to grow too slowly. As a result, objects often were missed at the beginning of a selection operation. Therefore, we perform a second row of hit-tests for the first input points with the current spot diameter after receiving 10 input points. Figure 21 shows a debugging view of this approach. This allows us to compensate for this initial delay without increasing the update rate and introducing the risk of erratic spot-size changes.

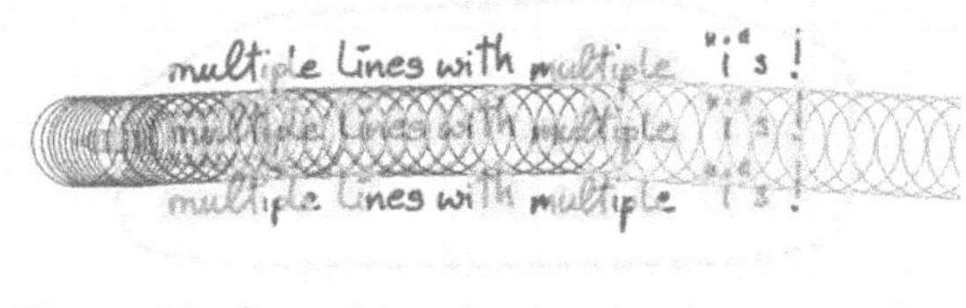

Figure 21: Smoothing the input values sometimes causes the spot size to grow too slowly (orange circles). This can be corrected after a sufficient number of values have been received (blue circles).

CONCLUSION & FUTURE WORK

In this paper, we have presented a new kind of selection technique, called *Harpooning*. *Harpooning* is designed especially for interactive whiteboard surfaces and is based on crossing objects using a speed dependent area cursor. A first user test showed that *Harpooning* resulted in significantly reduced selection times compared to *Tapping* and *Lassoing*. User-feedback showed that *Harpooning* results in high error rates that influence overall usability of the tool. During the study, we have discovered several error sources and we have presented solutions for each problem. We have started prolonged tests outside the lab. Gathered feedback will be collected to further improve of the tool.

For future work, we are also interested in how the tool can integrate with systems that facilitates fast selection of grouped objects [8]. Such a combination would enable users to select grouped objects quickly without sacrificing easy access to fine grain control of selection.

ACKNOWLEDGMENTS

This project is part of the Research Studio Austria NiCE, funded by the FFG, 818621. We would like to thank Florian Perteneder, Christian Rendl and Thomas Seifried for their help with the project. We also would like to thank our reviewers for their useful comments.

REFERENCES

1. Accot, J. and Zhai, S. 1997. Beyond Fitts' law: models for trajectory-based HCI tasks. In CHI '97, Steven Pemberton (Ed.). ACM, New York, NY, USA, 295-302.
2. Accot, J. and Zhai, S. 2002. More than dotting the i's - foundations for crossing-based interfaces. In CHI '02. ACM, New York, NY, USA, 73-80.
3. Apitz, G., Guimbretière, F. and Zhai, S. 2008. Foundations for designing and evaluating user interfaces based on the crossing paradigm. ACM Trans. Comput.-Hum. Interact. 17, 2, Article 9 (May 2008), 42 pages.
4. Brewster, S.A. 1998. Using Earcons to Improve the Usability of a Graphics Package. In HCI '98, Hilary Johnson, Laurence Nigay, and Chris Roast (Eds.). Springer-Verlag, London, UK, 287-302.
5. Buxton, W., Fiume, E., Hill, R., Lee, A. and Woo, C. 1983. Continuous Hand-Gesture Driven Input. Graphic Interface. 191-195.
6. Chapuis, O., Labrune, JB. and Pietriga E. 2009. DynaSpot: speed-dependent area cursor. In CHI '09. ACM, New York, NY, USA, 1391-1400.
7. Fitzmaurice, G., Khan, A., Piek R., Buxton, W. and Kurtenbach, G. 2003. Tracking menus. In UIST '03. ACM, New York, NY, USA, 71-79.
8. Grossman, T., Baudisch, P., and Hinckley, K. 2009. Handle Flags: efficient and flexible selections for inking applications. In GI '09. Canada, 167-174.
9. Guimbretière, F., Stone, M., and Winograd, T. 2001. Fluid interaction with high-resolution wall-size displays. In UIST '01. ACM, New York, NY, USA, 21-30.
10. Haller, M., Leitner, J., Seifried, T., Wallace, J. R., Scott, S. D., Richter, C., Brandl, P., Gokcezade, A., Hunter, S., 2010. The NiCE Discussion Room: Integrating Paper and Digital Media to Support Co-Located Group Meetings. In CHI '10, ACM, New York, NY, USA, 609-618.
11. Hinckley, K., Baudisch, P., Ramos, G., and Guimbretiere, F. 2005. Design and analysis of delimiters for selection-action pen gesture phrases in scriboli. In CHI '05. ACM, New York, NY, USA, 451-460.
12. Kabbash, P. and Buxton, W. 1995. The "prince" technique: Fitts' law and selection using area cursors. In CHI '95, ACM Press/Addison-Wesley Publishing Co., New York, NY, USA, 273-279.
13. Kurtenbach, G. and Buxton, W. 1991. Issues in combining marking and direct manipulation techniques. In UIST '91. ACM, New York, NY, USA, 137-144.
14. Lank, E. and Saund, E. 2005. Sloppy Selection: Providing an Accurate Interpretation of Imprecise Stylus Selection Gestures. Computers and Graphics. 29(4): 490-500.
15. Mizobuchi, S. and Yasumura, M. 2004. Tapping vs. circling selections on pen-based devices: evidence for different performance-shaping factors. In CHI '04. ACM, New York, NY, USA, 607-614.
16. Moran, T.P., Chiu, P. and Melle, W. 1997. Pen-based interaction techniques for organizing material on an electronic whiteboard. In UIST '97. ACM, New York, NY, USA, 45-54.
17. Plamondon, R. and Srihari, S. 2000. On-line and Offline Handwriting Recognition: A Comprehensive Survey. IEEE Pattern Analysis. 22(1), 63-84.
18. Rekimoto, J. 1997. Pick-and-drop: a direct manipulation technique for multiple computer environments. In UIST '97. ACM, New York, NY, USA, 31-39.
19. Ren, X., and Moriya, S. 2000. Improving selection performance on pen-based systems: a study of pen-based interaction for selection tasks. ACM Trans. Comput.-Hum. Interact. 7, 3 ,384-416.
20. Saund, E. and Lank, E. 2003. Stylus input and editing without prior selection of mode. In UIST '03. ACM, New York, NY, USA, 213-216.
21. Saund, E., Mahoney, J., Fleet, D., Larner, D. and Lank, E. 2002. Perceptual Organization as a Foundation for Intelligent Sketch Editing. AAAI Symposium on Sketch Understanding. 118-125.
22. Yin, J. and Ren, X. 2007. Investigation to line-based techniques for multi-target selection. In INTERACT'07, Springer-Verlag, Berlin, Heidelberg, 507-510.

No more Bricolage! Methods and Tools to Characterize, Replicate and Compare Pointing Transfer Functions

Géry Casiez[1,2,3] *and Nicolas Roussel*[2]
[1]LIFL, [2]INRIA Lille & [3]University of Lille
Villeneuve d'Ascq, France
gery.casiez@lifl.fr, nicolas.roussel@inria.fr

ABSTRACT
Transfer functions are the only pointing facilitation technique actually used in modern graphical interfaces involving the indirect control of an on-screen cursor. But despite their general use, very little is known about them. We present EchoMouse, a device we created to characterize the transfer functions of any system, and libpointing, a toolkit that we developed to replicate and compare the ones used by Windows, OS X and Xorg. We describe these functions and report on an experiment that compared the default one of the three systems. Our results show that these default functions improve performance up to 24% compared to a unitless constant CD gain. We also found significant differences between them, with the one from OS X improving performance for small target widths but reducing its performance up to 9% for larger ones compared to Windows and Xorg. These results notably suggest replacing the constant CD gain function commonly used by HCI researchers by the default function of the considered systems.

ACM Classification: H.5.2 [Information interfaces and presentation]: User interfaces - Graphical user interfaces.

General terms: Documentation, Experimentation, Human Factors, Measurement, Performance, Standardization

Keywords: Pointing, control-display gain functions, CD gain, pointer acceleration, transfer functions, toolkit

INTRODUCTION
Indirect control of an on-screen cursor with a separate device has been the prevalent way of pointing in graphical interfaces for many years. The mouse is undoubtedly the most popular pointing device in this context. As explained by Moggridge [20], it was not chosen simply because Engelbart invented it, but because it turned out to be the device that performed best for pointing and clicking on a display, outperforming everything else that was tried in early tests with users. More than forty years later, the mouse still provides a good match between human performance and the demands of desktop graphical interfaces [13], the touchpad offering a similar match on laptop configurations. Despite the current trend for tactile screens, indirect pointing will thus probably remain the prevalent paradigm for some time.

In indirect pointing configurations, movements in the control space can be mapped to different ones in the display space. We use the term *transfer function* to refer to the relationship between movements in the two spaces. It is very important to note that in order for this relationship to be meaningful, it has to be hardware-independent. All movements must thus be described using standard length and time units (e.g. meters) and not device-specific ones (e.g. mickeys and pixels). In the case of simple linear relations, the term *CD gain*[1] is commonly used to refer to the scale factor between the two spaces, e.g. $CDgain = V_{\text{display}}/V_{\text{control}}$ [8]. To be meaningful, this coefficient must be unitless, which will only be the case if the two factors involved in its computation are expressed using the same length and time units. The CD gain can be constant or dynamically adjusted over time based on control space kinetics or extrinsic information, for example. Whether static or dynamic, CD gain settings involve a tradeoff between gross and fine positioning [16]. High gains reduce the time it takes to approach a distant target but make it hard to precisely position the cursor on it. Conversely, low gains support precise positioning but increase the time to cover large distances.

It is generally assumed that in accordance with Meyer et al.'s *optimized initial impulse* model [19], the so-called "pointer acceleration" mechanisms implemented in modern desktops increase the CD gain as the user's hand or finger velocity increases. The transfer functions of Microsoft Windows, Apple OS X and Xorg (the X.Org Foundation server) are actually the only pointing facilitation mechanisms available to all users of these systems. But despite their general use, very little is known about them. Current knowledge on velocity-based transfer functions relies on evaluations of basic ones adapting the CD gain in discrete or continuous ways using low-order polynomials, e.g. [11, 14, 21]. The internal details and design rationales of the functions that we all use are mostly unknown. And with the notable exception of Casiez et al.'s work on Windows XP and Vista functions [8], their impact has never been studied.

This paper reports on efforts we made with the long-term goals of advancing this state of knowledge and bringing it

[1]The term *CD ratio* is also used and corresponds to the inverse of the gain.

in line with current practices. The paper is organized as follows. We first briefly review the related work, explaining how pointing facilitation research deals with transfer functions and what is known about them. We then explain what is actually involved from a system perspective when pointing on a desktop. We present `EchoMouse`, an HID device we created to characterize the transfer functions of any system, and `libpointing`, a toolkit that we developed to replicate and compare the ones used by Windows, OS X and Xorg[2]. We describe these functions and report on an experiment that compared the default one of the three systems. We conclude with a discussion and implications for future work.

RELATED WORK

Pointing transfer functions can be considered as low-level and general-purpose mechanisms for pointing facilitation. Before explaining what is known about them, it is interesting to look at how research on other pointing facilitation techniques takes them into consideration.

Transfer functions in other pointing facilitation research

As we explained, it is usually assumed that desktop systems dynamically adjust the CD gain based on movement speed. This behavior might well interfere with other pointing facilitation mechanisms, especially those that manipulate the CD gain, e.g. [23, 10, 5, 22]. As a consequence, one would expect researchers working on pointing facilitation to try to disable the system's transfer function, to precisely characterize it, or to systematically investigate its effect.

Transfer functions are usually treated as control variables, meaning they might influence a dependent variable but are not under investigation and are thus held constant from one test condition to another. One would expect a clear description of these control variables to ease the replication of a technique or experiment with different hardware configurations or operating systems, in case the control variable would in fact be a confounding one. However a review of the recent literature on pointing facilitation shows that the level of details provided is often incomplete or unclear.

Numerous authors report using a constant CD gain or ratio as a baseline condition or as a basis for their technique but fail to describe it with sufficient details. In [10], for example, Cockburn & Firth explain that the CD gain "*was set to a constant ratio of approximately 1:1.6*" in experiments running on a Linux system, but do not explain why they chose this particular value nor how they enforced it. The predictive pointing technique of the Delphian Desktop was evaluated by Asano et al. on Windows XP with a CD ratio "*set to a constant value of 0.5*" [2]. Again, the paper does not explain how this ratio was enforced. For the Bubble Cursor on the same system, Grossman & Balakrishnan say that "*mouse acceleration was set to 0, with a control-display ratio of 1/2*" [12]. The exact meaning of "*set to 0*" is unclear considering the Windows XP configuration interface (Figure 4), and we will see that a unitless constant ratio of 0.5 is not achievable through it (Figure 6). In their study of sticky targets, Mandryk & Gutwin said "*Windows pointer acceleration was turned off, and the baseline mouse gain was set to the midpoint*" [18]. The exact definition of this baseline is unknown which is unfortunate since the authors scaled it by 11 values between 0.05 and 1.0, CD gain being one of the experiment factors. In their own study of sticky icons, Worden et al. say that "*normal mouse gain was set at a constant 1 mickey to 3 pixels ratio for all conditions*" [23]. But as the mouse and display resolutions are not specified, this gain can not be expressed in a unitless hardware-independent way, which makes their results difficult to compare with those from other studies.

Enforcing a hardware-independent transfer function, even a constant gain, is actually quite difficult with current systems. Wobbrock et al. had to go to great lengths to disable Windows Vista's pointer acceleration and dynamically control the CD gain for their Angle Mouse study, for example. They acknowledge that "*although some on-line documentation discusses pointer ballistics in Windows, it does not contain sufficient information to establish the slider-to-gain mapping.*" [22]. A good way of enforcing a transfer function is to use a device not attached to the system cursor and an API that provides access to its raw data. As an example, Blanch et al. used the absolute coordinates of a puck on a Wacom tablet as input for their Semantic Pointing technique [5].

An alternative to enforcing a particular baseline is to use the default transfer function of the system. For the Ninja Cursors, Kobayashi & Igarashi say "*the mouse speed and acceleration rate were set to the Windows XP default values (middle speed, no acceleration)*" [15]. For DynaSpot, Chapuis et al. used "*the default X Window acceleration function*" [9]. As it is unclear whether these functions take into account specific characteristics of the devices, extensive details should be provided about them including their resolution (per length unit) and frequency. A problem with this approach is that it will be possible to replicate or reproduce the experiment only as long as the original system can be used.

In some cases, there is simply no way of knowing which transfer function was used. In [17], for example, MacKenzie & Isokoski only report using "*an optical USB Microsoft IntelliMouse with four buttons and a scroll wheel*" and an "*experimental software written in Java*". Mouse data was presumably provided to the Java application by the underlying operating system through its operative transfer function, but none of them is explicitly mentioned in the paper.

What is known about pointing transfer functions

An extensive review of the literature on transfer functions has been recently conducted by Casiez et al. [8]. Prior to their work, research on the effects of these functions on pointing performance had been largely inconclusive. In all constant CD gain studies, the range of gain evaluated was either small or had quantization problems. And the few dynamic transfer functions evaluated poorly resembled the ones used in modern systems, most of them involving a few discrete steps or simplistic low-level polynomials, e.g. [11, 14, 21].

Casiez et al. [8] showed there exists a wide range of constant CD gains for which performance is constant and provided a way to compute that range knowing the hardware and target widths and distances used in a particular context. They

[2]The source code for `EchoMouse` and `libpointing` is available from `http://libpointing.org/`.

also showed that the acceleration mechanisms of Windows XP resulted in faster pointing than constant gain functions: they found an average 3.3% improvement and up to 5.6% for small targets or long distances. In a different study, Casiez and Vogel showed that the impact of transfer functions on performance can be severe in the case of force input [7].

Windows XP mechanisms were re-implemented for the study described in [8] based on information extracted from the Windows registry and documentation publicly available from Microsoft [1]. However, the cursor controlled by this implementation was not in perfect sync with the system one due to missing details in the documentation. Figure 3 of Casiez et al.'s paper shows a plot of four Windows XP functions based on their custom implementation. It also shows a plot of six OS X functions that were estimated from the analysis of publicly available Apple source code, but not re-implemented.

POINTING: A SYSTEM PERSPECTIVE

Most if not all modern pointing devices conform to the *Human Interface Devices* (HID) class of the USB standard. This class covers a variety of equipments including keyboards, mice, touchpads and joysticks but also telephones, remote controls, barcode readers and voltmeters. HID devices are thus required to provide extensive descriptions of their characteristics to be properly recognized and used. Among other things, a pointing device description specifies for each axis whether transmitted values (called *counts*) are absolute or relative, linear or nonlinear, their byte size, their logical range, the corresponding physical range and the unit system and exponent used. The description also specifies the time interval that should be used when polling for data transfers.

The HID specification defines a simple *boot report format* for mice that allows to use them before the operating system is loaded, for low-level system configuration [3, p. 61]. This format describes movements along two axis with relative, linear, unitless counts encoded with one byte per axis, between -127 and +127. Most mice support this format and for many, it is also the one they use to report to the system once it is loaded. This format is also supported by touchpads, although they could provide an absolute location, so they can be used in place of a mouse even at boot time.

The polling interval is typically set to 8 ms for mice, leading to an update frequency of 125 Hz. For devices that specify their logical and physical range and their unit system and exponent, the resolution can be computed in counts per unit with: $Res = LogRange/(PhysRange * 10^{Exp})$. Unfortunately, many report formats including the boot one specify unitless values with no physical range, which makes this formula inapplicable. For these devices, systems usually assume a resolution of 400 CPI[3].

The fact that systems have no reliable way of knowing a pointing device's resolution is becoming more and more problematic as manufacturers not only propose high-resolution ones but also some where it is adjustable[4]. A higher resolution results in more counts reported for the same distance traveled by the device, by sending bigger values at the same rate or by reporting more often. High-resolution mice indeed use two-bytes values for each axis and can set a polling interval as low as 1 ms. A transfer function not aware of the resolution change or not taking time properly into account will inevitably misinterpret the reported counts and produce undesirable effects, the most common one being considerably amplified movements. This problem is so frequent that a lot of people equate the resolution of the device with the cursor speed, as illustrated by this text displayed in the mouse section of a consumer electronics retailer:

> *"Specified in DPI, the resolution corresponds to the speed of the mouse cursor on your screen. The higher it is, the less you will have to move the mouse for the same on-screen distance, though you will be less accurate."*

Changing the resolution of a pointing device or switching to one with a different resolution should not alter the mapping between movements in the control and display spaces. Changing or reconfiguring the transfer function should be the only way of doing that.

ECHOMOUSE

`EchoMouse` is an electronic device that we designed to measure a system's response to pointing movements received from an HID equipment. Based on a Microchip PIC (18LF14K50) programmed in C using the PICkit 2 development environment, it includes a switch and two LEDs for debugging purposes (Figure 1). Its program uses a mouse firmware provided by Microchip, so it appears as an ordinary HID mouse to the system. It has no motion sensor, though. We instead added a USB endpoint to the firmware to which a program can send an HID report to be echoed by the device on its mouse endpoint. Reports are expected and echoed in HID boot format. They are thus indistinguishable from genuine mouse reports and handled as such by the system.

We have used our `EchoMouse` to look into the transfer functions of Windows, OS X and Xorg with a specific program implementing the following procedure. After placing the

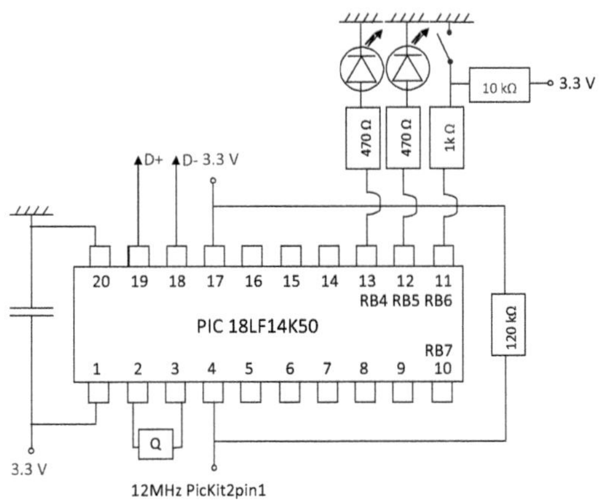

Figure 1: Electronic diagram of EchoMouse. The 3.3V can be easily generated from the 5V of the USB port using a voltage divider or a Zener diode.

[3]We will use CPI (*counts per inch*) and PPI (*pixels per inch*) instead of DPI to make a clear distinction between input and output resolutions.

[4]The resolution of the Logitech Gaming Mouse G500 can be adjusted between 200 and 5700 CPI, for example.

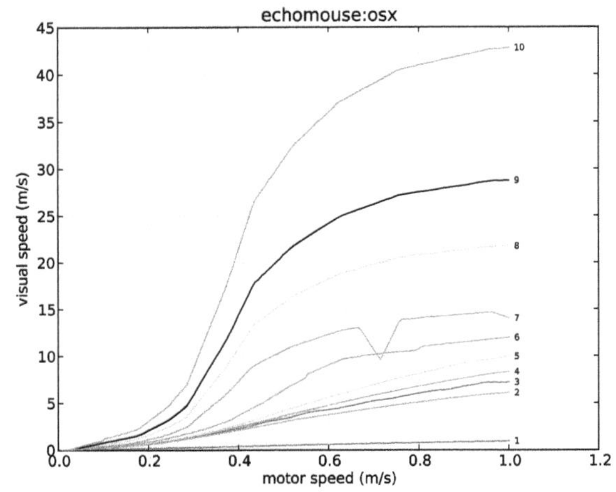

Figure 2: Speed plot for OS X 10.5.6 transfer functions ($n = 10$). Count and pixel values were converted to speed values considering the actual resolution of the monitor used and assuming a 400 CPI resolution for EchoMouse.

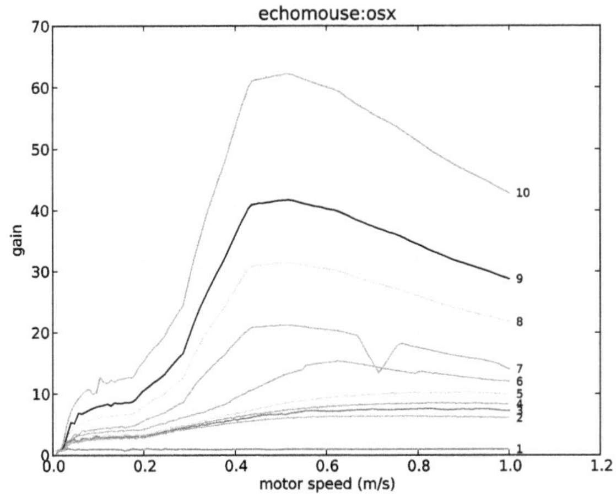

Figure 3: Gain plot of the data shown in Figure 2.

system cursor on the left edge of the screen, the program prepares an HID report describing a $(dx, 0)$ translation. It sends it n times to `EchoMouse` at 125 Hz, waits for a few milliseconds and polls the system for the new cursor position. It then divides the horizontal pixel distance traveled by the cursor by n and stores this number along with dx in a table. This procedure accounts for potential subpixel precision. When repeated for all dx between 1 and 127, it provides an extensional description of the transfer function used by the system. Repeating this for every pointer acceleration setting provides the descriptions of all the functions supported by the system.

Figures 2 and 3 illustrate the 10 transfer functions available in OS X 10.5.6 through the *Tracking* slider of the mouse preference pane shown on Figure 5. Figure 2 shows the speed in display space as a function of speed in control space. One can easily see with this plot that the functions used by OS X are not linear, can not be approximated by a single low-order polynomial and are likely defined in a piecewise fashion. The singularity observed in function 7 is inexplicable, however. And the differences between functions are not easy to perceive, especially at low speeds.

Figure 3 shows the CD gain as a function of speed in control space. This plot makes it easier to compare the functions at low speeds and to relate them to the movements in motor space, a CD gain of 1 corresponding to a horizontal line. The fact that some of the functions strongly decrease after a certain speed is hard to explain. We hypothesize that the functions were designed in a spatial space like the one of Figure 2 and that the designers were actually not aware of this slope change. The singularity observed in function 7 remains inexplicable. At this point, one can only hypothesize that the designers of the functions never tried to plot them.

`EchoMouse` allowed us to investigate the transfer functions used by three systems without spending too much time on their internals. Replicating the device is relatively easy. A similar but pure software approach is also probably achievable by developing fake mouse drivers, e.g. using `uinput` on Linux, or synthesizing low-level mouse motions, e.g. using the `SendInput` function on Windows. The `EchoMouse` approach is however restricted to observation, it can not alter the system functions. One can never be sure that the pseudo motions injected in the system have actually been processed when reading the cursor location. And one can hardly know if and which hardware or movement characteristics are taken into account by the system when applying the functions.

Although valuable for preliminary studies, an outside observation point is not enough to fully understand and compare the transfer functions used by modern desktop interfaces. In addition to `EchoMouse`, we thus developed `libpointing`, a toolkit that allows to replicate and compare them.

LIBPOINTING

The `libpointing` toolkit was designed with several goals in mind. First, we wanted a way of directly accessing HID pointing devices to bypass the system's transfer functions. Second, we wanted to replicate as faithfully as possible the transfer functions of Windows, OS X and Xorg. Third, we wanted the toolkit to run on these platforms to be able to compare our implementations to the genuine ones. And fourth, we wanted to support comparisons between the replicated functions and other ones.

The toolkit consists of about 10,000 lines of C++ developed on OS X 10.6, Ubuntu 10.10 and Windows XP, Vista and 7. Although parts of it use the Qt framework, care has been taken so that its essential components can be used with other GUI frameworks. A key aspect of `libpointing` is that it supports the use of URIs [4] to specify input and display devices as well as transfer functions. Combined with object factories, this makes it possible to (re)define at runtime the instances used by a program and contributes remarkably to the flexibility of the whole. The following summarizes the main other features of the toolkit.

Pointing devices

`PointingDevice` instances are created from URIs using the static `create` method of that class. Other methods allow to check whether a device is active, to obtain its resolution (in counts per inch), update frequency and URI, and to associate a callback to it. The callback will be executed every time the device has a motion or button event to report, passing it a timestamp, dx and dy values (in counts) and an integer coding the buttons states.

The toolkit provides direct access to any connected HID pointing device through platform-specific subclasses and URIs such as `osxhid:/USB/4600000/AppleUSBTCButtons`. The special URI `any:` matches any supported device and will list the available ones in the console if a debug option is passed on the query string. All HID `PointingDevice` objects support hot (re)plugging of the corresponding device. The toolkit also includes two pseudo-device subclasses for debugging and testing that can be instantiated with URIs such as `noisy:?cpi=400&hz=125` and `dummy:?cpi=800&hz=125`. The first one will execute the callback at the specified frequency to report movements synthesized by a 2D Perlin noise generator. The second one will never execute the callback but will return the specified values when queried for its resolution and update frequency.

Display devices

`DisplayDevice` instances are also created from URIs using a static `create` method. Other methods allow to obtain the horizontal and vertical bounds (in pixels), sizes (in inches or millimeters) and resolutions (in pixels per inch) as well as the refresh rate and the URI of a particular display.

URIs such as `osxdisplay:/69676098` and platform-specific subclasses provide access to the displays connected to the computer. A pseudo-device subclass is also available that will simply store the configuration values passed on the query string, e.g. `dummy:?ppi=96&hz=60`, and return them as expected when requested by the above methods.

Transfer functions

`TransferFunction` instances are created using a static `create` method from a URI, a `PointingDevice` and a `DisplayDevice`. Other methods allow to obtain the URI of a function, to clear its internal state and to apply it to dx_{in} and dy_{in} values (in counts) with a timestamp to produce dx_{out} and dy_{out} values (in pixels). The toolkit provides subclasses that correspond to different transfer functions. Care has been taken so that all implementations are platform-independent, i.e. all the transfer functions proposed by `libpointing` can be used on all the supported platforms. Although it imposes some constraints, we believe that having cross-platform implementations is important: a long-term goal for `libpointing` could be to serve as a living archive of the functions tried and used in research and commercial systems.

Three subclasses replicate the functions used by Windows (`windows:`), OS X (`osx:`) and Xorg (`xorg:`). The next section of the paper will describe these functions with extensive details. The special URI `system:` can be used to create the single appropriate instance of these subclasses that corresponds to the function used by the system. Configuration settings passed on the optional query string are applied to both the created instance and the system function.

Two other subclasses implement constant CD gain in both the naive and the right way. The first one simply multiplies the dx_{in} and dy_{in} values by a specified factor, e.g. `naive:?gain=2`, and returns the nearest integers as dx_{out} and dy_{out}. As this ignores the resolution of the input and output devices and multiplies counts to produce pixels, the effective unitless gain will most probably not be the one requested (it is usually higher, input devices having higher resolutions than displays). The second implementation (`constant:`) takes the resolutions into account to effectively produce a hardware-independent constant gain. It converts counts into distances, multiplies these distances by the specified factor and returns their pixel equivalent.

The toolkit provides various other subclasses, including a `sigmoid:` function and a `composition:` one, the latter allowing to compose an arbitrary number of functions. Adding a new function is simply a matter of creating a new subclass, implementing its `getURI`, `clearState` and `apply` methods and modifying the `TransferFunction::create` method.

Utilities

`libpointing` includes some test and debugging programs that allow to list the available devices and their characteristics, for example. The toolkit also includes a transfer function plotting tool written in Python using matplotlib. This tool proved quite useful as it provided some visual confirmation that our implementations of the Windows, OS X, and Xorg functions matched the data collected using `EchoMouse`. It was also used to plot all the curves shown in this paper.

The toolkit also includes an application that allows to test an arbitrary number of transfer functions at the same time specified by their URI as command-line arguments. The program creates an on-screen cursor (a small square) for each function, a single pointing device being used to control all of them. In addition to supporting informal comparisons between functions or between different settings of the same functions, this application proved again quite useful to compare our implementation of the Windows, OS X and Xorg functions with the system ones.

WINDOWS:, OSX: AND XORG: TRANSFER FUNCTIONS

As explained, one of our goals with `libpointing` was to replicate as faithfully as possible the transfer functions of Windows, OS X and Xorg. We not only wanted cursors controlled by our implementations to follow the system ones as closely as possible, but we also wanted to replicate the controls on the functions available to users from the relevant configuration interfaces. Our work was based on the documentation and source code publicly available from Microsoft, Apple and the Freedesktop community. This section presents the key findings that emerged from it.

The curves shown in the figures below have been plotted assuming the following pointing and display devices: `dummy:?cpi=400&hz=125`, `dummy:?ppi=96&hz=60`.

windows:

The transfer functions used in Microsoft Windows were redesigned for Windows XP, released in 2001. The rationales for this redesign and its general principles are described in a public document. Together with the configuration interface found in the "*Pointer Options*" tab of the "*Mouse Properties*" dialog (Figure 4), this document served as a starting point for our work. Note however that our experience was similar to that of Wobbrock et al. [22]: the information available was not sufficient to replicate the functions.

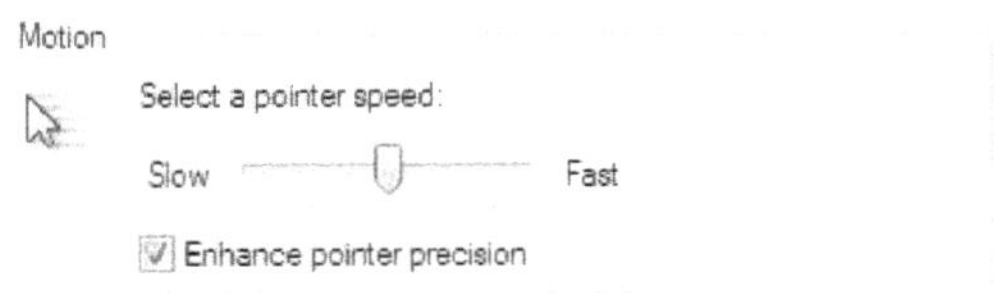

Figure 4: Windows 7 configuration interface with default settings. The same are used by Windows XP and Vista. No tooltip or help text is associated to these controls.

The transfer function code runs in an execution space where floating-point arithmetic is not available. The following equations illustrate how a (dx, dy) displacement in counts is transformed into pixel values when "*Enhance pointer precision*" is checked (Figure 4). Two important scale factors are used to convert count values to input speeds $(inConv)$ and output speeds to pixel values $(outConv)$. Computations for the y direction are omitted for brevity:

$$\begin{aligned}
mag &= max(|dx|, |dy|) + min(|dx|, |dy|)/2 && (1)\\
v_{in} &= mag \times inConv && (2)\\
gain &= lookup(v_{in}) \times pSpeed/10 && (3)\\
vx_{in} &= dx_{in} \times inConv && (4)\\
vx_{out} &= vx_{in} \times gain && (5)\\
px &= vx_{out} \times outConv && (6)\\
dx_{out} &= \lfloor px + rx \rfloor && (7)
\end{aligned}$$

The system computes a fixed-point approximation of the displacement vector magnitude (1). The magnitude is converted into an input velocity (2). A lookup table provides a base CD gain value for that velocity that is scaled by a factor ($pSpeed$) related to the "*pointer speed*" slider (Figure 4) to obtain the actual gain to apply (3). Each direction is then treated separately the following way. The directional input speed is computed (4) and multiplied by the gain to produce the output speed (5), which is then converted to a pixel displacement (6). The function returns the integral part (floor) of the sum of this displacement and the remainder of previous computations (7).

Although $inConv$ should be the quotient of the pointing device update frequency by its CPI resolution, empirical tests showed that it is always $1/3.5$. This constant value might be an approximation of 125/400, these numbers being common for mice. Empirical tests also showed that although $outConv$ should be the quotient of the display resolution by the pointing device update frequency, it is not the case either. Its actual value depends on the display resolution and frequency but also involves hardwired constants (96 PPI, 60 Hz, 150) and varies between system versions, XP and Vista differing from 7. Each of these three versions also uses a different algorithm to handle the x and y remainders: XP clears them when the pointer stops or changes direction, Vista clears them only when the pointer changes direction and 7 never clears them.

The lookup table that returns a base CD gain for a given device speed is stored in the Windows registry, so it should be possible to modify it. The position of the "*pointer speed*" slider (Figure 4) determines the value of the scale factor ($pSpeed$) applied on this base gain. Available values are: (slow) 1, 2, 4, 6, 8, 10 (default), 12, 14, 16, 18 and 20 (fast).

When "*Enhance pointer precision*" is unchecked, a naive constant CD gain is used. Based on the slider position, the available values for this gain are: (slow) 0.03125, 0.0625, 0.25, 0.5, 0.75, 1.0 (default, one pixel for one count), 1.5, 2.0, 2.5, 3.0 and 3.5 (fast). In this mode, no matter the system version, the remainders are never cleared.

The Windows transfer functions are available in `libpointing` through URIs such as `windows:<version>?slider=0&epp=true` where `<version>` can be one of `xp`, `vista` or `7`. The `slider` parameter encodes the slider position between -5 and +5 where 0 corresponds to the default position. The `epp` parameter indicates whether "*Enhance pointer precision*" is checked or not. Figure 6 shows the curves associated to each slider position, with and without enhanced pointer precision. Our implementation of these functions consists of about 200 lines of code. On XP, Vista and 7, a cursor controlled by it remains superimposed with the genuine one whatever movements are made. Our cursor can even respond to pointing device movement before the system cursor when the vertical synchronization of the display is disabled.

osx:

The source code for the internal parts of OS X that deal with pointing transfer functions is publicly available as part of the IOHIDFamily[5] project, the main concerned files being IOHIDSystem/IOHIPointing.cpp and IOHIDSystem/IOHIDSystem.cpp. From the archived versions of this project, it seems that the current pointer acceleration mechanisms first appeared in OS X 10.2, released in 2002. However, although the source code is available, the design rationales and principles of operation of these mechanisms are unknown. Figure 5 shows the related configuration interface, located in the "*Mouse*" pane of the system preferences. Note that from a user-perspective, the acceleration mechanisms are also badly documented, the tooltip associated to the slider being potentially misleading.

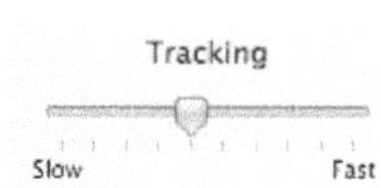

Figure 5: OS X 10.6.7 configuration interface for the mouse. A tooltip associated to the slider says "*Drag to adjust how fast you want the pointer to follow the movement of your mouse*".

[5]`http://opensource.apple.com/source/IOHIDFamily/`

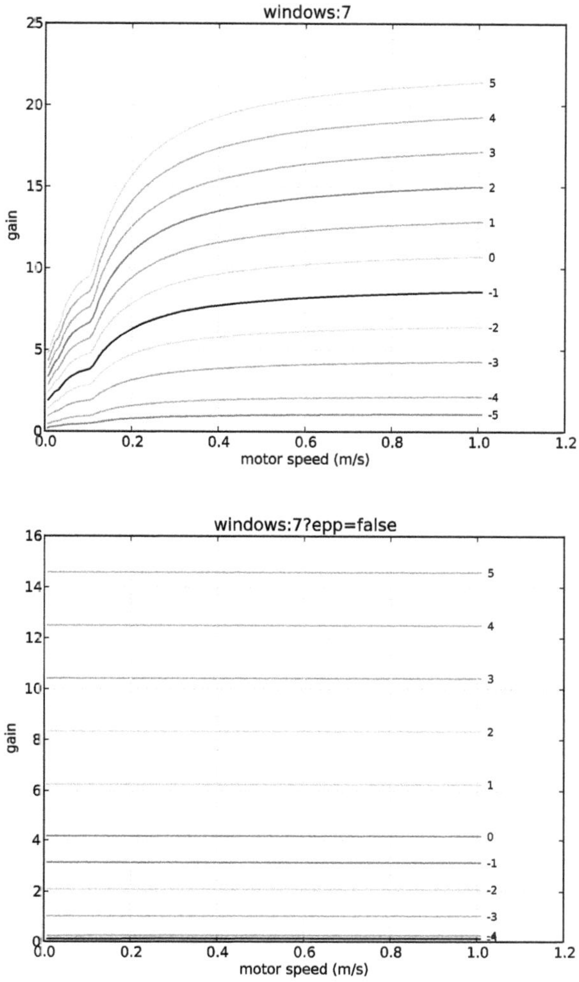

Figure 6: Windows 7 functions available through the interface shown in Figure 4 with and without enhanced pointer precision.

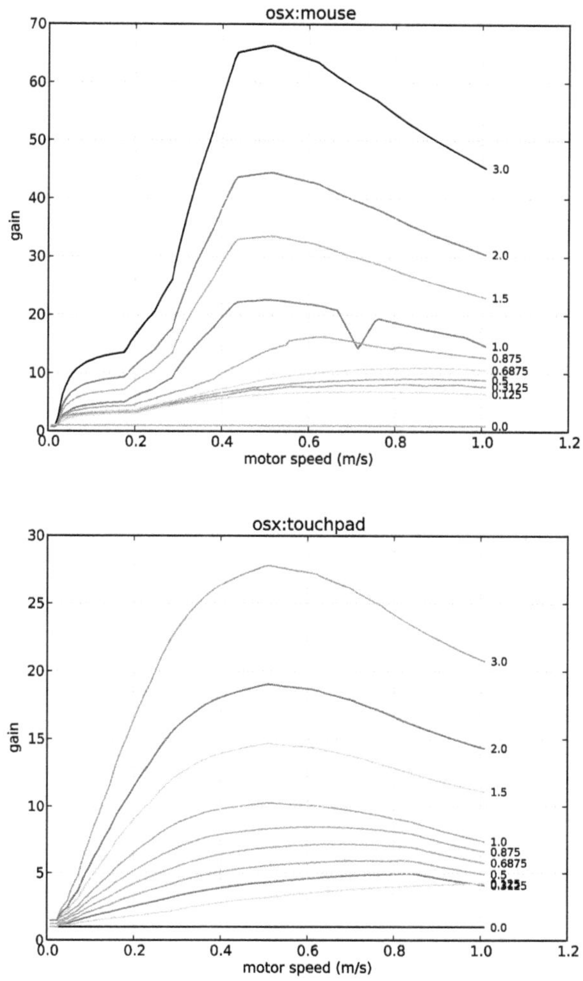

Figure 8: OS X 10.6.7 functions for mice (available through the interface shown in Figure 5) and touchpads.

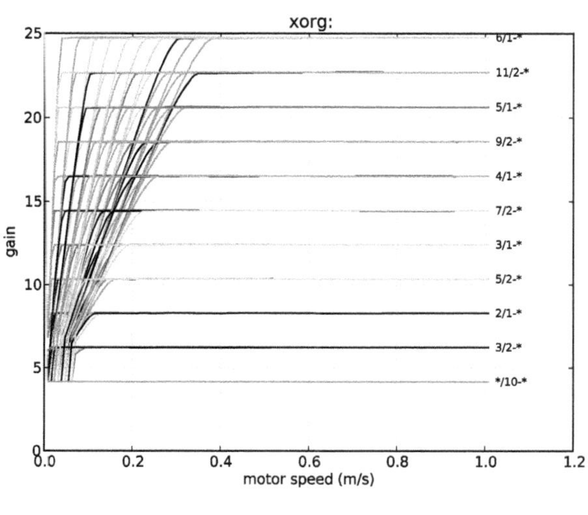

Figure 7: Xorg functions available in Ubuntu 10.10 through the interface shown in Figure 10.

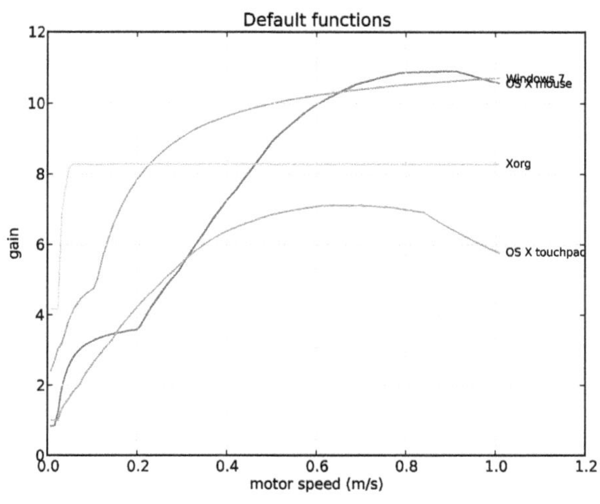

Figure 9: Default functions used by Windows 7, OS X 10.6.7 (mouse and touchpad) and Xorg.

It was relatively easy for us to isolate the portions of code from IOHIDFamily responsible for pointer acceleration (about 500 lines of code, mainly in IOHIPointing.cpp) and to add the necessary wrappers and definitions to make them compile on Windows and Linux. The basic operating principles followed by this code are also relatively simple and somewhat similar to those of Windows.

Each pointing device has an associated acceleration table provided by its driver (some also define a separate table for scrolling). This table specifies one or more curves defined by a series of segments and a *scale* level. The slider shown in Figure 5 allows users to specify a desired scale among the following: (slow) 0, 0.125, 0.3125, 0.5, 0.6875 (default), 0.875, 1, 1.5, 2, and 3 (fast). The system interpolates between the curves provided by the driver to create one that matches the desired scale and maps a vector magnitude to a CD gain value. Then for each (dx, dy) displacement, it computes an approximation of the vector magnitude using the same equation as Windows[6], uses the created curve to find the right CD gain, applies it to dx and dy, adds the previous remainders and returns the integral part of the result after updating the remainders. These remainders are never cleared.

The acceleration curves stored in device drivers are hardware-independent. When it interpolates between them, the system takes the resolution of the input device into account. However, it uses hardwired constants for the resolution of the display (96 PPI) and the frequency of the input and output devices (67 Hz). A detailed inspection of the drivers available on OS X 10.6.7 showed that several of them use the same tables. We identified two particular tables, one for mice and the other for touchpads, that seem to be used by all such devices that rely on Apple's drivers.

OS X transfer functions are available in `libpointing` through URIs such as `osx:<name or path>?scale=0.5`. The names `mouse` and `touchpad` can be used to load one of the generic acceleration tables that we found. A specific table can also be loaded from a file by specifying its path. The `scale` parameter encodes the desired scale. Figure 8 shows the curves associated to each slider position for generic mice and touchpads. Note that contrary to what it may seem in both cases, the unitless gain obtained for a scale of 0 is not always 1 but fluctuates between 0.9 and 1. From what we know, a constant CD gain is not achievable using these generic tables, even a naive one.

Although it can stay close in some situations, a cursor controlled by our `osx:` implementation does not remain superimposed with the genuine one. The reason appears to be some additional control mechanisms implemented in IOHIDSystem.cpp. Our current understanding is that these mechanisms feed the output of the function we just described into a trajectory prediction algorithm that schedules on-screen cursor updates synchronized with display refresh. No correction seems to be implemented in case a prediction was wrong, though. In effect, the whole acts as a low-pass filter on cursor movements. We hypothesize this explains the upward shift between the curves shown in Figure 3 and those in Figure 8 (above plot). Our present inability to schedule calls synchronized with display refresh prevents us from replicating these mechanisms, but we are currently investigating ways to circumvent this problem.

xorg:
The pointer acceleration mechanisms currently used by Xorg were introduced in 2008. The source code for these mechanisms is publicly available as part of the Xorg source tree[7]. It was again relatively easy for us to isolate the relevant portions of code (about 1500 lines of code, mainly in dix/ptrveloc.c) and to add the necessary wrappers and definitions to make them compile on Windows and OS X. This time, documentation for the design rationales and operating principles was also available[8], although a bit cryptic.

The changes introduced in Xorg in 2008 notably aimed at facilitating the exploration of transfer functions. The current architecture of the code supports 9 different *profiles* implemented within the new "*predictable*" scheme and the older "*lightweight*" scheme "*retained mostly for embedded scenarios*". Profiles can be considered as different transfer functions, although they share some common mechanisms and code. Numerous configuration settings are associated to them. But genericity and flexibility have a price: not only is the Xorg code for pointer acceleration much larger than the one used on other systems, but it is also far less readable.

The "*predictable*" scheme computes the euclidean distance corresponding to each displacement reported by the device and divides it by the time elapsed since the previous one. This instantaneous velocity is stored in a short history list ($n = 16$ by default) that is used to maintain a better estimation of the real pointing device velocity. Two adjustable settings also play an important part: *acceleration*, given as a fraction, and *threshold*. The first one defines a high value for the (naive) CD gain to be applied to displacements, considering a default low value of 1. The second one defines the minimum velocity that needs to be achieved to switch from the low gain to the high one. The active profile specifies how the estimated velocity will be used to determine the actual CD gain within these constraints. All computations are made with floating-point arithmetic. Remainders are preserved and never cleared.

The Xorg "*predictable*" transfer functions are available in `libpointing` through URIs such as `xorg:<profile>?accnum=2&accden=1&thr=4` where `<profile>` names one of the 9 available profiles, `accnum` and `accden` define the acceleration fraction and `thr` the threshold. On Ubuntu 10.10, a cursor controlled by our implementation remains superimposed with the genuine one.

It should be noted that a wide variety of command-line and graphical interfaces exists to configure the different profiles and their settings. Figure 10 shows the configuration interface available in the "*Pointer speed*" section of the "*Mouse preferences*" application of Ubuntu 10.10. Although the code that we use is not functionally limited to it, we will now fo-

[6]All computations are also made using fixed-point arithmetic.

[7]http://cgit.freedesktop.org/xorg/xserver/tree/

[8]http://xorg.freedesktop.org/wiki/Development/Documentation/PointerAcceleration

cus on the default profile used by Ubuntu ("*classic*") and the relevant settings that can be adjusted through this particular interface.

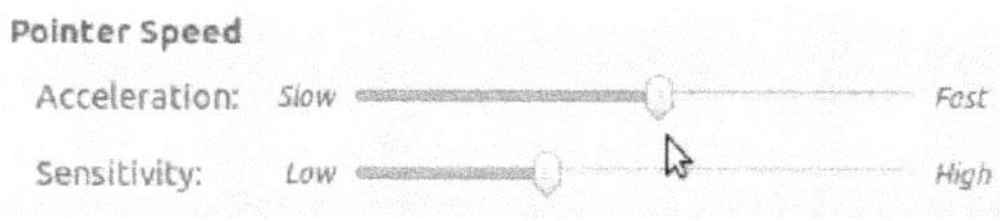

Figure 10: Ubuntu 10.10 configuration interface. A help page says about the first slider: "*Use the slider to specify the speed at which your mouse pointer moves on your screen when you move your mouse*". About the second: "*Use the slider to specify how sensitive your mouse pointer is to movements of your mouse*".

When the threshold is non-null, the "*classic*" profile implements a smooth transition between the low and high gain values. The sliders shown in Figure 10 only allow such configurations. As the label indicates, the upper slider controls the acceleration setting. When dragged, it feels like a continuous control but actually supports only a predefined set of values: (slow) 3/10, 4/10, 5/10, 6/10, 7/10, 8/10, 9/10, 10/10, 1/1, 3/2, 2/1 (default), 5/2, 3/1, 7/2, 4/1, 9/2, 5/1, 11/2, and 6/1 (fast). The bottom slider controls the threshold and actually feels like a discrete control. The available values are: (low) 1, 2, 3, 4 (default), 5, 6, 7, 8, 9, and 10 (high). In total, the interface shown in Figure 10 thus gives access to $19 \times 10 = 190$ configurations of the "*classic*" profile.

Figure 7 shows a plot of these 190 functions. As one would expect, the 90 functions with an acceleration setting lesser or equal than 1, those labeled */10-*, correspond to a naive constant gain of 1 (considering the 400 CPI and 96 PPI used for plotting the curves). Note that this is the only naive constant gain achievable through the interface shown in Figure 10 and that this interface does not allow to achieve a unitless constant gain.

Summary

Figure 9 shows the default transfer functions used by Windows, OS X and Xorg. Overall, despite a few differences, the different families have a lot in common.

The three systems take only partially into account the characteristics of the input and output devices. OS X is the only system that uses the real resolution of the input device (Windows assumes a 400 CPI resolution and Xorg does not use it). Xorg is the only system that takes input event times into account (the two others use harwired constant frequencies). Xorg completely ignores the display frequency and resolution while OS X uses hardwired constants for them (Windows varies on that topic).

All systems use a non linear function by default, but Windows and Xorg also support the use of naive constant gain functions. As the systems fail to properly take into account the resolution and frequency of the devices, none actually supports a unitless constant gain.

Windows and OS X both use fixed-point arithmetic. The three systems work with integer pixel coordinates but preserve the remainders to achieve subpixel precision when pointing. Windows 7, Mac OS X and Xorg never clear these remainders while they are cleared using different strategies on Windows XP and Vista.

The comparison of our custom cursors with the three system ones validated our Windows and Xorg implementations but revealed a slight difference for OS X presumably due to a trajectory prediction algorithm requiring information we are not yet able to provide.

EXPERIMENT

Our initial motivation for this experiment was to compare the performance of real-world transfer functions. Assuming they were probably used by many people and somewhat representative of theses systems, we decided to compare the default functions used by Windows, OS X and Xorg. We also added a constant CD gain function, as they are often used as a baseline for comparing pointing facilitation techniques.

Apparatus

A 400 CPI USB corded Logitech mouse was used as input device. A low-end model was preferred to a high-resolution one as 400 CPI is the default resolution considered by all systems. We used a 23" LCD display at a 1920×1200 resolution (98.5 PPI). The experiment was coded in C++ with the QT framework on a Windows 7 Professional machine with a NVidia GeForce GTX 460 graphics card. Our *libpointing* toolkit was used to get raw input from the mouse and apply the different transfer functions. Vertical synchronization of the display was disabled in order to be able to update our cursor's position at the mouse frequency (125 Hz). In this configuration, our controlled cursor was slightly in advance compared to the system one, which prevented any confounding effect of lag in the experiment.

Task

We used a reciprocal one dimensional pointing task (Figure 11). Each trial began after the previous target was successfully selected and ended with the selection of the current target. After a target was successfully selected, it turned grey and the next one (on the other side of the screen) turned green. If a participant missed a target, a sound was heard and an error was logged. Participants had to successfully select the current target before moving to the next one, even if it required multiple clicks. Participants used the left mouse button to select targets. After each block of trials, a cumulative error rate was displayed and a message encouraged participants to conform to an approximately 4% error rate by speeding up or slowing down.

Participants

Sixteen unpaid participants with a mean age of 30.6 (SD = 7.8, min = 23, max = 46) served in the experiment (15 male and 1 female, 13 right-handed and 3 left-handed). All participants worked most of their time with a computer. Three participants used exclusively OS X, four Windows 7, three Ubuntu 10.10. Two used Ubuntu 10.10 and Windows 7, two OS X and Windows 7, one Ubuntu 10.10 and OS X, and one Windows 7 and Ubuntu 10.10. Four participants used the mouse exclusively, two the touchpad and the remainder both devices. Among the sixteen participants, twelve kept the default settings for the mouse or touchpad while four slightly

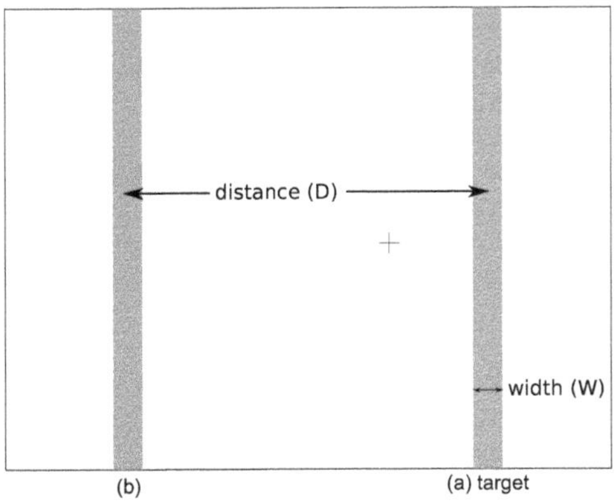

Figure 11: Experimental display. Targets were rendered as solid vertical bars equidistant from the center of the display in opposite directions along the horizontal axis. The target to be selected was colored green (a), and the previous one gray (b). The cursor was represented by a one-pixel-thick black cross 10 pixels wide.

increased the speed of their cursor by moving the slider in their configuration panel one or two ticks to the right.

Design

A repeated measures within-subjects design was used. The independent variables were the transfer function used (TF) and the target width (WIDTH).

Target distance was kept constant at 299.9 mm = 1,163 pixels. We decided for this moderate single distance because Casiez et al. had found stronger differences between constant CD gain and the Windows XP functions for small targets and long distances[9]. This decision was taken to reduce the duration of the experiment and to highlight the effect of WIDTH. The rationale was also that if no effect of TF was found with these settings, it would be likely that no such effect exists.

WIDTH was evaluated with four levels: W_{9pix} = 2.32 mm = 9 pixels, W_{6pix} = 1.55 mm = 6 pixels, W_{3pix} = 0.77 mm = 3 pixels, W_{1pix} = 0.26 mm = 1 pixel. Targets three pixels wide are common when resizing a window or clicking between two letters to position a text cursor. One pixel targets are less frequent but occur for example when selecting adjacent vertices or edges without zooming in vector drawing applications. The index of difficulty ranged from 7.0 to 10.2.

The transfer functions evaluated were constant CD gain of 1.5[10] (*Cst1.5*), the default Windows 7 function (*Win7*), the default OS X 10.6.7 function for mice (*OSX*) and the default Xorg function (*Xorg*). According to Casiez et al.'s method [8] and considering our experimental settings, the minimum gain value to prevent clutching was 30/30 = 1 and the maximum value that could be chosen given quantization problems and human limbs precision was equal to min(400/98.5, 0.26/0.2) = 1.3. The chosen CD gain value of 1.5 represents a good trade-off between these bounds and the CD gain value of 2 often used as a baseline in pointing experiments.

[9] The largest distance in [8] for a similar desktop configuration was 36 cm.

[10] Remainders were handled the same way as the other functions: they were never reset.

Participants were introduced to the task and had about 30 seconds to get used to it. They then completed three successive BLOCKS for each TF. Each BLOCK consisted of 24 trials: 6 repetitions of the 4 WIDTHS. WIDTHS were presented in decreasing order. The presentation order for TF was counterbalanced across participants using a balanced Latin Square design. Participants were encouraged to take a break after every 6 trials. They had to press the spacebar once they felt ready to start a new block. The desk was empty except for the keyboard and screen, and participants were instructed to use as much space as they wished to move the mouse. The experiment lasted approximately 15 minutes.

In summary, the experimental design was: 16 participants × 4 TF × 3 BLOCKS × 4 WIDTH × 6 trials = 4,608 total trials.

RESULTS

The dependent variables were the error rate and the movement time.

Error Rate

Targets that were not selected on the first attempt were marked as errors. Participants followed the instructions with an overall error rate of 4.1%. A repeated measures ANOVA showed a significant effect of WIDTH on error rate, the latter increasing as target width decreases ($F_{3,45}$=14.5, $p<0.001$). Pairwise comparisons showed significant differences between the smallest width and the three other widths (p=0.001; W_{1pix}: 9.7%, W_{3pix}: 2.8%, W_{6pix}: 1.7%, W_{9pix}: 2.1%).

Movement Time

Movement time is the main dependent measure and is defined as the time taken to move from a target to the next one and click on it. Targets marked as errors were removed from the timing analysis. We also considered trials at least three standard deviations away from the mean for each TF×WIDTH condition as outliers and removed them from the data analysis (1.6% of the trials).

A repeated measures ANOVA showed that the presentation order of TF had no significant effect or interaction on movement time, indicating that a within-participant design was appropriate. Repeated measures ANOVA showed a significant effect of BLOCK ($F_{2,30}$=14.2, $p<0.001$) on movement time. Pairwise comparisons showed a significant decrease in the movement time between the first block and the two remaining ($p<0.001$; Block 1: 2.05 s, Block 2: 1.93 s, Block 3: 1.94 s). The first block was thus removed from subsequent analysis.

Repeated measures ANOVA showed a significant main effect of TF ($F_{3,45}$=20.7, $p<0.001$)), WIDTH ($F_{3,45}$=244.4, $p<0.001$)) and a significant TF × WIDTH interaction ($F_{9,135}$=3.2, p=0.023)) on movement time (Figure 12). Post-hoc analysis showed significant differences between *Cst1.5* and the three other transfer functions ($p<0.001$, *Cst1.5*: 2.22 s, *OSX*: 1.86 s, *Win7*: 1.81 s, *Xorg*: 1.84 s). This shows that *Cst1.5* is more than 20% slower compared to the three default transfer functions. We did not control for clutching but according to the experimenter observation, it was infrequent for all conditions. When it occurred, it was at the beginning of the first block which was removed from the time analysis.

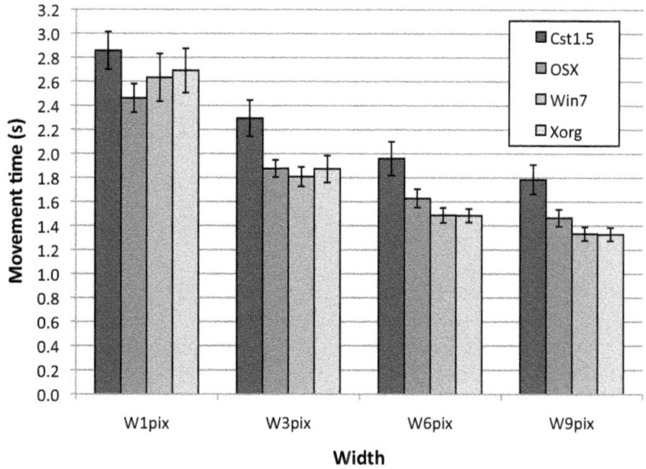

Figure 12: Mean movement time for TF and WIDTH, error bars representing 95% confidence interval.

For W_{9pix}, pairwise comparisons[11] showed significant differences (p<0.001) between *Cst1.5* and the three other transfer functions. We also observed significant difference (p=0.013) between *OSX* and *Win7* (*Cst1.5*: 1.78 s, *OSX*: 1.47 s, *Win7*: 1.33 s, *Xorg*: 1.33 s). For W_{6pix} pairwise comparisons showed significant differences (p<0.002) between *Cst1.5* and the other functions. *OSX* showed again significant difference (p=0.001) with *Win7* (*Cst1.5*: 1.96 s, *OSX*: 1.63 s, *Win7*: 1.48 s, *Xorg*: 1.48 s). For W_{3pix}, we again observed significant differences (p<0.002) between *Cst1.5* and the other functions. However, the significant difference between *OSX* and *Win7* disappears (*Cst1.5*: 2.29 s, *OSX*: 1.88 s, *Win7*: 1.81 s, *Xorg*: 1.87 s). For W_{1pix}, we observed significant differences (p<0.048) between *OSX* and *Cst1.5*, *Xorg* (*Cst1.5*: 2.85 s, *OSX*: 2.46 s, *Win7*: 2.63 s, *Xorg*: 2.69 s).

Our results show there is no single function that is best for all target widths. *Win7* and *Xorg* improve movement time by more than 9% compared to *OSX* and more than 24% compared to *Cst1.5* for widths 6 and 9 pixels. However, the difference with *OSX* disappears for 3 and 1 pixels targets. In contrast, *OSX* improves movement time by 13% compared to *Cst1.5* and 8% compared to *Xorg* for the 1 pixel target when the other functions do not show significant differences.

Qualitative Feedback

At the end of the experiment, participants were asked if they found some differences in the control of the cursor. All noticed there was a condition (*Cst1.5*) where they had to move the mouse over greater distances to reach targets and complained it was less comfortable than the other conditions. None of the participants was able to notice a difference between the three other conditions (*Win7*, *OSX* and *Xorg*).

DISCUSSION

The knowledge acquired by studying, replicating and comparing the transfer functions used by three different systems brings us to the following suggestions.

Choosing a Baseline Transfer Function

The use of a constant CD gain function as a baseline to compare with other techniques should be prohibited unless clearly justified. None of the prevalent systems uses such a function by default and it might not even be obtainable on some, like OS X. As we explained in the previous section, most participants of our experiment declared using the default settings of their system, and results from the experiment show that these default functions outperform a constant CD gain. We thus recommend to use the default transfer function of the considered system as a baseline condition.

Reporting Transfer Functions

To facilitate the replication or reproduction of pointing techniques and experiments, we recommend that researchers provide extensive details concerning the transfer function(s) they used.

If constant CD gains were used, we recommend to report them using unitless values in order to abstract them from hardware specifics. Detailing how a constant gain was achieved might also help detecting potential flaws in the methodology. As an example, it might be important to explain how remainders were handled as it remains unclear if they can affect performance. If a system function was used, the system and its particular configuration settings should be unambiguously described. A screen-shot is probably the most unambiguous way of reporting these settings. For completeness and as we have shown that some systems do not take them into account, we also recommend to report the resolution and frequency of both the input and output devices. For custom non linear functions, we recommend describing them using figures or tables with physical units mapping the device speed to the cursor speed or CD gain.

An alternative for describing transfer functions would be to use a notation based on URIs, similar to what we have started to do in `libpointing`. URIs are interesting because they allow to combine a class description, an instance description and optional parameters, e.g. `windows:vista?setting=2&epp=false`. They can be given fully expanded, with all possible parameters, or in a condensed form specifying only the ones differing from default values. If `libpointing` indeed turns into a living archive for transfer functions, we will certainly need some registry to standardize and officialize these notations.

In addition to the transfer function(s) used, the latency of the system might also be worthwhile to report as it can impact performance and might be a confounding variable. We acknowledge that measuring it is quite difficult. But some of the parameters that affect it can probably be described, such as the characteristics of the communication link between the input device and the computer, or the synchronization characteristics of the display.

Configuration Interfaces and Documentation

As we already stated, transfer functions should be defined in hardware-independent ways. Their implementation should thus be given either hardware-independent data, or the information to do the required conversions. In an ideal world, pointing device manufacturers would take full advantage of the HID specification to put all the necessary information in their device descriptions. Unfortunately, the reality is quite different... As systems are often forced to make educated

[11] Using Bonferroni correction for all post-hoc analysis.

guesses about device characteristics, we believe these should be visible and modifiable in the relevant configuration interfaces. Exposing wrongly estimated values should help raise the level of consciousness of the public about the difference between input resolution and cursor speed, for example.

Considering the different understandings of the current interfaces used for tuning the system transfer functions, even among researchers, we believe these interfaces should at least be properly documented if not completely redesigned.

CONCLUSION AND FUTURE WORK

In this paper, we presented a custom device and a toolkit that helped us characterize, replicate and compare the pointing transfer functions used on a daily basis by millions of people around the world. We showed in a controlled experiment that the default transfer functions used in Windows, OS X and Xorg outperform a constant CD gain similar to those used by most researchers. Our results also show a significant interaction between transfer function and target width suggesting that more work needs to be done to understand how these functions affect performance.

This work represents an important step in the understanding and study of pointing transfer functions. A long term goal is to improve the design of transfer functions by taking more into account the hardware characteristics (i.e. mouse vs. touchpad, desktop display vs. wall size display) and the motor capabilities of the users. This includes the study of management strategies for remainders which we hypothesize can be important for the selection of small targets. We are also interested in the study of the impact of the transfer function in relation with the task: a function performing well for pointing could degrade performance in other tasks like drawing, steering or executing command gestures, for example.

In the short term, we plan to study the interaction of the default transfer functions with pointing facilitation techniques manipulating CD gain, e.g. [5, 10, 23]. To our knowledge, these technique were only implemented on top of a constant CD gain and were also only evaluated against constant CD gains. We also plan to investigate the use of indirect mappings on multitouch interfaces. On this topic, Buxton recently said: "*one of the things that I see most neglected is any consideration of when to use relative vs absolute control and varying, including when and how to effectively and dynamically switch from one to the other, and when and how to dynamically adjust C:D ratio*" [6]. We could not agree more.

ACKNOWLEDGMENTS

We thank Damien Marchal and Mark Cranness for their help in the understanding of transfer functions and their contribution to `libpointing`.

REFERENCES

1. Pointer ballistics for Windows XP. Archived white paper, Windows Hardware Developer Center, Oct. 2002.
2. T. Asano, E. Sharlin, Y. Kitamura, K. Takashima, and F. Kishino. Predictive interaction using the Delphian Desktop. *Proceedings of UIST'05*, 133–141. ACM, 2005.
3. M. Bergman, T. Peurach, T. Schmidt, S. McGowan, J. Crowe, R. Dezmelyk, R. Zimmermann, M. Van Flandern, B. Nathan, M. Davis, and J. Rayhawk. Device class definition for human interface devices (HID). Version 1.11, USB Implementers' Forum, June 2001.
4. T. Berners-Lee, R. Fielding, and L. Masinter. Uniform Resource Identifier (URI): generic syntax. RFC 3986, IETF, Jan. 2005.
5. R. Blanch, Y. Guiard, and M. Beaudouin-Lafon. Semantic pointing: improving target acquisition with control-display ratio adaptation. *Proceedings of CHI'04*, 519–526. ACM, 2004.
6. W. Buxton, M. Billinghurst, Y. Guiard, A. Sellen, and S. Zhai. *Human input to computer systems: theories, techniques and technology*. 2011. Working draft, `http://www.billbuxton.com/inputManuscript.html`.
7. G. Casiez and D. Vogel. The effect of spring stiffness and control gain with an elastic rate control pointing device. *Proceeding of CHI'08*, 1709–1718. ACM, 2008.
8. G. Casiez, D. Vogel, R. Balakrishnan, and A. Cockburn. The impact of control-display gain on user performance in pointing tasks. *Human-Computer Interaction*, 23(3):215–250, 2008.
9. O. Chapuis, J.-B. Labrune, and E. Pietriga. DynaSpot: speed-dependent area cursor. *Proceedings of CHI'09*, 1391–1400. ACM, 2009.
10. A. Cockburn and A. Firth. Improving the acquisition of small targets. *Proceedings of HCI'03*, 77–80. BCS, 2003.
11. E. D. Graham. Virtual pointing on a computer display: non-linear control-display mappings. *Proceedings of GI'96*, 39–46. Canadian Information Processing Society, 1996.
12. T. Grossman and R. Balakrishnan. The bubble cursor: enhancing target acquisition by dynamic resizing of the cursor's activation area. *Proceedings of CHI'05*, 281–290. ACM, 2005.
13. K. Hinckley. Input technologies and techniques. A. Sears and J. A. Jacko, editors, *Human Computer Interaction Handbook (2nd edition)*. CRC Press, Sept. 2007.
14. H. D. Jellinek and S. K. Card. Powermice and user performance. *Proceedings of CHI'90*, 213–220. ACM, 1990.
15. M. Kobayashi and T. Igarashi. Ninja cursors: using multiple cursors to assist target acquisition on large screens. *Proceeding of CHI'08*, 949–958. ACM, 2008.
16. I. S. MacKenzie. Input devices and interaction techniques for advanced computing. W. Barfield and T. A. F. III, editors, *Virtual environments and advanced interface design*, 437–470. 1995.
17. I. S. MacKenzie and P. Isokoski. Fitts' throughput and the speed-accuracy tradeoff. *Proceeding of CHI'08*, 1633–1636. ACM, 2008.
18. R. L. Mandryk and C. Gutwin. Perceptibility and utility of sticky targets. *Proceedings of graphics interface 2008*, GI '08, 65–72. Canadian Information Processing Society, 2008.
19. D. E. Meyer, R. A. Abrams, S. Kornblum, C. E. Wright, and J. E. K. Smith. Optimality in human motor performance: Ideal control of rapid aimed movements. *Psychological Review*, 95(3):340–370, 1988.
20. B. Moggridge. *Designing interactions*. The MIT Press, Oct. 2006.
21. U. Tränkle and D. Deutschmann. Factors influencing speed and precision of cursor positioning using a mouse. *Ergonomics*, 34(2):161–174, 1991.
22. J. O. Wobbrock, J. Fogarty, S.-Y. S. Liu, S. Kimuro, and S. Harada. The Angle Mouse: target-agnostic dynamic gain adjustment based on angular deviation. *Proceedings of CHI'09*, 1401–1410. ACM, 2009.
23. A. Worden, N. Walker, K. Bharat, and S. Hudson. Making computers easier for older adults to use: area cursors and sticky icons. *Proceedings of CHI'97*, 266–271. ACM, 1997.

FingerFlux: Near-surface Haptic Feedback on Tabletops

Malte Weiss *Chat Wacharamanotham* *Simon Voelker* *Jan Borchers*

RWTH Aachen University
52056 Aachen, Germany
{weiss, chat, voelker, borchers}@cs.rwth-aachen.de

ABSTRACT
We introduce FingerFlux, an output technique to generate near-surface haptic feedback on interactive tabletops. Our system combines electromagnetic actuation with permanent magnets attached to the user's hand. FingerFlux lets users feel the interface before touching, and can create both attracting and repelling forces. This enables applications such as reducing drifting, adding physical constraints to virtual controls, and guiding the user without visual output. We show that users can feel vibration patterns up to 35 mm above our table, and that FingerFlux can significantly reduce drifting when operating on-screen buttons without looking.

ACM Classification: H5.2 [Information interfaces and presentation]: User Interfaces.—Haptic I/O.

General terms: Design, Human Factors, Experimentation

Keywords: Haptic feedback, Magnets, Actuation, Interactive Tabletops

Figure 1: FingerFlux provides attraction, repulsion, vibration, and directional haptic feedback on and near the surface using electromagnets in the table and a permanent magnet attached to the user's finger.

INTRODUCTION

Touchscreens allow users to directly manipulate objects on the screen with their fingers. This interaction heavily depends on the user's visual perception of the hand [8] and visual feedback from the screen [27]. Yet, there are situations in which vision is not available, such as entering text on a touchscreen while reading it off a piece of paper, or rejecting an incoming phone call while driving. When the visual sense is taken away, although the direction of hand movement is still accurate [5], the touches gradually drift from the target [4]. Using suitable haptic feedback reduces those errors, lowers subjective workload [17], increases attention [2], and improves motor learning [13].

The introduction of haptic feedback on touchscreen devices has received much attention [1, 11]. However, a common property of most approaches is creating *a posteriori* feedback: the haptic feedback begins *after* the surface is touched. To maintain input efficiency, drifting has to be compensated by algorithms that interpret uncertain input [20]. However, if the user is drifting too much, e.g., beyond the boundaries of a control she wants to press, there is no haptic feedback to realign her fingers anymore.

In this paper, we present a system that allows users to feel haptic feedback when hovering above the table, i.e., *before* they touch the surface. Our system is based on electromagnetic actuation [18, 25] in combination with permanent magnets attached to the user's hand. By attracting or repelling these permanent magnets, we create haptic feedback over a distance and guide the user when she approaches the surface.

After giving an overview on related work, we will explain our prototype design and describe example applications. Moreover, we provide evidence that users can feel haptic feedback above the table and that our technique significantly reduces drifting when operating buttons without looking. The paper closes with a discussion about limitations and a conclusion.

RELATED WORK

There are different classes of techniques that improve haptic feedback on touchscreens. The first generates haptic feedback *on the surface*. One of the early approaches are pin displays, e.g., [14], that display Braille characters by moving thin rods upwards from the surface. SmartTouch [12] is an electrocutaneous display which pulses small currents to the finger to generate haptic feedback. More recently, TeslaTouch [1] uses electrovibration to dynamically change perceived surface friction. MudPad [11] uses electromagnets to change the viscosity of magnetorheological fluids in the surface. These techniques can only create feedback while the user touches the surface.

Tangible user interfaces are physical objects that are used to represent and manipulate virtual data. They can provide rich haptic feedback and physical constraints [26]. Furthermore, they can act as mediator for dynamic haptic output [15, 24]. However, they have to be placed on the table explicitly, consume real estate, and are harder to use on small or non-horizontal surfaces.

Stationary devices like the PHANTOM [16] or Maglev Haptics [6, 23] can provide 3D haptic feedback to a user's fingertip. Similarly, exoskeletons attached to the user's arm [3], gloves [29], and electrodes that directly stimulate muscles in the user's hand [22] can create haptic feedback *above the surface*. Although these methods are effective in providing a priori feedback, stationary devices are difficult to use on interactive tables while the others require users to wear complex actuation systems or create local vibration feedback only. Arrays consisting of air-jet [21] or ultrasound emitters [10] create a 3D sensation in the air. Yet, these displays are limited in resolution and can only create a repulsion feedback. SenseableRays [19] uses a lightweight actuator, attached to the user's fingertip, which converts structured light to tactile patterns. Still, the proposed system can only produce vibration feedback.

Our technique is based on magnetism, which has been investigated for both output and input previously. On the output side, the seminal system Actuated Workbench uses an array of electromagnets to move magnetic pucks on a tabletop [18]. More recently, Madgets [25] supports actuating complex tangible controls and provides techniques to push physical objects in the vertical direction. On the input side, Hook et al. [9] employ an array of coils for detecting ferrous objects on a tabletop. Our hardware design is also inspired by Abracadabra [7] which tracks a magnet attached to a finger for precise input on small-screen devices.

The body modification artists has also explored the addition of a *magnetic sixth sense*. People implanted or glued magnets to their fingertips to be able feel electromagnetic fields. Furthermore, Wishnitzer et al. reported that gamblers used subcutaneous magnets to control dice containing magnets [28].

In contrast to previous approaches, FingerFlux can generate repulsion, attraction, vibration, and directional feedback on and above the surface, without mounting bulky equipment on the user's hand.

PROTOTYPE DESIGN

For electromagnetic actuation, we used the design of the Madgets table [25]. A discrete grid of 19 × 12 electromagnets allows for synthesizing a 2D matrix of magnetic fields. Each magnet (19.5 mm diameter × 34.5 mm height) contains 3,500 turns of enameled copper around an iron core. We drive the magnets at 40 V DC and 255 mA. Strength and polarization of each electromagnet can be controlled individually from software. A backlit LCD panel on top of the array provides graphical output.

Our system uses electromagnetic fields to generate feedback *beyond* the surface. Similarly to the input technique Abracadabra [7], we attached a permanent magnet to the user's finger (Fig. 1). Electromagnets in the table create magnetic fields that attract or repel these permanent magnets. Being attached to the user, they directly pass their force to the user's skin. We can, therefore, create haptic feedback in the near-surface volume above the table. Note that users do not have to move their fingers to feel the feedback.

For our prototype, we attach two cylindric neodymium magnets (10 mm diameter × 2 mm height) below the finger tip of the user's index finger using elastic tape. We observed that a rigid tape reduces the haptic sensation in the finger. Note that the two magnets could also be replaced with a single thicker one. For consistency, the same pole of the magnet always faces away from the finger surface.

It is also possible to generate multi-finger feedback by attaching magnets to more fingers. We created a prototype glove with magnets fixed to multiple parts of multiple fingers. However, those magnets attracting and sticking to each other made the glove difficult to wear. Yet, this effect is less severe if magnets are only put on the fingertips.

APPLICATIONS

Using our setup, we can apply two basic forces to the user's finger: attraction towards and repulsion away from one or more electromagnets beneath the surface. We prototyped a set of applications using a combination of these forces. In the following, we explain these applications, beginning with those requiring single magnets only to those that involve an entire array.

A Priori Feedback in Near-surface Interaction

Our technique allows users to feel electromagnetic force fields when hovering above the surface. Using a single magnet with repelling magnetic field, a designer can model a haptic bump. This simple technique can be used to let users feel the table interface without looking or to emphasize the state of an on-screen object. For example, a strong repelling force can signify a UI element which is currently unavailable like an inactive button. When the polarization of an electromagnet is quickly reversed repeatedly, the user feels a vibration pattern when approaching the electromagnet. Those patterns could indicate a system event or warn users before they trigger critical operations, e.g., an "Exit without saving" button could emit a vibration signal to avoid accidental presses. Beyond that, magnetic fields could be exploited as private output channel that only users wearing permanent magnets could perceive.

Reducing Drifting

When users interact with touch devices while focusing on different tasks, they tend to drift away from their targets [4, 15]. Unlike approaches that try to interpret uncertain input, e.g. [20], we can use attracting forces to realign the finger's trajectory before it touches the surface. One example is virtual buttons. To reduce drifting, we can attract the user's finger to each button's center. Repelling forces around the center increase this effect by pushing the finger away from the control's boundary (Fig. 2a). This feedback re-

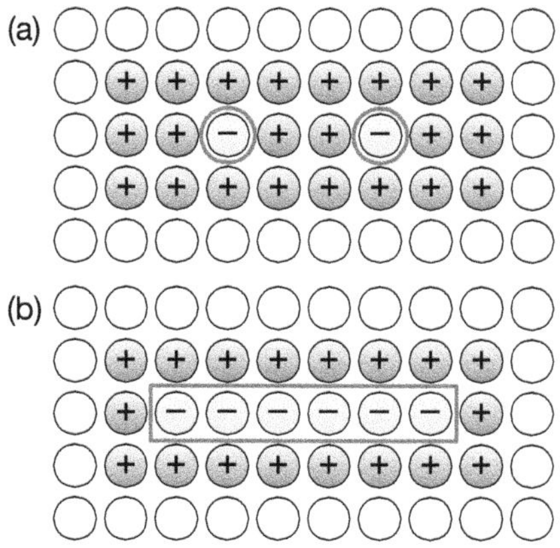

Figure 2: Actuation scheme with idle (white), attracting (green) and repelling electromagnetic fields (red). (a) Buttons (blue circles). (b) Slider (blue rectangle).

duces errors caused by accumulated drifting as will be shown in the Evaluation section. It is also straight-forward to apply this technique to transfer the snap-to-grid functionality known from GUIs to tabletops. For example, the table can attract the user's finger to points in a virtual grid when she approaches them.

Moderate Physical Constraints

By arranging attracting and repelling magnets in lines, we can create moderate physical constraints on the surface without using any physical widget, e.g., a virtual slider may use the actuation scheme in Fig. 2b. The user can slide to the left end or the right end smoothly. If she moves to the front, to the back, or beyond the endpoints, she needs to force her finger through the repelling magnetic field. Together with the ability to change these schemes dynamically, FingerFlux enables a richer interaction design. E.g., the size of this haptic slider could be changed on the fly, or an application could dynamically turn on detents by activating magnets beneath points of interest more strongly than other magnets.

Guiding the User

The Actuated Workbench [18] shows that electromagnetic arrays can create horizontal forces to move objects on tabletops. We can use the same method to create *directional* haptic feedback, e.g., if the user hovers her finger above the table and a nearby magnet is activated, her finger is either attracted towards or repelled from the target, depending on polarization. This allows application designers to guide the user across the table. An example is teaching gestures, or helping users with visual impairments to find an object on the screen.

Rendering Objects

An entire high-resolution magnet array would allow designers to even render lines and basic shapes using repelling magnetic fields. This could, e.g., help blind people to sense geographical information like a city map which otherwise would not be available on a touchscreen. By creating repelling fields with various strengths, the table could also simulate 2.5D objects in form of an elastic height map. Note that the array could only render smooth surfaces without sharp features due to the elliptical shape of magnetic fields.

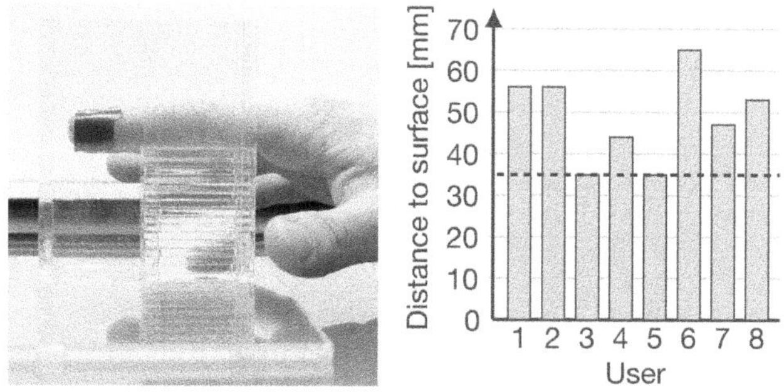

Figure 3: Near-surface haptic feedback test. Left: User test setup. Right: Distances from the surface at which each user reports random vibrations 100% correctly for all 10 trials.

EVALUATION

We conducted two user studies to prove our key contributions. Our first experiment evaluates to which extent FingerFlux provides near-surface haptic feedback. The second one tests if our system can influence input before the user touches the surface.

User Test 1: Height of Near-surface Haptic Volume

In our first user test, we determined the maximum height above the surface at which the haptic feedback can be perceived reliably. We chose a vibration feedback for this test, as our pilot study indicated that vibrations are easier to perceive than constant forces, probably due to the larger peak-to-peak amplitude of the force.

Test Setup. Fig. 3 (left) shows our test setup. An acrylic box which is opened towards the user contains a track for stacking acrylic plates. During the test, the stack of plates supports the finger of the user, so that the finger tip is directly above an electromagnet that we trigger. Each plate is 3 mm thick, except the bottommost plate which amounts to 5 mm. The acrylic plate stack allows us to control the distance from the fingertip to the surface via the number of stacked plates.

Participants. We tested eight users (age: 23–28 years, M = 25.6, SD = 2.10). One was female. All users but one were right-handed.

Procedure. We attached two cylindrical neodymium magnets (2 mm height × 10 mm diameter each) to the index finger of the user's dominant hand. The distance of the finger from the surface started at 20 mm. In each trial, the user hears two audio beeps, two seconds apart. Between the beeps, the system randomly creates either no signal at the electromagnet beneath the finger or a full-power signal with alternating polarization at 10 Hz. The latter causes permanent magnets at the finger to be attracted and repelled quickly, which can be perceived as vibration. After the second beep, the user reported to the instructor whether or not she felt the vibration. The instructor entered the answer into the software, and started the next trial. After 10 trials another 3 mm plate was placed on the stack, and the test repeated until the height of 65 mm has been tested. In total, each user performed 160 trials (10 trials × 16 height steps).

The test was double-blind: neither the user nor the instructor could see or hear whether the electromagnet produced a vibration signal or not. For each of the user's answers, the software checks whether it was correct or not. The maximum height that the haptic feedback is reliably sensed at is determined from the minimum of heights in which all users gave correct answers in all 10 trials.

Results. Fig. 3 (right) shows the results. All users were able to detect the vibration signal up to a height of 35 mm. User 6 even reliably differentiated signals up to 65 mm.

Discussion. Our results provide a proof of concept that electromagnetism can provide haptic feedback in a useful area above the surface. The volume is large enough to use the haptic channel as an output when hovering the finger above the surface. Nevertheless, designers should be reminded that the magnetic force attenuates quadratically to the distance from the surface. Accordingly, they should use smaller distances for haptic output.

The intensity of the haptic output and the maximum height depend on many hardware parameters, such as the size of the electromagnets, the voltage applied, the quality and size of the permanent magnets at the user's finger, and the temperature of the magnets. Individual differences between users also influence the maximum height.

User Test 2: Reducing Drifting

In our second study, we evaluated whether or not FingerFlux reduces drifting when pressing on-screen buttons without looking.

Test Procedure. As in the previous test, the user worn two neodymium magnets beneath her index finger of the dominant hand. For precise tracking of the finger, we used a Vicon optical tracking system[1] and glued a single retroreflective marker on top of the fingernail. Two circular buttons (25 mm diameter, 40 mm = 2 electromagnets gap) were displayed on the table surface. Users had to push the left and right button alternately without resting their hands on the surface (Fig. 4, left). The independent variable was the feedback condition:

- In the *non-haptic* condition, we did not create any electromagnetic fields.
- In the *haptic* condition, we created two attracting electromagnetic fields beneath each button center, and repelling fields around them (Fig. 2a).

Users performed both conditions consecutively, starting with the left button in each. Order of conditions was counterbalanced among users to prevent learning effects. Each condition consisted of 14 training presses and 44 measured presses. Each trial was a left button press, except the first press for which users hovered their fingers above the starting position before closing their eyes. We advised users before the training that they had to perform the measured period eyes-free so that they could memorize the movement during the training period. First, the users completed 7 trials in which they were allowed to look at the buttons. Then, they had to close their eyes and perform 22 trials.

[1]http://www.vicon.com

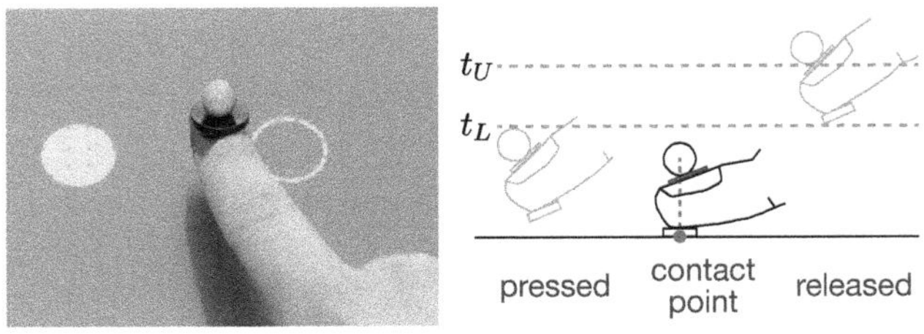

Figure 4: Drifting reduction test. Left: Test setup. Right: Contact point detection with upper (t_U) and lower (t_L) threshold for touch detection .

We measured the presses using the Vicon optical tracking system and a hysteresis thresholding. When the marker on the finger was moved below the lower threshold (15 mm), the button was considered as held down. When the user then moved the marker beyond the upper threshold (17 mm), the button was released. We considered the x-y-projection of the position closest to the surface as the *contact point* (Fig. 4, right). Since this contact point was slightly different among users, we measured the deviation based on the initial contact point of the left button where the user started.

The dependent variable was the *cumulative drift* [4] of the contact points. Following Brown et al., this is the Euclidean distance between the first contact point on the left button and each successive contact point for that button. Brown et al. show that the cumulative drift increases with trial numbers if no haptic feedback is present. We hypothesized that in our haptic condition, the cumulative drift would not increase along with trial numbers.

Participants. We tested 10 users (age: 23–29 years, M = 25.6, SD = 2.17). Two were female. All users were right-handed.

Results. The effect of haptic feedback can be seen from a trace of contact points such as the example shown in Fig. 5. The non-haptic condition is shown in bright red, and the haptic condition is shown in dark green. The arrows show the order of the trials. The contact points in the non-haptic feedback condition gradually drift downward. The contact points in the haptic feedback condition, however, are clustered together and do not show any consistent drifting direction.

As shown in Fig. 6, the increased cumulative drift in non-haptic condition, plotted in bright red, confirmed Brown et al.'s experiment [4], $F(1, 219) = 194.11$, $p < .001$, $r = 0.69$. In the haptic condition, plotted in dark green, however, the cumulative drift did not accumulate, $F(1, 219) = 3.51$, $p = .062$.

Discussion. Our results show that using electromagnetic force fields can significantly decrease drifting when operating virtual buttons in an eyes-free setting. As in the previous test, the attraction to the surface depends on the applied voltage and on the quality and size of the magnets involved. Furthermore, the position of the permanent magnet on the fingertip might influence touch performance. According to Holz and Baudisch [8], users rely on visual features to de-

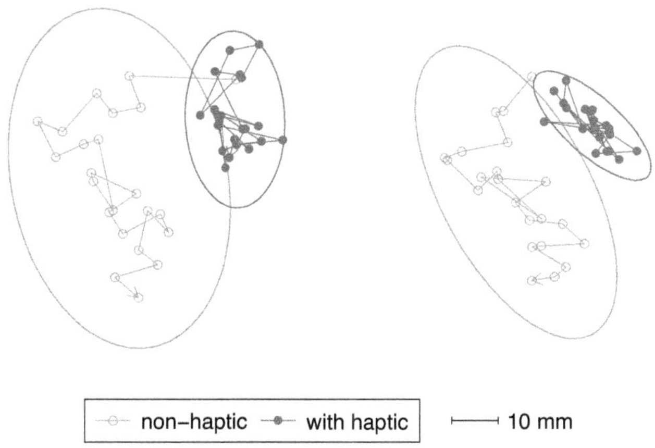

Figure 5: An example of contact points in the eyes-free user test. The ellipses superimpose the 95% confidence level of the normal-probability contours.

rive a mental model of where the actual contact point on the surface is. The electromagnet at the button's center, however, attracts the permanent magnets to a distinct position which does not necessarily match the user's mental model. Although this is not an issue in an eyes-free task, the interaction while looking could suffer from interfering visual and haptic models. This should be taken into account when attaching the permanent magnet to the finger.

DISCUSSION

Our prototype involves taping a magnet to the user's fingertip to maximize the perceived haptic feedback. While this preserves most pressure and shearing feedback when touching and dragging on the surface, this specific setup reduces the tactile sensation of the fingertip and might be impractical for ad-hoc use. However, more practical solutions are straightforward, such as wearing a glove or a thimble that places a magnet to the each side of the finger or on top of the fingertip. Also, a less direct input device, such as a stylus, is imaginable. In all cases, users have to wear an additional feedback device. Yet, this limitation can be worthwhile in many applications, e.g., when providing haptic feedback for blind people that could not feel the interface otherwise.

Haptic feedback is most effective when the magnet is hold parallel to the table. Rolling the finger around inverses the perceived force. However, we did not observe this inconvenient posture in our studies. Yet, in cases where tilting finger gestures are considered for input, or where a physical input device is used (e.g., a stylus with permanent magnet attached to its tip), orientation must be tracked, e.g., with an accelerometer, and magnetic fields must be adapted accordingly.

The strength and quality of the haptic experience also depends on the properties of the involved permanent and electromagnets. Beyond that, ergonomic constraints must be taken into account when designing the system. On the one hand, a large neodymium magnet at the user's finger enables strong feedback but may be inconvenient to wear. On the other hand, smaller permanent magnets need a higher electric power consumption for the same haptic effect.

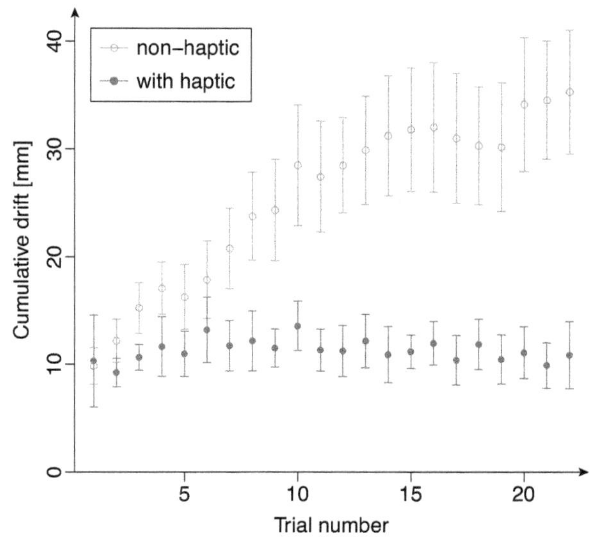

Figure 6: Comparison of drifting with and without haptic feedback. Inter-subject means of cumulative drift in each measured trial. Error bars represent inter-subject SE. Without haptic feedback, drifting increases in subsequent trials. With haptic feedback, it does not increases in subsequent trials.

The diameter and space of the electromagnets determine the haptic output resolution. While a smaller diameter allows designers to model smaller virtual controls, this also decreases the power of the electromagnets. A longer electromagnet or a different core material can compensate for this. Also, dynamically modulating the strengths of adjacent electromagnets can increase the haptic resolution. However, this requires precise tracking and high update rates of the electromagnetic array.

Electromagnets become warm when activated over a long time. The warmer an electromagnet is, the higher is its electrical resistance, and, therefore, the lower the force felt by the user. Cooling the array is essential to apply a constant force.

CONCLUSION AND FUTURE WORK

We presented FingerFlux, a system for creating near-surface haptic feedback in tabletop systems. Using electromagnetic actuation with permanent magnets on the user's finger tip, we are able to generate repulsion, attraction, vibration, and directional feedback on and above the table surface. Several potential applications using this feedback were presented. We have shown that the feedback is perceivable in a volume near the surface up to a height of 35 mm, and that it can reduce drifting when users operate on-screen controls in an eyes-free manner.

For future work, we want to explore the perceivable resolution of magnetic actuation patterns on different parts of the hand. We are also interested in evaluating the capabilities of the system to generate multi-finger haptic feedback. From an engineering perspective, we want to iterate practical designs that make wearing a magnet on the hand convenient but also preserve the natural tactile sensation when interacting with touchscreens. Finally, we intend to implement and evaluate applications that employ near-surface haptic feedback to augment productivity tasks.

ACKNOWLEDGMENTS
The German B-IT Foundation funded this work in part.

REFERENCES

1. O. Bau, I. Poupyrev, A. Israr, C. Harrison. TeslaTouch: electrovibration for touch surfaces. *Proc. UIST '10*, 283–292, 2010.
2. M. A. Baumann, K. E. MacLean, T. W. Hazelton, A. McKay. Emulating human attention-getting practices with wearable haptics. *Proc. HAPTICS '10*, 149–156, 2010.
3. M. Bergamasco, B. Allotta, L. Bosio, L. Ferretti, G. Parrini, G. Prisco, F. Salsedo, G. Sartini. An arm exoskeleton system for teleoperation and virtual environments applications. *Proc. ICRA '94*, 2:1449–1454, 1994.
4. L. E. Brown, D. A. Rosenbaum, R. L. Sainburg. Limb position drift: Implications for control of posture and movement. *J NEUROPHYSIOL*, 90(5):3105 –3118, 2003.
5. J. Gordon, M. F. Ghilardi, C. Ghez. Accuracy of planar reaching movements. I. independence of direction and extent variability. *EXP BRAIN RES*, 99(1):97–111, 1994.
6. T. Grieve, Y. Sun, J. M. Hollerbach, S. A. Mascaro. 3-D force control on the human fingerpad using a magnetic levitation device for fingernail imaging calibration. *Proc. EuroHaptics '09*, 411–416, 2009.
7. C. Harrison, S. E. Hudson. Abracadabra: wireless, high-precision, and unpowered finger input for very small mobile devices. *Proc. UIST '09*, 121–124, 2009.
8. C. Holz, P. Baudisch. Understanding touch. *Proc. CHI '11*, 2501–2510, 2011.
9. J. Hook, S. Taylor, A. Butler, N. Villar, S. Izadi. A reconfigurable ferromagnetic input device. *Proc. UIST '09*, 51–54, 2009.
10. T. Hoshi, M. Takahashi, T. Iwamoto, H. Shinoda. Noncontact tactile display based on radiation pressure of airborne ultrasound. *IEEE Trans. Haptics*, 3(3):155–165, 2010.
11. Y. Jansen, T. Karrer, J. Borchers. MudPad: tactile feedback and haptic texture overlay for touch surfaces. *Proc. ITS '10*, 11–14, 2010.
12. H. Kajimoto, M. Inami, N. Kawakami, S. Tachi. SmartTouch - augmentation of skin sensation with electrocutaneous display. *Proc. HAPTICS '03*, 40–46, 2003.
13. J. Lee, S. Choi. Effects of haptic guidance and disturbance on motor learning: Potential advantage of haptic disturbance. *Proc. HAPTICS '10*, 335–342, 2010.
14. J. Linvill, J. Bliss. A direct translation reading aid for the blind. *P IEEE*, 54(1):40–51, 1966.
15. N. Marquardt, M. A. Nacenta, J. E. Young, S. Carpendale, S. Greenberg, E. Sharlin. The haptic tabletop puck: tactile feedback for interactive tabletops. *Proc. ITS '09*, 85–92, 2009.
16. T. H. Massie, J. K. Salibury. The PHANTOM haptic interface: A device for probing virtual objects. *Proc. HAPTICS '94*, 55:295–301, 1994.
17. I. Oakley, M. R. McGee, S. Brewster, P. Gray. Putting the feel in 'look and feel'. *Proc. CHI '00*, 415–422, 2000.
18. G. Pangaro, D. Maynes-Aminzade, H. Ishii. The actuated workbench: computer-controlled actuation in tabletop tangible interfaces. *Proc. UIST '02*, 181–190, 2002.
19. J. Rekimoto. SenseableRays: opto-haptic substitution for touch-enhanced interactive spaces. *Proc. CHI EA '09*, 2519–2528, 2009.
20. J. Schwarz, S. Hudson, J. Mankoff, A. D. Wilson. A framework for robust and flexible handling of inputs with uncertainty. *Proc. UIST '10*, 47–56, 2010.
21. Y. Suzuki, M. Kobayashi. Air jet driven force feedback in virtual reality. *IEEE Comput. Graph. Appl.*, 25:44–47, 2005.
22. E. Tamaki, T. Miyaki, J. Rekimoto. Possessedhand: Techniques for controlling human hands using electrical muscles stimuli. *Proc. CHI '11*, 543–552, 2011.
23. B. Unger, R. Hollis, R. Klatzky. The geometric model for perceived roughness applies to virtual textures. *Proc. Haptics '08*, 3–10, 2008.
24. M. Weiss, C. Remy, J. Borchers. Rendering physical effects in tabletop controls. *Proc. CHI '11*, 3009–3012, 2011.
25. M. Weiss, F. Schwarz, S. Jakubowski, J. Borchers. Madgets: actuating widgets on interactive tabletops. *Proc. UIST '10*, 293–302, 2010.
26. M. Weiss, J. Wagner, Y. Jansen, R. Jennings, R. Khoshabeh, J. D. Hollan, J. Borchers. SLAP widgets: bridging the gap between virtual and physical controls on tabletops. *Proc. CHI '09*, 481–490, 2009.
27. D. Wigdor, S. Williams, M. Cronin, R. Levy, K. White, M. Mazeev, H. Benko. Ripples: utilizing per-contact visualizations to improve user interaction with touch displays. *Proc. UIST '09*, 3–12, 2009.
28. R. Wishnitzer, T. Laiteerapong, O. Hecht. Subcutaneous implantation of magnets in fingertips of professional gamblers-Case report. *PLAST RECONSTR SURG*, 71(3):473–474, 1983.
29. C. Wusheng, W. Tianmiao. Design of data glove and arm type haptic interface. *Proc. HAPTICS '03*, 422–427, 2003.

Force Gestures: Augmenting Touch Screen Gestures with Normal and Tangential Forces

Seongkook Heo and Geehyuk Lee
Department of Computer Science, KAIST
Daejeon, 305-701, South Korea
{leodic, geehyuk}@gmail.com

ABSTRACT

Force gestures are touch screen gestures augmented by the normal and tangential forces on the screen. In order to study the feasibility of the force gestures on a mobile touch screen, we implemented a prototype touch screen device that can sense the normal and tangential forces of a touch gesture on the screen. We also designed two example applications, a web browser and an e-book reader, that utilize the force gestures for their primary actions. We conducted a user study with the prototype and the applications to study the characteristics of the force gestures and the effectiveness of their mapping to the primary actions. In the user study we could also discover interesting usability issues and collect useful user feedback about the force gestures and their mapping to GUI actions.

ACM Classification: H5.2 [Information interfaces and presentation]: User Interfaces. - Input devices and strategies.

General terms: Design, Human Factors

Keywords: Touch input, force input, finger properties

INTRODUCTION

A touch screen allows users to manipulate objects on the screen directly with their fingers. Many touch screen gestures such as a swipe, a flick, or a pinch are intuitive as they are based on real-world gestures. However, a touch screen usually detects the position of touch points only, and ignores other physical properties of a finger gesture. The same finger movement on an object in the real world may be associated with different intentions depending on its normal and tangential forces. For instance, the same finger movement can be intended to turn a single page or to turn multiple pages, or to slide on a page depending on its normal and tangential forces. However, the touch screen cannot differentiate these gestures. A solution to deal with these types of gesture conflicts is to use modes, but this strategy usually complicates the user interface. Another solution is to use different numbers of fingers [1], but this is not the way we manipulate objects in the real world. A more fundamental solution will be to let a touch screen sense physical properties of a finger gesture beyond touch movements and discern the differences among similar gestures.

We explored new possibilities with a touch screen that can sense not only touch positions but also the touch force. In particular, we focused on the tangential component of the force, as common gestures such as underlining, page-turning, and multi-page turning gestures are differ in terms of the tangential component of the touch force. We implemented a prototype device that can sense the normal and the tangential component of the forces on the screen, designed 'force gestures' which differ in terms of both touch movements and force patterns, and conducted an experiment to verify the feasibility of this approach. Finally, we compiled strategies to map force gestures to different actions, implemented two force gesture applications, and evaluated the force gesture mappings by a user study.

RELATED WORK

Numerous studies have attempted to augment input actions by sensing additional physical properties such as force. Harrison et al. [5] added pressure sensors on a mobile device to detect flicking and grasping gestures. The pressure sensors were also used for handedness detection. Cechanowicz et al. [2] used force sensors to extend the input of a mouse and studied usability issues through experiments. They also suggested design recommendations based on the results of their experiments. Ramos et al. [11] undertook experiments to investigate the use of force with different types of visual feedback, finding that continuous visual feedback is necessary for a pressure widget. Ramos and Balakrishnan [10] presented a method of controlling a precision parameter with force, also presenting pressure marks, which augment pen gestures using force.

The force-sensing touch screen has a long history. In 1978, Herot and Weinzapfel [6] presented an interface that can sense the force vector applied to a screen via strain gauges around the touch surface. Minsky [7] implemented a system to sense force vectors and presented scenarios in which single finger gestures were detected by a screen. For multi-touch table settings, Davison and Han [4] implemented an object arrangement method using the pressure of the touch point. The pressure was estimated from the size of the touch area. Vision-based multi-touch tables can measure the shape of a touch area, and there have been attempts to obtain the orientation of a finger [14] and to differentiate two different types of touch [15].

The force-sensing mobile touch screen has a relatively short history. Clarkson et al. [3] investigated the possibility of using pressure as input for a mobile device. Miyaki and Rekimoto [8] added a force-sensitive resistor to a mobile device and proposed a zooming and scrolling method controlled by pressure. Research In Motion [12] released Blackberry Storm 2, which has four FSRs under the touch screen and used pressure information to distinguish a touch and a click. Roudaut et al. [13] proposed a method that enriched touch input without the use of additional sensors by distinguishing a touch input according to the movement patterns of touch points.

While a force-sensing touch screen has a long history and force sensing on a mobile touch screen has been studied, no research has investigated the use of tangential force on a mobile touch screen, which is the main focus of our paper.

IMPLEMENTATION

Prototype Device

We implemented a prototype touch screen that can sense normal and tangential forces. Before we arrive at the current prototype, we had to experience many trials and errors. At first, we took apart an iPod Touch and attempted to install sensors under the touch panel, but were never successful. The next strategy that we chose was to use the device as it is and add a structure around it for sensing. We made a frame that is basically in the same form as the one shown in Figure 1, and attached 11 force sensors under and by the device to sense normal and tangential forces applied on the screen. The main problem of this prototype was that it was not sensitive enough to detect small shear force by natural touch gestures. Also, the iPod Touch would be stuck on or between the sensors intermittently. These problems were solved by the structure shown in Figure 1.

The prototype consists of three parts: a frame with force sensors, an iPod Touch device, and a film plate to deliver a tangential force on the screen to sensors on the frame. The film plate has a thin acrylic frame that prevents the film from bending. The sensor frame has 12 sensors: four sensors on the bottom to measure normal force, and two sensors on each of the four sidewalls to measure the tangential forces. The sensor frame also incorporates a circuit board with a PIC18F4620 microcontroller with a 10-bit A-D converter. When a finger touches the screen, normal force is delivered to the four pressure sensors on the bottom of the frame through the iPod Touch while tangential force is delivered to side sensors through the film plate. We had to pay special attention to the friction between the film plate and the sensors on the frame and to the friction between the film plate and the device. To reduce this friction, we attached a Teflon tapes (X-Ray Zerofriction) onto the four edges of the iPod screen and on the force sensors.

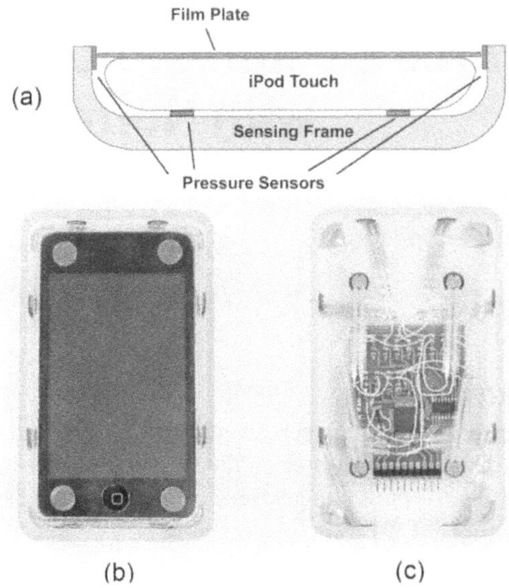

Figure 1: The prototype: (a) a cross-sectional view to show the sensing structure, (b) the top view of the prototype, and (c) the sensing frame.

The final prototype is in fact a result of much trial and error. The sensing structures given in Herot and Weinzapfel [6] or in Minsky [7] were not a suitable example for a small mobile touchscreen. The structure in Figure 1 was finally sensitive enough to sense the small shear force rendered by a finger slide on a slippery touch screen (approximately 0.3 N). We refrained from a hasty user study with an unsatisfactory prototype because we knew that a poor prototype is often the end of a new idea. We might have given up the current study discouraged by negative user feedback if we had enforced a user test with an immature prototype that required excessive force to the point of fatigue.

Signal Processing

A microcontroller samples sensor values via a 10-bit A-D converter at a sampling rate of 30Hz, and sends the sampled sensor values to a PC, which then forwards the sensor values to the iPod Touch via a Wi-Fi connection. All subsequent signal processing is done by the iPod Touch, including the initial calibration. Owing to gravity, the sensor values change as the attitude of the prototype device changes. In order to remove the effect of gravity, the device stores the sensor values at the onset of a touch gesture and uses them as reference points for all subsequent sensor readings. The system calculates forces on the four side walls by adding the values from two sensors located on the walls. A 2D tangential force vector can be obtained by comparing the forces on the left/right walls and the top/bottom walls. Normal force is calculated by adding the sensor values of the four sensors at the bottom of the sensing frame. The touch input now has a touch position and a 2.5-dimensional force vector. (2.5-dimensional because the normal force is non-negative.)

FORCE GESTURES

Designing Force Gestures

A touch gesture is defined by a series of touch points. We designed force gestures by augmenting touch gestures by adding the force properties of the tangential force and the normal force. The set of force gestures that we designed is summarized in Table 1. The two basic touch gestures, a tap and a slide, are augmented to the five force gestures, a tap, a press, a pivot, a slide, and a drag. A press gesture is similar to a tap gesture but should be performed with a stronger normal force. A drag gesture is similar to a slide gesture but should be performed with a stronger tangential force. A pivot gesture is similar to a drag gesture but should be performed without slippage. Note in Table 1 that the normal force condition for a drag gesture is yes/no, which means that a drag gesture may or may not be accompanied by a strong normal force. A strong tangential force, which is the main feature of a drag gesture, may be due to a strong normal force or due to a high friction coefficient since the tangential force is given by $F = \mu N$ where μ is the coefficient of friction between a finger and the screen and N denotes the normal force on the screen. In other words, a drag gesture may be performed with a large normal force and/or with a high friction, e.g., by using the finger pad rather than the fingertip.

Mapping Force Gestures

We formulated two strategies to design the interaction mappings of force gestures based on the hierarchical structure of the GUI and the physical mass of the corresponding physical metaphor of action.

Current GUI elements are structured in a hierarchical manner. For example, in the Cocoa framework, a window may contain a view of three panels with buttons and text fields. In this case, we can assume that the GUI component at the higher level of the hierarchy have more components and information compared to those at the lower level. Therefore, we can connect gestures with less force to the current level of actions and gestures requiring more force with actions at the higher hierarchy.

Many GUI actions have been designed with physical metaphors. For example, the slide gesture used in an e-book reader application comes from the position movement of turning the pages of a book. Navigation through chapters has a heavier metaphor. When there are series of actions with different metaphor masses, we can map force gestures for their force properties.

Force Gesture Applications

We implemented two applications, a web browser and an e-book reader, to explore the properties of force gestures. The gesture mappings for these applications are shown in Table 1.

Web Browser Application

The web browser application supports multiple tabs (Figure 2(a)). We mapped the force gestures to actions for the web browser using both the hierarchical and the physical mass strategy. In the hierarchical GUI structure, the application frame containing multiple tabs is at the highest level, tabs are at the next level, and web pages are under the tabs. Thus, light force gestures, sliding and tapping, are mapped to scrolling a page and selecting a link, respectively, since they are actions within a web page. The pivot gesture is mapped to navigating backward and forward, which are higher level actions than actions within a web page. The drag gesture is a heavy gesture, and therefore we mapped it to left/right navigation between tabs. To give an immediate feedback about a gesture, simple animation of a tab movement was provided. Dragging upward or downward was mapped with a physical-mass strategy. A dragging gesture is heavier than a sliding gesture, and therefore we mapped dragging upward or downward to scrolling to the bottom or the top of the page. Adding to favorites can be done with a press gesture, which is a metaphor of pinning something up.

E-book Reader Application

The e-book reader application was designed following the

Icon	Name	Position Movement	Normal Force	Tangential Force	Application Mappings			
					Web Browser		e-Book Reader	
	Tap	No	No	No	Select a link		Call menu	
	Press	No	Yes	No	Add to Favorites		Add Bookmark	
	Pivot	No/Little	Yes	Yes	↑	-	↑	-
					↓	-	↓	-
					←	Go Back	←	Thumb through pages to end (Rate Control)
					→	Go Forward	→	Thumb through pages to first (Rate Control)
	Slide	Yes	No	No	↑	Scroll Down	↑	-
					↓	Scroll Up	↓	-
					←	Scroll Right	←	Turn a page to Next
					→	Scroll Left	→	Turn a page to Prev
	Drag	Yes	No/Yes	Yes	↑	Scroll to Bottom	↑	Hide Table of Contents
					↓	Scroll to Top	↓	Show Table of Contents
					←	Switch to Next Tab	←	Turn Multiple Pages to Next
					→	Switch to Prev Tab	→	Turn Multiple Pages to Prev

Table 1: Force gestures: their icons, defining properties, and mappings to application actions.

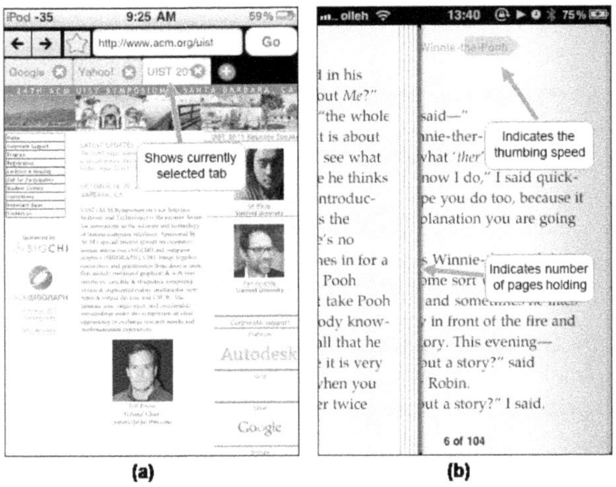

Figure 2: Screenshots of (a) the web browser and (b) the e-book application

Apple iBooks application (Figure 2(b)). A slide gesture was mapped to the action of turning a page, and a tap gesture was mapped to turning on or off an overlay menu. With this menu, users can add a bookmark, open the table of contents page, or navigate the e-book with a scroll bar. Force gestures are used to help users to navigate pages more efficiently. A drag gesture can be regarded as a slide gesture with stronger friction, i.e., it is like turning multiple pages. Thus, we mapped the drag gesture to the action of flipping multiple pages at a time. A visual feedback about the number of pages to be turned is provided at the edge of the page. Therefore, users can select the number of pages to turn, from one to five pages, by controlling force on the edge before dragging.

Thumbing through the book can be done in many e-book applications with a slider control. However, in the real world, thumbing through a book can be regarded as a rate control action rather than a position control action. Therefore, we mapped the pivot gesture to thumbing action. Users can thumb through the book at a varying speed by controlling tangential force in the pivot gesture. The magnitude of the tangential force is displayed on the screen as the length of an indicator in the shape of a pentagon. Dragging downward and upward on a page was mapped to show and hide the table of contents. The press gesture was mapped to the action of adding a bookmark, as the press gesture was mapped to adding to favorites in the browser application.

EVALUATION

Two experiments were conducted to test the feasibility of a prototype device and to study the usability properties of the force gestures.

Participants

Ten participants were recruited for the experiments. Three participants were female and all participants were right-handed. The mean age of the participants was 25.3 years old. One of the participants had little experience in using mobile devices equipped with a touch screen, while all others were experienced users.

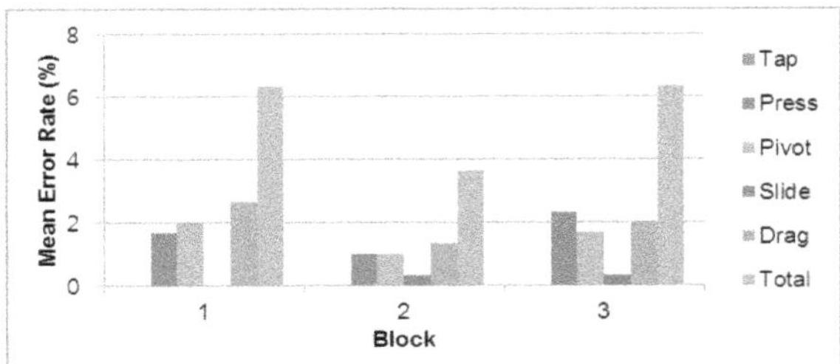

Figure 3: The mean error rates of the force gestures in the three blocks.

Experiment Settings

All experiments were done in a seated condition. Because every participant was right-handed, they were asked to hold the prototype device in their right hand and operate the touch screen with the thumb on that hand.

Feasibility Test

The first experiment was designed to test the basic feasibility of the prototype and the proposed force gestures. The experiment also aimed to discover the difficulties and error characteristics of the force gestures. Force gestures were recognized by a simple rule-based algorithm based on the attributes defined in Table 1. The classification rules were heuristically generated.

Tasks and Procedure

At the beginning of the experiment, simple instructions and a demonstration of the force gestures were given to the participants. After receiving the instructions, participants were asked to use force gestures until they became feel comfortable with input gestures, which did not take more than 5 minutes. When they felt that they were ready for the experiment, they started it. The task was to perform force gestures by following prompts randomly displayed on the screen. The recognized result was also displayed on the screen. The experiment consisted of 900 trials (10 participants x 3 blocks x 30 trials).

Results

Figure 3 shows the mean error rate for the three blocks of the feasibility study. Although the experiment was conducted immediately after a short practice period, users were able to input force gestures for approximately 93.6% of tasks from the first block, and the mean error rate of all blocks was approximately 5.4%. A drag gesture was the most error-prone for all blocks, responsible for 36.7% of all errors. Among the drag errors, 66.7% were recognized as pivot gestures; these errors resulted when the participants failed to slide their finger far enough to trigger a drag gesture. The second most error-prone gesture was a press gestures, with 66.7% press gestures recognized as tap gestures. The third was a pivot gesture, which was often misrecognized as a press gestures. We expect that these three most common types of error may be reduced with a proper visual feedback as these errors often occur when a movement distance, a normal force, or a tangential force failed to reach a threshold value.

Evaluating Force Gestures

To discover the usability issues related to the force gestures, we conducted an experiment with two applications that use force gestures.

Tasks and Procedure

The two applications of a web browser with tab browsing functionality and an e-book reader application were used for this task. After the feasibility test, participants were asked to use both applications. Instructions regarding the use of the applications with force gestures were given at the beginning of the experiment. While explaining the force gestures, we described the gestures figuratively. For the press gestures, mapped to the 'add to favorites' and 'add bookmark' actions, we instructed "press as though you are pinning something up.", while for drag gestures, we instructed them to "drag as though you're dragging paper pages".

For the web browser application, participants were asked to visit the news page at Google.com, a long page that requires scrolling to view. They were also asked to surf the web for about five minutes while using all of the available gesture hotkeys, as described in the previous section. With the e-book application, we demonstrated how to use force gestures and let the participants navigate a book freely with force gestures. As in the web browser application, they were asked to use all force gestures.

After the experiment, the participants completed a questionnaire with using a five-point Likert scale (1: strongly disagree, 5: strongly agree), answering about six questions about usability. These assessed the intuitiveness of the gestures, the ease of learning, the level of fatigue, the input difficulty, enjoyment, and their preference regarding the use of a force gesture over a conventional touch gestures. We also used interviews to discover possible usability issues, such as how a participant felt about the mapping direction of the force gestures, which was rated the most interesting gesture.

Results

The questionnaire results for the eight force gesture mappings as used in the two applications (four gestures for each application) are shown in Figure 4. The four gesture mappings listed above were used in the web browser application and four below were used in the e-book reader application. The participants agreed that the gesture mappings were intuitive and easy to learn.

We noted that the two gesture mappings of backward/forward and thumbing through pages were relatively difficult to learn, as they were triggered by the pivot gesture. According to the responses to the questions about fatigue and input difficulty we found that these two gesture mappings were difficult to input and that they led to user fatigue. One interesting aspect was that although the thumbing and the backward/forward actions were activated by the same force gesture, thumbing through pages was the most preferable gesture mapping of all, whereas the backward/forward was the least. We deduced the reason for this from the questionnaire result and from the comments during the interview. Thumbing through pages was rated highest in terms of enjoyment; it also received the most positive feedback in the interview.

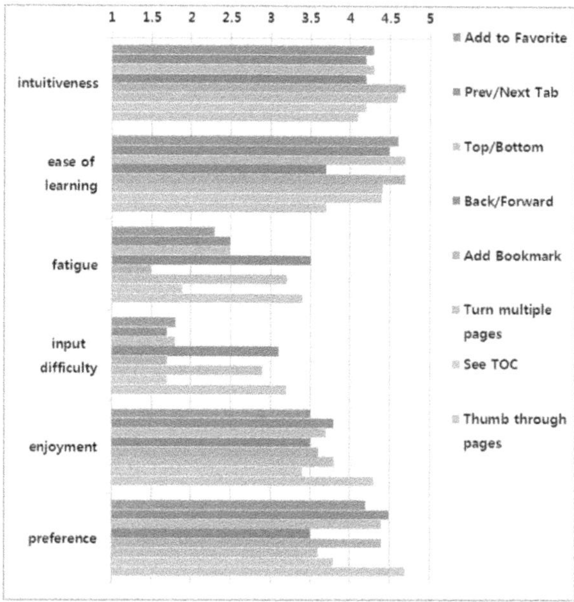

Figure 4: The questionnaire results for the eight force gesture mappings (on a 5-point Likert scale)

Turning multiple pages enables users to turn multiple pages at once while providing a method to choose the number of pages to turn. We observed that participants tended to choose the exact number of pages carefully and that they did not want to turn an arbitrary number of pages. We received many comments about this gesture. Participants stated, "I was stressed about the visual feedback showing the number of pages. The visual feedback urged me to select the exact number of pages." Another subject reported, "I would not use this function. If I need to turn many pages, I would simply thumb through them all".

The press gesture was used in two applications, for "add to favorites" and "add bookmark," which can be assumed to be similar in terms of the action required. However, the questionnaire result on fatigue showed a difference between the two actions; "add bookmark" was reported to be the gesture that led to the least fatigue, whereas "add to favorites" was rated relatively highly in this area. We could infer the reasoning behind comments such as, "I was worried when I added a page to my favorites because I would end up selecting a link if I failed to perform the press gesture. Going to an unwanted page is really annoying." Hence, the possibility of triggering an unintended action made participants apply more force to the screen.

During the interviews, the participants were asked questions about the direction mappings for gestures. We received various comments related to these questions, and most answers reported "no problem with the direction," but some of the participants expressed that they experienced confusion. Two participants reported that they were confused when they performed the drag up/down to scroll to bottom/top actions. One participant reported that he felt like he was holding a scroll bar, not the webpage itself. Two participants told us that they were confused about the tab change direction. Finally, one participant reported that the direction mapping for backward/forward actions was initially confusing.

DISCUSSION

Participants in the user study reported that the two actions, backward/forward navigation and thumbing through pages, were most difficult and caused the most fatigue. Note that both were actions associated with the pivot gesture. However, the user preferences of the two actions were markedly different. Backward/forward navigation was least preferred, while thumbing through pages was the most preferred. The backward/forward action may have been least preferred because it caused a lot of fatigue. Thumbing action, though it is basically the same as backward/forward navigation action in terms of gesture, may have been favored because it was rewarding, i.e., it enabled the control of the flipping rate, which was not possible before. Also, it may have been preferred because its conceptual mapping was adequate.

For the drag gesture, participants felt more fatigue when it was used for the multiple page-turn action than when it was used for previous/next-tab action. This may be that the drag gesture for turning multiple pages involves multiple levels. In order to hold a certain amount of pages, participants had to press the screen with a strong force, resulting in stronger friction between the finger and the screen. In particular, they experienced difficulty while adjusting the number of pages that they wanted to hold.

We explained all participants how to use force gestures with a short demonstration. Unlike finger movements, finger forces may have been invisible to the participants, and this may have confused them. In the first implementation, the e-book application did not give a feedback on the amount of tangential force applied to the device, and, for this reason, participants in the pilot study commented that it was hard to perform a thumbing action. Later, we added a tangential force indicator on top of the screen, and participants reported that it was much easier to use than before. We expect that a continuous visual feedback about applied forces will help users learn force gestures more easily.

CONCLUSION

We implemented a prototype touch screen device to detect force vectors and studied force gestures by designing two applications on the prototype. Through a user study, we verified the feasibility of force gestures and discovered valuable usability issues about using force gestures. We are currently investigating possible mappings between force gestures and GUI actions further with the goal of building a force gesture framework.

ACKNOWLEDGMENTS

This work was in part supported by the IT R&D program of MKE/KEIT. [10039161, Core UI technologies for improving Smart TV UX]

REFERENCES

1. Apple™, Magic Trackpad™ http://www.apple.com/magictrackpad/
2. Cechanowicz, J., Irani, P. and Subramanian, S., Augmenting the mouse with pressure sensitive input. In *Proc. CHI '07*, pp. 1385-1394.
3. Clarkson, E., Patel, S., Pierce, J. and Abowd, G. Exploring Continuous Pressure Input for Mobile Phones. In GVU Technical Report; GIT-GVU-06-20, 2006.
4. P. Davidson and J. Han, Extending 2D object arrangement with pressure-sensitive layering cues. In *Proc. UIST '08*, pp. 87-90.
5. Harrison, B., et al., Squeeze Me, Hold Me, Tilt Me! An Exploration of Manipulative User Interfaces, In *Proc. CHI '98*, pp. 17-14.
6. Herot, C. F. and Weinzapfel, G., One-point touch input of vector information for computer displays. In *Proc. SIGGRAPH '78*, pp. 210-216.
7. Minsky, M. R. Manipulating simulated objects with real-world gestures using a force and position sensitive screen. In *Proc. SIGGRAPH '84*, pp. 195-203.
8. Miyaki, T. and Rekimoto, J. GraspZoom: zooming and scrolling control model for single-handed mobile interaction. In *Proc. MobileHCI '09*, pp. 1-4.
9. Ramos, G. A. and Balakrishnan, R. Pressure marks. In *Proc. CHI '07*, pp. 1375-1394.
10. G. Ramos and R. Balakrishnan, Zliding: fluid zooming and sliding for high precision parameter manipulation. In *Proc. UIST '05*, pp. 143-152.
11. Ramos, G. A. et al. Pressure widgets. In *Proc. CHI '04*, pp. 487-494.
12. Research In Motion™ SurePress™ Technology http://www.rim.com/products/surepress/index.shtml
13. Roudaut, A. et al. MicroRolls: expanding touch-screen input vocabulary by distinguishing rolls vs. slides of the thumb. In *Proc. CHI '09*, pp. 927-936.
14. Wang, F. et al. Detecting and leveraging finger orientation for interaction with direct-touch surfaces. In *Proc. UIST '09*, pp. 23-32.
15. Wang, F. and Ren, X. Empirical evaluation for finger input properties in multi-touch interaction. In *Proc. CHI '09*, pp. 1063-1.

TapSense: Enhancing Finger Interaction on Touch Surfaces

Chris Harrison *Julia Schwarz* *Scott E. Hudson*

Human-Computer Interaction Institute and Heinz College Center for the Future of Work
Carnegie Mellon University, 5000 Forbes Avenue, Pittsburgh PA 15213
{chris.harrison, julia.schwarz, scott.hudson}@cs.cmu.edu

ABSTRACT

We present *TapSense*, an enhancement to touch interaction that allows conventional surfaces to identify the type of object being used for input. This is achieved by segmenting and classifying sounds resulting from an object's impact. For example, the diverse anatomy of a human finger allows different parts to be recognized – including the tip, pad, nail and knuckle – without having to instrument the user. This opens several new and powerful interaction opportunities for touch input, especially in mobile devices, where input is extremely constrained. Our system can also identify different sets of passive tools. We conclude with a comprehensive investigation of classification accuracy and training implications. Results show our proof-of-concept system can support sets with four input types at around 95% accuracy. Small, but useful input sets of two (e.g., pen and finger discrimination) can operate in excess of 99% accuracy.

ACM Classification: H.5.2 [Information interfaces and presentation]: User Interfaces - Graphical user interfaces; Input devices and strategies.

General terms: Human Factors

Keywords: Acoustic classification, tabletop computing, interactive surfaces, tangibles, tools, pens, stylus, finger, multi-user, touchscreen, collaborative, input.

INTRODUCTION

Computers are increasingly featuring direct touch interfaces, found in forms as diverse as kiosks and interactive tabletops, to tablet computers and handheld mobile devices. At present, finger input on touchscreens is handled very simplistically, essentially boiled down to an X/Y coordinate. However, human fingers are remarkably sophisticated, both in their anatomy and motor capabilities. We can form them into many poses and perform a wide variety of gestures.

We present an enhancement to touchscreen interaction that enables identification of the object used for input. Our system can recognize small sets of passive tools as well as discriminate different parts of the finger – tip, pad, knuckle and nail (Figure 1 and 2). The latter is especially valuable on mobile devices, where input bandwidth is limited due to small screens and "fat fingers" [16]. For example, a knuckle tap could serve as a "right click" for mobile device touch interaction, effectively doubling input bandwidth. Right-click-like functionality is currently achieved on touch surfaces with fairly unintuitive and un-scalable chording of fingers and tap-and-hold interactions. Finally, our approach requires no electronics or sensors to be placed on the user.

RELATED APPROACHES

Many technologies exist that have the ability to digitize different types of input. There are two main touch sensing approaches: active and passive.

The key downside of active approaches is that an explicit object must be used (e.g., a special pen), which is implemented with electronics (and batteries if not tethered). For example, pens augmented with infrared light emitters on their tips can be used on the commercially available Microsoft Surface [15]. There have also been efforts to move beyond pens, including, e.g., infrared-light-emitting brushes for painting applications [27]. Current systems generally do not attempt to discriminate among different pens (just perhaps pen from finger input). Variably-modulated infrared light enables identification, but requires specialized hardware. Additionally, ultrasonics can be used for input localization [19], and can provide pen ID as well. Capacitive coupling in [6,7] allows users or objects to be localized and identified, though this requires grounding plates or a physical connection to function.

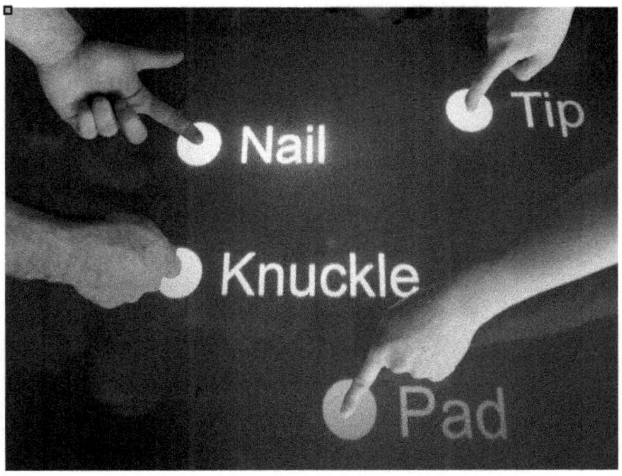

Figure 1. *TapSense* can classify different types of finger input.

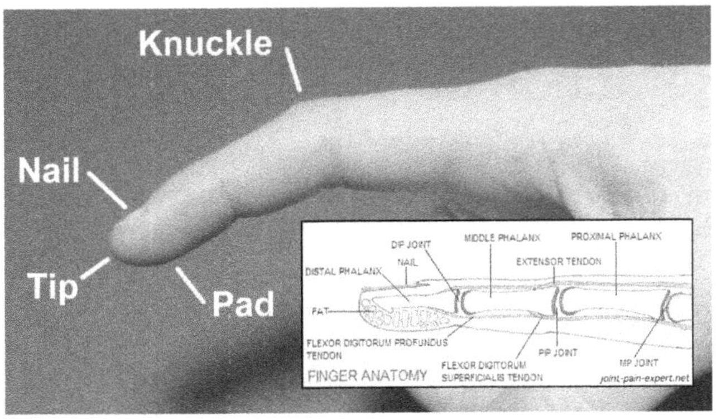

Figure 2. Different parts of the finger can be identified for use on touch surfaces.

Sensing based on electromagnetic resonance operates between active and passive. Although the tools and tangibles need not be powered, they contain a resonant coil that is excited by proximate EM fields, generated by the specialized tablet they operate on. Although highly capable, including the ability to provide ID, table-sized setups are prohibitively expensive at present. It is also possible to support object identification through a combination of RFID and vision processing [20], which offers greater scalability.

Fiducial markers are a truly passive approach. They provide the ID of an object through a uniquely patterned tag – often in a sticker form factor [17,24]. This method has been shown to be very capable – the only major drawback is the size of the marker, which in general, prevents placement on small surfaces like the tip of a pen. Fiducial markers can also work in a capacitive-sensing manner [26], allowing tags to be embedded in an object. Additionally, the shape of an object can be captured optically and used for classification (e.g., mice and keyboards in [12]).

In general, the aforementioned techniques require instrumentation of the object providing input, which is a non-starter for fingers. To side step this, Hambone [5] uses wrist-mounted acoustic sensors to classify finger-on-finger actions, such as pinching or flicking. Finger taps can also be localized on the body through acoustic fingerprinting [10]. However, the latter systems require sensors to be placed on the user (a key objective of *TapSense* was that users did not need to be instrumented). Without instrumentation, some areas of the finger can be determined through computer vision (e.g., pad vs. tip) [16,28]. Using accelerometers, soft and hard taps can be discriminated [13].

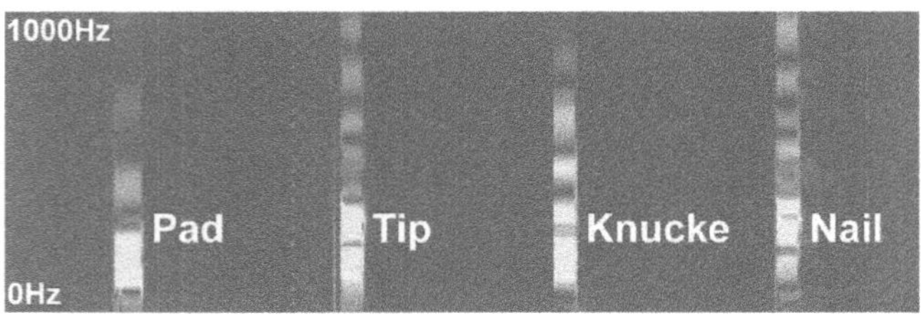

Figure 3. Spectrograms of our four finger input types.

Finally, The Interactive Window Project [21,22] uses time of flight to localize touch events on a large pane of glass. The work also briefly mentions that frequency distribution can be used to classify touch type, such as a finger vs. fist bash, an approach seemingly similar to *TapSense*. Unfortunately, no details are provided about classification or training. Further, no accuracy results are provided, making the system impossible to compare, evaluate, or improve upon.

SENSING AND PROCESSING

Our approach is comprised of two key processes operating in concert. The first is some method for detecting and tracking the position of input, either single- or multi-touch. A variety of existing technologies could be used, including optical, resistive, and capacitive touchscreens. The second component - and the chief contribution of this paper - listens, segments and classifies impacts on the interactive surface using acoustic features. It relies on the physical principle that different materials produce different acoustic signatures and have different resonant frequencies (Figure 3). Once a classification has been made, it is paired with the last event from the touch surface.

For acoustic sensing, we use a conventional medical stethoscope coupled with an inexpensive electret condenser microphone, seen in Figure 4 (many microphone technologies are suitable, as well as accelerometers). This is affixed to the surface of an input-capable display. This setup resembles [11], which uses the same sensor and also takes advantage of (solid) surface acoustic transmission, albeit with a different objective (gesture recognition on ad hoc surfaces vs. tip recognition on touchscreens).

When an object strikes the surface, an ensemble of mechanical vibrations propagate outward through the material. Typically, interactive surfaces use rigid materials, such as plastic or glass, which both quickly distribute and faithfully preserve the signal. As demonstrated in [10,21] (also passive acoustic based), the strength of taps does not need to be great. Indeed, one needs to tap no harder than required to type on a keyboard.

A key property of this approach is that items striking the surface do not require active components. Input objects are simply composed of different materials and are entirely passive.

Segmentation of input signals is straightforward. Stethoscopes naturally provide a high level of environmental noise suppression. This allows impacts to be readily segmented from any background noise with a simple amplitude threshold. Once the audio data for the impact has been captured, our software processes it, extracting a series of time-independent acoustic features.

We recommend sampling at 96KHz, using a sliding window of 4096 (the first 43ms of impact signal). An Fast Fourier Transform (FFT) of this window produces 2048 bands of frequency power; we discard all but the lower 500 bands, representing the acoustic power from 0 to ~10kHz (though the lower 1kHz is the most expressive; see Figure 3). We then down-sample this data into an additional vector of length 50 (i.e., buckets of ten), providing a different aliasing. We also include the average absolute amplitude, total absolute amplitude, standard deviation of the absolute amplitude, and center of mass for both the segmented input signal and the FFT (8 features). Lastly, we also calculate the fundamental frequency of the impact waveform. These features are largely based on those employed successfully in Skinput [10], which used a similar acoustic approach for localizing inputs on the skin.

This process yields 559 features, on which we rely for classification. We use a support vector machine (SVM) implementation provided by the Weka Machine Learning toolkit [9] (SMO; polynomial kernel with default parameters). A full description of SVMs is beyond the scope of this paper; see [3] for a tutorial (note: as will be discussed in more detail later, before the classifier can be used, it must first be trained on each class' acoustic signature).

Once a classification has been made, the resulting type is used to label an unassigned input point (digitized by one of many touch sensing technologies and reported to our software). This matching process could be done several ways – we found selecting the input event with the closest onset timestamp was sufficient. The entire classification process, starting from the onset of impact, can occur in approximately 100ms, allowing for real-time interaction.

In practice, this method appears to work fairly well, and enables several users with multiple input objects to work on a common surface simultaneously. However, there is one special case where this process breaks down and for which there is no immediate solution – timing collisions. In particular, if two objects strike the surface in sufficiently close temporal proximity, their acoustic signals will not be segmented separately, and therefore not allow for accurate classification.

The duration of this period is defined by four factors: 1) the aggressiveness of the segmenter (because we use time-independent acoustic features, classification could potentially use e.g., the first 10ms of audio), 2) the resonant frequencies of the impact material (lower frequencies take longer to dissipate), 3) the dampening of the surface (to dissipate previous impacts) and 4) the size of the surface (more mass takes longer to dampen). With a carefully selected input set (almost exclusively materials with higher frequency resonance), a safe separation between impacts could be roughly 300ms on a large surface, such as a table or wall.

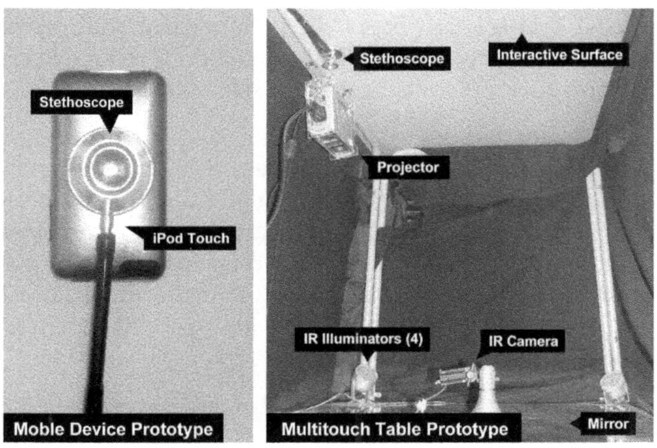

Figure 4. Chief components of our two prototype setups.

An alternative solution is to employ sophisticated algorithms that can localize impact sounds and separate them into distinct acoustic waveforms [1]. Although this is generally applied to environmental noises, such as speech, the principles should also apply to touch surfaces.

Fortunately, this issue is mostly moot on mobile devices, which, due to their small size and light weight, quickly diminish acoustic energy. Taps can occur as close as ~50ms apart on our mobile setup. Furthermore, mobile devices typically have a single user. This almost entirely eliminates the possibility of simultaneous impacts (the fastest the authors could double finger tap was 66ms - achieved in a contrived way).

PROOF-OF-CONCEPT SETUPS

To evaluate the scalability of our approach and better consider fruitful application areas, we constructed two proof-of-concept, *TapSense*-augmented, interactive surfaces: a hand-held mobile device and a full-sized multitouch table.

Mobile Device

To evaluate the performance of our approach on handheld devices, we instrumented an Apple iPod Touch (Figure 4). We use the iPod's 7.6 x 5.1 cm capacitive screen for input tracking. We connect our acoustic sensor to a conventional computer, which also runs our classifier and interface demos. To provide a graphical interface on the iPod, we simply VNC to the aforementioned computer. Although introducing some latency, this afforded us a common code base for our mobile device and multitouch table, enabling faster prototyping.

In a real product, a small microphone would likely be coupled to the screen at the cost of a few tens of cents. It may even be possible to use built-in microphones found in e.g., mobile phones. During early prototyping, it appeared that commercial devices applied various software/hardware filters for superior voice capture and ambient noise suppression, which degraded performance in the acoustic space we wished to use. However, with raw access to a device's microphone, it seems likely *TapSense* could be enabled with no additional hardware. Finally, it may be possible to realize superior sensing resolution through the use of multiple microphones [21,22].

Multitouch Table

We also built a tabletop multitouch setup (Figure 4) to 1) evaluate how *TapSense* scaled to larger surfaces, 2) consid-

Figure 5. Left: a directory of files; items can be opened or dragged using the traditional finger pad tap. Center: user alt-clicks a file with a knuckle tap, triggering a contextual menu. Right: User pad taps on the print option.

er collaborative applications (i.e., several collocated users), and 3) explore the uses and performance of handheld tools.

The tabletop surface consists of a 110 x 75 cm frosted glass sheet that provides a diffuse surface for both diffused illumination sensing [18] and graphical projection. In brief testing, plastics such as acrylic and polycarbonate appear to work just as well acoustically – we chose glass because of availably, low cost, and scratch resistance. Furthermore, the technique should function on curved or irregular interactive surfaces (e.g., [2]).

To create a table-like form factor, the glass surface is supported by a simple metal frame. To reduce undesirable chattering, the glass is supported on the frame by several rubber nubs. This also helped to isolate the touch surface from the support members and dampen mechanical energy from impacts. We centered our acoustic sensor above the interactive area, though many placements are possible.

FINGERS

Contemporary interactive surfaces generally treat finger touches as a single class of input (a partial exception to this is [16], which captures a high-resolution fingerprint image to infer the 3D "posture" of a finger; area of contact via optical sensing is used as an extra input dimension in [4,28]). However, this is a gross simplification - fingers are diverse appendages, both in their motor capabilities and their anatomical composition. Indeed, a single digit contains one major and two minor knuckles, a boney tip, a fleshy pad, and a fingernail – most of which can be readily discriminated by our acoustic approach. This ability to identify which part of the finger was used for input is unique to our system. Supporting additional dimensions of finger input has largely been ignored because instrumenting the user with active or passive components is invasive.

This approach has the potential to mitigate two significant problems faced in touch interaction:

1) Finger Overloading: At present, in order for a finger to perform different operations at a single point in space, it must be overloaded, typically triggered by a tap-and-hold period or chording of the fingers (e.g., two-finger-tap for right click). This often then triggers a transient contextual menu, which allows a user to select one of several actions. The power of contextual menus could be easily coupled to a finger "right click" (e.g., knuckle tap). The conventional finger pad tap could then operate as usual (selection, opening, dragging). The value of mice with two buttons is clear in desktop-class interaction. *TapSense* immediately enables this (and several additional click types) for touch screen input, with no user instrumentation. Figure 5 illustrates a simple sequence (see Video Figure for extended examples).

2) Breaking Out Functionality: An alternative to finger overloading is breaking functionality out into one or more buttons – for example, a button for minimizing a window and another for closing it. However, this is problematic for mobile devices with limited screen real estate.

TapSense offers a solution that entails no buttons. For example, the finger pad could operate as usual. However, a finger nail tap anywhere on the surface could trigger a minimization or "go back" action. Window maximization or "go forward" could be done similarly with a knuckle tap.

Example Finger Applications

TapSense is an enabling technique that can be used in a wide variety of application domains and use contexts. To help motivate our approach and underscore its utility, we developed several example applications we believe to be particularly interesting.

Soft keyboards on mobile devices are particularly problematic – there are many keys that need to be provided and very little space. In response, keyboards are typically broken up into several "pages" of keys, toggled with modal buttons. Not only does this add extra clicks to typing interactions, but also further crowds the small screen.

As a demonstration, we developed a *TapSense*-augmented soft keyboard that aimed to alleviate some of these problems. It features two key sets that operate in parallel, seen in Figure 6. To type a primary character, users can use their finger pad as usual. To type an alt character, a finger tip is used. Thus, users have access to the entire character set without having to switch pages. To backspace, the user can nail tap anywhere on the screen (i.e., no button necessary).

Another application we developed was a simple painting interface. To draw freehand, the user simply uses their finger pad like a brush. To draw line segments, a user tip

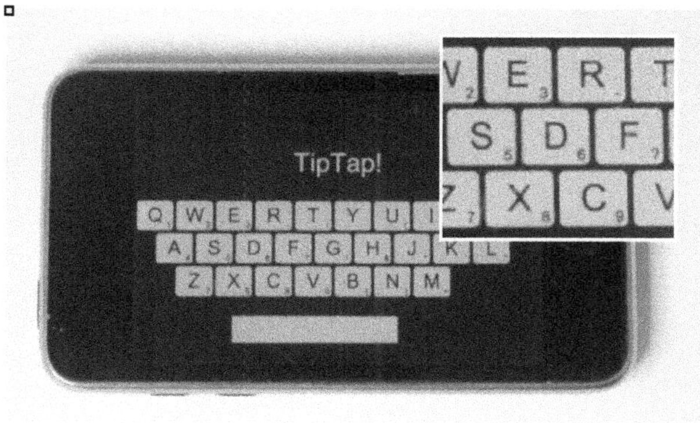

Figure 6. Our *TapSense*-augmented soft keyboard.

taps the screen and then drags to a desired location. To undo the last stroke, users can nail tap anywhere on the screen. This, like our keyboard demo, illustrates a simple way to remove modal buttons from the interaction and push this complexity to our highly dexterous fingers. Other interactions could involve rapid switching between tools (e.g., fill tool, erase tool) and modes (e.g., brush thickness, opacity, color).

Leveraging Existing Finger Behaviors

It is interesting to note that humans use different parts of their fingers in different ways – to scratch an itch, type on a keyboard, tap a co-worker on the shoulder, or knock on a door. With careful design, it may be possible to leverage these norms such that existing finger behaviors could be ported to and made relevant in digital domains.

For example, consider a system where a knuckle "knock" is used to open files or applications. A tap with the tip of the finger (i.e., poke) could be used to bring something to attention, perhaps maximized or given focus, whereas a fingernail "flick" could be used to minimize or delete an item. This functionality could operate in harmony with conventional finger-driven interfaces, which tend to rely on finger pads for pointing and "clicking".

PENS, POINTERS, STAMPS AND TOOLS

Humans have remarkable dexterity with handheld tools and, unsurprisingly, numerous research projects have introduced physical manipulators to interactive systems (see e.g., [14,15,17,23,25]). These often come in the form of pens, pointing devices, stamps (e.g., for instantiation) and miscellaneous tools (e.g., dials, sliders, guides).

Such items could easily incorporate acoustically-distinct materials, and be made small and pointy, like real pens and pencils. These would be extremely durable and inexpensive to mass produce. To accompany our multitouch table setup, we built a set of input objects, shown in Figure 7. These are simply different materials glued to the heads of dry erase markers, and were not specially engineered to achieve top performance.

Having even a small set of input objects could be valuable. For instance, painting applications on conventional interactive surfaces typically use a palette-based color mode selec-

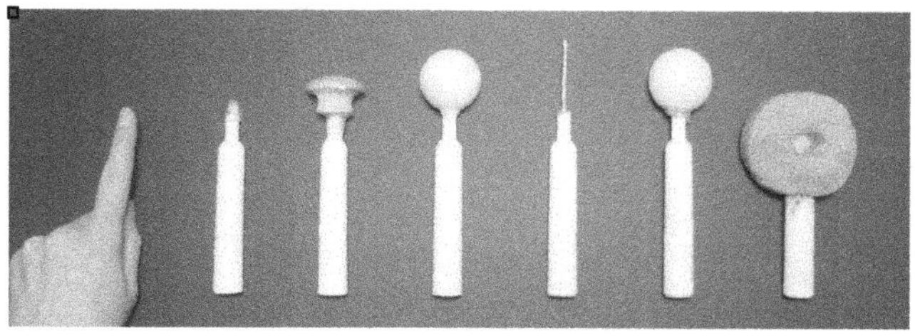

Figure 7. Finger and six tools with different materials affixed to their tips. Left to right: finger, polycarbonate nub, wood knob, acrylic ball, metal screw, ping-pong ball, foam.

tion. When a color is chosen, all users are forced to switch to this color. However, our system allows multiple users to pick up one of several color "brushes" and use them simultaneously (Figure 8). We also created a tool with different materials on each end, which could be used to draw and then flipped around to erase, like a pencil.

Another possibility is to assign users uniquely identified input tools. This would allow actions on a system to be attributed to a particular person (Figure 8) – a capability shared with [7]. This could be used for e.g., collaborative document editing, individualized undo stacks, and read/write permissions; see [8] for more complete discussion of techniques for collaboration in shared workspaces.

EVALUATION

To understand the feasibility and accuracy of our approach, we collected data from 18 participants. Nine participants (four female) completed the study on our prototype mobile device, and another nine participants (five female) completed the study using our multitouch table setup. Participants were paid $10 for their involvement.

For the mobile device, we evaluated an input set comprised of four finger locations: pad, tip, knuckle and nail (Figure 2). Two participants had long nails that prevented them from tapping with the boney tip of their fingers. No special changes were made for these users – they were simply allowed to tap using the tip of their nail (i.e. perpendicular to the touch surface, distinct from the nail tap, which required the hand to be palms-up). Anecdotally, users had no trouble performing these different taps, perhaps because they leverage existing finger behaviors (see section on left).

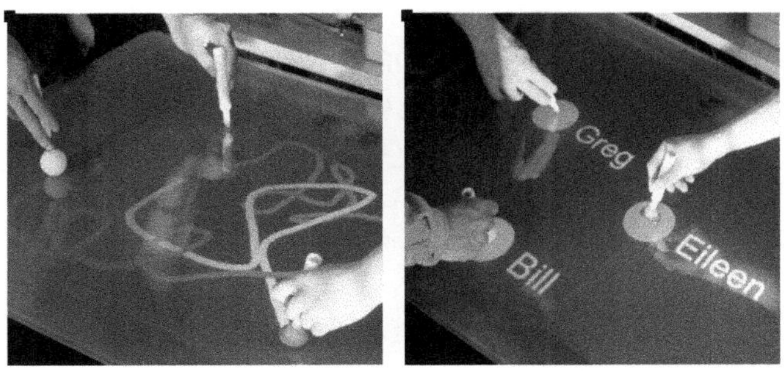

Figure 8. Left: tools representing different "brush" colors allow several users to paint simultaneously, without color or mode switching. Right: unique pens could allow interactive surfaces to identify which user was performing what action.

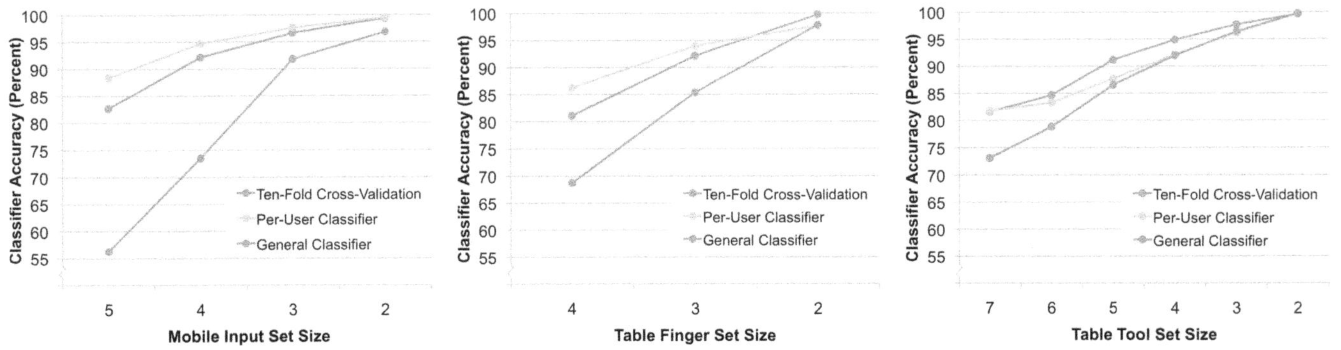

Figure 9. Classification accuracy results for input sets of different sizes. Three classification approaches are evaluated.

As an additional, fifth input type, we used an iPod compatible capacitive stylus (which uses conductive foam inside). Styli, although increasingly uncommon in mobile devices, have attractive qualities for some interactive applications [14,15]. For these applications, it would be useful to discriminate between finger and pen input.

For our multitouch table, two input sets were evaluated: our four finger types (tip, pad, knuckle and nail – Figure 2) and seven input tools (Figure 7). The finger was included in the latter tool set since it is unlikely an interactive surface would want to give up finger discrimination capability, even if several tools were present.

For each input type, participants were asked to provide ten taps to different locations on the screen. Participants completed this sequence four times, going through all input types first, before looping back around to complete the next round (this ensured better temporal independence). This produced 40 data points per input type. Although our classifier would likely benefit from additional training data, we found user boredom and fatigue became problematic in longer study durations. Thus, results presented in this paper should be considered as an accuracy lower bound.

This procedure produced, per participant, 200 data points for the *mobile input set*, 160 data points for the *table finger set*, and 280 data points for the *table tool set*. In total, 5760 tap events were collected.

RESULTS

The central questions we sought to answer in our evaluation were 1) the accuracy of our approach and 2) how large of an input set could be supported with this acoustic approach. To assess this, we purposely created input sets larger that what we believed our system could accurately classify. This allowed us to post-hoc prune down the input sets to analyze how performance would improve. Ultimately, this procedure allows a size of set vs. accuracy balance to be identified.

We evaluated the classification performance of the *mobile input set* at four different sizes: 5, 4, 3, and 2 input types. The process was initiated by including all five input types. In each subsequent round, we removed the input type with the least accuracy (i.e. highest confusion). The only location not allowed to be eliminated was the finger pad, as this was the standard pointing modality. The same procedure was used for the *table finger set* (4 types) and the *table tool set* (7 types). In the *table tool set*, the finger was not allowed to be eliminated; likewise for pad location in the *table finger set*.

Ten-Fold Cross Validation

To get a general sense of our system's performance, we conducted a conventional ten-fold cross-validation using all of our data (1800, 1440 and 2520 data points for the *mobile input set, table finger set* and *table tool set* respectively). However, this statistic tends to be generous, since train and test data sets can contain points from the same user and points adjacent in time (which will naturally tend to be more similar). Nonetheless, it provides a good baseline - this result is illustrated in Figure 9.

Per-User Classifiers

To better understand how our system would perform in the real world, we assessed the accuracy of user-specific classifiers. Specifically, we trained the SVM on three rounds of a user's input data, and tested on the fourth. We evaluated all

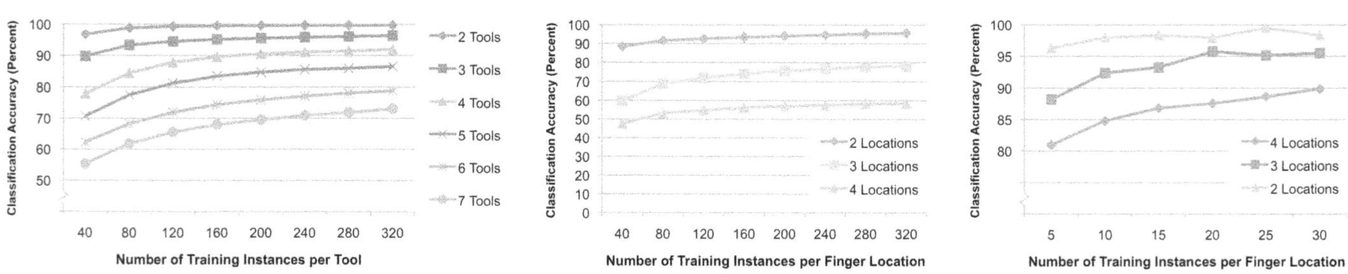

Figure 10. Left & middle: accuracy results using a general classifier. Right: accuracy results using a per-user classifier. The volume of training data was varied to see how performance was affected.

train/test combinations, and averaged the results per user (i.e. four-fold cross-validation). After computing this accuracy measure for our participants, we combined the means (see per-user plots in Figure 9).

Using all five types, the *mobile input set* achieves an accuracy of 88.3% (SE=1.7%). The tip type was the worst performing in the set, contributing 47.2% of the misclassifications. Anecdotally, the tip location appears to be the least well defined among users (compared to e.g., the knuckle), leading to higher variance. When tip is removed, accuracy jumps to 94.7% (SE=1.1%). A set containing just finger pad and the stylus achieves an average classification accuracy of 99.4% (SE=0.3%), or roughly one error in every 200 taps.

Turning to the *table finger set* - classification accuracy when using all four finger input types stands at 86.3% (SE=3.1%). As with the mobile device, tip is the worst performing; accuracy jumps to 94.0% (SE=1.4%) once tip is eliminated. Pad and nail are the best performing pair, with an average accuracy of 97.7% (SE=0.7%). Of note in the *table tool set*, finger and pen - perhaps the most common mixed-use modality (see e.g., [14,15]) - achieves 99.7% accuracy (SE=0.2%).

General Classifier

In this analysis, we evaluate system performance without per-user classifiers. In essence, we are simulating "walk up" users and estimating their performance without any training for that particular individual. We achieve this by combining data from eight users into a single aggregate training set, and then use a ninth user as the test (all combinations, i.e. nine-fold per-user holdout cross-validation).

Favorably, in the case of the *table tool set*, performance is as good as classifiers trained on a specific user (1% or less loss of accuracy at four or fewer items, well within statistical variation). This suggests the most important classification features are user-independent, and that the acoustic features of the objects are most influential.

This result was less true for the two finger-centric input sets. Given that different users have different fingers, it is not surprising per-user models would yield better results than a general classifier (per-user models also make more sense with mobile devices, as there is more opportunity and need to personalize to a single user). On average, the *mobile input set* and the *table finger set* saw their performance drop 12.1% compared to the per-user classifiers. However, this performance gap is mostly closed by the time the input sets have been reduced to just pad and nail; with 96.8% (SE=1.2%) and 97.8% (SE=1.5%) accuracy for the *mobile input set* and *table finger set* respectively (vs. 97.7%). The general classifier plots in Figure 9 illustrate the above accuracy results.

Volume of Training Data

A central question when building systems using machine learning is how much data is needed for training before accuracy levels off. In other words, where is the point where more training data is of marginal benefit? As an initial estimation of this point in our system, we analyze data from our worst-performing table setup.

We trained our classifier on incrementally larger sets of data, starting from 40 randomly selected instances per input type to 320. Our full data set is 360 points per type, but we withheld 40 points, all from a random single user, to serve as the test set on each fold. For each size input set, we did folds for every combination of users. This procedure ensured a single user's data was either in the test set or train set, but not both – allowing for a fair evaluation and numbers comparable to our general classifier results. Figure 10 (left and center) contains accuracy plots for each input set size in the table's tool and finger modalities.

The *table tool set* results suggest sets of two or three plateau rapidly, with perhaps only 200 data points needed for training. However, for tool sets of four or larger, no plateau is reached. The trajectory is clearly upward even when the classifier is utilizing our full data set for training (320 points). Thus, more training data may further improve accuracy. With thousands of training instances provided by a wide variety of users, it is conceivable our full tool set of seven types could operate at useable accuracies.

A different effect is seen with the *table finger set*. General classifier accuracy improves by an average of 6.0% from a training set of 40 to 80, but only another 6.1% from 80 to 320 data points. Unlike the *table tools set* results, however, the upward trajectory is modest. Expanding from 280 to 320 training instances improves accuracy a mere quarter of a percent on average. These results paint a clear picture: a general classifier using our current table setup and software implementation would seem unlikely to ever support finger sets above two – at least not at accuracies above 90%.

These results directly support our earlier hypothesis - that per-user classifiers are most appropriate (and ultimately needed) for finger-centric input sets. If we repeat our training volume analysis using a per-user classifier, the results are notably different (Figure 10, right). Ten random instances are used as the test set, leaving at most 30 instances for training. Foremost, even with remarkably small training sets - five instances per finger type - accuracies start above 80% with four finger input types. This compared to below 50% accuracy with a general classifier using 40 training instances from random users. With 30 training instances (a very small training set by any measure), accuracies exceed 90% for *table finger sets* of 2, 3 and 4 types.

Even more encouraging, perhaps, is the fact that the *table finger set* with four input types looks to have a strong and consistent upward trajectory (Figure 10, right). It seems likely our full input set (tip, pad, knuckle and nail) could achieve 95%+ accuracies if users supplied several hundred or more training instances. This would not be unreasonable if a setup is deployed in the home or workspace.

CONCLUSION

In this paper, we have presented our acoustic-based input classification approach called *TapSense*. It relies on the unique acoustic signatures different objects create when striking a touch surface. A support vector machine is used to classify impact instances using a series of time-independent acoustic features. Software then pairs the resulting classification with an input event tracked by a variety of possible digitizing technologies. A distinguishing feature of our approach is its ability to classify different types of finger input – specifically the pad, tip, knuckle and nail – opening new interaction opportunities for touch surfaces, especially those with limited surface area. Our user study showed the technique is immediately feasible, with accuracies in excess of 95%.

ACKNOWLEDGEMENTS

This work was funded in part by a Microsoft PhD Fellowship, a Graduate Research Fellowship from the National Science Foundation, and the Center for Future Work, Heinz College, Carnegie Mellon University.

REFERENCES

1. Asano, F., Goto, M., Itou, K. and Asoh, H. Real-time sound source localization and separation system and its application to automatic speech recognition. In *Proc. Eurospeech '01*. 1013-1016.
2. Benko, H., Wilson, A., and R. Balakrishnan, Sphere: multi-touch interactions on a spherical display. In *Proc. UIST '08*. 77-86.
3. Burges, C.J. A Tutorial on Support Vector Machines for Pattern Recognition. *Data Mining and Know. Disc.*, 2.2, June 1998, 121-167.
4. Cao, X., Wilson, A., Balakrishnan, R., Hinckley, K., and Hudson, S.E. ShapeTouch: Leveraging contact shape on interactive surfaces. In *Proc. TABLETOP '08*. 129-136.
5. Deyle, T., Palinko, S., Poole, E.S., and Starner, T. Hambone: A Bio-Acoustic Gesture Interface. In *Proc. ISWC '07*. 1-8.
6. Dietz, P.H., Harsham, B., Forlines, C., Leigh, D., Yerazunis, W., Shipman, S., Schmidt-Nielsen, B., and Ryall, K. DT controls: adding identity to physical interfaces. In *Proc. UIST '05*. 245-252.
7. Dietz, P. and Leigh, D. DiamondTouch: a multi-user touch technology. In *Proc. UIST '01*. 219-226.
8. Gutwin, C., Greenberg, S., Blum, R. and Dyck, J. Supporting Informal Collaboration in Shared Workspace Groupware. HCI Report 2005-01, U. Saskatchewan, Canada. 2005.
9. Hall, M., Frank, E., Holmes, G., Pfahringer, B., Reutemann, P., and Witten, I.H. The WEKA Data Mining Software: An Update. *SIGKDD Explor.*, 11,1. 2009.
10. Harrison, C., Tan, D., and Morris, D. Skinput: appropriating the body as an input surface. In *Proc. CHI '10*. 453-462.
11. Harrison, C. and Hudson, S.E. Scratch Input: Creating Large, Inexpensive, Unpowered and Mobile finger Input Surfaces. In *Proc. UIST '08*. 205-208.
12. Hartmann, B., Morris, M.R., Benko, H., and Wilson, A.D. Augmenting interactive tables with mice & keyboards. In *Proc. UIST '09*. 149-152.
13. Hinckley K. and Song, H. Sensor synaesthesia: touch in motion, and motion in touch. In *Proc. CHI '11*. 801-810.
14. Hinckley, K., Yatani, K., Pahud, M., Coddington, N., Rodenhouse, J., Wilson, A., Benko, H., and Buxton, B. Pen + touch = new tools. In *Proc. UIST '10*. 27-36.
15. Hinckley, K., Yatani, K., Pahud, M., Coddington, N., Rodenhouse, J., Wilson, A., Benko, H., and Buxton, B. Manual deskterity: an exploration of simultaneous pen + touch direct input. In *CHI '10 Ext. Abst.* 2793-2802.
16. Holz, C. and Baudisch, P. The generalized perceived input point model and how to double touch accuracy by extracting fingerprints. In *Proc. CHI '10*. 581-590.
17. Kaltenbrunner, M. and Bencina, R. ReacTIVision: a computer-vision framework for table-based tangible interaction. In *Proc. TEI '07*. 69-74.
18. Matsushita, N. and Rekimoto, J. HoloWall: designing a finger, hand, body, and object sensitive wall. In *Proc. UIST '97*. 209-210.
19. Mimio: http://www.mimio.com
20. Olwal, A. and Wilson, A.D. SurfaceFusion: unobtrusive tracking of everyday objects in tangible user interfaces. In *Proc. GI '08*. 235-242.
21. Paradiso, J.A. and Leo, C.K. Tracking and Characterizing Knocks Atop Large Interactive Displays. *Sensor Review*, 25(2), 2005, 134-143.
22. Paradiso, J., Hsiao, K., Strickon, J., Lifton, J., and Adler, A. Sensor Systems for Interactive Surfaces. *IBM Sys. Journal*, 39(3/4), Oct '00, 892-914.
23. Patten, J., Ishii, H., Hines, J., and Pangaro, G. Sensetable: a wireless object tracking platform for tangible user interfaces. In *Proc. CHI '01*. 253-260.
24. Rekimoto, J. and Saitoh, M. Augmented surfaces: a spatially continuous work space for hybrid computing environments. In *Proc. CHI '99*. 378-385.
25. Rekimoto, J. and Sciammarella, E. ToolStone: effective use of the physical manipulation vocabularies of input devices. In *Proc. UIST '00*. 109-117.
26. Rekimoto, J. SmartSkin: an infrastructure for freehand manipulation on interactive surfaces. *In Proc. CHI '02*. 113-120.
27. Vandoren, P., Van Laerhoven, T., Claesen, L., Taelman, J., Di Fiore, F., Van Reeth, F., and Flerackers, E. Dip - it: digital infrared painting on an interactive table. In *CHI '08 Ext. Abst.* 2901-2906.
28. Wang, F. and Ren, X. Empirical evaluation for finger input properties in multi-touch interaction. In *Proc. CHI '09*. 1063-1072.

Author Index

www.ingramcontent.com/pod-product-compliance
Ingram Content Group UK Ltd.
Pitfield, Milton Keynes, MK11 3LW, UK
UKHW051418290926
15471UKWH00009B/1666

9 781450 307161